International Conflict and Security Law

Sergey Sayapin · Rustam Atadjanov ·
Umesh Kadam · Gerhard Kemp ·
Nicolás Zambrana-Tévar · Noëlle Quénivet
Editors

International Conflict and Security Law

A Research Handbook

Volume 2

Editors
Sergey Sayapin
School of Law
KIMEP University
Almaty, Kazakhstan

Rustam Atadjanov
School of Law
KIMEP University
Almaty, Kazakhstan

Umesh Kadam
National Law School of India
Pune, India

Gerhard Kemp
Law and Social Sciences
University of Derby
Derby, UK

Nicolás Zambrana-Tévar
School of Law
KIMEP University
Almaty, Kazakhstan

Noëlle Quénivet
Bristol Law School
University of the West of England
Bristol, UK

ISBN 978-94-6265-517-1   ISBN 978-94-6265-515-7 (eBook)
https://doi.org/10.1007/978-94-6265-515-7

Published by T.M.C. ASSER PRESS, The Hague, The Netherlands www.asserpress.nl
Produced and distributed for T.M.C. ASSER PRESS by Springer-Verlag Berlin Heidelberg

© T.M.C. ASSER PRESS and the authors 2022
No part of this work may be reproduced, stored in a retrieval system, or transmitted in any form or by any means, electronic, mechanical, photocopying, microfilming, recording or otherwise, without written permission from the Publisher, with the exception of any material supplied specifically for the purpose of being entered and executed on a computer system, for exclusive use by the purchaser of the work.
The use of general descriptive names, registered names, trademarks, service marks, etc. in this publication does not imply, even in the absence of a specific statement, that such names are exempt from the relevant protective laws and regulations and therefore free for general use.

This T.M.C. ASSER PRESS imprint is published by the registered company Springer-Verlag GmbH, DE, part of Springer Nature.
The registered company address is: Heidelberger Platz 3, 14197 Berlin, Germany

Foreword

For much of the history of international law, the distinction between war and peace affected the laws that applied to a given situation, but was not a legal question itself. Oppenheim's magnum opus, for many editions, came in two volumes: the first on 'peace' and the second on 'war and neutrality'. Of the various transformations in the course of the twentieth century—including the end of colonialism, the rise of human rights, the shift to multilateralism—the prohibition on the use of force arguably affected the structure of international law in the most fundamental way.

As this important new work demonstrates, international conflict and security law today has gone far beyond the jus ad bellum and the jus in bello. Much as the United Nations Security Council's brief to address 'threats to international peace and security' expanded considerably in the euphoric 'new interventionism' of the early 1990s, the contributors interpret threats to human well-being broadly. It is now two decades since the September 11, 2001 attacks led the USA to conclude that it had more to fear from failing states than from conquering ones. Our own insight at this moment of pandemic is that shared biology renders us all vulnerable to diseases that pay no heed to borders. And, at least in the back of our minds, we know that the greatest threat our children will face is the sickening of the Earth itself.

Solving or resolving these and other problems demands cooperation, and the editors are to be congratulated for bringing together authors that span literal and metaphorical boundaries of geography and discipline. The resultant work—coincidentally, also published in two volumes—will be of interest to lawyers and diplomats, but also activists and officials, as well as anyone seeking to understand the evolving dangers confronting our shared world, and the tools and institutions needed to avert, mitigate, or survive them.

Singapore
October 2021

Simon Chesterman

Preface

As this two-volume book was being conceptualized in late 2017, it was the co-editors' starting point that threats to international peace and security were numerous and not necessarily military, and therefore, our exposition of international conflict and security law should go beyond the narrowly defined classical areas such as the use of force, the law of armed conflict, peacekeeping, refugee law, and international criminal law. Surprisingly enough, few book-length works have been written on the subject. One, edited by Burchill et al., is a collection of essays on selected topics of the conflict and security law.[1] Another one is a research handbook edited by White and Henderson focusing mostly on conflict prevention and the legality of resorting to the use of force.[2] The third book, written by White, constitutes an introduction to international conflict and security law dealing with the use of force, conflict situations, and peacetime security.[3] We departed from earlier approaches by highlighting a few key values protected by international law and then proceeding to discuss some of the most relevant aspects of international conflict and security law in an interdisciplinary manner. In the first volume, we examine values protected by relevant legal rules, as well as some key international institutions enforcing those rules, whereas the second volume deals with a few challenges to established rules, crimes under international law, and a handful of illustrative case studies. We believe that the ensuing developments, including the COVID-19 pandemic, confirmed the relevance of our basic perception and editorial approach.

We were lucky to assemble a team of contributors from literally all continents and all major legal systems of the world, in order to make the project truly international. In order for international law to be deserving of its name, it must be reflective of a

---

[1] Burchill R et al. (2005) International conflict and security law. Essays in memory of Hilaire McCoubrey. Cambridge University Press, Cambridge.

[2] White N, Henderson C (2015) Research handbook on international conflict and security law: Jus ad bellum, jus in bello and jus post bellum. Edward Elgar Publishing, Cheltenham, Northampton.

[3] White N (2014) Advanced introduction to international conflict and security law. Edward Elgar Publishing, Cheltenham, Northampton. Most recently, Geiß R, Melzer N (2021) The Oxford Handbook of the International Law of Global Security (Oxford University Press, Oxford) covered a broader range of topics.

variety of legal traditions and perspectives. Also, in order for international law to be effective, especially in such a sensitive area, as international security, it should take account of lawful interests of as many actors concerned as possible, including states, international institutions, and non-state actors. On account of the contemporary world realities, increasing attention is being paid to issues concerning international conflict and security from a variety of perspectives, such as political, legal, sociological, philosophical, economic, and cultural. One aspect of such renewed attention is that a sizable number of academic institutions have introduced either stand-alone courses that revolve around the general theme of international conflict and security, or integrated elements of these studies in general courses on public international law, international relations, political science, journalism, etc. Undergraduate and postgraduate students pursuing such studies will benefit from these volumes. Undoubtedly, even non-lawyers are often required to delve into legal dimensions of these issues. Apart from students, the present work will also profit those who work for think tanks, intergovernmental and non-governmental organizations dealing with peace, conflict and security related issues as well as armed forces, military academies, governments, and media houses.

The first volume is organized into three parts. Part I ("Protected Values") makes the point that mankind's security and welfare are based upon fundamental values both of a natural and positive character. The three inaugural chapters deal with the philosophy and sociology of international law: Rustam Atadjanov (Chap. 1) reflects on the idea of humanity, which transcends all international law, followed by Boris Kashnikov (Chap. 2) who dwells on the concept of self-determination, and Anthony Cullen with Kostiantyn Gorobets (Chap. 3) who introduce the rule of law theory. The next chapter (Chap. 4) written by Victor Ventura and Eduardo Filho, discusses the common heritage of mankind. Part I concludes with Anicée Van Engeland's chapter (Chap. 5) on the concept of cultural relativism in international human rights law.

Part II ("Law") explores the main areas of international conflict and security law. In Chap. 6, Onder Bakircioglu offers a useful overview of the legal regulation of the use of force. In the three following chapters, the UN Security Council is discussed: Rossana Deplano in Chap. 7 explores the Security Council's evolving role in the maintenance of international peace and security, Ben Murphy in Chap. 8 analyses the modalities of the Security Council sanctions, and Sabine Hassler in Chap. 9 explains the formalities of peace operations mandated by the Security Council. Joop Voetelink's following chapter (Chap. 10) on the Status of Forces Agreements explains the regime of extraterritorial deployment of state armed forces. Next, Melanie O'Brien (Chap. 11) introduces readers to international human rights law (IHRL), before international humanitarian law (IHL) is expounded on in a few chapters. In Chap. 12, Christine Byron explains the key concept of direct participation in hostilities (DPH). Jeroen van den Boogaard highlights the operational perspectives of the conduct of hostilities (Chap. 13) and explains the legal regime of the prohibition of chemical and biological weapons (Chap. 14). Next, Rustam Atadjanov (Chap. 15) turns to the status of nuclear weapons under international law, and Evhen Tsybulenko analyses the regulation of blinding laser weapons (Chap. 16) and vacuum weapons (Chap. 17). In Chap. 18, Evhen Tsybulenko and Anastassiya Platonova dwell on the legal regulation of new types of weapons, and Kubo Mačák in Chap. 19 completes the overview of Hague Law in his chapter on military space operations. In the next two chapters, Tara Smith (Chap. 20) analyses the effects of armed conflicts on the environment and natural resources, and Marina Lostal (Chap. 21) focuses on the protection of cultural property in armed conflicts. Next, after Sergey Sayapin's general introduction to international criminal law (ICL) (Chap. 22), Thomas Kruessmann (Chap. 23) goes into the particulars of anti-corruption law and action. Katja Samuel and Silvia Venier (Chap. 24) complete Part II with their chapter on the due diligence obligations of international organizations engaged in disaster management.

Part III ("Institutions") is devoted to universal and regional institutions, both intergovernmental and non-governmental, which are instrumental in enforcing international conflict and security law, and maintaining international and regional peace and security. Since such institutions are numerous, we had to be selective, and our approach to peace and security was broad and comprehensive enough to include institutions dealing with economic cooperation, education and culture, health care, and development. The first three chapters in this part relate to representative regional organizations with broad competences, including security issues: Ioannis Tzivaras' chapter (Chap. 25) on the Organization for Security and Cooperation in Europe (OSCE) is followed by Lehte Roots' chapter on the European Union (EU) (Chap. 26), and then by Ondrej Hamulak and Josef Valuch's overview (Chap. 27) of the Association of East Asian Nations (ASEAN). In the next chapter, Sultan Sakhariyev (Chap. 28) explains the mandate of the Collective Security Treaty Organization (CSTO). Whereas an overview of the International Criminal Court (ICC) is offered in the chapter on international criminal law, two chapters exemplify the action of "hybrid" tribunals: Olivier Beauvallet and Jeanne-Thérèse Schmit (Chap. 29) explain the operation of the Extraordinary Chambers in the Courts of Cambodia (ECCC), and Michail Vagias (Chap. 30) analyses other "hybrid" tribunals. Alison Bisset (Chap. 31) adds to the discussion an overview of post-conflict justice mechanisms. The next few chapters are devoted to universal institutions such as INTERPOL (Chap. 32 by Evhen Tsybulenko and Sebastian Suarez), UNESCO (Chap. 33 by Umesh Kadam), UNICEF and the WHO (Chaps. 34 and 35 by Nataliia Hendel), and the UNDP (Chap. 36 by Julio P. F. H. de Siqueira, Andrew Mtewa, and Daury César Fabriz). The part concludes with Heike Spieker's chapter (Chap. 37) on the International Red Cross and Red Crescent Movement, and a chapter on human rights NGOs and humanitarian NGOs (Chap. 38) written by Nataliia Hendel, Tymur Korotkyi and Roman Yedeliev.

The purpose of the second volume consists in placing the first volume's theory in practical contexts. Part IV ("Challenges") exemplifies a few threats calling for a creative and innovative application of existing rules. Tara Smith's inaugural chapter (Chap. 39) discusses the problem of climate change and is followed by a chapter on wildlife poaching as a threat to international peace and security by Federico Dalpane and Maria Baideldinova (Chap. 40). The next two chapters discuss the use of force in specific contexts: Elizabeth Chadwick in Chap. 41 discusses the use of force in pursuance of the right to self-determination, and Eki Omorogbe in Chap. 42 explores the African Union's action against mercenaries. Each of the final three chapters in

Part IV addresses an individual issue: Julio P. F. H. de Siqueira, Daury César Fabriz and Junio G. Homem de Siqueira in Chap. 43 discuss the rights of elderly and disabled persons in the context of security challenges, Stefanie Bock and Nicolai Bülte in Chap. 44 explore the politics of international justice, and Evelyne Schmid in Chap. 45 addresses the problem of poverty.

Part V ("Crimes") is devoted to crimes under international law and some transnational crimes. The "core" crimes under international law are addressed in accordance with Article 5 of the ICC Statute: in Chap. 46 Olivier Beauvallet with Hyuree Kim and Léo Jolivet discuss genocide, followed by Rustam Atadjanov (Chap. 47, on crimes against humanity), Gerhard Kemp (Chap. 48, on apartheid), Ewa Sałkiewicz Munnerlyn and Sergey Sayapin (Chap. 49, on war crimes), and Annegret Lucia Hartig (Chap. 50, on aggression). The subsequent chapters address military ecocide (Chap. 51 by Peter Hough), religious extremism (Chap. 52 by Sherzod Eraliev), human smuggling and human trafficking (Chap. 53 by Natalia Szablewska), and organized crime (Chap. 54 by Thomas Kruessmann).

Finally, Part VI ("Case Studies") discusses a few conflicts from geographic and thematic perspectives. The country case studies discussed are Cambodia (Chap. 55 by Natalia Szablewska), Myanmar (Chap. 56 by Melanie O'Brien), Northern Cyprus and the former Yugoslavia (Chaps. 57 and 58 by Ioannis Tzivaras), and Northern Ireland (Chap. 59 by Lauren Dempster). The thematic case studies include the "war on terror" (Chap. 60 by Rumyana Van Ark (nee Grozdanova)), an assessment of the Boko Haram crisis from Islamic and international humanitarian law perspectives (Chap. 61 by Muhammad-Basheer A. Ismail), reflections on the accountability of religious actors for religiously motivated conflicts, and on the accountability of the Catholic Church for clergy sex abuse (Chaps. 62 and 63 by Nicolás Zambrana-Tévar), and the role of international law in the prevention and resolution of possible conflicts over water in Central Asia (Chap. 64 by Hafeni Nashoonga).

As mentioned above, in international law the concepts of conflict and security are often understood narrowly. Such an approach fails to take into consideration a wider spectrum of situations and factors that create or mitigate conflicts or change their nature. Espousing this narrow stance often leads commentators to failing to grasp some of the intricacies of a specific conflictual situation and, consequently, to offer concrete, valuable legal solutions. Whilst in international affairs scholars have long accepted the multifaceted aspects of conflicts, legal pundits, constrained by the straightjacket of a rigid, often doctrinal interpretation of international law and a conservative United Nations Security Council, have been unable to move beyond the military/human/environmental security discursive framework. A broader view, as adopted by this book, is thus warranted. This endeavour is further met by bringing together scholars who are not only specialists in their field but also whose views reflect a worldwide variety of approaches towards the subject-matter.

Liberation from the conventional notions of "human security" and "conflict", as well as the legal, political, and social paradigms that inform them, requires humility and a sense of history. It also demands serious work on, and recognition of, the roles that the marginalized, the oppressed, and the colonized have played in the formation of an essentially hegemonic and triumphalist international system. For instance, not recognizing the crime of apartheid as a settler-colonialist continuity that fundamentally destroyed any sense of security and humanity of entire populations (and the dignity and self-respect of an entire continent), and by analysing *that* crime through a narrower (Western!) lens of twentieth century, post-Second World War human rights sensibilities, exposes the flaw at the heart of international (criminal) law. Our approach (as evidenced throughout the book, including the chapter on the crime of apartheid) is thus informed by perspectives from the marginalized (for instance, the disabled and the elderly in the context of IHL), gender perspectives, and a sense that we must with this book, in all humility and with critical awareness of its own limitations, create avenues that will lead to further debate, discussion, and serious intellectual work on the construction and deconstruction of notions of law, security, and human interests in the twenty-first century.

Social stability and the protection of individual rights, especially the right to life and property are considered common, probable, and desirable goals of any moral and legal system. The very existence of moral and legal norms presupposes and leads to the absence of arbitrariness, which is often present in any community where laws are replaced by the will and self-interests of those who have power and can impose it on those who have not. Law, therefore, leads in itself to security and to the absence of conflict. However, the more we learn about the causes of conflict and violence, the more we can tailor our legal system to ensure that conflicts are appropriately tackled, eliminating their exact causes, sensibly approaching those opposing interests in the community which are often behind outbursts of violence or present in any sustained situation of injustice and deprivation of individual and collective rights. Books on conflict and security law—such as this one—contribute to this study of how to remedy violence and attacks on human rights by examining specific types of conflicts and how the law can contribute to long-standing solutions.

We take this occasion to thank all contributors for their reflection and hard work. They made this book possible. Very special thanks are due to Prof. Simon Chesterman, Dean and Professor at the National University of Singapore, for his endorsing Foreword. English language editors at Scribendi (www.scribendi.com) were very helpful in proofreading selected chapters. KIMEP University (Almaty, Kazakhstan) should be credited for taking over the English language editing costs. We thank Dr. Chan Young Bang, President of KIMEP University, Dr. Joseph Luke, Acting Vice President for Academic Affairs, Mr. Yuri Fidirko, Vice President for Finance, Dr. Fred M. Isaacs, Associate Professor and Dean of KIMEP University's School of Law, and Dr. Claudio Lombardi, Assistant Professor and Research Director at the School of Law, for their continued support. We also thank Mr. Frank Bakker, Ms. Kiki van Gurp, and other colleagues at T.M.C. ASSER PRESS and the law team at Springer for their support for this project since its inception. Ms. Anna Margatova was helpful in formatting the manuscript and putting together the List of Abbreviations, and Ms. Dilnaz Israilova provided administrative assistance. We dedicate this book to our students and all friends of international law, in the hope that they will contribute to building a better and safer world.

Almaty, Kazakhstan	Sergey Sayapin
Almaty, Kazakhstan	Rustam Atadjanov
Pune, India	Umesh Kadam
Derby, UK	Gerhard Kemp
Almaty, Kazakhstan	Nicolás Zambrana-Tévar
Bristol, UK	Noëlle Quénivet
August 2021	

Contents

Part I Protected Values

1 **Humanity** 3
   Rustam Atadjanov

2 **Self-determination of Peoples** 27
   Boris Kashnikov

3 **The International Rule of Law** 47
   Anthony Cullen and Kostiantyn Gorobets

4 **The Common Heritage of Mankind** 67
   Victor Alencar Mayer Feitosa Ventura
   and Eduardo Cavalcanti de Mello Filho

5 **Human Rights: Between Universalism and Relativism** 93
   Anicée Van Engeland

Part II Law

6 **The Use of Force in International Law** 117
   Onder Bakircioglu

7 **The UN Security Council: From Preserving State
   Sovereignty to Protecting Humanity** 149
   Rossana Deplano

8 **UN Security Council Sanctions and International
   Peace and Security: Context, Controversies and (Legal)
   Challenges** 171
   Ben L. Murphy

9 **Peace(keeping) Operations: Soldiers Without Enemies?** 201
   Sabine Hassler

10	**The Status of Forces Agreements** Joop Voetelink	229
11	**International Human Rights Law** Melanie O'Brien	255
12	**Direct Participation in Hostilities** Christine Byron	277
13	**The Conduct of Hostilities** Jeroen C. van den Boogaard	301
14	**Chemical Weapons** Jeroen C. van den Boogaard	317
15	**Nuclear Weapons** Rustam Atadjanov	337
16	**Blinding Laser Weapons** Evhen Tsybulenko	367
17	**Fuel Air Explosive Weapons** Evhen Tsybulenko	379
18	**Current Issues of Hague Law** Evhen Tsybulenko and Anastassiya Platonova	389
19	**Military Space Operations** Kubo Mačák	399
20	**The Protection of the Environment and Natural Resources in Armed Conflict** Tara Smith	421
21	**The Protection of Cultural Property in Armed Conflict and Occupation** Marina Lostal	443
22	**Transnational and International Criminal Law** Sergey Sayapin	469
23	**International Anti-corruption Law** Thomas Kruessmann	503
24	**The Due Diligence Obligations of International Organisations Engaged in Disaster Management** Katja L. H. Samuel and Silvia Venier	527

Part III Institutions

25 Organization for Security and Co-operation in Europe (OSCE) 555
Ioannis P. Tzivaras

26 European Union (EU): Security, Conflict and Migration 575
Lehte Roots

27 Association of Southeast Asian Nations (ASEAN) 595
Jozef Valuch and Ondrej Hamuľák

28 Collective Security Treaty Organization (CSTO) 609
Sultan Sakhariyev

29 The Extraordinary Chambers in the Courts of Cambodia 619
Olivier Beauvallet and Jeanne-Thérèse Schmit

30 Other "Hybrid" Tribunals 633
Michail Vagias

31 Post-conflict Justice Mechanisms 651
Alison Bisset

32 INTERPOL 673
Evhen Tsybulenko and Sebastian Suarez

33 United Nations Educational, Scientific and Cultural Organization (UNESCO) 693
Umesh Kadam

34 United Nations International Children's Emergency Fund (UNICEF) 719
Nataliia Hendel

35 World Health Organization (WHO) 733
Nataliia Hendel

36 United Nations Development Programme (UNDP) 761
Julio Homem de Siqueira, Andrew G. Mtewa
and Daury César Fabriz

37 The International Red Cross and Red Crescent Movement 779
Heike Spieker

38 Human Rights NGOs and Humanitarian NGOs 813
Nataliia Hendel, Tymur Korotkyi and Roman Yedeliev

Part IV Challenges

39 Climate Change and Armed Conflict 841
Tara Smith

40	Poaching and Wildlife Trafficking as Threats to International Peace and Security	861
	Federico Dalpane and Maria Baideldinova	
41	The Use of Force in Pursuance of the Right to Self-determination	885
	Elizabeth Chadwick	
42	The African Region's Pushback Against Mercenaries	917
	Eki Yemisi Omorogbe	
43	International Humanitarian Protection to Disabled and Elderly People in Armed Conflict Zones	941
	Julio Homem de Siqueira, Daury César Fabriz and Junio G. Homem de Siqueira	
44	The Politics of International Justice	957
	Stefanie Bock and Nicolai Bülte	
45	Poverty	981
	Evelyne Schmid	

Part V Crimes

46	Genocide	1005
	Olivier Beauvallet, Hyuree Kim and Léo Jolivet	
47	Crimes Against Humanity	1031
	Rustam Atadjanov	
48	The Crime of Apartheid	1073
	Gerhard Kemp	
49	War Crimes	1093
	Ewa Sałkiewicz-Munnerlyn and Sergey Sayapin	
50	The Crime of Aggression: The Fall of the Supreme International Crime?	1111
	Annegret Lucia Hartig	
51	Military Ecocide	1139
	Peter Hough	
52	Religious Extremism	1161
	Sherzod Eraliev	
53	Human Smuggling and Human Trafficking	1181
	Natalia Szablewska	
54	Organized Crime	1207
	Thomas Kruessmann	

Part VI Case Studies

55 **Cambodia** 1229
    Natalia Szablewska

56 **Myanmar** 1257
    Melanie O'Brien

57 **Northern Cyprus** 1285
    Ioannis P. Tzivaras

58 **Former Yugoslavia** 1309
    Ioannis P. Tzivaras

59 **Northern Ireland: The Right to Life, Victim Mobilisation,
    and the Legacy of Conflict** 1333
    Lauren Dempster

60 **The "War on Terror"** 1359
    Rumyana van Ark

61 **Jihad Misplaced for Terrorism: An Overview of the Boko
    Haram Crisis from Islamic and International Humanitarian
    Law Perspectives** 1389
    Muhammad-Basheer A. Ismail

62 **Accountability of Religious Actors for Conflicts Motivated
    by Religion** 1421
    Nicolás Zambrana-Tévar

63 **The Children vs the Church: Human Rights and the Holy
    See in the Sex Abuse Crisis** 1443
    Nicolás Zambrana-Tévar

64 **The Role of International Law in the Prevention
    and Resolution of Possible Conflicts over Water in Central
    Asia: A Comparative Study with Special Reference
    to the European Union (EU)** 1473
    Hafeni Nashoonga

Editors and Contributors

About the Editors

Sergey Sayapin LLB, LLM, Dr. iur., Ph.D., is Associate Professor and Associate Dean at the School of Law, KIMEP University (Almaty, Kazakhstan). In 2000–2014, he held various posts at the Communication Department of the Regional Delegation of the International Committee of the Red Cross (ICRC) in Central Asia. His current research focuses on Central Asian and post-Soviet approaches to international law, international and comparative criminal law, human rights, and sociology of law. He regularly advises the Central Asian Governments as well as UNODC and the ICRC on international and criminal law and has recently joined Chatham House's expert pool. He is Sub-Editor for Central Asia of the *Encyclopedia of Public International Law in Asia* (Brill, 2021).

Rustam Atadjanov LLB, LLM, Dr. iur., Ph.D., is Assistant Professor of Public and International Law at KIMEP University School of Law (Almaty, Kazakhstan) since 2019 and Director of the Bachelor in International Law Programme. He is Graduate of the Karakalpak State University, Uzbekistan (2003), University of Connecticut School of Law, USA (2006), and University of Hamburg, Faculty of Law, Germany (2018). He formerly worked as Programme Responsible and Legal Adviser at the Regional Delegation of the International Committee of the Red Cross (ICRC) in Central Asia (2007–2014), dealing with international humanitarian law, public international law, and criminal law issues. His areas of expertise and research include public international law, international human rights law, international criminal law, international humanitarian law, theory of law and state, and constitutional law. He authored a monograph entitled *Humanness as a Protected Legal Interest of Crimes against Humanity: Conceptual and Normative Aspects* (T.M.C. ASSER PRESS/Springer, 2019) and published 20 academic and publicist articles, encyclopedic entries, and book reviews in a number of European and Asian academic journals. At KIMEP University's School of Law, he teaches public law and international law-related courses.

Umesh Kadam holds a LLM, M.Phil. (Education) and Ph.D. in International Law from Shivali University, Kolhapur, India, and LLM in International Law from University of London. From 1980 to 1998, he taught international law in various Indian law schools. From 1998 until 2008, he worked for the International Committee of the Red Cross (ICRC) as Regional Legal Adviser for the promotion and implementation of International Humanitarian Law in South Asia, Southeast and East Asia, and East Africa. Currently, he works as Visiting Professor in some Indian law schools. His areas of interest include international humanitarian law, international criminal law, and international migration law.

Gerhard Kemp obtained the BA, LLB, LLM, LLD degrees (Stellenbosch) and the International Legal Studies Certificate (Antwerp). He is Professor of international and transnational criminal justice at the University of Derby in the UK and serves on the executive committee of the Institute for Justice and Reconciliation in Cape Town, South Africa. He has published widely in the fields of international and transnational criminal justice, transitional justice, international humanitarian law, and comparative criminal law. He is Recipient of the Alexander von Humboldt research fellowship.

Nicolás Zambrana-Tévar studied law at the Complutense University in Madrid. He received an LLM degree from the London School of Economics and a Ph.D. from the University of Navarra. He worked as Lawyer for Freshfields Bruckhaus Deringer and Garrigues Abogados. He has been Member of several research groups on Business and Human Rights. He has also published in the field of law and religion in the *Journal of Church and State*, the *Oxford Journal of Law and Religion*, and *Ius Canonicum*.

Dr. Noëlle Quénivet (LLM Nottingham; Ph.D. Essex) is Associate Professor in International Law at the Bristol Law School of UWE (UK) where she has been working since 2006. Prior to that, she was Researcher at the Institute for International Law of Peace and Armed Conflict (Germany). She has extensively published in the field of International Humanitarian Law, International Criminal Law, and more specifically Gender and Children in Armed Conflict.

Contributors

Rustam Atadjanov School of Law, KIMEP University, Almaty, Kazakhstan

Maria Baideldinova School of Law, KIMEP University, Almaty, Kazakhstan

Onder Bakircioglu Leicester Law School, University of Leicester, Leicester, UK

Olivier Beauvallet Supreme Court Chamber, Pre-Trial Chambe, Extraordinary Chambers in the Courts of Cambodia, Phnom Penh, Cambodia

Alison Bisset Faculty of Law, University of Reading, Reading, UK

Editors and Contributors

Stefanie Bock Department of Law, Philipps University Marburg, Marburg, Germany

Christine Byron Cardiff University, Cardiff, Wales, UK

Nicolai Bülte Department of Law, Philipps University Marburg, Marburg, Germany

Eduardo Cavalcanti de Mello Filho Graduate Institute of International and Development Studies, Geneva, Switzerland;
University of Geneva, Geneva, Switzerland

Elizabeth Chadwick (Retired) Nottingham Trent University, Nottingham, UK

Anthony Cullen Middlesex University, London, UK

Federico Dalpane School of Law, KIMEP University, Almaty, Kazakhstan

Julio Homem de Siqueira Institute of Criminal Law Studies Alimena, University of Calabria, Rende, Italy

Junio G. Homem de Siqueira Rio Grande do Norte Federal Justice, Rio Grande do Norte, Brazil

Lauren Dempster School of Law, Queen's University Belfast, Belfast, Northern Ireland, UK

Rossana Deplano University of Leicester, Leicester, UK

Sherzod Eraliev Aleksanteri Institute, University of Helsinki, Helsinki, Finland

Daury César Fabriz Vitoria Law School, Vitoria, Brazil;
Brazilian Academy of Human Rights, Vitoria, Brazil

Kostiantyn Gorobets University of Groningen, Groningen, The Netherlands

Ondrej Hamuľák Faculty of Law, Palacký University Olomouc, Olomouc, Czech Republic;
TalTech Law School, Tallinn, Estonia

Annegret Lucia Hartig University of Hamburg, Hamburg, Germany

Sabine Hassler Bristol Law School, University of the West of England, Bristol, UK

Nataliia Hendel International Law and Comparative Law Department, International Humanitarian University, Odessa, Ukraine

Peter Hough Department of Politics, Middlesex University, London, UK

Muhammad-Basheer A. Ismail School of Law, University of Hull, Hull, England, UK

Léo Jolivet Organised crime, white collar crime and international cooperation division, Office of the Prosecutor, Orléans, France

Umesh Kadam Independent Consultant, Pune, India

Boris Kashnikov National Research University Higher School of Economics, HSE University, Moscow, Russian Federation

Gerhard Kemp Faculty of Law, University of Derby, Derby, United Kingdom; Humboldt Universität zu Berlin, Berlin, Germany

Hyuree Kim Supreme Court Chamber, Pre-Trial Chamber, Phnom Penh, Cambodia

Tymur Korotkyi Department of International Law and Comparative Law, National Aviation University, Kyiv, Ukraine

Thomas Kruessmann King's College London, London, UK; Global Europe Centre, University of Kent, Canterbury, UK

Marina Lostal School of Law, University of Essex, Colchester, UK

Kubo Mačák Law School, University of Exeter, Exeter, UK

Andrew G. Mtewa Malawi University of Science and Technology, Thyolo, Malawi

Ben L. Murphy School of Law and Social Justice, University of Liverpool, Liverpool, UK

Hafeni Nashoonga Independent Legal Consultant, Windhoek, Namibia

Eki Yemisi Omorogbe Law School, University of Leicester, Leicester, UK

Melanie O'Brien University of Western Australia, Perth, Australia

Anastassiya Platonova Tallinn University of Technology, Tallinn, Estonia

Lehte Roots School of Law, Governance and Society, Tallinn University, Tallinn, Estonia

Sultan Sakhariyev KIMEP University School of Law, Almaty, Kazakhstan

Katja L. H. Samuel GSDM, Southampton, UK

Sergey Sayapin School of Law, KIMEP University, Almaty, Kazakhstan

Ewa Sałkiewicz-Munnerlyn Akademia Krakowska AFM, Krakow, Poland

Evelyne Schmid Faculty of Law, Criminal Justice and Public Administration, University of Lausanne, Lausanne, Switzerland

Jeanne-Thérèse Schmit Paris Bar, France

Tara Smith School of Law, Bangor University, Wales, UK

Heike Spieker German Red Cross, Berlin, Germany

Sebastian Suarez Equinord—International Law Counsellors, Tallinn, Estonia

Natalia Szablewska The Open University Law School, Milton Keynes, United Kingdom;
Royal University of Law and Economics, Phnom Penh, Cambodia;
Humanitarian and Development Research Initiative, Western Sydney University, Sydney, Australia

Evhen Tsybulenko Faculty of Law, Tallinn University of Technology, Tallinn, Estonia;
Kyiv International University, Kyiv, Ukraine

Ioannis P. Tzivaras Department of Economics and Management, Open University of Cyprus (OUC), Nicosia, Cyprus

Michail Vagias The Hague University of Applied Sciences, The Hague, The Netherlands

Jozef Valuch Faculty of Law, Comenius University, Bratislava, Slovakia

Rumyana van Ark T.M.C. Asser Instituut, The Hague, The Netherlands;
University of Amsterdam, Amsterdam, The Netherlands

Jeroen C. van den Boogaard Ministry of Foreign Affairs, The Hague, The Netherlands;
University of Amsterdam, Amsterdam, The Netherlands

Anicée Van Engeland Defence Academy of the UK, Shrivenham, Swindon, UK

Silvia Venier GSDM, Southampton, UK;
Scuola Superiore Sant'Anna, Pisa, Italy

Victor Alencar Mayer Feitosa Ventura Brazilian National Agency for Agriculture, João Pessoa, Paraíba, Brazil;
Humberto Bezerra Law Firm LLP, João Pessoa, Brazil;
Center for Political-Strategic Studies of the Brazilian Navy, Rio de Janeiro, Brazil;
Brazilian Institute for the Law of the Sea (BILOS), Belo Horizonte, Brazil

Joop Voetelink Netherlands Defence Academy (NLDA), Breda, The Netherlands

Roman Yedeliev International Law Department, Taras Shevchenko National University of Kyiv, Kyiv, Ukraine

Nicolás Zambrana-Tévar School of Law, KIMEP University, Almaty, Kazakhstan

Abbreviations

AAA	American Anthropological Association
ACHPR	African (Banjul) Charter of Human and Peoples' Rights
ACWG	Working Group on Anti-Corruption
ANC	African National Congress
AP	Additional Protocol
APIM	Association Professionnelle Internationale des Médecins
ARSIWA	Articles on Responsibility of States for Internationally Wrongful Acts
ASA	Association of South East Asia
ASEAN	Association of Southeast Asian Nations
ASP	Assembly of States Parties
AU	African Union
AUC	African Union Commission
BWC	Biological Weapons Convention
CAH	Crime(s) against Humanity
CAJ	Committee on the Administration of Justice
CAR	Central African Republic
CAT	Convention against Torture
CBM	Confidence-building Measures
CCE Statute	Continuing Criminal Enterprise Statute
CCF	Commission for the Control of INTERPOL's Files
CEDAW	Convention on the Elimination of All Forms of Discrimination against Women
CEPPs	Childhood and Early Parenting Principles
CERD	Convention on the Elimination of Racial Discrimination
CERN	European Organization for Nuclear Research
CESCR	Committee on Economic, Social, and Cultural Rights
CFSP	Common Foreign and Security Policy
CHM	Common Heritage of Mankind
CIS	Commonwealth of Independent States

CITES	Convention on International Trade in Endangered Species of Wild Fauna and Flora
CIVCOM	Committee for Civilian Aspects of Crisis Management
CJEU	European Court of Justice
CNR	Council of National Nursing Association Representatives
COPs	Conferences of the Parties
COPUOS	Committee on the Peaceful Uses of Outer Space
CPP	Cambodian People's Party
CR(O)C	Convention on the Rights of the Child
CRPD	Convention on the Rights of Persons with Disabilities
CSCE	Conference on Security and Cooperation in Europe
CSDP	Common Security and Defence Policy
CSTO	Collective Security Treaty Organization
CTA	Central Tracing Agency
CTBT	Comprehensive Nuclear Test Ban Treaty
CTC	Counter Terrorism Committee
CWC	Chemical Weapons Convention
DARIO	Draft Articles on the Responsibility of International Organizations
DCCIT	Draft Comprehensive Convention on International Terrorism
DK	Democratic Kampuchea
DPH	Direct Participation in Hostilities
DRC	Democratic Republic of the Congo
EAC	Extraordinary African Chambers
EC	European Commission
ECCC	Extraordinary Chambers in the Courts of Cambodia
ECHR	European Convention on Human Rights
ECOSOC	United Nations Economic and Social Council
ECtHR	European Court of Human Rights
EDC	European Defence Community
EEAS	European External Action Service
EFA programme	'Education for All' programme
EIAP	Ebola Interim Assessment Panel
EITI	Extractive Industries Transparency Initiative
ENMOD	Convention on the Prohibition of Military or Any Other Hostile Use of Environmental Modification Techniques
ENVSEC	Environment and Security Initiative
EOKA	National Organization of Cypriot Fighters
EPHA	European Public Health Alliance
ESDP	European Security and Defence Policy
ESS	European Security Strategy
EU	European Union
EUMC	Military Committee of the European Union
FAE weapons	Fuel Air Explosive Weapons
FBI	Federal Bureau of Investigation

Abbreviations

FCPA	Foreign Corrupt Practices Act
FPA(s)	Framework Partnership Agreement(s)
GA	General Assembly
GAERC	General Affairs and External Relations Council
GC(s)	Geneva Convention(s)
GCPCA	Global Coalition to Protect Education from Attack
GDP	Gross Domestic Product
GNA	Government of National Accord
HCNM	High Commissioner on National Minorities
HDR	Human Development Report
HLRM	High-Level Reporting Mechanism
HRC	Human Rights Council/Human Rights Committee
HRCe	Human Rights Committee
HRW	Human Rights Watch
HVDP	High-Value Detainee programme
HVO	Croatian Defence Council
IAC(s)	International armed conflict(s)
IACHR	Inter-American Convention on Human Rights
IAComHR	Inter-American Commission on Human Rights
IAEA	International Atomic Energy Agency
IARC	International Agency for Research on Cancer
ICC	International Criminal Court
ICCPR	International Covenant on Civil and Political Rights
ICCWC	International Consortium on Combating Wildlife Crime
ICESCR	International Covenant on Economic, Social, and Cultural Rights
ICI	Imperial Chemical Industries
ICIDH	International Classification of Impairments, Disabilities, and Handicaps
ICJ	International Court of Justice
ICL	International Criminal Law
ICN	International Council of Nurses
ICPC	International Criminal Police Commission
ICPR	International Commission for the Protection of the Rhine
ICRC	International Committee of the Red Cross
ICSL	International Conflict and Security Law
ICTR	International Criminal Tribunal for Rwanda
ICTY	International Criminal Tribunal for the Former Yugoslavia
IDP(s)	Internally Displaced Person(s)
IED	Improvised Explosive Device
IFOR	NATO's Implementation Force
IFRC	International Federation of the Red Cross and Red Crescent Societies
IHL	International Humanitarian Law
IHR	International Health Regulations

IHRL	International Human Rights Law
ILA	International Law Association
ILC	International Law Commission
ILO	International Labour Organization
IMT	International Military Tribunal
IMTFE	International Military Tribunal for the Far East
INTERPOL	International Criminal Police Organization
IO(s)	International Organization(s)
IOCTA	Internet Organized Crime Threat Assessment
IOM	International Organization for Migration
IRM	Implementation Review Mechanism
ISA	International Seabed Authority
ISIL	Islamic State of Iraq and the Levant
ISIS	Islamic State of Iraq and Syria
ISU	Implementation Support Unit
JNA	Yugoslav People's Army
JTJ	Jama'at al-Tawhid wal-Jihad
KIA	Kachin Independence Army
KIO	Kachin Independence Organization
KKK	Ku Klux Klan
KNLA	Karen National Liberation Army
KNU	Karen National Union
KR	Khmer Rouge
LNA	Libyan National Army
LoAC	Law of Armed Conflict
LRA	Lord's Resistance Army
MDBs	Multilateral Development Banks
MDGs	Millennium Development Goals
MILAMOS	Manual on the International Law of Military Space Operations
MSF	Médicins Sans Frontières
NAPs	National Adaptation Plans
NATO	North Atlantic Treaty Organization
NCA	Nationwide Ceasefire Agreement
NCB(s)	National Central Bureau(s)
NESG	Nigerian Economic Summit Group
NGO(s)	Non-governmental organization(s)
NHRIs	National Human Rights Institutions
NIAC(s)	Non-international Armed Conflict(s)
NIEO	New International Economic Order
NIO	Northern Ireland Office
NLD	National League for Democracy
NNAs	National Nursing Associations
NP/APN Network	Nurse Practitioner/Advanced Practice Network
NSAG	Non-State Armed Group
NSs	National Red Cross or Red Crescent Societies

Abbreviations

NSW	New South Wales
NTC	Nuclear Terrorism Convention, International Convention for the Suppression of Acts of Nuclear Terrorism
OAU	Organization of African Unity
OCCRP	Organized Crime and Corruption Reporting Project
OCG(s)	Organized Criminal Group(s)
ODIHR	Office for Democratic Institutions and Human Rights
OECD	Organization for Economic Cooperation and Development
OHCHR	Office of the High Commissioner for Human Rights
OLAF	European Anti-Fraud Office
OP	Optional Protocol
OPCW	Organization for the Prohibition of Chemical Weapons
OPG	Open Government Partnership
OPONI	Office of the Police Ombudsman for Northern Ireland
OSB	Operation Sovereign Borders
OSCE	Organization for Security and Cooperation in Europe
OTP	Office of the Prosecutor
PAC	Pan Africanist Congress
PCIJ	Permanent Court of International Justice
PESCO	Permanent Structured Cooperation
PMCs	Private Military Companies
POW(s)	Prisoner(s) of War
PRK	People's Republic of Kampuchea
PSC	Political and Security Committee/Private security company
PTBT	Partial Nuclear Test Ban Treaty, Treaty Banning Nuclear Weapon Tests in the Atmosphere, in Outer Space and Under Water
PTC	Pre-Trial Chamber
R2P	Responsibility to Protect
RAF	Royal Air Force
RICO	Racketeer Influenced and Corrupt Organizations Act
RSS	Rashtriya Swayamsevak Sangh
RUSI	Royal United Services Institute for Defence and Security Studies
SAARC	South Asian Association for Regional Cooperation
SADF	South African Defence Force
SAR	International Convention on Maritime Search and Rescue
SAS	Special Air Service
SC	Security Council
SCO	Shanghai Cooperation Organization
SCSL	Special Court for Sierra Leone
SDGs	Sustainable Development Goal(s)
SGBV	Sexual and Gender-based Violence
SIS	Schengen Information System
SMCC	Strengthening Movement Coordination and Cooperation

SMM	Special Monitoring Mission
SOCTA	Serious and Organized Crime Threat Assessment
SOFA	Status of Forces Agreement
SPSC	Special Panels for Serious Crimes
STL	Special Tribunal for Lebanon
TEIA	Transboundary Environmental Impact Assessment
TEU	Treaty on the European Union
TFEU	Treaty on the Functioning of the European Union
TFSC	Turkish Federated State of Northern Cyprus
TMT	Turkish Resistance Organization
TOCTA	Transnational Organized Crime Threat Assessment
TPNW	Treaty on the Prohibition of Nuclear Weapons
TRC	Truth and Reconciliation Commission
TRNC	Turkish Republic of Northern Cyprus
TSK	Turkish Armed Forces
UDHR	Universal Declaration of Human Rights
UK	United Kingdom
UN	United Nations
UN.GIFT	United Nations Global Initiative to Fight Human Trafficking
UNAKRT	United Nations Assistance to Khmer Rouge Trials
UNBRO	United Nations Border Relief Operation
UNCAC	United Nations Convention against Corruption
UNCAT	United Nations Convention against Torture
UNCC	United Nations Compensation Commission
UNCDF	United Nations Capital Development Fund
UNCED	United Nations Conference on the Environment and Development
UNCHE	United Nations Conference on the Human Environment
UNCLOS	United Nations Convention on the Law of the Sea
UNCOPUOS	United Nations Committee on the Peaceful Uses of the Outer Space
UNCRC	United Nations Convention on the Rights of the Child
UNCTED	United Nations Counterterrorism Executive Directorate
UNDAF	United Nations Development Assistance Framework
UNDP	United Nations Development Programme
UNDRD	United Nations Declaration on the Right to Development
UNDS	United Nations Development System
UNEF	United Nations Emergency Force
UNEP	United Nations Environment Programme
UNESCO	United Nations Educational, Scientific and Cultural Organization
UNFCCC	United Nations Framework Convention on Climate Change
UNFICYP	United Nations Peacekeeping Force in Cyprus
UNFPA	United Nations Population Fund
UNGA	United Nations General Assembly

UNGPs	United Nations Guiding Principles on Business and Human Rights
UNHCR	United Nations High Commissioner for Refugees
UNICEF	United Nations International Children's Emergency Fund
UNMIK	United Nations Mission in Kosovo
UNODC	United Nations Office on Drugs and Crime
UNPOs	United Nations Peace Operations
UNPROFOR	United Nations Protection Force
UNSC	United Nations Security Council
UNSDG	United Nations Sustainable Development Group
UNTAC	United Nations Transitional Authority in Cambodia
UNTAET	United Nations Transitional Authority for East Timor
UNTOC	United Nations Convention against Transnational Organized Crime
UNV	United Nations Volunteers
UPR	Universal Periodic Review
US	United States
VCS	Vatican City State
VHP	Vishnu Hindu Parishad
VSS	Victims Support Section
WCESKT	World Commission on the Ethics of Scientific Knowledge and Technology
WCO	World Customs Organization
WHO FCTC	World Health Organization Framework Convention on Tobacco Control
WHO	World Health Organization
WMA	World Medical Association
WMD	Weapons of Mass Destruction
WTO	World Trade Organization
WWI	First World War
WWII	Second World War

Part IV
Challenges

Chapter 39
Climate Change and Armed Conflict

Tara Smith

Contents

39.1 Introduction	842
39.2 History of the Relationship Between Climate Change and Conflict	843
39.3 Anticipated Climatic Causes of Armed Conflict	844
39.3.1 Resource Scarcity	844
39.3.2 Migration and Geopolitical Tensions	846
39.3.3 Disputes Over Responses to Climate Change	847
39.4 Relevant International Law	848
39.4.1 International Humanitarian Law	848
39.4.2 International Climate Change Law	849
39.4.3 International Criminal Law	851
39.5 Future Developments	853
39.6 Conclusion	854
References	855

Abstract Climate change is one of the defining issues of our time, and there is a growing body of scientific research suggesting that it will cause an increase in armed conflicts in the future. However, this is by no means a foregone conclusion. In fact, the relationship between armed conflict and climate change is extremely complex and highly nuanced. This chapter traces the history of the connection between armed conflict and climatic conditions, before examining some of the ways in which climate change is expected to cause conflict in the future. It then examines the role that relevant fields of international law may play before concluding with a discussion of future developments likely to affect this issue going forward.

Keywords Climate change · Armed conflict · Resource scarcity · Migration · International law · Humanitarian law · International criminal law

---

T. Smith (✉)
School of Law, Bangor University, Wales, UK
e-mail: t.smith@bangor.ac.uk

© T.M.C. ASSER PRESS and the authors 2022
S. Sayapin et al. (eds.), *International Conflict and Security Law*,
https://doi.org/10.1007/978-94-6265-515-7_39

39.1 Introduction

Climate change is one of the most challenging issues of our time. Indeed, if global responses to the negative effects of climate change do not perform as expected over the coming decades, it may become the life-defining issue for generations to come,[1] just as armed conflict has been for generations past. There are many similarities between the anticipated disruption that climate change will cause and the extensive disruption that historical and contemporary armed conflicts have caused to date: competition for access to life-sustaining resources, migration of vulnerable populations to safer parts of the world, shifts in the power-balance at the international level and the knock-on effect that these circumstances and more have for an increasingly connected and globalized world. It is not an exaggeration, therefore, to connect the dots between climate change and armed conflict going forward, and it is certain prudent to study anticipated security risks with an open mind, and with an eye towards developing timely solutions to address contestable issues before they result in situations that cause harm to human life and the environment. Following that, relevant international law will be examined to determine the extent to which international law is equipped for future climate-related conflicts.

Although climate change is often perceived to be a threat multiplier[2]—a circumstance which increases the intensity or likelihood of threats that would have occurred anyway,[3] some scholars have attempted to make a more direct causal link between climate change and armed conflict to argue that some armed conflicts in the future will not happen but for the circumstances created by climate change.[4] This latter perspective is by no means a foregone conclusion, and indeed the scientific research underpinning such predictions has been robustly challenged. Nonetheless, even at this early stage in the development of knowledge pertaining to the link between climate change and future armed conflicts, there are many issues to explore and this chapter will touch on a number of key debates.

Climate change is a term that is used to refer to changes to the Earth's climate that have occurred and that will continue to occur as a result of carbon dioxide and other greenhouse gases that have been emitted since the industrial revolution. Increased levels of greenhouse gases cause a warming effect around the Earth, and the implications of this warming become more serious with every degree Celsius that the Earth's average temperature increases. Over the coming decades, climate change is expected to cause severe changes to weather systems around the world. An increase in natural disasters, from slow-onset disasters such as drought, to sudden-onset disasters brought about by increasingly intense storm systems, are consequences that may also be attributed to climate change. Furthermore, as a result of the increases to global average temperatures, ice is melting at an alarming rate, and this, along with other

---

[1] World Bank 2014.

[2] Saul 2009, p. 6.

[3] SIDA 2018.

[4] The link between climate change and conflict is complex, and it has been argued that climate change will mostly likely indirectly cause conflict. See arguments in Das 2015.

climate-related factors, is causing sea-levels to rise around the world, threatening life in low-lying island states, delta regions and coastal cities.[5]

This chapter will firstly trace the history of the relationship between climate change and armed conflict, examining ancient conflicts that have been linked to unusual climatic conditions and contemporary conflicts with links to environmental conditions that have been attributed to climate change that has occurred over the past 200 years or so. The discussion in the chapter will then proceed to examine a number of ways in which climate change is expected to cause armed conflict. Although there are many causal pathways, three of the most significant are explored. These include the relationship between climate change and resource scarcity, and the consequences for armed conflict to arise over access to these resources; the expected increase in global migration as a result of climate change and the potential for conflict to arise under those circumstances; and the potential for conflict to occur between states as a result of differentiated contributions to the global response to climate change. Finally, relevant future developments will be discussed.

39.2 History of the Relationship Between Climate Change and Conflict

Climate change has been linked to armed conflicts that have occurred throughout history. From pre-historic conflict between Neanderthals and Homo Sapiens driven by climate-related reductions in temperature and associated migratory patterns of early humans,[6] to the fall of the one of the world's first empires, the Akkadian Empire, as a result of a centuries-long period of drought in Mesopotamia approximately 4200 years ago;[7] from the collapse of the Mayan Empire as a result of changing rainfall patterns between 810 and 910 AD,[8] to human-induced climatic changes and their effect on the contemporary armed conflict in Syria[9] and Sudan[10]—there is no shortage of evidence to support claims of a direct correlation between climatic conditions and armed conflict. Indeed a recent study has identified a link between 9% of armed conflicts occurring between 1980 and 2010 and climate-related natural disasters.[11] The more severe and extreme the climatic conditions, the more likely it seems that increases in armed conflict will follow.[12]

---

[5] Intergovernmental Panel on Climate Change 2014.

[6] Some researchers refute the link between climate and conflict in these circumstances. See Staubwasser et al. 2018. Nonetheless the connection is still made. See Lee 2009.

[7] Cullen et al. 2000.

[8] Haug et al. 2003.

[9] Kelley et al. 2015.

[10] United Nations Environment Programme 2007, p. 8.

[11] Schleussner et al. 2016.

[12] Hsiang et al. 2013.

However, for every study that links armed conflict and climate change, there are many that refute the strength of the causal connection being made. For example, it has been asserted that emphasizing the link between climate change and the armed conflict in Syria displaces the responsibility to prevent such conflicts in the first place.[13] At best, it appears as though policy discussions are placing too much emphasis on empirical evidence that is not yet strong enough to provide a conclusive picture,[14] while largely ignoring evidence that paints a contradictory conclusion: that climatic challenges in the future may present opportunities for cooperation rather than conflict.[15] On balance, there are considerable options on the table to offset any potential climate-induced conflict long before armed violence becomes the response of choice for affected groups.[16] Therefore a more nuanced message about the connection between armed conflict and climate change is revealed by the empirical research into this issue, and hasty assumptions about the causal connection should be received with caution.

39.3 Anticipated Climatic Causes of Armed Conflict

There are a number of ways in which climate change is expected to increase instances of conflict, three of which will be discussed in this section. Firstly, research suggests that resource scarcity, such as that which occurs in situations of drought or in the aftermath of more sudden onset natural disasters, has been a causal factor in past conflicts and so resource scarcity that can be attributed to climate change may trigger violence rising to the level of armed conflict within and between communities[17] in the future. Secondly, migration caused by climatic conditions could exacerbate geopolitical tensions or ethnic rivalries, and in so doing precipitate conflict between disparate groups. Thirdly, inter-state disputes may arise over issues such as the unequal contribution of states to the global response to climate change, differentiated access to financial and technical resources which facilitate adaptation to the effects of climate change, or responsibility for irreparable loss and damage that may occur over time.

39.3.1 Resource Scarcity

Climate change is expected to have a negative impact on resource availability over the coming decades, and that, coupled with poor governance of dwindling resources,

---

[13] De Châtel 2014, p. 522.

[14] Theisen et al. 2013; Raleigh and Urdal 2007.

[15] Dinar et al. 2015; Van Jaarsveld Bronkhorst and Whande 2012.

[16] Gilmore et al. 2017; Buhaug et al. 2008

[17] Das 2016, p. 412.

may cause armed conflict.[18] Access to fresh water, food and land may become more restrictive than at present due to anticipated changes to weather patterns, increases to global and regional temperatures and sea-level rise. Indeed, many of the conflicts that are used as examples of the causative link between climate and conflict feature significant resource scarcity issues, frequently as a result of drought. Research suggests that drought may indeed contribute to the causation of armed conflict,[19] and increases in the frequency of climate change-induced drought are predicted over the coming century.[20] However drought has most frequently been identified as a factor in the causation of armed conflict where it affects very poor agriculturally dependent societies.[21] It is not a major trigger of conflict outside of these circumstances, and so general assertions that climate change will conclusively cause drought which will in turn conclusively cause armed conflict are simplistic and sensationalized caricatures of the expected reality.[22]

When there is scarcity in the supply of essential resources, when demand outstrips supply, competition for control of and access to these resources increases. It is this increased competition that is theorized to serve as the ultimate trigger for any subsequent armed conflict that occurs.[23] A contemporary example of resource scarcity that has the potential to ignite conflict can be found by examining the environmental circumstances surrounding Lake Turkana in Northern Kenya.[24] However, the vast majority of research into the link between resource scarcity and the causation of armed conflict suggests that natural resource scarcity is not a major factor in causing armed conflict.[25] In fact, a greater driver of armed conflict is likely to be the abundance of high value natural resources such as gemstones, minerals, oil and gas;[26] resources which climate change is unlikely to affect.

Nonetheless, resource scarcity is not expected to directly cause armed conflict if institutions which are responsible for anticipating issues that may trigger conflict over such resources are developed in a timely manner.[27] Indeed, the absence of functioning institutions or natural resource governance structures seems to be a much more significant factor contributing to conflict.[28] For the majority of imagined scenarios, a strategic approach will need to be developed in relation to different resources in

---

[18] See generally Evans 2011.

[19] Von Uexkull et al. 2016.

[20] Intergovernmental Panel on Climate Change 2014, pp. 51, 53

[21] Von Uexkull et al. 2016; Buhaug and Rudolfsen 2015.

[22] Indeed, the literature on resource scarcity and armed conflict appears to be inconclusive on the point. See Mildner et al. 2011.

[23] Hall and Hall 1998.

[24] Corcoran 2016.

[25] Theisen 2008; Raleigh and Urdal 2007; Benjaminsen et al. 2012; Klomp and Bulte 2013.

[26] Koubi et al. 2014; McNeish 2010.

[27] Fetzek and Mazo 2014.

[28] Bernauer and Siegfried 2012; Adano et al. 2012.

different contexts,[29] so that preventive securitization of these resources does not stimulate armed responses to gain access in the future.

39.3.2 Migration and Geopolitical Tensions

Although every armed conflict is a product of its own context-specific causative factors, a large proportion contain some element of socio-political tension or ethnic division. Some research suggests that these long-standing causes of armed conflict will be exacerbated by the challenging conditions brought about by climate change.[30] In other words, as the negative or adverse consequences of climate change increase over time, significant populations may be compelled to migrate to survive.[31] The term *climate refugee* is often used to describe individuals who will be forced to flee from the negative and dangerous effects of climate change much in the same way that refugees today have fled from persecution.[32] However, the definition of refugees in the 1951 Refugee Convention does not apply to climate induced migration. To be classified as a refugee, an individual must be fleeing from a well-founded fear of persecution.[33] This does not necessarily describe the reason for leaving a climate-affected location to move to a more environmentally hospitable location. Therefore, the term *climate refugee* currently has no legal value, highlighting the degree to which international law is ill-equipped to provide guidance to states if climate-related migration occurs on a large scale in the future.[34]

Changing climatic conditions may render certain parts of the world impossible to live in: for instance, sea-level rise is expected to severely affect low-lying coastal regions. Indeed, some small island states, such as Kiribati, have already planned for territorial loss by purchasing land on neighboring Fiji to accommodate its population in the event that the entire island falls below sea-level as a result of climate change.[35] Not every state will be able to provide for its population in this way, and so climate-induced migration is expected to occur, either as a result of resource scarcities rendering locations uninhabitable or very costly to live in, or as a result of slow- or sudden-onset natural disasters which may occur with more frequency as a result of changing climatic conditions.[36] Conflict may arise along migratory channels or in receiving states as a result of existing socio-political tensions exacerbated by the exceptional circumstances or as a result of major geopolitical changes and shifting

---

[29] Qasem 2010.

[30] Schleussner et al. 2016.

[31] Das 2016, p. 414.

[32] Ahmed 2018; Carrington 2016.

[33] UN General Assembly, Convention Relating to the Status of Refugees, 28 July 1951, United Nations Treaty Series, Vol. 189, p. 137, Article 1.

[34] Saul 2009, p. 11.

[35] Caramel 2014.

[36] Brzoska and Fröhlich 2016.

power dynamics caused by the redistribution of populations on a large scale around the world.[37]

However, research indicates that large scale movements of populations are unlikely to take place as a consequence of climate change to any great extent.[38] The threat of conflict being caused by climate-induced migration and over-population in 'lifeboat regions' is well-contested.[39] Therefore conflict caused by climate-induced migration is by no means a forgone conclusion, and just like contemporary migration issues around Europe, risks of armed conflict taking place, if anticipated, can be mitigated in good time.

39.3.3 Disputes Over Responses to Climate Change

Armed conflict may also occur as a result of the differentiated responses to climate change that are developed and implemented over the coming decades. These conflicts may relate to disproportionate contributions to the solution to climate change, or advantages gained by states failing to contribute sufficiently. Moreover, as technology develops, unilateral solutions to the effects of climate change may be developed, which if left unregulated as they are at present, may cause inter-state armed conflict over the control of such technologies.

There are many ways to quantify the extent to which each state is responsible for contributing to both the problem of and the solution to climate change.[40] Historically high greenhouse gas emitting states—those states whose development has been based on carbon intensive energy pathways from the time of the industrial revolution onwards—are obvious candidates to whom the greatest responsibility could be assigned. However emerging economies, such Brazil, Russia, India, Indonesia, China, and South Africa now feature quite high up on lists of contemporary greenhouse gas emitting states. Though unlikely, it is not unforeseeable that conflict may occur in the future between states on the grounds of a failure to contribute adequately to the global response to climate change when there is a perceived responsibility to do so. If some states perceive others to be in a position of advantage because their reductions to greenhouse gas emissions are disproportionately low, and particularly where the poorly-performing state may have been historically or contemporaneously responsible for a significant proportion of greenhouse gases that have been emitted globally to date, some level of conflict may ensue to either compel the poorly-performing state to mitigate adequately, or, more likely, to remove the advantage

---

[37] Burrows and Kinney 2016.

[38] Raleigh et al. 2008.

[39] Hendrixson and Hartmann 2018.

[40] Saul 2009, pp. 7–8. States, particularly developing states, are often perceived as having contributed least to the problem, and this has been raised in the UN Security Council—see Brown et al. 2007, p. 1143.

that they enjoy by failing to contribute adequately to the global response to climate change.

If technology develops sufficiently over the coming decades, geoengineering may become a strong option that states may wish to use to respond quickly to rising global temperatures that threaten to push the earth into a climatic tipping point, causing runaway irreversible climate change.[41] Geoengineering can be implemented in two main ways: through carbon dioxide removal technologies and through solar radiation management. While carbon dioxide removal is a relatively slow process, mirroring natural systems that remove carbon dioxide and other greenhouse gases from the atmosphere, solar radiation management involves radical steps to block or reflect sunlight away from the earth to induce a rapid cooling effect on global temperatures. If solar radiation management technologies were to be controlled by a single state or grouping of states, that would give them control of the global thermostat. In such a position, states could deploy solar radiation technologies in a way that was favourable to the climate as experienced on their territory, and perhaps disfavourable in another. The side-effects of geoengineering are at present unknown. Inter-state conflict may occur in circumstances where one state through the use of geoengineering causes harm to another state in this way. While a global conflict for control of sunlight is certainly a very remote possibility, it is worth noting nonetheless.

39.4 Relevant International Law

International climate change law and the laws of armed conflict are the two main fields of international law implicated by the connection between climate change and armed conflict. These will be explored in turn, as will the extent to which international criminal law may play a role in either deterring climate-related conflict or atrocities in the future.

39.4.1 International Humanitarian Law

The laws of armed conflict that are relevant to environmental protection during the conduct of hostilities are discussed in greater detail in Chap. 20.[42] Suffice it to say in this present chapter that the laws of armed conflict have not been designed to address the causes of conflict, merely to regulate the use of force by belligerents during the conduct of hostilities in situations of violence that can be defined as armed conflicts. Even at that, the level of protection is very difficult to ascertain with precision. For example, the United Nations Compensation Commission (UNCC)

---

[41] The Royal Society 2009.

[42] See Chap. 20 on Environment and Natural Resources by Smith.

was established in the aftermath of Iraq's occupation of Kuwait,[43] a conflict which resulted in substantial environmental damage and significant volumes of greenhouse gases being emitted into the atmosphere as a result of the attacks on oil wells in the Persian Gulf. However, the environmental damage was not a priority for the UNCC, and it certainly did not discuss the long-term, widespread or severe impacts on the global climate that relevant attacks caused.

However, one treaty in particular may be relevant to climate-induced conflicts in the future, particularly those discussed above which may involve geoengineering by states. The Environmental Modification Convention (ENMOD)[44] prohibits the use of the environment as a weapon during armed conflict. This treaty was developed in direct response to weather-manipulation techniques that were used by the United States in the conflict with Vietnam during the 1970s,[45] and it would certainly prohibit the use of geoengineering technology and climate modification techniques as a weapon in any future armed conflict.[46] In other words, even though states, or even a single state, may have the capacity to block sunlight from entering the Earth's lower atmosphere through sophisticated solar radiation management techniques, they would not be permitted to use these technologies as a strategic part of their methods and means of warfare in any future conflict.

Going forward, unless radical amendments are made to the laws of armed conflict, or unless very clear customary international law emerges, this body of law does not provide the strongest means of regulating or minimizing the environmental and human damage that might occur during climate-related conflicts in the future.

39.4.2 International Climate Change Law

International law developed to specifically respond to climate change is predominantly represented by the 1992 UN Framework Convention on Climate Change (UNFCCC) and its associated treaties, the 1997 Kyoto Protocol and the 2015 Paris Agreement.[47] Yet even though this is the principal legal regime that states have developed to coordinate their collective response to present and future climate-related challenges, it does not anticipate or address the threat of future conflict as a result of climate change in official decisions that have been taken to date. The 1992 UNFCCC has as its main objective 'stabilization of greenhouse gas concentrations in the atmosphere at a level that would prevent dangerous anthropogenic interference with the

---

[43] Discussed further in Chap. 20 on Environment and Natural Resources by Smith.

[44] Discussed further in Chap. 20 on Environment and Natural Resources by Smith.

[45] Discussed further in Chap. 20 on Environment and Natural Resources by Smith.

[46] Convention on the Prohibition of Military or Any Other Hostile Use of Environmental Modification Techniques, 10 December 1976, United Nations Treaty Series, Vol. 1108, p. 151.

[47] Although the 2016 Kigali Amendment to the 1987 Montreal Protocol 1522 United Nations Treaty Series 3; 26 ILM 1550 (1987) has also been viewed as contributing to the solution to climate change.

climate system'.[48] The Kyoto Protocol, intended to compel certain states deemed to be historically responsible for climate change to reduce their greenhouse gas emissions, did not refer to armed conflict.[49] The newest treaty in this system, the Paris Agreement, which compels all states to make a contribution to the solution to global climate change, does not refer to anticipated situations of armed conflict caused by climate change either. Parties to each treaty meet annually at Conferences of the Parties (COPs) to make binding decisions on the best way to achieve each treaty's objectives. However, even though the threat of climate-related armed conflict is often used to motivate states to make ambitious strides forward in developing solutions to climate change at COPs, no decisions have yet been adopted regarding the precipitation of armed conflict as a result of climate change.

Amongst the climate change treaties mentioned above, there is a significant emphasis on climate change mitigation to address the causes of climate change. However, it has been suggested that the greatest threat of future climate-related conflict will come not from a failure to mitigate, but from a failure to sufficiently adapt to the effects of climate change.[50] Adequate adaptation measures are an important factor in minimizing the risk of conflict,[51] as competition for resources or increased migration can be anticipated and planned for through adaptation plans. The Cancun Adaptation Framework was established by states in 2010 at the 16th Conference of the Parties (COP16) and it redressed the balance between adaptation and mitigation making them equal priorities going forward.[52] Under the Cancun Adaptation Framework, states are required to identify country-specific short- medium- and long-term climate change adaptation priorities in National Adaptation Plans[53] (NAPs). Anticipating and planning for issues that may be likely to contribute to the causation of armed conflict should be included in these plans to ensure that states anticipate and reduce the risk of mal-adaptation being a contributory factor to future violence.[54] In this way, the research on the link between climate change and armed conflict could be used not as conclusive proof that such conflicts will occur in the future, but as a means of predicting the kinds of environmental conditions that have been a contributing factor to conflicts in the past so that those conditions and the need to reduce the risk of violence occurring can be factored into National Adaptation Plans as early as possible.

---

[48] Article 2, United Nations Framework Convention on Climate Change, 20 January 1994, A/RES/48/189.

[49] Kyoto Protocol to the United Nations Framework Convention on Climate Change, UN Doc FCCC/CP/1997/7/Add.1, Dec. 10, 1997; 37 ILM 22 (1998).

[50] Das 2016, p. 412.

[51] Das 2016, p. 413.

[52] The Cancun Agreements: Outcome of the work of the Ad Hoc Working Group on Long-term Cooperative Action under the Convention, Decision 1/CP.16, para 13. Discussed also by Das 2016, p. 423. This balance has been subsequently reflected in the treatment of adaptation and mitigation in the Paris Agreement.

[53] The Cancun Agreements: Outcome of the work of the Ad Hoc Working Group on Long-term Cooperative Action under the Convention, Decision 1/CP.16, para 15.

[54] Das 2016, p. 424.

39.4.3 International Criminal Law

International criminal law, a body of law that was initially developed to respond to the devastating consequences of the Second World War, and which now prosecutes those individuals considered to be most responsible for genocide, crimes against humanity, war crimes and aggression, may be relevant to the deterrence of future situations of climate-related armed conflict or violence that can be attributed to climate change. The International Criminal Court was established in 2002 to act as the permanent forum for the prosecution of these four core crimes going forward.[55] Although none of the core crimes make direct reference to the security implications of climate change, they may each be interpreted purposefully in this regard to either deter individuals from committing climate-related genocide, crimes against humanity, war crimes or aggression.

Genocide is considered to be the crime of crimes,[56] and it prohibits the destruction in whole or in part of ethnic racial or religious groups.[57] One of the ways in which both the 1951 Genocide Convention and the 1998 Statute of the International Criminal Court envisage genocide being committed is by creating conditions of life that are calculated to bring about the destruction of the group being targeted.[58] It is not difficult to imagine how conditions of life may be inflicted as a result of climate change that may result in the destruction of national, racial, ethnic or religious groups. Indeed, in the early 1990s, Saddam Hussein's government deliberately drained the Mesopotamian marshlands which were home to the Marsh Arabs, a group who had participated in a failed uprising against the regime. The environmental destruction was viewed by some scholars as tantamount to genocide.[59] However, to prosecute an individual for genocide, they must have had the intention to destroy the particular group. Without this *dolus specialis*,[60] even if significant climate-related damage results in the destruction of a group, the crime of genocide will not have been committed.

Crimes against humanity have evolved significantly since they were first included in codified form in the statute of the International Criminal Tribunal for the former Yugoslavia in 1993. Now the International Criminal Court will prosecute individuals for committing crimes against humanity where there is evidence of widespread or systematic attacks against the civilian population and where those attacks result in

---

[55] Rome Statute of the International Criminal Court (last amended 2010), 17 July 1998, A/CONF.183/9.

[56] See Chap. 22 on Transnational and International Criminal Law by Sayapin.

[57] Article II, Convention on the Prevention and Punishment of the Crime of Genocide, 9 December 1948, United Nations, Treaty Series, vol. 78, p. 277; Article 6, Rome Statute of the International Criminal Court (last amended 2010), 17 July 1998, A/CONF.183/9.

[58] Article II(c), Convention on the Prevention and Punishment of the Crime of Genocide, 9 December 1948, United Nations, Treaty Series, vol. 78, p. 277; Article 6(c), Rome Statute of the International Criminal Court (last amended 2010), 17 July 1998, A/CONF.183/9.

[59] See arguments in Schwabach 2004, pp. 7–8.

[60] For further information see Ambos 2009.

the commission of certain enumerated crimes.[61] Relevant to the effects of climate change are the crimes against humanity of murder,[62] extermination,[63] deportation or forcible transfer of the population,[64] torture,[65] persecution,[66] or other inhumane acts.[67] While each of these crimes may be argued to have a climate-related dimension,[68] the limitations inherent in using crimes against humanity to either prevent climate-related atrocities or hold those most responsible for causing them accountable, is the requirement to demonstrate that the climate-related harm was caused in situations that amount to an 'attack'.[69] If 'attack' is interpreted to mean a course of mistreatment, as the International Criminal Tribunal for the former Yugoslavia have done,[70] then perhaps climate-related damage may be used to substantiate a prosecution for crimes against humanity, or at best to deter individuals from embarking on actions that would result in a course of climate-related mistreatment being inflicted on the civilian population in a widespread or systematic manner.

War crimes in international criminal law are derived from the laws of armed conflict that apply during international and non-international armed conflict. As discussed above, the laws of armed conflict do not protect the environment well. Under the jurisdiction of the International Criminal Court, individuals responsible for causing long-term, widespread, and severe damage to the environment during

---

[61] Article 7, Rome Statute of the International Criminal Court (last amended 2010), 17 July 1998, A/CONF.183/9.

[62] Article 7(1)(a), Rome Statute of the International Criminal Court (last amended 2010), 17 July 1998, A/CONF.183/9.

[63] Article 7(1)(b), Rome Statute of the International Criminal Court (last amended 2010), 17 July 1998, A/CONF.183/9.

[64] Article 7(1)(d), Rome Statute of the International Criminal Court (last amended 2010), 17 July 1998, A/CONF.183/9.

[65] Article 7(1)(f), Rome Statute of the International Criminal Court (last amended 2010), 17 July 1998, A/CONF.183/9.

[66] Article 7(1)(h), Rome Statute of the International Criminal Court (last amended 2010), 17 July 1998, A/CONF.183/9.

[67] Article 7(1)(k), Rome Statute of the International Criminal Court (last amended 2010), 17 July 1998, A/CONF.183/9.

[68] Most analyses of environmental crimes against humanity examine environmental situations more broadly, rather than climate change in particular. See Smith 2013 as an example.

[69] There is a difference between the concept of "attack" in crimes against humanity and "attack" in the laws of armed conflict. As a crime against humanity, an attack can be a course of mistreatment against civilian population. See Prosecutor v Dragoljub Kunarac, Radomir Kovac, and Zoran Vukovic, Appeal Judgment, 12 June 2002, para 86; Prosecutor v Fatimir Limaj, Haradin Bala, Isak Musliu, Trial Judgment, 30 November 2005, para 194.

[70] See Prosecutor v Dragoljub Kunarac, Radomir Kovac, and Zoran Vukovic, Appeal Judgment, 12 June 2002, para 86; Prosecutor v Fatimir Limaj, Haradin Bala, Isak Musliu, Trial Judgment, 30 November 2005, para 194.

international armed conflict[71] may be prosecuted for war crimes. The global environment in general, as well as more specific locations around the world, are anticipated to experience the effects of climate change more acutely and could be severely compromised as a result. Environmental damage caused during armed conflict in the future may more easily cross the required threshold harm in the future.

The crime of aggression was prosecuted at the International Military Tribunal at Nuremberg as crimes against peace, and it is generally understood to be underpinned in the present day by the international law on the use of force as represented by Article 2(4) of the Charter of the United Nations. There was initially no agreement about its inclusion in the Statute of the International Criminal Court in 1998, but subsequent negotiations[72] have included it in the Statute as Article 8 *bis* and the provision came into force on 17 July 2018. The crime of aggression is closely linked to the use of armed force by one state against another which results in a violation of the UN Charter.[73] The concept of 'armed force', if interpreted narrowly, precludes any application of the crime of aggression to climate-related environmental consequences. However, an expansive understanding of 'armed force' may indeed bring acts of environmental harm into the jurisdiction of the crime.[74]

39.5 Future Developments

Looking ahead, there are a number of future developments which may affect the legal regulation of climate-related conflicts, two of which will be mentioned here. Firstly, the International Law Commission has been exploring the issue of environmental protection in armed conflict since it was included in their current programme of work in 2013.[75] Although climate change as a cause of armed conflict has not featured significantly in their discussions of the issue to date, which they have considered from the pre-conflict,[76] *in bello*,[77] and post-conflict[78] perspectives, as well as in situations of occupation,[79] any guidelines or principles that are developed to enhance environmental protection in armed conflict should in some way prevent more damage than

---

[71] Article 8(2)(b)(iv), Rome Statute of the International Criminal Court (last amended 2010), 17 July 1998, A/CONF.183/9.

[72] Clark 2010, pp. 692–706; See also Kreß and Von Holtzendorff 2010.

[73] See Article 8 *bis*, Rome Statute of the International Criminal Court (last amended 2010), 17 July 1998, A/CONF.183/9.

[74] Although literature linking the crime of aggression to climate change is not yet that extensive useful analysis can be gleaned from the literature examining the notion of armed attacks in relation to the emerging threat of cyber warfare. See arguments in, for example, Ophardt 2010.

[75] International Law Commission, 'Protection of the Environment in Relation to Armed Conflict', http://legal.un.org/ilc/guide/8_7.shtml, accessed 30 August 2018.

[76] International Law Commission 2014.

[77] International Law Commission 2015.

[78] International Law Commission 2016.

[79] International Law Commission 2018.

is strictly necessary in future armed conflicts that take place in climate-compromised environments.[80]

Secondly, from an international criminal law perspective, although no prosecutions for environmental damage have yet taken place at contemporary international criminal courts and tribunals, that may be about to change. In 2016, the Office of the Prosecutor at the International Criminal Court issued a Policy Paper on Case Selection and Prioritisation, in which it was stated that attention will be given to prosecuting crimes perpetrated through environmental destruction in the future.[81] While this does not change the legal parameters of the crimes that fall within the jurisdiction of the International Criminal Court, it does mean that prosecutions in the future will deal with such crimes being committed through environmental damage, and climate-related environmental damage may feature over time.

39.6 Conclusion

In conclusion, the relationship between armed conflict and climate change is extremely complicated, and the scholarship supporting causal links between the two are consistently and convincingly challenged.[82] Although research has demonstrated that there may have been climatic causes to conflict from prehistoric times to the present, the causal link that this research makes between climatic factors and the creation of armed conflict is not irrefutable. When the relationship between climate change and armed conflict is broken down into specific causal pathways—for example through resource scarcity, increased migration, or inter-state disputes over unequal contributions to climate change solutions—it is clear that any perceived link between conflict and climate change is temporally remote, and highly preventable if anticipated issues are identified and addressed in good time. Indeed, some research suggests that preemptively viewing climate change as a security issue likely to trigger armed conflicts may be a 'self-fulfilling prophecy':[83] militarized responses governing scarce natural resources or migration issues may amplify tensions more than the environmental issues at the root of such problems.[84] However, just because the scientific research cannot conclusively establish a causal link between climate and conflict in the future does not mean that this will not happen.[85] As Das asserts

> The adverse consequences of climate change will not cause conflict in all situations, nor will it be the sole cause of armed conflict. It is the adverse impacts of climate change coalescing

---

[80] Guidance is being developed which relates to the prevention of environment-based conflicts. See for example United Nations Interagency Framework Team for Preventive Action 2012.

[81] Office of the Prosecutor at the International Criminal Court 2016, paras 7, 40, 41.

[82] Buhaug et al. 2014, p. 396: 'research to date has failed to converge on a specific and direct association between climate and violent conflict.'

[83] Gleditsch 2012, p. 3.

[84] Gleditsch 2012, p. 7.

[85] Smith and Vivekananda 2012, p. 78.

with existing divisions within society—whether political, economic, or social in nature—that could lead to or exacerbate violent conflict.[86]

The UN Security Council may have a leadership role to play in this regard in the future,[87] but other international processes can play a bigger part in mindfully mitigating against climate-related conflict. These processes include establishing appropriate adaptation responses and institution-building initiatives under the UNFCCC and Paris Agreement. Moreover, the global focus on achieving the 2015 Sustainable Development Goals, with their emphasis on climate change and peace and security, may also play a role in offsetting some of the factors that may contribute to conditions likely to foster climate-related conflict in the future. Indeed, even the concept of Responsibility to Protect may have a new role to play in compelling states to adhere to their international obligations to avoid mass atrocities caused as a result of climate change.[88] While climate change is not guaranteed to create additional conflict in the future, there is certainly enough evidence on the table to suggest that this issue needs to be taken seriously by the international community as a matter of priority. It is becoming more and more a possibility that wars will not just be fought on the earth, or for the earth, but for survival. The vast majority of climate-related conflicts that are predicted to occur in the future are eminently avoidable, and steps should be taken as a matter of priority in all related fields of international law to ensure that such conflicts are not allowed to erupt as a result of inaction.

References

Adano WR, Dietz T, Witsenburg K, Zaal F (2012) Climate Change, Violent Conflict and Local Institutions in Kenya's Drylands. 49(1) Journal of Peace Research 65–80

Ahmed B (2018) Who takes responsibility for the climate refugees? 10(1) International Journal of Climate Change Strategies and Management, 5–26

Ambos K (2009) What Does 'Intent to Destroy' Mean? 91(876) International Review of the Red Cross, 835–858

Benjaminsen T, Alinon K, Buhaug H, Buseth J, Gleditsch N (2012) Does climate change drive land-use conflicts in the Sahel? 49(1) Journal of Peace Research, 97–111

Bernauer T, Siegfried T (2012) Climate Change and International Water Conflict in Central Asia. 49(1) Journal of Peace Research 227–239

Brown O, Hammill A, McLeman R (2007) Climate Change as the "New" Security Threat: Implications for Africa. 83(6) International Affairs 1141–1154

Brzoska M, Fröhlich C (2016) Climate change, migration and violent conflict: vulnerabilities, pathways and adaptation strategies. 5(2) Migration and Development, 190–210

Buhaug H, Rudolfsen I (2015) A Climate of Conflicts? Conflict Trends 05, Peace Research Institute Oslo

Buhaug H, Gleditch NP, Theisen OM (2008) Implications of Climate Change for Armed Conflict. Paper presented at World Bank Workshop on Social Dimensions of Climate Change,

---

[86] Das 2016, p. 415.

[87] Motzfeldt Kravik 2018.

[88] See Chap. 7 on The UN Security Council: From Preserving State Sovereignty to Protecting Humanity by Deplano.

The World Bank, Washington DC, 5-6 March 2008, http://siteresources.worldbank.org/INT RANETSOCIALDEVELOPMENT/Resources/SDCCWorkingPaper_Conflict.pdf, accessed 24 September 2018

Buhaug H, Nordkvelle J, Bernauer T, Böhmelt T, Brzoska M, Busby JW, Ciccone A, Fjelde H, Gartzke E, Gleditsch NP, Goldstone JA, Hegre H, Holtermann H, Koubi V, Link JSA, Link PM, Lujala P, O'Loughlin J, Raleigh C, Scheffran J, Schilling J, Smith TG, Theisen OM, Tol RSJ, Urdal H, von Uexkull N (2014) One Effect to Rule Them All? A Comment on Climate and Conflict. 127 Climate Change 391–397

Burrows K, Kinney PL (2016) Exploring the Climate Change, Migration and Conflict Nexus. 13(4) International Journal of Environmental Research and Public Health, 443

Caramel L (2014) Besieged by the rising tides of climate change, Kiribati buys land in Fiji. The Guardian 1 July 2014, https://www.theguardian.com/environment/2014/jul/01/kiribati-climate-change-fiji-vanua-levu, accessed 24 September 2018

Carrington D (2016) Climate change will stir 'unimaginable' refugee crisis, says military. The Guardian, 1 December 2016, https://www.theguardian.com/environment/2016/dec/01/climate-change-trigger-unimaginable-refugee-crisis-senior-military, accessed 24 September 2018

Clark RS (2010) Amendments to the Rome Statute of the International Criminal Court Considered at the first review Conference on the Court, Kampala, 31 May-11 June 2010. 2(2) Goettingen Journal of International Law, 689–711

Corcoran B (2016) In Kenya, scarcity and drought are driving two tribes to go to war. The Irish Times, 30 July 2016

Cullen HM, deMenocal PB, Hemming S, Hemming G, Brown FH, Guilderson T, Sirocko F (2000) Climate change and the collapse of the Akkadian empire: Evidence from the deep sea. 28(4) Geology, 379–382

Das O (2015) Climate Change, the Environment and Armed Conflict. Bristol Law School Centre for Legal Research Working Paper No. 6, March 2015 http://www2.uwe.ac.uk/faculties/BBS/BUS/law/Law%20docs/climate-change-environment-armed-conflict.pdf, accessed 26 September 2018

Das O (2016) Climate change and armed conflict: Challenges and opportunities for maintaining international peace and security through climate justice. In: Abate RS (ed) Climate Justice: Case Studies in Global and Regional Governance Challenges. Environmental Law Institute, Washington, D.C.

De Châtel F (2014) The Role of Drought and Climate Change in the Syrian Uprising: Untangling the Triggers of the Revolution. 4 Middle Eastern Studies 521–535

Dinar S, Katz D, De Stefano L, Blankespoor B (2015) Climate change, conflict, and cooperation: Global analysis of the effectiveness of international river treaties in addressing water variability. 45 Political Geography, 55–66

Evans A (2011) Resource Scarcity, Climate Change and the Risk of Violent Conflict. World Development Report 2011 Background Paper, World Bank, http://siteresources.worldbank.org/EXTWDR 2011/Resources/6406082-1283882418764/WDR_Background_Paper_Evans.pdf, accessed 26 September 2018

Fetzek S, Mazo J (2014) Climate, Scarcity and Conflict. 56(5) Global Politics and Strategy 143–170

Gilmore E, Hegre H, Petrova K, Moyer J, Bowlsby D (2017) Projecting Conflict and Cooperation under Climate Change Scenarios: White Paper for Discussion Developed for IMPACTS World 2017 https://www.impactsworld2017.org/documents/298/IW2017_white_paper_C6.pdf, accessed 24 September 2018

Gleditsch NP (2012) Whither the Weather? Climate Change and Conflict. 49(1) Journal of Peace Research 3–9

Hall JV, Hall DC (1998) Environmental Resource Scarcity and Conflict. In: Wolfson M (ed) The Political Economy of War and Peace. Vol. 64 Recent Economic Thought Series. Springer, Boston, MA

Haug GH, Günther D, Peterson LC, Sigman DM, Hughen KA, Aeschlimann B (2003) Climate and the Collapse of Maya Civilization. 299(5613) Science, 1731–1735

Hendrixson A, Hartmann B (2018) Threats and burdens: Challenging scarcity-driven narratives of "overpopulation". Geoforum, https://doi.org/10.1016/j.geoforum.2018.08.009

Hsiang SM, Burke M, Miguel E (2013) Quantifying the Influence of Climate on Human Conflict. 341(6151) Science, doi: https://doi.org/10.1126/science.1235367

Intergovernmental Panel on Climate Change (IPCC) (2014) Climate Change 2014: Synthesis Report: Contribution of Working Groups I, II and III to the Fifth Assessment Report of the Intergovernmental Panel on Climate Change (Pachauri RK, Meyer LA (eds). IPCC, Geneva, Switzerland

International Law Commission (2014) Preliminary Report on the Protection of the Environment in relation to Armed Conflicts, A/CN.4/674 http://legal.un.org/docs/?symbol=A/CN.4/674, accessed 26 September 2018

International Law Commission (2015) Second Report on the Protection of the Environment in Relation to Armed Conflicts, Sixty-Seventh Session, A/CN.4/685, http://legal.un.org/docs/?symbol=A/CN.4/685, accessed 26 September 2018

International Law Commission (2016) Third Report on the Protection of the Environment in Relation to Armed Conflicts, Sixty-Eighth Session A/CN.4/700, http://legal.un.org/docs/?symbol=A/CN.4/700, accessed 26 September 2018

International Law Commission (2018) First report on protection of the environment in relation to armed conflicts by Marja Lehto, Special Rapporteur A/CN.4/720 http://legal.un.org/docs/?symbol=A/CN.4/720, accessed 26 August 2018

Kelley CP, Mohtadi S, Cane MA, Seager R, Kushnir Y (2015) Climate Change in the Fertile Crescent and Implications of the Recent Syrian Drought. 112(11) Proceedings of the National Academy of Sciences of the United States of America, 3241–3246

Klomp J, Bulte E (2013) Climate change, weather shocks, and violent conflict: a critical look at the evidence. 44(1) Agricultural Economics 63–78

Koubi V, Spilker G, Böhmelt T, Bernauer T, Buhaug H, Levy J (2014). Do natural resources matter for interstate and intrastate armed conflict? 51(2) Journal of Peace Research, 227–243

Kreß C, Von Holtzendorff L (2010) The Kampala Compromise on the Crime of Aggression. 8(5) Journal of International Criminal Justice 1179–1217

Lee JR (2009) A brief history of climate change and conflict. Bulletin of the Atomic Scientists https://thebulletin.org/2009/08/a-brief-history-of-climate-change-and-conflict/, accessed 24 September 2018

McNeish JA (2010) Rethinking Resource Conflict. World Development Report 2011 Background Paper http://web.worldbank.org/archive/website01306/web/pdf/wdr%20background%20paper%20-%20mcneish_0.pdf, accessed 24 September 2018

Mildner SA, Lauster G, Wodni W (2011) Scarcity and Abundance Revisited: A Literature Review on Natural Resources and Conflict. 5(1) International Journal of Conflict and Violence, 155–172

Motzfeldt Kravik A (2018) The Security Council and Climate Change – Too Hot to Handle? EJIL: Talk! 26 April 2018 https://www.ejiltalk.org/the-security-council-and-climate-change-too-hot-to-handle/, accessed 26 September 2018

Office of the Prosecutor at the International Criminal Court (2016) Policy Paper on Case Selection and Prioritisation, 15 September 2016, https://www.icc-cpi.int/itemsDocuments/20160915_OTP-Policy_Case-Selection_Eng.pdf, accessed 26 September 2018

Ophardt JA (2010) Cyber Warfare and the Crime of Aggression: The Need for Individual Accountability on Tomorrow's Battlefield. 9 Duke Law & Technology Review, 1–28

Qasem I (2010) Resource Scarcity in the 21st Century: Conflict or Cooperation? The Hague Centre for Strategic Studies and TNO Strategy and Change Paper No. 3 https://hcss.nl/sites/default/files/files/reports/Strategy_Change_PAPER_03_web.pdf

Raleigh C, Urdal H (2007) Climate change, environmental degradation and armed conflict. 26(6) Political Geography, 674–694

Raleigh C, Jordan L, Salehyan I (2008) Assessing the Impact of Climate Change on Migration and Conflict. Working Paper prepared for the World Bank Workshop on Social Dimensions of

Climate Change http://siteresources.worldbank.org/EXTSOCIALDEVELOPMENT/Resources/SDCCWorkingPaper_MigrationandConflict.pdf, accessed 24 September 2018

Saul B (2009) Climate Change, Conflict, and Security: International Law Challenges. University of Sydney Law School Legal Studies Research Paper No. 09/107, October 2009, http://ssrn.com/abstract=1485175, accessed 26 September 2018

Schleussner C, Donges JF, Donner RV, Schellnhuber HJ (2016) Armed-conflict risks enhanced by climate-related disasters in ethnically fractionalized countries. 113(33) Proceedings of the National Academy of Sciences of the United States of America 9216–9221

Schwabach A (2004) Ecocide and Genocide in Iraq: International Law, the Marsh Arabs, and Environmental Damage in Non-International Conflicts. 15 Columbia Journal of International Environmental Law and Policy, 1

SIDA (2018) The Relationship Between Climate Change and Violent Conflict. Working Paper, https://www.sida.se/contentassets/c571800e01e448ac9dce2d097ba125a1/working-paper---climate-change-and-conflict.pdf, accessed 25 September 2018

Smith T (2013) Creating a Framework for the Prosecution of Environmental Crimes. In: Schabas W, McDermott Y, Hayes N (eds) The Ashgate Companion to International Criminal Law: Critical Perspectives. Ashgate Publishing, 45–62

Smith D, Vivekananda J (2012) Climate Change, Conflict and Fragility: Getting the Institutions Right. In: Scheffran J et al. (eds) Climate Change, Human Security and Violent Conflict: Challenges for Societal Stability. Springer, 77–90

Staubwasser M, Drăgușin V, Onac BP, Assonov S, Ersek V, Hoffmann DL, Veres D (2018) Impact of climate change on the transition of Neanderthals to modern humans in Europe. 115(37) Proceedings of the National Academy of Sciences of the United States of America, 9116–9121

The Royal Society (2009) Geoengineering the Climate: Science, Governance and Uncertainty. https://royalsociety.org/~/media/Royal_Society_Content/policy/publications/2009/8693.pdf, accessed 24 September 2018

Theisen OM (2008) Blood and Soil? Resource Scarcity and Internal Armed Conflict Revisited. 45(6) Journal of Peace Research, 801–818

Thiesen OM, Gleditsch NP, Buhaug H (2013) Is climate change a driver of armed conflict? 117(3) Climatic Change 613–625

United Nations Environment Programme (2007) Sudan: Post-Conflict Environment Assessment. UNEP, Nairobi

United Nations Interagency Framework Team for Preventive Action, (2012) Toolkit and Guidance for Preventing and Managing Land and natural Resources Conflict: Renewable Resources and Conflict, http://www.un.org/en/events/environmentconflictday/pdf/GN_Renewable_Consultation.pdf, accessed 25 September 2018

Van Jaarsveld Bronkhorst S, Whande W (2012) Climate Change Adaptation, Conflict and Cooperation: A Diplomatic Approach for Africa? 10 April 2012, http://www.accord.org.za/publication/climate-change-adaptation-conflict-cooperation/, accessed 24 September 2018

Von Uexkull N, Croicu M, Fjelde H, Buhaug H (2016) Civil conflict sensitivity to growing-season drought. 113(44) Proceedings of the National Academy of Sciences of the United States of America 12391–12396

World Bank (2014) Turn Down the Heat: Confronting the New Climate Normal, http://documents.worldbank.org/curated/en/317301468242098870/pdf/927040v20WP00O0ull0Report000English.pdf, accessed 26 September 2018

Dr. Tara Smith is a Senior Lecturer in International Law and Human Rights at Bangor University, North Wales. She graduated with her Ph.D. from the National University of Ireland Galway in 2013 with her thesis titled 'The Prohibition of Environmental Damage during the Conduct of Hostilities in Non-International Armed Conflict' which she completed as a Doctoral Fellow at the Irish Centre for Human Rights. Prior to this, Dr. Smith graduated from University College Dublin in 2006 with a Bachelor of Civil Law, and the National University of Ireland Galway in 2007 with an LL.M in International Human Rights Law. Dr. Smith has also qualified as an Attorney-at-Law in New York. Dr. Smith's research explores contemporary challenges in international law and policy connecting climate change, armed conflict and environmental human rights.

Chapter 40
Poaching and Wildlife Trafficking as Threats to International Peace and Security

Federico Dalpane and Maria Baideldinova

Contents

40.1 Poaching and Wildlife Crime	862
40.2 Legal Framework	863
40.3 Poaching-Terror Link	865
40.4 Poaching and Regional Conflict	868
40.5 The Militarization of Conservation	872
40.6 A New Ecocentric Approach in International Law?	876
40.7 Conclusion	880
References	880

Abstract In recent years, wildlife crime has ceased being the exclusive concern of conservation specialists, and has entered the radar field of international policy and security circles. A controversy has arisen about the alleged role of elephant poaching and ivory trafficking in the funding of terrorism and regional conflicts. It has been suggested that ivory might play the same role of diamonds and other natural resources in fueling conflicts. War-like anti-poaching policies have been promoted as a way to deny terrorists and rebels the funds to continue their activities. A substantial critical literature seems to have debunked these claims, but the trend toward the militarization of conservation interventions becomes nonetheless more and more established. On the other hand, a positive development might be that poaching and wildlife trafficking started featuring in resolutions of the UN Security Council adopted under Chapter VII of the UN Charter. Further, in 2015 the UN General Assembly adopted a resolution on wildlife trafficking for the first time ever. We might be witnessing the early phases of an evolution of international law that could overcome the limitations of the current legal framework for combating wildlife crime.

Keywords Poaching · Wildlife trafficking · Wildlife crime · Ivory · Conservation · Africa · Terrorism · Green militarization

F. Dalpane (✉) · M. Baideldinova
School of Law, KIMEP University, Almaty, Kazakhstan
e-mail: dalpane@kimep.kz

M. Baideldinova
e-mail: maria@kimep.kz

40.1 Poaching and Wildlife Crime

The dead body of a rhinoceros, complete except for a bleeding wound where the horn used to be. Michael the gorilla, who was taught American Sign Language, "telling" humans a horrifying story about him as a helpless cub, witnessing his parents being caught and butchered by humans. An African baby-elephant remaining for days with his dead mother, trying to wake her up, after she was poisoned by poachers... These are the images that come to our mind when we think of poaching. But illegal hunting with its cruelty toward animals, and its dramatic impact on the environment and on development, turns out to be a source of an even bigger evil. Due to a rapidly growing demand, the traffic in live animals and their body parts has become a major source of income for transnational criminal networks. Enabled by state failure or state weakness and by widespread corruption, wildlife traffic has been recognized as a threat to regional stability, security, and human rights. Rebel or terrorist groups are suspected of financing themselves through wildlife trafficking, too; meanwhile, military operations aimed at fighting wildlife crime have introduced their own challenges, leading to frequent complaints of "militarization" of wildlife conservation.

In recent years there has been an increasing awareness of the interrelation between environmental issues and security (broadly defined). This chapter discusses some implications of poaching and wildlife trafficking for human security and international law. Further, it examines a recent development in international security law, which according to some commentators might prefigure a trend in the development of international law away from the traditional "anthropocentric" approach toward a new "ecocentric" approach.

The global illegal wildlife trade is generally estimated to be worth around 7–23 billion US dollars annually.[1] It includes poaching, trafficking in live animals or in dead specimens, and the sale of illegal products made from wildlife. It is a deadly global industry run by a variety of local and transnational criminal organizations, enabled by corrupt state officials, that connects problematic areas of the world with a growing demand in East Asia and in North America. There is big money to be made in wildlife crime on both ends of the trade: rhino horns, for example, are sold in Asia at $65,000 US dollars per kilogram, more than the price of gold and cocaine; African poachers are paid between $1000 and $9000 US dollars per kilogram, depending on their position within the poaching team.[2]

At the current rate of destruction, the African elephant could become extinct in one or two decades.[3] Even those who are less inclined to sentimentalism toward animals might agree that this outcome is highly undesirable. Countless animal and vegetal species, indeed, have already met with this fate through human activity, with many other species to follow soon.

---

[1] Nellemann 2016, p. 17.

[2] Lunstrum 2014, p. 821.

[3] France-Presse 2015; WWF-Belgique 2019.

The losses for the economies of the source states, too, are huge. When considering all forms of environmental crime including wildlife trafficking, losses of government revenues through lost tax income alone are estimated at 9–26 billion US dollars annually.[4] Of course, this estimate does not take into account the greater damage to ecosystems, economies, and societies. In many countries, wildlife crime is a major vehicle of criminal infiltration in state institutions. Wildlife crime undermines the rule of law, promotes corruption, impoverishes governments and local communities, and enriches transnational criminal networks. It is no wonder that even circles that were not traditionally involved in conservation, are increasingly focusing on environmental and wildlife crime. The following section outlines the relevant international legal framework.

40.2 Legal Framework

The international legal framework for combating poaching is inadequate, maybe pointing to a difficulty of the international community in acknowledging the gravity of wildlife crime. No treaty provides a definition of poaching or wildlife crime, and there is still no global legal instrument specifically against poaching and other wildlife crimes. Several international conventions are concerned with the conservation of wildlife,[5] but the main international legal instrument in the fight against illegal wildlife trade is still the CITES, the Convention on International Trade in Endangered Species of Wild Fauna and Flora, also known as the Washington Convention. The CITES is a multilateral treaty that regulates trade in endangered plants and animals, and animal specimens. It entered into force in 1975 and has 183 parties (mostly states and, since a 2013 amendment, also regional economic blocs like the European Union, which acceded in 2015[6]). A regional convention, known as the Lusaka Agreement, entered into force in 1996 to support the implementation of the CITES in Africa.[7] The CITES binds the parties to adopt domestic legislation to implement the convention at the national level, whether the parties are source, transit, or destination states.

---

[4] Nellemann 2016, p. 17.

[5] For example the Convention on Wetlands of International Importance Especially as Waterfowl Habitat, Feb. 2, 1971, 11 I.L.M. 963; the UNESCO Convention Concerning the Protection of the World Cultural and Natural Heritage, Nov. 16, 1972, 11 I.L.M. 1358; the Convention on the Conservation of Migratory Species of Wild Animals, June 23, 1979, 10 I.L.M. 15; the Convention on Biological Diversity (CBD), June 5, 1992, 1760 U.N.T.S. 79.

[6] The CITES is implemented in the European Union through a set of Regulations known as the EU Wildlife Trade Regulations. The most important are the Council Regulation (EC) No 338/97 on the protection of species of wild fauna and flora by regulating trade therein (known as the Basic Regulation), and the Commission Regulation (EC) No 865/2006 of 4 May 2006 laying down detailed rules concerning the implementation of Council Regulation (EC) No 338/97 on the protection of species of wild fauna and flora by regulating trade therein (known as the Implementing Regulation), and subsequent amendments.

[7] Lusaka Agreement on Co-operative Enforcement Operations Directed at Illegal Trade in Wild Fauna and Flora, https://lusakaagreement.org, accessed 25 February 2020.

More than 5000 species of animals and about 30,000 species of plants are protected by CITES. The trade of the species threatened with extinction, listed in Appendix I, is prohibited or allowed only exceptionally (if the national authority certify that the trade of animals or specimens does not endanger the survival of the species). The trade of other species, which are only potentially threatened with extinction, listed in Appendix II, is also subject to strict regulation. The Conference of the Parties meets every three years to discuss and adopt amendments. The latest meeting was held in Geneva, Switzerland, in August 2019.

Together with the CITES Secretariat, in 2010 four other organizations joined their efforts against wildlife crime in the International Consortium on Combating Wildlife Crime (ICCWC): INTERPOL, the United Nations Office on Drugs and Crime, the World Bank, and the World Customs Organization.[8]

Among the latest achievements of the ICCWC, in June 2019 INTERPOL and the World Customs Organization (WCO) coordinated Operation Thunderball, with operations against wildlife and timber crime across 109 countries that led to the arrest of almost 600 suspects and to the seizure of many thousands of live animals, wildlife parts, plants, and timber.[9]

Another recent operation against wildlife trafficking is Operation Blizzard (12 April–22 May 2019), a global operation jointly coordinated by INTERPOL and Europol against the illegal trade in reptiles, which resulted in about 4400 live animals seized and the identification of more than 180 suspects.[10]

In spite of the CITES's successes and its central role in the international legal framework of the fight against wildlife crime, the CITES is often criticized for a few shortcomings. First of all, as mentioned above, by design the CITES only regulates international trade: therefore, it does not regulate internal trade, and does not directly address wildlife crime. Furthermore, the CITES is not self-executing, and needs the states to adopt the necessary measures in their domestic legislations. Not all parties have done so yet; those who did, may have followed different approaches, with (logically) different outcomes: "Trade in a particular species can thus be legal in one country and illegal under CITES; or, conversely, it can be prohibited under national legislation and permitted under CITES".[11]

The design of the CITES, relying on national authorities to enforce the trade bans, or to exceptionally authorize the trade even of endangered species, is a liability especially in case of situations of political instability or even civil conflict. Unfortunately, this is a common occurrence in the source areas of several endangered species. Also, by design the CITES protects species, not habitats or ecosystems, which is arguably a more effective approach if the focus switches from trade to conservation. Others

---

[8] Official website: https://cites.org/eng/prog/iccwc.php, last accessed 12 November 2019.

[9] INTERPOL-WCO Joint Press Release Wildlife trafficking: organized crime hit hard by joint INTERPOL-WCO global enforcement operation, https://cites.org/eng/news/wildlife-trafficking-organized-crime-hit-hard-by-joint-interpol-wco-global-enforcement-operation_10072019, last accessed 8 January 2020.

[10] INTERPOL, https://www.interpol.int/en/News-and-Events/News/2019/Illicit-trade-in-reptiles-hundreds-of-seizures-and-arrests-in-global-operation, last accessed 8 January 2020.

[11] Haenlein and Smith 2016, Introduction.

have criticized the CITES as fundamentally flawed and ineffective for being a manifestation of cultural imperialism, a unilateral vehicle of Western values and attitudes to nature and wildlife conservation, which are often not shared by other cultures, and which should not be unreflectingly granted preference.[12]

Regardless of these limitations and criticisms, however, the CITES is playing an important role in the global fight against wildlife crime and has positively influenced even a few recent Resolutions of the General Assembly of the United Nations, which will be discussed in the last section of this chapter.

40.3 Poaching-Terror Link

Around 2012, the fight against poaching and wildlife crime, until then the preserve of conservation specialists, attracted the attention of the international security community.

In that period, a marked change in the approach to poaching and wildlife crime happened in U.S. government circles. Goodrich describes how the US Government embraced the link between security and wildlife trafficking between 2012 and 2015.[13] In 2012, then-Secretary of State Hillary Clinton requested the U.S. intelligence community to produce a report on the impact of large-scale wildlife trafficking on U.S. security interests.[14]

Simultaneously, the U.S. Department of State adopted a strategy to curb illegal wildlife trade, and on 1 July 2013 President Barack Obama issued Executive Order 13648 for Combating Wildlife Trafficking. This E.O. defined the fight against wildlife crime as a national priority and directed the administration to draft a National Strategy for Combating Wildlife Trafficking.

The National Strategy was released in February 2014.[15] This was going to have important consequences for the fight against wildlife crime and indeed for the public's perception of it. Poaching and illegal ivory trade were presented as sources of funding for certain terror organizations and rebel formations in Africa, and the consequence

---

[12] Jung 2017. For examples of the ongoing controversy about the CITES, see Conrad 2012; Bowman 2013. Nowak 2016 points out that the CITES essentially depends on implementation and cooperation at the state level, and that is where its main weaknesses lie. For recommendations on the furthering of wild animal welfare in international law, see Harrop 2013; White 2013.

[13] Goodrich 2015.

[14] The unclassified summary is available at U.S. National Intelligence Council Wildlife Poaching Threatens Economic, Security Priorities in Africa, 6 September 2013, http://www.dni.gov/files/doc uments/Wildlife_Poaching_White_Paper_2013.pdf, last accessed 10 January 2020. Ms. Clinton and former Ohio Governor John Kasich recently made a bi-partisan call for intensifying the fight against poaching and wildlife trafficking: "Hillary Clinton and John Kasich: We cannot cede ground on animal poaching", 2 February 2019, https://www.washingtonpost.com/opinions/hil lary-clinton-and-john-kasich-we-cannot-cede-ground-on-animal-poaching/2019/02/01/ea151808-24b7-11e9-ad53-824486280311_story.html, last accessed 7 December 2019.

[15] National Strategy for Combating Wildlife Trafficking, https://www.fws.gov/home/feature/2014/trafficking/national-strategy-wildlife-trafficking.pdf, last accessed 28 February 2020.

was drawn that, in order to stop terrorism, the international community needed to target wildlife crime as a matter of priority. A few variants of this narrative appeared, and were promptly relayed and amplified by ONGs and the media.

Many commentators indicate a much-cited 2013 report by the newly established conservation NGO Elephant Action League as a decisive factor in the linking of elephant poaching with terrorism. The report denounced the poaching of elephants and the sale of ivory as a major source of income for insurgents and terrorist organizations such as al-Shabaab. The report stated that al-Shabaab received up to 40% of its running costs through the illegal ivory trade alone. The obvious implication was that, in order to end conflicts in Africa and fight terror organizations, it was necessary to combat, with military means and tactics, poaching and the illegal wildlife trade. When, in September 2013, al-Shabaab associates attacked the Westgate shopping mall in Nairobi, killing 67 people and wounding about 200, the report suddenly gained in popularity. Soon high-profile politicians, wildlife conservation NGOs, news outlets, private security entrepreneurs, and even famous film directors like Kathryn Bigelow began propagating the idea of a nexus between ivory trafficking and terrorism. The poaching-terror link, however, would soon draw extensive criticism from academics, think tanks, and government officials.

Some U.S. government officials interviewed in March 2015 about the above-mentioned U.S. National Strategy for Combating Wildlife Trafficking expressed support but also expressed the concern that the framing of wildlife trafficking as a security issue, as done in the Strategy, could skew conservation efforts.[16]

Other commentators did not spare their criticism. In his eloquently titled article "Kathryn Bigelow and the bogus link between ivory and terrorism", conservationist Diogo Veríssimo warned about the risk for conservationists who embrace unsubstantiated but popular theories of becoming "the boy who cried wolf".[17]

In their 2015 report for the Royal United Services Institute for Defence and Security Studies (RUSI), Tom Maguire and Cathy Haenlein criticize a 2013 report by Elephant Action League that stated that al-Shabaab received up to 40% of its running costs through the illegal ivory trade alone.

The authors point out that the available evidence demonstrates that ivory trafficking occupies a very minor place in al-Shabaab's funding, and that the real culprits are transnational organized crime syndicates and corrupt state officials. The focus on al-Shabaab and other terror organizations is misleading and counterproductive, subtracting resources where they would be most needed. Also, an exclusive focus on military response against poaching teams would not solve the problem and would not touch the higher levels of the criminal organizations profiting from wildlife trafficking; they would replicate the failures of militarized anti-drug strategies aimed at the supply side. Instead, Maguire and Haenlein refer to a growing consensus that anti-poaching strategies "should combine hard-security, community-engagement and development programmes".[18]

---

[16] Goodrich 2015.

[17] Veríssimo 2015.

[18] Maguire and Haenlein 2015, pp. 38–39.

Haenlein, Maguire, and others returned on this issue in a 2016 book about poaching and security in Africa.[19] Haenlein and others find no evidence of a significant involvement of al-Shabaab[20] in poaching and ivory trafficking, or for the claim that these activities represent a major source of funding for al-Shabaab. Greater evidence for involvement in poaching and ivory trafficking, according to the authors, exists for the Sudanese Janjaweed and Joseph Kony's Lord's Resistance Army (LRA). The authors, however, conclude that the unsubstantiated linking of terrorism and poaching and ivory trafficking risks being completely misleading, failing both to disrupt the revenues of terror organizations and to hit the organized crime syndicates and the corrupt state officials who are the real culprits (p. 97).

Other authors showed themselves even more skeptical of the claims about LRA's involvement in poaching and ivory trafficking. Kristof Titeca and Patrick Edmond (University of Antwerp) discuss the first report on the 'LRA ivory–terrorism' link in Congo, which appeared in 2013.[21]

Titeca and Edmond argue that "[...] the 'ivory terrorism' narrative is not for practical conservation actors. It is a discursive tool for other agendas, such as raising funds or justifying interventions (for the advocacy organisations or the US government) or widening readership (for the media outlets reporting on this). The narrative lives in an echo-chamber, which is less concerned with local dynamics."[22] Further, the authors define the widely assumed link between ivory trafficking and LRA's terrorism in Garamba National Park (GNP) in the Democratic Republic of the Congo (DRC) as a "myth", which is conveniently exploited by a number of actors furthering particular agendas. They point out that military intervention against the LRA has worsened poaching, because state forces have themselves taken part in poaching. In the climate that followed the 9/11 attacks, the idea that by fighting poaching the states, NGOs, and private citizens could help fight terrorism was "too good to be true".[23] The outcome was that "Rather than helping both conservation and security, a focus on the LRA's poaching deflected attention from the much larger poaching threat from other actors, not to mention the related security dynamics."[24]

In 2016, Elephant Action League, renamed Earth League International, felt compelled to publish a defense of the controversial 2013 report.[25]

Authors Crosta and Sutherland qualify claims made in the 2013 report, and try to correct misunderstandings. In particular, they state the original 2013 report never claimed that ivory trafficking supplies up to 40% of al-Shabaab's total revenue; instead, the report claimed that ivory trafficking "could be supplying up to 40% of the funds needed to pay salaries to its fighters";[26] Crosta and Sutherland acknowledge that

---

[19] Haenlein and Smith 2016.

[20] Haenlein et al. 2016, p. 86.

[21] Titeca and Edmond 2019, p. 261. The report is by Agger and Hutson 2013.

[22] Titeca and Edmond 2019, p. 266.

[23] Titeca and Edmond 2019, p. 258.

[24] Ibid.

[25] Crosta and Sutherland 2016, pp. 24 and following.

[26] Crosta and Sutherland 2016, p. 28.

the majority of the ivory supply chain is controlled by organized criminal networks; still, al-Shabaab is certainly involved as well, and the 2013 report was the first to draw attention to it; and whatever the misunderstandings and the misinformation spread by some sources on the basis of the 2013 report, drawing attention to elephant poaching was certainly a positive outcome.[27]

In conclusion, the existing literature seems to corroborate the thesis that organizations such as al-Shabaab, the LRA, and Janjaweed may occasionally resort to elephant poaching and ivory trafficking, but in an opportunistic and sporadic manner. Elephant poaching and ivory trafficking do not represent a major source of revenue for these organizations; a much bigger source of revenue, at least for some of these organizations, appears to be the trafficking in charcoal.[28]

40.4 Poaching and Regional Conflict

In the past decade, poaching and wildlife crime have been recognized as a regular occurrence in many insurgencies and regional conflicts, especially in Africa. The exact role played by wildlife crime in African conflicts is still matter for debate, in part due to the difficulty of gathering evidence, but also due to the delay with which the international academic community and policy circles have acknowledged the role of wildlife natural resources, in contrast to other natural resources such as diamonds or rare minerals, which have been extensively treated in the literature about African conflicts. Regardless, poaching and wildlife trafficking feature prominently in a series of resolutions issued by the Security Council of the United Nations to address the ongoing conflicts in the Democratic Republic of Congo and in the Central African Republic. Because these resolutions are issued under Chapter VII of the UN Charter and declare the situation in both countries a continuing threat to international peace and security in the region, a commentator has argued that poaching and wildlife trafficking have de facto been recognized as a threat to international peace and security themselves.[29] While this claim may seem controversial, the inclusion of poaching and wildlife trafficking in Chapter VII UNSC resolutions is undoubtedly an exceptional novelty, which may prelude to further changes in the treatment of wildlife crime under international law.

After the Cold War, the UN Security Council has made frequent recourse to Chapter VII of the UN Charter to address various problematic situations.[30] The era of humanitarian interventions and UN peacekeeping had begun. The 1990s and early 2000s witnessed an expansion of the traditional meaning of "security", exemplified by the emergence of the concept of "human security". Furthermore, the traditional

---

[27] Crosta and Sutherland 2016, pp. 29, 31.

[28] As confirmed by UNEP and Interpol, see Haenlein and Smith 2016, pp. 21, 27–28. About the poaching-terrorism link, see also Felbab-Brown 2018.

[29] Peters 2014.

[30] About Chapter VII measures, see Shaw 2017, pp. 951–963.

concept of absolute state sovereignty was attacked on many fronts, and principles like "Responsibility to Protect" were introduced.[31] The end of the Cold War could not fail to impact also on the academic study of war. "Conflict diamonds" and "conflict natural resources" started attracting wide attention in the international scholarly community. Influential studies claimed that, in a post-ideological age, conflicts assume an increasingly opportunistic and predatory character, which blurs the distinction between politics and thuggery. Diamonds and other natural resources could no longer be considered as a mere means to finance wars waged for ideological reasons; the looting of diamonds and other natural resources had instead become one of the main reasons of the wars. More than financing wars, diamonds and other natural resources had become the real cause of wars, and could prolong them indefinitely.[32]

Attempting to end the Angolan Civil War (1975–2002), in 1998 the United Nations Security Council adopted Resolution 1173 and Resolution 1176, which imposed sanctions against Angola's UNITA party aiming at removing UNITA's ability to finance the war through the sale of diamonds. These measures, however, did not succeed in entirely removing this source of income for UNITA, so in 1999 the UNSC established expert panels to investigate the violations of the sanctions imposed against UNITA. The resulting report, known as the Fowler Report (2000), prompted the United Nations to set up a system for the certification of the origin of diamonds, with a view to interdicting the sale of diamonds as a means to finance rebel movements and insurgencies.

On 1 December 2000, the UN General Assembly adopted resolution 55/56 on "conflict diamonds". That resolution was motivated by the use of rough diamonds by rebel movements in Africa to finance their illegal activities, and it established a certification scheme for diamonds known as the Kimberley Process Certification Scheme,[33] to ensure that rebel movements could not profit from the sale of diamonds. The degree of success of this initiative is contested, but the idea that the regulation of trade in natural resources is key to any attempt to stop conflicts in Africa was definitively established.

As noted by Stéphane Crayne and Cathy Haenlein,[34] the academic literature that flourished since the 1990s on the role of natural resources in African conflicts has mostly overlooked wildlife derivatives such as ivory or rhino horns. As a consequence, say Crayne and Haenlein, instruments similar to those developed to control the diamond trade were never developed for ivory, and politicians and media alike basically reiterated vague notions about the presumed role of poaching and the illegal ivory trade in the funding of terrorism without solid evidence. Crayne and Haenlein do not intend to deny that warring parties in the Central African Republic of the 2010s might have occasionally resorted to poaching and ivory smuggling; but the scant evidence and the few studies available do not allow to substantiate the claim that poaching funds or "fuels" conflict.

---

[31] Shaw 2017, pp. 962–963.
[32] Kaldor 1999.
[33] Official website: https://www.kimberleyprocess.com.
[34] Haenlein et al. 2016, pp. 60–61.

Stéphane Crayne and Cathy Haenlein warn that many organizations are involved in poaching, as the experience in the CAR in the 2010s showed, but the attention of the public and of the policymakers is mostly focused on insurgent formations, overlooking crime syndicates and corrupt state officials.[35]

Further, the authors cite reports by UN Office on Drugs and Crime (UNODC), UNEP and INTERPOL, which demonstrated that the ivory trade does not bring sufficient economic resources to armed groups to finance conflicts, while the number of animals slaughtered in peace areas is a multiple of the number of animals slaughtered in conflict areas. Crayne and Haenlein conclude that it would be unrealistic not to use force, especially in conflict areas, but the international community must realize the tenuous role of the ivory trade in financing conflicts, and avoid distorted policies, which are not based on solid empirical evidence.[36]

In 2014, the UN Security Council adopted two resolutions, #2134 and #2136, dealing with the Central African Republic and the Democratic Republic of Congo respectively. What is notable in these resolutions is that, alongside the illicit exploitation of natural resources, wildlife poaching is mentioned for the first time, namely as a "destabilizing force", which contributes to threatening peace and security in the region. So reads Resolution 2134:

Preamble, para 7:

Noting the Kimberley Process Certification Scheme's temporary suspension of rough diamond trading by the CAR[37] and expressing concern that diamond smuggling and other forms of illicit natural resource exploitation, including wildlife poaching, are destabilizing forces in CAR, and encouraging the Transitional Authorities and the State Authorities to address these issues through all possible avenues.

Preamble, last paragraph (para 24):

Determining that the situation in the CAR constitutes a threat to international peace and security in the region.

Paragraph 37,

(d) providing support for armed groups or criminal networks through the illicit exploitation of natural resources, including diamonds and wildlife and wildlife products, in the CAR

Similarly, Resolution 2136 about the Democratic Republic of the Congo (DRC) reads:

Preamble, para 10:

Recalling the linkage between the illegal exploitation of natural resources, including poaching and illegal trafficking of wildlife, illicit trade in such resources, and the proliferation and trafficking of arms as one of the major factors fuelling and exacerbating conflicts in the Great Lakes region of Africa, and encouraging the continuation of the regional efforts of the ICGLR and the governments involved against the illegal exploitation of natural resources,

---

[35] Haenlein et al. 2016, p. 68.

[36] Ibid., pp. 70, 74.

[37] Rough diamond trading by the CAR was suspended by the Kimberley Process Certification Scheme from 2013 to 2015.

and *stressing*, in this regard, the importance of regional cooperation and deepening economic integration with special consideration for the exploitation of natural resources.

Preamble, para 20:

Determining that the situation in the DRC continues to constitute a threat to international peace and security in the region

Paragraph 4: sanction

(g) Individuals or entities supporting armed groups in the DRC through illicit trade of natural resources, including gold or wildlife as well as wildlife products.

Since UNSC Resolution 2121 of 2013, all subsequent Resolutions about the Central African Republican include a mention of poaching: Resolution 2121 (2013); Resolution 2127 (2013); Resolution 2134 (2014); Resolution 2196 (2015); Resolution 2217 (2015); Resolution 2262 (2016); Resolution 2301 (2016); Resolution 2339 (2017); Resolution 2387 (2017); Resolution 2399 (2018); Resolution 2448 (2018); Resolution 2488 (2019); Resolution 2499 (2019); Resolution 2507 (2020) of 31 January 2020 is the latest resolution on the CAR, and the last so far to mention poaching. Concerning the DRC, too, since Resolution 2136 (2014), all subsequent resolutions mention poaching: Resolution 2198 (2015); Resolution 2293 (2016); Resolution 2360 (2017); Resolution 2409 (2018); Resolution 2463 (2019); Resolution 2502 (adopted on 19 Dec 2019 and the last so far).

It may be difficult to quantify the exact contribution of poaching and wildlife trafficking to the fueling of regional conflicts and insurgencies, and it may be premature to suggest that international law is moving away from its traditional anthropocentric outlook (see in this chapter below); but the important fact is that poaching and wildlife crime did make a momentous, historical entrance into a core feature of modern international law, Chapter VII resolutions.

As mentioned earlier, the international community has been slow to consider the role of wildlife derivatives in regional conflicts, in contrast to what happened with diamonds and other natural resources. In the mid-2010s, however, some academics suggested that elephant tusks and rhinoceros's horns could be playing the same role of diamonds in precedent conflicts.[38] On 21 September 2015, the blog of the National Geographic published an open letter by Dr. Katarzyna Nowak, an anthropologist and a zoologist, to the United Nations General Assembly (UNGA). In the letter, Dr. Nowak made a plea for the formulation of a UNGA resolution on "conflict ivory", on the model of resolution 55/56 of 2000 about "conflict diamonds". A resolution on "conflict ivory" would highlight the role of wildlife crime in financing violence and destabilization and might facilitate the development of a convention on wildlife crime that would operate independently of CITES, with its focus on wildlife trade. The proposed resolution on "conflict ivory" would have to overcome the limitation to rebel movements to include all kinds of entities that profit from elephant poaching, like corrupt state officials or units of the armed forces.[39]

---

[38] White 2014.
[39] Nowak 2016.

For the time being, however, the United Nations has not taken up this call, and the assumption that ivory plays a role comparable to diamonds in the funding of African conflicts has met with criticism. For example Stéphane Crayne and Cathy Haenlein affirm that similar claims, unsupported by solid empirical evidence, risk spreading oversimplified narratives and ultimately skewing policies.[40]

40.5 The Militarization of Conservation

The recent turn toward the "securitization" or "militarization" of conservation efforts advocated by Western political and media circles matches conspicuous developments on the field, in Africa. In recent years, in several African states, a trend toward the involvement of armed forces and the use of military tactics and weapons against poachers, which started in the 1980s, has been further intensified. In some cases there has been an escalation of the level of violence. In several areas, units from the regular armed forces or paramilitary rangers confront poachers armed to the teeth. The fight against poaching does not limit itself to engage the poachers caught in the act, but includes invasive surveillance and intelligence gathering operations, which instill fear and resentment in local communities. The soundness of this militarized approach is heavily contested.

The political geographer Roderick Neumann offered one of the earliest and most radical criticisms of the militarization of conservation. In a 2004 article, Neumann probed into the discursive and ethical practices that legitimate anti-poaching shoot-to-kill policies. Such war-like tactics, according to Neumann, could only be justified by humanizing animals and denigrating and de-humanizing indigenous hunters, and criminalizing them as "poachers". As a consequence, human rights abuses and deadly violence against humans become widely accepted and normalized.[41]

Elizabeth Lunstrum (York University, Toronto) has introduced the term "green militarization" for "the use of military and paramilitary (military-like) actors, techniques, technologies, and partnerships in the pursuit of conservation".[42] While green militarization, a new and still relatively unknown phenomenon, is taking hold in many parts of the world, Lunstrum has described how poaching and conservation are recast as national security issues requiring a military response in particular with reference to the Kruger National Park in South Africa; there the contradictory situation can be observed that the natural environment, damaged by military activity in the past, is now the theater of military activities for its conservation. Due to the strategic location of the Kruger National Park and the South African Army's traditional mission of protecting the state borders against hostile neighbors, the South African Army has been enlisted also in anti-poaching activities in the Park with controversial results.[43]

---

[40] Haenlein et al. 2016, p. 74.
[41] Neumann 2004.
[42] Lunstrum 2014.
[43] Lunstrum 2014, 2015.

In the Kruger National Park, the militarization of conservation has led also to more than 300 suspected poachers killed between 2008 and 2013.[44]

Also, Lunstrum noted how green militarization benefits private military companies, which have become a protagonist of the post-Cold War security and conflict scenario and have now ample opportunities for "greenwashing".[45] Furthermore, once conservation for whatever reason incorporates military tactics, or involves the militarization of previously civilian forces, or enlists traditional military formations, militarization becomes permanent.[46] Importantly, Lunstrum noted that green militarization is supported by militaristic values and assumptions; it is, indeed, a new form of militarism.[47] In conclusion, Lunstrum identified some emerging trends in militarized approaches to wildlife protection, which are likely to be extended soon to other areas of environmental concern, possibly making of green militarization one of the defining characteristics of our age.[48]

In the conclusions to their book *Poaching, Wildlife Trafficking and Security in Africa*, Cathy Haenlein and M. L. R. Smith acknowledge that the use of force is necessary, but the question is one of balancing short-term action on the field against poachers with a long-term strategy against the destination markets and the wider networks that profit from wildlife trafficking. Another question that needs to be addressed is whether poaching and wildlife trafficking are a crime or an act of war. Certainly, a propensity for the "war" label has been shown to encourage militarized approaches to conservation, which may result ineffective. Beneficial, however, is that in the last years these issues have left the domain of pure "conservation issues" and have enter the radar field of the security and law enforcement communities. The involvement of the UNSC is also seen as a positive development.[49]

The misguided emphasis on insurgent formations and terrorist organizations should be replaced by an increased awareness of the potential of wildlife crime to contribute to the destabilization and criminal infiltration of the state, and to the failure of the rule of law, which is in itself one of the biggest threats to human security.

---

[44] Lunstrum 2014, p. 817.

[45] Lunstrum 2014, pp. 825, 829.

[46] Lunstrum 2014, pp. 825–826.

[47] Lunstrum 2014, pp. 826, 829. Brian Campbell and Diogo Veríssimo have made an interesting study of the use of military language or even militaristic rhetoric by Maltese environmental NGOs to explain and promote their efforts against hunters: Campbell and Veríssimo 2015.

[48] See also Büscher and Ramutsindela 2015; Büscher and Fletcher 2018; Büscher 2018; Fletcher 2018. Büscher and Ramutsindela 2015 propose to adopt the broader category of "green violence". Shaw and Rademeyer 2016 have questioned the analytical value of the term "green militarization" and called for a broader study of political and institutional change in relation to anti-poaching tactics beyond the conservation literature. Marijnen and Verweijen 2016 have studied the discursive techniques used to legitimize and "normalize" militarized conservation in the Virunga National Park (Democratic Republic of Congo).

[49] Haenlein and Smith 2016, pp. 134 and following.

Another prominent critic of militarized wildlife conservation strategies is Professor Rosaleen Duffy (University of Sheffield).[50] Duffy claims that the militarized approach, which seems to have become the preferred option in recent years, is misguided because it is based on an incorrect understanding of wildlife crime and on flawed intelligence about its main actors. The militarization of anti-poaching is ultimately counterproductive, according to Duffy and others, because it distorts conservation policies, damages local communities, picks the wrong targets, and wastes resources. Duffy mentions the alleged link between elephant poaching and the Somali terrorist organization al-Shabaab. In that case, in 2012 a conservation NGO that advocates strong measures against poaching, the Elephant Action League, posted on its website a report that linked elephant poaching and al-Shabaab. Duffy notes that report was only picked up by international media after the terror attacks at a Nairobi mall in late 2013.[51] Soon afterwards the idea was being embraced and relayed without much further investigation by many commentators, media, think tanks, and high political circles, as illustrated by statements by US Secretary of State Hilary Clinton and US President Barack Obama. Duffy points out two main flaws in this oversimplified approach. First, militias and rebels are often involved in poaching, but only as part of a wider military strategy; so anti-poaching strategies must also adopt a broader scope and comprehensively address regional stability. The second issue is the serious humanitarian fallout of aggressive anti-poaching tactics and shoot-to-kill policies adopted in several states. In certain situations, a greater use of force would only result in an escalation of the conflict between rangers and poachers, with local communities left to pay a high price. Furthermore, because poaching is to a great extent driven by demand in distant countries and controlled by powerful crime syndicates, arresting or killing increasing numbers of poachers might not be effective in curbing wildlife crime.[52]

Besides academics, also professionals on the field have expressed their concerns about the trend toward the militarization of conservation. In April 2017, the Game Rangers Association of Africa, a non-profit organization representing rangers from over 20 African countries, published a media statement on "The use of military and security personnel and tactics in the training of Africa's rangers".

The Association expressed there with utmost clarity the concern that foreign trainers with military background but lacking experience in Africa and understanding of the local environment, societies, and law, might be more harmful than helpful. The Rangers Association emphasized the need to have a solid understanding of the local conditions, which many foreign trainers lack, and stressed the difference between military and security work and the rangers' work. As examples of misguided foreign interventions the document mentions cases when foreign trainers taught rangers

---

[50] Duffy et al. 2015.

[51] Neme et al. 2013: "If the world needs another reason to get serious about combating elephant poaching, here's one: The attack by terrorists on Westgate Mall in Nairobi. Income from illegal ivory trafficking is a substantial funding source for the Shabab, the group that claimed responsibility for the attack".

[52] See also Duffy 2014, 2016, 2017; Duffy et al. 2015, 2017, 2019.

tactics, which are illegal in the relevant countries and would lead to the arrest of the rangers.

There is no silver bullet in conservation and an excessive emphasis on military techniques and equipment, undoubtedly driven by powerful economic interests, risks being counterproductive. Besides being inefficient in the struggle against poaching, military tactics risk alienating the very local communities, proper conservation depends on. The Rangers Associations lamented a lack of proper vetting of military trainers, and requested conservation agencies to appreciate the need to respect the states' sovereignty when introducing foreign military or security operatives.[53]

A comprehensive criticism of militarized conservation was made in 2019 by Professor Duffy and other experts. The authors offer several arguments to demonstrate that militarized conservation must be rejected. First of all, it does not address the real, deep causes of poaching and trafficking but only tackles the symptoms. The criminalization of poachers is ineffective or counterproductive, and perpetuates a colonial and racial narrative that distorts an objective understanding of poaching. Militarized conservation is morally simplistic; it unilaterally labels poachers as the "bad guys" and rangers as the "good guys", ignoring the many instances of environmental and human rights abuses committed by rangers; it undermines trust in conservation authorities and troubles local communities. In some cases, in Southern Africa, militarized conservation operations reproduce patterns of violence against rural populations, which are reminiscent of apartheid-era tactics. In some cases, state armed forces are heavily involved in poaching and wildlife trafficking themselves, and are seen as hostile by local populations. Major international conservation organizations sponsor repressive activities, including invasive intelligence gathering tactics, and compromise their declared moral codes by relying on former operatives from security and intelligence services. The preference given to militarized and hence more "spectacular" conservation interventions results in less and less resources being allocated to less marketable but more effective approaches. Duffy and the other authors conclude their article by an impassioned call to escape the tyranny of urgency, dictated by the prospective of extinction of animal species, and reflect "on the full range of implications of the militarisation of conservation, and its intersections with broader social, political and economic contexts".[54]

Other conservationists, more sympathetic to militarized law enforcement, and state officials involved in anti-poaching did not fail to respond to these criticisms, like Army Major General Johan Jooste (retired), a veteran of the South African Border War with Angola (1966–1989), who oversees all anti-poaching efforts in the Kruger National Park in South Africa;[55] Dr. Susan Canney, Director of the Mali Elephant Project and Research Associate at the Department of Zoology, University of Oxford,[56] Dr. Niall McCann, Director of Conservation at Animal Park Rescue.[57]

---

[53] Game Rangers Association of Africa 2017.
[54] Duffy et al. 2019, pp. 68–71.
[55] Jooste and Ferreira 2018.
[56] Canney 2017.
[57] McCann 2017.

Particularly relevant to a discussion of international law and wildlife crime seems to be an article by academics from Botswana who defend the country's controversial "shoot-to-kill" anti-poaching policy.[58] Authors Mogomotsi and Madigele briefly review the literature on the militarization and conservation and conclude that anti-poaching is a war, indeed a "just war", comparable to the war on terror. The shooting of poachers is not extra-judicial killing, but what happens in war: "We believe parks are war zones and that rules and principles of war ought to be implemented".[59]

The war against poachers is justified by the clear and present danger of extinction of many species, and is supported by its effectiveness. By adopting this approach in 2013, Botswana has already been able to reduce the loss of animals substantially. Mogomotsi and Madigele urge neighboring South Africa, which struggles to prevent the loss of animals, to adopt the same approach.

The authors are aware that wildlife conservation may be unpopular among local communities, and militarized conservation more so. They accept that militarized conservation should not replace but complement other approaches based on the involvement of local communities; but other approaches have proven to be ineffective to deter poachers; hence the justification for the shoot-to-kill policy. Other arguments in favor of such policy is that it is cheaper to enforce and more effective than enforcing CITES trade bans; and that the criminal prosecution of poachers is ineffective.

Mogomotsi and Madigele note that, like the fight against terrorism, even the fight against poaching is now commonly framed in terms of a "war on poaching". Therefore, the rules that apply to armed conflicts ought to apply to anti-poaching as well. The authors proceed to justify the killing of poachers under international humanitarian law. Basically, the killing of poachers is analogous to the killing of civilians who take part in hostilities, and therefore, however controversial, the killing of poachers is legal under international humanitarian law.

In conclusion, however, it is security expert Gretchen Peters who may have offered the best interpretation of militarized conservation in her discussion of the "curse of the shiny object": militarized counternarcotics tactics, shoot-to-kill anti-poaching policies, zero tolerance policing are all examples of counterproductive policies focusing on symptoms instead of addressing the deep causes of unwanted phenomena, which nonetheless are often preferred by policy makers for their high visibility.[60]

40.6 A New Ecocentric Approach in International Law?

In this chapter we have discussed how, in recent years, poaching and wildlife trafficking have ceased being the excessive concern of conservationists and trade regulators, and have attracted the attention of security specialists. Moreover, we have seen

---

[58] Mogomotsi and Madigele 2017.

[59] Mogomotsi and Madigele 2017, p. 54.

[60] Peters 2017.

how poaching and wildlife trafficking have made their entrance into international conflict and security law through the new practice of the UN Security Council of routinely mentioning poaching and wildlife trafficking in their resolutions about the Central African Republic and the Democratic Republic of Congo.

International lawyer Anne Peters has discussed the significance of these novel mentions of poaching and wildlife trafficking in UNSC resolutions adopted under Chapter VII. She pointed out that the UNSC implicitly qualified wildlife poaching and trafficking as a threat to peace.[61] Peters emphasized that the intervention of the UNSC was due to common anthropocentric motives (quelling human conflict), and not directly by a concern for wildlife *per se*. Peters considered the novel practice of the UNSC as a continuation of its previous practice concerning climate change, which the UNSC recognizes as relevant for peace and security since 2007. Peters, however, concluded her appraisal with moderate optimism, noting that the UNSC had not yet qualified climate change as a threat to peace, while it did so for poaching and wildlife trafficking; this, Peters hoped, could introduce a new, extended concept of security, which would not separate human security from the integrity of nature, because humans and animals "are ultimately in the same boat".[62]

An emerging, extended concept of security envisaged by Peters, which does not pit human security against nature and animals, is certainly desirable, but the experience of indigenous peoples and the conservation literature show that it is not so simple: often, human security and nature or wildlife security do conflict. Iconic, protected species like elephants may also be dangerous crop-destroying pests. Human communities are often evicted and displaced to make room for natural reserves. Subsistence hunters may be recast as poachers, and criminalized accordingly. Rural communities may experience abuses from rangers.[63]

We believe, however, that a new trend toward a less "anthropocentric" approach to the protection of the environment and of wild animals is indeed underway. The UN General Assembly has recently adopted a series of resolutions on the tackling of wildlife crime, starting with Resolution 69/314 of 30 July 2015, which addresses wildlife crime for the first time ever, and does it in the framework of an "ecocentric" language of biodiversity and sustainable development. We think it is worth quoting these pathbreaking documents extensively. UNGA Resolution 69/314 reads:

The General Assembly,

Reaffirming the intrinsic value of biological diversity and its various contributions to sustainable development and human well-being, and recognizing that wild fauna and flora in their many beautiful and varied forms are an irreplaceable part of the natural systems of the Earth which must be protected for this and the generations to come […]

Recognizing that illicit trafficking in wildlife contributes to damage to ecosystems and rural livelihoods, including those based on ecotourism, undermines good governance and the rule of law and, in some cases, threatens national stability and requires enhanced regional cooperation and coordination in response […]

---

[61] Peters 2014.

[62] Peters 2014.

[63] About conservation-induced displacement and human-wildlife conflict, see for example Witter 2013; Bocarejo and Ojeda 2016; Massé 2016; Lunstrum and Ybarra 2018; Vidal 2020.

Reaffirming its call for holistic and integrated approaches to sustainable development that will guide humanity to live in harmony with nature and lead to efforts to restore the health and integrity of the Earth's ecosystem, etc.

Similarly, resolution 70/301 of 9 September 2016 so begins:

The General Assembly,

Reaffirming the intrinsic value of biological diversity and its various contributions to sustainable development and human well-being, and recognizing that wild fauna and flora in their many beautiful and varied forms are an irreplaceable part of the natural systems of the earth which must be protected for this and the generations to come,

Remaining concerned, therefore, about the increasing scale of poaching and illegal trade in wildlife and wildlife products and its adverse economic, social and environmental impacts, etc.

Resolution 71/326 of 11 September 2017 reads:

The General Assembly,

Reaffirming the intrinsic value of biological diversity and its various contributions to sustainable development and human well-being, and recognizing that wild fauna and flora in their many beautiful and varied forms are an irreplaceable part of the natural systems of the Earth which must be protected for this generation and the generations to come,

Remaining concerned, therefore, about the increasing scale of poaching and illegal trade in wildlife and wildlife products and its adverse economic, social and environmental impacts,

Expressing serious concern over the extraordinarily detrimental levels of rhinoceros poaching and the alarmingly high levels of killings of elephants in Africa, as well as the illegal trade in other protected wildlife species […], which threaten those species with local extinction and, in some cases, with global extinction,

Underlining the need to take measures to prevent illegal timber harvesting, which leads to the decimation of rare timber species, in particular of rosewood, agarwood and sandalwood,

Recognizing that illicit trafficking in wildlife contributes to damage to ecosystems and rural livelihoods, including those based on ecotourism, undermines good governance and the rule of law and, in some cases, threatens national stability and requires enhanced transnational and regional cooperation and coordination in response,

Emphasizing that the protection of wildlife must be part of a comprehensive approach to achieving poverty eradication, food security, sustainable development, including the conservation and sustainable use of biological diversity, economic growth, social well-being and sustainable livelihoods,

Reaffirming its call for holistic and integrated approaches to sustainable development that will guide humanity to live in harmony with nature and lead to efforts to restore the health and integrity of the Earth's ecosystem, which will contribute the creation of a shared future based upon our common humanity,

[…]

Bearing in mind that the illicit trade in small arms and light weapons could be linked to illicit trafficking in wildlife, which may pose a serious threat to national and regional stability in some parts of Africa, etc.

Finally, UNGA Resolution 73/343 of 16 September 2019 reads:

The General Assembly,

[…]

Reaffirming further the intrinsic value of biological diversity and its various contributions to sustainable development and human well-being, and recognizing that wild fauna and flora in their many beautiful and varied forms are an irreplaceable part of the natural systems of the Earth which must be protected for this generation and the generations to come,

[…]

Remaining concerned, therefore, about the increasing scale of poaching and illegal trade in wildlife and wildlife products and its adverse economic, social and environmental impacts,

[…]

Reaffirming its call for holistic and integrated approaches to sustainable development that will guide humanity to live in harmony with nature and lead to efforts to restore the health and integrity of the Earth's ecosystem, which will contribute to the creation of a shared future based upon our common humanity,

[…]

Bearing in mind that the illicit trade in small arms and light weapons could be linked to illicit trafficking in wildlife, which may pose a serious threat to national and regional stability in some parts of Africa, etc.

Analogous language and approach are adopted also by the UNGA Resolution 74/221 of 19 December 2019 "Implementation of the Convention on Biological Diversity and its contribution to sustainable development":

Recognizing the important role of other biodiversity-related multilateral environmental agreements, including the Convention on International Trade in Endangered Species of Wild Fauna and Flora, in contributing to the conservation and sustainable use of biodiversity and in ensuring that no species entering into international trade is threatened with extinction, recognizing also the economic, social and environmental impacts of poaching and trafficking in wildlife, and noting the contribution of parties to and the secretariat of the Convention on International Trade in Endangered Species of Wild Fauna and Flora to the implementation of the Strategic Plan for Biodiversity 2011–2020, its 20 Aichi Biodiversity Targets and the Global Strategy for Plant Conservation, etc.

These five resolutions are definitively good news. They suggest at least the following ideas:

1. The United Nations has embraced an ecocentric approach to environmental protection, including wildlife conservation. Biological diversity is recognized intrinsic value, and living in harmony with nature is considered as essential for humanity;
2. the politically, economically, and socially destabilizing character of environmental crime, and in particular wildlife trafficking, is emphasized;
3. the United Nations emphasize the need to strengthen national capabilities to meet the requirements of three UN Conventions: the Convention on International Trade in Endangered Species of Wild Fauna and Flora, the Convention against Transnational Organized Crime, and the Convention against Corruption. The CITES, with its limitations, still remains the only instrument specifically devoted to wildlife.
4. these five UNGA resolutions refrain from using terms such as "threat to international peace and security". That may be due to deference to the Security Council in matters involving the potential application of Chapter VII of the UN Charter,

or even may be due to the intention to avoid the criticism of promoting the "securitization" or the "militarization" of wildlife conservation.
5. the resolutions underscore the need to combat wildlife crime both on the side of supply and on the side of demand;
6. the United Nations stresses the need to consider local communities not as antagonists but as "active partners" in wildlife conservation efforts, and urges to provide alternative livelihoods;
7. the United Nations will consider wildlife trafficking as a matter of concern on a permanent basis. The General Assembly, indeed, committed to periodically revisit the issue of wildlife trafficking and the implementation of these resolutions (currently every two years).

40.7 Conclusion

The outlook resulting from the analysis of the legal framework to combat wildlife crime, of the prevalent approaches to wildlife conservation, and of the literature, in a context of accelerating destruction of entire animal species through poaching, is bleak. No consensus has emerged on the most effective way to reduce poaching and ensure the survival of wildlife. The CITES, which is the only international legal instrument to combat wildlife crime, is criticized on many counts. Besides its ethical implications, the effectiveness of militarized conservation is heavily contested. An awareness is growing, however, that legal instruments and policies should evolve in the direction of a more "ecocentric" approach, realizing the intrinsic value of nature and wildlife, or at least realizing that humankind cannot thrive separated from nature or in opposition to nature. It is only in a difficult, open-ended process of learning that we set our hopes for wildlife and for humankind.

References

Agence France-Presse (2015) African Elephants Could Be Extinct in Wild within Decades, Experts Say. The Guardian, 24 March 2015. https://www.theguardian.com/environment/2015/mar/24/african-elephants-could-be-extinct-in-wild-within-decades-say-experts. Accessed 24 July 2020

Agger K, Hutson J (2013) Kony's ivory: how elephant poaching in Congo helps support the Lord's Resistance Army. Enough Project, The Resolve, Invisible Children, and the Satellite Sentinel Project (with DigitalGlobe), https://enoughproject.org/files/KonysIvory.pdf. Accessed 25 February 2020

Bocarejo D, Ojeda D (2016) Violence and Conservation: Beyond Unintended Consequences and Unfortunate Coincidences. Geoforum doi:https://doi.org/10.1016/j.geoforum.2015.11.001

Bowman M (2013) A Tale of Two CITES: Divergent Perspectives upon the Effectiveness of the Wildlife Trade Convention: A Tale of Two Cites. Review of European, Comparative & International Environmental Law, doi:https://doi.org/10.1111/reel.12049

Büscher B (2018) From Biopower to Ontopower? Violent Responses to Wildlife Crime and the New Geographies of Conservation. Conservation and Society doi:https://doi.org/10.4103/cs.cs_16_159

Büscher B, Fletcher R (2018) Under Pressure: Conceptualising Political Ecologies of Green Wars. Conservation and Society doi:https://doi.org/10.4103/cs.cs_18_1

Büscher B, Ramutsindela M (2015) Green Violence: Rhino Poaching and the War to Save Southern Africa's Peace Parks. African Affairs, doi:https://doi.org/10.1093/afraf/adv058

Campbell B, Veríssimo D (2015) Black Stork Down: Military Discourses in Bird Conservation in Malta. Human Ecology doi:https://doi.org/10.1007/s10745-015-9724-6

Canney S (2017) A response to "We need to talk about the militarization of conservation". Wild Foundation, 24 July 2017. https://www.wild.org/blog/green-european-journal-response. Accessed 19 November 2019

Conrad K (2012) Trade Bans: A Perfect Storm for Poaching? Tropical Conservation Science doi:https://doi.org/10.1177/194008291200500302

Crosta A, Sutherland K (2016) The White Gold of Jihad. The 2010-2012 groundbreaking investigation into al-Shabaab's link to ivory trafficking in Eastern Africa. Elephant Action League, https://earthleagueinternational.org/wp-content/uploads/2016/02/Report-Ivory-al-Shabaab-Oct2016.pdf. Accessed 4 January 2020

Duffy R (2014) Waging a War to Save Biodiversity: The Rise of Militarized Conservation. International Affairs doi:https://doi.org/10.1111/1468-2346.12142

Duffy R (2016) War, by Conservation. Geoforum doi:https://doi.org/10.1016/j.geoforum.2015.09.014

Duffy R (2017) We Need to Talk about the Militarisation of Conservation. Green European Journal, 20 July 2017. https://www.greeneuropeanjournal.eu/we-need-to-talk-about-militarisation-of-conservation. Accessed 19 November 2019

Duffy R et al. (2015) The Militarization of Anti-Poaching: Undermining Long Term Goals? Environmental Conservation doi:https://doi.org/10.1017/S0376892915000119

Duffy R et al. (2017) Foreign 'conservation Armies' in Africa May Be Doing More Harm than Good. The Conversation. 13 July 2017. http://theconversation.com/foreign-conservation-armies-in-africa-may-be-doing-more-harm-than-good-80719. Accessed 7 January 2020

Duffy R et al. (2019) Why We Must Question the Militarisation of Conservation. Biological Conservation doi:https://doi.org/10.1016/j.biocon.2019.01.013

Felbab-Brown V (2018) Wildlife and Drug Trafficking, Terrorism, and Human Security. PRISM 7 (4): 124–137

Fletcher R (2018) License to Kill: Contesting the Legitimacy of Green Violence. Conservation and Society, doi:https://doi.org/10.4103/cs.cs_16_148

Game Rangers Association of Africa (2017) Media Statement: The Use of Military and Security Personnel and Tactics in the Training of Africa's Rangers. 26 April 2017. http://www.gameranger.org/news-views/media-releases/170-media-statement-the-use-of-military-and-security-personnel-and-tactics-in-the-training-of-africa-s-rangers.html. Accessed 12 January 2020

Goodrich C (2015) Where did this link between security and wildlife trafficking come from? Global Wildlife Conservation Group, U. of Texas at Austin. https://sites.utexas.edu/wildlife/2015/05/07/where-did-this-link-between-security-and-wildlife-trafficking-come-from. Accessed 10 January 2020

Haenlein C, Maguire T, Somerville K (2016) Poaching, wildlife trafficking and terrorism. In: Haenlein C, Smith MLR (eds) Poaching, Wildlife Trafficking and Security in Africa: Myths and Realities. Whitehall Paper 86. Royal United Services Institute for Defence and Security Studies, London

Haenlein C, Smith M L R (eds) (2016) Poaching, Wildlife Trafficking and Security in Africa: Myths and Realities. Whitehall Paper 86. Royal United Services Institute for Defence and Security Studies, London

Harrop S R (2013) Wild Animal Welfare in International Law: The Present Position and the Scope for Development. Global Policy, doi:https://doi.org/10.1111/1758-5899.12086

Jooste J, Ferreira S M (2018) An Appraisal of Green Militarization to Protect Rhinoceroses in Kruger National Park. African Studies Quarterly 18 (1): 12–23

Jung B D (2017) The Tragedy of the Elephants. Wis. L. Rev. 695
Kaldor M (1999) New and Old Wars: Organized Violence in a Global Era. Polity Press, Cambridge
Lunstrum E (2014) Green Militarization: Anti-Poaching Efforts and the Spatial Contours of Kruger National Park. Annals of the Association of American Geographers, doi:https://doi.org/10.1080/00045608.2014.912545
Lunstrum E (2015) Conservation Meets Militarisation in Kruger National Park: Historical Encounters and Complex Legacies. Conservation and Society, doi:https://doi.org/10.4103/0972-4923.179885
Lunstrum E, Ybarra M (2018) Deploying Difference: Security Threat Narratives and State Displacement from Protected Areas. Conservation and Society, doi:https://doi.org/10.4103/cs.cs_16_119
Maguire T, Haenlein C (2015) An Illusion of Complicity: Terrorism and the Illegal Ivory Trade in East Africa. Royal United Services Institute for Defence and Security Studies, London
Marijnen E, Verweijen J (2016) Selling Green Militarization: The Discursive (Re)Production of Militarized Conservation in the Virunga National Park, Democratic Republic of the Congo. Geoforum, doi:https://doi.org/10.1016/j.geoforum.2016.08.003
Massé F (2016) The Political Ecology of Human-Wildlife Conflict: Producing Wilderness, Insecurity, and Displacement in the Limpopo National Park. Conservation and Society, doi:https://doi.org/10.4103/0972-4923.186331
McCann N (2017) Attacks on 'Militarized Conservation' Are Naive (Commentary). Mongabay Environmental News. 10 October 2017. https://news.mongabay.com/2017/10/attacks-on-militarized-conservation-are-naive-commentary. Accessed 19 November 2019
Mogomotsi G E J, Madigele P K (2017) Live by the Gun, Die by the Gun: An Analysis of Botswana's 'Shoot-to-Kill' Policy as an Anti-Poaching Strategy. South African Crime Quarterly, doi:https://doi.org/10.17159/2413-3108/2017/v0n60a1787
Nellemann Ch et al (eds) (2016) The Rise of Environmental Crime: A Growing Threat to Natural Resources, Peace, Development and Security. A UNEP-INTERPOL Rapid Response Assessment. United Nations Environment Programme, Nairobi, Kenya
Neme L et al. (2013) Terrorism and the Ivory Trade. Los Angeles Times. 14 October 2013. https://www.latimes.com/opinion/op-ed/la-oe-neme-ivory-poaching-terrorism-20131014-story.html. Accessed 19 November 2019
Neumann R P (2004) Moral and Discursive Geographies in the War for Biodiversity in Africa. Political Geography, doi:https://doi.org/10.1016/j.polgeo.2004.05.011
Nowak K (2016) CITES Alone Cannot Combat Illegal Wildlife Trade. South African Institute of International Affairs, Johannesburg
Peters A (2014) Novel Practice of the Security Council: Wildlife Poaching and Trafficking as a Threat to the Peace. EJIL: Talk! https://www.ejiltalk.org/novel-practice-of-the-security-council-wildlife-poaching-and-trafficking-as-a-threat-to-the-peace. Accessed 10 November 2019
Peters G S (2017) The Curse of the Shiny Object. PRISM 7 (1): 74–89
Shaw M N (2017) International Law, 8th edn. Cambridge University Press, Cambridge, UK/New York, NY/Port Melbourne, VIC/Delhi/Singapore
Shaw M, Rademeyer J (2016) A Flawed War: Rethinking 'Green Militarisation' in the Kruger National Park. Politikon, doi:https://doi.org/10.1080/02589346.2016.1201379
Titeca K, Edmond P (2019) Outside the Frame: Looking Beyond the Myth of Garamba's LRA Ivory–Terrorism Nexus. Conservation and Society, doi:https://doi.org/10.4103/cs.cs_18_145
Veríssimo D (2015) Kathryn Bigelow and the Bogus Link between Ivory and Terrorism. The Conversation, 17 January 2015. http://theconversation.com/kathryn-bigelow-and-the-bogus-link-between-ivory-and-terrorism-35864. Accessed 19 November 2019
Vidal J (2020) Armed ecoguards funded by WWF 'beat up Congo tribespeople'. The Guardian, 7 February 2020. https://www.theguardian.com/global-development/2020/feb/07/armed-ecoguards-funded-by-wwf-beat-up-congo-tribespeople. Accessed 29 February 2020
White N (2014) The Political Economy of Ivory as a "Conflict Resource". Peace and Conflict Studies Vol. 21, No. 2: 172–186

White S (2013) Into the Void: International Law and the Protection of Animal Welfare. Global Policy, doi:https://doi.org/10.1111/1758-5899.12076

Witter R (2013) Elephant-Induced Displacement and the Power of Choice: Moral Narratives about Resettlement in Mozambique's Limpopo National Park. Conservation and Society doi:https://doi.org/10.4103/0972-4923.125756

WWF-Belgique (2019) Sans action urgente, l'éléphant d'Afrique disparaîtra dans 20 ans. 19 November 2019. https://wwf.be/fr/actualites/sans-action-urgente-lelephant-dafrique-disparaitra-dans-20-ans. Accessed 24 July 2020

Federico Dalpane studied political and legal theory at the Universities of Bologna, Frankfurt am Main, and Berlin (Humboldt), and holds a doctorate in history of political thought from the Scuola Superiore Sant'Anna (Italy). He is Assistant Professor at the School of Law of KIMEP University (Kazakhstan), and a member of the International Center for Animal Law and Policy of the Autonomous University of Barcelona. Among his research interests are animals and the environment in political and legal theory.

Maria Baideldinova holds an LL.M from the Christian-Albrechts University of Kiel (Germany) and a Ph.D. from the Scuola Superiore Sant'Anna (Italy). Her academic background is private law but her passion is definitely animal law. Maria launched the first university course in animal law in the post-Soviet space at the School of Law of KIMEP University (Almaty, Kazakhstan) where she is Assistant Professor. She is involved in consultations with the Government of Kazakhstan for the reform of the country's legislation on animals. She is a member of the International Center for Animal Law and Policy of the Autonomous University of Barcelona, and an expert member of the Global Animal Law Association.

Chapter 41
The Use of Force in Pursuance of the Right to Self-determination

Elizabeth Chadwick

Contents

41.1 Introduction 886
41.2 The Use of Force 887
    41.2.1 General Issues Surrounding the Use of Force 888
    41.2.2 The Conflation of Military and Police Force 891
41.3 IHL Parameters Relevant to Self-determination 892
    41.3.1 Common Article 3 893
    41.3.2 Self-determination and 'Internationalised' Uses of Force 895
    41.3.3 Formalisation as 'International' 897
41.4 Forceful Self-determination as 'Terrorism' 900
    41.4.1 'Terrorist' Force and Self-determination 900
    41.4.2 Locating 'Terrorism' for Legal Purposes 904
    41.4.3 The Necessity of Forceful Struggle 906
    41.4.4 The Terrorism-Liberation Distinction 908
41.5 Conclusion 908
References 909

Abstract Self-determination is a UN principle, a legal norm, and an international right of all, *erga omnes*, yet the notion of a 'right' to use force in struggles to achieve it destabilises a geo-political environment based on sovereign states. Specifically, states hold the legal monopoly over the use of force. This discussion considers the legal approaches to liberation conflicts to achieve self-determination, first, by reference to the International Humanitarian Law of Armed Conflicts, and secondly, through a brief examination of domestic state approaches to acts of 'terrorism'. Although acts of terrorism today are viewed as never justifiable, it is argued that limiting a 'people' to passive resistance, alone, in the face of state-led gross oppression or threat, would entrench and reinforce mis-rule.

Keywords Self-determination · Use of force · International humanitarian law · Terrorism · ICRC · 1949 Geneva Conventions · Protocols of 1977 · Jurisdiction · Criminal law · Due process · Rights of defence

E. Chadwick (✉)
(Retired) Nottingham Trent University, Nottingham, UK

All too little understood, the uniqueness of the strategy lies in this: that it achieves its goal not through its acts but through the response to its acts.[1]

I know not what course others may take; but as for me, give me liberty or give me death![2]

41.1 Introduction

The right of 'peoples' to utilise force to achieve their self-determination is controversial in international relations. First, international law has never had a universally-accepted list of 'peoples' entitled to self-determination, or agreement as to the rights entailed by the concept of self-determination. Instead, consensus as to the use of force to achieve self-determination has had to await the outcome of specific liberation struggles. Secondly, 51 UN member states existed in 1945, when a third of the world's population was dependent on colonial states;[3] today, there are 193 UN member states.[4] Over 80% of casualties in post-1945 armed conflicts have occurred in non-international armed conflicts, most fought for self-determination.[5]

Thirdly, the international community cannot impose one single framework of governance on states. Moreover, international law does not prohibit rebellion and revolution, each of which differs in 'cause', e.g., 'legitimate' governance may not be 'representative'; territorial consolidation may exacerbate minority discrimination, and/or fantasies of genetic or national difference. In turn, when speaking of 'liberation' struggles, one must ask 'liberation from what'? To force out an invader or foreign occupier, to end gross oppression, to achieve greater political autonomy, and/or effect territorial secession?[6] Each rationale may provide a 'cause' prompting the outbreak of violent civil strife, such that a 'people' may seek its self-determination forcefully,[7] as recognised at international level since 1945.[8]

---

[1] Shariatmadari 2015 (quoting David Fromkin).

[2] Patrick Henry, St. John's Church, Richmond, Virginia, 23 March 1775.

[3] See UN undated-c, Declarations.

[4] UN undated-b, at a Glance.

[5] ICRC undated-a, Introduction.

[6] See, e.g., Milanovic 2017.

[7] Consider Kaempfer et al. 2018 ('self-determination initiative').

[8] E.g., the 1998 Good Friday or Belfast Agreement, http://education.niassembly.gov.uk/post_16/snapshots_of_devolution/gfa. See O'Carroll 2018. The Agreement enshrines the principle of self-determination, and permits a border poll on reunification.

Nonetheless, revolution remains an exceptional event, and states hold the legal monopoly on the use of force.[9] This means that non-state group violence is 'unauthorised' domestically, and likely to be viewed as 'unlawful' under state criminal law. Moreover, the contemporary 'terrorism-aware' international environment means that forceful struggles for self-determination are certainly not to be engaged in lightly. When combined with communications technologies, and sophisticated weaponry and military tactics, the idea of utilising force to achieve self-determination is likely to impact negatively on the maintenance of international peace and security.[10]

The use of force to achieve self-determination is often necessary, and remains fundamental in anchoring self-determination in the modern consciousness. Indeed, 'the idea that the use of violence is never justified ... is a doctrine that would deprive people of all weapons save passive resistance in the face of any oppression or threat, however terrible'.[11] Therefore, the viability of a 'right' to utilise force to achieve self-determination must depend on a competition between international legal limits on state uses of force, and the extent to which threatened governments respect those limits. To frame the issues otherwise is to put the cart before the horse.[12]

The normative and legal limits placed on state uses of force against their own home-grown rebels are certainly more flexible than force utilised between states. The wider juridical space reserved to states to utilise internal force is to enforce domestic good order. Inter-state alliance and geopolitical positioning also affect the parameters of existing legal limits. Accordingly, this discussion will highlight the central role of law when a 'people' utilises force to seek their self-determination. First, the legal restraints on force in the International Humanitarian Law of Armed Conflicts ('IHL') are introduced. Secondly, resort to domestic state terrorism prosecutions is considered. The respective advantages of each legal approach are addressed.

41.2 The Use of Force

An understanding of sovereign power over force reveals self-determination as inherently producing instability at both the international and internal legal levels. Specifically, many liberation conflicts, which should be viewed from the start as international armed conflicts, have in fact been 'internationalised' through external involvement of one sort or another. The sheer intensity of many liberation conflicts, and state unwillingness to show restraint against those deemed 'rebels', 'traitors',

---

[9] See Accordance with International Law of the Unilateral Declaration of Independence in Respect of Kosovo (Advisory Opinion) [2010] ICJ Rep, p. 403, paras 82–3 (entitlement to self-determination, and 'rights of revolution', expressly side-stepped). Consider Ku 2017 (secession remains contested).
[10] UN Charter, Article 1.
[11] Geras 1989, p. 186.
[12] Stephens 2010, p. 468.

and/or 'terrorists',[13] in turn, necessitated the insertion in 1977 of self-determination's exceptionalism into substantive IHL frameworks.

41.2.1 General Issues Surrounding the Use of Force

The 1945 UN Charter acknowledges state domestic control in Article 2(7), by incorporating the international principle of non-interference by states in the domestic affairs of each other.[14] States hold the legal monopoly on the domestic use of force, along with control over the mechanisms of forceful domestic coercion, meaning any unauthorised resort to domestic force or violence will normally be considered unlawful. The non-interference principle is fundamental, and both acknowledges and reinforces the ability of each state to control matters domestically largely as each sees fit. Sovereign autonomy includes the ability to choose the political and legal labels to specify and proscribe the domestic parameters of acts deemed 'criminal', and the detail of each state's domestic laws will differ. Sovereign autonomy thus enables states to promote specific aims via legal regulation, illustrating that state domestic criminal law may be of little utility when seeking multi-lateral resolution of problematic international issues, such as 'self-determination'.

41.2.1.1 The Destabilising Effects of Self-determination

State domestic control, internal rights of coercion, and the non-interference principle produce enclosure effects, but cannot insulate states entirely against 'rights' demands for self-determination.[15] Rather, self-determination instead exacerbates existing geopolitical frictions, particularly when demands are made by a trans-boundary 'people', whose cross-border existence can also destabilise wider regional interests.[16] Therefore, self-determination causes an inherent instability in interaction between law and politics, and between the international legal community and more localised elites.

The mechanics of substantiating contested rights entitlements also rest on codifications negotiated and agreed by states at the international level, the rights and procedures of which are then domestically implemented by states, first, as a matter of inter-state treaty obligation, and secondly, in accordance with each state's legal traditions. Once implemented, these international rights will be enforced vertically by governments, in accordance with local agendas, producing variations in approach to rights entitlements between states wherever there is no over-arching judicial authority.[17] In turn, any gaps in coverage create space between the external (diplomatic, political)

---

[13] See, e.g., Le Mon 2003.

[14] UN Charter, Article 2(7). Consider Tsagourias 2019 ('control as baseline of coercion').

[15] Regarding which, see Lorca 2014.

[16] See, e.g., Milanovic 2017.

[17] Such as the ECtHR, or the IACtHR.

and internal (coercive, political) spheres of sovereign state power,[18] thus prompting forceful struggles for self-determination.

No over-arching codifications exist however to provide concrete, substantive content to rights of self-determination, just as there are no centralised codifications detailing which 'peoples' are 'entitled' to such rights, and why. The principle and content of self-determination are left indeterminate, thus necessitating rights entitlements to be enunciated and claimed by self-identifying 'peoples', who in turn may need to utilise force against resistant government in order to be heard.

This approach to force and self-determination has been the norm for much of the UN era, for several reasons. First, geo-political friction surrounding self-determination was exacerbated during the Cold War by the US and USSR, which competitively funded a number of high-intensity Cold War 'proxy' conflicts. Secondly, a number of non-state violent actors, including Islamist fundaments,[19] who pursued non-traditional 'causes' had been visible since the early 1970s.[20] Once the 'Super Power' rivalry collapsed in the late 1980s, it was also hoped that new opportunities would arise to seek the peaceful resolution of long-standing liberation struggles.[21] However, the 9/11 (2001) atrocities instead focussed intense international activity on dealing with a variety of new, non-state violent actors.[22]

As the focus shifted to 'peacetime' (i.e., law-and-order) frameworks for dealing with international 'terrorism' rather than liberation 'wars', and the post-1945 military-industrial complex transitioned into the modern-day 'security-industrial and -technological' complex,[23] another alteration in focus was to the formation of national security partnerships, in which private and corporate actors were entrenched. This made it increasingly difficult to argue persuasively for a 'right' of 'peoples' to utilise force for any reason whatsoever.

41.2.1.2 IHL and the 'Exceptionalism' of Self-determination

Given that neither self-determination nor the identity of its rightful recipients is specified at the global level, the tardy-yet-premature insertion of self-determination into IHL's legal provisions remains a near-solitary event.[24] Specifically, IHL provisions

---

[18] See, e.g., Case C-266/16, Western Sahara Campaign UK, The Queen v Commissioners for Her Majesty's Revenue and Customs, Secretary of State for Environment, Food and Rural Affairs, ECLI:EU:C:2018:118; Azarova and Berkes 2018; Milanovic 2018; Hart 2015 (UN recognition of Western Saharan entitlement to self-determination). Consider Kattan 2018.

[19] See, e.g., Schultz 2012.

[20] Burke 2003, p. 5.

[21] At least 32 self-determination settlements achieved between 1988 and 2008. Weller 2008, p. 20.

[22] See, e.g., UN undated-d, Office of Counter Terrorism, and UN 2019a, Plan of Action to Prevent Violent Extremism.

[23] See, e.g., Bennett and Haggerty 2011; Schewe 2018. See also Yua 2019.

[24] Principally, in Protocol Additional to the Geneva Conventions of 12 August 1949, and relating to the Protection of Victims of International Armed Conflicts (Protocol I), 8 June 1977, Article 1(4). See, e.g., Macak 2018.

for international 'armed conflicts', which must be respected 'in all circumstances',[25] were revised and extended in 1977 to certain liberation struggles,[26] even though such conflicts had constituted the main type since 1945. Greater limits on force were also developed and codified separately for high-intensity civil wars.[27] These new codifications were intended to attract greater international attention to, and impose greater restraint on, all participants in such conflicts.

The inclusion of self-determination in IHL rules was not merely a 'revolutionary' event, but it occurred at the height of an intense era of anti-colonial liberation conflicts. High-intensity 'civil' wars traditionally were regulated pursuant to inter-state laws of war by analogy (largely, for purposes of laws of neutrality once international trade was disrupted by internal conflict),[28] but the UN Charter, in prohibiting the use of force between states in Article 2(4), had effectively allocated control over civil conflicts (which can provoke international conflicts) to states,[29] as per Article 2(7). Civil conflicts thus remain far less regulated by IHL,[30] as Charter provisions enable a higher degree of latitude in state strategic choice when utilising force domestically.[31]

This allows any evidence of domestic opposition to governmental authority to intensify perceptions in official circles of a need to react forcefully with state repression. Should force be utilised mutually, and become protracted or prolonged, the issue of an 'armed conflict' arises, the objective identification of which causes a great deal of political and doctrinal disagreement, due to its position of 'war' at the intersection of power politics and legal rules. For this reason, the International Law Association's (ILA) Use of Force Committee undertook a major study of the essential indicia of 'armed conflict'. It concluded in 2010 there were two:

(1) The existence of organised armed groups;
(2) Engaged in fighting of some intensity.[32]

---

[25] Article 1 common to the four Geneva Conventions of 12 August 1949, and Relating to the Protection of Victims of Armed Conflicts, states: 'The High Contracting Parties undertake to respect and to ensure respect for the present Convention in all circumstances'.

[26] Protocol 1, Article 1(4), provides that armed conflicts in which peoples are fighting against colonial domination, alien occupation or racist regimes are 'international armed conflicts'.

[27] Protocol Additional to the Geneva Conventions of 12 August 1949, and relating to the Protection of Victims of Non-International Armed Conflicts (Protocol 2), 8 June 1977, Article 1(1), applies to all armed conflicts occurring 'in the territory of a High Contracting Party, between its armed forces and dissident armed forces or other organized armed groups, which, under responsible command, exercise such control over a part of its territory as to enable them to carry out sustained and concerted military operations and to implement this Protocol'.

[28] See, e.g., ICRC 2016, para 360. See also Chadwick 2002, passim.

[29] Van Steenberghe 2015; Pustorino 2018.

[30] Via Article 3 common the four Geneva Conventions of 1949, Protocol 2, and customary IHL, ICRC undated-b, Customary IHL Database.

[31] See Beaumont 2012, pp. 26–7.

[32] ILA Use of Force Committee 2010, p. 2.

Once these minima are present, one or other level of IHL rules should apply, i.e., inter-state rules of armed conflict, the lesser rules for non-international conflicts,[33] and for either, customary IHL.[34]

Once invoked, the IHL treaty regime, both conventional and customary, includes a well-established distinction between combatants and civilians, to the effect that intentional attacks against civilians and their objects are prohibited, military attacks must be confined strictly to achieving 'lawful' military objectives,[35] while collateral damage and injury may be acceptable,[36] but only for so long as necessary and proportionate, not entailing unlawful means or methods. Moreover, compliance with IHL rules during any forceful struggle, including liberation struggles, should be adjudicated at the conclusion,[37] thus affecting the international recognition afforded to the victor.[38]

41.2.2 The Conflation of Military and Police Force

The state monopoly on the use of force is one of many sovereign governance legitimacies, regarding which the rule of law component remains the institutional reference point and touchstone of 'peacetime' frameworks of analysis. For example, the institutional and legal frameworks in place to restrain governmental force must operate non-discriminatorily, as non-discrimination is an essential tenet of the rule of law; otherwise, governmental domestic force is not adequately sourced.[39] In turn, the rule of law provides for differences in the meaning and operation of parameters of 'necessity' and 'proportionality' in law enforcement as opposed to military operations.[40] Specifically, peacetime law enforcement tasks are not ordinarily undertaken by the military,[41] and any employment of 'armed' force during peacetime is expected to be legitimate, necessary, proportionate, and sparing, with death inflicted only if absolutely necessary.

---

[33] As mirrored in Article 8(2)(a) and (b), and (d) and (e), respectively, 1998 Rome Statute of the International Criminal Court, https://www.icc-cpi.int/resource-library/Documents/RS-Eng.pdf.

[34] ICRC undated-b, Customary IHL Database.

[35] Protocol 1, Article 51(4) and (5), prohibits 'indiscriminate attack'. See, e.g., Bothe 2004. Article 52(2) defines lawful military objectives as 'limited to those objects which by their nature, location, purpose or use make an effective contribution to military action and whose total or partial destruction, capture or neutralisation, in the circumstances ruling at the time, offers a definite military advantage'.

[36] Geneva Protocol 1, Articles 51 and 52.

[37] See, e.g., Ambos 2018.

[38] ILA 2001/2008, Article 10, pp. 50–2. See, e.g., Crawford 2007, discussing, *inter alia*, Israel and Palestine, the dissolution of the USSR and Yugoslavia, German re-unification, and Chechen and Kosovan self-determination. Regarding Palestine, consider UNGA Resolution 181(2), UN Doc A/RES/181(II), 29 November 1947.

[39] A view approved by Stephens 2010, p. 503 n. 52, citing Tomuschat (citation omitted).

[40] See Watkin 2004.

[41] See, e.g., Stephens 2010.

Nonetheless, the shock prompted by '9/11' has seemingly diminished a number of related rule-of-law issues. For example, states today afford to each other a more mutually-acceptable permissiveness to utilise militarised law-and-order, or *military*[42] operatives and personnel against both civil disorder and 'terrorist' actors (however defined).[43] Moreover, states are utilising their armed forces, both abroad and domestically, to pursue criminal matters which have metamorphosed into national security ones.[44] This newer tendency, to conflate domestic crime and international political security, and to conflate police and military capabilities, threatens the long-standing demarcation between the prohibition of inter-state force in UN Charter Article 2(4), and of interference in state domestic affairs as per Charter Article 2(7).[45] It also is exacerbating controversial issues surrounding the transboundary use of force 'in self-defence' against a variety of non-state violent actors,[46] further risking the legal distinction between 'peacetime' contexts of police action (against domestic riots, isolated acts of violence, and the like), and military force utilised, e.g., in liberation struggles for self-determination.

The twin 'Geneva' virtues, of factually recognising belligerency, and of encouraging material reciprocity, are negatively impacted whenever law enforcement agencies are authorised to utilise deadly force anywhere against alleged 'terrorists',[47] while the peace-war dichotomy in international law is equally destabilised whenever the military is ordered to act under police control.

41.3 IHL Parameters Relevant to Self-determination

In 1949, the laws of armed conflict were revised and supplemented, including a provision for domestic conflicts, albeit at the most basic level. Four Geneva 'Red Cross' Conventions, Relating to the Protection of the Victims of Armed Conflicts,[48]

---

[42] Chatham House 2005, Principle 6, p. 11 (right of self-defence against non-state actors).

[43] See, e.g., Tams 2009; McCulloch and Pickering 2009.

[44] Stephens 2010, p. 456. See also Weisburd et al. 2010. Cf. Walker 2010.

[45] See, e.g., Laing 1973, p. 222, citing Brownlie 1973: 'UN organs do not permit Article 2(7) to impede discretion and decision when [self-determination] is in issue' (citation omitted). See also Lewis 2010; Thakur 2008, Chap. 22. Consider UNSC Resolutions 1674 of 28 April 2006, para 4 (R2P), 1973 of 17 March 2011, para 4 (Libya), and 2043 of 21 April 2012 (Syria).

[46] Chatham House 2005, Principle 6, p. 11. See also Nussberger and Fisher 2019 (claim, repeatedly rebutted, that strikes directed against an actor within the territory of another state are not a prohibited use of force against the territorial state); Nussberger 2019 ('attribution narratives' linking states with non-state violent actors); Gaggioli 2019.

[47] Consider Ishil 2019 ('no settled definition of "military activities"').

[48] Convention (I) for the Amelioration of the Condition of the Wounded and Sick in Armed Forces in the Field; Convention (II) for the Amelioration of the Condition of Wounded, Sick and Shipwrecked Members of Armed Forces at Sea; Convention (III) relative to the Treatment of Prisoners of War. Geneva; and, Convention (IV) relative to the Protection of Civilian Persons in Time of War. Full texts and commentaries available at https://www.icrc.org/en/war-and-law/treaties-customary-law/geneva-conventions.

were opened for signature and ratification on 12 August 1949.[49] Compliance was made automatic, omitting the former proviso 'only if all the belligerents are parties to the Convention'.[50] The first three conventions revised, updated and superseded earlier versions,[51] while the fourth is entirely new. Each convention applies to interstate armed conflicts,[52] but all contain an identical, or 'common' Article 3, inserted specifically to provide basic humanitarian protections in non-international armed conflicts.

41.3.1 Common Article 3

Common Article 3, 'a convention in miniature',[53] represents the absolute minimum humanitarian standard during any armed conflict.[54] In 1949, human rights laws were yet to be formulated, making Common Article 3 a precursor. Common Article 3 provides as follows:

> In the case of armed conflict not of an international character occurring in the territory of one of the High Contracting Parties, each Party to the conflict shall be bound to apply, as a minimum, the following provisions:
>
> (1) Persons taking no active part in the hostilities, including members of armed forces who have laid down their arms and those placed *hors de combat* by sickness, wounds, detention, or any other cause, shall in all circumstances be treated humanely, without any adverse distinction founded on race, colour, religion or faith, sex, birth or wealth, or any other similar criteria.

---

[49] Consider Burra 2019a, b ('African, Asian and Latin American states constituted almost half of the 59 participating States').

[50] The '*si omnes*' or 'general participation' clause. See, e.g., the 1907 Hague Convention IV Respecting the Laws and Customs of War on Land, Article 2. This convention did not apply formally during World War 1, due to non-ratification by Serbia and Montenegro. The very similar 1899 Hague Convention II was applicable. See Werner 1918, p. 96 n. 3, citing the Bulletin International des Sociétés de la Croix-Rouge (1918), pp. 25–6.

[51] Convention for the Amelioration of the Condition of the Wounded in Armies in the Field, Geneva, 22 August 1864; Additional Articles relating to the Condition of the Wounded in War, Geneva, 20 October 1868; Convention for the Amelioration of the Condition of the Wounded and Sick in Armies in the Field, Geneva, 6 July 1906; Convention for the Amelioration of the Condition of the Wounded and Sick in Armies in the Field, Geneva, 27 July 1929; Convention relative to the Treatment of Prisoners of War, Geneva, 27 July 1929; and, 'Hague law', so-called. Full texts available at https://ihl-databases.icrc.org/applic/ihl/ihl.nsf/vwTreatiesHistoricalByDate.xsp.

[52] Article 2 common to the four Geneva Conventions of 12 August 1949, states in pertinent part: 'the present Convention shall apply to all cases of declared war or of any other armed conflict which may arise between two or more of the High Contracting Parties, even if the state of war is not recognised by one of them'.

[53] ICRC 1952, Common Article 3, 'General'.

[54] Military and Paramilitary Activities in and against Nicaragua (Nicaragua v. United States of America) (Merits) (Judgment) [1986] ICJ Rep, p. 14, para 218 ('a minimum yardstick' to apply in all conflicts).

To this end, the following acts are and shall remain prohibited at any time and in any place whatsoever with respect to the above-mentioned persons:

(a) violence to life and person, in particular murder of all kinds, mutilation, cruel treatment and torture;
(b) taking of hostages;
(c) outrages upon personal dignity, in particular, humiliating and degrading treatment;
(d) the passing of sentences and the carrying out of executions without previous judgement pronounced by a regularly constituted court affording all the judicial guarantees which are recognised as indispensable by civilised peoples.

(2) The wounded and sick shall be collected and cared for.

An impartial humanitarian body, such as the International Committee of the Red Cross, may offer its services to the parties to the conflict.

The Parties to the conflict should further endeavour to bring into force, by means of special agreements, all or part of the other provisions of the present Convention.

The application of the preceding provisions shall not affect the legal status of the Parties to the conflict.

The trigger for implementing Common Article 3 is 'armed conflict'. Nonetheless, states remained reluctant to accept or acknowledge positive obligations of restraint, however minimal, in conflicts against 'rebels' and 'bandits', unless forced to do so by battlefield conditions.[55] The following agreed conditions proved influential in helping to formalise the article:

- That the *de jure* government has recognised the insurgents as belligerents; or
- that it has claimed for itself the rights of a belligerent; or
- that it has accorded the insurgents recognition as belligerents
- for the purposes only of the present Convention; or
- that the dispute has been admitted to the agenda of the UN Security Council or the General Assembly as being a threat to international peace, a breach of the peace, or an act of aggression.[56]

These and similar points simply nod to certain traditional patterns of behaviour,[57] reflecting recognition of a factual state of affairs.

In 1949, however, it was not yet anticipated that 'the equal rights and the self-determination of peoples'[58] might generate civil *armed conflict*, as such, i.e., in which the military would be called out 'under orders'.[59] Indeed, when compared to the ready resort to military force today for purposes of suppressing domestic unrest, e.g., during high-intensity public protests,[60] it is perhaps easier to understand why

---

[55] See, e.g., Meron 1983.
[56] ICRC 1952, Common Article 3, 'General'.
[57] See, e.g., Reydams 2006.
[58] UN Charter Articles 1(2) and 55.
[59] See generally, ILA Use of Force Committee 2010.
[60] See, e.g., Yua 2019.

such an obvious 'trigger' for Geneva obligations as use of the military could cause consternation at the highest political levels.

The Algerian 'War of Independence' from France (1954–1962) was a case in point.[61] That conflict was both a de-colonisation war, and a true 'civil' war between loyalist French Algerians and pro-independence insurrectionists. France preferred to characterise it throughout as 'terrorism', and reportedly employed torture widely, notably because '[t]he struggle against terrorism makes it necessary to resort to certain questioning techniques as the only way of saving human life and avoiding new attacks'.[62] At no point did France acknowledge the *de jure* applicability of the Geneva regime,[63] however minimal, but was forced by battlefield conditions to apply certain Geneva provisions, *de facto*, to its battlefield behaviour and treatment of prisoners, thus illustrating the importance of material, if not formal, reciprocity in treatment.

41.3.2   Self-determination and 'Internationalised' Uses of Force

Destabilisation of the peace-war dichotomy by the use of force for self-determination highlights a curious paradox regarding the vertical penetration of IHL during non-international armed conflicts in a state-centric world: in the event of an 'armed conflict', IHL ordinarily constitutes the *lex specialis*, trumping, where relevant, what otherwise would be the applicable *lex generalis* (peacetime law), as is now discussed.[64]

41.3.2.1   Legal Prioritisation

First of all, the IHL 'trump' does not 'ordinarily' occur during civil wars. The delegation by the UN Charter of domestic good order to states enables a state threatened with public disorder to delay the point at which it recognises the obligations of even

---

[61] See, e.g., Fraleigh 1971, p. 179.

[62] Lema 2005.

[63] Meyer 1989 (Algerian Provisional Government attempted in 1960 to accede to the 1949 Geneva Conventions).

[64] But see Prosecutor v. D. Tadic, Case No. IT-91-1-AR72, Decision on the Defence Motion for Interlocutory Appeal on Jurisdiction (Appeals Chamber), 2 October 1995, paras 113–18 (premise that 'international humanitarian law includes principles or general rules protecting civilians from hostilities in the course of internal armed conflicts'), and 134 ('customary international law imposes criminal liability for serious violations of Common Article 3').

the most minimal protections of Geneva Common Article 3,[65] to utilise its 'emergency' powers to derogate from its human rights obligations to the extent possible,[66] and to characterise the unrest as generated by 'terrorists' and 'rebels'. The main advantage to states of continuing domestic la, alongside the non-interference principle, is flexibility. When combined with the over-arching importance of international and regional peace and security, forceful domestic responses to internal unrest are more likely to be externally tolerated,[67] even in the thorny context of 'international' liberation conflicts. Therefore, it can be argued that not only did Cold War efforts to end colonialism endanger the peace-war dichotomy, but also, that extending IHL coverage to liberation 'causes' harmed the prioritisation of IHL over peacetime law, as is now discussed.

41.3.2.2 UNGA Resolution 2625 (XXV) (1970)

UNGA Resolution 2625 (XXV) of 24 October 1970 (the 'Friendly Relations' Declaration)[68] is arguably the most important step taken in treating certain liberation conflicts automatically as 'international'. Specifically, the conversion of liberation conflicts into 'international' ones not only better reflected the realities of anti-colonial conflicts, but also it encouraged much greater international attention on the force employed. Resolution 2625 provides in pertinent part as follows:

> [T]he territory of a colony or other non-self-governing territory has ... *a status separate and distinct* from the territory of the state administering it; and such separate and distinct status under the Charter shall exist until the people of the colony or non-self-governing territory have exercised their right of self-determination in accordance with the Charter .... [Emphasis added.]

Resolution 2625 thus controversially predicts the applicability of IHL in full in such struggles. Resolution 2625 also undermines the non-interference principle, as follows:

> Nothing ... shall be construed as authorising or encouraging any action which would dismember or impair, totally or in part, the territorial integrity or political unity of sovereign and independent states *conducting themselves in compliance with the principle of equal rights and self-determination of peoples ... and thus possessed of a government representing the whole people belonging to the territory without distinction as to race, creed or colour.* [Emphasis added.]

---

[65] Article 2(7) is without prejudice to 'the application of enforcement measures under Chapter VII' by the Security Council.

[66] Certain rights however are 'absolute'. ECHR Article 3 (prohibition of torture), Article 4(1) (prohibition of slavery or servitude), and Article 7 (no punishment without law). Oxbridge Notes n.d.

[67] See, e.g., Le Mon 2003.

[68] Declaration on Principles of International Law Concerning Friendly Relations and Cooperation Among States in Accordance with the Charter of the United Nations, 24 October 1970, UN Doc. A/RES/2625(XXV), https://www.refworld.org/docid/3dda1f104.html, agreed by consensus.

This conditionality in turn led some to argue that self-determination constituted a '*causus feodoris*', justifying force to right a wrong, because the highlighted clause provides legal and moral support to transform a denial of internal rights entitlements into rights of territorial secession.[69] The spirit of the doctrine of *uti possidetis* is also evident in Resolution 2625,[70] inasmuch as that doctrine premises rights on battlefield victory. What Resolution 2625 does not do is equate 'representative' with 'democratic' governance, while the exhortation to preserve *only* those states whose governments represent the people 'belonging' to the land smacks more of traditional national liberation theory, to oust invaders.[71]

Resolution 2625 would have explosive consequences, including UN General Assembly Resolutions 3070 (XXVIII) of 30 November 1973, and 3246 (XXIX) of 29 November 1974, which approved the right of peoples to use 'all available means' to achieve their self-determination. These and other related developments concerning force and self-determination made it glaringly evident that IHL required modernisation, which occurred in 1977, in Additional Protocol 1, applicable to international armed conflicts, and Additional Protocol 2 for non-international armed conflicts. States remained reluctant however to cede control over their internal affairs, and ratification of both protocols was initially slow.[72]

41.3.3 Formalisation as 'International'

Protocol 1, Article 1(4), specifically extends IHL in full to certain liberation conflicts, indirectly incorporating Resolution 2625 regarding their separate status, as follows:

> [*International* armed conflicts] include armed conflicts in which peoples are fighting against colonial domination and alien occupation and against racist regimes in the exercise of their right of self-determination. [Emphasis added.]

Protocol 1, Article 1(4), recognises the nominated liberation conflicts as international automatically,[73] catapulting their regulation, from the domestic to the international plane, and the *lex specialis* of IHL in its entirely. Further, the scope of Article 1(4) is also somewhat flexible. As noted by the ICRC, in 1977:[74]

> The expression "colonial domination" certainly covers the most frequently occurring case in recent years … . The expression "alien occupation" … covers cases of partial or total occupation of a territory which has not yet been fully formed as a state. Finally, *the expression "racist regimes" covers cases of regimes founded on racist criteria*. The first two situations

---

[69] Friedrich 2005, p. 248 (citations omitted).

[70] The *uti possidetis* doctrine conveys the international law principle that, subject to any contrary treaty provision, he who possesses territory at the end of war may hold it. See Case concerning the Frontier Dispute (Burkina Faso/Republic of Mali) [1986] ICJ Rep, 554, paras 20–6.

[71] See, e.g., Mishra 2017.

[72] See, e.g., Burra 2019a, b (India not party to either protocol).

[73] See, e.g., Lynk 2018.

[74] ICRC 1987, Article 1, para 112.

imply the existence of distinct peoples.[75] *The third implies, if not the existence of two completely distinct peoples, at least a rift within a people which ensures hegemony of one section in accordance with racist ideas.*[76] [Emphasis added.]

As noted above, states were slow initially to ratify the protocol.[77] Certain states were concerned the applicability of IHL in full now afforded international recognition of 'just causes', and would encourage 'terrorist charters'.[78]

In contrast, '[t]he justice of the cause does not make good, cannot transmute, moral atrocities committed in its name',[79] while any conflation of liberation conflict with 'terrorism' depends on multiple legalities. For example, liberation violence may notionally be viewed as 'just', if not necessarily as 'lawful'. The de-centralised, anarchic international legal order favours sovereign power over the labelling process, which can delay recognition of wider legal obligations. Moreover, IHL rules are ignored opportunistically wherever possible, often due to government concerns about 'lawful killing' by non-state fighters.[80] Geras notes presciently, in pertinent part,

> Wars are fought in the main between states and ... there must be enough of a common interest among them in having codes of rules for these to have evolved to the point they have. Few states, however, if any, can have an interest in drawing up, much less in observing, a comparable code of rules to govern possible revolutionary struggles against them. Oppressive regimes, it may therefore also be said, will use - do use, across the globe - the most savage forms of violence in the counter-revolutionary cause: use terror, torture, massacre.[81]

International pressure on the ICRC to clarify Article 1(4) was quickly brought to bear. In response, it re-assured that 'the mere existence of a government or resistance movement is not sufficient evidence of the international character of the conflict, nor does it establish that character'.[82] Further, Protocol 1 does not alter the legal status of either party in conflict, although it does in fact afford a means for 'peoples' to seek

---

[75] The ICRC adopts an 'ethnic' or 'minority' approach, and a 'civic' or political dimension for 'peoples'. ICRC 1987, Article 1, paras 103–6. Consider Guichard 2017 (competing Korean conceptions of body politic); Alcantara and Dick 2017.

[76] Genocide can occur during a racist/ethnic conflict. See, e.g., the Application of the Convention on the Prevention and Punishment of the Crime of Genocide (Bosnia and Herzegovina v. Serbia and Montenegro) [26 February 2007] ICJ Rep, 43 (Srebrenica massacre).

[77] As of September 2019, Protocol 1 has 174 state parties, and Protocol 2, 168.

[78] See, e.g., Gardam 1989.

[79] Geras 1989, p. 201.

[80] See Obradovic 2000 (Protocol 2, not terrorism, applicable to KLA-Serbia conflict).

[81] Geras 1989, p. 197. Consider Application no. 28761/11, Case of Al Nishiri v. Poland (Judgement) [24 July 2014] ECtHR (US-CIA interrogation techniques and black sites). Contrast R (on the application of (1) Freedom & Justice Party & Ors, (2) Yehia Hamed) (Appellants) v SOS for Foreign & Commonwealth Affairs, (2) Director of Prosecutions (Respondents) & Commissioner of Police of the Metropolis (Interested Party) & (1) Amnesty International, (2) Redress (Interveners) [2018] EWCA Civ 1719 (diplomatic immunity from prosecution for torture).

[82] ICRC 1987, Article 43, para 1662 (citation omitted). See Boelaert-Suominen 2000.

41 The Use of Force in Pursuance of the Right to Self-determination 899

international attention for their 'cause'.[83] Whether Protocol 1 actively encourages a people to adopt force is determined by 'events'.

Protocol 2 codifies better regulations for non-international armed conflicts than does Common Article 3, which Protocol 2 supplements. The central concern of Protocol 2 is to obligate states to show restraint during high-intensity civil wars. It accomplishes this by conditioning its material field of application to armed conflicts which

> [T]ake place in the territory of a High Contracting Party between its armed forces and dissident armed forces or other organised armed groups which, under responsible command, exercise such control over a part of its territory as to enable them to carry out sustained and concerted military operations and to implement this Protocol.[84]

A higher threshold of conflict intensity applies in Protocol 2 than in Common Article 3: 'internal disturbances and tensions, such as riots, isolated and sporadic acts of violence and other acts of a similar nature' are not covered.[85] Protocol 2, Article 3, preserves the state responsibility to re-establish domestic law and order, and conflict does not justify external intervention. Should neither protocol be deemed applicable, there remain only the minimal provisions of Common Article 3,[86] and customary IHL.[87]

One difficulty remains, however: who identifies an 'armed conflict'? Threatened governments resist invoking even Common Article 3, due largely to political consequences. Therefore, it is useful, once again, to consider the 2010 report of the ILA's Use of Force Committee, on the meaning in international law of 'armed conflict'. In finding the two essential indicia of 'armed conflict', highlighted earlier,[88] it specified the rule-of-law consequences for states of not recognising 'armed conflict', as such:

> States may not, consistently with international law, simply declare that a situation is or is not an armed conflict based on policy preferences.[89]

It can be seen therefore that there is plentiful international law and policy for the regulation of all participants in struggles for self-determination. What is lacking is the political will to recognise factual situations of domestic armed conflict, as such, and to implement IHL at the appropriate level. Instead, there has been a veritable

---

[83] For example, Eritrean post-war independence from Ethiopia brought international recognition, and an UN-supervised referendum in 1993; international supervision of Kosovo constituted 'deferred self-determination', until its 2008 Declaration of Independence. Chadwick 2015, pp. 843–4.

[84] Protocol 2, Article 1(2). See, e.g., Obradovic 2000. For case law examples illustrating 'responsible command', and capacity to implement IHL, see ILA Use of Force Committee 2010, pp. 20–1.

[85] Article 8(2)(d) and (f) ('war crimes'), 1998 Rome Statute of the International Criminal Court, https://www.icc-cpi.int/resource-library/Documents/RS-Eng.pdf, applies this threshold to all non-international armed conflicts.

[86] See, e.g., Hamdan v. Rumsfeld, 548 US (2006), 66 (Common Article 3 applicable to US-al Qaeda conflict in Afghanistan).

[87] ICRC undated-b, Customary IHL Database.

[88] ILA Use of Force Committee 2010, p. 1.

[89] ILA Use of Force Committee 2010, p. 2.

explosion of counter-terrorism provisions in recent decades blurring the 'cause' of many forceful 'rights' struggles, as is now discussed.

41.4 Forceful Self-determination as 'Terrorism'

It is a truism to state that self-determination is conflated with terrorism. Nonetheless, a strong state preference for analysing liberation struggles via the lens of terrorism can be attributed to the fact that '[f]ew states, … can have an interest in drawing up, much less in observing, a comparable code of rules to govern possible revolutionary struggles against them'.[90] This state preference also enables the *lex specialis* of IHL to be side-stepped, thereby obviating much international scrutiny, e.g., over judicial safeguards. Finally, the preference for domestic criminal law frameworks permits state flexibilities to be entrenched when implementing international anti-terrorism rules.

Violent acts, per se, are rarely determinative of the law subsequently applied, but must first be characterised and labelled. The conflation of self-determination and terrorism thus exposes state choices, whether as to legal sources or their content, when directing military/police enforcement operations. Variable, localised state domestic anti-terrorism provisions in turn place much heavier defence burdens on alleged perpetrators when faced with criminal prosecution or extradition, than do 'war crimes'.[91] The political advantages thereby afforded to states are multiplied during a liberation conflict, as local criminal laws are able to accomplish what international law cannot: the prohibition of revolution.[92] So long as protracted, sustained,[93] and organised[94] liberation violence can be prosecuted as 'terrorism', the lack of a global definition of 'terrorism' is a positive advantage.

41.4.1 'Terrorist' Force and Self-determination

Violence has throughout history been necessary in effecting system change. That modern IHL was developed during the Cold War era, in part to widen IHL applicability in civil struggles, reflects how reliance on IHL to regulate objectively-identified

---

[90] Geras 1989, p. 197.

[91] 'Terrorist' war crimes may be perpetrated only against civilian populations. Convention IV, Article 33; Protocol 1, Article 51(2); and, Protocol 2, Article 13(2). See also Convention IV Article 147.

[92] See, e.g., Top 2017 (instigators of secessionist Catalan charged with rebellion).

[93] Cf. the five groups of indicative factors, in Prosecutor v. Ljube Boskoski and Johan Tarculovski, IT-04-82-T, Judgement of 10 July 2008, para 199, and the three strict criteria utilised by Rodenhauser 2019.

[94] ICTY, The Prosecutor v. Dusko Tadić, IT-94-1-AR72, Appeals Chamber, Decision, 2 October 1995, https://casebook.icrc.org/case-study/icty-prosecutor-v-tadic, para 70.

situations of organised, protracted armed conflict thus stands in contrast to indiscriminate 'terrorist' violence, the indeterminacies of which continue to plague the international community, as is now discussed.[95]

41.4.1.1 Non-state Force, Self-determination, and Law

When seeking to differentiate terrorism and self-determination, the issue of force is the most problematic. A principle of self-determination is certainly long-standing,[96] being referred prior to emerging after both World Wars,[97] first, via the League of Nations Minorities Treaties, for use in newly-formed states,[98] and, secondly, within the UN principle of 'friendly relations among nations'.[99] In neither context however is there indicated any 'right' to utilise force. Moreover, the politics of self-determination may certainly be pursued by an ethnic minority,[100] but the underlying principle does not, per se, concern minorities. While a minority may adopt force to compel receipt of internal rights entitlements ('internal' self-determination), an entitlement to secede ('external' self-determination) is less likely.

The indeterminacy in the Charter regarding 'which' peoples are entitled to self-determination, 'how', precisely, they are to achieve it, and what rights entitlements are included, has not helped to strengthen anticipated UN goals, such as international peace and security.[101] UN provisions prohibiting the inter-state use of force except in self-defence,[102] reserving sovereign internal control to governments,[103] and imposing legal duties on states to prevent non-state violent actors have instead fostered the view that liberation movements are unlawful 'terrorism', leaving many struggles for self-determination at the mercy of governmental uses of over-whelming, excessive, 'peacetime' force.[104]

---

[95] Of interest, see, e.g., Feuerherd 2019; Gage 2011; Rappaport 2011.

[96] The self-determination canon is extensive. Weller 2008, Bibliography, pp. 171–224. Consider Lenin 1914/1972; Decision of the League of Nations on the Aaland Islands Including Sweden's Protest (Sept. 1921), AJIL 18: 777, [Sept. 1921] LNOJ 697, http://www.kulturstiftelsen.ax/trakta ter/eng_fr/1921a_en.htm; Laing 1993; Whitehall 2016.

[97] See, e.g., Lorca 2014.

[98] E.g., the Kingdom of the Serbs, Croats and Slovenes, formed in December 1918, and becoming Yugoslavia in 1929. Judah 2011.

[99] UN Charter, Articles 1(2) ('friendly relations among nations') and 55 ('creation of conditions of stability and well-being').

[100] See, e.g., 'Conference on Yugoslavia Arbitration Commission Opinions 2 and 3 on Questions arising from the dissolution of Yugoslavia [11 January and 4 July 1992]', reprinted in 31 I.L.M. 1488, 1497–8, and 1499–1500, respectively ('true' minorities may only claim a right to full political participation in an existing entity).

[101] See, e.g., Milanovic 2007; Abresch 2005, p. 765 (doubt as to the existence of a '*jus ad bellum* of internal conflict').

[102] UN Charter, Articles 2(4) and 51.

[103] As per Charter, Article 2(7), and the non-interference principle.

[104] Consider Syria in 2011. See, e.g., RULAC Geneva Academy 2019.

The human and social costs of violent civil 'rights' struggles are well-known, yet the UN's anti-colonial agenda has not always contributed to 'friendly relations among nations'. The promise of post-1945 self-determination originated in the 1941 Atlantic Charter,[105] agreed between US President Roosevelt and UK Prime Minister Churchill, a key component of which was for 'peoples' to seek to liberate themselves from outsider rule and occupation, and to oust invaders.[106] In 1946, eight UN member states (Australia, Belgium, Denmark, France, the Netherlands, New Zealand, the UK and the USA) identified 72 non-self-governing territories under their control, and 11 territories were placed under the stewardship of the Charter Trusteeship System.[107] As new states joined the UN, many having achieved their independence forcefully, self-determination gained content.

This does not assist however in sourcing a legal 'right' to utilise liberation force. In this context, it is also useful to consider the Charter's indeterminacy concerning self-determination, in comparison with its 'hard' rules prohibiting inter-state conflict and interference in the affairs of other states.[108] The non-anticipation in 1945 of the rapidly-unfolding liberation conflicts prospered mainly from the geo-strategic Super Power rivalry, as 'proxy' wars,[109] alongside which states began to agree a number of issue-specific, anti-terrorist conventions, starting in the early 1960s,[110] none of which employed the term 'terrorism'.

41.4.1.2 Terrorist-Liberation Conflation

Today, the right, *erga omnes*,[111] to self-determination is widely understood as denoting the *political* processes by which a 'people' may determine its way of life, including by forming a government and/or state,[112] but with the Cold War waning

---

[105] Atlantic Charter (14 August 1941), https://avalon.law.yale.edu/wwii/atlantic.asp ('[t]hird, they respect the right of all peoples to choose the form of government under which they will live; and they wish to see sovereign rights and self government restored to those who have been forcibly deprived of them').

[106] See, e.g., Currivan 1948 ('self-evident right of the Jewish people to be a … sovereign state').

[107] UN 2008a, pp. 298–304.

[108] Charter, Articles 2(4) and 2(7). See also Charter, Articles 24(1), 25, and Chapters VI and VII, respectively.

[109] See, e.g., Atomic Heritage Foundation 2018.

[110] UN 2008b (earlier documents on Prevention and Suppression of International Terrorism).

[111] Legal Consequences of the Construction of a Wall in the Occupied Palestinian Territory (Advisory Opinion) [2004] ICJ Rep, 136, para 88 (right *erga omnes*). Respect for the right to self-determination is an obligation *erga omnes*. East Timor (Portugal v. Australia), Judgment [1995] ICJ Rep, 90, p. 102, para 29; Barcelona Traction, Light and Power Company, Limited (Belgium v. Spain), Second Phase, Judgment [1970] ICJ Rep, 6, p. 32, para 33.

[112] Regional autonomy is thus included. UNGA Resolution 1541 (XV), of 15 December 1960 (three options for self-determination). See also the Declaration on the Granting of Independence to Colonial Countries and Peoples, UNGA Resolution 1514 (XV), of 14 December 1960; UN Resolutions 2625 (XXV), of 24 October 1970; and, 65/119, of 10 December 2010, on the Third International Decade for the Eradication of Colonialism (2011–2020). See generally UN undated-a,

in the 1980s, attempts to differentiate liberation conflicts and 'terrorism' began to falter.[113] The silencing of competing East-West liberation rhetoric revealed instead that the international *political* support for self-determination had in fact underpinned a widespread use of force in international life. It also became apparent that decades of Cold War rivalry in sponsoring self-determination conflicts had merely fostered an expectation of ever-increasing levels of violence.

Many liberation struggles ended once the Cold War ended, yet not all. The emergence of new funding sources,[114] alongside new, violent 'causes' and goals, merely blurred the picture further.[115] Today, with most 'classic' colonial situations resolved,[116] it can be stated with confidence that traditional 'justifications' for utilising violence to achieve self-determination have been superseded.[117] Similarly, many post-Cold War, non-state violent acts reflect far wider political issues than rights entitlements, leaving self-determination disregarded, if not forgotten entirely, in the contemporary era.

The transition in attitude at UN level includes UNGA Resolution 49/60 (1994),[118] as supplemented by Resolution 51/210 (17 December 1996),[119] both constantly referred to ever since in condemnations of 'terrorist' acts. The UN and its relevant agencies and committees continue to fill notional remaining gaps in anti-terror legal coverage at the international level.[120] Three anti-terror conventions with extremely broad definitions—on terrorist bombings, terrorist financing, and acts of nuclear terrorism[121]—have now permanently altered the scope and direction of global anti-terrorist commitments, strengthening a consensus regarding a 'right'—rather than a

---

and Decolonization. Consider Legal Consequences for States of the Continued Presence of South Africa in Namibia (South West Africa) (Advisory Opinion) [1971] ICJ Rep, pp. 16, 31; Kattan 2018.

[113] E.g., via the *uti possidetis* doctrine, noted above. See Abraham 2007 (spirited attack on *uti possidetis*).

[114] See, e.g., Howard and Traughber 2013.

[115] See, e.g., Stepanova 2009, p. 104.

[116] With some notable exceptions. See, e.g., Legal Consequences of the Separation of the Chagos Archipelago from Mauritius in 1965 (Advisory Opinion) [25 February 2019] ICJ General List, No. 169, https://www.icj-cij.org/files/case-related/169/169-20190225-01-00-EN.pdf (Chagos Islanders' right to self-determination breached in 1968 Mauritius decolonisation). Consider France Agence-Presse 2018; Reuters 2018; Anon 2018.

[117] Starting with UNGA Res. 40/61, of 9 December 1985, on measures to prevent international terrorism.

[118] UNGA Res. 49/60, of 9 December 1994, on Measures to eliminate international terrorism, https://undocs.org/en/A/RES/49/60. Resolution 49/60 mentions neither 'peoples' nor 'legitimate struggle'.

[119] UNGA Res. 51/210, of 17 December 1996, on Measures to eliminate international terrorism, https://undocs.org/en/A/RES/51/210.

[120] The source of geo-political friction. See, e.g., Bosworth-Davies 2008.

[121] The 1997 International Convention for the Suppression of Terrorist Bombings, the 1999 International Convention for the Suppression of the Financing of Terrorism, and the 2005 International Convention for the Suppression of Acts of Nuclear Terrorism, available at UN undated-d, Office of Counter Terrorism.

power or a licence—to use force in self defence against violent non-state groups.[122] One is nonetheless reminded of the rejection of the idea 'that the use of violence is never justified', because '… it is a doctrine that would deprive people of all weapons save passive resistance in the face of any oppression or threat, however terrible'.[123]

41.4.2 Locating 'Terrorism' for Legal Purposes

As already noted, a number of 'terrorist' conventions exist, mainly for prohibiting and prosecuting violent acts such as hijacking and hostage-taking,[124] while locating a definition in international customary law remains contentious.[125] Further, the General Assembly's Ad Hoc and Sixth (Legal) Committees have long worked on a Draft Comprehensive Convention on International Terrorism (DCCIT).[126] The DCCIT is mainly a technical, enforcement instrument, to supplement police and judicial cooperation, e.g., in extradition matters and mutual assistance. However, a consolidated text of the DCCIT, submitted in 2005 to the General Assembly,[127] still awaits finalisation,[128] due, *inter alia*, to the issue of inclusion or exclusion of violent liberation acts from its coverage. Specifically, what divides the developed and less developed worlds is whether liberation violence should be assessed under IHL, or, the state preference, through peacetime law.[129]

Depending on the outcome of this controversy, there is a danger in terrorist contexts that the *lex specialis*[130] will be trumped completely by the *lex generalis* of domestic law, endangering humanitarian restraint 'in all circumstances'.[131] Specifically, terrorist acts are always unlawful, but while non-state terrorist acts under peacetime law are 'crime',[132] they are unlawful under laws of armed conflict only

---

[122] Charter, Article 51. See, e.g., Chatham House (1 October 2005), Principle 6, p. 11. Contrast UNGA Resolution 3314 (XXIX), of 14 December 1974, on The Definition of Aggression, and, Article 8 bis, 1998 Rome Statute of the International Criminal Court (force utilised between states).

[123] Geras 1989, p. 186.

[124] Available at UN undated-d, Office of Counter Terrorism.

[125] Contrast Cassese 2006; Saul 2011.

[126] Draft comprehensive convention against international terrorism: Consolidated text, UNGA Doc A/59/894 (12 August 2005), 59th Sess., Item No. 148, Appendix II, https://undocs.org/en/A/59/894.

[127] See, e.g., Hmoud 2006.

[128] In January 2019, the Assembly tasked the UN's Sixth (Legal) Committee with establishing a working group, to attempt to finalise the DCCIT, and to consider convening a high-level conference under UN auspices, to agree it, https://www.un.org/en/ga/sixth/74/int_terrorism.shtml.

[129] Contrast Van Poecke 2019.

[130] Including during military occupations. See, e.g., Darcy and Reynolds 2010.

[131] Article 1 common to the four Geneva Conventions of 1949. Consider Clapham 2006.

[132] As reflected in the 1999 Financing Convention's purportedly 'exceptionless' definition of terrorism, substantially incorporated in UNSC Resolution 1373, of 28 September 2001, https://www.refworld.org/docid/3c4e94552a.html.

when utilised intentionally against civilians.[133] Cassese encapsulates this distinction succinctly:

> [A]ttacks by freedom fighters and other combatants in armed conflict, if directed at military personnel and objectives in keeping with IHL, are lawful and may not be termed terrorism. If instead they target civilians, they amount to terrorist acts (not, therefore, to war crimes) if their purpose is to terrorise civilians.[134]

This *legal* differentiation thus exposes the widening over recent decades of a *political* gap within the international and domestic legal spheres. Specifically, the latter is utilised to differentiate (discriminate) according to status, e.g., exempting from official censure uses of authorised force,[135] when in contrast, terrorising enemy combatants is an important tool in ending a war. Whenever the fact of an extant liberation conflict is ignored, legal issues surrounding *lawful* means and methods of armed conflict are side-stepped. Once a threatened state insists a conflict is 'terrorism',[136] the 'terrorists' (not the state agents) will be prosecuted for perpetrating violence. Third states, bound by the principle of non-interference, may simply look the other way.

Long-standing state conflation of 'terrorists' and 'freedom fighters' results from sovereign state power over force, yet, where states lead, non-state violent actors follow. Walzer highlights the ethics and 'political code[s] … roughly analogous to the laws of war' of early revolutionary groups,[137] asserting that:

> Tyrants taught the method [of terrorism] to soldiers, and soldiers to modern revolutionaries. … [T]errorism in the strict sense, the random murder of innocent people, emerged as a strategy of revolutionary struggle only in the period after World War II, that is, only after it had become a feature of conventional war.[138]

Assuming formal inter-state laws of war, and informal revolutionary codes, arose in tandem, e.g., during both World Wars in which the belligerents intentionally terrorised non-combatants,[139] the increasingly indiscriminate means and methods of warfare become obvious.[140] Those wars were 'total', as can seem the violence

---

[133] Geneva Convention IV of 1949, Article 33; Protocol 1 of 1977, Article 51(2); Protocol 2 of 1977, Article 13(2).

[134] Cassese 2006, pp. 955–6.

[135] See, e.g., Council of Europe 2005, para 83 ('[t]he Convention, therefore, leaves unaffected conduct undertaken pursuant to lawful government authority'). See Chadwick 2007.

[136] See, e.g., Syria, in its on-going civil war.

[137] Walzer 1977, p. 198.

[138] Walzer 1977, p. 198.

[139] E.g., the London 'Blitz' (September 1940–May 1941). Encyclopaedia Britannica (last updated 31 August 2019), https://www.britannica.com/event/the-Blitz. Consider ILA, Draft Convention for the Protection of Civilian Populations Against New Engines of War, Amsterdam, 1938, https://ihl-databases.icrc.org/applic/ihl/ihl.nsf/Treaty.xsp?action=openDocument&documentId=29DF95181E9CC0FDC12563CD002D6A9B, intended to protect the civilian population from bombardment.

[140] E.g., Allied high-altitude, carpet-bombing of the Ruhr Valley, Germany. Encyclopaedia Britannica (undated), https://www.britannica.com/event/World-War-II/Air-warfare-1942-43.

utilised in post-1945 liberation conflicts,[141] as fought by state militaries and demobbed former soldiers, both well-trained in the methods of unrestricted warfare. In turn, the conflation of 'terrorist' and 'freedom fighter' is but another sovereign flexibility today enabling the UN to create a complex, 'counter-terror' legal web, intended to snare *all* non-state violent actors.[142]

Moreover, and despite existing human rights and freedoms,[143] many states prefer to declare emergency powers and decrees during violent civil unrest.[144] These powers and decrees are notionally of finite duration, but risk entrenching reduced civil rights and judicial safeguards, hybridising the police and military, and instituting new layers of secrecy in criminal justice.[145] The UN's contemporary condemnation of *all* 'terrorist' acts as 'unjustifiable', under *any* circumstances, coupled with no global legal definitions, thus enable states to disregard what prompts domestic unrest in the first place, as is now discussed.

41.4.3 The Necessity of Forceful Struggle

The lack of global definitions only blurs distinctions between international terrorism and the right of 'peoples' to struggle for self-determination.[146] Further, the term 'terrorism' more denotes a 'characterisation',[147] while government rights over force make self-sanction for violence unlikely. As for liberation violence, it may be true that '[t]he justice of the cause does not make good, cannot transmute, moral atrocities committed in its name',[148] but condemnations of *all* non-state violence cannot explain '… a doctrine that would deprive people of all weapons save passive resistance in the face of any oppression or threat, however terrible'.[149] This paradox underlines the sheer desirability of state sovereign power at the heart of liberation struggles.

Indeed, the 9/11 era has reawakened 'the very old trend of resorting to the notion of "terrorism" to stigmatise political, ethnic, regional or other movements [governments] simply do not like',[150] but inter-state efforts to prevent terrorism are

---

[141] E.g., the use of napalm and agent orange during the Vietnam War, 1954–1975. Encyclopaedia Britannica (last updated 30 August 2019), https://www.britannica.com/event/Vietnam-War.

[142] A range of useful UN resources is in Dag Hammerskjold Library 2019. See generally UN 2019b.

[143] UN 2006, 2017.

[144] Nine ECHR state parties have to date derogated. ECHR 2019.

[145] See, e.g., Yub 2019 (invocation of colonial era 'Emergency Regulations Ordinance' will eradicate many fundamental rights and 'scare people with an atmosphere of war'). See also Barak-Erez and Waxman 2009–2010; Weigelt and Marker 2007, p. 377; Sari 2019.

[146] See, e.g., Weigand 2006.

[147] Shariatmadari 2015.

[148] Geras 1989, p. 201.

[149] Geras 1989, p. 186.

[150] UN 2005, para 56(a).

not new.[151] The 1937 Terrorist Convention was the first to frame the definition of terrorism as an attack against the state.[152] Anarchist-inspired political assassinations prompted its drafting,[153] alongside the first Convention for the Creation of an International Criminal Court,[154] neither ever in force. Article 1(2) of the Terrorism Convention defines 'acts of terrorism' as 'criminal acts directed against a State'. The 'state', as per Article 2, includes Heads of State, their families, other state agents, and public property. The public is mentioned in Article 2(3). The Terrorism Convention also attempts to alter traditional state neutrality regarding the perpetrators of political offences, inaugurating the link between terrorism and self-determination.[155]

The 1999 Terrorism Convention of the Organisation of African Union provides a more recent example of how regional codifications protect the state from challenge. 'Terrorist acts,' as per Article 1(3), include:

(a) any act which is a violation of the criminal laws of a State Party ... and is calculated or intended to: ...; or

   (iii) create general insurrection in a State; ... .

Therefore, it can be argued that a principal reason to prohibit *all* non-state violent acts, in contexts far beyond the *actus reus* and *mens rea* of ordinary criminal law, is the protection of the state.[156]

In contrast, the principle of equal rights and self-determination of peoples has been re-affirmed constantly during the UN era, including in the Preamble of the 1979 Hostages Convention.[157] At the regional level, self-determination struggles are acknowledged, e.g., in the 2004 Convention against Terrorism of the Co-operation Council for Arab States of the Gulf, the Arab Convention on the Suppression of Terrorism 1998 of the League of Arab States, the Convention on the Prevention and Combating of Terrorism 1999, and Protocol of 2004, of the Organisation of African Unity, and the Convention of the OIC On Combating International Terrorism 1999. As late as 2005, Duursma notes, the UN's Sixth Committee did not consider self-determination to involve terrorism.[158]

---

[151] See UN undated-d, Office of Counter Terrorism. See also UNSC Resolution 1566, of 8 October 2004.

[152] League of Nations, Convention for the Prevention and Punishment of Terrorism, 1937, 7 Hudson, International Legislation, No. 499, at 862, LNOJ 1934, pp. 23–34, World Digital Library, https://www.wdl.org/en/item/11579/.

[153] Keesings Archives, p. 1394 ('during the past 80 years more than 100 Monarchs, Presidents, and Heads of Government have been assassinated').

[154] 7 Hudson, International Legislation, No. 500, LNOJ 1934, pp. 37–51, respectively.

[155] Terrorism Convention Article 2 (extradition). See In re Castioni [1891] 1 QB 149, https://www.refworld.org/docid/48abd5390.html (Extradition Act 1870, 33 & 34 Vict., c. 52, political offence exception applied). Contrast ILC 2014.

[156] See, e.g., Council of Europe (16 May 2005), para 34 ('the new crimes introduced by the Convention ... do not require that a terrorist offence ... actually be committed').

[157] 1979 International Convention Against the Taking of Hostages (New York; 17 December 1979). See, e.g., Lambert 1990.

[158] Duursma 2008.

41.4.4 The Terrorism-Liberation Distinction

Terrorism (form of violence) and self-determination ('cause') are also distinguishable by their different means and methods. The use of unexpected and indiscriminate violence characterises contemporary terrorism. In contrast, struggles for self-determination entailing protracted or sustained armed conflict should be regulated by rules of IHL, the central principles of which rely on fundamental principles of targeting discrimination and distinction.

This particular distinction between force and 'cause' is relatively recent, however. During the early UN Charter era, wartime experience of 'total warfare' proved useful in otherwise unregulated liberation conflicts. The Geneva Protocols of 1977 put in place regulatory frameworks for such conflicts, yet by the end of the Cold War, international sentiment was hardening against the 'justness' of so-called forceful 'causes'. For example, para 1 of UNGA Res. 40/61 (9 December 1985), on measures to prevent international terrorism, 'unequivocally condemns, as criminal, all acts, methods and practices of terrorism wherever and by whomever committed'.

After 9/11, UN Security Council Resolution 1373, of 28 September 2001, pressed all Member States to ratify and enforce the provisions of the Financing Convention, and earlier terrorist conventions. The resolution ultimately has constructed a global criminal net over all 'terrorist' actors. The fraught question 'who is a terrorist?' remains however,[159] as do questions surrounding any automatic exemption of liberation fighters from prosecution for terrorism. Meanwhile, the hallmarks of *indiscriminate* violence utilised today by all violent actors are clearly evident. Randomness, 'death by chance', intimidation and fear are everyday experiences, as 'war' and 'peace' converge.

41.5 Conclusion

The foregoing discussion considered the right to use force in struggles for self-determination. It did so by reference to IHL regulation of liberation struggles, after which domestic law approaches to 'terrorism' were addressed. It was highlighted throughout that self-determination is a UN principle, a legal norm,[160] and a right of all, *erga omnes*. It has been noted that self-determination embraces older 'just causes', of colonial domination, alien occupation and racist regimes,[161] and a range of new 'causes', groups and rights claims.

---

[159] See, e.g., Käser and Wigger 2019 (terrorism a constantly evolving, dynamic phenomenon).

[160] Self-determination as a norm of customary international law emerged between 1965 and 1968. Legal Consequences of the Separation of the Chagos Archipelago from Mauritius in 1965 (Advisory Opinion) [25 February 2019] ICJ General List, No. 169, https://www.icj-cij.org/files/case-related/169/169-20190225-01-00-EN.pdf, paras 142 and 161.

[161] As per Protocol 1, Article 1(4). Contrast Chadwick 1996, 2011.

It has been argued that self-determination destabilises a geo-political environment based on sovereign states, which latter are to maintain domestic order, and hence, international peace and security. For this purpose, states hold the legal monopoly over the internal use of force, which the use of force by a 'people' to pursue self-determination disturbs. Nonetheless, as the UN anti-colonial agenda was achieved, in large part by the use of liberation force against recalcitrant administering states, IHL provisions were extended, first, in 1949, in Common Article 3, and secondly, in 1977, in Protocols 1 and 2. It has been argued that these developments reflected the realities of 'civil' armed conflicts, but also provided evidence of a new political willingness to ensure legal regulation of fratricidal warfare.

Nonetheless, civil and liberation conflicts continue to erupt worldwide, and to be treated as 'terrorism'. The difficulty remains that states are reluctant to acknowledge any legal rules applicable to 'rebels' other than those prohibiting 'terrorism'. This means the regulation of liberation conflicts, civil war and/or rebellion by IHL is too often a theoretical possibility, alone. Treating liberation violence as terrorism is also easier for states to process, as alleged perpetrators only have 'rights' (not absolute) to basic provisions of due process and defence. Moreover, identifications of non-international 'armed conflicts', as such, remain fraught with political dangers, despite the availability of the essential objective indicia of organised forces and protracted violence.

In conclusion, although today's hyper-terror-aware, geo-political environment is replete with condemnations at the highest levels of *all* non-state violence, the premise noted at various points, above, remains sound: liberation violence can be necessary, as a last resort to means of self-defence against gross oppression and mistreatment by states. To argue otherwise would be to entrench mis-rule without redress. Having said that, the force utilised in armed conflict is never unrestrained by law. Therefore, until the international community of states is willing and able to respect the rule of law during armed conflict, the use of force to achieve self-determination is likely to continue.

References

Abraham G (2007) "Lines upon Maps": Africa and the Sanctity of African Borders. Afr JI&CompL 15(1): 61
Abresch W (2005) A human rights law of internal armed conflict: The European Court of Human Rights in Chechnya. EJIL 16(4): 741
Alcantara C, Dick C (2017) Decolonization in a Digital Age: Cryptocurrencies and Indigenous Self-determination in Canada. Can JL&Soc 32(1): 19
Ambos K (2018) Another Challenge for Columbia's Transitional Justice Process: Aggravated Differentiated Treatment between Armed Forces and FARC. https://www.ejiltalk.org/another-challenge-for-colombias-transitional-justice-process-aggravated-differential-treatment-between-armed-forces-and-farc/
Anon (2018) Commentaire: Sauver la paix en Nouvelle-Caledonie. https://www.ouest-france.fr/reflexion/editorial/commentaire-sauver-la-paix-en-nouvelle-caledonie-6048545?utm_source=neo

lane_of_newsletter-generale&utm_medium=email&utm_campaign=of_newsletter-generale&
utm_content=20181102&vid=2614190&mediego_euid=2614190

Atomic Heritage Foundation (2018) Proxy Wars during the Cold War: Africa. https://www.atomic heritage.org/history/proxy-wars-during-cold-war-africa. Accessed 30 September 2019

Azarova V, Berkes A (2018) The Commission's Proposals to Correct EU-Morocco Relations and the EU's Obligation Not to Recognise as Lawful the "Illegal Situation" in Western Sahara. https://www.ejiltalk.org/the-commissions-proposals-to-correct-eu-morocco-relations-and-the-eus-obligation-not-to-recognise-as-lawful-the-illegal-situation-in-western-sahara/. Accessed 30 September 2019

Barak-Erez D, Waxman M C (2009 – 2010) Secret Evidence and the Due Process of Terrorist Detentions. Columb JTrans'IL 48: 3

Beaumont P (2012) Egypt's generals wait in wings as the revolutions turns messy. https://www. theguardian.com/world/2012/may/05/egypt-generals-wait-wing-revolution-messy. Accessed 30 September 2019

Bennett C, Haggerty K (eds) (2011) Security Games: Surveillance and Control at Mega-Events. Routledge, Abingdon

Boelaert-Suominen S (2000) The ICTY and the Kosovo conflict. IRRC 82(837): 217. https://www. icrc.org/en/doc/resources/documents/article/other/57jqd2.htm. Accessed 30 September 2019

Bosworth-Davies R (2008) The Influence of Christian Model Ideology in the Development of Anti-Money Laundering Compliance in the West and Its Impact, Post 9-11, Upon the South Asian Market: An Independent Evaluation of a Modern Phenomenon. JMoneyLaundrContr 11(2): 179

Bothe M (2004) Second Expert Meeting on the Notion of Direct Participation in Hostilities: Direct Participation in Hostilities in Non-International Armed Conflict. ICRC, The Hague. https://www.icrc.org/en/doc/assets/files/other/2004-05-expert-paper-dph-icrc.pdf. Accessed 30 September 2019

Brownlie I (1973) Principles of Public International Law. Clarendon Press, Oxford, p. 577

Burke J (2003) Al-Qaeda: Casting a Shadow of Terror. I.B. Taurus & Co. Ltd., London

Burra S (2019) India's Strange Position on the Additional Protocols of 1977. https://www.ejiltalk. org/indias-strange-position-on-the-additional-protocols-of-1977/. Accessed 30 September 2019

Burra S (2019) Was there the Third World in Geneva in 1949? https://www.ejiltalk.org/was-there-the-third-world-in-geneva-in-1949/. Accessed 30 September 2019

Cassese A (2006) The multifaceted criminal notion of terrorism in international law. JICrimJust 4(5): 933

Chadwick E (1996) Self-Determination, Terrorism and the International Humanitarian Law of Armed Conflict. Martinus Nijhoff Publishers, London

Chadwick E (2002) Traditional Neutrality Revisited: Law, Theory, and Case Studies. Kluwer Law International (Humanitarian Law Series Vol. 4), The Hague

Chadwick E (2007) The 2005 Terrorism Convention: A Flexible Step Too Far? Nottm LJ 16(2): 29

Chadwick E (2011) Self-Determination in the Post-9/11 Era. Routledge, Abingdon

Chadwick E (2015) National Liberation in the Context of Post- and Non-Colonial Struggles for Self-Determination. In: Weller M (ed) The Oxford Handbook of The Use of Force in International Law. OUP, Oxford

Chatham House (2005) Principles of International Law on the Use of Force By States in Self-Defence. https://www.chathamhouse.org/publications/papers/view/108106. Accessed 30 September 2019

Clapham A (2006) Human rights obligations of non-state actors in conflict situations. IRRC 88: 491

Council of Europe (2005) Explanatory Report of Europe Terrorism Convention, CETS No. 196, Warsaw. https://rm.coe.int/16800d3811. Accessed 30 September 2019

Crawford J (2007) The Creation of States in International Law, 2nd edn. OUP, Oxford

Currivan G (1948) Zionists Proclaim New State of Israel. https://archive.nytimes.com/www.nyt imes.com/library/world/480515israel-state-50.html. Accessed 30 September 2019

Dag Hammerskjold Library (2019) 'Counter-Terrorism: Quick Guide'. http://research.un.org/en/counter-terrorism (last updated 19 August 2019)

Darcy S, Reynolds J (2010) "Otherwise occupied": the status of the Gaza Strip from the perspective of international humanitarian law. JConfl&SecL 15(2): 211

Duursma J (2008) Definition of Terrorism and Self-Determination. HarvIRev (copy on file with author)

ECHR (2019) Press Unit Factsheet: Derogation in time of emergency. <http://www.echr.coe.int/Documents/FS_Derogation_ENG.pdf (last updated July 2019). Accessed 30 September 2019

Feuerherd P (2019) What Violent Acts Get Defined As Terrorism? https://daily.jstor.org/what-violent-acts-get-defined-as-terrorism/. Accessed 30 September 2019

Fraleigh A (1971) The Algerian Revolution as a Case Study in International Law. In: Falk R A(ed) The International Law of Civil War. John Hopkins Press, London

France Agence-Presse (2018) New Caledonia votes on independence from France in landmark test. https://www.theguardian.com/world/2018/nov/04/new-caledonia-voting-france. Accessed 30 September 2019

Friedrich J (2005) UNMIK in Kosovo: Struggling with Uncertainty. Max Planck Yearbook of United Nations Law 9: 225

Gage B (2011) Terrorism and the American Experience: A State of the Field. JAmHist 98(1): 73

Gaggioli G (2019) Soldier Self-Defense Symposium: Self-Defense in Armed Conflicts – The Babel Tower Phenomenon. https://opiniojuris.org/2019/05/03/soldier-self-defense-symposium-self-defense-in-armed-conflicts-the-babel-tower-phenomenon/. Accessed 30 September 2019

Gardam J (1989) Protocol 1 to the Geneva Conventions: A Victim of Short-Sighted Political Considerations? Melb ULRev 17: 107

Geras N (1989) Our Morals: the Ethics of Revolution. The Socialist Register 25: 185. https://socialistregister.com/index.php/srv/article/view/556. Accessed 30 September 2019

Guichard J (2017) In the Name of the People: Disagreeing over Peoplehood in the North and South Korean Constitutions. Asian JL&Soc 4: 405

Hart QC D (2015) Western Sahara goes to Europe. https://ukhumanrightsblog.com/2015/10/23/western-sahara-goes-to-europe/. Accessed 30 September 2019

Hmoud M (2006) Negotiating the Draft Comprehensive Convention on International Terrorism: Major Bones of Contention. JICrimJust 4: 1031

Howard R D, Traughber C (2013) The Nexus of Extremism and Trafficking: Scourge of the World or So Much Hype? JSOU Report 13/6. https://jsou.libguides.com/jsoupublications/2013

ICRC (undated-a) Introduction: Additional Protocol II of 1977. http://www.icrc.org/ihl.nsf/INTRO/475?OpenDocument. Accessed 30 September 2019

ICRC (undated-b) Customary IHL Database. https://ihl-databases.icrc.org/customary-ihl/eng/docs/home

ICRC (1952) Commentary to the First Geneva Convention. https://ihl-databases.icrc.org/applic/ihl/ihl.nsf/Comment.xsp?action=openDocument&documentId=1919123E0D121FEFC12563CD0041FC08. Accessed 30 September 2019

ICRC (1987) Commentary to the First Additional Protocol of 1977. https://ihl-databases.icrc.org/applic/ihl/ihl.nsf/Comment.xsp?action=openDocument&documentId=7125D4CBD57A70DDC12563CD0042F793. Accessed 30 September 2019

ICRC (2016) Commentary to the First Geneva Convention. https://ihl-databases.icrc.org/applic/ihl/ihl.nsf/Comment.xsp?action=openDocument&documentId=59F6CDFA490736C1C1257F7D004BA0EC. Accessed 30 September 2019

ILA (2001/2008) Draft Articles on Responsibility of States for Internationally Wrongful Acts, with Commentaries. http://legal.un.org/ilc/texts/instruments/english/commentaries/9_6_2001.pdf, Accessed 30 September 2019

ILA (2010) Use of Force Committee: Final Report on the Meaning of Armed Conflict in International Law, 15–20 August 2010. http://www.ila-hq.org/index.php/committees. Accessed 30 September 2019

ILC (2014) Final Report, Executive Summary: The obligation to extradite or prosecute (aut dedere aut judicare), 66th Sess., YbILC 2: Pt. 2. http://legal.un.org/ilc/texts/instruments/english/reports/7_6_2014.pdf. Accessed 30 September 2019

Ishil Y (2019) The Distinction between Military and Law Enforcement Activities: Comments on Case Concerning the Detention of Three Ukrainian Naval Vessels (Ukraine v. Russian Federation), Provisional Measures Order'. https://www.ejiltalk.org/the-distinction-between-military-and-law-enforcement-activities-comments-on-case-concerning-the-detention-of-three-ukrainian-naval-vessels-ukraine-v-russian-federation-provisional-measures-order/. Accessed 30 September 2019

Judah T (2011) BBC History: Yugoslavia: 1918 – 2003. http://www.bbc.co.uk/history/worldwars/wwone/yugoslavia_01.shtml, last updated 17 February 2011. Accessed 30 September 2019

Kaempfer C, Thirion S, Schmid E (2018) Switzerland Rejects a Popular Initiative "Against Foreign Judges". http://opiniojuris.org/2018/12/17/switzerland-rejects-a-popular-initiative-against-foreign-judges/. Accessed 30 September 2019

Käser H-J, Wigger B (2019) Commentary: The 2019 Swiss Security Network Exercise: More Than an Exercise. RUSI. https://rusi.org/commentary/2019-swiss-security-network-exercise-more-exercise. Accessed 30 September 2019

Kattan V (2018) "There was an elephant in the court room": Reflections on the Role of Sir Percy Spender (1897-1985) in the South West Africa Cases (1960-1966) after half a century. Leid JIL 31(1): 1

Ku J (2017) International Law Pays No Homage to Catalonia's Declaration of Independence. http://opiniojuris.org/2017/10/29/international-law-pays-no-homage-catalonias-declaration-independence/. Accessed 30 September 2019

Laing E A (1993) The Norm of Self-Determination, 1941–1991. 22 Int. Rel. 209

Lambert J J (1990) Terrorism and Hostages in International Law – A Commentary on the Hostages Convention 1979. CUP, Cambridge

Le Mon C J (2003) Unilateral Intervention by Invitation in Civil Wars: The Effective Control Test Tested. International Law and Politics 35: 741. https://ssrn.com/abstract=723182. Accessed 30 September 2019

Lema L (2005) Torture in Algeria. The report that was to change everything. https://www.icrc.org/en/doc/resources/documents/article/other/algeria-history-190805.htm. Accessed 30 September 2019

Lenin V I (1914/1972) The Right of Nations to Self-Determination, in Lenin's Collected Works, Vol. 22. Progress Publishers, Moscow

Lewis A (2010) The Responsibility to Protect: a new response to humanitarian suffering? e-International Relations (6 July 2010)

Lorca A B (2014) Petitioning the International: A "Pre-history" of Self-determination. EJIL 25(2): 497

Lynk M (2018) Prolonged Occupation or Illegal Occupant? https://www.ejiltalk.org/prolonged-occupation-or-illegal-occupant/. Accessed 30 September 2019

Macak M (2018) Wars of national liberation: The story of one unusual rule Pt. 1. https://blog.oup.com/2018/07/wars-national-liberation-unusual-rule-part-1/, 23 July 2018. Accessed 30 September 2019

McCulloch J, Pickering S (2009) Pre-crime and counter-terrorism: imagining future crime in the "war on terror". BritJCrim 49(5): 628

Meron T (1983) Notes and Comments: On the Inadequate Reach of Humanitarian and Human Rights Law and the Need for a New Instrument. AJIL 77(3): 589

Meyer (1989) Recent Publications. Interights Bulletin 4: 13

Milanovic M (2007) Lessons for human rights and humanitarian law in the war on terror: Comparing Hamdan and the Israeli Targeted Killings Case. IRRC 89: 373

Milanovic M (2017) A Footnote on Secession. https://www.ejiltalk.org/a-footnote-on-secession/. Accessed 30 September 2019

Milanovic M (2018) Western Sahara before the CJEU. https://www.ejiltalk.org/western-sahara-before-the-cjeu/. Accessed 30 September 2019

Mishra P (2017) How colonial violence came home: the ugly truth of the First World War. https://www.theguardian.com/news/2017/nov/10/how-colonial-violence-came-home-the-ugly-truth-of-the-first-world-war. Accessed 30 September 2019

Nussberger B K (2019) Language as Door-Opener for Violence? How a New "Attribution-Narrative" May Lead to Armed Confrontation between Iran, and the US and Saudi-Arabia. http://opiniojuris.org/2019/06/07/%EF%BB%BFlanguage-as-door-opener-for-violence-how-a-new-attribution-narrative-may-lead-to-armed-confrontation-between-iran-and-the-us-and-saudi-arabia/. Accessed 30 September 2019

Nussberger B, Fisher P (2019) Justifying Self-defence against Assisting States: Conceptualising Legal Consequences of Inter-State Assistance. https://www.ejiltalk.org/justifying-self-defense-against-assisting-states-conceptualizing-legal-consequences-of-inter-state-assistance/. Accessed 30 September 2019

Obradovic K (2000) International humanitarian law and the Kosovo crisis, IRRC 839, 30 September 2000. https://www.icrc.org/en/doc/resources/documents/article/other/57jqqb.htm. Accessed 30 September 2019

O'Carroll L (2018) Brexit: Sin Fein wants Northern Ireland vote in event of no-deal Brexit. https://www.theguardian.com/politics/2018/oct/15/sinn-fein-we-will-demand-referendum-on-northern-Ireland-in-event-of-no-deal-brexit. Accessed 30 September 2019

Oxbridge Notes (nd) Absolute Rights Notes. https://www.oxbridgenotes.co.uk/revision_notes/law-european-human-rights-law/samples/absolute-rights. Accessed 30 September 2019

Pustorino P (2018) May Third States Directly and/or Indirectly Intervene In the Syrian Armed Conflict? The principle of non-intervention in recent non-international armed conflicts. http://www.qil-qdi.org/principle-non-intervention-recent-non-international-armed-conflicts/. Accessed 30 September 2019

Rappaport D C (2011) Terrorism and the American Experience. JAmHist 98(1): 115

Reuters (2018) New Caledonia votes "non" to independence from France. https://www.theguardian.com/world/2018/nov/04/new-caledonia-votes-non-to-independence-from-france. Accessed 30 September 2019

Reydams L (2006) A la guerre comme à la guerre: patterns of armed conflict, humanitarian law responses and new challenges. IRRC 864. http://www.icrc.org/eng/resources/documents/article/review/review-864-p729.htm. Accessed 30 September 2019

Rodenhauser T (2019) Organizing Rebellion Symposium: Organizing Responses – A (Partial) Reply to the Blog Symposium'. http://opiniojuris.org/2019/09/23/organizing-rebellion-symposium-organizing-responses-a-partial-reply-to-the-blog-symposium/. Accessed 30 September 2019

RULAC Geneva Academy (2019) International Armed Conflicts in Syria. http://www.rulac.org/browse/conflicts/international-armed-conflict-in-syria, last updated 23 May 2019. Accessed 30 September 2019

Sari A (2019) Legal Resilience in an Era of Gray Zone Conflicts and Hybrid Threats, ECIL Working Paper 1. https://ssrn.com/abstract=3315682. Accessed 30 September 2019

Saul B (2011) Legislating from a Radical Hague: The UN Special Tribunal for Lebanon Invents an International Crime of Transnational Terrorism. Leid JIL 24: 677

Schewe E (2018) The World's New Private Security Forces. https://daily.jstor.org/the-world's-new-private-security-forces/?utm_term=TheWorld\u2019s

Schultz R H (2012) Strategic Culture and Strategic Studies: An Alternative Framework for Assessing al-Qaeda and the Global Jihad Movement. Joint Special Operations University Report 12-4. https://jsou.libguides.com/jsoupublications/2012. Accessed 30 September 2019

Shariatmadari D (2015) Is it time to stop using the word "terrorist"? https://www.theguardian.com/global/commentisfree/2015/jan/27/is-it-time-to-stop-using-the-word-terrorist. Accessed 30 September 2019

Stepanova E (2009) Islamist Terrorism in the Caucasus and Central Asia. In: Schmid A P, Hindle G F (eds) After the War on Terror: Regional and Multilateral Perspectives on Counter-Terrorism Strategy. RUSI Books, London

Stephens D (2010) Military involvement in law enforcement. IRRC 878: 453

Tams C J (2009) The Use of Force against Terrorists. EJIL 20(2): 359

Thakur R (2008) Humanitarian Intervention. In: Weiss TG, Daws S (eds) The Oxford Handbook on the United Nations. OUP, Oxford

Top S (2017) The European Arrest Warrant against Puigdemont: A feeling of deja-vu? https://www.ejiltalk.org/the-european-arrest-warrant-against-puigdemont-a-feeling-of-deja-vu/. Accessed 30 September 2019

Tsagourias N (2019) Electoral Cyber Interference, Self-Determination and the Principle of Non-Intervention in Cyberspace. https://www.ejiltalk.org/electoral-cyber-interference-self-determination-and-the-principle-of-non-intervention-in-cyberspace/. Accessed 30 September 2019

UN (undated-a) and Decolonization. https://www.un.org/dppa/decolonization/en. Accessed 30 September 2019

UN (undated-b) at a Glance. https://outreach.un.org/mun/content/un-glance. Accessed 30 September 2019

UN (undated-c) Declarations of the UN International Decades for the Eradication of Colonialism. The UN and Colonialization: International Decades for the Eradication of Colonialism. https://www.un.org/dppa/decolonization/en/history/international-decades. Accessed 30 September 2019

UN (undated-d) Office of Counter Terrorism: International Legal Instruments. https://www.un.org/en/counterterrorism/legal-instruments.shtml. Accessed 30 September 2019

UN (2005) Commission on Human Rights. Report of the Special Rapporteur: Promotion and Protection of Human Rights, 62nd session, agenda item 17, UN Doc E/CN.4/2006/98. https://www2.ohchr.org/english/bodies/chr/sessions/62/listdocs.htm. Accessed 30 September 2019

UN (2006) Secr-Gen'l Report: Uniting Against Terrorism: Recommendations for a global counter-terrorism strategy. https://www.un.org/en/events/pastevents/uniting_against_terrorism.shtml. Accessed 30 September 2019

UN (2008a) Department of Public Education. The United Nations Today: Basic Facts about the United Nations: Territories to which the Declaration on the Granting of Independence to Colonial Countries and Peoples continues to apply (as of 2007), ASDF, New York. https://www.un.org/ar/geninfo/pdf/UN.today.pdf. Accessed 30 September 2019

UN (2008b) International Instruments related to the Prevention and Suppression of International Terrorism. https://www.unodc.org/documents/terrorism/Publications/Int_Instruments_Prevention_and_Suppression_Int_Terrorism/Publication_-_English_-_08-25503_text.pdf. Accessed 30 September 2019

UN (2017) Security Council, Consolidated Sanctions List. https://www.un.org/securitycouncil/content/un-sc-consolidated-list, last updated 20 April 2017. Accessed 30 September 2019

UN (2019a) Counter-Terrorism Implementation Task Force: Plan of Action to Prevent Violent Extremism. https://www.un.org/counterterrorism/ctitf/en/plan-action-prevent-violent-extremism, last updated 17 August 2019. Accessed 30 September 2019

UN (2019b) Security Council, Counter-Terrorism Committee. https://www.un.org/sc/ctc/, last updated 30 August 2019. Accessed 30 September 2019

Van Poecke T (2019) The IHL Exclusion Clause, and why Belgian Courts Refuse to Convict PKK Members for Terrorist Offences. https://www.ejiltalk.org/the-ihl-exclusion-clause-and-why-belgian-courts-refuse-to-convict-pkk-members-for-terrorist-offences/. Accessed 30 September 2019

Van Steenberghe R (2015) The Alleged Prohibition on Intervening in Civil Wars Is Still Alive After the Airstrikes Against Islamic State and Iraq: A Response to Dapo Akande and Zachary Vermeer. https://www.ejiltalk.org/the-alleged-prohibition-on-intervening-in-civil-wars-is-still-alive-after-the-airstrikes-against-islamic-state-in-iraq-a-response-to-dapo-akande-and-zachary-vermeer/. Accessed 30 September 2019

Walker C (2010) Conscripting the public in terrorism policing: towards safer communities or a police state? CrimLRev 6: 441

Walzer M (1977) Just and Unjust Wars. Basic Books, New York

Watkin K (2004) Controlling the use of force: a role for human rights norms in contemporary armed conflict. AJIL 98(1): 17

Weigand T (2006) The Universal Terrorist: The International Community Grappling with a Definition. JICrimJust 4: 912

Weigelt K, Marker F (2007) Who is Responsible? The Use of PMCs in Armed Conflict and International Law. In: Jäger T, Kümmel G (eds) Private Military and Security Companies: Chances, Problems, Pitfalls and Prospects. Springer, Wiesbaden

Weisburd D et al (2010) Terrorist threats and police performance: a study of Israeli communities. BritJCrim 50(4): 725

Weller M (2008) Escaping the Self-Determination Trap. Martinus Nijhoff Publishers, Leiden

Werner G (1918) Les prisonniers de guerre. Hague Recueil 21: 56

Whitehall D (2016) A Rival History of Self-determination. EJIL 27(3): 719

Yua V (2019) China detains man who reportedly shared images of troops at Hong Kong border. https://www.theguardian.com/world/2019/sep/11/china-detains-taiwan-man-military-hong-kong-border. Accessed 30 September 2019

Yub V (2019) Hong Kong emergency law "marks start of authoritarian rule". https://www.theguardian.com/world/2019/oct/05/hong-kong-emergency-law-marks-start-of-authoritarian-rule. Accessed 30 September 2019

Elizabeth Chadwick (Retired) is a Reader and Associate Professor (Research) at Nottingham Trent University. Her main research and teaching interests lie in the related fields of international humanitarian law, the self-determination of 'peoples', international terrorism, and the law of armed neutrality. Among her publications, Elizabeth is the author of *Self-Determination in the Post-9/11 Era* (Routledge Research in International Law 2011), "Terrorism and self-determination" in Ben Saul (ed.), *Research Handbook on Terrorism and International Law* (Edward Elgar Publishers 2014) pp. 298–314, 'National Liberation in the Context of Post- and Non-Colonial Struggles for Self-Determination', in Marc Weller (ed.), *The Oxford Handbook of The Use of Force in International Law* (Oxford: OUP, 2015), pp. 841–858, and 'Neutrality revisited', in Rain Liivoja and Tim McCormack (eds.), *Routledge Handbook of the Law of Armed Conflict* (London: Routledge, 2016), pp. 455–473. She has also contributed the chapter on "Neutrality" in Tony Carty (ed.), *Oxford Bibliographies in International Law* (OUP 2014). She continues to teach, write and publish on these and other, related topics.

Chapter 42
The African Region's Pushback Against Mercenaries

Eki Yemisi Omorogbe

Contents

42.1 The OAU and the Challenge of Mercenaries (1963–2003) 918
42.2 The African Union and the Current Challenge (Since 2002) 923
    42.2.1 Libya (2019- to Date) 926
42.3 The Regulation of Mercenary Activity in Africa 927
    42.3.1 Current Treaties 927
    42.3.2 The Malabo Protocol (2014) 934
42.4 Conclusion 938
References 939

Abstract This chapter considers the response of the Organisation of African Unity (OAU, 1963–2003) and, its successor, the African Union (AU, since 2002) to mercenaries and their sponsors and the threats these pose to the peace, security and development of African states. (The AU existed alongside the OAU for a year, during a period of transition, AU Assembly, Decision on the Interim Period, AU Doc. Ass/AU/Dec. 1(I), July 9–10, 2002.) In so doing, it addresses the strategies of these organisations and examines the regional legal frameworks they have developed. It argues that these frameworks address key gaps in international law but are undermined by the definitions of mercenaries and the lack of adequate engagement with a new form of mercenarism, private military companies. The chapter concludes that a re-envisioning of the current legal framework could address remaining gaps and that a holistic approach is required to stop the recruitment and use of mercenaries in African states.

Keywords Organisation of African Unity · African Union · Mercenaries · Private Military Companies · Malabo Protocol · Armed Conflict · Coups · Unconstitutional Change of Government

---

E. Y. Omorogbe (✉)
Law School, University of Leicester, Leicester LE1 7RH, UK
e-mail: eyo1@le.ac.uk

© T.M.C. ASSER PRESS and the authors 2022
S. Sayapin et al. (eds.), *International Conflict and Security Law*,
https://doi.org/10.1007/978-94-6265-515-7_42

42.1 The OAU and the Challenge of Mercenaries (1963–2003)

A critical concern of the Organisation of African Unity (OAU, 1963–2003) was that Western states were using mercenaries to threaten the sovereignty, security and development of African states.[1] Certainly, during the decolonisation era and beyond, some governments of Western states, in pursuit of their geo-political and economic interests, recruited mercenaries for use in African territories.[2] Alongside that, mercenaries were hired through recruitment centres and advertisements in Western states or Rhodesia and South Africa, states pursuing racist policies.[3] In addition, the governments and agencies of these states gave support, often covertly, to mercenaries in the form of finance, arms, technology, training, and intelligence.[4] During the decolonisation era, mercenaries were used in the fight for apartheid and white minority rule in the states of Southern Africa.[5] In the immediate aftermath of independence of African states, mercenaries supported the secession of mineral rich provinces (notably the Katangan secession against Congo—now Democratic Republic of the Congo—1960–1963), threatening the economic viability of the new state. In the context of the Cold War, they fought proxy wars against Russia and Cuba on African territories and sought to influence the political direction of sovereign African states (Angola, 1975).[6] They propped up Western-friendly regimes against rebellions (Premier Tshombe of the Congo, 1964) and engaged in coups d'état against others (Comoros 1978 and 1995).[7] They rebelled against African governments which hired them (1966 and 1967 uprisings against President Mobutu Sese Seko of the Congo) aiming to install a more pliable regime (ex-Prime Minister Tshombe for whom they had fought for in the

---

[1] See as example, OAU Assembly, Resolution on Mercenaries (11–14 September 1967) OAU Doc. AHG Res. 49(IV); OAU Council of Ministers, Resolution on the Activities of Mercenaries in the Great Lakes Area and especially in Zaire (23 February–4 March 1979) OAU Doc. CM/Res 681 (XXXII) and Resolution on the Activities of Mercenaries in Zimbabwe and Namibia and Against the Front-Line States (23 February–4 March 1979) OAU Doc. CM/Res.695 (XXXII); Declaration on the Activities of Mercenaries in Africa (15–19 June 1971) OAU Doc. CM/St. 6(XVII).

[2] See 'Tshombe's Mercenaries; Congo Leader Uses Them for Immediate Action Against Rebels While Seeking African Aid', *New York Times*, 30 August 1964, p. 8 Section E.

[3] Gleijeses 2016, at 158; Taulbee 1985, at 342; Thobhani 1976, at 63–68; Tshombe Declares White Mercenaries Will Be Sent Home, *New York Times*, 5 September 1964, p. 1.

[4] Gleijeses 2016, at 156; Bonner R., 'U.S. Reportedly Backed British Mercenary Group in Africa' *New York Times*, 13 May 1998, p. 3 Section A.

[5] OAU Council of Ministers, Resolution on the Activities of Mercenaries in Zimbabwe and Namibia and Against the Front-Line States (23 February–4 March 1979) OAU Doc. CM/Res. 695 (XXXII).

[6] During an armed conflict between three opposing factions, the Popular Movement for the Liberation of Angola (MPLA), the National Union for the Total Independence of Angola (UNITA) and the National Front for the Liberation of Angola (FNLA). Russia's ally, the MPLA led by Antonio Agostinho Neto won and were subsequently recognised by the OAU as the legitimate government of Angola. See Taulbee 1985, at 341.

[7] 'Mercenary Unit is ready to fight rebels in Congo', *New York Times*, 25 August 1964 p. 1; Gleijeses 2016, at 156ff.

Katangan secession).[8] The activities of mercenaries proved disruptive even where unsuccessful. That includes the invasions and attempted coups (in Benin 1977, Sao Tome and Principe 1978 and Seychelles 1981).

These activities of mercenaries heightened the prospect of regional conflict. As example, in 1970, Dr. Mungai, Kenya's Foreign Affairs minister, called on the OAU and African states to intervene in defence of Guinea.[9] As he put it: "The time is now ripe for all of us to go out and fight against the aggression of imperialist dictatorship of Portugal, in order to liberate Guinea Bissau, Mozambique and Angola."[10] That call followed the attempted overthrow of the government of President Sekou Toure by a group of European and African mercenaries.[11] According to the ruling party, the Parti democratique de Guinee, these mercenaries were "fighting under the flag of Portuguese colonialism".[12] The concern about a common foe led Angola and Guinea Bissau to deploy 1600 troops in support of the government of President Manuel Pinto da Costa of Sao Tome and Principe following an attempted invasion by mercenaries.[13]

Throughout, the OAU condemned such activities. As part of that, the OAU Assembly (Assembly) in 1967 denounced events in Congo as aggression, rejected events in Guinea in 1970 as "treacherous aggression by Portugal", while the OAU Council of Ministers similarly censured as aggression mercenary activity in Benin in 1977 and Sao Tome and Principe in 1978.[14] In 1982, the Council of Ministers branded the attempted ouster of President France Albert Rene of Seychelles by mercenaries as "part of a worldwide strategy of international imperialism to destabilize and reconquer independent and sovereign African states" and South Africa's role in "planning, organising and financing this barbarous aggression" as part of that state's policy of expansionism in the African region.[15]

---

[8] See Taulbee 1985, at 341.

[9] Ministerial Statement, 'Kenya's Stand on Foreign Invasion of Guinea' (25 November 1970) at 970, ruinea'iberation movements, Kenya National Assembly Official Record (Hansard), 18 November 17–December 1970, at 2299–2300.

[10] Ibid., at 2299.

[11] Ibid., at 2297–2298.

[12] Keesing's Record of World Events: Vol. XVII (December 1970), Guinea: 'Repulse of Raids by "Mercenaries" and Guinean Exiles', p. 24353, http://web.stanford.edu/group/tomzgroup/pmwiki/uploads/1385-Keesings-1970-12-a-RRW.pdf. Accessed 31 July 2020.

[13] Seibert 2005, at 144–145.

[14] OAU Assembly, Resolution on Mercenaries (11–14 September 1967) OAU Doc. AHG Res. 49(IV), para 2, and OAU Council of Ministers, 'Resolution on Aggression and Invasion by Mercenaries Against the People's Republic of Benin, the Democratic Republic of Sao Tome and Principe' (Khartoum, Sudan, 7–18 July 1978) OAU Doc. CM/Res. 639 (XXXI).

[15] OAU Council of Ministers, 'Resolution on the Mercenary Aggression Against the Republic of Seychelles' (22–28 February 1982, Addis Ababa, Ethiopia) OAU Doc. CM/Res. 906 (XXXVIII), preamble and paras 2, 3 and 5.

Nevertheless, the OAU's preference was for the use of peaceful measures in response.[16] At the international level, the Assembly and the Council of Ministers repeatedly called on all states to deter their citizens from enlisting as mercenaries and requested that they criminalise the recruitment and training of mercenaries on their territories.[17] The Council of Ministers in 1971 called on states to arrest and transfer mercenaries back to the territorial state in which they have been active for prosecution.[18] With specific reference to the USA, France, UK, Germany, Portugal, Australia and Canada, the Council called on states to prosecute their nationals engaged in mercenary activity abroad.[19] At the regional level, the OAU established a regional criminal law framework (discussed below) against mercenaries and their sponsors. The AU was successful in encouraging specific African governments to expel mercenaries. As example, in 1964, the Assembly refused to consider Tshombe's request for a meeting to discuss the crisis in the Congo until he expelled the mercenaries his government had hired to combat rebels.[20] In 1978, the Council of Ministers expelled the Comoros delegation from the OAU in objection to the way its new government acceded to power. That followed the overthrow and assassination of President Ali Soilih by Bob Denard and his group of Western mercenaries and their installation of Ahmed Abdallah as President.[21] Comoros' membership in the OAU was reinstated in February 1979 after Denard was expelled from the state.[22] The OAU viewed the mercenaries operating in Africa with disdain.[23] In 1967, the OAU twice required the voluntary departure of mercenaries involved in the rebellion against President Mobutu in the Congo (coincidentally the OAU Chair at the time) under threat of

---

[16] OAU Council of Ministers, 'Resolution on Military Interventions in Africa and on Measures to be Taken Against Neo-Colonialist Manoeuvres and Interventions in Africa' (7–18 July 1978), OAU Doc. CM/Res. 641 (XXXI), paras 3–4.

[17] OAU Assembly, Resolution on Mercenaries (11–14 September 1967) OAU Doc. AHG Res. 49(IV), para 5; OAU Council of Ministers, Resolution on the Activities of Mercenaries in Zimbabwe and Namibia and Against the Front-Line States (23 February–4 March 1979) OAU Doc. CM/Res. 695 (XXXII), para 3, and Declaration on the Activities of Mercenaries in Africa (15–19 June 1971) OAU Doc. CM/St. 6(XVII).

[18] Ibid.

[19] OAU Council of Ministers, Resolution on the Activities of Mercenaries in Zimbabwe and Namibia and Against the Front-Line States (23 February–4 March 1979) OAU Doc. CM/Res. 695 (XXXII), para 3.

[20] 'Tshombe's Mercenaries; Congo Leader Uses Them for Immediate Action Against Rebels While Seeking African Aid', *New York Times*, 30 August 1964, p. 8 Section E; Tshombe Declares White Mercenaries Will Be Sent Home, *New York Times*, 5 September 1964, p. 1.

[21] World News Briefs, *New York Times*, 10 July 1978, p. 6 Section A.

[22] US Dept of State Bureau of African Affairs, AF Press Clips (1978), 'Foreign Leader of Coup Quits Comoros', *Washington Post*, 27 September 1978, lxi.

[23] See as example, OAU Assembly, Resolution on Mercenaries (11–14 September 1967) OAU Doc. AHG Res. 49(IV); OAU Council of Ministers, 'Resolution on the Mercenary Aggression Against the Republic of Seychelles' (22–28 February 1982, Addis Ababa, Ethiopia) OAU Doc. CM/Res. 906 (XXXVIII).

criminal proceedings.[24] That includes the option of repatriation to Europe on condition that the mercenaries would never return to the African continent.[25] In spite of these strategies, mercenaries continued to operate in Africa, and Western states (in particular ex-colonial powers) and South Africa continued to use them.[26]

However, the OAU's position was broadly aligned with that of the UN. Between 1960 and 2007, the UN General Assembly (UNGA) has issued more than 100 resolutions criticising mercenaries.[27] Specifically, the UNGA and the UN Security Council (UNSC) characterised as threats to the peace and criminal acts the use of mercenaries by colonial regimes against national liberation movements.[28] The UNGA declared the use of mercenaries in Portuguese administered territories as "colonial war being waged in African states" (1968).[29] It also declared the continuation of colonialism and policies of apartheid and racial oppression as international crimes and threats to the peace.[30] The UNSC referred to events in Benin as "aggression" (1977).[31] In resolution 2395 (XXIII) 1968, the UNGA called on UN member states to prevent the recruitment or training of mercenaries for use by colonial or racist regimes in independent African states on their territories. Regrettably, these lacked binding force—the UNSC resolutions were not made under UN Chapter VII powers and the UNGA resolutions are declarations.[32]

However, the UN resolutions have since been affirmed in the International Convention against the Recruitment, Use, Financing and Training of Mercenaries 1989 (UN Convention) which the UNGA adopted following a push by Nigeria, on behalf of African states, for an international treaty.[33] That Convention establishes that the use of mercenaries is of grave concern to all states and the recruitment, use, financing and

---

[24] OAU Assembly, Resolution on Mercenaries (11–14 September 1967) OAU Doc. AHG Res. 49(IV); Makinde A., 'European Mercenaries Asked to Sign a Declaration Never to Come Back to Africa, Rwanda' *YouTube* (November 1967).

[25] The ICRC assisted with their repatriation. International Committee of the Red Cross 1968, at 29–35 and International Committee of the Red Cross 1969, at 20–21.

[26] See 'Use of Mercenaries as a Means to Violate Human Rights and Impede the Exercise of the Right of Peoples to Self-Determination' UN Doc. A/RES/47/84 (1992).

[27] Percy 2007, at 373–374.

[28] SC on Seychelles: S/RES/ 496 (1981); S/RES/507 (1982). GA: 'Basic Principles of the legal status of the combatants struggling against colonial and alien domination and racist regimes' UN Doc. A/RES/3103 (XXVIII) (1973); 'Implementation of the Declaration on the Granting of Independence to Colonial Countries and Peoples' UN Doc. A/RES/2708 (XXV) (1970); 'Question of Territories under Portuguese administration' UN Doc. A/RES/2395 (XXIII) (1968); 'Declaration on the Granting of Independence to Colonial Countries and Peoples' UN Doc. A/RES/1514 (XV) (1960).

[29] 'Question of Territories under Portuguese administration' UN Doc. A/RES/2395 (XXIII) (1968), para 9.

[30] UNGA, 'Programme of Action for the Full Implementation of the Granting of independence to Colonial Countries and Peoples' A/RES/2621 (XXV) (1970).

[31] UN Docs. S/RES/405 (1977) and S/RES/419 (1977).

[32] Major 1992, at 149 and fn 198.

[33] Adopted under Resolution 44/34, 4 December 1989, U.N.T.S. vol. 2163, 75. See Percy 2007, at 370 n 10.

training of mercenary activities are grave crimes.[34] It imposes on member states a duty to disrupt the preparation of mercenary activity on their territories and requires them to criminalise the activities of persons, groups or organisations that encourage, instigate, organise or engage in mercenary activity.[35] The UN Convention came into force on 20 October 2001 after 22 states had ratified it. At February 2020, 36 states have ratified it, of which 11 are from the African region.[36] However, to date, no member of the UNSC has signed or ratified it. One reason is may be that they are reluctant to assume strict liability for the criminal conduct of their citizens.[37]

A critical point for regional peace came in 1998, four years after the ending of apartheid policies in South Africa, when the government adopted the Regulation of Foreign Military Assistance Act to prevent its nationals, citizens and other persons on its territory from recruiting, using, training, financing or engaging in mercenary activities on other African states.[38] In practice, however, mercenaries from South Africa and elsewhere continued to attempt to capture African state resources, with ex-African state collusion. As example, in March 2004, mercenaries led by Simon Mann (ex-British Special Air Services—SAS) and Nick du Toit (ex-South African Defence Forces, SADF) were involved in an attempt to oust President of Equatorial Guinea, Teodore Obiang Nguema (the Wonga coup) from office. The plan was to install to power Severe Moto, an exiled politician in return for cash and oil concessions in Equatorial Guinea.[39] The attempt was financed by, among others, Mark Thatcher, the son of Margaret Thatcher, the former Prime Minister of the UK. The governments of the UK, US, Spain and South Africa are suspected of involvement in the plot.[40] What is clear is that the UK government was informed of the plot in January 2004 but failed to warn Nguema.[41]

---

[34] UN Convention preamble, Articles 2, 5 and 12.

[35] Ibid., Article 6.

[36] Ratification Status: International Convention against the Recruitment, Use, Financing and Training of Mercenaries, https://ihl-databases.icrc.org/applic/ihl/ihl.nsf/States.xsp?xp_viewStates=XPages_NORMStatesParties&xp_treatySelected=530.

[37] Percy 2007, at 383–386.

[38] Act No. 15 of 1998, *Republic of South Africa Government Gazette*, Vol. 395, No.18912, Cape Town, 20 May 1998, para 2.

[39] See Bannerman L., 'Ely Calil, oil Tycoon behind Wonga coup, found dead after fall at mansion', *The Times*, 1 June 2018; McVeigh T., 'Ex-mercenary Nick du Toit tells of his five years in a 'living hell' and why he is ashamed of war', *The Observer*, 13 June 2010; Siddique H. and Tremlett G., 'Simon Mann pardoned over role in Equatorial Guinea plot', *The Guardian*, 2 November 2009.

[40] Pallister D., 'Mann accuses Mark Thatcher of key involvement in African coup plot', *The Guardian*, 19 June 2008; Leigh D., 'US link uncovered in Thatcher's coup plot role', *The Guardian*, 24 January 2005; Barnett A. and Bright M., 'Revealed: How Britain was told full coup plot', *The Observer*, 28 November 2004.

[41] Secretary of State for UK Foreign and Commonwealth Affairs, Jack Straw, 'Equatorial Guinea' HC Debates 9 November 2004, col. 632W.

42.2 The African Union and the Current Challenge (Since 2002)

The African Union (AU), a peace and security institution established in 2002 as successor to the OAU, shares the OAU's opposition to mercenaries in Africa. That is reflected in key principles of the AU Constitutive Act that prohibit political assassination, subversive activities and unconstitutional changes of government (Articles 4(o) and 4(p)), all of which are linked to mercenary activity in the African region. But it has its own additional challenges.

Central to these is the level of use of mercenaries by African actors, and the reasons for that reliance. African governments that supported liberation movements during the decolonization era have since used mercenaries against dissident groups. That may be related to the perception that the use of mercenaries by governments outside national liberation conflicts, or colonial or racist systems is less problematic.[42] But their use against rebel groups could be seen as impeding self-determination struggles in the state.[43] Certainly, Muammar Gaddafi, the Head of State of Libya, relied on Tuareg mercenaries to fight alongside state troops against the rebel National Transitional Council forces in 2011, during a conflict which began after state forces bombed civilian protesters.[44] In certain crises, all state parties have also relied on mercenaries. That is not a new phenomenon—ex-African mercenaries fought on the side of the government and the rebels during the Biafran civil war in Nigeria (1967–1970).[45] Critically, during the 2010–2011 post-election violence in Côte d'Ivoire between President Laurent Gbagbo and Allasane Ouattara, Gbagbo relied on Liberian mercenaries in an illegal attempt to remain in office after his defeat at democratic elections, while Liberian mercenaries were used by Ouattara to support his democratic ascension to power.[46] Similarly, opposition parties have relied on mercenaries to attempt regime change through coups d'état. Ostensibly, some of these actions are taken because of the oppressive nature of the government (Equatorial Guinea, 2017) or to reverse corruption and social and economic decline of the state (Sao Tome and Principe, 2003).[47] But the concern remains that an underlying objective is the seizure of control of state assets and natural resources. Irrespective, the Chairperson of the AU Commission (AUC), Moussa Faki and the UN Secretary-General, Antonio Guterres,

---

[42] Kinsey 2008, at 9; ICRC, 'IHL Rule 108: Mercenaries', https://ihl-databases.icrc.org/customary-ihl/eng/docs/v1_rul_rule108.

[43] On the point, see Kufuor 1999, at 203. UN Doc. A/HRC/18/32 (2011), at para 60.

[44] Keenan 2018, at 152; Francis 2007, at 165.

[45] Ibid.

[46] 'UN Expert Reports 'Alarming Resurgence' In Use Of Mercenaries To Violate Human Rights, Often In New, Novel Ways, In Statement To Third Committee', UN Press release GA/SHC/4023 (2011).

[47] 'Chad jails 11 'mercenaries' over Equatorial Guinea coup plot', *Punch*, 7 June 2019, https://punchng.com/chad-jails-11-mercenaries-over-equatorial-guinea-coup-bid; 'Equatorial Guinea 'stops coup attempt by mercenaries'', *BBC News*, 3 January 2018; Murphy J., 'Coup in Sao Tome', *CBS News*, 16 July 2003.

are agreed that the continuing activities of mercenaries is problematic for Africa's development and they have called for a range of measures in response, including the strengthening of legal regimes and ratification and implementation of existing treaties.[48]

A particular challenge for the AU is the shift by states in Africa (as elsewhere) since the 1990s towards using private military companies (PMCs) to fill security gaps.[49] Undoubtedly, PMCs can provide legitimate military and security services for governments including consultancy, advisory, logistics and support services and training including in weapons capability and operability to national armies.[50] But the direct participation of PMCs in hostilities is problematic. The UNGA's Working Group on the Use of Mercenaries as a Means of Violating Human Rights and Impeding the Exercise of the Right of Peoples to Self-Determination in its 2007 Report characterised that as a "modern form of mercenarism" and as "new modalities of mercenary-related activities".[51] The difficulty is that the staff of PMCs do not fit easily within the definition of mercenaries (below).[52] Nor does general international law regulate the activities of PMCs in armed conflicts—traditional international law presupposes that intervention in armed conflicts is the responsibility of state armed forces.[53] Further, PMCs are non-state parties and as such are not directly subject to human right obligations.[54] The result is that PMCs are rarely held accountable for their violations of international law.[55] It may be possible to take indirect action through the employing state as their obligations under human rights treaties remain.[56] But action against heads of African states and their senior government officials is unlikely as the AU in 2013 adopted a policy which protects these from proceedings before any international court or tribunal during their term of office.[57] An impunity gap clearly exists. Moussa Faki, the AUC Chair, has recommended the establishment of a regional framework for the regulation of PMC activities.[58]

Such regulation is important for the African region, particularly because PMCs echo the challenges of the past. At 2005, the majority of PMCs were from Angola, South Africa, France, U.K., U.S., Canada and Israel.[59] In Africa, PMCs typically

---

[48] UN Press Release SC/13688, 4 February 2019.

[49] Stinnett 2005, at 213–214.

[50] Arielli and Collins 2013, at 255.

[51] See Report of the Working Group on the Use of Mercenaries as a means of violating Human Rights and Impeding the Exercise of the Right of Peoples to Self-Determination, UN Doc. A/62/301 (2007), paras 26, 27, 68 and 69.

[52] Stinnett 2005, at 215–217; A/HRC/15/25 (2010), para 51.

[53] Stinnett 2005, at 211–212.

[54] A/HRC/15/25 (2010), at para 65.

[55] Ibid., paras 36–37 and 90.

[56] Ibid., para 40.

[57] *Decision on Africa's Relationship with the International Criminal Court*, AU Doc. Ext/Assembly/AU/Dec.1 (Oct. 2013), 12 October 2013, para 10(i).

[58] UN Press Release SC/13688, 4 February 2019.

[59] Stinnett 2005, at 222.

provide groups of foreign trained fighters to governments for use in putting down rebellions in return for cash and access to state resources.[60] These include:

- The Wagner Group, a Russian company which has been active since 2014. The concern is that it is acting as a vanguard for the geo-political and economic interests of Russia—it is reported to act only with the approval of the Russian government.[61] It has entered into contracts with more than 20 African states, including Central African Republic, Libya, Mozambique and Sudan.[62]
- Specialised Tasks, Training, Equipment and Protection International Limited (STTEP), a South African company established in 2006, which was employed by the government of Nigeria to fight against Boko Haram (2014–2015) and
- Executive Outcomes, a South African company which operated from 1989 to 1998, was employed by the governments of Angola against Savimbi/UNITA (1993–1996) and Sierra Leone against the Revolutionary United Front (1995–1997).[63] The government of Angola paid it USD 40 million per year for two years. More generally, Executive Outcomes paid its officers a salary, between 2000 and 12,000 per month.[64]

Additionally, PMCs in Côte d'Ivoire, Libya and Sierra Leone have also been accused of human rights violations against the civilians including summary execution, enforced disappearances, rape and torture.[65]

Regulation is crucial because the use of PMCs is likely to continue. One reason is their relative capability and effectiveness compared to some underfunded and under equipped national forces.[66] As illustration, the Nigerian army was under resourced and unable to provide an adequate response to Boko Haram, including as a result of the diversion of allocated state funds for private use by corrupt government officials and senior army officers.[67] Another is the unreliability of UN intervention in African crises. As Eeben Barlow, the founder of Executive Outcomes and STTEP put it: "Private military companies would not be necessary if national armies and the United Nations were actually able to fulfill their mandate. So I don't think the world should [p]lay the blame before us, they should go and look why we exist."[68]

---

[60] Musah and Fayemi 1999, at 23–24.

[61] 'Russia Africa summit: What's behind Moscow's push into the continent?', *BBC News*, 23 October 2019; Balestrieri S., 'Wagner Group: Russian Mercenaries Still Floundering in Africa', 19 April 2020, https://sofrep.com/news/wagner-group-russian-mercenaries-still-foundering-in-africa/.

[62] Ibid. (both).

[63] See Spearin 2009, at 1095–1107.

[64] Harding 1997, at 89.

[65] UN Expert Reports 'Alarming Resurgence' In Use Of Mercenaries To Violate Human Rights, Often In New, Novel Ways, In Statement To Third Committee, UN Press release GA/SHC/4023 (2011); Stinnett 2005, at 215.

[66] For a wider discussion, see Howe 2001.

[67] Bappah 2016, in particular at 149–150.

[68] 'Eeben Barlow: Inside the world of private military contractors', *Talk to Aljazeera*, 5 January 2020. See also Harding 1997, at 96–97.

42.2.1 Libya (2019- to Date)

The ongoing armed conflict in Libya, which began in 2019, highlights the current threats mercenaries (including staff of PMCs) and their sponsors pose to peace, security and development of states in the African region. Libya has the largest oil reserves in Africa and the ninth largest globally.[69] It has been under an arms embargo since the 2011 conflict. At that time, the UN Security Council under Resolution 1970 (2011) prohibited, *inter alia*, the provision of armed mercenary personnel and arms, military equipment and military vehicles in Libya.[70] At the heart of the 2019 conflict is a fight for state power between the UN recognized transitional Government of National Accord (GNA) led by Faiez Mustafa Serraj and the rebel Libyan National Army (LNA) led by General Khalifa Haftar. Each conflict party has relied on mercenaries from the African region—mercenaries from Chad support the GNA and mercenaries from Sudan back the LNA.[71] Each conflict party relies on ex-African states and their mercenaries. The Wagner Group supports the LNA, and the Russian government is reported to have covertly transferred 14 fighter jets to the Wagner Group for use in Libya.[72] Separately, Turkey supports the GNA and Russia supports the LNA and these states are recruiting and supporting Syrian mercenaries for use by the conflict parties in Libya.[73] The continuous breaching of the UN embargo is troubling.[74] The actions of Russia and Turkey have also led to concerns that African state territory is once again the site for proxy warfare of ex-African states in pursuit of their political and economic interests. In this respect, the escalation of tension between Russia and the U.S. is of concern.[75] That followed the blockade of the Sharara oilfield, one of the largest production areas, and Es Sider, the key oil export terminal, in June 2020 by the Wagner Group which enforced a shutdown of oil production facilities imposed earlier in the year by the LNA.[76] By end-July 2020, the shutdown and effects on oil

---

[69] 'NOC: Losses of Oil Exports Shutdown in Libya Exceed $7.47 Billion', *Libya Review*, 26 July 2020.

[70] S/RES/1970 (26 February 2011), para 9.

[71] Burke J. and Salih Z.M., 'Mercenaries flock to Libya raising fears of prolonged war' *The Guardian*, 24 December 2019.

[72] See Burke J. and Salih Z.M., 'Mercenaries flock to Libya raising fears of prolonged war' *The Guardian*, 24 December 2019; 'Russian Fighter Jets in Libya could increase civilian casualties, says US', *The New Arab (Alaraby)*, 19 June 2020.

[73] Trew B. and Biurhan R., 'Inside the murky world of Libya's mercenaries', *The Independent*, 15 June 2020; McKernan B. and Akoush H., 'Exclusive: 2000 Syrian fighters deployed to Libya to support government', *The Guardian*, 15 January 2020.

[74] Jordan and the United Arab Emirates (both support the LNA) are also reported to be systematically breaching the embargo in Libya. Wintour P., 'Libya arms embargo being systematically violated by UN States', *The Guardian*, 9 December 2019.

[75] See U.S. Embassy Libya, 'U.S. Embassy Regrets Foreign Interference Against Libya's Economy', *The Libya Observer*, 12 July 2020.

[76] Faucon B. and Malsin J., 'Russian Oil Grab in Libya Fuels US Russia Tensions' *Wall Street Journal* 26 July 2020.

exports overall had cost the Libyan economy USD 7.5 billion.[77] In providing the conflict parties with military assets and enhanced capabilities, mercenaries and their sponsors have enabled the prolongation of the conflict and undermined the prospect for peace.[78] As Moussa Faki, the Chair of the AUC, previously put it: "The continued flow of mercenaries and terrorists to the country, aggravates the state of destabilization and anarchy in Libya, while the multiplication of external interference does not help solve the crisis".[79]

It is clear that the peace, security and development of the African region continue to be impacted by the activities of mercenaries. As we shall see, the OAU and the AU have built criminal law frameworks which resist that, to different levels.

42.3 The Regulation of Mercenary Activity in Africa

The African region has been severely affected by the actions of mercenaries. In response to gaps in international law protection, the African regional organisations have developed legal frameworks which prohibit mercenaries and mercenarism. These legal frameworks highlight key challenges to the security of African states. Over time, the focus has shifted from the problems caused by colonial and racist regimes to that caused by the contestation for power within postcolonial African states.

42.3.1 Current Treaties

This part considers four key treaties which form the current regional framework against mercenaries. These are the Convention for the Elimination of Mercenaries in Africa (1972) and the Convention for the Elimination of Mercenarism in Africa (1977) each of which originated from within the OAU, and the Draft Convention on the Prevention and Suppression of Mercenarism 1976 which is the product of a group of international jurists. These provide various definitions of mercenaries and mercenarism under regional criminal law and clearly support the independence and self-determination of African states. The fourth treaty, the Non-Aggression and Common Defence Pact is from the AU period, and provides for a common legal and military response.

---

[77] 'NOC: Losses of Oil Exports Shutdown in Libya Exceed $7.47 Billion', *Libya Review*, 26 July 2020.
[78] Ibid.; *United Nations Support Mission in Libya: Report of the Secretary-General* UN Doc. S/2020/360 (5 May 2020), para 3; Golden R., 'African Union: War in Libya threatens the entire region', *The Libya Observer*, 29 February 2020.
[79] 'African Union's Brazzaville Summit Calls for a Pan-Libya Reconciliation Conference', *Almarsad*, 31 January 2020, https://almarsad.co/en/2020/01/31/african-unions-brazzaville-summit-calls-for-a-pan-libya-reconciliation-conference/.

42.3.1.1 OAU Convention for the Elimination of Mercenaries in Africa (1972)

In 1972, the OAU Council of Ministers put forward the Convention on the Prevention and Suppression of Mercenaries (1972 Convention).[80] That Convention was adopted by the Assembly in 1977 and it came into force on 22 April 1985 after 18 states had ratified it.[81] At the time of writing (end-July 2020), 22 states of the African region have ratified it. That means that 33 states remain outside it.[82]

In the 1972 Convention, the OAU for the first time provided a definition of mercenaries and a list of prohibited acts. Under that, a mercenary is 'anyone who is not a national of the state against which his actions are directed and is employed, enrols or links himself willingly to a person, group or organization whose aim is:

(a) to overthrow by force of arms or by any other means the government of that Member State of the Organization of African Unity;
(b) to undermine the independence, territorial integrity or normal working of the institutions of the said State;
(c) to block by any means the activities of any liberation movement recognized by the Organization of African Unity.'[83]

What is included within the term 'overthrow by force of arms or by any other means' is not defined. But it clearly would include acts outside armed conflict scenarios including assassinations and coups d'état. The Convention is silent as to whether inchoate acts are sufficient for the offence.

Critically, the OAU characterised as 'crimes against the peace and security of Africa' both the actions of mercenaries and those of individuals who recruit, train, finance or give protection to them.[84] The term 'crime against peace' is not defined in the Convention. But it can be read in conjunction with other key OAU resolutions and statements linking mercenary activities to conquest and expansion of territory, including in relation to Guinea (discussed above).

Under the Convention, member states are required to implement the Convention within national law (Article 3), extradite or prosecute offenders (Articles 5 and 6) and impose severe penalties on those found guilty of Convention offences (Article 4). Member states also owe a duty to prevent mercenary activity within their individual territory and outside it. As part of that, member states are required to prevent their nationals or residents from recruiting, training, financing, equipping or giving protection to mercenaries, and the transit of mercenaries or their equipment through their territories (Article 3). They must prohibit persons or organisations employing

---

[80] Article 1, OAU Convention for the Elimination of Mercenaries in Africa, O.A.U. Doc. CM/433/Rev.L, Annex 1 (1972) in force 22 April 1985. See also del Prado 2019, at 449–476 and Kinsey 2008, at 4.

[81] On this point, see Ettinger 2014, at 180–181.

[82] Ratification Status: OAU Convention for the Elimination of Mercenaries in Africa (1972), http://hrlibrary.umn.edu/instree/mercenaryratifications.html.

[83] OAU 1972 Convention, Article 1.

[84] Ibid., Article 2.

mercenaries from committing acts against OAU member states on their territory. States must also swiftly inform other OAU states of any plans and activities of mercenaries of which they are aware (Article 3).

42.3.1.2 OAU Endorsed Draft Convention on the Prevention and Suppression of Mercenarism (1976)

An appendix to and part of the 1972 Convention is the Draft Convention on the Prevention and Suppression of Mercenarism 1976 (Luanda Convention) that the OAU endorsed in 1977.[85] The Luanda Convention was produced by the International Commission of Inquiry on Mercenarism following their attendance at the first trial of mercenaries in Africa for international crimes. That trial took place before the Angolan People's Revolutionary Court in Luanda, Angola. Ten Europeans (nine British and one Irish national) and three Americans were found guilty of crimes of mercenarism and crimes against peace committed during an armed conflict in newly independent Angola in which Russia and the USA along with their respective allies supported opposing factions (1975–1976).[86] Four of these mercenaries were sentenced to death and the remaining were given terms of imprisonment ranging from 16 to 30 years.[87]

Reflecting its origin, the Luanda Convention criminalises mercenary activity against self-determination movements. It characterises mercenarism as an international crime and "part of a process of perpetuating by force of arms racist colonial or neo-colonial domination over a people or State" (preamble). The offence is committed when an actor intends to oppose a process of self-determination through violence and:

(a) organizes, finances, supplies, equips, trains, promotes, supports or employs in any way military forces consisting of or including persons who are not nationals of the country where they are going to act, for personal gain, through the payment of a salary or any other kind of material recompense;
(b) enlists, enrols or tries to enrol in the said forces;
(c) allows the activities mentioned in para (a) to be carried out in any territory under its jurisdiction or in any place under its control or affords facilities for transit, transport or other operations of the abovementioned forces.[88]

Assuming command over mercenaries or giving orders to mercenaries constitute aggravating factors of the offence inviting harsher penalties (Article 2). The mercenaries themselves are denied the status of combatants and prisoners of war on capture (Article 4), but they are entitled to due process of law (Article 9). That means that they

---

[85] OAU Convention for the Elimination of Mercenaries in Africa, O.A.U. Doc. CM/433/Rev.L, Annex II. On this point, see Kinsey 2008, at 16 endnote 39.
[86] See information in n 7.
[87] '4 Mercenaries are Executed in Angola', *New York Times*, 11 July 1976, p. 1.
[88] Article 1.

can be treated as common criminals. They can be prosecuted for being mercenaries as well as for crimes committed while acting in such capacity (Article 5).

The Luanda Convention provides that a wide range of actors can commit the offence of mercenarism and establishes the procedures for ensuring responsibility. In the event that individuals, groups or associations commit the offence, states party to the Convention can bring criminal proceedings under the territoriality and nationality principles of international law (Article 7). That leaves open prosecution by the state in which the mercenary acts, the state of nationality of the aggressor and the national state of any victim. Representatives of the states as well as States can commit the offence through their acts and through their omissions (Article 3). While representatives of states are to be punished, the international responsibility of the injurious state can be invoked by other states and before a competent international organisation (Article 3). Presumably, the state that is harmed and the victims are entitled to reparation for loss of life or other human rights abuse and material damage.

The Luanda Convention is aimed at preventing activities that undermine self-determination. In the round, it achieves its objective.[89] Its focus also provides an additional facet to the OAU framework. Read together, the characterization of mercenaries and mercenarism in the 1972 Convention and the 1976 Luanda Convention is limited to those acting against the interests of African states and governments, liberation movements and self-determination movements.[90] Additionally, the Luanda Convention focus on personal gain through salary or material recompense excludes persons whose primary motivation for participation in the combat arise from personal or public gain of a different nature. The effect is to protect African and Western foreigners fighting 'just wars' on behalf of African states and peoples including for liberation or self-determination, where non-material motivations are likely to be uppermost. It also has the dual effect of allowing African governments to give support to liberation movements while protecting that government from challenge by rebel groups.[91]

42.3.1.3 OAU Convention for the Elimination of Mercenarism in Africa (1977)

The third treaty is the Convention for the Elimination of Mercenaries in Africa which the Council of Ministers adopted in July 1977 (1977 Elimination Convention).[92] That also came into force on 22 April 1985, after 17 states had ratified it.[93] At the time of

---

[89] Ibid., 7.
[90] See Kinsey 2008, at 7–8.
[91] Ibid., 4.
[92] U.N.T.S. vol. 1490, I-25573.
[93] OAU, Convention for the Elimination of Mercenaries in Africa, OAU Doc. CM/817 (XXIX) Annex II Rev.1 (Libreville, 3 July 1977), Article 13(2).

writing, end-February 2020, 32 states have ratified it, meaning 23 states are outside it.[94]

The Elimination Convention characterises mercenarism as a crime. In that, it follows the 1972 OAU Convention and the 1977 Luanda Convention in providing that mercenarism is a grave breach and a 'crime[s] against peace and security in Africa'. The term 'crime against peace and security' is not defined in the Elimination Convention, but as discussed above, it is synonymous with the crime of aggression. Natural or legal persons—individuals, groups or associations, representatives of the state and the state, can commit the crime (Articles 1(2) and 1(3)). Although not specifically listed, that would include companies as these are legal persons. That means that this provision could be read to cover private military companies. The person commits the offence only if they intend to use armed violence to oppose the stability, territorial integrity, or self-determination of another state through, *inter alia*, recruiting, sheltering employing, financing, training, or assisting mercenaries, enlisting, enrolling, or attempting to enrol as mercenaries, allowing these activities on territory under control, and providing facilities for transit and transport (Article 1(2)). The Elimination Convention also provides for remedies. It provides for the extradition or prosecution of mercenaries on capture (Articles 3 and 4) and requires that severe penalties, including the death penalty, be imposed on perpetrators.

Significantly, Article 1(1) of the 1977 Elimination Convention provides the OAU's definition of mercenary. That is a person who satisfies all of the following cumulative conditions:

(a) is specially recruited locally or abroad in order to fight in an armed conflict;
(b) does in fact take a direct part in the hostilities;
(c) is motivated to take part in the hostilities essentially by the desire for private gain and, in fact, is promised, by or on behalf of a Party to the conflict, material compensation;
(d) is neither a national of a Party to the conflict nor a resident of territory controlled by a Party to the conflict;
(e) is not a member of the armed forces of a Party to the conflict; and
(f) is not sent by a State other than a Party to the conflict on official mission as a member of the armed forces of the said state.

That definition follows, in the main, the provisions on mercenaries found under Article 47(2) of Additional Protocol I to the 1949 Geneva Conventions (API) which was adopted after considerable pressure from African states.[95] API regulates conduct in international armed conflicts (IACs) for state parties, and improves on existing treaty and customary international law protections for civilians and combatants. The Diplomatic Conference on the Reaffirmation and Development of International Humanitarian Law Applicable in Armed Conflicts adopted it on 8 June 1978 and

---

[94] The most recent information available is at 15 June 2017, AU, 'Ratification Status: OAU Convention for the Elimination of Mercenarism', https://au.int/sites/default/files/treaties/37287-sl-oau_convention_for_the_elimination_of_mercenarism_in_africa_1.pdf.
[95] Fallah 2006, at 604–605; Percy 2007, at 370 n 9.

it entered into force on 7 December 1978. At the time of writing, end-July 2020, 174 states have ratified it of which 51 are from the African region.[96] API also addresses other critical challenges (historical and otherwise) of the African region. As example, it extends the definition of IACs to conflicts of self-determination and national liberation. API does not make clear what would fall under the definition of self-determination or national liberation movement. In practice, the UN has relied on determinations made by regional organisations within the relevant area.[97] The OAU certainly had a recognition policy in place.[98]

API denies to mercenaries the automatic status of legal combatants or POWs. The consensus is that this provision leaves open to states the granting of such status.[99] However, the Council of Ministers in 1977 seem to have otherwise interpreted this provision. According to the Council, the denial of the status of legal combatants during wars of national liberation under the Additional Protocols means that mercenaries could be subject to summary execution on capture.[100] The 1977 Declaration was made against the backdrop of the routine commission of gross violations by mercenaries against combatants against racist and colonial regimes on capture which the UNGA had described as 'inhuman' and inhuman treatment of civilians including in Congo and Zimbabwe as well as attacks on neighbouring states and refugee camps.[101] Irrespective, mercenaries would still be entitled to fundamental guarantees provided to illegal combatants under Article 75 of API and more generally under Common Article 3 of the Geneva Conventions 1949, which requires humane treatment and prohibits arbitrary killings and reflects customary international law. Crucially, the OAU in the Elimination Convention makes mandatory the removal of the status of combatant and POW status to mercenaries though use of the terms the terms "shall not enjoy" and "shall not be entitled" (Article 3). That means that mercenaries could be treated in law as common criminals.

The 1977 Elimination Convention is to be welcomed. It improves on API's definition of mercenaries in several key respects. Firstly, the Elimination Convention Article 1(1)(c) is silent on the requirement for the material compensation to be substantially in excess of that which persons of similar rank and function in the state army would be entitled found under API Article 47(2)(c). The Elimination Convention closes a potential gap relating to persons promised material gain commensurate

---

[96] ICRC, 'Ratification: API Protocol 1', https://ihl-databases.icrc.org/applic/ihl/ihl.nsf/States.xsp?xp_viewStates=XPages_NORMStatesParties&xp_treatySelected=470.

[97] Green 2008, at 79–80.

[98] See OAU position in the 1972 Convention, Article 1(c) and OAU Council of Ministers, Resolution on South Africa (23 February–4 March 1979, Nairobi, Kenya) OAU Doc. CM/Res. 698 (XXXII).

[99] Green 2008, at 141; Major 1992, at 146; Gillard 2006, at 563; ICRC, 'IHL Rule 108: Mercenaries', https://ihl-databases.icrc.org/customary-ihl/eng/docs/v1_rul_rule108.

[100] Resolution on the activities of Mercenaries in Zimbabwe and Namibia and Against the Front-Line States (23 Februrary–4 March 1979) OAU Doc. CM/Res. 695 (XXXII), preamble (i) and (iii).

[101] Ibid.; GA Res. 3103 (XXVIII) (1973), in particular at paras 1 and 3–4. On Congo, see Gleijeses 2016, 161; 'Basic Principles of the legal status of the combatants struggling against colonial and alien domination and racist regimes'. UN Doc. A/RES/3103 (XXVIII) (1973), preamble.

with national forces. But that has limited practical significance—mercenaries are usually paid substantially in excess of national troops.[102] But it relates only to interstate armed conflict—while the vast majority of conflicts in Africa since 1989 are intra-state—and is committed only where the aim is to oppose state stability, territorial integrity or a process of self-determination. That limits its applicability to more recent armed conflicts and violence. Although not fatal, the cumulative nature of the definition of mercenaries raises the evidentiary bar.[103] Moreover, determining the primary motivation of individual fighters is likely to prove challenging. The focus on material gain excludes persons motivated by other reasons, whether ideological, ethnic, religious, political or social.[104] In this, the 1977 Convention clearly follows the 1972 and 1976 Conventions in protecting foreigners motivated by injustice and non-material gain in fighting for liberation or self-determination movements. The 1977 Convention is particularly unsuited for a pushback against PMCs because of the requirement in Article (1)(1)(a) that the person be specially recruited to fight in an armed conflict as that generally is taken to mean recruitment for a specified armed conflict and because Article 1(1)(e) excludes those enrolled in the armed forces of a state. As we have seen, fighters are recruited by PMCs under agreements which avoid these and the political sensitivities involved is likely to make proof of their direct involvement in hostilities difficult to obtain (see discussion on PMCs above). A more nuanced definition of mercenaries therefore would enable better responses to the current needs of the African region.

42.3.1.4 The African Union Non-aggression and Common Defence Pact (2005)

The final treaty is the 2005 Non-Aggression and Common Defence Pact is a key part of the regional legal framework against mercenaries. It classifies as acts of aggression the sending of mercenaries by or on behalf of an AU member state or the provision of support to mercenaries which may carry out hostile acts against an AU member state of such gravity as to constitute, *inter alia*, the use of armed force against the sovereignty, territorial integrity and political independence of the state.[105] Under the Defence Pact, AU state parties agree to respond by all available means to aggression or threats of aggression against an AU state.[106] The term 'all available means' is

---

[102] Balestrieri S., 'Wagner Group: Russian Mercenaries Still Floundering in Africa', *SOFREP*, 19 April 2020, https://sofrep.com/news/wagner-group-russian-mercenaries-still-floundering-in-africa/; 'Russia Africa summit: What's behind Moscow's push into the continent?', *BBC News*, 23 October 2019; Malik S., 'How Nigeria engaged South African Mercenaries to Fight Boko Haram', *International Centre for Investigative Reporting*, 5 April 2006, https://www.icirnigeria.org/how-nigeria-engaged-south-african-mercenaries-to-fight-boko-haram/.

[103] Kinsey 2008, at 7.

[104] For a fuller discussion of API, see Percy 2007, at 367–397.

[105] AU Non-Aggression and Common-Defence Pact 2005 (adopted in Abuja, Nigeria 31 January 2005), Article 1.

[106] Ibid., Article 4(b).

not defined. It clearly covers the use of force in collective self-defence as the Pact provides that an attack or threat of attack on one AU state is to be treated as an attack on all AU states.[107] The term would also include the use of judicial measures. That conclusion is supported by a commitment for AU state parties to prosecute and arrest mercenaries when these pose a threat to a member state.[108]

More generally, under the Pact, AU states are required to prohibit their territories from being used for stationing, transit, withdrawal or incursions of mercenaries operating in the territory of another AU state.[109] Further, AU states agree to prevent their territories and their nationals from being used for encouraging or committing acts of subversion, hostility, or aggression which threaten the territorial integrity and sovereignty of an AU state or regional peace and security.[110]

42.3.2 The Malabo Protocol (2014)

The AU Assembly adopted the Protocol on Amendments to the Protocol on the Statute of the African Court of Justice and Human Rights in June 2014, ironically, in Malabo, Equatorial Guinea (Malabo Protocol). The Malabo Protocol will come into force after 30 AU states have ratified it. At mid-June 2020, no state has ratified it and only 15 states have signed it (Benin, Chad, Comoros, Congo, Equatorial Guinea, Ghana, Guinea Bissau, Kenya, Mauritania, Sao Tome and Principe, Sierra Leone, Togo and Uganda).[111] If it comes into effect, it would have significant impact on the African regional crime of mercenarism.

The Malabo Protocol follows the OAU's resolutions and the 2005 AU Defence Pact in prohibiting the use of mercenaries by one state in another. The Malabo Protocol provides that, subject to the gravity threshold, the sending or material support to armed bands, groups, irregulars or mercenaries which use force against another state and the sending by a state of armed bands or mercenaries to use force against another state can constitute aggression (Article 28M(B)(h)). The Malabo Protocol further provides that those in effective control of the state or organisation as well as state, group of states, organisation, organisations of states, non-state actors, and foreign entities can commit aggression (Articles 28M(A) and 28M(B)). The term 'organisation' is not defined. But it can be read to include business organisations.

---

[107] Ibid., Articles 2(b) and 2(c).

[108] Ibid., Article 6(b).

[109] Ibid., Article 5(c).

[110] Ibid., Article 5(b).

[111] AU, Ratification Status: 'Protocol on Amendments on the Protocol on the Statute of the African Court of Justice and Human Rights', https://au.int/sites/default/files/treaties/36398-sl-PROTOCOL%20ON%20AMENDMENTS%20TO%20THE%20PROTOCOL%20ON%20THE%20STATUTE%20OF%20THE%20AFRICAN%20COURT%20OF%20JUSTICE%20AND%20HUMAN%20RIGHTS.pdf. The most recent information available to the author is at 20 May 2019.

If that interpretation is correct, the Malabo Protocol could address the activities of private military companies in Africa.[112]

Significantly, the Malabo Protocol extends the definition of aggression to include the provision of material support. That would include the provision of technological, intelligence or training assistance (Article 28M (B)(h)).[113] In so doing, the Malabo Protocol improves on definitions of aggression in international treaties such as the Rome Statute of the International Criminal Court Article 8 *bis* 2 (adopted in June 2010) and the UNGA resolution 3314 (XIX) (1974) which exclude the material support from their definition of aggression and limit the range of perpetrators to those in effective control of the political and military structures of the state.[114] In that way, the Malabo Protocol better addresses the covert and indirect nature of the use of force by ex-African actors in African states. In addition, Article 28M(A) of the Malabo Protocol provides that aggression can be a manifest violation of the AU Constitutive Act *or* the UN Charter. In that, the Malabo Protocol departs from the Defence Pact which provides that aggression is a violation of the AU Constitutive Act *and* the UN Charter, and the Rome Statute which provide only for manifest violation of the UN Charter. It is clear that the AU reserves to itself the final determination of a given situation.

Outside of that, the Malabo Protocol builds on and in many ways extends existing regional and international treaties prohibiting mercenaries and mercenarism. That includes the International Convention against the Recruitment, Use, Financing and Training of Mercenaries 1989 (UN Convention), in force since 2001.

In relation to armed conflict scenarios, the Malabo Protocol uses the cumulative definition of mercenaries found under the 1977 Elimination Convention Article 1(1), API (1977) Article 47(2) and the UN Convention Article 1(1).[115] In line with the 1972 OAU Convention and the UN Convention, the Malabo Protocol recognises that mercenary activities also occur outside armed conflicts.[116] In doing so, the Malabo Protocol follows the UN Convention in extending the cumulative definition of mercenaries to persons recruited to participate in a concerted act of violence aimed at overthrowing a government or at undermining the constitutional order of a state or at undermining the territorial integrity of a state.[117] It also follows the UN Convention in outlawing the recruiting, financing and training of mercenaries.[118] Under each of these two treaties, those who attempt to participate in armed conflicts and concerted act of violence as well as direct participants fall within the definition

---

[112] Gillard 2006, at 542; ICRC, 'IHL Rule 108: Mercenaries', https://ihl-databases.icrc.org/customary-ihl/eng/docs/v1_rul_rule108.

[113] Schaak B.V., 'Immunity Before the African Court of Justice & Human & Peoples Rights – The Potential Outlier', *Just Security*, 10 July 2014, https://www.justsecurity.org/12732/immunity-african-court-justice-human-peoples-rights-the-potential-outlier.

[114] ICC, Official Records of the Review Conference of the Rome Statute of the ICC, Kampala, 31 May–11 June 2010, Doc. RC/9/11.

[115] Malabo Protocol Article 28H(1)(a).

[116] 1972 Convention Article 1, UN Convention Article 1(2) and Malabo Protocol Article 28H(1)(b).

[117] UN Convention Article 1(2) and Malabo Protocol Article 28H(1)(b).

[118] UN Convention Article 2 and Malabo Protocol Article 28H(2).

of mercenaries.[119] Significantly, Article 28N of the Malabo Protocol follows Article 4 of the UN Convention in outlawing the actions of accomplices. In doing so, they open up the prosecution of those who provide support services to mercenaries.[120]

But there are crucial differences. In relation to armed conflicts scenarios, the Malabo Protocol follows the Elimination Convention and omits the requirement found under API and the UN Convention that the material compensation be substantially in excess of that to which persons of similar rank and function in the state army would be entitled. Outside armed conflicts, the Malabo Protocol follows the UN Convention in characterising 'Assisting a group of persons to obtain power' as mercenary activity. A crucial difference is that the Malabo Protocol similarly characterises 'Assisting a government to maintain power'. In doing so, the AU addresses the refusal of incumbents to step down from office, a significant source of conflict in African states, including in Côte d'Ivoire.

Remarkably, the Malabo Protocol provides for a standing criminal chamber to be established within the existing African Court on Human and Peoples' Rights with jurisdiction over 14 crimes, including aggression and mercenarism. It is the first treaty to provide for regional jurisdiction over the crime, but it allows for national and sub-regional action in the alternative under the principle of complementarity. In contrast, the UN Convention provides that state parties can refer breaches (presumably each other's breaches) to the Secretary-General of the United Nations (Article 8). Aside from that, the UN Convention allows for action at the national level in providing that any person who commits such offences should be extradited or prosecuted under the nationality principles and the territoriality principles of international law (Articles 5, 9, 10 and 12) with prosecutions in national courts and according to local laws (see also Articles 8 and 14).

The Malabo Protocol is to be welcomed. But it is not perfect. The Malabo Protocol is silent on the issue of penalties. That is in contrast to the UN Convention that requires that states impose penalties on perpetrators which take into account the grave nature of the offences. The Malabo Protocol is also silent as to status whereas the UN Convention clearly denies to mercenaries the automatic status of combatants and POWs.[121] Its prohibition of the use of mercenaries to maintain power is to be welcomed and complements the AU's African Charter on Democracy, Elections and Good Governance Democracy Charter 2007 (Democracy Charter, in force since 2012) which prohibits coups and other forms of unconstitutional change including 'Any refusal by an incumbent government to relinquish power to the winning party or candidate after free and fair elections'.[122] But it contradicts the exclusion of Heads

---

[119] UN Convention Articles 3–4 and Malabo Protocol Article 28H(3).

[120] See generally, Report of the Working Group on the Use of Mercenaries as a means of violating Human Rights and Impeding the Exercise of the Right of Peoples to Self-Determination, UN Doc. A/62/301 (2007), para 71.

[121] UN Convention Article 16(b).

[122] Democracy Charter Article 23(4). The Democracy Charter has been in force since February 2012 after 15 states deposited their instruments of ratification. At end-July 2020, 34 African states have ratified the treaty. Ratification Status: African Charter on Democracy, Elections and

of States and senior officials from prosecution under Article 46A *bis* of the Malabo Protocol, and under the 2013 policy of the AU Assembly. That prohibition means that the court is limited to prosecuting the use of mercenaries by non-state actors, an uneven treatment that undermines the legitimacy of the framework.

Also problematic is that the Malabo Protocol limits the definition of mercenary to persons (Article 28H). Presumably, that is to be interpreted as natural persons. But the actions of states and private military companies have amplified the impact of mercenaries on African states. As we have seen, the Elimination Convention refers to all natural and legal persons. Alongside that, Articles 4–6 of the UNGA Convention includes states, persons, groups and organisations as potential perpetrators of mercenary activity. One way forward is to read Article 28H alongside Article 46C of the Malabo Protocol which excludes states from the overview of the court but enables jurisdiction over legal persons. One benefit is that Article 46C makes clear that the court would have jurisdiction over corporations. The general consensus is that the term includes business corporations.[123] If that interpretation is correct, Article 46C of the Malabo Protocol read in conjunction with Article 28H(2)—which criminalises recruiters, financers, users and trainers of mercenaries—or/and Article 28N—which relates to accessories takes us closer to a framework in which PMCs can be prosecuted for crimes of mercenarism. The challenge is the meeting each element of the definition of mercenaries.

Until the Malabo Protocol comes into effect, the 1977 OAU Elimination Convention and its annexes, the 1977 Luanda Convention and the 1972 OAU Convention, as well as the 2005 Defence Pact, remain the applicable regional treaties providing specifically for a response to mercenary activity. Under these, AU state parties have a strict duty to prosecute or extradite mercenaries when these pose a threat to another member state. Additionally, the regional treaties require the imposition of severe penalties at the national level, including capital punishment. The challenge to that is the trend away from capital punishment. Certainly, at December 2010, 38 of 54 AU states retain the death penalty for offences but 23 of those states choose not to use that sanction in practice.[124] With the exception of the trial of mercenaries in Luanda in 1976, the death penalty has generally not been imposed by African states for mercenary activity.

So far, African states have cooperated in bringing mercenaries to trial. Equatorial Guinea and Chad prosecuted those involved in the 2017 attempt for offences related to their mercenary activities.[125] Similarly, Equatorial Guinea, Zimbabwe and South

---

Good Governance Democracy Charter 2007, https://au.int/sites/default/files/treaties/36384-sl-AFRICAN%20CHARTER%20ON%20DEMOCRACY%2C%20ELECTIONS%20AND%20GOVERNANCE.PDF, the most current information available to the author is at 28 June 2019.

[123] Colvin and Chella 2012, at 299 and 302.

[124] 16 African states have abolished the death penalty, 38 states retain the death penalty but in 23 states that have not abolished, it is no longer the practice. African Commission on Human and Peoples' Rights Working Group on the Death Penalty in Africa 2011, at 21.

[125] 'Chad jails 11 'mercenaries' over Equatorial Guinea coup plot', *Punch*, 7 June 2019, https://punchng.com/chad-jails-11-mercenaries-over-equatorial-guinea-coup-bid/. But there are questions about due process in Equatorial Guinea, see Mendez 2019.

Africa prosecuted those involved in the 2004 Wonga coup plot. Zimbabwe also extradited Mann to Equatorial Guinea, where he and du Toit were sentenced to 34-years imprisonment each for their roles.[126] Although they did not serve much of their sentences, President Nguema pardoned them, Mann was deported to the UK.[127] These prosecutions reflect the importance of controlling mercenary activity to African states. But, they also underline the difference in approach to mercenaries used by incumbent governments of post-colonial African states.

42.4 Conclusion

The OAU, AU and their member states have led the development of regional and international legal frameworks against mercenaries and their co-conspirators which reflecting key challenges for the African continent and key gaps in international legal protection. Significantly, the most recent treaty, the African Union's Malabo Protocol (2014), links mercenarism to aggression, coups and unconstitutional maintenance of power and it provides for a regional criminal court for adjudicating cases. On balance, it more adequately addresses current challenges arising from the activities of mercenaries than international frameworks. However, its definition of mercenaries is too narrow and would exclude many protagonists including PMCs. Also problematic is the exclusion of heads of African states and senior government officials from prosecution. Whilst imperfect, the legal frameworks reflect the importance of a resolution of the activities of mercenaries (at least in theory). In practice however, AU states are reluctant to move forward with establishing the criminal court.

Going forward therefore, it may be more appropriate to devise a specific regime for mercenaries based on relevant and more nuanced provisions of the Malabo Protocol. One question is whether a change of nomenclature is necessary. Ettinger argues that the term 'mercenary' is loaded and stigmatising and suggests the title 'freelance militant' instead and for PMCs 'freelance companies'.[128] It is difficult to describe the activities of mercenaries in Africa in neutral terms. But a change in terms may be useful in gaining broader consensus for new treaties which allow for greater control of their activities.

However, a legal response alone will not address the use and recruitment of mercenaries in African states. As we have seen, the OAU and the AU have developed legal frameworks against mercenaries. In practice, however, mercenaries continue to be prevalent in intra-state armed conflicts and crises and the AU has tolerated the use

---

[126] 'A Short Trial, at Last; a British Mercenary on Trial in Equatorial Guinea' *The Economist* (US), 21 June 2008, vol. 387 Issue 8585, p. 58; Wines M., 'Thatcher's son pleads guilty in coup plot, avoiding Prison', *New York Times*, 14 January 2005.

[127] Three other South Africans were also pardoned for their part in the plot. McVeigh T., 'Ex-mercenary Nick du Toit tells of his five years in a 'living hell' and why he is ashamed of war', *The Observer*, 13 June 2010; Siddique H. and Tremlett G., 'Simon Mann pardoned over role in Equatorial Guinea plot', *The Guardian*, 2 November 2009.

[128] Ettinger 2014, at 183.

of mercenaries by post-colonial governments suppressing dissent. The dichotomy in approach undermines the rule of law, and it empowers oppressive regimes. It is therefore crucial that the AU lead in opposing the use of mercenaries by all sides, irrespective of any short-term benefit that use may bring.

The AU, UN and Equatorial Guinea, a target state of mercenary action, agree that the complex causes of conflicts in African states must be addressed if a solution is to be found to the issue of mercenaries.[129] Key triggers are the lack of development of more democratic institutions in states and a lack of respect for human rights and constitutional term limits by those in power. The AU is progressively addressing this through legal frameworks supporting democratic governments in Africa, at least in theory. In practice, however, the AU has been unwilling to criticise incumbents.[130] Unemployment and poverty are also triggers. The availability of a pool of recruits, in particular young men, from across African states for mercenary activities can be traced to these. It is important that the AU work with its members to put in place strategies that improve socio-economic opportunities.[131] The AU should be willing to challenge state leaders who redirect state funds for private ends and those who divert state funds and assets from social projects to mercenaries. As part of that, governments should be encouraged to strengthen their national armies rather than relying on mercenaries and PMCs. Finally, the AU and the UN should be willing to intervene, in particular where governments are using mercenaries against the people.

Without a holistic and effective approach, the peace, security and development of African states is likely to remain in jeopardy.

References

African Commission on Human and Peoples' Rights Working Group on the Death Penalty in Africa (2011) Study on the Death Penalty in Africa. Baobab Printers, Gambia
Arielli N, Collins B (2013) Conclusion: Jihadists, Diasporas and Professional Contractors – The resurgence of Non-state Recruitment since the 1980s. In: Arielli N, Collins B (eds) Transnational Soldiers. Palgrave Macmillan, pp 250–256
Bappah AY (2016) Nigeria's Military Failure against the Boko Haram Insurgency. African Security Review 25: 148–158
Colvin E, Chella J (2012) Multinational Corporate Complicity: A Challenge for International Criminal Justice in Africa. In: Nmehielle VO (ed) Africa and the future of international criminal justice. Eleven International Publishing, pp 297–318
del Prado JLG (2019) The Crime of Mercenarism. In: Jalloh CC, Clarke KM, Nmehielle VO (eds) The African Court of Justice and Human and Peoples' Rights. Cambridge University Press, pp 449–476
Ettinger A (2014) The mercenary moniker: Condemnations, contradictions and the politics of definition. Security Dialogue 45: 174–191

---

[129] UN Press Release SC/13688, 4 February 2019.

[130] See Keane F., 'There will be work for mercenaries in Africa until democracy replaces dictatorships', *The Independent*, 20 March 2004.

[131] See Burke J. and Salih Z.M., 'Mercenaries flock to Libya raising fears of prolonged war', *The Guardian*, 24 December 2019.

Fallah K (2006) Corporate actors: the legal status of mercenaries in armed conflict. International Review of the Red Cross 88: 599–610

Francis DJ (2007) Uniting Africa. Ashgate Publishing

Gillard EC (2006) Business goes to war: private military/security companies and international. International Review of the Red Cross 88: 525–572

Gleijeses P (2016) 'Flee! The White Giants are Coming!': The United States, the Mercenaries and the Congo 1964-1965'. In: Young T (ed) Readings in the International Relations of Africa. Indiana University Press, pp 153–164

Green LC (2008) The Contemporary Law of Armed Conflict, 3rd edn. Manchester University Press

Harding J (1997) The Mercenary Business: 'Executive Outcomes'. Review of African Political Economy 71: 87–99, at 96–97

Howe HH (2001) Ambiguous Order: Military Forces in African States. Lynne Rienner Publishers

International Committee of the Red Cross (1968) Annual Report 1967. ICRC, Geneva

International Committee of the Red Cross (1969) Annual Report 1968. ICRC, Geneva

Keenan J (2018) Why the Tuareg have been demonised. In: Tschudin A et al (eds) Extremisms in Africa. Fanele, South Africa

Kinsey C (2008) International Law and the Control of Mercenaries and Private Military Companies. Cultures and Conflicts. https://journals.openedition.org/conflits/11502. Accessed 31 July 2020

Kufuor KO (1999) The OAU Convention for the Elimination of Mercenarism and Civil Conflicts. In: Musah AF, Fayemi JK (eds) Mercenaries: An African Security Dilemma. Pluto Press, pp 198–209

Major MF (1992) Mercenaries and International Law. Georgia Journal of International and Comparative Law 22:103–150

Mendez J (2019) Preliminary Report on Mass Trial in Equatorial Guinea. American Bar Associations Center for Human Rights and Clooney Foundation for Justice TrialWatch Project. https://www.americanbar.org/groups/human_rights/reports/mass-trial-eg/. Accessed 31 July 2020

Musah AF, Fayemi JK (1999) Africa in Search of Security: Mercenaries and Conflicts – An Overview. In: Musah AF, Fayemi JK (eds) Mercenaries: An African Security Dilemma. Pluto Press, pp 13–42

Percy SV (2007) Mercenaries: Strong Norm, Weak Law. International Organization 61: 367–397

Seibert G (2005) Comrades, Clients and Cousins: Colonialism, Socialism and Democratization in Sao Tome and Principe. Brill Academic Publishers

Spearin C (2009) Back to the Future: The Lessons of History. International Journal 64: 1095–1107

Stinnett N (2005) Regulating the Privatization of War: How to stop private military firms from committing human rights abuses. Boston College International and Comparative Law Review 28: 211–224

Taulbee J (1985) Myths, Mercenaries and Contemporary International Law. California Western International Law Journal 15: 339–363

Thobhani AH (1976) The Mercenary Menace. Africa Today 23(3): 61–68

Dr. Eki Yemisi Omorogbe is a Lecturer at the University of Leicester. Her research is on African States and International Law. Eki founded and co-chairs the International Law and Policy in Africa Network (ILPAN). She is also a member of the African Union Law Research Network, and the African Expert Group on International Criminal Justice.

Chapter 43
International Humanitarian Protection to Disabled and Elderly People in Armed Conflict Zones

Julio Homem de Siqueira, Daury César Fabriz and
Junio G. Homem de Siqueira

Contents

43.1 Introduction	941
43.2 The Humanitarian Protection of Disabled People	942
43.3 The Humanitarian Protection of Elderly People	949
43.4 Conclusion	953
References	954

Abstract This chapter demonstrates that there is a deficit of international humanitarian protection of the rights of the elderly and disabled people in armed conflict zones. Although there is a significant list of rights for these individuals in practice there is no effective application. It lists and comments on most of the international documents which deal with the protection of such vulnerable groups and, using the data available, describes how states and international organizations materialize the rights of those people.

Keywords International public law · Humanitarian law · Disabled people · Elderly people · Armed conflict

43.1 Introduction

There are many issues concerning the rights of vulnerable groups. One is concerned with their protection during hostilities. The International Committee of the Red Cross (ICRC) understands international humanitarian law as a set of norms that seek

---

J. H. de Siqueira (✉)
Institute of Criminal Law Studies Alimena, University of Calabria, Rende, Italy

D. C. Fabriz
Vitoria Law School, Vitoria, Brazil

Brazilian Academy of Human Rights, Vitoria, Brazil

J. G. H. de Siqueira
Rio Grande do Norte Federal Justice, Rio Grande do Norte, Brazil

to limit the effects of armed conflicts and to protect people who are not or are no longer participating in hostilities and to restrict the means and methods of warfare.[1] The history of this public international law ramification is antique and has its roots in ancient civilizations when the *ius in bello* first appeared.[2] However, the history of its regulation is recent and can be confounded with the history of the ICRC. Both the Red Cross and the humanitarian law appeared intending to aid militaries and, later, civilians wounded in armed conflicts, by means of the Geneva Conventions—a series of four international treaties concluded between 1864 and 1949, amended by three Additional Protocols, two in 1977 and a third in 2005.[3] Therefore, when someone talks about humanitarian law, they have in mind the purpose of protecting the rights of individuals who take no part in armed conflicts but are subject to them, which is the case of civilians, children, elderly people and people with disabilities, for example. For these reasons, international humanitarian law is related to international conflict and security law.

This chapter analyses, from the international humanitarian approach, the protection of two vulnerable groups affected by hostilities in armed conflict zones: disabled people and elderly people. Both sections list and comment on most of the international instruments dealing with the protection of such groups and, using the data available, describe how states and international organizations materialize the rights of those people. Concluding remarks are offered at the end of the chapter.

43.2 The Humanitarian Protection of Disabled People

Let's begin with the humanitarian protection of disabled people. *Disability* is the inability of doing something. Although laypersons can easily say what disability is, specialists cannot.[4] Since there is no consensus, the closest to an agreement may be understanding disability as an inevitable element of human experience— a kind of human diversity.[5] Thus, disability can no longer be seen as a personal tragedy or disease but as a result of social injustice.[6] And this is especially true after World War II, when international instruments on human rights and humanitarian law strengthened the protection of human dignity. To understand this approach, it is important to understand the evolution of the perspectives around the term disability.

Impairment, disability and handicap are terms that were created, respectively in the mid-14th century, the 1570s and the 1650s.[7] Their meanings reveal different

---

[1] See the ICRC website at https://bit.ly/2CUfBy5. Accessed 20 July 2020.

[2] For the history of international humanitarian law, see, for example, Alexander 2015.

[3] See the four Conventions and three Additional Protocols at https://bit.ly/39RuLkc. Accessed 3 August 2020.

[4] Mitra 2006.

[5] Couser 2005.

[6] Diniz 2010; Bampi et al. 2010.

[7] See https://www.etymonline.com/. Accessed 17 August 2020.

kinds of disturbances, as can be seen in the manual of ICIDH: *impairments* are "concerned with abnormalities of body structure and appearance and with organ or system function, resulting from any cause; in principle, impairments represent disturbances at the organ level"; *disabilities* reflect "the consequences of impairment in terms of functional performance and activity by the individual; disabilities thus represent disturbances at the level of the person"; and *handicaps* are "concerned with the disadvantages experienced by the individual as a result of impairments and disabilities; handicaps thus reflect interaction with and adaptation to the individual's surroundings".[8] However, the history of their subjacent ideas is as old as the history of humankind.[9]

Some research found evidence that "shows not only that mobility impairments were common in ancient Greece, but also that, once they are indicated, they are difficult to ignore in the archaeological and written record".[10] References can be found in the works of Homer, Hesiod, Thucydides, Plutarch, Hippocrates, Pliny the Elder, Martial and St. Augustine, for example.[11] Evidence can also be found in material record, such as bioarchaeological evidence and vase painting: "a tomb from Capua in Italy dating to c. 300 BC provides not just for impairment, but also for accommodation, in the form of an adult man whose missing lower leg had been replaced by one of the earliest known prostheses".[12] On the one hand, there was public support "to individuals whose impairments precluded them from working" and, "in some exceptional situations, having an impairment was not a barrier to attaining power"; on the other hand, "care for persons with impairments would have been reserved for those few who were wealthy enough to afford it", so "disability for the vast majority of Greeks and Romans would have increased the extent to which they were marginalized and excluded from society and living in deprived economic conditions".[13]

This was very common to congenital impairments. However, for persons disabled by war, the situation was different, since "pensions were granted to soldiers who had been injured in battle, and food was provided to others with disabilities who could prove their economic need".[14] Thus, "the consequences of physical handicaps varied according to the context and to the individual".[15] Whether the ideas, as well as the preoccupation, have ancient roots, the same does not apply to the discussions about the models of disability, which appeared only in the 1970s.

The first known model is medical. Also referred to as the traditional perspective, it is inherently individualistic. Being underpinned by the notion of personal tragedy, it is rooted in the thought that disability is a bad omen or a punishment for a sin. This

---

[8] WHO 1976, p. 14.
[9] Braddock and Parish 2001.
[10] Sneed 2020, p. 1017.
[11] Goodey and Rose 2018.
[12] Sneed 2020, p. 1018.
[13] Braddock and Parish 2001, p. 15.
[14] Braddock and Parish 2001, p. 16.
[15] Edwards 1997, p. 43.

approach was common among ancient peoples during the medieval period. However, "despite the negative impact that widespread superstition had on people with disabilities during medieval times, there is evidence that other attitudes about disabilities, particularly mental illness, were also common," and there are records that these people "survived by relying on a variety of supports: family members, neighbours, employers, charitable institutions, and begging".[16] Another bias emerged during the Middle Ages whereby asylums for people with mental disabilities were established, since it was believed that some disabilities were divinely inspired,[17] and others were not (leprosy, for example).[18] Those asylums became mental hospitals in Europe during the low Middle Age, to isolate the disabled people from society and provide their care and treatment. Unfortunately, the view that disabilities were demonically inspired prevailed in the early modern period and influenced the traditional model of seeing disability.

From the Middle Ages to the 20th century, many treatments appeared to supposedly cure some types of disability as a disease. The treatments were provided by the hospitals for the insane (madhouses, lunatic asylums, mental hospitals, hospices). They included assaults on the body and the senses, as in the case of "phrenze"—being "drenched or played upon, alternately with warm and cold water"; also "their scalps were shaved and blistered; they were bled to the point of syncope; purged until the alimentary canal failed to yield anything but mucous; and, in the intervals, they were chained by the wrist or the ankle to the cell wall".[19] In the 1920s, shock therapies were developed and implemented, which included "the use of insulin, Metrazol and malaria to induce shock and, it was hoped, cure patients with mental illness".[20] These proceedings were very common due to forced (for the poor) or paid (for the wealthy) private confinements, since disabled people were seen as plagues. But this occurred only with mentally disabled people. Other disabilities such deafness, blindness and muteness received different attention, at least since the Modern Age,[21] when there were schools created, not hospitals for them.

While some were included, others were segregated from society—literally incarcerated in hospitals. In the late 1800s, "as treatment gave way to confinement and custodial care in larger facilities, cure rates concomitantly dropped, and psychiatrists reported that mental illness was largely incurable".[22] In this period, psychiatric institutions were opened not only for care/treatment, but also for studying such people and their experiences. This and other facts, such as migratory control, stressed disability more as a medical pathology. For example, in 1882, the United States Congress "banned the entrance into the country of 'lunatics, idiots or any person unable to care of himself or herself without becoming a public charge'". In 1903, legislation was

---

[16] Braddock and Parish 2001, pp. 18–19.
[17] Metzler 2018; Braddock and Parish 2001.
[18] Scalenghe 2018, pp. 76–80.
[19] Morton 1897, p. 125.
[20] Braddock and Parish 2001, p. 41.
[21] Vierestraete and Söderfeldt 2018.
[22] Braddock and Parish 2001, p. 33.

passed "prohibiting 'epileptics' from entering the country", and in 1907, "imbeciles" and the "feebleminded" were banned; the same occurred in Cuba between 1902 and 1933, and in Brazil in the early 1900s.[23] These facts also partially explain why many references to disabilities appeared in the first editions of the ICD.

According to Kudlick, "[i]ronically, the limited interest in disabled people coincided with a time when modern Western societies understood disability almost exclusively in medical terms".[24] The beginning of the paradigm shift began in the 1960s, recovering and expanding some social movements that occurred in the late 19th century.[25] With the advent of social history, such historians started to question the primacy of stories centred on doctors, paving the way for focusing attention not only on other healthcare professionals but also on patient-centred stories.[26] However, the shift has not been fully completed yet. The *pathology model of disability* persists even to this day, but fortunately, it does not reign absolute.

Initially, the WHO adopted a model that was more medical than social, employing as its basis the ICIDH.[27] According to it, the illness-related phenomena sequence is disease, impairment, disability, and handicap.[28] In other words, disability is seen as a consequence of disease, so the person must be subjected to specific medical care. This is particularly true when the definitions of *impairments* (organs' disturbances), *disabilities* (individuals' disturbances) and *handicaps* (disadvantages impaired or disabled individuals face in the interaction with and adaptation to their surroundings) are read.[29] For this, the medical model regards segregation, unemployment, low education, and other social problems that disabled people face as stemming from the inability of their injured body to perform productive work.[30] That is why it is seen as a problem of health care, with both individual health and public health implications.

Before the publication of the ICIDH, many organizations for the rights of persons with disabilities appeared, for example: the American Association on Intellectual and Developmental Disabilities (1876), the National Association of the Deaf (1880), Easter Seals (1916), the Canadian National Institute for the Blind (1918), the American Foundation for the Blind (1921), the American Diabetes Association (1939), and Disabled in Action (1970)—but none of them was composed and managed by disabled persons for disabled people as was the Union of the Physically Impaired Against Segregation, which was founded in the UK in 1972/74. The purpose of UPIAS was to redefine disability in terms of social exclusion as a form of social oppression, and despite not being fully adopted by the ICIDH, its proposal gained strength in the 1980s, when disability became "an experience of oppression shared

---

[23] Rembis 2018, pp. 90–91.
[24] Kudlick 2018, p. 108.
[25] Not exactly in this sense, but allowing this approach, see Patterson 2018.
[26] Kudlick 2018, p. 107.
[27] WHO 1976.
[28] WHO 1976, p. 11.
[29] WHO 1976, p. 14.
[30] Diniz 2010; Barcellos and Campante 2012.

by people with different types of injuries" facing social barriers that hindered their independence as human beings.[31]

This new concept is due to many factors that occurred between the 1930s and 1950s. One of them was "the mass 'euthanasia' policy for disabled people, defined as 'useless eaters', introduced by Germany's then Nazi Government in the 1930s and 40s", which led wealthy states (the United Kingdom, the United States and some in Europe) to soften their attitudes and policies toward the disabled and allowed "an expansion of community-based services provided by state and voluntary agencies and a proliferation of professional helpers underpinned by traditional deficit understandings of disability".[32] The medical advances are also responsible for this shifting, as well as disability activism, which took a larger-scale development in the 1950s, when "friends and parents of people with disabilities began organizing for more extensive services for people with disabilities in many parts of the world".[33]

According to the UN Department of Economic and Social Affairs, "the focus of the United Nations on disability issues shifted in the late 1950s from a welfare perspective to one of social welfare".[34] The chronology offered by the DESA shows that in the Sessions 7/1951, 8/1952 and 9/1953, the Social Commission focused on the problems of social rehabilitation of persons with disabilities and expressed interest in programmes for the promotion of services for these people, stressing their independent and productive role in society. In 1969, the UN General Assembly adopted the Declaration on Social Progress and Development, in which article 19(d) addressed: "the institution of appropriate measures for the rehabilitation of mentally or physically disabled persons, especially children and youth, to enable them to the fullest possible extent to be useful members of society".[35] In the 1970s, despite the international widespread of the concept of human rights for persons with disabilities, the UN focus on disability remained on rehabilitation of the individual, as can be seen in its Declaration on the Rights of Mentally Retarded Persons (1971),[36] its Social Committee's Resolution 1921 (LVIII) on Prevention of Disability and Rehabilitation of Disabled Persons (1975),[37] and its General Assembly Declaration on the Rights of Disabled Persons (1975).[38]

Adopted in 1976, the ICIDH came to improve the ICD by establishing an official international catalogue of impairments, disabilities and handicaps, as well as reinvigorating the biomedical model, updating it. With the ICIDH, the WHO did not fully accept UPIAS' new approach, but did not put its efforts aside.[39] The analysis of the ICIDH shows that it went beyond the standard hitherto followed by the ICD:

---

[31] Diniz 2010.
[32] Barnes 2012, p. 13.
[33] Braddock and Parish 2001, p. 44.
[34] See https://bit.ly/2QrcQYH Accessed 26 August 2020.
[35] See https://bit.ly/34CEFFY Accessed 26 August 2020.
[36] See https://bit.ly/3aYhiYs Accessed 26 August 2020.
[37] See https://bit.ly/2YACTRV Accessed 26 August 2020.
[38] See https://bit.ly/3b0GYDR Accessed 26 August 2020.
[39] Hutchinson 1995.

the WHO employed three different words to identify impairments, disabilities and handicaps.[40] The result is that the biomedical model left behind an almost mathematical bias to adopt a perspective in which the individual may have a disability, a personal injury that may not be handicapping, that is disabling or disadvantageous. Nevertheless, the ICIDH was more a variant of the medical model than a new model.

For two decades, from the 1980s to 2001, there were many debates about the concepts of injury, impairment, disability and handicap, culminating with the revision of the ICIDH in the 1990s. It was replaced by the ICF, which changed the perception of disability from a result of illness or injuries to a result of health issues.[41] That is to say, "the ICF embodies a conceptualization of disability, but unlike the others this conceptualization is grounded in the notion of human functioning: disability is parasitical on positive, multidimensional notions of human functioning".[42] With the ICF, the social model, which had never been adopted, was absorbed to compose a new model. Contrary to the ICIDH, the ICF adopts a complex assessment of the relationship between the disadvantages experienced by a person and the opportunities that the society offers.[43] It can be said, then, "that the ICF is the only fully worked-out, culturally and linguistically piloted, and evidence-based, classification of functioning and disability".[44] So the individualistic concept of disability (as a strictly personal issue) was abandoned and a broader concept, indicative of social participation restrictions, was adopted. The *new model* currently endorsed by the WHO is three-dimensional (psychological, social and medical), having no unique solutions to the issue of disability. It is called the biosocial model.

From this perspective, disability is a kind of lifestyle that claims the right to be in the world.[45] The right to be recognized and treated as a person, equal to all others, without any stigma. The Convention on the Rights of Persons with Disabilities (CRPD) endorsed exactly this model and made disability part of the human experience.[46] It requires that the States Parties shall take "all necessary measures to ensure the protection and safety of persons with disabilities in situations of risk, including situations of armed conflict, humanitarian emergencies and the occurrence of natural disasters" (article 11);[47] and "collect appropriate information, including statistical and research data, to enable them to formulate and implement policies to give effect to the present Convention" (article 31). In other words, CRPD recognized a need for humanitarian aid to protect, include and ensure citizen participation for disabled people. However, most state parties do not understand the new model adopted by CRPD, and continue to adopt and apply the medical model, that is, they

---

[40] Amiralian et al. 2000.
[41] Diniz 2010.
[42] Bickenbach 2012, p. 53.
[43] Diniz 2010; Diniz and Medeiros 2007.
[44] Bickenbach 2012, p. 53.
[45] Diniz 2010; Diniz et al. 2009.
[46] Dhanda 2008.
[47] CRPD is available at https://bit.ly/3eSLnJi. Accessed 28 July 2020.

see disability "as a deviation from the normal health status".[48] This humanitarian aid aimed at protecting and helping people who are not or are no longer participating in the hostilities of armed conflicts has been effective in many situations, notably in the assistance given to people in general, but it has been weak to the protection of vulnerable groups.

In 2015, the Humanity & Inclusion (formerly Handicap International) NGO published a report based on the results of a consultation with 484 disabled people, 118 organizations for the disabled and some humanitarian organizations. It was concluded that 75% of disabled people do not have adequate access to basic services such as access to health, psychosocial care, food assistance and water, sanitation and hygiene services; and that although some of these services or others considered as essentials are available, 32% of the people do not have information about their existence.[49] The report revealed that 61% of disabled people are assisted by persons from their own families, which is critical to their quality of life. This demonstrates why formal recognition, as well as good intentions, are not sufficient for the realization of rights. Furthermore, it is essential to underline that humanitarian crises increase the vulnerability of certain groups, such as old-aged and disabled people. Considered the estimate made by the WHO in 2018,[50] that 15% of the world's population has some kind of disability, which means more than one billion people, and that this number tends to increase after natural disasters or armed conflicts. The lack of protection is alarming.

The good news is that this scenario seems to be changing. The Charter on Inclusion of Persons with Disabilities in Humanitarian Action, launched by the WHS in 2016,[51] helped to encourage the realisation of concrete actions (workgroups, donations, collection of data, enlarging representativity).[52] In the same year, the UNHCR conducted a survey with the Humanity & Inclusion NGO in a field of Syrian refugees in Jordan to identify who among them would be considered as a disabled person. The survey used two types of questionnaires for the same group: while the traditional questionnaire identified 2.36% of disabled people, the Washington Group Questionnaire (WGQ) found 27.55%. How the information is obtained explains the difference. Reading the Humanity & Inclusion's documents and the WGQ website allow us to conclude that the WGQ does not make direct references to the term *disability* or its correlations that create a stigmatic situation, but employs a neutral language, which allows us to focus on the reported needs and difficulties of those people.[53]

Notwithstanding, while the civilians wounded in war are usually neglected, once they are seen as "an uncomfortable reminder of what many people usually wish to forget—violence, terror, sacrifice, privation and disability itself"; after the hostilities,

---

[48] Degener 2017, pp. 32–33.

[49] See https://bit.ly/305cm0a. Accessed 1 April 2019.

[50] See Disability and health. https://bit.ly/2EjT6n1. Accessed 1 April 2019.

[51] See Charter on Inclusion of Persons with Disabilities in Humanitarian Action. https://bit.ly/334i7wM. Accessed 1 April 2019.

[52] Alt 2018.

[53] See Disability data collection at https://bit.ly/2WSvHQ9. Accessed 28 July 2020.

disabled veterans, at least in Western societies, are valourised with symbolic significance by the state, "and they have been the beneficiaries of State and private support in many forms that would greatly help disabled civilians to become more independent, equal participants in society".[54] Whether many causes for such privilege can be pointed out, the main is that once "States have consolidated their legitimacy, and ruling elites have solidified their power through war and the maintenance of armies that provide a formal monopoly on violence", so "those who fight and die or suffer injury in armed forces serve as powerful symbolic instruments for evoking loyalty and sacrifice and for legitimizing that monopoly", what explains that "while disabilities have carried stigma in most societies throughout time, disability incurred in military service has, in sharp contrast, been formally honored".[55] In other words, while disabled civilians are seen as a topic, disabled veterans of war are treated as a tool. Then, the model's name has changed, but not the praxis.

This whole picture allows concluding that the protection of disabled people and the realization of their rights is not simple—especially in armed conflict scenarios. Despite the new model adopted, the UN still sees disability primarily as a health issue, secondarily as a human rights issue and, finally, as a development priority, according to the WHO global disability action plan 2014–2021.[56] This plan, even when it explains why disability is a human rights issue, addresses disability as an individual problem: "disability is also a human rights issue because adults, adolescents and children with disability experience stigmatization, discrimination and inequalities". Then, the consequences experienced are seen as a result of being a person with disabilities, not as the CRPD's model, the result of the barriers socially imposed.

43.3 The Humanitarian Protection of Elderly People

The other issue addressed by this chapter is the humanitarian protection of elderly people. Both disability and ageing have a strict and historical relation. In some ancient Roman works (e.g., Terentius, Cicero, Herodotus), references to old age as a sickness or a disease can be found.[57] Being a disease, its consequences could be impairments, disabilities or handicaps. This assertion is not held here.[58] But since there is no consensus on labelling ageing as a disease or not,[59] both understandings must be presented.[60]

The increase in life expectancy and the pursuit of healthy ageing have transformed a physiological fact into a kind of disease contributor. This must be explained.

---

[54] Gerber 2018, p. 477.
[55] Gerber 2018, p. 478.
[56] See https://bit.ly/3aZDCB2 Accessed 27 August 2020.
[57] Renstrom 2020.
[58] In the same way McCrory and Kenny 2018, 768; Renstrom 2020; Chmielewski 2017.
[59] Chmielewski 2020, p. 125.
[60] In fact, there are more than 300 theories of ageing. See Chmielewski 2017.

Recently, the WHO approved the ICD-11 (for mortality and morbidity statistics),[61] in which appears the extension code XT9T for ageing-related ("caused by pathological processes which persistently lead to the loss of an organism's adaptation and progress in older ages"), as well as other already existing codes that have relation to it, such as old age (MG2A) and age-related diseases (e.g., 5A81.1, 6D8Z, 8D64.2, 9B10.0, 9B60, 9B75.0, 9B78.3Z, 9B78.4, 9D00.3, AB54, EE40.Y, EJ20, EE40.31, MB21.0, and SD86). Although the existence of these codes "is not tantamount to formal recognition of ageing as a disease",[62] it does signal that the WHO understands ageing at least as a cause of some diseases. Then it is not too much to say that ageing can be the origin of disabilities. This view can be stated, since there are many diseases related to children, pregnancy, youth, men, women and so on, and many of them can be treated or cured. However, being a child, a man, or being pregnant do not necessarily mean having a disease. And this seems to be adopted by the WHO.

Once ageing is "a complex multifactorial process leading to loss of function, multiple diseases, and ultimately death," and "there are many theories explaining the origin of the overall process," as well as there are associations of it with genetic and epigenetic changes and with human diseases, some researchers have concluded that there are many potential benefits in recognizing it as a disease.[63] This sort of conclusion seems to target the same problem lived by the medical model of disability. Seeing ageing as a disease is tantamount to seeing disability as a disease; it looks like an individual's tragedy. And for the very same reasons this approach cannot be adopted.

In the *World Report on Ageing and Health,* the WHO affirms that loss of functional ability cannot be considered to classify a person as aged or not because its relation to the chronologic age is only vague and it is essential to observe the entire life cycle to better understand the aging process. The fact underlined is that many octogenarian adults have a physical capacity better than many people in their twenties. Therefore, although the chronological criterion is still the safest and the most employed, it is also necessary to observe the social and the biological/genetic criterion.[64] Thus, it can be said that the WHO adopts a health-oriented approach, which is based on the perception that if ageing is a dynamic, plastic and complex process, there is no cure for it.[65]

The recognition of older people's rights gained prominence in the international scene during the later decades of the 20th century. This fact accompanies a global trend of declared rights in international treaties, but seems to suffer from the same ineffectiveness as most positivized rights. This is the case with the laws for elderly people affected by armed conflicts. International discussions on issues related to elderly people's rights date back to the late 1960s.

---

[61] See https://bit.ly/2Qvwnaw Accessed 28 August 2020.

[62] The Lancet Diabetes & Endocrinology 2018, 587.

[63] E.g. Zhavoronkov and Bhullar 2015, pp. 1–2; Perlman 1954; Bulterjs et al. 2015; Gems 2015.

[64] World Report on Ageing and Health. https://bit.ly/2D2MNUc. Accessed 28 July 2020.

[65] Chmielewski 2017, p. 126.

In 1969, the UN proclaimed the Declaration on Social Progress and Development [resolution 2542(XXIV)], in which article 11(c) recognized the rights and guarantees of elderly people. In this same year, the UN decided that from the following year on, the rights of elderly people would be prioritised [resolution 2599(XXIV)]. From then on, the UN began to launch not only legal and policy instruments, but also actions on this issue, as can be highlighted in the resolutions 2842(XXVI), 3137 and 3138(XXVIII), 31/113, 32/131 and 132, 33/52, 34/153, 35/129, 36/20 and 30, 37/51, 38/27, 39/25, 40/30, 41/96, 42/51, 43/93, 44/67 and 76, and 45/106.[66] This last resolution dealt with the World Assembly on Ageing (1982), from which the UN launched an international agenda of public policies for the elderly, known as the *International Plan of Action on Ageing*.

The assembly represented a breakthrough. For the first time, the UN focus was placed on the ageing issue, and objectives were set to guarantee the socioeconomic security of elderly people and identify which opportunities they need to be integrated into, considering the development process of their respective countries. The *International Plan* has as a direct reference to the Human Rights Conference that was held in Tehran (1968). From the *International Plan*, which first appeared in Vienna, the ageing issue became part of the human rights agenda, inaugurating a new chapter. But the recommendations launched in 1982 were not implemented, since they depended on the allocation of resources, which were never foreseen. Despite this, some laws have emerged in many countries to protect elderly people.[67]

The 1990s were also prolific in terms of UN resolutions on the rights and opportunities for elderly people, as seen in resolutions 46/91, 47/5, 49/162, 50/114, 52/80, 53/109 and 55/58, which began the preparations for the Second World Assembly on Ageing, held in Madrid. At the beginning of the third millennium, several preparatory documents of the Madrid Assembly of 2002 were produced, such as the UN resolutions 56/118 and 228, as well as the subsequent resolutions 57/167 and 177, 58/134, 59/150, 60/135, 61/142, 62/130, 63/151, 64/132, 65/182, 66/127, 67/139 and 143, 68/134, 69/146, 71/164, 72/144 and 73/143. Most of these resolutions refer to the follow-ups of the Second Assembly, in a completely different context from that which took place in Vienna 20 years earlier.

The *Madrid International Plan of Action on Ageing* is based on three fundamental guidelines: active participation of the elderly in society, including efforts for development and the fight against poverty; the promotion of health and well-being in ageing; and the creation of a conducive and favourable environment for ageing.[68] Reading the *Madrid International Plan*,[69] it is possible to discern the differential and practically pioneering treatment given to elderly people in situations of armed conflict. Obviously, they were not completely helpless, since there is a significant list of rights for people in situations of armed conflict in the international normative

---

[66] All the UN resolutions can be accessed here https://bit.ly/3hoR0Ay. The first number is the session, the second is the instrument.

[67] Camarano and Pasinato 2004.

[68] Camarano and Pasinato 2004.

[69] Madrid International Plan is available at https://bit.ly/3jyq6Ip. Accessed 28 July 2020.

universe, such as the *Universal Declaration of Human Rights* of 1948 (UDHR) and the *Geneva Conventions* of 1949; however, there was no specific protection as given by the *Madrid International Plan*.

Besides both *International Plans* and the numerous UN resolutions, it is germane to note that there is no profusion of international instruments for elderly people. An online search reveals a few examples, such as the ILO Invalidity, Old-Age and Survivors' Benefits Convention 128/1967, the Old-Age Insurance Conventions 35 and 36/1933,[70] the ILO Invalidity, Old-Age and Survivors' Benefits Recommendations 43/1933 and 131/1967, and the Older Workers Recommendation 162/1980.[71] There is also the OAS Inter-American Convention on Protecting the Human Rights of Older Persons of 2015, which deals in its article 29 specifically with the issue of elderly people in situations of armed conflict. The other sources are treaties, declarations and conventions on human rights and humanitarian law in general.

It is worth considering that international treaties on human rights are comprehensive and generic, so their provisions must be specified by the policies' actors. For example, in the UDHR there is no clear reference to the elderly; however, although the terms elderly or old-aged are not employed, Article 25.1 recognizes that everyone has the right to a standard of living sufficient to ensure to them and their family health and well-being at any stage of their lives, including old age. Another example is the UN *International Covenant on Economic, Social and Cultural Rights* of 1966 (ICESCR), which follows the same trend, since there is not explicit protection to elderly people's rights, except from Article 9, which deals with the right to security, but it does not only cover the protection of the old-aged, as it is known. In this way, moreover, the OAS *American Declaration of Rights and Duties of Man* of 1948, in its article XVI, recognizes that everyone has the right to social security to be protected against the effects of ageing. It is important to note that these two international treaties are prior to 1969, the year that the UN decided on the importance of discussing, recognizing and realizing the rights of elderly people.

The analysis of these instruments allows affirming that a set of obligations were established, mainly to the states (they are the regularly expected policies' actors). However, it cannot be denied that the recognition of the elderly people´s rights, both in general as in the situations of armed conflicts, is deficient, so it only remains to use the generic instruments which therefore cover this portion of the population. Luckily, there are some international actors who work with and for elderly people, especially in situations of armed conflicts. HelpAge International is one of them.

HelpAge is a global network gathering more than 140 organizations, acting in at least 80 countries, with a large experience in the humanitarian crisis, providing old-aged people the right to enjoy dignity, health and safe lives. The data collected by it shows that armed conflicts, as well as natural disasters, have a disproportionate impact on elderly people, worsening the pre-existing marginalization, exclusion and abandonment, which is evidenced when old-aged people are left behind during those situations—and also with the increase of isolation, abuse and disrespect of

---

[70] ILO conventions are available at https://bit.ly/30Lb6ll. Accessed 28 July 2020.

[71] ILO recommendations are available at https://bit.ly/3jBlnpl. Accessed 28 July 2020.

fundamental rights; the exclusion from common shelters, absence of registration for receiving food/clothing/water, difficulties in reaching distribution points, inequality of food sharing within the family, lack of warm clothing, adequate places to sleep, and separation at the commons shelters; the difficulty in enjoying sanitary facilities; the malnutrition, lack of medical treatment, and difficulty in accessing appropriate health services, psychological support and rehabilitation.

In 2015, a survey carried out by HelpAge found that considering all the implemented projects between 2010 and 2014 (16,221), 154 (less than 1%) included at least one activity specifically aimed at the old-aged, of which 74 (48% of that 1%) were financed, and 855 (not much more than 5%) included at least one activity that mentioned the elderly among other vulnerable groups, of which only 439 (51%) were financed.[72] Between 2013 and 2014, Afghanistan, Democratic Republic of Congo, Senegal, Gambia and the Sahel Region were not contemplated by any project aimed at the old-aged, and none of the projects even mentioned them among the groups covered. In addition, only two donors consistently fund projects addressed to the needs of the elderly: ECHO and Japan. Beyond HelpAge, many other important actors can be found involved in this niche of humanitarian aid. Although the efforts of the ICRC, OHCHR, UNHCR, UNICEF, OCHA, WHO, national public health and development agencies, NGO Committee on Ageing, Age International and IFA are not specifically directed at one or another group.

This whole picture allows us to conclude that the protection of elderly people and the realization of their rights is not simple either—especially in armed conflict scenarios. Despite the WHO recognition on ICD-11 of ageing as a cause not as a disease, the UN still sees it—as occurring to disability—firstly as a health issue, second as a human right issue. This fact, plus the lack of concrete and effective protection, also results in a deficit of humanitarian aid.

43.4 Conclusion

In this chapter, a short survey of the concepts of disability and ageing and international instruments was carried out on the protection of the rights of elderly and disabled people in the context of humanitarian aid. Despite the lack of formal instruments aimed to protect them, there are concrete actions, few and low resourced, to improve the quality of life of these vulnerable groups that are not or are no longer participating in hostilities. The whole picture allows us to conclude that protection of these vulnerable groups and the realisation of their rights is not simple. It is necessary to take effective measures to ensure social commitment to creating adequate opportunities (or the means for them) so they can exercise their rights as they consider best for them and not in the way that others think is more appropriate. In addition, the

---

[72] Older people in emergencies: identifying and reducing risks. https://bit.ly/33gi2qf. Accessed 6 July 2020.

international subjects must be provoked to ensure these people's rights, especially in armed conflict scenarios.

References

Alexander A (2015) A short history of international humanitarian law. EJIL 26(1): 109–138.
Alt V (2018) Como incluir pessoas com deficiência em respostas humanitárias. Politike. https://bit.ly/39C8siq. Accessed 1 Apr 2019.
Amiralian MLT et al. (2000) The concept of disability. Rev Saúde Pública 34(1): 97–103.
Bampi LNS, Guilhem D, Alves ED (2010) Social Model: A New Approach of the Disability Theme. Rev Latino-Am Enfermagem 18(4): 816–823.
Barcellos AP, Campante RR (2012) A acessibilidade como instrumento de promoção de direitos fundamentais. In: Ferraz C V et al. (eds) Manual dos direitos da pessoa com deficiência. Saraiva, São Paulo.
Barnes C (2012) Understanding the social model of disability: past, present and future. In: Watson N, Roulstone A, Thomas C (eds) Routledge handbook of disability studies. Routledge, London.
Bickenbach JE (2012) The International Classification of Functioning, Disability and Health and its relationship to disability studies. In: Watson N, Roulstone A, Thomas C (eds) Routledge handbook of disability studies. Routledge, London.
Braddock DL, Parish SL (2001) An institutional history of disability. In: Albrecht G L, Seelman KD, Bury M (eds) Handbook of disability studies. Sage, London.
Bulterjs S, Hull RS, Björk VC, Roy AG (2015) It is time to classify biological aging as a disease. Front Genet 6: 205 (1–5).
Camarano AA, Pasinato MT (2004) O envelhecimento populacional na agenda das políticas públicas. In: Camarano AA (ed) Os novos idosos brasileiros: muito além dos 60? IPEA, Rio de Janeiro.
Chmielewski PP (2017) Rethinking modern theories of ageing and their classification: the proximate mechanisms and the ultimate explanations. Anthropol Rev 80(1).
Chmielewski PP (2020) Human ageing as a dynamic, emergent and malleable process: from disease-oriented to health-oriented approaches. Biogerontology 21: 125–130.
Couser GT (2005) Disability as diversity: a difference with a difference. Ilha do Desterro 48: 95–113.
Degener T (2017) A human rights model of disability. In: Blanck P, Flynn E (eds) Routledge Handbook of Disability Law and Human Rights. Routledge, London.
Dhanda A (2008) Constructing a new human rights lexicon: Convention on the Rights of Persons with Disabilities. SUR – International Journal of Human Rights 5(8): 42–59.
Diniz D (2010) O que é deficiência. Brasiliense, São Paulo.
Diniz D, Barbosa L, Santos WR (2009) Disability, human rights and justice. SUR – International Journal of Human Rights 6(11): 64–77.
Diniz D, Medeiros M (2007) Comments on the Portuguese translation of the International Classification of Functioning, Disability and Health. Cad. Saúde Pública 23(10): 2507–2510.
Edwards ML (1997) Deaf and dumb in Ancient Greece. In: Davis L (ed) The disability studies reader. Routledge, New York.
Gems D (2015) The aging-disease false dichotomy: understanding senescence as pathology. Front Genet 6: 212 (1–7).
Gerber DA (2018) Disabled Veterans and the Wounds of War. In: Rembis M, Kudlick C, Nielsen KE (eds) The Oxford Handbook of Disability History. OUP, London.
Goodey CF, Rose ML (2018) Disability History and Greco-Roman Antiquity. In: Rembis M, Kudlick C, Nielsen KE (eds) The Oxford Handbook of Disability History. OUP, London.
Hutchinson T (1995) The classification of disability. J [Br] Paediatr Assoc 73: 91–94.

Kudlick C (2018) Social History of Medicine and Disability History. In: Rembis M, Kudlick C, Nielsen KE (eds) The Oxford Handbook of Disability History. OUP, London.

McCrory C, Kenny RA (2018) Rebuking the concept of ageing as a disease. The Lancet Diabetes & Endocrinology 6(10): 768.

Metzler I (2018) Intellectual Disability in the European Middle Ages. In: Rembis M, Kudlick C, Nielsen KE (eds) The Oxford Handbook of Disability History. OUP, London.

Mitra S (2006) The capability approach and disability. J Disabil Policy Stud 16(4).

Morton TG (1897) The history of Pennsylvania Hospital 1751–1895. Times Printing House, Philadelphia.

Patterson L (2018) The Disability Rights Movement in the United States. In: Rembis M, Kudlick C, Nielsen KE (eds) The Oxford Handbook of Disability History. OUP, London.

Perlman RM (1954) The aging syndrome. Journal of the American Geriatrics Society 2(2): 123–129.

Rembis M (2018) Disability and the History of Eugenics. In: Rembis M, Kudlick C, Nielsen KE (eds) The Oxford Handbook of Disability History. OUP, London.

Renstrom J (2020) Is aging a disease? Available at https://bit.ly/2QAQog2 Accessed 28 August 2020.

Scalenghe S (2018) Disability in the Premodern Arab World. In: Rembis M, Kudlick C, Nielsen KE (eds) The Oxford Handbook of Disability History. OUP, London.

Sneed D (2020) The architecture of access: ramps at ancient Greek healing sanctuaries. Antiquity 94(376): 1015–1029.

The Lancet Diabetes & Endocrinology (2018) Opening the door to treating ageing as a disease. The Lancet Diabetes & Endocrinology 6(8): 587.

Vierestraete P, Söderfeldt Y (2018) Deaf-blindness and the Institutionalization of Special Education in Nineteenth-century Europe. In: Rembis M, Kudlick C, Nielsen KE (eds) The Oxford Handbook of Disability History. OUP, London.

WHO (1976) International classification of impairments, disabilities, and handicaps: a manual of classification relating to the consequences of disease. https://bit.ly/307aFiD. Accessed 28 July 2020.

Zhavoronkov A, Bhullar B (2015) Classifying aging as a disease in the context of ICD-11. Front Genet 6: 326 (1–8).

Julio Homem de Siqueira is a Junior Researcher at the Institute of Criminal Law Studies "Alimena", University of Calabria—Italy (2021–2022); Researcher in Public Law at Federal University of Rio Grande do Norte (UFRN, Brazil), State University of Minas Gerais (UEMG, Brazil) and Vitoria Law School (FDV, Brazil); LL.M at FDV; Member of the Centre of Intelligence for Preventing Repetitive Demands at Rio de Janeiro Federal Justice; Law Clerk at Rio de Janeiro Federal Justice.

Daury César Fabriz is an Associate Professor of Laws at Espirito Santo Federal University (UFES, Brazil); Full Professor at Vitoria Law School (FDV, Brazil); Lead Researcher at *State, Constitutional Democracy and Fundamental Rights* Research Group (FDV); Member of Latin American Net for Democratic Constitutionalism; Lawyer at Fabriz Lawyers; Sociologist.

Junio G. Homem de Siqueira is a Bachelor in Laws (FDV) and Electric Engineering (UFRN); Energy Engineer at USIMINAS (1977–1981); Energy Distribution Manager (1981–1984), Thermal Power Plant (1984–1986), Energy and Utilities (1986–2007) and Coke and Energy (2007–2008) at ArcelorMittal Tubarao (former Companhia Siderurgica de Tubarao), Brazil; Superintendent Director at Sun Coke Tubarao S/A (2007–2009), Brazil; Consultant Engineer; Law Clerk at Rio Grande do Norte Federal Justice.

Chapter 44
The Politics of International Justice

Stefanie Bock and Nicolai Bülte

Contents

44.1 Introduction	958
44.2 'Classical' Understanding of International Law and the First International Courts	959
44.3 The Special Status of the Area of International Humanitarian Law, International Criminal Law, and International Human Rights Law	961
44.3.1 Early International Criminal Prosecutions: Ascribing Individual Responsibility and Power Politics	961
44.3.2 The Development of International Human Rights Courts and the Empowerment of the Individual	963
44.3.3 The Modern International Criminal Law Courts: Between Power Politics and the Pursuit of Objectivity	965
44.4 The Work of International Courts: Between Justice and Politics	968
44.4.1 International Criminal Courts	968
44.4.2 International Human Rights Courts	975
44.5 Conclusion	977
References	978

Abstract The question as to what constitutes "justice" is one which cannot be easily answered; it is a very complex concept which becomes even more difficult when asked on the international stage. And while it has been acknowledged that there are several ways of achieving all kinds of justice, especially in the context of mass or state crimes, there is a tendency to focus on justice achieved in judicial proceedings. On the international level, this may be surprising since that form of justice presupposes the existence of international tribunals. Such tribunals, however, limit the concept of absolute State sovereignty insofar as their Member States are bound to respect and implement their decisions. The tense relation between sovereignty and politics on the one hand and the rule of law on the other invites to look at when and under which circumstances those courts are established and how they themselves deal with the political pressure stemming from the highly political surroundings they are cast in. While it seems that courts can contribute to ordering the international stage in a meaningful way, the fact that almost all disputes in international law have both

---

S. Bock (✉) · N. Bülte
Department of Law, Philipps University Marburg, Marburg, Germany
e-mail: stefanie.bock@jura.uni-marburg.de

© T.M.C. ASSER PRESS and the authors 2022
S. Sayapin et al. (eds.), *International Conflict and Security Law*,
https://doi.org/10.1007/978-94-6265-515-7_44

political and legal aspects, makes it questionable whether all of them are suitable for judicial solution.

Keywords Power Politics · Justice · International Tribunals · Human Rights Courts · International Criminal Court

44.1 Introduction

The question as to what constitutes "justice" is one which cannot be easily answered; it is a very complex concept with a—depending on the context in which it is used—normative, legal, philosophical, sociological, and/or political dimension. At the international level, things get even more complicated. Which behaviour, treatment or (state) reaction is considered just depends *inter alia* on cultural, historical, and linguistic perceptions as well as on moral concepts and values which—at least traditionally—develop in the national sphere within national public discourses.[1] Asking about the "Politics of International Justice" then adds another layer of complexity because it refers to the delicate relationship between power (politics) and justice.

One way to approach this broad topic is to focus on the establishment and work of judicial bodies tasked with the enforcement of international law, in particular human rights courts and international criminal tribunals.[2] These institutions with their formalized rules and procedures in a very stylized way go against the idea that international law is not really law *strictu sensu* but rather power politics.[3] They are based on the notion that international norms and treaties are binding and enforceable and thus—at least to some extent—opposed to the traditional idea that states are the sole and decisive subjects of international law.[4] A partially court-driven international justice system limits the idea of absolute sovereignty insofar as, although a state—as a matter of principle[5]—freely decides to become a party to a court, it still gives up some of its authority in that it is then bound by the decisions of that court. This holds in particular true for criminal courts and human rights courts in whose proceedings the individual is rhetorically employed to argue against absolute state sovereignty.[6] However, and despite the fact that international tribunals contribute to the juridification (and the corresponding de-politicization) of international law,

---

[1] Cf German Constitutional Court (Bundesverfassungsgericht—BVerfG), 2 BvE 2/08, 30 June 2009, para 249. English translation available at https://www.bundesverfassungsgericht.de/SharedDocs/Entscheidungen/EN/2009/06/es20090630_2bve000208en.html;jsessionid=A1B74FB2BBF455DA424B92EB92938460.2_cid392. Accessed 14 February 2022.

[2] For other international courts, see Alter et al. 2018.

[3] Cf the references in Janis 1984, pp. 62–63.

[4] Shaw 2017, pp. 156–157.

[5] The situation is different if the Security Council of the United Nations (UNSC) triggers international criminal investigation and prosecutions, cf infra, Sect. 44.3.3 and Sect. 44.4.1.2.

[6] Already the International Military Tribunal (IMT), 1 October 1946, p. 447. Cf also Bantekas and Oette 2013, p. 273, who stress that states often view individual complaints procedures as unwarranted criticism (and thus as an interference with their sovereignty).

they are nevertheless in various ways connected to and influenced by international power politics. The questions of when tribunals are established, who they address as legal subjects with rights and duties, which cases they deal with, and how their decisions are received and implemented—to give but a few examples—inevitably have a political dimension. They thus offer a revealing example to illustrate the dynamics of the politics of international justice.

The course of this chapter is as follows: First, the traditional, state-centric approach of international law is paradigmatically outlined using the International Court of Justice (ICJ) as an example (Sect. 44.2). We then go on to look at the changes in discourse that bring about the international courts after the two world wars, the development of international human rights and corresponding courts as well as the establishment of "modern" international criminal courts after the end of the Cold War (Sect. 44.3). Section 44.4 then deals with the "inner politics" of these institutions, how they are influenced by politics and how they react to such influences.

44.2 'Classical' Understanding of International Law and the First International Courts

In a positivist turn at the end of the 19th and the beginning of the 20th century, the idea emerged that only states could be the subjects of international law.[7] And although this view was argued against rather early on,[8] may be readily admitted it soon became the dominant theory.[9] Accordingly, the modern (post World War I) history of international courts and tribunals started in 1920 with the creation of a state-centric body: the Permanent Court of International Justice (PCIJ) attached to League of Nations,[10] which was replaced after World War II by the International Court of Justice (ICJ), the principal judicial organ of the United Nations (UN). The ICJ is, and the PCIJ was, an interstate tribunal, that is, both do not, or did not, try claims of individuals.[11] Their main[12] purpose is to decide on disputes between states by applying generally recognized and accepted rules of law[13] and thus to judicialize[14] international conflicts arising from competing national interests of sovereign states.

---

[7] Cf Manner 1952, p. 444.

[8] For instances in which international courts recognized individuals as (procedural) subjects in their own rights, see Menon 1992, pp. 158–165. For scholarly writing, cf the references in Soirila 2017, p. 1167.

[9] Menon 1992, p. 154; Soirila 2017, p. 1167.

[10] Article 14 Covenant of the League of Nations.

[11] Hudson 1922, p. 258; Article 34(1) Statute of the International Court of Justice (ICJ Statute). The PCIJ allowed "states or Members of the League of Nations" to be parties in cases before the Court, cf Article 34 Statute of the Permanent Court of International Justice (PCIJ Statute).

[12] Beside deciding on legal disputes between states (contentious cases), the ICJ may also give advisory opinions on legal matters to United Nations organs and specialized agencies.

[13] Scott 1921, p. 100.

[14] Hurd 2018, pp. 193, 196.

The questions the ICJ deals with are inevitably highly political in nature. Take for example the *Yerodia* Case, where the Court had to decide whether Belgian authorities had violated the sovereign rights of the Democratic Republic of the Congo by issuing an international arrest warrant against the then acting Congolese Minister for Foreign Affairs, *Abdoulaye Yerodia Ndombasi*, for alleged crimes constituting grave violations of international humanitarian law.[15] The binding character of the Court's decisions[16] and their underlying premise that political disputes involve legal questions that can be judicially solved necessarily touch upon state sovereignty. To preserve the role of states as dominant subjects of international law, however, the jurisdiction of the ICJ is strictly based on the concept of state consent, that is, the Court can deal with interstate conflicts only if the states involved have in one way or another[17] consented to its jurisdiction over the concrete case. Accordingly, the Court's decisions only apply *inter partes* and have no legally binding effect on other states.[18] In doing so, the ICJ regime adheres to the general idea of traditional international law that states cannot be bound by obligations other than those which they have freely committed themselves to. This also means that—as a general rule—the ICJ can exercise its dispute solving powers only if this is in the political interests of the conflicting parties: it is the free political decision of every state whether and to what extend (case-by-case referral, treaty-based consent or unconditional acceptance) they accept the Court's jurisdiction. In other words: the role and power of the ICJ largely depends on the willingness of the states to subject themselves to the rule of law and to refrain from pushing through their interest by means of power politics.

States also gatekeep the access to international institutions, i.e., they are in a position to decide who legally partakes on the international stage. As the PCIJ explained in its Danzig Decision of 1928:

> "[i]t may be readily admitted that, according to a well established principle of international law… an international agreement, cannot, as such, create direct rights and obligations for private individuals. But it cannot be disputed that the very object of an international agreement, according to the intention of the contracting Parties, may be the adoption by the Parties of some definite rules creating individual rights and obligations and enforceable by the national courts."[19]

The decision is being interpreted as upholding *"states' monopoly on access to the international system and their status as gatekeepers of international rights and duties."*[20] At the same time, this passage indicates *"that nothing can prevent the*

---

[15] ICJ, *Democratic Republic of the Congo v. Belgium,* Arrest Warrant of 11 April 2000, 11 April 2000.

[16] *Argumentum e contrario* from Article 59 ICJ Statute.

[17] Article 36 ICJ Statute distinguishes three different ways to accept the Court's jurisdiction: case-by-case consent, treaty-based consent and prior declaration of consent; cf in more detail Hurd 2018, 197 et seq.

[18] Article 59 ICJ Statute.

[19] PCIJ, *Jurisdiction of the Courts of Danzig,* Advisory Opinion, 1928 PC.I.J. (Ser. B) No. 15, 3 March 1928, pp. 17–18.

[20] Soirila 2017, p. 1167.

individual from becoming the subject of international rights if States so wish."[21] Indeed it seems that the PCIJ was of the view that only states were actors on the international stage, and that only through their (voluntary) decision others could become such actors.

44.3 The Special Status of the Area of International Humanitarian Law, International Criminal Law, and International Human Rights Law

The idea that states are the only subjects of international law, is, as indicated above, heavily stylized. And while it is futile, or at least outside the scope of this article, to consider all exceptions to it, one may look at the broader area that comprises of international humanitarian law, international criminal law, and international human rights law. All three areas strongly overlap and may even be considered as forming one whole.[22] This whole, in its rhetoric and to a lesser extent in reality, restricts the power of states by strengthening the role of the individual and introducing regulatory mechanisms which are—at least to some degree—independent from the will of the affected states.

44.3.1 Early International Criminal Prosecutions: Ascribing Individual Responsibility and Power Politics

During the first half of the 20th century, discussions on international law became very much influenced by the two world wars. And while the PCIJ held in its Danzig decision that states were the gatekeepers to the international stage, the political discourse had changed some ten years prior. The rhetoric of World War I was marked by an unprecedented demonization of the other side and propagandistic reports on war crimes and atrocities committed by "the enemy".[23] Consequently, the Ottoman Empire was being threatened with the prosecution of individuals should they not stop systematic crimes committed against the Armenian people, and representatives of the Allied Powers called to charge the German Emperor and members of the German government with mass murder and violations of the laws and customs of war.[24] After the end of World War I, both the Peace Treaties of Sèvres[25] and

---

[21] Menon 1992, p. 164.

[22] Highly critical of "splitting" these areas: Bassiouni 2018, p. 27.

[23] Conze 2014, p. 17.

[24] Hankel 2003, pp. 21–40.

[25] Articles 226–230 Treaty of Peace between the Allied and Associated Powers and Turkey (Treatise of Sèvres).

Versailles[26] provided for the establishment of international and national tribunals to try alleged war criminals. However, neither treaty actually led to international trials[27]—the Treaty of Sèvres never entered into force but was replaced by the Treaty of Lausanne. The latter did for political reasons no longer demand for the criminal prosecutions of Turkish officials,[28] and the attempt to prosecute the former German Emperor Wilhelm II also failed when he found refuge in the Netherlands where he died in 1941.[29]

Nevertheless, the very idea to attach individual criminal responsibility to violations of international law and thus to overcome the traditional state-centrist approach by recognizing individuals as addressees of international norms was revolutionary. This holds all the more true as it seems doubtful if the ascription of international duties to individuals was based on genuine state consent. The peace treaties demanded international prosecutions, and while the losing parties did sign the treaties (and, in doing so, formally accepted all peace conditions imposed on them), arguably this was not a truly free consent. For example, the Treaty of Versailles was very much a "take it or leave it" offer, with "leave it" being equal to being militarily overrun.[30] Thus it seems that—contrary to the later Danzig Decision of the PCIJ—the Peace Treaties of Sèvres and Versailles introduced the individual as an actor on the international stage independently from the will of their nation states.

The emancipation of international criminal law from state consent becomes even more obvious in the aftermath of World War II. The International Military Tribunal (IMT) in Nuremberg and the International Military Tribunal for the Far East (IMTFE) were established by unilateral declaration of the victorious powers[31] without asking for the (formal) consent of the losing sides. The tribunals may thus be regarded as a tool of power politics: they were specifically created to publicly try representatives of the defeated nations. This is particularly reflected in their limited jurisdiction which does not extend to alleged war crimes of the Allies (which is one of the main reasons why both the IMT and the IMTFE are criticized as victor's justice).[32] In addition, it seems that the selection of defendants was—at least in some instances—politically motivated.[33] The Japanese Emperor *Hirohito*, for example, was spared

---

[26] Articles 227–230 Treaty of Peace with Germany (Treaty of Versailles).

[27] The Treaty of Versailles, however, led to a series of national war crime trials before the German Supreme Court in Leipzig. In more detail on these so-called Leipzig Trials, which are widely criticised for their restrictive case selection and the lenient sentences, see Hankel 2003.

[28] Cf Cassese 1998, p. 2.

[29] In more detail, cf Schabas 2018; Hankel 2003, pp. 74–87.

[30] Conze 2018, pp. 369–370.

[31] The IMT was established through the London Agreement of 8 August 1945 between France, the United Kingdom, the United States, and the Soviet Union. The IMTFE was established by Special Proclamation by the Supreme Commander for the Allied Powers at Tokyo, General Douglas MacArthur.

[32] Cf Ambos and Bock 2012, p. 492 with further references.

[33] Ibid., pp. 497–498.

from prosecution probably because the Allied Powers needed him as a partner to preserve public order within Japan.[34]

44.3.2 The Development of International Human Rights Courts and the Empowerment of the Individual

In contrast to the internationalisation of criminal law, the development of human rights only started after World War II. Under the impression of the atrocities committed in its wake, political discourse began to address the question whether individuals do not only have duties, as evinced in (international) criminal prosecutions, but also (human) rights on the international level.[35] The first two treaties stemming from that discourse, the International Covenant on Civil and Political Rights (ICCPR) and the International Covenant on Economic, Social and Cultural Rights (ICESCR), recognize such rights but give individuals only limited powers to enforce them. The ICCPR, for example, initially provided only for an inter-state complaint system before the Human Rights Committee (HRC), which is—in line with the classical approach of the ICJ—based on state consent (Article 41 ICCPR). This eventually means that international human rights are—as a rule—not effectively implemented and enforced if states lack the political will to do so.[36] To strengthen the human rights system, the Optional Protocol to the ICCPR introduced in 1976 an individual complaints procedure. Nevertheless, the HRC remains a political body[37] and its findings on alleged human rights violations are not fully comparable in their legal effects to binding judicial decisions.[38]

In this regard, the position of the individual was further developed at the regional level. The European Convention on Human Rights (ECHR), the Inter-American Convention on Human Rights (IACHR), and the African (Banjul) Charter of Human and Peoples' Rights (ACHPR)[39] led to the establishment of human rights courts; all three treaties do not only provide for state complaints,[40] but also—albeit in varying degrees and different ways—empower individuals to access the courts and claim human rights violations.[41] A quick glimpse at the case load demonstrates the high

---

[34] In more detail Otomo 2011.

[35] The debate whether they did have rights before is irrelevant in this context: the debate about human rights can be considered a genuinely new one—as a then newly emerging area of law. See Janis 1984, pp. 62–63; Soirila 2017, p. 1167.

[36] McQuigg 2011, pp. 10–13; also Bantekas and Oette 2013, p. 201.

[37] Bantekas and Oette 2013, p. 201; also HRC 2008, para 11.

[38] Cf Bantekas and Oette 2013, p. 201; also HRC 2008, paras 11, 15, 17.

[39] Amended in 1998 by the Protocol to the African Charter on Human and People's Rights on the Establishment of an African Court on Human and People's Rights (Protocol ACHPR).

[40] Article 33 ECHR; Article 61 IACHR; Article 5 Protocol ACHPR.

[41] Under the ECHR, individuals can directly address the European Court of Human Rights (ECtHR) after having exhausted all domestic remedies available, Article 34, 35(1) ECHR. In contrast, the

practical importance of individual complaints. Inter-state applications are very rare;[42] as a rule, states do not risk to deteriorate relations with other states by accusing them of human rights violations.[43] Individual complaints, to the contrary, are frequently used and form the bulk of the Courts' work: in 2021 alone, the ECtHR, for example, received 44,250 individual applications.[44] They are an important cornerstone of an efficient human rights system[45] as the individual gets the opportunity to obtain a binding judgment that has to be aboded by and executed by the affected state.[46] In other words: a non-political player is granted the power to promote the rule of law and to use international law to restrict a state's freedom of action.[47]

Notably, the human rights courts have further strengthened the role of the individual by holding that at least certain human rights entail positive duties of protection and care. The right to life,[48] for example, does not merely oblige states to refrain from intentional, unlawful killings, but also to actively protect the lives of all persons within their jurisdiction.[49] This involves—in words of the ECtHR—the duty to *"secure the*

---

access of the individual to the Inter-American Court of Human Rights (IACtHR) is more indirect. The IACtHR provides for a two-stage process: After having exhausted all national remedies (Article 46(1)(a) IACHR), the individual may lodge a complaint with the Inter-American Commission (Article 44 IACHR) which will assess the merits of the claim and—if applicable—will try to reach a friendly settlement (Article 48(1)(f) IACHR). If this fails, the Commission may submit the case to the IACtHR. The Commission thus serves as a "gatekeeper" and the individual victim depends on the advocacy of the Commission; cf also Bantekas and Oette 2013, pp. 247–248. A similar approach is taken by the African Court on Human People's Rights (ACtHPR, Articles 55, 56 ACHPR; Article 5(1)(a) Protocol ACHPR). In addition, however, states may by special declaration accept the competence of the Court to hear individual complaints and thus grant the victims of human rights violations direct access to the ACtHPR, Articles 5(3), 34(6) Protocol ACHPR.

[42] Cf Bantekas and Oette 2013, p. 225; Ambos 2018, p. 81.

[43] One of the rare state complaints the ECtHR had to deal with was the application of the Georgian Government against the Russian Federation because of alleged arbitrary repression of Georgians living in Russia (ECtHR, *Georgia v. Russia (I)*, App No. 13255/07, 31 January 2019). In this case, the initiating of a formal complaint proceeding seems to have been a kind of last resort for a politically weak state (Georgia) to protect its citizens from alleged human rights violation through a very powerful one; it thus was a kind of David v. Goliath scenario.

[44] ECtHR, Analysis of statistics 2021, p. 4. Available at https://www.echr.coe.int/Pages/home.aspx?p=reports&c. Accessed 14 February 2022. 27,100 of the applications were identified as likely to be declared inadmissible; on the development of ECtHR's caseload, see Madsen 2018. In 2020, 23 cases were sent to the IACtHR by the Commission, which had received 2,448 petitions, http://www.oas.org/en/iachr/multimedia/statistics/statistics.html. Accessed 14 February 2022. The ACHPR in total has received 301 individual applications up until February 2022, https://www.african-court.org/cpmt/statistic. Accessed 14 February 2022. All figures were the latest available at the time of writing.

[45] Cançado Trindade 2011, pp. 27–32.

[46] See, e.g., Article 46(1) ECHR; Article 62(1) IACHR (if declared by the state); Article 30 Protocol ACHPR.

[47] On the gradual development before the ECtHR, see in this regard Madsen 2018, pp. 265–271.

[48] Article 2 ECHR; Article 4(1) IACHR; Article 4 ACHPR.

[49] ECtHR, *Lambert and Others v. France*, App No. 46043/14, 5 June 2015 (*Lambert and Others v. France*), para 117.

right to life by putting in place effective criminal law provisions to deter the commission of offences against the person"[50] and to provide for effective prosecutions of intentional killings.[51] Thus, individuals can invoke human rights to force states to criminalize and punish certain behaviours.[52] This is a remarkable limitation of state sovereignty and political discretion.

44.3.3 The Modern International Criminal Law Courts: Between Power Politics and the Pursuit of Objectivity

About the same time when international human rights law discovered its "offensive function"[53] and demanded criminal prosecutions of human rights violations, a "window of opportunity" opened for the creation of new international criminal tribunals, starting with the UN *ad hoc* tribunals, the International Criminal Tribunal for the Former Yugoslavia (ICTY)[54] in 1993 and the International Criminal Tribunal for Rwanda (ICTR)[55] in 1994. These were followed in the next decade by several hybrid tribunals,[56] which have a mixed national-international legal basis and are staffed with national and international personnel.[57] The political and legal circumstances under which the courts were established vary. The *ad hoc* tribunals were created through Security Council (UNSC) decisions under Chapter VII of the UN Charter; other courts are based on bilateral agreements between the affected states and the UN, are part of a transitional UN administration, or established by an occupying power.[58] Common to all, however, is the involvement of a political body, that is, the decision to set up a tribunal and to investigate international crimes committed

---

[50] ECtHR, *Kiliç v. Turkey*, App No. 22492/93, 28 March 2000, para 62. For the IACtHR, *Velásquez Rodríguez v Honduras* (Merits), 29 July 1988, para 166. For a comparative analysis of the development of the jurisprudence of both Courts, see Huneeus 2013, pp. 6–9, who also takes into account the different social-political environments the courts are working in, ibid., pp. 198–200.

[51] ECtHR, *Armani da Silva v. The United Kingdom*, App No 5878/08, 30 March 2016, paras 230, 233.

[52] On the corresponding turn in the use of human rights, which originally were intended to defend against a state and not as a basis to oblige the state to perform certain actions, cf Pinto 2018, p. 165.

[53] Ibid., pp. 165–166.

[54] Established through UNSC Res 827 (1993) 25 May 1993.

[55] Established through UNSC Res 955 (1994) 8 November 1994.

[56] In particular: the Special Panels of the Dili District Court (East Timor) 2000, the Special Court of Sierra Leone (SCSL) 2002, the Extraordinary Chambers in the Courts of Cambodia (ECCC) 2006, the Special Tribunal for Lebanon 2009, the International Residual Mechanism for Criminal Tribunals (MICT) 2012, the Extraordinary African Chambers 2013, African Court of Justice and Human Rights 2005.

[57] Ambos 2021, p. 62 et seq.

[58] Ibid., pp. 66–91.

in a certain situation of crises is (also) a political one.[59] This does not mean that international criminal proceedings necessarily require the consent of the state where the crimes are committed. UNSC Resolution 955 establishing the ICTR, for example, was adopted against the vote of Rwanda.[60] But without (powerful) political support, the creation of *ad hoc* or hybrid tribunals seems hardly possible.

Against this background, the creation of the International Criminal Court (ICC)—a treaty-based permanent body with potential universal reach—was linked with the hope to uncouple the international criminal justice system from power politics and to counteract the risk of arbitrary selectivity associated therewith. According to Article 12 Rome Statute,[61] a state becoming a party to the Rome Statute automatically accepts the Court's jurisdiction over the international core crimes with no possibility to opt out with regard to specific investigations.[62] In the absence of a Security Council referral, however, the ICC has no universal jurisdiction, but can only deal with a situation if the state, on the territory of which the alleged crimes have occurred, or the state of which the person accused is a national of has ratified the Rome Statute (Article 12 Rome Statute). Its jurisdictional reach thus depends on the number of state parties. Whether or not a state joins the ICC is first of all a political decision. Powerful states like the USA, China, and Russia have not ratified the Rome Statute—*inter alia* because they feared that the proceedings might become politicized and misused as a measure of lawfare in diplomatic conflicts.[63] This, on the other hand, can be an incentive for less powerful states to become a member of the Court, as the risk (or threat) of international prosecutions might be a measure to restrain power politics and to enforce international law vis-à-vis strong(er) political players.[64] At the same time, as *Nouwen* has shown, states supportive of the ICC have exercised pressure in particular on African States to ratify the Statute: the European Union, for example, *"made support of the Rome Statute an explicit condition for some development cooperation"*.[65] Moreover, *Nouwen* assumes that many developing countries *"felt that ratification of the Rome Statute was a useful and harmless way to belong to the club"*, but did not necessarily fully consider the implications of accepting the Court's jurisdiction.[66] One must, however, also take into account that at the same time states opposed to the Court, notably the USA, restricted foreign aid for states which ratified

---

[59] With regard to the establishment of the ICTY by the Security Council ICTY, AC, *The Prosecutor v. Dusko Tadic*, Decision on the Defence Motion for Interlocutory Appeal on Jurisdiction, IT-94-1, 2 October 1995, paras 13–25.

[60] In more detail: Akhavan 1996, pp. 504 et seq.

[61] Rome Statute of the International Criminal Court (Rome Statute).

[62] Schabas and Pecorella 2022a, para 13 et seq. States may, however, withdraw from the Rome Statute as a whole, cf Article 127 Rome Statute.

[63] Cf the overview of the respective discussion at the Rome Conference by Fernández de Gurmendi 1997, p. 181; Schabas and Pecorella 2022b, paras 11–12.

[64] Nouwen 2012, p. 163.

[65] Ibid., pp. 163–164.

[66] Ibid., pp. 164–165.

the Rome Statute.[67] The ICC therefore was created in a context in which states may not have been truly free in their decision whether or not they join the Court.

Within the framework of a (potentially) global court, the (politically sensitive) process of selecting situations for investigation becomes another layer. When creating an *ad hoc* or hybrid Tribunal, the acting institution specifies its jurisdiction in temporal, territorial, and, in some cases, personal regards[68] and, in doing so, limits it to specific predefined events. The ICC, to the contrary, has a kind of "dormant" jurisdiction over the territories and nationals of its Member States, which must be activated with regard to a concrete situation.[69] The questions of who should have the power to trigger the Court's jurisdiction and in particular the role of the Prosecutor was one of the most controversial during the negotiating process. The possibility of a freely acting Prosecutor sat odd with a number of delegations, which feared that he or she could misuse his or her competence to initiate politically motivated, unfounded investigations.[70] Their opponents, to the contrary, argued that *proprio motu* powers were essential for a strong and efficient Court, because without them, the ICC would not be able to prosecute international crimes when—for political or other reasons—the State Parties[71] and the Security Council[72] decided not to trigger the Court's jurisdiction. These states regarded an independent Prosecutor, who—acting as an impartial ministry of justice[73]—can decide at his or her own (judicial) discretion if a certain situation warrants international investigations, as an important means to de-politicize the Court.[74] As a compromise, the final Articles 13 (c), 15 Rome Statute vest the Prosecutor with *proprio motu* powers, but link it to an early control by the Pre-Trial Chamber (PTC), which must authorize the opening of a formal investigation.

---

[67] Nouwen 2012, p. 164.

[68] The ICTR, for example, is empowered to prosecute persons responsible for serious violations of international humanitarian law committed in the territory of Rwanda and Rwandan citizens responsible for such violations committed in the territory of neighbouring States between 1 January 1994 and 31 December 1994 (Article 1 ICTR Statute).

[69] Ambos and Bock 2012, p. 532 with further references.

[70] Schabas 2016, pp. 397–402; Schabas and Pecorella 2022b, paras 2 et seq.; Fernández de Gurmendi 1997 esp. p. 178.

[71] Trigger mechanism according to Article 13(a) Rome Statute.

[72] Trigger mechanism according to Article 13(b) Rome Statute.

[73] Cf ICC, OTP, *Situation in Uganda*, Prosecution's Reply under Rule 89(1) to the Applications for Participation of Applicants [...] in the Uganda Situation, ICC-02/04-85, 28 February 2007, para 32; Ambos and Bock 2012, p. 537.

[74] Fernández de Gurmendi 1997, p. 178; Schabas 2016, pp. 398–399; Ambos and Bock 2012, p. 533.

44.4 The Work of International Courts: Between Justice and Politics

Power politics do not only affect the creation of international courts. Rather, after having started their work, they automatically become part of international politics and are caught in a crossfire of political influences. This will be shown for international criminal courts (Sect. 44.4.1) and international human rights courts (Sect. 44.4.2) in turn.

44.4.1 International Criminal Courts

Although the number of international or internationalised criminal courts is considerably larger than those of international human rights courts, the number of proceedings is not. The ECtHR decides on more cases a year as the international criminal courts combined have in their history. International criminal prosecutions have been, and will remain, an exception if measured against all those cases potentially worthy of prosecution.[75] A number of reasons contribute to this, such as but not limited to: the unwillingness of states to investigate[76] or let investigate especially their own nationals,[77] the difficulty of investigations in conflict or post-conflict situations, as well the sheer number of international crimes committed on the one hand and the limited resources of international criminal tribunals on the other.[78]

The scarcity of international criminal proceedings has led authors to the conclusion that the justice achieved by international criminal proceedings has to be considered a limited resource, and therefore as a form of distributive justice.[79] International criminal courts (and in particular the respective Offices of the Prosecutor) are thus forced to make difficult selection decisions and prioritise certain situations (in case of the ICC), persons, and crimes for investigation and prosecution.[80] That these selection processes also have a political dimension becomes apparent if one looks at the subject matter of international criminal proceedings. Formally seen, they are concerned only with establishing individual criminal responsibility and do not discuss the responsibility of states. When compared to the state-centric human rights courts

---

[75] Bassiouni 2009, pp. 139–140.

[76] Cassese 1998, p. 7.

[77] Supra (note 27).

[78] Cf Ambos and Bock 2012, p. 538.

[79] Mégret 2015, p. 81; cf also Ambos 2016, p. 377; Hafetz 2018, pp. 147–152, who compares selectivity in international and domestic prosecutions.

[80] Cf also Ambos and Bock 2012, p. 538. In the proceedings against *Lubanga*, for example, the ICC Prosecutor focused on the war crime of conscripting, enlisting and using child soldiers (ICC, OTP, *Prosecutor v. Thomas Lubanga Dyilo*, Prosecutor's Information on an Investigation, ICC-01/04-01/06-170, 28 June 2006)—a decision that probably led to an impunity gap for other crimes allegedly committed by *Lubanga* and his armed forces.

and the ICJ, this might at a first glance create the impression that international criminal proceedings are less political in nature. One must, however, consider that, at least in theory, international prosecutors tend to focus on persons most responsible for the most serious crime,[81] i.e., the most senior (political and military) leaders in a given situation,[82] who often act on behalf or as representatives of states. If, for example, the ICTR convicts the former Minister for Family Welfare and the Advancement of Women, *Pauline Nyiramasuhuko*, of genocide,[83] her official position indicates that her actions can be attributed to Rwanda and that Rwanda bears state responsibility for genocide.[84] In a similar vein, the Committee of Prosecutors of the IMT agreed on the general selection rule that the defendants should represent the Nazi regime as a whole,[85] which indicates that they saw a close connection between state and individual responsibility.

Moreover, international criminal justice is seen by many as the pinnacle of international justice[86] and, therefore, being charged by an international criminal court bears a certain stigma.[87] It is therefore legitimate to ask why a certain person is prosecuted while another is not;[88] and as all selection processes run the risk of being politicised,[89] a coherent, rational, and transparent strategy for the selection and prioritisation of cases is of crucial importance for the credibility and acceptance of the international criminal justice system.[90] If prosecutions are not distributed more

---

[81] Cf, e.g., ICC, PTC II, *Situation in the Republic of Kenya*, Decision Pursuant to Article 15 of the Rome Statute on the Authorization of an Investigation into the Situation in the Republic of Kenya, ICC-01/09-19-Corr, 31 March 2010 (Kenya Article 15 decision), para 188; Article 1(1) Statute of the Special Court for Sierra Leone (*"prosecute persons, who bear the greatest responsibility"*); Article 1 Law on the Establishment of the Extraordinary Chambers in the Courts of Cambodia for the Prosecution of crimes committed during the Period of Democratic Campuchea (*"bring to trial senior leaders...and those who were most responsible for the crimes."*).

[82] ICC, PTC I, *Prosecutor v. Thomas Lubanga Dyilo*, Decision on the Prosecutor's Application for a warrant of arrest. Article 58, ICC-01/04-01/06-1-Corr-Red, 10 February 2006, para 63.

[83] ICTR, Trial Chamber (TC) II, *Prosecutor v. Nyiramasuhuko et al.*, ICTR-98-42-T, 24 June 2011.

[84] Cf also ICJ, *Bosnia and Herzegovina v. Serbia and Montenegro*, Application of the Convention on the Prevention and Punishment of the Crime of Genocide, 26 February 2007, para 223 where the ICJ when deciding on the responsibility of states *"in principle accept[ed] as highly persuasive relevant findings of fact"* made by the ICTY (which directly concern only the criminal responsibility of the individual accused).

[85] Ambos and Bock 2012, p. 492.

[86] Crit. Nouwen and Werner 2015, pp. 163–164.

[87] This is especially true for the ICC, which is designed as last resort (Article 17 Rome Statute), cf Mégret 2015, p. 82.

[88] Ibid., p. 86.

[89] See, for example, the decision of the ICTY Prosecutor not to investigate alleged war crimes committed by NATO Forces during "Operation Allied Forces" (as to the factual background and the legal findings, cf ICTY, Final Report to the Prosecutor by the Committee Established to Review the NATO Bombing Campaign Against the Federal Republic of Yugoslavia. Available at https://www.icty.org/en/press/final-report-prosecutor-committee-established-review-nato-bombing-campaign-against-federal (accessed 14 February 2022), which was criticized as politically motivated, cf Massa 2006; Colangelo 2003.

[90] Ambos and Bock 2012, p. 541; Ambos 2016, p. 378.

or less equally within a conflict, those belonging to the side most targeted may start resenting the targeting institution. The Nuremberg Trials with their one-sided focus on NS-perpetrators, for example, were commonly perceived as "victor's justice" in defeated Germany,[91] the ICTY had to face accusations of anti-Serb bias, the ICTR was criticised for neglecting crimes committed by the Tutsi-led Rwandan Patriotic Front,[92] and the ICC (which—for the time being—is predominantly concerned with situations in Africa) is regarded by some as a tool of Western neo-colonialism.[93]

In the following, we would like to illustrate the relation between power politics and the work of the international criminal tribunals in a little more detail with two recent examples from the ICC: the initiation of investigation in Afghanistan and the proceedings against *Omar al-Bashir*, the former President of Sudan.

44.4.1.1 The Afghanistan Decisions: Power Politics and the Interests of Justice

At the ICC, the Prosecutor enjoys a rather broad discretion to select situations and cases for investigation. In particular, it is up to the Prosecutor to determine if a case or the potential cases likely to arise out of certain situation[94] are grave enough to justify further action by the ICC[95] and whether or not prosecutions are in the "interests of justice".[96] The Office of the Prosecutor (OTP) has stressed several times that it is bound by the principles of independence (Article 42 Rome Statute) and objectivity (Article 54(1) Rome Statute) which require the Office to exercise its authority in full autonomy and unaffected by external (political) influences.[97] In the context of the discussion on the "African focus" of the ICC, however, it was questioned if the decisions of the OTP are indeed free from political considerations.[98]

In any case and as already indicated above, the Prosecutor acts under the judicial supervision of the PTCs, which are supposed to prevent a politically motivated misuse of prosecutorial powers. Up until recently, however, the PTCs have not interfered with the OTP's *proprio motu* investigations, and granted its requests to open investigations

---

[91] Cf already supra, Sect. 44.3.1.

[92] In more detail on how the *ad hoc* tribunals dealt with core crimes committed by the winning side: Peskin 2005.

[93] Cf e.g. Lugano 2017, pp. 10–14.

[94] In more detail on the objects of reference of the admissibility test in terms of Article 17 Rome Statute, Ambos 2016, pp. 274 et seq.

[95] Article 17(1)(d) Rome Statute.

[96] Article 53(1)(c) Rome Statute.

[97] Cf ICC, OTP, *Situation in the Democratic Republic of the Congo*, Prosecution's Reply on the Application for Participation 01/04-1/dp to 01/04-6/dp, ICC-01/04-84, 15 August 2015, para 32; ICC, OTP, Policy Paper on Preliminary Examinations 3 November 2013, paras 26–27; ICC, OTP, Policy paper on case selection and prioritisation, 15 September 2016, para 17.

[98] Cf supra, Sect. 44.3.3. While there might be reasons as to why this may not be a policy issue, there are other reasons behind it (Schabas 2016, p. 397); the distrust the Court, as a whole, faces from certain actors remains for the time being.

in Kenya,[99] Côte d'Ivoire,[100] Georgia,[101] and Burundi[102] without further ado.[103] It is, of course, possible that in these situations there were no issues regarding a possible politicisation of the OTP. Nevertheless, it seems noteworthy that in all these decisions the PTCs restrained their control powers insofar as they considered only the gravity of potential cases in the relevant situation, but did not engage in how this compared to the gravity of other situations potentially worthy of prosecution.[104]

This somewhat changed in the Afghanistan decision. For the first time, a PTC denied the Prosecutor's request for opening a *proprio motu* investigation.[105] Although the Chamber agreed that there were reasonable grounds to believe that crimes falling within the jurisdiction of the ICC had been committed not only by the Taliban and other armed groups, but also by Afghan and US military forces and the CIA,[106] it concluded that international proceedings would not serve the interests of justice. As the preliminary investigations in Afghanistan had been particularly long and difficult, the Chamber assumed that prosecutions were unlikely to succeed, and thus run the risk to frustrate the hopes of victims raised by the investigations.[107] The Prosecutor should, according to the PTC, invest her resources in situations which had *"more realistic prospects to lead to trials"*.[108]

This decision touches upon the difficult relationship between prosecutorial independence and judicial supervision and raises the question if and to what extent the PTC has the power to control discretionary decisions of the Prosecution.[109] In this

---

[99] Kenya Article 15 decision (note 82).

[100] ICC, PTC III, *Situation in the Republic of Côte d'Ivoire*, Corrigendum to 'Decision Pursuant to Article 15 of the Rome Statute on the Authorisation of an Investigation into the Situation in the Republic of Côte d'Ivoire.', ICC-02/11-14-Corr, 15 November 2011 (Côte d'Ivoire Article 15 decision).

[101] ICC, PTC I, *Situation in Georgia*, Decision on the Prosecutor's request for authorization of an investigation, ICC-01/15-12, 27 January 2016 (Georgia Article 15 decision).

[102] ICC, PTC III, *Situation in the Republic of Burundi*, Public Redacted Version of "Decision Pursuant to Article 15 of the Rome Statute on the Authorization of an Investigation into the Situation in the Republic of Burundi", ICC-01/17-X-9-US-Exp, 25 October 2017, ICC-01/17-9-Red, 25 October 2017 (Burundi Article 15 decision).

[103] Later also ICC, PTC III, *Situation in the People's Republic of Bangladesh/Republic of the Union of Myanmar*, Decision Pursuant to Article 15 of the Rome Statute on the Authorisation of an Investigation into the Situation in the People's Republic of Bangladesh/Republic of the Union of Myanmar, ICC-01/19-27, 14 November 2019.

[104] Schabas 2016, p. 394; cf also Poltronieri Rossetti 2019, pp. 589–590.

[105] ICC, PTC II, *Situation in the Islamic Republic of Afghanistan*, Decision Pursuant to Article 15 of the Rome Statute on the Authorisation of an Investigation into the Situation in the Islamic Republic of Afghanistan, ICC-02/17-33, 12 April 2019 (Afghanistan Article 15 PTC decision).

[106] Ibid., paras 47–48.

[107] Ibid., para 96.

[108] Ibid., para 95.

[109] In more detail Poltronieri Rossetti 2019; Mariniello 2019.

context more interesting, however, is that the PTC did not merely review the arguments of the Prosecutor,[110] but engaged itself in political considerations. Its decision not to authorise formal investigations in Afghanistan, was obviously influenced by power politics: When assessing the prospects of further action by the Court, the Chamber referred to the *"scarce cooperation obtained by the Prosecutor"*[111] and noted that *"subsequent changes within the relevant political landscape both in Afghanistan and key States (both parties and non-parties to the Statute), coupled with the complexity and volatility of the political climate still surrounding the Afghan scenario, make it extremely difficult to gauge the prospects of securing meaningful cooperation from relevant authorities for the future, whether in respect of investigations or of surrender of suspects."*[112] This accepts that opposition to the Court yields (positive) results and thus, sends the political message to states: if they resist the Court strongly enough, no investigations will take place, or proceedings will collapse.[113] The impression of political dependency associated therewith is strengthened by the delicate timing:[114] the PTC rendered its decision shortly after the United States had once again threatened the ICC with sanctions, if it started prosecuting US nationals, and had revoked the visa of the then Chief Prosecutor.[115]

Meanwhile, the decision of the PTC was squashed on appeal. The Appeals Chamber (AC) took the view that the PTC should have addressed only whether there is a reasonable factual basis to proceed with an investigation, but was not allowed to discontinue investigations because of its own "interests of justice" assessment. Insofar, the PTC is bound by the (positive) evaluation of the Prosecutor.[116] This decision is decisive for the division of power between the Prosecutor and the Pre-Trial Chambers. With regard to the risk of an undue politicisation of the ICC, it is even more important that the AC stated *obiter dicta* that the PTC's reasoning *"was cursory, speculative and did not refer to information capable of supporting it."*[117] These clear words may be understood as a warning to all organs of the Court

---

[110] In previous decisions, the PTCs had restricted themselves to assess the "interests of justice" only if the Prosecutor decided *not to* proceed because an investigation would not be in the interests of justice, Kenya Article 15 decision (note 81), para 63. See also para 24 footnote 35 of the decision. For the other situations, see Côte d'Ivoire Article 15 decision (note 100), para 207; Georgia Article 15 decision (note 101), para 58; Burundi Article 15 decision (note 102), para 190.

[111] Afghanistan Article 15 PTC decision (note 105), para 91.

[112] Ibid., para 94.

[113] This is not necessarily restricted to the most powerful states, see e.g. the collapse of the proceedings against *Ruto* and *Sang*, ICC, TC V(A), *Prosecutor v. William Samoei Ruto and Joshua Arap Sang,* Public redacted version of Decision on Defence Applications for Judgments of Acquittal, ICC-01/09-01/11-2027-Red-Corr, 5 April 2016; Poltronieri Rossetti 2019, p. 600.

[114] Jacobs 2019.

[115] Cf Simons and Specia 2019

[116] ICC, AC, *Situation in the Islamic Republic of Afghanistan,* Judgment on the appeal against the decision on the authorisation of an investigation into the situation in the Islamic Republic of Afghanistan, ICC-02/17-138, 5 March 2020, (Afghanistan Article 15 AC decision). The PTCs thus can only consider the "interests of justice" if the Prosecutor answers the questions on the "interests of justice" in the negative, according to Article 53(3) Rome Statute (see note 110).

[117] Ibid., para 49.

44.4.1.2 The Bashir Arrest Warrants: Dependency of International Courts on the Good Will of States

Another example for possible tensions between justice and politics are the investigations in the situation in Darfur, Sudan which was referred to the ICC by the UNSC and which is sometimes used to illustrate how "toothless" the ICC is even if it acts—at least at the outset—with the backing of the Security Council.[118] Indeed: although the ICC had issued arrest warrants against the (now, former) head of state, Mr. Omar al-Bashir, in 2009[119] and 2010,[120] respectively, the OTP did not yet manage to detain him.

The warrants caused political backlash. It was argued that they might interfere with a peace process for which the participation of the Sudanese government appeared necessary.[121] Especially the African Union, for a time France and Great Britain too, tried to convince the UNSC to suspend investigations and prosecutions for twelve months (Article 16 Rome Statute),[122] but failed to do so. Regardless of such attempts of influencing the Court from the outside, its first prosecutor seemed rather unimpressed by political considerations as well as *al-Bashir's* official capacity. Other voices added that, charging him would deprive him of agency and marginalize him, as similar charges before the ICTY had.[123] And while the second Prosecutor agreed with the former—she too considers irrelevant political considerations[124]—she had to accept that the latter has proven not to be true. In her 2014 report to the UNSC she stated that *"without stronger action by Security Council and State Parties,"* she would not be able to conduct proceedings against *al-Bashir*.[125] After the change in

---

[118] See e.g. the case study in Rodman 2019, pp. 34–37.

[119] ICC, PTC I, *Prosecutor v. Omar Hassan Ahmad Al Bashir*, Warrant of Arrest for Omar Hassan Ahmad Al Bashir, ICC-02/05-01/09-1, 4 March 2009.

[120] ICC, PTC I, *Prosecutor v. Omar Hassan Ahmad Al Bashir*, Second Warrant of Arrest for Omar Hassan Ahmad Al Bashir, ICC-02/05-01/09-95, 12 July 2010.

[121] For this and the rest of the paragraph, see Bosco 2014, pp. 142–148.

[122] Article 16 Rome Statute is in itself an interesting example for the interdependency between justice and power politics as it grants a political organ—the UNSC—the power to prevent or stop judicial proceedings for a renewable period of twelve months. This provision was deemed necessary to preserve the primary responsibility of the UNSC for maintaining peace, but it is not without risk for the political independence of the Court, for an overview of the relevant discussion during the negotiating process, see Bergsmo and Zhu 2022, paras 1 et seq. For reasons of space, we will not discuss this provision in more detail.

[123] Especially the cases against *Karadžić* and *Milošević*, cited in Rodman 2019, p 34.

[124] Supra, Sect. 44.4.1.1.

[125] ICC, OTP, Twentieth Report of the Prosecutor of the International Criminal Court to the UN Security Council Pursuant to UNSCR 1593 (2005), 12 December 2014 (OTP, Twentieth Report), especially paras 30–31. Available at https://www.icc-cpi.int/iccdocs/otp/20th-UNSC-Darfur-report-ENG.PDF. Accessed 14 February 2022.

government in Sudan and the—at least from media news apparent[126]—decision by the conflicting parties to surrender *al-Bashir* to the ICC, it remains to be seen if he will finally be prosecuted before the ICC. This however is not in the ICC's power to decide.[127]

As regards the relation between justice and politics, it is noteworthy that the main reason why the proceedings have not moved forward is the refusal of State Parties to arrest and surrender *al-Bashir*.[128] This led to several non-compliance proceedings under Article 87(7) Rome Statute.[129] In the context of visits of *al-Bashir* to Malawi, South Africa, and Jordan, the Chambers have taken a clear stance on the legal situation: Article 27(2) Rome Statute declares irrelevant the official capacity of any individual before the ICC, including sitting head of states.[130] This—so the Chambers—applies both vertically (between the Court and States Parties) and horizontally (between states). That Sudan is not a party to the Rome Statute was deemed irrelevant, because the UNSC referral demanded from Sudan to cooperate with the Court, which led the Chambers to the conclusion that *al-Bashir*'s absolute immunity could not be invoked as reason to refuse the execution of the Court's arrest warrants.[131] To hold otherwise would, in the view of the AC, endanger the Court's ability to prosecute heads of states which in turn would *"clearly be incompatible with the object and purpose"* of the Rome Statute.[132] And while these decisions show self-confidence insofar as the Chambers try to hold their ground against political actors and to assure the jurisdiction of the Court, they at the same time appear resigned as regards the

---

[126] Cf e.g. BBC News 2020.

[127] Cf however the OTP's more optimistic last report, Thirtieth Report of the Prosecutor of the International Criminal Court to the UN Security Council Pursuant to UNSCR 1593 (2005), 18 December 2019. Available at https://www.icc-cpi.int/itemsDocuments/2019-12-19-otp-report-UNSC-sudan-eng.pdf. Accessed 14 February 2022. The report was submitted before news emerged that the parties to the conflict had agreed to surrender *al-Bashir* to the ICC.

[128] For examples of visits to States not Party to the Rome Statute cf OTP, Twentieth Report (note 125), para 10.

[129] For an overview of the legal regime governing non-compliance with cooperation obligation, see Ambos 2016, pp. 596–600.

[130] ICC, PTC I, *Prosecutor v. Omar Hassan Ahmad Al Bashir*, Corrigendum to the Decision Pursuant to Article 87(7) of the Rome Statute on the Failure by the Republic of Malawi to Comply with the Cooperation Requests Issued by the Court with Respect to the Arrest and Surrender of Omar Hassan Ahmad Al Bashir, ICC-02/05-01/19-139-Corr, 13 December 2011, para 36.

[131] ICC, PTC II, *Prosecutor v. Omar Hassan Ahmad Al Bashir*, Decision under article 87(7) of the Rome Statute on the non-compliance by South Africa with the Request by the Court for arrest and surrender of Omar Al-Bashir (South Africa Article 87(7) decision), ICC-02/05-01/09-30, 26 July 2017, paras 76–83, especially 79. The States have justified their non-cooperation in the *al-Bashir* case with reference to Article 98(1) Rome Statute according to which the Court may not proceed with a request for surrender or assistance which would require the requested state to act inconsistently with respect to the State immunity of a third state. In more detail on the complex relationship between Article 27 and Article 98 of the Rome Statute, see Ambos 2016, pp. 617–625 with further references.

[132] ICC, AC, *Prosecutor v. Omar Hassan Ahmad Al Bashir*, Judgment in the Jordan Referral re Al-Bashir Appeal, ICC-02/05-01/09-397-Corr, 6 May 2019, para 124.

power of the ICC to enforce compliance: in particular, PTC II refrained from referring South Africa to the Assembly of State Parties or the UNSC *inter alia*[133] because in prior instances, such referrals had been fruitless and not resulted in any measure against the defaulting state.[134] In doing so, the Chamber has *de facto* acknowledged the (at least partial) dependency of the international (criminal) justice system on the goodwill of the respective political players.

44.4.2 International Human Rights Courts

Human rights courts work differently from their international criminal counterparts. As we have already indicated above, they do not (and do not have to) establish individual responsibility but state responsibility. As in case of the ICJ,[135] proceedings before human rights courts are thus often in the same vein politically sensitive. And while the possibility of individuals to file complaints is seen as a crucial means to de-politicize human rights courts and to increase the efficiency of the human rights system,[136] this does not change the fact that the courts work in a political environment and that their decisions may be regarded as an undue intervention in the internal affairs of the affected state. This can even be the case if a decision—at least at first glance—concerns rather technical procedural issues. In the case of *Neziraj v. Germany*, for example, the ECtHR found that German Courts had violated the right to a fair trial (Article 6(1) in conjunction with Article 6(3)(c) ECHR), when they dismissed the appeal of a defendant due to his absence, although his counsel was present and prepared to act on his behalf.[137] The Higher Regional Court of Celle, however, refused to change its practice[138] and stated that the ECtHR judgement *"fundamentally disregard[ed] the legal situation in Germany"* (which does not allow for criminal proceedings in absentia) and that the *"defendant's interest in letting himself be represented by a defence counsel in the main appeal proceedings...is not legally protected by Article 6(3)(c) ECHR."*[139]

The ECtHR is well aware that an efficient human rights system is dependent on the acceptance by the Member States and tries to balance the obligations arising out

---

[133] In addition, the Chamber stressed that South Africa's courts (including the Supreme Court of Appeal) themselves had decided that the State was in breach of its obligations under the Rome Statute and thus it *"appear[ed] that the Government of South Africa ha[d] accepted its obligations,"* South Africa Article. 87(7) decision (note 131), para 136.

[134] Ibid., para 138.

[135] See supra, Sect. 44.2.

[136] See supra, Sect. 44.3.2.

[137] ECtHR, *Neziraj v. Germany*, App No. 30804/07, 8 November 2012.

[138] Generally, on the obligation of German Courts to give effect to the Judgments of the ECtHR, BVerfG, 2 BvR 1481/04, 14 October 2004. English translation available at https://www.bundesverfassungsgericht.de/SharedDocs/Entscheidungen/EN/2004/10/rs20041014_2bvr148104en.html;jsessionid=D0A2447FAF20F7EA7D9DF4146110DF15.2_cid383. Accessed 14 February 2022.

[139] OLG Celle, 32 Ss 29/13, 19 March 2013—English translation according to Ambos 2018, p. 97.

of the ECHR with the sovereign interests of the Member States. Although the Court is of the view that *"the object and purpose of the Convention as an instrument for the protection of individual human beings require that its provisions be interpreted and applied so as to make its safeguards practical and effective,"*[140] it grants the Member States a "margin of appreciation"[141] and thus a degree of (political) discretion when implementing European human rights standards.[142] While this discretion is not unlimited and subject to the judicial control of the ECtHR,[143] it gives the member states some room to preserve their (divergent) cultural and legal traditions. The scope of the margin of appreciation depends on the individual circumstances of the case and the rights concerned;[144] it is particularly broad where there is *"no consensus within the Member States…either as to the relative importance of the interest at stake or as to the best means of protecting it"* or *"where the case raises sensitive moral or ethical issues,"*[145] i.e., in situations in which states have a special interest to uphold their national identities. The IACtHR—although generally more reluctant to defer to national authorities than its European counterpart[146]—has developed a similar mechanism of self-restraint: according to the idea of "subsidiary competence", the Court merely verifies *"whether the State authorities made a reasonable and sufficient weighing up between the two rights in conflict, without necessarily making an autonomous and independent weighing, unless the specific circumstances of the case require this"*[147] and thereby grants the national authorities a certain scope of discretion.[148]

That the political dimension of human rights can pose enormous challenges to international courts can be illustrated by the case of *Khamtokhu and Arsenchik v. Russia*.[149] The two applicants had been convicted in Russia for several serious offences and sentenced to life imprisonment. As the Russian Criminal Code exempts *inter alia* women from life imprisonment, the applicants claimed a violation of Article

---

[140] ECtHR, *Soering v. United Kingdom,* App No. 14038/88, 7 July 1989, para 87. In more detail on the "doctrine of effectiveness": Rietiker 2010, pp. 256–275.

[141] In more detail on the "margin of appreciation" doctrine: Follesdal 2017, pp. 362–368.

[142] The seminal case is ECtHR, *Handyside v. United Kingdom,* App No. 5493/72, 7 December 1976, paras 47–50.

[143] Ibid., para 49; cf also EtCHR, *Lambert and Others v. France* (note 49), para 148.

[144] ECtHR, *Schalk and Kopf v. Austria,* App No. 30141/04, 24 June 2010, para 98.

[145] ECtHR, *Stübing v. Germany,* App No. 43547/08, 12 April 2012, para 60. With regard to permitting the withdrawal of artificial life-sustaining treatment *Lambert and Others v. France* (note 49), para 147.

[146] In more detail, Tsereteli 2016. Cf in this context also Huneeus 2013, p. 5, who stresses that the ECtHR took up work in the context of a number of rich democratic states, whereas the IACtHR had and has to deal with states of varying democratic quality including dictatorships. Follesdal 2017 nevertheless favours the adoption of the ECtHR's "margin of appreciation" doctrine by the IACtHR.

[147] IACtHR, *Memoli v. Argentina,* Preliminary Objections, Merits, Reparations and Costs, 22 August 2013, para 140.

[148] In more detail: Tsereteli 2016, p. 1102.

[149] ECtHR, *Khamtokhu and Arsenchik v. Russia,* App Nos. 60367/08 and 961/11, 24 January 2017.

14 ECHR (prohibition of discrimination) due to an unjustified difference in treatment on the basis of gender. Russia countered that the only thing the applicants could achieve *"was a change in the Russian criminal law which would allow others, including women...to be given harsher sentences."* Even if the Court was to find a violation of Article 14 ECHR, this would be no reason for Russia to completely abolish life sentences.[150] Thereby, Russia implied that—in case of a violation decision—it would extend life imprisonment to women.[151] Although not perceived as being in themselves contrary to human rights standards, the ECtHR is rather critical of life sentences[152] and obviously did not want to give Russia a reason to tighten its criminal law measures. Therefore, it argued that—given the diversity in the national laws of the Member States on life imprisonment and in light of the social sensitivity of penal policy—Russia enjoyed a broad margin of appreciation in shaping and devolving its law on sentencing. And as the exemption of women from life imprisonment was considered *"social progress in penological matters"* (and thus a kind of justified positive discrimination), it was found by majority that there was no violation of Article 14 ECHR.[153] This is hardly compatible with the Court's general approach that only "very weighty reasons" can justify differences in treatment based exclusively on the ground of gender.[154] It rather seems that the ECtHR was ready to ignore a gender-based discrimination (and thus a human rights violation) to avoid undesirable political consequences.[155]

44.5 Conclusion

International justice and (power) politics are in various ways intertwined. Whether international tribunals are created, which cases they actually try and how their decisions are implemented also involve policy considerations. In order to uphold the rule of law and to contribute effectively to a judicialization (and thus limitation) of power politics, international tribunals depend on the support of states and international organisations. To ensure political acceptance, international tribunals have developed different mechanisms or strategies of self-restraint. This, on the one hand, respects the sovereign rights of states as the major subjects of international law and gives them—as can particularly be seen in the work of human rights courts—room for manoeuvre to preserve their national identities and cultural characteristics. On

---

[150] Cf ibid., para 42.

[151] Cf ibid., paras 3, 7.

[152] Ibid., paras 86–87; also ibid., *Concurring Opinion of Judge Nussberger*, para 1. Cf also ECtHR, *Vinter and Others v. United Kingdom,* App Nos. 66069/09, 130/10 and 3896/10, 9 July 2013, where the Court concluded that life imprisonment is only compatible with Article 3 ECHR (prohibition of torture) if there is a prospect of release and a possibility for review.

[153] *Khamtokhu and Arsenchik v. Russia* (note 149), paras 82–88.

[154] In detail ibid., *Joint Partly Dissenting Opinion of Judges Sicilianos et al.*; in the same vein ibid., *Concurring Opinion of Judge Nussberger*, para 1.

[155] Cf ibid., *Concurring Opinion of Judge Nussberger*.

the other hand, these self-restraint tendencies involve the risk that courts give in to external political pressure—as may have been the case in the Afghanistan decision of the ICC's PTC. International tribunals are thus faced with the challenge to find a balance between upholding the rule of law and the normative standards of international law and respecting sovereign policy decisions of states and other political players. However, as Judge Lachs of the ICJ noted already in 1986, as almost all disputes arising in international law have both political and legal aspects, not all of them may be suitable for judicial solution.[156]

References

Akhavan P (1996) The International Criminal Tribunal for Rwanda: the politics and pragmatics of punishment. American Journal of International Law 90:501–510

Alter KJ et al (2018) International court authority in a complex world. In: Alter KJ et al (eds) International court authority. Oxford University Press, Oxford, pp 3–23

Ambos K (2013) Treatise on international criminal law: volume I: foundations and general part. Oxford University Press, Oxford

Ambos K (2016) Treatise on international criminal law: volume III: international criminal procedure. Oxford University Press, Oxford

Ambos K (2018) European criminal law. Cambridge University Press, Cambridge

Ambos K (2021) Treatise on international criminal law: volume I: foundations and general part, 2nd edn. Oxford University Press, Oxford

Ambos K, Bock S (2012) Procedural regimes. In: Reydams L et al (eds) International prosecutors. Oxford University Press, Oxford, pp 488–541

Bantekas I, Oette L (2013) International human rights law and practice. Cambridge University Press, Cambridge

Bassiouni MC (2009) International criminal justice in historical perspective: the tension between states' interests and the pursuit of international justice. In: Cassese A (ed) The Oxford companion to international criminal justice. Oxford University Press, Oxford/New York, pp 123–142

Bassiouni MC (2018) Human rights and international criminal justice in the twenty-first century. The end of the post-WWII phase and the beginning of an uncertain new era. In: DeGuzman M, Amann DM (eds) Arcs of global justice. Essays in honour of William A. Schabas. Oxford University Press, Oxford, New York, pp 3–38

BBC News (2020) Omar al-Bashir: Sudan agrees ex-president must face the ICC. https://www.bbc.com/news/world-africa-51462613. Accessed 14 February 2022

Bergsmo M, Zhu D (2022) Article 16 - deferral of investigation or prosecution. In: Ambos K (ed) Rome Statute of the International Criminal Court: A Commentary, 4th edn. C.H. Beck, Munich, pp 933–944

Bosco D (2014) Rough justice: the International Criminal Court in a world of power politics. Oxford University Press, Oxford

Cançado Trindade AA (2011) The access of individuals to international justice. Oxford University Press, Oxford

Cassese A (1998) Reflections on international criminal justice. Modern Law Review 61:1–10

Colangelo AJ (2003) Manipulating international criminal procedure: the decision of the ICTY Office of the Independent Prosecutor not to investigate NATO bombing in the former Yugoslavia. Northwestern University Law Review 97:1393–1436

---

[156] ICJ, *Nicaragua v. United States of America,* Military and Paramilitary Activities in and against Nicaragua, 27 June 1986, Separate opinion of Judge Lachs, p. 168.

Conze E (2014) Frieden durch Recht. In: Safferling C, Kirsch S (eds) Völkerstrafrechtspolitik. Praxis des Völkerstrafrechts. Springer, Berlin, pp 9–26

Conze E (2018) Die große Illusion. Versailles 1919 und die Neuordnung der Welt. Siedler, Munich

Fernández de Gurmendi SA (1997) The role of the international prosecutor. In: Lee RS (ed) The International Criminal Court. The making of the Rome Statute: issues, negotiations and results. Kluwer Law International, The Hague/London/Boston, pp 175–188

Follesdal A (2017) Exporting the margin of appreciation: lessons for the Inter-American Court of Human Rights. International Journal of Constitutional Law 15:359–371

Hafetz J (2018) Punishing atrocities through a fair trial. International criminal law from Nuremberg to the age of global terrorism. Cambridge University Press, Cambridge/New York

Hankel G (2003) Die Leipziger Prozesse. Deutsche Kriegsverbrechen und ihre strafrechtliche Verfolgung nach dem Ersten Weltkrieg. Hamburger Edition, Hamburg

Hudson MO (1922) The Permanent Court of International Justice. Harvard Law Review 35:245–275

HRC (2008) General comment no 33. The obligations of states parties under the Optional Protocol to the International Covenant on Civil and Political Rights, CCPR/C/GC/33. Available at https://www2.ohchr.org/english/bodies/hrc/docs/CCPR.C.GC.33.pdf. Accessed 14 February 2022

Huneeus A (2013) International criminal law by other means: the quasi-criminal jurisdiction of the human rights courts. American Journal of International Law 107:1–44

Hurd I (2018) International organizations. Politics, law, practice, 3rd edn. Cambridge University Press, New York

Jacobs D (2019) Spreading the Jam – ICC Pre-Trial chamber rejects OTP request to open an investigation in Afghanistan: some preliminary thoughts on an ultra vires decision. https://dovjacobs.com/2019/04/12/icc-pre-trial-chamber-rejects-otp-request-to-open-an-investigation-in-afghanistan-some-preliminary-thoughts-on-an-ultra-vires-decision/. Accessed 14 February 2022

Janis MW (1984) Individuals as subjects of international law. Cornell International Law Journal 17:61–78

Lugano G (2017) Counter-Shaming the International Criminal Court's intervention as neocolonial: lessons from Kenya. International Journal of Transitional Justice 11:9–29

Madsen MR (2018) The European Court of Human Rights. From the Cold War to the Brighton Declaration and backlash. In: Alter KJ et al (eds) International court authority. Oxford University Press, Oxford, pp 243–274

Manner G (1952) The object theory of the individual in international law. American Journal of International Law 46:428–449

Mariniello T (2019) Judicial control over prosecutorial discretion at the International Criminal Court. International Criminal Law Review 19:979–1013

Massa A (2006) NATO's intervention in Kosovo and the decision of the Prosecutor of the International Criminal Tribunal for the former Yugoslavia not to investigate: an abusive exercise of prosecutorial discretion. Berkeley Journal of International Law 24:610–649

McQuigg RJA (2011) International human rights law and domestic violence. The effectiveness of international human rights law. Routledge, New York

Mégret F (2015) What sort of global justice is 'international criminal justice'? Journal of International Criminal Justice 13:77–96

Menon PK (1992) The international personality of individuals in international law: a broadening of the traditional doctrine. Journal of Transnational Law & Policy 1:151–182

Nouwen SMH (2012) Legal equality on trial: sovereigns and individuals before the International Criminal Court. Netherlands Yearbook of International Law 43:161–166

Nouwen SMH, Werner WG (2015) Monopolizing global justice: international criminal law as challenge to human diversity. Journal of International Criminal Justice 13:157–176

Otomo Y (2011) The decision not to prosecute the emperor. In: Tanaka Y et al (eds) Beyond victor's justice? The Tokyo war crimes trial revisited. Brill, Leiden, pp 63–78

Peskin V (2005) Beyond victor's justice? The challenge of prosecuting the winners at the International Criminal Tribunals for the Former Yugoslavia and Rwanda. Journal of Human Rights 4:213–231

Pinto M (2018) Awakening the leviathan through human rights law – how human rights bodies trigger the application of criminal law. Utrecht Journal of International and European Law 34:161–184

Poltronieri Rossetti L (2019) The Pre-Trial Chamber's Afghanistan decision. A step too far in the judicial review of prosecutorial discretion? Journal of International Criminal Justice 17:585–608

Rietiker D (2010) The principle of "effectiveness" in the recent jurisprudence of the European Court of Human Rights: Its different dimensions and its consistency with public international law – no need for the concept of treaty sui generis. Nordic Journal of International Law 79:245–277

Rodman KA (2019) When justice leads, does politics follow? The realist limits of prosecutorial agency in marginalizing war criminals. Journal of International Criminal Justice 17:13–44

Schabas WA (2016) The short arm of international criminal law. In: McDermott Y et al (eds) The Ashgate research companion to international criminal law. Critical perspectives. Taylor and Francis, London, pp 387–405

Schabas WA (2018) The Trial of the Kaiser. Oxford University Press, Oxford

Schabas WA, Pecorella G (2022a) Article 12 - preconditions to the exercise of jurisdiction. In: Ambos K (ed) Rome Statute of the International Criminal Court: A Commentary, 4th edn. C.H. Beck, Munich, pp 805–833

Schabas WA, Pecorella G (2022b) Article 13 - exercise of Jurisdiction. In: Ambos K (ed) Rome Statute of the International Criminal Court: A Commentary, 4th edn. C.H. Beck, Munich, pp 834–852

Scott JB (1921) Aim and purpose of an International Court of Justice. Annals of the American Academy of Political and Social Science 96:100–107

Shaw MN (2017) International law, 8th edn. Cambridge University Press, Cambridge

Simons M, Specia M (2019) U.S. revokes visa of I.C.C. prosecutor pursuing Afghan war crimes. New York Times. https://www.nytimes.com/2019/04/05/world/europe/us-icc-prosecutor-afghanistan.html. Accessed 14 February 2022

Soirila U (2017) Persons and things in international law and "law of humanity". German Law Journal 18:1163–1182

Tsereteli N (2016) Emerging doctrine of deference of the Inter-American Court of Human Rights? International Journal of Human Rights 20:1097–1112

Stefanie Bock is Professor for Criminal Law, Criminal Procedure, International Criminal Law and Comparative Law at the Philipps-Universität Marburg, Germany (since 2016), and Director of the International Research and Documentation Centre for War Crimes Trials (since 2017). Her main fields of research are international criminal law, European criminal law and comparative criminal law.

Nicolai Bülte is a research assistant at the professorship for Criminal Law, Criminal Procedure, International Criminal Law and Comparative Law (Prof. Dr. Stefanie Bock) at the Philipps-Universität Marburg, Germany. In his PhD, he researches the possibility of cultural relativism in the crimes of the Rome Statute. His research interests in general are domestic and international criminal law.

Chapter 45
Poverty

Evelyne Schmid

Contents

45.1 Introduction	982
45.2 Defining, Measuring and Framing Poverty	983
45.2.1 How Prevalent Is Poverty?	985
45.2.2 Different Views on the Causes of Poverty and Implications for Poverty Reduction Strategies	986
45.3 The Various Relationships between Poverty and Conflict	987
45.3.1 Poverty as a Cause or a Driver of Instability	988
45.3.2 Poverty as a Symptom and Consequence of Conflict	990
45.3.3 Poverty as a Result of Deliberate Harm	991
45.3.4 Poverty as a Subject of Transitional Justice	993
45.3.5 Poverty as a (Neglected) Concern in So-Called 'Post-Conflict' Measures	994
45.4 The International Legal and Policy Framework	996
45.5 Concluding Thoughts on the Role of International Law in Addressing the Relationship between Poverty and Conflict	999
References	1000

Abstract This chapter introduces readers to the literature on the relationship between poverty and conflict and the role of international law in addressing poverty. How political actors consider or neglect poverty concerns in the context of security studies matters. Poverty does not automatically lead to conflict and insecurity, but poverty and inequalities can be a crucial aspect in the explanation of conflict and post-conflict dynamics. Therefore, poverty should also be a consideration in the measures taken during conflicts, in transitional justice or post-conflict interventions. Indeed, international law provides a valuable normative framework that can be used to address poverty. At the same time, however, there is a dark side to international law where its norms and the ways in which they are used contribute to the maintenance of a world order in which most of the world's population remains poor.

Keywords Poverty · Inequality · (In)security · Armed conflict · Root causes · Transitional justice

---

E. Schmid (✉)
Faculty of Law, Criminal Justice and Public Administration, University of Lausanne, Lausanne, Switzerland
e-mail: evelyne.schmid@unil.ch

45.1 Introduction

In August of 2018, Kofi Annan passed away in my hometown of Berne, Switzerland. A little over ten years earlier, in the spring of 2006, I sat an undergraduate exam at the University of Geneva where we were asked to comment on Annan's report *In Larger Freedom*. I vaguely remember the exam and my answer even less, but I do have a vivid memory of the admiration with which our professor, the late Victor-Yves Ghebali, and the teaching assistants spoke of Annan's report. I agreed that they had good reasons to be enthusiastic about the report—Annan's diagnosis seemed convincing: security, development and human rights must go hand in hand if we want to prevent conflict and create a world 'in larger freedom'.[1] Annan recognized the strong links between poverty and conflict and tried to mobilize resources at the UN to ensure better coordination and more effective responses to threats that became known as human security. *In Larger Freedom* is a testimony to the influential *Human Development Report* of 1994 which is widely perceived as having shifted the discourse on security and development towards a more holistic notion of security. The concept of human security insists on freedom from fear and the necessity to integrate people's everyday concerns into a new concept that no longer focuses exclusively on military security.[2] Today, Annan's emphasis of the link between poverty, conflict and insecurity remains as relevant as it did in 2005. Across times and cultures, human beings have always tried to secure their economic well-being and livelihoods as part of their survival and dignity. Poverty means vulnerability both at the individual level but also at a macro-level: armed conflicts tend to take place in poor countries and unsurprisingly, conflict-affected countries tend to lose development opportunities.[3] Hence, it is undeniable that poverty and insecurity are inextricably linked.

The chapter begins by introducing the various definitions and measurements of poverty and underlines the importance of paying attention to the framing of this notion. The way we speak or write about poverty or the poor is never neutral. The core of the chapter is the analysis of the multifaceted links between poverty and conflict. When referring to conflict, I do not limit the analysis to the concept of armed conflict in international law, but I include broader instability and violence. Section 45.4 begins with an outline of the main sources and documents in international law that are relevant to poverty and it is followed by a conclusion at Sect. 45.5 with a reflection on the role of international law in relation to poverty and conflict.

---

[1] UN Secretary-General, In Larger Freedom: Towards Development, Security and Human Rights for all (21 March 2005) A/59/2005, para 14.

[2] United Nations Development Programme 1994, p. 1.

[3] Fearon and Laitin 2003, p. 82. Goodhand 2001, p. 4. Addison et al. 2013, p. 160.

45.2 Defining, Measuring and Framing Poverty

Various definitions of poverty have been proposed—each with some advantages and disadvantages. A common way to define poverty is by considering the income of a person and to measure whether this income falls below some minimum level necessary to meet basic needs. This approach relates to *absolute poverty*. Basic needs can be defined very narrowly as the needs required for a human being to survive physically, such as a minimum number of calories per day or a basic shelter. Alternatively, basic needs can be defined in broader terms to include all those resources which are needed to 'keep body and soul together'.[4] The advantage of defining poverty in absolute terms is the relative simplicity of the definition. It suffices to define a minimum threshold below which an individual is considered poor. Absolute poverty measurements allow for comparisons over time in order to assess whether changes in the number of absolutely poor persons are really due to changes in the distribution rather than changes in the poverty threshold. However, the concept of absolute poverty is criticized because absolute poverty measurements fail to take into account horizontal inequalities and are silent on the social relations and the opportunities of an individual.[5]

Relative poverty defines poverty by reference to the relative standard of living as compared to other members of a given social community at a specific time.[6] According to this approach, a person is poor if his or her living standards fall below a certain prevailing standard. In Luxembourg or Switzerland, a person could be relatively poor whereas a person with the same income would be considered rich in another context. Relative poverty definitions have the advantage of taking into account the socio-economic context of an individual. Nonetheless, it is more difficult to assess the evolution of poverty over time. As with absolute poverty, relative poverty is concerned with income or consumption and thus attracts some of the same criticism as the definition of absolute poverty. How much a person earns or consumes does not necessarily say much about the quality of the person's life.

Extreme poverty is defined as a particularly severe form of absolute poverty. Since 2015, the World Bank uses a standard of extreme poverty defined as a person having less than 1.90U$ a day (equivalent to 1 U$ in 2011 prices).[7] The purpose of a definition of extreme poverty is to assist political actors in setting the priorities towards helping those within a population who are most desperately in need of support. The standard to measure extreme poverty is controversial. Some consider that it is too low and that there should be a more nuanced range of poverty lines.[8] The

---

[4] Committee on Scottish Affairs (2000) First Report. https://publications.parliament.uk/pa/cm199900/cmselect/cmscotaf/59/5908.htm. Accessed 14 May 2020.

[5] Waglé 2014, p. 5450.

[6] Ibid., p. 5449.

[7] World Bank (2015) Global Poverty Line Update. http://www.worldbank.org/en/topic/poverty/brief/global-poverty-line-faq. Accessed 12 February 2022.

[8] Pritchett 2006, p. 1, arguing that the poverty line should be differentiated beyond a binary model of 'poor' and 'non-poor', distinguishing between destitute, extremely poor and globally poor people.

UN Special Rapporteur on extreme poverty and human rights, for instance, criticizes the fact that rigid measures based exclusively on income 'fail to capture the depth and complexity of extreme poverty and do not reflect the significant impact of poverty on the full enjoyment of human rights'.[9] The UN Human Rights Council took note of this proposal to define extreme poverty as a combination of income poverty, human development poverty and social exclusion.[10]

Poverty as exclusion has been suggested as an alternative (or complementary) approach to define poverty. According to this view, the poor are those whose socio-economic situation is such that they cannot fully take part in activities of the daily life of a community and 'interact freely with others'.[11] Taking social exclusion into account in the conceptual understanding of poverty has the advantage of broadening the attention beyond simple measures of income, assets or consumption. Those defining poverty in relation to social exclusion also look at whether a household has sufficient resources to meet needs related to social participation in a community and whether the individuals are able to function according to their own capabilities.[12] A criticism of this approach is that it fails to take into account the fact that poor people may well be integrated in a society, but in ways that perpetuate their poverty, e.g. by their unavoidable participation in highly imperfect markets and relationships of dependency or even exploitation.[13]

To understand the phenomenon of poverty, it is particularly instructive to consider how poor people themselves define poverty. When poor people are asked to define poverty, it becomes apparent that 'many factors converge to make poverty a complex, multidimensional phenomenon'.[14] Poor people refer to their vulnerability to rudeness, humiliation, and inhumane treatment by both private and public agents of the state from whom they seek help. They also allude to their inability to respect certain social norms,[15] the social exclusion and 'adverse incorporation'[16] all of which play a major role.

---

[9] UNESCO Poverty. http://www.unesco.org/new/en/social-and-human-sciences/themes/international-migration/glossary/poverty/. Accessed 14 May 2020. (A/HRC/7/15 (28 February 2008), para 23ff.

[10] Human Rights Council, Human Rights and Extreme Poverty (18 June 2008) A/HRC/RES/8/11, para 1.

[11] Böhnke and Silver 2014, p. 6065.

[12] Robeyns 2016. The so-called 'capabilities approach' has notably been developed by Martha Nussbaum: Nussbaum 2013.

[13] Hickey and du Toit 2007, p. 3f.

[14] Narayan-Parker et al. 2000, 26.

[15] Ibid., 31.

[16] Hickey and du Toit 2007, 1, the term 'adverse incorporation' builds on the literature on social exclusion but takes into account that the poor are often 'incorporated' into society but in ways that have adverse effects on their well-being.

45.2.1 How Prevalent Is Poverty?

Poverty continues to be prevalent, but some say that it is decreasing over time. In 2018, the UN Development Programme (UNDP) estimated that acute multidimensional deprivations occur in 105 countries and 1.3 billion people in these countries lived in multidimensional poverty between 2006 and 2016–17. Statistics measuring the proportion of the world's population living below a certain poverty line indicate a decline from 94% in 1820 to approximately 10% today.[17]

Researchers agree that poverty is not permanent but there is controversy about whether poverty really has been decreasing over the past two centuries. According to Hickel, the problem with the above-cited statistics is that they are based on measurements of a household's monetary resources, keeping in mind that this data is scarce for the 19th and most of the 20th century and that China disproportionally affects the statistical results and obscures the lack of progress elsewhere.[18] Several authors argued that 'the empirical evidence in favor of the view that global poverty is declining rests on a dubious methodology for counting the poor'.[19] Whether or not someone has an income is possibly a very unreliable indicator of the person's situation and opportunities. Arguably, where people can make a living in subsistence economies with access to land, resources and opportunities, they do not necessarily need a monetary income to have a satisfactory standard of living. Dispossession of land and livelihoods increases the reliance on wages, which results in an income. But this alone does not automatically indicate a reduction in poverty—far from it.[20] It is therefore important to reflect cautiously on statistical data in order to determine what the numbers really reveal.

It is particularly relevant for this chapter to note that poverty continues to be widespread in countries affected by conflict. The UN Food and Agriculture Organization and the World Food Programme recently presented a report to the UN Security Council measuring the prevalence of conflict-driven hunger in the eight countries and regions that have the world's highest burden of people in need of food. According to the authors, in five of these regions [Yemen, South Sudan, Afghanistan, Democratic Republic of the Congo and Central African Republic], 'the number of people experiencing acute food insecurity increased in the latter part of 2018 because of conflict, demonstrating that the link between conflict and hunger remains all too persistent'.[21]

---

[17] Roser (2018) Our World in Data. https://ourworldindata.org/wrong-about-the-world. Accessed 12 February 2022.

[18] Hickel (2019) Bill Gates Says Poverty Is Decreasing. He Couldn't Be More Wrong. https://www.theguardian.com/commentisfree/2019/jan/29/bill-gates-davos-global-poverty-infographic-neoliberal. Accessed 12 February 2022.

[19] Sonderholm 2012, p. 371 with further references.

[20] Keswell and Carter 2014, p. 260, finding an inverse relationship between land asset transfer and poverty. Hence, access to land contributed to decrease poverty in the studied population.

[21] FAO and World Food Programme, Monitoring Food Security in Countries with Conflict Situations (28 January 2019), p. iv.

45.2.2 Different Views on the Causes of Poverty and Implications for Poverty Reduction Strategies

There are broadly three groups of perspectives on the causes of poverty: poor decision-making, environmental causes or multicausal explanations.

First, some believe that poverty is the result of an individual's sub-optimal decisions (such as not saving enough by not foregoing immediate payoffs). In the most extreme free choice models, individuals control their own destiny and can thus be the cause of their own poverty.[22] In more nuanced accounts on the links between poor decision-making and poverty, researchers consider that suboptimal decisions can often be explained by factors that are not under the poor person's control.[23] These accounts rejoin multicausal explanations (see below).

Second, extreme environmental conditions can certainly cause or exacerbate poverty. If a large-scale meteorite impact would hit the earth, soil, crops, infrastructure would be destroyed, and poverty may be the result. Scenarios in which poverty results from (or is aggravated by) environmental changes should therefore not be dismissed. However, as the next section explains, studies caution against deterministic views.

A third and predominant group of accounts emphasize multicausal explanations for poverty and argue that there are structural conditions that affect different groups of people differently. Nobel Prize winner Amartya Sen explained in 1981 already, that the overall availability of food is not the most important factor in explaining how and why abject poverty and famine occurs but rather it is the question of who gets what type of entitlements and opportunities.[24] In 2018, de Waal argued that 'climate change makes some poor and vulnerable populations less food secure. But the risk of these insecurities turning into famine will depend on political decisions'.[25] He believes that climate change and environmental decay alone cannot explain famines and thus the worst forms of abject poverty. Yet, the political failure to mitigate or adapt to climate change does undoubtedly and strongly increase vulnerability: Fears of future deterioration can be seized by political actors taking dangerous political decisions with potentially violent outcomes, sometimes leading to conflict.[26] Such multicausal explanations are, in my view, the most convincing. Poverty is influenced by the social, physical and cultural context in which people live and which are governed by power dynamics. Moreover, other societal conditions such as gender, all play a role (see Sect. 45.3.2).

The framing of poverty has implications on the extent to which one believes that law is relevant to reduce poverty, or whether other approaches to poverty alleviation should be resorted to. Those who see multiple causes, including structural ones, as

---

[22] For a discussion of the various nuances of the views on the extent of poor people's personal responsibility for poverty, see Wolff et al. 2015, p. 43.

[23] E.g. Mani et al. 2013, p. 976, arguing that 'poverty itself reduces cognitive capacity'.

[24] Sen 1981.

[25] De Waal 2018, p. 172.

[26] Ibid., pp. 173–5.

a main explanation for poverty tend to understand poverty as a form of injustice. In this view, people are poor—at least in part—because they do not have the same opportunities to use their capabilities as others. In this account, the law should thus be used to enhance substantive equality, notably by enhancing social rights and protections against discriminations. A prominent example of the use of law to fight extreme deprivation comes from the Indian Supreme Court. In 2001, the highest Indian court found that starvation deaths in Rajasthan did not result from an absolute lack of food but from the fact that applicable domestic legislation on the release of grain stocks in times of famine was not properly enforced. The Supreme Court concluded that the right to life was violated given that there were excess stocks available that were not used to alleviate starvation.[27]

In times of conflict, the framing of poverty and the underlying assumptions on its cause further impact on whether poverty is seen as a violation of legal norms or as contextual background information. If we view poverty as the result of natural causes or simply as the common fate of societies facing a conflict, we tend to portray poverty as information about the background of an armed conflict and our approaches to alleviate poverty are likely to be framed primarily in relation to the humanitarian needs of the affected population. On the other hand, those who view poverty at least in part as the result of adverse human agency and thus potentially as a violation of human rights or even a crime are more likely to display poverty as a phenomenon on its own term and alongside other abuses getting attention from international lawyers.[28]

Before Sect. 45.4 turns to the international law instruments that address poverty, we will consider in the next section how poverty and conflict influence each other.

45.3 The Various Relationships between Poverty and Conflict[29]

Poverty, conflict and instability interrelate in various and often overlapping ways. The relations between them are multifaceted, context-dependent and multi-directional (implying, for instance, that poverty can exacerbate conflict and vice versa).

Conceptually, it is possible to group the relationships between poverty and conflict into five categories. First, poverty can cause, drive or exacerbate instability. Second, poverty can be a symptom and a consequence of conflict. Third, poverty can also be a phenomenon that is sometimes best described as the result of criminal intent or the deliberate infliction of poor living conditions to achieve a certain aim related to the conflict. Fourth, poverty can be a primary concern in the aftermath of conflict. Transitional justice actors can be confronted with questions of how they could or should

---

[27] Supreme Court of India, People's Union for Civil Liberties v. Union of India and Others, Writ Petition (Civil) No. 196/2001, India.

[28] Schmid and Nolan 2014, p. 376ff.

[29] Some of the ideas to structure this chapter go back to my previous work. I adapted selected parts of these previous texts for the purposes of this chapter. See notably Schmid 2017; Schmid 2020.

address poverty in transitional justice attempts. Fifth and lastly, a consideration of the relationship between poverty and conflict would not be complete without analysing the impact of 'post-conflict' economic measures on poverty, such as the impact of new fiscal policies, measures to attract foreign investment or social security reforms.

45.3.1 Poverty as a Cause or a Driver of Instability

Many have argued that poverty plays a role in the explanations behind armed conflicts and other forms of violence and instability.[30] Poverty and inequality can lead to discontent with the state and may lead to reinforcing existing cleavages that can cause, drive or exacerbate conflict. It should be noted that the literature on links between poverty and security concentrates almost exclusively on the intrastate level, i.e. conflicts within a single state but not conflicts involving two or more states (international armed conflicts). While there may be spillover effects at the regional level when a state faces a conflict caused, driven, or exacerbated by poverty, common explanations of international armed conflicts focus on factors other than poverty.[31]

Since the 1990s there is a debate as to what extent 'greed' or rather 'grievance' is the most pertinent explanations for the outbreak of civil war.[32] Those on the side of the explanations related to greed or a 'resource curse' argue that greedy politicians can mobilize armed violence when there is a sizable opportunity for economic enrichment (by exploiting national resources for example).[33] On the other hand, those adhering to explanations related to grievances claim that perceptions of poverty and inequality have important psychological effects. Perceptions of poverty may lead to grievances of the relatively poor and this mobilization of discontent increases the likelihood of conflicts.[34] Poverty can make a country more prone to armed conflict because poverty correlates with weaker institutions and a reduced capacity for the provision of public services and social security. Poverty lowers the opportunity costs for the recruitment of armed fighters and for the prolonged engagement of fighters.[35] As

---

[30] Amongst the most explicit writings in this regard, see Rice 2007; Braithwaite et al. 2016; Addison et al. 2013, p. 161. The latter authors suggest that context-specific factors influence the specific outcome (see also the next footnote).

[31] In a well-known book, Blainey evaluated the commonly discussed causes of interstate war and argued that nations start international armed conflicts 'when two nations decide that they can gain more by fighting than be negotiating', taking into account at least seven factors when making that assessment, including the state of the economy. (Blainey 1988, pp. 123 and 159). While poverty may have some influence on the decision-making to start or end a war, it is not a primary candidate for explaining interstate war.

[32] On the limitations of the research on the causes of civil war and the various variables that seem to influence whether a specific situation degenerates into a civil war, see Dixon 2009, p. 713ff for a review of the 'greed versus grievance' debate.

[33] Berdal and Malone 2000, p. 4.

[34] E.g. Collier et al. 2009. For the argument on the perception of poverty and the effect on mobilization, see Fair et al. 2018.

[35] Addison et al. 2013, p. 163.

James Fearon and David Laitin famously and convincingly argued in 2003, poverty increases the risk of insurgency, i.e. non-international armed conflict.[36]

Political scientists caution against deterministic and mono-causal explanations for the outbreak of conflicts and instability. An increased risk of insurgency does not yet mean that conflict will break out. Mark Duffield, for instance, advocates against simplistic assumptions on the association between conflict and poverty.[37] Many poor countries are relatively stable, and some relatively well-off countries can be marked with insecurity. Danielle Beswick and Paul Jackson review a number of studies showing that 'it is possible for individuals and societies to live in relative security despite levels of development that would be considered low on international indicators'.[38] Simplistic assumptions of a deterministic link between poverty and conflict should thus be avoided.

The common assumption that development cannot take place without security and conversely, that security cannot exist without development, deserves to be reassessed. There are several additional factors (such as failures of governance and state control, geography or regional stability) that play a role in explaining the outbreak of conflict.[39] Poverty is often 'just' one amongst several factors that drive conflict. As a consequence, it is important not to gloss over the socio-political nuances that influence whether a certain level of poverty or inequality leads to conflict. That said, it is fair to argue that widespread poverty and inequality tend to increase the population's dissatisfaction with the government and correlate with other indicators that point to possible danger. On that basis, the UN Committee on the Elimination of Racial Discrimination urged for disparities in socio-economic indicators or access to essential goods or services to be part of the aspects analyzed in the prevention of genocide[40] and conflict more broadly[41] and should be monitored in early warning strategies.[42]

The idea that development activities such as poverty alleviation can contribute to conflict-prevention is attractive. The so-called *securitization* of development, i.e. the labelling of poverty and development as concerns of security, 'lends a certain urgency to the need to intervene.'[43] Putting poverty on the security agenda is also morally justifiable given 'the limited political interest, at international, national, and

---

[36] Fearon and Laitin 2003, p. 88.

[37] Duffield 2014, p. 117ff, and notably p. 121ff.

[38] Jackson and Beswick 2018, p. 14. Referring notably to Duffield 2014.

[39] Jackson and Beswick 2018, p. 13.

[40] CERD Committee, Decision on Follow up to the Declaration on the Prevention of Genocide: Indicators of Patterns of Systematic and Massive Racial Discrimination, CERD/C/67/1, 14 October 2005), notably paras 14f.

[41] An Agenda for Peace: Preventive Diplomacy, Peacemaking and Peace-Keeping (17 June 1992) A/47/277, paras 15, 18 and 81.

[42] OHCHR (2016) Early Warning and Economic, Social and Cultural Rights. http://www.ohchr.org/Documents/Issues/ESCR/EarlyWarning_ESCR_2016_en.pdf. Accessed 14 May 2020.

[43] Duffield 2014, p. 122.

local levels'.[44] Nonetheless, as mentioned, care must be taken not to oversimplify the relationship between poverty and security.

45.3.2 Poverty as a Symptom and Consequence of Conflict

Unsurprisingly, conflict can increase poverty and therefore poverty constitutes a symptom and a consequence of conflict.[45] Conflicts usually imply a general decline in employment and economic activity, economic productivity and opportunities for most individuals and households to sustain themselves and thrive economically and socially. Young and able-bodied individuals are recruited, sometimes killed or injured; many do not receive the healthcare they need. Assets ranging from infrastructure to land and livestock are destroyed, pillaged or abandoned and what remains is often more difficult to trade. Moreover, some armed conflicts go hand in hand with the creation or strengthening of war economies relying sometimes on the extraction and trade of primary resources in ways that can threaten long-term stability.[46] The level of poverty of those that are already poor before the conflict is sometimes worsened. Unsurprisingly, conflict also creates educational and social security deficits, making it more difficult for survivors to get out of poverty or avoid that poverty being passed on to the next generations.

Armed conflict also goes hand in hand with other economic and human losses. A state in conflict can face economic sanctions or the suspension of cooperation agreements by trade partners, both of which can increase poverty. The UN Security Council might adopt sanctions under Chapter VII of the UN Charter (such as was the case in relation to Iraq or North Korea),[47] and such sanctions can aggravate poverty.[48]

Gender discrimination often exacerbates the consequences of conflict, both for direct and indirect victims. It is well known, for instance, that the family members of a disappeared person often face significant problems in accessing social security or are prevented from access to land or other forms of inheritance and may therefore, be confronted with (increased) poverty as a result.[49] In the absence of certainty about whether an individual has died (and thus, for instance, the possibility of getting a death

---

[44] Moore and Brunt 2013, p. 1. Similarly, Addison et al. 2013, p. 168. The authors write that 'the need to appease warring factions or to pacify potential 'spoilers' to peace detracts attention from the needs of the chronically poor'; see also p. 171: 'there is a moral imperative to support society's weakest members, and this too often goes missing, or is downgraded'.

[45] Justino 2006, p. 4ff.

[46] E.g. for recent evidence from Liberia, see Cheng 2018.

[47] The Situation between Iraq and Kuwait (6 August 1990) S/RES/661. Democratic People's Republic of Korea (22 December 2017) S/RES/2397.

[48] Committee on Economic, General Comment 8 on the Relationship between Economic Sanctions and Respect for Economic, Social and Cultural Rights UN Doc ID, (12 December 1997) para 3. So-called targeted sanctions try to avoid increasing the poverty of the general population by only targeting those responsible for abuses.

[49] A/HRC/30/38/Add.5.

certificate), family members face difficulties in obtaining pensions. These problems increase the vulnerability for poverty and are sometimes exacerbated by gender discrimination and stereotypes, particularly for women (e.g. women not being able to decide matters related to land or other assets without the consent of the husband who has disappeared, etc.). According to the former Deputy UN High Commissioner for Human Rights: 'In societies where gender-based discrimination in laws and policies hinders the full realization of the human rights of women and limits their autonomy and participation in aspects of public and political life, the social and economic impact of disappearances is felt more strongly and, in turn, renders women and their children more vulnerable to exploitation and social marginalization.'[50] Moreover, evidence shows that those who were exposed to violence during an armed conflict are more prone to face long-term poverty.[51]

45.3.3 Poverty as a Result of Deliberate Harm

Poverty is sometimes the result of criminal intent or other forms of adverse human agency. Unfortunately, humans have time and again inflicted poverty on others—often with certain political goals in mind. As a result, there exist situations in which poverty is inflicted for reasons related to the conflict and situations in which poverty is part of the facts that might lead to a criminal conviction for a war crime, a crime against humanity, genocide or another international crime.

In previous research, I presented evidence that all four groups of war crimes, at least eight of the crimes against humanity, genocide and other offences can overlap with violations of economic, social and cultural rights.[52] This evidence is relevant when we assess the relationship between poverty and conflict. Economic, social and cultural rights include rights such as the right to food, shelter, work, education and social security—to name just a few. Not every occurrence of poverty amounts to a violation of economic, social or cultural rights. However, when poverty is due to human rights violations, states incur international legal responsibility for wrongful acts and omissions.[53] In some instances, it is possible and legally accurate to conclude that the same factual scenario is both a human rights violation and simultaneously gives rise to an international criminal responsibility, i.e. the criminal responsibility of one or several specific individuals for an international crime such as a war crime or crimes against humanity. Contrary to widespread assumptions in the literature, contemporary international criminal law is capable of addressing at least some violations of economic, social and cultural rights and, therefore, some instances of poverty.

---

[50] OHCHR Protecting Women from the Impact of Enforced Disappearances, 14 December 2012. http://www.ohchr.org/EN/NewsEvents/Pages/ProtectingWomenFromImpactOfEnforcedDisappearances.aspx. Accessed 14 May 2020.
[51] Annan et al. 2011; Hegre et al. 2013.
[52] Schmid 2015. This section is also partially based on Schmid 2020.
[53] Schmid 2015, 45ff.

Some of the earliest materials on international criminal law already indicate that abuses related to the deliberate infliction of poverty have always been part of the thinking on international criminal law.[54]

Consider crimes against humanity. The legal development of this category of crimes was inspired by the international community's desire to punish mass abuses of human rights by states against their own citizens. Sadly, states have sometimes been involved in deliberately starving or otherwise depriving people of their livelihoods. The offence of forcible transfer, a crime against humanity, for instance, often goes hand in hand with measures that deliberately increase the poverty of the affected population, particularly forced evictions or discriminatory measures in the realm of people's access to jobs, conditions of survival and well-being.[55] The destruction of livelihoods, by burning victims' homes for example,[56] can constitute a serious deprivation of fundamental rights for the purpose of a persecution charge as a crime against humanity.[57] The hindrance of humanitarian assistance,[58] contaminating water sources[59] and withholding essential (and available) medicine, food[60] or water[61] to individuals under one's control are other straightforward examples of conduct that occurs in conflicts and that exacerbates poverty. Such abuses can potentially constitute both violations of social or economic rights and crimes against humanity (or genocide[62] or war crimes—depending on the legal qualification of the situation and the intent with which the conduct was inflicted).

Several war crimes can overlap with deliberate infliction of poverty. As an example, pillage, which is regarded as an ancient war crime, can amount to the infliction or exacerbation of poverty. The Trial Chamber II of the International Criminal Court, for instance, recognized that the theft of household items, food or livestock could have extremely serious consequences for the daily life of survivors and can constitute pillage.[63] As mentioned in Sect. 45.3, international humanitarian law, inter alia, specifically prohibits starvation as a method of war, the poisoning of water sources or, under certain conditions, the obstruction of humanitarian assistance.[64] International law criminalizes a number of prohibitions provided for in international humanitarian law. This means that certain activities are not only prohibited

---

[54] Further references and a more detailed analysis, ibid., chapters 4–7.

[55] Prosecutor v. Krajišnik, IT-00-39-T, 27 September 2006, ICTY, para 729.

[56] Prosecutor v. Kupreškić, IT-95-16-T, 14 January 2000, ICTY, para 336.

[57] Report of the Commission of Inquiry on Human Rights in the Democratic People's Republic of Korea (7 February 2014) A/HRC/25/CRP.1, paras 115ff and 1084.

[58] Second Decision on the Prosecution's Application for a Warrant of Arrest against Al Bashir, 12 July 2010, Pre-Trial Chamber I, ICC-02/05-01/09, ICC, para 35.

[59] Ibid., para 37f.

[60] Prosecutor v. Delalić, IT-96-21-T, 16 November 1998, ICTY, paras 1092ff.

[61] Ibid., paras 1097ff. United States of America v. Toshino et al., Case No. 154, 4 May 1948, US Military Commission at Yokohama, USA.

[62] Schmid 2015, chapter 6.

[63] Prosecutor v. Katanga, Judgment Pursuant to Article 74 of the Statute, 7 March 2014, Trial Chamber II, N° ICC-01/04-01/07, ICC, para 953.

[64] For an overview, see Giacca 2014; Müller 2013.

but amount to a war crime. Some war crimes are specific to armed conflicts of an international character, while others attract special legal consequences (so-called grave breaches). Additionally, there are war crimes that exist in all types of armed conflicts. The relationship between war crimes and poverty is particularly relevant when it comes to the legal status of starvation as a method of war because starvation is an extreme manifestation of poverty. Starvation as a method of war is listed as a war crime in international armed conflicts.[65] The same crime was not listed in the Rome Statute list of war crimes for non-international armed conflicts. The most plausible explanation for this gap is that the drafters forgot the inclusion of this crime at the late hours of the drafting of the Rome Statute, which is why Switzerland proposed to add starvation to the list of war crimes in non-international armed conflicts in the Rome Statute. In December 2019, the ICC Assembly of States Parties, by consensus, adopted an amendment which is now subject to ratification or acceptance.[66] This amendment eradicates any doubt on the status of this crime in both types of armed conflict.[67] In any event, even without this amendment, starvation as a method of war is, in my view, criminalized in non-international armed conflicts in customary international law.[68] A range of poverty-related scenarios can potentially be captured under the lenses of international criminal law. There is no legal justification for claiming that poverty can or should not be addressed by the existing mechanisms that rely on international criminal law, such as truth commissions with a mandate covering crimes against humanity or war crimes. This leads us to transitional justice.

45.3.4 Poverty as a Subject of Transitional Justice

Transitional justice denotes 'the full range of processes and mechanisms associated with a society's attempts to come to terms with a legacy of large-scale past abuses, in order to ensure accountability, serve justice and achieve reconciliation'.[69] International criminal law, human rights law and international humanitarian law are usually the main normative frameworks of transitional justice approaches. Given the manifold ways in which poverty is relevant to all three of these sub-branches

---

[65] Rome Statute of the International Criminal Court, 2187 UNTS 90, 17 July 1998 (entered into force 1 July 2002), Article 8(2)(b)(xxv).

[66] ICC-ASP, Resolution on amendments to article 8 of the Rome Statute of the International Criminal Court, ICC-ASP/18/Res.5 (6 December 2019). For a recent report on the criminalization of starvation in NIAC, see Global Rights Compliance 2019.

[67] For an outline of the debate, see Non-Paper Submitted by Switzerland: Proposed Amendments to Article 8 of the Rome Statute on the Inclusion of Starvation as a War Crime in Non-International Armed Conflicts (20 September 2018) ICC-ASP/17/35, Annex IV. The proposal followed the adoption of a resolution in which the Security Council strongly condemned starvation of civilians and the unlawful denial of humanitarian access. S/RES/2417 (24 May 2018).

[68] Schmid 2015, p. 200ff.

[69] Report of the SG on the Rule of Law and Transitional Justice in Conflict and Post-Conflict Societies (23 August 2004) S/2004/616, para 8.

of international law, transitional justice has ample leeway in considering poverty-related abuses and problems. Whether this is a good idea is subject to debate. Some have argued that transitional justice should focus on a limited set of civil and political rights in order to avoid overburdening transitional justice mechanisms and placing unavoidably high (and often unrealistic) expectations on transitional justice endeavors. Others have countered that the consideration of socio-economic aspects in transitional justice can be promising as such consideration puts poverty on the agenda of the post-conflict/transitional political debate.[70] Recent findings from empirical research conducted in Cambodia seem to support the latter view.[71]

45.3.5 Poverty as a (Neglected) Concern in So-Called 'Post-Conflict'[72] Measures

At the end of a conflict or in a transition towards a less violent situation, the affected state's authorities and/or external actors often take a range of measures with the aim to stabilize a fragile situation, to avoid the recurrence of conflict or to exit the alleged 'conflict trap'.[73] Decision-makers often hope to strengthen economic growth and to generate private investment through infrastructure development, foreign aid, trade liberalization, debt relief, currency stabilization or measures oriented towards influencing the affected state's fiscal policies. If all goes well, poverty can successfully be reduced by such measures.[74] But poverty reduction or a reduction of inequality does not follow automatically from such 'post-conflict' interventions.[75] There are at least two possible problems: First, much depends on the specific context and the concrete approaches taken by external and domestic actors. The economic well-being and capacity of the host state to reduce poverty does not increase immediately by macroeconomic policies in a (so-called) post-conflict environment. Second, when foreign investment does arrive, the effects are not automatically positive for everyone—there can be winners and losers within the affected state.[76] The effects of attempts to

---

[70] For an overview of this debate and references, see Schmid and Nolan 2014, p. 368ff.

[71] Destrooper 2018.

[72] The term 'post-conflict' has different meanings to different people and initiatives are sometimes framed in an overly optimistic post-conflict language although a country may still find itself in a situation of ongoing armed conflict or widespread violence. Afghanistan is a case in point: According to Daria Davitti, most of the initiatives to attract foreign investment to Afghanistan were and are couched in post conflict language despite the ongoing armed conflicts on its territory. Davitti 2019, p. 12. For the legal qualification of the situation, see RULAC Afghanistan (15 September 2021). http://www.rulac.org/browse/countries/afghanistan. Accessed 14 February 2022.

[73] Collier et al. 2003, chapters 5 and 6.

[74] Mercurio 2013, p. 67 'trade liberalization is a necessary step toward poverty reduction [but] it is not a sufficient step'.

[75] See notably the work of Langer et al. 2014.

[76] While the pie may increase, e.g. after opening a country to free trade, the distribution of the pie may be unequal within a society.

attract foreign investment can even be detrimental for security. According to Daria Davitti's literature review, 'if left unchecked, investment risks exacerbating volatile contexts (...) and entrenching power structures and systems which enable violence and perpetuate inequality'.[77] Moreover, she considers that such 'post-conflict' initiatives come '[a]t a time when both home and host countries are often ready to trade off human rights protections in the attempt to establish a legal and regulatory framework capable of signaling to foreign investors that the host country is ready to grant priority to investment protection'.[78] This can impede the respect, protection and realization of human rights, including the right to an adequate standard of living and thus harm the achievement (or even just recognition) of poverty-reduction objectives. If no attention is paid to the distributive effects of macroeconomic policies and their possible compensation, inequalities can be exacerbated, and grievances nurtured. On the other hand, empirical research indicates that redistributive social policies, in particular spending for health, social security and education, 'contributes to sustaining peace because the provision of social services reduces grievances by offsetting the effects of poverty and inequality in society' and can 'co-opt the political opposition and decrease the incentives for organizing a rebellion'.[79] Several studies indicate that social welfare spending and notably the provision of health-care and educational opportunities are prone to contribute to sustaining peace by reducing vulnerabilities.[80] According to Barbara Walter's findings from an analysis of all civil wars ending between 1945 and 1996, 'a higher quality of life and greater access to political participation' reduce the likelihood of renewed conflict.[81]

Another challenge of post-conflict measures is the fact that international donors sometimes 'channel their resources to disarmament, demobilisation, and reintegration (DDR) programmes aimed at ex-combatants' in the hope 'to appease warring factions'.[82] As Toni Addison, Kathryn Bach and Tim Braunholtz-Speight write, there is—here too—no automatic relationship between the end of an armed conflict and a specific impact on poverty. Rather, 'wartime politics' and other political considerations impact the poverty reduction agenda.[83] Sometimes, there is a peace agreement or a transitional arrangement that puts poverty reduction on the post-conflict agenda,[84] resulting in an influx of foreign aid and/or marginalized groups getting a seat at the negotiation table. Such changes can provide windows of opportunity for the reduction of poverty—but they are fragile and success is far from certain.[85]

---

[77] Davitti 2019, p. 22.

[78] Ibid.

[79] Taydas and Peksen 2012, p. 273.

[80] For an excellent overview of existing research, see Marks 2016. See also Addison et al. 2013, p. 177.

[81] Walter 2004, p. 371.

[82] Addison et al. 2013, p. 168.

[83] Ibid., p. 169.

[84] E.g. the Comprehensive Peace Agreement between the Government of Nepal and the Communist Party of Nepal, 22 November 2006.

[85] Addison et al. 2013, pp. 169–171.

Particular challenges arise when humanitarian assistance winds down and international attention fades. Ideally, the poor will 'see their situation improve when labour demand increases'.[86] But those injured during the war or marked by illness, old age, particularly women, young children, the elderly and those with disabilities are particularly vulnerable.

As Pablo de Greiff, the former UN Special Rapporteur on the promotion of truth, justice, reparation and guarantees of non-recurrence emphasized, civic and social trust are commonly assumed to be crucial for economic growth. According to him, development actors should, therefore, not exclusively be concerned with macro-economic indicators but should take a holistic and human-rights-sensitive approach because 'massive human rights violations lead to diminished agency', which in all likelihood is highly detrimental to development.[87] Justice and development concerns are thus often considered mutually reinforcing. However, the mere allusion to the discourse of human rights will not yield positive outcomes from a human rights perspective.[88] Rather, the literature suggests that post-conflict situations, or anything resembling a transition out of armed conflict, are times during which there are opportunities to (re)negotiate the social contract in a society.[89] And this is ideally done in a way that helps assure that all members of society feel they are citizens with individual rights and not simply victims or second- or third-class members of a community. Paying attention to the situation of all members of a society is a matter of justice,[90] but it is also a matter of 'sustaining peace'.[91]

In this section, we considered how poverty and conflict relate to each other. The next section shows that international lawyers have at their disposal a number of international law instruments addressing poverty.

45.4 The International Legal and Policy Framework

What does international law have to say about poverty? Let us consider the extent to which poverty is a concern of international law. The preamble of the UN Charter expresses the objectives of the founding states 'to promote social progress and better standards of life in larger freedom'.[92] Article 1 of the Charter stipulates that the

---

[86] Ibid., p. 171.

[87] de Greiff, Report of the Special Rapporteur on the Promotion of Truth, Justice, Reparation and Guarantees of Non-Recurrence (23 August 2013) A/68/345, paras 20ff.

[88] Alston 2002.

[89] de Greiff 2006, p. 465.

[90] Addison et al. 2013, p. 173.

[91] Review of the United Nations Peacebuilding Architecture (12 May 2016) A/RES/70/262, notably preambular paras 8f. See also (11 July 2017) A/HRC/35/19. The adoption of these two resolutions was prepared by Report of the Advisory Group of Experts on the Review of the Peacebuilding Architecture, Challenge of Sustaining Peace (30 June 2015) A/69/968–S/2015/490.

[92] Charter of the United Nations, 1 UNTS XVI, 26 June 1945 (entered into force 24 October 1945), preamble.

objectives of the United Nations are, inter alia, the maintenance of international peace and security and the employment of 'international machinery for the promotion of the economic and social advancement of all peoples'.[93] In a holistic view, and in line with Kofi Annan's approach to the interrelatedness of peace, security, freedom from fear and want, poverty is thus a core concern of the UN, including the Security Council. Indeed, the Security Council recognizes that massive deprivations can constitute a threat to international peace and security and thus warrant action under Chapter VII of the UN Charter.[94]

In addition to the link between poverty and the objectives of the UN, numerous international treaties address poverty, making it an international law issue. As Krista Nadakavukaren Schefer appropriately summarizes, there is no explicit 'right to be free from poverty' but the right to adequate food and water, the right to health, the right to adequate housing and the right to education 'can be particularly potent claims for relief' from poverty.[95] The International Covenant of Economic, Social and Cultural Rights includes the right to freedom from hunger and the right to an adequate standard of living.[96] Additionally, the treaties of the International Labour Organization protect against economic exploitation. The Convention of the Rights of the Child contains explicit obligations for states to 'assist parents and others responsible for the child to implement [the right to a standard of living adequate for the child's development].[97] In the preamble of the Convention on the Rights of People with Disabilities, states affirm that the recognition of rights of people with disabilities will contribute to eradicate poverty[98] and that, conversely, poverty has a negative impact on persons with disabilities.[99]

Other treaties at the international or regional level do not specifically mention poverty-related concepts but protect non-discrimination, procedural rights or the right to a home, privacy and family life. These protections have important repercussions for obligations in the realm of poverty.[100] It is also important to mention international law protections for human rights defenders because those fighting poverty are sometimes threatened, oppressed and otherwise victimized.[101] The struggle over social rights

---

[93] Ibid., article 1.

[94] See, e.g. S/RES/2417 (24 May 2018), para 4, recognizing that the unlawful denial of humanitarian access can be a threat to international peace or security. For the earliest example, see Somalia (3 December 1992) S/RES/794, notably third preambular paragraph.

[95] Nadakavukaren Schefer 2013, p. 8f.

[96] International Covenant on Economic, Social and Cultural Rights, GA Res. 2200a (XXI), 16 December 1966 (entered into force 3 January 1976), article 11.

[97] Convention on the Rights of the Child, GA Res. 44/25 (1989), 20 November 1989 (entered into force 2 September 1990), article 27.

[98] International Convention on the Protection and Promotion of the Rights and Dignity of Persons with Disabilities, GA Res. 61/106 (2006), preambular para m.

[99] Ibid, preambular para t.

[100] For a useful overview of how socio-economic rights, including poverty-related concerns, can be addressed in various legal fora, see Langford 2008.

[101] See, for instance, A/HRC/30/38/Add.5, para 54.

and the targeting of those raising 'fears about dearth' was already documented for the French revolution.[102]

Outside international human rights law, other sub-branches of international law address some issues related to poverty. International humanitarian law, applicable in armed conflicts, prohibits starvation as a method of war and prescribes that relief operations and assistance may not be targeted and furthermore consent to humanitarian relief must not be arbitrarily denied.[103] As mentioned in the previous section, the infliction of poverty can be covered by substantive definitions of international criminal law.[104] Poverty is also the subject of bilateral and multilateral treaties in which states, for instance, agree to cooperate on matters of poverty reduction.[105]

There are also relevant international law documents, which are not binding as treaties. Most notably, the Universal Declaration of Human Rights emphasizes the importance of civil, cultural, economic, political and social rights and affirms the idea of a world in which individuals are free from fear and from want.[106] The UN General Assembly has adopted a considerable number of resolutions, which deal explicitly with poverty.[107] The UN Human Rights Council has mandated a Special Rapporteur on human rights and extreme poverty[108] and regularly adopts resolutions concerning poverty.[109] In 1986, the General Assembly adopted the Declaration on the Right to Development[110] and proclaimed, in 2007, the second UN Decade for the Eradication of Poverty (2008–2017), which included the Millennium Development Goals.[111] In December 2012, the General Assembly took note, with appreciation, of the guiding principles on extreme poverty and human rights adopted by the Human Rights Council in its resolution 21/11 as a tool for states to reduce and eradicate poverty.[112] The General Assembly subsequently adopted the 2030 Agenda for Sustainable Development in 2015 with the aim to 'end poverty in all its forms and dimensions by 2030'.[113] A number of international legal sources and documents thus deal with poverty. But is international law adequate or sufficient to address

---

[102] Walton 2011, p. 169.

[103] ICRC Customary International Humanitarian Law, Rule 55. https://ihl-databases.icrc.org/customary-ihl. Accessed 14 May 2020.

[104] See above, Sect. 45.3.3.

[105] E.g. Additional Protocol to the Framework-Agreement on Cooperation between France and Brazil Concerning Decentralized Cooperation (Saint-Georges-De-L'oyapock, 12 February 2008), 2883 UNTS 121, p. 121.

[106] Universal Declaration of Human Rights, GA Res. 217a (III), A/810 at 71, 10 December 1948, preamble and in relation to poverty, see notably article 25.

[107] See the further references in the preambular paragraphs of, e.g., Human Rights and Extreme Poverty (6 February 2015) A/RES/69/183. Implementation of the Third United Nations Decade for the Eradication of Poverty (2018–2027) (22 January 2019) A/RES/73/246.

[108] The current mandate was renewed in 2020: (23 July 2020) A/HRC/44/13.

[109] See the references in ibid.

[110] Declaration on the Right to Development (4 December 1986) A/RES/41/128.

[111] United Nations Millennium Declaration (18 September 2000) A/RES/55/2.

[112] Human Rights and Extreme Poverty (6 February 2015) A/RES/69/183.

[113] The 2030 Agenda for Sustainable Development (21 October 2015) A/RES/70/1, para 24.

poverty and sustain peace or does international law itself contribute to poverty and insecurity? Some critical concluding remarks are in order.

45.5 Concluding Thoughts on the Role of International Law in Addressing the Relationship between Poverty and Conflict

In this chapter, we have considered the five main groups of relationships between poverty and conflict. We also noted that a variety of international law sources and documents have something to say about poverty. Yet, what is missing is the more controversial question about whether international law as such contributes to poverty, instability and conflict. It would be beyond the scope of this chapter to conclusively answer this question, but the chapter would be incomplete without at an attempt at an outline of the debate. Let us begin with the optimistic narrative. An optimist could say that international law has brought progress to humanity by outlawing the use of force between states and by setting up a rules-based system of dispute resolution, cooperation and collaboration in all sorts of domains of human activity. Hence, optimists could argue that international law helps reduce poverty by reducing inter-state conflicts and instability. But there are more pessimistic voices. In 2018, John Linarelli, Margot Salomon and Muthucumaraswamy Sornarajh published a book entitled 'the misery of international law' in which they claim that international law is part of the problem of poverty. They argue that international law furthers 'an allocation of advantages based on the power of the actors who control the making of the law' and who are able to set up a global capitalist architecture 'in a way that serves the powerful, creates instability, and produces insecurity particularly for those least able to bear financial (systemic) risk'.[114] According to these authors, international law substantially contributes to maintaining poverty that might in turn lead to conflicts and insecurity. Previously, Thomas Pogge argued that the affluent members of developed countries impose a burdensome global order on the world's poor and that this order is made up by the international legal framework of states and their role in global institutions.[115] In his view, at least some important parts of international law harm the poor and the normative order benefits the interests of rich members of developed countries. Pogge elaborated on the role of international law and responded firstly to those who deny that the design of the global institutional order worsens severe poverty, secondly to those who believe poverty would be even more widespread without the institutional order and finally to those who believe that international law is just not as good as it could be.[116]

---

[114] Linarelli et al. 2018, p. 272.

[115] Pogge 2008, p. 122.

[116] Pogge 2010, 419ff. The following review essay provides a useful starting point to appreciate Pogge's position and to review the important criticisms that have been made: Sonderholm 2012.

Between a very optimistic outlook and the pessimistic conclusions reached by authors such as Pogge, Linarelli, Salomon and Sornarajh, one can consider that both views are complementary. It seems reasonable to believe that international law has a stabilizing effect on international relations, but this does not negate the important critique that international law is itself very problematically entrenched with the self-interests of the powerful.[117]

Acknowledgement I thank Nitya Duella, BSc/MLaw, for efficiently proofreading the manuscript.

References

Addison T, Bach K, Braunholtz-Speight T (2013) Violent Conflict and Chronic Poverty. In: Shepherd A W, Brunt J (eds) Chronic Poverty. Palgrave, Basingstoke, pp 160–182.
Alston P G (2002) Resisting the Merger and Acquisition of Human Rights by Trade Law: A Reply to Petersmann. European Journal of International Law 13: 815–844.
Alston P G (2015) Extreme Inequality as the Antithesis of Human Rights. https://www.opengloba lrights.org/extreme-inequality-as-the-antithesis-of-human-rights/. Accessed 14 May 2020.
Annan J, Blattman C, Mazurana D, Carlson K (2011) Civil War, Reintegration, and Gender in Northern Uganda. Journal of Conflict Resolution 55: 877–908.
Berdal M, Malone D (2000) Introduction. In: Berdal M, Malone D (eds) Greed and Grievance: Economic Agendas in Civil Wars. Lynne Rienner, Boulder, pp 1–15.
Blainey G (1988) The Causes of War, 3rd edn. The Free Press, New York.
Böhnke P, Silver H (2014) Social Exclusion. In: Michalos A (ed) Encyclopedia of Quality of Life and Well-Being Research. Springer Netherlands, Dordrecht, pp 6064–6069.
Braithwaite A, Dasandi N, Hudson D (2016) Does Poverty Cause Conflict? Isolating the Causal Origins of the Conflict Trap. Conflict Management and Peace Science 33: 45–66.
Cheng C (2018) Extralegal Groups in Post-Conflict Liberia: How Trade Makes the State. Oxford University Press, Oxford.
Collier P, Elliott V L, Hegre H, Hoeffler A, Reynal-Querol M, Sambanis N (2003) Breaking the Conflict Trap: Civil War and Development Policy. Oxford University Press, Washington.
Collier P, Hoeffler A, Rohner D (2009) Beyond Greed and Grievance: Feasibility and Civil War. Oxford Economic Papers 61: 1–27.
Davitti D (2019) Investment and Human Rights in Armed Conflict: Charting an Elusive Intersection. Hart, Oxford.
de Greiff P (ed) (2006) The Handbook of Reparations. Oxford University Press, Oxford.
De Waal A (2018) Mass Starvation: The History and Future of Famine. Polity, Medford.
Destrooper T (2018), Neglecting Social and Economic Rights Violations in Transitional Justice: Long-Term Effects on Accountability. Journal of Current Southeast Asian Affairs 37: 95–124.
Dixon J (2009) What Causes Civil Wars? Integrating Quantitative Research Findings. International Studies Review 11: 707–735.
Duffield M R (2014) Global Governance and the New Wars: The Merging of Development and Security, 2nd edn. Zed Books, London.
Fair C, Littman R, Malhotra N, Shapiro J (2018) Relative Poverty, Perceived Violence, and Support for Militant Politics: Evidence from Pakistan. Political Science Research and Methods 6: 57–81.

---

[117] I would, however, emphasize that human rights law does not inherently fetishize growth (Linarelli et al. 2018, pp. 272–3). Rather, as the authors themselves write, socio-economic rights are sidelined and misappropriated (pp. 233, 240). See in this regard Alston 2015.

Fearon J D, Laitin D D (2003) Ethnicity, Insurgency, and Civil War. American Political Science Review 97: 75–90.

Giacca G (2014) Economic, Social, and Cultural Rights in Armed Conflict and Other Situations of Armed Violence. Oxford University Press, Oxford.

Global Rights Compliance (2019) The Crime of Starvation and Methods of Prosecution and Accountability: Accountability for Mass Starvation: Testing the Limits of the Law. The Hague.

Goodhand J (2001) Violent Conflict, Poverty and Chronic Poverty. Institute for Development Policy and Management, Manchester.

Hegre H, Karlsen J, Nygård H M, Strand H, Urdal H (2013) Predicting Armed Conflict, 2010–2050. International Studies Quarterly 57: 250–270.

Hickey S, du Toit A (2007) Adverse Incorporation, Social Exclusion and Chronic Poverty. Chronic Poverty Research Centre, Manchester.

Hickel J (2019) Bill Gates says poverty is decreasing. He couldn't be more wrong. https://www.theguardian.com/commentisfree/2019/jan/29/bill-gates-davos-global-poverty-infographic-neo liberal. Accessed 12 February 2022.

Jackson P, Beswick D (2018) Conflict, Security and Development: An Introduction. Routledge, London.

Justino P (2006) On the Links between Violent Conflict and Chronic Poverty: How Much Do We Really Know? Chronic Poverty Research Centre, Manchester.

Keswell M, Carter M R (2014) Poverty and Land Redistribution. Journal of Development Economics 110: 250–261.

Langer A, Stewart F, Venugopal R (2014) Horizontal Inequalities and Post-Conflict Development. Palgrave Macmillan, Basingstoke.

Langford M (ed) (2008) Social Rights Jurisprudence: Emerging Trends in International and Comparative Law. Cambridge University Press, Cambridge.

Linarelli J, Salomon M E, Sornarajah M (2018) The Misery of International Law: Confrontations with Injustice in the Global Economy. Oxford University Press, Oxford.

Mani A, Mullainathan S, Shafir E, Zhao J (2013), Poverty Impedes Cognitive Function. Science 341: 976.

Marks Z (2016) Poverty and Conflict. DFID, Birmingham.

Mercurio B (2013) Trade Liberalization and Poverty Reduction. In: Nadakavukaren Schefer K (ed) Poverty and the International Economic Legal System: Duties to the World's Poor. Cambridge University Press, Cambridge, pp 66–78.

Moore K, Brunt J (2013) Introduction. In: Shepherd A W, Brunt J (eds) Chronic Poverty Concepts, Causes and Policy. Palgrave Macmillan, Basingstoke, pp 1–6.

Müller A (2013) The Relationship between Economic, Social and Cultural Rights and International Humanitarian Law: An Analysis of Health-Related Issues in Non-International Armed Conflicts. Nijhoff, Leiden.

Nadakavukaren Schefer K (2013) Poverty, Obligations, and the International Economic Legal System. In: Nadakavukaren Schefer K (ed) Poverty and the International Economic Legal System: Duties to the World's Poor. Cambridge University Press, Cambridge, pp 3–15.

Narayan-Parker D, Patel R, Schafft K, Rademacher A, Koch-Schulte S (2000) The Definitions of Poverty. In: Narayan-Parker D (ed) Can Anyone Hear Us? Voices of the Poor. Oxford University Press, New York, pp 26–64.

Nussbaum M (2013) Creating Capabilities: The Human Development Approach. Belknap Press, Cambridge.

Pogge T W (2010) The Role of International Law in Reproducing Massive Poverty. The Philosophy of International Law 417–435.

Pogge T W M (2008) World Poverty and Human Rights: Cosmopolitan Responsibilities and Reforms. Polity, Cambridge MA.

Pritchett L (2006) Who Is Not Poor? Dreaming of a World Truly Free of Poverty. The World Bank Research Observer 21: 1–23.

Rice S (2007) Poverty Breeds Insecurity. In: Brainard L, Chollet D (eds) Too Poor for Peace?: Global Poverty, Conflict, and Security in the 21st Century. Brookings Institution Press, Washington, pp 31–49.

Robeyns I (2016) The Capability Approach. In: Zalta E N (ed) Stanford Encyclopedia of Philosophy. Stanford University, Stanford.

Roser M (2018) Our world in data. https://ourworldindata.org/wrong-about-the-world. Accessed 12 February 2022.

Schmid E (2015) Taking Economic, Social and Cultural Rights Seriously in International Criminal Law. Cambridge University Press, Cambridge.

Schmid E (2017) L'économie. In: Beauvallet O (ed) Dictionnaire encyclopédique de la justice pénale internationale. Berger-Levrault, Boulogne-Billancourt, pp 383–385.

Schmid E (2020) International Criminal Law and Social Rights. In: Binder C, Piovesan F, Úbeda de Torres A, Hofbauer J (eds) Research Handbook on International Law and Social Rights. Edward Elgar Publishing, Cheltenham, pp 519–534.

Schmid E, Nolan A (2014) 'Do No Harm'?: Exploring the Scope of Economic and Social Rights in Transitional Justice. International Journal of Transitional Justice 8: 362–382.

Sen A (1981) Poverty and Famines: An Essay on Entitlement and Deprivation. Clarendon Press/Oxford University Press, Oxford.

Sonderholm J (2012), Thomas Pogge on Global Justice and World Poverty: A Review Essay. Analytic Philosophy 53: 366–391.

Taydas Z, Peksen D (2012) Can States Buy Peace? Social Welfare Spending and Civil Conflicts. Journal of Peace Research 49: 273–287.

Waglé U (2014) Relative Poverty Rate. In: Michalos A (ed) Encyclopedia of Quality of Life and Well-Being Research. Springer Netherlands, Dordrecht, pp 5449–5451.

Walter B F (2004) Does Conflict Beget Conflict? Explaining Recurring Civil War. Journal of Peace Research Journal of Peace Research 41: 371–388.

Walton C (2011) Les Graines de la discorde : Print, Public Spirit, and Free Market Politics in the French Revolution. In: Walton C, Darnton R (eds) Into Print: Limits and Legacies of the Enlightenment. Penn Press, University Park PA, pp 158–174.

Wolff, J, Lamb E, Zur-Szpiro E (2015) A philosophical review of poverty. Joseph Rowntree Foundation, York.

World Bank (2015) Global Poverty Line Update. http://www.worldbank.org/en/topic/poverty/brief/global-poverty-line-faq. Accessed 12 February 2022.

Evelyne Schmid is professor of public international law at the University of Lausanne in Switzerland. Her book *Taking Economic, Social and Cultural Rights Seriously in International Criminal Law* (Cambridge Studies in International and Comparative Law, 2015) won the 2016 Christiane-Rajewsky award of the German Association for Peace and Conflict Studies. She was previously based at the Universität Basel, Bangor University and at the Graduate Institute of International and Development Studies (IHEID) and holds a Master of Arts in Law and Diplomacy of the Fletcher School (Tufts University). She also acted as the project coordinator for the International Criminal Court's Legal Tools Project at TRIAL in Geneva. She is currently Vice-President of the European Society of International Law (ESIL).

Part V
Crimes

Part V
Crimes

Chapter 46
Genocide

Olivier Beauvallet, Hyuree Kim and Léo Jolivet

Contents

46.1 Introduction	1006
46.2 The New Requirement of a Contextual Element	1009
46.2.1 Lack of Any Reference to A Contextual Element in the Rome Statute	1009
46.2.2 The Issue of the Elements of Crimes Requesting an Additional Condition	1010
46.3 Mens Rea: The Mental Elements	1013
46.3.1 "Intent"	1014
46.3.2 To "Destroy"	1015
46.3.3 The Protected Groups: National, Ethnical, Racial and Religious Groups	1016
46.3.4 In Whole "or in Part"	1017
46.3.5 "As Such"	1018
46.4 Actus Reus: Prohibited Acts	1019
46.4.1 Killing	1020
46.4.2 Causing Serious Bodily or Mental Harm to Members of the Group	1021
46.4.3 Deliberately Inflicting on the Group Conditions of Life Calculated to Bring about Its Physical Destruction in Whole or in Part	1023
46.4.4 Imposing Measures Intended to Prevent Births within the Group	1024
46.4.5 Forcibly Transferring Children of a Protected Group to Another Group	1026
46.5 Conclusion	1028
References	1029

Abstract Article 6 of the Rome Statute of the International Criminal Court incorporates the provisions of Article II of the Convention on the Prevention and Punishment of Genocide. While genocide has given rise to an abundance of international jurisprudence, in particular before the International Criminal Tribunal for Rwanda

---

O. Beauvallet (✉)
Extraordinary Chambers in the Courts of Cambodia, Phnom Penh, Cambodia
e-mail: beauvallet@un.org

H. Kim
Supreme Court Chamber, Pre-Trial Chamber, Extraordinary Chambers in the Courts of Cambodia, Phnom Penh, Cambodia
e-mail: Kim.hyuree@eccc.gov.kh

L. Jolivet
Organised crime, white collar crime and international cooperation division, Office of the Prosecutor, Orléans, France
e-mail: leo.jolivet@justice.fr

© T.M.C. ASSER PRESS and the authors 2022
S. Sayapin et al. (eds.), *International Conflict and Security Law*,
https://doi.org/10.1007/978-94-6265-515-7_46

and the International Criminal Tribunal for the former Yugoslavia, it has only been a matter to incidental debates within the Pre-Trial Chamber of the International Criminal Court when issuing arrest warrants. If the jurisprudence of the International Criminal Court remains to come, particularly in the consistent interpretation of the Statute and the Elements of Crimes, genocide is articulated in three components. A contextual element that remains to be confirmed and, if need be, circumscribed; an intentional element that jurisprudence now distinguishes by analysing two facets, one general and the other special; and a material element that appears to be fixed but that could accommodate new forms of underlying criminality.

Keywords Destruction · Contextual element · *Actus reus* · Killing · Serious bodily or mental harm · Conditions for physical destruction · Measures to prevent births · Forcible transfer of children · *Mens rea* · Intent to destroy · Protected group

46.1 Introduction

The destruction of a human group has always and universally aroused a powerful feeling of repulsion. Yet it had remained, as the former Prime Minister of the UK Winston Churchill put it, "a crime without a name" until Raphaël Lemkin coined the word genocide. In his book *Axis Rule in Occupied Europe*, Lemkin stated that "[b]y 'genocide', we mean the destruction of a nation or of an ethnic group", and further clarified that genocide is intended "to signify a coordinated plan of different actions aiming at the destruction of essential foundations of the life of national groups, with the aim of annihilating the groups themselves".[1]

While Lemkin's characterisation of such massacres was certainly a mark of legal achievement, it was not an unprecedented attempt. Lemkin himself immediately found a synonym for "genocide" in "ethnocide". During the revolutionary wars in France, Gracchus Babeuf had denounced the treatment of the catholic and royalist populations of the Vendée by the armies of the Republic, using a varied vocabulary.[2] In 1795, Fouquier Tinville, former chief prosecutor of the Paris Revolutionary Tribunal, was prosecuted for having abused his authority in constituting a *"système populicide"* to send tens of thousands of people to the guillotine.[3]

After Lemkin, the crime of genocide gradually appears in the jurisprudence of the Nuremberg military tribunals and in international texts. A first official definition is given by the UN General Assembly in its Resolution 96 of 11 December 1946, proclaiming that "[g]enocide is the denial of the right of existence of entire human groups, just as homicide is the denial of the right to live of individual human beings". The Convention on the Prevention and Punishment of the Crime of Genocide of 9 December 1948 is certainly a major recognition of the "crime of crimes" although

---

[1] Lemkin 1944, p. 79.

[2] Babeuf 2008. In his book, initially released in 1794, Babeuf used many terms including "populicide" (p. 125), "plébéicide" (p. 140) or "nationicide" (p. 219).

[3] See, e.g., Cambon 1795.

the crime of genocide is much more narrowly defined than in the previous texts. The evolution of the international relations largely explains this change in the perception of the concept as reaching consensus among the major powers in the post-war climate was considerably difficult. Nonetheless, Article VI of this Convention provided that the persons accused of genocide "shall be tried by a competent tribunal of the State in the territory of which the act was committed, or by such international penal tribunal as may have jurisdiction".[4] It is well-known that there was no immediate follow-up to this call for creation of an international criminal court competent to prosecute and adjudicate those responsible for genocide.

The signing of the Rome Statute of the International Criminal Court,[5] fifty years after the Genocide Convention, successfully established a complete legal mechanism, at the international level, integrating an instrument of repression. While, admittedly, "there is no hierarchy between the crimes under the Statute" for the *ad hoc* international Tribunals,[6] the crime of genocide appears at the top of the four crimes for which the International Criminal Court ("ICC") has been given jurisdiction. It is undoubtedly a crime that affects not only the group whose destruction is sought, but also humanity as a whole. The definition of the crime of genocide is the subject of a large consensus, as evidenced by the absence of substantial discussion on Article 6 at the Rome Conference.[7] The International Court of Justice (ICJ) recognised the definition of genocide set forth in Article II of the 1948 Genocide Convention as reflecting customary law,[8] and all the delegations quickly accepted a complete transposition of the "historical" definition of genocide.[9] Therefore, although their respective scopes must be dissociated, the Rome Statute appears to be the culmination of the Genocide Convention. The coherence between the Genocide Convention and the Rome Statute is twofold. Firstly, the Rome Statute completes the mechanism for the prevention and punishment of genocide by establishing a permanent judicial mechanism in charge of individual prosecutions. Secondly, the ICC has jurisdiction

---

[4] 1948 Convention on the Prevention and Punishment of the Crime of Genocide, 9 December 1948, 78 UNTS. 277 (hereinafter 1948 Genocide Convention), Article 6.

[5] 1998 Rome Statute of the International Criminal Court, 2187 UNTS. 90 (hereinafter Rome Statute).

[6] *Prosecutor v. Georges Rutaganda*, Appeals Chamber, Judgement, Case No. ICTR-97-21-A, 26 May 2003 (*Rutaganda Appeal Judgement*), para 590.

[7] Von Hebel and Robinson 1999, p. 89.

[8] *Reservations to the convention of the Prevention and Punishment of Genocide*, ICJ, Advisory Opinion of 28 May 1951 at para 1.5. This was confirmed in the *Application of the Convention on the Prevention and Punishment of the Crime of Genocide (Bosnia and Herzegovina v. Serbia and Montenegro)*, ICJ, Judgment of 26 February 2007, Judgment (*Bosnia and Herzegovina v. Serbia and Montenegro Judgement*), p. 43.

[9] United Nations Diplomatic Conference of Plenipotentiaries on the Establishment of an International Criminal Court, Rome, 15 June–17 July 1998, Part 2, Jurisdiction, Admissibility and Applicable Law: Bureau Proposal, Committee of the Whole, UN Doc. A/CONF.183/C.1/L.59, Article 5. It has been a matter of concern to maintain a consistent definition of genocide and avoid any risk of fragmentation, see, e.g., Fronza 2000. Even more so since the international criminal Tribunals had already produced a significant amount of case law on genocide.

only over natural persons[10] and the ICJ retains the assessment of the States' responsibility and failure to comply with their international obligations such as those in violation of the Genocide Convention.[11] In sum, although the definition of genocide set forth in Article 6 of the Rome Statute reproduces the 1948 international definition in its entirety, it remains autonomous and certainly complementary to the 1948 definition. In other words, the basis for prosecution before the ICC is to be found in the Rome Statute and not in the Genocide Convention itself. However, it should be emphasised that the interpretation of Article 6 of the Rome Statute is closely linked not only to that of Article II but also to the 1948 Genocide Convention as a whole. Indeed, the Preparatory Committee stated in 1997 that "in interpreting this Article [on genocide], it may be necessary to take into account other relevant provisions of the Convention on the Prevention and Punishment of the Crime of Genocide [...]".[12]

The jurisprudence of the ICC in this area is extremely rare and consists of less than a handful of decisions. As of 1 September 2020, out of 45 defendants before the Court (including 8 for the offences against the administration of justice), only one is prosecuted for genocide.[13] Three elements must be present for genocide to be constituted under the Rome Statute:

i. The victims must belong to the targeted group;
ii. the killing, causing serious bodily or mental harm, inflicting serious bodily or mental harm, inflicting harm to living conditions, interfering with births or forcibly transferring children must occur "as part of a pattern of such conduct directed against that group, or was itself capable of causing such destruction"; and
iii. the perpetrator must act with the intent to destroy, in whole or in part, the target group.[14]

Given that paucity of decisions, the present study includes a review of the case law produced by prior international Tribunals and courts. The elements characterising the crime will be discussed through a threefold legal analysis addressing the context (Sect. 46.2), the mental elements (Sect. 46.3) and the prohibited acts (Sect. 46.4).

---

[10] See Rome Statute, Article 25(1).

[11] A system of dual responsibility is contemplated in *Bosnia and Herzegovina v. Serbia and Montenegro Judgement*, paras 163 and 173.

[12] Decisions Taken by the Preparatory Committee at its Session Held from 11 to 21 February 1997, UN Doc. A/AC.249/1997/L.5, p. 3, footnote 3.

[13] *Prosecutor v. Omar Hassan Ahmad Al Bashir*, Pre-Trial Chamber I, Second Warrant of Arrest for Omar Hassan Ahmad Al Bashir, Case No. ICC-02/05-01/09-95, 12 July 2010 (*Al Bashir Second Arrest Warrant*).

[14] *Prosecutor v. Omar Hassan Ahmad Al Bashir*, Pre-Trial Chamber I, Decision on the Prosecution's Request for a Warrant of Arrest against Omar Hassan Ahmad Al Bashir, Case No. ICC-02/05-01/09-34, 4 March 2009 (*Al Bashir Decision on the Prosecution's Request for a Warrant of Arrest*), para 113.

46.2 The New Requirement of a Contextual Element

46.2.1 Lack of Any Reference to A Contextual Element in the Rome Statute

Expressis verbis, Article 6 of the Rome Statute states that "'genocide' means any of the following acts[15] committed with intent to destroy" a protected group.[16] It hence does not foresee any contextual requirement as an element of the crime of genocide. Specifically, it is not required that the conduct took place in the course of any conflict or attack in order to qualify as genocide. Moreover, it is an autonomous incrimination that does not depend on the qualification of other crimes in the situation in question.

While at Nuremberg, the crime of genocide was considered as war crimes and crimes against humanity, the Genocide Convention affirmed "that genocide, whether committed in time of peace or in time of war, is a crime under international law".[17] The Rome Statute conspicuously abandons any reference to the situation of conflict or peace, on the understanding that it is hardly reasonable to imagine the perpetration of a crime of genocide in a peaceful environment. Moreover, the former reference to the commission of the crime "in time of peace or war" did not introduce any difference in legal regimes. However, at the Rome Conference, at the initiative of the United States, it was first suggested that the moral element of genocide includes "a plan to destroy" the protected group in whole or in part.[18] It evolved in the course of the debates and then proposed "a widespread or systematic policy or practice".[19] The proposal was largely rejected on the grounds that it created an unnecessary additional condition to a well-accepted offence in its customary definition.[20] However, a consensus emerged recognising the notion of "plan" found among the Elements of Crimes.[21]

Within the meaning of Article II of the Genocide Convention, no requirement is formulated, relating to the existence of an armed conflict or a context of systematic attack, for the purpose of constituting genocide. Further, all the jurisprudence of the International Criminal Tribunal for Rwanda ("ICTR") and the International Criminal Tribunal for the former Yugoslavia ("ICTY") is unanimous in excluding any contextual element, as noted by the ICC Pre-Trial Chamber in the case of *Al Bashir*.[22] The Chambers of the ICTY have constantly affirmed that the existence

---

[15] See Sect. 46.3.

[16] See Sect. 46.4.

[17] 1948 Genocide Convention, Article I.

[18] Annex on Definitional Elements for Part Two, Crimes: Proposal Submitted by the United States of America, 19 June 1998, UN Doc. A/CONF.183/C.1/L.10, p. 1.

[19] Draft Elements of Crimes: Proposal Submitted by the United States of America, 4 February 1999, UN Doc., PCNICC/1999/DP.4, pp. 5–6.

[20] Schabas 2009b, p. 146.

[21] Article 6, The Crime of Genocide: Discussion Paper Proposed by the Coordinator, 25 February 1999, UN Doc. PCNICC/1999/WGEC/RT.1.

[22] *Al Bashir Decision on the Prosecution's Request for a Warrant of Arrest*, paras 119–120.

of a plan or policy is not a legal ingredient of the crime of genocide.[23] While "the existence of such a plan would be strong evidence of the specific intent requirement for the crime of genocide",[24] it remains only evidence supporting the inference of intent, and does not become a legal ingredient of the offence.[25] Hence, the existence of a plan or policy is not a legal requirement of the crime. However, in the context of proving specific intent, the existence of a plan or policy may become an important factor in most cases. The evidence may be consistent with the existence of a plan or policy, or may even show such existence, and the existence of a plan or policy may facilitate proof of the crime.[26]

46.2.2 The Issue of the Elements of Crimes Requesting an Additional Condition

Are the norms applicable in the Rome legal apparatus likely to call into question this absence of contextual element? According to Article 6 of the Elements of Crimes, for each of the acts in question, "[t]he conduct took place in the context of a manifest pattern of similar conduct directed against that group or was conduct that could itself effect such destruction". Judges are therefore left with a question relating to the hierarchical organisation of the standards.

While Article 21(1)(a) of the Rome Statute provides that "the Court shall apply in the first place, this Statute, Elements of Crimes and its Rules of Procedure and Evidence", and that Article 9(1) of the Statute provides that "Elements of Crimes shall assist the Court in the interpretation and application of Articles 6, 7, 8 and 8 bis", the Pre-Trial Chamber in the *Al-Bashir* case found no contradiction in the issue at hand:

> the definition of the crime of genocide, so as to require for its completion an actual threat to the targeted group, or a part thereof, is (i) not per se contrary to Article 6 of the Statute; (ii) fully respects the requirements of Article 22(2) of the Statute that the definition of the crimes "shall be strictly construed and shall not be extended by analogy" and "[i]n case of ambiguity, the definition shall be interpreted in favour of the person being investigated, prosecuted or convicted"; and (iii) is fully consistent with the traditional consideration of the crime of genocide as the "crime of the crimes"[27]

---

[23] *Prosecutor v. Vidoje Blagojević & Dragan Jokić*, Trial Chamber, Judgement, Case No. IT-02-60-T, 17 January 2005 (*Blagojević & Jokić Trial Judgement*), para 656.

[24] *Prosecutor v. Clément Kayishema & Obed Ruzindana*, Trial Chamber, Judgement, Case No. ICTR-95-1-T, 21 May 1999 (*Kayishema & Ruzindana Trial Judgement*), para 276.

[25] *Prosecutor v. Goran Jelisić*, Appeals Chamber, Judgement, Case No. IT-95-10-A, 5 July 2001 (*Jelisić Appeal Judgement*), para 48; *Prosecutor v. Radislav Krštić*, Appeals Chamber, Judgement, Case No. IT-98-33-A, 19 April 2004 (*Krštić Appeal Judgement*), para 225.

[26] *Jelisić Appeal Judgement*, para 48; *Prosecutor v. Radoslav Brđanin*, Trial Chamber, Judgement, Case No. IT-96-36-T, 1 September 2004 (*Brđanin Trial Judgement*), para 705.

[27] *Al Bashir Decision on the Prosecution's Request for a Warrant of Arrest*, para 133.

In a separate and partially dissenting opinion, Judge Anita Ušacka dissociated herself from such analysis, holding that at the stage of issuing an arrest warrant, the question of whether the requirement of a contextual element was consistent with the Statute did not arise. More fundamentally, she disagreed with the majority's contention that "the Elements of Crimes and the Rules must be applied unless the competent Chamber finds an irreconcilable contradiction between these documents, and the Statute on the other hand".[28] According to Judge Ušacka, "only the Statute outlines the operative definition of the crime".[29] Indeed, the principle of legality would be called into question if the Statute provided an ambiguous definition of the crime. The majority, however, observed that "according to this contextual element provided for in the Elements of Crimes, the conduct for which the suspect is allegedly responsible, must have taken place in the context of a manifest pattern of similar conduct directed against the targeted group or must have had such a nature so as to itself effect, the total or partial destruction of the targeted group".[30] For Judge Ušacka, assuming that this element falls within the definition of genocide before the ICC, "the plain meaning of the term 'manifest pattern' refers to a systematic, clear pattern of conduct in which the alleged genocidal conduct occurs".[31] Therefore, she disagreed with the meaning given to the term by the majority, which interprets it to mean that "the crime of genocide is only completed when the relevant conduct presents a concrete threat to the existence of the targeted group, or a part thereof".[32] In her view, the majority's interpretation of Article 6(c)(5) of the Elements of Crimes "converts the term into a 'result-based' requirement, which would then duplicate the purpose of the second part of the sentence, 'or was conduct that could itself effect such destruction.'"[33] The Pre-Trial Chamber of the ICC, by majority, found that "the protection offered by the penal norm defining the crime of genocide—as an ultima ratio mechanism to preserve the highest values of the international community—is only triggered when the threat against the existence of the targeted group, or part thereof, becomes concrete and real, as opposed to just being latent or hypothetical".[34] Limiting its intervention to the required standard of proof, the Appeals Chamber did not rule on the question of the introduction of the contextual element in the crime.[35] The validity of the required contextual element remains open at this time.

For the time being, the question gives rise to doctrinal controversy. Indeed, some authors consider that a contextual element composed of a manifest series of similar

---

[28] *Al Bashir Decision on the Prosecution's Request for a Warrant of Arrest, Separate and Partly Dissenting Opinion of Judge Anita Usacka*, para 17.

[29] Ibid., para 18.

[30] *Al Bashir Decision on the Prosecution's Request for a Warrant of Arrest*, para 123.

[31] *Al Bashir Decision on the Prosecution's Request for a Warrant of Arrest, Separate and Partly Dissenting Opinion of Judge Anita Usacka*, para 19.

[32] Ibid., footnote 26.

[33] Ibid., para 19. The footnote refers to Oosterveld and Garraway 2001, p. 46.

[34] *Al Bashir Decision on the Prosecution's Request for a Warrant of Arrest*, para 124.

[35] *Prosecutor v. Omar Hassan Ahmad Al Bashir*, Case No. ICC-02/05-01/09-73, Appeal Chamber, Judgement on the appeal of the Prosecutor against the "Decision on the Prosecution's Application for a Warrant of Arrest against Omar Hassan Ahmad Al Bashir", 3 February 2010.

behaviours is a necessary element.[36] These authors rely, in particular, on the argument that weighed heavily during the Rome negotiations, namely that it is difficult to conceive of a case of genocide that is not conducted as "a widespread and systematic policy". This analysis has sometimes been favourably received in jurisprudence.[37] It is, in short, unrealistic for an isolated individual to aim at the destruction of a group. Therefore, the special genocidal intention must materialise in a collective criminal project.

Other authors take the approach that the contextual element, albeit found in most cases of genocide, is not a constitutive element.[38] They note that such element is not required by the Rome Statute and that contextual analysis provides only the evidence of special intent.[39] Abundant jurisprudence with this approach can be found, including that of the ICJ, which provided that "[t]he *dolus specialis*, the specific intent to destroy the group in whole or in part, has to be convincingly shown by reference to particular circumstances, unless a general plan to that end can be convincingly demonstrated to exist [...]".[40]

The question ultimately goes deeper into criminal intent than the definition of an attack. Thus, the question of whether a widespread or systematic policy or pattern is required is closely linked to the specific intent to destroy one of the protected groups, in whole or in part.

Taking the view that the genocidal campaign is not a constituent element of genocide within the meaning of Article 6 of the Rome Statute, it is notable that the Elements of Crimes introduce an important distinction since the conduct must be part of a manifest pattern of similar conduct directed against that group, or could in itself produce such destruction. Therefore, if a single act of conduct is of such a nature as to pose a concrete threat to the existence of the group independently of the existence of a policy of genocide, the act committed by the perpetrator may be qualified as genocide.[41] In other cases, proof of intent could be established by a clear pattern of similar conduct.

---

[36] Schabas 2009a, pp. 243–256; Kreß 2005, p. 562.

[37] *Prosecutor v. Radislav Krštić*, Trial Chamber, Judgement, Case No. IT-98-33-T, 2 August 2001 (*Krštić Trial Judgement*), para 682.

[38] Ambos 2014, p. 17. The author refers to an abundant literature in the bibliography.

[39] *Jelisić Appeal Judgement*, para 48, and ICTY, *Prosecutor v. Goran Jelisić*, Trial Chamber, Judgment, Case No. IT-95-10-T, 14 December 1999 (*Jelisić Trial Judgement*), paras 100–101; *Krštić Trial Judgement*, para 225; *Prosecutor v. Popović et al.*, Trial Chamber, Judgement, Case No. IT-05-88, 30 January 2015, para 830; *Prosecutor v. Clément Kayishema & Obed Ruzindana*, Appeals Chamber, Judgement (Reasons), Case No. ICTR-95-1-A, 1 June 2001 (*Kayishema & Ruzindana Appeal Judgement*), para 138 and *Kayishema & Ruzindana Trial Judgement*, para 276; *Prosecutor v. Aloys Simba*, Appeals Chamber, Judgement, Case No. ICTR-01-76, 27 November 2007, para 260.

[40] *Bosnia and Herzegovina v. Serbia and Montenegro Judgement*, para 373.

[41] Cassese 2013, p. 124.

46.3 Mens Rea: The Mental Elements

The crime of genocide has two mental elements, namely the requisite 'general intent' relating to the underlying prohibited act directed against one of the protected groups and the 'specific intent'[42] (*dolus specialis*) "to destroy in whole or in part, [a protected group] as such" as provided in Article II of the Genocide Convention.[43] It is this specific intent that distinguishes genocide from all other crimes against humanity and contributes to its particular wrongfulness and seriousness as "an extreme and the most inhumane form of persecution".[44]

There are four basic components of the specific intent of genocide: the perpetrator must (i) intend (ii) to destroy (iii) a protected group defined by nationality, race, ethnicity or religion (iv) in whole or in part.[45]

---

[42] The following terms have been employed: 'special intent' (*Prosecutor v. Jean Paul Akayesu*, Trial Chamber, Judgement, Case No. ICTR-96-4-T, 2 September 1998 (*Akayesu Trial Judgement*), para 498; *Prosecutor v. Athanase Seromba*, Trial Chamber, Judgement, Case No. ICTR-2001-66-I, 13 December 2006, paras 175, 319); 'dolus specialis' (*Akayesu Trial Judgement*, para 498; *Prosecutor v. Juvénal Kajelijeli*, Trial Chamber, Judgment and Sentence, Case No. ICTR-98-44A-T, 1 December 2003 (*Kajelijeli Trial Judgement*), para 803; *Kayishema & Ruzindana Trial Judgement*, para 91; *Prosecutor v. George Rutaganda*, Trial Chamber, Judgement and Sentence, Case No. ICTR-96-3-T, 6 December 1999 (*Rutaganda Trial Judgement*), para 59; *Prosecutor v. Ignace Bagilishema*, Trial Chamber, Judgement, Case No. ICTR-95-1A-T, 7 June 2001 (*Bagilishema Trial Judgement*), para 55; *Prosecutor v. Alfred Musema*, Trial Chamber, Judgement and Sentence, Case No. ICTR-96-13-T, 27 January 2000 (*Musema Trial Judgement*), para 164); 'genocidal intent' (*Kayishema & Ruzindana Trial Judgement*, para 91); 'specific intent' (*Kajelijeli Trial Judgement*, para 803; *Kayishema & Ruzindana Trial Judgement*, para 91; *Bagilishema Trial Judgement*, para 55); 'specific genocidal intent' (*Bagilishema Trial Judgement*, para 55); 'exterminatory intent' (*Jelisić Trial Judgement*, para 83); 'specific intention' (*Akayesu Trial Judgement*, para 498; *Rutaganda Trial Judgement*, para 59). This terminological variety did not end with the *Jelisić* Appeals Chamber's preference for the term 'specific intent' (*Jelisić Appeal Judgement*, para 45). The Chamber stressed that it does not attribute to this term any meaning it might carry in national jurisdictions. See also *Brđanin Trial Judgement*, para 695. For an interchangeable use of 'dolus specialis' and 'specific intent', see *Prosecutor v. Milomir Stakić*, Trial Chamber, Judgement, Case No. IT-97-24-T, 31 July 2003 (*Stakić Trial Judgement*), para 520.

[43] Ambos 2009, p. 834; Cryer et al. 2018, p. 220.

[44] Ambos 2009, pp. 835–836; Cryer et al. 2018, p. 220; Evans 2018, p. 747.

[45] Schabas 2009a, p. 270.

46.3.1 "Intent"

46.3.1.1 Interpretation of the "Intent": Purpose-Based Approach v. Knowledge-Based Approach

There has been an ongoing debate of a purpose-based and a knowledge-based approach to the interpretation of the "intent" as provided in Article II of the Genocide Convention.[46]

Some commentators with the knowledge-based understanding propose to distinguish between the collective intent that is manifested in an overall genocidal policy, plan or campaign and the individual intent that needs only knowledge of such plan or campaign together with foresight or recklessness as to the occurrence of the planned destruction.[47]

However, a majority of commentators and the international Tribunals as well as the ICC apply the purpose-based standard and require that the perpetrator must act "with aim, purpose or desire to destroy a group".[48] The prevailing understanding is that in accordance with the intent of the drafters,[49] the specific intent of genocide is "a specific intention, as required as a constitutive element of the crime, which demands that the perpetrator clearly seeks to produce the act charged"[50] and it is thus "not sufficient that the perpetrator simply knew that the underlying crime would inevitably or likely result in the destruction of the group".[51]

46.3.1.2 Proving the Specific Intent

In the absence of extraordinary circumstances or a confession, the genocidal intent is difficult, even impossible, to determine directly.[52] A careful examination of the jurisprudence of the international tribunals indicates that the tribunals rely on inferences of genocidal intent from the surrounding circumstantial factors[53] including the actions and the words of the perpetrator, the scale and the general nature of the

---

[46] Vianney-Liaud 2014, p. 10; Evans 2018, p. 747; Ambos 2009, pp. 836–838.

[47] Cryer et al. 2018, p. 224. See Greenwalt 1999, p. 2288; Kreß 2005, p. 572; Schabas 2008, p. 954.

[48] Jessberger 2009, p. 105; *Krštić Appeal Judgement*, para 134; *Jelisić Appeal Judgement*, paras 46, 50; *Rutaganda Appeal Judgement*, para 524; *Akayesu Trial Judgement*, para 520.

[49] Jessberger 2009, pp. 106–107. See Draft of Genocide Convention Prepared by the Secretary-General in pursuance of Economic and Social Council Resolution dated 28 March 1947, UN Doc. E/447, 26 June 1947, p. 5, Article I(2). 'In this Convention, the word "Genocide" means a criminal act directed against any one of the aforesaid groups of human beings, with the purpose of destroying it in whole or in part, or of preventing its preservation or development'.

[50] *Akayesu Trial Judgement*, para 498.

[51] *Blagojević & Jokić Trial Judgement*, para 656.

[52] *Akayesu Trial Judgement*, para 523.

[53] Park 2010, p. 151; Berster 2014, p. 155. See e.g., *Akayesu Trial Judgement*, para 523.

atrocities committed, systematic targeting of the protected group, and the evidence suggesting that commission of the genocidal *actus reus* was consciously planned.[54]

46.3.2 To "Destroy"

The intention to destroy refers to physical or biological destruction.[55] Some academics, notably Raphael Lemkin, and national jurisdictions extend the scope of genocide to other forms of destruction such as the social assimilation of a group into another, or attacks on cultural characteristics which give a group its own identity may constitute genocide.[56] The Preamble to General Assembly Resolution 96(1) also states that genocide "results in great losses to humanity in the form of cultural and other contributions represented by these human amount to genocide". Furthermore, Judge Shahabuddeen of the ICTY Appeals Chamber, in his partially dissenting opinion of the Appeals Judgement in the *Krštić* case, notably interpreted the Statute of the Tribunal "to mean that, provided that there is a listed act (this being physical or biological), the intent to destroy the group as a group is capable of being proved by evidence of an intent to cause the non-physical destruction of the group in whole or in part, except in particular cases in which physical destruction is required by the Statute".[57]

However, cultural loss, in the absence of physical destruction, does not amount to genocide.[58] It is noteworthy that the International Law Commission, during the consideration of the draft Code of Crimes, addressed the issue and provided that the preparatory work as well as the text of the Convention clearly show that "the destruction in question is the material destruction of a group either by physical or by biological means, not the destruction of the national, linguistic, religious, cultural or other identity of a particular group".[59] Furthermore, such construction has been rejected as a matter of law by the international Tribunals and the International Court of Justice.[60]

The Chambers of the ICTY, in *Krštić*, held that customary international law limits the definition of genocide to the physical or biological destruction of all or part of the

---

[54] Park 2010, p. 152; Cryer et al. 2018, p. 222; Evans 2018, pp. 747–748. See e.g., *Prosecutor v. Siméon Ncamihigo*, Trial Chamber, Judgement, Case No. ICTR-01-63-T, 12 November 2008, para 331; *Prosecutor v. Athanase Seromba*, Appeals Chamber, Judgement, Case No. ICTR-2001-66-A, 12 March 2008 (*Seromba Appeal Judgement*), paras 177–182.

[55] Cryer et al. 2018, p. 224; Schabas 2009a, p. 271; Evans 2018, p. 748.

[56] See e.g., Lemkin 1944, pp. 79, 87–89; German Federal Constitutional Court, 2 BvR 290/99, 12 December 2000, para III(4)(a)(aa); Schabas 2009a, pp. 207–221.

[57] *Krštić Appeal Judgement*, Partial Dissenting Opinion of Judge Shahabuddeen, para 54.

[58] Cryer et al. 2018, p. 225; Evans 2018, p. 748.

[59] Yearbook of the International Law Commission. 1989. Volume 2, part 2, Report of the Commission to the General Assembly on the work of its 41st session, UN Doc. A/CN.4/SER.A/1989/Add.1 (Part 2), p. 102, para 4.

[60] Evans 2018, p. 748.

group and the attacks only on the cultural or sociological characteristics of a group in order to annihilate these elements which give to that group its own distinct identity would not fall under the definition of genocide.[61]

The ICJ, in the Bosnian Genocide case, confirmed that genocide was limited to physical or biological destruction of a group and noted that if the transfer of members of a group results in the splitting up of the group, that is not genocide unless done with an intent to physically destroy the group.[62] However, simultaneous attacks on the cultural and religious property and symbols of the targeted group with physical or biological destruction may legitimately be considered as evidence for establishing an intent to physically destroy the group.[63]

46.3.3 The Protected Groups: National, Ethnical, Racial and Religious Groups

The Genocide Convention provides a closed list that only "national, ethnic, racial and religious groups" are protected. While there are national jurisdictions that have adopted wider formulations of the protected groups in their domestic law,[64] it is precisely because of the rigours of the definition, and because of its focus on crimes aimed at the eradication of particular groups, that genocide is especially stigmatised.[65]

During the negotiation and since the conclusion of the Convention, there have been proposals to expand the list to include others, such as social and political groups, or that other groups come within the scope of genocide by virtue of customary international law, but these have all been unsuccessful.[66] While the Trial Chamber of the ICTR, in *Akayesu* case, considered that the Convention protects all stable and permanent groups and the Commission of Inquiry established at the request of the Security Council to investigate violations of international humanitarian law and human rights in Darfur stated that this expansive interpretation had become part and parcel of international customary law, this minority view that the Convention's list of groups is not exhaustive is not supported by jurisprudence other than *Akayesu*, nor by general state practice and *opinio juris*, and cannot be seen as reflective of current law since no other Trial Chamber of *ad hoc* Tribunals has followed the *Akayesu* approach and the Appeals Chamber and the ICC have consistently held that the four groups are the exclusive focus of the Genocide Convention.[67] As the ICJ has noted, "the

---

[61] *Krstić Trial Judgement*, para 580; *Krštić Appeal Judgement*, para 25.

[62] *Bosnia and Herzegovina v. Serbia and Montenegro Judgement*, para 344.

[63] *Bosnia and Herzegovina v. Serbia and Montenegro Judgement*, para 344.

[64] Cryer et al. 2018, p. 211.

[65] Schabas 2009a, p. 277.

[66] Cryer et al. 2018, p. 210; Evans 2018, p. 748.

[67] Cryer et al. 2018, pp. 210–211. See e.g., *Krštić Appeal Judgement*, paras 6–8; *Al Bashir Decision on the Prosecution's Request for a Warrant of Arrest*, 4 March 2009, paras 134–137.

essence of the intent is to destroy the protected group, in whole or in part, as such. It is a group which must have particular positive characteristics – national, ethnical, racial or religious [...]".

Further, it is well-recognised that the four groups were not given distinct and different meaning in the Convention. The Trial Chamber of the ICTY, in the *Krštić* case, stated that "[t]o attempt to differentiate each of the named groups on the basis of scientifically objective criteria would thus be inconsistent with the object and purpose of the Convention".[68]

46.3.4 In Whole "or in Part"

The term "in whole or in part" refers to the intent of the perpetrator, not to the result or the participation by an individual offender.[69] This aspect of the intention has caused considerable controversy since the ambit of the protections granted by the prohibition of genocide hinges on the scope of the relevant group.[70]

Firstly, it is widely accepted that genocide may be found to have been committed where the intent is to destroy the group within a geographically limited area.[71]

Concerning the meaning of "in part", the International Law Commission considered that "the crime of genocide by its very nature requires the intention to destroy at least a substantial part of a particular group".[72] This 'substantial part' interpretation is well entrenched in the jurisprudence of international tribunals which has established that it does not amount to genocide if the intention is to target a part which is less than 'substantial'.[73] The ICJ confirmed the substantial part interpretation in the Bosnian Genocide case by holding that:

> the intent must be to destroy at least a substantial part of the particular group. That is demanded by the very nature of the crime of genocide: since the object and purpose of the Convention as a whole is to prevent the intentional destruction of groups, the part targeted must be significant enough to have an impact on the group as a whole.[74]

In determining the meaning of the 'substantial' part, the Chambers of the ICTY and the Commission of Experts established by the Security Council in 1992 to investigate

---

[68] *Krštić Trial Judgement*, paras 555–556.

[69] Schabas 2009a, p. 277.

[70] Evans 2018, pp. 748–749; Cryer et al. 2018, p. 225.

[71] *Bosnia and Herzegovina v. Serbia and Montenegro Judgement*, para 199. See *Jelisić Trial Judgement*, para 83; *Krštić Trial Judgement*, para 590; *Prosecutor v. Sikirica et al.*, Judgement on Defence Motions to Acquit, Case No. IT-95-8-I, 3 September 2001, para 68; Report of the International Law Commission on the work of its 48th session, 6 May-26 July 1996. UN Doc. A/51/10, (hereinafter 1996 ILC Report), p. 125.

[72] 1996 ILC Report, p. 125.

[73] Berster 2014, p. 149; Cryer et al. 2018, p. 226; Evans 2018, p. 749; Schabas 2018, p. 279. See *Kayishema & Ruzindana Trial Judgement*, para 96.

[74] *Bosnia and Herzegovina v. Serbia and Montenegro Judgement*, para 198.

violations of international humanitarian law in the former Yugoslavia held that both criteria of quantity, relative and absolute, as well as quality, in terms of special skills or positions, may be considered.[75] Notably, the Appeals Chamber of the ICTY, in *Krštić*, found that "[i]f a specific part of the group is emblematic of the overall group, or is essential to its survival that may support a finding that the part qualifies as substantial".[76]

46.3.5 "As Such"

The preparatory work of the Genocide Convention discloses that any explicit reference to motive was excluded and the words "as such" were inserted as a compromise in order to reconcile the two diverging approaches in favour and against including a motivational component as an additional element of the genocide.[77] Therefore, these words should not be relied upon as evidence of the need for motive.[78]

The term "as such" clarifies the specific intent requirement of genocide.[79] The jurisprudence of international tribunals demonstrates that "[t]he victims of the crime must be targeted because of their membership in the protected group, although not necessarily solely because of such membership".[80] In other words, while personal motivation, such as financial benefit, for the perpetrator's participation in the crime is not relevant and does not prohibit a conviction for genocide, the perpetrator's discriminatory motive to destroy the group is intrinsic to the specific intent.[81]

While proof of motive is rarely required, in addition to proof of intent, as an element of an offence in domestic criminal law systems, the discriminatory nature of genocide necessitates that the perpetrator has a genocidal motive.[82] Therefore, evidence of discriminatory motive may play an integral, while not decisive by itself, role in assessing the specific genocidal intent.[83]

---

[75] Berster 2014, pp. 150–151; Cryer et al. 2018, p. 226; Bassiouni 1994, p. 279 at pp. 323–324.

[76] *Krštić Appeal Judgement*, para 12.

[77] *Prosecutor v. Eliézer Niyitegeka*, Appeals Chamber, Judgement, Case No. ICTR-96-14-A, 9 July 2004, (*Niyitegeka Appeals Judgement*), para 49; *Prosecutor v. Elizaphan and Gérard Ntakirutimana*, Appeals Chamber, Judgement, Case No. ICTR-96-10-A and ICTR-96-17-A, 13 December 2004 (*Ntakirutimana Appeal Judgement*), paras 304, 363; Cryer et al. 2018, p. 227; Schabas 2009a, p. 305; Berster 2014, p. 152.

[78] Cryer et al. 2018, p. 227; Quigley 2006, pp. 120–126.

[79] *Niyitegeka Appeals Judgement*, para 49; *Ntakirutimana Appeal Judgement*, paras 304, 363.

[80] Berster 2014, p. 152; *Niyitegeka Appeals Judgement*, para 49; *Ntakirutimana Appeal Judgement*, paras 304, 363.

[81] *Krštić Trial Judgement*, para 545; *Krštić Appeal Judgement*, paras 45; *Kayishema & Ruzindana Appeal Judgement*, para 161; *Prosecutor v. Milomir Stakić*, Appeals Chamber, Judgement, Case No. IT-97-24-A, 22 March 2006, para 45; *Jelisić Appeal Judgement*, para 49.

[82] Schabas 2009a, p. 305; Cryer et al. 2018, p. 227.

[83] Schabas 2009a, p. 305; Cryer et al. 2018, p. 227.

46.4 Actus Reus: Prohibited Acts

The crime of genocide refers to any criminal enterprise seeking the destruction, in whole or in part, of a particular kind of human group, as such, by the five prohibited acts exhaustively enumerated in Article II of the Genocide Convention.[84] Therefore, only these criminal acts provided in Article II(2)(a)–(e) may be considered for the purpose of the crime of genocide and any other non-enumerated criminal act committed, even with the intent to destroy, does not constitute genocide.[85]

The Genocide Convention prohibits these conducts insofar as they are directed against the members of a protected group and reflect the intent to destroy that group in whole or in part.[86] While Article II of the Genocide Convention refers to the direct victim of the prohibited acts in the plural form, except for para 2(c), which criminalise conduct targeting a group itself, the *actus reus* does not require the actual destruction of a substantial part of the group. Indeed, a prohibited act may be directed to only one or more member(s) of the group.[87] It is notable that the ICC Element of Crimes states, *inter alia*, that "[t]he perpetrator killed *one or more persons*".[88] Furthermore, the jurisprudence of the international Tribunals confirms this one victim requirement.[89] The Extraordinary Chambers of the Courts of Cambodia ("ECCC"), the latest internationalised jurisdiction to prosecute the crime of genocide, affirmed that in order "to establish the *actus reus* for genocide it is not required for there to be a numerical assessment of the number of people killed nor does it have a numeric threshold".[90]

---

[84] See *Krštić Trial Judgement*, para 550. The same five prohibited acts appear also in the Rome Statute for the purpose of the crime of genocide.

[85] Schabas 2009a, p. 175–176; Jessberger 2009, p. 94.

[86] See Sect. 46.3. See also *Application of the Convention on Prevention and Punishment of the Crime of Genocide (Croatia v. Serbia)*, ICJ, Judgment, 3 February 2015 (*Croatia v. Serbia Judgment*), para 149.

[87] Schabas 2009a, p. 179. Schabas 2000, p. 234. 'No acceptable rationale can justify why an individual murder, if committed with the intent to destroy a group 'in whole or in part', should not be qualified as genocide.'; Kreß 2006, p. 480. For a different view, see Cassese 2003, p. 102: Werle 2005, pp. 62–64.

[88] ICC Elements of Crimes, Article 6(b)(1).

[89] *Prosecutor v. Emmanuel Ndindabahizi*, Trial Chamber, Judgement and Sentence, Case No. ICTR-2001-71-I, 15 July 2004, para 471; *Musema Trial Judgement*. 'For any of the acts charged to constitute genocide, the said acts must have been committed against one or more persons because such person or persons were members of a specific group, and specifically, because of their membership in this group'; *Rutaganda Trial Judgement*, para 60; *Prosecutor v. Laurent Semanza*, Trial Chamber, Judgement and Sentence, Case No. ICTR-97-20-T, 15 May 2003 (*Semanza Trial Judgement*), para 316.

[90] ECCC, Case against Nuon Chea and Khieu Samphân, Trial Chamber, Case 002/2 Judgement, Case No. 002/19-09-2007/ECCC/TC, 16 November 2018, E465, para 796.

46.4.1 Killing

The killing of a person belonging to a protected group is a crime of genocide when committed with the intent to destroy the group.[91] While sub-paragraph (a) of the Genocide Convention in English refers to "killing" encompassing unintentional killing, the French version uses the word "*meurtre*", which translates as intentional homicide. The intent, which separates those two versions, is, therefore, the key factor in determining whether a "killing" may be punished as genocide. A Trial Chamber of the ICTR first deemed the word "killing" too general including both intentional and unintentional killings and found that sub-paragraph (a) should be interpreted in the sense of murder, *i.e.*, requiring a "homicide committed with intent to cause death" in light of the presumption of innocence and pursuant to the principle of interpretation *in dubio pro reo*.[92] Both the ICTY and the ICJ adopted a similar interpretation of the term "killing".[93] This reasoning later evolved, although to reach the same conclusion. A Trial Chamber of the ICTR stated that there is virtually no difference between "killing" and "*meurtre*" as the term "killing" is linked to the intent to destroy in whole or in part articulated in the Chapeau of Article II.[94] This linking of the killing and the intent to destroy, which seems to conflate the specific genocidal intent and the general intent of the underlying crime,[95] is also the basis for not requiring premeditation as a material element of the killing.[96]

It is possible to extract two material elements of murder from the *ad hoc* Tribunals' jurisprudence: (i) the victim must be dead, and (ii) the death resulted from an unlawful

---

[91] However, the murder of a non-member of the targeted group within the context of genocide cannot be considered an act of genocide under the Convention definition, see *Akayesu Trial Judgement*, para 710.

[92] *Akayesu Trial Judgement*, paras 500–501. See also *Rutaganda Trial Judgement*, para 50, *Musema Trial Judgement*, para 155; *Prosecutor v. Théoneste Bagosora et al.*, Trial Chamber, Judgement and Sentence, Case No. ICTR-98-41-T, 18 December 2008 (*Bogosora et al. Trial Judgement*), para 2117. 'Killing members of the group requires a showing that the principal perpetrator intentionally killed one or more members of the group'.

[93] For the ICTY interpretation *see Krstić Trial Judgement*, para 543; *Blagojević & Jokić Trial Judgement*, para 543. For the ICJ interpretation, see *Croatia v. Serbia Judgement*, para 156.

[94] *Kayishema & Ruzindana Trial Judgement*. Upheld in *Kayishema & Ruzindana Appeal Judgement*, para 151.

[95] See Sect. 46.3. See also, e.g., Cassese 2003, p. 103 where the author differentiates the *dolus specialis* and the intent for the underlying crimes, 'This intent amounts to *dolus specialis* that is, to an *aggravated criminal intention*, required *in addition* to the criminal intent accompanying the underlying offence (killing; causing serious bodily or mental harm; inflicting conditions of life calculated to physically destroy the group; imposing measures designed to prevent births within the group; forcibly transferring children'; Jessberger 2009, p. 97. *Croatia v. Serbia Judgment*, paras 186–187, which also distinguishes between *dolus specialis* and intent for the underlying crimes.

[96] *Kajelijeli Trial Judgement*, para 813. 'Given that the element of *mens rea* in the killing has been addressed in the special intent for genocide, there is no requirement to prove a further element of premeditation in the killing.' See also, e.g., *Semanza Trial Judgement*, para 319. *Prosecutor v. Jean de Dieu Kamuhanda*, Trial Chamber, Judgement, Case No. ICTR-95-54A-T, 22 January 2004, para 632.

act or omission of the accused or a subordinate.[97] This underlying crime may encompass suicide when the perpetrator's acts or omissions "induced the victim to take action which resulted in his death, and that his suicide was either intended, or was an action of a type which a reasonable person could have foreseen as a consequence".[98]

46.4.2 Causing Serious Bodily or Mental Harm to Members of the Group

Although the prevalent understanding is that the crime of genocide requires the death of the targeted group's members, sub-paragraph (b) envisions the commission of the crime of genocide by causing serious bodily or mental harm to at least one member of the group.[99] While the International Law Commission stated that bodily harm referred to "some type of physical injury" and mental harm to "some type of impairment of mental faculties",[100] a more specific definition of these terms came from the jurisprudence of the *ad hoc* Tribunals clarifying that the term "serious bodily harm" refers to "acts of sexual violence, serious acts of physical violence falling short of killing that seriously injure the health, cause disfigurement or cause any serious injury to the external or internal organs or senses".[101] On the other hand, serious mental harm is construed as a mental impairment that causes serious injury to the mental state of the victim,[102] which excludes minor or temporary impairment of mental faculties such as the infliction of strong fear or terror, intimidation or threat.[103]

The harm inflicted on the members of the group must be caused intentionally[104] and must be severe enough to qualify as genocide. In consequence, the effect of the inflicted harm should go beyond temporary unhappiness, embarrassment or humiliation and should instead be harm that results in a grave and long-term disadvantage

---

[97] *Akayesu Trial Judgement*, para 589.

[98] Schabas 2009a, p. 179, *Prosecutor v. Milorad Krnojelac*, Trial Chamber, Judgment, Case No. IT-97-25-T, 15 March 2002 (*Krnojelac Trial Judgment*), para 329 applied *mutatis mutandis* from crimes against humanity of murder to killing in the context of genocide.

[99] Jessberger 2009, p. 97. See also *Prosecutor v. Tharcisse Muvunyi*, Trial Chamber, Judgement and Sentence, Case No. ICTR-2000-55A-T, 12 September 2006, para 487. '[T]he various Trial Chambers have concluded that the intent of the framers [of the Genocide Convention, regarding the infliction of serious bodily or mental harm] was to punish serious acts of physical violence that do not necessarily result in the death of the victim'.

[100] 1996 ILC Report, p. 46, para 14.

[101] *Kayishema & Ruzindana Trial Judgement*, para 109, *Bogosora et al. Trial Judgement*, para 2117.

[102] *Prosecutor v. Mikaeli Muhimana*, Trial Chamber, Judgement and Sentence, Case No. ICTR95-1B-T, 28 April 2005, para 502.

[103] *Seromba Appeal Judgement*, para 46.

[104] 1996 ILC Report, p. 44, para 5. 'The prohibited acts enumerated in subparagraphs (a) to (e) are by their very nature conscious, intentional or volitional acts which an individual could not usually commit without knowing that certain consequences were likely to result. These are not the type of acts that would normally occur by accident or even as a result of mere negligence'; *Bosnia and Herzegovina v. Serbia and Montenegro Judgment*, para 186; Cassese 2003, p. 103.

to a person's ability to lead a normal and constructive life.[105] It, however, need not be an injury that is permanent or irremediable.[106] The text of sub-paragraph (b) does not require the harm to be of such a serious nature as to threaten its destruction in whole or in part.[107] Nonetheless, the international case law, following the International Law Commission's interpretation, made of this element of destruction a criterion regarding the assessment of the seriousness of the harm,[108] and specified that the threshold for the seriousness of the harm has to be assessed on a case-by-case basis and be met for every individual case.[109]

On this basis and under those conditions, rapes and sexual violence may constitute a crime of genocide. A Trial Chamber of the ICTR

> underscore[d] the fact that in its opinion, they constitute genocide in the same way as any other act as long as they were committed with the specific intent to destroy [...]. Indeed, rape and sexual violence certainly constitute infliction of serious bodily and mental harm on the victims and are even, according to the Chamber, one of the worst ways of inflicting harm on the victim as he or she suffers both bodily and mental harm. [...] These rapes resulted in physical and psychological destruction of Tutsi women, their families and their communities. Sexual violence was an integral part of the process of destruction, specifically targeting Tutsi women and specifically contributing to their destruction and to the destruction of the Tutsi group as a whole.[110]

As a supplement of examples, death threats during interrogation, alone or coupled with beatings, torture, inhumane or degrading treatment, persecution, deportation,[111] enslavement or starvation may be prosecuted under this count of genocide.

---

[105] *Krstić Trial Judgement*, para 513; Kreß 2006, p. 481.

[106] *Bogosora et al. Trial Judgement*, para 2117. 'The serious bodily or mental harm [...] need not be an injury that is permanent or irremediable.' See also *Prosecutor v. André Ntagerura et al.*, Trial Chamber, Judgement Sentence, Case No. ICTR-99-46-T, 25 February 2004, para 664; *Semanza Trial Judgement*, paras 320–322; *Musema Trial Judgement*, para 156; *Rutaganda Trial Judgement*, para 51; *Kayishema & Ruzindana Trial Judgement*, para 108; *Akayesu Trial Judgement*, para 502.

[107] See Schabas 2009a, p. 188. 'Yet, while sexual violence and rape may in fact have the effect of contributing in a significant manner to the destruction of a group in whole or in part, this is not what the text of para (b) requires. The prosecution need not demonstrate a cause and effect relationship between the acts of violence and the destruction of the group. The result that the prosecution must prove is that one or more victims actually suffered physical or mental harm. If this act is perpetrated with the requisite mental element, the crime has been committed'; Jessberger 2009, p. 97.

[108] 1996 ILC Report, p. 46, para 14. *Croatia v. Serbia Judgment*, para 157. See also *Prosecutor v. Krajišnik*, Trial Chamber I, Judgement, Case No. IT-00-39-T, 27 September 2006, paras 862–863. 'it follows that "failure to provide adequate accommodation, shelter, food, water, medical care, or hygienic sanitation facilities" will not amount to the *actus reus* of genocide if the deprivation is not so severe as to contribute to the destruction of the group, or tend to do so. Living conditions, which may be inadequate by any number of standards, may nevertheless be adequate for the survival of the group'; *Prosecutor v. Tolimir*, Trial Chamber II, Judgement, Case No. IT-05-88/2-T, 12 December 2012 (*Tolimir Trial Judgement*), para 738; *Seromba Appeal Judgement*, para 46.

[109] Jessberger 2009, p. 99. *Tolimir Trial Judgement*, para 738.

[110] *Akayesu Trial Judgement*, para 731.

[111] *Akayesu Trial Judgement*, para 504; *Krstić Trial Judgement*, para 513.

46.4.3 Deliberately Inflicting on the Group Conditions of Life Calculated to Bring about Its Physical Destruction in Whole or in Part

The drafters of the Genocide Convention certainly had in mind the atrocities committed during the Nazi genocide when they drafted sub-paragraph (c),[112] which foresees the possibility of the destruction of a group through calculated conditions of life. The conditions of life need only be "calculated" to bring the group, in whole or in part, to its physical destruction. Nonetheless, a clear distinction needs to be drawn between physical destruction and mere dissolution of a group.[113] The expulsion or deportation of a group or part of a group does not per se constitute a genocidal act as the dissolution of the group is not to be equated with physical destruction.[114] The same conclusion applies regarding the practice of "ethnic cleansing", which aims at creating an ethnically homogeneous territory and used to describe the expulsion of Muslims and Croats from their territory by the Serbs during the war of the former Yugoslavia. The ICJ summarised the issue in stating that ethnic cleansing

> can only be a form of genocide within the meaning of the Convention, if it corresponds to or falls within one of the categories of acts prohibited by Article II of the Convention. Neither the intent, as a matter of policy, to render an area "ethnically homogeneous", nor the operations that may be carried out to implement such policy, can as such be designated as genocide: the intent that characterises genocide is "to destroy, in whole or in part" a particular group, and deportation or displacement of the members of a group, even if effected by force, is not necessarily equivalent to destruction of that group, nor is such destruction an automatic consequence of the displacement. This is not to say that acts described as "ethnic cleansing" may never constitute genocide, if they are such as to be characterised as, for example, "deliberately inflicting on the group conditions of life calculated to bring about its physical destruction in whole or in part", contrary to Article II, para (c), of the Convention, provided such action is carried out with the necessary specific intent (dolus specialis), that is to say with a view to the destruction of the group, as distinct from its removal from the region.[115]

With regards to the proof of result, this provision must be distinguished from other provisions of Article II(2). Indeed, as it was explained for the first time in the *Eichmann* Case, for the purpose of this provision, whether the group was effectively destroyed is unimportant as the deaths that result from the conditions are covered by sub-paragraph (a) or (b).[116] As a consequence, the death of a group member is not a required element of the crime.

---

[112] See Schabas 2009a, p. 189. '[A]s France explained, '[t]o quote an historical example, the ghetto, where the Jews were confined in conditions which, either by starvation or by illness accompanied by the absence of medical care, led to their extinction, must certainly be regarded as an instrument of genocide. If any group were placed on rations so short as to make its extinction inevitable, merely because it belonged to a certain nationality, race or religion, the fact would also come under the category of genocidal crime'. Jessberger 2009, p. 100.

[113] *Stakić Trial Judgement*, para 519, *Krštić Appeal Judgement*, para 33.

[114] Schabas 2009a, p. 193.

[115] *Bosnia and Herzegovina v. Serbia and Montenegro Judgment*, para 190.

[116] *Attorney General v. Adolf Eichmann*, Supreme Court of Israel, Judgment, Criminal Appeal 336/61, 29 May 1962, para 196. 'We do not think that conviction on the second Count [*i.e.*, imposing

Although the ICC Elements of Crimes states that certain conditions of life inflicted upon one or more persons may constitute genocide, the wording of para (c) makes clear that the conditions shall be imposed on a group and not only on a single individual of this group. However, given that the partial destruction of the group is possible under this paragraph, the submission of part of the group to the destructive conditions of life can be considered as genocide.[117]

With respect to the "conditions of life", the international Tribunals' jurisprudence indicates that it encompasses the methods of destruction by which the perpetrator does not immediately kill the members of the group, but which, ultimately, seek their physical destruction.[118] Under the condition that they would lead to the destruction of the group in whole or in part, these methods comprise: subjecting a group of people to a subsistence diet, systematic expulsion from homes, the reduction of essential medical services below the minimum requirement,[119] and the withholding of sufficient living accommodation for a reasonable period.[120] The term was further interpreted as comprising circumstances that would lead the group members to a slow death such as lack of proper housing, clothing and hygiene or excessive work or physical exertion.[121] For instance, the ICC treated the "contaminat[ion] of the wells and water pumps of the towns and villages primarily inhabited by [the members of the targeted group]" under the genocide count in the *Al Bashir* Case.[122]

46.4.4 Imposing Measures Intended to Prevent Births within the Group

Sub-paragraph (d) refers to the biological genocide aiming at the destruction of the group by imposing measures intended to prevent births within the targeted group.[123] This provision certainly refers to not only the conducts of enforced sterilisation and castration that were committed by the Nazis during the Second World War, but also any measures that may result in the prevention of births, such as separation of the sexes, prohibition of marriages and forced birth control.[124] The ICJ provided that

---

living conditions calculated to bring about the destruction] should also include those Jews who were not saved, as if in their case there were two separate acts—first, subjection to living conditions calculated to bring about their physical destruction, and later the physical destruction itself.' See Schabas 2009a, p. 192.

[117] Kreß 2006, p. 481; Jessberger 2009, p. 101.

[118] *Akayesu Trial Judgement*, para 505.

[119] *Akayesu Trial Judgement*, para 505.

[120] *Kayishema & Ruzindana Trial Judgement*, para 116.

[121] Jessberger 2009, p. 101; Schabas 2009a, p. 191; *Kayishema & Ruzindana Trial Judgement*, paras 115–116.

[122] *Al Bashir Second Arrest Warrant*, p. 7.

[123] Jessberger 2009, p. 101; Schabas 2009a, p. 191.

[124] See *Akayesu Trial Judgement*, para 507–508; Jessberger 2009, p. 101; Schabas 2009a, p. 191.

conducts preventing births require the circumstances of the commission of those acts, and their consequences, to be such that the capacity of the group members to procreate is affected.[125]

Under certain circumstances, rape and sexual assault are akin to a measure preventing birth. In this regard, a Trial Chamber of the ICTR found that rape may be an example of a physical measure intended to prevent births within the group when it was committed with the intention to change the ethnic composition of the group. That is the case when the perpetrator commits rape to have the mother give birth to a child who will consequently not belong to its mother's group.[126] The measures intended to prevent the births may also be psychological as "rape can be a measure intended to prevent births when the person raped refuses subsequently to procreate".[127] Similarly, "members of a group can be led, through threats or trauma, not to procreate".[128]

The definition in sub-paragraph (d) refers only to "imposing measures" which entails two consequences. Firstly, the measures must be forcibly imposed on the group, which implies an element of coercion.[129] Therefore, the mere legalisation of abortion or a state policy aiming at lowering birth for social or other reasons does not reflect a genocidal intent.[130] Secondly, the successful reduction of birth is not a material element of the crime, and the imposition of measures suffices.[131] Regarding the *mens rea* related to the measures, unlike sub-paragraph (c), this provision does not require the measures to be "calculated" to destroy the group, but only "intended" to prevent births within the group. Moreover, in order to constitute genocide, it is not necessary that the perpetrator had the intent to prevent births totally.[132]

---

[125] *Croatia v. Serbia Judgment*, para 166.

[126] *Akayesu Trial Judgement*, para 507.

[127] *Akayesu Trial Judgement*, para 508.

[128] *Akayesu Trial Judgement*, para 508.

[129] Where an accused was found responsible of imposing measures to prevent births by signing various decrees curtailing marriages: *United States v. Ulrich Greifelt et al.*, (1948) 13 LRTWC 1 (United States Military Tribunal), p. 17, p. 28. '(vii) Impeding the Reproduction of Enemy Nationals Measures, concerning mainly inhabitants of Poland, were taken to prevent their reproduction and thus contribute to the destruction of non-German races. They took the form of various decrees, and were chiefly aimed at drastically curtailing marriages. [...] The defendant Ulrich Greifelt, as chief of the Main Staff Office and deputy to Himmler, was with the exception of Himmler, the main driving force in the entire Germanisation program. By an abundance of evidence it is established beyond a reasonable doubt [...] that the defendant Greifelt is criminally responsible for [...] hampering the reproduction of enemy nationals'.

[130] Jessberger 2009, p. 101 citing Werle 2005, at 597. See also 1996 ILC Report, p. 46, para 16.

[131] See ICC Elements of Crimes, Article 6(d).

[132] Boot 2002, para 422. 'In order to constitute genocide, it is not necessary that the perpetrator had the intent to prevent births totally [and], it will be sufficient that partial prevention is the purpose of the measures in question'.

46.4.5 Forcibly Transferring Children of a Protected Group to Another Group

The forcible transfer of children of a protected group to another group is punishable under sub-paragraph (e) of Article II of the Genocide Convention as constituting a "biological genocide",[133] although the drafters of the Genocide Convention at first envisioned this underlying crime as part of cultural genocide, a notion that the drafters explicitly excluded from the Convention.[134] The International Law Commission explained the criminalisation of such conduct by stating that "[t]he forcible transfer of children would have particularly serious consequences for the future viability of a group as such".[135] Indeed, when the children, who bear the responsibility to grow and carry on the group's culture, language and traditions, are transferred from their group to another, they are unable to carry out this preservation role, and the group is bound to face extinction.

The text of the provision suggests that, like sub-paragraphs (a) and (b) but unlike sub-paragraph (d), a proof of the actual transfer is required as a material element of the crime. However, a Trial Chamber of the ICTR found that this paragraph goes beyond the forcible physical transfer. Indeed, "as in the case of measures intended to prevent births, the objective [of this paragraph] is […] also to sanction acts of threats or trauma which would lead to the forcible transfer of children from one group to another".[136] Such interpretation was adopted and further clarified in the ICC Elements of Crimes, which states that the term "forcibly" is not restricted to physical force, but may include the threat of force or coercion, such as that caused by fear of violence, duress, detention, psychological oppression or abuse of power, against such person or persons or another person, or by taking advantage of a coercive environment.[137] The essential element is, therefore, that the transfer be involuntary in nature, where the relevant persons have no real choice.[138]

---

[133] 1996 ILC Report, p. 46, para 4.

[134] Jessberger 2009, p. 102–103; Schabas 2009, pp. 201–202. Kreß describes this crime as "situated at the border line with so-called cultural genocide". Kreß 2006, p. 484.

[135] 1996 ILC Report, p. 46, para 17.

[136] *Akayesu Trial Judgement*, para 509. See also *Musema Trial Judgement*, para 159; *Rutaganda Trial Judgement*, para 54; *Kayishema & Ruzindana Trial Judgement*, para 118.

[137] ICC Elements of Crimes, Article 6(e), footnote 5.

[138] *See, e.g., Blagojević & Jokić Trial Judgement*, para 617. 'The evidence establishes that the Bosnian Muslim refugees in Potocari did not have a genuine choice of whether to remain in or leave the Srebrenica enclave. This lack of a genuine choice was a result of the actions and behaviour of the officers and soldiers of the VRS towards the refugees. In particular the Trial Chamber observes the following evidence testimony:

– the widespread knowledge among the Bosnian Muslim refugees of serious crimes committed by members of the Bosnian Serb forces in Potocari,

– the organised, inhumane and frequently aggressive process of separating out and removing the male members of the population,

– the evidence regarding the conditions in Potocari during the nights of 11 and, in particular, 12 July,

Unlike deportation, the crime of forcible transfer does not require the displacement of children across the national border.[139] The displacement within the national territory suffices.[140] A controversial issue that divides the legal community is the minimum duration of the transfer as the Genocide Convention is silent as to the specific minimum period during which the children are transferred from one group to another. Some authors advocate against the permanency requirement on the basis that, for example, "the word 'transfer' marks a temporary activity rather than a lasting consequence" and that "doubts as to whether a short-term abduction of children could constitute a suitable means to destroy the group, in whole or in part, can be adequately dealt with on the level of genocidal intent".[141] Others assert that the transfer must be permanent and done with the intent to destroy the targeted group.[142] They explain that the group's social as well as biological existence are threatened when children are alienated from their cultural identity and argue that the children involved are unlikely to reproduce within their own group.[143] In this perspective, temporary measures are, by nature, unlikely to destroy the culture, language or tradition of a group if the children are bound to reintegrate into the group sooner or later. It is, however, noteworthy that the crime of forcible transfer, in general, does not encompass provisional measures, such as a temporary evacuation.[144]

– that many VRS soldiers were cursing at the Bosnian Muslim refugees, saying that they would be slaughtered';

Krnojelac Trial Judgement, paras 233, 475. 'The Trial Chamber finds that living conditions in the KP Dom made the non-Serb detainees subject to a coercive prison regime which was such that they were not in a position to exercise genuine choice. [...] Deportation is illegal only where it is forced. 'Forced' is not to be interpreted in a restrictive manner, such as being limited to physical force. It may include the threat of force or coercion, such as that caused by fear of violence, duress, detention, psychological oppression or abuse of power against such person or persons or another person, or by taking advantage of a coercive environment. The essential element is that the transfer be involuntary in nature, where the relevant persons had no real choice'; *Blagojević & Jokić Trial Judgement*, para 67, 'forcible transfer of the women, children and elderly is a manifestation of the specific intent to rid the Srebrenica enclave of its Bosnian Muslim population. The manner in which the transfer was carried out – through force and coercion, by not registering those who were transferred, by burning the houses of some of the people, sending the clear message that they had nothing to return to'.

[139] *Krstić Trial Judgement*, para 521; *Krnojelac Trial Judgement*, para 476.

[140] *Krstić Trial Judgement*, para 521. 'Both deportation and forcible transfer relate to the involuntary and unlawful evacuation of individuals from the territory in which they reside. Yet, the two are not synonymous in customary international law. Deportation presumes transfer beyond State borders, whereas forcible transfer relates to displacements within a State'; *Krnojelac Trial Judgement*, para 476 'The Trial Chamber considers it to be well established that forcible displacements of people within national boundaries are covered by the concept of forcible transfer'.

[141] Berster 2014, para 93.

[142] Jessberger 2009, p. 103; Werle 2005, p. 203.

[143] Werle 2005, p. 203.

[144] See *Prosecutor v. Mladen Naletilić and Vinko Martinović*, Trial Chamber, Judgement, Case No. IT-98-34-T, 31 March 2003, footnote 1362. 'The Commentary to the Geneva Convention IV holds "[unlike] deportation and forcible transfer, evacuation is a provisional measure", p. 280. The Chamber sees this as indicative of that deportation and forcible transfer are not by their nature provisional, which implies an intent that the transferred persons should not return'.

The victim of the crime must be a child. While the Genocide Convention does not define the term "children", the definition provided in the authoritative UN Convention on the Rights of the Child is most instructive: "children" are persons not having attained eighteen years of age, unless specified otherwise. This approach is endorsed in the text of the ICC Elements of Crimes, which explicitly states that children for the purposes of the crime of genocide are below eighteen years of age.[145] Additionally, the transfer of adults does not fall within this definition. However, such conduct may be punished under Article II(2)(c) of the Genocide Convention, or as a crime against humanity or a war crime.[146]

46.5 Conclusion

Raphaël Lemkin, who coined the word genocide, noted that he became interested in genocide, "because it happened so many times". One might recall the famous declaration of Zarathustra, Friedrich Nietzsche's prophet, that "man is the cruellest animal". However, as Lemkin pointed out, "only man has law. Law must be built".

As a consequence of the several horrendous massacres that mark the history of mankind, the crime of genocide has historically been given, early on within the scope of international law, high attention by the international community in comparison to other international crimes. The crime of genocide is not a mere act of cruelty, but a "denial of the right of existence of entire human groups, as homicide is the denial of the right to live of individual human beings, such denial of the right to existence shocks the conscience of mankind and results in great losses to humanity, and which is contrary to moral law".[147] What makes the crimes of genocide "the crime of crimes" is that it is committed with the intent to destroy a group. These specific features distinguish it from other international crimes and place it comparatively on another level of seriousness.

In this regard, the UN General Assembly, in its Resolution 96(1), "*[a]ffirm[ed]* that genocide is a crime under international law which the civilised world condemns, and for the commission of which principals and accomplices - whether private individuals, public officials or statesmen, and whether the crime is committed on religious, racial, political or any other grounds - are punishable; *[i]nvit[ed]* the Member States to enact the necessary legislation for the prevention and punishment of this crime". The awareness of the international community regarding the seriousness of this crime is further emphasised by the fact that following the Resolution, the prohibition of genocide is now a peremptory norm applying to all states and the community of states as a whole.

In an attempt to grasp the atrocity of the crime of genocide and avoid the dilution of seriousness attached to it by a lax application and an overuse of the term, it was

---

[145] ICC Elements of Crimes, Article 6(e)(5).

[146] 1996 ILC Report, p. 46, para 17.

[147] General Assembly of the United National, Resolution 96(1).

granted a narrow definition regarding both the elements of *actus reus* and the *mens rea* through Article II of the Genocide Convention. While the definition provided by the Convention, albeit the result of long debates, is not without unresolved questions and issues, the jurisprudence of the national, and more notably, the international(ised) Tribunals have identified and clarified the elements of the definition.

References

Ambos K (2009) What Does 'Intent to Destroy' in Genocide Mean? International Review of the Red Cross, Vol. 91, No. 876

Ambos K (2014) Treatise on International Criminal Law, Volume II: The Crimes and Sentencing. Oxford, Oxford University Press

Babeuf G (2008) La Guerre de Vendée et le système de dépopulation. Cerf Edition

Bassiouni C (1994) The Commission of Experts Established Pursuant to Security Council Resolution 780: Investigating Violations of International Humanitarian Law in the Former Yugoslavia. Criminal Law Forum 5:279–340

Berster L (2014) Article II. In: Tams CJ et al (eds) Convention on the Prevention and Punishment of the Crime of Genocide: A Commentary. Beck/Hart, London, pp. 79–156

Boot M (2002) Genocide, Crimes Against Humanity and War Crimes: Nullum Crimen Sine Lege and the Subject Matter Jurisdiction of the International Criminal Court. Intersentia nv

Cambon J (1795) Pièces originales du procès de Fouquier-Tinville et de ses complices. Imprimerie de Hacquart, Paris

Cassese A (2003) International Criminal Law. Oxford University Press

Cassese A (2013) International Criminal Law, 3rd edn. Oxford University Press

Cryer R, Friman H, Robinson D, Wilmshurst E (2018) An Introduction to International Criminal Law and Procedure. Cambridge University Press

Evans D (2018) International Law. Oxford University Press

Fronza E (2000) Genocide in the Rome Statute. In: Lattanzi F, Schabas W (eds) Essays on the Rome Statute of the International Criminal Court, Vol I. Il Sirente, Ripa Fagnano Alto, pp. 105–137

Greenwalt A (1999) Rethinking Genocidal Intent: The Case for a Knowledge-Based Interpretation. Columbia Law Review 99:2259–2294

Jessberger F (2009) The Definition and The Elements of the Crime of Genocide. In: Gaeta P (ed) Genocide Convention: A Commentary. Oxford University Press, pp. 87–111

Kreß C (2005) The Darfur Report and Genocidal Intent. Journal of International Criminal Justice 3:562–578

Kreß C (2006) The Crime of Genocide under International Law. International Criminal Law Review 6:461–502

Lemkin R (1944) Axis Rule in Occupied Europe: Laws of Occupation—Analysis of Government—Proposals for Redress. Carnegie Endowment for International Peace, Washington D.C.

Oosterveld V, Garraway C (2001) Elements of Genocide. In: Lee R S K, Friman H (eds) The International Criminal Court: Elements of Crimes and Rules of Procedure and Evidence. Transnational Publishers, Ardsley, NY

Park R (2010) Proving Genocidal Intent: International Precedent and ECCC Case 002. Rutgers Law Review 63:130–191

Quigley J (2006) The Genocide Convention: An International Law Analysis. Routledge, London/New York

Schabas W (2000) Genocide in International Law: The Crime of Crimes. Cambridge University Press

Schabas W (2008) State Policy as an Element of International Crimes. The Journal of Criminal Law and Criminology 98:953–982

Schabas W (2009) Genocide in International Law: The Crime of Crimes, 2nd edn. Cambridge University Press

Schabas W (2018) Genocide in International Law: The Crime of Crimes, 3rd edn. Cambridge University Press

Schabas W (2009) Article 6: Genocide. In: Triffterer O (ed) Commentary on the Rome Statute of the International Criminal Court. Observers' Notes, Article by Article. C.H. Beck/Hart/Nomos, Baden-Baden, pp. 127–143

Triffterer O (ed) (2009) Commentary on the Rome Statute of the International Criminal Court. Observers' Notes, Article by Article. Nomos, Baden-Baden

Vianney-Liaud M (2014) Controversy on the Characterization of the Cambodian Genocide at the Extraordinary Chambers in the Courts of Cambodia. International Crime Database Brief 8

Von Hebel H, Robinson D (1999) Crimes within the Jurisdiction of the Court. In Lee R S K (ed) The International Criminal Court: The Making of the Rome Statute—issues, negotiations, results. Kluwer Law International, The Hague, pp. 79–126

Werle G (2005) Principles of International Criminal Law. T.M.C. Asser Press, The Hague

Olivier Beauvallet is currently an international judge at the Pre-trial Chamber of the Extraordinary Chambers in the Cambodia Courts (ECCC) and at the Appeals Chamber of the Central African Republic Special Criminal Court (SCC). An investigative judge by background, he has also served as Special prosecutor in EULEX and the SITF. He holds a doctorate in law (EHESS Paris), and has authored various books and article on criminal and international criminal law. He participated in various international projects in Europe especially in the Balkans, Africa and Central Asia.

Hyuree Kim is a Legal Consultant and Greffier at the Pre-Trial Chamber and the Supreme Court Chamber, Extraordinary Chambers in the Courts of Cambodia.

Léo Jolivet is a Legal Officer at the Office of the Prosecutor (organised crime, white collar crime and international cooperation division) in Orléans, France and a former. Legal Consultant at the Pre-Trial Chamber, Extraordinary Chambers in the Courts of Cambodia.

The views expressed in this chapter do not reflect the opinion of any institutions the authors are working for or have worked for.

Chapter 47
Crimes Against Humanity

Rustam Atadjanov

Contents

47.1 Introduction	1032
47.2 Historical Development	1034
47.3 Contemporary Definition	1037
47.4 Protective Scope	1039
47.5 Contextual (Material) Elements	1042
47.5.1 International Element of the Crime	1043
47.5.2 Widespread or Systematic Attack	1046
47.5.3 Any Civilian Population	1049
47.5.4 Policy Element	1051
47.6 Individual Acts	1054
47.6.1 Murder	1055
47.6.2 Extermination	1056
47.6.3 Enslavement	1056
47.6.4 Deportation or Forcible Transfer of Population	1057
47.6.5 Imprisonment or Other Severe Deprivations of Liberty	1058
47.6.6 Torture	1059
47.6.7 Sexual Crimes	1060
47.6.8 Persecution	1060
47.6.9 Enforced Disappearance of Persons	1061
47.7 Relationship to Other Crimes Under International Law	1063
47.8 Current Open Issues, Challenges and New Developments	1065
47.9 Conclusion	1068
References	1070

Abstract Crimes against humanity represent one of the so-called "core crimes" or crimes under international law. They constitute mass crimes against a civilian population and may be the most commonly known among the different of types international crimes used for labeling mass atrocities almost every time when there is news that such have occurred. The phenomenon of crimes against humanity continues to sparkle lots of debates both scholarly and practical. The modern definition of crimes against humanity is firmly established in the Rome Statute of the International Criminal Court. Despite this, many important doctrinal and normative issues

---

R. Atadjanov (✉)
School of Law, KIMEP University, Almaty, Kazakhstan

© T.M.C. ASSER PRESS and the authors 2022
S. Sayapin et al. (eds.), *International Conflict and Security Law*,
https://doi.org/10.1007/978-94-6265-515-7_47

(e.g., protective scope, contextual element, policy requirement and civilian population) are actively debated in scholarship and practice. This chapter discusses the key contextual elements of crimes against humanity, as well as the individual criminal acts comprising them but not before briefly describing the historical origins and definitional evolution of crimes against humanity, reviewing their contemporary structure according to the existing treaty definition, and offering a succinct explanation as to what constitutes the truly protected interest of crimes against humanity. The chapter aims at providing the textbook's readership with a brief but comprehensive account of the main legal, substantive and normative aspects related to crimes against humanity including doctrinal challenges and also some new pertinent developments in the law.

Keywords crimes against humanity · Humanity · Humanness · Martens Clause · Laws of humanity · Core crimes · Crimes under international law · International criminal law · Rome Statute

47.1 Introduction

Crimes against humanity, along with genocide, war crimes and the crime of aggression, constitute the so-called core crimes or crimes under international law as understood in contemporary international criminal law. They are mass crimes against civilian population.[1] According to Werle, the most serious crimes against humanity encompass the killing of entire groups of people which is also characteristic of the crime of genocide.[2] However, crimes against humanity are not necessarily directed against a concrete group of people but against a civilian population as a whole and hence they constitute a wider category of crimes than genocide.[3] The prohibited individual acts amounting to crimes against humanity include not only such extreme criminal acts as murder and extermination but also other serious forms: enslavement by way of forced labor, expulsion of people from their native places, torture of political opponents, mass raping of defenseless women, enforced disappearance[4] and so on.

Perhaps crimes against humanity are a type of crimes under international law which are most commonly used for labeling mass atrocities almost every time there is news that those have occurred. This holds true for many regions in the world, from the European continent through Asia to Africa and Latin America.[5] The phrase "crimes against humanity" has acquired enormous resonance in the legal and moral discourse in the post-World War II world.[6] This is fully understandable given the

---

[1] Werle 2011, p. 391.

[2] Ibid.

[3] Ibid. See also further below the discussion in Sect. 47.8.

[4] Ibid.

[5] Atadjanov 2019, p. 4.

[6] Luban 2004, p. 86.

horrific atrocities and vast numbers of victims of the crimes committed by states against their own citizens since WWII. Just to name some: one million in Nigeria were killed in the 1960s, one million fell victim in Bangladesh in the 1970s, at least one million were murdered in Cambodia during the 1970s and 1980s, 800,000 killed in Rwanda back in 1993–1994, 500,000 killed in Liberia and Sierra-Leone, more recently, 3,000,000 in the Democratic Republic of the Congo (DRC) since 2005, and many more.[7] This tragic list is not exhaustive. And it is only during the last several decades that a legal prohibition of crimes against humanity at the international level has gradually emerged and has been shaped, with the last twenty years when the crimes' elements in international criminal law started to become established and better clarified.[8]

The establishment of crimes against humanity as a matter of positive law did not take place before 1945 when their first definition was included in the text of the Charter of the International Military Tribunal at Nuremberg. Article 6(c) of the Nuremberg Charter defined crimes against humanity as a constellation of prohibited acts committed against civilian populations.[9] This category of core crimes was added to the Charter in order to guarantee that many of the Nazis' most characteristic acts would not go unpunished, in particular, to include acts committed by Germans against other Germans which did not fall under the category of war crimes. Ever since this codification was made, the phenomenon of crimes against humanity continues to sparkle lots of debates scholarly and practical alike. Their historical development, practical application, material and mental elements, their protective scope, role in (international) law, pertinent jurisdiction (−s) and many other aspects have been a subject of both general and detailed analysis.

While the modern definition of crimes against humanity is firmly elaborated in the Rome Statute of the International Criminal Court,[10] some of their abovementioned aspects can hardly be considered as clear-cut or fully established and clarified in law and practice. A very good example is the question of protected interests. Humanity as a protected legal interest of crimes against humanity has never been defined from a positive legal perspective. No explicit and accepted definition of the word "humanity" currently exists in international legal documents or in international or domestic case-law. It appears that since the beginning of the twentieth century, its precise intrinsic meaning has been left to an intuitive understanding which is to a large extent conditioned by political, social, cultural, or possibly some other important factors.[11]

---

[7] Bassiouni 2011, p. 83.

[8] Atadjanov 2019, p. 4.

[9] Agreement for the Prosecution and Punishment of the Major War Criminals of the European Axis, Annex, 59 Stat. 1544, adopted 8 August 1945, 82 U.N.T.S. 279 (entered into force 8 August 1945, Article 6(c).

[10] Even so, it is far from being utmostly clear or consistent: Ambos, for example, reasons that the definition of crimes against humanity in modern instruments of ICL has been vague and inconsistent in many respects. See Ambos 2014, p. 47.

[11] Atadjanov 2019, p. 6.

This and other important doctrinal and normative issues such as, e.g., the question of context as a "qualifier" of an inhumane act as a crime against humanity, the controversial issue of the policy requirement as defined in the Rome Statute, the exact connotation of "civilian population", etc.[12] will be discussed in this chapter. Before proceeding to that discussion, the chapter briefly describes the historical origins and definitional evolution of crimes against humanity, reviews the contemporary structure of the crimes according to their modern definition in the Rome Statute, and offers the authors' own view as to what constitutes their valid protected legal interest. Moreover, it analyzes the key contextual elements of the crimes, along with their *mens rea*, prior to looking at each of the individual acts comprising crimes against humanity. The relevant and the most authoritative case-law on the subject is cited. Similarities and differences between crimes against humanity and other core crimes are also succinctly presented.

The chapter is thus aimed at providing the textbook's readership with a brief—as the format requirements allow—but hopefully comprehensive account of the main legal aspects related to crimes against humanity, their historical and substantive elements, normative and doctrinal challenges faced when dealing with crimes against humanity as well as some new relevant developments in the law. To several of those challenges and problematic issues the chapter will attempt to provide its own responses or possible solutions and/or explanations thereto.

47.2 Historical Development

The genesis for term "crimes against humanity" is derived from the so-called "laws of humanity" included by eminent international law expert Fyodor Martens into his famous "Martens Clause", a general provision incorporated into the Preambles of the Second Hague Convention of 1899 and the Fourth Hague Convention of 1907 on the Laws and Customs of War on Land.[13] The clause declares that in cases not otherwise covered in the convention(-s) the inhabitants and belligerents remain under the protection and the rule of the principles of the law of nations, as they result from the usages established among civilized peoples, from the *laws of humanity*, and the dictates of the public conscience.[14] However, the Martens Clause whose sphere of application was limited to the time of armed conflict did not yet indicate the possibility of the criminalization of violations against such laws of humanity.[15]

---

[12] See DeGuzman 2011, pp. 130–134.

[13] Atadjanov 2019, p. 4.

[14] Convention (IV) Respecting the Laws and Customs of War on Land (Hague IV), opened for signature 18 October 1907, entered into force 26 January 2010, in Schindler and Toman 1996, pp. 69–93; see also for reference Roberts and Guelff 2000; Atadjanov 2019, pp. 4–5; DeGuzman 2011, p. 121.

[15] Werle 2011, p. 392. Still, via the Martens Clause, it may well be said that crimes against humanity have important and deep roots in humanitarian law (see Chap. 22 by Sayapin for the textbook review of international humanitarian law). DeGuzman 2011, p. 121; Atadjanov 2019, pp. 28, 73 and 77.

The earliest reference to "crimes against humanity" as a *legal concept* is found in the Joint Declaration by France, Great Britain and Russia in 1915, in response to the mass killings of Armenians by the Ottoman Empire. It denounced "crimes against humanity and civilization" and warned perpetrators of personal responsibility.[16] Thus, the birth of the concept itself came as a result of tragic events characterizing a policy of oppression of a government against its own citizens and not its enemy combatants. These events can be collectively termed as the "Armenian massacres"; they are also known and often regarded as the "Armenian Genocide".[17]

However, there was no practical follow up to the Declaration; nothing came out of this initiative at the time. The Declaration proved to be merely exhortative. Although the three Allies recognized explicitly the individual responsibility of the heads of state, in this case the Ottoman Empire, they did not really envisage the actual punishment of the culprits. This condemnation of the Turkish government's actions turned out to be purely political in nature.[18]

A more structured and serious effort to prosecute those who were responsible for the atrocities against Armenians was undertaken with the establishment of the so-called "Commission of Fifteen", i.e., the Commission on the Responsibility of the Authors of the War and On Enforcement of Penalties. It was set up in January 1919 by the Paris Preliminary Peace Conference, for the purpose of inquiring into the responsibilities relating to the First World War.[19] Its Final Report went beyond its strict assigned tasks in considering the violations committed during the war, deciding instead to apply a more inclusive approach. Thus, the majority of the Commission of Fifteen came to the conclusion that the World War I was conducted by Germany, Turkey and Bulgaria using barbarous or illegitimate methods in breach of the established laws and customs of war as well as the *elementary laws of humanity*. The document further determined that "all persons belonging to the enemy countries … who have been guilty of offences against the laws and customs of war or the *laws of humanity* are liable to criminal prosecution." [emphasis added].[20]

Regrettably, just as it was the case before with the Joint Declaration, the practical implementation of the Report's conclusions on the violations of the laws of humanity was again doomed to fail, this time in a much more explicit manner. The reason was the position of the United States (USA) which was joined by the Japanese members of the Commission. It was expressed in the Memorandum of Reservations written by Mr. Robert Lansing (1864–1928) and Mr. James Brown Scott who took objection to the use of the term "laws of humanity" by the majority of the Commission.[21] The American members objected to the invocation of and references to the "laws and principles of humanity" in the Final Report on the grounds that as opposed

---

[16] United Nations War Crimes Commission 1948, p. 35; Atadjanov 2019, pp. 4–5.

[17] Atadjanov 2019, p. 77. This occurrence represents the second-most studied case of systematic mass-killings after the Holocaust. Ibid., p. 77, n. 201.

[18] Ibid., p. 78; DeGuzman 2011, p. 122.

[19] Atadjanov 2019, p. 80.

[20] Peace Conference 1920, pp. 115, 117.

[21] Ibid., pp. 127–151; Atadjanov 2019, p. 81; Geras 2011, p. 8–9; DeGuzman 2011, p. 122.

to the laws and customs of war "the laws and principles of humanity" are not "a standard certain" to be found in books of authority and in the practice of nations but they, instead, "vary with the individual" which factor "...should exclude them from consideration in a court of justice, especially one charged with the administration of criminal law."[22]

As a result of this strong difference in the Commission's opinions, the expressions "laws of humanity", "violations of the laws of humanity" and alike were not eventually included in the texts of the subsequent treaties (Treaty of Versailles and Treaty of Lausanne) or, even when included, the treaty would not be ratified and enforced (such as the Treaty of Sèvres).[23]

Whatever the big failures, one should not underestimate the role—historical, legal, and even philosophical, played by the above three important instruments: the Martens Clause, the Joint Declaration of 1915 and the 1919 Report of the Commission of Fifteen, in later developments. For example, considering that at the time there was no formulation to be positively found either in humanitarian law or elsewhere, the Commission's work, all its deficiencies notwithstanding, should be considered a rather bold and progressive development.[24] Furthermore, the influence of the list of acts drawn up in the Final Report would prove to be important in the process of elaborating the legal definitions during the preparatory work of the Nuremberg Charter in the aftermath of World War II.[25] Finally, one significant legal aspect should not be disregarded, either: considering these three sources, it may fairly be argued that crimes against humanity had already been enshrined in customary international law even before the adoption of the Nuremberg Charter in 1945.[26]

The first true international legal codification of crimes against humanity came with the adoption of the Charter of the Nuremberg International Military Tribunal, or Nuremberg Charter. The Tribunal's Charter was annexed to it.[27] It defined crimes against humanity as

> murder, extermination, enslavement, deportation, and other inhumane acts committed against any civilian population, before or during the war; or persecutions on political, racial or religious grounds in execution of or in connection with any crime within the jurisdiction of the Tribunal, whether or not in violation of the domestic law of the country where perpetrated.[28]

Strikingly enough, so far no precise record exists of how the term "crimes against humanity" was chosen by the drafters of the Nuremberg Charter. It is known that the term was selected by the Chief US Prosecutor at IMT, Robert Jackson who consulted,

---

[22] Peace Conference 1920, p. 134; Atadjanov 2019, pp. 81–82.

[23] Atadjanov 2019, p. 82.

[24] Ibid., p. 83.

[25] Ibid.

[26] Ambos 2014, p. 47.

[27] Agreement for the Prosecution and Punishment of the Major War Criminals of the European Axis, Annex, 59 Stat. 1544, adopted 8 August 1945, 82 U.N.T.S. 279 (entered into force 8 August 1945).

[28] Ibid., Article 6(c).

at least over that matter, with the great international law scholar Hersch Lauterpacht. But their deliberations and discussions were unfortunately left unrecorded.[29]

A more or less similar definition of crimes against humanity was included at the time into the Charter of the International Military Tribunal for the Far East (IMTFE Charter)[30] and the Allied Control Council Law No.10 (CCL).[31] Few national cases involving this category of crimes were considered as well as few international instruments dealing with acts pertaining to crimes against humanity were adopted in the period between the CCL and the adoption of the Statute of the International Criminal Tribunal for the Former Yugoslavia (ICTY) in 1993.[32] Some notable domestic cases include the trials of *Eichmann* (Israel), *Barbie* (France) and *Finta* (Canada).[33] The latest definitions of these crimes were included into the Statute of the International Criminal Tribunal for Rwanda (ICTR)[34] and the Rome Statute of the International Criminal Court (ICC).[35] Currently, there is no specific international treaty on crimes against humanity either, unlike the situation with, for example, the crime of genocide. Efforts presently are being undertaken on the side of the legal academic community to promote the adoption of such an international legal instrument.[36]

47.3 Contemporary Definition

Not much consideration was given to the principal issue of whether or not to include a provision on crimes against humanity into the Rome Statute of the ICC during the discussions at the UN Diplomatic Conference held in Rome in 1998. From the very beginning it appears that the State delegations have had no difficulty in agreeing in general that crimes against humanity were crimes serious enough to warrant their inclusion in the Court's Statute.[37]

It was much more challenging to reach a common compromise on the precise definition of these crimes. The various relevant precedents existing before the Rome Conference—the corresponding provisions of the Nuremberg and Tokyo Charters, the Allied CCL, the Statutes of the ICTY and ICTR as well as the draft projects worked out by the United Nations International Law Commission, were viewed as

---

[29] Atadjanov 2019, p. 5.

[30] Cryer and Boister 2008, pp. 7 et seq.

[31] Control Council Law No. 10, Article 6(c), full text available at https://www.legal-tools.org/doc/ffda62/pdf/, accessed 5 May 2020; Ferencz 1980, p. 48; Atadjanov 2019, p. 5.

[32] United Nations Security Council 1993, Annex to the Secretary General's Report, Article 5; Atadjanov 2019, pp. 5–6.

[33] Werle and Jessberger 2014, pp. 13–14, 130–134, paras 43, 348–353.

[34] United Nations Security Council 1994, Annex, p. 4, Article 3; Atadjanov 2019, p. 6.

[35] Rome Statute of the International Criminal Court, opened for signature 17 July 1998, 2187 UNTS 90 (entered into force 1 July 2002) (Rome Statute), Article 7.

[36] See Sadat 2011.

[37] Atadjanov 2019, pp. 121–122.

vague and contradictory. The Conference delegates insisted on a more exact and detailed definition, as the Court to be established would have to be vested with prospective jurisdiction, unlike the previous tribunals which had dealt with specific situations in the past.[38]

The definition finally agreed upon was formulated in what is now Article 7 of the Rome Statute:

> ... For the purpose of this Statute, "crime against humanity" means any of the following acts when committed as part of a widespread or systematic attack directed against any civilian population, with knowledge of the attack:
>
> (a) Murder;
>
> (b) Extermination;
>
> (c) Enslavement;
>
> (d) Deportation or forcible transfer of population;
>
> (e) Imprisonment or other severe deprivation of physical liberty in violation of fundamental rules of international law;
>
> (f) Torture;
>
> (g) Rape, sexual slavery, enforced prostitution, forced pregnancy, enforced sterilization, or any other form of sexual violence of comparable gravity;
>
> (h) Persecution against any identifiable group or collectivity on political, racial, national, ethnic, cultural, religious, gender as defined in para 3, or other grounds that are universally recognized as impermissible under international law, in connection with any act referred to in this paragraph or any crime within the jurisdiction of the Court;
>
> (i) Enforced disappearance of persons;
>
> (j) The crime of apartheid;
>
> (k) Other inhumane acts of a similar character intentionally causing great suffering, or serious injury to body or to mental or physical health. ..."[39]

Furthermore, in its paras 2 and 3 the article contains clarifications for different terms and elements of the crimes, and for the individual underlying acts constituting these crimes ("attack directed against any civilian population", "extermination", "enslavement", "deportation", "torture", and so on).[40] Perhaps, compared to other definitions of crimes against humanity in various legal instruments, either before or after the adoption of the Rome Statute, Article 7 represents the most restrictive one. Even a brief comparison between the notions of crimes against humanity laid down in customary international law and Article 7 demonstrates that it is mostly based on the former, also drawing heavily from the ICTY's case-law.[41]

According to Ambos, Article 7 of the Rome Statute represents both a codification and a progressive development of international law within the meaning of the United

---

[38] Ibid., p. 122; Lee 1999, pp. 90–91; see also in general Bassiouni 2005.

[39] Rome Statute, above n. 35, Article 7(1).

[40] Atadjanov 2019, pp. 122–123; for a detailed discussion of those and other elements, see also Schabas 2010, pp. 137–187; Boot 2002, pp. 468–532; Cassese 2002, pp. 373–377; Triffterer 2008, p. 117.

[41] Atadjanov 2019, p. 123.

Nations Charter[42] because it unites the distinct legal features which may be thought of as the "common law of crimes against humanity".[43] The article is also important because it is so far the only definition agreed upon and adopted by a relevant number of States; moreover, when States take measures to implement international criminal law (hence, ICL) in their domestic legislations dealing with crimes against humanity (even if those are not so numerous yet) they often look to Article 7 for guidance; it therefore already carries a significant authority.[44]

The structure of the crimes may be described in a rather general and simplistic way as follows. The material elements of crimes against humanity involve the commission of one of the acts which are quite meticulously described in Article 7(1) of the Rome Statute.[45] These individual underlying acts become crimes against humanity when they are committed within the framework of a widespread or systematic attack on any civilian persons.[46] The attack against a civilian population constitutes a contextual element of the crime. The mental element, or *mens rea*, involves an intentional and knowledgeable attitude, in accordance with Article 30 of the Rome Statute, towards the material elements of the crime, including the contextual element.[47]

Thus, the material part, or *actus reus* of the crime includes individual acts and, in a wider sense, the contextual element[48] while the mental part, or *mens rea* encompasses intent and knowledge *as per* the statutory law of the ICC. All these elements will be subsequently analyzed in Sects. 47.5, 47.6 and 47.7. Before doing so, another important element needs to be discussed which is the question of the protected interest or interests of the crime.

47.4 Protective Scope

The question of the exact protected legal interest(s) of crimes against humanity represents one of the most open and unresolved issues in ICL, first of all, on a normative plane. There are numerous normative visions and conceptual descriptions of crimes

---

[42] Ambos 2014, p. 49; Charter of the United Nations, opened for signature 26 June 1945, 1 U.N.T.S. XVI (entered into force 24 October 1945), Article 13.

[43] Ambos 2014, p. 49.

[44] Atadjanov 2019, p. 123; DeGuzman 2011, p. 126.

[45] Werle 2011, p. 396.

[46] Ibid.

[47] Ibid., p. 397; "intent and knowledge" as defined in the Rome Statute, above n. 35, Article 30.

[48] When it concerns the discussion of crimes against humanity, it has become an accepted format of explanation in the modern scholarship to present or highlight the context as a specific and special element of the crime "in its own right". This is due to the key role it plays in the qualification process for the material individual acts the commission of which must be accompanied by widespread or systematic nature of the attack against civilian population, in order to amount to a crime against humanity.

against humanity which compete for recognition in law, jurisprudence and scholarship.[49] The definitions and interpretations of the concept of crimes against humanity varied, to different degrees, from one project to another since their first codification in the Nuremberg Charter.[50] According to DeGuzman, almost every definition used by the various jurisdictions differed in some important aspects from the others.[51] Many questions still remain open as a result of this multiplicity of definitions and legal diversity; it reveals lack of universal consensus on the fundamental normative basis for crimes against humanity[52]—even if there is a modern and generally accepted definition of this type of crimes in the Rome Statute as discussed above.

This lack of consensus and resulting multiplicity of theoretical and normative descriptions is partly attributed to the absence of a comprehensive unified vision on the precise protected interest of crimes against humanity. While this was not the case with the generally used and common term of "humanity" which has several notions embedded under the one umbrella term ("mankind", "humaneness", "human nature"), no explicit and accepted definition of the word "humanity" currently exists in international legal documents or in international/domestic jurisprudence. It appears that since the beginning of the twentieth century, its precise intrinsic meaning has been left to an intuitive understanding in a big measure conditioned by political, social, cultural, or possibly some other important factors.[53]

There are presently many theories of crimes against humanity that discuss to varying degrees the nature of these crimes' protected interest (aside from those that consider the nature and manner of the assault, or the material elements).[54] Some argue that the offence's defining feature is the value that they injure, namely humaneness as a basic universal value.[55] Some focus on human diversity without which the very words "humanity" or "mankind" would lose their meaning.[56] Others, such as the theory proposed by May, advance that group-based harm violates a strong interest of the international community and thus harms humanity, or mankind itself (international harm principle).[57] One popular theoretical construction offered by Luban maintains that crimes against humanity attack one particular aspect of a human being namely his/her character as a political animal.[58]

---

[49] DeGuzman 2011, p. 128. Some of those descriptions are centered around the view on crimes against humanity as a threat to international peace and security; others are focused on their gravity and the negative effect they have on the "conscience of humanity" as mankind. Yet others include such a characteristic feature of these crimes as their group-based harm. Ibid., pp. 127–130.

[50] Atadjanov 2019, p. 125. The competing normative visions of crimes against humanity are well but not too inclusively described in deGuzman 2011, pp. 127–130.

[51] DeGuzman 2011, p. 127.

[52] Ibid.; Atadjanov 2019, p. 125.

[53] Atadjanov 2019, p. 6.

[54] Ibid., p. 9.

[55] Ibid., pp. 149–151.

[56] Ibid., pp. 146–151.

[57] Ibid., p. 10; May 2005, pp. 80–95.

[58] Atadjanov 2019, p. 10; Luban 2004, pp. 111–114.

The most significant questions with respect to the protective scope of crimes against humanity would be the following ones. The element of humanity is a fundamental concept. It is so both for the word's general (or non-legal) meanings as understood by mankind and for its more specific implications for crimes against humanity as a legal category. But then, what exactly is this "humanity" that is attacked by the acts that constitute the crimes in question? Is it "mankind", or "human dignity", or "human status", or "humaneness"? Furthermore, does "civilian population" as it figures in the definition of the crime represent "humanity" in its fullest meaning? If "humanity" comes up as a sort of blurred abstract entity and is so unclear, then what exactly makes "humanity" useful and justified within the context of the term "crimes against humanity"? The fundamental underlying question would be: what is it about the concept of humanity that puts all those divergent material acts (murder, extermination, enslavement, and others) under the one heading of "crimes against humanity"?[59]

This chapter's author has proposed his own theory explaining the protective scope of crimes against humanity based on the fundamental nature of the concept of humanity. Since the "humanity" attacked by crimes against humanity is a comprehensive concept, a theory describing such crimes must, by logical extrapolation, be comprehensive, too. In other words, crimes against humanity are harmful to human beings' most fundamental interests. Therefore, to describe them the umbrella concept encompassing all those interests must be fundamental and comprehensive. Such an umbrella concept avails itself of the form of "humanity" understood as humanness. It allows to reflect and explain all the elements characteristic of these crimes' protective scope, and it also allows to unite all the doctrinal components in the authoritative theoretical efforts undertaken before by different scholars and jurists to describe crimes against humanity.[60]

Following this logic, the theory of humanness may be presented as follows. The protected legal interest of crimes against humanity is humanity as humanness. Humanness is a human status, human condition, or quality of being human; in other words, it is what makes us human. Crimes against humanity are inhuman acts which attack each and every element of humanity, those elements being freedom, human dignity, civilized attitude, humanness and reason. The commission of these acts eventually aims at rendering their victims "inhuman", in the sense of depriving them of that very status.[61] All parts of this status come under attack, that is:

(1) the victims' individual freedom is denied;
(2) they are deprived of their human dignity;
(3) their civilized attitude is negated removing the link between the victims and mankind;
(4) their sentiment of active good will, or humaneness, ceases to exist by the commission of inhumane acts, and

---

[59] Atadjanov 2019, pp. 10–11.
[60] Ibid., p. 312.
[61] Ibid., p. 187.

(5) the victims' human nature in the form of reason is denied as well, since those acts do not allow them to possess the status of rational creatures anymore.[62]

From this conceptual definition it becomes clear what exact interests are under threat when these crimes under international law are committed. While some crimes—either international or domestic, may be said to be encroaching upon one or more of these elements, this theory maintains that crimes against humanity breach all of them. This breach is inflicted upon the whole humanity—as humanness, or human condition. That is why they are crimes against, precisely, humanity as such.[63] Furthermore, the current interpretation of the "civilian population" element of crimes against humanity suggests that there is no pressing need to rename this group of core crimes as "crimes against a civilian population" or rephrase it otherwise. "Crimes against humanity" already serves the purpose of denoting some of the worst and most serious criminal offences in international law while also carrying with it a strong emotional resonance.[64]

47.5 Contextual (Material) Elements

According to the meaning of Article 7(1) of the Rome Statute, crimes against humanity include only those crimes which are defined as "committed as part of a widespread or systematic attack directed against any civilian population". This contextual element represents a necessary requirement in order for a crime to be qualified as a crime against humanity. It is the so-called *chapeau* element of the crime; it is what makes the crime truly international by distinguishing it from domestic crimes such as murder, torture, rape, enslavement and so on.[65] Hence it may be called an international element of the crime.[66] The following subsections contain an analysis of the material elements of the context: widespread or systematic attack, any civilian population, and element of policy. It also briefly looks at an aspect no longer required in order to properly qualify these crimes but which figures oftentimes in many descriptions and explanations of crimes against humanity in legal and

---

[62] Ibid.

[63] Ibid.

[64] Atadjanov 2019, pp. 312–313. The issue of how the five constituting elements of humanness relate to the material part of the crime, i.e., the underlying individual acts, is analysed in Ibid., pp. 190–204.

[65] Ibid., p. 204.

[66] Ambos 2014, p. 55. With respect to the mental element of crimes against humanity, or *mens rea*: according to Werle and Jessberger, the perpetrator must be aware that a widespread or systematic attack against a civilian population is taking place and that her or his action is part of this attack; discriminatory motives are not required except for the individual act of persecution. See Werle and Jessberger 2014, pp. 346–347, paras 913–915.

scholarly sources.[67] But first, some general remarks are offered in order to explain the rationale behind the contextual element as an interpretative tool.

47.5.1 International Element of the Crime

As noted above, the contextual element may be dubbed "international" since its function is to distinguish domestic crimes from crimes under international law; in other words, "ordinary" from "extraordinary".[68] This is key in the process of qualification of crimes under international law since the contextual element renders a certain criminal conduct a matter of international concern[69] and hence allows for a proper legal interpretation of the criminal conduct concerned. According to Ambos, the precise nature of such international concern, or, in other words, the rationale for why these crimes are considered sufficiently significant to be dealt with at the international level—as opposed to domestic legal (i.e. judicial) systems–, would help greatly in the interpretation of crimes against humanity[70] which justifies a succinct consideration of this nature here.

One can distinguish two main reasons for why the international community[71] can treat a crime as a matter of international law.[72] The first one is the international character of a crime because it cannot be prosecuted effectively at a domestic level while States have a common interest in doing so (i.e., in it being prosecuted).[73] Two good examples of such crimes would be piracy and damaging submarine telegraph cables.[74] The second reason—and this needs to be dealt with in more detail here, is the extreme gravity or seriousness of certain criminal acts which are often accompanied by an inability or unwillingness of the domestic criminal systems concerned to (effectively and properly) prosecute[75] for the commission of such crimes. Accordingly, the particularly serious violations of human rights—individual and collective—by way of intentional action or inaction of state actors have been a grave concern of international law since the concept of human rights began developing at the end of the nineteenth century and, with the adoption of the United Nations Charter, has gained

---

[67] Cryer et al. 2010, pp. 234–235; Ambos 2014, pp. 50–55, 57; Werle 2011, p. 395; DeGuzman 2011, pp. 122–123.

[68] Ambos 2014, p. 55.

[69] Ibid.

[70] Ibid.

[71] "International community" could usefully be defined as "a global group of States bound together by common values". There are certainly risks inherent in describing this phenomenon since it has often been criticized as mainly a West-oriented body promoting primarily the national interests of politically powerful States. Hence the attempt of a universalist description here. Atadjanov 2019, p. 270.

[72] Ambos 2014, p. 55.

[73] Ibid.

[74] Ibid., pp. 55–56.

[75] Ibid., p. 56.

the status of "hard law".[76] Therefore, argues Ambos, it was a logical consequence to criminalize the worst violations of human rights coinciding with the gravest crimes that mankind knows.[77]

Certainly, the role of the common interest of States as constituent members of the international community must be recognized. But the protective scope of the crimes plays a critical part here, too. What flows out of the theory of humaneness very briefly introduced above in Sect. 47.4 is also the following. There is a crucial value element which is at play here and it—together with the serious nature of the attack, needs to be taken into account in the argumentation above. It is crucial because the very members of international community, i.e., States, are bound together by common values, values which they need to protect in order to survive. To understand the role of the value element, one can look at the doctrine of so-called *global social contract*.[78]

According to this doctrine, by entering into agreements (i.e., treaties), the individual members of the international community (i.e., States) create a general collective will in pursuit of common interests and values. Those represent the values protected under international law and include international peace, security, and well-being, fundamental human rights, equality and others. These values are worthy of being defended by a universal and inter-culturally recognized criminal law;[79] otherwise the very survival of the current system of States (i.e. the international community) comes under threat. Hence, the community members have a real common interest in protecting these values. As this community is held (or is to be held) together by common values, the nature of such values acquires a particular significance for determining why crimes against them are to be judged international.

Indeed, the difference between this view and that of some other scholars (such as Ambos[80]) lies in the nature of those values. If they put forward the realization and protection of human rights and human dignity as the central value to be ensured by international criminal law, the theory of humanness would propose *humanity* as the fundamental concept denoting the very human status of individuals. In that connotation, it serves as a foundational concept for all the human rights since it incorporates in itself the crucial elements needed for the protection and realization of the rights: freedom, dignity and reason. Because of that intrinsic or inherent nature of humanity, the universal or international normative order based on common values is possible without all the features typical of national communities: sovereign, governmental system, political elements, legislator, enforcement mechanisms and so on.[81]

Such a value-based approach links humanity to the idea of a normative international order. It constitutes a value judgement that expresses a *legal* necessity to

---

[76] Ibid.

[77] Ibid.

[78] For a helpful explanation of the theory of global social contract, see Neidleman 2012.

[79] Atadjanov 2019, p. 271.

[80] See in general Ambos 2013.

[81] Atadjanov 2019, pp. 270–271.

punish criminal conduct at the macro level, in order to protect the fundamental legal interest (humanness). At the same time, it avoids the possible accusation of being too idealistic or utopian: it does not call into picture a radical cosmopolitanism, trying to avoid, instead, the loud rhetoric of world citizenship; thus the existing system of the Nation-States still holds.[82] In that normative order, the gravest attacks against common values (in this case, humanness) would best be punished by the criminal law of the international order that is ICL. This is especially so considering the frequent inability or unwillingness of the domestic criminal systems to punish and prosecute for the attacks.

Now, the contextual element means that such serious transgressions against humanness should be committed in a widespread or systematic manner, according to Article 7(1) of the Rome Statute, for a criminal act to be deemed a crime against humanity. This is also part of the issue of the specific gravity of the crimes in question. That the contextual element functions in order to single out random acts of violence—which may be violating some but not all elements of humanness, from the scope of crimes against humanity, is not a speculation of the author but a repeatedly confirmed feature of the crimes' modern conventional *corpus delicti*, supported by authoritative case-law and scholarly literature.[83]

Ambos rightly argues that the gravity of a single crime is increased by the widespread or systematic commission of it because it multiplies the *danger* of the conduct of an individual perpetrator.[84] But there is also an important relationship between the requirement that the acts be carried out as widespread or systematic attacks and the protective scope of crimes against humanity which needs to be considered, too. This relationship consists of the negative effect that the crime (i.e. individual criminal act) has on the protected legal interest if the perpetrator commits it within this context as compared to domestic crimes. Unlike the latter case, the "systematic" and especially "widespread" attack[85] adds qualifiers which *magnify the negative damaging effect* the crime's commission has on the interests protected. That is so because, for example, the "widespread" attack involves the large scale of the attack as well as the number of victims which is often much higher compared to those of "equivalent" domestic crimes.[86] Furthermore, the seriousness of the attacks amounting to crimes against humanity is affirmed by their systematicity which signifies the organized nature of the acts of violence and the

---

[82] Ibid., p. 271.

[83] NMTs, *United States v. Josef Alstoetter*, Judgment, 4 December 1947, Case 3 (Justice Case); ICTY, *Prosecutor v. Tadić*, Judgment, 15 July 1999, IT-94-1-T, paras 646, 648, 653; ICTR, *Prosecutor v. Akayesu*, Judgment, 2 September 1998, ICTR-96-4-T, para 579; Ambos 2014, p. 56.

[84] Ambos 2014, p. 56.

[85] The element of widespread or systematic attack is discussed in the next subsection.

[86] ICTY, *Prosecutor v. Tadić*, Opinion and Judgment, 7 May 1997, IT-94-1-T, para 648; ICTR, *Prosecutor v. Kayishema et al*, Judgment and Sentence, 21 May 1999, ICTR-95-1-T, para 206. No numerical limit exists; thus the issue must be decided based on the individual facts of each case. Cryer et al. 2010, p. 236. See further Atadjanov 2019, p. 205.

improbability of their random occurrence; it may be expressed through patterns of crimes or non-accidental repetition of a similar criminal conduct on a regular basis.[87]

This author has argued elsewhere that because of the presence of the contextual element one can maintain that crimes against humanity entail grave humanitarian consequences.[88] This is not only in the sense of a direct damage to the victims but also in terms of damage to their lawful interests and rights. In other words, the constituent elements of humanness, i.e., freedom, dignity, civilized attitude, humaneness and reason seen separately do not represent *exclusive* protected interests of crimes against humanity. Ordinary crimes which contain similar material acts—murder, rape, torture, enslavement and so on, also attack those values and interests. However, because of the widespread and/or systematic nature of the attack (these elements are considered in the next sub-section as a matter of legal interpretation) against the civilian population which amounts to crimes against humanity all the constituent elements of humanness are damaged to a more serious degree that in the case of ordinary crimes.[89]

Therefore, it is not the isolated violation of human freedom or dignity or other aspects of humanness of victims that renders them victims of crimes against humanity but it is the contextual element of the attacks under question that does so.[90] It also follows that the above-noted argumentation by Professor Ambos on the international nature of crimes against humanity via their contextual element and gravity of individual acts constituting them holds but it may further be developed and even reinforced if we clarify the exact protected interests and values of crimes against humanity (i.e., "not just" human rights but more globally, their foundational elements encompassed in one holistic concept of humanness).

47.5.2 Widespread or Systematic Attack

Concerning the judicial interpretation and application in practice, the requirement of the widespread or systematic nature of the attack has been dealt with extensively, both in literature and jurisprudence.[91] This requirement was for the first time codified in international law in the Statute of the International Criminal Tribunal for Rwanda (ICTR).[92] It was subsequently introduced in the contemporary definition of crimes

---

[87] Ambos 2014, p. 60, ns. 109–110, citing relevant case-law; Atadjanov 2019, p. 205. However, open questions remain as to the preciseness and clarity of qualifiers "widespread" and "systematic" as we will see in the penultimate section.

[88] Atadjanov 2019, p. 205.

[89] Ibid., p. 205.

[90] Ibid., pp. 205–206.

[91] Some relevant authoritative scholarly sources include: Ambos 2014, pp. 59–63; Werle 2011, pp. 402–406; Cryer et al. 2010, pp. 236–237; Klamberg 2017, pp. 31–33; Triffterer and Ambos 2016, pp. 167–172; Shelton et al. 2005, pp. 212–213; Boas et al. 2008, pp. 51–53; Stahn 2019, pp. 57–58; Schabas 2007, pp. 101–102. The pertaining most relevant case-law is cited below.

[92] United Nations Security Council 1994, Annex, p. 4, Article 3.

against humanity in Article 7 of the Rome Statute as referred to in Sect. 47.3.[93] This concept, at the time of its emergence and adoption in the early 90s of the past century, was accepted as a convenient formulation suitable for the contextual threshold of crimes against humanity which would contribute to the clarity and consistency of the law.[94] It turned out to be the case, generally. However, as we will see further down, some problems persisted.

There was disagreement over whether these two criteria of "widespread" and "systematic" should be alternative or cumulative, during the negotiations on the Rome Statute.[95] The group of so-called "like-minded states" advocated an alternative relationship but a large number of the remaining delegations believed that the criteria had to be cumulative. In the end, an alternative linkage was accepted.[96] Article 7(1) contains an explicit requirement and uses a disjunctive: the attack must be either widespread *or* systematic. In other words, a prosecutor needs only to satisfy one or the other threshold,[97] not both. This has further been consistently supported by the leading international jurisprudence.[98]

The first element of the trio "widespread or systematic attack", the criterion of "widespread" represents a quantitative element.[99] The relevant sources, authorities and case-law indicate that in order to decide that the nature of the attack was "widespread" its (large) scale and the number of its victims must be taken into account.[100] For the sake of fairness, the widespread nature of the attack can also be

---

[93] No explicit requirement of a widespread or systematic attack has been included in the Statute of the International Criminal Tribunal for the Former Yugoslavia (ICTY). United Nations Security Council 1993, Annex to the Secretary General's Report, Article 5.

[94] See also Cryer et al. 2010, p. 236.

[95] Werle 2011, p. 403.

[96] Ibid., pp. 403–404.

[97] Cryer et al. 2010, p. 236.

[98] ICTY, *Prosecutor v. Tadić*, Judgment, 15 July 1999, IT-94-1-T, paras 646–648; ICTY, *Prosecutor v. Blaškić*, Judgment, 3 March 2000, IT-95-14-T, para 207; ICTY, *Prosecutor v. Kunarac et al*, Judgment, 22 February 2001, IT-96-23-T, para 427; ICTY, *Prosecutor v. Kordić et al*, Judgment, 26 February 2001, IT-95-14/2-T, para 23; ICTR, *Prosecutor v. Akayesu*, Judgment, 2 September 1998, ICTR-96-4-T, para 579; ICTR, *Prosecutor v. Kayishema et al*, Judgment and Sentence, 21 May 1999, ICTR-95-1-T, para 123; ICTR, *Prosecutor v. Rutaganda*, Judgment and Sentence, 6 December 1999, ICTR-96-3-T, paras 67–68; ICTR, *Prosecutor v. Musema*, Judgment and Sentence, 27 January 2000, ICTR-96-13-T, paras 202–203; ICTR, *Prosecutor v. Bagilishema*, Judgment, 7 June 2001, ICTR-95-1A-T, para 77.

[99] Werle 2011, p. 404.

[100] Ibid.; Cryer et al. 2010, p. 236; Ambos 2014, p. 61; ICC, *Prosecutor v. Bemba*, Decision on the Prosecutor's Application for a Warrant of Arrest against Jean-Pierre Bemba Gombo, 10 June 2008, ICC-01/05-01/08, para 33; ICC, *Prosecutor v. Katanga et al*, Decision on the Confirmation of the Charges, 30 September 2008, ICC-01/04-01/07, para 395; ICTY, *Prosecutor v. Kunarac et al*, Judgment, 12 June 2002, IT-96-23-A, para 94; ICTY, *Prosecutor v. Tadić*, Opinion and Judgment, 7 May 1997, IT-94-1-T, para 648; ICTY, *Prosecutor v. Blaškić*, Judgment, 29 July 2004, IT-95-14-A, para 101; ICTY, *Prosecutor v. Kordić and Čerkez*, Judgment, 17 December 2004, IT-95-14/2-A, para 94; ICTR, *Prosecutor v. Nahimana et al.*, Judgment, 28 November 2007, ICTR-99-52-A, para 920. All the cited cases draw on and follow the logic of the 1996 Draft Code of Crimes against Peace

derived from its extension over a broad geographic area, but that alone is not sufficient in order to satisfy this requirement; rather, a widespread attack may consist even of one single act, if a large number of civilians fall victim to it.[101]

The second element, the criterion of "systematic" constitutes a qualitative one.[102] It denotes the organized nature of the acts of violence which are committed, and therefore it serves to make sure that isolated acts are not punishable (as crimes against humanity).[103] However, it is the opinion of some authorities backed by several early cases of *ad hoc* tribunals, ICTY and ICTR, that the attack is systematic if it is based on a policy or a plan which directs or guides the individual perpetrators as to the object of the attack, i.e., the civilian population.[104] This position is based on the ILC's commentary regarding the same term but in a different context.[105]

Since 2002, i.e. the time when the judgment in the case of *Prosecutor v. Kunarac et al.* was issued, both ICTY and ICTR have departed from their earlier jurisprudence; they no longer require a plan or policy as prerequisite for a "systematic" attack.[106] Their argumentation for this consists in that there is no basis in customary international law for such a limited interpretation.[107] This is correct: even if the idea of a systematic attack suggests a methodical and organized action, while the attacks typically follow at least some form of preconceived plan, this does not make the existence of a plan or policy a necessary legal prerequisite for the crime.[108] In other words, the presence of a plan or policy is not an independent legal element of the crime. Instead, evidence of a pre-existing plan or policy can be useful in order to prove that a "systematic" attack occurred.[109]

The two criteria of "widespread" and "systematic" need only be present in the alternative, as discussed above and following the logic of Article 7(1) of the Rome Statute. However, in practice both elements are in general satisfied. Furthermore, both prerequisites refer only to the attack (reviewed immediately below) as a part

---

and Security of Mankind worked out by the UN International Law Commission, see International Law Commission 1996, p. 47, para 4.

[101] Werle 2011, pp. 404–405, citing relevant case-law of the ICC and ICTY in n. 61.

[102] Ibid., p. 405.

[103] Ibid.

[104] Ambos 2014, p. 59; ICTY, *Prosecutor v. Tadić*, Judgment, 15 July 1999, IT-94-1-T, para 648; ICTY, *Prosecutor v. Kunarac et al*, Judgment, 22 February 2001, IT-96-23-T, para 429; ICTR, *Prosecutor v. Akayesu*, Judgment, 2 September 1998, ICTR-96-4-T, para 580; ICTR, *Prosecutor v. Kayishema et al*, Judgment and Sentence, 21 May 1999, ICTR-95-1-T, para 123.

[105] Werle 2011, p. 405.

[106] Ibid.

[107] Ibid., pp. 405–406; the relevant case-law includes ICTY, *Prosecutor v. Kunarac et al.*, Judgment, 12 June 2002, IT-96-23, IT-96-23/1-A, paras 94, 98, 104; ICTY, *Prosecutor v. Krstić*, Judgment, 19 April 2004, IT-98-33, para 225; ICTY, *Prosecutor v. Blaškić*, Judgment, 29 July 2004, IT-95-14, paras 100, 120; ICTR, *Prosecutor v. Semanza*, Judgment, 20 May 2005, ICTR-97-20-A, para 269; ICTR, *Prosecutor v. Gacumbitsi*, Judgment of 7 July 2006, ICTR-2001-64-A, para 84; ICTR, *Prosecutor v. Nahimana et al.*, Judgment, 28 November 2007, ICTR-99-52-A, para 922; ICTR, *Prosecutor v. Seromba*, Judgment, 12 March 2008, ICTR-2001-66-A, para 149.

[108] Werle 2011, p. 406.

[109] Ibid.

of the contextual element, and they do not have to apply to each of the individual acts.[110]

The third element, the "attack", is defined in the Statute as "a course of conduct involving the multiple commission of acts referred to in paragraph 1 ..., pursuant to or in furtherance of a state or organizational policy."[111] This element describes a course of conduct involving the commission of acts of violence.[112] It must include the "multiple commission" of individual prohibited acts listed in Article 7(1) of the ICC Statute. But the "multiple commission" is a less strict requirement than a "widespread" attack[113] and it should not be confused with the latter.

Furthermore, the term "attack" is not used in the same sense as in the war crimes law;[114] it does not necessarily have to involve the use of armed force. In other words, a military attack is not necessary which is explicitly stated in the Elements of Crimes.[115] The attack may include any mistreatment of civilian population.[116] According to Werle, multiple commission is present both if the same act is committed many times and if different acts are committed.[117] Furthermore, the perpetrator does not need to act repeatedly himself or herself; a single act of intentional killing can constitute a crime against humanity if that act fits within the overall context.[118]

47.5.3 Any Civilian Population

This element is one of the key parts of the crimes' definition. As rightly noted by Cryer, the word "any" highlights the central innovation and *raison d'être* of crimes against humanity.[119] That the law of crimes against humanity also covers crimes by a State against its own subjects and not only protects enemy nationals is an established interpretation of this element.[120] The phrase "civilian population" encompasses *any* group of people linked by shared characteristics that in turn make it the target of an attack;[121] the nationality or affiliation of the victims is irrelevant. Hence, crimes

---

[110] Ibid.

[111] Rome Statute, above n. 35, Article 7(2)(a).

[112] Werle 2011, p. 402.

[113] Ibid.

[114] Cryer et al. 2010, p. 237.

[115] Assembly of States Parties 2002 Available at https://www.icc-cpi.int/resource-library/Docume nts/ElementsOfCrimesEng.pdf. Accessed 5 May 2020.

[116] Cryer et al. 2010, p. 237; Werle 2011, p. 403.

[117] Werle 2011, p. 403.

[118] Ibid..; ICTY, *Prosecutor v. Tadić*, Opinion and Judgment, 7 May 1997, IT-94-1-T, para 649. Werle cites as a good historical example the denunciation of a single Jew to the Gestapo, which was part of the process of excluding German Jews from cultural and economic life in the Third Reich. Werle 2011, p. 403, n. 54.

[119] Cryer et al. 2010, p. 241.

[120] Ibid., n. 65.

[121] Werle 2011, p. 398.

against humanity are directed against a civilian population as such, not merely at an individual.[122] As an example, the occupancy of a certain territorial area can be cited.

Regarding the term "civilian", an important consideration must be kept in mind. Crimes against humanity may occur both in war and in peacetime.[123] It is already a settled international jurisprudence that the character of a predominantly civilian population will not be altered by "the presence of certain non-civilians in their midst", i.e., the presence of hostile military forces among a predominantly civilian population does not change its character as "civilian".[124]

Indeed, the current interpretation of the "civilian population" element of crimes against humanity suggests that there is no pressing need to rename this group of core crimes as "crimes against civilian population" or rephrase it otherwise, in order to make it clearer or more concrete and/or specific. The term "crimes against humanity" already serves the purpose of denoting some of the worst and most serious criminal offences in international law.[125] Military personnel is not strictly excluded from the protected persons of these crimes, according to the progressive interpretation of "any civilian population": the population need only be predominantly civilian in nature and the term "civilian" includes also all those who are no longer taking part in hostilities during the commission of the crimes.[126]

According to Werle, the "attack" must target a civilian population, while the individual crime must target civilians,[127] which is the result of a correct logical reasoning. As noted above, the "civilian" character of the attacked population and persons applies both in war and in peacetime. Therefore, there arises the question of applicable law: the distinction cannot be made solely based on the rules and principles of IHL which applies only during the time of armed conflict. The latter specifically protects all persons not, or no longer taking part in hostilities.[128] Hence, in construing the term "civilian population" with respect to crimes against humanity,

---

[122] Ibid.

[123] Just as the "civilian" character of the attacked population and persons applies both in war and in peacetime. Ibid., p. 399.

[124] Ambos 2014, p. 64; ICTY, *Prosecutor v. Tadić*, Opinion and Judgment, 7 May 1997, IT-94-1-T, para 638; ICTY, *Prosecutor v. Mrkšić and Šljivančanin*, Judgment, 5 May 2009, IT-95-13-1-A, para 31; ICTY, *Prosecutor v. Blaškić*, Judgment, 29 July 2004, IT-95-14-A, para 113; ICTY, *Prosecutor v. Kupreškić et al.*, Judgement, 14 January 2000, IT-95-16-T, para 549; ICTY, *Prosecutor v. Kunarac et al.*, Judgment, 22 February 2001, IT-96-23-T, IT-96-23/1-T, para 325; ICTY, *Prosecutor v. Kordić et al.*, Judgment, 26 February 2001, IT-95-14/2-T, para 180; ICTY, *Prosecutor v. Krnojelac*, Judgment, 15 March 2002, IT-97-25-T, para 56; ICTR, *Prosecutor v. Akayesu*, Judgment, 2 September 1998, ICTR-96-4-T, para 582; ICTR, *Prosecutor v. Kayishema et al.*, Judgment and Sentence, 21 May 1999, ICTR-95-1-T, para 128; ICTR, *Prosecutor v. Rutaganda*, Judgment and Sentence, 6 December 1999, ICTR-96-3-T, para 72; ICTR, *Prosecutor v. Musema*, Judgment and Sentence, 27 January 2000, ICTR-96-13-T, para 207; ICTR, *Prosecutor v. Bagilishema*, Judgment, 7 June 2001, ICTR-95-1A-T, para 79.

[125] Atadjanov 2019, pp. 312–313.

[126] Ibid., p. 313.

[127] Werle 2011, p. 399.

[128] Ibid.; ICTY, *Prosecutor v. Kunarac et al.*, Judgment, 22 February 2001, IT-96-23-T, IT-96-23/1-T, para 425.

the purpose of protecting the fundamental rights of every human being against any form of systematic violation must be observed.[129]

In contrast to IHL, it is not significant to the protected status of civilians whether they are under the control of their own side or the opposing side. Therefore, present or former members of one's own armed forces, in particular, who are not protected by international humanitarian law can become direct objects of a crime against humanity.[130] As for the contexts outside armed conflicts, crimes against humanity are generally characterized by one-sided acts on the part of the state or other organized armed groups against a civilian population; here, holders of state or other organized power are not encompassed by the term "civilian population", if they wield this power against the civilian population.[131]

Concerning specifically the "population", it can be said that this term refers to a multiplicity of persons sharing common attributes; however, it is not necessary that the perpetrator attacks the "entire population of the geographical entity in which the attack is taking place (a state, a municipality or another circumscribed area)".[132] This criterion emphasizes rather the collective nature of the crime, therefore ruling out the attacks against individuals as well as isolated acts of violence.[133]

47.5.4 Policy Element

This contextual element represents one of the most controversial aspects of the law of crimes against humanity. Article 7(2)(a) explicitly states that the ""[a]ttack directed against any civilian population" means a course of conduct involving the multiple commission of acts against any civilian population, *pursuant to or in furtherance of a State or organizational policy to commit such attack*; ..." [emphasis added]. Ambos maintains that this codification reflects the international element's move from the war nexus requirement to state or organizational authority.[134] However, despite the existence of a positively written applicable provision in statutory law there has clearly been a divide in the authorities and the question of whether the policy element is an absolutely necessary element of crimes against humanity appears to remain controversial for some authors.[135]

---

[129] Werle 2011, p. 399.

[130] Ibid., pp. 401–402.

[131] Ibid., p. 402, citing ICTR, *Prosecutor v. Kayishema et al.*, Judgment and Sentence, 21 May 1999, ICTR-95-1-T, para 127.

[132] ICTY, *Prosecutor v. Kunarac et al.*, Judgment, 22 February 2001, IT-96-23-T, IT-96-23/1-T, para 424; Ambos 2014, p. 63.

[133] ICTY, *Prosecutor v. Tadić*, Opinion and Judgment, 7 May 1997, IT-94-1-T, para 644; Werle 2011, p. 398.

[134] Ambos 2014, p. 67. The historical war nexus requirement of crimes against humanity is discussed in the next subsection.

[135] E.g., Cryer et al. 2010, p. 237.

There is a conflict between classical and progressive views on the matter. The proponents of the former, traditional approach appear to rely on its correspondence to historical descriptions of the evolution of crimes against humanity's law (indeed, the majority of the crimes usually labeled "crimes against humanity" have involved state-generated policies).[136] One of the influential exponents of the "state-involvement" view, Professor Bassiouni, has maintained that "[b]y virtue of its nature and scale, CAH [a crime against humanity – R.A.] requires the use of governmental institutions, structures, resources, and personnel acting in reliance on their powers and resources without being subject to effective legal controls."[137] Bassiouni wraps his arguments around the relevance of state policy and his message is clear—it is the involvement of the state actor which makes these crimes "special".[138]

Another notable supporter of the classical view, Professor Schabas, argues for a "revival" of state policy as an element of these crimes against international law. He contends: "[c]oncerns that requiring a State policy will leave a so-called impunity gap are misplaced. ... The needs in prosecution are not a broadening of the definitions of international crimes, but rather a strengthening of international judicial cooperation mechanisms so as to facilitate bringing offenders to book for "ordinary" crimes."[139] Both Bassiouni and Schabas appear to agree that non-state actors are already adequately covered by domestic justice systems.[140]

Even if on its face this argumentation concerning non-state actors does seem logical, in reality, however, that simply might not be sufficient to hold them accountable for the commission of serious human rights violations and crimes against international law. The blatant examples of the atrocities having been and being committed by groups such as ISIS or Boko Haram support the conclusion that even if there are some provisions in the national legislation for punishing non-state actors they easily get away with impunity—just as the cases of the armed conflicts in Syria and Iraq demonstrate.[141]

On the other end of the scales are the advocates of a more progressive position such as Professor Werle. According to him, no additional "policy element" to limit the definition is called for under customary law.[142] Despite their initial hesitance, the *ad hoc* Tribunals eventually clearly stated that a policy is not a separate element in the definition of the crime, nor is it necessary in order to prove a systematic attack.[143]

---

[136] Atadjanov 2019, p. 161.

[137] Bassiouni 2011, p. 14.

[138] Atadjanov 2019, p. 162.

[139] Schabas 2008, p. 982.

[140] Atadjanov 2019, p. 162.

[141] Ibid., n. 96.

[142] Werle 2011, p. 406.

[143] Ibid., pp. 406–407; first stated in ICTY, *Prosecutor v. Kunarac et al.*, Judgment, 12 June 2002, IT-96-23, IT-96-23/1-A, para 98; later confirmed in ICTY, *Prosecutor v. Krstić*, Judgment, 19 April 2004, IT-98-33, para 225; ICTY, *Prosecutor v. Blaškić*, Judgment, 29 July 2004, IT-95-14, para 120; ICTY, *Prosecutor v. Kordić and Čerkez*, Judgment, 17 December 2004, IT-95-14/2-A, para 98; ICTR, *Prosecutor v. Semanza*, Judgment, 20 May 2005, ICTR-97-20-A, para 269.

With respect to the policy element's relevance for the definition of the crime under the ICC Statute, there are two possible approaches. The element can be seen as an effective limitation of the scope of the crime, or it may be treated simply as an elaboration of the crime's systematic character.[144] Here, the standards developed in the early case-law of the *ad hoc* Tribunals with regard to the "policy element" required for a systematic attack remain significant in the Rome Statute's interpretation. According to these standards, the criterion of policy does not require a formal programmatic determination. Instead, the term is interpreted broadly as a planned, directed or organized crime, as opposed to spontaneous and isolated acts of violence.[145]

The body responsible for the policy must be a specific entity, namely a state or organization.[146] The term "organization" definitely includes groups of persons that govern a specific territory or in any case can move freely there. But this territorial element is not necessary. Ultimately, any group of people can be categorized as an organization if it has at its disposal, in material and personnel, the potential to commit a widespread or systematic attack on a civilian population.[147]

The policy of a state or organization can consist of taking a leading role in the commission of the crime, but also in actively promoting the crime or in merely tolerating it.[148] If such a broad interpretation is followed, the policy element does nothing more than elaborate upon what is already included in the contextual element of the crime, i.e., a "systematic attack on a civilian population".[149]

As a leading authority, the jurisprudence of the International Criminal Court can be cited in support of this conclusion. In its first decisions on the issue, the Court correctly stated that the (state or organizational) policy element has no independent relevance as an element of the crime, but it may serve as evidence for the attack's systematic character.[150] Regarding the widespread attacks, the Rome Statute's element of policy adds a qualitative dimension. Hence, a "widespread" attack on a civilian population will not qualify as a crime against humanity unless it is committed pursuant to or in furtherance of a state or organizational policy.[151]

It is useful to briefly note on the aspect no longer required: the so-called nexus of crimes against humanity to armed conflict. Some of the key international sources such as the Nuremberg Charter and Tokyo Charter required a connection to war crimes or aggression, thus demanding some nexus to armed conflict.[152] At the time, it contributed to the argumentation in favour of introducing the dispositions of

---

[144] Werle 2011, p. 408.

[145] Ibid., citing ICTY, *Prosecutor v. Tadić*, Opinion and Judgment, 7 May 1997, IT-94-1-T, para 653.

[146] Werle 2011, p. 409.

[147] Ibid. In addition to paramilitary units, this particularly includes terrorist organizations. Ibid.

[148] Ibid., p. 410.

[149] Ibid.

[150] ICC, *Prosecutor v. Harun and Kushayb*, Decision, 27 April 2007, ICC-02/05-01/07, para 62; ICC, *Prosecutor v. Bemba Gombo*, Decision, 10 June 2008, ICC-01/05-01/08, para 33.

[151] Werle 2011, p. 411.

[152] Cryer et al. 2010, p. 234. As reader recalls, the Nuremberg Charter defined crimes against humanity as the listing of individual "… inhumane acts committed against any civilian population,

crimes against humanity into the Charter texts, in order to ensure that perpetrators do not escape criminal liability. But other important instruments, e.g., Allied Control Council Law No. 10, did not have such a requirement. A brief look at the relevant international treaty law shows that the armed conflict nexus was not required.[153] It seems well settled nowadays that the nexus to armed conflict is not required anymore; the majority of instruments and precedents oppose such an outdated link.[154] The limitation in the Nuremberg Charter is now generally seen as only a jurisdictional limitation.[155] This view is backed by domestic jurisprudence, international expert bodies as well as commentator writings.[156] Importantly, no requirement of armed conflict has ever appeared in subsequent definitions of crimes against humanity, and will probably not appear in treaty law in the future. That corresponds well to the progressive—but also realistic and objective, view of international criminal law: that crimes against humanity can be committed both during armed conflict and in peacetime.

47.6 Individual Acts

As it can be seen from the definition in Article 7(1) of the Rome Statute, there are eleven individual prohibited acts of crimes against humanity including the "other inhumane acts". This list of acts has gradually evolved over the tens of years. The first list, figuring in the Nuremberg Charter, comprised murder, extermination, enslavement, deportation, persecution and other inhumane acts.[157] Soon afterwards Control Council Law No. 10 added rape, imprisonment and torture.[158] The Statutes of the

---

before or during the war; or persecutions on political, racial or religious grounds *in execution of or in connection with any crime within the jurisdiction of the Tribunal.*" [emphasis added] Nuremberg Charter, above n. 27, Article 6(c).

[153] For example, Convention on the Prevention and Punishment of the Crime of Genocide, opened for signature 9 December 1948, 78 U.N.T.S. 277 (entered into force 12 January 1951) (Genocide Convention); Convention on the Non-Applicability of Statutory Limitations to War Crimes and Crimes Against Humanity, opened for signature 26 November 1968, UN GA Res. 2391 (XXIII) (entered into force 11 November 1970); International Convention on the Suppression and Punishment of the Crime of Apartheid, opened for signature 30 November 1973, 1015 U.N.T.S. 243 (entered into force 18 July 1976); Inter-American Convention on Forced Disappearance of Persons, adopted 6 June 1994, 33 ILM (1994) 1529 (entered into force 28 March 1996).

[154] Cryer et al. 2010, p. 235.

[155] Ibid., citing relevant legal and scholarly authorities.

[156] Cryer et al. 2010, p. 235; District Court of Jerusalem, *Attorney-General of the Government of Israel v. Eichmann*, Judgment, 12 December 1961, 36 ILR 5 (1968), p. 49; Cour de Cassation, *Fédération Nationale des Deportés et Internés Resistants et Patriots et al. v. Barbie*, Judgment, 20 December 1985, 78 ILR 124 (1988), p. 136; International Law Commission 1996, p. 96; Orentlicher 1991, pp. 2588–2590; passim Meron 1995; passim Van Schaack 1998.

[157] Nuremberg Charter, above n. 27, Article 6(c); Cryer et al. 2010, p. 245.

[158] Control Council Law No. 10, Article 6(c), available at https://www.legal-tools.org/doc/ffda62/pdf/. Accessed 5 May 2020.

ICTY and ICTR have followed the same expanded list.[159] In 1998, the ICC Statute added sexual slavery, enforced prostitution, forced pregnancy, other sexual violence, enforced disappearance and apartheid.[160]

The individual underlying acts do not need to be carried out against a big number of victims, in order to constitute a crime against humanity (with the exception of extermination).[161] A single act directed against a limited number of victims, or even against a single victim, may constitute a crime against humanity, but on condition that it forms part of a widespread or systematic attack.[162] The subsequent text briefly describes the individual crimes against humanity following the same order in which they are established in the Rome Statute.

47.6.1 Murder

The individual act of murder is established in Article 7(1)(a) of the Rome Statute of the ICC. This provision is based on Article 6(c) of the Nuremberg Charter, Article II(1)(c) of Control Council Law No. 10, Article 5(c) of the Tokyo Charter, Article 5(a) of the ICTY Statute and Article 3(a) of the ICTR Statute.[163] The crime of murder was seen during the negotiations on the Rome Statute as a crime which is clearly defined in the domestic legal systems of every State.[164] The crime's material element requires the perpetrator to have caused the death of another person through his or her conduct.[165]

As for the requisite mental element, it is present if the perpetrator is aware of the substantial likelihood that his or her actions will result in the death of the victim; such an outcome flows from relevant customary international law, as reflected in the settled jurisprudence of the *ad hoc* Tribunals.[166] It is not necessary for the perpetrator to have acted with premeditation, in accordance with pertinent and well-established case-law.[167]

---

[159] United Nations Security Council 1993, Annex to the Secretary General's Report, Article 5; United Nations Security Council 1994, Annex, p. 4, Article 3.

[160] Cryer et al. 2010, p. 245.

[161] Werle 2011, p. 413.

[162] Ibid., citing relevant *ad hoc* tribunals' jurisprudence.

[163] Werle 2011, p. 414.

[164] International Law Commission 1996, p. 48, para 7.

[165] Assembly of States Parties 2002, above n. 115; Werle 2011, p. 414.

[166] Werle 2011, p. 414, citing relevant case-law.

[167] According to Werle, it was long unclear whether the mental element of the crime required premeditation due to the French version of the crime against humanity of killing ("assassinat") and Article 6(c) of the Nuremberg Charter as well as Article 5(a) of the ICTY Statute and Article 3(a) of the ICTR Statute. Because of that the *ad hoc* Tribunals at first had difficulty in clearly delineating the mental element of killing in accordance with customary international law. Werle 2011, pp. 415–416. However, now the authoritative cases presume that, despite the French wording ("assassinat"), only the French term "meurtre" correctly characterizes customary international law. Those include, *inter*

47.6.2 Extermination

In accordance with Article 7(2)(b) of the Rome Statute, "extermination" includes the intentional infliction of conditions of life, inter alia the deprivation of access to food and medicine calculated to bring about the destruction of part of a population. This crime essentially consists in the creation of deadly living conditions amounting to widespread killings, and it targets groups of persons.[168]

It is important to distinguish extermination from both the crime against humanity of murder and the crime of genocide. Extermination is the act of killing on a large scale, and it differs from the former crime in that it requires an element of mass destruction.[169] Another difference from murder is that extermination expressly includes indirect means of causing death.[170]

As for genocide, there are significant overlaps between the two types of crimes. Indeed, as noted by Cryer, the concepts of killing or inflicting conditions of life calculated to bring about the destruction of part of a population are common to both extermination and genocide.[171] The major difference between the two is the special intent for the crime of genocide, i.e., the intent to destroy a group as such, required to qualify it as such. More than that, genocide can only be committed where there is intent to target one of four types of groups—national, ethnical, racial or religious.[172]

47.6.3 Enslavement

Enslavement comprises a classic crime against humanity whose modern formulation is established in Article 7(1)(c) of the Rome Statute.[173] This notoriously known crime can be generally defined as "exercising the powers attaching to the right of ownership over person(s)".[174] It may take many forms including purchasing, selling, lending, bartering, capturing, transporting, disposing of, trafficking (in women and children in particular), debt bondage practices, serfdom, forced marriage, forced labour, child exploitation and others.[175]

---

alia, ICTR, *Prosecutor v. Akayesu*, Judgment, 2 September 1998, ICTR-96-4-T, para 588; ICTR, *Prosecutor v. Rutaganda*, Judgment and Sentence, 6 December 1999, ICTR-96-3-T, para 79; ICTY, *Prosecutor v. Blaškić*, Judgment, 3 March 2000, IT-95-14-T, para 216.

[168] Ambos 2014, p. 84, cited in Atadjanov 2019, p. 192.

[169] Werle 2011, p. 416.

[170] Cryer et al. 2010, p. 247.

[171] Ibid.

[172] Ibid.

[173] Werle 2011, p. 420.

[174] Atadjanov 2019, p. 193; Cryer et al. 2010, p. 247; ICTY, *Prosecutor v. Kunarac et al.*, Judgment, 22 February 2001, IT-96-23-T, para 539.

[175] Atadjanov 2019, p. 193; Ambos 2014, p. 85; Cryer et al. 2010, pp. 247–248; Assembly of States Parties 2002, above n. 115, Article 7(1)(c), para 1, fn. 11; ICTY, *Prosecutor v. Kunarac*

The main element of the definition of enslavement is the "right of ownership" exercised by one person over another, which is confirmed by relevant case-law: the Trial Chamber of the ICTY found that "enslavement as a crime against humanity in customary international law consisted of the exercise of any or all of the powers attaching to the right of ownership over a person".[176] The indicative features of enslavement include: the control of someone's movement, control of physical environment, psychological control, measures taken to prevent or deter escape, force, threat of force or coercion, duration, assertion of exclusivity, subjection to cruel treatment and abuse, control of sexuality, and forced labour; buying, selling, trading, or inheriting a person or that person's labour or services could also be a relevant indicator.[177]

It must be stressed that lack of consent by the victims is not an element of the crime, because enslavement rather flows from claimed rights of ownership.[178] As for the mental part, the requisite *mens rea* consists in an intentional exercise of power attaching to the right of ownership.[179]

47.6.4 Deportation or Forcible Transfer of Population

Article 7(2)(d) of the ICC Statute defines deportation and forcible transfer of population as the "forced displacement of the persons concerned by expulsion or other coercive acts from the area in which they are lawfully present, without grounds permitted under international law."[180] Generally, "deportation" is regarded as referring to displacement across a border while "forcible transfer" refers to internal displacement.[181] Both must be forced in order to qualify as crimes against humanity; but the force does not have to consist of *physical* force: often it can involve the threat of force, duress, coercion (coercive acts), detention, psychological oppression, abuse of power and entails negative consequences, such as separation of the members of the same family, improper accommodation conditions and non-satisfactory conditions of hygiene, health, safety and nutrition, for the victims.[182]

---

et al., Judgment, 22 February 2001, IT-96-23, paras 732–742; ICTY, *Prosecutor v. Krnojelac et al.*, Judgment, 15 March 2002, IT-97-25-T, paras 193–195.

[176] ICTY, *Prosecutor v. Kunarac et al.*, Judgment, 22 February 2001, IT-96-23-T, IT-96-23/1-T, para 539; Ambos 2014, p. 85.

[177] Ambos 2014, p. 85.

[178] ICTY, *Prosecutor v. Kunarac et al.*, Judgment, 12 June 2002, IT-96-23, IT-96-23/1-A, para 120, cited in Ambos 2014, p. 85.

[179] Ibid., para 122.

[180] Werle 2011, p. 425.

[181] Cryer et al. 2010, p. 249; Atadjanov 2019, p. 194.

[182] Ibid.

In both cases—in deportation and in forcible transfer, the material element requires the physical transfer of persons from one territory to another (forced displacement).[183] The Elements of Crimes stipulate that the transfer of even one single person from a territory can be sufficient.[184] The difference between the two acts lies only in whether a border is crossed. Deportation means the transfer of one or more persons from one state's territory to another state's territory (i.e., a state border is crossed); in contrast, forcible transfer means the transfer of one or more persons within the same state's territory.[185]

There is one more significant issue to be noted here: the forced displacement must also be *unlawful* under international law.[186] Most or all States carry out legitimate acts of deportation on a frequent basis, and deportation of aliens not lawfully present in the territory is an established practice of States.[187]

47.6.5 *Imprisonment or Other Severe Deprivations of Liberty*

According to the Elements of Crimes, this underlying act means that the perpetrator imprisoned one or more persons of physical liberty, and the gravity of the conduct was such that it was in violation of fundamental rules of international law.[188] To constitute a crime against humanity, imprisonment must be arbitrary[189] which is present if there was no proper legal procedure.[190] Of equal importance is the fact that imprisonment achieves the status of a crime under international law only through its violation of the "fundamental rules" of international law.[191] According to Werle, the cases that come into play here are especially those involving deprivation of liberty without any legal basis or without regard for elementary rules of procedure.[192]

The term "imprisonment" encompasses cases where a person is literally "imprisoned" in an enclosed space and therefore he or she is prevented from moving to another place whereas cases categorized as other severe deprivations of physical liberty include those in which a person can continue to move in a specific area, e.g.,

---

[183] Werle 2011, p. 425.

[184] Assembly of States Parties 2002, above n. 115, Article 7(1)(d).

[185] Werle 2011, p. 425.

[186] Cryer et al. 2010, p. 249.

[187] Ibid., pp. 249–250.

[188] Assembly of States Parties 2002, above n. 115, Article 7(1)(e), paras 1 and 2; Atadjanov 2019, p. 195. The pertinent international jurisprudence consists of ICTY, *Prosecutor v. Kordić et al.*, Judgment, 17 December 2004, IT-95-14/2A, paras 279, 301–302, and ICTY, *Prosecutor v. Krnojelac et al.*, Judgment, 15 March 2002, IT-97-25-T, paras 111–114.

[189] Cryer et al. 2010, p. 249; Atadjanov 2019, p. 195.

[190] Werle 2011, p. 430.

[191] Ibid.; ICTY, *Prosecutor v. Kordić et al*, Judgment, 26 February 2001, IT-95-14/2-T, para 302.

[192] Werle 2011, p. 431, citing ICTY, *Prosecutor v. Kordić and Čerkez*, Judgment, 17 December 2004, IT-95-14/2-A, para 114, and ICTY, *Prosecutor v. Krnojelac*, Judgment, 15 March 2002, IT-97-25-T, para 115.

within a ghetto or concentration camp.[193] House arrest may also fall under this definition but the deprivation of liberty for a short period of time should not be viewed as "severe" in terms of the Rome Statute.[194]

47.6.6 Torture

The crime of torture represents a *jus cogens* prohibition and a recognized customary law norm that has been well established in numerous international legal instruments.[195] The Rome Statute's definition of torture as a crime against humanity goes as follows:

> ..."Torture" means the intentional infliction of severe pain or suffering, whether physical or mental, upon a person in the custody or under the control of the accused; except that torture shall not include pain or suffering arising only from, inherent in or incidental to, lawful sanctions; ...[196]

The Elements of Crimes further indicate that no specific purpose needs to be proven for this crime.[197] Moreover, there is also no specific capacity requirement which corresponds to the relevant case law.[198] The physical or mental pain or suffering must attain a minimum level of severity.[199] It is this severity which distinguishes torture from other forms of inhumane treatment which do not "attain a minimum level of severity".[200]

If the "pain or suffering" is the consequence of a "lawful sanction" (according to Article 7(2)(e) of the Rome Statute), for example, the death penalty in some domestic jurisdictions, the conduct will not qualify as torture.[201] To be lawful, a sanction must be imposed in a fair trial pursuant to the international minimum standards as codified, for example, in Articles 14 and 15 International Covenant on Civil and Political Rights.[202] Finally, the victim must be under the control of the perpetrator, that is, in a situation from which there is no escape while the perpetrator does not need to pursue a certain purpose.[203]

---

[193] Ibid., p. 430.
[194] Ibid.
[195] Atadjanov 2019, p. 195.
[196] Rome Statute, above n. 35, Article 7(2)(e).
[197] Assembly of States Parties 2002, above n. 115, Article 7(1)(f), n. 14.
[198] ICTY, *Prosecutor v. Kunarac et al.*, Judgment, 22 February 2001, IT-96-23-T, para 496; Ambos 2014, p. 90; Atadjanov 2019, p. 196.
[199] Ambos 2014, p. 92.
[200] Ibid., p. 91.
[201] Ibid., p. 92.
[202] Ibid.
[203] Ambos 2014, p. 92.

47.6.7 Sexual Crimes

The Nuremberg Charter did not contain acts of sexual violence as crimes against humanity as such, but they could be incorporated by way of the catch-all clause "other inhuman acts." Rape was soon after explicitly included in Control Council Law No. 10, and is also contained in the ICTY and ICTR Statutes as a separate crime.[204] However, other forms of sexual violence are not mentioned in these instruments; those can only be incorporated as other crimes against humanity or again through the catch-all phrase of "other inhuman acts".[205]

The Rome Statute brings in a significant clarification by bundling the crimes of sexual violence. Accordingly, this category of underlying acts includes several distinct crimes: rape, sexual slavery, enforced prostitution, forced pregnancy, enforced sterilization, or any other form of sexual violence of comparable gravity.[206] Each one of those was clarified in the Elements of Crimes also including the crime against humanity of sexual violence.[207] All of them are listed in one group of crimes due to the common element of sexual violence present in each act.[208]

47.6.8 Persecution

As I wrote elsewhere, the crime of persecution does not represent a self-standing criminal act in the Rome Statute.[209] The latter formulates it as follows:

> ...Persecution against any identifiable group or collectivity on political, racial, national, ethnic, cultural, religious, gender as defined in paragraph 3, or other grounds that are universally recognized as impermissible under international law, in connection with any act referred to in this paragraph or any crime within the jurisdiction of the Court; ...[210]

The instrument further defines the term "persecution" as "the intentional and severe deprivation of fundamental rights contrary to international law by reason of the identity of the group or collectivity".[211] The Elements of Crimes clarify several important constituent elements of persecution including the discriminatory grounds for targeting which are impermissible under international law.[212]

There are many examples of acts of persecution. Those include: murder, imprisonment, deportation; seizure, collection, segregation and forced transfer of civilians

---

[204] Werle 2011, p. 437.

[205] Ibid.

[206] Rome Statute, above n. 35, Article 7(1)(g). For a detailed discussion of each of these distinct crimes, see Werle 2011, pp. 438–443; Cryer et al. 2010, pp. 254–258; Ambos 2014, pp. 95–104.

[207] Assembly of States Parties 2002, above n. 115, Article 7(1)(f)1–6.

[208] Atadjanov 2019, p. 197.

[209] Ibid., p. 198.

[210] Rome Statute, above n. 35, Article 7(1)(h).

[211] Ibid., Article 7(1)(g).

[212] Assembly of States Parties 2002, above n. 115, Article 7(1)(h); Atadjanov 2019, p. 199.

47 Crimes Against Humanity 1061

to camps; calling-out of civilians, beatings and killings; attacks on property, destruction, looting and plunder of (private) property; physical and mental injury; unlawful detention, and more.[213]

Consisting in a so-called "umbrella crime", persecution may be said to be a unique crime (with the exception of the crime of apartheid) due to its connection with other underlying acts of crimes against humanity reviewed above and below, and other crimes under international law falling under the jurisdiction of the ICC, first and foremost, genocide and war crimes.[214] Indeed, persecution can only be committed by way of concrete acts or omissions which amount to grave human rights violations, expressed in "severe deprivations of fundamental rights contrary to international law".[215] Thus, for the crime of persecution to occur, this individual act should violate fundamental human rights and this violation must be severe.[216]

47.6.9 Enforced Disappearance of Persons

The crime against humanity of enforced disappearance is dealt with in Article 7(1)(i) of the Rome Statute:

> 'Enforced disappearance of persons' means the arrest, detention or abduction of persons by, or with the authorization, support or acquiescence of, a State or a political organization, followed by a refusal to acknowledge that deprivation of freedom or to give information on the fate or whereabouts of those persons, with the intention of removing them from the protection of the law for a prolonged period of time.[217]

The Elements of Crimes lays out the constituent material and mental elements of this crime against humanity.[218] The underlying act of enforced disappearance usually has more than one perpetrator due to the sophisticated nature of the crime[219] while there are also indirect special victims of the crime, in addition to direct victims, meaning the latter's friends and families.[220] Notwithstanding its complex details, the *actus reus* of the crime of enforced disappearance consists of two related acts: deprivation of liberty and omission of information as flows out from the Statute and Elements, with those acts having to be carried out with the authorization, support or acquiescence of the State or political organization.[221]

---

[213] Atadjanov 2019, p. 199. For more exhaustive lists of example acts of the crime of persecution as well as the relevant jurisprudence, see Ambos 2014, pp. 106–107; Cryer et al. 2010, p. 262.

[214] Atadjanov 2019, p. 199.

[215] Ibid.; ICTY, *Prosecutor v. Tadić*, Judgment, 7 May 1997, IT-94-1-T, paras 704–710; Ambos 2014, p. 105 and n. 451.

[216] Ambos 2014, p. 106.

[217] See also Werle 2011, p. 454.

[218] Assembly of States Parties 2002, above n. 115, Article 7(1)(i), paras 1–8.

[219] Cryer et al. 2010, p. 263.

[220] Ibid., p. 264; Atadjanov 2019, pp. 200–201.

[221] Ambos 2014, p. 111.

With respect to the crime's protective scope, it is the necessary component of deprivation of liberty that entails its attack on the victim's freedom; in some cases, even a lawful arrest or detention may fulfill the offense's *actus reus*.[222] That the conduct amounting to the crime of enforced disappearance violates the right to personal liberty has been recognized by important regional judicial mechanisms such as the Inter-American Court of Human Rights (IACHR) and the ECHR.[223]

As noted above, deprivation of liberty must occur at the behest of or with the approval of a state or political organization; in addition, it is necessary that no immediate information be provided upon request, for example by the victim's relatives, on the fate and whereabouts of the victim.[224] The mental element is governed by Article 30 of the Rome Statute.

47.6.9.1 The Crime of Apartheid

The crime against humanity of apartheid is formulated in the Rome Statute as follows:

> …inhumane acts of a character similar to those referred to in paragraph 1, committed in the context of an institutionalized regime of systematic oppression and domination by one racial group over any other racial group or groups and committed with the intention of maintaining that regime; …[225]

The criminal acts constituting apartheid in essence correspond to those underlying acts listed under the Article 7(1)(a)–(i) and (k) or must be similar to those acts.[226] However, there is an important distinguishing element of this particular crime: to qualify as a crime against humanity it ought to be committed in the context of an institutionalized regime of systematic oppression and domination by one racial group over any other racial group or groups while the perpetrator's intent should be to maintain such a regime by her conduct.[227]

The term "apartheid" (Afrikaans for "separateness") stands for the policy of racial segregation and discrimination pursued in South Africa after 1948.[228] The inclusion of the crime in the Rome Statute came out of a proposal by South Africa; since the apartheid regime there has eventually been abolished, the establishment of an independent crime of humanity of apartheid has primarily symbolic significance at present.[229]

---

[222] Assembly of States Parties 2002, above n. 115, Article 7(1)(i), fn. 26; Atadjanov 2019, p. 201.

[223] Atadjanov 2019, p. 201; see Ambos 2014, pp. 108–109, ns. 480–482 for the listing of relevant jurisprudence.

[224] Werle 2011, p. 455.

[225] Rome Statute, above n. 35, Article 7(2)(h).

[226] Ambos 2014, p. 114; Atadjanov 2019, pp. 201–202.

[227] Assembly of States Parties 2002, above n. 115, Article 7(1)(j)4–5; Atadjanov 2019, pp. 201–202.

[228] Werle 2011, p. 456.

[229] Ibid., p. 457; Cryer 2005, p. 259.

47.6.9.2 Other Inhumane Acts

The last individual act listed in the Rome Statute's enumeration of crimes against humanity is formulated as "other inhumane acts". It reads: "Other inhumane acts of a similar character intentionally causing great suffering, or serious injury to body or to mental or physical health."[230] The crime's constituent material and *mens rea* elements are further determined in the Elements of Crimes.[231]

"Other inhumane acts" represents a catch-all general provision for the cases which are not covered in Article 7's list of underlying acts of crimes against humanity (from paras "a" to "j").[232] Elements of Crimes determine that similar "character" refers to the nature and gravity of the act, as in the case of the crime of apartheid.[233]

As noted by Werle, it was agreed during the negotiations on the Rome Statute that it would continue to be impossible to enumerate all behaviors possibly rising to the level of and deserving punishment as crimes against humanity.[234] The Statute seeks to take account of reservations about the imprecision of a general clause type of catch-all provision by making the provision more precise than earlier rules.[235]

47.7 Relationship to Other Crimes Under International Law

This brief section looks at some major similarities and differences between crimes against humanity and other core crimes. Regarding the crime of genocide, the several similarities between it and crimes against humanity include: common historical roots (genocide was initially regarded as an odious form of crimes against humanity);[236] context of application: the two types of crimes apply both during peacetime and armed conflict;[237] both genocide and crimes against humanity encompass very serious offences;[238] as a rule the two crime categories do not constitute isolated events but are instead part of a larger context;[239] finally, even if there is no specific legal requirement that genocide and crimes against humanity are perpetrated by State-actors, the element of the State is very often present in the commission of both.[240]

---

[230] Rome Statute, above n. 35, Article 7(2)(k).

[231] Assembly of States Parties 2002, above n. 115, Article 7(1)(k).

[232] Atadjanov 2019, p. 203.

[233] Ibid.

[234] Werle 2011, p. 459.

[235] Ibid., pp. 459–460; ICC, *Prosecutor v. Katanga et al*, Decision on the Confirmation of the Charges, 30 September 2008, ICC-01/04-01/07, para 450.

[236] United Nations War Crimes Commission 1948, pp. 196–197; Cryer et al. 2010, p. 234.

[237] Atadjanov 2019, p. 283.

[238] Ibid.; Cassese 2003, p. 144.

[239] Atadjanov 2019, p. 284; cf. Jessberger 2009, p. 95.

[240] Atadjanov 2019, p. 284.

As for major differences, three may be noted. The first major difference lies in the objective elements of the two crimes: crimes against humanity have a broader scope since they include individual acts which are not encompassed by the existing definition of genocide.[241] The second difference consists in the international element of the crimes. For crimes against humanity that element consists of the widespread or systematic attack against a civilian population, or the so-called "contextual element" discussed in the preceding sections while for genocide the context of organized violence, i.e., international element of the crime, is linked to its *mens rea*: the violence comprises of the intended destruction of a protected group.[242] And the third main difference between the two crimes lies in the difference between their protected interests. In the case of genocide attacks, aside from threatening peace and security of the world, it is the people's groups' right to existence, individual interests and rights of the attacked groups' members as well as the victims' dignity.[243] In the case of crimes against humanity attack, as the reader may recall, it is humanness and its constituent elements of freedom, human dignity, humaneness, civilized attitude and reason, as well as fundamental human rights.[244]

Regarding the comparison between crimes against humanity and war crimes, the first group, again, encompasses some overlaps in the description and application of both as it was the case for genocide above. For example, a mass killing of civilians during armed conflict can constitute both types of crimes.[245] Moreover, the law of crimes against humanity which are committed in the context of an armed conflict continues to be shaped by the law of war.[246]

Looking at the significant differences between these crimes and war crimes (as an informative exercise) one can see that there are, indeed, many. It is possible to single out at least five of them. First, crimes against humanity may be committed in the absence of an armed conflict unlike war crimes which necessarily require this contextual element of the conflict.[247] Second, war crimes can occur as single isolated incidents while a context of widespread or systematic commission (i.e., contextual element) is required for acts to be deemed crimes against humanity.[248] Third, the law of crimes against humanity protects victims no matter their nationality or affiliation which is not the case for the former type: the law of war crimes primarily concentrates on protecting "enemy" nationals, or persons who are affiliated with the other party to the conflict.[249] Fourth, the law of crimes against humanity deals with

---

[241] Ibid., p. 285.

[242] Ibid.

[243] Tams et al. 2014, pp. 85–86.

[244] For a comparative analysis of the protective scopes of genocide and crimes against humanity, see Atadjanov 2019, pp. 286–291.

[245] Ibid., p. 296.

[246] Akhavan 2008, pp. 21, 22.

[247] Cryer et al. 2010, p. 233.

[248] Ibid.

[249] This is logically explained because originally the war crimes law was based on reciprocal premises between parties to the conflict. Ibid.; Atadjanov 2019, p. 296.

acts directed against a civilian population whereas war crimes law is concerned with the regulation of conduct on the battlefield against military objectives.[250] Finally, the latter are broader in their definition than war crimes: the inclusion of "other inhumane acts" in the modern definition in the Rome Statute coupled with the very detailed and complicated nature of the acts constituting the war crimes makes it so.[251]

Finally, with respect to the crime of aggression, there are just too many principal differences between this crime and crimes against humanity. Suffice it to mention four. The first (and the biggest) difference consists in that the former concerns directly the law on the legality of use of force, or *jus ad bellum*, hence raising the issues relevant to the international law of State responsibility for acts of aggression.[252] Second, aggression may be said to represent even a broader category of core crimes than crimes against humanity because it provides a favorable "environment" or "occasion", according to Cryer, for other crimes under international law to take place.[253] Third, the crime of aggression can only be committed on behalf of a State and as part of a State plan or policy unlike crimes against humanity, for which it can often be the case but not necessarily always so.[254] Finally, the crime of aggression is a leadership crime; it can be committed exclusively by those who occupy the decision-making positions in a State.[255]

As one can see from the foregoing comparative review, there are important distinguishing elements found in the modern (but also in the historical) definition of crimes against humanity in the law, compared to other core crimes. Such a review is done not only for comparative purposes; it can be useful in terms of better appreciating the scope and legal aspects of one of the most controversial but also topical and fascinating categories in contemporary international law.

47.8 Current Open Issues, Challenges and New Developments

Before concluding this chapter, it makes sense to point out at least some of the most compelling or topical questions still left largely unanswered or unaddressed in the modern treaty or customary law. Most of them have been dealt with in the scholarly literature, and the latter can provide many a useful direction towards possible solutions in law and practice.

Perhaps, at the current stage, the most imperative issue to note would be a practical one, from the perspective of the judicial necessity to qualify the crimes properly: what exactly constitutes a "widespread or systematic attack"? The interpretation of

---

[250] Cryer et al. 2010, p. 233.
[251] Frulli 2001, p. 330; Atadjanov 2019, p. 297.
[252] Atadjanov 2019, p. 301.
[253] Ibid.; Cryer et al. 2010, p. 317.
[254] Cryer et al. 2010, p. 318; Atadjanov 2019, p. 297.
[255] Cryer et al. 2010, pp. 318–319.

this contextual question remains open even if there do exist helpful points in the accumulated case-law. Despite the meanings attributed to "widespread", "systematic" and "attack" by authoritative judicial decisions as discussed in Sect. 47.5.2, the precise qualifiers are still lacking. Concerning "widespread", the questions would be: how many victims are required and how far must they be spread,[256] in order to characterise the criminal acts as crimes against humanity? The meaning of the term hence remains not fully clarified. Similar questions arise with respect to the level, quality and quantity of organization required for the attack to reach the threshold of "systematic".[257]

Aside from the problematic contextual elements of policy requirements and the interpretation of the civilian population already considered in the chapter, there is also a question relevant to the material scope of the crimes under review, namely, what criminal behavior qualifies as "persecution" and "other inhumane acts"?[258] The connection between persecution and another inhumane act that is required under the Rome Statute is a controversial restriction since it precludes convictions based on persecution alone. The restrictions imposed by the Statute in the determination of what constitutes "other inhumane act" are not exhaustive and the judges have considerable discretion to elaborate on that. How it will help overcome the challenge remains to be seen. Hence, the law can be said to be still evolving.[259]

Finally, the analysis made of another important aspect of crimes against humanity, i.e., their protected legal interests, in no way represents an established or resolved issue in law. Due to the lack of a universally recognized definition of what is being attacked by the acts constituting crimes against humanity, there are numerous normative visions and conceptual descriptions of crimes against humanity which compete for recognition in law, jurisprudence and scholarship as we have earlier noted in Sect. 47.4. The theory responding to this crucial question proposed by this author represents a conceptual and normative attempt at clarifying the protective scope of crimes against humanity. The challenge presented by the absence of a codified formulation of humanness in international law could be resolved by way of introducing a comprehensive definition of humanity into relevant legal instruments.[260] There is also no specific acting treaty on crimes against humanity which would address, in full or in part, the difficulties and challenges briefly looked at above.

In fact, the adoption of such a treaty is currently on the ongoing agenda of the UN International Law Commission having been introduced for the first time back in 2014. An overall objective for this topic of the Commission was to draft articles for what could become a comprehensive convention on the prevention and punishment of crimes against humanity.[261] Ultimately, the pertinent report proposed two draft articles: one on prevention and punishment of crimes against humanity and the other

---

[256] DeGuzman 2011, p. 130.

[257] Ibid.

[258] Ibid., pp. 133–134.

[259] Ibid., p. 134.

[260] See for corresponding argumentation Atadjanov 2019, pp. 314–315.

[261] Ibid., p. 112.

on the definition of such crimes.[262] They were distributed for gathering the respective comments from states. Since that time, the Commission proceeded on the basis of three reports of the Special Rapporteur; in 2016 it adopted a draft preamble, a set of 15 draft articles and a draft annex, together with commentaries thereto, on crimes against humanity, and decided to transmit the draft conclusions through the Secretary General to governments, international organizations and others, for comments and observations.[263] It is expected that the draft treaty would be reviewed by the UN General Assembly's Sixth Committee in Fall 2019.

It is certainly a welcome and encouraging development. The answer to the question of why the international community needs a treaty specifically dealing with crimes against humanity has already been responded by notable legal experts.[264] Thus, there are several arguments in favor of such an adoption. First, a specific treaty would define the crimes universally and contribute to the development of emerging norms.[265] Second, such a treaty would extend the reach of the rule of law on crimes against humanity beyond the ICC and international tribunals, implanting uniform definitions of crimes against humanity into the laws of states around the world; gradually, a global body of jurisprudence would develop which would define crimes against humanity in many countries.[266] Third, an international instrument would develop into customary international law and help establish, in the future, an international law of crimes against humanity which acquires the status of *jus cogens*.[267] Fourth, the convention would set forth provisions for interstate cooperation in enforcement, and by universalizing the law on crimes against humanity it could facilitate the adoption of pertinent extradition procedures and international judicial assistance.[268]

This argumentation could go on and on. Hopefully, once the work of the ILC is over and the project moves to the stage where a corresponding forum is set, i.e., if a diplomatic conference on the adoption of the treaty (Convention) is held, this important initiative of the global community may not end up adopting another instrument of international law which looks nice on paper but ineffective and unfulfilled in practice.[269] Therefore, it is important that as many states from all regions of the world are involved in this work as possible and that the commitments they undertake accordingly are fully realized. Such an objective is really difficult to achieve as history shows but then, as they say in a well-known proverb, nothing ventured, nothing gained.

---

[262] Ibid.

[263] Updated information on the activities, sessions and texts of the ILC regarding crimes against humanity and the draft Convention itself are available at http://legal.un.org/ilc/summaries/7_7.shtml. Accessed 5 May 2020.

[264] Sadat 2011, pp. 345–358.

[265] Ibid., p. 356.

[266] Ibid., pp. 356–357.

[267] Ibid., under slightly differing formulations.

[268] Ibid. For more additional argumentation in this respect see DeGuzman 2011, pp. 134–135.

[269] Stanton cites the International Convention on the Prevention and Punishment of the Crime of Genocide as an example of such a disappointing instrument which fate must be avoided in case of the Proposed Convention on Crimes against Humanity. See Ibid., 347–350.

47.9 Conclusion

As the discussion in the chapter has revealed, the concept of crimes against humanity in international conflict and security law is in no way rigid. Rather, it is a rather complex, and quite actively and dynamically developing phenomenon. In this regard DeGuzman notes that even if now this concept is more than a half-century old (see Sect. 47.2), the law of crimes against humanity remains riddled with doctrinal ambiguities and subject to fundamental normative disagreements.[270] Following this logic, one can say that the modern consensus on these crimes' treaty definition, i.e., in the Rome Statute of the ICC, represents a coin of two sides: it is a big diplomatic accomplishment and at the same time a missed opportunity for conceptual clarity and preciseness.

Be it as it may, the law does not constitute a static area. It evolves, at different speeds, and truly so for many important concepts in law including the core crimes. ICL is a dynamic phenomenon, in its treaty and customary law dimension as well as in international jurisprudence. That fully concerns crimes against humanity as well. The ongoing work of the ICC notwithstanding, all the hurdles and stumbling blocks the Court frequently faces provide hope that its case-law will continue contributing to the crystallization of the law of crimes against humanity. This takes into account that many of those accused in the cases considered by its Chambers are charged on this crime category.

Furthermore, the developments in treaty law in the future bring new hopes as looked at briefly in the preceding subsection. Of course, the convention would mandate the prevention and repression of crimes against humanity and establish a cooperative regime for addressing such crimes; therefore, if widely ratified, such a convention would play an important role in strengthening the legal regime or regimes governing crimes against humanity.[271] It is yet another valid argument in favour of the adoption of a treaty devoted exclusively to crimes against humanity. But even more than that, clarifying the definition and many other important aspects of crimes against humanity specifically at the international treaty level would turn out instrumental for the much-needed criminalization at the domestic level, too, providing points of reference and serving as guiding international legal provisions.[272]

As this author noted, again, in another work, it appears that the phrase "crimes against humanity are as old as humanity itself" has become a sort of a fashionable truism to be used by the scholarly authorities who research issues dealing with crimes against humanity.[273] It disturbingly suggests that, historically, violations against universal categories such as humanity have accompanied the evolution

---

[270] DeGuzman 2011, p. 134.

[271] Ibid., p. 135.

[272] Atadjanov 2019, p. 315.

[273] Ibid., p. 309. In this phrase "humanity" denotes its first meaning: "mankind".

47 Crimes Against Humanity   1069

of human civilization since the origin of mankind as we know it, demonstrating the long-lived nature of crimes against humanity as a historical phenomenon.[274]

The chapter reviewed and described the most significant aspects pertaining to crimes against humanity in ICSL. This review included the historical development of the concept of these crimes as a legal category, protected interests, their modern definition and the key elements of that definition as established in the Rome Statute of the ICC, such as the contextual elements, *actus reus* and *mens rea*. Their individual prohibited acts each looked at separately albeit succinctly, relationship to other "counterpart" core crimes, i.e., genocide, war crimes and the crime of aggression, as well as existing problematic issues and current positive developments in the law have been subsequently analyzed. The chapter hence tried to project a general picture of the current legal standing of crimes against humanity and the role they play as part of the material content of international criminal law and, by extension, of ICSL.

Professor Bassiouni noted in his seminal book that the viability of crimes against humanity as international crimes separate and apart from genocide and war crimes is a legal reality that no one can deny.[275] I would add that this is despite all the setbacks the history of law of crimes against humanity has repeatedly experienced, some of them noted earlier, with such vulnerability being owed to the ignorance and lack of attention of those who were in a position to shape and influence the evolution of international law. This contributed to the impunity of perpetrators which in turn negatively affected the conduct of other perpetrators in situations all over the world which produced a high level of victimization. Some horrifying numbers are cited in the introduction to the chapter. Bassiouni cites even more mind-boggling numbers of tens of millions of victims and mentions situations of armed conflict and other situations of violence starting from Afghanistan to Cambodia to Rwanda to the Former Yugoslavia and many more.[276] Most of those deaths fall within the meaning of crimes against humanity, indeed.

A very just question that springs to mind is the following: what does the future hold? Can the era of human rights in this century prevent the recurrence of horrible and senseless violence by man against man, as witnessed during World War II and thereafter?[277] The prospects are dim especially if one recalls the many grave challenges faced by international law of today. Some of those challenges include: the flagrant multiple violations of law (war crimes and crimes against humanity) committed by terrorist non-State actors such as ISIS; ongoing armed conflicts of a mixed nature, both international and non-international, including the conflicts in

---

[274] Ibid. Obviously, what is meant here by "crimes against humanity" was not a strictly legal denomination of the type of crimes and their appearance as defined in law but rather a moral and historical concept.

[275] Bassiouni 2011, p. 738.

[276] Ibid., p. 736.

[277] Ibid., p. 740.

Syria and Ukraine;[278] challenges presented due to real or potential violations of law by some State systems; rise of populism in certain regions of the world, and so on.[279]

Hence, a codification of crimes against humanity in a separate international legal instrument which would address and establish the key elements and aspects flowing out of the application of the law of crimes against humanity (e.g., prevention, cooperation between states, implementation, and much more) is only a welcome development. This is provided that the work is the result of a principled, unswerving and committed stance of the states taking part in the process of treaty drafting and corresponding negotiations, and not a politically motivated compromise which would produce a weak, insignificant and mostly declarative convention.

But going even beyond treaty-supporting arguments, and following Bassiouni's logic, it is clear that mankind needs an effective international criminal law which is able to express, safeguard and ensure the highest values of human civilization in the fair and impartial adjudication of international crimes.[280] This is not only the issue of an effective ICC, an institution which, to paraphrase Aristotle, would offer the same law whether in Athens or Rome, and apply equally to all peoples of the world, not only because it is law, but because it is "the right reason",[281] an idealistic view which is being gravely tested nowadays because of, again, the problems faced by the Court but also due to disappointments caused by it in its activities... It is also the question of a concerted effort of the global community, active work of civil society members, humanitarian actors, but first of all, states as subjects of international law. Given the existing hurdles in today's realities of the world, that effort is not an easy undertaking but was it ever?

References

Akhavan P (2008) Reconciling crimes against humanity with the laws of war. Human rights, armed conflict, and the limits of progressive jurisprudence. Journal of International Criminal Justice 21:6

Ambos K (2013) Punishment without a sovereign? The ius puniendi issue of ICL: A first contribution towards a consistent theory of ICL. Oxford Journal of Legal Studies 33:293

Ambos K (2014) Treatise on ICL, Vol. II. Oxford University Press, Oxford

Atadjanov R (2019) Humanness as a protected legal interest of crimes against humanity: Conceptual and normative aspects. T.M.C. Asser Press, The Hague

Bassiouni C (2005) The legislative history of the International Criminal Court: Introduction, analysis and integrated text, Vol. I. Transnational Publishers, Ardsley, New York

---

[278] The case of Ukraine involves, in terms of qualification, multiple legal regimes all caused by the crime of aggression committed by the Russian Federation and still ongoing: regime of occupation and international armed conflict in the Crimean Peninsula, international and non-international armed conflicts taking place in the Eastern Ukraine. See in general Sayapin and Tsybulenko 2018.

[279] Atadjanov 2019, p. 316.

[280] See Bassiouni 2011, p. 741.

[281] Ibid.

Bassiouni M (2011) Crimes against humanity: Historical evolution and contemporary application. Cambridge University Press, Cambridge

Boas G et al (2008) Elements of crimes under international law. Cambridge University Press, Cambridge

Boot M (2002) Genocide, crimes against humanity, war crimes: Nullum crimen sine lege and the subject matter jurisdiction of the International Criminal Court. Intersentia, Antwerp/Oxford/New York

Cassese A (2003) International criminal law, 3rd edn. Oxford University Press, Oxford

Cassese A et al (2002) The Rome Statute of the International Criminal Court: A commentary, Vol. I. Oxford University Press, Oxford

Cryer R (2005) Prosecuting international crimes. Selectivity and the international criminal law regime. Cambridge University Press, Cambridge

Cryer R, Boister N (eds) (2008) Documents on the Tokyo International Military Tribunal. Oxford University Press, Oxford

Cryer R et al (2010) An introduction to ICL and procedure, 2nd edn. Cambridge University Press, Cambridge

DeGuzman M (2011) Crimes against humanity. In: Schabas W, Bernaz N (eds) Routledge handbook of international criminal law. Routledge, London, New York, pp. 121–122

Ferencz B (1980) An international criminal court: A step toward world peace. Oceana Publications, London

Frulli M (2001) Are crimes against humanity more serious than war crimes? European Journal of International Law 2:12

Geras N (2011) Crimes against humanity: Birth of a concept. Manchester University Press, Manchester

International Law Commission (ILC) (1996) Report of the International Law Commission on the work of its forty-eighth session, 6 May–26 July 1996. GAOR A/51/10

Jessberger F (2009) The definition and the elements of the crime of genocide. In: Gaeta P (ed) The UN Genocide Convention: A commentary. Oxford University Press, Oxford

Klamberg M (ed) (2017) Commentary on the law of the International Criminal Court. Torkel Opsahl Academic EPublisher, Brussels

Lee R (1999) The International Criminal Court: The making of the Rome Statute. Issues, negotiations, results. Kluwer Law International, The Hague/London/Boston

Luban D (2004) A theory of crimes against humanity. Yale J. Int'l L. 29:85–167

May L (2005) Crimes against humanity: A normative account. Cambridge University Press, Cambridge

Meron T (1995) International criminalization of internal atrocities. American Journal of International Law, 89(3):554

Neidleman J (2012) The social contract theory in a global context. E-International Relations (E-IR) http://www.e-ir.info/2012/10/09/the-social-contract-theory-in-a-global-context/. Accessed 5 May 2020

Orentlicher D (1991) Settling accounts: The duty to prosecute human rights violations of a prior regime. Yale Law Journal 100:2537

Roberts A, Guelff R (2000) Documents on the laws of war, 3rd edn. Oxford University Press, Oxford

Sadat L (2011) Forging a convention for crimes against humanity. Cambridge University Press, Cambridge

Sayapin S, Tsybulenko E (eds) (2018) The use of force against Ukraine and international law. T.M.C. Asser Press, The Hague

Schabas W (2007) An introduction to the International Criminal Court, 3rd edn. Cambridge University Press, Cambridge

Schabas W (2008) State policy as an element of international crimes. Journal of Criminal Law and Criminology 98(3):953

Schabas W (2010) The International Criminal Court: A commentary on the Rome Statute. Oxford University Press, Oxford

Shelton D et al (eds) (2005) Encyclopedia of genocide and crimes against humanity, Vol. 1 (A-H). Thomson Gale, Farmington Hills

Schindler D, Toman J (eds) (1996) Des conflits armés: Recueil des conventions, résolutions et autre documents. Comité international de la Croix-Rouge, Geneva

Stahn C (2019) A critical introduction to international criminal law. Cambridge University Press, Cambridge

Tams C et al (2014) Convention on the prevention and punishment of the crime of genocide: A commentary. C.H. Beck/Hart/Nomos, Munich/Oxford/Baden-Baden

Triffterer O (2008) Commentary on the Rome Statute of the International Criminal Court, 2nd edn. C.H. Beck/Hart/Nomos, Munich

Triffterer O, Ambos K (2016) The Rome Statute of the International Criminal Court. A commentary, 3rd edn. C.H. Beck/Hart/Nomos, Munich

United Nations Security Council (1993) Resolution 827 adopted by the Security Council at its 3217th meeting on 25 May 1993. UN Doc. S/25704, Annex

United Nations Security Council (1994) Resolution 955 adopted by the Security Council at its 3453rd meeting on 8 November 1994. UN Doc. S/RES/955, Annex

United Nations War Crimes Commission (1948) History of the United Nations War Crimes Commission and the development of the laws of war. H.M.S.O., London

Van Schaack B (1998) The definition of crimes against humanity: Resolving the incoherence. Columbia Journal of Transnational Law 37:787

Werle G [Верле Г] (2011) Principles of International Criminal Law (translation into Russian) [Принципы международного уголовного права]. Fenix, TransLit, Odessa, Moscow

Werle G, Jessberger F (2014) Principles of international criminal law, 3rd edn. Oxford University Press, Oxford

Rustam Atadjanov LLB, LLM, Dr. iur., PhD is an Assistant Professor of Public and International Law at KIMEP University School of Law (Almaty, Kazakhstan) since 2019, and Director of the Bachelor in International Law Programme. He is a Graduate of the Karakalpak State University, Uzbekistan (2003), University of Connecticut School of Law, USA (2006), and University of Hamburg, Faculty of Law, Germany (2018). Rustam formerly worked as a Programme Responsible and Legal Adviser at the Regional Delegation of the International Committee of the Red Cross (ICRC) in Central Asia (2007–2014), dealing with international humanitarian law, public international law and criminal law issues. His areas of expertise and research include public international law, international human rights law, international criminal law, international humanitarian law, theory of law and state, and constitutional law. Rustam authored a monograph entitled Humanness as a Protected Legal Interest of Crimes against Humanity: Conceptual and Normative Aspects (T.M.C. Asser Press/Springer, 2019), and published 20 academic and publicist articles, encyclopedic entries and book reviews in a number of European and Asian academic journals. At KIMEP University´s School of Law, Rustam teaches Public Law and International Law-related courses.

Chapter 48
The Crime of Apartheid

Gerhard Kemp

Contents

48.1 Apartheid in Historical Context	1074
48.1.1 Introduction	1074
48.1.2 Apartheid and Settler-Colonialism	1075
48.1.3 The Policy and Legal Foundations of the System of Apartheid in South Africa	1077
48.1.4 Resisting Apartheid	1080
48.1.5 The Armed Struggle against Apartheid	1082
48.2 Political and Legal Responses to the System of Apartheid	1082
48.2.1 An Overview of International Instruments Declaring Apartheid to be a Crime against Humanity	1082
48.2.2 Defining the Crime of Apartheid	1084
48.3 Apartheid as a Crime against Humanity (and *Humanness*)	1087
48.4 Conclusion	1090
References	1090

Abstract South Africa's apartheid system (1948–1994) gained notoriety not only as an offensive, racist and oppressive domestic policy, but as a crime against humanity. Historically and conceptually apartheid should not be seen in temporally restrictive terms. It should rather be seen as a continuation and systematisation of settler-colonialism in Southern Africa. Apartheid as a criminal phenomenon is not parochially restricted to Southern Africa, but is now recognised as a crime against humanity, attracting criminal liability wherever it is committed. The criminalisation of apartheid as a crime against humanity prior to the adoption of the Rome Statute of the International Criminal Court is not uncontested, however that debate now seems moot in light of the current state of international criminal law.

Keywords Apartheid · Crimes against humanity · Colonialism · South Africa

---

G. Kemp (✉)
Faculty of Law, University of Derby, Derby, United Kingdom
e-mail: G.Kemp2@derby.ac.uk

Humboldt Universität zu Berlin, Berlin, Germany

© T.M.C. ASSER PRESS and the authors 2022
S. Sayapin et al. (eds.), *International Conflict and Security Law*,
https://doi.org/10.1007/978-94-6265-515-7_48

48.1 Apartheid in Historical Context

48.1.1 Introduction

Scholars and commentators generally mark 1948 as the birth year of the racist constitutional, legal and political system that came to be known as 'apartheid'.[1] This most infamous word in the Afrikaans language, literally translated, means 'separateness'. The system of apartheid which emerged in South Africa after the election victory of the National Party in 1948 should be seen as a continuation of the racist settler-colonialism introduced first by the Dutch in 1652 and thereafter by the British.[2] But apartheid was also more than the settler-colonial racism that one would find in the United States, Canada, New Zealand, Australia, and elsewhere. Apartheid was a very deliberate effort to use race as the defining principle in all aspects of South African economic, social, political and legal life.

In the two decades prior to, as well as after the 1948 election victory, the Afrikaner intelligentsia in the media, in cultural institutions, the churches and in the predominantly Afrikaans universities,[3] set about to produce the intellectual groundwork for what became the vast complex of legislative instruments that formed the legal basis for the apartheid system.[4] Superficially, apartheid shared the same kind of racism that one would find for instance in the segregated South of the United States. But apartheid turned out to be much more than petty racism and racial segregation. The endpoint for the apartheid thinkers was not just segregation of the different racial groups in everyday life, but indeed the balkanization of South Africa into separate political entities based on race, or, the so-called 'grand apartheid'.

The aim of this chapter is not to provide a comprehensive historical or sociological account of apartheid in South Africa. The aim is to provide an overview and discussion of the elements of the crime of apartheid under international law. But these elements can only be understood in the proper historical context of apartheid as a systemic phenomenon that dominated life in South Africa and the broader Southern African region for half a century. It should also be noted that, although the crime of apartheid is, first and foremost, associated with South Africa, its status as a crime against humanity is codified in the Apartheid Convention and provided for in the

---

[1] Lave 1994, at 484; Giliomee 2003a, at 495.

[2] The Cape of Good Hope was under Dutch control from 1652 to 1795. From 1795 to 1803 the Cape was occupied by British forces, but on 19 January 1806 the Cape finally surrendered to the British. In terms of the Convention of 13 August 1814 between Great Britain and the United Provinces of the Netherlands the Cape was ceded to Britain. The Cape Colony was thus established as part of the growing British Empire. For the text of the treaty, see Eybers 1918, at 19.

[3] The Afrikaner secular intelligentsia (including HF Verwoerd and others at Stellenbosch University) articulated the intellectual foundation and justification for apartheid, which historian Herman Giliomee described as a kind of 'racist paternalism and trusteeship', that is, the worldview that infantilised black people as unsophisticated, undeveloped, and in need of guidance and direction from whites. Giliomee 2003b, at 373–392.

[4] On the role of legal academics in the formation and perpetuation of the apartheid legal system, see Mcquid-Mason 1998, at 102–103.

Rome Statute of the International Criminal Court. It is by no means a parochial matter; rather, it forms part of one of the core crimes under international law. It is this legal fact which makes it appropriate to discuss apartheid beyond the contours of transitional justice. Apartheid is a crime against humanity, whether it was practiced in Southern Africa, or elsewhere.[5]

48.1.2 Apartheid and Settler-Colonialism

The first European settlement in what is today South Africa, was not initially intended to be a permanent settlement at all. The Europeans that settled at the Cape of Good Hope in 1652 were servants of the Dutch East India Company and their task was to establish and maintain a half-way establishment between Europe and the East, where sick persons could recuperate and where commercial vessels could be supplied with fresh produce grown in the Company's vegetable and fruit gardens. The early settlement was thus not supposed to become a colony in the traditional sense of the word. This is not to say that the bellicosity and violence associated with European colonial expansion throughout the globe was absent at the Cape. The initial settlement at the Cape was very small and with a very specific commercial mandate. Territorial conquest was not the primary goal. However, the seeds of colonial expansion and a sense of political and social identity independent from the Dutch East India Company were planted in 1657 when a small number of farmers who attained the status of free men or 'burghers' were allowed to establish their own smallholdings at some distance from the Company's main buildings; the fort and warehouses that would later become the nucleus of the future city of Cape Town. The small concession by the Company paved the way for the burghers to explore more fertile lands to the east of Cape Town, thus setting in motion the eventual settlement of modern South Africa by, first, the Dutch, and later, the British. Significantly for our purposes is the cultural and political consequences of that fateful concession by the Dutch East India Company in 1657; the establishment of a settler identity distinct from the Company bureaucrats. This newfound identity would later become the driving force and arch-narrator of Afrikaner nationalism; the cultural and ideological cynosure of apartheid.

The founding myth of Afrikaner identity is tied up with a sense of freedom; freedom from, first, the bureaucratic control of the Dutch East India Company and, later, freedom from the British controlled Cape Colony and other parts of South Africa, including the two Boer republics of the Orange Free State and Transvaal that were established by the Voortrekkers (Dutch speaking settlers who left the British controlled Cape Colony), but that were later defeated by the British in the Second Boer War of 1899–1902.

The fate of the First peoples, the native inhabitants of the western and northern parts of the Cape, and, towards the east and north of present-day South Africa,

---

[5] For more on apartheid beyond the Southern African context, see Dugard 2013, at 867–914.

the black African tribes, were intertwined with the intentions and designs of the European settlers, as was the case elsewhere in the world. But the very essence of apartheid as a denial of the humanity and freedom of people can be traced to the Cape burghers' determination that they could, in their quest for freedom, destroy and deny the freedom of fellow human beings. Again, this is by no means unique to the settler-colonial story of South Africa, but it needs to be pointed out to dispel the myth that apartheid was somehow a twentieth century derivative of European national-socialism.

While the Cape burghers cherished their own freedom, the same basic human right was denied the thousands of slaves that worked the lands of the Cape, first under Dutch and later under British control. On 28 August 1833 a bill for the emancipation of slaves in all the British dominions (including the Cape Colony) received the royal assent. In the Cape Colony slavery was abolished on 1 December 1834.[6] At the time, there were almost 40,000 slaves in the Cape Colony.[7]

Emancipation of the slaves at the Cape unfortunately did not result in a new era of equality and freedom for all. The black majority, in particular, were deliberately excluded from political and economic life; a precursor to the highly formalised system of apartheid that would follow in the twentieth century. In the Cape, the Glen Grey Act of 1894 was adopted as a legislative framework for labour and spatial planning, effectively excluding black people from any meaningful economic and social life in the Cape Colony. During the debate on the Glen Grey Act in the Cape Parliament, Cecil John Rhodes, who was Prime Minister of the Cape Colony from 1890 to 1896, made remarks that would later be echoed by the twentieth century apartheid ideologues:

> Every black man cannot have three acres and a cow, or four morgen and a commonage right. We have to face the question, and it must be brought home to them that in the future nine-tenths of them will have to spend their lives in daily labour, in physical work, in manual labour. This must be brought home to them sooner or later.[8]

The racist and exclusionary policies at the Cape under the British were precursors to what would later be formalised under Afrikaner nationalism as economic, social and legal apartheid; culminating in the notional statehood of the entities constituting the bantustans of 'Grand Apartheid'. Rhodes's vision of a permanent black underclass found further expression in the Natives Land Act of 1913 and the Native Trust Land Act of 1936 that were adopted by the parliament of the Union of South Africa— the dominion that came into existence when the four former British colonies of the Cape, Natal, Orange Free State and Transvaal merged into a unitary state that would later become the Republic of South Africa. Under the Land Acts of 1913 and 1936 black people were essentially denied the opportunity to become economically active property owners in their own country. More than 85% of South Africa's land was declared off-limits for prospective black property owners. The contours of the future

---

[6] Cape of Good Hope Ordinance 1 of 1835; Eybers 1918, at 38.

[7] Eybers 1918, at 38.

[8] Cecil John Rhodes, Speech at the Second Rereading of the Glen Grey Act to the Cape Parliament, 30 July 1894, available at https://www.sahistory.org.za/sites/default/files/glen_grey_speech.pdf.

'Grand Apartheid' scheme of bantustans (the bits and pieces of land that formed the rest of the 15% or so of South Africa's land) were thus established. The political and constitutional pieces of the apartheid puzzle were completed in 1970 with the Bantu Homelands Citizenship Act, in terms of which the majority of blacks were stripped of their South African citizenship.[9] They were henceforth to be citizens of the so-called 'independent homelands' or bantustans, but neither the legitimacy nor legality of these entities were ever accepted by the majority of black people in South Africa or by the international community.[10]

48.1.3 The Policy and Legal Foundations of the System of Apartheid in South Africa

The platform on which the National Party won the South African general election of 1948 paved the way for the adoption of a series of legislative and policy measures which, collectively and in terms of impact, formed the essential framework for the implementation of apartheid. South Africa at the time was no liberal democracy and was in terms of racial matters not dissimilar from countries like the United States (especially the segregated South), Australia and others. But segregation was more a fact of life; not yet state ideology. Racism, as in all settler-colonial societies, was pervasive, but not necessarily codified. The narrow election victory of the National Party in 1948 changed that. The institutionalisation and formalisation of segregation and racist policies to give effect to the National Party's policy of apartheid, were premised on a complex of laws that would govern every aspect of life, love and labour in South Africa for the next forty years. I will briefly note the most important of these statutes and how they have related to the core elements of apartheid.

The brutal logic of apartheid was premised on inflexible and strictly demarcated racial boundaries. Different racial groups had to be defined, classified and then kept apart as separate populations to be further dealt with by the apartheid state. This was not a horizontal 'separate but equal' charade, but a very obvious hierarchical process with the white population at the apex of the apartheid state; the net beneficiaries of power and privileges. To this end, and in short order, the National Party of Prime Minister DF Malan prioritised two pieces of legislation, the Prohibition of Mixed Marriages Act 55 of 1949, and the Population Registration Act 30 of 1950. The aim of the former was not only to keep the next generations racially separated and 'pure', but was also to satisfy the conservative religious lobby that formed such an important part of the National Party's constituency. A statement by dominee ('Reverend') PJS de Klerk in 1939, nine years before the National Party election victory, is emblematic

---

[9] Madlalate 2019, at 197–201.

[10] For UN resolutions condemning the Bantustan policies, see GA Res 2775, 26 UN GAOR, Supp (No 29) 39, UN Doc A/8429 (1971); GA Res 3411, 30 UN GAOR, Supp (No 34) 35, UN Doc A/10034 (1975). See also Richardson 1978, at 185–186.

of the theological rationale that was put forward for the adoption of the apartheid laws. On marriages between black and white South Africans, De Klerk wrote:

> Equalisation leads to humiliation of both races. Mixed marriages between higher civilized Christianized nations and lower nations militate against the Word of God…This is nothing less than a crime, particularly when we take note of the very clear lines of division between the races in our country. The Voortrekkers constantly guarded against such admixture and because of their deed of faith the [Afrikaner] nation was conserved as a pure Christian race up to this day.[11]

Apartheid ideology was based on the biological construct of race. None of the policies that the National Party had in mind would have been possible was it not for the next big piece of legislation that was adopted, namely the Population Registration Act, 1950.[12] This law provided the apartheid state with the legal tools to divide and classify the entire South African population into different racial groups. The categories were: white, coloured (persons of mixed racial background and certain groups of Asian descent, mainly Indian and Chinese), and Bantu (black African). The bureaucratic sounding name of the Act masked the day-to-day dehumanisation of thousands of individuals and families who were living in fear and uncertainty. Classification, one way or the other, had profound consequences in terms of virtually every aspect of an individual's educational opportunities, employment prospects, housing, access to public services and so much more. The Apartheid Museum in Johannesburg serves as a vivid reminder of the daily consequences of the policies that were made possible by the Population Registration Act. The separated entrances reproduced at the museum—one for *Blankes*/Whites and one for *Nie-Blankes*/Non-Whites—encapsulate the duality of apartheid: the white entrance through which the minority could enter their land of opportunity, access to power, the best education, land, capital and everything that an emerging post-war dominium, still within the British Commonwealth, could provide. The Non-White entrance, on the other hand, was not one that any individual would want to enter by choice. It was the entrance to a life of forced removals from land and urban areas, of job restrictions, poor education opportunities, daily acts of discrimination and humiliation, and increasing levels of state violence and oppression.

Racial classification made possible the spatial dimensions of apartheid. The Group Areas Act 41 of 1950 provided for the legal framework to divide South African towns and cities into white, coloured and black areas. The Act was by no means just a tool for *future* racialised spatial planning; it was also the law that made possible wholesale racial purges of previously vibrant multiracial suburbs in cities like Cape Town and Johannesburg, and it was the law that was used to create the vast townships for black and coloured South Africans forcibly removed from their homes and established communities, to be dumped in areas that were often far removed from the best economic and educational opportunities. Simply put, the Group Areas Act made it clear that the aim of apartheid was not just racial separation, but racial subjugation, with whites as the ultimate beneficiaries.

---

[11] Quoted in Lave 1994, at 498–499.
[12] Act 30 of 1950.

Even some defenders of apartheid found the blatant racist and dehumanising aspects suffered by black and coloured South Africans on a daily basis to be too much; for them apartheid was always about a noble universal claim of 'self-determination' which would manifest in self-government for the various racial and ethnic groups in South Africa. For them, apartheid was never supposed to be all about 'petty apartheid' (racial segregation in everyday life) but about the 'Grand Apartheid' of separate homelands for the different racial and ethnic groups. However, even the most charitable reading of the policy positions and legislative priorities of the National Party government could not ignore the racist and dehumanising designs and consequences apparent in the slew of statutes aimed at governing the lives of people on the basis of their skin colour. For example, the Reservation of Separate Amenities Act 49 of 1953 compelled local authorities to segregate all public amenities like recreational areas, beaches, public toilets and access points to public and government buildings. Even many privately owned businesses followed suit by providing for separate entrances or service counters for white and black customers.

While legislation like the above mentioned Reservation of Separate Amenities Act provided the legal basis for the daily humiliation of and discrimination against non-white South Africans, it is statutes like the Bantu Education Act 47 of 1953 that fundamentally impacted on the educational and economic prospects of generations of black South Africans. This statute very explicitly provided for unequal education and also centralised the education of black children and tertiary students in the hands of the National Party government in Pretoria, rather than in the provinces or in the private and religious sectors. The racist view that black children deserved no quality education because they were not destined to follow careers associated with the advanced 'European' part of the population, was widely held in National Party circles and can best be illustrated by the infamous statement on the subject by HF Verwoerd, who would later become Prime Minister of South Africa. On apartheid in education, Verwoerd stated:

> There is no place for [the Bantu] in the European community above the level of certain forms of labour…What is the use of teaching the Bantu child mathematics when it cannot use it in practice? That is quite absurd. Education must train people in accordance with their opportunities in life, according to the sphere in which they live.[13]

The implementation of apartheid in primary and secondary education was followed by apartheid in tertiary education. Under the Extension of University Education Act 45 of 1959, all institutions of higher learning, including former multiracial colleges and universities, were forced to implement race-based admission policies. South Africa's top universities were closed for non-white students, thus perpetuating the socio-economic impact of apartheid at the primary and secondary levels.

The deprivation of quality education for non-white South Africans was a major but by no means the only contributor to the further relegation of non-whites to the status of a permanent economic underclass. The ability of black South Africans to work and to move freely within the borders of the country was seriously curtailed by a plethora of

---

[13] https://www.thoughtco.com/apartheid-quotes-bantu-education-43436 (accessed 2 March 2020).

restrictions and policies, most notably the hated pass-laws, which were consolidated in 1952 in the Bantu (Abolition of Passes and Co-ordination of Documents) Act 67 of 1952. Large numbers of economically active and job-seeking black South Africans were effectively excluded from living or trying to make a living in the economic hubs and urban centres of South Africa. The apartheid rationale was clear: to keep the cities and towns as white as possible, thus laying the groundwork for what would be the real aim of the apartheid laws mentioned thus far—the creation of a white South African state, and then areas that were culturally and demographically deemed to be the nucleuses of future black self-governing territories (the 'homelands' and bantustans of Grand Apartheid). The unjust impact of these laws extended beyond the deprivation of liberty and freedom of movement of millions of black South Africans. It also criminalised all manner of technical violations of these laws and regulations, thus adding to the fear, dehumanisation and carceral aspects which were hallmarks of apartheid as a totalitarian system.

48.1.4 Resisting Apartheid

The political and legal system introduced by the National Party in 1948 brought radical change to South Africa. Given the prominent role of South African Prime Minister Jan Smuts in Britain's war effort against Nazi Germany in the Second World War, it was generally assumed that the Union of South Africa (as one of the so-called 'white dominions', the other being Canada, Australia and New Zealand) would stay on in the post-war continuation of the British Commonwealth. The election victory of DF Malan's National Party in 1948 came as a shock and set South Africa on the course to become a republic in 1961. At the Conference of Commonwealth Prime Ministers that was held in London in March 1961, the newly minted Republic of South Africa formerly requested to stay on in the Commonwealth, albeit now as a republic. This request was opposed by African states, India and Canada. The reason for their opposition to South Africa's request was that they could not reconcile South Africa's increasingly oppressive apartheid system with continued membership of the Commonwealth, even at a time when anti-colonialism and the struggle for freedom were gaining momentum in Africa and elsewhere.

While the Republic of South Africa encountered a rather chill reception on the international stage, domestic opposition to apartheid also intensified. The formation of the Union of South Africa in 1910 was always seen by South Africa's black liberation movements as a missed opportunity for the recognition of universal human rights and equality between black and white South Africans. Indeed, 1910 was seen as a missed opportunity to bring an end to centuries of colonialism, racism and oppression. The African National Congress (ANC), one of Africa's oldest liberation movements, which was formed in 1912 in the South African city of Bloemfontein, resolved to peacefully resist all efforts by the white minority government of the Union of South Africa to exclude the black majority from political decision making. The election victory of the National Party in 1948 and the intensification and formalisation of racist policies now known as apartheid, brought a sense of urgency to the ANC's and the broader Congress movement's resistance against apartheid. Their peaceful acts of resistance were, however, met with harsh responses by the apartheid state. The massacre at Sharpeville on 21 March 1960 was a turning point in the domestic resistance against apartheid. In turn, the brutality of the South African state's response to the domestic resistance against apartheid galvanised international opposition to apartheid and led to the increased international isolation of South Africa, including at the United Nations.

Domestically, the notion that apartheid could be defeated by means of peaceful resistance became increasingly unrealistic. The National Party government has made it at any rate clear that they were not interested in any form of meaningful engagement with organisations and movements representing the black majority. This was true long before the events at Sharpeville. For instance, in the 1950's a number of laws were adopted to suppress or prohibit certain political organisations, including those aligned with the ANC. The Suppression of Communism Act 44 of 1950 was ostensibly aimed at the spreading of the communist ideology. In reality it prohibited any doctrine which sought to bring about 'any political, industrial, social or economic change ... by the promotion of disturbance or disorder by unlawful acts or omissions.'[14] The vagueness and scope of the definition of 'communism' was by design; it was meant to herd domestic opposition to apartheid by the ANC and its allies in the labour movement, the other Congress organisations and parties and organisations on the Left, all into one amorphous and easy to demonise adversary that could conveniently be targeted by the oppressive state.

In 1955, at a gathering in Kliptown, Johannesburg, the Freedom Charter was adopted as a blueprint for a democratic, non-racial, non-sexist and egalitarian South Africa; the antithesis of the policy of apartheid.[15] Given the socialist policy proposals that were also contained in the Freedom Charter (*inter alia* the nationalisation of banks and mines) it was not difficult for the apartheid state to respond with the broad anti-communist prosecutorial tools provided for in legislation such as the Suppression of Communism Act, as well as with vaguely defined common law crimes such as treason. As a result several prominent anti-apartheid activists were arrested and tried, only to be acquitted. The National Party Government was temporarily humiliated in the courts, but did enjoy a tactical victory of sorts, in that many of the prominent leaders of the Congress Movement, including Oliver Tambo and Nelson Mandela, spent several years in court rather than with their political movement where they could organise against apartheid.

---

[14] Article 1(1)(b).
[15] Kemp 2017, at 422.

48.1.5 The Armed Struggle against Apartheid

The National Party's realisation of their republican dream in 1961 coincided with heightened opposition against apartheid. The ANC and the breakaway Pan Africanist Congress (PAC), which was established as a more radical Africanist liberation movement as opposed to the ANC which was, as per the Freedom Charter, committed to non-racialism, realised that the emboldened National Party government would only become more committed to apartheid and was not to be persuaded by peaceful resistance. The ANC therefore created an armed wing, Umkhonto we Sizwe ('Spear of the Nation') to carry out acts of violence and sabotage against government targets. Young black South Africans were sent by Umkhonto for military training in the Soviet Union, sympathetic African states, and, later, also in states like the German Democratic Republic ('East Germany'), which were supportive of the liberation struggle.

In response to the more radical and violent opposition to apartheid, the National Party government adopted harsh new laws, including the Sabotage Act of 1962 and detention without trial measures in terms of the Criminal Procedure Amendment Acts. By 1963 both the ANC and the PAC were banned under the Unlawful Organisations Act. This ban would only be lifted in 1990 after FW de Klerk's historic speech in the last white parliament; a political act which set in motion the negotiations that ended official apartheid and led to the adoption of South Africa's first democratic constitution in 1993.

48.2 Political and Legal Responses to the System of Apartheid

48.2.1 An Overview of International Instruments Declaring Apartheid to be a Crime against Humanity

The escalating levels of violence on both sides of the South African conflict, as well as the growing international revulsion against the apartheid state's policies of oppression and systemic human rights violations, brought the issue of apartheid to the centre of international law and politics. At the International Court of Justice (ICJ) in The Hague, South Africa had to defend the application of apartheid policies in South West Africa (Namibia), a territory then under South African occupation and administration. In New York, at the United Nations, there was growing political agreement that apartheid was morally reprehensible, prompting the UN General Assembly to adopt the International Convention on the Suppression and Punishment of the Crime of Apartheid in 1973. This was the most comprehensive, but by no means only, international declaration that apartheid constituted a crime against humanity. The General Assembly had at several occasions adopted resolutions condemning apartheid as a crime against humanity.[16] Even the Security Council, where South Africa could sometimes rely on the explicit or passive support of the United Kingdom and the United States, agreed that apartheid is a crime against the conscience and dignity of mankind.[17] Security Council Resolution 556 of 13 December 1984 unequivocally stated that apartheid is a crime against humanity.

Apart from the Apartheid Convention, there are a number of other international instruments that also recognise apartheid as a crime against humanity. The Convention on the Non-Applicability of Statutory Limitations to War Crimes and Crimes against Humanity[18] provides that 'inhuman acts resulting from the policy of apartheid are condemned as crimes against humanity.'[19] The Draft Code of Crimes against the Peace and Security of Mankind (1991)[20] includes apartheid as a crime against the peace and security of mankind. The 1996 Draft Code[21] did not reference apartheid as a distinct international crime, but the Draft Code listed conduct that specifically constitute crimes against humanity, including the following:

> A crime against humanity means any of the following acts, when committed in a systematic manner or on a large scale and instigated or directed by a government or by any organisation or group: ...(f) institutionalised discrimination on racial, ethnic or religious grounds involving the violation of fundamental human rights and freedoms and resulting in seriously disadvantaging a part of the population.[22]

At the regional level, the Organisation of African Unity and its successor, the African Union, has a long history of opposing apartheid. The Preamble to the African Charter on Human and Peoples' Rights therefore affirms that member states have a duty to 'achieve the total liberation of Africa, the peoples of which are still struggling for their dignity and genuine independence, and undertake to eliminate colonialism, neo-colonialism, apartheid [and] Zionism'.[23]

Despite a request by the International Committee of the Red Cross, the crime of apartheid was not included in the Statutes of the UN *ad hoc* tribunals, the ICTY and the ICTR.[24] The drafting of the Rome Statute of the International Criminal Court led to a different result, and, at the behest of South Africa (supported by several states) the crime of apartheid was ultimately included as a crime against humanity.[25]

---

[16] See, for instance, GA Res 2189; GA Res 2202; GA Res 39/72A; GA Res 2074.

[17] UNSC Res 392, 19 June 1976; and subsequently, UNSC Res 418 (1977); UNSC Res 473 (1980); UNSC Res 591 (1986).

[18] UNTS, Vol. 754, p. 73.

[19] Article I(b).

[20] Report of the International Law Commission, 43rd Secs, UN GAOR, Supp No 10, at 255, UN Doc A/46/10 (1991).

[21] Reproduced in: Yearbook of the International Law Commission 1996, vol. II, Part Two.

[22] Article 18(f).

[23] 27 June 1981, OAU doc CAB /LEG/67/3 rev. 5, 21 ILM 58 (1982).

[24] Eden 2014, at 184.

[25] Eden 2014, at 185.

48.2.2 Defining the Crime of Apartheid

The International Convention on the Suppression and Punishment of the Crime of Apartheid provides for the following extended definition:

> For the purpose of the present Convention, the term "the crime of apartheid", which shall include similar policies and practices of racial segregation and discrimination as practised in southern Africa, shall apply to the following inhuman acts committed for the purpose of establishing and maintaining domination by one racial group of persons over any other racial group of persons and systematically oppressing them:
>
> (a) Denial to a member or members of a racial group or groups of the right to life and liberty of person:
>
> (i) By murder of members of a racial group or groups;
>
> (ii) By the infliction upon the members of a racial group or groups of serious bodily or mental harm, by the infringement of their freedom or dignity, or by subjecting them to torture or to cruel, inhuman or degrading treatment or punishment;
>
> (iii) By arbitrary arrest and illegal imprisonment of the members of a racial group or groups;
>
> (b) Deliberate imposition on racial group or groups of living conditions calculated to cause its or their physical destruction in whole or in part;
>
> (c) Any legislative measures and other measures calculated to prevent a racial group or groups from participation in the political, social, economic and cultural life of the country and the deliberate creation of conditions preventing the full development of such group or groups, in particular by denying to members of a racial group or groups basic human rights and freedoms, including the right to work, the right to form recognized trade unions, the right to education, the right to leave and to return to their country, the right to a nationality, the right to freedom of movement and residence, the right to freedom of opinion and expression, and the right to freedom of peaceful assembly and association;
>
> (d) Any measures, including legislative measures, designed to divide the population along racial lines by the creation of separate reserves and ghettos for the members of a racial group or groups, the prohibition of mixed marriages among members of various racial groups, the expropriation of landed property belonging to a racial group or groups or to members thereof;
>
> (e) Exploitation of the labour of the members of a racial group or groups, in particular by submitting them to forced labour;
>
> (f) Persecution of organizations and persons, by depriving them of fundamental rights and freedoms, because they oppose apartheid.[26]

The Rome Statute of the International Criminal Court, as noted above, provides that 'the crime of apartheid' is a crime against humanity when committed 'as part of a widespread or systematic attack directed against any civilian population, with knowledge of the attack'.[27] For this purpose the crime of apartheid means 'inhumane acts of a character similar to those referred to in para 1 [of Article 7], committed in the context of an institutionalized regime of systematic oppression and domination

---

[26] Article II of the International Convention on the Suppression and Punishment of the Crime of Apartheid (1973). Reproduced in Van den Wyngaert 2011, at 413–414.

[27] Rome Statute of the ICC, Article 7(1)(j).

by one racial group over any other racial group or groups and committed with the intention of maintaining that regime.'[28]

It was noted that, for purposes of individual criminal liability, the Rome Statute is the first legal instrument that criminalises apartheid in line with the principle of legality.[29] This view is in contrast to the view that apartheid was a crime under international law even before the adoption of the Rome Statute. South Africa's own Truth and Reconciliation Commission (TRC) considered apartheid to be a crime against humanity.[30] This determination by the TRC was made before the finalisation of the Rome Statute. The TRC referred to the various UN General Assembly and Security Council resolutions, the Apartheid Convention as well as other international instruments as legal and normative support for the view that apartheid has been a crime against humanity at least since the early 1970's.

It is true that many, if not most, of the instruments referred to by the TRC were either non-binding resolutions, or were not drafted in the clear and unambiguous language expected of a criminalisation provision that would satisfy the legality principle. It is also true that many would object to the argument that, in the absence of an international criminal law treaty, apartheid should nevertheless be viewed as a crime under customary international law.[31] The gist of the objection regarding the customary status of apartheid as a crime against humanity, is that the supposed universal condemnation of apartheid as a crime against humanity via the Apartheid Convention, was not followed through with universal ratification, thus illustrating the lack of universal *opinio juris* regarding apartheid as a crime against humanity.[32]

Since there has never been an attempt, either in a South African court, or in an international tribunal, to prosecute an individual for the crime of apartheid, one can only speculate what a court or tribunal would make of the legal arguments on both sides of the debate. A number of post-TRC prosecutions and attempted prosecutions of apartheid era crimes (including allegations of war crimes) came before the courts in South Africa, but none of these concerned the crime of apartheid as a crime against humanity. The crime of apartheid was at any rate, and for obvious reasons, not a crime under South African law and the ANC-led government did not make it a priority to adopt laws on the matter till 2002, when South Africa incorporated the Rome Statute of the International Criminal Court via domestic legislation, thus making the crime of apartheid as a crime against humanity part of statutory criminal law in South Africa—but not retroactively. The Constitutional Court of South Africa did note on occasion, albeit *obiter dicta*, that 'the practice of apartheid constituted crimes against humanity and some of the practices of the apartheid government constituted war crimes.'[33] The matter before the Constitutional Court concerned a number of procedural issues, the only relevant substantive issue being the question of whether

---

[28] Article 7(2)(h).
[29] Eden 2014, at 189.
[30] TRC Report (1998) Vol. I, at 94.
[31] Eden 2014, at 178–179 and 191.
[32] Eden 2014, at 179.
[33] *S v Basson* 2005 (1) SA 171 (CC) at para 37.

the trial court was correct to have quashed charges against the accused on the ground that the applicable law did not criminalise conspiracies to commit crimes beyond the borders of South Africa. The accused, a medical doctor, was at the relevant times an employee of the apartheid government and the allegation was that he was responsible for murder and other gross human rights violations in neighbouring countries and as part of the apartheid military's war efforts. The point was raised that prosecutorial decisions (including decisions whether to prosecute apartheid-era crimes) must be viewed through the proper constitutional lens. The Constitutional Court stated:

> [The] state's obligation to prosecute offences is not limited to offences which were committed after the Constitution came into force but also applies to all offences committed before it came into force. It is relevant to this enquiry that international law obliges the state to punish crimes against humanity and war crimes. It is also clear that the practice of apartheid constituted crimes against humanity and some of the practices of the apartheid government constituted war crimes. We do not have all the details before us but it does appear that the crimes for which the accused was charged may well fall within the terms of this international law obligation. In the circumstances, it may constitute an added obligation upon the state. We conclude therefore that the question of the quashing of the charges in this case also raises a constitutional issue.[34]

It should be noted that, despite the Constitutional Court's opening of the door to a possible prosecution of an individual for apartheid as a crime against humanity, nothing came of it. Not this case, nor any other criminal case, was pursued on the basis of apartheid as a crime against humanity.[35] Apartheid-era crimes like murder and other serious human rights violations were prosecuted, but then as 'ordinary' crimes under South African domestic criminal law.[36]

Regardless of where one stands on this issue, the clear trend since 1973 was to not only object to apartheid in vague diplomatic or political terms, but to refer to it as a crime against humanity. That was the view of a significant part of the international community. The fact that Western states may not have shared this view cannot nullify the legislative groundwork that was been done by African states and their allies and supporters in the UN General Assembly.

The TRC noted in its Report that the 'recognition of apartheid as a crime against humanity remains a fundamental starting point for reconciliation in South Africa'.[37] The fact that no individuals were prosecuted for this international crime was the result of a deliberate choice by both the international community and by the major parties to the post-apartheid negotiations that paved the way for democratisation in South Africa. Indeed, the TRC noted that 'there was no call for trials by the international community during or after the peaceful transition from apartheid to democracy between 1990 and 1994. It was recognised that the National Party had

---

[34] *S v Basson* para 37.

[35] For a comprehensive discussion, see Gevers 2018, at 25–49.

[36] *Rodrigues v National Director of Public Prosecutions*, Case no 76755/2018, 3 June 2019 (Gauteng High Court, Johannesburg). In this case, the high court rejected the applicant's application for a permanent stay of prosecution of an apartheid-era murder case. The killing of the victim was linked to the apartheid state's nefarious activities in the 1970s.

[37] TRC Report (1998) Vol I, at 94.

become an active participant in this transition and that the South African situation was no longer a threat or a potential threat to international peace. At former State President De Klerk's second appearance before the Commission in May 1997, the Commission placed on record its recognition of the vital role Mr De Klerk had played in the dismantling of the apartheid system.'[38]

Unfortunately, this confidence in FW de Klerk's role in South Africa's transition has not aged too well. In February 2020, De Klerk came under severe criticism for statements issued by his Foundation, echoing similar statements by the former president that he had uttered in 2015, which denied that apartheid was a crime against humanity. De Klerk later apologised for the pain caused by the statement, but the prevailing view in South Africa is that De Klerk has significantly damaged if not destroyed his legacy as one of the architects of post-apartheid South Africa.[39]

48.3 Apartheid as a Crime against Humanity (and *Humanness*)

The National Party government had always maintained that the policy of apartheid was a domestic issue; outside the purview of scrutiny by the international community. This response, based on Article 2(7) of the UN Charter (the principle of non-interference), was supplemented with the political calculation that the international community's (especially the West's) concern about apartheid was rather muted and more symbolic than real. The events at Sharpeville, and the subsequent intensification of the apartheid state's security response to the opposition to apartheid, changed not only the tone but also the substance of the international community's response. As noted by Skinner, the earlier UN resolutions (before 1966) contained words like 'regret' and 'concern'; but as the human rights situation in South Africa became more dire, the UN resolutions also became more serious. Apartheid was now condemned as 'reprehensible and repugnant to human dignity' and the international community was called upon to act more decisively, and this included calls for sanctions against South Africa.[40] Indeed, perhaps no other state's domestic policy attracted more scrutiny than apartheid South Africa after Sharpeville. The UN Special Committee Against Apartheid produced a significant volume of condemnations of the racist and discriminatory policies of apartheid in general, and the security state's abuses of criminal and security law to repress opposition to apartheid, in particular.[41]

---

[38] TRC Report (1998) Vol I, at 94, fn 30.

[39] See commentary by Kajaal Ramjathan-Keogh. Daily Maverick, 21 February 2020. https://www.dailymaverick.co.za/article/2020-02-21-south-africa-apartheid-crimes-against-humanity-and-the-rule-of-law-quo-vadis/.

[40] Skinner 2019, at 137.

[41] https://africanactivist.msu.edu/organization.php?name=Special%20Committee%20Against%20Apartheid. More than 50 of the most important statements and records of the Committee can be

The post-Sharpeville UN resolutions, and the statements and reports by the Special Committee in particular, served as normative precursors to the adoption of the Apartheid Convention in 1973. The adoption of this Convention truly served as a turning point. Whether or not one takes the view that the Convention actually criminalised apartheid under international law, the fact is that the norm against apartheid became a lot less rhetorical and political and a lot more legal in tone, posture and substance.[42] At the heart of this progression was the idea that apartheid was more than a series of human rights violations; it was more than instances of racial discrimination; indeed, it truly represented a fundamental outrage against the notion of human dignity, of being human. That is to say, apartheid is a crime against humanity *par excellence*.

Atadjanov pointed out that there are several definitions of the word 'humanity', including the most commonly used understanding of the concept, namely that of 'humanity' as 'humankind', or, 'the aggregation of all human beings, as a collectivity'.[43] A second approach to the concept of humanity is to focus on the 'quality of being human, or humanness, or the very human condition itself'.[44] There is also a third approach that focuses on humanity as a virtue, and is strongly associated with the humanist tradition, with the broader humanitarian movement, and with attributes and traits like compassion and humaneness.[45] Atadjanov makes the case that crimes against humanity affect 'the quality of being human, or humanness, or the very human condition itself'.[46] To this end the author employs the protected interest theory (the German doctrine of *Rechtsgut*).[47]

What I find appealing about Atadjanov's work on humanness as protected legal interest for purposes of crimes against humanity, is that it not only explains the appropriate normative basis for the criminalisation of crimes against humanity, but it also neutralises a common strategy of those who want to minimise or relativise the characterisation of conduct as crimes against humanity. An example of the latter is the 2015 statement by FW de Klerk, repeated by his Foundation in 2020, that essentially rejected the proposition that apartheid is a crime against humanity since, as a policy, it did not compare to 'genuine crimes against humanity—which have generally included totalitarian repression and the slaughter of millions of people'. De Klerk clearly pushed the idea that crimes against humanity is all about the number of victims killed. He stated:

> By contrast, 23 000 people died in South Africa's political violence between 1960 and 1994 of whom fewer than 4 000 were killed by the security forces. Most of the rest of the deaths occurred in the conflict between the IFP and the ANC. In Kenya, the British interned more

---

accessed at: https://africanactivist.msu.edu/browse_results.php?category=media&member=Documents&org=Special%20Committee%20Against%20Apartheid&.

[42] Skinner 2019, at 139.

[43] Atadjanov 2019, at 19.

[44] Atadjanov 2019, at 19.

[45] Atadjanov 2019, at 19–20.

[46] Atadjanov 2019, at 27.

[47] For the author's working hypothesis, see Atadjanov 2019, at 29–30.

than 320 000 people during the Mau Mau uprising and hanged more than a thousand Mau Mau members. In Algeria the French killed more than 140 000 people in a war that claimed some 700 000 lives.[48]

The focus on numbers of victims (people killed) for purposes of the characterisation of a system as a crime against humanity obscures the true normative basis of the crime. De Klerk's red herring of apartheid's relative low numbers of victims (understood to be people killed) is offensive in its own right, but is the type of construction of apartheid as an 'immoral but not criminal' system that is exposed by an emphasis on *humanness* as a protected legal interest for purposes of crimes against humanity. That is also why South Africa's TRC process, which focused on 'gross human rights violations' between 1960 and 1994, rather than on the systemic aspects of apartheid, can be viewed as flawed. Although the TRC Report stated that apartheid is a crime against humanity, the bulk of the Report, as well as the processes before the Amnesty Committee, contributed to the narrative that apartheid was really about acts of police brutality, torture and a number of killings, rather than the criminality of the system as a whole and with due regard to the historical antecedents of settler-colonialism. If we look at the substance of apartheid as a system; the day to day indignities, the systemic deprivation of generations of non-white South Africans of economic opportunities, quality education, and the chance to live their lives as fellow human beings, we get a sense of the true criminal character of apartheid as a systemic violation of the legal interest of humanness.

Pointing out the substantive and temporal limitations of South Africa's TRC mandate and process is not to minimise the importance of the findings of gross human rights violations by the TRC, or of the general statements about apartheid as a crime against humanity (even if those statements were of a preambular and contextual nature, rather than legal findings in the strict sense of the word). The human rights orientation of the TRC's mandate and findings is at any rate a good connecting point to the notion that crimes against humanity (such as apartheid) are *inhuman* conduct that 'violate the fundamental interests of human beings as such, across all cultural specifics and differences'.[49] Drawing on the work of the political theorist Norman Geras, and political philosopher Massimo Renzo, Atadjanov points out that crimes against humanity are really a denial of the victim's status as a human being.[50] The threshold of seriousness is not numerical, but rather the substantive question of whether the relevant conduct seriously affected the victim's status as a human being. Apartheid as a system, and the plethora of laws, practices and rules that affected non-white South Africans on a daily basis and generationally, certainly denied millions of people their status as human beings. From the daily indignities suffered by individual black and coloured South Africans, to the collective humiliation and disruption suffered by whole groups and communities, apartheid was all

---

[48] https://www.politicsweb.co.za/news-and-analysis/afrikaans-identity-under-huge-pressure--fw-de-kler.

[49] Atadjanov 2019, at 143.

[50] Atadjanov 2019, at 142–145.

about white supremacy and the denial that black and coloured South Africans were human beings that could live free and with dignity just as their white compatriots.

48.4 Conclusion

The protected interest of humanness finds clear expression in the criminalisation of apartheid as a crime against humanity in the Rome Statute of the International Criminal Court. Article 7(2)(h) of the Statute defines apartheid as 'inhumane acts of a character similar to those referred to in para 1, committed in the context of an institutionalized regime of systemic oppression and domination by one racial group over any other racial group or groups and committed with the intention of maintaining that regime'. The condemnation of apartheid as a crime against humanity has gained further recognition in the work of the International Law Commission (ILC). The Draft articles on Prevention and Punishment of Crimes Against Humanity[51] recognises apartheid as a crime against humanity[52] and has followed the basic construction of the Rome Statute.

Apartheid is a racist and dehumanising *system*. The systemic nature of apartheid is underscored in its inclusion within the construct of crimes against humanity. The Commentary on the ILC's draft articles reinforces this, and notes that an individual who commits one of the prohibited acts (including apartheid), 'can commit a crime against humanity; the individual need not have committed multiple acts; but the individual's act must be "part of" a widespread or systematic attack directed against any civilian population.'[53]

References

Atadjanov R (2019) Humanness as a protected legal interest of crimes against humanity. T.M.C. Asser Press, The Hague

Dugard J (2013) Apartheid, international law, and the occupied Palestinian Territory. European Journal of International Law 24: 867–914

Dugard J (2018) Confronting apartheid. Jacana, Auckland Park

Eden P (2014) The role of the Rome Statute in the criminalisation of apartheid. Journal of International Criminal Justice 12: 171–191

Eybers GW (1918) Select Constitutional Documents Illustrating South African History 1795–1910. Routledge & Sons, London

---

[51] Draft articles on Prevention and Punishment of Crimes Against Humanity, with Commentaries (2019), Adopted by the International Law Commission at its seventy-first session, in 2019, and submitted to the General Assembly as part of the Commissioners' report covering the work of that session (A/74/10). For the Report with commentaries to the draft articles, see Yearbook of the International Law Commission, 2019, Vol II, Part Two.

[52] Draft articles on Crimes Against Humanity, Article 2(1)(j).

[53] Draft articles on Crimes Against Humanity, Commentary on Article 2, para 37.

Gevers C (2018) Prosecuting the crime against humanity of apartheid: Never, again. African Yearbook on International Humanitarian Law 25–49

Giliomee H (2003a) The Afrikaners. Tafelberg, Cape Town

Giliomee H (2003b) The making of the apartheid plan, 1929–1948. Journal of Southern African Studies 29: 373–392

Kemp G (2017) South Africa's (possible) withdrawal from the ICC and the future of the criminalization and prosecution of crimes against humanity, war crimes and genocide under domestic law: A submission informed by historical, normative and policy considerations. Wash Univ Glob Stud Law Rev 16:411–438

Lave TR (1994) A nation at prayer, a nation in hate: Apartheid in South Africa. Stanford Journal of International Law 30:483–524

Madlalate R (2019) Dismantling apartheid geography: Transformation and the limits of law. Constitutional Court Review 9: 195–217

Mcquid-Mason D (1998) Truth and Reconciliation Commission submissions by the Society of University Teachers of Law and Certain Law Schools. The South African Law Journal 115: 102–103

Richardson HJ (1978) Self-determination, international law and the South African Bantustan policy. Columbia Journal of Transnational Law 17: 185

Skinner S (2019) Ideology and criminal law—Fascist, National Socialist and Authoritarian Regimes. Hart, Oxford

Van den Wyngaert C (2011) International Criminal Law—A collection of international and regional instruments, 4th edn. Martinus Nijhoff, Leiden

Gerhard Kemp obtained the BA, LLB, LLM, LLD degrees (Stellenbosch) and the International Legal Studies Certificate (Antwerp). He is professor of international and transnational criminal justice at the University of Derby in the United Kingdom and serves on the executive committee of the Institute for Justice and Reconciliation in Cape Town, South Africa. He has published widely in the fields of international and transnational criminal justice, transitional justice, international humanitarian law, and comparative criminal law. He is a recipient of the Alexander von Humboldt research fellowship.

Chapter 49
War Crimes

Ewa Sałkiewicz-Munnerlyn and Sergey Sayapin

Contents

49.1 A Brief History of International Prosecutions for War Crimes	1094
49.2 The Concept and Elements of War Crimes	1097
49.3 Classification of War Crimes	1099
49.3.1 War Crimes against Protected Persons	1099
49.3.2 War Crimes against Protected Objects	1100
49.3.3 War Crimes Related to Unlawful Methods of Warfare	1100
49.3.4 War Crimes Related to Unlawful Means of Warfare	1101
49.4 Perpetrators and Victims	1102
49.4.1 Perpetrators	1102
49.4.2 Victims	1103
49.5 Prosecutions and Amnesty	1105
49.6 Conclusion	1106
References	1107

Abstract War crimes are the most comprehensive category of crimes under international law. As criminal violations of international humanitarian law (IHL), they are widely penalised under domestic laws, including on the basis of the principle of universal jurisdiction, and are within the jurisdiction of the International Criminal Court (ICC). This chapter highlights the key milestones in the evolution of individual criminal responsibility for war crimes, and offers an overview of the concept under international criminal law (ICL).

Keywords individual criminal responsibility · International Criminal Court (ICC) · international criminal law (ICL) · international humanitarian law (IHL) · universal jurisdiction · war crimes

---

E. Sałkiewicz-Munnerlyn
Akademia Krakowska AFM, Krakow, Poland

S. Sayapin (✉)
School of Law, KIMEP University, Almaty, Kazakhstan
e-mail: s.sayapin@kimep.kz

49.1 A Brief History of International Prosecutions for War Crimes

The history of wars is as long as human history.[1] However, the first recoded international war crimes trial took place only in 1474, whereby an *ad hoc* tribunal in the Holy Roman Empire tried Peter von Hagenbach, a German knight, on charges of command responsibility. He was found guilty of war crimes committed during the occupation of Breisach, and was beheaded.[2] In the 19th century, a doctrinal codification of the laws and customs of war was carried out by a German-American legal scholar Franz (Francis) Lieber, and promulgated by the US President Abraham Lincoln as Instructions for the Government of Armies of the United States in the Field (General Order No. 100, also known as the "Lieber Code") on 24 April 1863.[3] At the international level, important codifications were carried out in the Hague Conventions of 1899 and 1907.[4] After World War I, the Treaty of Versailles, in Articles 227–230, provided for the arrest and trial of German officials accused of war crimes.[5] The resulting Leipzig War Crimes Trials were based on German criminal law, and essentially were domestic trials.[6] After World War II, the four major Allied powers—France, the Soviet Union, the United Kingdom, and the United States—set up an International Military Tribunal (IMT) in Nuremberg, to prosecute and punish the major war criminals of the European Axis. In 1945–1946, the IMT carried out a combined trial of senior political and military Nazi leaders as well as several Nazi organisations.[7] The Nuremberg Charter established, in Article 6(b), the IMT´s jurisdiction with respect to war crimes, as follows:

> War crimes: namely, violations of the laws or customs of war. Such violations shall include, but not be limited to, murder, ill-treatment or deportation to slave labour or for any other purpose of civilian population of or in occupied territory, murder or ill-treatment of prisoners of war or persons on the seas, killing of hostages, plunder of public or private property, wanton destruction of cities, towns or villages, or devastation not justified by military necessity [...]

After the 1945–1946 Nuremberg trial, lower-ranking Nazi war criminals were brought to justice during the so-called follow-up Nuremberg trials, a series of 12 trials carried out until mid-1949 on the basis of the Control Council Law No. 10.[8]

In July 1945, the Potsdam Declaration was adopted, in which the Republic of China, the United Kingdom, and the United States demanded Japan's "unconditional surrender" (para 13) and stated that "stern justice sh[ould] be meted out to all

---

[1] Cryer et a.l 2014, p. 264; Hathaway et al. 2019, pp. 54–113; Werle and Jessberger 2020, pp. 443–449.

[2] Umarkhanova and Sayapin 2021, p. 23.

[3] Cryer et al. 2014, p. 270; Werle and Jessberger 2020, pp. 444–445.

[4] Werle and Jessberger 2020, pp. 446–448.

[5] Sandoz 2008, pp. 297–298.

[6] Werle and Jessberger 2020, p. 4.

[7] Cryer et al. 2014, p. 270; Sandoz 2008, p. 302; Werle and Jessberger 2020, pp. 6–10.

[8] Werle and Jessberger 2020, pp. 12–13.

war criminals" (para 10). At the Moscow Conference held in December 1945, the Soviet Union, the United Kingdom, and the United States made arrangements for the occupation of Japan, and Supreme Commander of the Allied Powers, General MacArthur, was authorised to "issue all orders for the implementation of the Terms of Surrender, the occupation and control of Japan, and all directives supplementary thereto".[9] Accordingly, in January 1946, General MacArthur issued a special proclamation that established the International Military Tribunal for the Far East (IMTFE).[10] Article 2 of the IMFTE Charter enabled MacArthur to appoint judges to the IMTFE from the countries that had signed Japan's Instrument of Surrender, India, and the Commonwealth of the Philippines. Each of these countries appointed prosecutors to indict the defendants. In accordance with Article 5(b) of the Tokyo Charter, the IMTFE was to try Japan's supreme military and civilian leaders for war crimes committed during World War II, and concisely defined as follows:

Conventional War Crimes: Namely, violations of the laws or customs of war [...]

After the end of the Cold War, the UN Security Council established two international *ad hoc* Tribunals, to enable the prosecution of individuals for crimes under international law committed, respectively, during conflicts in the former Yugoslavia and Rwanda. The International Criminal Tribunal for the Former Yugoslavia (ICTY) was established by the UN Security Council Resolution 827(1993) on 25 May 1993. The ICTY Statute contained two provisions pertaining to war crimes committed in international armed conflicts. Thus, Article 2 listed the grave breaches of the 1949 Geneva Conventions:

The International Tribunal shall have the power to prosecute persons committing or ordering to be committed grave breaches of the Geneva Conventions of 12 August 1949, namely the following acts against persons or property protected under the provisions of the relevant Geneva Convention:

(a) wilful killing;
(b) torture or inhuman treatment, including biological experiments;
(c) wilfully causing great suffering or serious injury to body or health;
(d) extensive destruction and appropriation of property, not justified by military necessity and carried out unlawfully and wantonly;
(e) compelling a prisoner of war or a civilian to serve in the forces of a hostile power;
(f) wilfully depriving a prisoner of war or a civilian of the rights of fair and regular trial;
(g) unlawful deportation or transfer or unlawful confinement of a civilian;
(h) taking civilians as hostages.

In turn, Article 3 criminalised violations of Hague Law:

The International Tribunal shall have the power to prosecute persons violating the laws or customs of war. Such violations shall include, but not be limited to:

---

[9] See Report of the Meeting of the Ministers of Foreign Affairs of the Union of Soviet Socialist Republics, the United States of America, the United Kingdom, para VII(B)(5).

[10] On the prosecution of war crimes by the Tokyo Tribunal, see Cryer 2016, Werle and Jessberger 2020, pp. 10–11.

(a) employment of poisonous weapons or other weapons calculated to cause unnecessary suffering;
(b) wanton destruction of cities, towns or villages, or devastation not justified by military necessity;
(c) attack, or bombardment, by whatever means, of undefended towns, villages, dwellings, or buildings;
(d) seizure of, destruction or wilful damage done to institutions dedicated to religion, charity and education, the arts and sciences, historic monuments and works of art and science;
(e) plunder of public or private property.

The International Criminal Tribunal for Rwanda (ICTR) was established by the UN Security Council Resolution 955(1994) on 8 November 1994, and its Statute was designed for the circumstances of a non-international armed conflict. Article 4 of the Statute criminalised violations of Article 3 common to the 1949 Geneva Conventions and of Additional Protocol II (1977):

> The International Tribunal for Rwanda shall have the power to prosecute persons committing or ordering to be committed serious violations of Article 3 common to the Geneva Conventions of 12 August 1949 for the Protection of War Victims, and of Additional Protocol II thereto of 8 June 1977. These violations shall include, but shall not be limited to:

(a) Violence to life, health and physical or mental well-being of persons, in particular murder as well as cruel treatment such as torture, mutilation or any form of corporal punishment;
(b) Collective punishments;
(c) Taking of hostages;
(d) Acts of terrorism;
(e) Outrages upon personal dignity, in particular humiliating and degrading treatment, rape, enforced prostitution and any form of indecent assault;
(f) Pillage;
(g) The passing of sentences and the carrying out of executions without previous judgement pronounced by a regularly constituted court, affording all the judicial guarantees which are recognized as indispensable by civilized peoples;
(h) Threats to commit any of the foregoing acts.

Article 8 of the Rome Statute of the International Criminal Court (ICC) represents the most complete modern codification of war crimes.[11] The Rome Statute categorises war crimes by reference to the nature of a conflict (international or non-international), and to sources of IHL underlying the respective war crimes (see *infra* Sect. 49.2).

---

[11] Cryer et al. 2014, p. 270.

49.2 The Concept and Elements of War Crimes

There is no single document in international law defining and codifying all war crimes.[12] However, there is a common understanding to the effect that a war crime, irrespective of whether it is committed by a member of the military personnel or a civilian, in an international or non-international armed conflict, is (1) a breach of a treaty-based or customary rule of international humanitarian law (IHL), and (2) the breach must be "serious".[13] Treaty-based IHL consists of two comprehensive areas—the Law of Geneva (comprising the four Geneva Conventions of 1949 for the Protection of Victims of War, and their three Additional Protocols of 1977 and 2005[14]), and Hague Law (comprising numerous texts prohibiting or restricting the use of certain means and methods of warfare[15]). Article 147 of the Fourth Geneva Convention of 1949 explains what is meant by "grave breaches" for the purpose of the Convention:

> Grave breaches [...] shall be those involving any of the following acts, if committed against persons or property protected by the present Convention: wilful killing, torture or inhuman treatment, including biological experiments, wilfully causing great suffering or serious injury to body or health, unlawful deportation or transfer or unlawful confinement of a protected person, compelling a protected person to serve in the forces of a hostile power, or wilfully depriving a protected person of the rights of fair and regular trial prescribed in the present Convention, taking of hostages and extensive destruction and appropriation of property, not justified by military necessity and carried out unlawfully and wantonly.

The First, Second, and Third Geneva Conventions of 1949 and Additional Protocol I of 1977 contain similar provisions defining grave breaches for their respective purposes.[16] In turn, under customary international law, war crimes are serious violations of IHL committed in the context of, and in connection with, an international or non-international armed conflict.[17] According to the *Tadic* Appeal Decision, "an armed conflict exists whenever there is a resort to armed force between States or protracted armed violence between governmental authorities and organized armed groups or between such groups within a State".[18] IHL applies from the beginning of an armed conflict to a general conclusion of peace in the case of an international armed conflict (IAC), or to a peaceful settlement in the case of a non-international armed conflicts (NIAC). Importantly, in order to distinguish NIACs from internal unrest, internal tensions or banditry, IHL requires that NIACs should be prolonged, have a minimum level of intensity, and that the parties involved should be organised

---

[12] Bassiouni 2003, p. 141.
[13] Henckaerts and Doswald-Beck 2005, p. 568; Hathaway et al. 2019, pp. 82–91.
[14] Cryer et al. 2014, p. 265; Sandoz 2008, pp. 304–306; Werle and Jessberger 2020, pp. 445–446.
[15] Cryer et al. 2014, p. 265; Sandoz 2008, pp. 295–297; Werle and Jessberger 2020, pp. 446–447. See also Chap. 18 by Tsybulenko and Platonova.
[16] See Article 50 of the First Geneva Convention, Article 51 of the Second Geneva Convention, and Article 130 of the Third Geneva Convention. See also Sandoz 2008, p. 306.
[17] Werle and Jessberger 2020, pp. 463–472.
[18] Quoted in Werle and Jessberger 2020, p. 460.

to a minimum degree.[19] Traditionally, war crimes were violations of IHL rules regulating only IACs.[20] The ICTY Appeals Chamber decision in the *Tadic* case was the first one acknowledging that war crimes could also be committed in NIACs.[21]

As a rule, only serious violations of IHL amount to war crimes and entail individual criminal responsibility.[22] A serious violation is a grave deviation from an IHL rule protecting important values, which involves serious consequences for the victim. The jurisprudence of the ICTY clarified the common definitional elements of war crimes as follows:

1. the violation must constitute an infringement of a rule of international humanitarian law;
2. the rule must be customary in nature of, if it belongs to treaty law, the required conditions must be met [...].
3. the violation must be 'serious', that is to say, it must constitute a breach of a rule protecting important values, and the breach must involve grave consequences for the victim [...];
4. the violation must entail, under customary or conventional law, the individual criminal responsibility of the person breaching the rule.[23]

The most comprehensive codification of war crimes is currently found in Article 8 of the Rome Statute of the ICC, where four categories of war crimes are distinguished:[24]

1. grave breaches of the Geneva Conventions of 12 August 1949 (Article 8(2)(a));
2. other serious violations of the laws and customs applicable in international armed conflict, within the established framework of international law (Article 8(2)(b));
3. serious violations of Article 3 common to the four Geneva Conventions of 12 August 1949 (Article 8(2)(c));
4. other serious violations of the laws and customs applicable in armed conflicts not of an international character, within the established framework of international law (Article 8(2)(e)).

This codification usefully takes into account developments in customary international law as well as relevant case law of the ICTY and the ICTR. All war crimes included in Article 8 of the ICC Statute require evidence of four main elements, in addition to the mental element as defined in the Statute's Article 30:[25]

(a) a *prohibited act* (such as murder, causing bodily injury, or rape);

---

[19] Werle and Jessberger 2020, pp. 468–469.

[20] Cryer et al. 2014, p. 272; Werle and Jessberger 2020, p. 456.

[21] Cryer et al. 2014, p. 273; Werle and Jessberger 2020, pp. 456–457.

[22] Werle and Jessberger 2020, p. 453.

[23] *Prosecutor v Tadic* (Decision on the Defence Motion for Interlocutory Appeal on Jurisdiction), Case No. ICTY-94-1-AR72, 2 October 1995, para 94.

[24] Cf. Cryer et al. 2014, p. 285; Sandoz 2008, p. 310.

[25] On the mental element of war crimes, see Werle and Jessberger 2020, pp. 476–478.

(b) committed against *protected persons* (such as those taking no direct part in hostilities);
(c) during an international or non-international armed conflict;[26]
(d) with a *nexus* between the armed conflict and the act committed.[27]

The ICC has jurisdiction in respect of war crimes "in particular when committed as part of a plan or policy or as part of a large-scale commission of such crimes" (Article 8(1)).[28] It means that as a rule, in accordance with the principle of complementarity (cf. Article 17 of the ICC Statute), war crimes should be investigated and prosecuted by domestic systems of criminal justice. For this, the elements of war crimes must be implemented in relevant domestic penal laws.[29] Notably, not all domestic systems of criminal justice require IHL violations to be "serious", in order for them to qualify as war crimes.[30] In such domestic contexts, all violations of IHL are potentially criminalised. Domestic systems of criminal justice often make war crimes subject to the principle of universal jurisdiction, which enables a state to prosecute a person who committed a crime under international law irrespective of where the crime was committed,[31] in addition to other bases of criminal jurisdiction.[32]

49.3 Classification of War Crimes

Based on values protected by the specific IHL rules, war crimes may be categorised into (1) war crimes against protected persons; (2) war crimes against protected objects; (3) war crimes related to unlawful methods of warfare; and (4) war crimes related to unlawful means of warfare.[33]

49.3.1 War Crimes against Protected Persons

War crimes within this category are directed against victims who are members of a protected group as defined in the four 1949 Geneva Conventions. Generally, these are persons not taking a direct part in hostilities, in particular civilians or

---

[26] Cryer et al. 2014, p. 276.

[27] Cryer et al. 2014, pp. 281–282.

[28] However, note that the Court itself ruled that "the statutory requirement of either large-scale commission or part of a policy [was] not absolute". *Judgment on the Prosecutor's Appeal Against the Decision of Pre-Trial Chamber I,* Case No. ICC-01/04, Situation in the Democratic Republic of the Congo, 13 July 2006, para 70.

[29] Sandoz 2008, pp. 318–321; Sayapin 2020, pp. 45–46.

[30] Henckaerts and Doswald-Beck 2005, p. 569.

[31] Hovell 2018, pp. 433–436; Kluven 2017, pp. 1–38; Sandoz 2008, pp. 319–320.

[32] Cryer et al. 2014, pp. 53–56.

[33] Cf. a classification of war crimes in Cryer et al. 2014, p. 265. See also May 2007, pp. 17–20.

persons no longer able to fight as a result of illness, injury, detention or for any other reasons, including combatants who have laid down their weapons. Examples of relevant war crimes include wilful killing (Article 8(2)(a)(i)), torture or inhuman treatment, including biological experiments (Article 8(2)(a)(ii)), violence to life and person, in particular murder of all kinds, mutilation, cruel treatment and torture (Article 8(2)(c)(i)), taking of hostages (Articles 8(2)(a)(viii) and 8(2)(c)(iii)), intentionally directing attacks against the civilian population as such or against individual civilians not taking direct part in hostilities (Articles 8(2)(b)(i) and 8(2)(e)(i)), committing rape, sexual slavery, enforced prostitution, forced pregnancy, enforced sterilization, or any other form of sexual violence constituting a grave breach of the Geneva Conventions or their common Article 3 (Articles 8(2)(b)(xii) and 8(2)(e)(vi)), conscripting or enlisting children under the age of fifteen years into the national or other armed forces or groups or using them to participate actively in hostilities (Articles 8(2)(b)(xvi) and 8(2)(e)(vii)), and others.

49.3.2 War Crimes against Protected Objects

Article 48 of Additional Protocol I draws a distinction between military objectives and civilian objects. It is prohibited to direct attacks against civilian objects, which are defined in Article 52(1) of Additional Protocol I as all objects which are not military objectives. Accordingly, the ICC Statute criminalises, for example, intentionally directing attacks against civilian objects, that is, objects which are not military objectives (Article 8(2)(b)(ii)), attacking or bombarding, by whatever means, towns, villages, dwellings or buildings which are undefended and which are not military objectives (Article 8(2)(b)(v)), intentionally directing attacks against buildings dedicated to religion, education, art, science or charitable purposes, historic monuments, hospitals and places where the sick and wounded are collected, provided they are not military objectives (Articles 8(2)(b)(ix) and 8(2)(e)(iv)).

49.3.3 War Crimes Related to Unlawful Methods of Warfare

Unlawful methods warfare are ways of conducting hostilities, which are inconsistent with the basic rules of IHL. According to Article 35(1) of Additional Protocol I, "in any armed conflict, the right of the Parties to the conflict to choose methods and means of warfare is not unlimited". The ICJ confirmed this customary rule in its Advisory Opinion on the Legality of the Threat or Use of Nuclear Weapons to the effect that "methods and means of warfare, which would preclude any distinction between civilian and military targets, or which would result in unnecessary suffering to combatants, are prohibited".[34] Consistent with this, Article 8 of the ICC Statute includes war crimes such as making improper use of a flag of truce, of the flag or of the military insignia and uniform of the enemy or of the United Nations, as well as of the distinctive emblems of the Geneva Conventions, resulting in death or serious personal injury (Article 8(2)(b)(vii)), declaring that no quarter will be given (Article 8(2)(b)(xii)), intentionally using starvation of civilians as a method of warfare by depriving them of objects indispensable to their survival, including wilfully impeding relief supplies as provided for under the Geneva Conventions (Article 8(2)(b)(xxv)), or, in non-international armed conflicts, killing or wounding treacherously a combatant adversary (Article 8(2)(e)(ix)).[35] Importantly, on 6 December 2019, the ICC Statute was unanimously amended to the effect of criminalising "[i]ntentionally using starvation of civilians as a method of warfare by depriving them of objects indispensable to their survival, including wilfully impeding relief supplies" in NIACs (Article 8(2)(e)(xix)).

49.3.4 War Crimes Related to Unlawful Means of Warfare

According to the ICRC, means of warfare include "weapons, weapon systems and platforms employed for the purposes of attack in an armed conflict".[36] Additional Protocol I prohibits in Article 35(2) the use of weapons, projectiles and materials of war, which are likely to cause superfluous injury or unnecessary suffering. In line with this, the ICC Statute criminalises employing poison or poisoned weapons (Articles 8(2)(b)(xvii) and 8(2)(e)(xiii)), employing asphyxiating, poisonous or other gases, and all analogous liquids, materials or devices (Articles 8(2)(b)(xviii) and 8(2)(e)(xiv)), employing bullets which expand or flatten easily in the human body, such as bullets with a hard envelope which does not entirely cover the core or is pierced with incisions (Articles 8(2)(b)(xix) and 8(2)(e)(xv)), and employing weapons, projectiles and material and methods of warfare which are of a nature to cause superfluous injury or unnecessary suffering or which are inherently indiscriminate in violation of the international law of armed conflict (Article 8(2)(b)(xx)). Notably, the ICC Statute makes no specific mention of biological and chemical weapons and other weapons of mass destruction, as these are subject to separate legal regimes.[37]

On 14 December 2017, the ICC Statute was amended to the effect of introducing three new war crimes related to unlawful means of warfare both in IACs and NIACs:

---

[34] *Legality of the Threat or Use of Nuclear Weapons, Advisory Opinion*, I.C.J. Reports 1996, p. 226, para 95.

[35] See Sayapin 2008.

[36] See ICRC 2021.

[37] Cryer et al. 2014, p. 271. See also Chap. 14 by Jeroen van den Boogaard (on chemical weapons) and Chap. 15 by Rustam Atadjanov (on nuclear weapons).

employing weapons that use microbial or other biological agents, or toxins, whatever their origin or method of production (Articles 8(2)(b)(xxvii) and 8(2)(e)(xvi)), employing weapons, the primary effect of which is to injure by fragments which in the human body escape detection by X-rays (Articles 8(2)(b)(xxviii) and 8(2)(e)(xvii), and employing laser weapons specifically designed, as their sole combat function or as one of their combat functions, to cause permanent blindness to unenhanced vision, that is, to the naked eye or to the eye with corrective eyesight devices (Articles 8(2)(b)(xxix) and 8(2)(e)(xviii)).

49.4 Perpetrators and Victims

49.4.1 Perpetrators

War crimes can only be committed by individuals, not by legal entities. International criminal tribunals held after World War II that both combatants and civilians could be held responsible for committing war crimes.[38] The ICTY Prosecution in the *Delalic* case stated that "it is not even necessary that the perpetrator be part of the armed forces, or be entitled to combatant status in terms of the Geneva Conventions, to be capable of committing war crimes during international armed conflict".[39] The ICTR was initially more demanding regarding a nexus between the acts of the perpetrator and the armed conflict[40] but the Appeals Chamber ruled in the *Akayesu Case* in the Judgment of 1 June 2001 that "international humanitarian law would be lessened and called into question if it were to be admitted that certain persons be exonerated from individual criminal responsibility for a violation of common Article 3 under the pretext that they did not belong to a specific category".[41] There are authors who argue that it is necessary to prove the link between the perpetrator and one of the parties to an armed conflict. In that case, a civilian could only be held responsible for war crimes when he or she is sufficiently linked to a party to the conflict.[42] However, this condition would be inconsistent with Articles 49/50/129/146 of the 1949 Geneva Conventions, which require member states to prosecute and punish all persons who commit grave breaches. Moreover, there is no such restriction in the ICC Elements

---

[38] See, for example, *Prosecutor v Musema*, Judgment and Sentence, Case No. ICTR-96-13-A, 27 January 2000, paras 274 et seq; *Prosecutor v Semanza*, Judgment and Sentence, Case No. ICTR-97-20-T, 15 May 2003, para 358. See also Cryer et al. 2014, p. 282.

[39] *Prosecutor v Delalic et al* (Celebici case appeal judgment), Case No. ICTY, IT-96-21-A, 20 February 2001, para 325.

[40] *Prosecutor v Akayesu*, Judgment, Case No. ICTR-96-4-T, 2 September 1998, para. 640; *Prosecutor v Kayishema and Ruzindana*, Judgment, Case No. ICTR-95-1-T, 21 May 1999, paras 173–176.

[41] *Prosecutor v Akayesu*, Judgment, Case No. ICTR-96-4-A, 1 June 2001, para 443.

[42] Arnold 2002, pp. 344–359.

of Crimes,[43] and no one objected to the statement made during the negotiations at the Rome Conference that war crimes could be committed by both members of armed forces and civilians.

49.4.2 Victims

An act constitutes a war crime when its victim is a person protected under IHL. Potentially, both civilians and members of the armed forces can be victims of war crimes.[44] The 1949 Geneva Conventions protect several categories of persons:

- the wounded and sick in armed forces in the field, medical and religious personnel (Articles 13 and 24 of the First Geneva Convention of 1949);[45]
- the wounded, sick and shipwrecked members of armed forces at sea, medical, religious and hospital personnel of hospital ships and their crews (Articles 12, 36 and 37 of the Second Geneva Convention of 1949);[46]
- prisoners of war (Article 4 of the Third Geneva Convention) and persons whose liberty has been restricted for reasons related to a non-international armed conflict;[47]
- civilians and inhabitants of occupied territories (Article 4 of the Fourth Geneva Convention).[48]

Civilians and civilian groups are protected in both international and non-international armed conflicts. In international armed conflicts, the determination of whether a person belongs to a party to the conflict is formally based on the nationality of the person. The Fourth Geneva Convention explicitly states in Article 4(1) that "[p]ersons protected are those [...] in the hands of a Party to the conflict or Occupying Power of which they are not nationals". For this reason, it was argued during proceedings at the ICTY that war crimes could only be committed against individuals of a different nationality than that of the offender, which meant that Bosnian Serbs could not be considered "protected persons" under the Fourth Geneva Convention, because the authors of crimes committed against them were also Bosnian nationals.[49] The ICTY Appeals Chamber ruled that the nationality approach did not comply with "modern inter-ethnic armed conflicts such as that in the former Yugoslavia", and that "new States are often created during the conflict and ethnicity rather than nationality

---

[43] Dörmann 2003, pp. 34, 391–393.

[44] Cryer et al. 2014, pp. 283–284. See also May 2007, pp. 44–47.

[45] See also Articles 8–20 of Additional Protocol I, Articles 7–12 of Additional Protocol II (1977).

[46] See also Articles 21–31 of Additional Protocol I, Article 11 of Additional Protocol II (1977).

[47] See also Articles 44–45 of Additional Protocol I, Article 5 of Additional Protocol II (1977).

[48] See also Articles 50–51 of Additional Protocol I, Articles 13, 14 and 17 of Additional Protocol II (1977).

[49] *Prosecutor v Tadic*, Opinion and Judgment, Case No. ICTY-94-1, 7 May 1997, paras 118, 595.

may become the grounds for allegiance [...] to a party to the conflict and, correspondingly, control by this party over persons in a given territory may be regarded as the crucial test".[50]

The nationality requirement was criticised in the doctrine and jurisprudence of international criminal courts, because in war crimes cases where the victims belonged to an ethnic or religious group different from that of the offender but shared the same nationality, the elements of the crimes would not be present.[51] In order to determine whether persons involved in international armed conflicts have protected status, one should allow for an extensive interpretation of Article 4(1) of the Fourth Geneva Convention ("of which they are not nationals"). Notably, the ICC abandoned the nationality approach in *Prosecutor v Katanga et al.*[52] It has been suggested to extend the scope of Article 4(1) by including other criteria, such as religious beliefs, when it could be a decisive factor in the conflict.[53]

The situation is different in NIACs, because the nationality approach does not affect the application of the concept of war crimes in internal armed conflicts. In NIACs, the law of war crimes applies to members of a state's armed forces or organised armed groups and their adversaries sharing the same nationality.[54] Article 3 common to the 1949 Geneva Conventions, applicable in armed conflicts of a non-international nature, provides protection to "[p]ersons taking no active part in the hostilities including members of armed forces who have laid down their arms and those placed 'hors de combat' by sickness, wounds, detention or any other cause". Article 4 of Additional Protocol II also contains guarantees applicable to "[a]ll persons who do not take a direct part or have ceased to take part in hostilities [...]". The question of what exactly constitutes direct participation in hostilities (DPH) is one of the most controversial issues in IHL. The ICTY ruled in *Prosecutor v Tadic* that the decisive element in concluding whether a person was a potential victim of a war crime consisted in whether he or she took a direct part in hostilities at the time of the targeting.[55] In the absence of more detailed regulation in treaty law, the ICRC explored the concept of DPH in an *Interpretive Guidance*.[56]

---

[50] *Prosecutor v Tadic*, Judgment, Case No. ICTY-94-1, 15 July 1999, para 166.

[51] Ambos 2014, p. 149.

[52] *Prosecutor v Katanga et al.* Decision on the confirmation of charges, Case No. ICC-01/04-01/07, 30 September 2008, para 289.

[53] Ambos 2014, p. 149.

[54] La Haye 2008, p. 119.

[55] *Prosecutor v Tadic*, Opinion and Judgment, Case No. ICTY-94-1, 7 May 1997, para 615.

[56] See Melzer 2010. See also Chap. 12 on DPH by Byron.

49.5 Prosecutions and Amnesty

The rule that states must investigate war crimes and prosecute suspects is established as one of customary international law applicable in both international and non-international armed conflicts:

> Rule 158. States must investigate war crimes allegedly committed by their nationals or armed forces, or on their territory, and, if appropriate, prosecute the suspects. They must also investigate other war crimes over which they have jurisdiction and, if appropriate, prosecute the suspects.[57]

It means that usually, states exercise jurisdiction with respect to war crimes in domestic courts based on their national laws. Alternatively, states must exercise universal jurisdiction, which is obligatory for grave breaches of the 1949 Geneva Conventions and Additional Protocol I. States are under the obligation to search for persons who committed or ordered others to commit grave breaches of IHL, or extradite them, based on the 1949 Geneva Conventions.[58] The ICRC Study on Customary IHL recalls that the obligation to investigate and prosecute persons who have allegedly committed war crimes is regulated by multilateral ICL, IHRL, and IHL treaties, and applies to acts committed in both IACs and NIACs.[59] Many states have implemented this obligation in their national laws.[60] The UN Security Council reaffirmed the obligation to investigate and prosecute suspects with respect to attacks on peacekeeping personnel, and to crimes committed in NIACs like Afghanistan, Kosovo, and several African contexts.[61] The UN General Assembly has, on its part, stressed this obligation in its resolutions, which can be interpreted to mean that states consider it as an established principle that war crimes must be investigated and prosecuted.[62] Also, the General Assembly adopted resolutions specifically calling upon states to investigate and punish persons responsible for sexual violence in armed conflicts.[63] The UN Commission on Human Rights—a predecessor to the UN Human Rights Council—adopted resolutions demanding the investigation and prosecution of persons suspected of IHL violations in the context of a few conflicts in Africa, Chechnya, and the former Yugoslavia.[64]

A number of states are known to have issued amnesties with respect to war crimes committed in NIACs but these decisions were either set aside by domestic or regional courts, or criticised by the international community.[65] Such reactions show that there

---

[57] Henckaerts and Doswald-Beck 2005, p. 607.

[58] See Article 49 of the First Geneva Convention, Article 50 of the Second Geneva Convention, Article 129 of the Third Geneva Convention, and Article 146 of the Fourth Geneva Convention.

[59] Henckaerts and Doswald-Beck 2005, p. 608.

[60] Werle and Jessberger 2020, p. 450.

[61] Henckaerts and Doswald-Beck 2005, pp. 608–609.

[62] Henckaerts and Doswald-Beck 2005, p. 609.

[63] Henckaerts and Doswald-Beck 2005, p. 609.

[64] Henckaerts and Doswald-Beck 2005, p. 609.

[65] Werle and Vormbaum 2018, pp. 67–81.

is an obligation under customary international law to investigate war crimes allegedly committed in NIACs, and to prosecute suspects if appropriate:

> Rule 159. At the end of hostilities, the authorities in power must endeavour to grant the broadest possible amnesty to persons who have participated in a non-international armed conflict, or those deprived of their liberty for reasons related to the armed conflict, with the exception of persons suspected of, accused of or sentenced for war crimes.[66]

Similarly, Article 6(5) of Additional Protocol II creates an obligation for the authorities in power to endeavour to grant an amnesty at the end of hostilities. The authorities in power are not obliged to grant an amnesty at the end of hostilities but they are bound to consider the feasibility of doing so. The ICRC Study on Customary IHL recalls that the granting of such amnesties was encouraged by the UN Security Council,[67] the UN General Assembly,[68] and regional organisations such as the EU, OSCE and NATO.[69] However, it is generally accepted that amnesties should not apply to persons suspected of having committed war crimes or other crimes under international law, and that such persons are not entitled to the refugee status. For example, the President of the UN Security Council emphasised in his Statement of 14 October 1994 that "persons involved in [serious breaches of international humanitarian law could not] achieve immunity from prosecution by fleeing [Rwanda]", and that "the provisions of the Convention relating to the status of refugees [did] not apply to such persons".[70] In 1995, the Special Prosecutor of Ethiopia stated in the *Mengistu and Others* case that it was "a well-established custom and belief that war crimes and crimes against humanity [were] not subject to amnesty".[71] In 1998, the ICTY judgment reaffirmed in the *Furundzija* case with respect to torture that amnesty might not apply to war crimes.[72] The UN General Assembly expressed similar views in the Declaration on Territorial Asylum of 14 December 1967, and in Resolution 3074 (XXVIII) on principles of international co-operation in the detection, arrest, extradition and punishment of war criminals of 3 December 1973.

49.6 Conclusion

War crimes are a well-established area of ICL. They have a solid basis both in the Law of Geneva and Hague Law, and have been codified in the Statutes of several international criminal tribunals. Article 8 of the ICC Statute is the most comprehensive international codification of war crimes in ICL, which takes into account prior

---

[66] Henckaerts and Doswald-Beck 2005, p. 611.

[67] Henckaerts and Doswald-Beck 2005, p. 612.

[68] Henckaerts and Doswald-Beck 2005, p. 612.

[69] Henckaerts and Doswald-Beck 2005, p. 612.

[70] Statement by the President of the Security Council, S/PRST/1994/59, p. 2.

[71] Henckaerts and Doswald-Beck 2005, p. 613.

[72] Henckaerts and Doswald-Beck 2005, pp. 613–614.

normative developments and case law. In the future, the doctrine of the war crimes law will be guided by the case law of the ICC as well as that of "hybrid" tribunals.[73] War crimes have also been implemented in many domestic penal laws, which enables states to prosecute for alleged war crimes committed by their nationals, on their territories, and, as the case may be, in accordance with the principle of universal jurisdiction.

More work should be done to further extend the war crimes regime to NIACs. Currently, under the ICC Statute, the range of war crimes penalised in IACs is considerably broader than in NIACs, and more crimes should be included within the latter category, with due regard to customary international law. Likewise, more states, especially in the Islamic world, should be encouraged to ratify the ICC Statute, with a view to expanding the ICC's territorial and personal jurisdiction.

The development of modern technologies will, in the next years, entail an according evolution of the war crimes law.[74] Notable international actors such as NATO recognised cyberspace as an operational domain,[75] and there is general agreement to the effect that relevant principles and rules of IHL apply to cyber operations carried out during conventional armed conflicts, as well as to "pure" cyber conflicts.[76] Lawyers should work together with IT specialists, in order to reduce impunity for cyber crimes,[77] since proving individual responsibility in the context of cyber attacks is a major issue.[78]

References

Ambos K (2014) Treatise on International Criminal Law, Volume II: The Crimes and Sentencing. Oxford University Press, Oxford
Arnold R (2002) The Liability of Civilians under International Humanitarian Law's War Crimes Provisions. Yearbook of International Humanitarian Law 5: 344–359
Atadjanov R (2018) War Crimes Committed During the Armed Conflict in Ukraine: What Should the ICC Focus On? In: Sayapin S, Tsybulenko E (eds) The Use of Force against Ukraine and International Law: Jus Ad Bellum, Jus In Bello, Jus Post Bellum, T. M. C. Asser Press, The Hague, pp. 385 – 407
Bassiouni MC (2003) Introduction to International Criminal Law. Transnational Publishers, Inc., Ardsley
Cryer R (2016) Then and now: command responsibility, the Tokyo Tribunal and modern international criminal law. In: Sellars K (ed) Trials for International Crimes in Asia. Cambridge University Press, Cambridge, pp. 55–74

---

[73] On some immediate priorities for the ICC with respect to war crimes, see Atadjanov 2018. See also Chap. 30 by Vagias.
[74] See Valuch and Hamulak 2018.
[75] See Schmitt 2021.
[76] Werle and Jessberger 2020, p. 462.
[77] See generally Sayapin 2021.
[78] Werle and Jessberger 2020, p. 462.

Cryer R, Friman H, Robinson D, Wilmshurst E (2014) An Introduction to International Criminal Law and Procedure, 3rd edn. Cambridge University Press, Cambridge

Dörmann K (2003) Elements of War Crimes under the Rome Statute of the International Criminal Court: Sources and Commentary. Cambridge University Press, Cambridge

Hathaway O, Strauch P, Walton B, Weiberg Z (2019) What is a War Crime? Yale Journal of International Law 44: 54 – 113

Henckaerts JM, Doswald-Beck L (2005) Customary International Humanitarian Law, Volume I: Rules. Cambridge University Press, Cambridge

Hovell D (2018) The Authority of Universal Jurisdiction. EJIL 29: 427 – 456

ICRC (2021) Means of Warfare, https://casebook.icrc.org/glossary/means-warfare. Accessed 8 August 2021.

Kluven T (2017) Universal Jurisdiction in Absentia Before Domestic Courts Prosecuting International Crimes: A Suitable Weapon to Fight Impunity? Goettingen Journal of International Law 8: 7–38

La Haye E (2008) War Crimes in Internal Armed Conflicts. Cambridge University Press, Cambridge

May L (2007) War Crimes and Just War. Cambridge University Press, Cambridge

Melzer N (2010) Interpretive Guidance on the Notion of Direct Participation in Hostilities under International Humanitarian Law. ICRC, Geneva

Sandoz Y (2008) Penal Aspects of International Humanitarian Law. In: Bassiouni MC (ed) International Criminal Law, 3rd edition, Volume I: Sources, Subjects and Contents. Koninklijke Brill NV, Leiden, pp 293–321

Sayapin S (2008) A Development in International Law or a Misnomer: Who is the Combatant Adversary Referred to in Article 8(2)(e)(ix) of the Rome Statute of the International Criminal Court? Humanitäres Völkerrecht—Informationsschriften, pp. 21:130–133

Sayapin S (2020) Crimes against the Peace and Security of Mankind in the Revised Edition of the Criminal Code of the Republic of Uzbekistan. RCEEL 45:36–58

Sayapin S (2021) Russian Approaches to International Law and Cyberspace. In: Tsagourias N, Buchan R (eds) Research Handbook on International Law and Cyberspace, 2nd edn. Edward Elgar Publishing, Cheltenham (forthcoming)

Schmitt M (2021) International Law at NATO's Brussels Summit. https://www.ejiltalk.org/international-law-at-natos-brussels-summit/. Accessed 8 August 2021.

Umarkhanova D, Sayapin S (2021) Mezhdunarodnoye ugolovnoye pravo [International Criminal Law]. Ministry of Justice of the Republic of Uzbekistan/Tashkent State University of Law, Tashkent

Valuch J, Hamulak O (2018) Cyber Operations During the Conflict in Ukraine and the Role of International Law. In: Sayapin S, Tsybulenko E (eds) The Use of Force against Ukraine and International Law: Jus Ad Bellum, Jus In Bello, Jus Post Bellum. T.M.C. Asser Press, The Hague, pp. 215 – 235

Werle G, Jessberger F (2020) Principles of International Criminal Law, 4th edn. Oxford University Press, Oxford

Werle G, Vormbaum M (2018) Transitional Justice: Vergangenheitsbewältigung durch Recht. Springer, Berlin

Dr. Ewa Sałkiewicz-Munnerlyn is a university lecturer, Akademia Krakowska AFM (Krakow, Poland).

Sergey Sayapin LLB, LLM, Dr. iur., PhD is an Associate Professor and Associate Dean at the School of Law, KIMEP University (Almaty, Kazakhstan). In 2000–2014, he held various posts at the Communication Department of the Regional Delegation of the International Committee of the Red Cross (ICRC) in Central Asia. His current research focuses on Central Asian and post-Soviet approaches to international law, international and comparative criminal law, human rights, and sociology of law. Dr. Sayapin regularly advises the Central Asian Governments as well as UNODC and the ICRC on international and criminal law, and has recently joined Chatham House's expert pool. He is sub-editor for Central Asia of the Encyclopedia of Public International Law in Asia (Brill, 2021).

Chapter 50
The Crime of Aggression: The Fall of the Supreme International Crime?

Annegret Lucia Hartig

Contents

50.1 Introductory Remarks 1111
50.2 The Hypothesis of Nuremberg: The Supreme International Crime 1112
50.3 The Marginalization of the Crime of Aggression after Nuremberg 1115
    50.3.1 The Retarding Moments of the Resurrection of the Crime of Aggression 1115
    50.3.2 The Consensual Jurisdiction of the ICC in the Absence of a Security Council Referral 1117
    50.3.3 The Domestic Enforcement Conundrum 1121
50.4 Conclusion: Do Not Bite the Hand That Feeds You 1131
References 1132

Abstract Starting from the hypothesis of Nuremberg that labels the crime of aggression as the 'supreme international crime', this article assesses its validity and describes developments in international criminal law that seem to suggest the current marginalization of aggression among the crimes under international law. The fall of the crime of aggression will be illustrated by the retarding moments before it became a defined and internationally enforceable crime, by the comparatively restricted jurisdiction of the International Criminal Court and by the legal controversies surrounding its domestic implementation and prosecution.

Keywords Crime of aggression · Supreme international crime · International military tribunal · International Criminal Court · Domestic jurisdiction · Immunities · Cooperation

50.1 Introductory Remarks

It seems to be a *conditio sine qua non* of articles on the crime of aggression, to reproduce the famous words of the International Military Tribunal (IMT) that gives aggression a prominent position among the crimes under international law: '[T]o initiate a war of aggression…is not only an international crime; it is the supreme international crime differing only from other war crimes in that it contains within

---
A. L. Hartig (✉)
University of Hamburg, Hamburg, Germany

© T.M.C. ASSER PRESS and the authors 2022
S. Sayapin et al. (eds.), *International Conflict and Security Law*,
https://doi.org/10.1007/978-94-6265-515-7_50

itself the accumulated evil of the whole.'[1] Despite this description of the formerly known 'crime against peace' or 'war of aggression', the crime of aggression fell dormant right after the post-World War II trials. The formal resurrection took place in 2010 and 2018 when a definition of the crime was included in the Statute of the International Criminal Court (ICC Statute)[2] and the activation of its jurisdiction became effective.[3] The inserted Article 8*bis*(1) of the ICC Statute defines the crime of aggression as 'the planning, preparation, initiation or execution, by a person in a position effectively to exercise control over or to direct the political or military action of a State, of an act of aggression which, by its character, gravity and scale, constitutes a manifest violation of the Charter of the United Nations'.[4] The definition, in particular, the leadership clause and the high threshold of a manifest violation of the UN Charter, essentially reflects the idea born in Nuremberg.[5] While the formal resurrection gives cause for hope, various developments in the field of international criminal law seem to indicate that the 'supreme crime' at Nuremberg became today the 'odd crime out'. This chapter aims to describes the indicators of the fall of the crime of aggression.

50.2 The Hypothesis of Nuremberg: The Supreme International Crime

The IMT has put forward the hypothesis to perceive the crime of aggression as the supreme international crime that contains within itself the accumulated evil of the whole. The sentences preceding the famous *dictum* give a subtle hint of the aggravated wrong of aggression. After asserting that the charges of aggressive war are 'charges of utmost gravity', the IMT claims that 'war is essentially an evil thing' in reference to the consequences that are 'not confined to the belligerent states alone, but affect the whole world'.[6] This suggests that world peace-shattering nature of aggression and not the mere violation of state sovereignty is the reason why it was considered as the greatest wrong.[7] Similarly, *Dinstein* interprets the 'supreme international crime' label as pointing to the unpredictable nature and the devastating effects of war which is a 'cataclysmic event' that can in no way be waged 'as if it were a chess game'.[8]

---

[1] International Military Tribunal, Judgment of 1 October 1946, in *The Trial of German Major War Criminals. Proceedings of the International Military Tribunal sitting at Nuremberg, Germany*, Part 22 (22 August 1946 to 1 October 1946), at 421.

[2] See ICC Statute, Art. 8*bis*.

[3] See Assembly of States Parties, Resolution ICC-ASP/16/Res.5, 14 December 2017.

[4] Art. 8*bis*(2) ICC Statute continues by defining the 'act of aggression'.

[5] On the differences to the definition of the crime against peace, see McDougall 2017.

[6] International Military Tribunal, *supra note* 1, at 421.

[7] In the same vein, Mégret 2017, at 1414.

[8] Dinstein 2017, para. 360.

'In the nature of things', he asserts, 'blood and fire, suffering and pain, are the concomitants of war'.[9]

An analysis of the legal consequences of the aggressive use of armed force supports the destructive and dangerous nature of aggression beyond the violation of state sovereignty. First, it is difficult to imagine the use of armed force against another state in manifest violation of the UN Charter that does not amount to an armed conflict and thereby triggers the application of international humanitarian law. International humanitarian law outlaws but also legalizes certain forms of violence against combatants and civilians, the former can be killed as legitimate targets and the latter as collateral damage. In that sense, the crime of aggression creates the justification for killings which would otherwise be criminal.[10]

Second, it is difficult to imagine the use of armed force in manifest violation of the UN Charter that does not reach the threshold of an 'armed attack' in the sense of Article 51 UN Charter. This is why the crime of aggression allows the victim state to legally strike back in self-defense and thus creates the risk of escalation. It may be argued that the legal use of armed force in self-defense has an appeasing function. The restrictive framing of Article 51, however, reveals that even such use of force shall be excluded as far as possible 'in view of the typical dangers of escalation which are connected with mutual uses of armed force'.[11] The particularly destructive force of interstate armed conflicts is backed by empirical evidence. While interstate armed conflicts comprise only 16.7% of all armed conflicts since 1946, they account for nearly 67% of all battlefield deaths since 1989.[12] The crime of aggression should therefore protect from the destructive nature of interstate use of armed force whose initiation was in manifest violation of the UN Charter.

From a broader perspective, it is often said that the crime of aggression is the 'mother of all crimes'[13] that creates the permissive environment for the commission of other crimes. The Human Rights Committee, however, has lately affirmed the *ipso facto* wrong of aggression irrespective of the subsequent compliance of international humanitarian law or the commission of other crimes by stating: 'acts of aggression as defined in international law, resulting in deprivation of life, violate ipso facto article 6 [right to life] of the Covenant [on Civil and Political Rights].'[14] Recent examples of genocide, crimes against humanity and war crimes demonstrate that they are often committed as 'motherless children' without the prior commission of a crime of aggression.[15] On the other hand, the partial dependency of crimes against humanity from the crime of aggression under the IMT Charter and the realities of

---

[9] Ibid. Similarly, Cassese 1999, S. 146.

[10] In the same vein, Mégret 2017, at 1420 et seq. Ohlin 2017.

[11] Nolte and Randelzhofer 2012, para. 6.

[12] See Grover 2019, at 166, who relies on the UCDP database.

[13] Similarly, Cryer et al. 2019, at 302. For a critical assessment of this assumption, see Mégret 2017, 1416 et seq.

[14] See para. 70 of Human Rights Committee, General Comment No. 36, Article 6: Right to life, 3 September 2019, CCCPR/C/GC/36.

[15] In the same vein, Wrange 2017, at 7. For these examples, see Mégret 2017, at 1417.

World War II may explain why aggression was labelled as the 'mother of all crimes'.[16] According to Article 6(c) of the IMT Charter, crimes against humanity required to be committed 'in execution of or in connection with any crime within the jurisdiction of the Tribunal', i.e. war crimes or the crime of aggression.[17] It is also a matter of fact that the German aggression of neighboring countries was paired with the massive commission of war crimes and crimes against humanity.

This has led *Mégret* to conclude that the entire characterization as the supreme crime 'was quite tailored to the needs and visions of the Allies' as it describes a particular historical reality where the crime of aggression was indeed followed by other crimes.[18] Similarly, *Schabas* assumes that the 'supreme international crime' jargon may have been of strategical nature.[19] He asserts that '[a]ggressive war was a kind of prosecutorial magic bullet' that did not require to prove the chain of criminal liability up through the ranks to convict those most responsible.[20] To take up Schabas' thought, one may argue that 'supreme international crime' rather made reference to the supreme ranks than to the supreme wrong. Indeed, the allegedly 'supreme crime' was not always followed by the 'supreme penalty'. Whenever aggression was the only crime a person was convicted of in Nuremberg, that person was not sentenced to death.[21] The voiced criticism suggests that Nuremberg's 'supreme international crime' language is not universally applicable to crimes of aggression, but rather reflective of a pragmatic approach to address the particular wrong of the Nazis.

Another explanation for the IMT's emphasis on the supreme wrong of aggression may have been to subtly disguise the tension with the principle of *nullum crimen, nulla poena sine lege*.[22] There is no crime and no punishment without law. This principle was the objection most frequently raised to the Nuremberg trials, in particular to the crime of aggression.[23] While war making was unlawful by the time of World War II, it was unclear whether it was also criminal.[24] The IMT, however, asserted that the *nullum crimen* principle was a 'principle of justice' that had no application to the present facts as those who in defiance of treaties and assurances had attacked neighboring States must have known that they were doing wrong.[25] In these circumstances, it continued, it was not unjust to punish them, it would rather

---

[16] Similarly, ibid. at 1416 et seq.

[17] On the legal nature of the nexus requirement, see Ambos 2013, vol II, at 50 et seq.

[18] Mégret 2017, at 1416 et seq.

[19] Schabas 2004, at 31 et seq.

[20] Ibid.

[21] Ibid., at 30; Schuster 2003, at 12.

[22] Also known as rule against retroactive law or prohibition of ex post facto law.

[23] See also the objections on behalf of the defendants in IMT, judgment of 1 October 1946, *supra note* 1, at 444. See also Kelsen 1947, at 164; Schmitt 1994, at 23 et seq.; Weigend 2012, at 45.

[24] Kelsen 1945, at 6. For an overview, see Jeßberger 2017, at 294 et seq. In favor of the criminality of aggression at that time, Glueck 1946, at 34. For a contrary view, see Jescheck 1952, at 236 et seq.; 416; Schmitt 1994, at 182 with further references.

[25] International Military Tribunal, *supra note* 1, at 444.

be unjust if this wrong was allowed to go unpunished.[26] It thereby referred to the defendants' potential knowledge of the wrong ('must have known') and employed arguments of substantive justice.[27] It seems as if the utmost gravity of the crime of aggression reduced the leap between illegality and criminality to such a negligible size that allowed to overcome the tension with the *nullum crimen* principle. The foreseeability of doing wrong in the sense of engaging in illegal conduct paired with the fact that waging an aggressive war is a conduct of 'utmost gravity' precludes aggressors from invoking 'legitimate confidence'[28] in engaging in innocent conduct. Labelling aggression as the 'supreme crime' may have been a desperate attempt of the IMT to overcome the tension with the *nullum crimen* principle.[29]

Thus, it is debatable whether the label as the 'supreme international crime' accurately reflects the utmost gravity of aggression, or whether it was only of strategic nature to capture the wrong of the Nazis and to disguise the tension with the *nullum crimen* principle.

50.3 The Marginalization of the Crime of Aggression after Nuremberg

Despite the hypothesis of Nuremberg, the subsequent developments in international criminal law seem to marginalize the crime of aggression to the 'odd crime out'. The fall of the 'supreme international crime' shall be exemplified by the retarding moments of the resurrection of the crime of aggression, the consensual jurisdiction of the International Criminal Court, and the particularities of domestic enforcement.

50.3.1 The Retarding Moments of the Resurrection of the Crime of Aggression

Soon after its official birth in Nuremberg, the crime of aggression somehow sank into oblivion.[30] For comparative reasons, one may refer to the progress achieved in the criminalization of genocide and the codification of international humanitarian law in the 1940s. The momentum created by World War II led to the adoption of the Genocide Convention in 1948[31] and the Fourth Geneva Convention in 1949,[32] but

---

[26] Ibid.
[27] Cassese 2008, at 39.
[28] Tomuschat 2006, at 835.
[29] See also the explanations given by Kelsen 1945, at 6 et seq.
[30] Jeßberger 2017, at 297 et seq.
[31] Convention on the Prevention and Punishment of the Crime of Genocide, 9 December 1948.
[32] Geneva Convention relative to the Protection of Civilian Persons in Time of War, 12 August 1949.

did not end up in a definition of the crime of aggression. Admittedly, the underlying prohibition of the use of force became the cornerstone of the UN Charter in 1945. Moreover, the UN General Assembly was eager to perpetuate Nuremberg's revolutionary idea of holding individuals criminally responsible. This led to the adoption of Resolution 95 in 1946[33] affirming the Nuremberg Principles and of Resolution 177 in 1947[34] entrusting the International Law Commission (ILC) with the formulation of these principles. The ILC fulfilled this task in 1950, but abstained from defining aggression.[35] The impetus brought by World War II was thus lost without ensuring that the 'supreme crime' was fully defined.

In 1974, Resolution 3314 of the UN General Assembly did not come up with a definition for the purpose of individual criminal responsibility either. It approved a definition of the underlying *state* act of aggression, to guide the UN Security Council in its determinations in accordance with Article 39 UN Charter.[36] The only vague allusion to individual criminal responsibility may be Article 5(2) of the annex of the resolution that provides that a 'war of aggression is a crime against international peace' and that '[a]ggression gives rise to international responsibility'.[37] At best, this can be interpreted as confirming the Nuremberg dictum, but it fails to make a defining step further.

The end of the Cold War as well as the atrocities committed in Rwanda and the Former Yugoslavia created another momentum for the development of international criminal law but neglected the crime of aggression. Due to the lack of an interstate conflict, there was no need to include aggression into the Statute of the newly established International Criminal Tribunal for Rwanda.[38] Its inclusion into the Statute of the International Criminal Tribunal for the former Yugoslavia was not significantly discussed, although the use of force during the secessionist movements would have given rise to questions related to *ius ad bellum*.[39]

When states established the International Criminal Court (ICC) in Rome in 1998, they failed to agree on a definition of the crime of aggression. They included a placeholder in Article 5(2) of the Statute that postponed the task to define the crime and to set out the conditions under which the court shall exercise jurisdiction. Ironically, the special status of 'supreme international crime' became its status as a 'crime in waiting'.[40] The placeholder was removed at the Review Conference in Kampala in

---

[33] UN General Assembly, Resolution 95 (I), 11 December 1946.

[34] UN General Assembly, Resolution 177 (II), 21 November 1947.

[35] Principle VI only mirrors the language of Article 6(a) IMT Charter, see International Law Commission, Principles of International Law Recognized in the Charter of the Nürnberg Tribunal and in the Judgment of the Tribunal (1950). For a full account of the work of the ILC, see Crawford 2017.

[36] See operative para. 4, UN General Assembly Resolution 3314 (XXIX), 14 December 1974. In detail, see Bruha 2017.

[37] See also Kreß 2018, at 4; Solera 2007, at 200; Dinstein 2017, para. 388.

[38] McDougall 2013, at 40.

[39] See Mahony 2015, at 1079; Zolo 2007, at 804 et seq. For the reasons not to include the crime of aggression, see Matheson and Scheffer 2016, at 187.

[40] Jeßberger 2017, at 299.

2010 by Article 8*bis*(1) of the ICC Statute which finally provides for a definition of the crime of aggression.[41]

Still, 2010 did not mark the end of the delay tactic. States adjourned the activation of the ICC's jurisdiction over the crime of aggression by inserting two cumulative conditions.[42] Before the ICC may exercise jurisdiction with respect to crimes of aggression, they required 'the ratification or acceptance of the amendments by thirty States Parties'[43] and 'a decision to be taken after 1 January 2017 by the same majority of States Parties as is required for the adoption of an amendment to the Statute'.[44] While the 30th ratification was achieved on 26 June 2016,[45] the activation decision proved to be more complicated.[46] After heated debates at the 16th session of the Assembly of States Parties (ASP) in 2017, it was decided to activate the Court's jurisdiction over the crime of aggression as of 17 July 2018.[47] Twenty years after the adoption of the ICC Statute, the crime of aggression finally became a crime prosecutable under the regime of the ICC. As we will see, the long dormancy of the crime will often be held against it and perpetuate the marginalization of the crime of aggression.

50.3.2 The Consensual Jurisdiction of the ICC in the Absence of a Security Council Referral

The consensual[48] jurisdiction of the ICC over the crime of aggression is another feature indicating the marginalization of the 'supreme international crime' to the 'odd crime out'. The Kampala Amendments[49] and later the Resolution adopted at the 16th session of the ASP in 2017[50] provide for a jurisdictional regime over the crime of aggression that considerably deviates from the one over genocide, crimes against humanity and war crimes.

The first deviation concerns the prosecution of nationals of non-states parties. In case of a state referral[51] or a *proprio motu* investigation[52] Article 12(2)(a) of the ICC Statute normally allows the prosecution of nationals of non-states parties as

---

[41] For the definition, see *supra*.

[42] See Understanding no. 3, Resolution RC/Res.6, 11 June 2010, Annex III.

[43] See ICC Statute, Articles 15*bis*(2) and 15*ter*(2).

[44] See ICC Statute, Articles 15 *bis*(3) and 15 *ter*(3).

[45] For the status of ratifications, see https://treaties.un.org/.

[46] On the difficult negotiations, see Kreß 2018; Hartig 2018; Trahan 2018, at 211 et seq.; Weisbord 2019, at 169 et seq.

[47] Operative para. 1, Assembly of States Parties, Resolution ICC-ASP/16/Res.5, 14 December 2017.

[48] See also Kreß and Holtzendorff 2010, at 1212: 'The (Softly) Consent-Based Pillar'.

[49] Resolution RC/Res.6, 11 June 2010.

[50] Assembly of States Parties, Resolution ICC-ASP/16/Res.5, 14 December 2017.

[51] See ICC Statute, Article 13(a).

[52] See ICC Statute, Article 13(c).

long as the crimes were committed on the territory of a state party.[53] For the transboundary crime of aggression, however, this was ruled out by Article 15*bis*(5) which excludes from the jurisdiction of the ICC any crime of aggression when committed by a national of a non-state party or on its territory. Admittedly, the prosecution of nationals of non-states parties absent a Security Council referral[54] and state consent has long been subject to criticism irrespective of the crimes in question.[55] Whenever a person commits a crime on the territory of another state, however, the person cannot rely on the lacking consent of his or her national state to evade prosecution. Neither can this person evade prosecution by the ICC in case the territorial state has legitimized the ICC by ratifying the ICC Statute regardless of whether his or her national state is a party to the Statute.[56] Interestingly, this basic understanding of territorial jurisdiction[57] in Rome disappeared in Kampala. The time lapse allowed to play the consent card again and led to Article 15*bis*(5) which prevents jurisdiction over nationals of non-states parties even if they aggressed a ratifying state party.[58]

The second deviation is also consent-related. It excludes nationals of states parties that have not given prior consent to the jurisdiction of the ICC in case of a state referral or a *proprio motu* investigation. The outstanding question is 'only' how the principle of consent is operationalized.

On its face, Article 15*bis*(4) of the ICC Statute establishes an opt-out system, a system of *passive* consent by stating: 'The Court may, in accordance with article 12, exercise jurisdiction over a crime of aggression, arising from an act of aggression committed by a State Party, unless that State Party has previously declared that it does not accept such jurisdiction by lodging a declaration with the Registrar.' By default, nationals of states parties appear to be 'in' the Court's jurisdictional regime.[59] The idea behind passive consent was to bridge the gap between those in favor of the unmodified application of Article 12(2) and those preferring a regime

---

[53] See ICC Statute, Article 12(2)(a).

[54] For the jurisdiction upon Security Council referral, see ICC Statute, Article 15*ter*.

[55] See, e.g. the statements on the Afghanistan situation by Trump D, Remarks to the 73rd Session of the United Nations General Assembly (NYC, 25 September 2018), https://www.whitehouse.gov/briefings-statements/remarks-president-trump-73rd-session-united-nations-general-assembly-new-york-ny/; Bolton J, Protecting American Constitutionalism and Sovereignty from International Threats. Speech at the Federalist Society (Washington, D.C., 10 September 2018), https://www.justsecurity.org/60674/national-security-adviser-john-bolton-remarks-international-criminal-court/ https://www.justsecurity.org/60674/national-security-adviser-john-bolton-remarks-international-criminal-court/https://www.justsecurity.org/60674/national-security-adviser-john-bolton-remarks-international-criminal-court/, both accessed 1 November 2019. For a similar U.S. position during the drafting of the ICC Statute, see Scheffer 1999, at 26.

[56] See also Schabas and Pecorella 2016, para. 16; Similarly, Cassese et al. 2002, at 1911.

[57] On the principle of territorial jurisdiction, see Cryer et al. 2019, at 52 et seq.

[58] Aggressive nationals of non-states parties can still face trial if the UN Security Council refers a situation, Art. 15*ter* of the ICC Statute. The possibility of a subsequent *ad hoc* consent to the jurisdiction of the ICC on the basis of Article 12(3) is controversial. In favor Zimmermann and Freiburg 2016, para. 24; Cryer et al. 2019, at 313. In contrast, see Akande and Tzanakopoulos 2018, at 954 et seq.; Barriga and Blokker 2017, at 656.

[59] Trahan 2018, at 204; Wenaweser and Barriga 2015, at 292.

of active consent in Kampala.[60] According to the first group, the ratification of the amendments by the victim state (as one of the territorial states under Article 12(2)(a)) would have sufficed even if the aggressive state party did not consent.[61] According to the second group, only nationals of states parties that have given consent through ratification should fall under the jurisdiction absent Security Council referral.[62] Article 15*bis*(4) provides a compromise: The ratification of the amendments by the victim state suffices, the consent of the aggressor state is presumed in the absence of a previous opt-out.[63] Such an opt-out system normally works on the basis of shame. Although one provides an emergency exit, the hope is that its use is politically too costly.[64] To Kenya, however, which had previously threatened to leave the Court,[65] an opt-out declaration did not seem overpriced.[66] For all other states, a draft resolution at the 16th session of the ASP in December 2017 aimed at reducing the embarrassing effect of a formal opt-out by lowering the requirements for such a declaration.[67]

But instead of accepting this soft opt-out regime, the ASP adopted a resolution that seems to render Article 15*bis*(4) of the ICC Statute almost meaningless.[68] It provides in operative paragraph 2 that 'in the case of a State referral or *proprio motu* investigation the Court shall not exercise its jurisdiction regarding a crime of aggression when committed by a national or on the territory of a State Party that has not ratified or accepted these amendments.'[69] An isolated reading suggests a U-turn towards an opt-in regime whereby the nationals of states parties are not 'in' the jurisdictional reach of the Court unless their state has ratified the amendments. A combined reading with Article 15*bis*(4) of the ICC Statute leads to the absurd result of an opt-in-opt-out system. States could shield their aggressive leaders twice, by refusing to ratify the amendments and by later opting out.[70] Worse than a simple opt-in system, this result is incompatible with the described genesis of the Kampala

---

[60] Kreß and Holtzendorff 2010, at 1213; in detail, see Wenaweser and Barriga 2015, at 288 et seq. See also Report of the Facilitation on the Activation of the Jurisdiction of the International Criminal Court over the Crime of Aggression of 27 November 2017, ICC-ASP/16/24, at 5 et seq.

[61] See Annex II, Paper submitted by Liechtenstein (April 2017), Report of the Facilitation on the Activation of the Jurisdiction of the International Criminal Court over the Crime of Aggression of 27 November 2017, ICC-ASP/16/24, at 22.

[62] Ibid.

[63] See Kreß and Holtzendorff 2010, at 1214.; Barriga and Blokker 2017, at 655.

[64] On the political costs of an opt out, see Foley 2015, at 68; McDougall 2018, at 334.

[65] See, e.g., Ssenyonjo 2017, at 56 et seq.

[66] See Kenya, Declaration of Non-Acceptance, 15 October 2015, https://www.icc-cpi.int/iccdocs/other/2015_NV_Kenya_Declaration_article15bis-4.pdf. Accessed 1 November 2019.

[67] For the different options of softly opting out, see OP 1(a), [Draft resolution] Activation of the Jurisdiction of the Court over the Crime of Aggression, 13 December 2017, ICC-ASP/16/L.9, https://ejiltalk.org/wp-content/uploads/2018/01/ICC-ASP-16-L9-ENG-CoA-resolution-13Dec17-2200.pdf (last visited 20 December 2019). For a critique, see Hartig 2018; Stürchler 2018. Similarly, Ferencz 2018, at 3.

[68] Similarly, Zimmermann and Freiburg-Braun 2019, paras 359 et seq.; Clark 2020, para. 46.

[69] Assembly of States Parties, Resolution ICC-ASP/16/Res.5, 14 December 2017.

[70] Clark 2020, para. 45.

compromise. Afraid of postponing the activation decision *ad infinitum*,[71] however, states preferred to swallow the bitter pill and adopted operative paragraph 2 under the pressure of France and the UK.[72]

This absurd result is partly due to the birth defect of the ICC Statute. The placeholder in Article 5(2) and its subsequent replacement by Article 8*bis*, 15*bis* and 15*ter* gave those argumentative leverage that preferred a system of active consent for the crime of aggression.[73] 'Any amendment to articles 5,6,7 and 8' allow to assume the application of Article 121(5) whose second sentence spells out the active consent regime as reflected in operative paragraph 2. Although states parties in Kampala tried to emphasize the *lex specialis* nature of the amendments to avoid the application of Article 121(5) second sentence, the long dormancy of the crime of aggression has facilitated amnesia at the ASP in 2017.

It remains to be seen how the ICC will deal with the incompatibility between the drafting history of Article 15*bis*(4) and the language of the ASP resolution. This ultimately depends on whether Article 15*bis*(4) is clear on its face[74] and on the legal value of operative paragraph 2.[75] Interestingly, the resolution adds a third operative paragraph that leaves some 'constructive ambiguity'[76] on whether states parties as the 'masters of the treaty' were able to *de facto* delete Article 15*bis*(4) by way of an ASP resolution. It reaffirms 'paragraph 1 of article 40 and paragraph 1 of article 119 of the Rome Statute in relation to the judicial independence of the judges of the Court'. It is worth noting that Article 119 was precisely drafted to resolve conflicts of competences between the ASP, the ICC and other courts.[77] Thus, there is 'a glimmer of hope'[78] that whatever the ASP agreed on in operative paragraph 2, it is primarily up to the ICC to settle the question on the limits of its jurisdiction.[79]

For the purpose of this chapter it suffices, however, to emphasize the consensual nature of the jurisdiction of the ICC over aggressors of states parties irrespective of whether one requires active consent by the aggressor state via ratification (operative paragraph 2 of the ASP resolution prevails) or its passive consent via the absence of lodging an opt-out declaration (Article 15*bis*(4) of the ICC Statute prevails). Both operationalizations of the consent principle confirm a jurisdictional regime *à la carte* and the marginalization of the crime of aggression.

---

[71] Trahan 2018, at 213.

[72] Kreß 2018, at 11 et seq. See Akande and Tzanakopoulos 2018, at 942. See already Hartig 2018. In the same vein, Trahan 2018, at 214; Weisbord 2019 at 172.

[73] See Kreß and von Holtzendorff 2010, at 1195 et seq.

[74] In that vein, Trahan 2018, at 232.

[75] As a subsequent agreement or practice, it would be only one factor relevant to the contextual interpretation of Article 15*bis*(4). As a supplementary means of interpretation, it would be at the same interpretative level as the preparatory work of Article 15*bis*(4). See also the discussion of Akande and Tzanakopoulos 2018, 943 et seq.; Stürchler 2018; Grover 2019, at 163.

[76] On the practice of treaty negotiators in applying constructive ambiguity, see Hafner 2013, at 107 et seq.

[77] Clark 2016, paras 1 et seq.

[78] Clark 2020, para. 45.

[79] Similarly, Trahan 2018, at 216; Akande and Tzanakopoulos 2018, at 942.

50.3.3 The Domestic Enforcement Conundrum

Besides the poor prospects of trying aggressors at the ICC, the prospects of holding them accountable at the national level are not promising either. The reluctance to ensure domestic enforcement[80] of the criminalization of aggression seems to be another factor that clashes with its label as 'supreme international crime'.

States may be discouraged from implementing the crime of aggression because of several controversial questions that may be summarized as the domestic enforcement conundrum. It is for example subject to debate whether the principle of complementarity, one of the driving forces behind domestic implementations,[81] applies to the crime of aggression. And even if it applied, some question the right of states other than the aggressor state to exercise jurisdiction. Finally, legal and practical challenges, in particular immunities may impair the domestic enforcement of the criminalization of aggression.

50.3.3.1 The Principle of Complementarity and Understanding 5

Although the principle of complementarity[82] is one of the cornerstones of the ICC Statute,[83] its application to the crime of aggression has occasionally been put into question,[84] namely whether states are primarily responsible for prosecuting the crime of aggression and the ICC only complementary to national criminal jurisdiction.[85]

Before the ICC has been established, the ILC proposed *exclusive* and not complementary jurisdiction of an international criminal court over the crime of aggression except for the jurisdiction of the aggressor state.[86] At the Kampala Conference, these reservations about the domestic prosecution of aggression were particularly voiced by the United States.[87] For the Special Working Group on the Crime of Aggression, that met before the Kampala Conference, however, no problems seemed to arise

---

[80] Enforcement shall be understood in a broader sense, referring to the legislative act of criminalizing aggression, to the measures of the judiciary to adjudicate aggression and to the attempts of the executive to ensure its enforcement in the technical sense.

[81] Kleffner 2009, at 309 et seq.

[82] See ICC Statute, preambular para. 10, Articles 1, 17, 18, 19 and 20.

[83] See *Lubanga* (ICC-01/04-01/06), Decision on the Practices of Witness Familiarization and Witness Proofing, 8 November 2006, para. 34, fn. 38.

[84] van Schaack 2012; Veroff 2016; Ruys 2017, at 27 et seq.

[85] For a definition of complementarity, see *Lubanga* (ICC-01/04-01/06), Decision on the Practices of Witness Familiarization and Witness Proofing, 8 November 2006, para. 34, fn. 38.

[86] See Commentary to Article 8, para. 2, International Law Commission, Draft Code of Crimes Against the Peace and Security of Mankind with Commentaries (1996).

[87] Statement by Legal Adviser Koh H H at the Review Conference, 4 June 2010, as reproduced in Koh and Buchwald 2015, at 274. See the similar concerns expressed by in Commentary to Article 8, para. 14, International Law Commission, Draft Code of Crimes Against the Peace and Security of Mankind with Commentaries (1996).

from the provisions on complementarity being applicable to the crime of aggression.[88] Implicitly, the applicability of the principle to the crime of aggression has been affirmed in Kampala by adding Article 8*bis* in Article 20(3), which is referred to in Article 17(1)(c) of the Statute as one of three scenarios[89] where the ICC shall not exercise its complementary jurisdiction.[90]

The implicit affirmation seems to stand in contrast to understanding 5 to the Kampala Amendments.[91] To reflect the concerns of the United States, it states: "It is understood that the amendments shall not be interpreted as creating the right or obligation to exercise domestic jurisdiction with respect to an act of aggression committed by another State."[92] According to *van Schaack*, it aims at discouraging states from criminalizing and prosecuting aggression domestically.[93] According to *Kreß* and *von Holtzendorff* , in contrast, it states the obvious, the ICC Statute does not create the right or obligation for any state with respect to domestic legislation and adjudication.[94] Indeed, the principle of complementarity does not create an obligation but only a strong incentive for domestic implementation.[95] In any case, it seems to be far-fetched to ascribe a modifying effect to understandings that are of such low importance that they do not even require ratification,[96] especially if this would affect essential treaty provisions, such as the principle of complementarity. The divergent views ultimately demonstrate that negotiators made use of 'constructively ambiguous' language that was acceptable for all, including for those that do not want to neutralize the *de facto* incentivizing effect of the Statute.

In any case, the incentive to domestic implementation and prosecution in order to avoid scrutiny by the ICC[97] may be less pronounced due to the limited possibilities of the Court to adjudicate aggression without the help of the often-paralyzed Security Council. States do not need to implement and prosecute the crime of aggression out of fear, if their nationals do not fall within the Court's reach anyway.[98] It is open

---

[88] See 2004 Princeton Report, in Barriga and Kreß 2012, at 433 et seq.

[89] See Schabas and El Zeidy 2016, para. 23; But see van Schaack 2012, at 155 perceiving the first two scenarios as implicating the principle of complementarity and the third only as a consideration of the principle of *nebis in idem*; Kleffner 2009, at 118 et seq.

[90] McDougall 2013, at 314 et seq.

[91] Review Conference, Resolution RC/Res.6 of 12 June 2010.

[92] See Understanding 5, Review Conference, Resolution RC/Res.6 of 12 June 2010, Annex III.

[93] van Schaack 2012, at 161.

[94] Kreß and von Holtzendorff 2010, S. 1216; Similarly, Clark 2010, 705 fn. 57; Wrange 2017, S. 720; In the same vein, Jurdi 2013, S. 144; McDougall 2013, S. 314.

[95] Werle and Jeßberger 2014, para. 375; Cryer et al. 2019, at 80; But see Kleffner 2009, at 344.

[96] See paras 1 and 3, Review Conference, Resolution RC/Res.6 of 11 June 2010. Similarly, Jurdi 2013, at 144 et seq. On the legal nature of the understandings in general, see Heller 2012; Akande and Tzanakopoulos 2018.

[97] See Stahn 2019, at 226.

[98] For the consensual jurisdiction, see Sect. 50.3.2.

to speculations whether this is why only 13 states[99] have implemented the crime of aggression since Kampala.

50.3.3.2 Controversy on the Forms of Domestic Jurisdiction

Besides the failed attempts to contest the applicability of the principle of complementarity to the crime of aggression, the uncertainty about the legally available forms of jurisdiction may be another factor that prevents states from progressive implementation.

As understanding 5 to the Kampala Amendments and the 1996 Draft Code of the ILC try to suggest, only the jurisdiction of the aggressor state seems to be uncontroversial. From the perspective of the United States and the ILC, the jurisdiction by a state other than the aggressor state would be 'contrary to the fundamental principle of international law *par in parem imperium non habet*' which forbids an equal to have authority over an equal.[100] Translated into specific forms of jurisdiction, this means that the aggressor state can exercise jurisdiction on the basis of the territoriality principle[101] and the active personality principle.[102] From a practical perspective, however, it should be recalled that the prosecution of state-organized crimes by the state of nationality has never been perceived as a promising avenue,[103] and realistically requires a regime change.[104]

From a legal perspective, it seems to conflict with the principle of territorial jurisdiction to interpret the *par in parem* principle as denying victim states the right to exercise jurisdiction. The crime of aggression is by its very nature a transboundary crime which is committed in the aggressor state (on whose territory the conduct occurs) and the victim state (on whose territory at least the consequences of the conduct occur).[105] Neither the early implementers[106] nor the post-World War II codifiers[107] seem to have restricted their provisions on territorial jurisdiction. Finally, the criminal proceedings in response to the Russian-Ukrainian conflict demystify the *par in parem* objection. As the alleged victim state, Ukraine did not feel prevented

---

[99] See Hartig 2019: Afghanistan, Austria, Croatia, Czech Republic, Ecuador, Estonia, Finland, Germany, Liechtenstein, Luxembourg, North Macedonia, Samoa and Slovenia.

[100] See *supra note* 86.

[101] On the principle of territoriality, see Ambos 2013, vol III, at 211 et seq.

[102] On the active personality principle, see Ambos 2013, vol III, at 217 et seq.

[103] Gaeta 2012, at 597; Weigend 2005, at 973 See already *United States v. Wilhelm List et al.*, U.S. Military Tribunal, 19 February 1948, in Trials of War Criminals Before the Nuremberg Military Tribunals Under Control Council Law No.10, Vol. 11 (1950), at 1241.

[104] Similarly, Strapatas 2010, at 459 et seq. Clark 2011, 725 fn. 17; Wrange 2017, at 742.

[105] Clark 2015 at 792; McDougall 2013, at 315. See also 2008 SWGCA Report (November), in Barriga and Kreß 2012, paras 28-29; 2009 SWGCA Report, in Barriga and Kreß 2012, paras 38-39.

[106] Hartig 2019.

[107] Reisinger Coracini 2017, at 1067 et seq.

from convicting former president Yanukovych *in absentia* in January 2019[108] and two Russian servicemen in April 2016[109] for their participation in the commission of a crime of aggression, although the courts indirectly sat in judgment over the Russian state act of aggression. Instead of referring to a principle of rather vague origin and functioning,[110] the underlying[111] sovereign equality of states represents the better benchmark for assessing the legality of victim state jurisdiction. The sovereignty of another equal state, however, does not prevent a state from exercising its sovereign right to criminal jurisdiction, at least whenever one of the constituent elements of the offence have taken place on its territory.[112] Translated into specific forms of jurisdiction, the victim state may exercise jurisdiction on the basis of the principle of territoriality, the protective principle and depending on whether one perceives individuals as victims of the crime of aggression,[113] the principle of passive personality.[114]

Another unconvincing objection to the jurisdiction of the victim state may be made in reference to the consensual jurisdiction of the ICC absent Security Council referral. The argument goes as follows: If the jurisdiction of the ICC is perceived as consent-based and derivative in nature,[115] states also need the consent of the aggressor state for the exercise of original jurisdiction.[116] The consensual jurisdiction of the ICC would only reflect the imperfection of domestic jurisdiction. *Newton* describes this symmetry with the maxim: *Nemo plus iuris transferre potest quam ipse habet*, nobody can transfer more rights than he or she possesses.[117] As the drafting history of the Kampala Amendments shows, however, there was 'widespread support'[118] for the unmodified application of the no-consent regime of Article 12, enabling the ICC to exercise jurisdiction as long as the victim state had ratified the amendments. The ultimately adopted consensual jurisdictional regime simply reflects a political choice

---

[108] See <https://www.theguardian.com/world/2019/jan/25/ukraine-ex-president-viktor-yanukovych-found-guilty-of-treason>, accessed 8 January 2020.

[109] Sayapin 2018.

[110] See Dinstein 1966, at 408.

[111] Orakhelashvili 2015, at 209; Yang 2012, at 55; Strapatas 2010, at 453.

[112] See *The Case of the S.S. 'Lotus'*, Permanent Court of International Justice, Judgment of 7 September 1927, PCIJ ser. A, no. 10, at 23; Jeßberger 2011, at 231; Ambos 2013, vol III, at 213.

[113] Which seems to be possible in light of U.N. Human Rights Committee, General Comment No. 36, Article 6: Right to life, 3 September 2019, CCCPR/C/GC/36, para. 70.

[114] On the protective principle and the passive personality principle, see Ambos 2013, vol III, at 220 et seq.

[115] It may also be argued that the ICC exercises the original *ius puniendi* of the international community whose interest in international peace is affected by crimes under international law, see Stahn 2016, at 447; Werle and Jeßberger 2014, para. 213.

[116] For a similar reasoning on the basis of the Kampala outcome, see Koh and Buchwald 2015, at 275 et seq.

[117] Digest 50, 17, 54. See Newton 2016; For a powerful response, see Stahn 2016.

[118] Clark 2010, at 705. See also Paper submitted by Liechtenstein (April 2017), in Report of the Facilitation on the Activation of the Jurisdiction of the International Criminal Court over the Crime of Aggression of 27 November 2017, ICC-ASP/16/24, Annex II, at 20 whereby one half of the delegations wanted a no-consent regime.

among the legally available designs of jurisdiction.[119] Moreover, exact symmetry between international and national jurisdiction seems to run counter to the principle of complementarity. The ICC and national courts act in a complementary and not a congruent way, their jurisdictional reach does not need to match completely.

The *par in parem* principle and the consensual jurisdiction may also be held against third states exercising universal jurisdiction. Whether international law offers states the right to exercise universal jurisdiction over the crime of aggression is fairly controversial. Universal jurisdiction describes the jurisdiction of third states irrespective of any link between the crime and the prosecuting state.[120]

The 'somewhat ambiguous'[121] Lotus case of 1927 offers the classical starting point for determining the international legal framework relevant for domestic criminal jurisdiction.[122] While some interpret Lotus as providing domestic legislative freedom as long as there is no prohibitive rule under international law,[123] others question today's validity and require instead the existence of a permissive rule under international law for the extension of domestic criminal jurisdiction to matters with a foreign element.[124]

To be on the safe side, states better prove the existence of a permissive rule, which may be found under customary international law. This requires the establishment of general practice and *opinio iuris*.[125] It is however difficult to identify sufficient examples of direct state practice on universal jurisdiction over the crime of aggression.[126] Admittedly, there is some at the legislative level in form of the early implementations by Samoa, North Macedonia as well as Cyprus and arguably

---

[119] For a similar distinction between the legally available and practically possible jurisdictional regime as discussed in Rome, see Scharf 2001, at 77.

[120] Werle and Jeßberger 2014, para. 218 ; Cryer et al. 2019, at 56 et seq. ; Principle 1(1), The Princeton Principles on Universal Jurisdiction (2001).

[121] See Ambos 2013, vol III, at 207.

[122] See *The Case of the S.S. 'Lotus'*, Permanent Court of International Justice, Judgment of 7 September 1927, PCIJ ser. A, no. 10. For a detailed analysis, see Jeßberger, 2011, at 198 et seq.

[123] Dissenting Opinion van der Wyngaert to *Case Concerning the Arrest Warrant of 11 April 2000*, International Court of Justice, judgment of 14 February 2002 ICJ, Arrest Warrant, para 51: 'It follows from the "Lotus" case that a State has the right to provide extraterritorial jurisdiction on its territory unless there is a prohibition under international law.' See also Scharf 2012, at 379 et seq.

[124] Jeßberger 2011, at 203 et seq.; Kreß 2002, at 831; Ryngaert 2008, at 29; Cryer et al. 2019, at 51.

[125] See ICJ Statute, Article 38(1)(b).

[126] Jeßberger 2018, at 198 et seq.; Cryer et al. 2019, at 57; Akande 2010, at 35; Oeter 2013, at 120 et seq.

by Austria, Luxemburg and Liechtenstein,[127] which established universal jurisdiction over the crime of aggression.[128] On the other hand, Germany,[129] Finland and Croatia did not extend their provisions on universal jurisdiction, applicable to genocide, crimes against humanity and war crimes, to the crime of aggression.[130] There are also some examples from the Post-World War II codifiers that seem to establish universal jurisdiction over the crime of aggression.[131] Nonetheless, these examples do not provide sufficient aggression-specific state practice.

It is argued here that instances of state practice do not need to exist as regards the crime of aggression in particular.[132] Provided customary international law is to be ascertained by an inductive method, it suffices to establish the customary right to exercise universal jurisdiction over the crime of aggression on the basis of existing state practice in respect of *other* crimes. Understood as moving from the specific to the general, induction requires—by definition—a form of generalization. If a customary right to universal jurisdiction was assessed for each crime individually, the outcome would be easily objectionable. To put it mildly, the political context and nature of crimes under international law are not the ideal breeding ground for inflationary state practice.[133] This is why state practice on crimes under international law should form a joint pool of cases from which to extract the factors probably relevant to the general rule to apply.[134] The inductively obtained general rule can then be applied by way of deduction to the crime of aggression, provided it shares the legally relevant factors.[135] Such a combined inductive-deductive approach does not seem to be excluded by the ILC whereby the assessment of general practice and *opinio iuris* 'does not preclude a measure of deduction as an aid'.[136]

---

[127] Given that the jurisdiction of these three states is dependent upon the receipt and denial of a request for extradition, some tend not to describe it as universal jurisdiction, but 'representation principle' or 'vicarious administration of justice'. See, e.g. Reydams 2003, 34 et seq.

[128] For Hartig 2019, at 492. For Cyprus, see Reply of the Permanent Mission of the Republic of Cyprus to the United Nation on the Scope and Application of the Principle of Universal Jurisdiction, Sixth Committee of the UN General Assembly, 74th session, https://www.un.org/en/ga/sixth/74/universal_jurisdiction.shtml, accessed 20 January 2020.

[129] For the reasons, see German Government Draft, BT-Drs. 18/8621, at 12 et seq.

[130] Hartig 2019, at 491.

[131] Reisinger Coracini 2017, at 1068 et seq.

[132] Another way of addressing the low number of hard state practice is suggested by *Kreß*. He contends that customary law rules can be deduced from well-established principles underlying these instances of state practice if they naturally flow from such principles. See Written Observations of Professor Claus Kreß as *amicus curiae*, ICC, Al Bashir (Jordan), 18 June 2018, ICC-02/05-01/09 OA2, para. 9; Kreß 2002, at 836.

[133] Only 61 universal jurisdiction cases resulted in a completed trial between 1961 and 2017, see Langer and Eason 2019, at 788.

[134] Bleckmann 1977, at 505.

[135] Ibid. at 506.

[136] In detail see Commentary to Draft Conclusion 2, para. 5, International Law Commission (2018) Draft Conclusions on Identification of Customary International Law, with Commentaries, UN Doc. A/73/10.

It is beyond the scope of this chapter to analyze in detail existing state practice on universal jurisdiction over genocide, crimes against humanity and war crimes.[137] The quintessential rule scholars seem to extract is twofold.[138] From a normative perspective, states have the right to exercise universal jurisdiction if crimes harm the fundamental interests of the international community. Secondly, there seems to be a pragmatic justification for universal jurisdiction. Crimes that fall under the scope of universal jurisdiction are likely to go unpunished. When exercising universal jurisdiction, states are therefore filling an accountability gap.

Universal jurisdiction over the crime of aggression seems to be justified both from a normative and pragmatic perspective. Normatively, the crime of aggression directly affects the fundamental interests of the international community in international peace and security.[139] This is established by the labelling of its predecessor 'crime against peace', Article 1(1) of the UN Charter that equates the underlying act of aggression with 'other breaches of the peace' and the lengthy discussion in Kampala about the concurrent competency of the Security Council to determine the 'existence of any threat to the peace, breach of the peace, or act of aggression'.[140]

The crime of aggression also meets the pragmatic endeavor of universal jurisdiction. As the restricted jurisdiction of the ICC suggests, impunity for aggression is likely to remain the rule. Absent a Security Council referral and provided one perceived the opt-in-opt-out regime as the prevailing one, the ICC could only prosecute if aggression occurred in a conflict between the 39 ratifying states parties.[141] Around half of them are states from Europe, rated as the 'most peaceful region in the world'.[142] Combined with the fact that the first users of force in militarized interstate disputes are primarily non-states parties,[143] the number of cases falling under the jurisdiction of the ICC remains small. From a pragmatic perspective, the described accountability gap and the global endeavor to end impunity for crimes under international justify the exercise of universal jurisdiction over the crime of aggression.

To further support the presumed applicability of the general rule to exercise universal jurisdiction to the crime of aggression, one may refer to the IMT practice.

---

[137] For studies on universal jurisdiction, see Langer and Eason 2019; Amnesty International (2012), Universal Jurisdiction. A Preliminary Survey of Legislation Around the World—2012 Update; Trial International (2019), Evidentiary Challenges in Universal Jurisdiction Cases. Universal Jurisdiction Annual Review 2019. See also the work of the Sixth Committee of the UN General Assembly, 'The Scope and Application of the Principle of Universal Jurisdiction' since its Sixty-Fourth Session, which documents replies by states, https://www.un.org/en/ga/sixth/74/universal_jurisdiction.shtml, accessed 20 January 2020. For an analysis of state practice, see e.g. Kreß 2002, at 832 et seq.

[138] Jeßberger 2011, at 271 et seq.; Ambos 2013, vol III, at 225; Sadat and Carden 2000, at 407 fn. 156; Bassiouni 2001, at 96 et seq. Kreß 2002, at 936 et seq., 837; Weigend 2005, at 971 et seq.

[139] 'International peace and security' is mentioned 33 times in the UN Charter.

[140] Werle and Jeßberger 2014, para. 1479.

[141] For the list of ratifying states, see https://treaties.un.org/.

[142] See Institute for Economics & Peace, World Peace Index 2019, at 6, http://visionofhumanity.org/app/uploads/2019/07/GPI-2019web.pdf, accessed 20 January 2020.

[143] At least according to Brown 2014, at 663 who looked at conflicts between 1946 and 2001.

Some perceive the IMT as having applied universal jurisdiction in the interest of the international community delegated by the countries that ratified the 1946 London Agreement.[144] While some reject this view arguing that the Occupying Powers exercised the territorial jurisdiction of the defeated Germany,[145] both perceptions are not mutually exclusive. Different forms of jurisdiction may overlap.[146] It suffices to perceive the IMT as *also* exercising the *ius puniendi* of the international community over aggression to infer from this precedent a right of states to exercise universal jurisdiction.

50.3.3.3 Escalation 2.0 at the International Law Commission on Immunities

The successful reduction of the impunity gaps for aggression does not only depend on the design of the domestic jurisdictional regime but also upon legal and practical obstacles to domestic prosecution, such as conflicting immunities.

Aggressors that are *per definitionem* 'in a position effectively to exercise control over or to direct the political or military action of a State',[147] may often enjoy immunities or exemptions under domestic and international law.[148] Among those under international law with a barring effect on victim and third state jurisdiction, immunity *ratione personae* and immunity *ratione materiae* deserve closer scrutiny.[149]

Interestingly, immunity of state officials from foreign criminal jurisdiction is currently under consideration by the ILC.[150] The non-applicability of immunity *ratione materiae* in respect of crimes under international law led to an unprecedented divide among its members. It ultimately deviated from its usual consensual *modus operandi* and provisionally[151] adopted Draft Article 7 by vote[152] which states in its paragraph 1:

'Immunity ratione materiae from the exercise of foreign criminal jurisdiction shall not apply in respect of the following crimes under international law: (a) crime of genocide;

---

[144] In detail, see Scharf 2012, at 374 et seq.; Clark 2011, at 732. Similarly, Simons 1990, at 58; Nsereko 1999, at 101. For the features of the IMT that evince its universal jurisdiction, see Schwelb 1946, at 208 et seq.; McDougall 2013, at 317 et seq.

[145] See Kelsen 1947, at 167; Bassiouni 2001, at 91. But see Woetzel 1960, at 79 et seq.; McDougall 2013, at 318.

[146] See the conclusion of Scharf 2012, at 379. Similarly, Wright 1947, at 48 et seq.

[147] See ICC Statute, Article 8*bis*(1).

[148] Those are only relevant if the aggressor state decides to prosecute its own nationals. Constitutional immunities are technically unable to bar proceedings before foreign courts, Fox and Webb 2013, at 541.

[149] In detail, see ibid. at 537 et seq.

[150] For the current status, see https://legal.un.org/ilc/guide/4_2.shtml. Accessed 2 February 2020.

[151] The final adoption takes place after the second reading of all draft articles.

[152] On 20 July 2017, 21 members voted in favor, eight against, one member abstained. See https://legal.un.org/ilc/guide/4_2.shtml. Accessed 2 February 2020. Voting is a rare at the ILC, see Tladi 2019, at 171; Šturma 2019, at 36.

(b) crimes against humanity; (c) war crimes; (d) crime of apartheid; (e) torture; (f) enforced disappearance.'[153]

If states perceive the silence of Draft Article 7 on aggression as reflective of customary international law, this may have serious implications on the domestic prosecution of aggression. Unlike immunity *ratione personae*, immunity *ratione materiae* does not cease after a state official has left office.[154] Aggressors could not be held accountable by foreign courts after they left office unless the aggressor state waived immunity. Victim or third state jurisdiction would not have a significant advantage over the criminal prosecution by the aggressor state, but depend on the noble interest of the aggressor state in criminal accountability.

The conservativism of the ILC, that resonates through Draft Article 7, is quite striking. In face of the continuous efforts of the small group of 'persistent objectors'[155] within the ILC that challenged the existence of sufficient state practice in respect of *any* crime under international law,[156] it was difficult enough to keep the less controversial crimes in the list. To be fair, a truly conservative approach would have required to list the crime of aggression as the first crime in respect of which immunity *rationae materiae* does not apply. This seems to be inherent in Nuremberg's revolutionary idea of holding individuals accountable for serious violations of international law, which was primarily linked to the IMT's main charge, the crime of aggression. The contradiction between immunities and the inner logic of international criminal law is described by the IMT as follows:

> "The principle of International Law, which under certain circumstances protects the representatives of a State, cannot be applied to acts which are condemned as criminal by International Law. The authors of these acts cannot shelter themselves behind their official position in order to be freed from punishment in appropriate proceedings."[157]

The passage of the IMT is sometimes said to be relevant for prosecutions by international courts only. The general language of the *dictum* suffices, however, to emphasize its universal validity, also for domestic jurisdiction. Others perceive this passage as only referring to the substantive defense of the irrelevance of official capacity. Yet it appears to be almost ahistorical to make a firm distinction between immunity *ratione*

---

[153] See A/CN.4/L.893. For the reasons why the crime of aggression was not included, see Special Rapporteur Escobar Hernández C (2016), Fifth Report on Immunity of State Officials from Foreign Criminal Jurisdiction, International Law Commission, A/CN.4/701, paras 222 et seq.; Statement of the Chairperson of the Drafting Committee, Rajput A, International Law Commission, 20 July 2017, at 7 et seq.

[154] International Law Commission, Draft Article 6(2) provisionally adopted by the Drafting Committee at the sixty-seventh Session, 29 July 2015; Fox and Webb 2013, at 564.

[155] This is how Gómez-Robledo untechnically described the ILC members that constantly oppose draft Article 7, see International Law Commission, Provisional Summary Record of the 3486th meeting of 19 July 2019, A/CN.4/SR.3486, at 10.

[156] See International Law Commission, Report of the Sixty-Ninth Session in 2017, A/72/10, at 181 et seq. See also the symposium on 'The Present and Future of Foreign Official Immunity', in AJIL 2018:112, 1 et seq., where most of the contributors are those members that opposed Draft Article 7.

[157] International Military Tribunal, *supra note 1*, at 447.

materiae and the irrelevance of official capacity, even if this distinction is nowadays reflected in Article 27 of the ICC Statute.[158] Special Rapporteur *Escobar* has rightly noticed that the mere procedural nature of immunity *ratione materiae* is 'difficult to support in absolute terms'.[159] It is not uncommon to describe immunity *ratione materiae* as a substantive defense that prevents any individual criminal responsibility from accruing.[160] This seems to be in line with the early beginnings of international criminal law where the substantive defense of irrelevance of official capacity and the non-applicability of immunities were not systematically distinguished. The IMT itself used the concepts interchangeably, when it cited Article 7 of the IMT Charter (irrelevance of official capacity) and subsequently stated that 'he who violates the laws of war cannot obtain immunity'.[161] And even today, this polysemic use is not uncommon. For the non-applicability of immunities, scholars and the International Court of Justice still rely, with some variations, on Article 7 of the IMT Charter, Article 6 of the IMTFE Charter, Article II (4) (a) of the Control Council Law No. 10 and Principle III of the Nuremberg Principles,[162] although these provisions linguistically cover the irrelevance of official capacity only. In its Commentary to Article 7 of the 1996 Draft Code of Crimes, the ILC still pointed out that the 'absence of any procedural immunity' is an 'essential corollary of the absence of any substantive immunity or defence'.[163]

In comparison to interpreting Nuremberg as providing a right to exercise universal jurisdiction over aggression, perceiving it as a precedent for the non-applicability of immunity *ratione materiae* to the crime of aggression seems to be even more straightforward. This is why state practice on the non-applicability of immunity *ratione materiae* to crimes under international law must be perceived as a continuation of the Nuremberg legacy which is primarily based on the prosecution of state officials for aggression. Thus, unless stated otherwise, the non-applicability of immunity *ratione materiae* to the crime of aggression shines through any prosecution of state officials for crimes under international law. It is therefore difficult to separate the state practice on genocide, crimes against humanity and war crimes from the stable aggression-related foundation laid in Nuremberg.

---

[158] Even scholars do not necessarily perceive Article 27(1) of the ICC Statute as only referring to the irrelevance of official capacity. See Triffterer and Burchard 2016, para. 26; Similarly, Gaeta 2002, at 990.

[159] See Special Rapporteur Escobar Hernández C (2016), Fifth Report on Immunity of State Officials from Foreign Criminal Jurisdiction, International Law Commission, A/CN.4/701, para. 150. See also Ambos 2013, vol I, at 410; Wrange 2017, at 722.

[160] See Cassese 2008, 303 et seq.; Werle and Jeßberger 2014, para 724; see also Principle 5 and the respective commentary, in The Princeton Principles on Universal Jurisdiction (2001), at 31 and 48.

[161] See International Military Tribunal, *supra note* 1, at 447. See also Special Rapporteur Escobar Hernández C (2016), Fifth Report on Immunity of State Officials from Foreign Criminal Jurisdiction, International Law Commission, A/CN.4/701, para. 150 who has noticed this 'polysemic use' in case law. For a critical view, see O'Keefe 2015, para. 10.73.

[162] See e.g. Gaeta 2002, at 981; *Case Concerning the Arrest Warrant of 11 April 2000*, International Court of Justice, judgment of 14 February 2002 ICJ, Arrest Warrant, para. 58.

[163] See Commentary to Article 5, para. 6, International Law Commission, Draft Code of Crimes Against the Peace and Security of Mankind with Commentaries (1996).

To put an end to the enduring myth of a lack of direct state practice on the non-applicability of immunity *ratione materiae* with respect to the crime of aggression,[164] it shall be recalled that aggression trials against Germany and Japanese officials took place after World War II before Chinese,[165] Soviet,[166] Polish[167] and American[168] courts.[169] A more recent example for domestic aggression trials are the proceedings against the former military servicemen *Alexandrov* and *Yerofeyev* of the Russian armed forces before a Ukrainian Court in 2016.[170] Moreover, there have been few verbal acts by states at the at the Sixth Committee of the UN General Assembly that criticize the exclusion of the crime of aggression from Draft Article 7.[171] While this may not suffice to reach the threshold of *general* state practice, the Nuremberg legacy and any state practice echoing it can be used in support of the non-applicability of immunity *ratione materiae* with respect to the crime of aggression.

50.4 Conclusion: Do Not Bite the Hand That Feeds You

Despite the mantra-like repetition of its label as the 'supreme international crime', the crime of aggression has lost the glamour of Nuremberg. It neither benefitted from the impetus brought by the end of World War II and the Cold War nor from the initial magic of the ICC's beginning. Its long dormancy has allowed to question the validity of standard accessories of crimes under international law, such as the complementary mandate of the ICC and primary task of states to prosecute it, universal jurisdiction or the non-applicability of immunity *ratione materiae*. In addition to the developments as outlined in the chapter, the dormancy has also facilitated to silence the crime of aggression in initiatives on interstate cooperation. To date, the draft convention for

---

[164] See, e.g. Special Rapporteur Escobar Hernández C (2016), Fifth Report on Immunity of State Officials from Foreign Criminal Jurisdiction, International Law Commission, A/CN.4/701, para. 222.

[165] Such as the trials against Sakai, Isogai, Tani and Tanka.

[166] Such as the trials against Wehrmacht Generals. For a summary, see Ginsburgs 2000.

[167] Such as the trial against Greiser.

[168] Such as the follow-up trials with crime of aggression charges before the U.S. Military Tribunals in the *I.G. Farben* case, the *Krupp et al.* case, the *von Weizäcker et al.* case and the von *Leeb et al.* case. However, one may question the relevance of these cases for the question of immunities as the tribunals have been established by occupying powers, see below and Kreicker 2007, vol I, at 194.

[169] The fact that they prosecuted former German state officials without considering immunities may indicate their non-applicability. On the other hand, one may discuss whether factors such as the nature of the tribunals or the surrender of Germany and Japan may render the question of immunities obsolete.

[170] Sayapin 2018, at 1097. According to *Sayapin*, immunity was only invoked in respect of war crimes, but it is very likely that the Court would have rejected functional immunity as it alluded to state responsibility held by Russia elsewhere in the judgment.

[171] In 2017 and 2018, three states of the General Assembly openly welcomed the exclusion of the crime of aggression from the list of Draft Article 7 (Czech Republic, Hungary and Belarus) and six states criticized it (Germany, Ukraine, Portugal, Slovenia, Estonia and Nicaragua).

mutual legal assistance and extradition in domestic prosecution of atrocity crimes as proposed by the 'mutual legal assistance initiative',[172] the European Network of Contact Points in respect of persons responsible for the crime of genocide, crimes against humanity and war crimes,[173] and Europol,[174] for example, fail to reconsider the exclusion of the crime of aggression from their mandate. From a purely practical perspective, interstate cooperation is more concerned with crimes that are statistically significant. The high threshold of a manifest violation of the UN Charter will leave the number of potential aggression cases relatively low. Nonetheless, states would be well advised to be better equipped against future aggressors and to avoid fragmentation between the 'quadriga of crimes' under the ICC Statute. If states keep on omitting the crime of aggression whenever they list 'core crimes' or 'atrocity crimes', there seems to be a risk that the formerly known 'supreme international crime' will lose its status as one of the four crimes under international law. In the same vein, genocide, crimes against humanity and war crimes risk to lose the supportive device of Nuremberg. It was the revolutionary idea of Nuremberg, that 'crimes against international law are committed by men, not by abstract entities' and the crime of aggression was the was crime the judges had primarily in mind. Marginalizing the crime of aggression may thus destabilize the very foundations of international criminal law.

References

Akande D (2010) Prosecuting Aggression: The Consent Problem and the Role of the Security Council. Law and Armed Conflict Working Papers, Oxford Institute for Ethics.
Akande D, Tzanakopoulos A (2018) Treaty Law and ICC Jurisdiction over the Crime of Aggression. Eur J Int Law 29: 939–959
Ambos K (2013) Treatise on International Criminal Law. Oxford University Press, Oxford, vol I-III
Barriga S, Blokker N (2017) Conditions for the Exercise of Jurisdiction Based on State Referrals and Proprio Motu Investigations. In: Kreß C, Barriga S (eds) The Crime of Aggression: A Commentary. Cambridge University Press, Cambridge, vol I, pp 652-674
Barriga S, Kreß C (eds) (2012) The Travaux Préparatoires of the Crime of Aggression. Cambridge University Press, Cambridge
Bassiouni MC (2001) Universal Jurisdiction for International Crimes. Historical Perspectives and Contemporary Practice. Virginia Journal of International Law 42:81–162.
Bassiouni MC (2011) Crimes Against Humanity. Historical Evolution and Contemporary Application. Cambridge University Press, Cambridge
Bleckmann A (1977) Zur Feststellung und Auslegung von Völkergewohnheitsrecht. ZaöRV 37:504-529

---

[172] See Article 2 of the Draft Convention on International Cooperation in the Investigation and Prosecution of the Crime of Genocide, Crimes against Humanity and War Crimes (version 02/10/2019), https://www.centruminternationaalrecht.nl/mla-initiative, accessed 8 January 2020.

[173] See Article 2 of the Draft Convention on International Cooperation in the Investigation and Prosecution of the Crime of Genocide, Crimes against Humanity and War Crimes (version 02/10/2019), https://www.centruminternationaalrecht.nl/mla-initiative, accessed 8 January 2020.

[174] Annex I, Regulation (EU) 2016/794 of the European Parliament and of the Council of 11 May 2016.

Brown D (2014) Why the Crime of Aggression will not Reduce the Practice of Aggression. International Politics 51:648-670

Bruha T (2017) The General Assembly's Definition of the Act of Aggression. In: Kreß C, Barriga S (eds) The Crime of Aggression: A Commentary. Cambridge University Press, Cambridge, vol I, pp 142–177

Cassese A (1999) The Statute of the International Criminal Court: Some Preliminary Reflections. Eur J of Int Law 10:144–171

Cassese A (2008) International Criminal Law, 2nd edn. Oxford University Press, Oxford

Cassese A, Gaeta P, Jones J (2002) The Rome Statute: A Tentative Assessment. In: Cassese A et al. (eds) The Rome Statute of the International Criminal Court: A Commentary. Oxford University Press, Oxford, pp 1901–1914.

Clark R S (2010) Amendments to the Rome Statute of the International Criminal Court Considered at the First Review Conference on the Court, Kampala, 31 May-11 June 2010, Goettingen. J. Int'l L. 2:689-711

Clark R S (2011) Complementarity and the Crime of Aggression. In: Stahn C, El Zeidy M M (eds) The International Criminal Court and Complementarity: From Theory to Practice. Cambridge University Press, Cambridge, pp 721–744

Clark R S (2015) The Crime of Aggression. In: Stahn C (ed) Law and Practice of the International Criminal Court. Oxford University Press, Oxford, pp 778-800

Clark R S (2016) Article 119. In: Triffterer O, Ambos K (eds) Rome Statute of the International Criminal Court: A Commentary, 3rd edn. C.H. Beck, Munich

Clark R S (2020) Exercise of Jurisdiction over the Crime of Aggression: International Criminal Court (ICC). Max Planck Encyclopedia of Public International Law. https://opil.ouplaw.com/home/mpil, accessed 10 January 2020.

Crawford J (2017) The International Law Commission's Work on Aggression. In: Kreß C, Barriga S (eds) The Crime of Aggression: A Commentary. Cambridge University Press, Cambridge, vol I, pp 233–243

Cryer R, Robinson D, Vasiliev S (2019) An Introduction to International Criminal Law and Procedure. 4th edn. Cambridge University Press, Cambridge

Dinstein Y (1966) Par in Parem non Habet Imperium. Israel Law Review, 1:407-420

Dinstein Y (2017) War, Aggression and Self-Defence, 6th edn. Cambridge University Press, Cambridge

Ferencz D M (2018) Aggression is no Longer a Crime in Limbo. Torkel Opsahl Academic EPublisher, FICHL Policy Brief Series No. 88

Foley B J (2015) Mobilising Law on the Side of Peace: Security Council Reform and the Crime of Aggression. In Linton S et al. (eds) For the Sake of Present and Future Generations. Essays on International Law, Crime and Justice in Honour of Roger S. Clark. Brill Nijhoff, Leiden, pp 52–71

Fox H, Webb P (2013) The Law of State Immunity, 3rd edn. Oxford University Press, Oxford

Gaeta P (2002) Official Capacity and Immunities. In: Cassese A et al. (eds) The Rome Statute of the International Criminal Court: A Commentary. Oxford University Press, Oxford, pp 975-1002

Gaeta P (2012) The Need Reasonably to Expand National Criminal Jurisdiction over International Crimes. In: Cassese A (ed) Realizing Utopia. The Future of International Law. Oxford University Press, Oxford, pp 596-606

Geneuss J (2013) Völkerrechtsverbrechen und Verfolgungsermessen. Nomos, Baden-Baden

Ginsburgs G (2000) Light Shed on the Story of *Wehrmacht* Generals in Soviet Captivity. Criminal Law Forum 11:101-120

Glueck S (1946) The Nuremberg Trial and Aggressive War. Knopf, New York

Grover L (2019) Activating the Crime of Aggression Amendments: A Look Ahead. In: Werle G, Zimmermann A (eds) The International Criminal Court in Turbulent Times. T.M.C. Asser Press, The Hague, pp 156–172

Hafner G (2013) Subsequent Agreements and Practice: Between Interpretation, Informal Modification, and Formal Amendment. In: Nolte G (ed) Treaties and Subsequent Practice. Oxford University Press, Oxford, pp 105-122

Hartig A (2018) Dubious negotiations in New York: Did France and the UK come to blow it up? https://ilg2.org/author/annegretlhartig/, accessed 10 January 2020

Hartig A (2019) Post Kampala: The Early Implementers of the Crime of Aggression. J Int Crim Justice 17:485–493

Heller K J (2012) The Uncertain Legal Status of the Aggression Understandings. J Int Crim Justice 10:229–248

Jescheck H-H (1952) Die Verantwortlichkeit der Staatsorgane nach Völkerstrafrecht. Röhrscheid, Bonn

Jeßberger F (2011) Der transnationale Geltungsbereich des deutschen Strafrechts. Grundlagen und Grenzen der Geltung des deutschen Strafrechts für Taten mit Auslandsberührung. Mohr Siebeck, Tübingen

Jeßberger F (2017) The Modern Doctrinal Debate on the Crime of Aggression. In: Kreß C, Barriga S (eds) The Crime of Aggression: A Commentary. Cambridge University Press, Cambridge, vol I, pp 287-306

Jeßberger F (2018) Implementing Kampala: The New Crime of Aggression under the German Code of Crimes against International Law. In: Böse M et al. (eds) Justice Without Borders. Brill Nijhoff, Leiden, pp 180–201

Jurdi N N (2013) The Domestic Prosecution of the Crime of Aggression After the International Criminal Court Review Conference: Possibilities and Alternatives. Melbourne J Int L 14:129-148

Kelsen H (1945) The Rule Against Ex Post Facto Laws and the Prosecution of the Axis War Criminals. Judge Advocate Journal 3:1–11

Kelsen H (1947) Will the Judgment in the Nuremberg Trial Constitute a Precedent in International Law? Int L Quarterly 1:153–171.

Kleffner J K (2009) Complementarity in the Rome Statute and National Criminal Jurisdictions. Oxford University Press, Oxford

Koh H H, Buchwald T F (2015) The Crime of Aggression: The United States Perspective. American J Int Law 109:257-295

Kreicker H (2007) Völkerrechtliche Exemtionen, vol I-II. Duncker & Humblot, Berlin

Kreicker H (2017) Immunities. In: Kreß C, Barriga S (eds) The Crime of Aggression: A Commentary. Cambridge University Press, Cambridge, vol I, pp 675–703

Kreß C (2002) Völkerstrafrecht und Weltrechtspflegeprinzip im Blickfeld des Internationalen Gerichtshofs. ZStW 114:818–849.

Kreß C (2018) On the Activation of ICC Jurisdiction over the Crime of Aggression. J Int Crim Justice 16:1–17

Kreß C, von Holtzendorff L (2010) The Kampala Compromise on the Crime of Aggression. J Int Crim Justice 8:1179-1217

Langer M, Eason M (2019) The Quiet Expansion of Universal Jurisdiction. Eur J of Int L 30:779–817

Mahony C (2015) The Justice Pivot: U.S. International Criminal Law Influence from Outside the Rome Statute. Georgetown J Int L 46:1071-1134

Matheson M J, Scheffer D (2016) The Creation of the Tribunals. American J of Int L 110:173–190

McDougall C (2013) The Crime of Aggression. Cambridge University Press, Cambridge

McDougall C (2017) The Crimes Against Peace Precedent. In: Kreß C, Barriga S (eds) The Crime of Aggression: A Commentary, vol I. Cambridge University Press, Cambridge, pp 49-112

McDougall C (2018) Protecting Civilians by Criminalising the Most Serious Forms of the Illegal Use of Force: Activating the International Criminal Court's Jurisdiction over the Crime of Aggression. In: Lattimer M, Sands P (eds) The Grey Zone. Civilian Protection Between Human Rights and the Laws of War. Hart Publishing, Oxford, pp 377-396

Mégret F (2017) What is the Specific Evil of Aggression? In: Kreß C, Barriga S (eds) The Crime of Aggression: A Commentary, vol II. Cambridge University Press, Cambridge, pp 1398-1453

Newton M A (2016) How the International Criminal Court Threatens Treaty Norms. Vanderbilt J Transnat L 49:371–432

Nolte G, Randelzhofer A (2012) Article 51. In: Simma B et al. (eds) The Charter of the United Nations: A Commentary, 3rd edn. Oxford University Press, Oxford

Nsereko D (1999) The International Criminal Court: Jurisdictional and Related Issues. Criminal Law Forum 10:87–120Oeter S (2013) Das Verbrechen der Aggression, die Konferenz von Kampala und das deutsche Strafrecht. In: Jeßberger F, Geneuss J (eds) Zehn Jahre Völkerstrafgesetzbuch. Bilanz und Perspektiven eines 'deutschen' Völkerstrafrechts. Nomos, Baden-Baden, pp 101–122

Oeter S (2013) Das Verbrechen der Aggression, die Konferenz von Kampala und das deutsche Strafrecht. In: Jeßberger F, Geneuss J (eds) Zehn Jahre Völkerstrafgesetzbuch. Bilanz und Perspektiven eines 'deutschen' Völkerstrafrechts. Nomos, Baden-Baden, pp 101–122

Ohlin J D (2017) The Crime of Bootstrapping. In: Kreß C, Barriga S (eds) The Crime of Aggression: A Commentary, vol II. Cambridge University Press, Cambridge, pp 1454-1479

O'Keefe R (2015) International Criminal Law, Oxford University Press (The Oxford International Law Library), Oxford

Orakhelashvili A (2015) Research Handbook on Jurisdiction and Immunities in International Law. Edward Elgar Publishing, Cheltenham

Reisinger Coracini A (2017) (Extended) Synopsis: The Crime of Aggression under Domestic Criminal Law. In: Kreß C, Barriga S (eds) The Crime of Aggression: A Commentary, vol II. Cambridge University Press, Cambridge, pp 1038-1078

Reydams L (2003) Universal Jurisdiction. International and Municipal Legal Perspectives. Oxford University Press, Oxford

Ruys T (2017) Justiciability, Complementarity and Immunity: Reflections on the Crime of Aggression. Utrecht Law Review 13:18-33

Ryngaert C (2008) Jurisdiction in International Law. Oxford University Press, Oxford

Sadat L N, Carden S R (2000) The New International Criminal Court: An Uneasy Revolution, Georgetown Law Journal 88:381–474

Sayapin S (2018) A Curious Aggression Trial in Ukraine. Some Reflections on the Alexandrov and Yerofeyev Case. J Int Crim Justice 16:1093–1104

Schabas W A (2004) Origins of the Criminalization of Aggression: How Crimes Against Peace Became the 'Supreme International Crime'. In: Politi M, Nesi G (eds) The International Criminal Court and the Crime of Aggression. Ashgate, Hants, pp 17-32

Schabas W A (2016) The International Criminal Court: A Commentary on the Rome Statute, 2nd edn. Oxford University Press, Oxford

Schabas W A, El Zeidy M M (2016) Article 17. In: Triffterer O, Ambos K (eds) Rome Statute of the International Criminal Court: A Commentary, 3rd edn. C.H. Beck, Munich

Schabas W A, Pecorella G (2016) Article 12. In: Triffterer O, Ambos K (eds) Rome Statute of the International Criminal Court: A Commentary, 3rd edn. C.H. Beck, Munich

Scharf M P (2001) The ICC's Jurisdiction Over the Nationals of Non-Party States: A Critique of the U.S. Position. Case Western Reserve J Int L 64:68–117

Scharf M P (2012) Universal Jurisdiction and the Crime of Aggression. Harvard Int L J, 53: 357-389

Scheffer D (1999) The United States and the International Criminal Court. American J Int L 93:1-123

Schick F B (1947) The Nuremberg Trial and the International Law of the Future. American J Int L 41:770–794

Schmitt C (1994) Das internationalrechtliche Verbrechen des Angriffskrieges und der Grundsatz 'Nullum crimen, nulla poena sine lege'. In: Quaritsch H (ed) [author, insert title publication], Duncker & Humblot, Berlin

Schuster M (2003) The Rome Statute and the Crime of Aggression: A Gordian Knot in Search of a Sword. Criminal Law Forum 14:1–57

Schwelb E (1946) Crimes Against Humanity. British Year Book of International Law 23:178–226

Simons W B (1990) The Jurisdictional Bases of the International Military Tribunal at Nuremberg. In: Ginsburgs G, Kudriavtsev VN (eds) The Nuremberg Trial and International Law. Nijhoff, pp 39–59

Solera O (2007) Defining the Crime of Aggression. Cameron May, London

Ssenyonjo M (2017) The Implementation of the Proprio Motu Authority of the Prosecutor in Africa. In: Jalloh C, Bantekas I (eds) The International Criminal Court and Africa. Oxford University Press, Oxford, pp 38-63

Stahn C (2016) The ICC, Pre-Existing Jurisdictional Treaty Regimes, and the Limits of the Nemo Dat Quod Non Habet Doctrine. A Reply to Michael Newton. Vanderbilt J Transnat L 49:443–454

Stahn C (2019) A Critical Introduction to International Criminal Law. Cambridge University Press, Cambridge

Strapatas N (2010) Complementarity and Aggression: A Ticking Time Bomb? In: Stahn C, van den Herik L (eds) Future Perspectives on International Criminal Justice. T.M.C. Asser Press, The Hague

Stürchler N (2018) The Activation of the Crime of Aggression in Perspective. https://www.ejiltalk.org/the-activation-of-the-crime-of-aggression-in-perspective/, accessed 10 January 2020

Šturma P (2019) The Rome Statute of the ICC and the Recent Works of the International Law Commission. In: Šturma P (ed) The Rome Statute of the ICC at its Fifteenth Anniversary. Achievements and Perspectives. Brill Nijhoff, Leiden, pp 27–41

Tladi D (2019) The International Law Commission's Recent Work on Exceptions to Immunity: Charting the Course for a Brave New World in International Law? Leiden J Int L 32:169–187

Tomuschat C (2006) The Legacy of Nuremberg. J Int Crim Justice 4:830–844

Trahan J (2018) From Kampala to New York—The Final Negotiations to Activate the Jurisdiction of the International Criminal Court over the Crime of Aggression. Int Crim L Rev 18:197–243

Triffterer O, Burchard C (2016) Article 27. In: Triffterer O, Ambos K (eds) Rome Statute of the International Criminal Court: A Commentary, 3rd edn. C.H. Beck, Munich

van Schaack B (2012) Par in Parem Imperium Non Habet: Complementarity and the Crime of Aggression. J Int Crim Justice 10:133-164

Veroff J (2016) Reconciling the Crime of Aggression and Complementarity: Unaddressed Tensions and a Way Forward. Yale L J 125:730-772

Weigend T (2005) Grund und Grenzen universaler Gerichtsbarkeit. In: Arnold J et al. (eds) Menschengerechtes Strafrecht. Festschrift für Albin Eser zum 70. Geburtstag. C.H. Beck, Munich, pp 955–976

Weigend T (2012) 'In General a Principle of Justice': The Debate on the 'Crime against Peace' in the Wake of the Nuremberg Judgment. J Int Crim Justice 10:41–58

Weisbord N (2019) The Crime of Aggression. The Quest for Justice in an Age of Drones, Cyberattacks, Insurgents, and Autocrats. Princeton University Press, Princeton

Wenaweser C, Barriga S (2015) Forks in the Road: Personal Reflections on Negotiating the Kampala Amendments on the Crime of Aggression. In: Linton S et al. (eds) For the Sake of Present and Future Generations. Essays on International Law, Crime and Justice in Honour of Roger S. Clark. Brill Nijhoff, Leiden, pp 281–297

Werle G, Jeßberger F (2014) Principles of International Criminal Law. Oxford University Press, Oxford

Werle G, Jeßberger F (2020) Vor §§ 3 ff. In: Rissing-van Saan R et al. (eds) Strafgesetzbuch. Leipziger Kommentar: Großkommentar, 13th edn. De Gruyter, Berlin

Woetzel R K (1960) Nuremberg Trials in International Law. Frederick Praeger

Wrange P (2017) The Crime of Aggression, Domestic Prosecutions and Complementarity. In: Kreß C, Barriga S (eds) The Crime of Aggression: A Commentary, vol I. Cambridge University Press, Cambridge, pp 704-751

Wright Q (1947) The Law of the Nuremberg Trial. American J Int L 41:38-72

Yang X (2012) State Immunity in International Law. Cambridge University Press, Cambridge

Zimmermann A, Freiburg E (2016) Article 15 *bis*. In: Triffterer O, Ambos K (eds) Rome Statute of the International Criminal Court: A Commentary, 3rd edn. C.H. Beck, Munich

Zimmermann A, Freiburg-Braun E (2019) Aggression under the Rome Statute. C.H. Beck, Munich

Zolo D (2007) Who is Afraid of Punishing Aggressors?: On the Double-Track Approach to International Criminal Justice. J Int Crim Justice 5:799–807

Annegret Lucia Hartig is a PhD Candidate and former Researcher at the University of Hamburg. She worked on the revision process of the textbooks Principles of International Criminal Law and Völkerstrafrecht by Gerhard Werle and Florian Jeßberger. She holds a German law degree (first state exam) from Humboldt-Universität zu Berlin, a LL.M. in International Criminal Law from the joint program of the University of Amsterdam and Columbia Law School, and a Maîtrise en Droit from the University of Paris II. She is writing her PhD thesis on the domestic implementation of the crime of aggression under the supervision of Professor Florian Jeßberger and was a visiting scholar at Columbia Law School.

Chapter 51
Military Ecocide

Peter Hough

Contents

51.1 Introduction 1140
51.2 The History of Military Ecocide 1140
    51.2.1 Offensive Ecocide 1141
    51.2.2 Defensive Ecocide 1144
    51.2.3 Collateral Damage: Indirect Military Environmental Degradation 1145
51.3 The Militarization of the Environment 1146
51.4 History of International Law on Military Ecocide 1149
51.5 Normative Progress in Criminalizing Military Ecocide 1154
51.6 Conclusion 1158
References 1159

Abstract Military ecocide, the destruction of the natural environment in the course of fighting or preparing for war, has a long history and remains a prominent feature of contemporary conflicts. Efforts to prohibit this in International Law were initiated after the US' notorious defoliation campaign in the Vietnam War in the 1960s and have developed since then. Whilst legal ambiguities and the defence of military necessity have limited the application of this body of law the proscription of ecocide has, nevertheless, progressed and looks set to develop further. Normative change driven by scientists, environmentalists and legal experts has raised awareness of and stigmatized such practises to the extent that recourse to the worst excesses of ecocide now appears to have lessened and some recompense for past crimes has been made. Military activities, though, continue to inflict a heavy cost on the environment and the drive for a more explicit legal prohibition of this has grown.

Keywords ecocide · Scorched Earth · Agent Orange · environment

P. Hough (✉)
Department of Politics, Middlesex University, London, UK
e-mail: P.Hough@mdx.ac.uk

© T.M.C. ASSER PRESS and the authors 2022
S. Sayapin et al. (eds.), *International Conflict and Security Law*,
https://doi.org/10.1007/978-94-6265-515-7_51

51.1 Introduction

This chapter reviews the progression of international legal efforts to prohibit militarily-induced ecocide; the deliberate or inadvertent destruction of the natural environment in the course of fighting or preparing for war. Ecocide is a term that has also come to be applied to the criminal and industrial destruction of the environment—such as through illegal deforestation or the dumping of toxic waste—but this review will confine itself to military-induced degradation.

There is a long history of military-induced environmental degradation and it is a facet of warfare that has generally worsened over time with the advent of more devastating and poisonous forms of weaponry. Such devastation has often been justified on the grounds of military necessity in ways that could not so readily be done if the casualties were human where, as illustrated in other chapters, a large body of international law offers some restraint. The perennial problem of the natural environment being valued only instrumentally (for its human utility) rather than intrinsically (in its own right) has been apparent throughout history in the recourse to military strategies such as scorching the earth, altering freshwater supplies or strategic deforestation.

However, many and an increasing number of people do value the environment for its own sake, as is evidenced by the rise of ecocentric domestic policy since the 1960s. In particular it is scientific evidence that has convinced most people of the need for ecocentric restraints on human behaviour. Despite the popular portrayal of environmentalists as mystic, tree-huggers it should not be forgotten that the green movement in the 1960s was kick-started by the emergence of ground-breaking, rational and convincing scientific evidence. In particular, US marine biologist Rachel Carson's magnum opus *Silent Spring* proved that the widespread use of organochlorine pesticides, following their discovery in the 1940s, in the fight against disease-carrying and crop-consuming insects was also polluting streams and killing wildlife.[1] As a consequence of this, the use of insecticides and herbicides began to be constrained in the US and then elsewhere even though they were serving human interests. One of the first focusses for this burgeoning environmental movement was the ecocentric (as well as anthropocentric) consequences of the US military deployment of organochlorine herbicides in the jungles of the Vietnam War. Whilst, fifty years on, military ecocide continues to feature in military campaigns the legal and normative prohibition of such practises has progressed. This has occurred in roughly the same timescale as the general advance of political ecologism, again largely due to the efforts of scientists and campaigners in highlighting the issue to the public.

51.2 The History of Military Ecocide

The destruction of nature in the course of war can occur as part of an offensive or defensive strategy or, less directly, as collateral damage.

---

[1] Carson 1962.

51.2.1 Offensive Ecocide

The 'scorched earth' destruction of the crops or livestock of the enemy is a strategy that has been deployed in wars since ancient times. It formed part of many international conquests, such as by the Romans in the Punic Wars against Carthage, and also in the course of domestic counter-insurgency campaigns, such as in the Normans' 'Harrying of the North' after annexing England in the 11th Century. In the modern era similar methods were still being deployed by US in the Philippines from 1898–1902 to undermine nationalist resistance from jungle-based guerrilla units. Domestic alarm at how this intervention, initially sold to the American public as liberating the Filipinos from the Spanish, had become a typically brutal colonization prompted criticism from prominent domestic quarters. Most notably, the likes of former President Grover Cleveland, business tycoon Andrew Carnegie and literary great Mark Twain expressed outrage at President Roosevelt's war methods as part of the American Anti-Imperialist League, perhaps the first manifestation of an anti-ecocide movement.

With the advent of the synthetic organochlorine pesticides that were the catalyst for *Silent Spring* and environmentalism, offensive ecocide was able to move beyond the razing of food sources to include the tactical destruction of tree cover. The British were the first to undertake a strategy of 'industrialized chemical defoliation' as a military tactic in the early 1950s during the 'Malayan Emergency'. The acidic herbicide formulations 2,4,5-T,[2] and 2,4-D[3] (later combined in *Agent Orange* used by the US in Vietnam) were used to clear lines of communication and food crops in the struggle against communist insurgents. With Imperial Chemical Industries (ICI) providing the technical advice, British and Malayan government troops in 1952 despatched fire-engines spraying mixtures of these herbicides along many key roads. The strategy was not successful and after seven months it proved more effective, both economically and practically, to remove vegetation by hand and the spraying was stopped. In the following year, though, the use of herbicides as an aid to fighting the guerrillas was restarted with the more traditional goal of destroying food crops grown by the communist forces in jungle clearings.[4] The environmental costs of this British ecocide are unclear. Since this episode pre-dated the political ecology era, the sorts of scientific studies which later highlighted the environmental and health damage resulting from similar spraying operations in Vietnam, never took place.

The application of herbicides was far more widespread in the subsequent Cold War battlefields of Vietnam, with an estimated 80 million litres of 2,4,5-T 2,4-D, picloram, and cacodylate blended in a variety of mixtures—including the notorious *Agent Orange*—and sprayed on jungle foliage from military aircraft between 1962 and 1971 in the most infamous ever systematic military assault on the environment. US scientists have estimated that 10% of Vietnam's inland forests, 36% of

---

[2] 2,4,5-Trichlorophenoxyacetic acid.
[3] 2,4-Dichlorophenoxyacetic acid.
[4] Connor and Thomas 1984.

her mangrove forests, and 3% of cultivated land were seriously damaged by the programme codenamed 'Operation Ranch Hand'.[5] This scale of ecological damage indirectly affected the health of millions of Vietnamese by reducing the quality of their nutritional intake and creating internally-displaced persons susceptible to disease. More directly deadly were the cases of acute poisoning by herbicides. In particular dioxin, which arises as a by-product in the manufacture of 2,4,5-T, is one of the most toxic chemicals known and an estimated 170 kg. of this was sprayed over Vietnam and the neighbouring countries of Laos and Cambodia.[6] Dioxin is severely toxic in several dimensions. It is teratogenic (causes birth defects), hepatoxic (liver), mutagenic, carcinogenic, a skin-irritant, and known to increase cholesterol levels in blood. Many studies have linked instances of such symptoms amongst Vietnamese residents and their offspring with the sprayings.[7] Whilst proving direct causality is difficult for some conditions, the evidence is unambiguous with regards to liver damage due to dioxin exposure. A study led by Do Thuc Trinh found that: 'Chronic hepatitis was more than ten times as prevalent among those subjects who had been directly exposed to military herbicides (more than a decade previously) than among those who had not'.[8]

Despite some initial uncertainties in the scientific data relating to dioxin exposure, the US's defoliation campaign in Vietnam, Cambodia, and Laos was quickly and roundly condemned by the American scientific community and many international statesmen, as well as environmental campaigners. The American Association for the Advancement of Science in 1969 set up a Herbicide Assessment Commission to investigate the effects of Operation Ranch Hand made up of four leading domestic scientists, of whom the most prominent was Arthur Westing. Westing's background was as a botanist and forest ecologist but the fact that he had also served in the US military, seeing action as an artillery officer in the Korean War, equipped him with insights on both sides of the military-environment equation. Westing described the US defoliation campaign in Vietnam as causing; 'widespread, long-lasting, and severe disruptions of perennial croplands, and of farmlands—that is to say of millions of hectares or the natural resource base essential to an agrarian society'.[9] Westing's writings also advocated the need to criminalize and prosecute such acts, most notably in the 1974 article 'Proscription of Ecocide';

> '... what is urgently required at this time is the establishment of the concept that widespread and serious ecological debilitation- so called ecocide- cannot be condoned.[10]

Westing here was utilizing the term 'ecocide' probably first employed by fellow US scientist Arthur Galston in 1970. Galston was a biologist central to the discovery of the defoliant qualities of 2,4,5-T who later became alarmed at how his work had

---

[5] NAS 1974, 5–6.
[6] Ibid., vii–9.
[7] Franklin 2003.
[8] Westing 1984, 166.
[9] Westing 1989, 337.
[10] Westing 1974, 26.

come to be put into practise and wrote critically about how Operation Ranch Hand was destroying Vietnamese river ecosystems.[11] Continued pressure by the Herbicide Assessment Commission, including a petition signed by 5000 scientists (of whom 17 were holders of Nobel prizes), led to the termination of the campaign in 1971, fuelled in particular by US public horror at evidence of appalling birth defects occurring in the Vietnamese population.[12]

Criticism of US ecocide, though, did not end with the termination of Operation Ranch Hand. In particular, high-profile international political expression of this view was given when Swedish Prime Minister Olaf Palme, after meeting Westing for a briefing on the subject, used this term indirectly to denounce the Vietnam defoliation programme at the 1972 United Nations Conference on the Human Environment (UNCHE) at Stockholm. Palme did not explicitly cite the US in his address at Stockholm but proceeded to do so overtly in several speeches in the following months.[13] The US administration used the threat of pulling out of UNCHE to avert any direct reference to Operation Ranch Hand in the official principles and paperwork that came out of the conference but Palme's continued criticism prompted Nixon to suspend full diplomatic relations with Stockholm for several months; an extraordinary situation for two Western democracies to find themselves in.

No compensation has ever been forthcoming for any of the Vietnamese, Cambodian or Laotian victims of birth deformities, liver damage or other ailments attributable to Operation Ranch Hand despite appeals from these governments. In fact the only victims to have been compensated for this are soldiers who fought on the side responsible. War veterans from the US, Australia, and New Zealand, who have suffered subsequent skin and liver disorders or birth defects in their offspring, won a long battle for compensation in 1979, when a US Federal Judge ruled that they could sue the companies responsible for the manufacture of Agent Orange. Over 45,000 people have since claimed a share of $180 million in damages from Dow and six other chemical firms. Dow agreed to this settlement in the face of public pressure and mounting legal costs, but have still never formally admitted that the various illnesses incurred by the veterans were directly related to Agent Orange and other herbicide mixtures sprayed in Vietnam.

Despite the controversy over Operation Ranch Hand the policy nevertheless served to inspire other governments and armed groups engaged in conflicts in woodland or arid terrain susceptible to tactical manipulation. Mimicking the tactics used in Vietnam the Indonesian government in the late 1960s conducted what may have been the worst case of deforestation in history in seeking to quell insurgencies in Borneo and West Kalimantan.[14] Similarly, during the 1980s civil war in El Salvador the government bombed agricultural lands and forests in seeking to deny guerrilla forces a base and sustenance. Partly as a consequence of this El Salvador today is almost completely deforested.

---

[11] Cook et al. 1970.
[12] Hay 1982, 151.
[13] Ibid., 165.
[14] Peluso and Vandergeest 2011.

In a different form of domestic ecocide Saddam Hussein of Iraq added deliberate desertification to his long list of environmental and human crimes in diverting the courses of the rivers Tigris and Euphrates in order to drain marshland areas that were home to the Shia 'Marsh Arabs', after they had initiated an uprising against his rule in 1991. This act of ecological ethnic cleansing drained around 90% of the region's marshes and also depleted its population from 250,000 to around 40,000.[15] Saddam's 'hydro-terrorism' doubtless served as an inspiration to ISIS who, in 2015, dammed sections of the Euphrates in order to dehydrate their opponents in the Syrian Civil War.

51.2.2 Defensive Ecocide

The 'backs to the wall' destruction of your own resources to prevent an invading enemy making use of them is also a well-established military tactic. Perhaps most famously, Russian forces in 1812 retreated from the invading French army whilst razing their own arable lands in an ultimately successful strategy that paved the way for Napoleon's disastrous 'retreat from Moscow', which led to his downfall. This Russian strategy was learned from British military leader Wellington who two years earlier, in alliance with Portuguese guerrilla forces, had resisted a French invasion in a similar manner in the Peninsular War.

By the 20th century industrial rather than arable might had become the main determinant of military power but scorching the earth could still have its uses. During World War Two the British took responsibility for rendering uninhabitable the islands of Norway's Svalbard archipelago (Spitsbergen) in order to limit German interest in its coalfields (despite Norwegian opposition). Consequently, the German presence on the Arctic islands was limited to the manning of a few weather stations. In a different and more dramatic form of defensive ecocide the Yellow River was deliberately flooded in 1938 by the Chiang Kai-shek government in China in resisting the Japanese invasion of Manchuria. In doing so the Chinese succeeded in slowing down the invaders, by creating a bigger barrier and destroying potential food supplies, but did so to the cost of hundreds of thousands of their own citizens' lives. More recently defensive ecocide, more spiteful than strategic, featured in the Gulf War when Saddam's forces set fire to hundreds of oil wells whilst retreating from Kuwait in 1991, some of which burned for several months. Oil was also deliberately leaked into the Persian Gulf by the Iraqi troops.

---

[15] Weinstein 2005, 715.

51.2.3 Collateral Damage: Indirect Military Environmental Degradation

Environmental degradation due to war can also occur more indirectly as a result of the general destruction of battle. The aforementioned Manchurian war was, in fact, a multi-faceted environmental (and human) horror show. The Japanese used chemical and biological weaponry in a brutal invasion and then, once their defeat in the Second World War became apparent, abandoned remaining munitions across northeastern China to prevent them falling into Allied hands. Shells containing chemicals such as mustard gas and phosgene were dumped in fields, lakes, and rivers prompting a slow-burning disaster which has killed or disabled thousands of Chinese in the decades that have followed. Elsewhere during World War Two 'total war' mass bombing campaigns were of such a scale and nature that environmental catastrophes were, of course, inevitable.

In spite of the revival of limited and just war principles since World War Two and the Cold War 'collateral ecocide' has still been apparent in the supposedly more strategic strikes of recent conflicts. In 2006, for example, between 20,000 and 30,000 tonnes of oil polluted a large stretch of the Eastern Mediterranean Sea and coastline after Israel bombed the Jiyeh power station during the Lebanon War against Hezbollah.[16] Similarly, during the 1999 Kosovan War NATO included amongst its strategic bombing targets several chemical plants and fossil fuel facilities knowing this would inevitably pollute waterways and the atmosphere. The campaign led to the significant pollution of the Danube and also released many toxic and carcinogenic chemicals into the ground and air. Most notorious was the targeting of the major Serbian petrochemical and fertilizer plants at Pancevo. NATO acknowledged the environmental consequences of these strikes but asserted that military necessity justified some collateral fall-out since the plants were a key source of the Serb regime's military power. The advent of radioactive and highly persistent chemical 'depleted uranium' to coat munitions shells has also served to add a new form of long-term pollution to the spoils of recent wars, such as in Kosovo and Iraq. More generally, greenhouse gasses, chlorofluorocarbons, mercury, sulphur dioxide and nitrous oxide emissions are also now part of the common collateral damage of contemporary bombing campaigns.[17]

Battlefield destruction can also render arable land and other natural resources useless to humanity and other life forms. In addition to the effects of pollution and defoliation, millions of craters today mark the agricultural belts of Vietnam and Laos as a consequence of a combination of deliberate and collateral military actions by the US in the 1960s. Many French and Belgian World War One battlefields remain barren today a century on. Resource depletion through over-utilization is another typical consequence of war. The appropriation of food and fuel by invading troops

---

[16] CoE 2011.
[17] Sanders 2009, 71–2.

is the most predictable form of this phenomenon but excessive strain can also be put on the home resources of invading forces.

Environmental degradation can also occur more indirectly as a result of sudden influxes of refugees fleeing war. For example, 38 km^2 of forest in the Kivu Province of the Democratic Republic of Congo were lost within three weeks of the arrival of Rwandan refugees fleeing genocide in the mid-1990s.[18] As well as being worsened deliberately, deforestation can also be accelerated as a consequence of countries literally rebuilding after a conflict. Many Iraqi city trees were felled for fuel in the aftermath of the US-led invasion of 2003 and it is also known that Afghan water supplies and vegetation were seriously damaged and depleted following the onset of war in 2001.[19] Wild animals are also frequent casualties of war. Gorilla numbers in the Democratic Republic of Congo are known to have fallen as a consequence of that country's persistent civil conflict, both through direct killings and more indirectly as a result of the destruction of their habitat through deforestation.[20] For a timeline of some of the major incidences of environmental damage due to instances of modern war, see Table 51.1.

51.3 The Militarization of the Environment

It is not just actual war which can prompt environmental damage but the whole phenomenon of defence and military preparation. The scale and nature of the Cold War greatly intensified the traditional ecological side-effects associated with this. The rise of nuclear weapons testing, mass military exercises and the global proliferation of military bases came with significant costs, many of which are still being counted. The Soviet testing of nuclear weapons and dumping of the waste from this was particularly extensive in its peripheral regions such as the northern reaches of Siberia. At least 130 tests were carried out in the Soviet Arctic between 1955 and 1970, prompting landslides and depositing radioactive materials in the soil, water, ice and air.[21] Environmental damage was also inflicted on parts of the Soviet empire during the Cold War. For example, Soviet military camps occupied nearly 2% of Estonia and left behind significant water and soil pollution in that country on their withdrawal, three years after independence in 1994. No compensation for pollution by oil, cadmium, lead, uranium and general waste was ever paid in a clean-up that the Estonian government claimed cost them $4 billion.[22]

US militarism at home and particularly in its overseas outposts has also carried significant environmental costs. Again in the Philippines, realpolitik and imperial neglect saw the Subic Bay naval base become the scene of a notorious ecological

---

[18] UNEP 2002.

[19] CoE 2011; Sheehan 2003.

[20] Kalpers 2001.

[21] Glasby and Voytekhovsky 2010, 20.

[22] Auer 2004, 119–121.

51 Military Ecocide

Table 51.1 Timeline of some major incidences of environmental damage in modern war

1810 Peninsular War: British and Portuguese in defending against French invasion
1812 'Retreat from Moscow': Russians defending against French invasion
1812–13 South American War of Independence: Argentine patriots defending against Spanish / Royalists
1817–18 Sri Lankan Great Rebellion—British colonial suppression of uprising
1864 'March to the Sea': US Unionists (Sherman) against Confederates in the Civil War.
1867–69 US (Sherman) extermination of the Buffalo to subjugate native Americans
1898–1902 US-Philippine War: US colonial suppression of uprising
1900 2nd Boer War: British against Boers in power struggle over South Africa
1922 Greco-Turk War: Greeks in Western Anatolia in retreat
1938 Manchurian War: Chinese flooding in defending against Japanese invasion
1941 World War Two: Soviets in defending against German invasion
1941 World War Two: British in Spitsbergen to render useless to German invasion
1944–5 World War Two: Germans in retreat from Soviets in Northern Norway and Finland
1945 Manchurian War: Japanese dumping of chemical weapons
1952 'Malayan Emergency': British and Malayan government suppressing leftist insurgency
1962–69 Vietnam War: US intervention against leftist insurgency
1967 Indonesia government suppression of insurgencies in Borneo and West Kalimantan
1980–90 Salvadoran Civil War: government suppression of leftist insurgency
1981–2 Guatemalan Civil War: government suppression of leftist insurgency
1990 Gulf War: Iraq (Saddam) in retreat from Kuwait
1991 Iraqi government (Saddam) suppression of uprising by 'Marsh Arabs'
1999 East Timorese secession from Indonesia: pro-government militia in retreat
1999 Kosovan War: pollution from NATO bombing of Serbia
1999–2009 Chechen Wars—pollution from Russian bombing

(continued)

Table 51.1 (continued)

1810 Peninsular War: British and Portuguese in defending against French invasion
2003–08 Darfur Crisis: Sudanese government and Janjaweed militia against Darfurians
2006 Lebanon War: pollution from Israeli bombing
2006–09 Sri Lankan Civil War: government suppression of Tamil insurgency
2011 Libyan Civil War: Government (Gadaffi) suppression of rebels in Benghazi.
2014–15 Syrian Civil War: Insurgents (ISIS) river diversion against government and slashed earth v Kurds.

Source The author

disaster which featured the wilful pollution of allowing human waste to be dumped directly into the sea without sewage treatment. The Philippine government claimed compensation for such pollution but the Americans never payed and abandoned the base in 1991 whilst pointing to the 1947 Military Bases Agreement between the two countries absolving them of any legal responsibility. In domestic politics American military exceptionalism is also apparent with the Pentagon exempted from being reported on by the Environmental Protection Agency and, hence, never having been held accountable for known instances of pollution by solvents, fuels and munitions near military bases well above state limits for other industries.[23]

In a different facet of ecocide the military securitization of the environment can sometimes take the form of a kind of 'nationalization of nature' with wild 'badlands' tamed by force. Tropical woodlands have regularly featured in conflicts as both the arenas and symbols of resistance. Much of the resistance to the Japanese invasions in South East Asia during the Second World War was jungle-based and this also came to be the stage for insurgencies against European colonial rule after 1945. Hence, as well as carrying out deforestation for tactical reasons, many governments consciously came to construct their woodland as 'jungle' so as to invoke notions of lawlessness, danger and insecurity that required the assertion of sovereign control through enforced land purchases, coerced population movements and the establishment of permanent military bases.[24] This was very much the case with the aforementioned governmental deforestations in Indonesia and El Salvador.

In a more general sense it should also always be remembered that there is a significant ecological side-effect to the sheer existence of the military-industrial complex. Sanders, for example, has estimated that the US military consumes a quarter of the world's jet fuel and is responsible for around 5% of global greenhouse gas emissions.[25]

---

[23] Schettler 1995.

[24] Peluso and Vandegeest 2011.

[25] Sanders 2009, 50, 61, 68.

51.4 History of International Law on Military Ecocide

A body of International law proscribing military ecocide has steadily evolved since the 1970s but there is little precedent for enforcing this legislation. Explicit references to the environment were not made in the war laws of the Geneva or Hague Conventions prior to the 1970s, despite their extensive evolution from the 19th Century. The second Hague Convention of 1907, though, does declare as illegal military methods which; 'destroy or seize the enemy's property, unless such destruction or seizure be imperatively demanded by the necessities of war'. In more general terms, the centuries old tradition of Just War, upon which the Geneva and Hague Conventions are built, can be seen as helping safeguard the environment since the notion of 'limited war', which proscribes the escalation of conflicts beyond their specific purposes and acts of pure retribution and spite, logically must apply also to the destruction of nature beyond military necessity. International arms control law can similarly be suggested to proscribe ecocide, in principle at least. The 1925 Geneva Protocol on Chemical Weapons (and its effective contemporary successor the 1993 Chemical Weapons Convention), whilst driven by humanitarian rather than environmental concerns, in outlawing the military use of toxins inherently makes wilful pollution illegitimate. For a timeline regarding International Law and military ecocide, see Table 51.2.

That the wanton destruction of land (and buildings) is contrary to international law was confirmed at the Nuremberg war trials at the close of the Second World War. German General Lothar Rendulic was prosecuted by the International Military Tribunal for his command of scorched earth raids in Finnmark, Norway when in retreat from the Russian army. Rendulic was actually acquitted, as the Tribunal accepted that he genuinely believed the destruction to be militarily-justified, but a precedent that such acts could amount to an international crime was, nonetheless, established.[26] Another German General, Alfred Jodl, was convicted and hanged for several war crimes amongst which was culpability for ordering scorched earth tactics in Finnmark for which no military justification could be found. The UN War Crimes Commission at Nuremberg also confirmed that German plundering of Polish forestry constituted a war crime under Article 55 of the 1907 Hague Convention (case 7150).[27] Military ecocide was more acute in the 'War in the East' but national interest and an early manifestation of Cold War realpolitik ultimately trumped humanitarian concerns when it came to prosecuting Japanese war crimes for this. The Tokyo War Crimes Trials did not properly address the Japanese deployment and dumping of chemical and biological weapons in Manchuria, largely because of the US's desire to keep such knowledge to themselves and out of the hands of the Soviet Union.

Japan's actions in Manchuria were clearly counter to the Hague Convention and Geneva Protocol but the will to implement these instruments was not apparent, as it also had not been a few years earlier when appeasement saw Mussolini's chemical assault on Abyssinia essentially overlooked by the League of Nations in 1935. The effective death knell of the Geneva Protocol came when it became apparent that the

---

[26] Boas and Schabas 2003, 293.

[27] Brady and Re 2018, 116.

Table 51.2 Timeline of international law and military ecocide

C3rd–C13th	Evolution of Just War principles within Christianity and Islam proscribe excessive military damage
1868	Declaration of St Petersburg by European powers outlawing explosive bullets includes agreed principle that only military targets should be considered legitimate
1899	First Hague Convention on Laws of War—article IV (ii) outlaws use of poison gas by great powers (except US)
1907	Second Hague Convention—article 23(g) outlaws 'wanton destruction'
1925	Geneva Protocol to Hague Convention outlaws chemical weapons
1948	Nuremburg War Trials establish scorched earth tactics without clear military purpose are illegal
1969	General Assembly Resolution 2603 states that all military applications of chemicals (including defoliants) is contrary to the 1925 Geneva Protocol
1976	Convention on the Prohibition of Military or any Hostile Use of Environmental Modification Techniques (ENMOD)
1977	Geneva Conventions on War Protocol I Articles 35 and 55 outlaw 'widespread, long—term and severe' military damage to the environment
1981	UN General Assembly Resolution 36/150 condemns Israeli canal plan because of its implications for Jordan in the context of their dispute
1990	Cairo Declaration on Human Rights in Islam Resolution Article 3b outlaws military destruction of crops or livestock
1991	UN Security Council Resolutions 687 and 692 prosecute Iraq government for environmental destruction in invasion of Kuwait
1992	UN General Assembly Resolution 47/37 states that military ecocide is contrary to International Law
1992	UN Conference on Environment & Development—Rio Declaration Principle 24 affirms that the environment should be respected in warfare
1993	Chemical Weapons Convention outlaws use and possession of chemical weapons
1995	Organization of African Union Conference of Ministers of Health Resolution 14(5) outlaws destruction of crops in war
1999	International Criminal Court Statute 8(2) b (iv) lists excessive damage to the environment as a war crime

Source The author

huge advances in chemical synthesis in the 1940s and '50s had rendered it redundant by the time an attempt came to prosecute the US for Operation Ranch Hand on the basis of a 1969 General Assembly request. The US were not a party to the protocol but had indicated a willingness to ratify (and later did so in 1975). Nevertheless in their defence US Secretary of State Rogers stated that the 1925 Geneva Protocol did *not* cover chemical herbicides on the grounds that the chemicals used were not known in 1925 and that their military aim was to kill plants not humans.

Despite not producing a prosecution Operation Ranch Hand did prove the catalyst for the emergence of international law specifically dealing with military ecocide as East-West relations improved with the US withdrawal from Vietnam. In the spirit of detente, the Americans and Soviets actually cooperated in formulating a draft for what would become the 1976 Convention on the Prohibition of Military or any Hostile Use of Environmental Modification Techniques (ENMOD Convention). Moscow, able to capitalize on the controversy that had emanated from Operation Ranch Hand, initiated the idea of an 'ecocide convention' and Washington, having terminated the strategy in 1971 and then the whole war four years later, had no strategic need to risk the reputational loss of allowing the Soviets to claim the moral high ground. ENMOD was adopted by Resolution 31/72 of the United Nations General Assembly in 1976 and opened for signature the following year. Parties to the ENMOD Convention undertake not to use environmental manipulation that would have 'widespread, long-lasting or severe effects as the means of destruction, damage or injury to any other State Party' (Article I).

Simultaneous to the negotiation of ENMOD a Protocol to the Geneva War Conventions dealing with ecocide was also agreed. Protocol I additional to the Geneva Conventions, agreed in 1977, includes two Articles dealing directly with the dangers that modern warfare poses for the environment.

Article 35 - Basic rules

3. It is prohibited to employ methods or means of warfare which are intended, or may be expected, to cause widespread, long-term and severe damage to the natural environment.

Article 55 - Protection of the natural environment

1. Care shall be taken in warfare to protect the natural environment against widespread, long-term and severe damage. This protection includes a prohibition of the use of methods or means of warfare which are intended or may be expected to cause such damage to the natural environment and thereby to prejudice the health or survival of the population.

2. Attacks against the natural environment by way of reprisals are prohibited.

By 2018 Protocol I had been ratified by some 174 states but notable amongst non-parties were the US, India, Israel, Iran, Pakistan, Turkey and Libya. Far less universal than Protocol I, ENMOD by 2018 had 78 parties (though this does include the United States).

Taken together parties to the twin ecocide instruments are prohibited from attacking, destroying, removing, or rendering useless objects indispensable to the survival of the civilian population, such as foodstuffs, agricultural areas and drinking water supplies. Protocol I is the more ecological of the twin instruments since its aim is to protect the environment from war whilst ENMOD is really humanitarian as it seeks to prohibit the use of the environment as a weapon in war. ENMOD is limited by the stipulation that such manipulation of the environment must be 'widespread, long-lasting or severe' ('WLS') to be deemed illegal, which clearly is open to wide interpretation. Nevertheless, it has the advantage of being worded in such a way that gives it the potential to outlaw war-making methods not yet devised.[28] Hence the sort of defence used by the US against prosecution for Operation Ranch Hand under the Geneva Protocol would not stand up in the event of a country being prosecuted under ENMOD (although this could not happen in this particular instance since the Convention does not permit retrospective jurisdiction). Indeed, it was international concern

---

[28] Roberts and Guelff 2000, 407–418.

that the US strategy in Vietnam could evolve to include tactics such as deliberate flooding and the manipulation of the weather that did much to inspire ENMOD.

The general multilateral optimism that permeated international relations in the aftermath of the Cold War reinvigorated international efforts to prevent ecocide and this manifested itself in response to the oil pollution that marked the Gulf War. Hence, in 1991, the Security Council held Iraq liable for ecocide in their invasion of Kuwait through the adoption of Resolution 687, confirming that they were:

> liable under international law for any direct loss, damage, including environmental damage and the depletion of natural resources, or injury to foreign Governments, nationals and corporations, as a result of Iraq's unlawful invasion and occupation of Kuwait.[29]

On the basis of this the Kuwaiti government and others filed claims against Iraq for damages to natural resources and related public health concerns. The UN Compensation Commission (UNCC), comprising 59 lawyers from 40 states, was subsequently established by Security Council Resolution 692 in May 1991 to adjudicate the amount of damages payable by Iraq. Three Commissioners on a panel assessing environmental damages subsequently distributed compensation to numerous individual, corporate and state claimants including the governments of Iran, Jordan, Saudi Arabia and Syria in addition to Kuwait.[30] Hence the Saddam government became the first and, to date, only international entity to be successfully prosecuted for military ecocide.

As a corollary of this Iraqi prosecution, the UN General Assembly in November 1992 adopted a resolution on 'The protection of the environment in time of conflict', which stated that the 'destruction of the environment not justified by military necessity and carried out wantonly, is clearly contrary to international law'.[31] In the 1996 Nuclear Weapons Case, an advisory opinion of the International Court of Justice on the legality of these weapons, further credence was given to the notion that military ecocide was contrary to customary international law. Written statements to this effect were provided for the court by governments including: Sweden, New Zealand, Samoa, Marshall Islands, Solomon Islands, Zimbabwe, Rwanda, Lesotho, Ukraine and Iran. In further developments, in 1992 and 1993, the UN Secretary General submitted two reports on the protection of the environment which paved the way for a General Assembly resolution mandating the International Committee of the Red Cross (ICRC) to encourage the inclusion of their guidelines on the protection of the environment during conflict in military manuals.[32] Consequently, many countries have adapted ICRC drafted principles into their rules of engagement for armed forces.

A further legal milestone for ecocide came with the adoption of Article 8(2)(b)(iv) in the statutes of the International Criminal Court in 1999, which lists as a war crime:

---

[29] S/RES/687 (1991) 8 April.
[30] Payne 2016, 725–6.
[31] A/RES/47/37.
[32] A/RES/49/50.

intentionally launching an attack in the knowledge that such attack will cause widespread, long-term and severe damage to the natural environment which would be clearly excessive in relation to the concrete and direct overall military advantage anticipated.

However, whilst this makes individual criminal responsibility for ecocide clearly established in international law, the statute suffers from the same lack of precision as the Geneva Protocol and ENMOD in terms of determining what constitutes 'excessive damage'.[33] Hence, to date, no individual or government has been prosecuted specifically for military ecocide under the Hague Convention, ENMOD or through the ICC.

In illustration of the difficulties inherent in establishing the burden of proof, some cases of military ecocide that have been brought have failed to generate prosecutions. A case was presented to the International Criminal Tribunal for Yugoslavia (ICTY) (a special *ad hoc* UN court set up to try crimes committed in the wars of the Yugoslav secession) by the Serbian government against NATO bombing raids in the Kosovan War but was dismissed by the ICTY committee on the basis that it did not exceed the WLS threshold. Similarly, the Eritrea-Ethiopia Claims Commission, set up in 2000 as part of the Algiers Peace Agreement ending the conflict, rejected a claim from Addis Ababa for compensation from the Eritreans for damages to natural resources on the grounds of insufficient evidence. However in doing so, the Commission did not refute Ethiopia's right to make such a claim.[34]

In other areas international laws that could potentially limit ecocide military exceptionalism is apparent. The 1993 Prevention of Major Industrial Accidents Convention, for example, does not apply to military installations. Similarly, military vessels are excluded from the large body of maritime safety and pollution laws nurtured by the UN's International Maritime Organization. The Arctic Council, an intergovernmental organization that has produced a range of soft and hard laws on environmental and shipping issues covering the region since the mid-1990s, also has it written into its rules of procedure that military matters are off the table. It is much the same story across the world with 'national security' invariably trumping health and safety or environmental concerns.

Reflecting international relations as a whole, early 1990s international solidarity against Saddam has proved to be something of a false dawn for prosecuting military ecocide and the efforts of campaigners and UN experts have hence sought to improve the implementation of existing legislation and develop new instruments. Through its Environmental Cooperation for Peacebuilding programme, the United Nations Environment Programme (UNEP) has worked with the International Committee of the Red Cross in seeking to strengthen international laws protecting the environment during times of conflict. This work came together and was showcased in 2009 in an International Day for Preventing the Exploitation of the Environment in War and Armed Conflict on the 6th November. The event emphasized the need to clarify and enforce existing laws and made some particular recommendations including the following: (1) Give greater clarity to the 'widespread, long-term and severe'

---

[33] Peterson 2009; Jha 2014, 213–4.
[34] Plakokefalos 2017, 263.

(WLS) threshold; *severe* should be taken to mean environmental impacts over several hundred square kilometres and *long term* should be considered to be a period of several months or over a season. (2) Establish new laws to demilitarize important ecosystems, which should be determined at the outset of conflict. (3) Laws should deal with civil as well as inter-state wars. (4) Environmental crimes should be referable to The Permanent Court of Arbitration and be more directly included in the ICC Statutes.

Alongside these legal developments, a campaign for a more comprehensive and unambiguous UN treaty on ecocide, picking up the mantle from Westing in the early 1970s, has gathered momentum over recent years, led by British lawyer Polly Higgins. This campaign, launched in 2008, seeks to end the ambiguities around military (and industrial) necessity by establishing ecocide as a crime under customary international law (like genocide and torture) and more clearly opening it up to ICC prosecution. Celebrities, politicians and the Morales government of Bolivia are amongst those who have pledged their support for this cause which has set a deadline of 2020 for the codification of a new treaty.[35] Higgins submitted this proposal to the UN's International Law Commission in 2010 and they have subsequently produced three reports which have been presented at the UN General Assembly. The third report, presented in 2016, made the case for a single instrument to address military ecocide unambigiously:

> …there exists a substantive collection of legal rules that enhances environmental protection in relation to armed conflict. However, if taken as a whole, this collection of laws is a blunt tool, since its various parts sometimes seem to work in parallel streams. A holistic approach to the implementation of this body of law seems to be lacking at times. In addition, there are no existing or developed tools or processes to encourage States, international organizations and other relevant actors to utilize the entire body of already applicable rules.[36]

Higgins simultaneously was instrumental in the setting up of the 'End Ecocide in Europe' campaign from 2012 which seeks to get the EU Commission to draft a Directive criminalizing corporate and military damage to the environment. The movement was the first to take advantage of a new EU participatory democracy scheme, the European Citizens Initiative, under which signatures can be gathered to trigger new policies to be considered for proposal by the Commission in Brussels. The petition was discussed in the European Parliament in 2015 and continues to be advocated by Greens and other political groups in Brussels.

51.5 Normative Progress in Criminalizing Military Ecocide

The campaign aim of a UN Treaty on ecocide by 2020 looks like an ambition unlikely to be achieved but the popular support and attention gathered by this movement is maybe as important as establishing a clear legal platform for prosecution. As previous

---

[35] Higgins 2010.
[36] ILC 2016.

chapters have shown, the precedent for enforcing the conventions on genocide, torture and war crimes against humans is limited but the near universal acknowledgement of these as offences has still made them less likely to occur today than in the 'total war' era of the 20th Century. Implementing moral international laws is inherently difficult in a sovereign state system but few would deny that overall progress has been made in advancing both human rights and environmental principles over recent decades. Huge gaps and problems with implementation remain but sovereign states have come to be restrained on the basis of humanitarian and ecological values as they have crystallized in the form of international treaties and the 'soft law' rules of looser international regimes. The principle that military ecocide is unacceptable has, in line with this, come to be much better acknowledged. This has been reaffirmed at several high profile intergovernmental fora, including at the UN Conference on the Environment and Development (UNCED) in 1992, where Principle 24 of the Rio Declaration unambiguously states that; 'warfare is inherently destructive of sustainable development. States shall therefore respect international law providing protection for the environment in times of armed conflict and cooperate in its further development, as necessary.'

Whilst the advent of the 2nd Cold War in the 1980s slowed the progress in advancing the proscription of ecocide made in the détente era, some normative evolution still occurred in relation to the Arab-Israeli dispute. Long before New World Order optimism had come to inform international relations General Assembly Resolution 36/150 in 1981 condemned Israeli plans to construct a canal linking the Mediterranean to the Dead Sea, because of its environmental impact on Jordan (as well as the political ramifications for Palestinian independence), with only the US and Israel voting against. On the basis of this UNEP's Governing Council made several statements condemning Israeli actions that caused environmental damage to their Palestinians and their Arab neighbours and reaffirmed the General Assembly position on the canal in 1983.

Post-Cold War optimism, though, boosted the normative evolution of proscribing military ecocide by advancing the *idea* of environmental protection in war and UNEP have been central to this. The Disasters and Conflicts Programme offers services and advice on: post-crisis environmental assessment, post-crisis environmental recovery, environmental cooperation for peacebuilding and disaster risk reduction which have been utilized in Afghanistan, The Congo, Sierra Leone, Nigeria and Ukraine. UNEP also lead ENVSEC, an initiative established in 2003 linking it with the United Nations Development Programme, Organization for Security and Cooperation in Europe and other intergovernmental organizations in researching the environmental impacts of war. In 2006 for example, at the request of the Lebanese government, ENVSEC carried out a scientific assessment of the environmental impact of the Israeli invasion of 2006 and submitted a detailed report just four months after the ceasefire.[37]

Intergovernmental fora outside of the UN system have also taken up the cause of exposing and stigmatizing military ecocide. The Parliamentary Assembly of the Council of Europe have called for the environment to be more explicitly cited in

---

[37] UNEP 2007.

Geneva Protocol I and argued that the conflicts in Bosnia-Herzegovina and Chechnya should have seen prosecutions mounted on the basis of that legal instrument.[38] This body, representing all of Europe bar the dictatorship of Belarus, have also called for the general strengthening of existing international legislation on ecocide and for greater funding for UNEP and ENVSEC in the carrying out of environmental impact assessments on conflict zones.

Whilst the Iraqi compensation to Kuwait represents the one clear legal ecocide case we can see some small steps being taken by other culpable but unprosecuted governments to make amends for historic environmental war crimes. The Japanese government in 1997, having denied knowledge of the chemical weapons used in Manchuria for over half a century, finally entered into talks with the Chinese government over how to remedy the damage. This led to a 1999 memorandum committing Tokyo to a plan to locate and destroy some 700,000 abandoned weapons at a cost of over $500 million that they continue to work on.[39]

The US have also taken some steps to atone for Operation Ranch Hand, whilst accepting no legal liability. In 1975, on the full termination of the Vietnam War, Executive Order 11850 renounced the military use of herbicides 'as a matter of national policy'. Nevertheless, thirty year on from this, the US position was still that; 'there is no basis for any of the claims of plaintiffs under the domestic law of any nation or state or under any form of international law'.[40] However, the persistence of a campaign by Vietnamese victims and the fact that US war veterans suffering from dioxin exposure have received compensation from the chemical manufacturers has made this a difficult position to sustain and maintained pressure on Washington. Hence in 2012, whilst still not accepting liability, the US initiated a clean-up of ecological damage by dioxin in Vietnam. Washington gave $43 million to two American firms working in conjunction with the Vietnamese Defence Ministry in an operation Hanoi hope to complete by 2020. In 2016 the US also agreed to pay for the clean-up of unexploded ordnance in Laos. Partial atonement was also apparent in 2012 when the US returned to Subic Bay in the Philippines in 2015 in preparation for the re-opening of their naval base. However, in re-establishing military relations with their former colony, the Americans were now cooperating with an independent government that was not willing to accept being literally 'crapped on' as a price of their protection. The Subic Bay Metropolitan Authority now provides Philippine oversight of the US naval presence and has helped highlight concerns at the dumping of waste and even hosted maritime pollution conferences.

Realpolitik could be said to underpin these cases of atonement since 21st Century US foreign policy still values South East Asian influence and better Japanese relations with Beijing make economic and security sense, but moral pressure has undoubtedly played a part. Global civil society has been influential with groups like the Alliance for Bases Clean Up (ABC) (formerly known as the People's Task Force for Bases Clean Up (PTFBC)) and the Vietnamese Association of Victims of Agent Orange

---

[38] CoE 2011.
[39] BBC 2004.
[40] USDC 2005, 233.

(who have led the legal campaign) presenting the US with a reputational incentive to act. The Manchuria case presents perhaps the clearest illustration of how normative forces can influence governments both by shaming and encouragement. The Chinese came to throw their weight behind the Chemical Weapons Convention by recognizing that abandoning their own small stockpile (a condition of ratification) would be a price worth paying in order to remedy a festering environmental and health sore and also secure a moral victory over their old adversary. At the same time the Japanese, as champions of arms control on the international stage, felt compelled to confront their past demons and make some reparation for the sins of their grandparents.[41]

It is no coincidence that political ecology rose to prominence at the same time as the backlash against the US intervention in Vietnam and the growth of the powerful green social movement since then has given impetus to the anti-ecocide campaign. Environmental conservation is now part of the political mainstream in most developed democracies. The populism of this perspective is increasingly apparent also in non-democratic settings, with a clear example being the implementation of a range of anti-pollution measures by the Chinese government over recent years in the face of public protest at the growing levels of smog in many cities. We can also see evidence from political evolution in many states that public demands on government are not always self-serving and anthropocentric. Ecocentricism has been apparent in much domestic policy and law on the environment since the US responded to Rachel Carson's critique and restricted the use of DDT in the 1960s, even though the use of the organochlorine as a pesticide had been successful in increasing food yields. More specifically the criminalization of ecocide is making inroads in domestic law. In recent years domestic courts, such as in France and Belize, have passed verdicts against corporations for 'industrial ecocide'.[42] Bolivia in 2011 enacted a 'law of mother earth'[43] giving legal protection to their environment and, three years earlier, Ecuador amended their constitution to include this.[44] Guatemala in 2015 then became the first state to establish an 'Environmental Crimes Court' specifically to defend nature.

The maturation of law and politics in this way can also be observed at the global level as the globalization of ideas and ethics advances, aided in particular by global civil society and global epistemic communities of transnational experts usually working within the UN system. The existence of 'global ethics' can be seen in the development of human rights law and in many other dimensions of global law and policy, as seen throughout this volume. The reform of the World Bank, from being an advocate of 'unreconstructed liberalism' into a more socially and environmentally-oriented set of institutions, is a clear example of such normative change. The World Bank now routinely considers the environmental or social cost of any development project, as well as its economic viability, before granting it its seal of approval. This metamorphosis occurred through the development of a different epistemic community working within the system of organizations making up the

---

[41] Frieman 2004.
[42] TOTALSA v France 2008; Belize v Westerhaven 2009.
[43] Bolivia 2011.
[44] Ecuador 2008.

'bank', largely in response to civil society criticism. An emergent global discourse has promoted the normative change that has seen principles like a right to health and concrete aims such as the Sustainable Development Goals become established on the international stage not directly equitable with national interests. Promoted by an epistemic community of scientists, lawyers and expert campaigners, respected as acting outside of parochial state interests by an ever more enlightened global public, environmental rights can be understood as part of this progression. Whilst it is hardly likely to be eradicated, it is difficult to imagine anything other than there coming to be more international awareness of and an increased desire to restrict military ecocide.

51.6 Conclusion

Military necessity will probably always be cited as trumping environmental concerns during times of crisis on the grounds of national interest, but this is not to say that moral restraints cannot advance. As illustrated in previous chapters, whilst democracy and human rights continue to be compromised on the grounds of military necessity International Humanitarian Law (IHL) has nonetheless advanced overall in recent decades. Just War principles continue to be sidestepped in contemporary conflicts but they have, nevertheless, greatly advanced in the years since the end of the Cold War. In addition, globalization makes national reputations more important than ever and exposes illegality and immorality more easily than ever. In this way moral laws and norms tend not to unravel once established. The recent US and Japanese ecocide clean-up operations also show that the passage of time, both in terms of the accumulation of moral pressure in support of victims and in creating 'distance' for the perpetrator, can permit steps to be taken in making amends for historical crimes. Inevitably, governments will continue to carry out acts of ecocide if they feel they can get away with it but they are increasingly unlikely to get away with it, even if only reputationally rather than legally. As with IHL, though, the codification of unambiguous legal restraints on military ecocide would go further in strengthening natures defences.

However, as is the case in many facets of environmental politics and Public International Law, the high profile military ecocide catastrophes are but the tip of the iceberg. We may be unlikely to witness again anything comparable to Operation Ranch Hand or the burning oilfields of the Persian Gulf but beneath the surface of much international attention lies a huge military-industrial complex eating up the earth's resources and spitting and belching out what it does not need. Establishing ecocide as a war crime is important but only part of the fight to protect nature.

References

Auer M (2004) Restoring Cursed Earth: Appraising Environmental Policy Reforms in East Europe and Russia. Rowman & Littlefield, Oxford
Boas G, Schabas W (2003) International Criminal Law. Developments in the Case Law of the ICTY. Martinus Nijhoff, Leiden
Bolivia (2011) Law of Mother Earth. Law 071
Brady H, Re D (2018) Environmental and Cultural Heritage Crimes: the Possibilities Under the Rome Statute. In: Bose M, Bohlander M, Klip A, Lagodny O (eds) Justice Without Borders: Essays in Honour of Wolfgang Schomburg. Brill Nijhoff, Leiden: 103–136
BBC (2004) WW2 Bombs Unearthed in China 19 June http://news.bbc.co.uk/1/hi/world/asia-pacific/3822007.stm (accessed 31 January 2016)
Carson R (1962) Silent Spring. Penguin, Harmondsworth
Connor S, Thomas A (1984) How Britain Sprayed Malaya With Dioxin. In: Sahabat Alam Malaysia (eds) Pesticide Dilemma in the Third World. A Case Study of Malaysia
Cook RE, Haseltine W, Galston AW (1970) 'What have we done to Vietnam?' In: Weisberg B (ed) Ecocide in Indochina: the ecology of war. Canfield Press, San Francisco, 89–94
Council of Europe (CoE) (2011) Armed Conflicts and the Environment. Report of the Committee on the Environment, Agriculture and Local and Regional Affairs, Doc 12744 17 October; Parliamentary Assembly of the Council of Europe, Strasbourg
Ecuador (2008) Rights for Nature. Constitution, adopted 28 September
Franklin H (2003) Agent Orange and Cancer. An Overview for Clinicians. Environmental Carcinogens 53(4): 245–255
Frieman W (2004) China, Arms Control and Non-Proliferation. Routledge, London/New York
Glasby G, Voytekhovsky (2010) Arctic Russia: Minerals and Resources. Geoscientist 8
Hay A (1982) The Chemical Scythe- Lessons of 2,4,5,T and Dioxin. Plenum Press, New York
Higgins P (2010) Eradicating Ecocide: Laws and Governance to Prevent the Destruction of our Planet. Shepheard-Walwyn, London
ILC (2016) Third report on the protection of the environment in relation to armed conflicts Submitted by Marie G. Jacobsson, Special Rapporteur, United Nations General Assembly 3 June
Jha U (2014) Armed Conflict and Environmental Damage. Vij books, New Delhi
Kalpers J (2001) Armed Conflict and Biodiversity in Sub-Saharan Africa: Impacts, Mechanisms and Responses. In: Armed Conflict and Biodiversity in Sub-Saharan Africa. Biodiversity Support Program, Washington, D.C.
National Academy of Sciences (1974) The Effects of Herbicide in South Vietnam, Part A Summary and Conclusion. NAS, Washington, D.C.
Payne C (2016) Legal Liability for Environmental Damage. The United Nations Compensation Committee and the 1990-1991 Gulf War. In: Bruch C, Muffett C, Nichols S (eds) Governance, Natural Resources and Post-Conflict Peacebuilding. Routledge, London
Peluso N, Vandergeest P (2011) Taking the Jungle Out of the Forest. In: Peat R, Robbins P, Watts M (eds) Global Political Ecology. Routledge, London/New York
Peterson I (2009) The Natural Environment in Times of Armed Conflict: A Concern for International War Crimes Law? Leiden Journal of International Law 22(2): 325–343.
Plakokefalos I (2017) Responsibility for Environmental Damage in Jus Post Bellum. The Problems of Shared Responsibility. In: Stahn C, Iversen J, Easterday J (eds) Environmental Protection and Transition from Conflict to Peace. Oxford University Press, Oxford
Roberts A, Guelff R (2000) Documents on the Laws of War, 3rd edn. Oxford University Press, Oxford
Sanders B (2009) The Green Zone: the Environmental Costs of Militarism. AK Press, Oakland
Schettler T (1995) Reverberations of Militarism: Toxic Contamination, the Environment, and Health. Medicine and Global Survival, 2(1).
Sheehan N (2003) The Aftermath of an Invasion: A field report from Nasiriyah. Warchild, 1 May
UNEP (2002) GEO-3: Global Environment Outlook 3. Earthscan, London

UNEP (2007) Lebanon: Post Conflict Environmental Assessment. UNEP, Nairobi

USDC (2005) "Agent Orange" Product Liability Litigation. Memorandum Order and Judgement, MDL no. 381 10 March. United States District Court, New York

Weinstein T (2005) Prosecuting Acts that Destroy the Environment: Environmental Crimes or Humanitarian Atrocities? Georgetown International Law Review 17: 607–722

Westing A (1974) Proscription of Ecocide. Science and Public Affairs 26: 24–27

Westing A (1984) Herbicides in War-the Long Term Ecological and Human Consequences. Taylor & Francis, London

Westing A (1989) Herbicides in Warfare: the Case of Indochina. In: Bourdeau P, Haines JA, Klein W, Krishna Murti CR (eds) Ecotoxicology and Climate. John Wiley, Chichester: 337–357

Peter Hough is an Associate Professor in International Politics at Middlesex University, London. He holds a degree and Masters degree in International Relations from the London School of Economics and a PhD in International Relations from City University, London. Peter has published widely in the areas of global environmental politics and human security. He is the author of *Understanding Global Security* (2004, 2008, 2013, 2018 4th edn) the *Arctic in International Politics: Coming in From the Cold* (2013) and *Environmental Security* (2014, 2021 2nd edn).

Chapter 52
Religious Extremism

Sherzod Eraliev

Contents

52.1 Religion and Violence	1162
52.2 Religious Extremism	1163
52.3 Fundamentalism versus Extremism	1166
52.4 Extremism in Judaism	1167
52.5 Extremism in Christianity	1168
52.6 Extremism in Islam	1169
52.7 Extremism in Buddhism	1172
52.8 Extremism in Hinduism	1173
52.9 Human Rights and Countering Religious Extremism	1174
52.10 Conclusion	1176
References	1176

Abstract This chapter analyses the use of violence in the name of religion. Religious extremism is an ideology of certain movements, groups, individuals in denominations and religious organizations, characterised by adherence to extreme interpretations of dogma. It also involves methods of action by these parties to achieve their goals and spread their views and influence. The purpose of religious extremism is a fundamental reform of the existing religious system as a whole or of any significance of its component. Achieving this goal involves deep transformations of the social, legal, political, moral and other foundations of the society associated with the religious system. Religious fundamentalism is meticulous adherence to the strict interpretation of religion, while religious extremism goes further by including violent action to ensure this adherence. Following this analysis, the chapter provides a brief account of extremist actions taken in the name of Judaism, Christianity, Islam, Buddhism and Hinduism. It then discusses the balance between countering religious extremism and ensuring human rights.

Keywords religious fundamentalism · religious extremism · terrorism

---

S. Eraliev (✉)
Aleksanteri Institute, University of Helsinki, Helsinki, Finland
e-mail: sherzod.eraliev@helsinki.fi

© T.M.C. ASSER PRESS and the authors 2022
S. Sayapin et al. (eds.), *International Conflict and Security Law*,
https://doi.org/10.1007/978-94-6265-515-7_52

52.1 Religion and Violence

Is violence inherent in religion? Or is religion used to justify violence? Why do people of different faiths resort to violence in the name of their religion? The debate on the link between religion and violence has not yet been settled.

Mark Juergensmeyer, a well-known scholar of religion and violence, has argued that a post-colonial collapse of confidence in Western models of nationalism and the rise of globalisation led to the rise of "religious nationalism" after the end of the Cold War.[1] On the other hand, David Rapoport, one of the leading experts on terrorism, developed a 'four waves of religious terrorism' theory, according to which each wave is a cycle of about 40 years with a precipitating event, signature tactics and weapons and an inevitable gradual decline that culminates in the birth of another wave. In 2004, Rapoport wrote that the current wave, the 'religious wave', started around 1979. According to Rapoport, the current wave of terrorism is mostly associated with Islam, but it also includes terrorism by Christianity and other religious groups.[2] Whatever period is used to indicate the rise of violence in the name of religion, the contemporary world has witnessed shocking religious extremism of unprecedented form and scale. This is in addition to the horrific, sometimes decades-long, incidents of violence that humanity witnessed in the name of religion in medieval times.

Does religion lead to violence? Selengut argued that "violence is part of religion, something that emerges from deeply experienced religious faith and living history. War and politics are the venues for religious values."[3] Selengut claimed that members of religious communities are simply unable to accept and deal with the reality of contemporary societies and thus become susceptible to the use of violence encouraged by their charismatic leaders.[4] Supporting this idea, Pearce claimed that religious conflicts are more intense than other types of conflicts.[5]

However, Juergensmeyer argued the opposite, insisting that violence "happens only with the coalescence of a peculiar set of circumstances—political, social and ideological—when religion becomes fused with violent expressions of social aspirations, personal pride, and movements for political change."[6] For Guiora, the problem of violence is not inherent in religion; "rather, it is the view of a religious extremist regarding his or her own belief system."[7] Having analysed more than 100 ethno-religious minorities, Fox also argued that religious institutions tend to inhibit peaceful opposition unless there is a sufficient level of perceived threat to religious institutions or the religion itself.[8]

---

[1] Juergensmeyer 1993, 1996.
[2] Rapoport 2004, p. 61.
[3] Selengut 2003, p. 152.
[4] Ibid., p. 152.
[5] Pearce 2005, p. 349.
[6] Juergensmeyer 2000, p. 10.
[7] Guiora 2009, p. 12.
[8] Fox 1999, p. 119

Defining religion as one of the "central defining characteristics" of civilisations, Samuel Huntington's famous "clash of civilisations" concept argued that future wars would be fought not between countries, but between cultures and civilisations.[9] Contemporary scholars have widely criticised the attribution of violence to all religions. It should also be stressed that religious extremists are in conflict with both internal and external enemies: "While they may confront 'civilizational' adversaries, their primary enemies are often those within their own tradition."[10]

Iannaccone provided an economic perspective in explaining the resilience of religious groups. He held that rational citizens can opt for violence because extremist groups may offer unusually great opportunities to potential members. Extremist groups provide their members with "hope for the future, benefits for the present, and insurance against misfortune" in the case of financial setbacks or health problems.[11] Berman and Iannaccone argued that religious sects, which are good at producing both spiritual and material goods for members, often become major suppliers of social services, political action and coercive force when governments function poorly.[12]

Whether religion incites violence or groups and individuals justify their acts of violence with the cause of gods, religious extremism is a serious challenge to peace and prosperity in the contemporary world. As Guiora put it, religious extremism is "the greatest danger faced by the liberal state today."[13]

52.2 Religious Extremism

Although there is an increasingly wide use of the term 'religious extremism', it does not have a single agreed-upon meaning. Scholars, government authorities and international organisations have defined it differently. In its most general form, extremism is characterised by a commitment to extreme views and actions, radically denying the norms and rules that exist in society.

The essence of religious extremism is the denial of the moral and ethical values of traditional societies. It also relies on dogmatic foundations and aggressive propaganda of worldview aspects that contradict traditional universal values. This is manifested particularly in the desire of the adherents of a particular faith to spread their religious ideas and norms to the whole society.

Religious extremism is a complex social phenomenon that exists in three interrelated forms:

1. as a state of consciousness (social and individual), which is characterised by signs: hyperbolisation of a religious idea, nihilism and fanaticism;

---

[9] Huntington 1996.
[10] Barkun 2003, p. 60.
[11] Iannaccone 1999, p. 20.
[12] Berman and Iannaccone 2005, p. 21.
[13] Guiora 2009, p. IX.

2. as an ideology (religious doctrine, characterised by an unambiguous explanation of the problems of the existing world and the suggestion of simple ways to solve them, dividing the world into "good" and "evil"), giving a dominant position to one aspect of being that does not correspond to the hierarchy of values accepted in society, ignoring and levelling others' norms;
3. as a set of actions to implement religious doctrines.

In other words, religious extremism refers to an ideology of certain movements, groups, individuals in denominations and religious organisations, characterised by adherence to extreme interpretations of dogma, but it also refers to methods of action to achieve their goals, spreading their views and influence.

> Religious extremism is when the actor believes that his or her tenets and principles are infallible and that any action, even violence, taken on behalf of those beliefs is justified. The action can be directed both at people of other faiths (or those of no faith), as well as members of the same religion who have violated the extremist's understanding of how their religion is to be practiced.[14]

The purpose of religious extremism is the fundamental reform of the existing religious system as a whole or of a significant part of its components. The realisation of this goal is connected with a deep transformation of the social, legal, political, moral and other foundations of society associated with the religious system.

There is also a difference between how government officials and international organisations (such as the United Nations) have used the term extremism. UN organisations have used the term 'violent extremism', while government officials have opted for 'extremism', arguing that 'violent extremism' was a tautology because extremism is inherently violent. Thus, according to government officials in some parts of the world, merely holding extremist beliefs without necessarily acting on them is indictable within the state justice system. In contrast, the UN and civil society representatives have been careful not to judge beliefs that citizens hold dear as violent in nature or as grounds for prosecution.[15]

The use and scale of violence in the name of faith have differed from one religion to another. However, despite important differences in ideology, composition and targets, groups and individuals practising religious extremism also share a number of characteristics:

(a) Deliberate targeting—with the objective of inflicting harm—of civilians, both individuals and communities, based on their identity;
(b) A lack of tolerance for multiple narratives that challenge their fundamentalist belief system;
(c) A related and violent disregard for civic discourse, culture, scientific or rational thought, human rights, due process, and the traditional and modern embodiments of law and authority;
(d) References to symbols, whether religious (Sharia law, the Bible) or otherwise (such as the Swastika);

---

[14] Ibid., p. 10.
[15] IPI 2019.

(e) In some cases, a rejection of the nation-state or at least of existing boundaries;
(f) In other cases, a glorification of the nation-state is linked to a rhetoric of supremacy of one people/class over others (as was the case with the Nazis, the Pol Pot regime, and the Knights of the Ku Klux Klan);
(g) The presentation of individual or group objectives in nihilistic, millenarian or apocalyptic terms, rather than as realizable political objectives (albeit with the caveat that, for many leaders of violent extremist groups, these lofty statements often disguise more practical aspirations for power or territorial control);
(h) The systematic discrimination and abuse of women and their subordination through rape, enslavement, abduction, denial of education, forced marriage, or sexual trafficking, which has been part of the ideology or practice of several violent extremist groups.[16]

Religious extremism is manifested not only in a religious environment; it is often directed against the secular state, the existing social system, and the laws and norms in it. Religious extremism has manifestations in the fields of politics, culture and interethnic relations. In these cases, it acts as a religious motivator or religious ideological design of political and nationalist extremism, etc. Slogans, appeals, ideological actions of extremist religious organisations are addressed, as a rule, not to reason, but to people's feelings and prejudices, designed for uncritical, emotional perception, blind adherence to customs and traditions, and the crowd effect. Violent extremist actions are aimed at spreading fear, suppressing opponents psychologically and causing shock in society.

The social environment of religious extremism consists mainly of marginalised and disadvantaged groups within society who experience a feeling of dissatisfaction with their situation, who feel uncertain about the future, and fear undermining or losing their national or confessional identity.

Religious extremism can take different forms. Intra-confessional extremism targets co-believers for departing in their view from what extremists consider to be the true, original path of their faith. Examples include Christian fundamentalists in the United States in the 1980s and 1990s attacking abortion clinics or militants of the Islamic State executing other Muslims. Another form of religious extremism is the targeting of other faiths and/or their representatives. Ethno-religious extremism occurs when representatives of a particular ethnic group and faith are involved in discriminating and persecuting other ethnic and/or religious groups. Fundamentalist Hindus in India and Buddhists in Myanmar are examples.

These types of religious extremism are often mixed in nature and do not appear in a pure form. The purpose of religious extremism is radical reform of the existing religious system as a whole or of a significant part of its components. Realisation of this purpose is connected with the tasks of deep transformation of the social, legal, political, moral and other foundations of society associated with the religious system.

---

[16] UNDP 2016, pp. 12–13.

Religious violence is undertaken not only for strategic reasons but also to accomplish a symbolic purpose. Mark Juergensmeyer called religious extremism a 'performance violence,' which is played out before audiences and therefore meant to be witnessed because of its symbolic meaning.[17]

52.3 Fundamentalism versus Extremism

There is confusion regarding the use of terms related to religion and violence. Scholars, government officials, the media and international organisations sometimes use the terms 'fundamentalism' and 'extremism' interchangeably. Although they are often used and understood as synonyms, they are not. To determine the difference, let us first explain what fundamentalism is.

The term fundamentalism was initially used to describe the conservative movement within Protestantism in the United States during the late 19th and early 20th centuries, which saw modernisation as a threat. Between 1910 and 1915, the most active of these individuals wrote a series of pamphlets called *The Fundamentals* (hence the name fundamentalists), in which they outlined what they saw as the fundamental, non-negotiable aspects of the Christian faith.[18]

Several scholars have offered definitions of religious fundamentalism. However, the most comprehensive, although criticised by some other academics, explanation of the issue was provided by the Fundamentalism Project, which resulted in five volumes of work from 1991 to 1995. The authors of the project attributed several characteristics to religious fundamentalism, including:

- Reaction to the marginalisation of religion;
- Selectively accepting some sides of modernity (such as technology), while refusing others (ideological underpinnings such as relativism, secularism and pluralism);
- Manicheism; that is, dividing the world into light and dark, good and evil; absolutism and inerrancy of their sacred texts (e.g., Bible, Torah, Koran, etc.),
- Messianism, etc.[19]

Marty and Appleby defined religious fundamentalism as "a distinctive tendency— a habit of mind and a pattern of behaviour—found within modern religious communities and embodied in certain representative individuals and movements … a religious way of being that manifests itself as a strategy by which beleaguered believers attempt to preserve their distinctive identity as a people or group."[20]

Haynes understands that religious fundamentalists share the following characteristics:

---

[17] Juergensmeyer 2013, p. 280.
[18] Emerson and Hartman 2006.
[19] Marty and Appleby 1995.
[20] Marty and Appleby 1992, p. 34.

- they fear that their preferred religiously oriented way of life is under attack from unwelcome secular influences or alien groups;
- their aim is to create traditionally oriented, less modern(ised) societies;
- as a result, many pursue campaigns in accordance with what they believe are suitable religious tenets in order to change laws, morality, social norms and, in some cases, domestic and/or international political configurations;
- many are willing to engage the ruling regime politically in various ways if the regime appears to be encroaching into areas of life—including education, gender relations and employment policy—that religious fundamentalists believe are an integral part of their vision of a religiously appropriate society, one characterised by a certain kind of 'pure' moral climate;
- they may also actively oppose co-religionists who they believe are excessively lax in upholding their religious duties, as well as followers of rival or opposing religions whom they may regard as misguided evil, even satanic.[21]

As we can see, a fundamentalist is someone who believes in a strict interpretation and application of his or her religion's holy texts. Another strand of scholars also attributes to fundamentalists the use of violence when deemed necessary. For example, Pratt argued that a fundamentalist has gone through a passive (normative) to an assertive (hard-line) phase before reaching the last impositional (activist) fundamentalist phase.[22] At this level, fundamentalists can resort to intimidation and coercion as well as to violent and destructive actions.[23] However, when a fundamentalist resorts to violence, he or she will have already become radicalised into violent extremism. Hence, fundamentalism is still an utmost devotion. As Pfarrkirchner put it, extremism is misuse of religion, often but not always resulting in violence, and fundamentalism is meticulous adherence to a set of beliefs.[24] Moreover, given that the concept of "radicalisation into violent extremism" is well established in academia, extremism already assumes violence.[25]

52.4 Extremism in Judaism

The obvious manifestation of religious extremism in Judaism is religious Zionism. This ideology was born in the second half of 19th century in Western Europe. Zionists believed that Jews' right to "Eretz Yisrael" (the Land of Israel) was permanent and inalienable and that every Jew must strive to settle the land promised to Israelites by God. A noted scholar Al-Modhaki explained that "Zionism was not merely a political movement by secular Jews. It was actually a tool of God to promote His divine

---

[21] Haynes 2009, pp. 161–162.
[22] Pratt 2007.
[23] Ibid.
[24] Pfarrkirchner 2010.
[25] See, for example, Borum 2012a, 2012b; Vergani et al. 2018.

scheme, and to initiate the return of the Jews to their homeland—the land He promised to Abraham, Isaac and Jacob."[26] The State of Israel was founded in 1948. The Six-Day war in 1967 and Israel's occupation of the Golan Heights and the Gaza Strip gave birth to the neo-Zionist movement. Contemporary neo-Zionists advocate the settlement of newly occupied lands by Jewish families despite international criticism.

One of the leading organisations promoting neo-Zionism was Gush Emunim, which was formally established only in 1974. Gush Emunim actively propagated and organised the settlement of Occupied Territories and the West Bank by Jewish families despite their forced removal by Israeli authorities. Ozzano noted that the movement did not have the cycles of mobilisation typical of other extremist groups. "On the one hand, it has always been marked out by a sort of permanent mobilisation ..., on the other, its activities have been deeply influenced by the emergence of phenomena such as the two Intifadas and the peace process."[27]

Attacks by Arabs on new Jewish settlements gave birth to so-called 'price tag attacks'. Jewish ultra-nationalists conducted acts of vandalism against Palestinians, Israeli Arabs, Christians and Israeli security forces as retaliation for resistance to the settlement. These acts included violent attacks on minorities, burning mosques and fields, and incursions into Palestinian villages.[28]

Another movement that has taken an extreme form in Judaism is Haredi Judaism, which seeks to interpret Jewish law and values strictly, regarding them as opposed to modern values and practices. Members of this movement are referred to as ultra-Orthodox Jews. Haredi Judaism is a fundamentalist reaction to societal changes, including modernity, secularisation and emancipation.[29] Haredi Jews are often criticised for their extreme views on women's status in society: abuse and domestic violence is widespread. Some Haredi women are required to wear a burqa, including a veil covering the face.[30]

52.5 Extremism in Christianity

Although it may appear that Christian extremism has disappeared and given way to Islam over the last half a century, this is not the case. As Pratt put it, "in the contemporary world there is evidence of an upsurge in fundamentalist mentality and groupings within Christianity sufficient to suggest that fundamentalist extremism is not just the province of Islam but that Christianity is also able to produce similar extreme ideology and related actions."[31]

---

[26] Al-Modhaki 2010, p. 104.
[27] Ozzano 2009, p. 140.
[28] Btselem 2017.
[29] Finkelman 2011; Fisher 2016.
[30] Cares and Cusick 2012.
[31] Pratt 2010, p. 454.

Extremists in Christianity justify their violent actions through their own interpretations of the Bible. Probably the first manifestations of Christian extremism in the early modern era were related to the events of the so-called Gunpowder Plot, when English Catholics made a failed attempt to assassinate Protestant King James I in 1605. In America, the reactivated Ku Klux Klan (KKK) organisation in the 1910s was explicitly anti-Catholic. Basing its ideology in Protestant Christianity, the organisation targeted Jews, Catholics and other social or ethnic minorities, as well as those individuals that members found 'immoral'.[32] KKK members believed that Jesus was a Klansman and the purpose of cross burnings, apart from intimidating targets, was to show respect for Jesus Christ.[33]

Although there was a decline in the use of violence in the name of Christianity in the mid-20th century, a wave of violence emerged in the 1980s. Anti-abortion movements grew, mostly in the United States, but also in Canada, Australia and New Zealand. Members of the Army of God in the United States engaged in kidnapping, stalking, assault, murder, arson, bombings and destruction of property in the 1980s and 1990s.

While anti-abortion extremists targeted both Christians and non-Christians, the last decade has witnessed a rise in violence against Muslims. In November 2011, Anders Breivik shot dead 69 participants of a summer camp in Norway (Breivik was anti-Islam; however, these victims were not necessarily Muslims). In March 2019, Brenton Tarrant killed 51 mosque attendants in Christchurch, New Zealand.

As Stockwell wrote, "today, many fundamentalists have been at the forefront of the so-called 'culture wars' in America, insisting that Christians should become involved politically to save America as a Christian land."[34]

52.6 Extremism in Islam

Islamic extremists see secularism as the root of the contemporary world's problems; they believe that peace and justice can be achieved only by returning to the original version of Islam.

The first manifestations of extremism in Islam are attributed to the Kharijites of the seventh and eighth centuries. The Kharijites strongly criticised other Muslims who, in their opinion, did not fully abide by Islam. Radical Kharijites declared that those who disagreed with their position were apostates and launched periodic military attacks against mainstream Muslim communities until the late 8th century.[35]

Syed Abul A'la Maududi (1903–1979) was one of the first influential Muslim thinkers to pioneer the politicization of Islam and pressed for the strict application of the *Sharia* in state affairs. In 1947, Maududi moved from India to Pakistan and

---

[32] Al-Khattar 2003.
[33] Neal 2009.
[34] Stockwell 2006, p. 10.
[35] Armstrong 2000.

influenced the establishment of the Islamic State of Pakistan in 1956. A prolific scholar and promoter of Islam, he wrote more than 120 books and pamphlets. In his writings and speeches, Maududi argued that *jihad* was a central tenet of Islam and called for Muslims to start a *jihad* against Western secularism. For Maududi, Muslims had no choice but to "capture State Authority" since "a pious cultural order can never be established until the authority of Government is wrested from the wicked."[36] Haynes, a scholar of religious fundamentalism, maintains that "Maududi's ideas about the Islamic state are widely regarded as the basic foundation for the political, economical, social and religious system of any Islamic country that wishes to live under Islamic law."[37]

Maududi's ideas profoundly influenced Sayyid Qutb (1906–1966), an Egyptian Islamic scholar and activist who was an active member of the *Ikhvan al-Muslimin* (the Muslim Brotherhood). Author of two dozen books, Sayyid Qutb advocated *Sharia* rules in state governance. He criticised the Muslim world for not living up to the standards of Islam, and he especially criticised the Western world. He was particularly critical of the society and culture of the United States for being materialistic and obsessed with violence and sexual pleasure.[38]

Consecutive defeats of Arab countries during wars against Israel (especially the Six-Day War of 1967), the Islamic revolution in Iran and the Soviet intervention in Afghanistan (fuelled by Western support of anti-Soviet mujahedeen) contributed to the alienation and radicalisation of certain groups among Muslim activists. For many of them, Western hegemony—manifested first by colonialism and imperialism and then via global capitalist economic control—was a key factor in the growth of Islamism.[39]

As Haynes explained, "what they [Muslim activists] share in common … is a shared sense that the West—because of its expansionism and perceived disdain for religion in general and Islam in particular—is a key problem for Muslims around the world."[40] Marranci observed "a general feeling among Muslims, both living in the West as minorities and in Muslim-majority countries, that Islam is under attack, both in its physical embodiment of the ummah (see the cases of Iraq, Afghanistan, Palestine and Chechnya, among others) as well as culturally and politically."[41]

Esposito outlined Islamic extremism's 'ideological worldview' as follows:

1. Islam is a total and comprehensive way of life; religion is to be integrated into politics, law and society.
2. The failure of Muslim societies is due to their departure from the straight path of Islam and their acceptance of Western values and secularism.
3. Renewal of society requires a return to Islam, the Quran and the teachings of the prophet Muhammed.

---

[36] Mofidi 2014, p. 166.
[37] Haynes 2009, p. 163.
[38] Khatab 2006.
[39] Akbar 2002.
[40] Haynes 2009, p. 164.
[41] Marranci 2009, p. 151.

4. Western-inspired civil codes must be replaced by Islamic law.
5. Although Westernisation is condemned, science is not, although science is to be subordinated to Islamic beliefs and values.
6. The process of Islamisation requires a struggle against corruption and social injustice (jihad).[42]

Today, Islamic extremism is manifested most notably by remnants of ISIS, al-Qaeda (Arabian Peninsula), Taliban (Afghanistan, also active in Pakistan), Jabhat Fateh al-Sham (Syria), Boko Haram (Nigeria), al-Shabaab (Somalia). It seeks to create an Islamic state (*Caliphate*) that is ruled by Sharia.

The attacks of September 11, 2001, also referred to as 9/11, are the single deadliest terrorist act in contemporary history: al-Qaeda members launched a series of attacks against the United States, in which 19 terrorists hijacked four passenger airlines. Two crashed into the World Trade Center buildings in New York, the third crashed into the Pentagon, and the fourth plane fell into a field on its way to Washington, DC. The attacks killed 2,977 people and injured more than 6,000 others.[43] The United States announced al-Qaeda and its leader Osama bin Laden as the perpetrators of the terrorist attacks and responded by launching air strikes on Taleban targets in Afghanistan, which had given safe haven to al-Qaeda. By that time, bin Laden was already on the United States' designated list of wanted terrorists who had committed a series of terrorist attacks in 1990s, including the bombing of United States embassies in Kenya and Tanzania. The invasion of Afghanistan marked the start of the United States Global War on Terror.[44] Bin Laden said that United States support of Israel, the presence of United States troops in Saudi Arabia, and sanctions against Iraq were al-Qaeda's motives for the attacks.[45]

The case of the IS, or the ISIL—the Islamic State of Iraq and the Levant—is the most profound example of religious extremism in the contemporary world. In 2014, as a Salafist militant organisation, IS founded a non-recognised state in a large territory of Iraq and Syria until its defeat in early 2019.

The IS started in 1999 as a small group called Jama'at al-Tawhid wal-Jihad (JTJ), under the leadership of Abu Musab al-Zarqawi. When the United States occupied Iraq in 2003, JTJ militants became a major insurgency group under the name of al-Qaeda in Iraq. The withdrawal of American troops from Iraq and the start of the civil war in neighbouring Syria in 2011 created a power vacuum that was exploited by the militants. Having captured large territories in Iraq and Syria, the group announced the creation of the Islamic State as a worldwide Caliphate in June 2014. In late 2014, the group held more than 100,000 square kilometres of territory, with a population of nearly 12 million, mostly in Iraq and Syria, where it sought to enforce Sharia law.[46] The IS continued to draw foreign fighters from several countries for the duration of the conflict. Approximately 30,000 fighters from at least 85 countries (including

---

[42] Esposito 2005, p. 165.
[43] CNN 2019.
[44] Boyle 2008.
[45] CBC 2004.
[46] RAND 2017.

North Africa, Central Asia, China, Russia and Western Europe) joined the Islamic State.[47] The IS also had a meticulous bureaucratic and financial system and a strong online media presence in different languages.[48]

The IS fought Syrian government forces, Syrian rebel groups, the Iraqi military and militias, and Kurdish Peshmerga groups. An international coalition led by the United States supported anti-IS forces with air strikes against IS posts, supplies, weapons and training. The Russian military also supported the Syrian government, launching limited air strikes on IS targets in Syria. International intervention had an impact on the hostilities and IS increasingly lost territory over the course of several years. The last IS territory was seized in Syria in March 2019. However, at the time of writing, the group is reorienting to a decentralised, guerrilla-style insurgency, carrying out attacks through sleeper cells, not only in Iraq and Syria but also in other parts of the world.[49]

International organisations, including the United Nations, hold the IS responsible for committing war crimes, crimes against humanity, genocide and systematic human rights abuses. These include executions, torture, amputations, ethno-sectarian attacks, rape and sexual slavery imposed on women and girls.[50]

52.7 Extremism in Buddhism

Non-violence is at the heart of Buddhist thinking and behaviour. One of its main ideas is found in Buddha's sermon: "Even if thieves carve you limb from limb with a double-handed saw, if you make your mind hostile you are not following my teaching."[51]

Contemporary figures such as the 14th Dalai Lama (Nobel Peace Prize laureate) have preached peace. However, like every other world religion, Buddhism has not always lived up to its principles of non-violence. In fact, Buddhists have engaged in wars for centuries.[52]

The civil war in Sri Lanka (1983–2009) between the mostly Buddhist Sinhalese majority and the Hindu Tamil minority cost 50,000 lives. There have been a series of anti-Muslim riots in Sri Lanka, India and Thailand causing several deaths and hundreds of injuries. However, the Rohingya crisis in Myanmar shows how a seemingly pacifist religion can be used for extremist purposes.

Muslim and Buddhist communities in Myanmar have been in tension for decades. Rohingya, Muslims of the country's Rakhine province, have been discriminated

---

[47] NBER 2016.
[48] CISAC 2019.
[49] Ibid.
[50] UN 2018.
[51] BBC 2009, para 27–29.
[52] Jerryson 2013.

against and persecuted by both the majority Buddhist population and the government. Buddhist extremist groups, including the MaBaTha and the anti-Muslim 969 movement, regularly attack Muslim communities and call for their expulsion from the country.

In October 2016, following an attack on a security post in Myanmar that left nine police officers dead, Myanmar's armed forces launched a crackdown on unarmed Muslims. These attacks caused more than 1000 civilian deaths and forced tens of thousands to flee their villages.

In August 2017, a Rohingya militant group carried out an attack on government military and police outposts, killing more than 70 people. In response, the government military forces launched a brutal crackdown on Rohingya villages, causing more than 700,000 people to flee the country to neighbouring Bangladesh. Buddhist groups participated actively in the violence. International organisations reported that authorities were involved in indiscriminate killings and in the burning of the Rohingya people.[53] UN Human Rights Commissioner called the situation "a textbook example of ethnic cleansing".[54]

52.8 Extremism in Hinduism

Anti-British sentiment in India in the early 20th century led to the rise of not only the secular Congress movement, but also of the Hindu nationalist movement collectively known as the Sangh Parivar. Its central organisation, Rashtriya Swayamsevak Sangh (RSS), proclaims an ideology of Hindutva aimed at ensuring the predominance of Hinduism in Indian society and subjugating Muslims and Christians, who comprise 17% of India's population.[55]

Sangh Parivar supporters fiercely opposed and criticised the partition of the subcontinent into India and Pakistan in 1947. The movement's racism and religious chauvinism brought it into conflict with other strands of Hinduism, especially those preached by Mahatma Gandhi, who was assassinated in 1948 by a former RSS member.

Today, the RSS is a large paramilitary organisation with millions of members. Its educational section, the Vidya Bharati, has some 20,000 educational institutes, with 100,000 teachers and two million students. Other Sangh Parivar organisations include the Bajrang Dal and the Vishnu Hindu Parishad (VHP), which engage in propaganda, virulent hate campaigns and sometimes violence against religious minorities. The VHP was formed in 1964 to unite Hindu groups and serve as the RSS's bridge to sympathetic religious leaders. It has sought to radicalise Hindus by claiming that they are under threat from an "exploding" Muslim population and a spate of Christian conversions. The VHP organised nationwide demonstrations in 1992 that culminated

---

[53] Amnesty 2017.
[54] UN 2017.
[55] Marshall 2004.

in the destruction of the Ayodhya mosque by Hindu mobs (Marshall 2004). Bajrang Dal, which was founded in 1984 and was responsible for the total demolition of Babri mosque in Ayodhya in 1992, currently has approximately 2,500 cells across the country.[56]

Sangh Parivar have profoundly opposed conversions from Hinduism. There have been reports of attacks on Christian missionaries. These attacks include murders of missionaries and priests, sexual assaults on nuns, ransacking of churches, desecration of cemeteries and Bible burnings. In 1999, Hindu extremists burned alive an Australian Christian missionary who had worked with leprosy patients with his two young sons (Marshall 2004). One report claimed that, within the last seven years, Hindu extremists, in the name of protecting cows, have conducted 168 attacks that have left 46 people dead.[57] International organisations, including the United Nations Human Rights Office, Human Rights Watch and Amnesty International, have raised concerns over discrimination and violence against religious and ethnic minorities in India.

The Bharatiya Janata Party (BJP), which won parliamentary elections in 1998 and 2014, is reportedly tied to the RSS, VHP and Bajrang Dal. A new victory of the BJP in parliamentary elections in early 2019 was seen by some analysts as a triumph of Hindu nationalism.[58]

52.9 Human Rights and Countering Religious Extremism

In response to the rise of terrorism incidents, national governments have developed new laws and tightened policies to counter violent extremism. This has led to debates among scholars, journalists, civil society activists, government officials and representatives of international organisations regarding how a state must counter religious extremism while ensuring the rights of religious people. Drawing a line between violent extremism and idiosyncratic but non-violent religious practices has raised serious discussions, especially in Western countries.

Proponents of religious freedom and human rights have criticised government authorities for abusing human rights in the name of countering terrorism and extremism. At the same time, governments have an obligation to protect their citizens from terrorist attacks and the incitement of such acts motivated by extremism and violence. As Guiora noted:

> The decision to protect harmful religious practices rather than the individual endangers vulnerable members of society. It, frankly, reflects an unjustified defence of extremism by government reflecting misguided priorities largely predicated on a disturbing failure to understand harm posed by extremism. That decision, however, represents a failure of the larger

---

[56] Griswold 2019.
[57] Ibid.
[58] Foreign Affairs 2019.

responsibility owed by the nation-state; the duty owed paradigm requires protecting individuals from extremists and extremism. In that sense, the danger emanating from government's failure to minimize the potential threat of extremism is no less potent than the harm caused by extremists.[59]

Since there is no universally agreed-upon definition of terrorism and extremism, the United Nations sees that definition as the prerogative of member states, as long as they are consistent with states' obligations under international human rights law.[60] Although anti-extremism laws in most countries do not raise concerns, there may still be room for state authorities to abuse the rights of citizens. International organisations have expressed concerns that vague definitions of "extremism" give governments in authoritarian countries the opportunity to interfere in religious practices and persecute those believers they perceive as a threat to the regime.

For example, China is often criticised for abusing the rights of the ethnic and religious minorities of Uighurs in the name of fighting religious extremism, one of the "three evil forces". Chinese authorities have detained hundreds of thousands of Muslim-minority Uighurs, whom the government has identified as extremists, in so-called re-education camps, where authorities force individuals to abandon their religion. "Regional legislation identifies 15 types of behaviours the government views as extremist, such as wearing an 'abnormal' beard, wearing a veil, or following halal practices (Muslim dietary laws)."[61]

Russia's anti-extremism policies have also raised concerns. For years, Russian authorities have mainly targeted Muslim activists in fighting extremism, ranging from Hizb ut-Tahrir to Tabligh Jamaat, as well as individuals who do not necessarily have a group affiliation. However, there has recently been a crackdown on Christian denominations that do not belong to the Russian Orthodox Church, including Jehovah's Witnesses and Scientologists.[62] Several countries, including some in Central Asia, have been criticised for persecuting all forms of Islam, except the officially sanctioned one.

On the other hand, anti-blasphemy laws, which are especially prevalent in the Middle East and North Africa, have also raised concerns. Blasphemy—defined as speech or actions that are considered contemptuous of God or the divine—has led not only to persecution by government authorities, but also, in particular cases, to mob violence.[63]

---

[59] Guiora 2014, p. 22.
[60] UN 2015.
[61] USCIRF 2019, p. 4.
[62] Kravchenko 2018.
[63] Pew 2016.

52.10 Conclusion

Human history in any society is intertwined with religion. Religion has played an important, sometimes decisive, role in the development of countries for centuries. Despite the rise of secularisation, it will continue to play an important role in the future, as proven by developments in recent decades.

For its important role in a society, religion is and will be used by religious groups and leaders to achieve political goals. When political means are exhausted or deemed undesirable in the pursuit of these goals, religious groups or individuals will resort to the use of violence. Thus, extremists normalise violence to achieve goals. What is peculiar to religious extremism is that extremists often target not only those whom they perceive as enemies (enemies can be competing religious denominations, groups within their own denomination or political institutions) but also civilian bystanders.

Although Islam is often blamed for inciting the use of violence by extremists, this is not the whole picture. Violence has been committed in the name of Christianity, Judaism, Buddhism and Hinduism, too. It is the confluence of global political, social and economic processes that, at this point in history, makes Islam more prone to be used by extremists.

States and societies must actively use all means to curb religious extremism in order to minimise its material and moral damage on individuals. At the same time, countering religious extremism must not be used to justify violations of human rights.

Organisations like the UNDP and the OSCE recommend a developmentalist approach in countering religious extremism, which, along with law enforcement, includes the promotion of inclusive development, tolerance and respect for diversity. The effectiveness and legitimacy of the state's actions against extremism will be undermined if the state uses its power in violation of international human rights standards.[64]

References

Akbar MJ (2002) The shade of swords: Jihad and the conflict between Islam and Christianity. Routledge, London/New York.
Al-Khattar AM (2003) Religion and terrorism: An interfaith perspective. Praeger, London.
Al-Modhaki A (2010) I will meet you at the crossroads. Baheth For Studies, Beirut.
Amnesty (2017) Myanmar: Crimes against humanity terrorize and drive Rohingya out. https://www.amnesty.org/en/latest/news/2017/10/myanmar-new-evidence-of-systematic-campaign-to-terrorize-and-drive-rohingya-out/ Accessed 25 September 2019.
Armstrong K (2000) Islam: A short history. The Modern Library, New York.
Barkun M (2003) Religious violence and the myth of fundamentalism. Totalitarian Movements and Political Religions, 4(3), 55–71.
BBC (2009) Buddhism and war. https://www.bbc.co.uk/religion/religions/buddhism/buddhistethics/war.shtml Accessed 25 September 2019

---

[64] OSCE 2014.

Berman E, Iannaccone LR (2005) Religious extremism: The good, the bad, and the deadly. NBER Working Paper: https://www.nber.org/papers/w11663 Accessed 25 September 2019.

Borum R (2012a) Radicalization into violent extremism I: A review of social science theories. Journal of Strategic Security, 4(4), 7–36.

Borum R (2012b) Radicalization into Violent Extremism II: A review of conceptual models and empirical research. Journal of Strategic Security, 4(4), 37–62.

Boyle MJ (2008) The war on terror in American grand strategy. International Affairs, 84(2), 191–209.

Btselem (2017) Settler violence: Absence of law enforcement. Btselem, 11 November 2017, https://www.btselem.org/settler_violence Accessed 25 September 2019.

Cares A, Cusick G (2012) Risks and opportunities of faith and culture: The case of abused Jewish women. Journal of Family Violence (27), 427–435. https://www.haaretz.com/israel-news/.premium-women-of-the-wall-demands-government-inquiry-into-violent-attacks-at-western-wall-1.7003709.

CBC (2004) Bin Laden claims responsibility for 9/11. https://www.cbc.ca/news/world/bin-laden-claims-responsibility-for-9-11-1.513654, 29 October 2004, accessed 25 September 2019.

CISAC (2019) The Islamic State profile. Stanford Center for International Security and Cooperation: https://cisac.fsi.stanford.edu/mappingmilitants/profiles/islamic-state#text_block_18356 Accessed 25 September 2019.

CNN (2019) September 11 terror attacks fast facts. https://edition.cnn.com/2013/07/27/us/september-11-anniversary-fast-facts/ Accessed 25 September 2019.

Emerson MO, Hartman D (2006) The rise of religious fundamentalism. Annual Review of Sociology, 32, 127–144.

Esposito JL (2005) Islam: The straight path, rev. 3rd edn. Oxford University Press, New York/Oxford.

Finkelman Y (2011) Ultra-Orthodox/Haredi education. In: Miller H, Grant LD, Pomson A (eds) International handbook of Jewish education. Springer, Dordrecht, pp. 1063–1080.

Fisher N (2016) The fundamentalist dilemma: Lessons from the Israeli Haredi case. International Journal of Middle East Studies, 48(3), 531–549. doi:https://doi.org/10.1017/S0020743816000477

Foreign Affairs (2019) The roots of Hindu nationalism's triumph in India. (September/October) https://www.foreignaffairs.com/articles/india/2019-09-11/roots-hindu-nationalisms-triumph-india Accessed 25 September 2019.

Fox J (1999) Do religious institutions support violence or the status quo? Studies in Conflict & Terrorism, 22, 119–139.

Griswold E (2019) The violent toll of Hindu nationalism in India. The New Yorker. https://www.newyorker.com/news/on-religion/the-violent-toll-of-hindu-nationalism-in-india Accessed 25 September 2019.

Guiora AN (2009) Freedom from religion: Rights and national security. Oxford University Press, Oxford/New York.

Guiora AN (2014) Tolerating intolerance: The price of protecting extremism. Oxford University Press, Oxford/New York.

Haynes J (2009) Religious fundamentalisms. In: Haynes J (ed) Routledge handbook of religion and politics. Routledge, London/New York, pp. 159–173.

Huntington SP (1996) The clash of civilizations and the remaking of the world order. Simon & Schuster, New York.

Iannaccone LR (1999) Religious extremism: Origins and consequences. Contemporary Jewry, 20(1), 8–29.

IPI (2019) Preventing violent extremism while promoting human rights: Toward a clarified UN approach.: International Peace Institute, New York. https://www.ipinst.org/wp-content/uploads/2019/07/1907_PVE-While-Promoting-Human-Rights.pdf Accessed 25 September 2019.

Jerryson M (2013) Buddhist traditions and violence. In: Juergensmeyer M, Kitts M, Jerryson M (eds) The Oxford handbook of religion and violence. Oxford University Press, Oxford, pp. 41–66.

Juergensmeyer M (1993) The new Cold War? Religious nationalism confronts the secular state. University of California Press, Berkeley/Los Angeles/London.
Juergensmeyer M (1996) The worldwide rise of religious nationalism. Journal of International Affairs, 50(1), 1–20.
Juergensmeyer M (2000) Terror in the mind of God: The global rise of religious violence. University of California Press, Berkeley/Los Angeles/London.
Juergensmeyer M (2013) Religious terrorism as performance violence. In: Juergensmeyer M, Kitts M, Jerryson M (eds) The Oxford handbook of religion and violence. Oxford University Press, Oxford, pp. 280–292.
Khatab S (2006) The political thought of Sayyid Qutb: The theory of Jahilliyah. Routledge, London/New York.
Kravchenko M (2018) Inventing extremists: The impact of Russian anti-extremism policies on freedom of religion or belief. USCIRF, Washington, DC. https://www.uscirf.gov/sites/default/files/Inventing%20Extremists.pdf Accessed 25 September 2019.
Marranci G (2009) Understanding Muslim identity: Rethinking Fundamentalism. Palgrave Macmillan, Basingstoke/New York.
Marshall P (2004) Hinduism and terror. Hudson Institute. https://www.hudson.org/research/4575-hinduism-and-terror Accessed 25 September 2019.
Marty ME, Appleby SR (eds) (1992) The glory and the power: The fundamentalist challenge to the modern world. Beacon Press, Boston.
Marty EM, Appleby SR (eds) (1995) Fundamentalisms Comprehended. University of Chicago Press, Chicago.
Mofidi S (2014) Political religion: Outcome and continuity of religious fundamentalism. IMPACT: International Journal of Research in Applied, Natural and Social Sciences, 2(5), 161–168.
NBER (2016) What explains the flow of foreign fighters to ISIS? National Bureau of Economic Research: https://www.nber.org/papers/w22190 Accessed 25 September 2019.
Neal LS (2009) Christianizing the Klan: Alma White, Branford Clarke, and the art of religious intolerance. Church History, 78(2), 250–378.
OSCE (2014) Preventing terrorism and countering violent extremism and radicalization that lead to terrorism: A community-policing approach. Vienna. https://www.osce.org/secretariat/111438?download=true Accessed 25 September 2019.
Ozzano L (2009) Religious fundamentalism and democracy. Politics and Religion, 127–153.
Pearce S (2005) Religious rage: A quantitative analysis of the intensity of religious conflicts. Terrorism and Political Violence, 17(3), 333–352.
Pew (2016) Which countries still outlaw apostasy and blasphemy? Pew Research Center: https://www.pewresearch.org/fact-tank/2016/07/29/which-countries-still-outlaw-apostasy-and-blasphemy/ Accessed 25 September 2019.
Pfarrkirchner R (2010) Religious fundamentalism is not the problem. Matador. https://matadornetwork.com/bnt/religious-fundamentalism-is-not-the-problem/ Accessed 1 September 2019.
Pratt D (2007) Religious fundamentalism and extremism: A paradigm analysis. New Zealand Association for the Study of Religions Biennial Conference. Queenstown. https://researchcommons.waikato.ac.nz/handle/10289/754 Accessed 25 September 2019.
Pratt D (2010) Religion and terrorism: Christian fundamentalism and extremism. Terrorism and Political Violence, 22(3), 438–456.
RAND (2017) Rolling back the Islamic State. RAND, Washington. https://www.rand.org/pubs/research_reports/RR1912.html Accessed 25 September 2019.
Rapoport DC (2004) The four waves of modern terrorism. In: Cronin AK, Ludes J (eds) Attacking terrorism: Elements of a grand strategy. Georgetown University Press, Washington, DC, pp. 46–73.
Selengut C (2003) Sacred fury: Understanding religious violence. Altamira, Walnut Creek, CA.
Stockwell C (2006) Fundamentalisms and the Shalom of God: An analysis of contemporary expressions of fundamentalism in Judaism, Christianity and Islam. IAPCHE, Granada, pp. 1–29.

UN (2015) Plan of action to prevent violent extremism. https://www.un.org/en/ga/search/view_doc.asp?symbol=A/70/674 Accessed 24 September 2019.

UN (2017) UN human rights chief points to 'textbook example of ethnic cleansing' in Myanmar. https://news.un.org/en/story/2017/09/564622-un-human-rights-chief-points-textbook-example-ethnic-cleansing-myanmar#.WfJRrltSy70 Accessed 25 September 2019.

UN (2018) First report of the Special Adviser and Head of the United Nations Investigative Team to promote accountability for crimes committed by Da'esh/Islamic State in Iraq and the Levant. New York: UN. https://www.un.org/sc/ctc/wp-content/uploads/2018/11/N1837464_EN.pdf Accessed 25 September 2019.

UNDP (2016) Preventing violent extremism through promoting inclusive development, tolerance and respect for diversity: A development response to addressing radicalization and violent extremism. UNDP, New York. https://www.undp.org/content/dam/norway/undp-ogc/documents/Discussion%20Paper%20-%20Preventing%20Violent%20Extremism%20by%20Promoting%20Inclusive%20%20Development.pdf Accessed 25 September 2019.

USCIRF (2019) Legislation factsheet: Anti-extremism laws. US Commission on International Religious Freedom, Washington, DC. https://www.uscirf.gov/sites/default/files/Legislation%20Factsheet%20-%20Extremism.pdf Accessed 25 September 2019.

Vergani M, Iqbal M, Ilbahar E, Barton G (2018) The three Ps of radicalization: push, pull and personal. A systematic scoping review of the scientific evidence about radicalization into violent extremism. Studies in Conflict & Terrorism, 1–32. doi:https://doi.org/10.1080/1057610X.2018.1505686

Sherzod Eraliev is Academy of Finland postdoctoral researcher at the Aleksanteri Institute for Russian, East European and Eurasian Studies, University of Helsinki. He holds a PhD from the University of Tsukuba, Japan (2018). His research interests include religion and migration, religious extremism, migration in Eurasia, state and society relations in Central Asia.

Chapter 53
Human Smuggling and Human Trafficking

Natalia Szablewska

Contents

53.1 Introduction 1182
    53.1.1 The Main Differences Between Human Smuggling and Human Trafficking 1183
53.2 Human Smuggling 1184
    53.2.1 Legal Framing 1185
    53.2.2 Maritime Migrant Smuggling 1188
53.3 Human Trafficking 1193
    53.3.1 Legislative Framework 1194
    53.3.2 Human Trafficking as a Form of Modern Slavery 1196
53.4 Human Trafficking and Smuggling in Conflict 1199
    53.4.1 International Jurisprudence 1201
53.5 Conclusion 1202
References 1204

Abstract Human smuggling and human trafficking are part of mixed migration flows, which are defined as complex population movements concerning both regular (i.e. documented) and irregular (i.e. undocumented) migrants. Even though migration rates have been steady since the 1990s, the forced displacement of people is on the rise worldwide. There are often similarities between the trafficking and smuggling of people, but the profiles of the persons affected and, consequently, the legal responses differ. It is important therefore to distinguish, in law and in practice, between human smuggling and trafficking, even though both are considered a form of organised crime. Yet, despite their different legal status, they are often conflated, including by law enforcement agencies, courts and support service providers, which leads to unsatisfactory protection and services being offered to trafficked and smuggled persons who find themselves in situations of vulnerability. This chapter provides an overview of the legal framework on migrant smuggling, with a particular focus on

---

N. Szablewska (✉)
The Open University Law School, Milton Keynes, United Kingdom
e-mail: natalia.szablewska@open.ac.uk

Royal University of Law and Economics, Phnom Penh, Cambodia

Humanitarian and Development Research Initiative, Western Sydney University, Sydney, Australia

maritime migrant smuggling, followed by human trafficking, which is further considered in the context of modern slavery legislation. The final section examines human trafficking and human smuggling in conflict and the corresponding jurisprudential developments in international criminal law.

Keywords Human trafficking · Human smuggling · Modern slavery · Maritime migrant smuggling · Irregular migration · Armed conflict

53.1 Introduction

The stories of human trafficking of minors for sexual exploitation or attempts of maritime migrant smuggling ending with boats capsizing and never reaching their destinations have captured the imagination of the general public across the world. However, these stories present only part of what is a much more complex and nuanced reality for those travelling on perilous migration routes, including the victims of human trafficking and smuggled persons.

Inequality and natural or manmade disasters, as well as conflicts, tend to be the main triggers for forced and irregular (or undocumented) migration worldwide. It is estimated that nearly ten per cent of the world's population is displaced from their homes,[1] including an estimated 11 million undocumented migrants residing in the United States (US)[2] and further millions in Pakistan, Iran, Africa, Europe and Southeast Asia.[3] Human trafficking and migrant smuggling are part of mixed migration flows, defined by the International Organization for Migration (IOM) as "[c]omplex migratory population movements...as opposed to migratory population movements that consist entirely of one category of migrants".[4]

The reality of human trafficking is that it affects every country, whether as a country of origin, transit or destination or a combination thereof, and, similar to smuggling, it is a worldwide phenomenon. The human trafficking flows and smuggling routes tend to be from less- to more-prosperous countries and regions, but domestic trafficking in persons is on the rise.[5] The trafficking and smuggling of persons are clandestine activities generating a substantial income for organised criminal networks, which is estimated to be US$150.2 billion a year for traffickers,[6] and the estimated economic return from migrant smuggling in 2016 was US$5.5–7 billion.[7] Thus, both are seen as profitable, and hence growing, forms of organised

---

[1] United Nations High Commissioner for Refugees (UNHCR) 2018.
[2] Krogstad et al. 2017.
[3] International Organization for Migration (IOM) 2018b.
[4] IOM 2011, p. 63.
[5] See UNODC 2018b.
[6] FATF 2018, p. 13.
[7] UNODC 2018a, p. 5.

crime, including for terrorist organisations, as they offer viable sources of terrorism financing.[8]

There are a number of commonalities between human trafficking and human smuggling, but, in law and in practice, they differ. The complexity of distinguishing these practices is further exacerbated by the often-interchangeable use by media and policy outlets of terms such as (modern) slavery, slavery-like practices or forced labour, which, again, are interrelated but not necessarily the same. Thus, sensitive treatment of these different practices is required, as well as consequent recognition of their distinct legal status. In order to comprehend what ultimately is a complex system where different branches of international law and national laws intersect, it is necessary to briefly look at the main differences between human trafficking and smuggling first, before these two are explained in more detail in the subsequent sections.

53.1.1 The Main Differences Between Human Smuggling and Human Trafficking

The distinction between the trafficking and smuggling of persons is relatively new. In 1994, the IOM defined human trafficking as an illegal international border crossing involving a voluntary movement and offering financial gain for the trafficker,[9] which was relatively close to the contemporary definition of smuggling. It was only in 2000, when the UN Protocol to Prevent, Suppress and Punish Trafficking in Persons, Especially Women and Children (the Trafficking Protocol) was enacted, that the legal distinction between these two crimes became cemented. The main differences between these two crimes relate to consent, transnationality and the assessment of victimhood.

The key distinguishing factor is that a person can consent to being smuggled, whereas victims of trafficking can never consent to their own exploitation. However, in practice, the matter of consent is often difficult to ascertain in relation to migrant smuggling, as, once en route, a smuggled migrant might withdraw their consent but still be forced to continue. Moreover, a person who consented to and procured their own smuggling can become a victim of human trafficking at the different stages of smuggling, including at the destination, once their circumstances change.[10]

Another difference is that smuggling requires international border crossing, which is not required for human trafficking. Thus, whether a victim of trafficking is moved across or within a state's borders is irrelevant for the crime to occur if other elements of the crime are present (see Sect. 53.3). Further, even though neither a smuggled

---

[8] See, for instance, FATF 2018.
[9] Cited in Laczko 2005, p. 10.
[10] See, for instance, Reports of the Special Rapporteur on Trafficking in Persons, especially Women and Children, UN Doc. A/HRC/32/41, 3 May 2016, para 16 and UN Doc. A/HRC/29/38, 31 March 2015, para 11.

migrant nor a trafficked person is criminalised for the fact of being smuggled or trafficked, smuggling is often perceived as a 'victimless crime' (it is a crime against a state), whereas human trafficking never is. That is not to say that smuggled migrants do not suffer, as the conditions in which they are transported can be dangerous and their work is often abusive, with the IOM estimating that 40,000 migrants died or went missing between 2000 and 2014, with more than half of those trying to reach Europe.[11] Thus, even though smuggled migrants are not recognised as victims per se, the situation in which they find themselves might constitute human rights abuses, and they might be victims of crime in certain circumstances.

This chapter will begin by providing an overview of the legal framework on human smuggling (Sect. 53.2), with a particular focus on migrant smuggling in the maritime context (Sect. 53.2.2). This will be followed by an introduction to the crime of human trafficking at the international level (Sect. 53.3), as well as in the context of modern slavery legislation (Sect. 53.3.2). The next section (53.4) will examine human trafficking and smuggling in conflict and will look at international criminal jurisprudence in relation to the corresponding potential modes of prosecution. The final section will provide a summary of the chapter.

53.2 Human Smuggling

Attitudes towards human (or people or migrant) smuggling need to be placed within the wider context of the territorial sovereignty of states, where it is within states' purview to prescribe, as a matter of national policy and domestic legislation, who has the right to enter their territory and on what grounds. Thus, in most cases, states have some form of border control that acts as a barrier to non-nationals entering (or sometimes nationals leaving) without the permission to do so, usually in the form of entry (or exit) visas. Such restrictions on transnational mobility are nothing new and have existed since political boundaries were introduced, but such restrictions have also created demand for services in migrant smuggling. For example, in the context of the Mediterranean region, free-flow migration between North Africa and Southern Europe was relatively easy until Spain and Italy introduced Schengen Visas for North Africans in the early 1990s, which increased irregular migration in the region and, in turn, amplified border securitisation.[12] Thus, what is in fact relatively new is the criminalisation and penalisation of smuggling, which have been increasing worldwide.

Thus, perceptions of people smuggling were not always as they are today. Historically, smuggling across borders was often the only way for people to escape oppressive regimes or persecution. Jews escaping Nazi Germany during World War II or

---

[11] IOM 2014.

[12] Van Liempt 2016.

defectors from East Germany (and often other parts of the Eastern Bloc)[13] to West Germany during the Cold War relied on smugglers, who were perceived as 'saviours' and 'enablers' of migration. Even though the social context of contemporary migrant smuggling is very similar, as it mostly occurs in response to persecution, war, demand for cheap labour, poverty and states' restrictions on human mobility, and so smugglers continue to provide often the only alternative, attitudes have changed: "[s]mugglers are nowadays…perceived much more as criminals than before".[14] However, the shift in the (legal and social) framing of the issue as predominantly an 'illegal' activity involving organised crime and, consequently, harsher policies on migrant smuggling has been instigated by the reality of migrant smuggling, where violence, including sexual violence, kidnapping and robbery, against refugees and other migrants by smugglers is estimated to account for between 50 and 76% of all incidents.[15]

53.2.1 Legal Framing

At the end of 1998, the United Nations General Assembly (UNGA) established an intergovernmental ad hoc committee[16] with a mandate to develop an international framework to combat international organised crime.[17] With the support of the majority of states, in 2000, the UN Convention Against Transnational Organized Crime (UNTOC) was introduced,[18] supplemented by three Protocols dealing with the trafficking of persons, the smuggling of migrants, and the trafficking in firearms.

The Protocol Against the Smuggling of Migrants by Land, Air and Sea (the Smuggling Protocol) defines 'smuggling' as a form of organised crime involving "the procurement, in order to obtain, directly or indirectly, a financial or other material benefit, of the illegal entry of a person into a State Party of which the person is not a national or a permanent resident", where an "illegal entry" is understood to mean "crossing borders without complying with the necessary requirements for legal entry into the receiving State".[19]

"Procurement" is not defined in the Protocol, but, in line with the general meaning of the word, it would include acts of organising, facilitating, enabling, promoting or otherwise materially supporting a person's entry into a country without permission when that person is neither a national nor a permanent resident of that country (as

---

[13] The Eastern Bloc (often referred to also as the Soviet Bloc or Communist Bloc), consisted of countries in Eastern Europe, East Asia and Southeast Asia that were under the influence of the Soviet Union during the Cold War (1947–1991).

[14] Van Liempt 2016, p. 3.

[15] Horwood et al. 2018, pp. 122–123.

[16] Ad Hoc Committee on the Elaboration of a Convention against Transnational Organized Crime, established by the UNGA Resolution 53/111 (1998), https://www.unodc.org/unodc/en/treaties/CTOC/background/adhoc-committee.html. Accessed 28 August 2019.

[17] See the UNGA Resolution 53/111 (20 January 1999).

[18] Adopted by the UNGA Resolution 55/25 (15 November 2000).

[19] Article 3(a) and (b) respectively.

defined under Article 3(b)). Thus, smuggling constitutes an illegal border crossing at the request of the migrant, where the smuggler is usually paid by the migrant (or someone on their behalf) to achieve that aim, after which the involvement of the smuggler ceases.

In Europe, the first attempt to legally regulate smuggling came in 2000 with a proposal by the French government to the European Commission for a 'Framework Decision on Strengthening the Penal Framework for Preventing the Facilitation of Unauthorized Entry and Residence'.[20] This was considered part of an agenda to "combat the aiding of illegal immigration both in connection with unauthorised crossing of the border in the strict sense and for the purpose of sustaining networks which exploit human beings" and aimed to supplement "other instruments adopted in order to combat illegal immigration, illegal employment, trafficking in human beings and the sexual exploitation of children".[21]

In the Asia and Pacific region, the Bali Process on People Smuggling, Trafficking in Persons and Related Transnational Crime (the Bali Process) was established in 2002 to support collaboration and information sharing to address the issues of people smuggling, human trafficking and related crimes in the region.[22] The Bali Process, guided by the Bali Process Declaration (2018)[23] and led by Indonesia and Australia, has 49 members, including intergovernmental organisations such as the UN High Commissioner for Refugees and the IOM. Since 2015, in response to the Bay of Bengal migrant smuggling crisis, involving thousands of migrants from Myanmar and Bangladesh being stranded at sea or whose bodies were uncovered in mass graves in South Thailand, resulted in "a new focus on combating the crime of migrant smuggling in the [Association of Southeast Asian Nations (ASEAN)][24] region" and was a trigger point for the ASEAN to consider migrant smuggling as "one of the transnational crimes that falls under its purview".[25]

At the international level, mirroring the regional level, smuggling is predominantly seen as part of transnational organised crime, which has affected the level of support deemed appropriate for smuggled persons, as well as the assessment of their culpability. The framing of the problem as one of 'organised crime', has also had consequences for assessing the motivations of smugglers and, consequently, establishing corresponding legal responses.

It needs to be noted that smuggling that does not involve an organised criminal group still remains punishable.[26] According to UNTOC, an organised criminal group

---

[20] See https://eur-lex.europa.eu/legal-content/EN/ALL/?uri=CELEX%3A32002F0946. Accessed 27 August 2019.

[21] Ibid., at (2) and (5) respectively.

[22] For more information, see https://www.baliprocess.net/.

[23] Declaration of the Seventh Ministerial Conference of the Bali Process on People Smuggling, Trafficking in Persons and Related Transnational Crime, 7 August 2018.

[24] For more information, see https://asean.org/.

[25] UNODC 2018d, p. 1.

[26] UNTOC, Article 34(2); Smuggling Protocol, Article 4; see also UNODC 2004, Part 3, Chap. I, para 20, p. 334.

is a "structured group" consisting of three or more persons who have been part of that group for a certain period of time and have acted in a concerted fashion to commit the crime (as defined in UNTOC) for the purpose of obtaining a financial or other material benefit.[27] Thus, profits are the main motive for organised criminal groups, with other objectives such as control or power being secondary, but the definition is broad as to the level of affiliation of its members and their role within the group.

The offences under UNTOC need to be transnational in nature (as per Article 3(2)); under Article 3 of the Smuggling Protocol, the offences include migrant smuggling as well as the facilitation of illegal entry and document fraud offences enabling migrant smuggling or illegal stay. Article 6 of the Smuggling Protocol prescribes conduct to be criminalised by the state parties, thus requiring the conduct to be committed intentionally for financial or other gain.

It is required, therefore, that offences under the Protocol must be shown to have been committed with the purpose of obtaining, directly or indirectly, a "financial or other material benefit".[28] This might involve bribing, rewarding and offering privileges or services (including sexual services), thus covering both economic and non-economic benefits. There are, however, exemptions in relation to humanitarian assistance, when acting on the basis of family ties or when support is provided by religious groups or non-governmental organisations.[29]

Aggravating circumstances are listed in Article 6(3) of the Smuggling Protocol and constitute those that "endanger, or are likely to endanger, the lives or safety of the migrants concerned", as well as those that would be considered "inhuman or degrading treatment, including for exploitation, of such migrants".[30] The list is not exhaustive, and thus state parties are free to include additional aggravating circumstances in their domestic legislation. As explained earlier, the involvement of an organised group is not considered a constitutive element of the crime of smuggling but is often considered an aggravating circumstance.

Under the Smuggling Protocol, being smuggled is not a crime, and thus the smuggled person should not be prosecuted for the fact of being smuggled,[31] nor, when applicable, should their asylum claims be negatively affected as a result of resorting to smuggling.[32] However, the Protocol does not prevent the state parties from introducing criminal offences under their domestic legislation for document fraud, illegal entry or illegal residence. In the context of maritime migrant smuggling (Sect. 53.2.2),

---

[27] Article 2.

[28] Article 3(a).

[29] See UNGA, 'Interpretative notes for the official records (travaux préparatoires) of the negotiation of the United Nations Convention against Transnational Organized Crime and the Protocols thereto', UN Doc. A/55/383/Add.1, 2000, para 88.

[30] The meanings of "inhumane" or "degrading" are not defined in the Smuggling Protocol, but there already exists extensive international and domestic jurisprudence in relation to these terms in the context of human rights law and as defined in Article 7 of the International Convent on Civil and Political Rights (ICCPR) (1966) 999 UNTS 171. See also the UNODC 2010, p. 43.

[31] Article 5.

[32] Article 19; see also the UN Convention on the Status of Refugees (1951) 189 UNTS 150, Article 31.

even states that are not parties to UNTOC or the Smuggling Protocol should refrain from the detention or arrest of migrants who have not entered their territorial waters and have not violated their domestic immigration laws, and states are required to render assistance to any person or vessel in distress at sea, including those carrying irregular migrants.[33]

UNTOC prescribes assigning liability not only to natural but also legal persons (such as corporations or charitable organisations). Article 10 specifies that the liability of legal persons, which can often shield natural persons from liability, can be criminal, civil or administrative, and sanctions should be "effective, proportionate and dissuasive", ranging from criminal to non-criminal, including monetary sanctions. Article 11(2)–(4) of the Smuggling Protocol establishes the responsibility of commercial carriers for verifying whether "all passengers are in possession of the travel documents required for entry into the receiving State",[34] but where the person reasonably believed that the documentation presented was the travel documents required for lawful entry into the country concerned, such liability will be waived.[35]

In response to global legal changes, as well as increased land border controls, since 2009, smuggling activities have shifted towards sea crossing, in particular across the Red and the Arabian Seas and along the Mediterranean Sea route.[36] The next section will therefore focus on the situation of maritime migrant smuggling, as it poses a specific conceptual and practical challenge for states.

53.2.2 Maritime Migrant Smuggling

Part II of the Smuggling Protocol deals with the smuggling of migrants by sea, with Article 7 prescribing that "State Parties shall cooperate to the fullest extent possible to prevent and suppress the smuggling of migrants by sea, in accordance with the international law of the sea." Thus, the key treaty, incorporating many provisions of prior international instruments in this area, is the UN Convention on the Law of the Sea (UNCLOS). UNCLOS does not directly deal with the protection of migrants at sea, beyond the basic humanitarian rescue provisions, but rather concerns the delineation of the sea into maritime zones and states' responsibilities in relation to those.

In the maritime context, states' jurisdiction is defined by maritime zones, giving the states the right to prescribe, enforce and implement laws within their territorial waters. Maritime zones are measured from the state's baseline ("the low-water line

---

[33] See UN Convention on the Law of the Sea (UNCLOS) (1982) 1833 UNTS 397, Article 98(1), but it needs to be noted that the application of this provision has been challenged given recent increase in vessels at sea in need of rescue. See also Papastavridis 2013, p. 23.

[34] Article 11(3).

[35] See UNODC 2010, pp. 59–60.

[36] UNODC 2018a.

along the coast")[37] and are divided into five main zones: internal waters and territorial seas, where states have exclusive territorial jurisdiction; and contiguous zone, exclusive economic zone (EEZ) and high seas, where the freedom of navigation and flag state[38] jurisdiction apply. Thus, states can pursue their domestic immigration laws freely within their territorial seas and, to some extent, their contiguous zone, whereas the flag states enjoy exclusive jurisdiction over vessels on the high seas,[39] with some limited exceptions.[40]

"Interception" in this context is understood to mean "all measures applied by a State, outside its national territory, in order to prevent, interrupt or stop the movement of persons without the required documentation crossing international borders by land, air or sea, and making their way to the country of prospective destination".[41] Depending on the flag of the intercepted vessel and in which maritime zone the interception has taken place, states have different competencies.[42]

Traditionally, under UNCLOS and customary international law, a state's jurisdiction over a vessel with migrants on the high seas was limited, unless given such permission by the flag state or exercising it within the limited exceptions,[43] even if that ship was heading towards the state's territorial waters. However, given the "evolving environment in which refugee protection has to be provided" and the rise in human trafficking and smuggling, it has been increasingly recognised that states have "a legitimate interest in controlling irregular migration"; thus, where there are reasonable grounds to believe that the vessel is transporting irregular migrants, it has become more accepted that such a vessel can be intercepted by a non-flag state.[44] In response to the rise in the death toll in the Mediterranean Sea, the UN Security Council Resolution 2312 (2016) extended the authority of states, initially established by Resolution 2240 (2015), to inspect vessels believed to have been used for migrant smuggling or human trafficking from Libya.[45]

In cases where the vessel does not fly a flag, which is not that uncommon in relation to vessels carrying irregular migrants, states have more options to engage with and intercept such vessels and the individuals on board. In the context of the European Union (EU), the statelessness of vessels has been used by member states

---

[37] UNCLOS, Article 5.

[38] Meaning the country where the ship is registered and, under UNCLOS Article 27, that country has responsibility, including criminal jurisdiction, over the ship even when the ship is outside the territorial waters of the flag state.

[39] See also *The Case of the SS Lotus (France v. Turkey)* (Judgment), Permanent Court of International Justice, 7 September 1927.

[40] Gallagher and David 2014, p. 273.

[41] UNHCR 2000, para 10.

[42] It is beyond the scope of this chapter to discuss in detail the legal implications for each of the maritime zones, but for an in-depth overview see IOM 2018a.

[43] These would include: when the vessel is engaged in piracy (UNCLOS, Article 105); slave trading (UNCLOS, Articles 99 and 110(1)(b)); and unauthorised broadcasting (UNCLOS, Articles 109(4) and 110).

[44] UNGA 2003.

[45] UN Security Council (UNSC) Resolution S/RES/2312 (6 October 2016).

as the legal basis for interception on the high seas.[46] There has reportedly been also a rise in recent years in the use of so-called 'ghost ships', where the crew abandons the vessel before it reaches its destination, forcing a rescue operation to save those on board. One such example in 2015, when the cargo ship Ezadeen, flying under a Sierra Leone flag, with 450 people on board, mainly Syrian asylum seekers, was intercepted by the Italian coastguards.[47]

Once a vessel enters a foreign state's port or territorial waters, it "put[s] [itself] within the territorial sovereignty of the coastal State"[48] and thus becomes subject to domestic laws and regulations (the same as people who enter a foreign territory).[49] However, even in cases of interception outside states' territorial waters, states still have obligations towards those they exercise 'effective control' over,[50] including under international human rights law,[51] international refugee law (including the principle of *non-refoulement*) and international customary law. In such circumstances, states' obligations arise not under territorial but extra-territorial jurisdiction. The matter of the application of the law extra-territorially, particularly in relation to international human rights law, has been a topic of intense legal and political debate, and not exclusively in relation to the interception of irregular migrants at sea.

In the context of the International Covenant for Civil and Political Rights (ICCPR), the United Nations Human Rights Committee in its General Comment No. 31 asserted the general rule of the extra-territorial application of human rights obligations, stating that:

[T]he enjoyment of Covenant rights is not limited to citizens of State Parties but must also be available to all individuals, regardless of nationality or statelessness, such as asylum seekers, refugees, migrant workers and other persons, who may find themselves in the territory or subject to the jurisdiction of the State Party. This principle also applies to those *within the power or effective control* of the forces of a State Party acting outside its territory, regardless of the circumstances in which such power or effective control was obtained.[52]

The Smuggling Protocol also contains mandatory protection provisions[53] and a saving clause preventing other international rules, including human rights obligations, from being diluted in the process of implementing the provisions of the

---

[46] See, for instance, Tejera 2011.

[47] J. Hooper, 'Abandoned ship Ezadeen with 450 migrants on board being towed to Italy', *The Guardian* (International edition), 02 January 2015. www.theguardian.com/world/2015/jan/02/abandoned-cargo-vessel-migrants-towed-italy-traffickers. Accessed 28 August 2019.

[48] Churchill and Lowe 1999, p. 54.

[49] See also McDorman 2000.

[50] For a legal evaluation of the concept of 'effective control' in the context of Australia's obligations towards asylum seekers and refugees, see Szablewska and Ly 2017.

[51] However, some human rights treaties do not include jurisdiction clauses thus, arguably, these have only territorial scope, i.e. the International Covenant on Economic, Social and Cultural Rights (ICESCR) (1966) 993 UNTS 3 and the Convention on the Elimination of All Forms of Discrimination against Women (CEDAW) (1979) 1249 UNTS 13. See also Khaliq 2015.

[52] UN Human Rights Committee (HRC) 2004, para 10, emphasis added.

[53] See Article 8(5).

Protocol.[54] Thus, an extra-territorial application of human rights obligations is widely considered to apply to all cases of person interception carried out at sea.[55] This has also been confirmed in the jurisprudence of the European Court of Human Rights, which, in the case of *Medvedyev and Others v. France*, held that:

> [The] special nature of the maritime environment...cannot justify an area outside the law where ships' crews are covered by no legal system capable of affording them enjoyment of the rights and guarantees protected by the Convention which the States have undertaken to secure to everyone within their jurisdiction, any more than it can provide offenders with a 'safe haven'."[56]

However, not all legal questions in relation to the extra-territorial application of human rights, particularly in relation to maritime migrant smuggling, have been fully settled, and states often act in contravention of those obligations.

In Australia, in response to the rise in maritime migrant smuggling, under the Operation Sovereign Borders (OSB),[57] Australian coastguards return intercepted vessels to international waters,[58] which has met with widespread criticism for putting the lives of migrants at risk and flouting Australia's international obligations, including under the Smuggling Protocol and the principle of *non-refoulement*,[59] which bars states from returning an alien to a place where they would likely face persecution or their life would be threatened.[60] There have also been reports of Australian navy officers being endangered when migrants on board those vessels threatened to set the vessels alight, as well as cases of post-traumatic stress disorder resulting from delaying rescue operations until vessels reach Australian waters and when these operations result in the drowning of migrants or pushing boats back, knowing that the lives and safety of passengers would be jeopardised.[61] Pushing or towing boats back by Australian authorities to the territorial waters of Indonesia also violates Indonesia's territorial sovereignty.[62]

---

[54] Article 19.

[55] See also Klug and Howe 2010.

[56] *Medvedyev and Others v. France* (Judgment), Application no. 3394/03, para 81, 29 March 2010.

[57] For more information, see http://osb.homeaffairs.gov.au.

[58] See also IOM 2016.

[59] But it must be noted that Australia has denied that the principle of non-refoulement has extra-territorial application or that it applies outside the territorial seas, see *CPCF v. Minister for Immigration and Border Protection* (Judgment), Case No. S169/2014, High Court of Australia, 28 January 2015.

[60] See, for instance, the Convention on the Status of Refugees, above n 32, Article 33(1).

[61] See 'Royal Australian Navy personnel open up about trauma of seeing asylum seekers die at sea', *ABC News*, 02 December 2014. https://www.abc.net.au/news/2014-12-02/navy-personnel-open-up-about-border-protection/5933260. Accessed 28 August 2019; see also Schloendhardt and Craig 2015.

[62] See Report of the Special Rapporteur of the Human Rights Council on extrajudicial, summary or arbitrary executions, 'Unlawful death of refugees and migrants', UN Doc. A/72/335, 2017, in particular para 33.

In cases of vessels in distress on the high seas, states have an obligation – as opposed to arguably a right in situations of interception – to search and rescue.[63] Nevertheless, states often fail in this regard, which can be due to states' unwillingness to engage but also because of the lack of effective collaboration between states.[64] Such failures will most likely be a violation of international obligations to search and rescue (under UNCLOS and international customary law) as well as to coordinate rescue operations by the states that are parties to the International Convention on Maritime Search and Rescue (the SAR Convention).[65]

Rescue situations are often complicated even further when there is a clash of different international obligations, as happened in 2001 in the case of the MV Tampa, a Norwegian cargo vessel, which involved Australia's coastal state jurisdiction, Indonesia's SAR jurisdiction[66] and Norway's flag jurisdiction. Australia denied the Tampa entry to its waters to disembark the 438 people it had rescued from a sinking Indonesian fishing boat in the Indian Ocean.[67] This incident resulted in amendments to the SAR Convention,[68] as well as prompted Australia to introduce the Pacific Solution policy, involving an offshore processing system for asylum seekers,[69] which has attracted much international condemnation for the widespread human rights violations of those detained.[70]

There have been many more examples in recent years where migrant smuggling has resulted in migrants' lives being lost,[71] often due to insufficient or even the absence of assistance or rescue by states, despite states bearing international obligations in this regard under different international law regimes, including human rights, refugee and maritime laws.

---

[63] UNCLOS, Article 98(2).

[64] For instance, in a 2011 incident, 63 irregular migrants died as a result of a "catalogue of failures" of Italy, Malta, NATO and two commercial fishing vessels in responding to distress calls, see Parliamentary Assembly of the Council of Europe (PACE) 2012.

[65] 1979 (as amended in 1998) 1403 UNTS, Article 3.1.1.

[66] Under the SAR Convention 'search and rescue region' (SRR) regime, see para 2.1.4.

[67] For more on the legal issues surrounding the incident, see Szablewska and Karim 2013.

[68] Maritime Safety Committee, 'Review of Safety Measures and Procedures for the Treatment of Persons Rescued at Sea', A.920(22), 2002. See also the non-legally binding guidance introduced by the IMO, 'Guidelines on the treatment of persons rescued at sea', MSC.167(78), 2004, Annex 34.

[69] For an overview of Australian refugee and asylum seekers policy, see Szablewska 2014.

[70] For example, HRC, 'Consideration of Reports by State Parties under Article 40 of the Covenant, Concluding Observations of the Human Rights Committee: Australia', UN Doc. CCPR/C/AUS/CO/5, 2009; Committee Against Torture, 'Concluding Observations on the Combined Fourth and Fifth Periodic Reports of Australia', UN Doc. CAT/C/AUS/CO/4-5, 2014; UNHCR, 'Monitoring Visit to the Republic of Nauru, 7–9 October 2013', 2013.

[71] See, for instance, UNODC 2018a.

53.3 Human Trafficking

Human trafficking (or trafficking in persons or trafficking in human beings[72]) is a global phenomenon that is as much a political issue as it is a social issue. Given its clandestine nature, its true extent will most likely never be known, but, according to recent estimates by the ILO and the Walk Free Foundation, there were 24.9 million victims of forced labour and sexual exploitation at any moment in time in 2016.[73] At the outset, however, it needs to be noted that "[d]ifferent patterns of trafficking emerge in different parts of the world along with different forms of exploitation",[74] and thus even though anti-trafficking responses need to be coordinated locally, trans-regionally and globally, different approaches are often required to address the geographical specificities.[75] Some studies, however, indicate that anti-trafficking efforts often fail to sufficiently account for these differences, which can lead to further marginalisation and stigmatisation of actual and potential victims and thus be ultimately ineffective.[76]

According to the recent global report by the UN Office on Drugs and Crime (UNODC), women and girls continue to be the main victims of trafficking (72%), trafficked mainly for the purposes of sexual exploitation, forced marriage and domestic servitude.[77] The most commonly reported form of human trafficking in the EU is trafficking for sexual exploitation, with 95% of registered victims being women and girls.[78] Thus, human trafficking is considered a gendered issue and a form of gender-based violence, as it disproportionately affects women.[79] However, the reporting of the trafficking of men has been increasing, and, according to the most recent estimates, over half of the victims of forced labour are men.[80]

Even though there is no 'universal' profile of a victim of human trafficking, so anyone can potentially fall victim to trafficking, there are a number of factors that contribute to or increase vulnerability to trafficking, including socioeconomic background, gender, disability, marginalisation, discrimination, age and education level. As is the case with irregular migration in general, poverty, unemployment, escaping persecution and conflict are the main 'push' factors driving people from their

---

[72] The latter term is used in the Council of Europe Convention on Action Against Trafficking in Human Beings (the Warsaw Convention) (2005) CETS No.197.

[73] International Labour Organization (ILO) and Walk Free Foundation 2017.

[74] UNODC 2018b, p. 11.

[75] On human trafficking in Australasia, see Szablewska 2018; in the European context, see Stoyanova 2017.

[76] See, for instance, Szablewska and Kubacki 2018.

[77] UNODC 2018b.

[78] European Institute for Gender Equality, 'Gender-Specific Measures in Anti-Trafficking Actions', 2018. https://eige.europa.eu/rdc/eige-publications/gender-specific-measures-anti-trafficking-actions-report. Accessed 28 August 2019.

[79] On the more nuanced approach to gender and 'gendering' of human trafficking, see Vijeyarasa 2015.

[80] UNODC 2018b.

home countries. On the other hand, employment opportunities, political stability and prospects for a better life in the destination (usually wealthier) country are the main 'pull' factors.[81] This makes migrants, in particular undocumented migrants, prone to exploitation and increases their vulnerability to being abused by unscrupulous recruiters, smugglers and traffickers.

A victim of trafficking might start as a person looking for legal, or otherwise, opportunities to migrate abroad but might end up in a situation of trafficking or akin to slavery. Their irregular legal status is key for keeping the victim from reporting to the local authorities due to fear of retaliation from the traffickers, fear of being deported by the authorities or the victim having low trust in law enforcement authorities. Thus, the line between an illegal migrant (e.g. through smuggling) and a victim of trafficking can be thin, and it can shift over time.

The global approach to human trafficking is based on four key pillars: protection (of victims of trafficking), prosecution (of offenders), prevention (by addressing vulnerabilities) and partnerships (between the different bodies and sectors of society at the national, regional, trans-regional and global levels). Additionally, in the context of the UN 2030 Agenda for Sustainable Development,[82] covering 17 goals and 169 targets, the international community has committed to end modern slavery by 2030 (specifically targets 5.2, 8.7 and 16.2). Moreover, the Global Compact for Safe, Orderly and Regular Migration, in Objective 10, calls for specific measures to prevent, combat and eradicate human trafficking in the context of international migration.[83]

A global initiative involving various stakeholders, including governments, business, academia, civil society and the media, was launched in March 2007, marking the 200th anniversary of the abolition of the trans-Atlantic slave trade. The UN Global Initiative to Fight Human Trafficking (UN.GIFT), through engagement with state and non-state actors, aims to reduce the vulnerability of potential victims of human trafficking and the demand for exploitation in all its forms, ensure a sufficient level of protection for victims, and safeguard the prosecution of perpetrators.[84]

53.3.1 Legislative Framework

Under the Trafficking Protocol, which is the main international instrument regulating anti-trafficking efforts worldwide,[85] state parties are called upon to reduce

---

[81] Ibid.

[82] For more information see https://sustainabledevelopment.un.org/?menu=1300.

[83] For more information see https://www.iom.int/global-compact-migration.

[84] For more information see http://www.ungift.org/.

[85] See also the Universal Declaration of Human Rights (1948) 217 A (III), Article 4; ICCPR, Article 8; CEDAW, Article 6; Convention on the Rights of the Child (CRC) (1989) 1577 UNTS 3, Article 35; Convention on the Rights of All Migrant Workers and Members of their Families (1990) A/RES/45/158, Article 11; see also the Convention for the Suppression of the Traffic in Persons and of the Exploitation of Prostitution of Others (1949) A/RES/317.

the demand for trafficked labour.[86] The Trafficking Protocol has one of the highest ratification rates and, as of September 2019, 174 member states have ratified or acceded to it, in addition to several states introducing domestic legislation to that effect. There are also corresponding regional instruments: the Council of Europe Convention on Action Against Trafficking in Human Beings (2005); the ASEAN Convention Against Trafficking in Persons, Especially Women and Children (2015); and the South Asian Association for Regional Cooperation (SAARC) Convention on Preventing and Combating Trafficking in Women and Children for Prostitution (2002), in addition to other non-binding principles, guidelines and model laws in other regions and globally.[87]

The definition of human trafficking in the Trafficking Protocol relies on three constitutive elements: the 'act' (including transportation, transfer or receipt), the 'means' (such as the threat or use of force or other forms of coercion) and the 'purpose' (including, *inter alia*, the exploitation of the prostitution of others or other forms of sexual exploitation, forced labour, slavery or slavery-like practices, and the removal of organs).[88] In the case of child victims, there is no requirement for the 'means' to be present.[89] As noted earlier, the 'consent' of the victim is rendered irrelevant when any of the means have been present or, putting it differently, valid consent needs to be informed and given freely, and thus the presence of duress or coercion or any other 'means' listed in Article 3(a) negates it as a basis for a criminal defence.[90]

Unlike for migrant smuggling, there is no requirement for national border crossing to have occurred; in fact, the UNODC estimates that, nowadays, the majority of victims of human trafficking are exploited within their country of origin.[91] Furthermore, the involvement of an organised group is not an element of the crime, even if in practice it might be the case, particularly in relation to trafficking in persons for the removal of organs.[92]

An often-held assumption is that traffickers rely predominantly on physical restraint to exploit their victims. In reality, however, emotional or psychological control is as, if often not more, effective. In a UNODC Issue Paper on the abuse of a position of vulnerability, it was noted that:

> [T]raffickers are becoming increasingly adept at recognizing and manipulating vulnerability to create dependencies, expectations and attachments. Indeed, the use of other more 'tangible' or 'direct' means such as force and violence was noted to have decreased in recent years, as more subtle strategies of abuse of vulnerability are refined.[93]

---

[86] Article 9.

[87] See, for instance, UNHCR, 'Recommended Principles and Guidelines on Human Rights and Human Trafficking,' UN Doc. E/2002/68/Add. 1, 2003.

[88] Trafficking Protocol, Article 3(a).

[89] Ibid., Article 3(c).

[90] See also UNODC 2014.

[91] UNODC 2018b, p. 41.

[92] UNODC 2018b.

[93] UNODC 2013, p. 84.

The concept of the "abuse of a position of vulnerability", one of the 'means', is considered the key element for the identification of victims. However, it lacks a clear definition; consequently, its varied interpretations, including in national legislation and jurisprudence, have caused some controversy.[94]

Under the Trafficking Protocol, the non-criminalisation of trafficking victims is not specifically addressed, but Article 2(b) instructs state parties to "protect and assist" the victims, which would indicate that states should adopt a victim-centred approach and refrain from criminalising the victim. To that end, in 2009, the Working Group on Trafficking in Persons, advising the Conference of the Parties to the UNTOC, recommended that:

> [W]ith regard to ensuring the non-punishment and non-prosecution of trafficked persons, State Parties should: (a) Establish appropriate procedures for identifying victims of trafficking in persons and for giving such victims support; (b) Consider, in line with their domestic legislation, not punishing or prosecuting trafficked persons for unlawful acts committed by them as a direct consequence of their situation as trafficked persons or where they were compelled to commit such unlawful acts...[95]

Following the implementation of the non-punishment principle in Europe,[96] it has now been accepted widely that trafficking victims should not be penalised or punished for illegal conduct committed while under the control or undue influence of the traffickers.[97]

53.3.2 Human Trafficking as a Form of Modern Slavery

Human trafficking is not a new phenomenon. In one form or another, abuses of vulnerability and the exploitation of others have existed throughout human history. In the past, slavery was a practice of exercising complete control over others, where it was legal for a person to be considered 'property' that could be sold and bought.[98] Eventually, slavery was outlawed by most nations. In 1926, under the auspice of the

---

[94] Further on this point in the context of sex work, see Bradley and Szablewska 2016.

[95] UN Conference of the Parties to the United Nations Convention against Transnational Organized Crime, Working Group on Trafficking in Persons, Report on the Meeting of the Working Group on Trafficking in Persons held in Vienna on 14 and 15 April 2009, UN Doc. CTOC/COP/WG.4/2009/2, 2009, para 12.

[96] See the Warsaw Convention, above n 72, Article 26; the EU Directive 2011/36 (5 April 2011), Article 8 which prohibits not only the conviction but also brining charges against the victim of trafficking; Organization for Security and Co-operation in Europe (OSCE), Addendum to the Action Plan to Combat Trafficking in Human Beings, PC.DEC/1107/Corr.1, Sect. IV, 2013, para 2.6.

[97] See, for instance, ICAT 2020.

[98] On the history of slavery see, for example, Bales 2004.

League of Nations, the Convention to Suppress the Slave Trade and Slavery[99] was passed, supplemented by the 1956 UN Convention on the Abolition of Slavery.[100]

Nevertheless, the same or similar forms of exploitation of vulnerability continue, including in the form of human trafficking. Human trafficking is seen as a form of 'modern slavery' or 'modern-day slavery', meaning that human trafficking is considered an exploitative practice akin to slavery, but not all forms of slavery are human trafficking. Arguably, there is a difference between slavery as was historically practised and modern-day human trafficking, as the latter does not require complete ownership but merely exercising control or undue influence over the victim once the other elements of the crime are present. However, in practical terms, the matter of 'demand' has been a key driving force in both practices.

The demand for cheap labour, services (including sexual services) and 'donors' in the context of the orphanage industry[101] is considered the main 'pull' factor. Given that, according to the ILO's estimates, some 64% (16 million) of the victims of forced labour worldwide are in the private economy,[102] addressing the demand requires involving businesses in anti-modern-slavery efforts. Certain industries, such as agriculture, mining, fashion and hospitality, are considered high risk for modern slavery practices throughout their operations and supply chains, making the private sector a key player in combating modern slavery. Further, under the UN Guiding Principles on Business and Human Rights (UNGPs),[103] business entities have a responsibility to respect human rights, including acting to prevent, mitigate and, when necessary, remedy such violations. Thus, a number of countries have been working with the business community to strengthen their domestic regulatory frameworks pertaining to modern slavery and other human rights violations in supply chains.

As there is no universal definition of 'modern slavery', states are free to define the term in their domestic legislation, as long as it does not contravene established obligations, including those under the Trafficking Protocol. A number of countries have introduced specific legislation dealing with modern slavery in supply chains, including in the United Kingdom (UK) the Modern Slavery Act (2015), in the US state of California the Transparency in Supply Chains Act (2010) and in Australia the Commonwealth (Cth) and the New South Wales (NSW) Modern Slavery Acts (2018),[104] as well as those with mandatory human rights 'due diligence' legislation,[105] like the French Duty of Vigilance Act (2017) and the Dutch Child Labour Due Diligence Law (2019).

---

[99] 60 LNTS 253.

[100] The Supplementary Convention on the Abolition of Slavery, the Slave Trade, and Institutions and Practices Similar to Slavery, 226 UNTS 3.

[101] On orphanage trafficking or 'paper orphaning', see Van Doore 2016.

[102] ILO and the Walk Free Foundation 2017, p. 10.

[103] UNHCR 2011.

[104] At the time of writing, the NSW Act is not yet in force.

[105] That is requiring companies to account for how they address their adverse human rights impacts; see also the UNGPs: Principles 15 and 17.

The UK was the first country to introduce a national modern slavery reporting requirement for large businesses, which was based on a sector-specific reporting regime introduced in 2010 in California. The UK Act consolidated a number of existing human trafficking and slavery offences and thus arguably made the application of the law more straightforward. The Act established an Independent Anti-Slavery Commissioner to support and encourage good practice in the prevention of modern slavery, as well as introduced a new statutory defence for (slavery or trafficking) victims compelled to commit criminal offences.[106]

The Cth Act in Australia was modelled on the UK Act and was the first national legislation providing a definition of modern slavery, which refers to all forms of trafficking in persons and debt bondage (as defined under Division 271 of the Criminal Code and Article 3 of the Trafficking Protocol); slavery and slavery-like offences (as defined under Division 270 of the Criminal Code), such as forced labour and forced marriage; and the worst forms of child labour (as defined under Article 3 of the ILO Convention[107]).[108] However, there are some differences among modern slavery legislation. For example, in contrast to the UK and the NSW Acts, the Cth Act does not provide for the function of an Independent Anti-Slavery Commissioner, nor does it prescribe penalties for non-compliance with the reporting requirements.[109]

Governments introducing legislation directly combating modern slavery supports the states' direct obligations in relation to human rights, as they have an obligation to prevent slavery (or enslavement), servitude and forced labour[110] committed by private individuals or entities, as well as to protect those at risk. The Working Group on Contemporary Forms of Slavery also pointed out that "transborder trafficking of women and girls for sexual exploitation is a contemporary form of slavery and constitutes a serious violation of human rights law".[111] Thus, human trafficking is a serious crime that can involve violations of human rights, ranging from freedom from slavery and forced labour;[112] protection from exploitation, violence and abuse;[113] freedom of movement;[114] the right to work and rights at work;[115] and the right to health.[116] Combating human trafficking requires a human rights-based approach, which entails shifting conceptualisation of the problem as only, or even predominantly, a national

---

[106] See http://www.legislation.gov.uk/ukpga/2015/30/contents/enacted

[107] ILO Convention (No. 182) concerning the Prohibition and Immediate Action for the Elimination of the Worst Forms of Child Labour (1999) C 182.

[108] Sec. 4.

[109] For an analysis of the Australia's Modern Slavery Act, see Nolan and Frishling 2019.

[110] See the European Convention on Human Rights (1950) ETS 5, Article 4; ICCPR, Article 8; American Convention on Human Rights (1969) OAS Treaty Series No 36, Article 6; African Charter on Human and Peoples' Rights (1981) 1520 UNTS 363, Article 5.

[111] Report of the Working Group on Contemporary Forms of Slavery, Recommendation 4, UN Doc. E/CN.4/Sub.2/1998/14, 1998.

[112] ICCPR, Article 8.

[113] ICCPR, Article 20; CRC, Article 19.

[114] ICCPR, Articles 12 and 13.

[115] ICESCR, Articles 6 and 7.

[116] ICESCR, Article 12(1).

security matter to a broader perspective requiring greater focus on the human rights protection of victims and development efforts.

53.4 Human Trafficking and Smuggling in Conflict

Armed groups, criminal groups and private individuals engage in human trafficking and smuggling during armed conflicts, and the nexus between these practices and financing terrorism and/or conflict has been increasingly examined and scrutinised.[117] Migrant smuggling is often a "stepping stone to human trafficking",[118] when the person cannot pay the smuggler or is trapped in economic exploitation,[119] and often results in people being sold for forced labour, which amounts to human trafficking.

Armed conflicts drastically increase the risk of human trafficking and other forms of modern slavery, as they exacerbate the vulnerability of people, in particular women, children, refugees and other displaced persons, to exploitation at the hands of traffickers or armed groups.[120] The recruitment and participation of children in war efforts, even though illegal,[121] is a lucrative industry and can be strategically rewarding for armed groups.[122]

At the UN level, the nexus between human trafficking and conflict was formally recognised in 2016 when the UN Security Council (UNSC) passed Resolution 2331, noting the particular vulnerability of women and children to human trafficking and recognising "the connection between trafficking in persons, sexual violence and terrorism and other transnational organized criminal activities" in conflict and post-conflict situations.[123] The following year, the UN Secretary General's Report on human trafficking in armed conflict situations echoed that women and children are

---

[117] See, for example, UN Security Council Counter-Terrorism Committee Executive Directorate, 'Identifying and exploring the *nexus between* human trafficking, terrorism, and terrorism financing', 2019. https://www.un.org/sc/ctc/wp-content/uploads/2019/02/HT-terrorism-nexus-CTED-report.pdf. Accessed 28 August 2019; also Report of the Special Rapporteur on contemporary forms of slavery, including its causes and consequences, 'Current and emerging forms of slavery', UN Doc. A/HRC/42/44, 2019, para 19.

[118] UN Security Council Counter-Terrorism Committee Executive Directorate, above n 117, p. 12.

[119] CARITAS, 'Trafficking in Human Beings in Conflict and Post-Conflict Situation', 2015, p. 6. http://antitrafficking.am/wp-content/uploads/2015/10/2research_action_trafficking_in_human_beings_and_conflicts_en_10_juin_2015_pdf.pdf. Accessed 28 August 2019.

[120] In the context of the Syrian conflict see International Centre for Migration Policy Development (ICMPD) 2015.

[121] See Additional Protocols I (1125 UNTS 3) and II (1125 UNTS 609) to the 1949 Geneva Conventions (1967), Articles 72(2) and 4(3)(c) respectively; Rome Statute of the International Criminal Court (Rome Statute) (1998) 2187 UNTS 90, Article 8(2)(b)(xxvi) and (e)(vii); CRC, Article 38(2); see also the Option Protocol to the CRC (2000) A/RES/54/263.

[122] See, for instance, UNODC 2018b.

[123] S/RES/2331 (20 December 2016), p. 1.

disproportionately affected by trafficking.[124] Subsequently, the UNSC adopted Resolution 2388 (2017), which emphasised member states' obligations to strengthen and support national investigations and prosecutions of human trafficking in conflict.[125] In addition, in its most recent global report on trafficking, the UNODC highlighted the correlation between human trafficking and conflict.[126]

Organised groups use human trafficking to terrorise and control local populations. As noted by the UN Rapporteur on Human Trafficking, human trafficking is used in a systematic manner against civilian populations as criminal groups "take advantage of the breakdown of the rule of law to carry out the dirty business of trafficking in persons and become more powerful and dangerous".[127] Examples include Sierra Leone's civil war, where women were trafficked to become 'bush wives'[128] or, more recently, the abductions and enslavement of Yazidi women, who were bought and sold in 'slave auctions', including on the internet, by the fighters of the Islamic State of Iraq and the Levant (ISIL, also known as Da'esh).[129] In Nigeria, Boko Haram, along with other terrorist organisations, have been found to traffic children for soldiering purposes and women for forced prostitution to provide sexual services to the fighters, as well as to generate income to finance these groups.[130] The same armed criminal groups are often involved in multiple transnational organised crimes involving the trafficking of various types of 'commodities', ranging from drugs and firearms to humans. In the case of Libya, armed groups were found to have profiteered from human smuggling and trafficking, which overlapped with weapons, petroleum and gold trafficking.[131]

There has also been growing cognisance that there is a link between sexual and gender-based violence (SGBV) taking place during conflict and conflict-related human trafficking for sexual exploitation. Even though not all forms of SGBV constitute human trafficking, the latter is an example of the former. There are, therefore, also correlations between the distinct legal regimes created to tackle these crimes. However, as international jurisprudence indicates, there is still some way to go before the nature and impact of human trafficking, and other forms of modern slavery, in armed conflict are fully addressed, especially in the context of SGBV.

---

[124] UNSC, Report of the Secretary-General on Trafficking in Persons in Armed Conflict Pursuant to Security Council Resolution 2331, UN Doc. S/2017/939, 2017.

[125] 2017, UN Doc. S/RES/2388.

[126] UNODC 2018b; see also UNODC 2018c.

[127] UN Special Rapporteur on Trafficking in Persons, 'Statement to the Security Council Open Debate on Maintenance of international peace and security: trafficking in persons in conflict situations', 2017. https://www.ohchr.org/en/NewsEvents/Pages/DisplayNews.aspx?NewsID=22431&LangID=E. Accessed 28 August 2019.

[128] See, for example, Coulter 2009.

[129] UN Human Rights Council 2016.

[130] See, for instance, United States Department of State, 'Trafficking in Persons Report – Nigeria', 2018.

[131] UNSC, Final Report on the Panel of Experts on Libya Established Pursuant to Resolution 1973, UN Doc. S/2017/466, 2011.

53.4.1 International Jurisprudence

Human trafficking is not codified as a separate offence in any of the statutes of current or past international courts or tribunals but instead has been linked to some of the established 'associated' offences. The Charters of the International Military Tribunals (IMTs) at Nuremberg and Tokyo recognised 'enslavement' as a crime against humanity.[132] The International Criminal Tribunal for the Former Yugoslavia (ICTY) also held that 'sexual enslavement' could be a form of crime against humanity.[133] The Special Court for Sierra Leone (SCSL) found in the case of the former Liberian president, Charles Taylor, that 'sexual slavery' constituted an international crime.[134]

The Rome Statute of the International Criminal Court (the Rome Statute) includes 'enslavement'[135] (defined, *inter alia*, as an exercise of power in "the course of *trafficking* in persons, in particular women and children")[136] and 'sexual slavery'[137] as a crime against humanity, as well as 'sexual slavery' as a war crime.[138] The first case put before the International Criminal Court (ICC) where charges of sexual violence were part of the indictment was the case against Germain Katanga, a Congolese militia leader.[139] However, even though there was evidence of rape and sexual slavery being committed, he could not be connected to these crimes and, ultimately, was acquitted on those grounds. In July 2019, the ICC found Bosco Ntaganda guilty of 18 counts of war crimes and crimes against humanity, including sexual slavery, committed in the Democratic Republic of the Congo between 2002 and 2003.[140]

However, even though the constitutive elements of international crimes, such as 'enslavement' and 'sexual slavery' (as defined in the Rome Statute) are often linked to human trafficking, the definition of human trafficking under the Trafficking Protocol is based on distinct legal requirements. Human trafficking under the Trafficking Protocol does not require transboundary crossing (as is often the reality in the context of conflict) or even for it to take place during an armed conflict (as is the case for war crimes), nor needs to be committed "as part of a widespread or systematic attack directed against any civilian population"[141] (the contextual element of crimes against humanity). Thus, as rightly pointed out by Piotrowicz, "[t]he true significance of classifying trafficking as a crime against humanity lies more in emphasising the gravity

---

[132] IMT Charter (Nuremberg), Article 6; IMT Charter (Tokyo), Article 5(c).

[133] *Prosecutor v. Kunarac, Kovac and Vukovic*, Case Nos. IT-96-23-T and IT-96-23/1-T, Appeals Chamber, 12 June 2002, para 515.

[134] *Prosecutor v. Charles Ghankay Taylor (Judgement Summary)*, SCSL-0 3-1-T, 26 April 2012.

[135] Article 7(1)(c).

[136] Article 7(2)(c), emphasis added.

[137] Article 7(1)(g).

[138] Article 8(2)(b)(xxii).

[139] *Prosecutor v. Germain Katanga*, ICC-01/04-01/07, 27 March 2017.

[140] *Prosecutor v. Bosco Ntaganda*, ICC-01/04-02/06, Trial Chamber VI, 8 July 2019.

[141] Rome Statute, above n 121, Article 7.

of the offence than in the practical matter of successfully prosecuting traffickers",[142] and whether occurring in times of peace or conflict.

Unsurprisingly, then, in a 2016 office policy paper, the then-ICC Prosecutor Fatou Bensouda identified human trafficking as one of the serious crimes under national law that her office wished to focus on.[143] In 2017, she indicated the possibility of investigating migrant smuggling and human trafficking in relation to the Libyan conflict, had the jurisdictional requirements been met.[144] More recently, she re-affirmed her desire to initiate a policy paper that would bring modern slavery within the Rome Statute legal framework.[145] Thus, there is scope in the future for human trafficking, and modern slavery more widely,[146] to be addressed more directly in international criminal law.

53.5 Conclusion

Even though global migration rates are considered to have been steady since the 1990s,[147] the number of undocumented or irregular migrants, as well as the forced displacement of people, is on the rise worldwide. Many of the irregular migrants do not fall under the established legal categories for protection, which exposes them to additional hardship or denial of assistance. Yet, most irregular migrants face dangers and human rights infringements, which requires inter-state and inter-agency cooperation, including better information and data sharing, as well as improving consistency and compatibility between international, regional and national legislation and law enforcement activities.

Human smuggling and human trafficking are part of mixed migration flows. They often happen along the same routes, there are a multiplicity of factors driving them and they are considered forms of transnational organised crime. However, despite the commonalities, there are differences, both practical and legal, between these two crimes, including in relation to consent, transnationality and the victim status in criminal justice responses (Sect. 53.1.1). Nonetheless, these two crimes are often conflated, including by law enforcement, courts and service providers, which often

---

[142] Piotrowicz 2012, p. 185.

[143] Office of the Prosecutor, 'Policy paper on case selection and prioritisation', 2016. https://www.icc-cpi.int/itemsDocuments/20160915_OTP-Policy_Case-Selection_Eng.pdf. Accessed 27 August 2019.

[144] ICC, 'Statement of the ICC Prosecutor to the UNSC on the situation in Libya', 2017. https://www.icc-cpi.int/Pages/item.aspx?name=170509-otp-stat-lib. Accessed 27 August 2019.

[145] Fatou Bensouda, 'Remarks at the 17th session of the Assembly of States Parties', 2018. https://www.icc-cpi.int/itemsDocuments/20181205-otp-statement.pdf. Accessed 27 August 2019.

[146] Note also the findings of the China Tribunal, a people's tribunal, on 17 June 2019, that forced organ harvesting committed against certain minorities in China constitutes a crime against humanity, see https://chinatribunal.com/wp-content/uploads/2019/07/ChinaTribunal_-SummaryJudgment_17June2019.pdf. Accessed 28 August 2019.

[147] See, for instance, the study by Azose and Raftery 2019.

leads to inadequate provision of support and assistance being offered to trafficked and smuggled persons who find themselves in situations of vulnerability.

The matter of person smuggling is a complex and multi-faceted problem, requiring global cooperation, but, as discussed in the example of maritime migrant smuggling (Sect. 53.2.2), this is challenging because of the often-conflicting concerns and interests. Even though the Smuggling Protocol offers a solid basis for combating the organised crime of smuggling and associated offences, it might be insufficient to deal with the current global migrant smuggling crisis. The 'human element' requires coordinated approaches that account for the specific context, including the fact that smuggling is often "an integral part of the refugee experience",[148] where desperation and necessity are largely the driving forces behind the migrant smuggling phenomenon, involving organised crime or not.

Human trafficking, like other forms of modern slavery, is an exploitation of vulnerability; thus, factors increasing a person's vulnerability, including (gender and other types of) inequalities, poverty and marginalisation, heighten the risk of trafficking. Addressing these vulnerabilities is key for supressing this crime, which at its root is a complex social problem. Despite the wider recognition of the non-punishment provision, whereby trafficking victims are not penalised for crimes committed while under the control or undue influence of the traffickers, trafficking victims are often denied protection and assistance and frequently are treated by authorities as 'illegal' migrants, which they are not.

Situations of conflict or post-conflict increase the risk of migrant smuggling and human trafficking, which are often used by organised criminal groups to finance terrorism. Women, children, people displaced internally by war, and refugees in formal or informal camps have been particularly targeted by traffickers and smugglers. The breakdown of the rule of law and the collapse of political, social and economic structures increase vulnerability to forced labour or sexual slavery and, in the case of children, to forced marriage and armed combat. In the aftermath of conflict, seeking justice for the victims of human trafficking through international criminal justice institutions, including the ICC, is viable but subject to it being linked to the established associated international crimes of 'enslavement' and 'sexual slavery' (Sect. 53.4.1).

The *problematique* of human smuggling and trafficking elucidates the need to enforce the principle that states not only bear international obligations in relation to state-sanctioned human rights violations but also have positive obligations to prevent and regulate the activities of private persons or entities whose actions might bring about such violations. Thus, legislative and policy responses to human trafficking and smuggling, even though often inconsistent across the different national and regional efforts, are nevertheless an important step to ensuring that those at risk, or already harmed in the process, of trafficking or smuggling are protected.[149] Moreover, states

---

[148] Grewcock 2010, p. 15.

[149] See, for instance, UNGA, New York Declaration for Refugees and Migrants, UN doc. A/RES/71/1, 2016.

should invest more effort in mitigating the wider socioeconomic drivers leading to, as well as caused by, human smuggling and human trafficking.

References

Azose JJ, Raftery AE (2019) Estimation of emigration, return migration, and transit migration between all pairs of countries. Proceedings of the National Academy of Sciences 116(1):116–122

Bales K (2004) New Slavery: A Reference Handbook (2nd Ed). ABC-CLIO, Santa Barbara

Bradley C, Szablewska N (2016) Anti-Trafficking (ILL-)Efforts: The Legal Regulation of Women's Bodies and Relationships in Cambodia. Social & Legal Studies 25(4): 461–488

Churchill R, Lowe V (1999) The Law of the Sea, 3rd edn. Manchester University Press, Manchester

Coulter C (2009) Bush Wives and Girl Soldiers: Women's Lives through War and Peace in Sierra Leone. Cornell University Press, Ithaca, NY

Financial Action Task Force (FATF) on Money Laundering (2018) Financial Flows from Human Trafficking. FATF, Paris

Gallagher AT, David F (2014) The International Law of Migrant Smuggling. Cambridge University Press, New York

Grewcock M (2010) 'Scum of the Earth?' People Smuggling, Criminalisation and Refugees. Human Rights Defender 19(3):14–16

Horwood C, Forin R, Frouws B (eds) (2018) Mixed Migration Review 2018. Highlights. Interviews. Essays. Data. Mixed Migration Centre, Geneva

Inter-Agency Coordination Group against Trafficking in Persons (ICAT) (2020) Issue Brief: Non-Punishment of Victims of Trafficking. https://www.unodc.org/documents/human-trafficking/ICAT/19-10800_ICAT_Issue_Brief_8_Ebook.pdf. Accessed 30 May 2020

International Centre for Migration Policy Development (ICMPD) (2015) Targeting Vulnerabilities: The Impact of the Syrian War and Refugee Situation on Trafficking in Persons – A Study of Syria, Turkey, Lebanon, Jordan and Iraq. ICMPD, Vienna

International Labour Organization and Walk Free Foundation (2017) The Global Estimates of Modern Slavery: Forced Labour and Forced Marriage. ILO, Geneva

International Organization for Migration (2011) Glossary on Migration, 2nd edn. IOM, Geneva

International Organization for Migration (2014) Fatal Journeys: Tracking Lives Lost during Migration. IOM, Geneva

International Organization for Migration (2016) Bay of Bengal and Andaman Sea Crisis Response. IOM, Bangkok

International Organization for Migration (2018a) Protection of Migrants at Sea. IOM, Bangkok

International Organization for Migration (2018b) World Migration Report 2017. IOM, Geneva

Klug A, Howe T (2010) The concept of State jurisdiction and the applicability of the non-refoulement principle to extraterritorial interception measures. In: Bernard R, Mitsilegas V (eds) Extraterritorial Immigration Control: Legal Challenges. Brill Nijhoff, Leiden, pp 69–102

Krogstad JM, Passell JS, Cohn D (2017) Five Facts about Illegal Immigration in the U.S. Fact Tank. Pew Research Institute. http://pewrsr.ch/2pqs0RS. Accessed 28 August 2019

Khaliq U (2015) Jurisdiction, Ships and Human Rights Treaties. In: Ringbom H (ed) Jurisdiction over Ships: Post-UNCLOS Developments in the Law of the Sea. Brill Nijhoff, Leiden, pp 324–361

Laczko F (2005) Data and Research on Human Trafficking. International Migration 43(1/2): 5–16

McDorman TL (2000) Regional port State control agreements: Some issues of international law. Ocean and Coastal Law Journal 5(2):207–225

Nolan J, Frishling N (2019) Australia's Modern Slavery Act: Towards Meaningful Compliance. Company and Securities Law Journal 37:104–126

Papastavridis E (2013) Issue paper: Combating transnational organized crime at sea. UNODC, Vienna

Parliamentary Assembly of the Council of Europe (PACE) Committee on Migration, Refugees and Displaced Persons (2012) Lives lost in the Mediterranean Sea: Who is responsible? PACE, Strasbourg

Piotrowicz R (2012) State's Obligations under Human Rights Law towards Victims of Trafficking in Human Being: Positive Developments and Positive Obligations. International Journal of Refugee Law 24(2):181–201

Schloendhardt A, Craig C (2015) Turning back the boats: Australia's Interdiction of Irregular Migrants at Sea. International Journal of Refugee Law 27(4): 536–572

Stoyanova V (2017) Human Trafficking and Slavery Reconsidered: Conceptual Limits and States' Positive Obligations in European Law. Cambridge University Press, Cambridge

Szablewska N (2014) Illegal immigrants, asylum seekers and Australia's international obligations: the debate goes on. Australian Law Journal 88(10): 707–714

Szablewska N (2018) Human Trafficking in Australasia. In: Piotrowicz R, Rijken C, Uhl BH (eds) Routledge Handbook of Human Trafficking. Routledge, Abingdon/New York, pp 78–92

Szablewska N, Karim S (2013) Protection, Solutions, Prevention and International Cooperation: Refugee Perspective. In: Islam MR, Bhuiyan JN (eds) Introduction to Refugee Law. Brill, Geneva, pp 189–213

Szablewska N, Kubacki K (2018) Anti-Human Trafficking Campaigns: A Systematic Literature Review. Social Marketing Quarterly 24(2): 104–122

Szablewska N, Ly R (2017) Regional collaborative responses to the global migration crisis: refugee law, human rights and shared state responsibility. Australian Law Journal 91(3): 186–197

Tejera AD (2011) The interception and rescue at sea of asylum seekers, refugees and irregular migrants. Council of Europe Parliamentary Assembly, Strasbourg

UN General Assembly (2003) Conclusion on protection safeguards in interception measures. UN, New York

UN High Commissioner for Refugees (2000) Interception of Asylum-Seekers and Refugees: The International Framework and Recommendations for a Comprehensive Approach. UNHCR, Geneva

UN High Commissioner for Refugees (2018) Global Trends: Forced Displacement in 2017. UNHCR, Geneva

UN Human Rights Committee (2004) General Comment No. 31 on Nature of the General Legal Obligation Imposed on States Parties to the Covenant. CCPR/C/21/Rev.1/Add. 1326

UN Human Rights Council (2016) "They came to destroy": ISIS Crimes Against the Yazidis, A/HRC/32/CRP.S

UN Human Rights Office of the High Commissioner (2011) Guiding Principles on Business and Human Rights. UNHCR, New York/Geneva

UN Office on Drugs and Crime (2004) Legislative Guide to the United Nations Convention Against Transnational Organized Crime and the Protocol Thereto. UN publication, Sales No. E.0000000

UN Office on Drugs and Crime (2010) Model Law against the Smuggling of Migrants. UN, New York

UN Office on Drugs and Crime (2013) Abuse of a Position of Vulnerability and Other Means within the Definition of Trafficking in Persons. UNODC, Vienna

UN Office on Drugs and Crime (2014) Issue Paper: The Role of 'Consent' in the Trafficking in Persons Protocol. UNODC, Vienna

UN Office on Drugs and Crime (2018a) Global Study on Smuggling of Migrants. UN Publication, Sales No. E.18.IV.9

UN Office on Drugs and Crime (2018b) Global Report on Trafficking in Persons 2018. UN publication, Sales No. E.19.IV.2

UN Office on Drugs and Crime (2018c) Global Report on Trafficking in Persons 2018, Booklet 2: Trafficking in persons in the context of armed conflict. UN publication, Sales No. E.19.IV.2

UN Office on Drugs and Crime (2018d) Migrant Smuggling in Asia and the Pacific: Current Trends and Challenges. UNODC, Bangkok

Van Doore K (2016) Paper Orphans: Exploring Child Trafficking for the purpose of Orphanages. International Journal of Children's Rights 24:378–407
Van Liempt I (2016) A Critical Insight into Europe's Criminalisation of Human Smuggling. Swedish Institute for European Policy Studies 3: 1–12
Vijeyarasa R (2015) Sex, Slavery and the Trafficked Women. Routledge, London/New York

Natalia Szablewska PhD GradCertAP, Dip(IHL), BSc(Econ)(Hons), LLB(Hons) is a legal scholar and social scientist with 20 years of experience spanning the public sector, governmental and non-governmental organisations and academia in five countries. She is Professor in Law and Society at The Open University Law School (United Kingdom), Adjunct Professor at the Royal University of Law and Economics (Cambodia) and Adjunct Fellow at the Humanitarian and Development Research Initiative, Western Sydney University (Australia). Her research is interdisciplinary in nature and she employs gender- and human rights-based approaches to examine issues relating to forced migration, modern slavery and, more widely, socioeconomic (in)equalities in post-conflict societies. Natalia has published widely for academic and non-academic audiences, and her academic work has appeared in leading journals and publishers in several disciplines.

Chapter 54
Organized Crime

Thomas Kruessmann

Contents

54.1 Introduction 1207
54.2 Origins of the Concept 1209
54.3 Construction of a Crime and Design of Criminal Law Offenses 1211
    54.3.1 The U.S. Experience 1211
    54.3.2 Modern Approaches to Constructing Organized Crime Offenses 1213
54.4 The Police View on Organized Crime 1218
    54.4.1 Introduction 1218
    54.4.2 Europol 1218
    54.4.3 Interpol 1220
    54.4.4 Other International Organizations' Voices 1221
54.5 "Leaks", Civil Society and Investigative Reporting 1222
54.6 Relevance of Organized Crime for International Conflict and Security 1223
54.7 Conclusion 1224
References 1225

Abstract Organized crime is a complex construct. Although there is now much agreement that it poses a threat to conflict and security, its manifestations are diverse and wide-ranging. The purpose of this chapter is to point out the historic origins of the concept and show how during the past two decades it was adapted to a variety of societal conditions.

Keywords Crime · Europol · Interpol · Investigative reporting · Organized crime

54.1 Introduction

In most countries, organized crime is considered to be an enhanced version of regular crime. The general idea is that it is a rational, commercially-driven type of wrongdoing, and that where it resorts to violence, threats or illicit influence (corruption), its overall goal is to maximize profit. Furthermore, it is committed not by single persons or groups of persons, but by highly professional enterprise-like structures.

T. Kruessmann (✉)
Global Europe Centre, University of Kent, Canterbury, UK

© T.M.C. ASSER PRESS and the authors 2022
S. Sayapin et al. (eds.), *International Conflict and Security Law*,
https://doi.org/10.1007/978-94-6265-515-7_54

So, in many ways it is described as a kind of "mega crime", infinitely more sinister, aggressive, and harder to destroy.

When approaching the topic of organized crime, it is important to distinguish the criminological definition from the one used in law to either define an offense or to build competences, e.g. in the area of criminal investigations. Last but not least, there is a colloquial use of the term that is neither scientific nor based on law, but a category of discourse in the media that is often alarmist and used to capture the attention of politicians and the police.

The connections between organized crime, international security and conflict are not evident at first sight. Unless imagining some James-Bond-type conspiracy of criminals attempting to wrestle control over the planet from governments, a large number of organized crime-related offenses takes place on the local level and targets the general population and various businesses. By undermining regular sectors of the economy, there is the fear that such crimes become a feature of the affluent lives of many in the global North. For instance, due to the aging of populations in Europe, it is increasingly attractive for "gangs" from neighboring lower-income countries to engage in cross-border property crime, targeting the elderly in their single houses and robbing whatever valuables can be found. If this happens in the community, a profound feeling of insecurity is engendered. Unlike bicycle theft which is also widespread in most cities, property-related housing crime stirs up the notion of being unsafe and renders the concept of organized crime committed by "others" (e.g. foreign gangs, "gypsies", migrants and refugees) credible. The Academic Advisory Group that accompanied the 2017 Europol Serious and Organized Crime Threat Assessment (SOCTA) aptly notes that "it is important to also recognise the lived experience of contact with criminality by European citizens, which may be removed from the headline grabbing dramatic event. Even 'organized crime'—a highly flexible construct—is often far more mundane than the dramaturgical killings and extortion that dominate the popular imagery."[1]

It is also hard to imagine how organized crime may affect international security. One plausible example is that the widespread fires in Siberia and the Amazon rain forest in 2019 are connected to criminal groups who use the fires to promote their commercial interests. The loss of forest wilderness and the actual effects of the fires on the climate are now stirring emotions worldwide, and it is not unlikely that the conflicts will spill over onto the inter-state level, e.g. the G7 or G20. Another example of possibly state-sponsored organized crime can be seen in the democracy movement in Hong Kong. It was rumoured that when young men dressed in white T-shirts started to beat up Hong Kong demonstrators, they were members of Chinese triads—organized crime groups—sent by the Communist Party from mainland China.

Organized crime is definitely not self-explanatory and the way it is constructed tells a lot about the uses that this construction is put to. The following will be an attempt to contextualize the concept and show its relevance for the wider notions of conflict and security.

---

[1] Comment by Academic Advisors, available at <https://www.europol.europa.eu/newsroom/news/crime-in-age-of-technology---europol's-serious-and-organized-crime-threat-assessment-2017>.

54.2 Origins of the Concept

The popular fascination with organized crime goes back to the United States' (U.S.) experience of the early 20th century when crime figures such as Al Capone created business-like structures and used corruption and violent intimidation to bring municipal governments under their control.[2] Even before the Prohibition era, cities like New York and Chicago were deeply under the influence of so-called mobsters, and bootlegging, illegal gambling, prostitution, drug sale etc. created fortunes in cash money. The profitability of this business was only increased when in the Prohibition era (1920–1933) the sale of alcohol was made illegal. When the Federal Bureau of Investigation (FBI) finally launched its counter-attacks, the ensuing battle reached epic proportions, aptly depicted in many Hollywood movie productions. In fact, without the Hollywood representation, organized crime would have remained a largely unknown episode of U.S. crime history. Interestingly, at the same time in Europe and in other parts of the world there were no such constellations to be observed. Urban centres such as Berlin, London or Paris, to name but a few, had their share of gangs, but nowhere did an image emerge that would be as powerful as the one in the U.S.[3]

This picture of organized crime is closely connected to some developments specific to the U.S. In the 19th and early 20th century, there was no other country that experienced immigration on a scale like the U.S. The massive inflow of refugees from hunger-stricken (Irish potato famine 1845–1849), impoverished and war-torn Europe created a fertile breeding ground for criminal gangs. Despite the idea of the U.S. being a melting pot of nationalities, immigrants often remained in tightly knit neighborhoods on the East coast and in Midwestern cities. Polish, Jewish, Irish and last but not least Italian communities established themselves at the fringes of the existing middle-class urban populations, and young members of the "families" soon began to venture into criminal businesses, using crime also as a means of moving upwards socially. At this early stage, ethnic belonging and family ties created an important asset for trust among gang members and safeguarded their operations against law enforcement control. Against this general background, Italian "mafia-style" organized crime became paradigmatic of what organized crime was meant to be: basically a cultural practice imported by immigrants (refugees), and first and foremost an adaptation of the centuries-old criminal practices prevalent in the impoverished South of Italy. Not surprisingly, one prominent way of understanding organized crime in the U.S. was to describe it as an "alien conspiracy".

When in the early 1990s the Cold War came to an end, the notion of organized crime experienced a sudden revival. U.S. and European attitudes in this era were distinctly different, but both combined to make the 1990s the era of organized crime. Its renaissance and depiction as a global threat lasted approximately until the terrorist attacks of 9/11. Since then Islamic terrorism has largely superseded organized crime as the crime threat number one.

---

[2] For more on the US background, see Woodiwiss 2003.

[3] On the history of organized crime in Europe, see the contributions in Fijnaut and Paoli 2004, at 21–238.

In the U.S., the end of the Cold War and the disintegration of the Soviet Union almost immediately created the image of "Russian organized crime" threatening the country.[4] As we know today, the *perestroika* years created an amalgam of company directors, semi-criminal entrepreneurs posing as directors of cooperatives, and young and ambitious Komsomol members who all participated in the "free for all" voucher privatizations that led to the concentration of enormous wealth in the hands of a few. But instead of referring to those contemporaneous criminal developments, the point of reference for "Russian organized crime" became the traditional criminal hierarchies, called *vory v zakone* (thieves-in-law) that emerged in the early Soviet Union and were characteristically formed under the system of Stalin repressions. Not entirely a folk myth, their importance was largely inflated and it appeared that they had lived through the Soviet Union only to be set free and roam the U.S. As if by reflective instinct, Russian-dominated neighborhoods of New York City such as Brighton Beach became the focal point of attention. Another focus was "Armenian organized crime" that was seen as encroaching upon the U.S. via the California émigré neighborhoods of Glendale. By comparison, "Georgian organized crime", which under President Shevardnadze was truly threatening Georgian statehood, did not make it onto the map of U.S. organized crime threats, simply because there were no pronounced Georgian diaspora communities in the country. It is also interesting to see that Canada, which had a very strong share of the Ukrainian diaspora, responded to possible organized crime threats in a much more relaxed manner.

In Europe, the demise of the Soviet Union came a few years after the establishment of the Schengen space of free movement in 1985. While the police of the then European Community (EC) Member-States had no significant cross-border capacities at the time and Europol was still years away from being created,[5] there was an increasing feeling of anxiety in the face of changes in the East and the perceived openness of the European continent. It was frequently argued that "Russian organized crime", equipped with the latest technologies and quickly connecting to their foreign counterparts, would have no problem manoeuvring the Schengen space while national police forces had to stop at the national borders. From among the EC Member States, Germany, due to its re-unification experience, was expected to have the most pronounced encounter with "Russian organized crime", but in reality the only visible sign of organized criminal activity came from the Vietnamese *gastarbeiter* who had been working in the GDR under more than modest circumstances and had developed a specialization in smuggling cigarettes. The large inflow of ethnic Germans from Kazakhstan, by contrast, did not trigger an organized crime wave. It was perhaps only the myth of Berlin and also of Vienna as a stomping ground for undercover agents where large Russian communities had settled and a fair share of organized crime activity was expected.

Emphasizing the transatlantic dimension in the renaissance of the concept of organized crime is by no means an accident. It is here where the perceived threat

---

[4] Finckenauer and Waring 1998.

[5] Although officially launched in 1999, Europol dates back to the Europol Drugs Unit (EDU) that was created in 1993.

created funding opportunities and spawned comprehensive research that materialized in a large number of handbooks and companions published in the first decade of the 2000s and beyond.[6] A lot of these handbooks pursue the approach of defining organized crime along ethnic lines. Therefore, there is now a rich treatment of all types of organized crime in all the different regions of the world. In some cases, there is a certain dynamic visible according to which the point in writing about organized crime becomes the identification of ever newer, ever more sinister organized crime threats, e.g. Nigerian organized crime when in fact the local crime scene in Nigeria had been outside the scope of interest of non-African criminologists for decades. So, without being too critical, there was certainly a bubble in research on organized crime around the turn of the century, and it is fair to say that the interest in the topic has been decreasing in the 21st century ever since. This can also be seen in such new terminology that connects organized crime to some other crime threat, such as "serious and organized crime" or "organized and emerging crime".[7]

Nowadays, the so-called migration crisis in Europe has refocused the attention on the lives of migrants. Migration to Europe is by no means a new phenomenon, and the failures of integration policies have helped to spawn new anti-foreigner populist movements in many countries. The "parallel worlds" in which migrants often live have been the subject of study for many years. Now, there is a renewed concern about "clan criminality", a term currently often used in Germany, to understand the role of far-flung "families" stemming mostly from the Middle East. While they engage in crime with a significant amount of societal harm, it is difficult to characterize them using the established categories of "organized crime". Very often, they clash violently over "family matters". While their origin, language and customs serve as a strong shield against police observation, they do not share the rational and calculating instincts often ascribed to organized crime figures. Arguably, in their raw energy, love of status and conspicuous consumption they are much closer to the original U.S. organized crime than to the sterile concepts of globally acting villains that we know of today.

54.3 Construction of a Crime and Design of Criminal Law Offenses

54.3.1 The U.S. Experience

From the earliest days of Al Capone, the difficulty for law enforcement was how to collect the evidence to prove the role of the criminal kingpin when the actual offenses were committed by lowly thugs. In the early 19th century, witnesses who

---

[6] See Allum et al. 2010; Allum and Gilmore 2011; Beare 2003, 2013; Paoli 2014; Reichel and Albanese 2014; Sheptycki 2014; Mitsilegas et al. 2019.

[7] Interpol 2017.

might point out the role of the criminal mastermind were often intimated by brute force or outrightly killed. Later, intimidation took on more subtle forms like threats to relatives. This still is a particularly efficient tool when considering that in the world of migrant families some relatives are still at home and their whereabouts known in the local communities.

Given the complex nature of organized crime, it is an ongoing challenge how to design criminal offenses that are capable of dealing with the problem that the criminal masterminds often pose as successful businessmen and there is hardly a way to connect them to the actual offenses committed by members of their organization. An indirect, yet ultimately successful approach was offered by U.S. law enforcement after many attempts of bringing direct charges against Al Capone: it was by going after his money and charging him with tax evasion. The same approach is still underlying modern money-laundering offenses: nowadays, it is sufficient to prove that money stems from a list of predicate offenses without showing that the person to be charged actually committed the offenses. But while tax offenses in the 1930s were relatively easy to prove, nowadays the hiding and layering of criminal money has turned anti-money laundering investigations into a game of hide and seek. Highly paid law firms are consulting their criminal clients into ever more sophisticated ways of moving money around the world. Investigators, even in the highly-specialized Financial Intelligence Units, are often at a disadvantage. Glimpses into the financial networks of organized crime have been offered recently by the various "leaks" of confidential material offered by anonymous whistle-blowers.

How to tackle organized crime figures directly, but still using an indirect approach, has been a point of debate in the U.S. since the 1960s. A major breakthrough was achieved when so-called RICO legislation was adopted. RICO stands for "Racketeer Influenced and Corrupt Organizations Act" and refers to the provisions that were introduced into federal law by the 1970 Organized Crime Control Act. Under RICO, a person who has committed "at least two acts of racketeering activity" drawn from a list of 35 crimes—27 federal crimes and 8 state crimes—within a 10-year period can be charged with racketeering if such acts are related in one of four specified ways to an "enterprise". The gist of RICO is that it is not necessary to prove in court the actual commission of the predicate offense, but showing that the person engaged in a pattern of "racketeering" activity over a certain period of time. The actual list of predicate offenses for "racketeering" include all standard offenses associated with organized crime. Later, a large number of States adopted state RICO legislation.

Although there was scepticism at first, RICO led to a large number of criminal convictions of all the major New York "mafia" families. Up until these days, it continues to be used as an attractive tool in the strategies of law enforcement. A number of countries worldwide have followed suit and adopted similar tools. The only disadvantage is that a RICO offense is highly complex and does not always meet the level of dual criminality that is often a precondition for mutual legal assistance.

Next to RICO, another constructive approach was first tried in the U.S.: criminalizing membership in a criminal organization without needing to prove the actual commission of a crime. The Continuing Criminal Enterprise Statute (commonly referred to as the CCE Statute or The Kingpin Statute) is a U.S. federal law that targets large-scale drug traffickers who are responsible for long-term and elaborate drug conspiracies. Unlike the RICO Act, which covers a wide range of organized crime enterprises, the CCE statute covers only major narcotics organizations. The statute makes it a federal crime to commit or conspire to commit a continuing series of felony violations of the Comprehensive Drug Abuse Prevention and Control Act of 1970 when such acts are taken in concert with five or more other persons. For a conviction under this statute, the offender must have been an organizer, manager, or supervisor of the continuing operation and have obtained substantial income or resources from drug violations.

54.3.2 Modern Approaches to Constructing Organized Crime Offenses

54.3.2.1 United Nations

Moving from the narrower to the wider, let us first look at how organized crime came to be defined by international law. Compared to the anti-corruption movement that originated in the U.S. and spawned a number of regional conventions, only to see the UN Anti-Corruption Convention adopted in the early 2000s, there was no similarly broad agenda in the area of organized crime. Organized crime in the U.S. was mostly seen as a domestic problem, with international dimensions primarily in the area of drug trade. For this reason, the U.S., as part of its "war on drugs", pushed the adoption of the UN Convention against Illicit Traffic in Narcotic Drugs and Psychotropic Substances (UN Anti-Drug Convention), to effectively become the first universal instrument to tackle one type of organized crime. The Convention was adopted in December 1988 and entered into force in November 1990. It currently has 191 parties.

Technically, the UN Anti-Drug Convention does not offer a definition of organized crime and does not call for the criminalization of organized crime *per se*. Although State-Parties recognize "the links between illicit traffic and other related organized criminal activities which undermine the legitimate economies and threaten the stability, security and sovereignty of States",[8] the obligation to criminalize certain types of behavior in Article 3 focuses on concrete activities, such as production, distribution, etc. But the Convention makes sure that the criminalization must also extend to the organization, the management or financing of any of the activities mentioned above.[9] Furthermore, subject to constitutional principles and the basic concepts of its legal system, State Parties shall criminalize "participation in, association or conspiracy to commit, attempts to commit and aiding, abetting, facilitating and counselling the commission of any of the offenses established in accordance with

---

[8] Preamble UN Anti-Drug Convention.
[9] Article 3(1) (a) (v) UN Anti-Drug Convention.

this article."[10] The criminalization provisions of the UN Anti-Drug Convention thus do not go as far as RICO or Continuing Criminal Enterprise concepts known from the U.S., but they extend the conventional provisions to the maximum. Organized crime in proper terms comes in as part of a list of optional aggravating circumstances, including among others

- the involvement in the offense of an organized criminal group to which the offender belongs;
- the involvement of the offender in other international organized criminal activities.[11]

From this somewhat restrained approach, the international community went in one step to the maximum of rolling out a universal convention committed to the fight against organized crime: the UN Convention against Transnational Organized Crime and the Protocols Thereto (UNTOC), signed in December 2000 and entered into force in 2003. Currently, there are 190 parties to this Convention (as of April 2020).[12] The three additional protocols supplementing the Convention are: (1) Protocol to Prevent, Suppress and Punish Trafficking in Persons, Especially Women and Children, (2) Protocol against the Smuggling of Migrants by Land, Sea and Air, and (3) Protocol against the Illicit Manufacturing of and Trafficking in Firearms, Their Parts and Components and Ammunition. It is *a priori* limited to "transnational" organized crime, defined in Article 3(2) UNTOC as a situation where

- it is committed in more than one State;
- it is committed in one State but a substantial part of its preparation, planning, direction or control takes place in another State;
- it is committed in one State but involves an organized criminal group that engages in criminal activities in more than one State; or
- it is committed in one State but has substantial effects in another State.

The limitation on "transnational" organized crime is arguably not a very serious one because in the specific understanding of the 1990s, as explained, the common expectation was for organized crime to be a transnational threat. Domestic crime would probably not even merit the label of organized crime, if it did not have a transnational element in it.

For the purpose of constructing organized crime offenses, UNTOC first gives a general definition of what it considers to be an "organized criminal group" (OCG).[13] It defines it as a "structured group of three or more persons, existing for a period of time and acting in concert with the aim of committing one or more serious crimes or offences established in accordance with this Convention, in order to obtain, directly or indirectly, a financial or other material benefit." A "serious crime" is defined as

---

[10] Article 3(1) (c) (iv) UN Anti-Drug Convention.

[11] Article 3(5) (a) and (b) UN Anti-Drug Convention.

[12] <https://treaties.un.org/pages/ViewDetails.aspx?src=TREATY&mtdsg_no=XVIII-12&chapter=18&clang=_en>. For a commentary, see McClean 2007.

[13] Article 2 lit. (a), (b) and (c) UNTOC.

any offense punishable by a maximum deprivation of liberty of at least four years or a more serious penalty. Finally, "structured group" is to be understood as a "group that is not randomly formed for the immediate commission of an offence and that does not need to have formally defined roles for its members, continuity of its membership or a developed structure". This definition can, of course, easily be criticized from a criminological point of view,[14] but as in any attempt to arrive at a universal definition, there need to be choices made. The given definition is more equivocal on what it does *not* require than what it considers important. For instance, in calling for the group of people to be "structured" it is not clear what is meant by this in a positive way. The definition only clarifies that it is not to be understood in an ideal-type requirement of being hierarchical and there does not need to be a membership basis. It should also not be created *ad hoc*, but then the structure does not need to be "developed". This type of openness leaves the legislator's will a lot of room for manoeuvre.

Building on this general definition of OCG is the criminalization provision in Article 5 UNTOC. It consists of two parts. In the first part,[15] it requires State Parties to choose one or two models of criminalization separate from criminalizing the actual criminal activity:

- agreeing with one or more other persons to commit a serious crime for a purpose relating directly or indirectly to the obtaining of a financial or other material benefit and, where required by domestic law, involving an act undertaken by one of the participants in furtherance of the agreement or involving an organized criminal group;
- conduct by a person who, with knowledge of either the aim and general criminal activity of an OCG or its intention to commit the crimes in question, takes an active part in:
  a. criminal activities of the OCG;
  b. other activities of the OCG in the knowledge that his or her participation will contribute to the achievement of the above-described criminal aim.

The first option is actually not about criminalizing an OCG at all; rather it extends criminality to the earliest beginning of the coming to an agreement to commit an organized crime-type offense. Normally, it is the concept of attempt that marks the earliest beginning of criminality, and national criminal law would, as a rule, require at least some preliminary act to avoid the criminalization of "evil thoughts". Asking State Parties to consider moving the earliest stage of criminality to an even earlier point is an approach that is not specific to combating organized crime. In a number of jurisdictions there have been calls for such changes in criminal justice policy, and they are usually tantamount to blurring the borderlines between criminal and police law. Traditionally, and for a number of good reasons, criminal law is reactive to some kind of wrongdoing, and it does not entail prognostic elements, as classical police law (in the German doctrinal sense) does. So, arguing that there is an increased danger in the

---

[14] The debate on what constitutes organized crime in a proper criminological understanding is probably never-ending.

[15] Article 5(1) (a) UNTOC.

mere agreement to commit an organized crime-type offense would create an offense under criminal law that is going against some of the most fundamental divisions in purpose and function between criminal and police law. Besides, it will raise issues of evidence that are difficult to solve, unless the parties to the agreement have made it in writing or kept notes about it.

The second option is the one that is most closely related to the idea of the continuing criminal enterprise. It criminalizes any type of conduct that presents an active contribution to any of the criminal activities of the OCG, provided that there is as a specific subjective element of either knowledge or intent. In the second part of Article 5 UNTOC, State Parties are obliged to criminalize the "organizing, directing, aiding, abetting, facilitating or counselling the commission of serious crime involving an organized criminal group".[16]

All in all, the criminalization requirements of UNTOC appear to be very tight, at least on paper. Problems of implementation may emerge, as common law jurisdictions gravitate more towards a conspiracy approach and civil law jurisdictions to a criminal association approach.[17] But it is still unclear how effective the criminalization provisions are actually implemented in the national legal systems. In the UN system, a review mechanism for UNTOC and its supplementary protocols was envisaged in Article 32 UNTOC, but unlike the Implementation Review Mechanism (IRM) for UNCAC, it took the Conference of Parties to UNTOC more than 10 years to come up with a mechanism. In fact, it was only in October 2018 that the Conference established the detailed legal basis.[18] The result is a severely watered-down version of monitoring: it is a purely intergovernmental, non-intrusive process that is non-adversarial and non-punitive. There will be self-assessment questionnaires for each of the instruments in the preparatory phase, followed by country reviews performed by two other states that are State Parties to UNTOC. The reviews will be based on a clustering exercise that combines in advance all provisions of the relevant instruments into certain topical clusters. For example, the first cluster will deal with criminalization and jurisdiction. While this UNTOC IRM is only taking shape, there are of course no results yet.

54.3.2.2 European Approaches

In defining organized crime for criminalization purposes, the blueprint delivered for the UNTOC approach did actually come from the EU. Based on the 1997 Action

---

[16] Article 5(1) (b) UNTOC.

[17] See the Legislative Guide for the Implementation of the United Nations Convention against Transnational Organized Crime at para 71, available at <https://www.unodc.org/documents/treaties/Legislative_Guide_2017/Legislative_Guide_E.pdf>.

[18] Resolution 9/1, see <https://www.unodc.org/unodc/en/organized-crime/intro/revew-mechanism-untoc.html>.

Plan to Combat Organized Crime,[19] the EU in a Joint Action of 21 December 1998[20] called upon its Member States to consider making it a criminal offense to participate in a criminal organization in the Member States of the EU. The definition of "criminal organization" largely coincided with the OCG definition later adopted by UNTOC, but it adopts a slightly different "mission statement": for the offenses to be committed, it suffices that they are an end in themselves and must not necessarily constitute "a means of obtaining material benefits and, where appropriate, of improperly influencing the operation of public authorities." In addition, Article 5 (2) Joint Action provides that "nothing in this joint action shall prevent a Member State from making punishable conduct in relation to a criminal organization which is of broader scope than that defined in Article 2(1)." This possibility for lawmakers to define a broader purpose of organized crime groups than just "obtaining a material benefit" (in UNTOC parlance) is quite important. In Austria, for example, there had been very contentious claims and litigation that organized animal rights activists could be charged with constituting an organized criminal group.

Almost ten years later, on 24 October 2008, the EU[21] adopted a Framework Decision "On the Fight against Organized Crime" that repealed the aforementioned Joint Action. The new Framework Decision throws its weight behind the UNTOC approach, obliging Member States to adopt the criminalization provision exactly as foreseen by UNTOC for the sake of facilitating mutual recognition of judgments and judicial decisions and police and judicial cooperation in criminal matters.[22] Nevertheless, Member States shall remain free to "classify other groups of persons as criminal organizations, for example, groups whose purpose is not financial or other material gain."[23] As the formal UNTOC IRM has not yet been launched, the EU subsequently commissioned a study on the implementation of the Framework Decision in the EU Member States. The results which were published in 2015 confirmed that with the exception of Denmark and Sweden, all Member States had transposed the key elements of the Framework Decision and introduced a self-standing offense of participation in a criminal organization and/or conspiracy to commit offenses.[24]

---

[19] Official Journal C 251 of 15 August 1997, pp. 1–16.

[20] Joint Action of 21 December 1998 adopted by the Council on the basis of Article K.3 of the Treaty on European Union, on making it a criminal offence to participate in a criminal organization in the Member States of the European Union. Official Journal L 351 of 29 December 1998, p. 1–3.

[21] Later in 2011, Council of Europe Recommendation Rec(2001)11 concerning guiding principles on the fight against organized crime reiterated the UNTOC approach for Council of Europe Member States. See <https://rm.coe.int/16804c0f57>.

[22] Para 3 Preamble, Council Framework Decision 2008/841/JHA of 24 October 2008 "On the Fight against Organized Crime". Official Journal L 300 of 11 November 2008, p. 42–45. See also the critical comments by Calderoni 2008.

[23] Para 4 Preamble, ibid.

[24] DiNicola et al. 2015.

54.4 The Police View on Organized Crime

54.4.1 Introduction

Normal police practice is usually far away from the concerns of international law. Arguably, when it comes to understanding organized crime, police practitioners have developed an "I know it when I see it" approach. They are not guided by dogmatic concerns, but show a hands-on attitude that is more or less the same in all countries. Police practitioners were also quite pragmatic in coping with the opening up of the Schengen space and cultivated close personal networks especially in border regions. It was rather politicians and public lawyers who superimposed cooperation frameworks like Europol. These arrangements do follow an administrative rationality and have the potential to evolve into effective organizations with functioning judicial oversight, but at the time and in the short run they profoundly complicated the day-to-day police work.[25] Nowadays, the situation around police cross-border cooperation has much improved, but judging by the experience of joint investigation teams,[26] cajoling national police forces into co-operation can still be widely observed.

In the following, we shall feature some of the key reports on the development of organized crime, mostly based on police information. Apart from Europol and Interpol with their access to aggregate data from national police forces, a number of international organizations have tried to "enter the ring" by producing their own brand of situation report or threat assessment, inviting police practitioners and academics to co-author. It appears that this competition for attention is another by-product of the hype around new threats. Over the years, this activity has died down and, in all fairness, only the Europol SOCTA has established itself as the most central source of information for an overall perspective. Detailed criminological research is needed, and there are still miles to go between the matter-of-fact police statistics and the highly nuanced research on crime as presented by the social sciences.

54.4.2 Europol

Europol, which on 1 July 2019 celebrated its 20th birthday, is now one of the main police resources in the fight against organized crime worldwide. In its analytical work, it focuses on crime threat assessments. Unlike some national police offices like the German *Bundeskriminalamt* which publishes annual organized crime situation reports,[27] the Europol threat assessments are pro-active risk-based analyses that aim to prioritize upcoming threats based on available data not only from the 27 Member

---

[25] Krüßmann 2009, pp. 410–412.

[26] Krüßmann 2020.

[27] See <https://www.bka.de/DE/AktuelleInformationen/StatistikenLagebilder/Lagebilder/Organisierte Kriminalitaet/organisiertekriminalitaet_node.html>.

States, but also from dozens of third countries with whom Europol has entered into agreements on information exchange. There are currently two types of threat assessments available:

- A "Serious and Organized Crime Threat Assessment" (SOCTA) was first published in 2013. It comes out every four years, so the current SOCTA dates back to 2017.[28]
- An "Internet Organized Crime Threat Assessment (IOCTA) was first published in 2011; since 2014 it appears annually.[29]

Due to the large amount of information, it is impossible to give a full overview of all SOCTAs and IOCTAs. Suffice it to have a critical look at the SOCTA 2017. When it was published under the title "Crime in the Age of Technology", the following key findings were highlighted:[30]

- More than 5000 international OCGs with more than 180 nationalities are currently under investigation in the EU.
- The number of OCGs that are involved in more than one criminal activity (poly-criminal) has increased sharply over the last years (45% compared to 33% in 2013).
- For almost all types of organized crime, criminals are deploying and adapting technology with ever greater skill and to ever greater effect. This is now, perhaps, the greatest challenge facing law enforcement authorities around the world, including in the EU.
- Cryptoware (ransomware using encryption) has become the leading malware in terms of threat and impact. It encrypts victims' user generated files, denying them access unless the victim pays a fee to have their files decrypted.
- Document fraud has emerged as a key criminal activity linked to the migration crisis.
- Document fraud, money laundering and the online trade in illicit goods and services are the engines of organized crime.

SOCTA 2017, like many other similar reports, is plagued by the issue of defining OCGs. While committing to the UNTOC definition, Europol nevertheless contends that "this definition does not adequately describe the complex and flexible nature of modern organized crime networks."[31] While it is hard to disagree, the matter-of-fact should be distinguished from the sensationalist. From the very invention of the concept of organized crime, it had the air of the "mega crime", of something ultimately more dangerous than ordinary crime because it was committed by

---

[28] See <https://www.europol.europa.eu/activities-services/main-reports/serious-and-organized-crime-threat-assessment>.

[29] See <https://www.europol.europa.eu/activities-services/main-reports/internet-organized-crime-threat-assessment>.

[30] <https://www.europol.europa.eu/newsroom/news/crime-in-age-of-technology---europol's-serious-and-organized-crime-threat-assessment-2017>.

[31] SOCTA 2017, 13.

enterprise-like organizations. Later, when in fact not so many hierarchically structured organizations were found, it was argued that OCGs were becoming even more dangerous because they were shedding their institutional features and turning into networks. This observation is surely not wrong, but it is not in the range of the extraordinary. Just as companies are turning into networks, with large numbers of employees working in a mobile way and using the office only as a "docking station", members of OCGs will go about their criminal goals not in the old ways of the 1990s. Absolute increases in numbers, even if communicated in good faith, can only be understood against the background of the methodology how the data are collected. And here, as the Academic Advisory Group rightly comments, artificial administrative and geographical boundaries are still preventing police from coming to a holistic understanding of areas of criminal activity.

In the area of specific crimes that are posing threats in the present time and more so in the future, the era of digitalization will of course lead to new dimensions of cybercrime. In the more detailed SOCTA 2017 sections, it becomes clear that organized crime is still ranging from the banal to the sensationalist. Organized property crime and fraud of all types are everyday phenomena of life, and it is not surprising that they remain in the spotlight. All types of illicit commerce, from smuggling of migrants to trafficking in human beings to trafficking in firearms and drugs are also not really new phenomena. What clearly stands out is a heightened understanding that there are three "engines" to serious and organized crime: document fraud, online trade in illicit goods and services, and money laundering. It is surely helpful to move away from sensationalist claims and to understand the "machinery" by which organized crime is run.

54.4.3 Interpol

As the world's largest and oldest international police organization, Interpol's activities are centered around three global crime programs: Counter-terrorism, Organized and Emerging Crime, and Cybercrime. To each of these areas it has devoted strategies covering the time period 2016–2020. The Global Strategy on Organized and Emerging Crime's overarching aims[32] are to enable the Interpol member countries to target and disrupt transnational criminal networks and to identify, analyze and respond to emerging criminal threats. To address this two-fold challenge, the Strategy outlines four interconnected "action streams":

- identification of criminal networks;
- illegal trafficking and illicit markets;
- enabling crimes and criminal convergence;
- illicit flows of money and assets.

---

[32] <https://www.interpol.int/Crimes/Organized-crime>.

It is interesting to see that the Strategy does not bother much with the definition of OCGs, but uses the term "criminal network" right away. It does so by outrightly stating that "traditional structures headed by powerful kingpins controlling niche crimes are increasingly replaced by loose, flexible criminal networks that shift operations and modify their business models based on opportunities, incentives, profitability and demand."

Within its Global Strategy on Organized and Emerging Crime, Interpol focuses on three projects to encourage national and international enforcement bodies to exchange operational data, best practice and lessons learned with a view to dismantling specific groups. The choice of projects is quite revealing of the areas in which Interpol sees a priority need for international collaboration:

- Asian organized crime;
- Latin American organized crime;
- Eurasian organized crime.

The information which is available on Interpol's website does, of course, not go very deep. But it provides an interesting snapshot on what member countries are willing to devote their resources to.

54.4.4 Other International Organizations' Voices

Among the major international organizations, the Council of Europe has had a chequered history in dealing with organized crime. Against the background of UNTOC, it adopted a Convention on Action against Trafficking in Human Beings in 2005 which entered into force three years later. Article 2 explains that the Convention shall apply to all forms of trafficking in human beings, whether national or transnational, whether or not connected with organized crime. It therefore goes beyond the UNTOC Supplementary Protocol in more than one way. By comparison, in the field of smuggling of migrants, the area of the second UNTOC Supplementary Protocol, the Council of Europe has been quite slow to leave its mark. With the migration crisis in Europe in full sway, it created a Working Group on the Prevention of Smuggling of Migrants only in 2017.[33] Naturally, the European Convention on Human Rights is applicable to the plight of migrants, but so far it did not help to counteract the criminalization of sea rescue operations which were depicted as facilitating the OCGs of smugglers.

Beyond immediate action in the field of international law, the Council of Europe has for several years produced its own series of Organized Crime Situation Reports. There are reports for 2000 and 2001 available on the internet,[34] and a third one for

---

[33] <https://rm.coe.int/090000168078b519>.

[34] For 2000, see <https://www.coe.int/t/dg1/legalcooperation/economiccrime/organizedcrime/Report2000E.pdf>, for 2001, see <https://www.coe.int/t/dg1/legalcooperation/economiccrime/organizedcrime/Report2001E.pdf>.

2004 is behind a pay wall. But this type of reporting has been discontinued. More recently in December 2014, the Council of Europe unveiled a so-called White Paper on Transnational Organized Crime.[35] Elaborated by an *ad hoc* Drafting Group on Transnational Organized Crime created in 2012, it sets out to identify areas in which the criminal justice response to transnational organized crime is still lacking and where the involvement of the Council of Europe could make a difference. Ultimately, it identified 5 key areas in which a more coherent approach, under the guidance of the Council of Europe, could address existing deficiencies:

- Enhancing international co-operation through networks;
- Special investigative techniques;
- Witness protection and incentives for co-operation;
- Administrative synergies and co-operation with the private sector;
- Recovery of assets.

It is not clear, however, whether there has been any follow-up action.

Last but not least, it should be mentioned that UNODC in 2010 published a Transnational Organized Crime Threat Assessment (TOCTA).[36] The report has obviously been a one-shot operation because there are no follow-up reports available. Compared to even the Europol 2013 SOCTA, it appears to be less discriminatory in highlighting the major crime threats. Rather, it is a broadband treatment of various types of trafficking (human beings, drugs, firearms, environmental resources, and counterfeit products), smuggling of migrants, cybercrime, maritime piracy and a quite innovative concluding chapter entitled "Regions under stress: When TOC threatens governance and stability".

54.5 "Leaks", Civil Society and Investigative Reporting

Recently, a new source of information has helped to shed light on the dimensions of organized crime: "leaks" like the so-called Panama Papers or Paradise Papers opened up a fascinating view into the world of offshores, beneficiaries and illicit financial flows. While using all these instruments is not necessarily illegal or even a sign of organized crime, the materials contain a large share of information on actual money-laundering practices. Beyond the one-time effects of the leaks which are often brought about by anonymous informers, the leaks also created a change in the journalistic profession. Investigative journalism has again become important, and there is now the International Consortium of Investigative Journalists[37] as a resource to analyze large amounts of data. Another important force in investigations

---

[35] <https://edoc.coe.int/en/organized-crime/6837-white-paper-on-transnational-organized-crime.html>.

[36] <https://www.unodc.org/unodc/en/data-and-analysis/tocta-2010.html>.

[37] <https://www.icij.org/>.

is the private network Bellingcat[38] which specializes in tracing online information. Finally, the Organized Crime and Corruption Reporting Project (OCCRP)[39] provides a platform for investigative journalism on organized crime that presents unrivalled stories on organized crime worldwide.

54.6 Relevance of Organized Crime for International Conflict and Security

Organized crime, due to the flexibility of the underlying concept, has been expanded and broadened to include ever new types of criminal activity to its portfolio. One assumption, however, has remained unchanged: it is described as an evil force outside the state, threatening and perhaps undermining it for strategic reasons, but in essence a kind of "underworld" as opposed to the "upperworld" of statehood and legality. Furthermore, from being a mere crime threat, it has been described as a threat to the state and to the security not only of single states, but of entire regions.[40] On the whole, the rise of the concept of organized crime cannot be explained outside the internationalization and globalization of crime threats in general.[41] Organized crime is thus a prime example of what in the social sciences is called "securitization", i.e. the process of state actors transforming subjects into matters of "security": an extreme version of politicization that enables extraordinary means to be used in the name of security.[42]

The approach of distinguishing a criminal underworld from an upperworld of statehood and legality is challenged by a strand in the research that is rooted in the critical social sciences. A number of researchers have devoted themselves to the question whether and under what circumstances the state itself or part of its executive structures can turn into criminal actors and how to distinguish "state crimes" from "organized crime" beyond the fact that the state is an organized entity *per se*. Starting from research into the origins of statehood and the understanding of states as "protection rackets"[43] or "stationary bandits",[44] there is an intriguing field of research that is basically concerned with classifying the ingredients of criminal states and the counterforces such as a strong sense of rule of law, independent courts, openness to human rights, an active civil society, etc. While it is not necessary to summarize this research strand in greater detail,[45] one important take-away point is that there are many shades of grey between upperworld and underworld, not least because the state

---

[38] <https://www.bellingcat.com/>.
[39] <https://www.occrp.org/en>.
[40] Carrapiço 2011, p. 19; UNODC 2010, 221.
[41] See Natarajan 2010 and Mitsilegas et al. 2015.
[42] Buzan et al. 1998.
[43] Tilly 1997a, b, p. 167.
[44] Olson 1993.
[45] See the overview by Karstedt 2014 with many references.

in its law-making function is controlling the definition of legality to a large extent. An example for this is the smuggling of migrants. While there is no human right to migration and the international governance of migration is still not very developed, the distinction between "irregular" and "illegal" migration is incumbent on each state and its criminal laws. Thus, any commercial structure facilitating the migration of people in an organized way is easily turned into organized crime and there are no rules in international law prescribing the limits to criminalization.

States are by no means victims of organized crime, but contribute to its expansion in a number of ways. One classical argument from the 1990s was that organized crime is adept in exploiting differences in regulation. Any unwillingness to join the harmonization train could thus easily be labelled as giving organized crime an entry point. In addition, the various offshore jurisdictions worldwide that allow for discreet corporate and banking services have spawned a multi-billion industry that is difficult to reign in. While it is true that illicit financial flows and money laundering are mostly on paper and do not necessarily bring organized crime structures to the countries concerned, the abundance of superyachts in the Mediterranean speaks a different language.

Recently, the debate around states inviting so-called investors and offering them citizenship or residence in exchange for a certain amount of investment in the country has finally reached the point that at least the EU has begun to take action.[46] Earlier reporting by the OCCRP had claimed that a good number of EU member states are effectively selling citizenship and residence without due controls, thus inviting shady figures and their families to come and live in the EU. Some of these schemes involve large profit margins for intermediaries, and there is little transparency about who is actually benefiting from the process. In this way, so-called "golden passport" and "golden visa" schemes have turned into powerful engines of inviting suspected criminals into the EU and profiting certain office-holders and people affiliated with them who are charged with implementing the programs. Needless to say that states in this way are actually contributing to the increase of insecurity.

54.7 Conclusion

Over the past decades, the spread of the concept of "organized crime" has acted as a Trojan horse in bringing down the defences of national criminal law. While the benefits of securitizing new criminal threats have remained vague and are clearly tangible only for police itself who have received an enormous boost in competences and capabilities, there is a profound loss of security on the level of individual citizens.

---

[46] Based on the EU Commission's Report "Investor Citizenship and Residence Schemes in the European Union" of 23 January 2019 [COM(2019) 12 final], a Group of Member State Experts on Investor Citizenship and Residence Schemes was created that is investigating the issue in the course of the year 2019. For more information, see <https://ec.europa.eu/info/files/report-commission-european-parliament-council-european-economic-and-social-committee-and-committee-regions-investor-citizenship-and-residence-schemes-european-union_en>.

The reason is that when securitizing certain threats, the international community (mostly represented by politicians and diplomats) is not interested in factoring in the entire system of counter-principles, checks and balances, limitations and practical proportionality rules that the national systems have developed in the course of the centuries. Securitization works by flagging threats and by creating "solutions" in the interest of global security, paying lip-service to the observance of human rights at best.

What emerges is a paradox situation. Criminal law in the national context is the strongest weapon that a state can wield. It is considered the *ultima ratio* of state intervention in the lives of citizens. And in order to be legitimate, it needs to satisfy the highest standards of legality, proportionality, internal consistency, and also due process in the way charges are brought, all of which have the goal of protecting the presumed offender against any undue state intervention. When "organized crime" becomes the driving force for changes in the architecture of the international security system, it takes advantage of all the achievements that liberal thinking has brought forward without adding any protective layers in return. Securitization thus enhances collective security only in the short-term: while the foundations of criminal law rest on the strength of the nations' legal systems, the increasing use of the internationalization strategy will subvert the strength of this very criminal law.

References

Allum F, Gilmour S (2011) Routledge Handbook of Transnational Organized Crime. Routledge, London

Allum F, Longo F, Irrera D, Kostakos PA (2010) Defining and Defying Organized Crime. Routledge, London

Beare ME (2003) Critical Reflections on Transnational Organized Crime, Money Laundering, and Corruption. University of Toronto Press, Toronto

Beare ME (2013) Transnational Organized Crime. Ashgate, Burlington

Buzan B, Wæver O, de Wilde J (1998) Security: A New Framework for Analysis. Lynne Rienner Publishers, Boulder

Calderoni F (2008) A Definition that Could Not Work: The EU Framework Decision on the Fight against Organised Crime. European Journal of Crime, Criminal Law and Criminal Justice, 16: 3, 265–282

Carrapiço H (2011) Transnational Organized Crime as a Security Concept. In: Allum F, Gilmour S (eds) Routledge Handbook of Transnational Organized Crime. Routledge, London, 19–35

DiNicola A, Gounev P, Levi M, Rubin J, Vettori B (2015) Study on Paving the Way for Future Policy Initiatives in the Field of Fight against Organized Crime: The Effectiveness of Specific Criminal Law Measures Targeting Organized Crime. European Union, Brussels

Fijnaut C, Paoli L (2004) Organised Crime in Europe. Concepts, Patterns and Control Policies in the European Union and Beyond. Springer, Dordrecht

Finckenauer J, Waring EJ (1998) Russian Mafia in America. Immigration, Culture and Crime. Northeastern University Press, Boston

Interpol (2017) Global Strategy on Organized and Emerging Crime. Interpol, Lyon

Karstedt S (2014) Organizing Crime. The State as Agent. In: Paoli L (ed) The Oxford Handbook on Organized Crime. Oxford University Press, 303–320

Krüßmann T (2009) Transnationales Strafprozessrecht. Nomos, Baden-Baden

Krüßmann T (2020) Besondere Formen der grenzüberschreitenden Zusammenarbeit, Vol 10. In: Hatje A, Müller-Graff P-C (eds) Enzyklopädie Europarecht, 2nd edn. Nomos, Baden-Baden

McClean D (2007) Transnational Organized Crime: A Commentary on the UN Convention and its Protocols. Oxford University Press

Mitsilegas V, Alldridge P, Cheliotis L (2015) Globalisation, Criminal Law and Criminal Justice. Theoretical, Comparative and Transnational Perspective. Hart Publishing, Oxford/Portland

Mitsilegas V, Hufnagel S, Moiseienko A (2019) Research Handbook on Transnational Crime. Edward Elgar, Cheltenham

Natarajan M (2010) International and Transnational Crime and Justice. Cambridge University Press, Cambridge

Olson M (1993) Dictatorship, Democracy and Development. The American Political Science Review 87:3, 567–576

Paoli L (2014) Oxford Handbook of Organized Crime. Oxford University Press, Oxford

Reichel P, Albanese J (2014) Handbook of Transnational Crime and Justice, 2nd edn. Sage Publications, Thousand Oaks

Sheptycki JWE (2014) Transnational Organized Crime. Sage Publications, Thousand Oaks

Tilly C (1997a) War Making and State Making as Organized Crime. In: Tilly C (ed) Roads from the Past to the Future. Rowman and Littlefield, Oxford, 165–192

Tilly C (1997b) Roads from the Past to the Future. Rowman & Littlefield, Lanham

UNODC (2010) The Globalization of Crime. A Transnational Organized Crime Threat Assessment. UNODC, Vienna

Woodiwiss M (2003) Transnational Organized Crime: The Strange Career of an American Concept. In: Beare ME (ed) Critical Reflections on Transnational Organized Crime, Money Laundering, and Corruption. University of Toronto Press, Toronto, 1–34

Prof. Dr. Dr. h.c. Thomas Kruessmann LLM (King's College) is co-ordinator of the Erasmus+ Capacity Building in Higher Education Project "Modernisation of master programmes for future judges, prosecutors, investigators with respect to European standard on human rights" for Ukraine and Belarus with the University of Graz. As President of the Association of European Studies for the Caucasus, he devotes himself to European Studies in the wider Caucasus region, including by acting as series editor of the book series "European Studies in the Caucasus". Prof. Kruessmann is a German-qualified lawyer with extensive legal practice in one of Vienna's leading law firms. He is founding director of the Russian, East European and Eurasian Studies Centre at the University of Graz (2010–2015) and Visiting Professor at Kazan Federal University (2015–2016). Beyond the Caucasus, his research interests extend to issues of comparative, European and international criminal law, gender and the law as well as corruption and compliance.

Part VI
Case Studies

Chapter 55
Cambodia

Natalia Szablewska

Contents

55.1 Introduction 1230
55.2 The Legacy of the Past 1231
    55.2.1 The Pre-1975 Period 1232
    55.2.2 The Post-1975 Period 1233
55.3 Post-Conflict Reconstruction 1234
    55.3.1 Peace Agreement 1234
    55.3.2 Post-UNTAC 1235
55.4 Extraordinary Chambers in the Courts of Cambodia 1236
    55.4.1 Structure and Composition 1237
    55.4.2 Overview of the Applicable International and Domestic Laws 1238
    55.4.3 Case Law 1241
55.5 The Current Justice System and Political Climate in Cambodia 1243
    55.5.1 The Justice System 1243
    55.5.2 The Political Climate 1245
    55.5.3 The ECCC's Contribution to the Development of the Rule of Law
           in Cambodia 1247
55.6 Conclusion 1250
References 1251

Abstract Since gaining its independence from France in 1953, Cambodia has endured nearly 30 years of conflict, followed by a precarious road towards recovery and socioeconomic development. Cambodia represents a complex case where historic and modern-day foreign interventionism coupled with geopolitical conditions contributed to the outbreak of a civil war, leading to the rise to power of the Khmer Rouge regime (1975–1979), bringing about mass killings and resulting in a ten-year foreign occupation. Cambodia's modern-day legal and political systems continue to be impacted by the brutal legacy of its past. From the 1990s onwards,

---

N. Szablewska (✉)
The Open University Law School, Milton Keynes, UK
e-mail: natalia.szablewska@open.ac.uk

Royal University of Law and Economics, Phnom Penh, Cambodia

Humanitarian and Development Research Initiative, Western Sydney University, Sydney, Australia

© T.M.C. ASSER PRESS and the authors 2022
S. Sayapin et al. (eds.), *International Conflict and Security Law*,
https://doi.org/10.1007/978-94-6265-515-7_55

the involvement of the United Nations, the dispensation of foreign aid and the establishment of the Extraordinary Chambers in the Courts of Cambodia, a hybrid court to try atrocities committed during the Khmer Rouge era, have had a positive effect on strengthening the rule of law and (re)building the legal and judicial system in the country. At the same time, these events have inadvertently contributed to the emergence and consolidation of the *ruling elite*, which, in turn, has weakened the democratisation process and stalled the advancement of the rule of law in Cambodia.

Keywords Cambodia · Cambodian law · Extraordinary Chambers in the Courts of Cambodia · Rule of law · Khmer Rouge · Transitional justice

55.1 Introduction

Cambodia offers a unique case of multiple conflicts—ranging from civil war and foreign intervention to protracted violence—that altogether lasted for nearly 30 years and led to over 2.5 million deaths.[1] After regaining its independence from France in 1953, the (first) Kingdom of Cambodia was led by Prince Norodom Sihanouk, and it benefited from the 1954 Geneva Accords, aiming to end the conflict in Indochina, which recognised Cambodia's neutrality and military autonomy. However, the internal struggle for power, widespread corruption and the Vietnam War contributed to Cambodia descending into a civil war in 1970, which lasted until 1975, when the Khmer Rouge, a military faction inspired by communist ideology, assumed power. Their demise in 1979 was facilitated by the Vietnamese invasion and resulted in Cambodia's occupation for the next ten years. Peace negotiations commenced in 1989, culminating in a peace accord signed in 1991 ending the Vietnam–Cambodia war; nonetheless, the civil war continued, with light fighting between 1989 and 1993,[2] which from 1993 until 1998 transformed into infighting between the different political factions seeking to (re)gain power and influence over the country. Even though this period in Cambodian history can be divided into five distinct periods, the reality of the internal situation combined with external influences under a complex set of circumstances makes it difficult to clearly delineate the boundaries of the overlapping and intermingling conflicts.

There is no denying that Cambodia has come a long way from being a war-torn country to a country taking steps on a road towards recovery and socioeconomic development. Cambodia managed to halve its poverty rate in 2011, exceeding its Millennium Development Goal poverty target,[3] which continues to steadily fall as

---

[1] Brogan 1998, p. 155.

[2] Even though the official ceasefire was reached in 1975, skirmishes between the Khmer Rouge supporters and government forces lasted until the late 1990s.

[3] World Bank (2018) 'Poverty has fallen, yet many Cambodians are still at risk of slipping back into poverty, new report finds'. www.worldbank.org/en/news/press-release/2014/02/20/poverty-has-fallen-yet-many-cambodians-are-still-at-risk-ofslipping-back-into-poverty. Accessed 9 September 2019.

economic growth continues to rise.[4] However, its human rights record and its quest for (political, social, economic and gender) equality remain dismal. Cambodia continues to be a country in transition, where 65% of its population is under 30 years of age,[5] which presents certain challenges to the country's labour market. It is ranked 146 out of 189 countries according to the United Nations (UN) Human Development Index,[6] as well as 162 out of 180 in the Corruption Perceptions Index,[7] which suggests that Cambodia's rule of law and democracy are still fragile, despite the 13-year long operation of the Extraordinary Chambers in the Courts of Cambodia (ECCC),[8] a hybrid tribunal established to try crimes committed during the Khmer Rouge period. According to the 2020 Rule of Law Index, measuring the strength of the rule of law, Cambodia ranks 127, which is far behind its neighbouring Thailand (71) and Vietnam (85), with only Venezuela ranking lower.[9]

This chapter begins by placing Cambodia's contemporary political and legal developments within the context of the mass atrocities committed in the second half of the 1970s, often referred to as genocide or simply *utopian madness*, as only then might it become possible to fully comprehend the current legal and socioeconomic developments in Cambodia. This is followed by focusing briefly on the post-conflict reconstruction efforts led by the UN through its various aid programmes, before turning attention to the establishment and operation of the ECCC. The final part offers an overview the current justice and political systems and outlines the ECCC's legacy in the development of the rule of law in Cambodia.

55.2 The Legacy of the Past

It is beyond the scope of this chapter to provide a full overview of the rich and complex history of what has been officially known since 1993 as the (second) Kingdom of Cambodia. In addition, the lack of written documentation of the early periods, along with many of the documents being destroyed in the conflicts that followed, makes it difficult to establish the exact facts or build an accurate picture of the past. However, it is important to place the current developments in Cambodia in their wider political and historical contexts.

---

[4] See, for instance, World Bank, 'Cambodia', https://www.worldbank.org/en/country/cambodia/overview#1.

[5] See, for instance, UN in Cambodia, 'About Cambodia', http://kh.one.un.org/content/unct/cambodia/en/home/who-we-are/about-cambodia.html.

[6] UN Development Programme 2018.

[7] Transparency International 2019.

[8] See ECCC, https://www.eccc.gov.kh/en/about-eccc.

[9] World Justice Project 2020.

55.2.1 The Pre-1975 Period

The history of Cambodia is conventionally associated with the creation of the Khmer (or Angkor) Empire in 802 CE, which was a powerful Hindu–Buddhist country in Southeast Asia that lasted for over 600 years. During its peak, between the eleventh and the thirteenth centuries, the Angkor Empire is believed to have been the world's largest preindustrial settlement.[10] The demise of the Khmer Empire by the fifteenth century is traditionally linked to the interventionism of foreign powers—a thesis that has been challenged by recent geoarchaeological studies offering an alternative explanation of a more gradual, "complex and protracted transformation".[11] Irrespective of the reasons for the Angkor Empire's decline, the past has been an important factor in the creation of Khmer identity, where Cambodia's once powerful status has been a source of pride and a powerful aspect of modern nation-building.[12]

Upon request from the Cambodian King, Norodom Prohmbarirak, Cambodia became a French protectorate within French Indochina in the late nineteenth century, which lasted for 90 years, with a short spell of Japanese occupation (1941–1945) during World War II. Cambodia regained its independence from France in 1953, which also marked the beginning of the troubled or *dark* period in its modern history. The Indochina Wars, in particular the Vietnam War (1955–1975), affected Cambodia and the neighbouring Kingdom of Laos and created conditions that contributed to the rise of communist ideology and the anti-American movement. Cambodia remained neutral in the war between the United States (US) and the Republic of Vietnam (South Vietnam) against the Democratic Republic of Vietnam (North Vietnam) until 1970, when a pro-American government (headed by General Lon Nol) was installed in Cambodia, overthrowing Prince Norodom Sihanouk, who went into exile in China until 1975.

Following the coup, the country became a republic, and a civil war erupted between the Republican government (supported by the US and South Vietnamese governments) and the Communist Party of Kampuchea (who later became known as the Khmer Rouge). As part of the Vietnam War, the US dropped more than 500,000 tons of bombs on Cambodia,[13] which resulted in nearly half of the population being displaced and driven to the cities[14] and a significant amount of farmland being destroyed. That period was also marked by accusations of rampant corruption and internal fighting for power, which led Lon Nol to resign and flee the country into exile on 1 April 1975. On 17 April, Phnom Penh fell to the Khmer Rouge. This also marked the beginning of an international armed conflict between Cambodia and Vietnam.[15]

---

[10] Evans et al. 2007.

[11] Pennya et al. 2018, p. 4871; see also Evans 2016.

[12] See, for instance, Yong and Chhoy 2000.

[13] Kiernan 1989.

[14] International Committee of the Red Cross 1999.

[15] ECCC, *Case of KAING Guek Eav alias Duch*, Trial Judgment, 26 July 2010, Case No. 001/18-07 2007/ECCC/TC (*Case 001*), pp. 63–64. Both countries officially recognised the existence of

55.2.2 The Post-1975 Period

Led by Pol Pot, who was educated in France and became a member of the Communist Party there,[16] the Khmer Rouge assumed power in 1975 and immediately started to introduce far-reaching policies underpinned by a communist/Marxist ideology to create an agrarian utopia or "radical communist community".[17] If 1970 was a turning point in the history of modern Cambodia, 1975 was a 'Year Zero' (*chhnam saun*), where the old culture and traditions were replaced by the new revolutionary culture.[18] This involved the mass forceable displacement of the population from urban areas to the countryside to create a classless agrarian society living and working in agricultural communes, which was induced by a gradual introduction of the collectivisation of land and the abolishment of land deeds, taxes, private property, schools, newspapers and religious practices. To that end, it also required breaking the traditional familial and community ties and pledging full allegiance to the *Angkar* (the 'Organisation' or 'Centre').

The Khmer Rouge policy relied on the concept of 'the enemy', in particular from 1977 onwards, pitting urban dwellers against peasant population, intellectuals against the uneducated, rich against poor, children against parents, and collectively against all those who did not contribute to the goals of the *Angkar* (i.e. the 'enemies' of the Revolution, *kmang*). Offences, whether economic or social, were widely defined; for instance, stealing food (to survive in the famine-ridden country) was considered counter-revolutionary.

The Constitution of Democratic Kampuchea,[19] promulgated on 5 January 1976, declared to "represent...and defend...the people's justice...the democratic rights and liberties of the people, and condemn...any activities directed against the people's state or violating the laws of the people's state" (Article 9) and proclaimed "complete equality among all Kampuchean people in an equal, just, democratic, harmonious, and happy society", defining men and women as "fully equal in every respect" (Article 13). Despite these commitments, over a million people died in less than four years as a consequence of the regime's policies,[20] including due to mass executions in the "killing fields", starvation, malnutrition or illness, and some 20% of property was destroyed.[21]

The fall of the Khmer Rouge was brought about by Vietnamese military intervention in late 1978. This was largely a reaction to the escalation of border clashes and

---

international conflict only from the end of December 1977. During that time there were also military skirmishes on the border with the Thai forces, but of much lower intensity.

[16] D. Chandler (1999) Pol Pot. *Time Asia Magazine*.
https://web.archive.org/web/20110203010225/http://www.time.com/time/asia/asia/magazine/1999/990823/pol_pot1.html. Accessed 9 September 2019.

[17] McLellan 1999, p. 137.

[18] This was a reference to the 'Year One' in the French Revolution. See also Ponchaud 1978.

[19] Signed 19 December 1975 (entered into force 5 January 1976).

[20] Brogan 1998, p. 155.

[21] Shawcross 1979, p. 222.

armed confrontation between the armed forces of the two nations, including Pol Pot's troops' incursions into Vietnamese territory and diplomatic relations being broken off between the countries in 1977. However, the roots of the animosity between the nations can be traced to the fifteenth century and, to a large extent, continues to exist today. Hanoi took control over Phnom Penh from the Khmer Rouge in January 1979, and a new pro-Vietnamese (and backed by the Soviet Union) government was installed in 1985, with Hun Sen as Prime Minister.

The long history of international interventionism and the legacy of the 1970s conflict can assist in explaining Cambodians' general distrust of the government and the legal system, which in the past was created simply to support the government and its brutal policies.[22] This, in turn, has had a continuous impact on post-conflict reconstruction efforts and the political and legal reforms that have taken place in Cambodia since.

55.3 Post-Conflict Reconstruction

The formal involvement of the UN in Cambodia started in the 1950s, with Cambodia joining the UN Children's Fund (UNICEF) in 1951 and becoming a member of the UN in 1955.[23] During the Democratic Kampuchea period, the UN's operation in the country was suspended. After 1979, following the fall of the Khmer Rouge, the international community and the UN started playing an active role in peace negotiations and bringing about a ceasefire, along with introducing the largest of their kind, at the time, humanitarian and political support programmes. Today, there are 16 UN programmes and funds, in addition to other UN Specialised Agencies and related organisations, operating in Cambodia.[24] It is also estimated that, after Rwanda, Cambodia has the highest number of non-governmental organisations per capita in the world.[25]

55.3.1 Peace Agreement

The UN Security Council considered the situation in Cambodia in early 1979, but any potential action of the Security Council was stalled by the disagreement between the five permanent members (the US, the United Kingdom, the Soviet Union, France and

---

[22] Luco 2002.

[23] See UN, 'Member states', https://www.un.org/en/member-states/.

[24] See UN in Cambodia, 'UN entities in Cambodia', http://kh.one.un.org/content/unct/cambodia/en/home/who-we-are/un-entities-in-cambodia-.html.

[25] R. Ven (2015) Cambodia prepares NGO law. *Khmer Times*. www.khmertimeskh.com/news/8200/cambodia-preparesngo-law. Accessed 22 May 2019.

China). It was thus left to the General Assembly to lead, for the next decade, the international community's efforts to withdraw foreign power from and restore peace in Cambodia, with the International Conference on Kampuchea being convened in 1981. In early 1982, in response to the massive humanitarian crisis, relief assistance for the hundreds of thousands of Cambodians displaced along the Thailand–Cambodia border was introduced via the UN Border Relief Operation (UNBRO), which, as it had no separate budget, relied on the support of donors, including the US, France, Australia, Canada and the European Commission.[26]

In 1988, representatives of the Phnom Penh government (the People's Republic of Kampuchea, led by Hun Sen) and Cambodian opposition parties (forming a coalition, the National Government of Cambodia, led by Prince Norodom Sihanouk) met informally in Indonesia, which eventually led to the Paris Conference in 1989. This time was marked by intense international diplomatic activity and Vietnamese troops gradually withdrawing from Cambodia as a result of financial pressures and extensive criticism from the international community.

The Paris Conference on Cambodia concluded with the Agreements on a Comprehensive Political Settlement of the Cambodia Conflict,[27] known as the Paris Peace Agreements, on 23 October 1991. The Paris Agreements established the UN Transitional Authority in Cambodia (UNTAC)[28] to ensure the implementation of the agreements, and its mandate related to human rights, civil administration, military arrangements and the maintenance of law and order, among others. The UNTAC's initial deployment started on 15 March 1992. UNTAC temporarily shared power with the different Cambodian factions combined into the Supreme National Council of Cambodia, which was "the unique legitimate body and source of authority in which, throughout the transitional period, the sovereignty, independence and unity of Cambodia [were] enshrined".[29]

55.3.2 Post-UNTAC

The mandate of UNTAC ended in September 1993, when the Constitution of the Kingdom of Cambodia (the Cambodian Constitution) was promulgated and the first democratic elections were held, with an astounding voter turnout of nearly

---

[26] Morey 2014, pp. 96–97.

[27] These included a Final Act and three instruments: The Agreement on a Comprehensive Political Settlement of the Cambodia Conflict; The Agreement concerning the Sovereignty, Independence, Territorial Integrity and Inviolability, Neutrality and National Unity of Cambodia; and The Declaration on the Rehabilitation and Reconstruction of Cambodia.

[28] See UNTAC, https://peacekeeping.un.org/sites/default/files/past/untac.htm.

[29] Paris Peace Agreements 1991, above n 29, Section III, Article 3.

87%.[30] The elections resulted in a hung parliament, with the royalist FUNC-INPEC[31] winning, followed by the Cambodian People's Party (CPP), led by Hun Sen, and monarchy being restored with Norodom Sihanouk as king. In 1994, the new government announced amnesty,[32] leading to thousands of Khmer Rouge guerrillas surrendering.[33]

From this point on, the focus of the international community shifted to post-conflict reconstruction and peace-building. The first UN Development Assistance Framework (UNDAF) was introduced in 2001, and, following the adoption of Millennium Development Goals (MDGs) in 2000, the Royal Government of Cambodia began to adapt the MDGs to the Cambodian context. In its second progress report on the implementation of the MDGs in 2003, the government reaffirmed that "[t]he efforts by the royal government to meet the [Cambodian MDG] targets constitute important steps toward the fulfilment of a number of its international human rights obligations".[34] Against this backdrop, a tribunal to try crimes committed during the Democratic Kampuchea period was established, which has been operating for the last 14 years.

55.4 Extraordinary Chambers in the Courts of Cambodia

An UN-backed hybrid tribunal, known as the Extraordinary Chambers in the Courts of Cambodia (ECCC) or Khmer Rouge Tribunal, was created through an agreement between the Cambodian government and the UN. The law on the establishment of the ECCC for the prosecution of crimes committed during the period of Democratic Kampuchea (the ECCC Law) was promulgated on 10 August 2001 and amended in 2004,[35] and the ECCC started its operation in 2006. By that time, however, many of the senior leaders had died, including Pol Pot, who passed away of seemingly natural causes in 1998 with no justice being sought against him.

The delay was caused by multiple factors. In 1997, the UN and the Cambodian government initiated a dialogue, after the UN received a request from the Cambodian Co-Prime Minister asking for assistance in bringing the responsible persons to

---

[30] Inter-Parliamentary Union 1993.

[31] Standing for: Front uni pour un Cambodge indépendant, neutre, pacifique et coopératif.

[32] Royal Government of Cambodia, The Law on Outlawing the Group of Democratic Kampuchea, 7 July 1994.

[33] It was not until 1999 that the Khmer Rouge ceased to exist, by which time its members defected, surrendered, got arrested or died, see *Cambodia Tribunal Monitor* (n.d.) Chronology of the Khmer Rouge Movement. https://www.cambodiatribunal.org/history/cambodian-history/chronology-of-the-khmer-rouge-movement/. Accessed 9 September 2019.

[34] Council for the Development of Cambodia 2003, p. 4.

[35] Law on the Establishment of Extraordinary Chambers in The Courts of Cambodia for The Prosecution of Crimes Committed during the Period of Democratic Kampuchea, (entered into force 27 October 2004), NS/RKM/1004/006 (the *ECCC Law*).

justice.[36] Yet, the negotiations were protracted and marked by disagreements, which prolonged the process. As a result, an agreement was not reached until six years later. The first question was on the most suitable form of justice mechanism, with a truth commission and tribunal being given main consideration.[37] However, there was concern whether a Cambodian court could guarantee independence, impartiality and neutrality. Despite the Cambodian government wanting to create a tribunal within its domestic justice system, the UN introduced a hybrid tribunal under its administration, asserting that the Cambodian judicial system was too weak to meet international criminal justice standards.[38]

55.4.1 Structure and Composition

The ECCC receives technical support and assistance through the UN Assistance to Khmer Rouge Trials (UNAKRT).[39] It is defined as *hybrid* because it applies both Cambodian and international law, as well as combines Cambodian and international judges, prosecutors and defence lawyers (with two-thirds being Cambodian staff and a third being UN and international staff). The official working languages of the tribunal are Khmer, English and French. The Chambers of the ECCC operate according to Cambodian procedural law,[40] and the ECCC has adopted Internal Rules to "consolidate applicable Cambodian procedures for proceedings before the ECCC", providing additional rules where the "existing procedures do not deal with a particular matter, or if there is uncertainty regarding their interpretation or application, or if there is a question regarding their consistency with international standards."[41]

The ECCC operates within the framework of a civil law system;[42] consequently, victims play a central role in the court's proceedings as civil parties and complainants.[43] The Victims Support Section (VSS) is key in ensuring effective participation by assisting victims with training and information regarding their

---

[36] UN Assistance to the Khmer Rouge Trials 1997.

[37] Ciorciari and Heindel 2014.

[38] Linton 2002.

[39] See UNAKRT, http://www.unakrt-online.org/.

[40] Agreement between the UN and the Royal Government of Cambodia concerning the prosecution under Cambodian law of crimes committed during the period of Democratic Kampuchea, signed on 6 June 2003, 2329 UNTS 117 (entered into forces 29 April 2005) (the *ECCC Agreement*), Article 12; the ECCC Law, above n 36, Article 33 (new).

[41] ECCC Internal Rules 2015, Preamble.

[42] Under the French protectorate and until 1975, a French-modelled civil law system operated in Cambodia, and some argue that Cambodian law combines influences from French, German and Japanese legal systems, see, for instance, Kong 2012.

[43] ECCC Internal Rules 2015, Rule 12.

rights and legal developments at the ECCC.[44] The VSS is also vested with the implementation of reparation initiatives and other non-judicial mechanisms.[45]

Also typical for a civil law system, judges play a more active role, compared with other international criminal tribunals, by leading the selection of witnesses, controlling the questioning of witnesses and often questioning witnesses themselves. The Co-Investigating Judges open a case upon request by the Co-Prosecutors, the facts of which are then investigated, and the case is either sent to trial or dismissed by the Co-Investigating Judges. According to Article 14 (new) of the ECCC Law, the super-majority must be applied for any decision to investigate, try or convict. This creates a system whereby any decision must be co-decided by both national and international Co-Investigating Judges.[46]

Any appeals of the closing order or any other decision of the Co-Investigating Judges can be heard before the Pre-Trial Chamber. Once hearings have been completed, following the presentation of the case by the parties, as well as the examination of witnesses and other evidence, the decision of the guilt or otherwise of the accused is handed down by the Trial Chamber. The Co-Prosecutors, the defence and the civil parties can appeal the decision of the Trial Chamber to the Supreme Court Chamber, with the decision of the latter being final.[47]

55.4.2 Overview of the Applicable International and Domestic Laws

The jurisdiction of the ECCC is confined to prosecuting "senior leaders of Democratic Kampuchea" or "those who were most responsible for the crimes and serious violations of Cambodian penal law, international humanitarian law and custom, and international conventions recognized by Cambodia".[48] However, neither the ECCC Agreement nor the ECCC Law provides a definition of "senior leaders of Democratic Kampuchea" or "those who were most responsible". To that end, the Group of Experts for Cambodia, established pursuant to General Assembly Resolution 52/135 (1998),[49] concluded that "any tribunal focus upon those persons most responsible for the most serious violations of human rights during the reign of [Democratic Kampuchea]...would include senior leaders with responsibility over the abuses as

---

[44] See VSS, http://vss.eccc.gov.kh/index.php?option=com_content&view=article&id=17%3Avictim-support-section&catid=14%3Avss&lang=en

[45] ECCC 2013.

[46] See also Jarvis 2016.

[47] ECCC Law, above n 37, Article 36 (new).

[48] ECCC Agreement, above n 42, Article 1.

[49] UN General Assembly 2018.

well as those at lower levels who are directly implicated in the most serious atrocities."[50] Thus, and in line with the jurisprudence of other tribunals,[51] establishing a threshold involves looking at the gravity of the crimes committed and the level of responsibility of the accused, which might include factors such as the level of participation in the alleged crimes and their rank or position.[52]

The burden of proof lies on the Co-Prosecutors to prove the guilt of the accused, and the Chamber must be convinced "beyond reasonable doubt" of the guilt to convict the accused.[53] However, it needs to be noted that the French version of Internal Rule 87(1) states that, as translated, "[i]n order to convict the accused, the Chamber must have the *intimate conviction* of the guilt of the accused."[54] The onus of proof on the Co-Prosecutors is the same in both versions, but the standard of proof differs between the English version ("beyond reasonable doubt") and the French version ("intimate conviction"), and these are not in fact the same. As the former concept derives from a common law system and the latter from a civil law system, their basis and aims differ. The Trial Chamber addressed this discrepancy in its first case:

> [T]he basis of this finding is expressed differently in common law and civil law systems, and within the different language versions of Internal Rule 87(1)…Despite these conceptual differences, the Chamber has adopted a common approach that has evaluated, in all circumstances, the sufficiency of the evidence. Upon a reasoned assessment of evidence, any doubt as to guilt was accordingly interpreted in the accused's favour.[55]

The Chamber's approach was reaffirmed in the second case (Case 002/01).[56] However, it remains debatable whether the favouring of the common law approach in relation to the standard of proof is fully justifiable, given that the ECCC's domestic legal framework is based on civil law.

The ECCC has the jurisdiction to try crimes of torture, murder and religious persecution under the 1956 Cambodian Penal Code; genocide; crimes against humanity; grave breaches of the 1949 Geneva Conventions; the destruction of cultural property during an armed conflict; and crimes against internationally protected people under the 1961 Vienna Convention on diplomatic relations. However, the scope of the ECCC's subject matter jurisdiction has caused some controversy.

According to Article 15 of the International Covenant on Civil and Political Rights,[57] the principle of legality provides that "no one shall be held guilty of any

---

[50] UN General Assembly and Security Council 1999, para 110.

[51] See, for instance, International Criminal Tribunal for the former Yugoslavia, *Prosecutor v Lukić and Others*, Decision on referral of case pursuant to rule 11bis with confidential annex A and annex B, 5 April 2007, Case No. IT-98-32/1-PT, paras 27–28.

[52] UN Security Council 2002, para 42; see also UN Commission on Human Rights 1999, para 14.

[53] ECCC Internal Rules 2015, Rule 87(1).

[54] Original text: "Pour condamner l'accusé, la Chambre doit avoir *l'intime conviction* de sa culpabilité" [emphasis added].

[55] Case 001, Trial judgement, above n 16, para 45.

[56] ECCC, *Case of NUON Chea and Others*, Trial Judgement, 7 August 2014, Case No. 002/19-09-2007/ECCC/TC (*Case 002*), para 22.

[57] International Covenant on Civil and Political Rights, open for signature 16 December 1966, 999 UNTS 171 (entered into force 23 March 1976) (the *ICCPR*).

criminal offences on account of any act or omission which did not constitute a criminal offence, under national or international law, at the time when it was committed". Thus, offences and modes of liability charged before the ECCC must have existed under either national or international law at the time of the alleged criminal conduct: that is, occurring between 17 April 1975 and 6 January 1979.

In the first case before the ECCC, the defence filed a motion to challenge the application of the 1956 Cambodian Penal Code as a source of applicable law, claiming that the statute of limitations of crimes granted under the Code had expired before the ECCC Law (Article 3 and Article 3 (new)) extended the limitation period for 30 years. The Trial Chamber's Cambodian and international judges agreed that in certain circumstances, such as in the case of a country's instability, the limitation period could be suspended for a certain period of time, but they could not agree (3–2) on whether, as argued by the national judges, given that there was no judicial system between 1975 and 1979, the statute of limitations did not run during that time[58] and hence whether the limitation period for domestic crimes had been extinguished before the adoption of Article 3 of the ECCC Law in 2001. As no super-majority was reached, the Trial Chamber was not able to "consider the guilt or innocence of the accused with respect to domestic crimes."[59] However, the international judges concluded that, as there was significant overlap between the elements of the domestic and international crimes charged against the accused, "this finding has had no impact on the Chamber's evaluation of the totality of the accused's criminal culpability, or on the sentence ultimately imposed".[60] The validity of Article 3 (new) under the principle of non-retroactivity was raised again in the second case, where the Trial Chamber held that it was not able to try domestic crimes in relation to the accused due to the deficiencies in the closing order to support domestic crime allegations,[61] and thus it was "unnecessary for the Chamber to otherwise determine the applicability of domestic crimes before the ECCC".[62] Thus, the validity of Article 3 (new) continues to remain uncertain.[63]

There was a further legal challenge in relation to the existence of crimes against humanity, as an international crime, at the relevant time. The Supreme Chamber, agreeing with the Trial Chamber, confirmed in the first case that in order for a charged offence to fall within the ECCC's subject matter jurisdiction, it must be either "explicitly or implicitly" provided for in the ECCC Law, as well as have existed under Cambodian or international law between 17 April 1975 and 6 January 1979.[64]

---

[58] Case 001, above n 16, Decision on the defence preliminary objection (statute of limitations on domestic crimes), 26 July 2010, para 16.

[59] Ibid., para 56.

[60] Ibid., para 55.

[61] Case 002, above n 58, Decision on defence preliminary Objection (statute of limitations on domestic crimes), 22 September 2011, para 15.

[62] Ibid., para 23.

[63] In the third (*Case 003*) and fourth (*Case 004*) case, the accused have been charged with offences under the 1956 Penal Code, see Sect. 55.4.3 below.

[64] Case 001, above n 16, para 98.

The Supreme Chamber did not consider the applicability of crimes against humanity under Cambodian law, as "it was not prohibited under [national] law at the applicable time".[65] Turning its focus to international law, the Supreme Chamber debated the historical development of the concept, concluding that "the atrocities committed by belligerents during World War I helped lay the conceptual framework whereby crimes against humanity became positive international law in the aftermath of World War II".[66] It further observed that the definition provided under Article 5 of the ECCC Law largely mirrors the definition in the 1945 International Military Tribunal (IMT) Charter.[67] National and regional courts have subsequently interpreted the 1950 Nuremberg Principles[68] underlying the IMT, established to try Nazi Party members following World War II, as reflective of customary international law prior to 1975.[69] The Supreme Chamber recognised that even though the IMT judgments did not constitute binding precedent for the ECCC, the IMT Charter and General Assembly Resolution 95(I) (1946),[70] affirming the Nuremberg Principles, established sufficient evidence of the existing principle of international criminal law[71] as reflective of the state practice and *opinio juris* at the relevant time.[72] Accordingly, the Supreme Chamber confirmed that the offence of crimes against humanity applied under the ECCC's temporal jurisdiction.[73]

55.4.3 Case Law

The ECCC has so far convicted three accused: in Cases 001 and 002 (severed into 0002/01 and 0002/02). The first ECCC judgment was against Kaing Guek Eav, alias Duch, former Chairman of the Khmer Rouge S-21 Security Centre in Phnom Penh. The Trial Chamber found the defendant guilty of crimes against humanity, including murder, extermination, enslavement, torture and other inhuman acts by inflicting serious bodily and mental harm, and grave breaches of the 1949 Geneva Conventions committed at the S-21 (Tuol Sleng) and S-24 (Choeung Ek and Prey Sar) Security Centres. Duch was sentenced to 35 years imprisonment, following the Supreme Chamber overturning the Trial Chamber's sentence of life imprisonment.

The second case was separated in 2011 by the Trial Chamber due to the number of issues, including the life expectancy of the accused and the complexity of the

---

[65] Ibid., fn 188, p. 51.

[66] Case 001, above n 16, para 102.

[67] Annex to the Agreement for the prosecution and punishment of the major war criminals of the European Axis, 82 UNTS 280.

[68] International Law Commission 1950.

[69] Case 001, above n 16, para 103.

[70] UN General Assembly (1946) Resolution 95(I) (1946), UN Doc A/RES/95.

[71] Cf Kelsen 1947, pp. 153–171.

[72] Case 001, Appeal Judgement, above n 16, para 93.

[73] Ibid., para 104.

indictment.[74] The first of the cases, known as Case 0002/01, was against Nuon Chea (former Chairman of the Democratic Kampuchea National Assembly and Deputy Secretary of the Communist Party of Kampuchea), Khieu Samphan (former Head of State of Democratic Kampuchea), Ieng Sary (former Minister of Foreign Affairs) and Ieng Thirith (former Minister of Social Affairs in Democratic Kampuchea). The latter two defendants passed away during the trial proceedings.[75] Those still standing trial were found guilty of crimes against humanity, namely murder, extermination, political persecution and other inhuman acts of forced transfer and attacks against human dignity. In the second trial, Case 0002/02, additional charges were put forward and, in 2018, the accused were found guilty of crimes against humanity of murder, extermination, enslavement, deportation, imprisonment, torture, persecution on religious, racial and political grounds, enforced disappearance, forced marriage and rape, and genocide of Cham and Vietnamese victims. The accused were sentenced to life imprisonment in both cases.

In 2009, the international Co-Prosecutor initiated Cases 003 and 004. Initially, there were two accused in Case 003: Meas Muth and Sou Met, but the latter defendant passed away in 2015 and the judicial investigation against him was terminated. The key allegations against Muth (alleged Central Committee Member, General Staff Deputy Secretary, and Secretary of Division 164 and the Kampong Som Autonomous Sector) include crimes against humanity, grave breaches of the 1949 Geneva Conventions and violations of the 1956 Cambodian Penal Code.

Case 004 was severed into three case files: 004 remains against Yim Thith (alleged Secretary and Deputy Secretary of various Zones and Kirovong District), with Case 004/01 being created against Im Chaem (alleged Preah Net Preah District Secretary and Northwest Zone Sector 5 Deputy Secretary) and 004/02 being against Ao An (alleged Central Zone Deputy Secretary and Sector 41 Secretary). In the case against Yim Thith, the key allegations are of genocide of the Khmer Krom and crimes against humanity, including persecution against the so-called "17 April people", East Zone evacuees, Northwest Zone cadres and their families and subordinates, as well as the Khmer Krom and Vietnamese, and other inhumane acts, including forced marriage, grave breaches of the Geneva Conventions of 1949 and violations of the 1956 Cambodian Penal Code.

In the case files against Im Chaem and Ao An, the Co-Investigating judges disagreed as to whether the accused were subject to the jurisdiction of the ECCC, as they were neither "senior leaders" nor the "most responsible" officials of the Khmer Rouge regime. It is not under dispute that the accused would not fall under the first category, but the definition of the "most responsible" individuals continues to pose a legal challenge, despite the recommendation of the Group of Experts (as discussed earlier).[76]

---

[74] Williams 2015.

[75] ECCC (n.d.) Accused person Ieng Thirith dies. https://www.eccc.gov.kh/en/articles/accused-person-ieng-thirith-dies. Accessed 9 September 2019; and ECCC (n.d.) Accused person Ieng Sary dies. https://www.eccc.gov.kh/en/articles/accused-person-ieng-sary-dies. Accessed 9 September 2019.

[76] See also DeFalco 2014.

The future of the pending cases remains uncertain. The Cambodian government, particularly Prime Minister Hun Sen, has not been supportive of extending the ECCC's operation beyond Case 002 to avoid "[the] war and chaos [that] could ensue if the court continued to pursue additional cases."[77] However, the ongoing public support for the ECCC might influence the government's position in this respect.[78] Beyond the cases tried and pending, the establishment of the ECCC has been widely perceived as a milestone development and indicative of Cambodia's commitment to providing accountability and to combating the impunity for crimes committed during the period of Democratic Kampuchea.[79] Moreover, the wider purpose of the tribunal, beyond facilitating justice, reconciliation and forgiveness, has been to create a model court for judicial reform in Cambodia and to advance the rule of law.[80]

55.5 The Current Justice System and Political Climate in Cambodia

In order to assess the legacy of the ECCC, its operation must be placed within the wider legal and political climate, which, despite the fall of the Khmer Rouge over 40 years ago, continues to shape modern Cambodia.

55.5.1 The Justice System

Not only did the "autogenocidal"[81] regime act in a manner suggesting that it assumed that it would likely never be held accountable for its atrocities, but it has also been estimated that only four to six lawyers survived the purges of the Khmer Rouge regime,[82] with others either managing to flee or being outside the country in 1975.[83] This

---

[77] Kuch N. (2015) Hun Sen warns of civil war if ECCC goes beyond "limit". *The Cambodia Daily*. https://www.cambodiadaily.com/news/hun-sen-warns-of-civil-war-if-eccc-goes-beyond-limit-78757/. Accessed 07 March 2019.

[78] See, for instance, Ly 2017.

[79] Cambodia is so far the only ASEAN country that has ratified the Rome Statute of the International Criminal Court, open for signature 17 July 1998, 2187 UNTS 90 (entered into force 1 July 2002).

[80] See Royal Government of Cambodia of the Third Legislature of National Assembly, Council for Development of Cambodia, Rectangular Strategies for Growth, Employment, Equity, and Efficiency in Cambodia Phase I, 2004.

[81] This concept assumes genocide committed by the same group as the victims, and in this case against the majority of Cambodian population. The term was used by the UN Special Rapporteur, Abdelwahab Bouhdiba, see UN Commission on Human Rights 1979.

[82] See also Donovan 1993, providing an estimate of "six to ten legal professionals remain[ing] alive in Cambodia" in 1979, p. 445; See also Neilson 1996.

[83] See, for instance, Postlewaite S. (1995) The law that cobbles the lawyers. *The Phnom Penh Post*. https://www.phnompenhpost.com/national/law-cobbles-lawyers. Accessed 15 June 2019.

was part of the wider policy targeting the middle class and intellectuals, including lawyers, doctors, teachers, journalists, artists and students. During the period of Democratic Kampuchea, the judicial system of Cambodia was dismantled, and even though Article 9 of the Constitution of Democratic Kampuchea stipulated establishing "people's courts", there were no courts, judges or trials.[84] Consequently, there was no functioning judicial system in place to ensure justice and procedural fairness—a gap that has been not easy to close since.

After the collapse of the Khmer Rouge, some lawyers returned from exile, but an entire generation was lost, which has had a dire effect on the legal profession in Cambodia, as well as in terms of the legal education and training of future lawyers, prosecutors and judges. The government of the People's Republic of Kampuchea, established in 1979 by the Socialist Republic of Vietnam and its Cambodian allies, began to restore a formal education system. This included reopening the *école de formation des cadres administratifs et judiciaires*, where training programmes were conducted in 1982 and 1986, but its success was thwarted by the lack of "training equipment…quality textbooks…permanent faculty, the poor quality of professional skills, low salaries, and so on".[85] Progress was slow, particularly in relation to reviving legal education, which was also because, typical for a socialist regime, the law was largely devalued.[86]

In the late 1980s, legal and judicial reforms accelerated, but they were largely crippled by the lack of resources and funding. Consequently, in the early 1990s, Cambodia was governed "almost exclusively by the executive branch of government, through the medium of executive degrees and regulations", including in the areas of substantive criminal law and ownership of property.[87] Unsurprisingly, then, Dolores Donovan, a US visiting professor in Cambodia in 1992, lamented that "the enactment of legislation [was] a matter of the highest priority, rivalled only by the need to educate and field enough legal professionals to render Cambodia's legal system operational".[88]

Today, there are 21 law schools in the country, with the Royal University of Law and Economics admitting in the 2018–2019 academic year nearly 5,500 law students across its Khmer-, English- and French-based Bachelor of Law degrees, which is the largest law faculty in Cambodia. The Bar Association of the Kingdom of Cambodia (BAKC) reportedly admits some 50 lawyers a year through an entrance exam and an unspecified number of applicants based on their legal background and experience.[89] Even though the number of law graduates is encouraging, few become legal counsels; consequently, there continues to be a shortage of practising lawyers and permanent legal services, which currently exist in only 14 of the 25 provinces.[90] There is also

---

[84] Chandler 2000.

[85] Peou 2000, p. 96.

[86] See Donovan 1993; Butler 1983.

[87] Donovan 1993, p. 448.

[88] Ibid., p. 449.

[89] Cited in International Bar Association 2015, p. 49.

[90] International Bridges to Justice n.d.

an under-representation of minorities and women in the judiciary, with the most recent statistics showing that only around 14% of judges and 13% of prosecutors[91] (including two judges and one prosecutor at the Supreme Court),[92] and 21.5% of lawyers[93] are women.

Progress with the legislative framework needs to be noted, in that more than 500 laws, including a criminal code, criminal procedure code, civil code and civil code of procedure, and more than 40,000 sub-degrees have been adopted since 1993.[94] The more recent adoption of the Code of Ethics for Judges (2014) and the creation of three additional regional appeal courts, in operation since April 2019, demonstrate that steps continue to be taken to progress the rule of law in Cambodia.[95] However, the inflation of legislation and regulations might lead to the weakening of the already weak legal enforcement, which, coupled with the lack of information dissemination among the legal profession and general public, could in fact make the judicial system even less effective. Arguably, it is not merely the number of new regulations being introduced, or even the commitments made to legal reforms, but rather strengthening the application and enforcement of the existing laws, along with raising awareness of the legal rights and capacity-building of the legal profession, that could bring about a tangible change to the operation of the rule of law in Cambodia. However, the legal developments in Cambodia cannot be divorced from its political climate, which has also been wrapped in the legacy of the past, as it has a key bearing on the legal and judicial developments in the country.

55.5.2 The Political Climate

Modern Cambodia is a constitutional monarchy based on a liberal multi-party democracy system.[96] Separation of the executive, legislative and judicial powers is granted under the Constitution to safeguard citizens' rights and ensure accountability of the government.[97] However, in practice, the executive holds significant influence over the other branches of the government.[98] The close proximity between the judiciary

---

[91] Mattes et al. 2020; see also 'Women in the law: enhancing leadership, opportunities, and knowledge' programme https://www.womeninlaw-kh.org/#/

[92] See Bar Association of the Kingdom of Cambodia, 'Name-list of Supreme Court judges and prosecutors' (in Khmer), https://www.bakc.org.kh/index.php/en/2020-02-02-04-05-54/2020-02-02-05-51-51#.

[93] Ibid., 'Statistics of lawyers' (in Khmer), https://www.bakc.org.kh/index.php/en/2020-02-02-04-06-24.

[94] See Cambodian National Assembly (in Khmer), http://national-assembly.org.kh.; see also a blog (in Khmer), collating data on Cambodian law, http://laws-page.blogspot.com/p/blog-page_26.html.

[95] See also Phun and Reyes-Kong 2016.

[96] Constitution of the Kingdom of Cambodia, signed 21 September 1993 (entered into force 24 September 1993) (the *Cambodian Constitution*), Article 1.

[97] Ibid., Article 51.

[98] Phun and Reyes-Kong 2016.

and the executive is not necessarily that surprising, given Cambodia's history of socialist rule, which typically relies on the unity of powers as central for the socialist legal and political theory.[99] That being said, some of the difficulties in developing the rule of law and independent legal profession have been linked with a "deliberate rejection of the concept of a state governed by the rule of law".[100]

The current government or ruling party has been in power for over 30 years: that is, it has had uninterrupted control over the longest period of peace in Cambodia's modern history since gaining its independence from France.[101] Starting with the liberalisation of the Cambodian economy in the late 1980s, there have been corresponding legal changes to facilitate the macro-economic restructuring, including in public-sector management and public and private finance reforms geared towards the growth of the private sector, trade and economic integration.[102] This required introducing legal reforms, in particular allowing for private ownership, which was abolished under the Khmer Rouge. With the enactment of the Land Law in 1992,[103] economic transition became possible. However, these rapid socioeconomic changes, along with nearly total reliance on foreign aid post-1979, required creating certain structures, influencing the emergence of and consolidating the "ruling elite".[104]

Prime Minister Hun Sen, a former Khmer Rouge cadre himself,[105] has praised his "win-win" policy, where the defecting Khmer Rouge were allowed to join the government, for bringing an end to the conflict in Cambodia and laying the basis for Cambodia's current social and economic growth, as "[p]eace is the main and the most important prerequisite for building economic foundation and social development".[106] There is no denying that the ruling party has demonstrated a commitment to addressing and solving some of the pressing societal issues, including through the Rectangular Strategy for Growth, Employment, Equality and Efficiency, a socioeconomic policy agenda currently in its fourth phase, and other initiatives, such as the National Social Protection Policy Framework (2016–2025), focusing on reducing economic and financial vulnerability.

Unsurprisingly, the government's political agenda on economic growth and development has earned the public's trust and support. However, the government's lack of tolerance towards activities deemed as provoking political instability or social unrest[107] and accusations of widespread corruption and nepotism,[108] as well as civil

---

[99] See, for instance, Donovan 1993; Furtak 1986.

[100] Ghai 2010, p. 42.

[101] See also Future Forum 2017.

[102] Sok 2010.

[103] Signed 10 August 1992 (entered into force 13 October 1992).

[104] Cock 2010.

[105] Encyclopedia of World Biography n.d.

[106] Office of the Council of Ministers 2019.

[107] Cohen et al 2016.

[108] Human Rights Watch 2015.

rights violations, including the freedom of expression and a free press,[109] have met with less-sympathetic responses, including internationally. Consequently, claims of shrinking democratic space in Cambodia have shifted Cambodia's foreign policy towards closer cooperation with China.[110] Chinese investment in Cambodia has been increasing rapidly and, undoubtedly, has contributed to economic growth and generated employment but has also caused growing public resentment due to the loss of livelihood, the exploitation of natural resources and increasing human rights violations, including workers' rights.

55.5.3 The ECCC's Contribution to the Development of the Rule of Law in Cambodia

The UN Human Rights Office of the High Commissioner (OHCHR) in Cambodia has assisted the ECCC in its commitment to promote the rule of law and build the legal profession "through creating a 'demonstration effect'—by evincing the independence and impartiality of proceedings and the credibility of its process—as well as by actively engaging in programs that ensure the effective transfer of knowledge, skills and practices from the ECCC to the national legal sector."[111] Thus, the legacy of the tribunal, beyond its primary goal, is seen in three areas: strengthening the rule of law within the society; developing and supporting legal education; and influencing the 'law in action' by, for example, running 'test' cases in the national system using the ECCC's jurisprudence or practice.[112]

The ECCC has been perceived, both domestically and internationally, as a model for courts in Cambodia[113] by raising legal standards, particularly in relation to victims' participation, upholding the rights of the accused and consolidating the roles of civil parties and reparations, as well as making "significant strides in raising expectations of the administration of justice in Cambodia, and promoting greater transparency and accountability in justice processes".[114] The positive impact of its

---

[109] For example, *The Cambodia Daily*, one of few independent newspapers in Cambodia, closed in September 2017 due to accusations of tax fraud, see *The Cambodia Daily* (2019) The Cambodia Daily to close after 24 years. https://www.cambodiadaily.com/cambodia-daily-close-24-years/. Accessed 15 May 2019.

[110] See, for instance, Future Forum 2016.

[111] Office of the United Nations High Commissioner for Human Rights (OHCHR) (n.d.) Promotion of ECCC legacy, n.p. http://cambodia.ohchr.org/en/rule-of-law/promotion-eccc-legacy. Accessed 25 June 2019.

[112] Ibid.

[113] See, for instance, Cambodian Deputy Prime Minister Sok An cited in ECCC 2012; Coughlan et al. 2012.

[114] OHCHR, above n 115.

work has been acknowledged by the Cambodian government, which, despite its opposition to continuing with Cases 003 and 004, endorses the ECCC as instrumental for the development of the rule of law and the wider legal reforms.[115]

However, beyond these affirmations, judging such success is very difficult, as there is no common definition of the *rule of law*, as it operates differently depending on the legal and political systems in place.[116] Thus, assessing the rule of law should go beyond studying state institutions or the national statutory framework to examining a nation's beliefs, norms, expectations, values and attitudes towards the rule of law.[117] In that sense, in common perception, the ECCC has largely contributed to its prescribed goals. A 2018 report on victim participation in Cambodia's transitional justice process, despite indicating a low level of factual knowledge of the ECCC and Cases 001 and 002, reported a high level of perception of the ECCC's independence (76.3%) and trust (90.2%), as well as a broad desire for the tribunal to continue with Cases 003 and 004 (80.2%).[118]

That being said, it is difficult to unequivocally establish the cause–effect relationship between people's perceptions and the legacy of a hybrid tribunal. A 2010 study of the ECCC found that support for the rule of law by the local population had been widespread in Cambodian society even before the trials began: "[t]he public support for the rule of law might have been a cause of the establishment of the ECCC rather than a consequence of it."[119] This can be explained in that those who are denied the protection of the rule of law have stronger aspiration for it, regardless of how that society accommodates and operates it in practice.[120] Further support for this thesis can be found in a 1999 country report on Cambodia, part of the International Committee of the Red Cross's worldwide consultation on the rules of war, where it was found that the three most common grounds on which respondents based their beliefs that atrocities committed against civilians were "wrong" included being against the law (56%), against religious principles (23%) and against human rights (21%).[121] In addition, the majority of the respondents (64%) noted that violations of international law should be punished, including by prosecuting the wrongdoers, with 54% of respondents favouring an international criminal court over a Cambodian court.[122] Thus, even prior to the ECCC's establishment, the Cambodian people had a strong sense of justice and a desire for the rule of law, despite the complete breakdown of the legal and judicial system during the period of Democratic Kampuchea.

---

[115] See, for instance, Royal Government of Cambodia, Council for Development of Cambodia, Rectangular Strategies for Growth, Employment, Equity, and Efficiency Phase III, 2013.

[116] The International Commission of Jurists (ICJ) regards the rule of law "as a living concept permeating several branches of the Law and having great practical importance in the life of every human being...", see ICJ 1959, p v. On the history and the development of the concept of the rule of law, see Tamanaha 2004.

[117] Ryan and McGrew 2016.

[118] Williams et al. 2018, pp. 63–65.

[119] Gibson et al. 2010, p. 380.

[120] Ibid.

[121] International Committee of the Red Cross 1999, p. 14.

[122] Ibid., p. 33.

There have also been voices pointing to a more limited impact of the ECCC's legacy, in particular its secondary goals. For example, according to a report by the Open Society Justice Initiative, the ECCC has had limited impact on Cambodia's culture of impunity for "the politically connected".[123] It is argued that, since the establishment of the ECCC, the development of the rule of law in Cambodia has proven illusory or modest at best.[124] This could be attributed mainly to the fact that the ECCC itself has encountered several challenges to upholding international standards of fair trials due to the lack of political will to fully support its work, the lack of sustained funding and the lack of a systematic programme of professional capacity-building, as well as being largely ineffective in preventing political interference in its key decisions, all of which would have consolidated the common perception that the legal institutions, including the judiciary, in Cambodia are not fully independent.[125] A similar conclusion was drawn by the then UN Special Rapporteur on the Situation of Human Rights in Cambodia, Surya Subedi, noting that:

> Overall, the situation of the judiciary in Cambodia has not fundamentally changed since 2010. Despite some progress, the pace of judicial reform remains very slow. The challenges are the same, namely lack of independence, problems of capacity, lack of resources, widespread corruption, all resulting in a lack of confidence by the general public in the ability of the court system to provide effective remedies when human rights violations occur.[126]

In 2015, the International Bar Association's Human Rights Institute published a report in response to Cambodia's new laws[127] establishing the executive's and the legislature's control over the judiciary, providing a gloomy picture of the issues facing the judiciary in Cambodia:

> Corrupt influence – political and financial – appears to be exerted at will over all judicial activities. Trainee judges are asked for bribes in order to enter onto professional training and those judges who are members of the incumbent Cambodian People's Party (CPP) are favoured for appointments and promotions. It is widely acknowledged that court decisions are dictated by financial and political pressures on judges: cases in which the authorities have an interest are consistently resolved in their favour and in other cases, the party able to offer the largest bribe to a judge or clerk will almost certainly win the case, regardless of the merits.[128]

The independence of the judiciary, which *nota bene* is enshrined in the Cambodian Constitution,[129] is critical, as it is "a pre-requisite to the rule of law and a

---

[123] Ryan and McGrew 2016, p. 12.

[124] Ibid.

[125] Ibid. See also Coughlan et al. 2012. Further on the legacy of the ECCC, see Cambodian Human Rights Centre and the Bar Association of the Kingdom of Cambodia 2013.

[126] Cited in Ryan and McGrew 2016, p. 52.

[127] The Law on the Organization and Functioning of the Supreme Council of the Magistracy; The Law on the Status of Judges and Prosecutors; and The Law on the Organization and Functioning of the Courts, which were passed by the National Assembly on 23 May 2014, see also *Radio Free Asia* (2014) Cambodia's Parliament passes laws "threatening judicial independence". www.rfa.org/english/news/cambodia/laws-05232014201001.html. Accessed 22 May 2019

[128] International Bar Association 2015, p. 7.

[129] Article 128 (new) states that "[t]he Judicial power shall be an independent power".

fundamental guarantee of a fair trial".[130] Thus, it is troubling not only that the judiciary in Cambodia is not truly independent but also that this lack of independence infringes on the further development of the rule of law and the administration of justice in Cambodia.

Considering current developments in the country, major steps have been taken towards creating a more *just* legal and judicial system, which undoubtedly can be attributed to the work of the ECCC. However, Cambodia is an example of a post-conflict country where the *legal* transformation has been less linear and, subsequently, the durability of the rule of law and legal legacy efforts, despite the progress being made, continue to be inadequate.

55.6 Conclusion

The brutal legacy of the past continues to unfold in Cambodia today. Multiple conflicts of different types ravaged the country for nearly 30 years after it gained independence from France in the early 1950s. Even though the civil war under the Khmer Rouge regime ended nearly 40 years ago, Cambodia continues to be a country in transition: transitional justice processes, including the ECCC, remain in operation, and it continues on a path of recovery and socioeconomic development.

The role of international law and international institutions has been critical in (re)building the rule of law and the administration of justice in Cambodia, and it "remains a country profoundly influenced and shaped by the international community".[131] With the establishment of the ECCC, judicial reforms and capacity-building of the legal profession have accelerated. In 2014, the UN Special Rapporteur on the Independence of Judges and Lawyers, Gabriela Knaul, commended "the efforts made by Cambodia to promote judicial reforms".[132] However, the independence of the judiciary in Cambodia has been curtailed by laws passed in 2014 that provide wide-reaching control to the executive and the legislature over the judiciary (see Sect. 55.5), despite the Cambodian Constitution protecting their separation.

Some of these issues could be explained by Cambodia's history, as laws and courts were abolished during the reign of the Khmer Rouge, and it was only in 1994 that a law on the judiciary was promulgated. However, they could also be seen as part of a wider policy to stronghold the power by the ruling party, not only over the judiciary but over every sector of society. The ruling party has been in power for over 30 years and has been accused of maintaining power through intimidation and repression, leading it to be accused of being an "autocracy"[133] or "increasingly dictatorial".[134] Allegations of corruption and repressions and abuses of human rights, including undermining

---

[130] UN Office on Drugs and Crime 2002, Value 1: Independence, p. 3.
[131] International Bar Association 2015, p. 67.
[132] Knaul 2014, p. 4.
[133] International Bar Association 2015.
[134] Human Rights Watch 2018.

the freedom of expression, a free press and the right to peaceful assembly, have become widely reported. In the long term, even if relative peace has been secured, the direction taken by the government will affect Cambodia's future.

The ECCC has played a major role in shaping Cambodia's legal framework; however, it has faced its share of criticism, with the key one being that only two cases have reached the trial phase, despite it being in operation since 2006 and costing nearly US$300 million.[135] Thus, unsurprisingly, the question of *has it been worth it?* is often invoked. Moreover, the ECCC has faced some similar issues as the rest of the judiciary in Cambodia, or, rather, it has not been able to shield itself from the vices that it has been vested to tackle, including allegations of the executive, or the international community, "routinely attempt[ing] to influence" its work.[136] Thus, even though the ECCC's legacy must be acknowledged, the extent to which it has fulfilled its goals, both primary and secondary, particularly in relation to strengthening the rule of law and capacity-building of the legal profession in Cambodia, might in fact be more modest than had been hoped.

Postscript

In mid-2020 the Supreme Court Chamber of the ECCC decided to terminate Case 004/02 and, at the end of 2021, terminated Case 003 and Case 004 due to the absence of enforceable indictments.

References

Brogan P (1998) World conflicts. The Scarecrow Press Inc., Lanham, Maryland
Butler WE (1983) Soviet law. Butterworths, London
Cambodian Human Rights Centre and the Bar Association of the Kingdom of Cambodia (2013) Implementation of the ECCC legacies for domestic legal and judicial reform. Phnom Penh
Chandler D (2000) Voices from S-21: Terror and history in Pol Pot's secret prison. University of California Press, California
Ciorciari J D, Heindel A (2014) Hybrid justice: The Extraordinary Chambers in the Courts of Cambodia. University of Michigan Press, Ann Arbor
Cock AR (2010) External actors and the relative autonomy of the ruling elite in post-UNTAC Cambodia. Journal of Southeast Asian Studies 41(2):241-265
Cohen D, Tan K, Nababan A, Reyes-Kong FSD (eds) (2016) Update on the rule of law for human rights in ASEAN: The path to integration. Human Rights Resource Center, Indonesia
Coughlan J, Ghouse S, Smith R (2012) The legacy of the Khmer Rouge Tribunal: Maintaining the status quo of Cambodia's legal and judicial system. Amsterdam Law Forum 4(2):16-35
Council for the Development of Cambodia (2003) Human development report. http://www.cdc-crdb.gov.kh/cdc/cmdgs_en.pdf. Accessed 22 May 2019
Defalco RC (2014) Case 003 and 004 at the Khmer Rouge Tribunal: The definition of "most responsible" individuals according to international criminal law. Genocide Studies and Prevention: An International Journal 8(2):45-65

---

[135] See ECCC, 'Frequently asked questions about the ECCC', https://www.eccc.gov.kh/en/about-eccc/faq.
[136] International Bar Association 2015, p. 60.

Donovan DA (1993) Cambodia: Building legal system from scratch. The International Lawyer 27(2):445-454
ECCC (2012) Introduction to the Khmer Rouge trials, 5th edn. ECCC Publication
ECCC (2013) ECCC reparation program 2013-2017: For the victims of the Khmer Rouge regime 1975-1979. http://vss.eccc.gov.kh/images/stories/2014/Reparation.pdf. Accessed 9 September 2019
ECCC (2015) Internal Rules (Rev.9), as revised on 16 January 2015. https://www.eccc.gov.kh/en/document/legal/internal-rules. Accessed 9 September 2019
Encyclopedia of World Biography (n.d.) Hun Sen. https://www.encyclopedia.com/history/encyclopedias-almanacs-transcripts-and-maps/hun-sen. Accessed 9 September 2019
Evans D (2016) Airborne laser scanning as a method for exploring long-term socio-ecological dynamics in Cambodia. Journal Archaeological Science 74:164-175
Evans D, Pottier C, Fletcher R, Hensley S, Tapley I, Milne A, Barbetti M (2007) A comprehensive archaeological map of the world's largest preindustrial settlement complex at Angkor, Cambodia. Proceedings of the National Academy of Sciences of the United States of America 104(36): 14277-14282
Future Forum (2016) An overview and analysis of the current political situation in Cambodia. https://www.futureforum.asia/app/download/13343252/2016+Political+Analysis+-+SUMMARY.pdf. Accessed 10 September 2019
Future Forum (2017) Moving beyond the January 7 narratives: Briefing note. https://www.futureforum.asia/app/download/12451094/Future+Forum+-+_Moving+Beyond+the+January+7+Narratives_+Briefing+Note+%28January+2017%29_ENG.pdf. Accessed 10 September 2019
Furtak RK (1986) The political systems of the socialist states: An introduction to Marxist-Leninist regimes. Wheatsheaf
Ghai Y (2010) Access to land and justice: Anatomy of a state without the rule of law. In: Ghai YCBE, Cottrell J (eds) Marginalized communities and access to justice, 1st edn. Routledge, New York, pp 37-59
Gibson JL, Sonis J, Hean S (2010) Cambodian's support for the rule of law on the eve of the Khmer Rouge Trials. International Journal of Transitional Justice 4(3):377-396
Human Rights Watch (2015) Cambodia: 30 years of Hun Sen violence and repression. https://www.hrw.org/news/2015/01/13/cambodia-30-years-hun-sen-violence-repression. Accessed 22 May 2019
Human Rights Watch (2018) Cambodia's dirty dozen: A long history of rights abuses by Hun Sen's generals. https://www.hrw.org/report/2018/06/27/cambodias-dirty-dozen/long-history-rights-abuses-hun-sens-generals. Accessed 9 September 2019
International Bar Association (2015) Justice versus corruption: Challenges to the independence of the judiciary in Cambodia. http://ticambodia.org/library/wp-content/files_mf/1443694998JusticevcorruptioninCambodiaAug2015.pdf. Accessed 9 September 2019
International Bridges to Justice (n.d.) Cambodia. https://www.ibj.org/where-we-work/cambodia/. Accessed 9 September 2019
International Commission of Jurists (ICJ) (1959) The rule of law in a free society: A report on the International Congress of Jurists. ICJ, New Delhi
International Committee of the Red Cross (ICRC) (1999) Country report: Cambodia - ICRC worldwide consultation on the rules of war. Reported by Greenberg Research, Geneva
International Law Commission (1950) Principles of international law recognized in the Charter of the Nuremberg Tribunal and in the judgment of the Tribunal, UN Doc A/CN.4/34
Jarvis H (2016) Trials and tribulations: The long quest for justice for the Cambodian genocide. In: Meisenberg SM, Stegmiller I (eds) The Extraordinary Chambers in the Courts of Cambodia. T.M.C. Asser Press, The Hague, pp 13-44
Kelsen H (1947) Will the judgment in the Nuremberg Trial Constitute a Precedent in International Law? International Law Quarterly 1(2):153-171
Kiernan B (1989) The American bombardment of Kampuchea, 1969-1973. Vietnam Generation 1(1): 4-41

Knaul G (2014) Intervention by the United Nations Special Rapporteur on the independence of judges and lawyers. Presentation at the International Bar Association's Human Rights Institute Press Conference 'Cambodia's Draft Judicial Laws', 15 July, Phnom Penh. www.ibanet.org/Document/Default.aspx?DocumentUid=6499E34F-B76A-4CF5-89D8-3E798D8461EE. Accessed 9 September 2019

Kong P (2012) Overview of Cambodian legal and judicial system. In: Hor P, Kong P, Menzel J (eds) Introduction to Cambodian law. Konrad Adenauer Stiftung, Phnom Penh, pp 10-11

Linton S (2002) New Approaches to International Justice in Cambodia and East Timor. IRRC 84(845):93-119

Luco F (2002) Management of local conflicts in Cambodia: An anthropological approach to traditional and new practices. UNESCO, Phnom Penh

Ly R (2017) Prosecuting the Khmer Rouge: Views for the inside. In: Buckley-Zistel S, Mieth F, Papa M (eds) After Nuremberg. Exploring multiple dimensions of the acceptance of international criminal justice. International Nuremberg Principles Academy, Nuremberg

Mattes D, Ngouv MS, Kum S (2020) Compendium report: Women in the law. RULE Centre for the Study of Humanitarian Law and Sandford Centre for Human Rights and International Justice, Phnom Penh

McLellan J (1999) Many petals of the lotus: Five Asian Buddhist communities in Toronto. University of Toronto Press, Toronto

Morey RD (2014) The United Nations at work in Asia: An envoy's account of development in China, Vietnam, Thailand and South Pacific. McFarland & Company, North Carolina

Neilson KE (1996) They killed all the lawyers: Rebuilding the judicial system in Cambodia. Occasional Paper Series, Centre for Asia Pacific Initiatives, Canada

Office of the Council of Ministers (2019) Remark Samdech Techo Hun Sen. The 75th Session of the UN-ESCAP on Empowering People and Ensuring Inclusiveness and Equality. https://pressocm.gov.kh/en/archives/53373. Accessed 15 June 2019

Pennya D, Halla T, Evans D, Polkinghornec M (2018) Geoarchaeological evidence from Angkor, Cambodia, reveals a gradual decline rather than a catastrophic 15th-century collapse. Proceedings of the National Academy of Sciences of the United States of America 116(11): 4871-4876

Peou S (2000) Intervention and change in Cambodia: Towards democracy? Silkworm Books, Chiang Mai

Phun V, Reyes-Kong FSD (2016) Cambodia. In: Cohen D, Tan K, Nababan A, Reyes-Kong FSD (eds) Update on the rule of law for human rights in ASEAN: The path to integration. Human Rights Resource Centre, Indonesia, pp cxix-clxxiii

Ponchaud F (1978) Cambodia: Year zero (Amphoux N (translator)). Holts Rinehart and Winston, New York

Ryan H, McGrew L (2016) Performance and perception: The impact of the Extraordinary Chambers in the Courts of Cambodia. Open Society Foundations, New York

Shawcross W (1979) Sideshow: Kissinger, Nixon and the destruction of Cambodia. Simon and Schuster, New York

Sok S (2010) Legal system of Cambodia. Presentation at the Royal University of Law and Economics, Phnom Penh, 21 June. https://www.soksiphana-private.com/public/uploads/Lecture_on_Cambodian_Legal_System_for_the_University_San_Francisco_Fullbright.pdf. Accessed 10 September 2019

Tamanaha BZ (2004) On the rule of law: History, politics, theory. Cambridge University Press, Cambridge

Transparency International (2019) Corruption perceptions index, country profile: Cambodia. https://www.transparency.org/country/KHM. Accessed 1 June 2020

UN Assistance to the Khmer Rouge Trials (1997) Letter dated 21 June 1997 from the First and Second Prime Ministers of Cambodia addressed to the Secretary-General of the United Nations. http://www.unakrt-online.org/documents/letter-dated-21-june-1997-first-and-second-prime-ministers-cambodia-addressed-secretary. Accessed 14 March 2019

UN Commission on Human Rights (1979) Question of the violation of human rights and fundamental freedoms in any part of the world, with particular reference to colonial and other dependent countries and territories, UN Doc E/CN.4/SR.1510

UN Commission on Human Rights (1999) Resolution 1999/76 (1999), E/CN.4/RES/1999/76

UN Development Programme (2018) Human development reports, statistical update 2018. http://hdr.undp.org/en/2018-update. Accessed 9 September 2019

UN General Assembly and Security Council (1999) Identical letters dated 15 March 1999 from the Secretary-General to the President of the General Assembly and the President of the Security Council. UN Doc. A/53/850-S/1999/231. Annex ("Report of the Group of Experts for Cambodia established pursuant to General Assembly Resolution 52/135", 18 February 1999)

UN General Assembly (1946) Resolution 95(I) (1946), UN Doc A/RES/95

UN General Assembly (2018) Situation of human rights in Cambodia, UN Doc. A/RES/52/135

UN Office on Drugs and Crime (2002) Bangalore Principles of Judicial Conduct (as revised at the Round Table Meeting of Chief Justices held at the Peace Palace). www.unodc.org/pdf/crime/corruption/judicial_group/Bangalore_principles.pdf. Accessed 10 September 2019

UN Security Council (2002) Letter dated 17 June 2002 from the Secretary-General addressed to the President of the Security Council, UN Doc. S2002/678, Enclosure ("Report on the judicial status of the International Criminal Tribunal for the Former Yugoslavia and the prospects for referring certain cases to national courts")

Inter-Parliamentary Union (1993) Cambodia, Parliamentary Chamber: Constituent Assembly. http://www.ipu.org/parline-e/reports/arc/2051_93.htm. Accessed 9 September 2019

Williams S (2015) The severance of Case 002 at ECCC: A radical trial management technique or a step too far? JICJ 13(4):815-843

Williams T, Bernath J, Tann B, Kum S (2018) Justice and reconciliation for the victims of the Khmer Rouge? Victim participation in Cambodia's transitional justice process. Centre for Conflict Studies, Marburg/Centre for the Study of Humanitarian Law, Phnom Penh/Swisspeace, Bern

World Justice Project (2020) Rule of law index. https://worldjusticeproject.org/sites/default/files/documents/WJP-ROLI-2020-Online_0.pdf. Accessed 1 June 2020

Yong T, Chhoy YH (2000) Cambodian identity: Land, history, culture and civilization, state and governance, and society. Harvard-Yenching Institute, Phnom Penh

Other Documents

Agreement between the UN and the Royal Government of Cambodia concerning the prosecution under Cambodian law of crimes committed during the period of Democratic Kampuchea, signed on 6 June 2003, 2329 UNTS 117 (entered into forces 29 April 2005)

Natalia Szablewska Ph.D., GradCertAP, Dip(IHL), BSc(Econ)(Hons), LLB(Hons) is a legal scholar and social scientist with 20 years of experience spanning the public sector, governmental and non-governmental organisations and academia in five countries. She is Professor in Law and Society at The Open University Law School (United Kingdom), as Adjunct Professor at the Royal University of Law and Economics (Cambodia) and Adjunct Fellow at the Humanitarian and Development Research Initiative, Western Sydney University (Australia). Her research is interdisciplinary in nature and she employs gender- and human rights-based approaches to examine issues relating to forced migration, modern slavery and, more widely, socioeconomic (in)equalities in post-conflict societies. Natalia has published widely for academic and non-academic audiences, and her academic work has appeared in leading journals and publishers in several disciplines.

Chapter 56
Myanmar

Melanie O'Brien

Contents

56.1 Myanmar: A State of Colonialism, Conflict and Coups	1257
56.1.1 Terminology	1258
56.1.2 Myanmar as a State: A Turbulent History	1259
56.2 Constant Conflict	1262
56.2.1 Conflict Case Study Examples: Karen and Kachin	1265
56.3 The Rohingya Genocide	1266
56.4 Myanmar's Conflicts and Genocide in International Law	1269
56.4.1 The Universal Periodic Review	1271
56.4.2 The United Nations Security Council	1271
56.4.3 International Court of Justice	1272
56.4.4 International Criminal Court	1275
56.5 Conclusion	1277
References	1278

Abstract This chapter discusses conflict and security issues in the state of Myanmar. Myanmar is a state with a history of colonisation, conflict, coups, military leadership, and mass atrocities. This chapter provides a brief history of Myanmar's conflict and insecurity, summarising the turbulent history of the Burmese state. The focus of the chapter is on the current security and international law concerns in Myanmar. It thus discusses the conflicts with ethnic minority peoples, and examines the Rohingya genocide, finally engaging with the specific international law framework and developments with regards to the conflicts and the genocide.

Keywords Myanmar · Rohingya · Genocide · Colonialism · Conflict · Karen · Kachin · International Court of Justice · International Criminal Court

56.1 Myanmar: A State of Colonialism, Conflict and Coups

Myanmar is a state with a history of colonisation, conflict, coups, military leadership, and mass atrocities. Myanmar is a prominent case study for 'conflict and

---

M. O'Brien (✉)
University of Western Australia, Perth, Australia
e-mail: melanie.obrien@uwa.edu.au

© T.M.C. ASSER PRESS and the authors 2022
S. Sayapin et al. (eds.), *International Conflict and Security Law*,
https://doi.org/10.1007/978-94-6265-515-7_56

security'; it is a state with an abundance of historical and ongoing conflict and (in)security issues, including armed conflict and genocide, which this chapter will explore, in the context of relevant international law. This chapter provides a brief history of Myanmar's conflict and insecurity, summarising the turbulent history of the Burmese state, centring on colonisation, coups and conflict. The focus then shifts to the ongoing conflicts with minority groups, and the Rohingya genocide, a significant human security process that has been pervasive in Myanmar's history of the late 20th and early 21st centuries, with global impact caused by over one million refugees fleeing Myanmar. These conflicts and the genocide against the Rohinyga consist of significant violations of international law. The chapter finishes by exploring the relevant international law framework in the context of these conflicts and the Rohingya genocide, considering Myanmar's treaty obligations, customary law obligations, and current international court proceedings relating to the atrocities against the Rohingya It will demonstrate that, even with an infamously 'hermit' state such as Myanmar, international law remains relevant and continues to provide an avenue by which state and individual accountability for violations of international law can be achieved.

56.1.1 Terminology

Naming conventions in Burmese history have changed over time. This chapter will refer to the state as Myanmar, but also refer generally to 'the Burmese state', and use the title 'Burma' when referring to the pre-1989 state, when the state's name was changed to 'Myanmar' by the military leadership. The city of Rangoon is now referred to as Yangon; and the city of Pagan (the centre of the Pagan Kingdom) is now called Bagan. The major ethnic group in Myanmar were historically called 'Burmese' or 'Burmans'; they are here referred to historically as 'Burman' and by current terminology as 'Bamar'; they speak Burmese, a Sino-Tibetan language.[1] 'Rakhine state' will be used for the current administrative region; its historical name, 'Arakan', will be used where appropriate.[2] Other names used throughout the chapter will also note alternative or former names, where relevant. 'Tatmadaw' is the Burmese term for the military.

---

[1] 66–75% of the population are Bamar: Mills 2000, p. 267. A more recent figure is 68%. See Thawnghmung and Furnari 2019, p. 133.

[2] Rohingya people still use the terms Burma and Arakan; author's interviews with 21 Rohingya women in refugee camps, Bangladesh, November 2019 [University of Western Australia Ethics RA/4/20/5737].

56.1.2 Myanmar as a State: A Turbulent History

The Burmese state has a long history of multi-ethnicity, particularly in the regions to the north and east of the central Irrawaddy region. Many of these ethnic groups live in regions that sit across the border of Myanmar and neighbouring states;[3] that is, ethnic groups who have long resided in the region are not bound by the national boundaries created in the 1900s.[4] Over 100 languages are represented in the ethnic minorities.[5] While a complete history of the Burmese state is outside the scope of this chapter, it is worth drawing attention to three of the most significant eras in Burmese history.

The Burman Pagan Kingdom ruled from the 9th to 13th Century, "probably the first largely ethnic-Burman state".[6] Its power has led to many subsequent rulers seeking to trace their lineage to this era, as representation of their own legitimacy for ruling Burma. The current military leadership has also glorified the Pagan period, rebuilding pagodas from this era.[7] It was during the Pagan Kingdom that most people adopted Buddhism, although religious diversity and cultural pluralism continued.[8]

Another prominent era was the Konbaung Dynasty, 1752–1885, during which Burma became a major regional power, founding Mandalay as the state's capital.[9] The Konbaung Dynasty fought wars with Siam neighbours, and with the British, until the British took Arakan state in 1826 and then all of Burma in 1886. This led to the third significant era, British colonialism, until Burma's independence in 1948.[10]

The current era, since the 1948 independence, has been fraught with conflict (which will be discussed in the following section). Burma became independent in 1948, with government headed by Prime Minister U Nu. This was a shaky time as Burma attempted to situate itself as a nation-state,[11] and in March 1962, General Ne Win led a military coup, abolishing the federal system and nationalising the economy. Burma became a single-party state, and independent newspapers were banned. States that had been given independence under the British, such as Karenni state, were invaded by the Burmese army and forced under the central government.[12] In 1974, a new constitution was introduced, forming a People's Assembly headed by Ne Win and other former military leaders. By 1987, the economy and social structures were suffering, with a currency devaluation triggering anti-government

---

[3] Ibrahim 2018, p. 18.

[4] A perfect practical example of Anderson's 'imagined communities' theory of the nation-state. See Anderson 2006.

[5] Mills 2000, p. 267.

[6] Ibrahim 2018, p. 21.

[7] Ibid., p. 21.

[8] Ibid., p. 22.

[9] Ibid.

[10] For a detailed political and economic history of Burma/Myanmar from the 1800s until 2008, see Taylor 2009. A more social history focused history is found in Steinberg 2001.

[11] See Taylor 2009, Chapter 5, for a discussion of the pre-1962 political and economic situation.

[12] Leading to the ongoing conflicts as discussed in Sect. 56.2.; Kyaw and Nwe 2019.

riots. Further riots in 1988 led to the deaths of thousands, and declaration of martial law in 1989. It was in 1989 that Burma was renamed Myanmar.

1989 was also the year that Aung San Suu Kyi, leader of the National League for Democracy (NLD), was first put under house arrest. Suu Kyi was to live under house arrest for six years, but was again placed many times under lengthy periods of house arrest, until her final release in 2010. Suu Kyi's final release represented what was hopefully perceived to be the transition to democracy for Myanmar, with a civilian government sworn in in 2011. However, it was really only nominally civilian, with the Tatmadaw still in control. Elections were held in 2012, with the Suu Kyi-led NLD winning by a substantial margin. In 2012, the government claimed to abolish media censorship, but the reality remains that journalists are not free to report, with two Reuters reporters arrested in 2017 for reporting on the Rohingya situation, only released in May 2019 after significant international pressure.[13] Another election was held in 2015, with Suu Kyi's NLD winning enough seats to form a government. Suu Kyi holds the title State Counsellor, a position similar to prime minister, and yet it is evident that the military remain the dominant leaders in Myanmar. The exile-led politics and resistance to human rights violations of the 1990s[14] had led to some elements of rights restoration in Myanmar, but not a true human rights- and rule of law-focused democracy.[15]

Suu Kyi became a human rights icon, due to the decades she spent fighting for democracy in Burma, and being held under house arrest for doing so. She won the Nobel Peace Prize in 1991. However, after her release and inclusion in Myanmar's government, she has received a significant amount of criticism for not speaking out against violence committed by the Tatmadaw, but rather specifically publicly denying the genocide being committed against the Rohingya and supporting the Tatmadaw.[16] In December 2019, Suu Kyi expressly argued before the International Court of Justice (ICJ) that Myanmar was not committing genocide, refusing (along with all members of Myanmar's legal team) to use the term Rohingya in her statements.[17] There have been calls for her to be stripped of her Nobel Prize, although the committee declined to do so.[18]

Thus, Myanmar remains a hermit state, disengaged with international law and human rights (see Sect. 56.4 below). The hope of a sweeping change to democracy and human rights that the 2011/12 elections and governmental overhaul would bring has disappeared. The Burmese remain a people restricted in their rights, particularly free speech, the restriction of which remains a key requirement for the Tatmadaw to continue committing war crimes and genocide. Controlling the media (including social media) allows the Tatmadaw to peddle extensive propaganda and hate speech

---

[13] See the Reuters dedicated page on the reporters, their story and their arrest, available at Reuters, Myanmar reporters, https://www.reuters.com/subjects/myanmar-reporters. Accessed 5 March 2020.

[14] Taylor 2009, pp. 425–433.

[15] Crouch 2019a; Steinberg 2001, pp. 80–83.

[16] Ware and Laoutides 2018.

[17] See Sect. 56.4.2 for detail on the ICJ case.

[18] Reuters 2018.

to ensure that the majority population groups support the 'security actions' against minority groups such as the Rohingya.[19] With revered rights icon Suu Kyi no longer providing leadership on human rights, there is no voice speaking out in a country to lead people away from the propaganda and hate speech. To the contrary, the Bamar people blindly follow Suu Kyi, including her rhetoric against the Rohingya.[20]

Impunity exists for abuses by the state, whether by the military in the context of conflict and genocide, or by the police more generally.[21] The state regulates religion, restricting minorities' right to freedom of religion.[22] The right to freedom of assembly (in the form of protest and demonstrations) is restricted by law and in practice never allowed.[23] The media is also controlled by the government, restricted by law, prohibited from criticising the government.[24] Debate over legislative and constitutional change, in 2015 and 2019, revolves around "aspirations for civilian rule, federalism and democracy in Myanmar".[25]

Myanmar is also struggling to develop economically. A recent, extensive UN report revealed that the Tatmadaw controls a substantial amount of business throughout Myanmar, particularly the ruby and jade mining industries, which are significant income earners for Myanmar.[26] The investigation found that the Tatmadaw is also involved in business throughout Myanmar in a wide variety of areas: construction, manufacturing, insurance, tourism, banking, communications and more. All of these economic holdings and actions were deemed to be connected to human rights abuses and mass atrocities, violating human rights law, international humanitarian law (IHL) and the Genocide Convention.[27]

In November 2020, elections were held in Myanmar. Due to the results providing overwhelming support for the civilian wing of the government led by Suu Kyi, the Tatmadaw alleged election fraud. Based on this allegation, on 1 February 2021, the Tatmadaw staged a coup to nullify the election results. Members of the civilian government were detained. The coup was unpopular with the general population, which began ongoing large street protests against the coup. Martial law was declared, and thousands of people arrested.[28] The Tatmadaw responded with force, opening fire on protestors, including shooting people in the head in what has been suggested

---

[19] Dolan and Gray 2014, pp. 10–11.

[20] An organiser of a support protest for Myanmar in its case against The Gambia in the International Court of Justice (see Sect. 56.4.2) said "[w]e must show our unity. If a country's leader says a lemon is sweet, we have to say it is sweet." Naing and Aung 2019.

[21] Cheesman 2019.

[22] Crouch 2015; Kyaw 2019b; Walton et al. 2015.

[23] Crouch 2016, p. 233.

[24] Ibid., p. 233.

[25] Crouch 2019b.

[26] Human Rights Council 2019a.

[27] Ibid., see Sect. 56.4 for more detail about Myanmar's international law obligations.

[28] Human Rights Watch 2021.

are targeted killings.[29] The violence escalated daily, and drew condemnation from states (including through sanctions)[30] and UN entities, with the UN Special Adviser on the Prevention of Genocide and UN High Commissioner for Human Rights jointly calling on the UN Security Council to take action.[31] Weller notes that the "coup has now returned the situation back to 1990", namely with the elected parliament unable to function, politicians arrested, and allegations of torture.[32] The coup and subsequent violent crackdown resulted in the violation of a number of human rights, including the right to vote, freedom of association and assembly, freedom from torture, the right to fair trial and the right to life. It is clear then, as of 2021, that the democratic future of Myanmar is distant, along with the compliance of Myanmar with international law norms.

56.2 Constant Conflict

Since independence in 1948, the Burmese state has been in civil war, with political, economic and ethnic bases for the conflict.[33] Through usually described as 'low-level' conflict, there have been political and ethnic groups "militarily contesting the state for control of territory",[34] with at least 40 non-state groups in conflict with the government since independence.[35] As of 2015, there were about 21 non-state armed groups in Myanmar. The groups differ in "size, legitimacy, and objectives".[36] For example, some groups have nationalist goals, "explicit political agendas, and provide education and healthcare services within the areas under their control".[37] Other groups are self-focused, carrying out financing activities such as drug production and trafficking. Some groups have no armed forces; others as few as a few hundred combatants; while major groups, such as the United Wa State Army, have about 30,000 armed personnel.[38] The main fronts of conflict are Kachin state (the Kachin people), Kayah state (the Karenni people), Kayin state (the Karen people),

---

[29] 'Myanmar coup: Dozens killed as army opens fire on protesters during deadliest day', BBC, 28 March 2021 https://www.bbc.com/news/world-asia-56546920. Accessed 30 March 2021.

[30] VOA News 2021; UK FCDO 2021.

[31] Joint Statement by UN Special Adviser on the Prevention of Genocide and UN High Commissioner for Human Rights—on Myanmar, https://www.un.org/sg/en/content/note-correspondents-joint-statement-un-special-adviser-the-prevention-of-genocide-and-un-high-commissioner-for-human-rights-myanmar. Accessed 30 March 2021. At the time of the joint statement, the UN Security Council had only released a statement, on 10 March 2021 (S/PRST/2021/5), condemning the violence against peaceful protestors.

[32] Weller 2021.

[33] Farrelly 2014.

[34] Taylor 2009, p. 433.

[35] Thawnghmung and Furnari 2019, p. 134.

[36] Ibid., p. 137.

[37] Ibid.

[38] Ibid.

and Shan state (the Shan people).[39] In this chapter, the Rohingya situation will not be considered a conflict; the genocide of the Rohingya people in Rakhine state will be discussed below.[40]

The conflict in Myanmar has generally been separatist, and along ethno-nationalist identity lines. The conflict stems from inequality, suppression, and power imbalance, and steeped in complex historic social realities, including

> decades of rule by highly centralised and militarized governments which have suppressed the cultural and political rights of the country's minorities and extracted their resources without sharing the profits with local communities.[41]

Writing on the Kachin conflict, Laoutides and Ware determine that

> 'ethnicity' has become the outward manifestation of a conflict far more deeply underpinned by issues of political rights and distribution, state power versus decentralization, the quest for equality and freedom, and the question of who constitutes the demos in Myanmar's future democracy.[42]

Within this frame, territory is seen as inherently connected to a nationalistic sense of identity. Groups fight for ideologies (anti-capitalist communism), democratic regime change, citizenship and human rights.[43] Mills also writes of an authoritarian, conservative and masculine military regime repressing women, particularly ethnic minority women.[44] This suppression, exclusion, marginalisation and insecurity (along with significant sexual violence against women) has pushed many women to support or join independence organisations or their armed groups.[45] These descriptions can be applied to any of the conflicts in Myanmar (as well as the Rohingya genocide).

While nationalist identity and territory issues have a long history, with frequent wars between nominally independent kingdoms, two turning points in the Twentieth Century led to the conflicts that continue today. The first was British colonialism and the subsequent British-controlled independence structure, under which an arbitrary border was drawn around Burma, giving the Burmese authority over previously independent ethnic groups.

The second turning point was the change in 1962 to military dominance over all of that designated Burmese territory. An empirical study by Laoutides and Ware, including of state officials, found that most people "agree that there has been institutionalized discrimination against all minorities",[46] with perception "that 'the Burman

---

[39] Kayah state was formerly Karenni state; Kayin state was formerly Karen state. Other groups in conflict include the Chin, Mon and Rakhine peoples. See Ibid.

[40] The Myanmar authorities present the Rohingya issue as 'terrorism' and 'insurgencies', and thus position it outside the peace process in the country. See Crouch 2019b.

[41] Thawnghmung and Furnari 2019, p. 133.

[42] Laoutides and Ware 2016, p. 49.

[43] Thawnghmung and Furnari 2019, p. 133.

[44] Mills 2000.

[45] Hedström 2016. Yet women are still excluded from combat roles and political participation. See Hedström 2017; Hedström 2015; and from the peace process, see Khen and Nyoi 2014.

[46] Laoutides and Ware 2016, p. 54.

elite' and military are trying to homogenize identity to achieve their ideological ideal of a strong nation-state".[47]

The period of 1989–1997 saw multiple ceasefire agreements made between the Burmese government and various independence entities and their armed groups. 17 major ceasefires covered the regions of Shan, Kayah, Kachin, Kayin and Rakhine.[48] All but one ceasefire agreement were unwritten, existing more as an understanding of future constitutional settlement leading to disarmament. Most groups refused to surrender their arms, and many were converted into police and militias.[49] However, these ceasefires were ultimately unsuccessful, with conflict recommencing at various times in different states. This is likely due to the fact that during the ceasefire period, the Tatmadaw undertook extensive extractive and infrastructure projects, which had harmful environmental and social ramifications on local populations, and they took territory and revenue-generating enterprises away from the independence groups.[50]

Since 2012, a peace process has been ongoing, for "recognised ethnic armed groups".[51] By mid-2012, the government had renewed ceasefire agreements with 13 armed groups.[52] In 2015, a Nationwide Ceasefire Agreement (NCA) was made between the Myanmar government and various Ethnic Armed Organisations (EAOs).[53] The signing of the NCA was overseen by, inter alia, the United Nations. Despite being promoted as a multi-lateral and inclusive agreement, the government refused to invite six organisations to participate and sign. This led other invited organisations to withdraw from the process.[54] Eight groups signed on to the NCA, including the Karen National Union (KNU), but this did not include some major groups such as the United Wa State Army or the Kachin Independence Army (KIA).

Yet, despite the NCA and subsequent 'national conferences' on the peace process,[55] the peace process languishes and conflict continues, with recent reporting of incidences related to Kachin, Shan, Karen, Rakhine and Mon conflicts.[56] The lack of success of ceasefires in Myanmar is palpable, best summarised by Thawnghmung and Furnari:

> [O]fficial responses to armed groups have consistently failed to address the roots of these conflicts. They have largely been temporary, ad-hoc reaction, which have not only failed to address long-held resentments against the central government and the military, but have rather deepened and perpetuated existing grievances, and created new ones.[57]

---

[47] Ibid., p. 55. See more discussion on this in Sect. 56.4.1.

[48] For a full table of major ceasefire agreements, see Taylor 2009, p. 437. Only one related to Rakhine; the majority were for groups in Shan, Kachin and Kayah.

[49] Taylor 2009, p. 438.

[50] Thawnghmung and Furnari 2019, p. 135.

[51] Crouch 2019b. See Sect. 56.4.2 for more detail on the ICJ case.

[52] For details on the peace processes before 2015, see Kipgen 2015.

[53] Ganesan 2015.

[54] Institute for Security and Diplomacy Policy 2015, pp. 5–6.

[55] Wilson 2017.

[56] See e.g. Naing 2020; Weng 2019; Human Rights Watch 2019.

[57] Thawnghmung and Furnari 2019, p. 134.

Over the decades, the conflicts have been rife with human rights abuses and atrocities, including ubiquitous sexual violence against girls and women, trafficking of women into China, the forced displacement (internally and across borders) of hundreds of thousands of people, recruitment and use of child soldiers, extrajudicial killings, forced labour and torture, all committed by the Tatmadaw with impunity.[58] The government also prevents humanitarian aid access to conflict and genocide areas, particularly Rakhine state, meaning populations are not able to access food, sanitary supplies and healthcare.[59] Recent positive developments include the adoption of the Child Rights Law (criminalising grave violations against children) and the ratification in 2019 of the Optional Protocol to the Convention on the Rights of the Child on the involvement of children in armed conflict.[60]

Ethnic armed groups have also been accused of committing violations of international humanitarian law, including enforced disappearances, forcible recruitment and extortion, the recruitment and use of child soldiers, and the use of landmines.[61] Since 2003, ten non-state armed groups have signed one or more Deeds of Commitment with Geneva Call, taking steps to implement these commitments. Six have signed the landmine ban deed; five have signed the child protection deed; and two have signed the prohibition of sexual violence deed. Only one group, the Chin National Front/Chin National Army, has signed all three; and only the Karen National Union (KNU)/Karen National Liberation Army (KNLA) has signed two (children protection and sexual violence).[62] As non-state actors cannot be party to treaties, by signing and implementing these deeds, the non-state armed groups are committing to uphold specific requirements of international humanitarian law. A number of the non-state armed groups including the KNU/KNLA have also engaged with the UN, with the KIA releasing 25 child soldiers.[63]

56.2.1 Conflict Case Study Examples: Karen and Kachin

Kachin and Karen are two examples of states that remain in armed conflict, despite the NCA, with the conflict "stoked by large-scale development projects and disputes over natural resources".[64]

---

[58] Human Rights Watch 2019; Amnesty International 2018; Baulk 2017; Bugher 2017; Kamler 2015; Women's League of Burma 2014; International Human Rights Law Clinic 2009.

[59] Human Rights Watch 2019; Amnesty International 2018.

[60] Report of the Secretary-General: Children and armed conflict, UN Doc. A/74/845-S/2020/525, 9 June 2020, para 130.

[61] Amnesty International 2018; Cathcart 2016.

[62] See Geneva Call, Where we Work, https://www.genevacall.org/where-we-work/. Accessed 5 March 2020.

[63] Report of the Secretary-General: Children and armed conflict, UN Doc. A/74/845-S/2020/525, 9 June 2020, para 133.

[64] Human Rights Watch 2019.

Soon after Burmese independence, the political group KNU and its armed wing, the KNLA, were formed, launching a campaign for self-determination. The KNU did not participate in the ceasefires of the 1990s, and was particularly and heavily targeted by the Tatmadaw after that time. The KNU finally signed a peace agreement with the government in 2012, and was the largest ethnic independence group to sign up to the NCA in 2015.[65] The KNU is one of the NCA groups, but does not necessarily support the government, and recently specifically noted it did not support the government in its defence before the ICJ, noting similarities between the operations against the Rohingya and previous government operations against the Karen people.[66]

The Kachin conflict has been on and off since 1962, based on independence claims by the Kachin people, with the two most significant entities being the Kachin Independence Organisation (KIO) and its armed wing, the Kachin Independence Army (KIA). In 1994, a signed ceasefire agreement was made (the only written, signed one of all the ceasefire agreements), and this lasted for 17 years, until armed conflict resumed in June 2011.[67] Conflict between the KIO/A and the Tatmadaw since 2011 has "centred around the control of resources and resource trade corridors", which indicates that ethnicity is not necessarily the only driving factor of the conflict.[68] Independence remains a strong motivator, with one study finding the Kachin "intense passion about their inability to exercise governance over what they consider to be 'their' communities and territory' is very strong".[69] The Kachin conflict has been a particular motivator for trafficking in women and girls to China as forced brides.[70] There are long-term internally displaced persons (IDP) camps, with thousands of civilians fleeing aerial bombing and heavy artillery shelling.[71]

56.3 The Rohingya Genocide

The Rohingya are one of the many ethnic groups living in Myanmar. Their history in the land extends back hundreds of years, with at least definitive evidence that they were living there in the late eighteenth century,[72] and eight century temple inscriptions indicating the Indo-Aryan roots of the Rohingya.[73] They are based in Rakhine state, on the western coast of Myanmar, along the border with Bangladesh

---

[65] Brenner 2018.

[66] Kean 2019.

[67] Sadan 2015.

[68] Laoutides and Ware 2016, p. 48. For women, their participation is about suppression, insecurity and inequality. See Hedström 2016.

[69] Laoutides and Ware 2016, p. 55.

[70] Human Rights Watch 2019; Hedström 2016, pp. 82–83.

[71] Human Rights Watch 2019. In 2016, Fortify Rights estimated over 100,000 civilians were displaced by the KIA-Tatmadaw conflict since 2011. Fortify Rights 2016.

[72] Wade 2019, pp. 108–109; Ibrahim 2018, pp. 24–25.

[73] Ibrahim 2018, p. 21.

56 Myanmar

and close to India. The Rakhine state was previously known as Arakan, a region separated from the rest of Burma by a mountain range. The term 'Rakhine' comes from the Rakhine people, who have Tibeto-Burmese ancestry and moved from central Burma to Arakan in around 1000AD. The Arakan region's history vacillates between independence, connections with Burma and rule over Bangladesh, although generally the area was formally independent until the late 18th Century.[74] Most recently, Arakan was included in British colonial Burma in 1948, at which point its name changed to Rakhine.[75] This arbitrary administrative decision to include Arakan in Burma rather than British India or Pakistan (specifically, East Pakistan, which was to become Bangladesh in 1971) is a significant contributing factor to the current ethnic tensions and genocide.

Following the 1962 military coup, by the 1970s, the Rohingya were experiencing persecution. Military attacks including killings, rape and burning of villages forced over 200,000 Rohingya to flee Myanmar in 1978, and another 250,000 in 1991. There have been waves of displacement and return marked by violence and growing suspicion towards the Rohingya by the Rakhine-based Buddhists and the national (military and civilian) governments. Over one million Rohingya have fled Myanmar since the 1970s.[76]

Over the decades, the Myanmar government has created an identity of a majority 'race' in the Burmese nation state (the Bamar); those who do not fit this acceptable identity are deemed a threat to the security of this identity and nationhood. There is a long history of categorisation of 'races' within Myanmar and suppression of minority ethnicities, including in pre-colonisation kingdoms, during colonisation and in the current military leadership.[77] "Holding a minority identity in Myanmar is in itself political", as assimilation and unity of ethnic groups has been part of the Burmese state for centuries, under which an ethnic group's identity is seen as anti-Burmese.[78] These challenges have been experienced by the Rakhine people, who have themselves felt threatened by previous regimes, a fact that has contributed to their own contribution to the persecution of the Rohingya.[79]

Rohingya are referred to as 'Bengali'—intended as a derogatory term in the Burmese context. They are also dehumanised in the state-run media, including being referred to as 'fleas'.[80] As the government controls the media, the Burmese people have little to no access to alternative narratives, instead being bombarded with hate speech about the threat of the Rohingya people, accusing the Rohingya of fabricating lies about the violence perpetrated against them.[81]

---

[74] Ibid., p. 23.
[75] Ibid., p. 18.
[76] Amnesty International 2017c, p. 8; Fortify Rights 2015, pp. 8–9.
[77] Wade 2019, pp. 101–107.
[78] Cho 2017.
[79] Wade 2019, pp. 101–107.
[80] Oo 2016a; 2016b.
[81] Hogan and Safi 2018; Lee 2019; Serrato 2018.

Specific laws and policies have been implemented to 'legalise' the persecution of the Rohingya. In 1982, the Citizenship Law was passed. This law authorised citizenship only to a specific list of minority groups living in Myanmar—excluding the Rohingya, who were thus not entitled to citizenship. It is a law born from the idea of there being a dominant and superior Bamar race, and that minorities and foreigners (who may be one and the same) are inferior.[82] Since 1994, the Myanmar government has refused to issue Rohingya children with birth certificates. In 2013, the government issued a report that stated "the rapid population growth of the Bengalis [Rohingya] [is] an extremely serious threat".[83] Consequently, in 2015, as part of a package of 'Race and Religion Protection Laws', the Population Control Healthcare Bill passed, aimed to restrict the reproductive freedoms of the Rohingya through forced 'birth spacing' and forced use of contraceptives.[84]

In addition to these, the Rohingya experience pervasive and daily violations of their human rights. Their freedom of movement is restricted; Rohingya are not permitted to travel without a permit—which is rarely, if ever, granted. They are isolated and segregated in their villages and into detention camps and ghettos. Denial of citizenship to the Rohingya has resulted in the violation of various human rights: Rohingya are not permitted to participate in public service or political life, or to vote. Their employment rights and options are severely limited, although they are subject to forced labour by the military. Rohingya are also denied access to education.

Access to food has also become a significant problem, with the Rohingya having little or no access to food sources within Myanmar. Rohingya have been fenced into their village and left to starve.[85] Violence carried out by the military or sanctioned by the military has included looting of Rohingya food, burning of their crops and stealing or killing Rohingya herd animals. The government has denied access to humanitarian aid, including various UN aid programmes.[86] Rohingya are also denied access to healthcare. No local doctors or other healthcare workers provide services for Rohingya, and healthcare from humanitarian organisations is little where it is available; as early as 2014, Médecins Sans Frontières was expelled from northern and eastern Rakhine state.[87]

Beyond this, Rohingya experience regular violence, carried out by the Myanmar military, police, sanctioned militia, and even the local community. Violence ranges from having rocks thrown at them by their Rakhine neighbours to massacres and executions by the military, carried out by shooting, stabbing, burning and beating.

---

[82] Kyaw 2015; 2019a.

[83] Republic of the Union of Myanmar, Final Report of Inquiry Commission on Sectarian Violence in Rakhine State (8 July 2013), http://www.burmalibrary.org/docs15/Rakhine_Commission_Report-en-red.pdf. Accessed 5 March 2020.

[84] Human Rights Watch 2015; Carstens 2017; Crouch 2016.

[85] Wade 2019, p. 25.

[86] Htusan 2020; McPherson 2018.

[87] MSF, 'Myanmar (Burma)', https://msf.org.au/country-region/myanmar-burma. Accessed 18 August 2020. See also Hodal 2014.

Sexual violence is also pervasive, usually perpetrated as gang rape.[88] One study of refugee women found 52% of those surveyed were victims of violence, although this is no doubt a conservative number.[89] In 2018, it was estimated that 16,000 babies of rape had already been born in the refugee camps in Bangladesh.[90] In 2019, the UN concluded that sexual violence and rape are specifically used by the Tatmadaw as a tactic of genocide, demonstrating genocidal intent.[91]

In addition to the burning of crops, soldiers also burn entire villages, using petrol and rocket launchers. Sometimes buildings are burned with people still inside. Satellite imagery clearly shows destruction of entire Rohingya villages, with neighbouring Rakhine villages untouched.[92]

Of the more than one million Rohingya who have fled Myanmar since the 1970s, as of August 2019, 911,566 Rohingya refugees are in the refugee camps in the Cox's Bazar area of Bangladesh.[93] Other refugees are situated in states including Malaysia, India, and the United Arab Emirates. Their situation is precarious, particularly in the major Cox's Bazar camps, where there are significant issues accessing healthcare and communicable diseases are rife, girls and women are subject to sexual violence,[94] and access to even basic food and water is a daily challenge.[95] Women and girls are being trafficked from Myanmar and Bangladesh to Malaysia, sold as forced wives, after being promised a life better than in the IDP and refugee camps.[96]

56.4 Myanmar's Conflicts and Genocide in International Law

With regards to the conflicts and genocide discussed above, this raises issues of international human rights law, IHL, and international criminal law. As a hermit

---

[88] Human Rights Watch 2017.

[89] OHCHR 2017a. A US State Department report noted over 50% of those interviewed had witnessed sexual violence. US Department of State 2018.

[90] UNICEF 2018.

[91] Human Rights Council 2019b, paras 94–95 (hereinafter gender-based violence in Myanmar).

[92] Amnesty International 2017a; 2017b. There are many reports about the Rohingya genocide, providing details of the discrimination and violence. See e.g. ibid.; Amnesty International 2017b; Human Rights Council 2018; Green et al. 2015; Green et al. 2018; Lowenstein 2015; OHCHR 2017a; 2017b; Fortify Rights 2019; Smith 2018; US Department of State 2018; UNICEF 2018; Human Rights Watch 2013. See also Ibrahim 2018; Zarni and Cowley 2014.

[93] Inter Sector Coordination Group (ISCG), ISCG Situation Report: Rohingya Refugee Crisis, Cox's Bazar (31 August 2019) https://reliefweb.int/report/bangladesh/iscg-situation-report-rohingya-refugee-crisis-cox-s-bazar-august-2019. Accessed 5 March 2020.

[94] Chynoweth 2018.

[95] For details about healthcare access and food security, see the regular Situation Report. ISCG, Situation Report: Rohingya Crisis, https://www.humanitarianresponse.info/en/operations/bangladesh. Accessed 5 March 2020.

[96] SUHAKAM and Fortify Rights 2019.

Table 56.1 Relevant Myanmar Treaty Ratifications

Treaty	Year of Ratification/Accession
Hague Convention for the Protection of Cultural Property	10 February 1954
Hague Protocol for the Protection of Cultural Property	10 February 1954
Convention on the Prevention and Punishment of Genocide	14 March 1956
Convention on the Rights of the Child (CRC)	15 July 1991
Geneva Conventions	25 August 1992
Convention on the Elimination of All Forms of Discrimination Against Women (CEDAW)	22 July 1997
Convention on the Rights of Persons with Disabilities (CRPD)	7 December 2011
Optional Protocol (OP) to the CRC on the Sale of Children, Child Prostitution and Child Pornography	16 January 2012
Convention on the Prohibition of Biological Weapons	1 December 2014
Convention Prohibiting Chemical Weapons	8 July 2015
International Covenant on Economic, Social and Cultural Rights (ICESCR)	6 October 2017
OP to the CRC on the Involvement of Children in Armed Conflict	27 September 2019

state, Myanmar has minimal engagement in and with international law. The starting point, then, is looking at which treaties Myanmar is a state party to. As demonstrated in the above table, Myanmar is a state party to few relevant treaties (Table 56.1).

Instruments that are conspicuously missing from this list, include key treaties such as the International Covenant on Civil and Political Rights, and the Additional Protocols to the Geneva Conventions (particularly Additional Protocol II, which regulates non-international armed conflict). Also notable is the fact that Myanmar has not accepted any inquiry procedures or individual complaints procedures under human rights law, despite the existence of these procedures for the COC, CEDAW, CRPD and the ICESCR. This demonstrates that Myanmar's engagement with international law is nominal.

This section will examine four different options for accountability (state or individual) with regards to violations of international law committed by Myanmar; violations that specifically relate to conflict and security. These processes demonstrate that, although Myanmar's engagement with international law is limited, there are means and methods under which Myanmar can be forced to engage with international law, and may be held to account for breaches of international law, although acknowledging that these processes are not without challenges. The mechanisms presented in this section are the Universal Periodic Review (UPR), the United Nations Security Council (UNSC), the International Court of Justice (ICJ) and the International Criminal Court (ICC). The two UN-based processes have been selected because the UPR is a mechanism which applies to all member states of the UN; and the UNSC can pass binding resolutions under Chapter VII of the UN Charter. With regards to the courts discussed here, the ICJ's jurisdiction is applicable to all member states of the UN and there is currently a case pending before that court against Myanmar; and the ICC is the court of last resort for individual criminal accountability when it is otherwise non-existent and there is also a case pending before the ICC related to crimes against the Rohingya.

56.4.1 The Universal Periodic Review

Myanmar is subject to the UPR procedure in the Human Rights Council,[97] and has been through the process twice, in 2011 and 2015.[98] In 2011, little attention was paid to the significant issues such as the Rohingya, where the focus within the Rohingya discussion only considered the denial of citizenship rights to the Rohingya. In 2015, many states did specifically mention the violation of human rights of the Rohingya. Various states made multiple recommendations concerning the prevention and cessation of the violations of Rohingya human rights. These were of general and specific focus, such as discrimination, human trafficking, and participating and voting in elections. In 2011, there were six mentions of the Rohingya; in 2015 there were 45. However, in both UPRs, Myanmar's response to all recommendations regarding the Rohingya was that such recommendations "did not enjoy the support of Myanmar". This is a clear manifestation of a main weakness of the UPR procedure: that it results only in 'recommendations' without any enforcement mechanism.[99]

56.4.2 The United Nations Security Council

A (UNSC response, such as passing a resolution, is a possibility for international action against Myanmar in response to Myanmar's violations of international law. However, this is not a promising option, because the Permanent Five states' veto powers include Russia and China, who have interest in blocking any resolution condemning or taking action against Myanmar. In particular, China, a neighbouring state, has economic interests, including gas pipelines through Myanmar, and thus protects Myanmar and its sovereignty.[100] While individual states such as the USA and Australia have enacted sanctions against individual members of the Tatmadaw, there is little to no likelihood that global sanctions will be enforced by the UNSC, nor

---

[97] For more detail on the UPR, see Chap. 11 on International Human Rights Law by the present author.

[98] Human Rights Council, Report of the Working Group on the Universal Periodic Review: Myanmar, 23 December 2015, Thirty-first Session, UN Doc. A/HRC/31/13; Human Rights Council, Report of the Working Group on the Universal Periodic Review: Myanmar, 24 March 2011, Seventeenth Session, UN Doc. A/HRC/17/9.

[99] Collister 2015, p. 115. See also Chap. 11 on International Human Rights Law by the present author.

[100] TNI 2019.

any more serious decisions such as intervention. UNSC members visited Bangladesh and Myanmar in 2018, particularly to observe the Rohingya situation. They stated that they were "struck by the scale of the humanitarian crisis and remain gravely concerned by the current situation", but the visit resulted in nothing further than this statement.[101] After the International Court of Justice (ICJ) preliminary measures order (see below), the UNSC met to discuss issuing a statement about the binding nature of the ICJ's order on Myanmar. However, China and Vietnam refused the issuance of a joint statement, so no UNSC statement was issued. Instead, the EU UNSC member states called for Myanmar to comply with the ICJ's order.[102] This confirms that, even in the face of an ICJ ruling, China is still unwilling to call on Myanmar to stop atrocities.

56.4.3 International Court of Justice

With regards to state responsibility, Myanmar can be held accountable for its violations of human rights and IHL treaty law, and the Genocide Convention, as well as any relevant customary international law.[103] However, the applicable IHL treaty law is minimal, because only the Cultural Property Protection instruments, the Chemical Weapons Convention and Common Article 3 of the Geneva Conventions apply to non-international armed conflict (NIAC). Proceedings could be commenced in the ICJ by any other state party to the relevant conventions, alleging a breach of the said instrument.[104] Likewise, where any of the conduct of Myanmar amounts to a breach of customary international law, such as the commission of war crimes[105] or genocide, any state could commence proceedings before the ICJ.

In November 2019, The Gambia filed proceedings against Myanmar in the ICJ, alleging breaches of Myanmar's obligations under the Genocide Convention and requesting the Court to order Myanmar to cease these internationally wrongful acts, ensure perpetrators of genocide are punished, provide reparations to victims

---

[101] United Nations Security Council, Security Council Press Statement on Security Council Visit to Bangladesh, Myanmar (9 May 2018), https://www.un.org/press/en/2018/sc13331.doc.htm. Accessed 5 March 2020.

[102] AP, 'UN Takes No Action on Order Against Myanmar on Rohingyas', *The New York Times*, 4 February 2020.

[103] For example, a 2019 UN report on sexual violence by the Tatmadaw specifically frames this conduct as violations of the human rights treaties that Myanmar is a state party to. See Gender-Based Violence in Myanmar, paras 98 and 144.

[104] Becker 2018; O'Brien 2020.

[105] Not all IHL rules apply to NIAC; see the ICRC Customary IHL Database for specific IHL customary rules applying to NIAC. ICRC, Customary IHL Database, https://ihl-databases.icrc.org/customary-ihl/eng/docs/home. Accessed 5 March 2020.

56 Myanmar

of the Rohingya genocide, and offer assurances and guarantees of non-repetition of violations of the Genocide Convention.[106]

The Gambia also requested urgent provisional measures, the hearings for which were held in December 2019. The provisional measures request that Myanmar shall immediately act to prevent genocidal acts; ensure any military, paramilitary or irregular armed units or any other persons under its control, do not commit genocide; not destroy or render inaccessible any events related to the Rohingya genocide; provide access to UN investigative mechanisms; not take any action to aggravate the dispute between the Gambia and Myanmar; provide a report to the Court on all measures taken within four months of the order.[107] Myanmar's arguments against the request included several jurisdictional considerations, and the claim that if there are crimes being committed, they are not genocide, but 'excesses' of the military in an armed conflict.[108]

In January 2020, the ICJ ruled on the provisional measures. Four of Gambia's six requested provisional measures were unanimously granted:

1. Myanmar shall "take all measures within its power to prevent the commission of all acts within the scope of Article II of [the Genocide Convention]" (where Article II is the definition of genocide).
2. Myanmar shall ensure that its military and other armed groups under its control, direction or influence, do not commit, conspire to commit, incite, attempt or be complicit in Article II acts.
3. Myanmar "shall take effective measures to prevent the destruction and ensure the preservation of evidence related to allegations of acts within the scope of Article II of the Convention".
4. Myanmar must submit a report to the ICJ about its activities implementing the order, the first within four months of the order, and then subsequently every six months until the final decision is rendered.[109]

While this is only a provisional measures order, there were significant elements within the order. Firstly, the ICJ held that the Rohingya "appear to constitute a protected group within the meaning of Article II of the Genocide Convention".[110] This is important recognition of the status of the Rohingya as a distinct minority group, particularly in the context that Myanmar, in its provisional measures arguments in December 2019, did not use the word 'Rohingya', instead referring to

---

[106] *Application of the Convention on the Prevention and Punishment of the Crime of Genocide (The Gambia v. Myanmar)*, ICJ, Application Instituting Proceedings and Request for the Indication of Provisional Measures, 11 November 2019.

[107] Ibid.; and see verbatim record of daily hearings, particularly Verbatim record 2019/20 of 12 December 2019, during which The Gambia summarised the provisional measures request.

[108] See *Application of the Convention on the Prevention and Punishment of the Crime of Genocide (The Gambia v. Myanmar)*, ICJ, Verbatim records 2019/19 (11 Dec 2019) and 2019/21 (12 Dec 2019).

[109] *Application on the Convention of the Prevention and Punishment of the Crime of Genocide (The Gambia v. Myanmar)*, ICJ, Order of 23 January 2020, p. 25 para 86.

[110] Ibid., p. 16, para 52.

'Muslims'. This has been reported to have already had an impact, with the media in Myanmar reportedly now using the term Rohingya openly.[111]

The second crucial aspect of the ruling is that the ICJ confirmed that any state party to the Genocide Convention may bring proceedings against another state party, even if they are not a specially affected state.[112] This affirms the status of the Genocide Convention as a special treaty that represents a common interest to prevent and punish genocide. However, it is impossible to assess the compliance of Myanmar with the provisional orders, as the ICJ has not made Myanmar's reports public, despite there being no legal reason for secrecy of these reports.[113]

ICJ cases usually take years from the initial filing to final decision. The *Bosnia and Herzegovina v Serbia and Montenegro (Genocide)* Case took 14 years from filing to final decision.[114] Initially, the ICJ set quite short time-limits for the filing of initial pleadings, requiring The Gambia to submit their Memorial by 23 July 2020 and Myanmar their Counter-Memorial by 25 January 2021. Such a tight timeframe was noted by the Court to be due to "the exceptional circumstances of the case and its gravity".[115] This demonstrates that the Court is acknowledging the seriousness of the situation, with an ongoing genocide that the Court has a role in stopping. This may be due in part to the lack of success of the provisional measures in the *Bosnia and Herzegovina v Serbia and Montenegro (Genocide)* Case, which did not prevent the Srebrenica genocide, and is no doubt a motivating factor for the Court to make a final decision on the merits.[116] However, submissions within such a tight timeframe have proven to be unachievable by the parties. On 18 May 2020, following an application filed by The Gambia, the ICJ granted an extension to the respective time limits for The Gambia and Myanmar to file the Memorial and Counter-Memorial.[117] On 20 January 2021, Myanmar filed preliminary objections to the ICJ's jurisdictions, and Gambia has until 20 May 2021 to respond to these objections.[118]

---

[111] M. Smith, Twitter, https://twitter.com/matthewfsmith/status/1220748639007580163. Accessed 5 March 2020.

[112] *Application on the Convention of the Prevention and Punishment of the Crime of Genocide (The Gambia v. Myanmar)*, ICJ, Order of 23 January 2020, p. 13, para 41.

[113] Abbott et al. 2020.

[114] The initial filings of which were in 1993 and final decision in 2007: *Application on the Convention of the Prevention and Punishment of the Crime of Genocide (Bosnia and Herzegovina v. Serbia and Montenegro)*, ICJ, Application instituting proceedings 20 March 1993; *Application on the Convention of the Prevention and Punishment of the Crime of Genocide (Bosnia and Herzegovina v. Serbia and Montenegro)*, ICJ, Judgment of 26 February 2007.

[115] *Application on the Convention of the Prevention and Punishment of the Crime of Genocide (The Gambia v. Myanmar)*, ICJ, Fixing of Time-Limits for the Filing of the Initial Pleadings 28 January 2020.

[116] DeWeese 1998.

[117] Extensions were granted from 23 July 2020 to 23 October 2020 for The Gambia, and from 25 January 2021 to 23 July 2021 for Myanmar; *The Gambia v Myanmar*, ICJ, Order of 18 May 2020, Extension of time-limits: Memorial and Counter-Memorial, General List No.178.

[118] *The Gambia v Myanmar*, ICJ, Order of 28 January 2021, Fixing of time-limit: Written statement of observations and submissions on preliminary objections, General List No.178.

56.4.4 International Criminal Court

Under international criminal law, individuals are held responsible for the commission of mass atrocities, whether through domestic criminal law or international criminal courts and tribunals. It is of course unlikely that the Myanmar government and military will ever hold itself accountable for the commission of war crimes and genocide. Thus, the only real option is international criminal justice. The challenge here is that Myanmar is, unsurprisingly, not a state party to the Rome Statute of the International Criminal Court (ICC).[119] The ICC's jurisdiction extends only to the territory of a state party, crimes committed by a national of a state party, or situations referred to the Court by the UNSC. Thus the ICC has no jurisdiction by the first two means over crimes committed in Myanmar, leaving only the possibility of a UNSC referral. However, as noted above, action by the UNSC is unlikely given China's support for Myanmar.

In response to this jurisdictional impediment, in 2018 the ICC Prosecutor began a process that is heading towards allowing the ICC to exercise jurisdiction over some crimes committed in Myanmar against the Rohingya. Firstly, the Office of the Prosecutor (OTP) formally requested the ICC's Pre-Trial Division to determine whether the ICC has jurisdiction over the crime against humanity of deportation of the Rohingya from Myanmar to Bangladesh. This request was based on the fact that Bangladesh is a state party to the ICC, and therefore the ICC has jurisdiction over crimes committed within its territory. The request argued that the crime of deportation contains a "legal requirement that the victim is forced to cross an international border... In circumstances where the enforced border-crossing takes the victim directly into the territory of another State, this legal element [of the crime] is completed in that second State."[120] Thus, the OTP argued that at least one legal element of the crime was committed in Bangladesh, in accordance with legal principles that require only part of a crime to occur on a state's territory.[121]

The ICC responded that it does have jurisdiction, agreeing that the definition of deportation requires crossing a border to another state, thus permitting ICC jurisdiction where the other state is a state party to the Rome Statute.[122] The Court also suggested that there would be jurisdiction over the crimes against humanity of persecution and other inhumane acts.[123] Consequently, in 2019, the OTP made a request for authorisation of an investigation into "the Situation in Bangladesh/Myanmar in

---

[119] 1998 Rome Statute of the International Criminal Court 2187 UNTS 90.

[120] Prosecution's Request for a Ruling on Jurisdiction under Article 19(3) of the Statute, Case No. ICC-RoC46(3)-01/18-1, 9 April 2018, para 13; see also paras 26–27. For procedural commentary, see Vagias 2018.

[121] Ibid., paras 28–50.

[122] Decision on the "Prosecution's Request for a Ruling on Jurisdiction under Article 19(3) of the Statute", Case No. ICC-RoC46(3)-01/18-1, Decision of 6 September 2018. For commentary, see Colvin and Orchard 2018; Guilfoyle 2018; Hale and Rankin 2018; Pedersen 2019; Vagias 2018; 2019.

[123] Ibid., paras 60, 64, 71–73.

the period since 9 October 2016 and continuing", where at least one element of the crimes occurred in Bangladesh.[124]

The only crimes detailed in the request are the crimes against humanity of deportation, persecution (on the grounds of ethnicity and/or religion) and other inhumane acts. However, in November 2019, Pre-Trial Chamber III (PTC) of the ICC authorised the OTP to investigate the situation in Bangladesh/Myanmar, and provided a wide scope, materially and temporally. The material scope is authorised to include "*any crime* within the jurisdiction of the Court committed at least in part on the territory of Bangladesh, or on the territory of any other State Party… if the alleged crime is sufficiently linked to the situation as described".[125] Thus, the ICC specifically stated that the Prosecutor is not restricted to those events and crimes identified in the Prosecutor's Request or in the jurisdiction decision. The Prosecutor has been given authorisation to investigate other crimes against humanity or any other of the crimes under the jurisdiction of the court.[126]

With regards to the *ratione temporis* jurisdiction, the Chamber noted that the Rome Statute entered into force on 1 June 2010, and thus authorised the investigation to include crimes committed from the date of entry into force onwards.[127] The PTC also authorised investigation into crimes commenced before 1 June 2010, provided the crimes continued after that date.[128]

The PTC further provided some leeway with the territorial scope of the investigation, permitting the Prosecutor to extend investigation to "alleged crimes committed at least in part on the territory of other States Parties… insofar as they are sufficiently linked to the situation as described… irrespective of the nationality of the perpetrators".[129] This means that the Prosecutor may investigate the situation of Rohingya refugees in Rome Statute state parties other than Bangladesh. However, this is unlikely to occur, as the majority of Rohingya refugees not in Bangladesh are located in non-state parties, such as Pakistan, Saudi Arabia and Malaysia.[130]

Due to jurisdictional limitations under which the OTP can only prosecute crimes with at least one element occurring in Bangladesh, the OTP's focus to date has been only on the three crimes against humanity mentioned above. Crimes of genocide were not included in the request, although it can be hoped that, given the wide ambit given by the Pre-Trial Chamber, the OTP will nonetheless include this in

---

[124] Situation in the People's Republic of Bangladesh/Republic of the Union of Myanmar, Request for Authorisation of an Investigation Pursuant to Article 15, Case No. ICC-01/09, 4 July 2019.

[125] Decision Pursuant to Article 15 of the Rome Statute on the Authorisation of an Investigation into the Situation in the People's Republic of Bangladesh/Republic of the Union of Myanmar, Case No. ICC-01/19, 14 November 2019, p. 54.

[126] Ibid.

[127] Ibid., p. 56.

[128] Ibid.

[129] Ibid., pp. 53–54.

[130] While Malaysia is not a state party to the ICC, it is an example state of where Rohingya have fled, finding themselves without support or means of sustenance and being forcibly assimilated. See Hoffstaedter and O'Brien 2017. For a useful visualisation of the location of the majority of Rohingya refugees, see Asrar 2017.

its investigation and potential future charges. Genocidal crimes can be argued to continue with the mass exodus of refugees across a border, particularly the crimes of inflicting conditions of life designed to bring about the group's physical destruction (continued through horrendous refugee camp conditions such as disease, starvation and rape), and causing serious bodily or mental harm (including dealing with the conditions in refugee camps or living as an unwanted migrant).

56.5 Conclusion

As evidenced by the discussion in this chapter, there are serious issues with the application of international law in and by Myanmar. Myanmar is party to very few treaties in the field of human rights law, IHL and international criminal law. This means that there are limited obligations on Myanmar to behave in a manner consistent with human rights and rule of law. It is a country ruled by military for decades, a power structure that, despite the alleged democratic and partially civilian nature of the state since 2012, has not changed, and the events of 2021 instead are a reversal away from civilian democracy to full military authoritarian rule. Human rights throughout Myanmar are limited,[131] and atrocities are commonplace, committed by government forces and sanctioned militias. War crimes continue to be committed by the Tatmadaw in the non-international armed conflicts taking place (with more commitment to IHL being demonstrated by non-state armed groups than the government); for the Rohingya, discrimination has morphed into genocide; and the 2021 coup has seen thousands detained and hundreds killed. Myanmar's legal system has not helped; rather, some of Myanmar's internal laws passed in recent years have exacerbated conflicts.[132]

Human rights mechanisms have been toothless against the disinterest of Myanmar. The UNSC is impotent while Myanmar has a very close relationship with P5 member, China.[133] It is unlikely that any action would be taken against Myanmar for war crimes committed in its non-international armed conflicts, especially given its few treaty obligations in this field. Thus, we are left with a hermit state with powerful friends, that cares little about how it is perceived outside its borders and thus conducts minimal engagement with international law, certainly not following the obligations it does have. However, with action being taken in the ICJ and the ICC, this demonstrates some hope for accountability for Myanmar and its military at least for the atrocities being committed against the Rohingya. For now, the outcomes of those cases remain to be seen, including whether or not Myanmar would comply with any arrest warrants issued or rulings handed down. It is only repeating what many other scholars and NGOs, and the UN, have said to note that there is a clear need for Myanmar to adopt a true "democratic framework that genuinely protects the human rights and equality

---

[131] Steinberg 2001, pp. 83–93.
[132] Crouch 2016, p. 224.
[133] Aung and McPherson 2020.

of every citizen of Myanmar without any discrimination".[134] States need to put far more pressure on Myanmar to respect international law and to cease human rights violations and atrocity crimes. The 2021 coup is a perfect opportunity for states to take action against Myanmar, not just for the human rights abuses during the coup, but all of the atrocities committed throughout the country.

References

Abbott K, Becker MA, Gelinas-Faucher B (2020) Rohingya Symposium: Why So Secret? The Case for Public Access to Myanmar's Reports on Implementation of the ICJ's Provisional Measures Order. http://opiniojuris.org/2020/08/25/rohingya-symposium-why-so-secret-the-case-for-public-access-to-myanmars-reports-on-implementation-of-the-icjs-provisional-measures-order/. Accessed 30 March 2021

Amnesty International (2017a) 'My world is finished' - Rohingya targeted in crimes against humanity in Myanmar. https://www.amnesty.org/download/Documents/ASA1672882017ENGLISH.PDF. Accessed 5 March 2020

Amnesty International (2017b) Myanmar: Scorched-earth campaign fuels ethnic cleansing of Rohingya from Rakhine state. https://www.amnesty.org/en/latest/news/2017/09/myanmar-scorched-earth-campaign-fuels-ethnic-cleansing-of-rohingya-from-rakhine-state/. Accessed 5 March 2020

Amnesty International (2017c) "Caged Without a Roof" Apartheid in Myanmar's Rakhine State. ASA 16/7484/2017. https://www.amnesty.org/en/documents/asa16/7484/2017/en/. Accessed 18 August 2020.

Amnesty International (2018) Myanmar 2017/2018. https://www.amnesty.org/en/countries/asia-and-the-pacific/myanmar/report-myanmar/. Accessed 5 March 2020

Anderson B (2006) Imagine communities: Reflections on the origin and spread of nationalism, rev. edn. Verso, New York/London

Asar S (2017) Rohingya crisis explained in maps. Al Jazeera. https://www.aljazeera.com/indepth/interactive/2017/09/rohingya-crisis-explained-maps-170910140906580.html. Accessed 5 March 2020

Aung TT, McPherson P (2020) Myanmar, China ink deals to accelerate Belt and Road as Xi courts an isolated Suu Kyi. Reuters. https://www.reuters.com/article/us-myanmar-china/myanmar-china-ink-deals-to-accelerate-belt-and-road-as-xi-courts-an-isolated-suu-kyi-idUSKBN1ZH054. Accessed 5 March 2020

Baulk D (2017) Performing accountability: Understanding the Myanmar military's impunity for human rights violations, Paper presented at the CHGS Conference Proceedings, Clark University

Becker M A (2018) The situation of the Rohingya: Is there a role for the International Court of Justice? https://www.ejiltalk.org/the-situation-of-the-rohingya-is-there-a-role-for-the-international-court-of-justice/. Accessed 5 March 2020

Brenner D (2018) Inside the Karen insurgency: Explaining conflict and conciliation in Myanmar's changing borderlands. Asian Security 14:83-99

Bugher M (2017) Crimes in Myanmar: The campaign for accountability and a UN Commission of Inquiry. Paper presented at the CHGS Conference Proceedings, Clark University

Carstens C (2017) Religion. In: Simpson A, Farrelly N, Holliday I (eds) Routledge Handbook of Contemporary Myanmar. Routledge, Abingdon, pp. 126-135

Cathcart G S (2016) Landmines as a form of community protection in Eastern Myanmar. In: Cheesman N, Farrelly N (eds) Conflict in Myanmar: War, politics, religion. ISEAS Yusof Ishak Institute, Singapore, pp. 121–136

---

[134] Khan 2016, p. 345.

Cheesman N (2019) Routine impunity as practice (in Myanmar). Human Rights Quarterly 41:873-892

Cho V (2017) Ethnicity and identity. In: Simpson A, Farrelly N, Holliday I (eds) Routledge Handbook of Contemporary Myanmar. Routledge, Abingdon, pp. 43-52

Chynoweth S (2018) 'It's happening to our men as well': Sexual violence Against Rohingya men and boys. https://www.womensrefugeecommission.org/gbv/resources/1664-its-happening-to-our-men-as-well. Accessed 5 March 2020

Collister H (2015) Rituals and implementation in the Universal Period Review and the human rights treaty bodies. In: Charlesworth H, Larking E (eds) Human Rights and the Universal Periodic Review: Rituals and Ritualism. Cambridge University Press, Cambridge, pp. 109-125

Colvin V, Orchard P (2018) The Rohingya jurisdiction decision: a step forward for stopping forced deportations. Aust J Int'l Aff 73:16-21

Crouch M (2015) Constructing religion by law in Myanmar. The Review of Faith & International Affairs 13:1-11

Crouch M (2016) Legislating reform? Law and conflict in Myanmar. In: Farrelly N, Cheesman N (eds) Conflict in Myanmar: War, politics, religion. ISEAS Yusof Ishak Institute, Singapore, pp. 221-242

Crouch M (2019a) The constitution of Myanmar: A contextual analysis. Hart, London

Crouch M (2019b) Illiberalism and democratic illusions in Myanmar. https://www.newmandala.org/illusions-in-myanmar/. Accessed 5 March 2020

DeWeese G S (1998) The failure of the International Court of Justice to effectively enforce the Genocide Convention. Denv J nt'l & Pol'y 26:625-654

Dolan T, Gray S (2014) Media and Conflict in Myanmar. United States Institute for Peace. https://www.usip.org/publications/2014/01/media-and-conflict-myanmar. Accessed 18 August 2020.

Farrelly N (2014) Cooperation, contestation, conflict: Ethnic political interests in Myanmar today. South East Asia Research 22:251-266

Fortify Rights (2015) Persecution of the Rohingya Muslims: Is Genocide Occurring in Myanmar's Rakhine State? Allard K. Lowenstein International Human Rights Clinic, Yale Law School. https://www.fortifyrights.org/downloads/Yale_Persecution_of_the_Rohingya_October_2015.pdf. Accessed 18 August 2020.

Fortify Rights (2016) Five years of war: A Call for peace, justice, and accountability in Myanmar. https://www.fortifyrights.org/mya-inv-js-2016-06-09/. Accessed 5 March 2020

Fortify Rights (2019) 'Tools of genocide': National verification cards and the denial of citizenship of Rohingya Muslims in Myanmar. https://www.fortifyrights.org/mya-bgd-rep-2019-09-03/. Accessed 5 March 2020

Ganesan N (2015) Ethnic insurgency and the nationwide ceasefire agreement in Myanmar. Asian Journal of Peacebuilding 3:273-286

Green P, MacManus T, de la Cour Venning A (2015) Countdown to annihilation: Genocide in Myanmar. http://statecrime.org/data/2015/10/ISCI-Rohingya-Report-PUBLISHED-VERSION.pdf. Accessed 5 March 2020

Green P, MacManus T, de la Cour Venning A (2018) Genocide achieved, genocide continues: Myanmar's annihilation of the Rohingya. http://statecrime.org/data/2018/04/ISCI-Rohingya-Report-II-PUBLISHED-VERSION-revised-compressed.pdf. Accessed 5 March 2020

Guilfoyle D (2018) The ICC pre-trial chamber decision on jurisdiction over the situation in Myanmar. Aust J Int'l Aff 73:2–8 =

Hale K, Rankin M (2018) Extending the 'system' of international criminal law? The ICC's decision on jurisdiction over alleged deportations of Rohingya people. Aust J Int'l 73:22–28Aff

Hedström J (2015) Gender and Myanmar's Kachin conflict. https://www.newmandala.org/gender-and-myanmars-kachin-conflict/. Accessed 5 March 2020

Hedström J (2016) A feminist political economy analysis of insecurity and violence in Kachin State. In: Farrelly N, Cheesman N (eds) Conflict in Myanmar: War, politics, religion. ISEAS–Yusof Ishak Institute, Singapore, pp 67–90

Hedström J (2017) The political economy of the Kachin revolutionary household. The Pacific Review 30:581-595

Hodal K (2014) Burma tells Medécins Sans Frontières to leave state hit by sectarian violence. The Guardian. https://www.theguardian.com/world/2014/feb/28/burma-medecins-sans-frontieres-rakhine-state. Accessed 18 August 2020.

Hoffstaedter G, O'Brien M (2017) The Rohingya genocide does not end at Myanmar's borders. Religion and Ethics. http://www.abc.net.au/religion/articles/2017/09/20/4737378.htm. Accessed 5 March 2020

Hogan L, Safi M (2018) Revealed: Facebook hate speech exploded in Myanmar during Rohingya crisis. The Guardian. https://www.theguardian.com/world/2018/apr/03/revealed-facebook-hate-speech-exploded-in-myanmar-during-rohingya-crisis. Accessed 5 March 2020

Htusan E (2020) Briefing: The growing emergency on Myanmar's newest battleground. The New Humanitarian. https://www.thenewhumanitarian.org/news/2020/02/18/Myanmar-Rakhine-conflict-Arakan-army-displacement-internet-shutdown. Accessed 19 August 2020.

Human Rights Council (2018) Report of the detailed findings of the Independent International Fact-Finding Mission on Myanmar, 17 September 2018, Thirty-ninth Session, 10–28 September 2018, UN Doc A/HRC/39/CRP.2

Human Rights Council (2019a) The economic interests of the Myanmar military: Independent International Fact-Finding Mission on Myanmar, 5 August 2019, Forty-second Session, 9-27 September 2019, UN Doc. A/HRC/42/CRP.3

Human Rights Council (2019b) Sexual and gender-based violence in Myanmar and the gendered impact of its ethnic conflicts, 22 August 2019, Forty-second Session, 9–27 September 2019, UN Doc. A/HRC/42/CRP.4

Human Rights Watch (2013) 'All you can do is pray'. Crimes against humanity and ethnic cleansing of Rohingya Muslims in Burma's Arakan state. https://www.hrw.org/report/2013/04/22/all-you-can-do-pray/crimes-against-humanity-and-ethnic-cleansing-rohingya-muslims. Accessed 5 March 2020

Human Rights Watch (2015) Burma: Reject Discrimination Population Bill (16 May 2015). https://www.hrw.org/news/2015/05/16/burma-reject-discriminatory-population-bill. Accessed 5 March 2020

Human Rights Watch (2017) 'All of my body was pain': Sexual violence against Rohingya women and girls in Burma. https://www.hrw.org/sites/default/files/report_pdf/burma1117_web_1.pdf. Accessed 5 March 2020

Human Rights Watch (2019) Myanmar events of 2018. https://www.hrw.org/world-report/2019/country-chapters/burma. Accessed 5 March 2020]

Human Rights Watch (2021) Martial Law in Myanmar a Death Knell for Fair Trials. https://www.hrw.org/news/2021/03/16/martial-law-myanmar-death-knell-fair-trials. Accessed 30 March 2021.

Ibrahim A (2018) The Rohingyas: Inside Myanmar's genocide, 2nd edn. Hurst & Company, London

Institute for Security and Diplomacy Policy (2015) Myanmar's nationwide ceasefire agreement. http://isdp.eu/publication/myanmars-nationwide-ceasefire-agreement/. Accessed 5 March 2020

International Human Rights Law Clinic (2009) Crimes in Burma. http://hrp.law.harvard.edu/wp-content/uploads/2009/05/Crimes-in-Burma.pdf. Accessed 5 March 2020

Kamler E M (2015) Women of the Kachin conflict: Trafficking and militarized femininity on the Burma-China border. Journal of Human Trafficking 1:209-234

Kean T (2019) KNU rejects reports armed groups will support govt over ICJ case. Frontier Myanmar. https://frontiermyanmar.net/en/knu-rejects-reports-armed-groups-will-support-govt-over-icj-case. Accessed 5 March 2020

Khan H M (2016) Threat perceptions in the Myanmar–Bangladesh borderlands. In: Farrelly N, Cheesman N (eds) Conflict in Myanmar: War, politics, religion. ISEAS–Yusof Ishak Institute, Singapore, pp 333–350

Khen S I, Nyoi M Y H (2014) Looking at the current peace process in Myanmar through a gender lens. https://www.swisspeace.ch/publications/reports/looking-at-the-current-peace-process-in-myanmar-through-a-gender-lens. Accessed 5 March 2020

Kipgen N (2015) Ethnic nationalities and the peace process in Myanmar. Social Research: An International Quarterly 82:399-425

Kyaw N N (2015) Alienation, discrimination, and securitization: Legal personhood and cultural personhood of Muslims in Myanmar. The Review of Faith & International Affairs 13:50-59

Kyaw N N (2019a) Adulteration of pure native blood by aliens? Mixed race kapya in colonial and post-Colonial Myanmar. Social Identities 25:345-359

Kyaw N N (2019b) Regulating Buddhism in Myanmar: The case of deviant Buddhist sects. In: Jamal A A, Goh D P S, Neo J L (eds), Regulating religion in Asia: Norms, Modes, and Challenges. Cambridge University Press, Cambridge, pp. 169-186

Kyaw N W H, Nwe S S (2019) From margin to center: Experiences of political and social marginalization of ethnic minorities in Karenni state. https://www.fes-myanmar.org/publications/. Accessed 5 March 2020

Laoutides C, Ware A (2016) Reexamining the centrality of ethnic identity to the Kachin conflict. In: Farrelly N, Cheesman N (eds) Conflict in Myanmar: War, politics, religion. ISEAS–Yusof Ishak Institute, Singapore, pp. 47–66

Lee R (2019) Extreme speech in Myanmar: The role of state media in the Rohingya forced migration crisis. International Journal of Communication 13:3203-3224

Lowenstein A K (2015) Persecution of the Rohingya Muslims: Is genocide occurring in Myanmar's Rakhine state? http://www.fortifyrights.org/downloads/Yale_Persecution_of_the_Rohingya_October_2015.pdf. Accessed 5 March 2020

McPherson P (2018) UN says it is still denied 'effective access' to Myanmar's Rakhine. Reuters. https://www.reuters.com/article/us-myanmar-rohingya-un/un-says-it-is-still-denied-effective-access-to-myanmars-rakhine-idUSKCN1L616F. Accessed 18 August 2020

Mills J (2000) Militarism, civil war and women's status: A Burma case study. In: Edwards L, Roces M (eds) Women in Asia: Tradition, modernity and globalisation. Allen & Unwin, St Leonards

Niang S (2020 Four Rohingya children killed in blast in Myanmar's Rakhine state. Reuters. https://www.reuters.com/article/us-myanmar-rohingya-explosion/four-rohingya-children-killed-in-blast-in-myanmars-rakhine-state-idUSKBN1Z61K1. Accessed 5 March 2020

Niang S, Aung T T (2019) Suu Kyi's loyalist rally for Myanmar leader before genocide trial. Reuters. https://www.reuters.com/article/us-myanmar-rohingya-justice/suu-kyis-loyalists-rally-for-myanmar-leader-before-genocide-trial-idUSKBN1Y61AA. Accessed 5 March 2020

O'Brien M (2020) The Rohingya crisis: Accountability for decades of persecution. In: Eski Y (ed) Genocide and victimology. Routledge, Abingdon [forthcoming]

OHCHR (2017a) Flash Report: Report of OHCHR mission to Bangladesh: Interviews with Rohingyas fleeing from Myanmar since 9 October 2016. United Nations Office of the High Commissioner for Human Rights

OHCHR (2017b) Report of OHCHR mission to Bangladesh: Interviews with Rohingyas fleeing from Myanmar since 9 October 2016. Retrieved from https://docs.google.com/viewer?url=%3A%2F%2Fwww.ohchr.org%2FDocuments%2FCountries%2FMM%2FFlashReport3Feb2017.pdf. Accessed 21 February 2022

Oo K M (2016a) A flea cannot make a whirl of dust, but-. The Global New Light of Myanmar. http://www.globalnewlightofmyanmar.com/a-flea-cannot-make-a-whirl-of-dust-but/. Accessed 5 March 2020

Oo K M (2016b) The thorn needs removing if it pierces! The Global New Light of Myanmar. http://www.globalnewlightofmyanmar.com/the-thorn-needs-removing-if-it-pierces/. Accessed 5 March 2020

Pedersen M B (2019) The ICC, the Rohingya and the limitations of retributive justice. Aust J Int'l Aff 73:9-15

Reuters (2018) Aung San Suu Kyi won't be stripped of Nobel peace prize despite Rohingya crisis. The Guardian. https://www.theguardian.com/world/2018/aug/30/aung-san-suu-kyi-wont-be-stripped-of-nobel-peace-prize-despite-rohingya-crisis. Accessed 5 March 2020

Sadan M (2015) Ongoing conflict in Kachin state. In: Singh D (ed) Southeast Asian Affairs. Institute of Southeast Asian Affairs, Singapore, pp 246–259

Serrato R (2018) Buddhist nationalists used Facebook to fuel hate speech in Myanmar. https://democracy-reporting.org/buddhist-nationalists-used-facebook-to-fuel-hate-speech-in-myanmar/. Accessed 5 March 2020

Smith M (2018) 'They gave them long swords': Preparations for genocide and crimes against humanity against Rohingya Muslims in Rakhine state, Myanmar. http://www.fortifyrights.org/downloads/Fortify_Rights_Long_Swords_July_2018.pdf Accessed 5 March 2020

Steinberg D I (2001) Burma: The state of Myanmar. Georgetown University Press, Washington D.C.

SUHAKAM and Fortify Rights (2019) 'Sold like fish': Crimes against humanity, mass graves, and human trafficking from Myanmar and Bangladesh to Malaysia from 2012 to 2015. https://drive.google.com/file/d/1bWRWUddQ7k1_iptBpUfGoLtgxnGXJLPw/view. Accessed 5 March 2020

Taylor R H (2009) The state in Myanmar. University of Hawai'i Press, Honolulu

Thawnghmung A M, Furnari M (2019) Anti-state armed groups in Myanmar: Origins, evolution and implications. In: Schreer B, Tan A T H (eds) Terrorism and insurgency in Asia: A contemporary examination of terrorist and separatist movements. Routledge, Milton, pp. 133-146

TNI (2019) Selling the Silk Road Spirit: China's Belt and Road Initiative in Myanmar. Transnational Institute 22: November. https://www.tni.org/en/selling-the-silk-road-spirit. Accessed 19 August 2020.

UNICEF (2018) More than 60 Rohingya babies born in Bangladesh refugee camps every day–UNICEF. https://www.unicef.org/press-releases/more-60-rohingya-babies-born-bangladesh-refugee-camps-every-day%E2%80%93-unicef. Accessed 5 March 2020

United States Department of State (2018) Documentation of atrocities in Northern Rakhine state. https://bd.usembassy.gov/documentation-of-atrocities-in-northern-rakhine-state/. Accessed 5 March 2020

UK FCDO (2021) UK sanctions further Myanmar military figures for role in coup: 25 February 2021. https://www.gov.uk/government/news/uk-sanctions-further-myanmar-military-figures-for-role-in-coup-february-25-2021. Accessed 30 March 2021

Vagias M (2018) The Prosecutor's request concerning the Rohingya deportation to Bangladesh: Certain procedural questions. LJIL 31:981-1002

Vagias M (2019) Case No. ICC-RoC46(3)-01/18, Decision on the 'Prosecution's Request for a Ruling on Jurisdiction Under Article 19(3) of the Statute'. AJIL 113:368-375

VOA News (2021) US, EU Impose Sanctions on Myanmar Coup Leaders. https://www.voanews.com/east-asia-pacific/us-eu-impose-sanctions-myanmar-coup-leaders. Accessed 30 March 2021

Wade F (2019) Myanmar's enemy within: Buddhist violence and the making of a Muslim 'other', 2nd edn. Zed Books, Croydon

Walton M J, McKay M, Mar Mar Kyi D K (2015) Women and Myanmar's 'Religious Protection Laws'. The Review of Faith & International Affairs 13:36–49

Ware A, Laoutides C (2018) Aung San Suu Kyi's extraordinary fall from grace. The Conversation. http://theconversation.com/aung-san-suu-kyis-extraordinary-fall-from-grace-104250. Accessed 5 March 2020

Weller M (2021) Myanmar: Testing the Democratic Norm in International Law. EJIL:Talk! https://www.ejiltalk.org/myanmar-testing-the-democratic-norm-in-international-law/. Accessed 30 March 2021

Weng L (2019) Myanmar army seizes ethnic mon armed group's base on Thai border. The Irrawaddy. https://www.irrawaddy.com/news/burma/myanmar-army-seizes-ethnic-mon-armed-groups-base-thai-border.html. Accessed 5 March 2020

Wilson T (2017) Why a national peace agreement is important for Myanmar. Asia & the Pacific Policy Studies 4:141-146

Women's League of Burma (2014) Same impunity, same patterns: Sexual abuses by the Burma army will not stop until there is a genuine civilian government. https://burmacampaign.org.uk/media/same_impunity_same_patterns.pdf. Accessed 5 March 2020

Zarni M, Cowley A (2014) The slow-burning genocide of Myanmar's Rohingya. Pacific Rim Law & Policy Journal 23:683-754

Melanie O'Brien (BA/LLB, GDLP, LLM, Ph.D., GCTT) is Associate Professor of International Law at the University of Western Australia, an award-winning teacher of International Humanitarian Law, Public International Law, and Legal Research. Her research examines the connection between human rights and the genocide process; and sexual exploitation by peacekeepers. She is President of the International Association of Genocide Scholars (IAGS) and co-convened the 2017 IAGS conference at University of Queensland. Melanie has conducted fieldwork and research across six continents. She is an admitted legal practitioner, and a long-term member of the International Humanitarian Law Committee of the Australian Red Cross. Melanie has previously worked at several Australian universities; the National Human Rights Institution of Samoa; and the Legal Advisory Section of the Office of the Prosecutor at the International Criminal Court. She is the author of *Criminalising Peacekeepers: Modernising National Approaches to Sexual Exploitation and Abuse* (2017, Palgrave) and tweets @DrMelOB.

Chapter 57
Northern Cyprus

Ioannis P. Tzivaras

Contents

57.1 Introduction: From Colony to Independence	1286
57.2 Cyprus Issue between Zurich and London	1287
57.3 The Establishment of Cyprus Democracy in 1960 and the Greco-Turkish Cyprus Republic	1288
57.4 The Period 1960–1963: The Post-Independence Breakdown	1289
57.5 From the Inter-Communal Disputes to the Breakdown of Constitutional Order	1289
57.6 On the Road to the Conflict of 1974: Inter-Communal Negotiations	1291
57.7 The First Intervention (Attila I) (July 1974)	1293
57.8 The Second Intervention (Attila II) (August 1974)	1294
57.9 Negotiations between Communities, Motherlands and the UN Involvement	1296
57.9.1 From "High-Level Agreements" to "Interim Agreement"	1296
57.9.2 From the "Draft Framework Agreement" to "Confidence Building Measures"	1297
57.9.3 The Annan Plan	1298
57.9.4 The New Era of Negotiations: The Cyprus Issue after Annan	1300
57.10 TRNC's Matters on State and Statehood and International Law	1301
57.11 Conclusion	1302
References	1303

Abstract The Cyprus issue is inseparably connected with the ongoing dispute between Greek Cypriots and Turkish Cypriots. Its starting point was the Turkish invasion of the Cyprus Republic in 1974. The outbreak of war in Cyprus is a multi-faceted issue, involving several parameters, causes and events. The proclamation of the Cyprus Republic was a temporary, even undesirable, development for both the Greek-Cypriot and Turkish-Cypriot Community. Despite the importance of the anti-colonial struggle, the majority of the Greek community fought for a union with Greece. On the contrary, the Turkish community wanted the division of the island between Greece and Turkey. The Cyprus war and, beyond that, the Cyprus issue are thorny, multi-dimensional problems, with many views and approaches directly connected with the bi-communal status quo. The Cyprus conflict created a number of lost opportunities and highlighted the absence of political realism, polarization and

I. P. Tzivaras (✉)
Department of Economics and Management, Open University of Cyprus (OUC), Nicosia, Cyprus
e-mail: ioannis.tzivaras@ouc.ac.cy

ideological constraints that put up barriers to a peaceful solution. This is illustrated by the fact that, since the start of negotiations on the settlement of the Cyprus issue, to date, the road to resolution is not easy, given its multifactorial nature.

Keywords Cyprus Republic · Cyprus Issue · Greek-Cypriots · Turkish-Cypriots · Bi-communal · Bi-zonal · London-Zurich Agreements · Intervention · Green Line · Annan · Referendum · Self-determination · Statehood

57.1 Introduction: From Colony to Independence

In 1878, after several conflicts and different occupiers, the Ottoman Empire ceded the administration of Cyprus to Great Britain. After the 1923 Treaty of Lausanne, Cyprus was a British protectorate; in 1925, it was proclaimed a Crown colony. Following that period, a number of Cypriot-triggered demands for independence and self-determination were recorded.[1]

In the late 19th century, a decisive movement started to emerge to determine whether a union with Greece (also known as enosis) was desired.[2] The consensus on this issue was clear in 1949, when 96% of Greek Cypriots voted in a plebiscite to unite with Greece. The British administration converted this dispute from colonial to ethnic, between Greek Cypriots and Turkish Cypriots, but soon the colonial policies promoted ethnic polarization. It was characteristic that in 1950, Archbishop Makarios, the leader of the Greek Cypriots, arranged a clandestine plebiscite in favour of union with the Greek state, a matter the Greek government referred to the UN in 1954, while the Turkish government favoured the maintenance of the *status quo* in Cyprus, with the support of Great Britain.[3]

In 1955, after tensions rose from British occupation, Greek Cypriots began an armed revolt against colonial leadership under the leadership of Colonel Georgios Grivas. This dispute was organized by the National Organization of Cypriot Fighters (also known as EOKA) and comprised right-wing Greek Cypriot nationalists who premised their agenda on the Great Idea and the union with Greece.[4] EOKA commenced four years (1955–1959) of guerrilla warfare against the British occupation in a coordinated series of armed attacks and sabotages against governmental and military installations in Nicosia, Larnaca, Limassol and Famagusta, in order to free Cyprus from foreign rule and "hellenize" the state through the union of Cyprus with Greece.[5] The armed campaign by EOKA for union with Greece and the Turkish Cypriot response for partition ("Taksim") brought a regime of supervised

---

[1] Faustmann and Peristianis 2006; Solomou and Faustmann 2010.

[2] Symeonides 2003, pp. 442–444; Hatzimihail 2013, pp. 39–42; Emerson 1960, pp. 295–325; Coughlan and Mallinson 2006, pp. 575–604.

[3] Faustmann 1999.

[4] Demetriou 2012, pp. 391–420.

[5] Hatzivassiliou 1997.

independence by the three guarantor powers.[6] Cyprus became an international issue and developed into an unresolved one, beyond Great Britain, between Greece and Turkey. This dispute rapidly led to a violent intercommunal conflict inside Cyprus.[7]

In contrast, the colonial secret services urged Turkish Cypriots to build their own clandestine organization, which became known as Volkan and, since 1957, as the Turkish Resistance Organization (also known as Türk Mukavemet Teşkilatı or TMT), which was formed to protect the Turkish Cypriots from EOKA threat.[8] TMT began to advocate a proposal on the division of the island into two certain geographical areas, each controlled by one of the communities,[9] with the aim of protecting Turkish Cypriots' identity against the Greek Cypriot enosis. The colonial authorities were increasingly at odds with the Turkish community, which had taken up arms in an attempt to secure the island's partition between Turkey and Greece.

In 1958, the Macmillan Plan was announced whereby a partnership between the two communities and the governments of Greece, Turkey and the United Kingdom was proposed. The plan was accepted by Turkey and Turkish Cypriots. Furthermore, in early October 1959, British authorities captured a Turkish ship named *Deniz* carrying weapons and ammunition for TMT. It was a special sign and a challenge, as well, for the relations between the two communities.

57.2 Cyprus Issue between Zurich and London

Given that Cyprus was on the verge of a civil interethnic war and that several attempts failed to secure a solution for the Cyprus issue, Great Britain, Greece and Turkey, for the first time, discussed the concept of an independent Cyprus and agreed to abandon any enosis or Taksim vision. Consequently, the two governments, represented by their foreign ministers, championing the rights of their own national communities in Cyprus, met at a conference held in February 1959 in Zurich, where it was agreed that an independent Cyprus should be created under Greece and Turkey's protection. The Zurich Conference produced an agreement based on a set of fundamental principles for the construction of a bi-communal independent, integral and unitary state, in which the public power would be shared by the two Cypriot Communities, with the agreement that certain areas of Cyprus should be retained under the United Kingdom's sovereignty.[10]

After the conclusion of the agreement in February 1959 in Zurich, a second round of negotiations started at Lancaster House in London on 17 February 1959. This second agreement was ratified and signed by the Prime Ministers of Great Britain, Greece and Turkey and by the leaders of the two Cypriot communities. Hence,

---

[6] Kalotychos 1998; Richter 2010.
[7] Holland 1999.
[8] Alleman 1958, pp. 9–12.
[9] Broome and Anastasiou 2012, pp. 293–324.
[10] Dodd 2010, pp. 86–98.

it should be clarified that the Zurich-London Agreements included a number of fundamental instruments and protocols, among other items. The most profound were the Basic Structure of the Republic of Cyprus; the Treaty of Guarantee, concluded between the Republic of Cyprus, Greece, Turkey and the United Kingdom; and the Treaty of Alliance, between Cyprus Republic, Greece and Turkey.[11]

57.3 The Establishment of Cyprus Democracy in 1960 and the Greco-Turkish Cyprus Republic

The transition period between February 1959 and August 1960 gave a self-government system organised under British supervision in an attempt to summarise the three sources of the Cyprus conflict, namely enosis, Taksim and colonialism.[12] After Greek and Turkish communities reached an agreement on a Constitution after the Zurich-London Agreements, on 16 August 1960, Cyprus gained independence and became a sovereign bi-ethnic republic, albeit in a limited way.[13] After the proclamation of independence, the notion of self-determination referred rather to a desire for sovereignty.[14]

After the first elections held to choose a president, vice president and members of representatives,[15] the democracy of Cyprus, as a non-unitary state, was founded on a dominant bi-communal basis in which the Greek Cypriots and the Turkish Cypriots were equally recognized but separate communities that had the status of co-founders and equal partners in their effort to run the new state.[16] Archbishop Makarios, from the Greek Cypriot community, and Fazil Küçük, from the Turkish Cypriot community, became the President and the Vice President of the Cyprus Republic. Given the enmity between EOKA and TMT and, in general, the relationship between Greek and Turkish communities, the new republic and its bicommunal governance had no specific provisions for unitary mechanisms and peaceful interethnic relations at the civil society level.

Given the bicommunal provisions and the practice in the case of Cyprus, the rise of ethnocentric nationalism was the main cause of the Cyprus conflict.[17] Both Greek Cypriot and Turkish Cypriot nationalism recognized Cyprus as a particular obstacle to their unitary agendas respectively. These binary aspirations were the core parameter that, in such circumstances, constituted the peace plan as a non-sustainable one.[18]

---

[11] Hoffmeister 2006, pp. 4–6.

[12] Sonyel 2003, pp. 12–14; Stephen 2000, pp. 4–10; Dodd 1998.

[13] Macris 2003.

[14] Richmond 2002, pp. 163–190; Tocci 2003, pp. 71–96.

[15] Drousiotis 2008, pp. 23–25.

[16] Stavrinides 1999, pp. 53–55.

[17] Attalides 1979, pp. 38–42; Papadakis 1998, pp. 149–164; Doob 1986, pp. 383–396.

[18] Beckingham 1957, pp. 165–174; Bryant 2004; Nevzat 2005.

57.4 The Period 1960–1963: The Post-Independence Breakdown

The Republic of Cyprus was an independent state and had been a member of the UN since 21 September 1961.[19] The 1960 Constitution, as a peace treaty, was a peculiar legal text with a complex and dysfunctional structure as a direct result of the compromise that emerged from the negotiations in Zurich and London, which was an essential regime of guaranteed independence.[20]

As a result, the constitutional text created an intense bicommunism, impeding the rational functioning of the state. The intercommunal mistrust was clearly observable and sharing powers were unthinkable and unworkable.[21] The Constitution, far from attempting to bring together the two Communities, perpetuated their separateness by setting up theoretical and technical rigorous bi-communalist provisions to represent two different communalist sets of arrangements instead of an independent and unified Cypriot set.[22]

Almost three years after independence, and given the complexity and multiplicity of the Constitution itself, Cyprus faced a constitutional crisis and, beyond major functional measures, problems raised from disputes over the sharing of civil services, the boundaries of the separate Greek Cypriot and Turkish Cypriot municipalities, as well as matters of taxation law and similar practices.[23]

After several problems and arguments that came up by the implementation of the Constitution and the legislative veto system, on 30 November 1963, President Makarios announced his intention to seek the amendment of the Constitution, putting forward a set of 13 proposals of constitutional revisions.[24] The amendment proposal concerned the smoothing of the relations between the Greek and Turkish communities, as well as the proper implementation of the Constitution and the elimination of impediments to the rational functioning of the Government.[25] It was characteristic that both Turkey and the Turkish Cypriots rejected the proposal.

57.5 From the Inter-Communal Disputes to the Breakdown of Constitutional Order

After the President's proposals about the Constitution amendment, Greek Cypriots believed that the Constitution prevented enosis with Greece and that the rights given to

---

[19] Adams 1966, pp. 475–490.
[20] Trimikliniotis 2015, pp. 247–266; Anastasiou 2008; Fouskas and Tackie 2009.
[21] Dodd 1993, pp. 6–8; Foley 1964.
[22] Markides 1977, pp. 86–89; Salem 1992, pp. 117–126.
[23] Weston-Markides 2001, pp. 128–130.
[24] Crawshaw 1964, pp. 428–435.
[25] Faustmann and Ker-Lindsay 2009, pp. 63–82.

Turkish Cypriots were too extensive. Based on that, the Greek Cypriots launched the Akritas Plan, which aimed at reforming the constitutional rules in favour of the Greek Cypriot part. After the rejection of the proposals by both the Turkish Government and the Turkish Cypriot community, the Turkish representation withdrew from the Cypriot government. As a result, the power-sharing government fell apart—along with the Constitution itself—a situation that born the "doctrine of necessity" on the government's functionality.[26] Nevertheless, the Republic continued to exist as a single international entity, with the collapse of power sharing, and was practically controlled by the Greek-Cypriot Community.

Prior to both the United States and the United Kingdom's efforts to appease both Greece and Turkey and their attempts to solve the Cyprus Issue before its escalation into an armed conflict, inter-communal violence erupted in Nicosia on 21 December 1963, where two Turkish Cypriots were killed at an incident involving the Greek Cypriot police forces, an incident that was the cause for the spread of violence in many areas of the island.[27]

Turkish members of the government, the House of Representatives, and members of the Army, police and civil service left their positions along with Turkish Cypriots and withdrew into Turkish quarters of areas around Nicosia and Famagusta, which were turned into armed enclaves. On 27 December, Great Britain, Greece and Turkey launched an interim peacekeeping force, the Joint Truce Force, to monitor the ceasefire and maintain order, which began the implementation of the Green Line Agreement.[28]

In general, in 1964, Turkey tried to intervene in the Cyprus Republic in response to the on-going intercommunal fighting. In January 1964, Great Britain called a conference in London in an attempt at a rapprochement between the two communities, which failed to make any headway towards abating the crisis. In the following months, violent incidents took place in various parts of Cyprus, especially near Paphos, Morphou, Nicosia, Ayios Vasilios and Erenköy and Limassol.[29] In March 1964, after Security Council Resolution 186,[30] the United Nations established the UN Peacekeeping Force in Cyprus (UNFICYP),[31] in order to act as an observer in the on-going crisis,[32] to contribute to the restoration of law and order and a return to normal conditions.[33]

---

[26] Kombos 2015; Emilianides 2019.

[27] Borowiec 2000, pp. 52–54.

[28] Ker-Lindsay 2006, pp. 561–572; Demetriou 2006, pp. 55–77; Calame and Charlesworth 2009.

[29] Ehrlich 1966, pp. 1021–1098; Demetriou 2007, pp. 987–1006.

[30] United Nations Security Council (1964) Resolution 186: The Cyprus Question, 4 March 1964, http://unscr.com/en/resolutions/186. Accessed 12 March 2020.

[31] United Nations Security Council (2020) Report of the Secretary-General 23: United Nations Operation in Cyprus, 7 January 2020, https://www.securitycouncilreport.org/un-documents/cyprus/. Accessed 12 September 2020. Beattie 2007.

[32] White 1993, pp. 241–247; Joseph 1985, pp. 113–116.

[33] Ker-Lindsay 2004, pp. 47–49; Necati-Ertekun 1983, pp. 13–17.

At the same time, the Turkish government threatened President Makarios about the military intervention of Turkey in order to protect the rights and the security of the Turkish Cypriots. United States President Lyndon Johnson informed Turkish Prime Minister, İsmet İnönü, on 6 June 1964, that the United States government would not approve the use of force in any intervention Turkey might take in Cyprus Republic[34] and recalled the two sides for peaceful negotiations. After President Makarios' request for military assistance to the USSR and Egypt, the parties agreed to a permanent ceasefire on 10 August 1964 after many killings and enforced displacements.[35]

Simultaneously, the UN Security Council recommended the designation of mediators to be in charge of peacekeeping efforts.[36] After the failure of Tuomioja's, Acheson's I & II, Plaza's and Vance's Plans as well as the attempt of Secretary General's Special Representative for Cyprus, Carlos Bernades, Security Council necessitate a series of UN Resolutions calling, *inter alia*, for respect of independence, sovereignty and territorial integrity of Cyprus Republic.[37]

57.6 On the Road to the Conflict of 1974: Inter-Communal Negotiations

In April 1967, a coup by a group of colonels brought Greece under a military dictatorship,[38] development that complicated the relationship between Greece and the Greek Cypriot Community.[39] During this period, the armed forces of Grivas were stronger than ever, in addition to the reduction provided by the Treaty of Alliance, where many of them had infiltrated into Cyprus, beyond the National Guard, which comprised a respectable number of soldiers.

A new series of attacks was carried out against Turkish Cypriots by EOKA members.[40] Given the well-planned attacks upon the Turkish Cypriot quarter of Boğaziçi and the village of Geçitkale, the Greek-Cypriot forces succeeded in cutting off the Turkish Cypriots in the south of the island from those in the north part.

In November 1967, Cyprus witnessed its most severe bout of intercommunal fighting since 1964.[41] In response to an attack on Turkish Cypriot villages in southern Cyprus, Turkey bombed Greek Cypriot forces. After several clashes between Greek Cypriots and Turkish Cypriots in villages near Limassol and Larnaca from July to August 1967, in response to attacks in Turkish Cypriot villages in the south, Greek

---

[34] Nicolet 2001; Stearns 1992, pp. 86–88.
[35] Stergiou 2007, pp. 83–106.
[36] Richmond 2001, pp. 102–104; Claude 2001, pp. 246–248; Papandreou 1970, pp. 99–101.
[37] Gary 1981, pp. 244–286; Negatigil 1993, pp. 174–182.
[38] Woodhouse 1991, pp. 293–295.
[39] Danopoulos 1982, pp. 257–273.
[40] Camp 1980, pp. 43–69.
[41] Demetriou 2007, pp. 987–1006.

Cypriot forces were bombed. Meanwhile, Greece agreed to recall General Grivas, the commander of the Greek Cypriot National Guard, to reduce its forces to Cyprus. A NATO mediation was the reason for the withdrawal of Greece's troops from Cyprus, which was completed on 16 January 1968.[42]

Given that inter-communal violence did not stop in 1964, but continued in 1967 and 1968, the Turkish Cypriots established the Provisional Turkish Cypriot Administration on 28 December 1968. It was a move that completely sealed the separation of the two communities.

After the Greek Cypriot elections held in July 1970, in 1971, the high command of the Turkish armed forces launched a coup in Turkey against the backdrop of political fractionalization and economic instability, placing the Turkish state under military rule. These developments marked a radicalization of the nationalism of both governments, a situation that played an important role on the issue of intercommunal disorder.[43]

While tensions between Greek Cypriots and Turkish Cypriots subsided after 1967, dangerous new conflicts arose among members of the Greek Cypriot Community. President Makarios abandoned the union with Greece in favour of an attainable solution with the Turkish Cypriot Community, whereas a large part of Greek Cypriots continued to believe that the only legitimate solution was the enosis with Greece.[44] General Grivas, who secretly returned to Cyprus, reestablished EOKA-B, which repeatedly tried to overthrow President Makarios. On his death in 1974, the organization fell under the control of Dimitrios Ioannides, a member of the Junta in Athens, who was determined to bring about union with Greece.

In July 1974, Makarios requested that the Greek military dictatorship remove all Greek officers from Cyprus who had been plotting covert actions and undermining his authority. On 15 July 1974, the Greek Cypriot National Guard enacted a coup against President Makarios on the grounds of union with Greece.[45] Nicos Sampson assumed the Presidency and he was declared the new President of the Republic on 16 July.[46] It must be noted that, consequently, the coup provided Turkey with the opportunity to make an intervention in Cyprus under the provisions of the London and Zurich Treaties of Guarantee.[47]

The UN involvement, as both peacemaker and peacekeeper, was connected to various unsuccessful negotiations in an attempt to bridge the political divisions between the two communities.[48] From May 1968 until 1974, several intercommunal rounds of talks began under the UN auspices for the constitutional problem on the basis of an integral and independent republic, but they all failed to establish a peace frame. The willingness to cooperate and the different approaches to the state problem,

---

[42] Richmond 1998, pp. 67–73, 108–110.

[43] Broome and Anastasiou 2012, pp. 293–324; Gokalp 1959; Tachau 1959, pp. 262–272.

[44] Panteli 1990, pp. 223–225.

[45] Crawshaw 1978; Mavratsas 1997, pp. 718–737.

[46] For an overview of the origins of the conflict, see generally Stephen 2000.

[47] Kassimeris 2008, pp. 256–273.

[48] Newman 2001, pp. 123–129.

from both Greek Cypriots and Turkish Cypriots, were the main causes of the failure of negotiations between them.[49] This was justified by the fact that the Greek Cypriots were trying to maintain total control of the government, while the Turkish Cypriots were trying to maintain regional autonomy in their enclaves.

57.7 The First Intervention (Attila I) (July 1974)

On 15 July 1974, the National Guard, with the support of Greek Junta, stormed the Presidential Palace and Makarios fled to Malta and from there to London, via the British base of Akrotiri. The same day, in the Meeting of the Turkish National Security Council, Finance Minister Deniz Baykal suggested a military intervention in Cyprus, an opinion that revealed the strategic Turkish policy on Cyprus Issue.[50] Despite its obligation as a protector of the Turkish Cypriot minority and as a guarantor of the Republic of Cyprus, Turkey decided to act unilaterally and began a military intervention[51] on 20 July 1974, with the support of Turkish Prime Minister Ecevit.[52]

Given the refusal of Great Britain to participate in the intervention[53] and the fact that Greece was informed of the concentration of Turkish landing forces in Turkish ports close to Cyprus, Turkey made use of its right as a guaranteeing power, based on Article 4 of the Treaty of Guarantee.[54] Turkish Armed Forces (TSK) invaded Cyprus by heavily armed troops who landed in Kyrenia, and the Turkish Air Force began bombing Greek positions.

It was an invasion that took place to protect the Turkish Cypriots and guarantee the independence of Cyprus.[55] Turkey took the initiative to intervene, by the use of military force, because such an act was considered to be a safeguard against the union with Greece, the protection of its co-nationals and the advantage of the Turkish state to have access to the Mediterranean.

In response, many Turkish Cypriots of the enclave of Limassol surrendered to the Cypriot National Guard, while, at the same time, areas around Famagusta and Morphou Bay were occupied by Greek Cypriots. It is characteristic that during this period, many Greek Cypriots were imprisoned in Adana and Saray Prisons, along with many Turkish Cypriots in various prison camps around Cyprus. Turkish military forces established a narrow corridor linking the north of Nicosia and occupied the north Turkish Cypriot enclave. Greek Cypriots lost the entire north coast and the Karpas peninsula, as well as the region of the eastern port city of Famagusta.

---

[49] Stavrou-Michael 2009, pp. 7–36.

[50] Barkey and Gordon 2002, pp. 83–93.

[51] It must be noted that Greek-Cypriots refer to this as an invasion and Turkish-Cypriots as a Peace Operation.

[52] Birand 1985, pp. 48–55; Drousiotis 2006.

[53] Burke 2017.

[54] Hadjipavlou 2007, pp. 349–365; Loizides 2007, pp. 172–189.

[55] Asmussen 2008.

After a ceasefire was implemented by the election of Glafkos Clerides as the President of Cyprus Republic, Great Britain called both sides for further discussion on 25 July—without any positive measures.[56] Subsequent negotiations took place from 8 to 14 August in Geneva, where Greece demanded the withdrawal of the Turkish armed forces to the ceasefire line and Turkey demanded the partition of the island.[57]

57.8 The Second Intervention (Attila II) (August 1974)

On 16 August 1974, Turkey launched a second intervention to provide assurance for the members of the Turkish Cypriot community, where the Turkish forces in Cyprus increased to 40,000, which resulted in the Turkish occupation of 36% of Cyprus.[58] This movement was clearly a violation of international law and divided Cyprus between the "Green Line" by the *de facto* partition of the Republic and the creation of a separated political entity in the North.

This act resulted in the creation of a federated Turkish state despite UN recognition of the sovereignty of the Republic of Cyprus according to the terms of its independence in 1960.[59] The events of 1974 altered the balance of power between the two communities and coupled their institutional separation with geographical and physical separation.[60] The invasion was accompanied by mass crimes and after the intervention, around 180,000 Greek Cypriots moved from the north part to the areas in the south that were controlled by the Cypress government. Furthermore, 50,000 Turkish Cypriots moved to the south enclaves of Turkish armed forces, and around 7,000 Turkish Cypriots moved into British sovereign bases as refugees.[61]

Based on the above-mentioned, Turkey was found guilty by the European Commission of Human Rights for the violation of rights and freedoms and, in particular, for deprivation of liberty, mass killings, ill treatment, crimes against sexual dignity and deprivation of life of many members of the Greek Cypriot community and for many violations of a number of Articles of the European Convention of Human Rights. It must be noted that the mass population shift made Cyprus one of the nations with the highest number of internationally displaced persons and hundreds of people remain uncountable for.[62] Moreover, plenty of atrocities were committed against members of the Turkish Cypriot community, especially killings, deprivation

---

[56] Clerides 2008.

[57] Crawshaw 1978, pp. 392–394.

[58] Borowiec 2000, pp. 2–4; Souter 1984, pp. 657–674.

[59] Fouskas 2001, pp. 98–127; Anastasiou 2002, pp. 581–596; Polyviou 1980.

[60] Solsten 1991, pp. 170–172.

[61] Kovras 2014, pp. 43–66; Berg 2007, pp. 210–213; Constantinou and Richmond 2005, pp. 65–84; Loizos 1981.

[62] Paul 2014, pp. 129–141.

of life and imprisonment, torture and sexual crimes. This was in addition to the destruction of monuments of cultural heritage for both sides.

With mediation from the United Nations Security Council, the United States government, and diplomatic assistance from Greek Prime Minister Karamanlis, the parties agreed to a ceasefire. That was in parallel with actions both by Greek Cypriots and Turkish Cypriots, which resumed military hostilities on 14 August 1974 and, as a result, Turkish Cypriots occupied a part of northern Cyprus, a conflict which caused approximately 5,000 victims and 250,000 displaced persons.[63]

As a result of the Turkish operation in August 1974, on 1 October 1974, the Turkish Cypriot administration was transformed into the Turkish Cypriot Autonomous Administration. President Makarios returned to power on 7 December 1974, accompanied by a United States arms embargo against Turkey after the proclamation of the Turkish Cypriot Federated State in the north; the UN General Assembly demanded the withdrawal of foreign armed forces from Cyprus.

After the military operations in 1974, the UN Security Council 353[64] called upon all states to respect the territorial integrity, independence and sovereignty of the Republic and demanded an end to military intervention in Cyprus. The guarantor powers called to enter into further negotiations to restore a peace frame in Cyprus. Two conferences held in Geneva during 1974 and five rounds of intercommunal talks in Vienna during April 1975 and February 1976 failed to produce any positive results.

On 13 February 1975, the Council of Ministers and the Legislative Assembly of Turkish Cypriot Administration proclaimed the establishment of the Turkish Federated State of Northern Cyprus (TFSC) as a bargaining chip in negotiating a higher degree of autonomy for the members of the Turkish-Cypriot community occupied by Turkish forces. Both the Council and the Assembly emphasized the determination to oppose all attempts against Cyprus partition with any other state and resolved to establish a separate administration.

Later, the Vienna Talks came to an agreement concerning the population's transfer from north to south and *vice versa*, a situation that divided the Cyprus Republic into two distinct zones: Greek Cypriots to the South and Turkish Cypriots to the North.[65] This separation remains to this day and cements the absence of a single Cypriot identity.

---

[63] Black 1977, pp. 43–67; Fischer 2001, pp. 307–326; Mendoza 1981, pp. 244–286.

[64] United Nations Security Council (1974) Resolution 353: Cyprus, 20 July 1974, http://unscr.com/en/resolutions/353. Accessed 26 April 2019.

[65] Faiz 1999, pp. 175–187.

57.9 Negotiations between Communities, Motherlands and the UN Involvement

57.9.1 From "High-Level Agreements" to "Interim Agreement"

After the *de facto* ethnic division of Cyprus in 1974, the Cyprus issue entered a political and diplomatic stalemate.[66] Based on the results of the legislative elections which were held on 5th September 1976, in early 1977, President Makarios and the Turkish Cypriot leader Rauf Denktaş agreed on a UN facilitated frame concerning a High Level Agreement to a common future solution of the Cyprus issue. This frame was based on a bi-zonal federal government structure, which became the reference point for future proposals.[67]

During this period, Turkish Cypriots insisted on a federative government system and in 1975, the Turkish Federated State of Cyprus was proclaimed. The Greek Cypriot side had to accept a federal solution and suggested a multi-cantonal federation with an effective government in contrast to the Turkish Cypriot proposal, which was founded on the construction of a bi-zonal federation with a weak central government. In 1977, the leaders of the Greek Cypriot and Turkish Cypriot Communities signed the Four Guidelines, based on the notion of a bi-communal and politically equal federal Republic, a proposal which was rejected due to the different view of the communities on the matter of the confederation.[68]

In 1978, the Nimitz Plan was revealed, which proposed a bi-zonal federation with concessions, especially from the Turkish Cypriot Community. This plan was rejected by the Greek Cypriot Community. By the death of Makarios, the election of President Spyros Kyprianou was accompanied, beyond a new High Level Agreement, with the UN new draft submission for the resumption of peace frame in 1979, which was the so called Ten-Point Agreement. The Ten-Point Agreement was the basis for further negotiations between the two communities.

In November 1981, UN Secretary General Kurt Waldheim drafted an evaluation paper, known as the Interim Agreement, as a framework for negotiations. The plan was evaluated on a three-region federal structure—a Greek Cypriot, a Turkish Cypriot, and a federal district—a plan that was rejected by both sides.

---

[66] Ker-Lindsay 2011, pp. 32–46.
[67] Mirbagheri 1998, pp. 95–98; Denktaş 1988.
[68] Mallinson 2009, pp. 737–752.

57.9.2 From the "Draft Framework Agreement" to "Confidence Building Measures"

After all the above-mentioned events and following several years of minimal progress, the situation led to the dissolution of TFSC and the unilateral declaration of the independent Turkish Republic of Northern Cyprus (TRNC) on 15 November 1983, which was only recognized by Turkey. The UN, in Resolution 541 (1983), immediately declared TRNC legally invalid and requested, by conducting many resolutions, for the withdrawal of the 'purported state'.

The Council of Europe also continued to recognize the government of the Republic of Cyprus as the sole legitimate government of Cyprus and called for respect for the territorial integrity of Cyprus. After the establishment of TRNC, and under pressure from the United States and the United Kingdom, the UN abandoned "mini package" approaches to the Cyprus issue in favour of a comprehensive and viable solution.[69] Hence, in 1984, UN Secretary General Perez de Cuellar produced the Draft Framework Agreement, which provided, in general, a vital and comprehensive opportunity both for Greek Cypriots and Turkish Cypriots to move forward to a federal solution.[70]

Despite the fact that both Turkish Cypriot and Greek Cypriot Communities initially found this solution acceptable and stated their satisfaction, the Greek Cypriot side announced that this agreement was unacceptable. In order to continue the intercommunal peace negotiations, the UN Secretary General organized two rounds of talks with each community separately, in November and December 1985 and in February and March 1986. The new Draft Framework Agreement was presented as a compromise to a bicommunal state to both sides on 29 March 1986, but without any result.

The intercommunal negotiations came to a halt after 1986 due to the presidential elections in the Greek Cypriot community in February 1988, where Kyprianou lost the elections and George Vassiliou became the third president of the Greek Cypriot Community. The UN Security Council adopted Resolution 649[71] which was, perhaps, the most balanced Resolution regarding the Cyprus Republic. By symmetrical analysis, the two communities were to be treated as equal partners, a parameter that was adopted during the next rounds of negotiations, in order to give a solution on a basis concerning a prospective bi-communal federal republic.

In August 1992, UN General Secretary Boutros-Ghali announced a "Set of Ideas", which was a detailed plan with respect to territorial adjustments, and suggested a federal system on a power-sharing structure, a proposal which was also rejected by both sides.[72] After reporting to the Security Council, on 24 November 1992, the UN Secretary General came up with the "Confidence Building Measures", which provided advantages for both communities in order to reach an overall agreement,

---

[69] Van Hook 2007.

[70] Tamkoç 1988, pp. 122–125.

[71] United Nations Security Council (1990) Resolution 649: Cyprus, 12 March 1990, http://unscr.com/en/resolutions/649. Accessed 12 June 2019.

[72] Bolukbasi 1995, pp. 460–482.

measures that were taken into account in May 1993 in New York, under the UN auspices.

In the months that followed, tensions started to grow between the two Communities, especially after the Corfu European Council on 24-25 June 1994, when the EU confirmed that Cyprus would be included in the next wave of European enlargement.[73] Following that, on 5 July the European Court of Justice imposed restrictions on the exports of goods from Northern Cyprus into the EU.[74] Beyond that, in December 1996, the European Court of Human Rights delivered a landmark decision ruling that Turkey was an occupying power in Cyprus. This case was about Titina Loizidou, a woman refugee from Kyrenia, who was judged to have been unlawfully denied the control of her property by Turkey,[75] where the Court decided that the property issue in Northern Cyprus fell within Turkey's jurisdiction and responsibility.[76] Also, the European Court of Human Rights, in its judgment of 10 May 2001 in the Cyprus v. Turkey case, concluded that the international community does not recognize the TRNC as a sovereign state under International Law.

57.9.3 The Annan Plan

It was characteristic that in the late 1990s, TRNC and Turkey changed their official policy on a federal solution to a demand on a confederal state and the establishment of two sovereign states. After all, the new UN Secretary General, Kofi Annan, tried to bring a new dynamism to the Cyprus issue.[77] After four years during which there were not any rounds of negotiations between the two communities, the two community leaders met in New York and Geneva between July and August of 1997. This time, the EU opened negotiations with the Greek Cypriot Community; the two sides disagreed and the Turkish side left the negotiating table on 3 December 1999.[78]

After EU pressure concerning the enlargement calendar, the UN put forth a plan on the Cyprus issue in November 2002, known as the Annan Plan. This plan had been the most detailed solution plan on the Cyprus issue that ever put on table, internalizing all the major milestones reached by the two communities from the beginning of the negotiations.[79] In an attempt to reactivate the peace process and to fill the gap in all

---

[73] Yesilada and Sozen 2000, pp. 272–278; Liaris 1998, pp. 38–41; Nugent 2000, pp. 131–150; Iseri 2004, pp. 125–143; Brewin 2001; Theophanous 1995, pp. 74–87; Bozkurt 1995.

[74] Talmon 2001, pp. 735–737; Botswain 1996, pp. 93–119.

[75] European Court of Human Rights, Loizidou v. Turkey, Preliminary Objections, 23 March 1995 (GC), 310, (Ser. A) (Application no. 15318/89).

[76] Oxman and Rudolf 1997, pp. 532–537; Talmon 2001, pp. 727–750; Bora 2013, pp. 28–57.

[77] Menelaou 2019, pp. 29–61; Broome 1997, pp. 381–407.

[78] Bahceli 1997, pp. 203–222.

[79] Coufoudakis and Kyriakides 2004.

the framework agreements, the Plan was modified twice, in December 2002 and in February 2003, respectively, to incorporate all the demands from both sides.[80]

The Annan Plan proposed the creation of a united Cyprus Republic by the establishment of a federation of two constituent states—the Greek Cypriot state and the Turkish Cypriot state—joined together by a federal government, as well as by a federal constitution and constitutions for each constituent state. At the Hague, the UN Secretary General summoned the community leaders to finalize the negotiations process. Denktaş rejected the UN plan and objected to putting it to a referendum, while the newly elected Tassos Papadopoulos accepted the idea of a referendum.

However, the two sides failed to reach an agreement at the Hague Conference in March 2003.[81] After the Hague, with Turkey's consent, the Turkish Cypriot leader decided on lifting restrictions on citizen movement across the Green Line. As a result, Greek Cypriots flooded to the northern part of the island, which was abandoned in 1974, while Turkish Cypriots crossed into the Greek Cypriot south. Both the EU and the UN saw the period between the anticipated entry of Cyprus into the EU and the failed Hague negotiations as an opportunity to reach a successful decision on the Cyprus Issue. On 10 February 2004, the UN Secretary General invited the two sides in New York to recommence negotiations.

Given the election of Mehmet Ali Talât as the Prime Minister of TRNC, the opening of the Green Line and the EU-UN diplomatic activity, both Turkish Cypriot and Greek Cypriot leaders agreed to the UN proposal for rapid negotiations in order to reach a peaceful and effective solution. The negotiations transferred to Nicosia between February and March of 2004, and rapidly, both Greece and Turkey joined negotiations in Bürgenstock, Switzerland, with negotiations leading to the 5th Annan Plan as a feasible plan that tried to secure the fundamental needs of the two sides.[82] Particularly, the fifth and final version of the Plan entailed a number of considerable improvements and some positive ways to address all the concerns of both communities.[83]

The plan was set up in a separate referendum in April 2004.[84] In the referendum, taking into account the campaigns of Talât and Papadopoulos, the Greek Cypriot electorate voted 75.8% against the Annan Plan and, on the other hand, the Turkish Cypriot electorate voted 64.9% in favour of it. It is characteristic that this referendum did not prevent the Greek Cypriot Community under the Republic of Cyprus from becoming an EU Member in May 2004.[85]

In 2006, Kofi Annan's adviser, Ibrahim Gambari, started a new initiative, also known as the Gambari Process. Based on this, Papadopoulos and Talât agreed on a politically equal bi-communal federation. The Process also included the establishment of technical committees to deal with other practical issues. However, there was

---

[80] Palley 2005.
[81] Kaymak 2009, pp. 143–158; Moulakis 2007, pp. 531–556.
[82] Hannay 2005, pp. 190–196.
[83] Trimikliniotis 2009, pp. 107–121.
[84] Christoforou 2005, pp. 85–104.
[85] Pericleous 2009; Amaral 2019.

no consensus on the functionality of those committees, a process that ended without any significant progress for both sides.

57.9.4 The New Era of Negotiations: The Cyprus Issue after Annan

The failure of the Annan Plan was a great shock for both the Cypriot communities and the European and international communities. For many years until then, there were no new rounds of negotiations and little expression of interest from the UN or the communities in pushing forward with Cyprus issue talks.[86] Given the problems concerning the state structure and power sharing between the two Communities, territory issues, guarantees, property, economic and other relevant issues, after many years of negotiations, in February 2008, Dimitris Christofias, leader of the left-wing Progressive Party of the Working People (AKEL), was elected to the Presidency of the Republic of Cyprus.[87]

Together with Mehmet Ali Talât, the leader of the Republican Turkish Party, there was a favourable opportunity for comprehensive negotiations between leaders under the same ideological roof, with the strong support of Greek Prime Minister George Papandreou, Turkish Prime Minister Recep Tayyip Erdoğan and Alexander Downer, the UN Special Adviser on Cyprus. During the meetings of the two leaders from September 2008 to April 2010, Christofias and Talât reached convergence by the establishment of technical committees and working groups in order to cover all the matters that needed to be negotiated. Significant progress was made in the areas of governance and power sharing, the capital of the economy, and EU issues.

In September 2011, the Republic of Cyprus began investigations of hydrocarbons in its Exclusive Economic Zone, with Turkey describing the development as illegal. Talât was succeeded by Derviş Eroğlu, a right-wing politician, with whom Christofias had several meetings concerning the Cyprus issue. After the rejection of the package of Greek Cypriot proposals, in their meeting at Greentree, Long Island in New York between 21 and 24 January 2012, both sides claimed that no progress was made during this period. When Cyprus assumed the Presidency of the EU in the second fall of 2012, Turkey froze any parameters for substantive negotiations.

In February 2013, Nikos Anastasiades was elected to the Presidency of the Republic. On 11 February 2014, Anastasiades and Eroğlu agreed on a joint declaration concerning the establishment of a bi-zonal and bicommunal federation. The two communities agreed upon certain measures for the future revitalization of the Famagusta region, while reaffirming US support for the exercise of sovereign rights for the Republic of Cyprus.

2014 was marked by intensified United States involvement in the process with Vice President Joe Biden's visit, the replacement of UN Secretary General's Special

---

[86] Michael 2007, pp. 587–604.
[87] Adams 1971.

Adviser Alexander Downer by Norway's former Foreign Minister Espen Barth Eide, the suspension of intercommunal talks due to Turkish challenges with the adoption of the Directive concerning "NAVTEX", and the launch of sea investigations by the seismic vessel Barbaros in the Cyprus Exclusive Economic Zone.

With the unanimous support of members of the National Council, President Anastasiades sent a letter to the UN Secretary General suspending his participation in the talks. Mustafa Akinci's election to the Turkish Cypriot leadership in 2015 gave new impetus to the intercommunal negotiations.[88] In November 2016, at the World Economic Forum in Davos, Anastasiades and Akinci, together with UN Secretary General Ban Ki-moon, emphasized that there was a great chance to reunite the island. Negotiations continued intensively with the decision to meet at the Mont Pelerin resort in Switzerland. After two rounds of the summit, the two leaders were unable to achieve the necessary convergence on the criteria for territorial adjustments that would pave the way for the final act of the talks.

The Greek Cypriot and Turkish Cypriot leaders resumed negotiations in early 2017 in Geneva in order to find an answer to all the questions concerning territorial, property, economic and security disputes between the two communities. Talks held in Crans Montana, Switzerland, were unable to make the necessary concessions to reach a final settlement. As a result, the long-sought bicommunal federal solution for the Cyprus Republic has remained elusive.[89]

57.10 TRNC's Matters on State and Statehood and International Law

Definitely, the Cyprus issue attracted great concern at the international level and challenged the international community, especially when Turkey took military action in the summer of 1974[90] and brought the UN in to manage the peacemaking processes. Many legal arguments have been reached concerning the responsibility of the Turkish state and the *de facto* recognition of TRNC under International Law.

On the one hand, it can be said that the unilateral declaration of independence was a grave breach of the Treaty of Guarantee and the TRNC is definitely illegal and not a state, based on the international ;aw rules and norms, where there is no justification for the Turkish occupation. On the other hand, it must be noted that as of November 1983, the Treaty was not valid, and the declaration of independence was not a breach of its provisions. So, based on that, it can be said that neither this unilateral declaration of independence nor the creation of TRNC were of relative significance in establishing a new order nor in creating a new state situation that better amounts to the criteria of statehood and the recognition of it as a sovereign

---

[88] Moutsis 2017, pp. 116–130.
[89] Urea 2019, pp. 87–96.
[90] Richmond 1999b, pp. 239–253; Chrysostomides 2000; Ker-Lindsay 2014, pp. 7–14.

state,[91] based on the criteria for statehood contained in the Montevideo Convention of the Rights and Duties of States.[92]

In this context, TRNC is located on a definite territory in the northern part of the island with certain boundaries and is inhabited by Turkish Cypriots, which constitute a permanent population. These parameters are synthesized by a government that has exercised total control since the state's declaration in 1974. With regard to democratic and governing accountability, TRNC has a government that is able to exercise effective control of its own territory and a constitution that grants its citizens a range of civil and political liberties and freedoms.[93] In the case of the capacity of the state to enter into international relations with other states, it must be said that the term "capacity" is not a criterion for statehood because it is a conflation of the requirements of government and independence.[94]

It must be highlighted that the recognition of an entity as a state that was created by the unlawful use of force is directly forbidden under international law, a principle that can be applied on TRNC. From a legal perspective, the right of Turkish intervention is abolished under Article 4 of the Treaty of Guarantee on the basis that this provision does not authorise military action or the use of force, and it is inconsistent, over Article 2(4) of the UN Charter and, consequently, *void ab initio* under Article 103 of the Charter. So, beyond the clearly defined territory with a certain population and a government with full internal autonomy and external independence in its international relations, TRNC, on the grounds of recognition of states, is a result of illegal use of military force, incompatible with the fundamental principles of customary international law.[95] So, it can be concluded that TRNC cannot be regarded as a sovereign state, but as a *de facto* administrated entity within the recognized confines of the Republic of Cyprus and dependent upon Turkish assistance.[96]

57.11 Conclusion

From its establishment as a bi-communal independent republic in 1960, the Cyprus Republic was a victim of a mixed situation between the communities as well as international factors. It is given that both communities are held responsible for the destabilization and the lack of trust and willingness to change. Additionally, it is not easy to reach a settlement between two different ethnic groups. The threat of war and the consequences of the Turkish intervention of 1974, despite the UN-patrolled buffer zone across the entire length of the island, led to a continuous but unproductive round

---

[91] Vidmar 2013b; Igarashi 2002; Crawford 2006; Vidmar 2013a, pp. 101–149; Richmond 1999a, pp. 42–63.

[92] Crawford 1976, pp. 93–182; Evriviades 1975, pp. 227–264.

[93] Tamkoç 1988.

[94] Blay 1983, pp. 90–91.

[95] Necatigil 1993, pp. 288–290; Safety 2011.

[96] Shaw 2018, pp. 155–209.

of negotiations, that was unsuccessful in producing an agreement. It is characteristic that the absence of any type of violence, since the beginning of the negotiations, does not obligingly signal the presence of a peace frame due to the total absence of ethnic cooperation.

Behind the dark shadows of an ethnopolitical war, peace-building created a sustained dialogue on the peace process forward in the Cyprus Republic. The overcoming of many challenges collided into nationalist matters on a sustainable, fragile peace. The dynamic of the transition from a divided democracy to an integrated future was faced by internal and external roadblocks. The Cypriot ethnic conflict and its remains are looking for an essential political solution, given the transition from peacemaking to peacebuilding, so that peace will have a chance to succeed in a common and unitary future.

The challenge for any type of reunification will be to embrace a new political and international order in an attempt to transform the political arrangement into an evolutionary and productive process, with respect to the fundamental principles that establish a functional and united state. Between a feasible solution and a painful compromise for the future conduct of internal and international negotiations, several points should be considered by flexible and subjective proposals.

Practically, this means that the solution will be based on a united state, with respect to the differences of the communities and the erasure of any regional hegemonism, in order to serve international peace and security, with respect to all basic international rules in observance to the tumultuous past of Cyprus, which offers plenty of lessons for the future. In the absence of progress towards a Cyprus settlement, the Greek Turkish relationship in Cyprus will remain tense.

References

Adams T (1966) The First Republic of Cyprus: A Review of an Unworkable Constitution. Western Political Quarterly 19(3): 475–490

Adams T (1971) AKEL: The Communist Party of Cyprus. Hoover Institution Press, Stanford, California

Alleman F R (1958) Cyprus: Calm before New Storm. New Leader 41: 9–12

Amaral J (2019) Making Peace with Referendums: Cyprus and Northern Ireland. Syracuse University Press, Syracuse, New York

Anastasiou H (2002) Communication across Conflict Lines: The Case of Ethnically Divided Cyprus. Journal of Peace Research 39(5): 581–596

Anastasiou H (2008) The Broken Olive Branch: Nationalism, Ethnic Conflict and the Quest for Peace in Cyprus. Syracuse University Press, New York

Asmussen I (2008) Cyprus at War. Diplomacy and Conflict during the 1974 Crisis. I. B. Tauris, London

Attalides M (1979) Cyprus: Nationalism and International Politics. Q Press, Edinburgh

Bahceli T (1997) The Lure of Economic Prosperity versus Ethno-Nationalism: Turkish Cypriots, the EU Option and the Resolution of Ethnic Conflict in Cyprus. In: Keating M, McGarry J (eds) Minority, Nationalism and the Changing International Order. Oxford University Press, Oxford, pp 203–222

Barkey H J, Gordon P H (2002) Cyprus: The Predictable Crisis. National Interest 66: 83–93

Beattie C (2007) The Bulletproof Flag: How a Small UN Force Changed the Concept of Peacekeeping Forever. Optimum Publishing International, Maxville, Ottawa

Beckingham F (1957) Islam and Turkish Nationalism in Cyprus. Die Welt des Islams 5(1): 165–74

Berg E (2007) Examining Power-Sharing in Persistent Conflicts: De Facto Pseudo-Statehood versus De Jure Quasi-Federalism. Global Society 21(2): 199–217

Birand M A (1985) Thirty Hot Days. Rustem, Nicosia

Black N (1977) The Cyprus Conflict. In: Suhrke A, Garner-Noble L (eds) Ethnic Conflict in International Relations. Praeger Publishers, New York, pp 43–67

Blay S K N (1983) Self-Determination in Cyprus: The New Dimensions of an Old Conflict. Australian Yearbook of International Law 2: 67–100

Bolukbasi S (1995) Boutros-Ghali's Cyprus Initiative in 1992: Why Did it Fail? Middle Eastern Studies 31(3): 460–482

Bora E (2013) Cyprus in International Law. Ankara Bar Review 1: 28–57

Borowiec A (2000) Cyprus: A Troubled Island. Praeger, Westport, CT/London

Botswain T (1996) Perceptions of Cyprus as European. In: Charalambous J et al (eds) Cyprus and the European Union: A Challenge. University of North London Press, London, pp 93–119

Bozkurt M (1995) Die Beziehung der Turkei zur Europaische Union. Peter Lang, Frankfurt am Main

Brewin C (2001) The European Union and Cyprus. Eothen Press, Huntingdon

Broome J B (1997) Designing a Collective Approach to Peace: Interactive Design and Problem-Solving Workshops with Greek Cypriot and Turkish Cypriot Communities in Cyprus. International Negotiation 2(3): 381–407

Broome J B, Anastasiou H (2012) Communication across the Divide in the Cyprus Conflict. In: Landis D, Albert D R (eds) Handbook of Ethnic Conflict: International Perspectives. Springer, Berlin/Heidelberg, pp 293–324

Bryant R (2004) Imagining the Modern: The Cultures of Nationalism in Cyprus. I. B. Tauris, London

Burke J (2017) Britain and the Cyprus Crisis of 1974: Conflict, Colonialism and the Politics of Remembrance in Greek Cypriot Society. Routledge, London/New York

Calame J, Charlesworth E (2009) Divided Cities: Belfast, Beirut, Jerusalem, Mostar and Nicosia. University of Pennsylvania Press, Philadelphia

Camp G (1980) Greek-Turkish Conflict over Cyprus. Political Science Quarterly 95(1): 43–69

Christoforou C (2005) South European Briefing: The Vote for a United Cyprus Deepens Divisions: The 24 April 2004 Referenda in Cyprus. South European Society and Politics 10(1): 85–104

Chrysostomides K (2000) The Republic of Cyprus: A Study in International Law. Martinus Nijhoff Publishers, The Hague/Boston

Claude N (2001) United States Policy towards Cyprus, 1945–1974: Removing the Greek-Turkish Bone of Contention. Bibliopolis, Mannheim und Möhnesee

Clerides G (2008) Negotiating for Cyprus: 1993–2003. Harrassowitz Verlag, Berlin

Constantinou C, Richmond O (2005) The Long Mile of Empire: Power, Legitimation and the UK Bases in Cyprus. Mediterranean Politics 10(1): 65–84

Coufoudakis V, Kyriakides K (2004) The Case against the Annan Plan. Lobby for Cyprus, London

Coughlan R, Mallinson W (2006) Enosis, Socio-Cultural Imperialism and Strategy: Difficult Bedfellows. Middle Eastern Studies 41(4): 575–604

Cranshaw N (1978) The Cyprus Revolt: An Account of the Struggle for Union with Greece. George Allen and Unwin, London

Crawford R J (1976) The Criteria for Statehood in International Law. British Yearbook of International Law 48(1): 93–182

Crawford R J (2006) The Creation of States in International Law, 2nd edn. Oxford University Press, Oxford

Crawshaw N (1964) Cyprus: Collapse of the Zurich Agreement. World Today 20(8): 428–435

Danopoulos C (1982) The Greek Military Regime (1967–1974) and the Cyprus Question: Origins and Goals. Journal of Political and Military Sociology 10(2): 257–273

Demetriou O (2006) Freedom Square: The Unspoken Reunification of a Divided City. Hagar Studies in Culture, Polity and Identities 7(1): 55–77

Demetriou O (2007) To Cross or Not to Cross? Subjectivization and the Absent State in Cyprus. Journal of the Royal Anthropological Institute 13(4): 987–1006

Demetriou C (2012) Political Radicalization and Political Violence in Palestine (1920-1948), Ireland (1850–1921) and Cyprus (1914–1959). Social Science History 36(3): 391–420

Denktaş R R (1988) The Cyprus Triangle. K. Rustem and Brother, London

Dodd C H (1993) The Political, Social and Economic Development of Northern Cyprus. Eothen Press, Huntingdon

Dodd C H (1998) The Cyprus Imbroglio. Eothen Press, Huntingdon

Dodd C (2010) The History and Politics of the Cyprus Conflict. Macmillan Publishers Limited, New York

Doob W L (1986) Cypriot Patriotism and Nationalism. Journal of Conflict Resolution 30(2): 383–396

Drousiotis M (2006) Cyprus 1974: Greek Coup and Turkish Invasion. Bibliopolis, Mannheim und Möhnesee

Drousiotis M (2008) The First Partition: Cyprus, 1963-1964. Alfadi Press, Nicosia

Ehrlich T (1966) Cyprus, the 'Warlike Isle': Origins and Elements of the Current Crisis. Stanford Law Review 18(6): 1021–1098

Emerson R (1960) From Empire to Nation: The Rise to Self-Assertion of Asian and African Peoples. Beacon Press, Boston

Emilianides C A (2019) Constitutional Law in Cyprus, 2nd edn. Wolters Kluwer, The Hague

Evriviades M L (1975) The Legal Dimension of the Cyprus Conflict. Texas International Law Journal 10: 227–264

Faiz M (1999) The Population Issue in North Cyprus. Cyprus Review 20(2): 175–187

Faustmann H, Peristianis N (2006) Britain in Cyprus. Colonialism and Post-colonialism 1878–2006, Bibliopolis. Mannheim and Möhnesee

Faustmann H, Ker-Lindsay J (2009) The Origins and Development of the Cyprus Issue. In: Ker-Lindsay J, Faustmann H (eds) The Government and Politics in Cyprus. Peter Lang, Bern, pp 63–82

Faustmann H (1999) Divide and Quit? British Colonial Policy in Cyprus 1878–1960 Including a Special Survey of the Transitional Period: February 1959–August 1960. Mateo, Mannheim

Fischer J R (2001) Cyprus: The Failure of Mediation and the Escalation of an Identity-Based Conflict to an Adversarial Impasse. Journal of Peace Research 38(3): 307–326

Foley C (1964) The Legacy of Strife: Cyprus from Rebellion to Civil War. Penguin Books, New York

Fouskas K V (2001) Reflections on the Cyprus Issue and the Turkish Invasions of 1974. Mediterranean Quarterly 12(3):98–127

Fouskas K V, Tackie O A (2009) Cyprus: The Post-Imperial Constitution. Pluto Press, London

Gary M (1981) Mediation as an Instrument of International Crisis Management: Cyprus as a Case Study. Yale Journal of World Public Order 7: 244–286

Gokalp Z (1959) Turkish Nationalism and Western Civilization. Columbia University Press, New York

Hadjipavlou M (2007) The Cyprus Conflict: Root Causes and Implications for Peacebuilding. Journal of Peace Research 44(3): 349–365

Hannay D (2005) Cyprus: The Search for a Solution. I. B. Tauris, London

Hatzimihail E N (2013) Cyprus as a Mixed Legal System. Journal of Civil Law Studies 6(1): 37–96

Hatzivassiliou E (1997) Britain and the International Status of Cyprus, 1955–1959. University of Minnesota Press, Minneapolis

Hoffmeister F (2006) Legal Aspects of Cyprus Problem: Annan Plan and EU Accession. Martinus Nijhoff Publishers, Leiden/Boston

Holland R (1999) Britain and the Revolt in Cyprus, 1954–59. Clarendon Press, Oxford

Igarashi M (2002) Associated Statehood in International Law. Kluwer Law International, The Hague/London/New York

Iseri E (2004) A Comparative Assessment of the United Nations and European Union's Roles in the Resolution of Cyprus Conflict: The Scale of Partiality-Impartiality. Turkish Review of Balkan Studies 9: 125–143

Joseph S J (1985) Cyprus: Ethnic Conflict and International Concern. Peter Lang, New York

Kalotychos V (1998) Cyprus and its People: Nation, Identity and Experience in an Unimaginable Community, 1955-1997. Westview Press, Boulder

Kassimeris C (2008) Greek Response to the Cyprus Invasion. Small Wars & Insurgencies 19(2): 256–273

Kaymak E (2009) The Turkish Cypriot Views on Annan V. In: Varnava A, Faustmann H (eds) Reunifying Cyprus: The Annan Plan and Beyond. I. B. Tauris, London, pp 143–158

Ker-Lindsay J (2004) Britain and the Cyprus Crisis, 1963–64. Bibliopolis, Mannheim und Möhnesee

Ker-Lindsay J (2006) The Joint True Force in Cyprus, December 1963-March 1964. In: Faustmann H, Peristianis N (eds) Britain in Cyprus: Colonialism and Post-Colonialism 1878–2006. Bibliopolis, Mannheim und Möhnesee, pp 561–572

Ker-Lindsay J (2011) The Cyprus Problem: What Everyone Needs to Know. Oxford University Press, Oxford

Ker-Lindsay J (2014) Resolving Cyprus: New Approaches to Conflict Resolution. I. B. Tauris, London

Kombos K (2015) The Doctrine of Necessity in Constitutional Law. Sakkoulas Publishers, Athens-Thessaloniki

Kovras I (2014) Truth Recovery and Transitional Justice: Deferring Human Rights Issues. Routledge, London/New York

Liaris E (1998) A European Solution: Opportunity for Rapprochement in Cyprus. Harvard International Review 20(1) (1998): 38–41

Loizides G N (2007) Ethnic Nationalism and Adaption in Cyprus. International Studies Perspectives 8: 172–189

Loizos P (1981) The Heart Grown Bitter: A Chronicle of Cypriot War Refugees. Cambridge University Press, Cambridge

Macris N (2003) The 1960 Treaties on Cyprus and Selected Subsequent Acts. Bibliopolis, Mannheim und Möhnesee

Mallinson W (2009) Cyprus, Britain, the USA, Turkey and Greece in 1977: Critical Submission or Submissive Criticism? Journal of Contemporary History 44(4): 737–752

Markides C K (1977) The Rise and Fall of the Cyprus Republic. Yale University Press, New Haven CT

Mavratsas C (1997) The Ideological Contest between Greek Cypriot Nationalism and Cypriotism, 1974-1995. Ethnic and Racial Studies 20(4): 718–737

Mendoza G (1981) Mediation as an Instrument of International Crisis Management: Cyprus as Case Study. Yale Journal of World Public Order 7: 244–286

Menelaou I (2019) A Historical Account of the Cyprus Problem and the Annan Plan: A Unique Opportunity or an Unwelcome Solution? Acropolis 3: 29–61

Michael M (2007) The Cyprus Peace Talks: A Critical Appraisal. Journal of Peace Research 44(5): 587–604

Mirbagheri F (1998) Cyprus and International Peacemaking. C. Hurst & Company, London

Moulakis A (2007) Power-Standing and Its Discontents: Dysfunctional Constitutional Arrangements and the Failure of the Annan Plan for a Reunified Cyprus. Middle Eastern Studies 43(4): 531–556

Moutsis I (2017) Turkish Cypriot Identity after 1974: Turkish Cypriots, Turks of Cyprus or Cypriots? Synthesis 10: 116–130

Necati-Ertekun M (1983) The Cyprus Dispute and the Birth of the Turkish Republic of Northern Cyprus, 2nd edn. Oxford University Press, Oxford

Necatigil M Z (1993) The Cyprus Question and the Turkish Position in International Law, 2nd edn. Oxford University Press, Oxford

Nevzat A (2005) Nationalism amongst the Turkish-Cypriots: The First Wave. Oulu University Press, Oulu

Newman E (2001) The Most Impossible Job in the World: The Secretary-General and Cyprus. In: Richmond O, Ker-Lindsay J (eds) The Work of the UN in Cyprus. Palgrave Macmillan, Basingstoke, pp 123–129

Nicolet C (2001) United States Policy towards Cyprus, 1954–1974. Bibliopolis, Mannheim und Möhnesee

Nugent N (2000) EU Enlargement and the Cyprus Problem. Journal of Common Market Studies 38(1): 131–150

Oxman H B, Rudolf B (1997) Loizidou v. Turkey. American Journal of International Law 9: 532–537

Palley C (2005) An International Relations Debacle: The UN Secretary-General's Mission of Good Offices in Cyprus 1999-2004. Hart Publishing, Oxford

Panteli S (1990) The Making of Modern Cyprus: From Obscurity to Statehood. Interworld Publications, London

Papadakis Y (1998) Greek Cypriot Narratives of History and Collective Identity: Nationalism as a Contested Process. American Ethnologist 25(2): 149–164

Papandreou A (1970) Democracy at Gun Point. Andre Deutsch, London

Paul A (2014) Cyprus and the Never-Ending Search for a Solution. Caucasus International 3(4): 129–141

Pericleous C (2009) The Cyprus Referendum. A Divided Island and the Challenge of the Annan Plan. I. B. Tauris, London

Polyviou P (1980) Cyprus, Conflict and Negotiation, 1960–1980. Duckworth, London

Richmond O (1998) Mediating in Cyprus: The Cypriot Communities and the United Nations. Routledge, New York

Richmond O (1999a) Ethno-Nationalism, Sovereignty and Negotiating Positions in the Cyprus Conflict: Obstacles to a Settlement. Middle East Studies 35(3): 42–63

Richmond O (1999b) The Cyprus Conflict: Changing Norms of International Society and Regional Disjunctures. Cambridge Review of International Affairs 13(1): 239–253

Richmond O (2001) UN Mediation in Cyprus, 1963-64. In: Richmond O, Ker-Lindsay J (eds) The Work of the UN in Cyprus: Promoting Peace and Development. Palgrave Macmillan, London, pp 102–126

Richmond O (2002) Decolonisation and Post-Independence Cause of Conflict: The Case of Cyprus. Civil Wars 5(3): 163–190

Richter H (2010) A Concise History of Modern Cyprus, 1878–2009. Verlag Franz Phillip Rutzen, Ruhpolding

Safty A (2011) The Cyprus Question: Diplomacy and International Law. iUniverse, Bloomington

Salem N (1992) The Constitution of 1960 and its Failure. In: Salem N (ed) Cyprus: A Regional Conflict and its Resolution. St. Martin's Press, New York

Shaw M (2018) International Law, 8th edn. Cambridge University Press, Cambridge

Solomou E, Faustmann H (2010) Colonial Cyprus 1878–1960. Selected Readings. University of Nicosia Press, Nicosia

Solsten E (1991) Cyprus: A Country Study. Library of Congress, Washington

Sonyel S (2003) Cyprus: The Destruction of a Republic and its Aftermath (1960–1974). Cyprus Republic, Nicosia

Souter D (1984) An Island Apart: A Review of the Cyprus Problem. Third World Quarterly 6(3): 657–674

Stavrinides I (1999) Isle of Discord: Nationalism, Imperialism and the Making of Cyprus Problem. C. Hurst & Company, London

Stavrou-Michael M (2009) Resolving the Cyprus Conflict: Negotiating History. Palgrave Macmillan, New York

Stearns M (1992) Entangled Allies: U.S. Policy towards Greece, Turkey and Cyprus. Council on Foreign Relations Press, New York

Stephen M (2000) The Cyprus Question: A Concise Guide to the History, Politics and Law of the Cyprus Question. Northgate Publishers, London

Stergiou A (2007) Soviet Policy towards Cyprus. Cyprus Review 19(2): 83–106

Symeonides S S (2003) The Mixed Legal System of the Republic of Cyprus. Tulane Law Review 78(1): 441–456

Tachau F (1959) The Face of Turkish Nationalism as Reflected in the Cyprus Dispute. Middle East Journal, 13(3): 262–272

Talmon S (2001) The Cyprus Question before the European Court of Justice. European Journal of International Law 12(4): 727–750

Tamkoç M (1988) The Turkish Cypriot State: The Embodiment of the Right to Self Determination. K. Rustem & Brother, London

Theophanous A (1995) Cyprus and the European Union: From Customs Union to Membership. Cyprus Review 7(2): 74–87

Tocci N (2003) Self-determination in Cyprus: Future Options within a European Order. In: Coppoeters B, Sakwa R (eds) Contextualizing Secession: Normative Analysis in Comparative Perspective. Oxford University Press, Oxford, pp 71–96

Trimikliniotis N (2009) Annan V: Rethinking the Viability of the Constitutional Arrangement and its Future Importance. In: Varnava A, Faustmann H (eds) Reunifying Cyprus: The Annan Plan and Beyond. I. B. Tauris, London, pp 107–121

Trimikliniotis N (2015) Beyond Secessionism in Cyprus: A Federal Remedial Reconstruction. In: Belser E M et al (eds) States Falling Apart? Secessionist and Autonomy Movements in Europe. Stampfli, Bern, pp 247–266

Urea T (2019) Cyprus Dispute. Revue des Sciences Politiques, 64: 87–96

Van Hook L (2007) Foreign Relations of the United States, 1969–1976. Volume XXX: Greece, Cyprus, Turkey, 1973–1976. United States Government Printing Office, Washington

Vidmar J (2013a) Democratic Statehood in International Law: The Emergence of New States in Post-Cold War Practice. Hart Publishing, Oxford/Portland, OR

Vidmar J (2013b) Territorial Integrity and the Law of Statehood. George Washington International Law Review 44: 101–149

Weston-Markides D (2001) Cyprus 1957–1963: From Colonial Conflict to Constitutional Crisis. University of Minnesota Press, Minnesota

White N D (1993) Keeping the Peace: The UN and the Maintenance of International Peace and Security. Manchester University Press, Manchester/New York

Woodhouse C M (1991) Modern Greece. Faber and Faber, London

Yesilada A B, Sozen A (2000) Negotiating a Resolution to the Cyprus Problem: Is Potential European Union Membership a Blessing or a Curse? International Negotiation 7(2): 272–278

Ioannis P. Tzivaras earned the LLM and PhD degrees from the Faculty of Law at Democritus University of Thrace (Greece). He is a Tutor at the Open University of Cyprus' Department of Economics and Management.

Chapter 58
Former Yugoslavia

Ioannis P. Tzivaras

Contents

58.1 Introduction: A Brief History Before the War	1310
58.2 On the Road to War: First Steps to Yugoslavia's Disintegration	1312
58.3 The First Phase: The Beginning of the Dissolution of Yugoslavia and the Rise of Ethnic Tensions	1314
58.4 The Second Phase: Self-Determination and the End of Yugoslavia	1315
58.4.1 The War in Slovenia	1316
58.4.2 The War in Croatia	1316
58.4.3 The War in Bosnia–Herzegovina	1318
58.5 The Dayton Peace Agreement	1321
58.6 The Question on Ethnic Cleansing and the International Criminal Tribunal for the Former Yugoslavia	1322
58.7 Conclusion	1326
References	1327

Abstract The armed conflict in former Yugoslavia has been the result of a multifunctional process between politics, ideology and the interaction of international actors. The gradual transition from communism to nationalism was accompanied by a particular surge of violence and hatred in the context of the creation of a Greater Serbia. The War in Yugoslavia was the bloodiest war in modern European history since World War II. From Slovenia to Bosnia, the dispersal of the armed conflict was heinous and had similar effects. The commission of crimes that constituted ethnic cleansing and the creation, for the first time, of the International Criminal Tribunal for former Yugoslavia proved the wide range of crimes that took place and set up the basis of the strengthening of International Humanitarian Law, as well as International Criminal Law.

Keywords Federal Republic of Yugoslavia · Bosnia-Herzegovina · Croatia · Slovenia · nationalism · disintegration · ethnic cleansing · Srebrenica · Dayton · ICTY · self-determination · secession

---

I. P. Tzivaras (✉)
Department of Economics and Management, Open University of Cyprus (OUC), Nicosia, Cyprus
e-mail: ioannis.tzivaras@ouc.ac.cy

© T.M.C. ASSER PRESS and the authors 2022
S. Sayapin et al. (eds.), *International Conflict and Security Law*,
https://doi.org/10.1007/978-94-6265-515-7_58

58.1 Introduction: A Brief History Before the War

The Yugoslav state, the former Kingdom of Serbs, Croats and Slovenes, was created after World War I as a multinational community of ethnicities, languages and religions that needed to find an effective way to live in peace under the modern concept of national self-determination.[1] In 1941, Yugoslavia was occupied by German armed forces[2] and a bitter conflict ensued between the Croat state, which was supported by the Germans, and resistance movements, such as the nationalist Chetnik Detachments of the Yugoslav Army, under the leadership of Dragoljub Mihailovi and the Communist Partisan Movement of Josip Broz Tito.[3]

It is characteristic that, with the decisive support of Stalin and under the principles of Lenin's Soviet centralism, the Communist Partisan Movement struggled not only for national liberation, but also for the socio-political transformation of the country, achieving the development of a pan-Yugoslav movement that managed to reach all Yugoslavia by recruiting members from different ethnic groups.[4]

Yugoslavia existed as a federation of six republics (Slovenia, Croatia, Serbia, Montenegro, Bosnia-Herzegovina and Macedonia) since the end of Yugoslavian Civil War (1941–1945), between the Croatian Revolutionary Movement, also known as Ustaša, Chetniks and Yugoslav Partisans,[5] until its dissolution in the early 1990s. From the end of World War II, Tito's Communist Partisan Movement[6] had been trying to unite the six republics, having achieved ethnic group interaction.[7] In October 1944, units of the Soviet army alongside Partisan units released Belgrade, while Chetniks' armed forces crashed after the War (mainly in May 1945) and the members of Ustaša who were either surrendered or arrested, were executed. In August 1945, the Communist Party of Yugoslavia established the People's Front of Yugoslavia (Narodni Front, NOF), a political scheme involving organizations and individuals who had fought with the Partisans during the liberation struggle, represented by Tito. After the elections on 11 November 1945, the People's Front accounted for 85% of the votes and the new government, along with the Constituent Assembly of Yugoslavia, officially abolished monarchy and declared the democratic character of the Federal People's Republic of Yugoslavia, consisting of six Republics and two autonomous regions, Kosovo and Vojvodina.[8]

The new Yugoslav Government allied with the Soviet Union under Stalin and followed the Stalinist Soviet model of economic development and bureaucratic centralism, some aspects of which, such as the public works and the road network, were remarkable. The tensions with the West were intense as Yugoslavia joined the

---

[1] Freeman 2019, pp. 1–8; Rady 1996, pp. 379–390.
[2] Crampton 2002, pp. 119–123.
[3] Judah 2000, pp. 116–121; Hofbauer 2001, pp. 20–22.
[4] Bataković 1995, pp. 25–41.
[5] Glenny 1996, pp. 144–152.
[6] Šuster 1999, pp. 65–69.
[7] Lampe 2000, pp. 201–202.
[8] Tanner 1997, pp. 176–178.

Communist Information Bureau (Cominform), which controlled the Eastern Block—a fact that led to the distrust of Yugoslavia by the United States, and the early phase of the Cold War began with Yugoslavia following an aggressive foreign policy.[9]

Among several issues that have arisen due to the peculiarities of the region and the international relations of the Yugoslav state, a question about Yugoslav ethnicities arose. In general, the Communist Party itself shaped the ideology of Yugoslavism and socialist patriotism[10] by claiming that all Yugoslav nations had contributed to the war against the Axis Powers who occupied and partitioned the state.[11] Based on the concept of a "Brotherhood of Nations and Unity of the Working Class", the Communists claimed that different nations of Yugoslavia had united in a common struggle and thus had legitimized the future unity of multi-ethnic Yugoslavia.

In 1948, the breakup of the Communist Party with the Soviet Union and the expulsion of Yugoslavia from Cominform led to economic and political separation from its allies and, as a result, to the breakdown of Yugoslavia's economy. In this period, there was a radical reorganization of the agricultural economy and the retribution of wealth from Croatia and Slovenia to the other four states through the state investment mechanism in the context of the Yugoslavian path to socialism.[12] It is noteworthy that Tito, after the breakup with the Soviet Union, reached out to the West and, especially, the United States, which welcomed isolation from the Soviets and began to support Yugoslavia, especially militarily and financially.

The enactment of the new Constitution in 1953 was characteristic of that period, with the election of Tito as President of the Republic and the creation of a new political and economic system based on a socialist template (named Titoism). In 1963, the nation changed its official name to the Socialist Federal Republic of Yugoslavia. Furthermore, the period between 1966 and 1980 was, moreover, peculiar to the Yugoslav Federation. A series of unsuccessful economic reforms aiming at market socialism were recorded over this period, which led to student rebellions against economic reforms in 1968, mainly in Belgrade, as well as Zagreb, Sarajevo and Ljubljana.[13]

During this time, Tito gave more liberties to the individual republics and recognized Vojvodina and Kosovo as autonomous provinces. The Croatian Spring, which took place in 1971 as a leading political and cultural movement emerging from the League of Communists of Croatia,[14] had to do with economic, political and cultural reforms. It mainly began with a declaration concerning the nature and the position of the Croatian language in 1967 and continued with a student strike at the University of Zagreb in 1971.

As a result, in 1974, a new federal constitution was ratified, which basically protected the self-management system of the republics from state interference and

---

[9] Swain 2010, pp. 641–663; Hunt 2013, pp. 38–39.

[10] Marolov and Stojanovski 2014, pp. 432–438.

[11] Ramet 1995, pp. 206–208.

[12] Allcock 2000, pp. 132–147.

[13] Fichter 2016, pp. 99–121.

[14] Spehnjak and Cipek 2007, pp. 255–297; Pickering and Baskin 2008, pp. 521–540.

expanded their representation in all electoral and policy forums.[15] The ratified Constitution weakened and collapsed the federal character of Yugoslavia, as well as the collective governance system, giving more autonomy to the Yugoslav republics and the Yugoslav democratic decentralization, and recognizing the regional interests, nationalism and the provinces' right to secession.[16] In other words, the republics and the autonomous regions of Vojvodina and Kosovo gained greater independence and control over decisions made at the federal level, a status that enhanced the nationalism of the constitutive nations and the empowerment of the right of self-determination.

Tito's death in May of 1980 highlighted fundamental problems in Yugoslavia: divergent ethnic interests and ethnic tensions, the inefficiency of economy, and the problematic united Yugoslavian institutional structure. The Republic's power was dispersed from the type of federal government to a type of collective presidency and, furthermore, both the fall of communism and the reunification of the Federal Republic of Germany assisted in the deterioration of political rearrangements and instability in Yugoslavia.

58.2 On the Road to War: First Steps to Yugoslavia's Disintegration

Since the establishment of the Kingdom of Yugoslavia as a multi-ethnic and multi-cultural nation, a continuous effort for the creation of a unified State has been observed, contradicting Yugoslavia's volatile and disobedient nature and despite ethnic strife being regarded as a major part of the Yugoslavian history.[17] The seeds of the war in Yugoslavia, which was the first classical war in the European mainland since 1945 and one of the most devastating humanitarian crises in the last two decades, partly lie in domestic and international developments in the 1980s that dictated Yugoslavia's future.[18]

Tito's death, the end of the period when the country had been thriving financially, and the economic transition to a market economy—taking into account the worldwide economic crisis of the 1980s—were the first essential parameters for the seeds of war, along with the rise of nationalism and the role of the international politics.[19] That period provided the Yugoslav political leadership with the opportunity of democratization of the country and the liberalization of the economy, combined with the end of the Cold War, which allowed Yugoslavia's geopolitical significance to emerge and transformed the country's key role at the international level.[20] By the end of 1980s, Yugoslavia looked more like a confederation due to the increase in

---

[15] Vevjoda 1996, pp. 9–27.
[16] Irving 2008, pp. 149–178.
[17] Gallagher 2003, pp. 50–59; Cohen 1993, pp. 106–114; Jović 2001, pp. 101–120.
[18] Gagnon 2004, pp. 1–30.
[19] Krizan 1994, pp. 47–68.
[20] Gow 1997, pp. 25–28.

the autonomy of the federal states and policies with respect to the main political and economic issues.

The beginning of the 1990s is perhaps the most critical period in Yugoslavia's post-Cold War history.[21] Given that Tito succeeded in keeping peace over the multi-ethnic Yugoslavian republic by ensuring no ethnic group domination, the sharp rise of nationalism in the Yugoslav republics proved that for more than forty years the communist solution to the national question had been temporary, and owed, indeed, to the distinct nationalist policies struggling for primacy—especially Serbian centralism, ethnocentrism, and Croatian separatism. These two policies did, in fact, preordain the failure of a liberal and unified Yugoslavia.

More analytically, the Yugoslavian state was destabilised by an unmanageable and unreformable political and financial crisis.[22] However, the election of Slobodan Milosević as the President of Serbia during the collapse of communism in Eastern Europe caused a strengthening of Serbian nationalism and hegemony in other republics, in particular in Slovenia and Croatia. It must be said that when Milosević came to power, he never openly rejected Yugoslavism and he was committed to keeping Tito's image alive. Yet, later, he turned to a nationalist movement and a national homogenization.

In general, by the end of communism, no political party was able to successfully mobilize a cohesive platform for Yugoslavia as a society of equal citizens and rights, with separatist nationalism[23] still characteristically apparent. The process of dissolution began with the rise of Slobodan Milosević in Serbia and the drafting of the Memorandum of the Academy of Arts and Sciences of Serbia, known as the SAAS Memorandum, under which Serbia, in fact, separated its political perspectives from the other republics in Yugoslavia.[24] The anti-bureaucratic revolution in Serbia and Montenegro dovetailed into an ethnic conflict between the Albanian and the Serbian populations within the province.[25]

Milosevic, riding a wave of Serbian nationalism, took advantage of the power void by using military and political strength, and by January 1989, he had gained control of Montenegro and the formerly autonomous regions of Vojvodina and Kosovo. Kosovo, in particular, became Milosevic's launching pad in his quest to extend his nationalist power to the rest of Yugoslavia, and the rise of nationalism was identified as a new source of legitimization. These combined as factors in the Slovenian and Croatian struggles for independence and the Serbian need for the reunification of eight million Serbs.[26]

The 14th Congress of the Yugoslavian League of Communists in 1990 led to the dissolution of the Communist Party following the fall of communism in Eastern Europe. After the withdrawal of Slovenian and Croatian delegations and the multi-party elections in all republics separately, an advantage was given to nationalist

---

[21] Ramet 2004, pp. 731–763.
[22] Basta 2010, pp. 92–110.
[23] Hayden 2008, pp. 487–516.
[24] Mihailović and Krestić 1995.
[25] Pavlaković 2005, pp. 13–55; Blagojević 2000, pp. 212–246.
[26] Scharf 1997, pp. 21–36.

platforms in Slovenia and Croatia. These platforms promised to protect their separate nationalist interests, where the rebranded former communist parties emerged victorious in Serbia and Montenegro. It should also be highlighted that, after these political fermentations, other republics put forward their plans for sovereignty and greater political pluralism.

58.3 The First Phase: The Beginning of the Dissolution of Yugoslavia and the Rise of Ethnic Tensions

The end of the Yugoslav state was marked by the bloody Yugoslav wars and the division of the multinational state into smaller entities, where the new regime was marked by a rise of nationalist sentiment as a source of political legitimacy.[27] The dissolution of Yugoslavia took place in two phases. The first was in 1991 at the end of war in Croatia and the second was between 1992 and 1995 during the assignment of the General Framework Agreement for Peace in Bosnia-Herzegovina in Dayton.

After the dissolution of the Communist Party and the rise of nationalist platforms in Yugoslavia's republics, the idea of the Federation began to fall apart. Nationalism replaced communism as the dominant force in the Balkans. This is evidenced by the fact that the single-party system was abandoned in 1990 and a multi-party election system was held in all the Republics, whereas in Serbia and Montenegro, communists emerged victorious while in the other four Republics, elections were won by nationalist parties.

The victory of nationalist forces, especially in Croatia and Slovenia, created a new political situation in regard to the future of the relationship of the republics with Yugoslavia. Most political parties refused to make a plan about the reestablishment of Yugoslavia as a strong confederation; instead, disassociation was suggested. A proposal that concerned the transformation of Yugoslavia into a confederation and the recognition of Yugoslav republics as subjects of international law was rejected by Milošević, who argued that if a republic claimed a right to self-determination, then ethnic Serbs should also enjoy this right.

It was noteworthy that, after a series of inflammatory statements from all sides, the Croatian Parliament voted in favour of a new Constitution on 22 December 1990, which changed the status of ethnic Serbs in Croatia to an ethnic minority. The opposite views on the negotiations about the Constitution held by the newly elected governments in the republics[28] led to the beginning of a crisis on 15 May 1991, a date that found the country without a Head of State. A series of talks were held between the leaders of the six republics and the autonomous regions; they considered the question of the ethnic security dilemma, but no agreement was reached, except between Bosnia-Herzegovina and Macedonia, which cooperated to find a solution on a confederation basis.

---

[27] Blitz 2006; Silber and Little 1996.
[28] Hayden 1999, pp. 34–87.

58.4 The Second Phase: Self-Determination and the End of Yugoslavia

In general, the right of self-determination began as a political principle[29] and was quickly transformed into a binding principle of international law, commonly regarded as a *jus cogens* rule, endowed with a customary character, related both to the issue of the formation of a nation and to its civil rights and liberties, and as a universal rule that applies to countries, nations and peoples as collectivities.[30] In contrast, secession can be permitted in extraordinary cases of mass violations of human rights affecting a specific population for religious, ethnic or racial reasons.

Due to the recognition of the tension between self-determination and territorial integrity of states, it is submitted that the right of self-determination is a universal right and should be defined both in internal and external aspects. Also, it must be said that in the context of international peace and security, the right of self-determination must be balanced with sovereignty and territorial integrity.

The transformation of the political principle of self-determination and the establishment of this principle in different modes of implementation as internal and external aspects of self-determination must be connected with the dissolution of the Socialist Federal Republic of Yugoslavia and the relevant civil armed conflict. As noted already, the Yugoslav population consisted of a large number of non-homogenous ethnic groups.[31] The transition from communism to nationalism highlighted the growing ethnic tensions into a civil war, which widened the scope where self-determination by succession was possible.[32]

To examine the legality of the right of self-determination in the case of Yugoslav secession, it must be taken into consideration that the Federal Yugoslav Constitution included strict provisions that gave the Republics the right to secede. Referendums held in at least three Republics of the Federation, including Croatia, Slovenia and Macedonia, gave the expressed desire of the peoples of the above-mentioned states to be independent. These parameters played, *inter alia*, a particular role in the beginning of an ethnic civil war.[33] Based on this, the secessionist application of the right of self-determination would legally apply to the case of Yugoslavia.[34]

---

[29] Crawford 2006, pp. 10–38; Fisch 2015, pp. 118–119; Abulof 2015, pp. 488–497; Raič 2002, pp. 237–238.
[30] McWhinney 2007, pp. 8–10; Musgrave 2000, pp. 235–245.
[31] Radan 2001, pp. 160–161.
[32] Levdai 1991, pp. 252–258.
[33] Vladisavljević 2004, pp. 390–398.
[34] Schöpflin 2006, pp. 13–29; Hayden 1996, pp. 783–801.

58.4.1 The War in Slovenia

On 23 December 1991, Slovenia held a referendum on disassociation and seizure of border crossings; Croatia followed on 19 May 1991, disregarding warnings by both the United States and the European Community, steeply increasing the ethnic tensions. On 25 June 1991, Croatia and Slovenia unilaterally declared independence from the Yugoslav Republic,[35] just four days after the visit of the United States Foreign Minister. This movement did not rush the international community to recognize those republics, a situation which triggered an intervention of the Yugoslav People's Army and the beginning of a brief but violent armed conflict, generally referred to as the Ten-Day War (27 June–7 July)—the war that marked the beginning of the Yugoslav wars.[36]

In June, the Slovenian Territorial Defense Force and members of the Yugoslav People's Army[37] (JNA) were blockaded in combat and a Croatian Serb militia launched an attack against Croats.[38] Given that few JNA troops were deployed for the operation and the fact that Milosević had accepted, months earlier, the Slovenian succession and the preparation of Slovenian armed forces, the short Slovenian conflict led to the Brioni Declaration of 7 July 1991, which was signed by Croatia, Slovenia and Yugoslavia. This agreement sought to create a safe environment in which further negotiations on the future of Yugoslavia could take place, putting an end to hostilities in the Ten-Day War in Slovenia and giving certain solutions on other issues, such as, among others, the control over its border crossings and custom revenues and air-traffic control. It is noteworthy that with the victory of the Slovenian forces eleven days after the Declaration, the federal government pulled out the JNA soldiers and their equipment from Slovenia, but there was not any mitigating impact on fighting in Croatia.[39]

58.4.2 The War in Croatia

This period was also stigmatized by ethnic tensions in Croatia and the Croatian War of Independence, known as the Homeland War, as well as several violent incidents that broke out throughout the country.[40] Croatia proclaimed its independence from Yugoslavia on the same day as Slovenia, but Croatia's withdrawal from the Yugoslav Federation was not bloodless.[41] When the Croatian government claimed its sovereignty, the sizeable ethnic Serb minority in Croatia openly rejected the authority

---

[35] Rich 2011, pp. 36–65.
[36] O'Shea 2005, pp. 15–29; Isaković 2000, pp. 38–41; Rizman 2005, pp. 57–60.
[37] Hoare 2004, pp. 60–64.
[38] Ahrens 2007, pp. 42–47.
[39] Prunk 1997, pp. 24–28.
[40] Job 2002, pp. 125–131; Malesević 2002; Irving 1997, pp. 30–43.
[41] Magas 1991, pp. 33–37.

of the Croatian state, claiming the right to remain within Yugoslavia. In the beginning, sporadic interethnic incidents developed between Serb paramilitary forces and the Croatian Police.

With the involvement of JNA paramilitary forces and Serbia, the Serb minority rebelled and cut off Serbian populated regions from the rest of the Croatian state, in line with the declaration of Slobodan Milosević about the superiority of Serbs and that all the Serbs must live in a greater Serbia.[42] The Croatian Serb paramilitary armed forces, militia from Serbia and members of JNA worked in close cooperation to violently cleanse Croats and non-Serbs from its territory, where the result was the death of more than 10,000 people from July to December.[43]

Given the Declaration of the Serbian Autonomous Oblast of Krajina, as a self-proclaimed Serbian autonomous region that demanded to remain in union with Serbia, on 28 February 1991, after a referendum, the Serb National Council declared this region to be independent from Croatia and a constitutive part of the unified territory of Serbia.[44] With the involvement of the JNA army, the conflict over the control of Krajina soon escalated into open war—a clash between two defined camps, Serbs and Croats.[45] The conflict spread soon amongst the Serb Army of Krajina, paramilitary forces from Serbia and the Croatian military. Major incidents of this conflict were the siege of Vukovar by the Serbs and the assault on Dubrovnik. In addition to the mass killings, many Serbs were forced to leave their homes as a parameter of an unlawful deportation in a large-scale ethnic cleansing. It must be said that several negotiations were managed and administered by the European Community concerning ceasefire agreements, but they had already collapsed due to political compromises.[46]

It is characteristic that by the end of 1991, one-third of Croatia was under the control of Serb paramilitary forces, openly supported by the Yugoslav Army and as a result, more than 270,000 people, mainly Croats, were displaced. The Croatian war officially ended after two, in total, operations carried out by the Croatian military forces—Operation Flash in May 1995 and Operation Storm in August of the same year. More analytically, in the first operation, Croatian forces regained control over territories in Western Slavonia and in the second Operation, regained occupied territories in Croatia. As a result, the advancement of Croatian forces caused thousands of Croatian Serbs to flee either to Serb-controlled territories in Bosnia-Herzegovina or Serbia.

After the failure of Yugoslavia and the negotiations conducted by the European Community, the United Nations were summoned to mediate with a peace plan. The Vance Plan negotiated in November 1991 was designated to implement a ceasefire, the demilitarization of the Yugoslav People's Army and Croatian Serbs, and the return of refugees, as well as to create conditions for negotiations on a permanent

---

[42] Bjelajać and Žunec 2009, pp. 249–252; Ramet 1996.
[43] Fisher 2006.
[44] Gagnon 2004, pp. 32–47.
[45] Lefebvre 1995, pp. 45–57.
[46] Biondich 2004, pp. 439–442.

settlement to avoid the break-up of Yugoslavia.[47] The Implementation Agreement was signed in Sarajevo, accepted by Belgrade, Croatia and JNA, and supervised by the United Nations Protection Force (UNPROFOR).[48]

It must be said that this plan left the armed conflict unresolved and Milosević used the arrival of the peacekeeping troops as a mechanism for consolidating his military nationalist gains in Croatia, given the ongoing crisis in neighbouring Bosnia.[49] The war in Croatia effectively ended in the fall of 1995 when Croatia re-asserted its authority over the entire territory.

58.4.3 The War in Bosnia–Herzegovina

In general, the conflict in Bosnia-Herzegovina is regarded to have been the deadliest of all conflicts in the disintegrating Yugoslav Federation.[50] The Carrington-Cutileiro Plan and the European Community Peace Conference in February 1992 were failed attempts to prevent Bosnia from sliding into war. The Bosnian War from April 1992 to November 1995 was the latest sign that the Yugoslav Federation had been on a route towards an inevitable collapse.[51]

In spite of proper pre-war relations in the population's mixed ethnic composition of Bosnian Muslims, Bosnian Serbs, Bosnian Croats and other nationalities,[52] Croatia triggered a war with Bosnia in that period resulting in Bosnia—the most ethnically heterogeneous republic—becoming the main target of ethnic cleansing.[53] In a fragile peace frame, in early March 1992, the majority of Bosnians voted for independence. Immediately after the referendum, the Serbian local militia set up roadblocks that blockaded Bosnia's major cities. As a result, many Serbs left Sarajevo and a separate Bosnian-Serb Parliament was set up.[54]

In April 1992, Radovan Karadžić quite methodically led Bosnian-Serb forces and the Serbian minority on an armed quest to gain control of as much territory as possible, giving priority to the eastern part of Bosnia in hopes that a possible union with Serbia could be materialized. With the support of JNA units and a Chetnik militia, Serbian forces began a systematic persecution campaign against non-Serbs and forced Muslims to leave their homes, mostly targeting Srebrenica, Tuzla, Zepa and Sarajevo. The siege of Sarajevo was the beginning of the ethnic cleansing of Bosnian Muslims that went beyond other incidents of terror by all other ethnicities in the area; many killings, the use of sexual violence and the creation of concentration

---

[47] Marijan 2012, pp. 103–123.
[48] Nambiar 2001, pp. 172–179.
[49] Sell 2002, pp. 155–160.
[50] Cohen 1996, pp. 119–134; Tabeau and Bijak 2005; Bryant 1993; Rogel 1998.
[51] Slack and Doyon 2001, pp. 154–159.
[52] Jansen 2007, pp. 199–204; Wesselingh and Vaulerin 2003, pp. 45–49; Calić 1996, pp. 87–93.
[53] Sloan 1998, pp. 27–35.
[54] Ali and Lifschultz 1994, pp. 367–401.

camps became a bloody reality. During the Bosnian conflict, ethnic cleansing took place in many phases during the ethnic homogenization process.[55] The conflict turned into a three-sided fight for territories, with civilians from all ethnicities becoming victims of heinous crimes.

During the summer of 1992, the humanitarian crisis in Bosnia-Herzegovina led the deployment of UN peacekeeping forces to facilitate the delivery of humanitarian relief. From April 1992 until the departure of Serbs from Sarajevo, it was characteristic that Bosnian-Serbs had consolidated their power over the majority of Eastern Bosnia-Herzegovina via the commencement of a massive wave of population displacements. 750,000 Muslims were targeted through a combination of selected massacres, imprisonments, crimes against sexual dignity and expulsion of non-Serbs, especially in Visegrád, Sanski Most, Bratunarac, Zvornik, Prijedor, Foča and Bjelogorci (Rogatica).[56]

In January 1993, the UN Special Envoy, Cyrus Vance and the European Community's representative, Lord Owen, began negotiations on a peace proposal with Bosnia. The Vance-Owen Peace Plan called for a split of Bosnian territory through the establishment of a decentralized state into ten cantons, operating from Sarajevo, in which the three major ethnic groups would be equally recognized as constituent units; it laid out certain details about how those cantons would function in relation to each other and to the central government.

After a series of negotiations, in April 1993, the Plan was widely criticized and rejected by the Bosnian Serbs and Croats, fearing the possibility of Muslim-Croat domination in the central government as well as for cutting off the land corridor in northern Bosnia and the obstruction of the Serbian zone to the Serb Republic.[57] In fact, the proposed plan was not acceptable to any local actors and did not generate consensus within the international community. Furthermore, it reflected the unwillingness of the international community to pursue certain measures to protect Bosnia-Herzegovina.

After the Vance-Owen Plan was abandoned, the peace proposal was replaced in June 1993 by the Owen-Stoltenberg Plan.[58] This proposal was drawn up by Presidents Milosević and Tuđman, and aimed to divide Bosnia into a union of three, in total, ethnic republics, in which Bosnian Serb forces would be allotted 52% of Bosnia-Herzegovina's territory, Muslims would be given 30% and Bosnian Croats would receive 18%—a proposal that was rejected by the Bosnian government. This plan gave a green light to the international community to proceed with the forcible division of Bosnia-Herzegovina.

Bosnia, at this time, received UN aid by the designation of "safe zones" in order to not be attacked by the Serbian forces. Nevertheless, Bosnian Serb advances forced the Muslim population to shelter in enclaves. The details of this are that in May 1993,

---

[55] Sell 2000, pp. 179–202.
[56] Toal and Dahlman 2011, pp. 103–105.
[57] Dulić 2005, pp. 309–312.
[58] Goodby 1996, pp. 501–523.

Security Council Resolution 824,[59] pursuant to Resolutions 713 (1991)[60] and 819 (1993)[61] and acting under the provisions of Chapter VII of the UN Charter, declared six "safe" towns against hostile acts and other armed attacks, such as Sarajevo, Žepa, Tuzla, Srebrenica, Goražde and Bihać. UNPROFOR was tasked with securing those areas, but the safe areas mandate was never enforced.

In April 1993, in parallel with NATO's air strikes, Bosnian Croat forces began to move against Muslims in Bosnia-Herzegovina, where Mostar was destroyed.[62] NATO began Operation Deny Flight as the enforcement of a UN no-fly zone over Bosnia-Herzegovina, which played a significant role in the use of air power and the prevention of fixed-wing aircraft from flying over restricted air space in Bosnia.

In February 1994, after an explosion in Sarajevo's marketplace, the United States, the European Community and NATO demanded the Serbs remove artillery from the area. Russia seized the opportunity and, taking advantage of its relationship with the Serbs, agreed to replace Serbs in the exclusion zone with Russian forces, turning the International Conference on the Former Yugoslavia (ICFY) into the focal point for a new round of negotiations.

In March 1994, the US brokered the Washington Agreement, which established, among others, an agreement between Bosnia, Bosnian Croats and Croatia to establish a federation between Croats and Muslims in Bosnia. The Contact Group tried to inject a new momentum into the peace process, and in July 1994, a set of proposals concerning the assignment of 51% of the territory to Croat-Muslim Federation and 49% to Bosnian Serbs was presented.

The Belgrade and the Bosnian government accepted the plan, but the Bosnian Serbs rejected it. In April 1994, NATO employed the first air strikes against Bosnian Serb forces to halt a Serb attack on the UN safe area of Goradze. In the spring of 1994, a new mediation group, also known as the Contact Group, which consisted of diplomats from Russia, Great Britain, France, the United States and Germany and representatives from the European Community, were making steady efforts towards a settlement of the armed conflict in Bosnia-Herzegovina.[63]

In January 1995, President Tuđman decided to terminate the UN operation in Croatia, a parameter that also affected the war in Bosnia. After Serbs ignored the UN's order to remove heavy weapons around Sarajevo, on 25 May, aircrafts destroyed a Serbian ammunition dump near Pale. During the summer of 1995, war in Bosnia escalated, as in July Serbian forces defied the UN and overran two "safe" areas in eastern Bosnia, Zepa and Srebrenica.

---

[59] United Nations Security Council (1993) Resolution 824: On Treatment of Certain Towns and Surroundings in Bosnia and Herzegovina as Safe Areas, 6 May 1993. https://digitallibrary.un.org/record/166133. Accessed 28 June 2020.

[60] United Nations Security Council (1991) Resolution 713: Socialist Federal Republic of Yugoslavia, 25 September 1991. http://unscr.com/en/resolutions/713. Accessed 13 October 2020.

[61] United Nations Security Council (1993) Resolution 819: Bosnia and Herzegovina, 16 April 1993. http://unscr.com/en/resolutions/819. Accessed 10 October 2020.

[62] Belloni 2007, pp. 125–128.

[63] Kalyvas and Sambanis 2005, pp. 191–230.

At that time, the most heinous ethnic cleansing since World War II[64] took place in Srebrenica,[65] where around 8000 Muslims were massacred and around 30,000 were forcibly deported under the supervision of the Bosnian-Serb commander Ratko Mladić and paramilitary units of the Bosnian-Serb Army, the Drina Corps.[66] On 24 July 1994, Croatia agreed to provide military assistance to Bosnia, where Croatian troops attacked Serbian positions and on 4 August, Croatian forces launched an attack and retook Krajina, which was under Croatian-Serbian control; as many as 200,000 Croatian-Serb refugees poured into Bosnia.

After the withdrawal of UNPROFOR forces from Goražde in late August, NATO, aided by the Croatian Defence Council (HVO), launched an extensive air strike campaign, known as Operation Deliberate Force, with large-scale bombings against Bosnian-Serb military targets,[67] pushing the war to its conclusion. United States President Bill Clinton launched a new diplomatic initiative by sending Richard Holbrooke to negotiate for the ending of the war.[68]

Based on the Contact Group Plan, Holbrooke's proposal had to do with the remains of Bosnia within its borders and the possession of 49% by Serbia and 51% by Croatia and Muslims. In September 1995, Serbia, Croatia and Bosnia accepted an agreement on ending the armed conflict in Bosnia-Herzegovina and agreed that there would be a Bosnian state with a federal constitution and relative constitutional principles.[69]

58.5 The Dayton Peace Agreement

The Bosnian War came to an end in November 1995 with the General Framework Agreement for Peace in Bosnia-Herzegovina. The Agreement was negotiated at Wright-Patterson Air Force Base in Dayton, Ohio, and formally signed in Paris on 14 December 1995.[70] The Accord gave an agenda for peace and the contracting parties, including the Presidents of the Republic of Serbia, the Republic of Croatia and the Republic of Bosnia-Herzegovina, the United States' and the United Kingdom's delegates, EU Representatives and the Foreign Minister of Russia, agreed for peace, stability and security in the region and, in order, to endorse regional balance in former Yugoslavia.[71]

The Peace Accords contained a General Framework Agreement for Peace (GFAP) and eleven supporting Annexes, which aimed to end the hostilities, implement the

---

[64] Mojzes 2011, pp. 175–185; Eyal 1995, pp. 29–33.
[65] Delpla et al. 2012, pp. 12–13.
[66] Bellucci and Isernia 2003, pp. 173–218.
[67] Harris 1996, pp. 132–133.
[68] Mass 2002, pp. 71–88.
[69] Haskin 2006, pp. 13–15.
[70] Holbrooke 1998, pp. 231–314; Malcolm 1994, pp. 234–235; Caplan 2005, pp. 95–120; Lazić 1999, pp. 4–9; Oliver 2005, pp. 83–88; Parenti 2000, pp. 50–58.
[71] Caplan 2000, pp. 213–232; Chollet 2005; Bose 2002, pp. 1–3; Vladisavljević 2004, pp. 390–398.

military Annexes and to establish a central Bosnian government. The Agreement mandated monitoring by a wide range of international bodies and international organizations on the implementation of the terms of the Accord. NATO's Implementation Force (IFOR), as a multinational peace enforcement in Bosnia-Herzegovina known as Operation Joint Endeavor, was responsible for the implementation of military aspects of the Agreement, taking over the armed forces of UNPROFOR from the period December 1995 to December 1996. Also, it must be noted that NATO, beyond IFOR, was held responsible to the UN for carrying out the Dayton Peace Accords.

Furthermore, the Dayton Agreement created, as an immediate result, the Office of the High Representative for Bosnia-Herzegovina, which was charged with the task of civil implementation of the Agreement, representing the countries that were involved in the Dayton Accords, through the Peace Implementation Council—an Office that was strengthened its duties by the Bonn Powers in 1997. Also, the OSCE was charged with organizing the first free elections in 1996.[72]

In general, the Dayton Agreement, as a temporary measure, was aimed at moving the states from an early post-conflict stage to a phase of consolidation and reconstruction as a conflict resolution negotiation and a peace-building process. Given the extensive interaction of international actors, it must be said that the Agreement also created a decentralized and complicated governmental system through state-identity building.[73]

58.6 The Question on Ethnic Cleansing and the International Criminal Tribunal for the Former Yugoslavia

The atrocities carried out in Croatia and later in Bosnia-Herzegovina urged the international community to act. Since the beginning of the war, the UN followed the situation, and established an *ad hoc* International Criminal Tribunal for the former Yugoslavia (ICTY), on the basis of Chapter VII of the UN Charter.[74] The Tribunal—the first international criminal tribunal since Nuremberg and Tokyo Military Tribunals—was established in response to mass atrocities and in order to prosecute persons responsible for serious violations of international humanitarian law that took place, *ratione loci*, in the territory of the former Yugoslavia, and especially Bosnia-Herzegovina and Croatia, after 1 January 1991. Under the Statute, the law applicable by the ICTY was based on rules of conventional and customary international law,[75] including, *ratione materiae*, horrendous and appalling crimes

---

[72] Hartwell 2019, pp. 443–469; Chandler 2005, pp. 336–349.

[73] Sumantra 2002, pp. 214–217; Keane 2001, pp. 59–62; Yourdin 2003, pp. 59–74.

[74] Morris and Scharf 1995, pp. 395–405.

[75] According to the Tribunal's Statute, "That part of international humanitarian law which has indisputably become customary international law is the law applicable to armed conflicts, namely: the Geneva Conventions of 12 August, 1949, the Fourth Hague Convention and the rules concerning

concerning grave breaches of the Geneva Conventions of 1949, violations of the laws or customs of war, genocide and crimes against humanity.[76] All these violations entailed individual criminal responsibility under the provisions of Article 7 of the Statute of the Tribunal.[77]

The ICTY was a UN tribunal, cited in The Hague that, in an efficient and transparent international justice norm, dealt with international crimes from 1991 to 2017, charged more than 160 persons, and irreversibly changed the landscape of international criminal and international humanitarian law. The Tribunal also proved that those suspected of bearing individual or collective responsibility for atrocities committed during Yugoslavian armed conflicts could be called to account against members of various ethnic groups in Serbia, Bosnia-Herzegovina, Croatia, Macedonia and Kosovo.[78]

It is noteworthy that the ICTY, beyond justifying its own existence and the resources invested in it,[79] dealt with a significant number of cases concerning crimes committed by Serbs and Bosnian Serbs and brought charges against individuals for crimes committed against Serbs and other members of various ethnic groups. Furthermore, the Tribunal made a certain impact on the former states of Yugoslavia through its contribution to ending impunity and paving the way for conciliation on a road to strengthening the rule of international law and, especially, international criminal law.

Most cases before the ICTY had to do with crimes that constituted ethnic cleansing, especially in the area of Bosnia-Herzegovina, given that a universally accepted definition of ethnic cleansing, which would precisely describe the practice in its entirety, does not exist. In particular, this term first appeared in international terminology in 1992, when the UN Commission on Human Rights and the Committee for the Prevention of Discrimination and the Protection of Minorities

---

the laws and conventions of war on land of 1907, the Convention of 9 December, 1948 for the prevention and suppression of the crime of genocide and the Statute of the Military Tribunal of Nuremberg of 8 August, 1945".

[76] Feinberg 2006, pp. 87–113; Van Sliedregt 2009, pp. 183–200.

[77] According to Article 7 para 1 of the Statute: "1. A person who planned, instigated, ordered, committed or otherwise aided and abetted in the planning, preparation or execution of a crime referred to in articles 2–5 of the present Statute, shall be individually responsible for the crime. 2. The official position of any accused person, whether as Head of State or Government or as a responsible Government official, shall not relieve such person of criminal responsibility nor mitigate punishment. 3. The fact that any of the acts referred to in articles 2–5 of the present Statute was committed by a subordinate does not relieve his superior of criminal responsibility if he knew or had reason to know that the subordinate was about to commit such acts or had done so and the superior failed to take the necessary and reasonable measures to prevent such acts or to punish the perpetrators thereof. 4. The fact that an accused person acted pursuant to an order of a Government or of a superior shall not relieve him of criminal responsibility, but may be considered in mitigation of punishment if the International Tribunal determines that justice so requires".

[78] Pocar 2008, pp. 665–667; Radan 2001, pp. 244–245.

[79] Milanović 2016, pp. 233–259.

condemned the acts in the former Yugoslavia as acts of ethnic cleansing.[80] In the case of Bosnia-Herzegovina, compared to genocide, this term was described as a planned and intentional deportation of members of a group who are in some aspects different from the dominant majority, such as in race, ethnic origin, religion, etc., in a certain geographical territory.[81]

Contrary to genocide, which concerns a set of crimes committed with the special intent (*dolus specialis*) to destroy, in whole or in part, a particular group, where victims are not killed for their acts or omissions but because they belong to one of the protected groups,[82] ethnic cleansing can be linked to the expulsion of a group from a specific geographical context, given the fact that the victims are recognized not as independent entities but as members of a national, ethnic or religious group.[83]

Given that the displacement of a population can be described as ethnic cleansing and that there are certain connective issues between it and genocide, it is pointed out that there are obvious similarities between the policy and the purpose of genocide as a result of ethnic cleansing.[84] It is a fact that the term "ethnic cleansing", though not being an independent crime under the principles of International Law and not specifically provided from Article II of the Convention on Genocide, provided that the conditions of that provision are fulfilled, may constitute genocide.

In the *Case of the Application of the Convention on the Prevention and Punishment of the Crime of Genocide* (Bosnia and Herzegovina v. Serbia and Montenegro),[85] the ICJ considered that there were obvious similarities between the policy pursued during the genocide and the policy of ethnic cleansing. In particular, the Court ruled that ethnic cleansing can be classified as genocide if the acts provided for in Article II of the Convention are fulfilled and there is a specific intent to destroy the group as such.[86] This view was also adopted in both the *Vučković Case* before the Supreme

---

[80] United Nations Commission on Human Rights (1992) Report of the 2nd Special Session, 30 November-1 December 1992, Economic and Social Council, Official Records, 1992. U.N. Doc. E/1992/22/84/Add.2. http://hr-travaux.law.virginia.edu/document/cped/e199222add2/nid-2455. Accessed 3 October 2020.

[81] Bell-Fialkoff 1993, pp. 110–121; Bell-Fialkoff 1996; Sokolovic 2005, pp. 115–130.

[82] May 2010, pp. 91–107; Tatz 2003, pp. 1–42; Chirot and McCauley 2006, pp. 11–50.

[83] Damrosch 1998, pp. 256–279; Tournaye 2003, pp. 447–449.

[84] United Nations Commission on Human Rights (1995) Situation of Human Rights in the Republic of Bosnia and Herzegovina, the Republic of Croatia and the Federal Republic of Yugoslavia (Serbia and Montenegro), 51st Session, E/CN.4/RES/1995/89, 8 March 1995. https://ap.ohchr.org/documents/alldocs.aspx?doc_id=4363. Accessed 9 September 2020; United Nations General Assembly (1993) The Situation in Bosnia Herzegovina, 47th Session, G.A. Res. 47/121, U.N. Doc. A/RES/47/121, 7 April 1993. https://undocs.org/en/A/RES/47/121. Accessed 3 August 2020.

[85] International Court of Justice (1996) Application for Revision of the Judgment of 11 July 1996 in the Case concerning Application of the Convention on the Prevention and Punishment of the Crime of Genocide (Bosnia and Herzegovina v. Yugoslavia), Preliminary Objections (Yugoslavia v. Bosnia and Herzegovina), para 190.

[86] Lyman 1993, pp. 193–196.

Court of Kosovo[87] and the *Jorgić Case* before the Federal Constitutional Court of Germany.[88]

It could, therefore, be argued that the committed crimes in former Yugoslavia, and the fact that the Bosnian genocide can mean either the genocide committed by the Serb forces in Srebrenica 1995 or the ethnic cleansing during the 1992–1995 Bosnian War,[89] showed that the policy of ethnic cleansing was carried out in certain geographical areas and was aiming at the elimination or partial physical extermination of the particular ethnic group of Bosnian Muslims, which would be carried out by clearing specific areas.[90] It must be noted that ethnic cleansing is not explicitly foreseen as an independent crime, and this is only when the clarification of acts that are identified in its meaning are analysed on the basis of other international crimes and under the respect of crimes consisting genocide, war crimes and crimes against humanity in an organized action plan, aimed at neutralizing, in a short or long term, the national identity of the victims with massively and systematically intent.[91]

Especially in the case of Bosnia-Herzegovina, there is controversy as to whether there had been a planned intention not only to ethnically cleanse specific territories but also to liquidate non-Serbs inhabitants in the effort to gain absolute control over claimed territories through Serbian high command. It is characteristic that violent acts or omissions perpetrated to genocide, as defined in the 1948 UN Convention,[92] identified within the preplanned scenario, pointing at the alleged genocidal nature of the Serbian operations and their aggressive intention against Bosnia-Herzegovina.[93]

As mentioned above, the 1948 legal definition of genocide seems, in the case of the Yugoslavian civil war, to be too broad compared to ethnic cleansing. Beyond the numerous policy similarities between genocide and ethnic cleansing and given that the two crimes may occur in parallel under certain circumstances, the Yugoslavia conflict and the ICTY judgments gave the differentiation of those crimes concerning the difference between genocidal planned extermination and the removal of an ethnic group or nation from a specific territory. In the case of ethnic cleansing in the territory of the former Yugoslavia, there was identification between the scope of ethnic cleansing and the dynamism of the armed conflict through the deeply rooted ethnic hatred and the nations involved.[94]

It was significant that the ICTY broke the tradition of impunity of war crimes by putting individuals in front of their responsibilities and holding them accountable,

---

[87] Supreme Court of Kosovo (2001) Vučković Case, Federal Republic of Yugoslavia (Serbia and Montenegro), 31 August 2001, para 135.

[88] Federal Constitutional Court (1997) Jorgić Case Germany, 4th Chamber of the Second Senate, Judgment of 26 September 1997, para 132–135.

[89] Thackrah 2008, pp. 81–82; Mirković 1999, pp. 26–37.

[90] Mann 2005, pp. 1–33; Midlarsky 2005, pp. 129–134; Gutman 1996.

[91] Petrović 1994, pp. 342–344; Jamieson 1999, pp. 139–140.

[92] Convention on the Prevention and Punishment of the Crime of Genocide, G.A. Res. 260 (III), 9 December 1948. *See* Schabas 2009, pp. 105–108; Byron 2004, pp. 143–177; Wagner 2003, pp. 419–431.

[93] Gow 2003.

[94] Bax 2000, pp. 16–29.

raising charges against heads of states, prime ministers, army commanders, political leaders and members of the governments and bringing justice to victims.

58.7 Conclusion

The break-up of Yugoslavia as an umbrella-state in the 1990s has attracted a plethora of legal and political analyses. With the deep roots of the Balkan conflict, its fragile condition due to interethnic tensions and disagreements, and given the transition from communism to nationalism claims and the state's nature and structure, Yugoslavia was conceived as a particular political experiment through violence and repression.

The dissolution of the common Yugoslav identity and the state collapse were accompanied by ineffective and complicated federal governance and the demonetization of the regime, supporting a decentralized federation or a centralized state under Serbia's control—a situation which ended Yugoslavia through a horrific and violent conflict with great atrocities and the creation of new independent states through the break-up.

Given the missed chances between 1991 and 1992 to avoid the armed conflict, the international community was unprepared for the outbreak of nationalist interstate violence and failed to assure minority rights; its effectiveness depended on the willingness of Yugoslav states and their policies on specific aspects of the armed conflict. Beyond that, not only was it the transition from communism to an open market and democracy, but also the rise of nationalism that led Yugoslavia to this violent dissolution.

Multiple causal factors concerning a continuing economic and political crisis, many cultural differences, institutional and constitutional problems (especially after 1974), the ratification of the new Constitution, the role of states, as well as the role of the international factors that changed the international situation through the confusion of international responses, all accompanied the unwillingness of the republics to make the necessary compromises in order to keep Yugoslavia from falling apart and the dissolution of the Yugoslav state and shaped the last years of Yugoslavia before its breakdown in 1991.

Ethnic cleansing, other inhuman practices and war crimes were the central elements of the civil war, especially in Bosnia-Herzegovina, and an inhuman tool for the implementation of the nationalist geostrategic plans and the creation of a superior national state through the ethnic structure. Given the complexity of the Yugoslavian civil war, the intensity of crimes perpetrated in the name of the ethnic homogenization of controlled territories was changing into brutally armed clashes in order to expel ethnically different populations, with unique characteristics, from a specific territory.

The dissolution of Yugoslavia gave a certain paradigm on the issue of the right of self-determination and the secession of the new states from an, internationally recognized, unitary state. But this is not the main issue. It must be said that the War in Yugoslavia set an important example regarding the sensitive issue of international peace and security as the first heinous armed conflict in the Balkans after World War II and the activation of international criminal justice, bringing to justice all those responsible for committing mass war crimes against persons protected by the laws and the values of International Humanitarian Law.

References

Abulof U (2015) The Confused Compass: From Self-Determination to State-Determination. Ethnopolitics 14(5): 488–497

Ahrens G H (2007) Diplomacy on the Edge: Containment of Ethnic Conflict and the Minorities of the Conferences in Yugoslavia. Woodrow Wilson Center Press, Washington D.C.

Ali R, Lifschultz L (1994) Why Bosnia? Third World Quarterly 15(3): 367–401

Allcock B J (2000) Explaining Yugoslavia. Columbia University Press, New York

Basta K (2010) Non-ethnic Origins of Ethnofederal Institutions: The Case of Yugoslavia. Nationalism and Ethnic Politics 16(1): 92–110

Bataković D (1995) Nationalism and Communism. The Yugoslav Case. Serbian Studies 9(1): 25–41

Bax M (2000) Warlords, Priests and the Politics of Ethnic Cleansing: A Case Study from Rural Bosnia Herzegovina. Ethnic and Racial Studies 23(1): 16–29

Bell-Fialkoff A (1993) A Brief History of Ethnic Cleansing. Foreign Affairs 72: 110–121

Bell-Fialkoff A (1996) Ethnic Cleansing. MacMillan, London

Belloni R (2007) State Building and International Intervention in Bosnia. Routledge, New York/London

Bellucci P, Isernia P (2003) Massacring in Front of a Blind Audience? Italian Public Opinion and Bosnia. In: Sobel R et al (eds) International Public Opinion and the Bosnia Crisis. Lexington Books, Lanham, MD, pp 173–218

Biondich M (2004) Croatia. In: Frucht C R (ed) Eastern Europe: An Introduction to the People, Lands and Culture. ABC Clio, Santa Barbara/Denver/Oxford, pp 413–476

Bjelajać M, Žunec O (2009) The War in Croatia, 1991-1995. In: Ingrao W, Emmert A T (eds) Confronting the Yugoslav Controversies: A Scholar's Initiative. Purdue University Press, West Lafayette, pp 233–272

Blagojević M (2000) The Migrations of Serbs from Kosovo during the 1970s and 1980s: Trauma and/or Catharsis. In: Popov N (ed) The Road to War in Serbia: Trauma and Catharsis. Central European University Press, Budapest, pp 212–246

Blitz K B (2006) War and Changes in the Balkans. Nationalism, Conflict and Cooperation. Cambridge University Press, Cambridge

Bose S (2002) Bosnia after Dayton. Nationalist Partition and International Intervention. Hurst and Company, London

Bryant L (1993) The Betrayal of Bosnia. University of Westminster, London

Byron C (2004) The Crime of Genocide. In: McGoldrick D et al (eds) The Permanent International Criminal Court: Legal and Policy Issues. Hart Publishing, Oxford/Portland, OR, pp 143–177

Calić M J (1996) Kriek und Frieden in Bosnien-Herzegowina. Edition Suhrkamp, Frankfurt am Main

Caplan R (2000) Assessing the Dayton Accord: The Structural Weakness of the General Framework Agreement for Peace in Bosnia and Herzegovina. Diplomacy and Statecraft 11(2): 213–232

Caplan R (2005) Europe and the Recognition of New States in Yugoslavia. Cambridge University Press, Cambridge

Chandler D (2005) From Dayton to Europe. International Peacekeeping 12(3):336–349

Chirot D, McCauley C (2006) Why not Kill them all? The Logic and Prevention of Mass Political Murder. Princeton University Press, Princeton

Chollet D (2005) The Road to the Dayton Accords. Palgrave Macmillan, New York

Cohen J L (1993) Broken Bonds. The Disintegration of Yugoslavia. Westview Press, San Francisco
Cohen J L (1996) Serbia's Secret War: Propaganda and the Deceit of History. Texas University Press, College Station, TX
Crampton R J (2002) The Balkans since the Second World War. Longman, London
Crawford R J (2006) The Creation of States in International Law, 2nd edn. Oxford University Press, Oxford
Damrosch L F (1998) Genocide and Ethnic Conflict. In: Wippman D (ed) International Law and Ethnic Conflict, Cornell University Press. Ithaca, New York, pp 256–279
Delpla I et al (2012) Investigating Srebrenica. Berghahn Books, New York
Dulić T (2005) Utopias of Nation: Local Mass Killings in Bosnia and Herzegovina, 1941-42. Uppsala University Press, Uppsala
Eyal J (1995) The War in Yugoslavia: Some Preliminary Lessons. RUSI Journal 140(2): 29–33
Feinberg G (2006) The International Criminal Tribunal for the Former Yugoslavia: The Establishment and Evaluation of a Unique Concept in International Justice Administration. War Crimes, Genocide and Crimes against Humanity 2: 87–113
Fichter M (2016) Yugoslav Protest: Student Rebellion in Belgrade, Zagreb and Sarajevo in 1968. Slavic Review 75(1): 99–121
Fisch J (2015) A History of the Self-Determination of Peoples: The Domestication of an Illusion. Cambridge University Press, Cambridge
Fisher S (2006) Political Change in Post-Communist Slovakia and Croatia. From Nationalist to Europeanist. Palgrave Macmillan, London/New York
Freeman M (2019) The Right to Self-Determination: Philosophical and Legal Perspectives. New England Journal of Public Policy 31(2): 1–8
Gagnon V P (2004) The Myth of Ethnic War. Serbia and Croatia in the 1990s. Cornell University Press, Ithaca, London
Gallagher T (2003) The Balkans after the Cold War: From Tyranny to Tragedy. Routledge, New York/London
Glenny M (1996) The Fall of Yugoslavia: The Third Balkan War, 3rd edn. Penguin Books, London
Goodby J E (1996) When War Won out: Bosnian Peace Plans before Dayton. International Negotiation 1(3): 501–523
Gow J (1997) Triumph of the Lack of Will: International Diplomacy and the Yugoslav War. Hurst and Company, London
Gow J (2003) The Serbian Project and its Adversaries: A Strategy of War Crimes. Hurst and Company, London
Gutman R (1996) Witness to Genocide. MacMillan Publishing, New York
Harris P (1996) Cry Bosnia. Interlink Books, New York
Hartwell L (2019) Conflict Resolution: Lessons from the Dayton Peace Process. Negotiation Journal 35(4):443–469
Haskin M J (2006) Bosnia and Beyond: The Quiet Revolution that wouldn't go Quietly. Algora Publishing, New York
Hayden M R (1996) Imagined Communities and Real Victims: Self-Determination and Ethnic Cleansing in Yugoslavia. American Ethnologist 23: 783–801
Hayden M R (1999) Blueprints for a House Divided: The Constitutional Logic of the Yugoslav Conflicts. University of Michigan Press, Ann Arbor
Hayden M R (2008) Mass Killings and Images of Genocide in Bosnia, 1941-5 and 1992-5. In: Stone D (ed) The Historiography of Genocide. Palgrave Macmillan, London, pp 487–516
Hoare M A (2004) How Bosnia Armed. Saqi Books, London
Hofbauer H (2001) Balkan Krieg: Zehn Jahre Zerstörung Jugoslawiens. Promedia, Vienna
Holbrooke R (1998) To End a War. Random House, New York
Hunt M (2013) The World Transformed: 1945 to the Present. Oxford University Press, Oxford
Irving J (1997) Ultranationalist Ideology and State-Building in Croatia, 1990-1996. Problems of Post-Communism 44(4): 30–43

Irving J (2008) The Croatian Spring and the Dissolution of Yugoslavia. In: Cohen J L, Dragović-Soso J (eds) State Collapse in South-Eastern Europe: New Perspectives on Yugoslav Disintegration. Purdue University Press, West Lafayette, pp 149–178

Isaković Z (2000) Identity and Security in Former Yugoslavia. Ashgate, Aldershot

Jamieson R (1999) Genocide and the Social Production of Immorality. Theoretical Criminology: 131–146

Jansen S (2007) Remembering with a Difference: Clashing Memories of Bosnian Conflict in Everyday Life. In: Bougarel X et al (eds) The New Bosnian Mosaic: Identities, Memories and Moral Claims in a Post-War Society. Ashgate, Aldershot, pp 199–210

Job C (2002) Yugoslavia's Ruin: The Bloody Lessons of Nationalism. Littlefield Publishers, New York

Jović D (2001) The Disintegration of Yugoslavia: A Critical Review of Explanatory Approaches. European Journal of Social Theory 4(1): 101–120

Judah T (2000) The Serbs: History, Myth and the Destruction of Yugoslavia, 2nd edn. Yale University Press, New Haven

Kalyvas N S, Sambanis N (2005) Bosnia's Civil War: Origins and Violence Dynamics. In: Collier P, Sambanis N (eds) Understanding Civil War. Evidence and Analysis. World Bank, Washington, DC, pp 191–230

Keane R (2001) Reconstructing Sovereignty: Post-Dayton Uncovered. Ashgate, London

Krizan M (1994) New Serbian Nationalism and the Third Balkan War. Studies in East European Thought 46: 47–68

Lampe R J (2000) Yugoslavia as History. Twice there was a Country. Cambridge University Press, Cambridge

Lazić M (1999) Protest in Belgrade. Winter of Discontent. Central European University Press, Budapest

Lefebvre S (1995) The Former Yugoslavia: War Termination Prospects and Hypotheses. Stanford Journal of International Affairs 4(1):45–57

Levdai P (1991) Yugoslavia without Yugoslavs: The Roots of the Crisis. International Affairs 67(2): 251–261

Lyman B L (1993) Beyond the 1948 Convention: Emerging Principles of Genocide in Customary International Law. Maryland Journal of International Law and Trade 17: 193–226

Magas B (1991) The War in Yugoslavia. RUSI Journal 136(4): 33–37

Malesević S (2002) Ideology, Legitimacy and the New State: Yugoslavia, Serbia and Croatia. Routledge, London

Malcolm N (1994) Bosnia. A Short History. Macmillan General Books, London

Mann M (2005) The Dark Side of Democracy: Explaining Ethnic Cleansing. Cambridge University Press, Cambridge

Marijan D (2012) The Sarajevo Ceasefire: Realism or Strategic Error by the Croatian Leadership? Review of Croatian History 7(1): 103–123

Marolov D, Stojanovski S (2014) About the Terms 'Yugoslavia', 'Balkanization' and 'Third Balkan War'. International Journal of Sciences: Basic and Applied Research, 18(2): 432–438

Mass P (2002) Paying for the Powell Doctrine. In: Mills N, Brunner K (eds) The New Killing Fields: Massacre and Politics of Intervention. Basic Books, New York, pp 71–88

May L (2010) Identifying Groups in Genocide Cases. In: May L, Hoskins Z (eds) International Criminal Law and Philosophy. Cambridge University Press, Cambridge, pp 91–107

McWhinney E (2007) Self-Determination of Peoples and Plural-Ethnic States in Contemporary International Law. Martinus Nijhoff Publishers, Boston/Leiden

Midlarsky I M (2005) The Killing Trap: Genocide in the Twentieth Century. Cambridge University Press, Cambridge

Mihailović K, Krestić V (1995) Memorandum of the Serbian Academy of Sciences and Arts: Answers to Criticisms. Serbian Academy of Sciences and Arts, Belgrade

Milanović M (2016) The Impact of the ICTY on the former Yugoslavia: An Anticipatory Postmortem. American Journal of International Law 110(2): 233–259

Mirković D (1999) On Destruction and Self-Destruction of Croatian Serbs: A Preliminary Draft for a Study of Genocide. South Slav Journal 20(1):26–37

Mojzes P (2011) Balkan Genocides: Holocaust and Ethnic Cleansing in the Twentieth Century. Rowman and Littlefield, Lanham, Maryland

Morris V, Scharf P M (1995) An Insider's Guide to the International Criminal Tribunal for the Former Yugoslavia. A Documentary History and Analysis. Transnational Publishers, Irvington on Hudson

Musgrave D T (2000) Self Determination and National Minorities. Oxford University Press, Oxford

Nambiar S (2001) UN Peacekeeping Operations in the Former Yugoslavia: From UNPROFOR to Kosovo. In: Thakur R, Schnabel A (eds) United Nations Peacekeeping Operations: Ad hoc Missions, Permanent Engagement. United Nations University Press, Tokyo/New York/Paris, pp 167–181

Oliver I (2005) War and Peace in the Balkans. The Diplomacy of Conflict in the Former Yugoslavia. I. B. Tauris, London/New York

O'Shea B (2005) The Modern Yugoslav Conflict 1991–1995. Perception, Deception and Dishonesty. Routledge, London

Parenti M (2000) To Kill a Nation: The Attack on Yugoslavia. Verso, London/New York

Pavlaković V (2005) Serbia Transformed? Political Dynamics in the Milosević Era and After. In: Ramet P S, Pavlaković V (eds) Serbia since 1989: Politics and Society under Milosević and After. University of Washington Press, Seattle, pp 13–55

Petrović R (1994) Ethnic Cleansing: An Attempt at Methodology. European Journal of International Law 5: 342–359

Pickering M P, Baskin M (2008) What is to be done? Succession from the League of Communists of Croatia. Communist and Post-Communist Studies 41: 521–540

Pocar F (2008) Completion or Continuation Strategy? Appraising Problems and Possible Developments in Building the Legacy of the ICTY. Journal of International Criminal Justice 6: 655–665

Prunk J (1997) The Origins of an Independent Slovenia. In: Fink-Hafner D, Robbins R J (eds) Making a New Nation: The Formation of Slovenia. Dartmouth Publishers, Aldershot/Brookfield, pp. 21–32

Radan P (2001) The Break-up of Yugoslavia and International Law. Routledge, London/New York

Rady M (1996) Self-Determination and the Dissolution of Yugoslavia. Ethnic and Racial Studies 19(2): 379–390

Raič D (2002) Statehood and the Law of Self-Determination. Kluwer Law International, The Hague

Ramet P S (1995) Social Currents in Eastern Europe: The Sources and Consequences of the Great Transformation. Duke University Press Books, Durham

Ramet P S (1996) Balkan Babel: The Disintegration of Yugoslavia from the Death of Tito to Ethnic War. Westview Press, Boulder

Ramet P S (2004) Explaining the Yugoslav Meltdown: Chapter 1. Journal of Nationalism and Ethnicity 32(4): 731–763

Rich R (2011) Recognition of States: The Collapse of Yugoslavia and the Soviet Union. European Journal of International Law 4(1): 36–65

Rizman R M (2005) (Un)certain Path: The Problems of Democratic Transition and Consolidation in Slovenia. Texas University Press, College Station TX

Rogel C (1998) The Breakup of Yugoslavia and the War in Bosnia. Greenwood Press, Westport CT

Schabas WA (2009) Genocide in International Law. The Crime of Crimes, 2nd edn. Cambridge University Press, Cambridge

Scharf P M (1997) Balkan Justice: The Story behind the First International War Crimes Trial since Nuremberg. Carolina Academic Press, Durham, NC

Schöpflin G (2006) Yugoslavia: State Construction and State Failure. In: Blitz K B (ed) War and Change in the Balkans: Nationalism, Conflict and Cooperation. Cambridge University Press, Cambridge, pp 13–29

Sell L (2000) The Serb Flight from Sarajevo: Dayton's First Failure. East European Politics and Societies 14(1): 179–202

Sell L (2002) Slobodan Milosević and the Destruction of Yugoslavia. Duke University Press, Durham, North Carolina

Silber L, Little A (1996) The Death of Yugoslavia. Penguin Books, London

Slack A, Doyon R (2001) Population Dynamics and Susceptibility for Ethnic Conflict: The Case of Bosnia and Herzegovina. Journal of Peace Research 38(2): 139–161

Sloan E C (1998) Bosnia and the New Collective Security. Greenwood Publishing Group, Westport CT

Sokolovic D (2005) How to Conceptualize the Tragedy of Bosnia: Civil, Ethnic, Religious War or...? War Crimes, Genocide and Crimes against Humanity 1(1): 115–130

Spehnjak K, Cipek T (2007) Dissidents, Opposition and Resistance: Croatia and Yugoslavia, 1945–1990. Journal of Contemporary History 39(2): 255–297

Sumantra B (2002) Bosnia after Dayton: Nationalist Partition and International Intervention. Oxford University Press, Oxford

Šuster Z (1999) Historical Dictionary of the Federal Republic of Yugoslavia. Scarecrow Press, London

Swain G (2010) The Cominform: Tito's International? The Historical Journal 35(3): 641–663

Tabeau E, Bijak J (2005) War-Related Deaths in 1992-1995 Armed Conflicts in Bosnia and Herzegovina: A Critique of Previous Estimates and Recent Results. European Journal of Population 21: 187–215

Tanner M (1997) Croatia: A Nation Forged in War. Yale University Press, New Haven CT

Tatz C (2003) With Intent to Destroy: Reflecting on Genocide. Verso, London/New York

Thackrah J R (2008) Routledge Companion to Military Conflict since 1945. Taylor and Francis, London

Toal G, Dahlman C (2011) Bosnia Remade: Ethnic Cleansing and its Reversal. Oxford University Press, Oxford

Tournaye C (2003) Genocidal Intent before the ICTY. International and Comparative Law Quarterly 52: 447–462

Van Sliedregt E (2009) System Criminality at the ICTY. In: Van der Wilt H, Nollkaemper A (eds) System Criminality in International Law. Cambridge University Press, Cambridge, pp 183–200

Vevjoda I (1996) Yugoslavia 1945-91: From Decentralization without Democracy to Dissolution. In: Vevjoda I, Dyker D (eds) Yugoslavia and After. Longman, London, pp 9-27

Vladisavljević N (2004) Yugoslavia's Successor States. In: Calvert P (ed) Border and Territorial Disputes of the World. John Harper Publishing, London, pp 390–398

Wagner M (2003) The ICC and its Jurisdiction: Myths, Misperceptions and Realities. Max Planck Yearbook of United Nations Law 7: 409–512

Wesselingh I, Vaulerin A (2003) Bosnie, la Mémoire a Vif : Prijedor, Laboratoire de la Purification Ethnique. Buchet-Chastel, Paris

Yourdin C (2003) Society Building in Bosnia: A Critique of Post-Dayton Peacebuilding Efforts. Journal of Diplomacy and International Relations 4(2): 59–74

Ioannis P. Tzivaras earned the LLM and PhD degrees from the Faculty of Law at Democritus University of Thrace (Greece). He is a Tutor at the Open University of Cyprus Department of Economics and Management.

Chapter 59
Northern Ireland: The Right to Life, Victim Mobilisation, and the Legacy of Conflict

Lauren Dempster

Contents

59.1 Introduction	1334
59.2 Background: Human Rights and the Northern Ireland Conflict	1336
59.3 Rights in Practice: Northern Ireland, the ECtHR, and Article 2	1338
59.3.1 Northern Ireland and Article 2 ECHR: The Right to Life	1339
59.4 The Rhetoric of Rights: Victim Mobilisation and Article 2 Compliant Investigations	1344
59.4.1 Opposition to Human Rights Language in Northern Ireland	1349
59.5 Conclusion	1353
References	1354

Abstract Article 2 of the European Convention on Human Rights has become an important tool utilised by relatives of those killed by state forces during the conflict in Northern Ireland in their campaigns for truth and justice. Of particular significance has been the jurisprudence which resulted from a series of cases which emanated from Northern Ireland: *McCann, Jordan, Kelly, McKerr* and *Shanaghan v. UK*. With these judgments the European Court of Human Rights (ECtHR) established a positive obligation on states to protect life, and a number of procedural obligations which states must meet in order for an investigation into deaths to be considered effective. This chapter examines the ECtHR's response to the use of lethal force in Northern Ireland and the resulting jurisprudence. In addition, it analyses the role played by relatives of those killed in bringing these cases to Strasbourg in the first place. Finally, it explores some of the challenges around utilising a human rights framework in the context of Northern Ireland.

Keywords Right to Life · Northern Ireland · lethal force · victims · mobilisation · human rights

L. Dempster (✉)
School of Law, Queen's University Belfast, Belfast, Northern Ireland, UK
e-mail: Lauren.Dempster@qub.ac.uk

59.1 Introduction

In 1998, the Good Friday Agreement was signed, bringing to an end some three decades of conflict in Northern Ireland. While this Agreement made provision for (among others) the establishment of a devolved assembly in Northern Ireland, the development of North-South relations on the island of Ireland, reform of the police service, and the release of prisoners, limited space was given over to considering how best to address the legacy of the conflict.[1] Rather than the establishment of an overarching transitional justice mechanism incorporating prosecutions, truth recovery, and reconciliation-focused measures, Northern Ireland has instead experienced a 'piecemeal' approach to its past.[2] This has included the establishment of The Office of the Police Ombudsman for Northern Ireland (OPONI), public inquiries, coronial inquests, the Historical Enquiries Team (HET), a police-led review of conflict-related deaths, investigations into alleged wrongful convictions by the Criminal Cases Review Commission, litigation efforts by families of those killed both in domestic courts and at the European Court of Human Rights (ECtHR), and community- and civil society-led story-telling, truth recovery, and oral history projects.[3] This 'piecemeal' approach has been criticised by some, both as an overall approach,[4] and with respect to specific elements or institutions.[5] In 2016, Pablo de Greiff, UN Special Rapporteur on the promotion of truth, justice, reparation and guarantees of non-recurrence, concluded in his report on the UK that 'despite the multiplicity of efforts undertaken' the past 'has not been properly and completely addressed.' As a result, it 'still disrupts the country's present.'[6]

There have been four attempts to develop an overarching series of mechanisms to address the legacy of the conflict. In 2006, the NGO Healing Through Remembering (HTR) produced a report, *Making Peace with the Past*, which detailed a range of options for addressing the past. In 2007, the Consultative Group on the Past released its recommendations, which drew upon the HTR document and a widespread consultation process. In 2013, the Northern Ireland political parties engaged in a talks process, chaired by US diplomats Richard Haass and Meghan O'Sullivan, but failed to reach agreement. All-party talks resumed in 2014 and in December of that year, the Stormont House Agreement (SHA) was concluded. It proposed the establishment of

---

[1] Some of the ideas discussed in this chapter emerged during my time as Postdoctoral Research Fellow on two research projects: AH/N001451/1 Voice, Agency and Blame: Victimhood and Imagined Community in Northern Ireland and ES/N010825/1 Apologies, Abuses and Dealing with the Past.

[2] Bell 2002; Bell et al. 2004; McEvoy and Ellison 2003.

[3] McEvoy and Bryson 2016.

[4] See e.g. Bell 2002; McEvoy and Ellison 2003; and McEvoy and Bryson 2016.

[5] See e.g. Lundy 2009 with regards to the HET; Duffy 2010; Lawther 2013; McGovern 2013; and Rolston 2006 on the challenges of truth recovery; Committee on the Administration of Justice (CAJ) 2015 on impunity; Breen-Smyth 2009 and Jankowitz 2018 on the definition of victimhood and issues of victim hierarchy; Lundy and Rolston 2016 on the role of apology; Requa and Anthony 2008 on the coronial inquest system; Quirk 2013 on the Criminal Cases Review Commission.

[6] United Nations General Assembly 2016.

four mechanisms aimed at addressing the legacy of the conflict, including a Historical Investigations Unit and an Independent Commission on Information Retrieval.[7] A public consultation on these proposals, including draft legislation, was completed in 2018 and, in July 2019, the UK government published a summary of responses received.[8] In January 2020, the British government made a commitment to introduce legislation to address the legacy aspects of the SHA within 100 days. However, in March 2020, the government shifted its position quite dramatically in response to the introduction of a Bill to set a time limit of five years for prosecutions for UK armed forces members who have served overseas.[9] The Secretary of State for Northern Ireland, Brandon Lewis MP, stated in a Written Ministerial Statement (WMS) that legacy issues would be addressed by the government in a way that ensures 'equal treatment of Northern Ireland veterans and those who served overseas.' Furthermore, 'while the principles underpinning the draft [SHA] Bill...remain, significant changes will be needed to obtain a broad consensus for the implementation of any legislation.'[10] The WMS, according to the human rights NGO The Committee on the Administration of Justice (CAJ), 'signalled the unilateral abandonment of the commitment to implement the Stormont House Agreement.'[11] In an October 2020 report, the House of Commons Northern Ireland Affairs Committee criticised this shift in the government's approach, highlighting a lack of provision of policy detail following the publication of the WMS, the lack of 'meaningful consultation' with victims' groups or other key stakeholders, and the absence of guidance on practical issues relating to the purpose and operation of the proposed new body.[12]

Rather than giving an overview of these various mechanisms, institutions, and proposals (a task which has been done by others),[13] this chapter will instead focus on one element of efforts to 'deal with' the past in Northern Ireland. Specifically, it will examine the key role played by Article 2 of the European Convention on Human Rights (ECHR) both as a legal framework for legacy related litigation and as part of broader mobilisation efforts by victims seeking truth and justice. In 1998, signatories to the Good Friday Agreement (Belfast Agreement/GFA) declared: 'we firmly dedicate ourselves...to the protection and vindication of the human rights of all.'[14] The Agreement is argued to have given 'recognition to an argument which human rights campaigners had been pushing for many years. Namely that issues of human rights are central to any successful resolution of the Northern Ireland

---

[7] Ibid.
[8] Northern Ireland Office 2019.
[9] McEvoy et al. 2020.
[10] Hansard House of Commons 2020. See also McEvoy et al. 2020.
[11] Committee on the Administration of Justice 2020. See also McEvoy et al. 2020.
[12] House of Commons Northern Ireland Affairs Committee 2020.
[13] See McEvoy and Bryson 2016 and McEvoy et al. 2020.
[14] The Belfast Agreement (10 April 1998). https://assets.publishing.service.gov.uk/government/uploads/system/uploads/attachment_data/file/1034123/The_Belfast_Agreement_An_Agreement_Reached_at_the_Multi-Party_Talks_on_Northern_Ireland.pdf. Accessed 3 March 2022.

conflict.'[15] Just as 'human rights became intrinsic to the language and politics of the peace process,'[16] unsurprisingly, so too have they emerged as a central component in efforts to address the legacy of past violence. As will be examined in this chapter, this role has been two-fold: directly, through engagement with the European Court of Human Rights (ECtHR) and the rights enshrined in the ECHR, and indirectly, through the adoption of the language of human rights into the parlance of debate on how to most effectively address the legacy of the conflict.

This chapter will first provide some background to the Northern Ireland conflict, with particular focus on the role of human rights. Then it will examine the ECtHR's response to lethal force killings by state forces in Northern Ireland, and the resulting jurisprudence. This will be followed by an analysis of how victims and survivors of the conflict have utilised a human rights framework in their efforts to seek truth and justice. A central element to this is the emergence of demands for Article 2 compliant investigations into historical killings. Finally, this chapter will analyse some of the challenges to the use of this human rights framework.

59.2 Background: Human Rights and the Northern Ireland Conflict

Described as 'the most violent in 50 years of Western European history,'[17] the conflict in Northern Ireland resulted in the deaths of over 3600 individuals [18] and injuries of an estimated 8383 to 100,000 people.[19] Although this chapter focuses on human rights violations resulting from the conflict, it must be noted that the violence in Northern Ireland was (for some) a reaction to underlying inequalities. Key issues included inequality of treatment of the minority Catholic population in both the private and public sector, in areas such as housing, employment and education, and a lack of trust in the police by this same community.[20] This chapter focuses on killings by state forces, however these killings constitute a minority (9.9%) of conflict-related deaths.[21] The Provisional Irish Republican Army was responsible for the majority of deaths (47.5%). Smaller Irish Republican non-state armed groups were responsible for just over 10% of deaths. Pro-British state, Loyalist paramilitaries were responsible for 29.9% of deaths.[22] Killings by non-state armed groups therefore comprise the majority of conflict-related deaths, and are examined elsewhere.[23] Of the 9.9% (367)

---

[15] Livingstone and Harvey 1999.

[16] Harvey 2015, p. 49.

[17] Campbell et al. 2003, p. 325.

[18] Bell 2002; McKittrick et al. 2007.

[19] Breen-Smyth 2012.

[20] See e.g. Dickson 2010; Grech 2017; Livingstone and Harvey 1999.

[21] Figures taken from McKittrick et al. 2007.

[22] Ibid.

[23] See e.g. Dempster 2019; Fay et al. 1999; Lawther 2014b; Jankowitz 2018; McKittrick et al. 2007.

of killings attributed to state forces, the British Army and Royal Ulster Constabulary (Northern Ireland's police force) were responsible for 6.5% and 1.4% of deaths respectively.[24] Between 1969 and 1974 (the most violent period of the conflict) 188 people were killed by state forces—169 of these by the regular military. 65% of these individuals were undisputedly unarmed at the time they were killed. In only 12% of cases were the individuals confirmed to have been armed. The remaining 23% comprise cases in which the individual was possibly armed, or in which the armed status is either unknown or disputed.[25]

As is well established, when challenging violence by armed groups, states may engage in practices which limit the rights that their citizens normally enjoy.[26] Northern Ireland was no exception. Since its inception, the jurisdiction had 'existed in an almost permanent "state of emergency".'[27] Although 'there was never wholesale impunity,'[28] and both the UK and the Republic of Ireland have 'demonstrated at least some commitment to legality,'[29] human rights violations undoubtedly featured as part of both states' responses to political violence.[30] The IRA and Loyalist ceasefires of 1994 raised expectations that the measures which were alleged to infringe on rights would end as 'the rationale for such measures had now gone, and with it, the reasoning went.'[31] However, by the late 1990s international criticism of rights abuses in Northern Ireland was on the increase. While 'considerable sympathy' existed for the UK and the challenges it faced in seeking to address the violence, UN bodies and international human rights NGOs increasingly vocalised their concern and criticised the UK's counter-terrorism measures and the infringement of these measures on human rights—in particular the right to life and prohibition of torture.[32] Some 20 years after the ceasefires, Nils Muižnieks, then Council of Europe Commissioner for Human Rights, stated: 'there has been virtual impunity for the state actors' involved in cases of killings concerning British military personnel: 'the issue of impunity is a very, very serious one…This is not just an issue of dealing with the past; it has to do with upholding the rule of law in general.'[33]

---

[24] McKittrick et al. 2007.

[25] Ní Aoláin 2000. See also McEvoy 2017. Please note that these figures relate to deaths that have been directly attributed to members of the security services and they do not include cases of collusion (see McEvoy 2017, footnote 6). As defined by Judge Peter Cory, collusion involves army or police forces 'ignoring or turning a blind eye to the wrongful acts of their servants or agents or supplying information to assist them in their wrongful acts or encouraging them to commit wrongful acts' (Cory 2004).

[26] See e.g. Boyle 1982.

[27] Campbell et al. 2003.

[28] Bell 2002, p. 1098.

[29] Boyle 1982.

[30] See Dickson 2010 for a detailed analysis. See also Livingstone and Harvey 1999.

[31] Mageean and O'Brien 1998, p. 1500.

[32] Livingstone and Harvey 1999, p. 1.

[33] BBC News 2014 and Northern Ireland Human Rights Commission 2017.

59.3 Rights in Practice: Northern Ireland, the ECtHR, and Article 2

For Boyle, writing in 1982, 'the emergency in Northern Ireland...has not prevented important proceedings under the Convention.'[34] Indeed, prior to the 1980s conflict in Turkey, Northern Ireland provided more 'test cases' for Strasbourg than anywhere else in Europe.[35] Its conflict was at the centre of both the first decision made by the Court (*Lawless v. Ireland*), and the first inter-state case to result in a judgment (*Ireland v. UK*).[36] Despite the frequency of Northern Ireland conflict cases coming before the European Court, Strasbourg's approach (at least in these early cases) has been described as 'cautious',[37] with the outcome of *Lawless* argued to have set a troubling precedent.[38] In this case, the European Commission on Human Rights concluded that Lawless's detention in the Republic of Ireland in 1957 without trial was a breach of the ECHR. However, this derogation was permitted as a state of public emergency existed at the time.[39] This 'reasonably government-friendly, pronouncement,'[40] Dickson contends, 'left a deep and not entirely beneficent impact on the jurisprudence subsequently emanating from Strasbourg,'[41] establishing, as it did, that states facing a 'public emergency' were to be allowed a wide margin of appreciation as regards how best to respond.[42]

Ní Aoláin argues that, during the 1980s, the approach of Strasbourg to a number of Northern Ireland cases demonstrated an 'unwillingness to articulate exacting standards of behaviour for State agents who had killed citizens during the course of their duties.'[43] This 'relatively 'hands-off' approach,' Bakircioglu and Dickson suggest, has over time become 'much more interventionist.'[44] Unsuccessful applications lodged during the 'hands-off' phase related to claims of religious discrimination, fair trial rights, and allegations regarding the behaviour of security forces.[45] That these applications were unsuccessful was, however, not solely a result of Strasbourg's perceived reluctance to challenge the state. For Dickson, a key factor in the failure of these early applications was that 'the claims were not formulated and managed carefully enough.'[46] As argued by McEvoy, one result of the 'quietism'

---

[34] Boyle 1982, p. 159.
[35] Dickson 2010.
[36] Bakircioglu and Dickson 2017.
[37] Dickson 2010, p. 37.
[38] Ibid. See also Doolan 2001.
[39] Doolan 2001.
[40] Dickson 2010, p. 37.
[41] Ibid., p. 34.
[42] Doolan 2001.
[43] Ní Aoláin 2002, p. 3.
[44] Bakircioglu and Dickson 2017, p. 266.
[45] Ibid.; Dickson 2010.
[46] Dickson 2010, p. 51.

of many in the legal profession during the civil rights campaigns of the 1960s was that 'the level of technical skill amongst lawyers, certainly with regard to the use of the European Convention on Human Rights, was questionable.'[47] Furthermore, a range of limitations within the Convention on admissibility rendered getting cases accepted in the first place difficult.[48]

Later, more successful, applications relating to the right to life, the right to a fair trial, the right to liberty, and the right not to be ill-treated were more sympathetically addressed by the ECtHR.[49] This shift in Strasbourg's approach can be seen through the changing approach to right to life cases, as examined in the next section. Although not the focus of this chapter, it must be noted that many of the principles which were established in the Northern Ireland-related cases have been influential across Europe and beyond.[50] 'Cases emerging out of the conflict in Northern Ireland have had a profound effect on the development of the European Court's approach to Article 2 of the Convention.'[51]

59.3.1 Northern Ireland and Article 2 ECHR: The Right to Life

Article 2 case law 'provides an illustration of dramatic change in Strasbourg's recognition of a right'.[52] Dickson (in 2010) summarised the relevance of Article 2 to the conflict thus:

> the provision was not frequently invoked during the early years...the applicants who did invoke it were not successful...the Article has come into its own only during the last 10 or 15 years...cases connected with Northern Ireland have been extremely important in the development of the European Court's jurisprudence on the right to life.[53]

Prior to *McCann v. UK*,[54] cases alleging that British security forces had breached the right to life were declared inadmissible for a range of reasons, including a lack of evidence, that security forces were acting in self-defence, or—as in the case of Bloody Sunday—being lodged out of time.[55] Dickson has described the approach of Strasbourg as displaying a 'reluctance...to 'second-guess' the decisions of governments, and of military authorities' when involved in counter-terrorism efforts.[56]

---

[47] McEvoy 2011, p. 359.
[48] Dickson 2010.
[49] Bakircioglu and Dickson 2017. See also Dickson 2010.
[50] Dickson 2010.
[51] Ibid., p. 275. See also Winter 2013.
[52] Requa 2012.
[53] Dickson 2010, p. 225.
[54] *McCann v. UK* (1996) 21 EHRR 97. For analysis see e.g. Dickson 2010; Ní Aoláin 2002; Winter 2013.
[55] Bakircioglu and Dickson 2017.
[56] Dickson 2010, p. 233.

McCann v. UK is argued to have constituted a 'breakthrough'[57] or 'sea-change'[58] in this regard. This case resulted from the killing of three unarmed members of a Provisional IRA Active Service Unit (Mairead Farrell, Daniel McCann and Sean Savage) by SAS soldiers in Gibraltar in March 1988. The Court held that although the soldiers believed it was necessary (in light of the information they had been given) to shoot the suspects to prevent them from detonating a bomb, it questioned a number of elements of the case: why the authorities did not detain the three at the border—rather than allowing them to enter Gibraltar; the failure to consider that the intelligence assessment which indicated that the bomb could be detonated via a remote control from a distance could have been wrong; and that the soldiers automatically used lethal force. In its judgment the Court emphasised the 'absolutely necessary' and proportionality requirements of Article 2: 'the force used must be strictly proportionate to the achievement of the aims.'[59] With this judgment the Court established a positive obligation on states to protect life.[60] For Ní Aoláin, 'the right to life emerged from the *McCann* decision as a strict scrutiny right subject to enhanced review.'[61] The 'contentious' *McCann* decision, Ní Aoláin argues, was 'the precursor to' the outcome of a group of 2001 decisions on the right to life.[62] When considered alongside an emerging Article 2 jurisprudence emanating mostly from Turkey,[63] the *McCann* decision was demonstrative of 'a willingness by the Court to be far more proactive in articulating State obligations to protect the right to life.'[64]

On 4 May 2001, the ECtHR issued a series of decisions on cases relating to Northern Ireland, establishing as it did so a number of procedural obligations which states must meet when investigating deaths.[65] In the cases of *Jordan*,[66] *Kelly*,[67] *McKerr*[68] and *Shanaghan v. UK*,[69] the court held that by failing to carry out thorough and effective investigations into the deaths of 12 individuals, the state had violated their right to life.[70] The Court's findings with regards the requirements for an Article 2-compliant investigation constitute, for Dickson, 'perhaps the single most important development in European human rights standards attributable to applications

---

[57] Bakircioglu and Dickson 2017, p. 275.
[58] Ní Aoláin 2002, p. 3.
[59] *McCann v. UK* (1996) 21 EHRR 97, paras 200–214 and 149.
[60] Sicilianos 2016; Bakircioglu and Dickson 2017.
[61] Ní Aoláin 2002, p. 3.
[62] Ibid., p. 1.
[63] Ibid.; Hadden 2004.
[64] Ibid., p. 1.
[65] Bakircioglu and Dickson 2017.
[66] *Jordan v. UK* (2003) 37 EHRR 2.
[67] *Kelly v. UK* App No 30054/96.
[68] *McKerr v. UK* (2002) 34 EHRR 20.
[69] *Shanaghan v. UK* App 37715/97.
[70] Ní Aoláin 2002.

resulting from the conflict in Northern Ireland.'[71] Ní Aoláin similarly has described these as the Court's 'most significant judgments to date on the right to life.'[72]

While each of these cases involved separate fact-specific concerns,[73] collectively these cases 'raised strikingly similar issues about the inadequacies of the investigations following death at the hands of the state,'[74] highlighting 'a number of systemic failings in the investigative and prosecutorial processes.'[75] These included criticisms of the Coroners Courts, the police, and the Director of Public Prosecutions (DPP). Criticisms of the Coroners Courts included that: inquiries into controversial deaths were too limited; those involved in the use of force could not be compelled to give evidence; there were delays in holding inquiries; legal aid was not provided for some families of the deceased; and that public interest immunity certificates were used to suppress information on key issues.[76] Criticisms of the police focused on the lack of independence between those investigating cases and those police and soldiers who were implicated in the events being investigated. The DPP was criticised by the ECtHR for demonstrating insufficient transparency and accountability with regards to prosecution decisions.[77] The response to this set of killings also highlighted the lack of any effective sanction to hold accountable police and military personnel involved in such incidents, and the inadequacy of compensation as the sole remedy for right to life violations.[78]

In the aftermath of these Article 2 judgments, Bell and Keenan suggest:

> an optimist could have expected two things: first, that adequate investigations would now ensue in these particular cases, and others like them; and second, that the institutional failings identified by the Court would form a blueprint for holistic change relating to police, prosecution, and coroner practices, aimed at ensuring an effective investigation.[79]

These judgments prompted the UK government to adopt a 'package of measures' which, it claimed, would constitute human rights-compliant, effective, independent investigations.[80] This package included changes to the Coroners Courts, police accountability mechanisms, and the DPP.[81] Some changes have been made. For example, it is now judges, rather than government ministers, who decide on the necessity (or not) of protecting a document from disclosure under a public interest immunity certificate; information related to an inquest is now disclosed to all parties in advance of the inquest taking place; and, since 2002, witnesses who are suspected

---

[71] Dickson 2010, p. 268.

[72] Ní Aoláin 2002, p. 1.

[73] Anthony and Mageean 2007. See Ní Aoláin 2002; Bakircioglu and Dickson 2017; Dickson 2010; Early et al. 2016 for details of each case.

[74] Ní Aoláin 2002, p. 5.

[75] Anthony and Mageean 2007.

[76] Ibid.

[77] Ní Aoláin 2002; Dickson 2010; Anthony and Mageean 2007.

[78] Ní Aoláin 2002.

[79] Bell and Keenan 2005, pp 73–74.

[80] CAJ 2015.

[81] Anthony and Mageean 2007; Bell and Keenan 2005; Ní Aoláin 2002.

of involvement in a death can be compelled to attend the inquest.[82] However, Bell and Keenan's 'optimist' is likely to have been disappointed. The changes have been described as 'piece-meal and minimalist,'[83] and a number of criticisms of the practical feasibility and impact of these reforms have emerged.

In terms of feasibility, for Lord Chief Justice, Sir Declan Morgan:

> the Article 2 investigatory obligations in the legacy cases pose huge problems particularly in relation to the requirement of reasonable expedition. If the existing legacy inquests are to be brought to a conclusion under the present system, someone could easily be hearing some of these cases in 2040.[84]

In 2015, Belfast based human rights NGO the Committee on the Administration of Justice (CAJ) reported that:

> serious limitations…have become apparent in relation to these mechanisms…Elements of the package have been shown not to have the necessary independence, effectiveness or impartiality to investigate state actors. Even those mechanisms which have been independent have faced limitations on their powers, delay or obstruction in undertaking their work.[85]

With regards the impact of the 'package of measures', Dickson has highlighted a range of both individual measures (related to each of the four 2001 cases) and overarching issues which have yet to be adequately addressed.[86] The changes were 'essentially prospective in effect'.[87] The package focused only on reforming institutions with a view to future investigations—there were to be no new investigations into the cases which prompted the Strasbourg judgments.[88] Since the 2001 decisions, the ECtHR has held in a number of decisions that the requirements for a proper investigation have not been met.[89] Even in such cases, there remains no obligation under domestic law for an Article 2 compliant investigation to be held.[90] These difficulties result in part from the interpretation of the Human Rights Act 1998 (HRA) and the question of whether the UK government is required to hold Article 2 compliant investigations into these cases if deaths had taken place prior to the HRA coming into force in 2000.[91] For Ní Aoláin, the ECtHR decisions of 2001 'do not come close to any form of oversight for the significant number of outstanding lethal force killings.'[92] CAJ suggests that this was a deliberate move on the part of the UK government:

---

[82] Dickson 2010, see pp. 271–273 for the impact of the package of measures.

[83] Bell and Keenan 2005, p. 75.

[84] Morgan 2016, p. 91. See also e.g. Requa and Anthony 2008; Committee on the Administration of Justice 2015; Larkin 2016; Requa 2012 for an analysis of the Coronial inquest system.

[85] CAJ 2015, p. i.

[86] Dickson 2010.

[87] Anthony and Mageean 2007, pp. 191–192.

[88] Bell and Keenan 2005; Anthony and Mageean 2007.

[89] Bakircioglu and Dickson 2017.

[90] Dickson 2010. In *Brecknell v. UK* it was held that the state has an obligation to trigger a fresh investigation if new evidence is available (see McEvoy 2017).

[91] Anthony and Mageean 2007; Bell and Keenan 2005; Requa 2012. See also Re: McQuillan, McGuigan and McKenna (2021) UKSC 55.

[92] Ní Aoláin 2002, p. 10.

the evidence does not support a conclusion that a 'package of measures' is being deployed in good faith by the UK Government…Rather, it points to a common purpose between the UK government and elements within the security establishment to prevent access to the truth and maintain a cover of impunity for state agents.[93]

To date, the ECtHR has not ruled that security forces in Northern Ireland violated the negative duty not to take life,[94] nor has it required the UK government to introduce more specific legislation regarding the use of force by security forces.[95] Dickson summarises thus:

the European Convention's adjudication and enforcement organs have not done all that they could have done to ensure that human rights have been fully protected during the Northern Ireland conflict: the Convention is still not completely 'fit for purpose' in that sense. In truth, the Convention has proved itself to be something of a blunt instrument in a highly conflicted society.[96]

In 2015, the UN Human Rights Committee reported:

The Committee remains concerned that, a considerable time after murders…have occurred, several inquiries into these murders have still not been established or concluded, and that those responsible for these deaths have not yet been prosecuted…The State party should conduct, as a matter of particular urgency given the passage of time, independent and impartial inquiries in order to ensure a full, transparent and credible account of the circumstances surrounding violations of the right to life in Northern Ireland.[97]

The result of these various challenges and weaknesses is that the Article 2 jurisprudence which emerged in Strasbourg, 'has not significantly benefited the families of the victims of killings in Northern Ireland itself.'[98] Furthermore, these criticisms 'have raised a broader concern about whether the UK is in systemic breach of its international obligations and whether it is institutionally capable of accommodating the demands of Article 2 ECHR.'[99]

In addition, the Council of Europe's Committee of Ministers has become increasingly exasperated with the UK's response to the ECtHR's findings in these cases. The Committee last issued an interim decision into the *McKerr* group of cases in 2009, at that time deciding to resume consideration of these cases at subsequent meetings.[100] Since 2015, the UK has been using the SHA as its response to the Article 2 failings identified by the ECtHR.[101] And yet, as examined above (49.1) the SHA

---

[93] CAJ 2015, p. 124.
[94] Bakircioglu and Dickson 2017.
[95] Dickson 2010.
[96] Dickson 2010, p. 4.
[97] UN Human Rights Committee 2008.
[98] Dickson 2010, p. 225.
[99] Anthony and Moffett 2014, p. 399.
[100] Council of Europe Committee of Ministers 2009.
[101] See e.g. Secretariat of the Committee of Ministers 2015; Council of Europe Committee of Ministers 2015; Secretariat of the Committee of Ministers 2017; Secretariat of the Committee of Ministers 2019.

has yet to be implemented. At the 1355th meeting of the Committee of Ministers in September 2019, the Deputies 'recalled with profound regret that the investigations and related litigation in the cases of *McKerr, Shanaghan, Jordan, Kelly and Others* and *McCaughey and Others* have still not been completed' and 'reiterated their serious concerns about the delay in the establishment of the Historical Investigations Unit (HIU) and other legacy institutions and underlined that…it is imperative that the authorities ensure that effective Convention-compliant investigations can be conducted.'[102] Following delays on submission by the UK government of information relating to the investigation into the murder of Pat Finucane, and the 'lack of detail' on the legacy approach set out in the WMS (see 49.1), in September 2020, the Committee of Ministers 'strongly urged' the UK 'to act, within the shortest possible timeframe, on their obligation to put an end to the type of violation identified by the Court in the present cases and to secure compliance with the requirements of Article 2 of the Convention,' setting a deadline of December 2020 for the provision of the requested information by the UK.[103]

What the ECtHR judgments on Article 2 have done, however, is to provide the families of those whose loved ones were killed at the hands of the state with a jurisprudence that they can (and do—see below) draw on in their campaigns for truth and justice. There have been some developments, for example investigations by both OPONI and the HET (since dissolved) are (or were, in the case of the HET)[104] required to meet international human rights standards and to comply with Article 2 ECHR. This means they must be completely independent of those who are, or potentially are, under investigation. They must also involve the family of the person killed.[105] As McGovern contends, 'this is the result of a long struggle by human rights activists and lawyers and successful challenges to earlier investigations in cases brought from Northern Ireland to the European Courts.'[106]

59.4 The Rhetoric of Rights: Victim Mobilisation and Article 2 Compliant Investigations

Advocacy groups and others seeking to effect change may utilise human rights strategies and adopt human rights language in order to better promote their cause.[107] In

---

[102] Council of Europe Committee of Ministers 2019.

[103] Council of Europe Committee of Ministers 2020. See also Committee on the Administration of Justice 2020. The execution of the judgment in the case of *McCann* was noted as closed by the Committee of Ministers in March 1996 (Council of Europe Committee of Ministers 1996). See also Dickson 2010, pp. 257–258 on *McCann* and pp. 271–272 on the McKerr group.

[104] The HET was criticised for a lack of independence when investigating state violence and was closed in 2014 (Jankowitz 2018; see Lundy 2011 and Lundy and Rolston 2016 for an analysis of the HET).

[105] McGovern 2013.

[106] Ibid., p. 11.

[107] Martens 2006; Mertus 2007. See also Keck and Sikkink 1998.

particular, groups trying to draw attention to a specific wrong might frame their cause in human rights terms.[108] Human rights, we are told, have 'an expressive dimension, in terms of the construction, articulation, and legitimization of norms, values, identities, and lifestyles.'[109] As Ignatieff argues: 'if human rights has not stopped the villains, it certainly has empowered bystanders and victims.'[110]

During the Northern Ireland conflict and since, groups of victims and survivors, human rights organisations, and journalists have raised 'a series of issues relating to accountability for the past, with respect to both State and non-State actors.'[111] The cases examined above would not have come to the attention of the ECtHR were it not for the efforts of the relatives of those who had been killed, often supported by human rights organisations, in particular CAJ.[112] The individual complaint procedure became the 'primary vehicle' for pursuing cases which alleged an Article 2 violation, with the majority of these cases emanating from Northern Ireland.[113] Despite its flaws, the *Lawless* case did make Irish people aware that the ECHR provided a route for addressing alleged human rights violations.[114] The development of the jurisprudence around Article 2 in the years since is the culmination of years of work:

> The development of Article 2's procedural aspect itself stands testimony to the difficulties of holding state actors accountable domestically. Over the years, families, lawyers, and NGOs had cooperated in a wide variety of strategies aimed at holding state actors accountable domestically and internationally.[115]

As Harvey contends, 'the discourse of human rights plays a prominent role in Northern Ireland's transitional context.'[116] In this section, the role of the families of those killed by state forces in pursuing human rights cases will be examined, and the value of human rights as a mobilising framework explored.

To consider one case, *McCann*, relatives of those killed in Gibraltar first called on the Irish government to take an inter-state case against the UK. The mothers of Sean Savage and Daniel McCann asked in a statement: 'We ask the Taoiseach…to stand up to the British Government and what it is doing to Irish people. We appeal to you…to use your power. We urge you to expose the truth about what happened in Gibraltar.'[117] In 1989, the families of those killed announced that they would be taking a civil action against the British Government. Mairead Farrell's brother, Niall, told journalists: 'If we want to take this case to the European Court of Human Rights we've got to exhaust all the domestic remedies. So therefore we will take it

---

[108] Mertus 2007.
[109] Stammers 2003, p. 299.
[110] Ignatieff 2001, p. 8.
[111] Bell 2002, p. 1128.
[112] Felner 2012; Mallinder 2019; McEvoy 2011; Winter 2013.
[113] Ni Aoláin 2000, p. 193.
[114] Dickson 2010.
[115] Bell and Keenan 2005, p. 72.
[116] Harvey 2015, p. 47.
[117] Cusack 1988. See also The Irish Times 1988.

to the High Court…'[118] After calling again on the Irish government to bring a case, in 1991, relatives of the three killed on Gibraltar lodged an individual application against the UK with the European Commission for Human Rights, seeking a decision as to whether or not the British state had violated Article 2.[119]

The example of *McCann* speaks to Ignatieff's contention that: 'Human rights has gone global by going local, embedding itself in the soil of cultures and worldviews independent of the West, in order to sustain ordinary people's struggles against unjust states and oppressive social practices.'[120] While Northern Ireland is very much in 'the West', human rights have developed a utility in the local context for challenging the behaviour of a Western, democratic state. As will be examined, the rhetoric of rights—and specifically the positive obligations of Article 2—has become a valuable tool utilised by those who lost loved ones during the conflict in cases involving state forces directly or where there are allegations of state collusion with loyalist or republican paramilitaries. For Curtis, the 'rhetoric and practice' of rights 'are not neatly separable.'[121] As will be explored, while the language of human rights, Article 2, and independent investigation has become central to many families' campaigns for truth and justice, this is very much a reflection of the practical reality of what they need and want.

As Lady Hale has said, for families, their efforts to engage Article 2 have often resulted from a desire to know the truth of what happened to their relative:

> The families of the dead have wanted to know whether these killings were in reality done in necessary self-defence, or for the protection of others, or whether they were the result of an official or unofficial 'shoot to kill' policy.[122]

In statements to the media, the families of those killed on Gibraltar gave several reasons as to why they wanted to take the case to Strasbourg. Seeking 'a thorough and impartial investigation,' the families believed that the ECtHR was 'the proper judicial forum to examine all the evidence, without restrictions.'[123] Members of the group spoke of the value of having an opportunity to 'highlight internationally' the killings.[124] In the aftermath of the ECtHR's judgment, the families of the three individuals killed described this as a 'complete vindication' of their belief that the killings were unnecessary and unjustifiable.[125]

As the Gibraltar families' statements make clear, the perceived impartiality of the ECtHR was valued. This is evident from statements relating to other cases of lethal killing. With regards the families of those killed at Loughgall,[126] who requested that

---

[118] The Irish Times 1989a.

[119] *McCann and Others v. The United Kingdom* Application no. 18984/91.

[120] Ignatieff 2001, p. 7.

[121] Curtis 2014, p. 8.

[122] Hale 2016, p. 20.

[123] The Irish Times 1989b.

[124] Cusack 1988. See also The Irish Times 1988.

[125] Moriarty 1995.

[126] *Kelly v. UK* App No 30054/96.

CAJ lodge a case with the European Commission of Human Rights, CAJ remarked that the case: 'requires independent and impartial investigation. The experience of the families of the deceased has been that such investigation is not available in Northern Ireland.'[127] Hugh Jordan, whose son Pearse (an unarmed IRA member) was shot and killed by the police in 1992, said of the ECtHR: 'We believe that this is the only means open to us to get at the truth surrounding our son's murder.'[128] For Curtis, 'one reason why human rights discourse has proved so politically powerful...is the way it resonates with people's subjective understandings of their experiences.'[129] It is evident from the statements made by these families that the value of human rights in shining a light on the foggy mechanics of state action lies in the perceived transparency, independence, and thoroughness of the Strasbourg institutions, in comparison to what the families expected from the domestic justice system. Here we see the 'expressive dimension'[130] of rights in practice, as the families at once seek justice, and draw attention to the challenges they face doing so at home.[131]

As examined above, in cases where force is used resulting in loss of life, Article 2 ECHR places an obligation on states to conduct a full, open, and effective investigation.[132] Just as 'effective official investigation' became 'the mantra' for the *Jordan, Kelly, McKerr,* and *Shanaghan* judgments,[133] so too has it become a mantra for many victims of the conflict and those who support them. 'The phrase "Article 2 compliant inquest" has become an accepted part of legal discourse.'[134] Furthermore, the phrase has become a regular part of the discourse of the wider group of stakeholders engaged in efforts to address the legacy of the past, including relatives of those killed. For example, in June 2019, the sister of a man shot and killed in Ballymurphy in 1971 spoke at a rally for action on dealing with the past: 'every family deserves...an Article 2 inquest.'[135] Another relative of one of those killed in Ballymurphy said in 2014: 'We need a properly funded independent Article 2 compliant inquest.'[136]

Families of those killed by representatives of the state have used Article 2 requirements to both bolster their calls for investigation, and to provide a benchmark for what they expect from any investigation. For instance, following the 2001 judgments examined above, the father of Billy Wright, a leader of the Loyalist Volunteer Force who was murdered in prison in 1997, deployed the Article 2 requirements to support his claim that he should have access to the police investigation file:

---

[127] The Irish Times 1995.
[128] Cowley 1992.
[129] Curtis 2014, p. 147.
[130] Stammers 2003, p. 299.
[131] Of course, the efforts of these families did not end at Strasbourg. Many have continued to campaign on these issues, as examined by Bell and Keenan 2005.
[132] Anthony and Mageean 2007.
[133] Ní Aoláin 2002, p. 6.
[134] Larkin 2016, p. 161. See also Harvey 2018.
[135] McCurry 2019.
[136] Black 2014.

It is my contention that I should have access to the murder file...My rights under Article 2 of the European convention are of course engaged in this respect...I...believe a series of judgments made by the European Court of Human Rights on May 4 this year have altered the legal position on this matter. Therefore, I am returning to the High Court.[137]

In 2011, the family of Denis Donaldson, an IRA informer who was murdered in 2006, told reporters: 'In order to be effective, thorough, independent and compliant with our family's rights under Article 2 of the ECHR, any investigation of Denis' murder must examine the identities, motivations, activities, links, communications and movements of' Donaldson's former handler.[138]

In July 2019, the Northern Ireland Office (NIO)[139] released its report on the responses received to the public consultation on the legislation designed to implement the Stormont House Agreement.[140] Over 17,000 responses were received by the NIO. These were submitted by individuals, organisations, and groups. This summary of responses indicates the importance of independent, effective investigation. Concerns with the current system for dealing with the past included a lack of transparency and the need for reform to work more effectively. With regards the SHA proposals, many responses highlighted the importance of independence and 'some respondents noted' the need for institutions 'to be human rights compliant in their operation.'[141] Some organisations raised concerns that previous investigations which were not Article 2 compliant might not be reinvestigated unless new evidence is available. With regards all the proposed institutions, 'almost all respondents insisted on the need to ensure independence and transparency.'[142]

Although, as noted above, human rights have 'empowered' those impacted by past harms,[143] Wilson emphasises that it is important not to assume 'that human rights are either a governmental "ethics of power" or a grassroots, emancipationist "weapon of the weak".'[144] Rather, as Ignatieff contends:

> we need to stop thinking of human rights as trumps and begin thinking of them as a language that creates the basis for deliberation...rights are...the shared vocabulary from which our arguments can begin.[145]

Encounters with national and international legal institutions have arguably encouraged relatives of those killed by state actors to (as Merry examines in the context of women affected by domestic violence), 'adopt a rights consciousness' and begin to

---

[137] The Belfast Telegraph 2001.

[138] Madden and Finucane 2011.

[139] The NIO is the UK government department responsible for overseeing the devolution settlement in Northern Ireland (NI), representing NI interests at UK government level, and representing UK interests in NI.

[140] Northern Ireland Office 2019.

[141] Ibid., p. 13.

[142] Ibid., p. 19.

[143] Ignatieff 2001, p. 8.

[144] Wilson 2006, p. 78. See also Merry 2006.

[145] Ignatieff 2001, p. 95.

see themselves as 'rights-bearing subjects'.[146] Human rights can, McEvoy argues, 'provide a practical and normative basis for grass-roots justice work in communities which have been affected by conflict and violence.'[147] Article 2 has come to provide such a basis for 'justice work' in the Northern Ireland context. As illustrated by the examples above, the Article 2 jurisprudence that emerged from Strasbourg has come to serve as a motivational frame—a 'call to arms' or 'rationale for action'.[148] As a motivational frame, Article 2 functions as a 'prod to action'[149] in efforts to motivate the state to act.

Effective motivational framing, however, relies on the use of frames which are accessible to many,[150] and the Article 2 frame is one which—in Northern Ireland—has encountered some opposition. Although, as Mallinder proposes, the language of human rights may be employed in order to imply a position that is 'neutral, non-partisan and non-political,'[151] in reality 'rights are inescapably political because they tacitly imply a conflict between a rights holder and a rights "with-holder," some authority against which the rights holder can make justified claims.'[152] Although in a democratic state, the activities of human rights organisations may be perceived as less political, in a divided society, 'the politics of advocating for rights often becomes more visible and contested. This is particularly the case where human rights obligations to investigate and prosecute are applied to politically motivated past crimes.'[153] This is very much the case in Northern Ireland, where the emergence of human rights as a mobilising frame has not been welcomed by all.

59.4.1 Opposition to Human Rights Language in Northern Ireland

For Curtis, human rights are 'used for war by other means in Northern Ireland.'[154] This results in part from the origins of the use of human rights language in that context. In commentary on events in Northern Ireland between the 1920s and 1960s, the language of 'human rights' was not a common feature.[155] As a result of emerging civil rights activism in Northern Ireland in the 1960s, Curtis contends, 'rights of different kinds…became the lingua franca for political demands.'[156] Much of the

---

[146] Merry 2003, p. 344.
[147] McEvoy 2007, p. 429.
[148] Benford and Snow 2000; Snow and Benford 1988.
[149] Snow and Benford 1988, p. 202.
[150] Ibid.
[151] Mallinder 2019, p. 13.
[152] Ignatieff 2001, p. 67.
[153] Mallinder 2019, p. 14.
[154] Curtis 2014, p. 216.
[155] Dickson 2010.
[156] Curtis 2014, p. 4.

discourse of the 1960s focused on 'civil rights', and in the 1970s and 1980s on economic rights.[157] It was from the 1990s that the language shifted to political and human rights.[158] This history of 'rights talk' in Northern Ireland is one that has 'simultaneously furthered liberatory projects and reproduced, even exacerbated, profound ethnopolitical divisions.'[159] During the civil rights campaign, 'the experience of the nationalist community within the state of Northern Ireland was forcefully articulated in the language of rights.'[160] As a result, for many of the Protestant community, civil rights and the language of rights became associated with the Nationalist community.[161]

This perceived bias in the use of rights language (see further below) was only entrenched further with the turn to violence. By the late 1960s, the civil rights movement 'had been usurped by a paramilitary movement that had different aims and used different methods.'[162] The rise of the IRA, in addition to other Republican and Loyalist paramilitary groups, 'contaminated…perfectly laudable demands' for better human rights protections, by themselves engaging in human rights violations.[163] At that time, many human rights activists believed that only governments could perpetrate violations of human rights. CAJ, formed in 1981, made the decision to monitor only violence perpetrated by the state, rather than paramilitaries—a decision it reiterated in 1991 following Amnesty International's extension of its remit to cover abuses by non-state armed groups.[164] As a result, by 1981 the concept of human rights had become 'a propaganda tool in a war of words between all sides to the conflict in Northern Ireland.'[165]

Since the ceasefires, human rights discourse has become 'embedded in broader debates about the legitimacy of violence and the culpability of different actors in the conflict. These debates…reinforce public perceptions of human rights talk as a selective and partial form of politics.'[166] This has manifested in what Harvey describes as a 'unionist scepticism' about human rights initiatives.[167] As Mallinder contends:

> Unionists have responded negatively to human rights work that seeks to hold the State to account. Unionists generally view the State as a benign, and even deified, entity. As a result, Unionists are often resistant to measures that seek to restrict the exercise of governmental power…In addition, Unionist self-identity is closely aligned to the State. Thus, Unionists

---

[157] Ibid. See also Dickson 2010.
[158] Curtis 2014.
[159] Ibid., p. 202.
[160] Mageean and O'Brien 1998, p. 1503.
[161] Curtis 2014. See also Mallinder 2019.
[162] Dickson 2010, p. 21.
[163] Ibid., p. 21.
[164] Dickson 2010; Felner 2012; Mallinder 2019; McEvoy 2001.
[165] Dickson 2010, p. 22.
[166] Curtis 2014, p. 146.
[167] Harvey 2018, p. 12.

resist the work of CAJ and other human rights practitioners in monitoring and criticising the State.[168]

As a result of this 'self-identification' with the British state, some Unionists equate human rights activism which challenges the actions of the state with an 'anti-Unionist' stance, and ally human rights activists with a Nationalist perspective.[169] One of the themes of this critique examined in Mallinder's analysis is that human rights standards are being applied 'in a narrow and selective manner that disadvantages members of their community.'[170] Such a perspective is encapsulated by the contention of former DUP MLA Nelson McCausland: 'Article 2 of the European Convention on Human Rights is interpreted in Northern Ireland so as to prioritise cases involving the State, the Army and the RUC over the greater number of cases, which involve the Provisional IRA and other organisations.'[171]

This comment by McCausland exemplifies a perspective shared by others in Northern Ireland. Many of the families of those killed by the state have campaigned for decades, and their efforts should not be undermined, however their efforts to make visible crimes of the state 'have also at times created new exclusions and hierarchies of victims'[172]—or at least the perception of such. Unionist politicians and Unionist-aligned victims' groups 'argue that CNR [Catholic Nationalist Republican] communities and the Irish government wish to impose a hierarchy that prioritizes victims of state violence.'[173] This apparent division, or hierarchy, in part results from:

> the public-private divide that underlies much of human rights law: while the victims of state violence have the option of relying upon the right to life under Article 2 of the European Convention on Human Rights ECHR when seeking redress, that Article cannot be directly invoked against non-state actors who were responsible for the much greater number of deaths during the conflict.[174]

One result of this tension in the Northern Ireland context has been the emergence of two forms of rhetoric: one of human rights, and the other the 'rhetoric of "victims" rights.'[175] The discourse of human rights has become bound up with competition and disagreement over who constitutes a 'legitimate target' or an 'innocent victim.'[176] For example, following a decision to defer signing off on a plan to address the backlog of legacy inquests, First Minister Arlene Foster told the BBC: 'Unfortunately a lot of innocent victims feel that their voice has not been heard recently and there has been

---

[168] Mallinder 2019, p. 17.
[169] Ibid. See also Lawther 2014a.
[170] Ibid., p. 23. See also McEvoy et al. 2020.
[171] McCausland 2017.
[172] Curtis 2014, p. 148.
[173] Jankowitz 2018, p. 9. As Jankowitz analyses, others believe that victims of state violence have been neglected, and victims of paramilitary violence prioritised.
[174] Anthony and Moffett 2014, p. 396.
[175] Curtis 2014, p. 162.
[176] Ibid., p. 163. Issues of victim hierarchy in Northern Ireland have been examined in, e.g., Bell 2002; Brewer and Hayes 2012; Ferguson et al. 2010; Hearty 2019; Jankowitz 2018; Lawther 2014b.

an imbalance in relation to state killings as opposed to paramilitary killings...the rights of innocent victims are very key in this and I will not allow any process to rewrite the past.'[177] In 2015, following a High Court decision not to allow the release of a prisoner for St Patrick's Day, the victims campaigner Kenny Donaldson stated: 'this issue goes to the heart of whose rights come first—the rights of innocent victims or the rights of convicted terrorists/criminals.'[178]

As Jankowitz highlights, 'debate about the SHA has centred around perceived imbalances in approaches to victims of state and nonstate violence.'[179] This perception of partiality is evident in the responses to the NIO consultation. Alongside calls for 'independence' in the NIO summary of consultation responses are a similar number of references to the need for investigations to be balanced and proportionate.[180] In Mallinder's analysis of publicly available submissions made by Unionist political parties and organisations aligned to them to the NIO Consultation and to two parliamentary inquiries on dealing with the past in Northern Ireland, a key emerging theme was the need for investigative decisions to be taken in a 'balanced' way.[181] That legacy investigations to date have been 'imbalanced' is a key component of a narrative that has emerged (particularly in Britain) in which 'inquests, investigations and prosecutions constitute a 'witch-hunt' directed specifically against former members of the British security forces and in particular British soldiers.'[182] However, McEvoy et al. contend that the 'witch-hunt' argument is not supported by evidence and, in reality, 'the reason for the higher number of state-related cases requiring an effective investigation is the widespread acceptance by criminal justice and legal professionals that they were not properly investigated in the first place.'[183] If decisions relating to investigation and prosecution were to be made in a way that reflects that the vast majority of conflict related deaths were perpetrated by paramilitary organisations, this would represent 'a significant divergence from existing Northern Irish and international standards,' with implications for 'equality before the law, independence and impartiality in the administration of justice, and non-discrimination.'[184] In McEvoy et al.'s analysis, any potential approach which seeks to tip this perceived imbalance in favour of the security forces (e.g. the introduction of a statute of limitations for security forces; requiring Attorney General consent for the prosecution of

---

[177] McCurry 2016.
[178] Erwin 2015.
[179] Jankowitz 2018, p. 7.
[180] Northern Ireland Office 2019.
[181] Mallinder 2019.
[182] McEvoy et al. 2020, p. 8.
[183] McEvoy et al. 2020, p. 10. Between 1970 and 1973, deaths caused by soldiers were investigated by the Royal Military Police rather than Northern Ireland's police service, and in 2013, then PSNI Chief Constable Mark Baggott ordered that all 238 military killings should be reviewed, following the publication of a report which was highly critical of the work of the Historical Enquiries Team (McEvoy et al. 2020).
[184] Mallinder 2019, p. 32.

former soldiers; basing prosecutions on whether the weapon was 'lawfully supplied') would be incompatible with the UK's human rights obligations.[185]

59.5 Conclusion

Recourse to the ECHR has been an important avenue for families of those killed by state forces during the conflict in Northern Ireland. The resulting Article 2 jurisprudence, in particular around the requirement to hold an independent investigation into state killings, has become a valuable tool. This exists because families of those killed, their lawyers, and human rights organisations have campaigned for years—sometimes decades—for truth and justice. Via the 'package of measures', 'the ECHR litigation…provided a catalyst for the development of dealing with the past mechanisms in Northern Ireland…human rights law, institutions and actors have played a significant role in pressuring the United Kingdom to investigate Troubles-related offences.'[186] The language of human rights, and in particular the 'mantra' of Article 2 compliant independent investigation has become an important currency in efforts to have the legacy of the past addressed.

However, many families are still waiting, and still campaigning. Wilson contends that there is a 'crucial distinction between what governments do with human rights and what social movements seek to achieve through them.'[187] As analysed above, there is still no requirement for the state to hold Article 2 compliant investigations into cases in which the ECtHR has found that one was not carried out. And, where cases taken to the ECtHR have witnessed success, this has been a slow process. For instance, the decision in *McCann* came some seven years after the killings on Gibraltar had taken place. Dickson questions how many lives might have been saved if the judgment had come sooner, and its lessons absorbed into police and army practice.[188]

Furthermore, as examined above, the political nature of rights has manifested in Northern Ireland to create a perception—amongst some—that human rights claims are used by those who are 'anti-Unionist',[189] and that a hierarchy of victimhood has emerged with victims of state killings prioritised over those killed by paramilitaries. As a result, valid calls for independent investigations have been dismissed as politically motivated, seeking to rewrite the past, and prioritising some victims over others. This contestation has manifested, in the recent NIO Consultation, in a combination of calls for independence and balance in addressing the legacy of the past. This arguably only emphasises the need for a comprehensive approach to

---

[185] McEvoy et al. 2020.
[186] Mallinder 2019, p. 15.
[187] Wilson 2006, p. 78.
[188] Dickson 2016.
[189] Mallinder 2019.

addressing the legacy of the past—one in which the needs of victims from all sides can be addressed.

Human rights can become 'key benchmarks' for measuring progress,[190] and the Strasbourg case law has 'made a significant difference to attempts to deal, in a principled way, with the legacies of the past,'[191] with Article 2 jurisprudence providing a template for how to effectively investigate killings involving the state. However, to make progress on human rights issues, there is a need for both grassroots, victim-led efforts and for the law to take rights seriously.[192] The SHA legislation has the potential to bring together these two elements, if independence is embedded into the mechanisms it establishes, and—of course—if it is implemented.

Post Scriptum

The legal landscape surrounding legacy issues in Northern Ireland is a changing one. The contents of this chapter reflect the context at the time of writing (2019) and early revisions (2020). One key development since that time is the publication of Command Paper 498 in July 2021 by the UK government. This Command Paper proposes 'a sweeping and unconditional amnesty' which would end all judicial activity related to the legacy of the conflict, including inquests, civil actions, and prosecutions.[193]

References

Anthony G, Mageean P (2007) Habits of mind and 'truth telling': Article 2 ECHR in post-conflict Northern Ireland. In: Morrison J, McEvoy K, Anthony G (eds) Judges, transition and human rights. Oxford University Press, Oxford, pp 181–200
Anthony G, Moffett L (2014) Northern Ireland: law, politics, and the 'problem of the past'. Eur Public Law 20:395–406
Bakircioglu O, Dickson B (2017) The European Convention in conflicted societies: the experience of Northern Ireland and Turkey. Int Comp Law Q 66:263–294
BBC News (2014) UK must pay for Troubles killings investigations says European official. 6 November 2014
Bell C (2002) Dealing with the past in Northern Ireland. Fordham Int'l LJ 26:1095–1147
Bell C, Campbell C, Ní Aoláin F (2004) Justice discourses in transition. Social & Legal Studies 13:305–328
Bell C, Keenan J (2005) Lost on the way home? The right to life in Northern Ireland. J Law Soc 32:68–89
Benford R, Snow D (2000) Framing processes and social movements: An overview and assessment. Annu Rev Sociol 26:611–639
Black R (2014) Exhumation of Army victim's body ordered. Belfast Telegraph, 19 December 2014
Boyle K (1982) Human rights and political resolution in Northern Ireland. Yale J Int Law 9:156–177
Breen-Smyth M (2009) Hierarchies of pain and responsibility: Victims and war by other means in Northern Ireland. Tripodos 25:27–40

---

[190] McEvoy 2007, p. 430.
[191] Harvey 2018, p. 15.
[192] Merry 2003.
[193] The Model Bill Team 2021, p. 4.

Breen-Smyth M (2012) The needs of individuals and their families injured as a result of the Troubles in Northern Ireland. Report commissioned by WAVE Trauma Centre

Brewer J, Hayes B (2012) Victims as moral beacons: victims and perpetrators in Northern Ireland. Contemporary Soc Sci 6:73–88

Campbell C, Ni Aolain F, Harvey C (2003) The frontiers of legal analysis: reframing the transition in Northern Ireland. Mod Law Rev 9:68–77

Committee on the Administration of Justice (CAJ) (2015) The Apparatus of Impunity? Human Rights Violations and the Northern Ireland Conflict. CAJ, Belfast

Committee on the Administration of Justice (CAJ) (2020) Submission to the Committee of Ministers from the Committee on the Administration of Justice (CAJ) in relation to the supervision of the cases concerning the action of the security forces in Northern Ireland. CAJ, Belfast

Cory P (2004) Cory Collusion Inquiry Report—Pat Finucane. The Stationery Office, London

Council of Europe Committee of Ministers (1996) 559th meeting (DH) Decisions adopted and Records. CM/Del/Dec/Act (96) 559

Council of Europe Committee of Ministers (2009) Interim Resolution. CM/ResDH(2009)44[1]

Council of Europe Committee of Ministers (2015) 1222nd meeting of the Ministers' Deputies, Decision Cases No. 23. CM/Del/Dec(2015)1222/23

Council of Europe Committee of Ministers (2019) 1340th meeting of the Ministers' Deputies. CM/Del/Dec(2019)1340/H46-30

Council of Europe Committee of Ministers (2020) 1377bis meeting of the Ministers' Deputies. CM/Del/Dec(2020)1377bis/H46-44

Cowley M (1992) Proceedings against RUC over death of son initiated. The Irish Times, 8 December 1992

Curtis J (2014) Human rights as war by other means. University of Pennsylvania Press, Philadelphia

Cusack J (1988) Taoiseach asked to act on Gibraltar. The Irish Times, 13 May 1988

Dempster L (2019) Transitional justice and the 'disappeared' of Northern Ireland: Silence, memory, and the construction of the past. Routledge, Abingdon

Dickson B (2010) The European Convention on Human Rights and the conflict in Northern Ireland. Oxford University Press, Oxford

Dickson B (2016) The planning and control of operations involving the use of lethal force. In: Early L, Austin A, Ovey C, Chernishova O (eds) The right to life under Article 2 of the European Convention on Human Rights: Twenty years of legal developments since McCann v. the United Kingdom. Wolf Legal Publishers, Oisterwijk, pp 47–59

Doolan B (2001) Lawless v. Ireland (1957-1961): The first case before the European Court of Human Rights: an international miscarriage of justice? Ashgate, Aldershot

Duffy A (2010) A truth commission for Northern Ireland? Int J Transitional Justice 4:26–46

Early L, Austin A, Ovey C, Chernishova O (eds) (2016) The Right to Life under Article 2 of the European Convention on Human Rights: Twenty Years of Legal Developments since McCann v. the United Kingdom. Wolf Legal Publishers, Oisterwijk

Erwin A (2015) Relief for victim's family as release of IRA killer stalled. Belfast Telegraph, 14 March 2015

Fay M, Morrissey M, Smyth M (1999) Northern Ireland's troubles: The human costs. Pluto, London

Felner E (2012) Human rights leaders in conflict situations: A case study of the politics of 'moral entrepreneurs. J Hum Rights Practice, 4:57–81

Ferguson N, Burgess M, Hollywood I (2010) Who are the victims? Victimhood experiences in postagreement Northern Ireland. Political Psychology, 31:857–886

Grech O (2017) Human rights and the Northern Ireland conflict: law, politics and conflict 1921–2014. Routledge, Abingdon

Hadden T (2004) Punishment, amnesty and truth: legal and political approaches. In: Guelke A (ed) Democracy and ethnic conflict advancing peace in deeply divided societies. Palgrave MacMillan, Basingstoke, pp 196–217

Hale B (2016) Issues relating to the beginning and end of life. In: Early L, Austin A, Ovey C, Chernishova O (eds) The Right to Life under Article 2 of the European Convention on Human

Rights: Twenty Years of Legal Developments since McCann v. the United Kingdom. Wolf Legal Publishers, Oisterwijk, pp 19–28

Hansard House of Commons (2020) Written Ministerial Statement, 18th March 2020 Vol 673

Harvey C (2015) Bringing Humanity Home: A Transformational Human Rights Culture for Northern Ireland? In: McAlinden A, Dwyer C (eds) Criminal justice in transition: The Northern Ireland context. Hart Publishing, Oxford, pp 47–66

Harvey C (2018) Mutual Respect? Interrogating Human Rights in a Fractured Union. King's Law Journal 29:216–241

Hearty K (2019) Victims who have done nothing or victims who have done nothing wrong: Contesting blame and 'innocent victim' status in transitioning societies. British J Criminology, 59:1119–1138

House of Commons Northern Ireland Affairs Committee (2020) Addressing the Legacy of Northern Ireland's Past: the Government's New Proposals (Interim Report). House of Commons, 26 October

Ignatieff M (2001) Human rights as politics and idolatry. Princeton University Press, New Jersey

Jankowitz S (2018) The 'Hierarchy of Victims' in Northern Ireland: A Framework for Critical Analysis. Int J Transitional Justice 12:216–236

Keck ME, Sikkink K (1998) Activists Beyond Borders. Cornell University Press, London

Larkin JF (2016) Dialogue at cross-purposes? The Northern Ireland inquest and Article 2 of the European Convention on Human Rights. In: Early L, Austin A, Ovey C, Chernishova O (eds) The Right to Life under Article 2 of the European Convention on Human Rights: Twenty Years of Legal Developments since McCann v. the United Kingdom2. Wolf Legal Publishers, Oisterwijk, pp 161–170

Lawther C (2013) Denial, silence and the politics of the past: unpicking the opposition to truth recovery in Northern Ireland. Int J Transitional Justice 21:157–177

Lawther C (2014a) Truth, Denial and Transition: Northern Ireland and the Contested Past. Routledge

Lawther C (2014b) The construction and politicisation of victimhood. In: Lynch O, Argomaniz J (eds) Victims of terrorism: A comparative and interdisciplinary study. Taylor and Francis, London, pp 10–30

Livingstone S, Harvey CJ (1999) Human rights and the Northern Ireland peace process. Eur Hum Rights Law Rev 1–12

Lundy P (2009) Exploring home-grown transitional justice and its dilemmas: A case study of the historical enquiries team, Northern Ireland. Int J Transitional Justice 3:321–340

Lundy P (2011) Paradoxes and challenges of transitional justice at the 'local' level: Historical enquiries in Northern Ireland. Contemporary Social Science 6:89–105

Lundy P, Rolston B (2016) Redress for past harms? Official apologies in Northern Ireland. Int J Hum Rights 20:104–122

Madden & Finucane (2011) 'Statement from Family of Denis Donaldson'. Madden & Finucane solicitors. https://madden-finucane.com/2011/04/07/statement-from-family-of-denis-donaldson/. Accessed 12 Nov 2019

Mageean P, O'Brien M (1998) From the margins to the mainstream: Human rights and the Good Friday Agreement. Fordham Int Law J 22:1499–1538

Mallinder L (2019) Metaconflict and international human rights law in dealing with Northern Ireland's past. Cambridge Int Law J 8:5–38

Martens K (2006) Professionalised representation of human rights NGOs to the United Nations. Int J Hum Rights 10:19–30

McCausland N (2017) Only Sinn Fein could contest election on an anti-corruption ticket and keep a straight face. Belfast Telegraph, 26 January 2017

McCurry C (2016) Foster: Why I blocked plans to speed up Troubles probes. Belfast Telegraph, 4 May 2016

McCurry C (2019) Campaigners march over Troubles killings. Belfast Telegraph, 10 June 2019

McEvoy K (2001) Human rights, humanitarian interventions and paramilitary activities in Northern Ireland. In: Harvey C (ed) Human rights, equality and democratic renewal in Northern Ireland. Hart Publishing, Oxford, pp 215–249

McEvoy K (2007) Beyond legalism: Towards a thicker understanding of transitional justice. J Law and Society 34:411–440

McEvoy K (2011) What did the lawyers do during the 'war'? Neutrality, conflict and the culture of quietism. Mod Law Rev 74:350–384

McEvoy K (2017) Amnesties prosecutions and the rule of law in Northern Ireland. House of Commons Defence Select Committee

McEvoy K, Bryson A (2016) Justice, truth and oral history: Legislating the past 'from below' in Northern Ireland. Northern Ireland Legal Quarterly 67:67–90

McEvoy K, Ellison G (2003) Criminological discourses in Northern Ireland: Conflict and conflict resolution. In: McEvoy K, Newburn T (eds) Criminology, conflict resolution and restorative justice. Palgrave Macmillan, Basingtoke, pp 51–88

McEvoy K, Holder D, Mallinder L, Bryson A, Gormally B, McKeown G (2020) Prosecutions, Imprisonment and The Stormont House Agreement: A Critical Analysis of Proposals on Dealing with the Past in Northern Ireland

McGovern M (2013) Inquiring into collusion? Collusion, the state and the management of truth recovery in Northern Ireland. State Crime 2:4–29

McKittrick D, Kelters S, Feeney B, Thornton C, McVea D (2007) Lost lives: The stories of the men, women and children who died as a result of the Northern Ireland Troubles. Mainstream Publishing, Edinburgh/London

Merry SE (2003) Rights talk and the experience of law: Implementing women's human rights to protection from violence. Hum Rights Q 25:343–381

Merry SE (2006) Transnational human rights and local activism: Mapping the middle. American Anthropologist 108:38–51

Mertus J (2007) The rejection of human rights framings: The case of LGBT advocacy in the US. Hum Rights Q 29:1036–1064

Morgan D (2016) 'Legacy inquests' in Northern Ireland. In: Early L, Austin A, Ovey C, Chernishova O (eds) The Right to Life under Article 2 of the European Convention on Human Rights: Twenty years of legal developments since McCann v. the United Kingdom. Wolf Legal Publishers, Oisterwijk, pp 87–92

Moriarty G (1995) Solicitor says use of lethal force must be looked at. The Irish Times, 28 September 1995

Ní Aoláin F (2000) The politics of force: conflict management and state violence in Northern Ireland. Blackstaff Press, Belfast

Ní Aoláin FN (2002) Truth telling, accountability and the right to life in Northern Ireland. Eur Hum Rights Law Rev 5:572–590

Northern Ireland Human Rights Commission (NIHRC) (2017) Advice of the Northern Ireland Human Rights Commission on the House of Common's Defence Committee report on 'Investigations in fatalities in Northern Ireland involving British military personnel'. NIHRC, Belfast

Northern Ireland Office (2019) Government publishes summary of responses to Legacy Consultation [Press release, available at: https://www.gov.uk/government/news/government-publishes-summary-of-responses-to-legacy-consultation] Accessed 18 July 2020

Quirk H (2013) Don't mention the war: the Court of Appeal, the Criminal Cases Review Commission and dealing with the past in Northern Ireland. Mod Law Rev 76:949–980

Requa M (2012) Keeping up with Strasbourg: Article 2 obligations and Northern Ireland's pending inquests. Public Law 1–9

Requa M, Anthony G (2008) Coroners, controversial deaths, and Northern Ireland's past conflict. Public Law 1–7

Rolston B (2006) Dealing with the past: pro-state paramilitaries, truth and transition in Northern Ireland. Hum Rights Quarterly 28:652–675

Secretariat of the Committee of Ministers (2015) 1222 meeting (10–12 March 2015) (DH)—Communication from the authorities (12/01/2015) concerning the McKerr group of cases against the United Kingdom (Application No. 28883/95)—Information made available under Rule 8.2.a of the Rules of the Committee of Ministers. DH-DD(2015)81

Secretariat of the Committee of Ministers (2017) 1288th meeting (June 2017) (DH) Communication from the United Kingdom concerning the case of MCKERR v. the United Kingdom (Application No. 28883/95). DH-DD(2017)530

Secretariat of the Committee of Ministers (2019) 1340th meeting (March 2019) (DH)—Communication from the United Kingdom concerning the McKerr group of cases v. the United Kingdom (Application No. 28883/95). DH-DD(2019)164

Sicilianos L-A (2016) Out of harm's way: positive obligations under Article 2 of the European Convention on Human Rights. In: Early L, Austin A, Ovey C, Chernishova O (eds) The Right to Life under Article 2 of the European Convention on Human Rights: twenty years of legal developments since McCann v. the United Kingdom. Wolf Legal Publishers, Oisterwijk, pp 29–46

Snow D, Benford R (1988) Ideology, frame resonance, and participant mobilization. International Social Movement Research, 1: 197–217

Stammers N (2003) Social Movements, Human Rights, and the Challenge to Power. Proc ASIL Annu Meet 97:299–301

The Belfast Telegraph (2001) Wright's father calls for file on murder. Belfast Telegraph, 26 November 2001

The Irish Times (1988) Barry calls for inquiry to dispel doubts about killings. The Irish Times, 3 October 1988

The Irish Times (1989a) Families of Gibraltar trio to seek damages. The Irish Times, 7 March 1989

The Irish Times (1989b) Gibraltar families repeat call for European hearing. The Irish Times, 21 June 1989

The Irish Times (1995) Human rights group lodges case of SAS killings with commission. The Irish Times, 12 October 1995

The Model Bill Team (2021) Addressing the Legacy of Northern Ireland's Past: The Model Bill Team's Response to the NIO's Proposals. https://www.dealingwiththepastni.com/assets/Model-Bill-Team-Response-to-the-UK-Government-Command-Paper-on-Legacy-in-NI-Final-3.09.21-(1).pdf. Accessed 3 March 2022

United Nations General Assembly (2016) Report of the Special Rapporteur on the promotion of truth, justice, reparation and guarantees of non-recurrence on his mission to the United Kingdom of Great Britain and Northern Ireland, 17 November. A/HRC/34/62/Add.1

United Nations Human Rights Committee (2008) Concluding observations of the Human Rights Committee, United Kingdom of Great Britain and Northern Ireland, 21 July. CCPR/C/GBR/CO/6

Wilson RA (2006) Afterword to 'Anthropology and Human Rights in a New Key': The social life of human rights. Am Anthropol 108:77–83

Winter J (2013) Abuses and activism: The role of human rights in the Northern Ireland conflict and peace process. Eur Hum Rights Law Rev 1:1–9

Lauren Dempster is a Lecturer in the School of Law, Queen's University Belfast, Belfast, Northern Ireland.

Chapter 60
The "War on Terror"

Rumyana van Ark

Contents

60.1 Introduction	1360
60.2 The Post 9/11 Securitisation and the 'War on Terror' Paradigm	1362
60.2.1 Domestic Securitisation	1362
60.2.2 International Securitisation	1364
60.3 Designing the 'War on Terror'	1367
60.3.1 The Complementarity of International Humanitarian Law and International Human Rights Law	1368
60.3.2 The 'War on Terror' as an Armed Conflict	1371
60.3.3 The Concept of Armed Conflict within International Law	1374
60.3.4 The 'War on Terror', Core IHL Protections and Individual Terror Suspects	1378
60.4 The post 9/11 Securitisation Catalysts and the Legacy of the 'War on Terror'	1381
60.5 Conclusion	1383
References	1384

Abstract Following the events of 11 September 2001 (9/11), the prevention and pre-emption of acts of terrorism has become a priority. At international level, through a series of Resolutions and the establishment of a new Committee, the UN Security Council contributed to the development of a transnational environment accommodative of wide-ranging and collaborative counter-terrorism measures. Domestically, states such the United States and United Kingdom, engaged in immediate and determined legislating. Existing criminal and counter-terrorism legislation was updated and expanded while at the same time new Acts and measures were being introduced in an equally swift manner. Despite these substantial legislative changes however considerable legal and political effort was devoted by the US in particular to construct a transnational counter-terrorism campaign known as the 'War on Terror'. As a political paradigm, this 'war' was used to justify the military operations in Afghanistan and Iraq. As a legal paradigm, the 'War on Terror' was designed to construct an environment within which the applicability of the relevant international norms was either severely restricted or uncertain. In the years following the events of 9/11, the

R. van Ark (✉)
T.M.C. Asser Instituut, The Hague, The Netherlands
e-mail: R.Grozdanova@asser.nl

University of Amsterdam, Amsterdam, The Netherlands

US 'War on Terror' gradually came to define the first decade of the 21st century. Almost 20 years on since its start, its legacy continues to be felt.

Keywords Securitisation · War on Terror · Terrorism · Armed conflict · Human rights · Humanitarian law · Counter-terrorism

60.1 Introduction

Following the events of 11 September 2001 (9/11), the prevention and pre-emption of acts of terrorism has become a priority at domestic and international[1] level. Through resolutions such as 1368,[2] 1373,[3] 1624[4] and 2249,[5] the United Nations Security Council (UNSC) has urged states to take 'all necessary' measures to prevent acts of terrorism both individually and collectively. Some of the measures suggested have included more traditional counter-terrorism methods such as bi- and multi-lateral agreements to prevent and supress acts of terrorism.[6] The UNSC additionally placed emphasis on more contemporary methods of countering terrorism such as the freezing of funds, assets and any other economic resources of individuals suspected of or having committed acts of terrorism.[7] The Security Council Counter Terrorism Committee (CTC) was specifically created to improve the ability of UN Member States to prevent terrorist acts within and outside their own country as well as monitor compliance with its founding Resolution, UNSC Resolution 1373.[8] The overall approach of the UNSC post 9/11 indicated a willingness to facilitate a transnational environment accommodative of wide-ranging and collaborative counter-terrorism measures.[9]

---

[1] Despite the number of signed Conventions prohibiting certain acts of terrorism in discrete circumstances, there is, however, no single codified definition of terrorism in international law.

[2] This Resolution was adopted on 12 September 2001 in the immediate aftermath of the events of September 11. UN Doc. S/RES/1368 (2001).

[3] Adopted on 28 September 2001, this Resolution expressly reaffirmed Resolutions 1269 (1999) and 1368 (2001). UN Doc. S/RES/1373 (2001).

[4] Adopted on 14 September 2005 two months after the events on 7 July 2005 in the United Kingdom. UN Doc. S/RES/1624 (2005).

[5] Adopted on 20 November 2015 following the attacks in Paris on 13 November 2015. UN Doc. S/RES/2249 (2015).

[6] UN Doc. S/RES/1373 (2001).

[7] See further the text of Resolutions such as 1373 and 1624. In addition, in accordance with state obligations under Resolution 1373, the global initiative of the Counter-Terrorism Committee Executive Directorate (CETD), launched in 2012, has been aimed at assisting UN Member States to set up effective asset freezing mechanisms. Further details of the initiative are available at https://www.un.org/sc/ctc/focus-areas/financing-of-terrorism/. Accessed 16 September 2020.

[8] Please refer to the Counter Terrorism Committee's outline of their mandate available at https://www.un.org/sc/ctc/about-us/. Accessed 16 September 2020.

[9] For similar arguments see for example Talmon 2005 and Powell 2007.

Domestically, the United States (US) adopted a number of new Acts and/or amendments to existing counter-terrorism and security legislation. The swift introduction of comprehensive counter-terrorism laws such as the 2001 USA Patriot Act or modifications of existing legislation have reshaped[10] the relationship between the state and the individual terrorist suspect. However, these additional domestic legislative measures were not deemed sufficient to counter the threat posed by terrorism. The considerable legal and political effort devoted by the US to construct multi-faceted and multi-front counter-terrorism responses based on their assessment of the post 9/11 terrorism threat also resulted in the creation of the transnational counter-terrorism campaign known as the 'War on Terror'.

As a political paradigm, this 'war' was used to justify the military operations in Afghanistan and Iraq. The beginning of the 'War on Terror' was announced by George W Bush in his State of the Union address on 21 September 2001—a mere ten days after the events of 9/11.[11] He expressly noted that the 'US would pursue nations that provide aid or safe haven to terrorism' thus linking any potential invasions with the 'War on Terror'. In its subsequent National Security Strategies, the US described states such as Iraq and Afghanistan as 'rogue states', which 'sponsor terrorism around the globe'.[12] As a legal paradigm, the 'War on Terror' was designed to construct an environment within which the applicability of the relevant international norms was either severely restricted or uncertain. The wealth of academic, legal and political debate focusing on the post 9/11 state compliance with international legal obligations and the impact on individual human rights during the use of expansive counter-terrorism measures attests to the transformative effect of this paradigm.[13]

The discussion that follows in Sect. 60.2 will outline the highly securitised environment within which the 'War on Terror' paradigm was created and operationalised. The post 9/11 legislative fever—both domestically and internationally—should not be perceived as entirely shocking or unpredictable. Historically, terrorist events such as those in Northern Ireland for example, have resulted in limitations of individual rights and civil liberties.[14] However, as will be discussed below, the events of 9/11 provoked such an immense shock and uncertainty that the US had to be seen to respond as muscularly as possible. In their eagerness to both assuage fears of further similarly devastating attacks and restore a sense of security, the US sought to reduce the applicability of the international humanitarian and human rights law provisions to the extent that individuals, captured and detained on suspicions of terrorism involvement, were denied almost all recourse to legal protections. The manner in which the US attempted to justify this approach will be the focus of Sect. 60.3. Section 60.4

---

[10] Roach 2011 and Jenkins et al. 2014.

[11] George W. Bush 'State of the Union Address' *The Guardian* 21 September 2001. http://www.theguardian.com/world/2001/sep/21/september11.usa13. Accessed 16 September 2020.

[12] See for example the 2002 National Security Strategy of the United States of America, full text available at https://2009-2017.state.gov/documents/organization/63562.pdf. Accessed 16 September 2020.

[13] For a short selection, see Bellamy 2008; Poynting and Whyte 2012; Ni Aolain and Gross 2013; Davis and De Londras 2014 and Roach 2015.

[14] See for example Dickson 2010 and Blackbourn 2014.

will then address the triggers or catalysts behind the decision-making that led to the creation of the 'War on Terror' paradigm and its various aspects. Understanding these catalysts is important in order to assess the impact and legacy of the 'War on Terror'. The by now entrenched perception that it is justifiable to curtail the rights of individual terror suspects together with the corollary argument that human rights provisions limit the abilities of states to pre-empt and respond to acts of terrorism are arguably two of the most enduring legacies.

60.2 The Post 9/11 Securitisation and the 'War on Terror' Paradigm

While counter-terrorism laws since September 2001 have considerably altered the relationship between the individual terror suspect and the state, the tensions between liberty and security, between normalcy and emergency[15] have nevertheless felt familiar to an extent.[16] What has, however, been the distinctive characteristic of the post 9/11 security exigency is how security[17] appears to have become more intrinsically associated with pre-empting acts of terrorism and detaining individual terrorist suspects than with more traditional crime prevention. Another distinguishing feature has been the US response to the threat posed by terrorism. Following the events of 9/11, the US has extensively relied on a number of international organisations as well as state allies such as the UK and many others in order to embark on a worldwide multi-front campaign against terrorism. The immediate domestic and international responses, as reflected on below, aptly illustrate the perceived uniqueness of 9/11 and contextualise the extraordinariness of the 'War on Terror'. What is perhaps of even more significance is how some of the measures recommended by the UNSC and NATO have had an important role in the construction of the 'War on Terror' paradigm (see Sect. 60.3).

60.2.1 Domestic Securitisation

The domestic US legislative response to the events of 9/11 was embodied by the USA Patriot Act 2001 (Patriot Act). The Patriot Act, codified into law a mere 45

---

[15] The term 'emergency' here and throughout this chapter reflects the texts of Article 4 of the International Covenant on Civil and Political Rights and Article 15 of the European Convention on Human Rights both of which refer to a public emergency threatening the life of the nation. For an academic discussion on what constitutes an emergency, see for example Gross and Ni Aolain 2001, Dyzenhaus and Thwaites 2007 and Greene 2018.

[16] On this point, see Ramraj et al. 2014. For further discussions on liberty/security debate and previous state responses to terrorism, see Dickson 2010 and Taylor Saito 2008.

[17] Defined as the ability of a state to protect its citizens from internal and external threats: Goold and Lazarus 2007, p. 57.

days after 9/11,[18] aimed to 'deter and punish terrorist acts in the United States and *around the world*' and 'to enhance law enforcement investigatory tools'.[19] Surveillance and physical powers under existing legislation such as the Foreign Surveillance and Intelligence Act of 1978 and the Electronic Communications Privacy Act of 1986 were expanded.[20] Under Section 214 in particular and Title II of the Patriot Act in general, government agencies were allowed to gather 'foreign intelligence information' from both US and non-US citizens. Title IV of the Patriot Act—Border Security—has amended the Immigration and Nationality Act of 1952 (INA) to expand the law enforcement and investigative powers of the US Attorney General[21] and the Immigration and Naturalisation service.[22]

Under Section 411 of the Patriot Act, non-US nationals or aliens who endorse or espouse terrorist activity or have persuaded others to support such activity are prevented from entering the US. The spouse or child of such an alien would similarly be restricted from travelling into the US. Thus, by relying on immigration legislation as part of counter-terrorism measures, the Patriot Act—similar to UNSC Resolution 1373, which will be discussed further below—has made express links between the prevention and pre-emption of terrorism with immigration status.

In addition, despite the existence of approximately 150 definitions of terrorism in federal law,[23] the definition of 'terrorist activity' was expanded to include actions involving the use of any dangerous device other than explosives and firearms as well as the solicitation of funds for a terrorist organisation and of individuals to engage in terrorist activity.[24] Overall, the US legislative response to 9/11 has resulted in the permanent expansion of the pre-emptive security capabilities of various agencies to the detriment of individual civil liberties and protections.[25] Yet, this legislative response should be distinguished from the Executive's response, which resulted in the creation of the 'War on Terror' legal and political paradigm and the authorisation of deeply problematic counter-terrorism measures within it—namely the High-Value Detainee programme (HVDP) and its core components.[26]

---

[18] The Act was signed into law by President George W Bush on 26 October 2001 following very brief discussions in both Houses of Congress. Please refer to http://georgewbush-whitehouse.arc hives.gov/news/releases/2001/10/images/20011026-5.html. Accessed 16 September 2020.

[19] Uniting and Strengthening America by Providing Appropriate Tools Required to Intercept and Obstruct Terrorism (USA PATRIOT ACT) Act of 2001 https://www.gpo.gov/fdsys/pkg/BILLS-107 hr3162enr/pdf/BILLS-107hr3162enr.pdf Accessed 16 September 2020. (emphasis added)

[20] See for example Sections 202, 207, 216 and 217 of the USA Patriot Act of 2001.

[21] See for example Subtitle A, Section 401.

[22] See for example Subtitle A, Section 402 and 403.

[23] Perry 2003.

[24] See Subtitle B, Section 411.

[25] On this point see further Roach 2011, p. 238.

[26] These include 'enhanced interrogations', extraordinary rendition and *incommunicado* detentions in black sites across the world. See further the full text of John Yoo's Memorandum Opinion for the Deputy Counsel to the President entitled 'The President's Constitutional Authority to Conduct Military Operations against Terrorists and Nations Supporting Them' available at https://www.justice.gov/file/19151/download. Accessed 16 September 2020. See also the infamous 2003

However, it was not just the domestic US approach that contributed to the creation of a highly securitised environment within which pervasive and stringent counter-terrorism legislative and Executive measures became the norm. The response by the relevant international bodies played a similarly significant role. Both the UNSC and NATO made decidedly important—and influential—interventions, which have changed the landscape when it comes to states' international responsibilities in respect of countering terrorism.

60.2.2 International Securitisation

Two UNSC Resolutions led the international response to the events of 9/11. Resolutions 1368[27] and the subsequently quite influential 1373,[28] adopted shortly after the acts of terrorism on 9/11, have reaffirmed the 'inherent right of individual or collective self-defence' of states. Both have expressed readiness and determination by the UNSC to take 'all necessary steps' to combat all forms of terrorism. Resolution 1373 in particular urged states to intensify the exchange of operational information and to cooperate to prevent acts of terrorism particularly through bi- and multilateral arrangements and agreements.[29] Further, the Resolution made an express link between refugee status and terrorism by noting that states should ensure that terrorists do not misuse refugee status.[30] The Resolution is seen as one of the drivers behind the post 9/11 trend to rely on immigration provisions and, in particular, those relating to transfers and detention as well as the more widespread use of contemporary methods of counter-terrorism such as asset freezing and other financial measures as part of states' counter-terrorism toolkit.[31]

More significantly perhaps Resolution 1373 has been described by the then President of the UNSC as the 'first step' in the UNSC legislating for the 'rest of the United Nations' membership'.[32] The reasoning behind this statement lies in the distinction between classic individualised resolutions and new generic resolutions

---

Torture Memo by John Yoo and Jay Bybee as discussed in 'The Torture Memos, 10 Years Later', *The Atlantic* 6 February 2012 https://www.theatlantic.com/national/archive/2012/02/the-torture-memos-10-years-later/252439/. Accessed 16 September 2020. Also Goldsmith 2009 and Goldsmith 2012.

[27] UN Security Council Resolution 1368, UN Doc. S/RES/1368 (2001).

[28] Security Council Resolution 1373 (2001) adopted 28 September 2001.

[29] Ibid.

[30] UN Security Council Resolution 1624, UN Doc. S/RES/1624 (2005) similarly expressly noted that the protections of the 1951 Refugee Convention including *non-refoulement* should not extend to an individual who is suspected of acts contrary to the purposes and principles of the UN.

[31] Goldstone 2005, p. 165. See also Robinson 2005, p. 308 and Luban 2005, p. 249.

[32] Press Conference by Security Council President, 2 April 2004, full text available at https://www.un.org/press/en/2004/pleugerpc.DOC.htm. Accessed 16 September 2020. See also Talmon 2005, p. 175; Alvarez 2003a, 2003b, p. 241; Krisch 2003, p. 883 and Alvarez 2003a, p. 874.

such as 1373.[33] Classic UNSC resolutions are expressly or implicitly limited in time until the specific purpose for which they are adopted—usually to secure performance of an obligation or the cessation of an internationally wrongful act by the addressee—is accomplished.[34] In comparison, the language of UNSC Resolution 2249[35] suggests that at present there does not seem to be no end to the fight against international terrorism.[36] With this Resolution, UN member states were urged to take all necessary measures to 'redouble and coordinate their efforts to prevent and suppress terrorist acts'. Additionally, the hallmark of any legislative resolution is the general and abstract character of the obligations imposed.[37] As noted by the Columbian delegate to the UNSC specifically in relation to Resolution 1373, it 'does not name a single country, society or group of people'.[38] In other words, the obligations in law-making resolutions are phrased in neutral language, apply to an indefinite number of cases, and are not usually limited in time.[39] While these obligations may well be triggered by a particular situation, conflict, or event, they are not restricted to it and are hence akin to obligations entered into by states in international agreements.[40]

Concomitantly to the UNSC affirmation of states' individual and collective right to self-defence, on 12 September 2001, NATO invoked the principle of collective self-defence under Article 5 of the North Atlantic Treaty.[41] This was the first invocation of this Article since the adoption of the North Atlantic Treaty.[42] A subsequent NATO Press Release declared, '*if it is determined* that this attack was directed from abroad against the United States, *it shall be regarded* as an action covered by Article 5 of the Washington Treaty'.[43] On the basis of this phrasing, the NATO invocation of Article 5 was initially considered to be provisional. Following a number of classified briefings by the US, however, the conditional clause was removed. In October 2001, the NATO Allies declared a unanimous assessment that the 9/11 attacks had been directed against the US from abroad thus activating Article 5 provisions.[44] Eight

---

[33] Talmon 2005, p. 177.

[34] Ibid., p. 176.

[35] UN Doc. S/RES/2249 (2015).

[36] Talmon 2005, p. 176.

[37] Ibid., p. 176.

[38] Quoted in 'U.N. Measure Requires Every Nation to Take Steps Against Terrorism' *The Los Angelis Times* 28 September 2001.

[39] Talmon 2005, p. 176.

[40] Ibid., pp. 176–179.

[41] North Atlantic Treaty 1949, full text available at https://www.nato.int/cps/en/natolive/official_texts_17120.htm. Accessed 16 September 2020.

[42] Committee on Legal Affairs and Human Rights, *Secret Detentions and Illegal Transfers of Detainees involving Council of Europe Member States*, AS/Jur (2007) 36, p. 16.

[43] Statement by the North Atlantic Council, Press Release (2001) 124 of 12 September 2001, full text available at http://www.nato.int/docu/pr/2001/p01-124e.htm. Accessed 16 September 2020. (emphasis added)

[44] Statement by the NATO Secretary General, Lord Robertson, NATO Press Release of 08 October 2001, full text available at http://www.nato.int/DOCU/pr/2001/p01-138e.htm. Accessed 16 September 2020.

measures, deemed to improve transborder counter-terrorism efforts, were agreed upon and were to be relied on either individually or collectively.[45] Amongst the adopted measures were the enhancement of intelligence cooperation and sharing and provision of assistance to NATO Allies, who are or may be subject to increased threat of terrorism.

Rather than the extensiveness of the measures itself, what is perhaps of more significance is that these were agreed upon at the request of the US.[46] According to NATO procedures, the International Staff have the responsibility to draft documents and resolutions.[47] The language of these particular measures was reportedly drafted, re-drafted and put forward by the US unilaterally.[48] Article 5 does accommodate the undertaking of individual self-defence measures and NATO did outline that while any collective action would be decided by the North Atlantic Council, the US could also carry out *independent actions*, consistent with its rights and obligations under the UN Charter.[49] However, the departure from the regular NATO procedures and the involvement of the US in the drafting process suggests that (a) there was an acceptance of the uniqueness of events on 9/11 and (b) the adopted measures would be of some operational significance. A report by the Council of Europe's Committee on Legal Affairs and Human Rights[50] suggests that there were additional components of the NATO measures that have remained classified adding to the perceived 'extraordinariness' of the post 9/11 security emergency.[51]

The invocation of Article 5 of the NATO Treaty and the adoption of UNSC resolutions such as 1368 and 1373 has influenced the adoption and further development of expansive international, regional and domestic counter-terrorism measures as well as contributed to the post 9/11 securitisation. The above outlined measures could be seen as necessarily broad due to the perceived nature of the terrorism

---

[45] Statement to the Press by NATO Secretary General, Lord Robertson, on the North Atlantic Council Decision On Implementation Of Article 5 of the Washington Treaty following the 11 September Attacks against the United States, 04 October 2001, full text available at http://www.nato.int/docu/speech/2001/s011004b.htm. Accessed 16 September 2020.

[46] Ibid.

[47] Buckley 'Invoking Article 5', *NATO Review* full text available at http://www.nato.int/docu/review/2006/issue2/english/art2.html. Accessed 16 September 2020.

[48] Committee on Legal Affairs and Human Rights, *Secret Detentions and Illegal Transfers of Detainees involving Council of Europe Member States*, AS/Jur (2007) 36, p. 18.

[49] 'NATO and the Scourge of Terrorism: What is Article 5?' 18 February 2005, full text available at http://www.nato.int/terrorism/five.htm. Accessed 16 September 2020.

[50] Committee on Legal Affairs and Human Rights, *Secret Detentions and Illegal Transfers of Detainees involving Council of Europe Member States*, AS/Jur (2007) 36, p. 19.

[51] The term 'emergency' here and throughout this chapter reflects the texts of Article 4 of the International Covenant on Civil and Political Rights and Article 15 of the European Convention on Human Rights. For a judicial discussion what constitutes an emergency, please refer to cases such as *Lawless v Ireland* (No 3) [1961] ECHR 2, *Ireland v the United Kingdom* [1978] ECHR 1 and more recently *A. and Others v the United Kingdom,* Application no. 3455/05, Judgment of 19 February 2009 as well as *Landinelli Silva v Uruguay,* Case No. 34/1978, Views adopted on 8 April 1981. In addition, refer to UN Human Rights Committee General Comment No. 29.

threat immediately following the events of 9/11. Yet, the development of an international security and counter-terrorism regime through the CTC and certain UNSC resolutions,[52] the engagement in international law making in matters of security[53] and the multi-layered impact on domestic legislation suggests that the events of 9/11 were approached as unique opportunity to significantly strengthen security and counter-terrorism provisions.

Overall, the period of intense securitisation post 9/11 created an environment within which comprehensive and stringent counter-terrorism prevention measures became more common across domestic legislation[54] and arguably more acceptable. As Sect. 60.3 will illustrate, the US sought to exploit—and further entrench—this environment by adopting the language and paradigm of war in the context of combatting terrorism. In other words, despite the swiftly increasing range of legislative means through which a state could detain an individual terror suspect and restrict their (alleged) activities, a transnational and multi-actor campaign to combat terrorism was also deemed necessary. More significantly perhaps, the determinations made by the UNSC and NATO contributed to the creation of the 'War on Terror' legal and political paradigm.

60.3 Designing the 'War on Terror'

For nearly a decade, the so-called 'War on Terror' and its various fronts dominated legal and political debates leaving a legacy, which can still be felt in domestic and international counter-terrorism approaches.[55] At the height of this 'war', the US was involved in military operations in Iraq and Afghanistan and relying on up 54 other states to operationalise[56] the extraordinary rendition circuits, undertake 'enhanced interrogations' and/or provide detention facilities as part of the HVDP. In the context of the latter, this 'war' was designed to provide operational spaces for these clandestine counter-terrorism operations. The first step in creating these spaces was George W. Bush's Address to the Nation equating the 9/11 attacks to an act of war against the US.[57] Shortly after his Address to the Nation, Military Order of 13 November 2001 identified international humanitarian law (IHL) as the only applicable legal standard to the counter-terrorism operations due to be undertaken by the US.[58] The Order stated that the actions of international terrorists including Al Qaeda had created a

---

[52] See also Ramraj 2014.

[53] See further Happold 2003 and Szasz 2002 as well as Klabbers et al. 2009.

[54] See for example Donohue 2008; Ramraj et al. 2012; and Masferrer and Walker 2013.

[55] See for example Jenkins et al. 2014.

[56] See further The Open Society Justice Initiative 2013 and UN General Assembly 2010.

[57] President George W Bush in September 2001 in an address to a joint session of Congress. Please see further 'Transcript of President Bush's Address', *CNN News* 21 September 2001.

[58] Military Order of November 13, 2001, Federal Register, Vol. 66, No. 222.

state of armed conflict, which required the use of US Armed Forces.[59] Further, in order to protect the US and its citizens, conduct effective military operations and prevent future acts of terrorism, the US would detain and try individuals subject to this Order for violations of the laws of war and other applicable laws by military tribunals.[60]

In a subsequent 2002 Memorandum, George W. Bush, stated that the 'War on Terror' had ushered in a new paradigm, which, while requiring a new approach towards the laws of war, should be consistent with the principles of the Geneva Convention.[61] International human rights protections were not referred to or noted as relevant to HVDP or other components of the 'War on Terror' within these documents. It is important to assess this position with reference to the relevant jurisprudence of the International Court of Justice (ICJ) and the European Court of Human Rights (ECtHR). While states have a tendency to seek limitations of—through either interpretation or emergency legislation—their human rights and international obligations, the extent to which the US sought to restrict the applicability of the relevant international standards was arguably extraordinary.

60.3.1 The Complementarity of International Humanitarian Law and International Human Rights Law

Contrary to the US position, the protections offered by international human rights law (IHRL) and IHL are complementary.[62] If a conflict arises between the provisions of these two legal regimes and their applicability to a particular situation, the relevant *lex specialis* should be identified and applied.[63] Thus, the operation of IHL within an international or non-international armed conflict as the *lex specialis* does not exclude the continued applicability of IHRL as *lex generalis*.[64] This is the approach adopted by the ICJ and subsequently confirmed in the jurisprudence of the ECtHR.

---

[59] Ibid.

[60] Ibid.

[61] Memorandum on Humane Treatment of Taliban and al Qaeda Detainees, The White House, 7 February 2002. Full text http://www.pegc.us/archive/White_House/bush_memo_20020207_ed.pdf. Accessed 16 September 2020.

[62] Report of the Working Group on Arbitrary Detention, UN Doc. E/CN.4/2006/7, para 70. See also Report by the Special Rapporteur, *Extrajudicial, Summary or Arbitrary Executions*, UN Doc. E/CN.4/2005/7, para 50.

[63] *Legality of the Threat or Use of Nuclear Weapons, Advisory Opinion*, International Court of Justice (ICJ), 8 July 1996, para 25 and *Advisory Opinion Concerning Legal Consequences of the Construction of a Wall in the Occupied Palestinian Territory*, International Court of Justice (ICJ), 9 July 2004, paras 108–111.

[64] Ibid.

In its Advisory Opinion on *The Legality of the Threat or Use of Nuclear Weapons*,[65] the ICJ was asked by the UN General Assembly to assess whether the threat or use of nuclear weapons is permitted in any circumstances under international law. The ICJ noted that in order to answer the question set, it must decide what the relevant law is within the corpus of international law norms.[66] In its considerations, the Court focused on the right to life as guaranteed under Article 6 of the International Covenant on Civil and Political Rights (ICCPR) and whether the applicable international law regarding the use of nuclear weapons stemmed from the ICCPR or the laws of armed conflict. The argument that the ICCPR was directed to the protection of human rights in peacetime rather than the unlawful loss of life during hostilities was also noted.[67]

The ICJ stated however that the protections of the ICCPR do not cease during an armed conflict unless and to the extent that there have been derogations under Article 4 of the ICCPR. The Court proceeded to advise that as the right to life is non-derogable, in principle the right not to be arbitrarily deprived of one's life also applies in hostilities.[68] However, the test of what is an arbitrary deprivation of life is to be determined by the relevant *lex specialis* namely the law applicable in armed conflict as it is specifically designed to regulate the conduct of hostilities. Thus, whether a particular loss of life is arbitrary contrary to Article 6 ICCPR can only be decided by reference to the law of armed conflict rather than the terms of the ICCPR itself.[69]

In a subsequent Advisory Opinion while considering the rules and principles of international law applicable to measures taken by Israel—*The Legal Consequences of the Construction of a Wall in the Occupied Palestinian Territory*[70]—the ICJ rejected the argument that the human rights instruments to which Israel was party were not applicable to the occupied territory. The ICJ referred to its Advisory Opinion on *Nuclear Weapons* and noted more generally that the protections afforded under human rights conventions do not cease during an armed conflict unless there has been a permissible derogation such as one under Article 4 ICCPR.[71] The Court further noted that there are three possible scenarios with regards to the relationship between IHL and IHRL: (1) 'some rights may be exclusively matters of international humanitarian law', (2) 'others may be exclusively matters of human rights law' and (3) 'yet others may be matters of both these branches of international law'.[72] In answering

---

[65] *Legality of the Threat or Use of Nuclear Weapons, Advisory Opinion*, International Court of Justice (ICJ), 8 July 1996.

[66] Ibid., para 24.

[67] Ibid.

[68] Under Article 6.1 of the ICCPR the right to life is defined thus: "Every human being has the inherent right to life. This right shall be protected by law. No one shall be arbitrarily deprived of his life." http://www.ohchr.org/en/professionalinterest/pages/ccpr.aspx. Accessed 16 September 2020.

[69] Ibid., para 25.

[70] *Advisory Opinion Concerning Legal Consequences of the Construction of a Wall in the Occupied Palestinian Territory*, International Court of Justice (ICJ), 9 July 2004.

[71] Ibid., para 106.

[72] Ibid., para 106.

the particular question set to it, the ICJ noted that it had to consider human rights as *lex generalis* and international humanitarian law as *lex specialis*. This decision was reaffirmed in the ICJ judgment in the *Armed Activities on the Territory of the Congo*.[73]

The ECtHR has taken a similar view in its jurisprudence in the 2001 case of *Al-Adsani v. the United Kingdom*[74] and subsequently in the 2009 case of *Varnava v. Turkey*.[75] More recently, the ECtHR has reaffirmed that IHRL and IHL can apply concurrently with reference to the jurisprudence of the ICJ in *Hassan v. the United Kingdom*.[76] In its decision, the ECtHR held that both the ECHR and IHL must be interpreted in harmony with other rules of international law.[77] The ECtHR acknowledged its previous case law and the jurisprudence of the ICJ before proceeding to state that during an armed conflict ECHR provisions continue to apply; however, the provisions needed to be interpreted with reference to the applicable IHL protections.[78]

The ICJ and ECtHR's discussion of the relationship of *lex specialis* and *lex generalis* in the context of IHL and IHRL provisions is helpful in understanding the minimum baseline of protections to be afforded to individuals during an armed conflict. In all of the above cases the ICJ (reaffirmed by the ECtHR) expressly stated that human rights provisions continue to operate during an armed conflict. In comparison, the applicability of IHL is conditional on the presence of either an international or a non-international armed conflict. Under Article 4 of the ICCPR, a state party can derogate from certain provisions during an officially declared public emergency threatening the life of the nation.[79] A state of declared war or an armed conflict would satisfy the criteria for derogation. Thus, while the rules of IHL are applicable in the particular or special circumstances of an armed conflict, they do not displace entirely the protections afforded by IHRL. Rather, the operation of IHL can have a role in the application of human rights standards such as in interpreting what 'arbitrary' is or expanding on the grounds allowing for detention of individuals.[80]

However, despite the above jurisprudence, in 2006, while addressing the UN Committee against Torture, John Bellinger[81] reaffirmed the US position that IHL was the relevant *lex specialis* governing the US detention operations in Guantanamo

---

[73] *Democratic Republic of Congo (DRC) v. Uganda*, Judgment 19 December 2005.

[74] Application no. 35763/97, Judgment 21 November 2001.

[75] Applications Nos. 16064/90, 16065/90, 16066/90, 16068/90, 16069/90, 16070/90, 16071/90, 16072/90 and 16073/90, Judgment 18 September 2009.

[76] Application no. 29750/09, Judgment 16 September 2014.

[77] Ibid., para 102.

[78] Ibid., para 104.

[79] Article 4, International Covenant on Civil and Political Rights.

[80] For a detailed discussion in relation to grounds for detention, please refer to the *Hassan v. the United Kingdom*, Application no. 29750/09, Judgment 16 September 2014.

[81] Legal Adviser of the US Department of State and head of the US delegation to the Committee against Torture.

Bay, Afghanistan and Iraq.[82] While acknowledging the similarity between certain IHL and IHRL protections, he explicitly restated this position twice in his address.[83] Further, when referring to the provisions of the UN Convention against Torture (UNCAT), John Bellinger expressly stated that at the conclusion of negotiations on UNCAT the US had clearly noted that UNCAT was not intended to apply during an armed conflict. He emphasised that if UNCAT were applicable to armed conflicts, this would result in an overlap of different treaties and undermine efforts to eradicate torture.[84] A similar view was adopted towards the obligations of the ICCPR.

Thus, the overall position endorsed by the US post 9/11 in relation to its international legal obligations appears to be as follows: when IHL is operating as *lex specialis*, IHRL is deemed not applicable. However, in seeking to severely restrict the operation of IHRL and IHL in respect of its 'War on Terror', the US did not just focus on the principles of *lex specialis* and *lex generalis*. Following the determination that IHL as the applicable *lex specialis* fully displaced the operation of IHRL, the US then proceeded to adopt a very narrow interpretation of the language, text and scope of the concept of 'armed conflict' as well as other core provisions in order to limit its obligations under the four Geneva Conventions.[85]

60.3.2 The 'War on Terror' as an Armed Conflict

On 13 November 2001, the then US President George W. Bush declared that the attacks carried out on 9/11 were on 'a scale that has created a state of armed conflict'.[86] This determination was made on the basis that the terrorist attacks were 'a sufficiently organised and systematic set of violent actions', which have reached a level of intensity amounting to an armed conflict.[87] While construing IHL as the only relevant legal framework, the US Attorney General's Office stated that a declaration of war was not required to create a state of war or to subject persons to the laws of war.[88] In

---

[82] US Meeting with UN Committee against Torture, Opening Remarks by John Bellinger, full text available at https://2001-2009.state.gov/g/drl/rls/rm/2006/66062.htm. Accessed 16 September 2020.

[83] Ibid.

[84] Ibid.

[85] The full text of the Geneva Conventions is available at https://www.icrc.org/en/war-and-law/treaties-customary-law/geneva-conventions. Accessed 16 September 2020.

[86] Military Order of Nov. 13, 2001, 66 Fed. Reg. 57, 833 § 1(a) (Nov. 16, 2001).

[87] Memorandum Opinion for the Counsel to the President, Opinions of the Office of Legal Counsel, Vol 25, 6 November 2001. The role of the Office of Legal Counsel is to provide legal advice to the President and Executive Branch agencies. The Office also drafts legal opinions of the Attorney General, provides its own written opinions and oral advice in response to requests from the Counsel to the President, the various agencies of the Executive Branch, and offices within the Department. Please see further http://www.justice.gov/olc. Accessed 16 September 2020.

[88] Ibid.

addition, the US could be engaged in an armed conflict with a non-state actor.[89] The scale of the 9/11 attacks, the number of casualties and necessary military response required were found to be sufficient to create a state of war *de facto*, which allowed the application of IHL.[90]

IHL applies in 'all cases of declared war and any other armed conflict' of either international or non-international character.[91] Even if IHL was the only applicable legal framework, the US would still be obligated to comply with the rules governing transfers of protected individuals and treat detainees humanely. However, by relying on a very narrow interpretation of domestic and international legal sources, the US challenged the core understanding of the concept of armed conflict in order to create a legal environment within which the 'War on Terror' was the relevant conflict. In other words, this was a novel type of armed conflict to which core IHL provisions were not applicable. In order to achieve this, the US claimed that the operation of IHL is in actuality more malleable than the texts of the four Geneva Conventions suggest. By fashioning a broad rhetorical fault line[92] within the international legal framework in this manner, the US aimed to create spaces of legal uncertainty within which expansive counter-terrorism activities such as the HVDP and extraordinary rendition could operate—or, to put it differently, operationalise core aspects of the 'War on Terror'.

This fault line was created as follows. On 18 September 2001, a Joint Resolution by the US Senate and House of Representatives authorised the use of the US Armed Forces as a response to the events of 9/11.[93] Under Section 2 of the Resolution, the US President was permitted to use all necessary and appropriate force against nations, organisations or persons considered to have been involved in the 9/11 attacks.[94] The determination of whether a state, organisation or an individual had planned, aided, authorised or committed the terrorist acts rested with the President.[95] On 20 September 2001 while declaring a global war on terrorism, then President George

---

[89] Ibid.

[90] Ibid.

[91] The full texts of Common Article 2 and 3 and the four Geneva Conventions are available at https://www.icrc.org/en/war-and-law/treaties-customary-law/geneva-conventions. Accessed 16 September 2020.

[92] For a discussion on the concept of fault lines within the international legal framework and fault lines of legitimacy in particular, please refer to Charlesworth and Coicaud 2010. In this chapter, fault lines are described as simultaneously being zones of fracture within the legal framework and opportunities for adjustment of the law.

[93] Joint Resolution To Authorize the Use of United States Armed Forces against those Responsible for the Recent Attacks launched against the United States, Public Law 107-40, 107th Congress, Sept. 18, 2001 [S.J. Res.23].

[94] Ibid.

[95] Ibid.

W. Bush also stated that this would be a lengthy multifaceted campaign involving US military and intelligence services.[96]

At the core of the 'War on Terror' legal paradigm was the assessment by the Office of the Legal Counsel that the terrorist attacks of 9/11 amounted to an armed conflict triggering the applicability of the four Geneva Conventions.[97] By relying on relevant domestic provisions and legal precedents, the Memorandum stated that where an organised force has engaged in a campaign of violence that reaches a sufficient level of intensity, the US President could regard such a campaign as an armed conflict justifying the operation of IHL.[98] In addition, the determination whether the laws of war applied in this context was also within the purview of the President.[99] This was the first step in determining whether IHL was applicable to the 'present conflict with terrorist forces'.[100]

The Memorandum then assessed the relevant international legal standards. With reference to previous terrorist attacks attributed to Al Qaeda,[101] it was argued that the events of 9/11 were the culmination of a 'lengthy and sustained campaign' against military and civilian targets in the US.[102] Viewed from this perspective, the 9/11 attacks were said to be part of a systematic campaign of hostilities rather than an isolated or sporadic event. Thus, the terrorist attacks of 9/11 were sufficient to create a *de facto* state of war triggering the operation of IHL. In addition, the scale of the military response following the Joint Congress Resolution and the declaration of war by President Bush further justified the conclusion that IHL could be invoked.

The final factor considered was NATO's immediate response to 9/11 as discussed in Sect. 60.2. Following an initial provisional invocation of Article 5 of the North Atlantic Treaty, in October 2001 the NATO Allies declared a unanimous assessment that the 9/11 attacks activated the Article's provisions.[103] This was described as a factor 'virtually conclusive in itself' in establishing that the attacks of 9/11 reached the level of hostilities required to be classified as an armed conflict.[104] This determination was made without any reference to the US involvement within NATO, which appears to have strongly influenced the invocation of Article 5 in the first place.[105]

---

[96] Please refer to the Address to Congress and the American People by George W. Bush on 20 September 2001, full text available at http://www.history2u.com/bush_war_on_terror.htm. Accessed 16 September 2020.

[97] Memorandum Opinion for the Counsel to the President, Opinions of the Office of Legal Counsel, Vol 25, 6 November 2001, pp. 1–23.

[98] Ibid., p. 24.

[99] Ibid., pp. 6, 7, 29, 33.

[100] Ibid.

[101] The events referred to were the bombings of the World Trade Centre in 1993, Khobar Towers in Saudi Arabia in 1996, US embassies in Kenya and Tanzania in 1998 and the U.S.S. Cole in 2000.

[102] Memorandum Opinion for the Counsel to the President, Opinions of the Office of Legal Counsel, Vol 25, 6 November 2001.

[103] Ibid.

[104] Memorandum Opinion for the Counsel to the President, Opinions of the Office of Legal Counsel, Vol 25, 6 November 2001, p. 29.

[105] Ibid.

60.3.3 The Concept of Armed Conflict within International Law

A brief overview of what constitutes an armed conflict is important in order to put the above statements into context. Under Common Article 2 of the Geneva Conventions, IHL and its protections apply to 'all cases of declared war and any other armed conflict' which may arise between two or more states signatories to the Geneva Conventions.[106] In addressing the concept of armed conflict, the 1960 Conventions Commentary notes that the use of this wording was chosen deliberately in order to avoid uncertainties or disputes.[107] Any difference arising between two states, which leads to the involvement of members of the military forces, would thus amount to an armed conflict within the meaning of Common Article 2 even when one of the parties denies that a state of war exists.[108] The phrase '*de facto* hostilities'[109] was relied on in the 1960 Commentary to describe what would also trigger the application of Common Article 2 of the Geneva Conventions. Isolated events involving force and requiring a response by members of the armed forces were expressly noted as not amounting to either an international or non-international armed conflict.[110] Under Common Article 3, the provisions of the Geneva Conventions are extended to armed conflicts of a non-international character. More recently, an armed conflict has been found to exist when states resort to the use of armed force or when there is protracted armed violence between governmental forces and organised armed groups.[111]

The 1960 Commentary acknowledges that the phrasing might be too vague, however it notes that isolated events involving the use of force and requiring a response by members of the armed force would not trigger the operation of Article 2 or 3.[112] What is within the scope of Article 3 however are 'armed conflicts, with *armed forces* on either side engaged in *hostilities*—conflicts, in short, which are in many respects similar to an international war, but take place within the confines

---

[106] International Committee of the Red Cross (ICRC), *Geneva Convention for the Amelioration of the Condition of the Wounded and Sick in Armed Forces in the Field (First Geneva Convention)*, 12 August 1949, 75 UNTS 31, International Committee of the Red Cross (ICRC), *Geneva Convention for the Amelioration of the Condition of Wounded, Sick and Shipwrecked Members of Armed Forces at Sea (Second Geneva Convention)*, 12 August 1949, 75 UNTS 85, International Committee of the Red Cross (ICRC), *Geneva Convention Relative to the Treatment of Prisoners of War (Third Geneva Convention)*, 12 August 1949, 75 UNTS 135 and International Committee of the Red Cross (ICRC), *Geneva Convention Relative to the Protection of Civilian Persons in Time of War (Fourth Geneva Convention)*, 12 August 1949, 75 UNTS 287.

[107] Pictet 1960, pp. 35–37.

[108] Ibid.

[109] Ibid., p. 23.

[110] Ibid.

[111] *Prosecutor v. Dusko Tadić aka "Dule" (Decision on the Defence Motion for Interlocutory Appeal on Jurisdiction)*, IT-94-1, International Criminal Tribunal for the former Yugoslavia (ICTY), 2 October 1995, para 70.

[112] Pictet 1960, pp. 35–37.

60 The "War on Terror"

of a single country'.[113] In the *Tadić* case, the International Tribunal for Former Yugoslavia (ICTY) adopted a similar interpretation and referred to extended armed violence between organised armed groups within a state.[114] The core aim of Common Article 3 during such a conflict is to provide a minimum baseline of protections for individuals no longer engaging in hostilities. These protections have been interpreted as being automatically applicable without prior determination as to the nature of the conflict.[115]

In the subsequent ICTY case of *Haradinaj*,[116] the ICTY elaborated on the criteria for non-international armed conflict. The Trial Chamber when discussing armed groups, emphasised characteristics such as the existence of a General Staff with the powers to appoint commanders, give directions and issue public statements on behalf of the organisation, and the capacity to issue ceasefire orders as well as conclude ceasefire agreements.[117] Furthermore, the ability to engage in armed clashes across a certain territory was interpreted as an indicator of a sufficient level of organisation.[118] The Appeals Chamber concluded that an armed conflict could only exist between parties that are sufficiently organised to confront each other with *military* means.[119]

The concept of armed conflict as defined and interpreted above is not easily reconciled with the arguments that a large-scale terrorist attack could amount to a conflict triggering IHL obligations. State practice suggests that acts of terrorism do not amount to an armed conflict.[120] This approach is supported by the Venice Commission findings that the activities of terrorist networks such as sporadic bombings and other violent acts and ensuing counter-terrorism responses (even when military units are engaged) do not amount to an armed conflict.[121] Similarly, Article 1 of Additional Protocol II to the Geneva Conventions UN Convention on Conventional Weapons states that isolated and sporadic acts of violence and other acts of

---

[113] Ibid., p. 37. (emphasis added)

[114] *Prosecutor v. Dusko Tadić aka "Dule" (Decision on the Defence Motion for Interlocutory Appeal on Jurisdiction)*, IT-94-1, International Criminal Tribunal for the former Yugoslavia (ICTY), 2 October 1995, para 70.

[115] Ibid., p. 35.

[116] *Prosecutor v. Ramush Haradinaj, Idriz Balaj and Lahi Brahimaj*, Case No. IT-04-84-T, ICTY, 3 April 2008.

[117] Ibid., paras 55–57.

[118] Ibid.

[119] Ibid., para 60.

[120] This is expressly stated in UK Ministry of Defence Law of Armed Conflict Manual—UK Ministry of Defence, *The Manual of the Law of Armed Conflict* (2004, Oxford; Oxford University Press), p. 31. The manual also refers to the French government's approach in 1954–1956 during the Algerian uprising. Domestic law was exclusively relied on to address the uprising until June 1956 when only Common Article 3 was formally accepted as applicable.

[121] Venice Commission, *Opinion on the International Legal Obligations of Council Member States in Respect of Secret Detention Facilities and Inter-State Transport of Prisoners*, Opinion no. 363/2005, CDL–AD (2006), para 78.

similar nature do not constitute an armed conflict.[122] The US nonetheless deviated from this established practice and interpreted the 'War on Terror' to be an armed conflict exclusively governed by IHL.

While assessing the general applicability of IHL, the US adopted a very strict and narrow reading of the text of the Geneva Conventions and attaching Commentary.[123] The US analysis of the concept of armed conflict appears to have followed very closely, if not mirrored exactly, certain language used within the Commentary in order to illustrate that the events of 9/11 were not an isolated incident but rather a part of ongoing hostilities.[124] The attacks of 9/11 were described thus: the culmination of a widespread and sustained campaign of hostilities, which required the engagement of US troops on a massive scale.[125] In other words—these were not isolated or sporadic events but rather *de facto* hostilities, which would engage IHL.[126] Protracted armed violence between governmental forces and organised armed groups has been found to trigger the applicability of IHL.[127]

The decision to declare a 'war' on terrorism has been criticised as a normative and pragmatic error.[128] Yet, the above definitions provided by the ICTY are broad enough to encompass conflicts between a state and a terrorist group provided that the latter is sufficiently organised and more importantly capable of sustaining military operations.[129] The core question that needs to be examined is whether various acts attributed to Al Qaeda are sufficiently related to each other to be interpreted as acts of war in the same conflict.[130] The US Executive determination that it is at war with Al Qaeda and international terrorist groups in general has been criticised on the basis that it lacks any geographical delimitation.[131] Even if the attacks on the World Trade Centre in 1993, Khobar Towers in Saudi Arabia in 1996 and US embassies in Kenya and Tanzania in 1998 could be attributed to Al Qaida or categorised as linked, serious questions nonetheless arise as to the geographical proximity and temporal closeness of these attacks.[132] The identification of one core target—Al Qaeda and its affiliates—does not help to delimit the location of war but rather seems to broaden it. For the 'War on Terror' to amount to an armed conflict under IHL, there should be

---

[122] International Committee of the Red Cross (ICRC), *Protocol Additional to the Geneva Conventions of 12 August 1949, and relating to the Protection of Victims of Non-International Armed Conflicts (Protocol II)*, 8 June 1977, 1125 UNTS 609.

[123] Pictet 1960.

[124] See above n. 109.

[125] Memorandum Opinion for the Counsel to the President, Opinions of the Office of Legal Counsel, Vol 25, 6 November 2001, p. 28.

[126] *Ibid.*, pp. 1, 31.

[127] *Prosecutor v. Dusko Tadić aka "Dule" (Decision on the Defence Motion for Interlocutory Appeal on Jurisdiction)*, IT-94-1, International Criminal Tribunal for the former Yugoslavia (ICTY), 2 October 1995, para 70.

[128] Habermas 2006, pp. 14–15.

[129] Lehto 2010, p. 508.

[130] Ibid., p. 508.

[131] Ibid., p. 509.

[132] Ibid.

a more specified geographical connection and more substantial or closer temporal links.

Nevertheless, these four benefits of the paradigm of war can arguably explain why the US adopted the language of war and then contended that IHL is the only applicable legal framework. As part of a war, it is permissible to use lethal force against enemy troops regardless of the degree of involvement such troops have with the enemy thus vastly expanding the number of individuals who can be legitimate targets.[133] Further, collateral damage, which is the unintended but foreseen killing of non-combatants, is permissible as part of operations against military targets provided the principle of proportionality is followed.[134] Quite significantly, the requirements in relation to evidence and proof in terms of detaining individuals or subjecting them to other restrictive practices are far less stringent than in comparison with the criminal justice system.[135] Thus, an enemy combatant can be captured and imprisoned without having to reach the beyond reasonable doubt standard of proof. Finally, within the context of war, legitimate targets are those who are considered to pose a threat and cause harm rather than only those who have already caused harm.[136] Under the Military Order of 13 November 2001,[137] the individuals subject to it were non-US citizens who had been determined (a) to be or have been members of Al Qaeda, (b) to be or have been engaged in aiding, abetting or conspiring to commit acts of international terrorism or have aimed to cause adverse effects on the US and (c) to have knowingly harboured such individuals.[138] Individuals whose capture and detention was in the interest of the US were also subject to the Order.[139] The access of these individuals to the protections of core IHL provisions was then severely restricted.

---

[133] Section 52 of Protocol Additional to the Geneva Conventions of 12 August 1949, and relating to the Protection of Victims of International Armed Conflicts (Protocol I) outlines what military objectives are. International Committee of the Red Cross (ICRC), *Protocol Additional to the Geneva Conventions of 12 August 1949, and relating to the Protection of Victims of International Armed Conflicts (Protocol I)*, 8 June 1977, 1125 UNTS 3. For some commentary of the Additional Protocol with reference to the 'War on Terror', see Luban 2002, p. 9.

[134] Section 51 of Protocol Additional to the Geneva Conventions of 12 August 1949, and relating to the Protection of Victims of International Armed Conflicts.

[135] Luban 2002, p. 9.

[136] Ibid.

[137] Military Order of Nov. 13, 2001, 66 Fed. Reg. 57, 833 § 1(a) (Nov. 16, 2001).

[138] Ibid., Section 2 (a)(1).

[139] Ibid., Section 2 (a)(2).

60.3.4 The 'War on Terror', Core IHL Protections and Individual Terror Suspects

Common Article 3,[140] or as it has also been described a 'Convention in miniature', expresses the fundamental core principles governing all four Geneva Conventions.[141] It applies automatically without a prior determination of the nature of the conflict and sets a compulsory minimum standard ensuring the humane treatment of detained individuals.[142] In assessing the applicability of Common Article 3, the ICTY in *Prosecutor v. Tadić*[143] found that the rules contained in the Article applied outside the narrow geographical context of the actual zone of combat operations.[144] In addition, the Tribunal found that the character or nature of a conflict was irrelevant to the applicability of the minimum baseline obligations of Common Article 3.[145] This interpretation was challenged on the basis that it ignored the text and context within which Common Article 3 (and the Geneva Conventions) was ratified by the US.[146] According to the US, Common Article 3 obligations traditionally applied to internal conflicts within one territory between a State Party and an insurgent group amounting to a large-scale civil war rather than to all forms of armed conflict not covered by Common Article 2.[147]

Thus, having developed a multi-faceted argument that the events of 9/11 activated the laws of war, the US proceeded to severely restrict the protections afforded to individuals captured, detained and potentially subject to capture, transfer and detention under IHL. This was achieved through a determination that while the 'War on Terror' was the relevant armed conflict, it was a type of armed conflict not expressly

---

[140] International Committee of the Red Cross (ICRC), *Geneva Convention for the Amelioration of the Condition of the Wounded and Sick in Armed Forces in the Field (First Geneva Convention)*, 12 August 1949, 75 UNTS 31, International Committee of the Red Cross (ICRC), *Geneva Convention for the Amelioration of the Condition of Wounded, Sick and Shipwrecked Members of Armed Forces at Sea (Second Geneva Convention)*, 12 August 1949, 75 UNTS 85, International Committee of the Red Cross (ICRC), *Geneva Convention Relative to the Treatment of Prisoners of War (Third Geneva Convention)*, 12 August 1949, 75 UNTS 135 and International Committee of the Red Cross (ICRC), *Geneva Convention Relative to the Protection of Civilian Persons in Time of War (Fourth Geneva Convention)*, 12 August 1949, 75 UNTS 287.

[141] Pictet 1960, p. 33.

[142] Ibid. See also published text on ICRC official website here https://ihl-databases.icrc.org/applic/ihl/ihl.nsf/Comment.xsp?action=openDocument&documentId=230CD134A931BD55C12563CD00422E11#:~:text=Article%203%2C%20which%20has%20been,other%20provisions%20of%20the%20Convention. Accessed 16 September 2020.

[143] *Prosecutor v. Dusko Tadić aka "Dule" (Decision on the Defence Motion for Interlocutory Appeal on Jurisdiction)*, IT-94-1, International Criminal Tribunal for the former Yugoslavia (ICTY), 2 October 1995.

[144] Ibid., para 69.

[145] Ibid., para 102.

[146] Memorandum from John Yoo, Deputy Assistant Attorney General and Robert J. Delahunty, Special Counsel to William J. Haynes II, General Counsel, Department of Defence, available at http://www.justice.gov/olc/docs/memo-laws-taliban-detainees.pdf. Accessed 16 September 2020.

[147] Ibid., p. 7.

governed by either Common Article 2 or 3 of the Geneva Conventions. Concurrently, the US proceeded to restrict other specific IHL protections linked to the operation of Common Articles 2 and 3. In a 2002, U.S. Department of Justice Memorandum (DoJ Memo) advocated that the provisions and protections afforded under Geneva Convention III were not applicable to detainees associated with Al Qaeda.[148]

It was reiterated that as the 'novel' nature of the conflict precluded the operation of Common Article 3, the military treatment of members of Al Qaeda was thus not restricted or governed by Common Article 3.[149] §948a Military Commissions Act of 2006 defined two categories of combatants—lawful enemy and unlawful enemy combatants. Lawful enemy combatants were deemed to be subject to the U.S. Code[150] and by proxy the Geneva Conventions; unlawful enemy combatants were however subject to a trial by a military commission under the Act and could not invoke the protections of the Geneva Conventions.[151] Individuals who were linked to Al Qaeda, the Taliban or associated forces were specifically listed as falling under the category of unlawful enemy combatant.[152] The result was that individual terrorist suspects captured and detained during military operations within the 'War on Terror' were effectively denied the protections afforded by Common Article 3.

In this context, the decision in *Hamdan v. Rumsfeld*[153] is of particular significance.[154] Mr. Hamdan was captured in Afghanistan in 2001 and subsequently transferred to Guantánamo Bay in 2002.[155] In 2003 he was deemed eligible for trial by a military commission for then-unspecified crimes. In 2004 he was charged with conspiracy to commit offences triable by a military commission. After a number of cases in the lower courts, the Supreme Court found that Common Article 3 affords minimal protection to individuals associated with either a signatory or a non-signatory of the Conventions who are involved in a conflict on the territory of a signatory.[156] The Court further disagreed with the contention of the US government that the conflict with Al Qaeda did not fall within the scope of the Geneva Conventions.[157] It noted that the term 'conflict not of an international character' under

---

[148] Memorandum from John Yoo, Deputy Assistant Attorney General and Robert J. Delahunty, Special Counsel to William J. Haynes II, General Counsel, Department of Defence, available at http://www.justice.gov/olc/docs/memo-laws-taliban-detainees.pdf p. 10. Accessed 16 September 2020.

[149] Ibid., p. 1.

[150] The relevant provisions are outlined in Title 10, Subtitle A, Part II, Chapter 47 U.S. Code.

[151] §948b(2)(g) and §948c Military Commissions Act of 2006.

[152] §948a(1)(i).

[153] 548 U.S. 557 (2006).

[154] The decision in *Hamdan* followed the earlier Supreme Court rulings in *Hamdi v. Rumsfeld* 124 S. Ct. 2633 (2004) and *Rasul v. Bush* 124 S. Ct. 2686 (2004). In both cases, the Court found that Guantánamo Bay detainees are entitled to a meaningful opportunity to contest the factual basis for their detention before a neutral decision maker and to invoke the jurisdiction of the US federal courts.

[155] *Hamdan v. Rumsfeld* 548 U.S. 557 (2006).

[156] *Hamdan v. Rumsfeld* 548 U.S. 557 (2006).

[157] Ibid., p. 65.

Common Article 3 was applied in contradistinction to a conflict between nations, which was demonstrated by the fundamental logic of the Convention's provisions.[158] The phrase should thus be read in its literal meaning and interpreted as having as wide a scope as possible.[159] The Court did acknowledge that the scope and application of Common Article 3 and in particular the meaning of 'not of an international character' was not expressly defined within the text of the Conventions. However, its meaning has been explained by additional treatises and commentaries relied on by the US Supreme Court itself.

The Court's decision has been criticised on the basis that it has not clarified the legal status of the conflict to which IHL applies.[160] In particular, while sustained references were made to the term 'war' and the applicability of IHL, there appeared to be limited engagement with the status of the relevant conflict and by proxy the appropriate status of the parties involved in the conflict.[161] The goal of Common Article 3 is to protect core humanitarian values for both state and non-state actors hence conflicts which fall under the scope of Common Article 3 should be formally recognised.[162] Consequently, until a formal judicial determination on the particular conflicts, which fall within the mandate of Common Article 3 is made, states can continue to interpret the application of Common Article 3 in a manner restricting Geneva Convention obligations. This is another problematic legacy of the 'War on Terror'.

In conclusion, having put forward a number of legal arguments severely restricting the general applicability of the relevant international legal norms and the accessibility of specific legal protections, the US proceeded to operationalise various components of the 'War on Terror'. A number of reports and cases are now available, in which the egregious nature of the counter-terrorism measures utilised within HVDP and the extraordinary renditions circuits has been discussed.[163] What these reports and cases crystalize is that despite the adoption of very comprehensive and stringent domestic legislative measures and procedures as well as transnational cooperation through NATO and the UNSC, the US consciously chose to engage in a number of clandestine and unaccountable transnational security policies operating outside the established legal framework.[164] This line of decision-making raises the question of what are the drivers behind a particular counter-terrorism approach. To put this question in a slightly different manner—why did the US consider its expansive and comprehensive legislative measures as insufficient to combat the threat of terrorism

---

[158] Ibid., p. 67.

[159] Ibid., p. 68. The US Supreme Court referred to a number of Geneva Convention III commentaries in discussing this point.

[160] Ni Aolain 2006–2007, p. 1546.

[161] Ibid., p. 1551.

[162] Ibid., p. 1560.

[163] See further Venice Commission, *Opinion on the International Legal Obligations of Council of Europe Member States in Respect of Secret Detention Facilities and Inter-State Transport of Prisoners*, Opinion no. 363/2005 CDL-AD (2006) 009.

[164] On this point, see for example Cole 2009, pp. 146–148 and Roach 2011, pp. 238–308. The Open Society Justice Initiative 2013.

thus opting to develop and rely on the 'War on Terror' paradigm with all of its components? This rather salient question will be the focus of Sect. 60.3.

60.4 The post 9/11 Securitisation Catalysts and the Legacy of the 'War on Terror'

In 2003, David Dyzenhaus noted that the US and a number of other states were gripped by a 'moral panic' following the events of 9/11.[165] While periods of moral panic are not new to societies—particularly in the context of national security emergencies—what tends to change is the episode, person or group of persons, which becomes defined as a threat to society.[166] The object of the panic can be quite novel; however it can also be something which has been in existence for a long time and has suddenly reappears in the limelight.[167] While the threat of terrorism and public acts of terrorism are certainly not new, as discussed above, the events of 9/11 have been perceived as unique and the threat by international terrorist organisations as unprecedented. This approach to the events of 9/11 could be explained by the correlation between the volatility or intensity of the moral panic and the Executive's decisions taken as a response to the event resulting in the panic.[168]

The events of 9/11—the scale of destruction, the callousness of the attack and the number of casualties—arguably touched a chord with the international community in a manner previous terrorist attacks have not.[169] The multi-faceted and multi-front response led by the US has been forceful; as noted by then President George W. Bush himself: 'every means of diplomacy, every tool of intelligence, every instrument of law enforcement, every financial influence, and every necessary weapon of war' was to be used for 'the destruction and the defeat of the global terror network'.[170] The ensuing 'War on Terror' has resulted in severe and lengthy restrictions of the rights and liberties of individual terrorist suspects and has perhaps permanently recalibrated[171] the relationship between such suspects and the state; moreover as the expansive domestic legislative and other measures suggest this recalibration has

---

[165] Dyzenhaus 2003, p. 2.

[166] Cohen 2002, p. 1. See also Tushnet 2003 and Young 2007.

[167] Cohen 2002, p. 1.

[168] Ibid., *p. xxxii.*

[169] Jenkins et al. 2014, p. 5.

[170] Please see further 'Transcript of President Bush's Address', *CNN News* 21 September 2001 available at http://edition.cnn.com/2001/US/09/20/gen.bush.transcript/. Accessed 16 September 2020.

[171] The concept of 'downward recalibration' of rights has been discussed in detail in De Londras 2011 and Fenwick 2010.

affected not only those who are suspected of terrorist activity but also those who may become a terrorist.[172]

Jenkins has argued that the entrenched post 9/11 moral panic and lingering fear of whether/when another attack might occur, has challenged both the ability of the state to provide security and the integrity of the international order in a world increasingly reliant on transnational networks.[173] Thus, the US and other states had to be seen to respond forcefully; the ensuing domestic and international securitisation and transnational intelligence and political cooperation have been some of the results.[174] There is arguably a (strong) link between the intense moral panic, which gripped the US, and the announcement of and subsequent engagement in a multi-front transnational counter-terrorism campaign. However, there are other factors, which also need to be examined to understand what drove the construction of the 'War on Terror' as a whole as well as separate counter-terrorism measures within it.

In recent years, there have been many speculations over the Executive's legal interpretation and decision-making, particularly in relation to matters of national security.[175] The debates on how and why the Executive arrives at a certain understanding of its legal constraints and the extent to which expansive national security and counter-terrorism measures proposed by the Executive can be adequately restrained by existing legal obligations have persevered.[176] Within the moral panic following 9/11 one of key legal questions for the US Executive arguably would have been what is the proper—i.e. within the existing international and domestic legal commitments—response to terrorism. This question would likely have been followed by another—would a strictly legislative approach be sufficient to effectively respond to 9/11 and pre-empt future terrorist threats? As discussed above, the US opted for a multi-faceted and multi-front transnational counter-terrorism campaign with the Executive approach, particularly in relation to the interpretation of the applicability and scope of certain international legal obligations, being heavily criticised. Some of the measures adopted as part of the 'War on Terror' such as components of the HVDP have been consistently referred to as unlawful[177] and have subsequently been dismantled.[178] However, as noted by Dyzenhaus, all institutional

---

[172] See for example Duffy 2015; Donohue 2008; Ramraj et al. 2012; Masferrer and Walker 2013. See also UK Counter Extremism and Safeguarding Bill 2016 and the UK Investigatory Powers Act 2016.

[173] Jenkins et al. 2014, p. 9.

[174] Ibid.

[175] Ingber 2013, p. 19.

[176] Ibid. See also Posner 2006; Posner and Vermeule 2007; Sunstein 2004; Cole 2003; Bickel 1986 and Kavanagh 2011.

[177] For commentary, see for example Wilson 2005, Duffy 2015 and Venice Commission, *Opinion on the International Legal Obligations of Council of Europe Member States in Respect of Secret Detention Facilities and Inter-State Transport of Prisoners*, Opinion no. 363/2005 CDL-AD (2006) 009 amongst many others.

[178] Executive Order 13491 revoked all executive directives, orders, and regulations including but not limited to those issued to or by the CIA between 11 September 2001 and January 2009. Thus, in effect, secret detention facilities were no longer to be used, enhanced interrogation was prohibited,

actors involved in the proposal, implementation and assessment of national security measures—the Executive in particular—tend to demonstrate a compulsion of legality or the compulsion to justify all acts of state as having a legal basis or the authority of law.[179]

In constructing its 'War on Terror' paradigm, the US Executive put forward extensive legal arguments in support of its interpretation of the general (in)applicability of the human rights framework, (ir)relevance of specific humanitarian law provisions to individuals captured and detained within the 'War on Terror'. Overall, the US aimed to provide legal justification for all key and distinct components of its 'war' as well as create an environment within which the applicability of the relevant human rights and humanitarian law provisions was uncertain or severely restricted. The liability limiting determination that the 'War on Terror' is a novel type of armed conflict is an illustration of how the US sought to provide a veneer of legality for the severe restriction on individual rights of terrorist suspects. The manner in which this veneer of legality has been constructed demonstrates an ever more perfunctory approach to international legal obligations by the US—an approach which arguably has become entrenched as evidenced by more recent comments by the current US administration.[180]

60.5 Conclusion

The expansive development of the international human rights and humanitarian law frameworks post-1945 has been one of the defining features of the 20th century. The number of signed conventions, treaties and associated documents indicates states' normative acceptance of their international legal obligations. Following the events of 9/11, these obligations have tended not to be a priority when set against national security concerns.[181] As the creation and operation of the US 'War on Terror' illustrates, in order to engage in this expansive transnational counter-terrorism campaign,

---

the full protections of Geneva Conventions I-IV and all other relevant international provisions were made available to remaining detainees. Extraordinary renditions—subject to improved monitoring mechanisms to prevent ill treatment—have however remained an available counter-terrorism tool for the US. Special Task Force on Interrogations and Transfer Policies Issues: Its Recommendations to the President, Department of Justice (Office of the Attorney General), 24 August 2009 (updated on 15 September 2014), full text available at https://www.justice.gov/opa/pr/special-task-force-interrogations-and-transfer-policies-issues-its-recommendations-president. Accessed 16 September 2020.

[179] Dyzenhaus 2008; for further discussion on legalism and legality, please refer to Fuller 1949; Shklar 1964; Shapiro 2011; and Dyzenhaus 2006.

[180] 'US quits 'biased' UN Human Rights Council' *BBC News* 20 June 2018, full text available here https://www.bbc.com/news/44537372 Accessed 16 September 2020 and Schwirtz, M. 'At the United Nations, Fears of a 'New World Disorder' as Trump Returns' *The New York Times* 24 September 2018, full text available here https://www.nytimes.com/2018/09/24/world/united-nations-united-states-trump-isolationism.html. Accessed 16 September 2020.

[181] See for example Gearty 2013; Wilson 2005; Brems 2011; UN General Assembly 2010 amongst many texts making this argument.

the US sought to severely restrict individual rights protections and limit the applicability of international human rights law both through legislative means and Executive decisions.

This 'War' could not have been fully operationalised without the conducive environment created by the intense international securitisation led by the UNSC and NATO however. Both organisations strongly encouraged states to engage in bi- and multi-lateral arrangements to fight terrorism, bi- and multi-lateral intelligence cooperation and exchange of information and individual or collective assistance to combat the threat of terrorism. Through the so-called law making UN Security Council Resolution 1373, the creation of the Security Council Counter Terrorism Committee and the first invocation of Article 5 of the North Atlantic Treaty, these bodies demonstrated willingness to facilitate a transnational environment accommodative of expansive counter-terrorism measures. It is within this atmosphere focused on pre-empting, preventing and muscularly responding to the threat of Al Qaeda and international terrorism in general that the US 'War on Terror' became a defining paradigm in the decade following the events of 9/11. The language and most components of this 'War on Terror' may no longer be in use. Its legacy however continues to cast a deep shadow.

References

Books, (Online) Articles and Chapters in Books

Alvarez JE (2003a) Hegemonic International Law Revisited. American Journal of International Law 97:873–888

Alvarez JE (2003b) The UN's 'War' on Terrorism. International Journal of Legal Information 31:238–250

Bellamy AJ (2008) Fighting Terror: Ethical Dilemmas. Palgrave Macmillan, New York

Bickel AM (1986) The Least Dangerous Branch: The Supreme Court at the Bar of Politics. Yale University Press, New Haven

Blackbourn J (2014) Anti-terrorism Law and Normalising Northern Ireland. Routledge, London

Brems E (2011) Transitional Justice in the Case Law of the European Court of Human Rights. The International Journal of Transitional Justice 5:282

Charlesworth H, Coicaud J M (2010) Fault Lines of International Legitimacy. Cambridge University Press, Cambridge

Cohen S (2002) Folk Devils and Moral Panics. Routledge, New York

Cole D (2003) Enemy Aliens: Double Standards and Constitutional Freedoms in the War on Terrorism. W.W. Norton & Co., New York

Cole D (2009) English Lessons: Analysis of UK and US Responses to Terrorism. Current Legal Problems 62:136–167

Committee on Legal Affairs and Human Rights, Secret Detentions and Illegal Transfers of Detainees involving Council of Europe Member States, AS/Jur (2007) 36

Davis FD, De Londras F (2014) Critical Debates on Counter-Terrorism Judicial Review. Cambridge University Press, Cambridge

De Londras F (2011) Detention in the 'War on Terror': Can Human Rights Fight Back? Cambridge University Press, Cambridge

Dickson B (2010) The European Convention on Human Rights and the Conflict in Northern Ireland. Oxford University Press, Oxford

Donohue L (2008) The Cost of Counter-Terrorism: Power, Politics and Liberty. Cambridge University Press, Cambridge

Duffy H (2015) The 'War on Terror' ad the Framework of International Law. Cambridge University Press, Cambridge

Dyzenhaus D (2003) Humpty Dumpty Rules or the Rule of Law: Legal Theory and the Adjudication of National Security. Australian Journal of Legal Philosophy 28:1–30

Dyzenhaus D (2006) The Constitution of Law; Legality in a Time of Emergency. Cambridge University Press, New York

Dyzenhaus D (2008) Introduction: Legality in a Time of Emergency. Windsor Review of Legal & Social Issues 24:1–4

Dyzenhaus D, Thwaites R (2007) Legality and Emergency – The Judiciary in a Time of Terror. In: Lynch A, MacDonald E, Williams G (eds) Law and Liberty in the War on Terror. The Federation Press, Sydney, pp 9–27

Fenwick H (2010) Recalibrating ECHR Rights and the Role of the HRA post 9/11: Reasserting International Human Rights Norms in the 'War on Terror'? Current Legal Problems 63:153–234

Fuller L L (1949) The Case of the Speluncian Explorers. Harvard Law Review 62:616–645

Gearty C (2013) Liberty and Security. Polity Press, Cambridge

Goldsmith J (2009) The Terror Presidency: Law and Judgment inside the Bush Administration. W.W. Norton & Company, New York

Goldsmith J (2012) Power and Constraint. W.W. Norton & Company, New York

Goldstone R (2005) The Tension between Combating Terrorism and Protecting Civil Liberties. In: Wilson R A (ed) Human Rights in the 'War on Terror'. Cambridge University Press, Cambridge, pp. 157–169

Goold BJ, Lazarus L (2007) Security and Human Rights. Hart Publishing, Portland OR

Greene A (2018) Permanent States of Emergency and the Rule of Law: Constitutions in an Age of Crisis. Hart Publishing, Oxford

Gross O, Ni Aolain F (2001) Emergency, War and International Law—Another Perspective. Nordic Journal of International Law 70:29–63

Habermas J (2006) The Divided West. Polity Press, London

Happold M (2003) Security Council Resolution 1373 and the Constitution of the United Nations. Leiden Journal of International Law 16:593–610

Ingber R (2013) Human Rights, National Security, and Executive Branch Legal Decisionmaking. Administrative and Regulatory Law News 38:19

Jenkins D, Jacobsen A, Henriksen A (2014) The Long Decade: How 9/11 Changed the Law. Oxford University Press, Oxford

Kavanagh A (2011) Constitutionalism, Counter-Terrorism and the Courts: Changes in the British Constitutional Landscape. International Journal of Constitutional Law (ICON) 9:172–199

Klabbers J, Peters A, Ulfstein G (2009) The Constitutionalization of International Law. Oxford University Press, Oxford

Krisch N (2003) The Rise and Fall of Collective Security: Terrorism, US Hegemony, and the Plight of the Security Council. In: Walter C, Voneky S, Roeben V, Schorkopf F (2003) Terrorism as a Challenge for National and International Law: Security versus Liberty. Springer, Berlin, pp 879–908

Lehto M (2010) War on Terror—Armed Conflict with Al-Qaida? Nordic Journal of International Law 78:499–511

Luban D (2002) The War on Terrorism and the End of Human Rights. Philosophy & Public Policy Quarterly 22:9–14

Luban D (2005) Eight Fallacies about Liberty and Security. In: Wilson R A (ed) Human Rights in the 'War on Terror'. Cambridge University Press, Cambridge, pp 242–258

Lynch A, MacDonald E, Williams G (2007) Law and Liberty in the War on Terror. The Federation Press, Sydney

Masferrer A, Walker C (2013) Counter-Terrorism, Human Rights and the Rule of Law. Edward Elgar, Gloucester
Ni Aolain F (2006–2007) *Hamdan* and Common Article 3: Did the Supreme Court Get it Right? Minnesota Law Review 91:1523–1561
Ni Aolain F, Gross O (2013) Guantanamo and Beyond. Cambridge University Press, Cambridge
Perry N (2003) The Numerous Federal Legal Definitions of Terrorism: The Problem of Too Many Grails. Journal of Legislation 30:249–274
Pictet JS (1960) Commentary on the Geneva Conventions 12 August 1949. International Committee of the Red Cross, Geneva
Posner R (2006) Not a Suicide Pact: The Constitution in a Time of National Emergency. Oxford University Press, New York
Posner E A, Vermeule E (2007) Terror in the Balance: Security, Liberty, and the Courts. Oxford University Press, New York
Powell C H (2007) The Legal Authority of the United Nations Security Council. In: Goold B J, Lazarus L (eds) Security and Human Rights. Hart Publishing, Portland, pp. 157–184
Poynting S, Whyte D (2012) Counter-Terrorism and State Political Violence: The 'War on Terror' as Terror. Routledge, London
Ramraj V (2014) Counter-Terrorism's Engagement with Transnational Legality. In: Jenkins D, Jacobsen A, Henriksen A (eds) The Long Decade: How 9/11 Changed the Law. Oxford University Press, Oxford, pp. 121–137
Ramraj VV, Hor M, Roach K, Williams G (2012) Global Anti-Terrorism Law and Policy. Cambridge University Press, Cambridge
Roach K (2011) The 9/11 Effect: Comparative Counter-Terrorism. Cambridge University Press, New York
Roach K (2015) Comparative Counter-Terrorism Law. Cambridge University Press, Cambridge
Robinson M (2005) Connecting Human Rights, Human Development and Human Security. In: Wilson R A (ed) Human Rights in the 'War on Terror'. Cambridge University Press, Cambridge, pp. 308–317
Shapiro S J (2011) Legality. Harvard University Press, Cambridge, MA
Shklar J (1964) Legalism. Harvard University Press, Cambridge, MA
Sunstein C (2004) Minimalism at War. Supreme Court Review 47–109
Szasz P (2002) The Security Council starts Legislating. American Journal of International Law 96:901–905
Talmon S (2005) The Security Council as World Legislature. American Journal of International Law 99:175–193
Taylor Saito N (2008) From Chinese Exclusion to Guantánamo Bay: Plenary Power and the Prerogative State. University Press of Colorado, CO
The Open Society Justice Initiative (2013) Globalizing Torture: CIA Secret Detention and Extraordinary Rendition. GHP Media, Inc., New York
Tushnet M (2003) Defending *Korematsu*?: Reflections on Civil Liberties in Wartime. Wisconsin Law Review 23:273–307
UN General Assembly (2010) Joint Study on Global Practices in Relation to Secret Detention in the Context of Countering Terrorism of the Rapporteur on the Promotion and Protection of Human Rights and Fundamental Freedoms while Countering Terrorism; the Special Rapporteur on Torture and Other Cruel, Inhuman or Degrading Treatment or Punishment; the Working Group on Arbitrary Detention the Working Group on Enforced or Involuntary Disappearances UN Doc. A/HRC/13/42
Walter C, Voneky S, Roeben V, Schorkopf F (2003) Terrorism as a Challenge for National and International Law: Security versus Liberty. Springer, Berlin
Wilson RA (2005) Human Rights in the 'War on Terror'. Cambridge University Press, Cambridge
Young J (2007) The Vertigo of Late Modernity. Sage Publications, London

Cases, Advisory Opinions, Judgments, Protocols and Other Documents

A. and Others v the United Kingdom, Application no. 3455/05, Judgment of 19 February 2009
Advisory Opinion Concerning Legal Consequences of the Construction of a Wall in the Occupied Palestinian Territory, International Court of Justice (ICJ), 9 July 2004
Al-Adsani v. the United Kingdom, Application no. 35763/97, Judgment 21 November 2001
Democratic Republic of Congo (DRC) v. Uganda, Judgment 19 December 2005
Hamdan v. Rumsfeld 548 U.S. 557 (2006)
Hamdi v. Rumsfeld 124 S. Ct. 2633 (2004)
Hassan v. the United Kingdom Application no. 29750/09, Judgment 16 September 2014
International Committee of the Red Cross (ICRC), *Geneva Convention for the Amelioration of the Condition of the Wounded and Sick in Armed Forces in the Field (First Geneva Convention),* 12 August 1949, 75 UNTS 31
International Committee of the Red Cross (ICRC), *Geneva Convention for the Amelioration of the Condition of Wounded, Sick and Shipwrecked Members of Armed Forces at Sea (Second Geneva Convention),* 12 August 1949, 75 UNTS 85
International Committee of the Red Cross (ICRC), *Geneva Convention Relative to the Treatment of Prisoners of War (Third Geneva Convention),* 12 August 1949, 75 UNTS 135
International Committee of the Red Cross (ICRC), *Geneva Convention Relative to the Protection of Civilian Persons in Time of War (Fourth Geneva Convention),* 12 August 1949, 75 UNTS 287
International Committee of the Red Cross (ICRC), *Protocol Additional to the Geneva Conventions of 12 August 1949, and relating to the Protection of Victims of International Armed Conflicts (Protocol I),* 8 June 1977, 1125 UNTS 3
International Committee of the Red Cross (ICRC), *Protocol Additional to the Geneva Conventions of 12 August 1949, and relating to the Protection of Victims of Non-International Armed Conflicts (Protocol II),* 8 June 1977, 1125 UNTS 609
Ireland v the United Kingdom [1978] ECHR 1
Jurisdiction), IT-94-1, International Criminal Tribunal for the former Yugoslavia (ICTY), 2 October 1995
Landinelli Silva v Uruguay, Case No. 34/1978
Lawless v Ireland (No 3) [1961] ECHR 2
Legality of the Threat or Use of Nuclear Weapons, Advisory Opinion, International Court of Justice (ICJ), 8 July 1996
Military Commissions Act of 2006
Prosecutor v. Dusko Tadić aka "Dule" (Decision on the Defence Motion for Interlocutory Appeal on Prosecutor v. Ramush Haradinaj, Idriz Balaj and Lahi Brahimaj, Case No. IT-04-84-T, ICTY, 3 April 2008
Rasul v. Bush 124 S. Ct. 2686 (2004)
Report by the Special Rapporteur, Extrajudicial, Summary or Arbitrary Executions (2005) UN Doc. E/CN.4/2005/7
Report of the Working Group on Arbitrary Detention (2006) UN Doc. E/CN.4/2006/7
UN Human Rights Committee (HRC), CCPR General Comment No. 29: Article 4: Derogations during a State of Emergency, UN Doc. CCPR/C/21/Rev.1/Add.11 (2001)
UN Security Council Resolution 1368, UN Doc. S/RES/1368 (2001)
UN Security Council Resolution 1373, UN Doc. S/RES/1373 (2001)
UN Security Council Resolution 1624, UN Doc. S/RES/1624 (2005)
UN Security Council Resolution 2249, UN Doc. S/RES/2249 (2015)
Uniting and Strengthening America by Providing Appropriate Tools Required to Intercept and Obstruct Terrorism (USA PATRIOT ACT) Act of 2001
Varnava v. Turkey Applications Nos. 16064/90, 16065/90, 16066/90, 16068/90, 16069/90, 16070/90, 16071/90, 16072/90 and 16073/90, Judgment 18 September 2009

Venice Commission (2006) Opinion on the International Legal Obligations of Council Member States in Respect of Secret Detention Facilities and Inter-State Transport of Prisoners, Opinion no. 363/2005, CDL-AD (2006)

Dr. Rumyana van Ark (nee Grozdanova) is a Post-Doctoral Researcher in Terrorism, Counter-Terrorism and Human Rights at the T.M.C. Asser Instituut/University of Amsterdam. She holds a PhD in Law from the University of Durham, an LLM in Criminology and Criminal Justice from University College Dublin and a BA (Hons.) Legal Studies with Business by Nottingham Trent University. Her research focuses on the evolving relationship between the individual (terror suspect) and the state following acts of terrorism. She is currently co-authoring a book on *Children's Rights, 'Foreign Fighters' and Counter-Terrorism: The Children of Nowhere.*

Chapter 61
Jihad Misplaced for Terrorism: An Overview of the Boko Haram Crisis from Islamic and International Humanitarian Law Perspectives

Muhammad-Basheer A. Ismail

Contents

61.1 Introduction	1390
61.2 Boko Haram: Its Emergence, Causes and Organisational Structure	1391
61.2.1 Emergence of Boko Haram	1391
61.2.2 Causes of Boko Haram Crisis	1392
61.2.3 Organisational Structure of Boko Haram	1393
61.3 Terrorism, Jihad and Boko Haram	1395
61.3.1 Defining Terrorism	1396
61.3.2 Defining Jihad	1397
61.3.3 Is Boko Haram Engaged in Jihad?	1398
61.3.4 Can Boko Haram Declare Jihad?	1400
61.3.5 Is Boko Haram Engaged in an Internal Armed Conflict under IHL?	1401
61.4 Basic Principles of Islamic Law of Jihad and IHL	1403
61.4.1 Principle of Military Necessity	1403
61.4.2 Principle of Distinction	1404
61.4.3 Principle of Proportionality	1405
61.4.4 Principle of Humanity	1406
61.5 Trial of Boko Haram Suspects in Domestic Courts or before the International Criminal Court	1409
61.6 Conclusion	1414
References	1415

Abstract The Boko Haram mayhem has not only become a national disaster for the Nigerian state but has gradually metamorphosed into what has now become almost a regional catastrophe. It has been argued though that Boko Haram embraced terrorist activities as a result of the gross socio-economic injustice and unfairness that has painfully become so endemic in Nigeria. The situation becomes more of a concern when people hide behind religious doctrine to perpetrate gruesome and nefarious acts. Should activities be structured around terrorism under the pretext that one is embarking on Islamic and mandatory acts of *jihad*? This question continuously agitates the minds of Muslims and some non-Muslims alike. This chapter

---

M.-B. A. Ismail (✉)
School of Law, University of Hull, Hull, England, UK
e-mail: m.a.ismail@hull.ac.uk

will examine the activities of Boko Haram within the perimeters of Islamic law (the legal system which Boko Haram ostensibly seeks to establish in Northern Nigeria) and international humanitarian law with a view to assessing the compatibility or otherwise of Boko Haram's activities with the two legal regimes. This chapter also examines whether Boko Haram can genuinely claim any justification for its activities by relying on the principles of jihad under the Islamic law of armed conflict. The chapter further examines the propriety of prosecuting the leadership of Boko Haram for war crimes and crimes against humanity before the International Criminal Court (ICC) as opposed to Nigerian courts.

Keywords International humanitarian law · Islamic law · Terrorism · Jihad · International law · Boko Haram

61.1 Introduction

The Boko Haram mayhem has not only become a national disaster for the Nigerian state but also gradually metamorphosed into what has now become almost a regional catastrophe. It has been argued though that Boko Haram embraced terrorist activities as a result of the gross socio-economic injustice and unfairness that has painfully become so endemic in Nigeria. The situation becomes more of a concern when people hide behind religious doctrine to perpetrate gruesome and nefarious acts. This chapter contends that activities need not be structured around terrorism under the pretext that one is embarking on Islamic and mandatory act of *jihad*. This contention raises question that continuously agitates the mind of Muslims and some non-Muslims alike.

The chapter examines the activities of Boko Haram within the perimeter of Islamic law (the legal system which Boko Haram ostensibly seeks to establish in Northern Nigeria), and international humanitarian law with a view of assessing the compatibility or otherwise of Boko Haram's activities with the two legal regimes. It is argued in this chapter that the Islamic law of armed conflict and international humanitarian law are compatible in their condemnation of the terrorist activities of the Boko haram. The chapter further argues that Boko Haram's claim to engage in the Islamic jihad cannot be justified under the Islamic law of armed conflict. In investigating the propriety of prosecuting members of Boko Haram for war crimes and crimes against humanity before the International Criminal Court (ICC) as opposed to Nigerian courts, the chapter argues that the interest of justice will be well served by bringing such trials before the ICC considering the serious nature of the terrorist acts of Boko Haram, coupled with the unwillingness and inability of the Nigerian government to carry out proper investigation and diligent prosecution.

61.2 Boko Haram: Its Emergence, Causes and Organisational Structure

The catastrophe created by Boko Haram will, no doubt, pass for being one of the worst global crises. This section examines how Boko Haram came into existence and grew into becoming a monstrous terrorist organisation. It also examines the formation of the group and the structural platform upon which the group operates.

61.2.1 Emergence of Boko Haram

The emergence of Boko Haram in Nigeria was indeed remarkable in the sense that it shook the economic, social and political strata of the Nigerian state since 2009. The colossal nature of that challenging moment culminated into various legal implications, which crave for solutions from the international and Islamic law perspectives. The flamboyant display of acts of terrorism under the disguise of Islamic jihad by a group that calls itself *Jama'at Ahl us-Sunnah li'd-Da'wah wa'l-Jihad,* but popularly identified within the media and by the people as 'Boko Haram'[1] had gained notoriety. The name *Jama'at Ahl us-Sunnah li'd-Da'wah wa'l-Jihad,* which has been translated in Arabic to mean 'Congregation of People of Sunnah for Preaching and Struggle' came into the lime-light after an attack on the Bauchi prison in September, 2010. Interestingly, 'Boko Haram' has been loosely translated from the local Hausa language as 'Western education is forbidden', perhaps due to its intense aversion to anything Western and interaction with it. Considering the origin of the word 'Boko Haram', one would see that it is made up of two words that emanate from Hausa and Arabic languages—'Boko' from the Hausa language and 'Haram' from the Arabic language. 'Boko' has often been wrongly translated as if it has a link with the English word 'Book'. In Hausa linguistic, 'Boko' stands for a fraud, a sham or the Western kind of education. On the other hand, 'Haram' in Arabic signifies 'forbidden' rather than 'sinful' or 'ungodly'.

The Boko Haram group was supposedly established in Maiduguri, in the North-Eastern part of Nigeria by Muhammad Yusuf in 2002.[2] Initially, the group started its

---

[1] See Roman 2012, pp. 37–15. See generally Newman 2013.

[2] According to the historical account given by Andrew Walker, as at 2002 there was no group known as Boko Haram; instead there was a group known as the "Nigerian Taliban", established by Muhammad Ali. The group ostracized itself to a village called Kanama, near the Nigeria-Niger border in Yobe State. Because of a dispute in December 2003 between the group and the police which later led to an invasion of its mosque by the army that claimed the lives of about seventy members of the group, including Muhammad Ali, a few survivors of the group subsequently formed a group that was to be known as *Jama'at Ahl us-Sunnah li'd* under the leadership of Muhammad Yusuf in 2004. See Walker n.d. There is yet another contention that Boko Haram has been in existence since 1995 under the leadership of one Lawan Abubakar, who, after having embarked on further studies at the University of Madinah, Saudi Arabia, Muhammad Yusuf then took over leadership of the group from. See Isioma 2011.

preaching activities sometime in 2002 as a peaceful organisation with no intention to impose its politico-religious views on anyone in the country.[3] The group later abandoned its non-violence posture and embraced violence, which consequently became, not only a national disaster, but a transnational catastrophe. This change appeared to have been instigated when its leader, Muhammad Yusuf, was killed by the Nigeria Police Force in July 2009 in what was widely considered an extra-judicial killing.[4]

61.2.2 Causes of Boko Haram Crisis

The Boko Haram crisis in Nigeria has been attributed and linked to various causes ranging from political, economic and social factors to reason of religious fundamentalism. Some are of the view that the poverty rate in Northern Nigeria, which currently stands at 75%, compared with the Southern part of the country with 27%, might have provided a fertile ground for Boko Haram to grow.[5] The Oxford Research Group gave a typical example of Bornu State, which happens to be the birth-place of Boko Haram '83% of young people are illiterate; 48.5% of children do not go to school.'[6] The fact that Nigeria witnessed the eruption of religious violence in one of the most socio-economically deprived parts of the country should, therefore, not be a surprise. The Research Director of the Nigerian Economic Summit Group (NESG), gave a clear summary of one of the causes of Boko Haram crisis:

> The increasing poverty in Nigeria is accompanied by increasing unemployment. Unemployment is higher in the north than in the south... Government statistics show that the northern states have the highest proportion of uneducated persons. If you link a lack of education and attendant lack of opportunities to a high male youth population, you can imagine that some areas are actually a breeding ground for terrorism.[7]

The emergence of Boko Haram has also been linked to the argument of an unending clash of civilizations particularly between Islamic and Western civilisations.[8] It has almost become the trend that anything that has 'Islamic' as a qualifying adjective thus appears to be like a sort of bogeyman, which is combat ready to be in a furious contest with Western hegemony.[9] This contention, in a way, lends credence to Huntington's 'Clash of Civilizations' where he argues, in the course of examining the conflict that exists between Islam and the West, which seems to be endless, that

---

[3] See Hill 2012, p. 26. It was also the contention of Shehu Sanni, a Human Right activist that Boko Haram could not be said to be violent until the extra judicial killing of its leader, Muhammad Yusuf in 2009.

[4] Smith 2009.

[5] Thomson 2012, p. 49.

[6] See Rogers 2012, pp. 1–5.

[7] Cited in Rogers 2012, p. 4.

[8] See Onyebuchi and Chigozie 2013, p. 44.

[9] Wa Baile 2011, p.11.

'so long as Islam remains Islam and the West remains the West, this fundamental conflict between two great civilizations and ways of life will continue to define their relations in the future even as it has defined them for the past fourteen centuries.'[10] This hypothesis tends to reaffirm the clash of civilizations considering the on-going Boko Haram crisis among other problems in the Muslim states.[11]

61.2.3 Organisational Structure of Boko Haram

It is important to consider the level of sophistication displayed in numerous attacks by Boko Haram; their ability to hit their targets in several places all at once; and their competence to send new recruits for trainings in foreign countries.[12] The structural organisation of Boko Haram is mainly decentralised, and as such, seems amorphous in nature. Therefore, one may need to examine the hierarchical structure of Boko Haram setting; the command rules and the ability to enforce its discipline among its members; the weapons used by the group; its capability to prepare and execute co-ordinated attacks; and the number of its force.[13]

Boko Haram had a command structure that almost look like a professional military command[14] with Muhammad Yusuf as the spiritual head and commander in chief. He was assisted by two deputies, namely: Abubakar Shekau and Mamman Nur.[15] During the reign of Muhammad Yusuf, Boko Haram could be said to have a clear chain of command, which was headed by him.[16] Since the demise of Yusuf in 2009, Abubakar Shekau took over the leadership of the group, and operated in conjunction with the *Shura* council consisting of 30 members. The *Shura* council is a decision-making body that decides matters that are central to the strategy of the group and commands the group's regional cells.[17] At the state-level, the group had commanders in some states in Nigeria[18] who were directly responsible to Shekau, and each of the states' commanders had various local government commanders under their control.[19] With Shekau formally pledging allegiance to the so-called Islamic State of Iraq and

---

[10] Huntington 1996, p. 212.
[11] Mang 2014, p. 85.
[12] Solomon 2015, p. 89.
[13] Comer and Mburu 2015, p. 80.
[14] See Omeni 2020, p. 132.
[15] Varin 2016, p. 66.
[16] Ibid.
[17] Comolli 2015, p. 61.
[18] Such states include Kano, Sokoto, Borno, Kaduna, Yobe, Katsina and Bauchi. See Varin 2016, p. 66.
[19] Hollingsworth and Kemedi 2015, p. 208.

Syria (ISIS)[20] under the leadership of Abubakr Al-Baghdadi on March 2015,[21] Boko Haram tactically adopted an organisational structure that could be said to be a prototype of ISIS with 'an operational coordination which has progressively tightened up'.[22]

In 2015, the core fighters in Boko Haram were estimated to be in the range of 7000 to 10,000.[23] During 2016 and in the early part of 2017, there occurred a drastic reduction in the number of Boko Haram fighters due to the overwhelming strength of the Nigerian troops.[24]

Tracing the fountain of Boko Haram's funds, may be, however, complex. Some believe that Boko Haram had its sources of income from members of the group, donations from politicians, contributions from government functionaries and businessmen from within Nigeria[25] and links to al-Qaeda[26] and other well-financed groups in some Arab countries.[27] For instance, the Inter-governmental Action Group Against Money Laundering in West Africa raised an observation that Boko Haram has its funding partly from 'private donors and misapplied charitable donations'.[28] It was rumoured that the Nigerian government recently paid millions of dollars to secure the release of some Chibok girls that were kidnapped in 2014.[29]

The Nigerian military, with the assistance of neighbouring forces from Chad, Niger and Cameroon had regained territory formerly held under the control of Boko Haram. Regardless of this defeat, the terror emanating from Boko Haram activities has neither been abated nor diminished. Boko Haram still remains active and controls some areas around Mandara Mountains, which are within the outskirts of Gwoza town, by intermittently attacking dwellers of nearby villages, travellers and, in most cases, sending suicide bombers to detonate their devices within unsuspecting crowds.[30]

---

[20] The Islamic State of Iraq and Syria (ISIS) is also alternatively known as the Islamic State of Iraq and the Levant (ISIL), which the Arabs generally refer to as Daesh. It is a militant Islamist organisation which was formed in 1999 by Abu Musa al-Zarqawi under the leadership of Abubakar al-Baghdadi. It formerly exercised control over some key cities in Western Iraq following the capture of Monsul and the Sinjar massacre. See Arango 2014.

[21] See Boffey 2015.

[22] Iocchi 2015, p. 205.

[23] Dorrie 2015.

[24] See Onuoha and Oyewole 2018, pp. 6–8.

[25] See Comolli 2015, pp. 78–79. The US government officials confirmed that Boko Haram continuously received sponsorship from a highly-placed politician in Bornu from around 2007 up till 2009.

[26] Al-Qaeda, as the name indicates, is a broad-based multi-national Islamist organisation under the leadership of the late Osama bin Laden. It was founded in 1988.

[27] See Ryder 2015, p. 167.

[28] Inter-Governmental Action Group Against Money Laundering in West Africa (GIABA) 2010, p. 94.

[29] Burke 2016.

[30] MacEachern 2018, pp. 54–155.

The rate at which the principles of international humanitarian law (IHL) and Islamic law have been continuously violated by Boko Haram under a misconceived notion of waging the 'Islamic jihad' in the Northern part of Nigeria is gruesomely alarming. The several bombings and killings that took place in Abuja,[31] Bornu,[32] Kaduna,[33] Jos[34] and Kano[35] serve as a reminder of the callous and dangerous activism of Boko Haram. The abduction of more than 200 school girls at the Government Secondary School, Chibok, Bornu State by Boko Haram in April 2014 received a unified condemnation both nationally and internationally.[36] The colossal loss of human lives resulting from the terrorist acts perpetrated by Boko Haram since its inception in 2009, is over 27,000 with monumental humanitarian crisis that has rendered 1.8 million homeless.[37] The description given by President Buhari that 'Boko Haram is a typical example of small fires causing large fires'[38] cannot be far from been accurate.[39]

These indiscriminate killings of civilians consisting of women, children and elderly, coupled with the shocking disappearance of people, were perpetrated without regard to human dignity which is held in high esteem in both Islamic law and IHL.

61.3 Terrorism, Jihad and Boko Haram

The two terms, 'terrorism' and 'jihad' have, in the past few decades, been given a synonymous meaning by some commentators due to the prevailing internal conflicts in most Muslim States. Terrorism has now been notoriously associated with Muslim fighters.[40] The perception of jihad and terrorism needs to be properly contextualised in their distinct perspectives so that one does not wallow endlessly in the murky cesspit of this misconception.

---

[31] There were series of attacks in Abuja which Boko Haram claimed responsibility for, such as the June 16, 2011 suicide bomb blast of the Police Headquarters; the August 26, 2011 suicide bombing of the United Nations building where more than 200 lives were lost; bomb blast was also recorded in Zuba Park killing 70 people. See Aljazeera 2011.

[32] There were multitude of attacks by Boko Haram in Bornu State, the most recent of which happened on 16 February 2019 where 8 people were killed and several injured. See Aljazeera 2019.

[33] See Tarpel 2014.

[34] See The Sun 2015.

[35] See Mamah et al. 2012.

[36] BBC Africa 2014.

[37] See Human Rights Watch 2017, 391; see also VOA News 2018.

[38] Independent 2015.

[39] Ismail 2015, p. 19.

[40] Khan 2006, p. 187.

61.3.1 Defining Terrorism

The word terrorism is a concept that has become notoriously difficult to define.[41] It has persistently suffered from a lack of universally accepted definition, which has impeded the ability to comprehend and properly explain the term.[42] As far back as 1988, Schmid and Jongman documented 109 various and distinct definitions of terrorism.[43] It is necessary to focus on the legal and more specifically international law, rather than political meaning of terrorism.

There are some definitions that can still be taken on board. According to Schachter, terror is said to be a 'threat or use of violence in order to create extreme fear and anxiety in a target group so as to coerce them to meet political (or quasi-political) objectives of the perpetrators.'[44] Bassiouni offers the following definition:

Individual or collective coercive conduct employing strategies of terror violence which contain an international element or are directed against an internationally protected target and whose aim is to produce a power-oriented outcome.[45]

It is, however, the view of the author that the criteria set out in Bassiouni's definition appears to have been fulfilled by the Nigerian Terrorism (Prevention) Act, 2011 as covering act which is deliberately done with malice to: (i) unduly compel a government or international organization to perform or abstain from performing any act; (ii) seriously intimidate a population; (iii) seriously destabilize or destroy the fundamental political, constitutional, economic or social structure of a country or international organization; or (iv) otherwise influence such government or international organization by intimidation or coercion.[46]

The general understanding from these definitions of terrorism is that terrorist acts should contain some of or all these elements. Firstly, terrorists often resort to terrorism by using violence to intimidate or instil fear mainly to advance a political objective. Secondly, they always make civilians (not taking a direct part in the hostilities) their prime targets. Thirdly, terrorism is all about communication, which thrives on successful transmission through communication infrastructure. Terrorists, as we know, rely on the strength and the 'power of Internet, which they use for propaganda, recruiting, and instruction, among other purposes.'[47] Fourthly, terrorists also employ the tactics of psychology and fear with the aim of 'creating an atmosphere of fear, anxiety, and collapse in an attempt to exploit the subsequent emotional reaction for political purposes'[48] which may eventually lead to the killing of civilians in an indiscriminate manner. And lastly, terrorism is generally conducted by non-state actors (that is not to say states may not engage in the act of terrorism). One may

---

[41] Berkebile 2017, p. 5.
[42] Ismail 2016, p. 140.
[43] Schmid and Jongman 2005, pp. 5–6.
[44] Schachter 1991, p. 163.
[45] Bassiouni 1975, p. xiv.
[46] See s.1(2) (a) and (b).
[47] Smith 2015, p. 13.
[48] Ibid, 14.

therefore conclude that the indiscriminate violence committed by non-state actors against civilians, which is meant to inculcate fear in people, qualifies as terrorism.

It is obvious that international humanitarian law (IHL) does not make any provision for the definition of terrorism, but it prohibits most acts that will commonly be considered as terrorist in nature during armed conflicts.[49] The basic principle of the IHL is the total prohibition of indiscriminate, premeditated or direct attacks on civilians and civilian objects.

61.3.2 Defining Jihad

Jihad, as a concept, has suffered from multiple misunderstanding both from the self-acclaimed jihadists who would rather see jihad as a justification to perpetrate their nefarious activities, and some Western commentators who view jihad as a synonym for terrorism.[50] There are yet other writers who perceive jihad to mean '*harb al-muqaddasah*,' which means 'holy war' against the non-Muslims, even though the phrase '*harb al-muqaddasah*' is not to be found in the Quran or the Prophetic sayings.[51] The theoretical meaning and practical understanding of the jihad concept is far from these misperception and misuse ascribed to it.

The word 'jihad' is an Arabic expression that is derived from the verb *jahada*, which means to strive or exert oneself in doing something good or abstaining from doing something bad to the best of one's ability.[52] Basically, the concept of jihad signifies self-exertion and peaceful persuasion for the sake of God in contradistinction to violence or aggression.[53] During the early days of Islam, jihad was understood as a kind of clarion call to submit everything a person has towards the service of Islam, which may also necessitate the use of force in self-defense, if the need arises. Even at that, the spiritual dimension of the use of jihad was more prominent among the Muslims in the time of Prophet Muhammad. Jihad has not only become a 'state doctrine which legitimized pre-emptive self-defense and justified conquest',[54] it has now moved to a new level where it is invoked as justification for the struggle for power. The assertion made by Bassiouni vividly points to the fact that:

---

[49] For example, Article 33 of the Fourth Geneva Convention 1949 provides that 'collective penalties and likewise all measures of intimidation or of terrorism are prohibited.' See also Article 51, paragraph 2, of Additional Protocol I and Article 13, paragraph 2, of Additional Protocol II to the Geneva Conventions which prohibit categorically prohibit all acts aimed at perpetrating terror the civilians thus: 'Acts or threats of violence the primary purpose of which is to spread terror among the civilian population are prohibited'.

[50] See Silverman 2002, p. 78.

[51] Badawi 2003, p. 38. See also Esposito 2002, p. 27.

[52] Al-Dawoody 2011, p. 76.

[53] Ismail 2015, n 33, p. 25.

[54] Bassiouni 2008, p. 2.

[J]ihad as political violence has become nothing more than a revolutionary doctrine to justify those who engage in it by appealing to the legitimacy of their self-proclaimed ends.[55]

Jihad has, since the late twentieth and twenty-first centuries, gained tremendous currency among resistance groups, liberation forces, and so-called terrorist movements, all using it to legitimise their cause and as a means of stimulation to their followers.[56] With all these groups wanting to ascribe jihad to their respective causes based on their different understandings and interpretations, one is therefore put in a kind of quagmire in deciding whose interpretation is correct, and who among them is or are manipulating the tenets of jihad to legitimise and justify violence on a tremendous scale.

61.3.3 Is Boko Haram Engaged in Jihad?

The adherents of the Boko Haram kind of 'jihad' are convincingly prepared to sacrifice their lives in the name of enforcing the so-called 'religious instructions', which often lead to multiple loss of lives and properties. It is usually common for the Boko Haram militant group to invoke and rely on some Islamic injunctions to justify their 'jihadi' activities.[57] The so-called jihad embarked upon by Boko Haram has come under serious scrutiny from non-Muslim and Muslim commentators. Can jihad, as perceived by Boko Haram, be said to be compatible with the basic principles of Islamic jihad and IHL?

Boko Haram has persistently and consistently proclaimed its engagement in Islamic jihad despite numerous condemnations of its nefarious and inhuman activities from Muslim authorities worldwide.[58] One of the statements reportedly made by the leader of the Boko Haram, Shekau, warning the Nigerian government in the following words: 'Do not think jihad is over. Rather jihad has just begun'[59] is a confirmation of Boko Haram's conviction of the religiousness of its engagement. Non-state actors, in the form of militants, now increasingly rely on jihad, albeit wrongly, 'to justify attacks on civilians and civilian objects in ... fighting the perceived "far" enemy *(al-'aduw al-baid)* and "near" enemy *(al 'aduw al-qarib)*.'[60] It is one thing for Boko Haram to ascribe the Islamic jihad to its various activities, it is yet another to examine whether those activities are in strict compliance with the fundamental objectives of the Islamic legal system and core principles of jihad.

We must understand that Islamic law distinguishes what is now known as international armed conflicts (IACs) and non-international armed conflicts NIACs) in

---

[55] Ibid. 63.

[56] Esposito 2002, p. 26.

[57] Some of the Qur'anic injunctions quoted out of context to legitimise violence are: Qur'an 4:74–76; 4:84; 9:5; 9:13–15; 9:38–39; 9:111; 2:190–191; 2:216; 22:39–40; and 8:39.

[58] See Ainoko 2017.

[59] Tattersall and Maclean 2010.

[60] Sseyonjo 2012, p. 26. See also Al-Dawoody 2017, p. 996.

IHL, though using different terms to describe them. International armed conflicts, in Islamic jurisprudence, are generally referred to as Islamic jihad or Islamic law of *qital*, which indicate war situations between a Muslim and a non-Muslim state. Non-international armed conflicts, going by the views of Muslim jurists, are categorised into four, namely: *qital al-bughah*—fighting against rebels; *qital hiraabah*—fighting against terrorists or highway robbers; *hurub al-riddah*—wars of apostasy; and *qital al-khawarij*—fighting against violent religious fanatics.[61] We will focus more on *qital hiraabah* and *qital al-bughah* with a view to clearing any misgiving in the usage of the two terms.

It is important to distinguish jihad from *hiraabah* and *baghy* so as to contextualise rightly Boko Haram. It is instructive to stress that the concept of jihad has nothing in common with both *hiraabah* and *baghy*, since the two belong to a class of punishable offences under Islamic law. Some Islamic law scholars are of the view that the meaning of *hiraabah* could be extended to include acts of terrorism,[62] most especially if one considers the broad definition given by the famous Muslim jurist, Ibn Hazm, who defines a *hiraaba* offender as:

> [O]ne who puts people in fear on the road, whether or not with a weapon, at night or day, in urban areas or in open spaces, in the palace of a caliph or a mosque, with or without accomplices, in the desert or in the village, in a large or small city, with one or more people … making people fear that they'll be killed or have money taken or be raped … whether the attackers are one or many.[63]

Therefore, *irhab*, which is a derivation of *hiraabah*, can be seen as a form of attack on the civilian population by some group of people, otherwise referred to as terrorists. This position has been adopted by the Kingdom of Saudi Arabia, as well as other Muslim states, in a counterterrorism report that was submitted to the United Nations Security Council that

> In the Islamic Shariah, which the Kingdom applies and from which it derives its statutes, crimes of terrorism are included among the crimes of hirabah. The severest of penalties are applied to these crimes in the Islamic Shariah, as set forth in the Holy Koran [Koran 5:33].[64]

Baghy, on the other hand, is a kind of rebellion mainly against the authority of the Muslim states, rather than the civilians. In other words, *baghy* relate to political revolt against the leader, which makes it most appropriate to refer to *baghy* as a 'political uprising by specific group of people the *imam* [the leader].'[65] Thus, *baghy* will be more applicable to political uprising orchestrated by a particular group of people against the state authority without purposefully harming the civilians, unlike *hiraabah* which targets the civilians.[66] The punishments for the two criminal offences

---

[61] Al-Dawoody 2017, p. 1001.

[62] See Nafi 2004, pp. 80–82.

[63] Quoted in Quraish 2000, p.130.

[64] Report of the Kingdom of Saudi Arabia Submitted Pursuant to Paragraph 6 of Security Council Resolution 1373 (2001) Concerning Counter-terrorism, at 5, U.N. Doc. S/2001/1294 (26 December 2001).

[65] Sharif 2015

[66] El Fadl 1990, p. 151.

are not similar; more so, because of the serious nature of *hiraabah*, it appears to be more severe in punishment than *baghy*.[67]

It is obvious from the above meanings of *hiraabah* and *baghy* that the activities of the Boko Haram group align more with the meaning of *hiraabah* rather than with the concept of jihad. It is crucial to note that jihad recognises and agrees with the basic principles underlying IHL, which are military necessity, humanity, distinction and proportionality.[68] Before discussing the basic principles applicable to IHL and jihad, it is important to first examine whether Boko Haram satisfies the requirement for declaring or initiating jihad.

61.3.4 Can Boko Haram Declare Jihad?

The call for jihad, right from the period of the Prophet of Islam, in the seventh century, until what appeared, though arguably, to be the last official jihad initiated by the Ottoman Empire during the First World War, was strictly within the prerogative of Muslim states.[69] There is consensus amongst both classical and modern Islamic jurists that the decision to initiate military jihad or the use of force in self-defense to combat an actual invasion or a threat of aggression on a Muslim territory rests solely with state authority.[70] A renowned Hanbali scholar, Abdullah ibn Qudamah, was emphatic in his remark that 'declaring Jihad is the responsibility of the Ruler and consists of his independent legal judgment.'[71] Basically, jihad concerns one of the issues of public safety, which necessarily requires the approval or consent of those in position of authority among the Muslims owing to its sensitive character. To initiate or declare jihad without the authority to do so will be considered, under Islamic law, as an act of disobedience which could eventually result into terrorist activities.

Boko Haram, we must not forget, is a non-state actor operating within the geographical entity called Nigeria. Although, Boko Haram claims severally that it is engaged in jihad, which means that one would expect the group to comply with all relevant rules regulating armed conflict under Islamic law. Evidently, Nigeria was not under any threat of invasion or attack by any other country that could have justified resort to a defensive jihad. According to the consensus of Muslim jurists, Boko Haram or any organisation, party or group does not have the authority to initiate or declare jihad within a Muslim state.[72] The power to declare jihad, generally, is the sole prerogative of the state.[73] It must be noted, however, that non-state actors

---

[67] Penalty for *hiraabah*, see Qur'an 5:33–34, but for *baghy*, there is no specific punishment either in the Qur'an or Sunnah.

[68] These are discussed in Sects. 61.4.1–61.4.4 of this chapter.

[69] See Phares 2005, p. 44.

[70] See Ismail 2016, p. 151; Sseyonjo 2012, p. 15; and Shah 2013, p. 358.

[71] See Ibn Qudamah 1972, p. 184.

[72] Bulac 2004, p. 71.

[73] See Ismail 2016, p. 152; Shah 2008, p. 23.

or group of individuals will only have the authority to declare jihad in a situation where physical attack or invasion is imminent on the state and the Head of state is incapable or refuses to initiate jihad for the protection of the lives and properties of its inhabitants.[74] A good example of this is the Russian invasion of Afghanistan in 1979. The failure of the Afghan authority to declare jihad gave legitimacy to the declaration of jihad by the various Afghan leaders, which drew large support from Muslims around the world. Based on the activities of Boko Haram, it is important to ascertain whether Boko Haram is a party in a non-international armed conflicts (NIACs) under the international humanitarian law (IHL). This will be discussed in the next section.

61.3.5 Is Boko Haram Engaged in an Internal Armed Conflict under IHL?

The international humanitarian law (IHL), otherwise known as the law of armed conflict is the law that applies in the situation of an armed conflict, which therefore makes it important in the determination whether a situation qualifies as an armed conflict. According to the *Tadic* Case,[75] an armed conflict is said to exist 'whenever there is a resort to armed force between States or protracted armed violence between governmental authorities and organised armed groups or between such groups within a State.'[76] Legally, armed conflicts are classified into two types, namely international armed conflicts (IACs) and non-international armed conflicts (NIACs).

An armed conflict is international when, according to Common Article 2 to the Geneva Conventions, one or more States have recourse to armed force against another State, 'even if the state of war is not recognised by one of them.'[77] Once the armed forces of two States attack each other, the armed conflict automatically becomes an international armed conflict.[78]

To understand the concept of a non-international armed conflict, recourse must be had to the provisions of Common Article 3 of the Geneva Conventions and Article 1 of Additional Protocol II of the Geneva Conventions. According to Common Article 3, an 'armed conflict not of an international character occurring in the territory of one of the High Contracting Parties' is considered to be another category of conflict. Once there is an armed conflict within a state involving the government of the state and its opponents who are not the armed forces of another state, such conflict will be regarded as a non-international armed conflict.[79] Taken a cursory look at the

---

[74] See Ibid.

[75] *The Prosecutor v. Dusko Tadic*, Decision on the Defence Motion for Interlocutory Appeal on Jurisdiction, IT-94-1-A, 2 October 1995.

[76] Ibid., para.70.

[77] See Common Article 2 to the Geneva Conventions of 1949.

[78] Dinstein 2016, p. 36.

[79] Solis 2016, p. 163.

provisions of Common Article 3 to the Geneva Conventions, all non-international armed conflicts appear to be governed by its rules. However, Article 1 of Additional Protocol II gives a narrow threshold of application of its provisions by defining a non-international armed conflict as one:

> which take[s] place in the territory of a High Contracting Party between its armed forces and dissident armed forces or other organized armed groups which, under responsible command, exercise such control over a part of its territory as to enable them to carry out sustained and concerted military operations and to implement this Protocol.

Apparently, from the above definition, conflicts between groups do not fall within the ambit of the provisions of Article 1 of Additional Protocol II as it only applies 'to conflicts in which at least one of the parties is a government—or to be more precise, conflicts between an organized armed group and the armed forces of a High Contracting Party.'[80] What this implies is that it is possible to have a non-international armed conflict falling within the scope of Common Article 3 without necessarily attaining the threshold imposed by Article 1 of Additional Protocol II.

Whether an insurgence necessarily amounts to a non-international armed conflict can only be assessed on a case-by-case basis.[81] It is paramount that we determine whether the Boko Haram crisis amounts to disturbances, riots, tensions and unrests or a non-international armed conflict considering the meaning under Common Article 3 to the Geneva Conventions and Additional Protocol II. Having demonstrated in this chapter that Boko Haram is not just an organised group with a strong command and a distinct hierarchical leadership structure, the group also has the competence and capability to initiate, plan and execute systematic and coordinated attacks as well as the ability to enforce its orders, recruit, train and arm its fighters.[82] We must not forget also that Boko Haram was able to control territories within the Nigerian state, and in some instance, had forces outnumbering 'the Nigerian security forces, forcing many of them to abandon their positions and flee into neighbouring Cameroon.'[83] It is important to consider the two criteria put forward by the International Committee of the Red Cross (ICRC) when advancing discussion of this type that:

> Non-international armed conflicts are *protracted armed confrontations* occurring between governmental armed forces and the forces of one or more armed groups, or between such groups .... The armed confrontation must reach *a minimum level of intensity* and the parties involved in the conflict must show *a minimum of organization*.[84]

The understanding from the above quote is that these two criteria (the intensity of the violence and the organisation of the parties) are purposefully designed to differentiate an armed conflict from 'banditry, unorganized, and short-lived insurrections or terrorist activities, which are not subject to international humanitarian law.'[85]

---

[80] Serralvo 2015, p. 31.

[81] Tsagourias and Morrison 2018, p. 1.

[82] Discussion concerning the organisational structure of Boko Haram is contained in Sect. 61.2.3; and Boko Haram being an organised group is also contained in Sect. 61.5 of this chapter.

[83] Ibanga and Archibong 2018, p. 147.

[84] International Committee of the Red Cross 2008, p. 5.

[85] *Tadic,* above n 59, para.

Therefore, taken the organisational level of Boko Haram and the degree of intensity of its violence into account, one could conclude by saying that Boko Haram has attained the threshold of a non-international armed conflict. This conclusion has been well supported by the finding of the International Criminal Court (ICC), whose Prosecutor's (Fatou Bensouda's) report reads thus:

[T]he Office has considered the hierarchical structure of Boko Haram; its command rules and ability to impose discipline among its members; the weapons used by the group; its ability to plan and carry out coordinated attacks; and the number of Boko Haram forces under command. The Office has concluded that Boko Haram fulfils a sufficient number of relevant criteria to be considered an organised armed group capable of planning and carrying out military activities.[86]

The Office of the Prosecutor further concludes that 'the required level of intensity and the level of organization of parties to the conflict necessary for the violence to be qualified as an armed conflict of non-international character appear to have been met.'[87]

61.4 Basic Principles of Islamic Law of Jihad and IHL

The law of armed conflict as indicated by international humanitarian law (IHL) is based on four basic principles. It is not a coincidence that going through the gamut of Islamic law relating to jihad, these principles are similarly well pronounced. They are military necessity, distinction, proportionality and humanity. We will examine these basic principles in the context of Boko Haram's activities with the view to ascertaining whether they are compatible with the two legal regimes—Islamic law and international humanitarian law.

61.4.1 Principle of Military Necessity

According to the long-established principle of military necessity, a belligerent or party to an armed conflict is permitted to use any means and methods of war which are not prohibited by the law of armed conflict and are required in order to lead to the complete or partial submission of the enemy at the earliest possible moment with the minimum expenditure of life and resources.[88] In other words, military necessity entails the attainment of some perceptible military dominance over and above the enemy. The principle of military necessity further operates to restrict acts which are not otherwise illegal but yet not necessary for the achievement of the legitimate

---

[86] ICC 2013, para. 215.
[87] Ibid, para. 218.
[88] See UK British Ministry of Defence 2004, p. 383. See also Otto 2012, p. 216.

purpose of the conflict.[89] Though military necessity has not received any codification in the Geneva Conventions or Additional Protocol II, it has, however, gained customary international law status based on the statement reportedly made by the International Law Commission that military necessity forms one of the 'obligations arising out of a peremptory norm of international law, i.e., a norm from which no derogation is permitted.'[90] The principle of military necessity, according to Islamic law of jihad, is paramount in armed conflict. We must note that military necessity, in Islamic law of armed conflict, may be invoked for the protection of public interest i.e. *maslaha* and justification of reprisals, i.e. reciprocity in case the laws of war are violated by the enemy.[91] As mentioned in some provisions of the Qur'an—2:190; 2: 193; 22:39; and 9:36, fighting against injustices and for the removal of mischief are considered as military objectives for waging jihad.[92] For instance, Qur'an 2:193 says 'Keep on fighting against them until mischief ends and the way prescribed by Allah prevails.' Qur'an 22:39 provides that 'Permission (to fight) has been granted to those [believers] for they have been wronged …'. Going by these verses, once the mischief or injustices (wrongs) have ceased to exist, meaning that military objectives have been achieved, hence jihad should come to an end. Embarking on additional operations that cause collateral damages, unnecessary suffering and destruction of properties are prohibited in armed conflicts both under Islamic law and IHL.

61.4.2 Principle of Distinction

During armed conflicts, military objectives are considered legitimate targets, which means that a clear distinction must be drawn between military objectives or combatants (or civilians taking a direct part in the hostilities) on the one hand and civilian objects and civilians on the other hand. It is one of the cardinal principles of IHL that 'the protection of the civilian population and civilian objects and [to establish] the distinction between combatants and non-combatants'[93] must be observed. Article 13(2) of Additional Protocol II is unequivocal in its pursuit of the principle of distinction that parties involved in conflicts should ensure that '[t]he civilian population as such, as well as individual civilians, shall not be the object of attack.' It further stresses that [a]cts or threats of violence the primary purpose of which is to spread terror among the civilian population are prohibited.' Many other instruments, such as Article 2(1) of the 2001 Protocol III to the Convention on Certain Conventional Weapons and Article 8(2)(e)(i) of the Statute of International Criminal Court emphatically prohibit attacks against civilian population.

---

[89] Dinstein 2016, p.16.

[90] Sandoz et al. 1987, p. 392. Also see Common Article 3 of the Geneva Conventions.

[91] Hashmi 2003, pp.146–47.

[92] See Vanhullebusch 2015, pp. 22–23. See also Shah 2011, p.73.

[93] Advisory Opinion on the *Legality of the Threat or Use of Nuclear Weapons,* [1996] *ICJ Rep.* 226, at 257.

The two primary sources of Islamic law of jihad, i.e. the Qur'an and *Sunnah* (the prophetic traditions), strictly adhere to the principle of distinction. The Qur'an categorically condemns attacks on innocent civilians stating: 'Fight in the way of Allah those who fight you but do not transgress. Indeed, Allah does not like transgressors.'[94] The Qur'an clearly sets up humanitarian limitations during armed conflicts that must necessarily be adhered to by warriors.[95] Prophet Muhammad was reported, in different occasions, to have instructed his companions concerning the ethics and rules of war. For example, in one of the battles where Prophet Muhammad saw a slain woman, he disappointedly said: 'she certainly could not have been fighting'.[96]

Similar to the provisions contained in Article 13(2) of Additional Protocol II non-combatants or civilians in Islamic law of jihad include women, children, the elderly, the infirm, monks in monasteries or people sitting in places of worship, diplomats and merchants. Incapacitated combatants who are no longer fighting due to injury sustained or sickness also benefit from these immunities.[97] It is a well-established rule in the Islamic law of jihad that there must not be indiscriminate attacks or killing of civilian populations, particularly those that are not directly involved in the armed conflicts. To harm or kill them will amount to a violation of the basic principles of Islamic law of jihad.

Boko Haram has been infamously known to target civilians and unintended victims in its various operations. Boko Haram maintains a policy to launch intentional attacks against civilians perceived as 'disbelievers' as declared in a video recording by Shekau saying 'anyone who supports the "disbelievers" (meaning anyone supporting democracy or western values) is … an enemy to us and a target to our forces and we will enslave him and sell him in the markets.'[98] While admitting the fact that 'Boko Haram is one of the worst devastating terrorist organizations in the world',[99] the group was reported to have recorded the deadliest attack on the civilian population leaving more than 6,000 dead in 270 different attacks in 2015 alone.[100]

61.4.3 *Principle of Proportionality*

It is worth mentioning that proportionality, despite its importance, is not referenced in Additional Protocol II, however, it can be found in customary international law and recently, in treaty law applicable to non-international armed conflicts. For instance, Article 3(8)(c) of the Amended Protocol II to the Convention of Certain Conventional Weapons specifically prohibits the indiscriminate use of weapons as contained in the

---

[94] Qur'an 2:190.
[95] Engeland 2016, p. 247.
[96] Abu Dawud Sulaiman bin Ash'ath 2008, pp. 295–296.
[97] Munir 2011, p. 25.
[98] ICC 2015.
[99] Urmacher and Sheridan 2016.
[100] Ibid.

treaty 'which may be to cause incidental of civilian life, injury to civilians, damage to civilian objects, or a combination thereof, which would be excessive in relation to the concrete and direct military advantage anticipated.'[101] The principle requires that the collateral damage caused to the civilians by the military operations must be proportional by limiting the overall level of destruction to life and property.[102] In other words, the losses, as a result of military action, should not be excessive in comparison to the expected military advantage.[103] Proportionality arises when military action is directed toward combatants and military objectives or civilians who take part directly in hostilities, and as a result of the attack, civilian objects are destroyed and civilians harmed.

Islamic law of jihad accords with the principle of proportionality in IHL. Islamic law requires that the principle of proportionality must be held in high esteem. This is demonstrated in some Qur'anic verses, like: Qur'an 16:126, 40:40, 42:40, 5:2 and 74:38. For example, Qur'an 16:126 was revealed purposely to entrench the principle of proportionality when Prophet Muhammad reacted furiously and bitterly after he found the mutilated body of his uncle, Hamzah, during the battle of Uhud. The body was without ears and nose, the stomach was rift open, with the liver missing. In a vengeful mood, Prophet Muhammad said: 'If God gives me victory over them [Quraysh], I will mutilate thirty of their men.'[104] It was on this occasion that God revealed that:

> Hence, if you have to respond to an attack, respond only to the extent of the attack levelled against you; but to bear yourselves with patience is indeed far better for [you, since God is with] those who are patient in adversity.[105]

The above verse came to lay the foundation of the principle of proportionality and in addition, the prohibition of mutilation.

61.4.4 Principle of Humanity

The principle of humanity otherwise known as the concept of unnecessary suffering applies mainly to combatants. The essence of the principle is codified in Article 4(1) Additional Protocol II:

All persons who do not take a direct part or who have ceased to take part in hostilities ... are entitled to respect for their person, honour and convictions and

---

[101] More examples are contained in a number of Military Manuals, such as Nigeria, Military Manual (1994), p. 42, § 11; Australia, Defence Force Manual (1994), § 535; Belgium, Law of War Manual (1983), p. 26; Benin, Military Manual (1995), Fascicule III, p. 14; Cameroon, Instructors' Manual (1992), p. 83; Colombia, Instructors' Manual (1999), p. 19; Kenya, LOAC Manual (1997), Precis No. 4, p. 1 etc.

[102] Tsagourias and Morrison 2018, p. 50. See also Gardam 2004, p. 30.

[103] See Solis 2016, p. 294. See also Shah 2011, p. 73.

[104] Ibn Ishaq 1997, p. 387.

[105] Quran 16:126.

religious practices. They shall in all circumstances be treated humanely, without any advanced distinction. It is prohibited to order that there shall be no survivors.

The general prohibition of the infliction of suffering, injury, or destruction not actually necessary for the accomplishment of a legitimate military purpose stands at the core of the concept of humanity.[106] It means that once a legitimate military purpose has been achieved, it therefore becomes unnecessary and superfluous to inflict further suffering or injury. For instance, a continuous attack of a wounded or captured enemy soldier will serve no military purpose. The principle of humanity also confirms the immunity of civilians from attacks, since direct attacks on the civilians will serve no military purpose.[107]

Islamic law of jihad similarly upholds and respect the principle of humanity during and after war. We must not forget that the hallmarks of God's creation, regardless of their disparity, constantly and consistently remain respect for all members of humanity. This principle is well-affirmed in the Islamic law of armed conflict with various authority emanating from the two primary sources of the Islamic jurisprudence. The humanitarian and moral dispositions are expressly emphasised in various Qur'anic verses.[108] Humanity has been endowed with great dignity according to Qur'an 17:70 amongst others, which states:

> Now, indeed, We have conferred dignity on the children of Adam, and borne them over land and sea, and provided for them sustenance out of the good things of life, and favoured them far above most of Our creation.

The humanitarian and moral dispositions of Islamic law, especially during armed conflict, are well-exemplified in the statements and instructions of Prophet Muhammad and his righteous Caliphs to their Islamic armies. Prophet Muhammad, in accordance with Qur'an 16:126, proscribed mutilation (or maiming) of bodies.[109] 'Umar Ibn 'Abdul Aziz[110] in his letter to one of the rulers under his Caliphate, wrote: 'We have been informed that when the Prophet of Allah, (peace be upon him) sent any military company, he used to tell them: '... [W]age war against the disbelievers [those who have attacked the Muslims]. Do not be deserters, nor commit perfidy, nor mutilate (your enemy). Do not kill a new born. Repeat this to your armies and companies, it's God's will, Peace be upon you'.'[111]

The directives given by 'Ali ibn Abi Talib (the fourth Caliph after Prophet Muhammad) to his soldiers are very instructive and relevant to the humanitarian inclination of the Muslim soldiers. He was reported to have said: 'If you defeat them, do not kill a man in flight, do not finish off a wounded man, do not uncover a pudendum, or mutilate the dead, do not rip open a curtain or enter a house without

---

[106] See UK Ministry of Defence 2004, *Manual*, para. 2.4, 23.

[107] Blank and Noone 2019, pp. 45-46.

[108] See Qur'an 2:190, 40:40, 42:40 and 16:126.

[109] Al-Bukhari, Vol. 3, Book 43, Number 654. (Narrated by 'Abdullah bin Yazid Al-Ansari).

[110] 'Umar ibn 'Abdul Aziz otherwise known as 'Umar II was the eighth Umayyad Caliph who reigned between 22 September 717 and February 720.

[111] Related by Imam Malik. See Jalal-u-din al-Sayuti n.d., p. 7.

permission, do not take any of their property, and do not torture or harm their women even though they may insult your leaders.'[112]

Following the concept of humanity in the Islamic law of armed conflict, Islamic soldiers are enjoined to minimise suffering by abstaining from reckless use of force that exposes life and property to unnecessary destruction. Enemy soldiers who have been incapacitated due to injury, sickness or disability cannot be killed rather, they are to be treated as non-combatants since they are not in a position to fight any more. This humane consideration during armed conflict has been epitomised by Prophet Muhammad during the conquest of Makkah when he instructed that 'wounded shall not be killed, anyone who turns his back and runs away from fighting shall not be chased, prisoner shall not be killed, and whosoever shuts his door shall be immune.'[113] To harm or kill them will be deemed as inflicting torture and unnecessary suffering on them with no military justification.

Suicide attacks, as we know, are often shrouded in treachery and perfidy. A suicide bomber will not openly display his or her suicide vest or dangerous weapons before the attack; such vest and weapons are usually concealed. Suicide attacks run contrary to the basic principles of humanity, distinction and proportionality, and, as such, cannot be said to be sanctioned by Islamic law.[114] A suicide bomber has been rightly said to commit five crimes in Islamic law by Munir, namely: killing civilians, mutilating them by blowing them up, violating the trust of the enemy's soldiers and civilians, committing suicide and, finally, destroying civilian objects or property.[115]

Sadly, the recent rate at which children, mostly girls, are been used for suicide attacks by Boko Haram, particularly in crowded markets, mosques and camps for internally displaced people in the Northeast of Nigeria has now become increasingly alarming. Boko Haram has not only been in the forefront of using children as suicide bombers, it has now become infamous as 'the first terrorist group in history to use more women suicide bombers than men.'[116]

The rate at which the principles of international humanitarian law and Islamic law have been violated and continue to be violated by Boko Haram under a misconceived notion of waging the 'Islamic jihad' in the Northern part of Nigeria has been gruesome and of great concern. As demonstrated, the activities of Boko Haram run contrary to the basic principles of both IHL and the Islamic law of armed conflict. Such violations, undoubtedly, provides a justifiable ground for the prosecution of Boko Haram suspects. The question left to be determined now is whether the national courts of Nigeria or the International Criminal Court should have jurisdiction in the trial of Boko Haram suspects.

---

[112] Syed Razi n.d., 573.

[113] Bayhaqi 1414/1994, p. 181.

[114] See Qur'an 2:195. See also Qur'an 4:29 "… And do not kill yourselves [or one another]. Indeed, Allah is to you ever Merciful".

[115] Munir 2008, p. 89.

[116] See Kriel 2017.

61.5 Trial of Boko Haram Suspects in Domestic Courts or before the International Criminal Court

The Boko Haram crisis which started as an intra-state armed conflict with the Nigerian government, has taken its war far beyond the territorial sovereignty of Nigeria. Its hostilities have now spilled over into neighbouring states, such as Cameroon, Niger and Chad, thus turning into a major regional conflict. Regardless of this development, the conflict still remains a non-international armed conflict in as much as all the states concerned pull forces together to wage hostilities only against the insurgents.[117] Mostly, states do exercise maximum restraint in recognising terrorist organisations as subjects of international law so as not to ascribe political legitimacy to them.[118] The fact that international lawyers seldom accept non-state actors as subjects of international law is understandable, since they are not entitled to benefit from rights and duties that flow from legal international dispensation. This explains why an armed conflict cannot be said to exist between a state and non-state terrorist organisation.[119]

We must not forget that the Rome Statute gives the national courts of state parties the jurisdiction to prosecute and punish perpetrators of international crimes, thereby leaving the ICC with jurisdiction based on the principle of complementarity. What this principle signifies is that the ICC resumes jurisdiction in the event where the concerned state is unable, due to one reason or another, to prosecute and punish the perpetrators of international crimes.[120]

First, we need to understand that in Nigeria, ss. 32 and 33 of the Terrorism (Prevention) Act, 2011 give the Federal High Court the exclusive jurisdiction to prosecute and possibly impose penalties on terrorist offenders. The Rome Statute of International Criminal Court (Rome Statute), which came into force on 1 July 2012, was ratified by Nigeria on 27 September 2001.[121] The Rome Statute gives the International Criminal Court (ICC) the jurisdiction to prosecute 'international crimes'—aggression, genocide, crimes against humanity, and war crimes.[122] At the same time, the Rome Statute recognises the domestic jurisdiction of state parties to prosecute international crimes. The preamble of the Statute categorically provides that state parties recall 'that it is the duty of every State to exercise its criminal jurisdiction over those responsible for international crimes.' However, it appears that the ICC may not have jurisdiction to prosecute the offence of terrorism unless it falls within any of those crimes mentioned in Article 5 of the Rome Statute.

The argument advanced by some commentators that terrorist groups, the like of Boko Haram, should be prosecuted at the ICC as a way of ensuring universal justice through the conviction of terrorists by the international community is worth given

---

[117] Dinstein 2016, p. 36.
[118] Nielsen 2011, p. 190.
[119] Goppel 2013, p. 88.
[120] Malekian 2011, p. 352.
[121] See International Criminal Court n.d.
[122] See Articles 5, 6, 7 and 8 of the Rome Statute.

proper consideration.[123] This argument seems to be more convincing considering the international elements inherent in the crime of terrorism. It is obvious that Boko Haram is not an agent of the Nigerian state, and more so, the Rome Statute gives primacy to national prosecution.

Some group of individuals have been recognised to overwhelmingly partake in operations having devastating effects on civilians in conflicts that may be described as non-international and, in most cases, international in character.[124] A typical example is the Hutu civilians that were instigated to commit genocide and other crimes against humanity (CAH) against the Tutsi civilians during the Rwanda crisis. Individuals belonging to both Tutsi and Hutu were eventually found guilty for committing CAH.[125] Since 2013 up until January 2015, Boko Haram gained control of territory by establishing its authority in a number of towns in the East of Northern Nigeria.[126] It was also reported that the militant group went as far as to capture territory in Bornu, Adamawa and Yobe States, and made Gwozao[127] its capital.[128] Boko Haram having had control of territory with a sizeable population and in possession of military strength, appears to give justification in support of jurisdiction for the ICC in the prosecution of crimes allegedly committed by members of the Boko Haram. This contention tends to align with Bassiouni's submission that:

> [W]henever such groups acquired characteristics similar to those of a state, such as controlling a given territory or exercising control over a given civilian population, and whose structure, whether civilian, military, or both, is capable of developing a policy similar to that of a state, the responsibility for CAH [crime against humanity] should be extended to such groups.[129]

Article 7(2)(a) of the ICC requires that the attack must be 'pursuant to or in furtherance of a State or organizational policy to commit such attack.' It must be noted, however, that the condition of having a link with a State or a group is not required for war crimes.[130] As stated in the Nuremberg judgment that 'crimes against international law are committed by men, not by abstract entities, and only by punishing individuals who commit such crimes can the provisions of international law be enforced'.[131] The provisions of Article 7(2)(a) indicate that the commission of crimes against humanity

---

[123] Vagts 2003, p. 325.

[124] Mullins 2010, p.67.

[125] Bassiouni 2011, p. 40.

[126] See Zirker 2015, pp. 44–45.

[127] Gwozao is a town within Bornu State, which is believed to be inhabited by close to half a million people.

[128] See Magstadt 2016, p. 263.

[129] Bassiouni 1999, p. 275.

[130] Fitzpatrick 2016, p. 112.

[131] International Military Tribunal (Nuremberg) Judgment and Sentences, reprinted in (1947) 41 American Journal of International Law 172, at 221.

may not necessarily be under the direction of state officials, but could also be by 'organizations'.[132] In *Prosecutor v. Bemba*,[133] the Pre-Trial Chamber pronounced that the word 'organizational' may be 'groups of persons who govern a specific territory or ... any organization with the capability to commit a widespread or systematic attack against civilian population.'[134] Arsanjani also viewed that the latter word in subparagraph 2(a) encompasses 'such groups as terrorist organizations and organizations of insurrectional or separatist movements.'[135] It is crucial to determine whether such organizational policy could be identified with Boko Haram. The identification will depend not only on the attribute of the element organization' but also, rather, 'on whether a group has the capability to perform acts which infringe on basic human values'.[136] The Chamber, in the case *The Prosecutor v. William Samoei Ruto, Henry Kiprono Kosgey and Joshua Arap Sang*[137] recalls that the following factors may be taken into consideration in determining whether a group qualifies as an organization under the Article 7(2)(a) of the Rome Statute:

> (i) whether the group is under a responsible command, or has an established hierarchy; (ii) whether the group possesses, in fact, the means to carry out a widespread or systematic attack against a civilian population; (iii) whether the group exercises control over part of the territory of a State; (iv) whether the group has criminal activities against the civilian population as a primary purpose; (v) whether the group articulates, explicitly or implicitly, an intention to attack a civilian population; (vi) whether the group is part of a larger group, which fulfils some or all of the abovementioned criteria.[138]

The Chamber further concludes that the above factors should not be seen as 'a rigid legal definition, and do not need to be exhaustively fulfilled.'[139] One will want to conclude that all the highlighted points from (i)—(vi) are identifiable with Boko Haram at one point or the other.

Considering the provisions of Article 5 of the Statute of International Criminal Tribunal of the former Yugoslavia (ICTY Statute), Article 3 of the International Criminal Tribunal for Rwanda (ICTR Statute), and Article 7 of the Rome Statute, one may want to assume that these provisions indicate that individuals unrelated to the State may be prosecuted for crimes against humanity.

Aside from Boko Haram having exercised control over a given territory and over a section of the civilian population in Nigeria, the willingness and ability of the Nigerian government to diligently prosecute suspects of Boko Haram for international crimes must be resolute and remain unquestionable considering its relevance

---

[132] Klamberg 2017, p. 62.

[133] Decision on Confirmation of Charges, 15 June 2009, ICC-01/05-01/08-424.

[134] Ibid., para. 81.

[135] Arsanjani 1999, p. 31.

[136] *Prosecutor v. Muthaura, Kenyatta and Ali,* Decision on the confirmation of charges, 23 January 2012, para. 112.

[137] *The Prosecutor v. William Samoei Ruto, Henry Kiprono Kosgey and Joshua Arap Sang,* Decision on the confirmation of charges, 23 January 2012.

[138] Ibid., para. 185.

[139] Ibid.

to state's jurisdictional competence. This assertion goes in line with the preamble of the Rome Statute, which states that 'the most serious crimes of concern to the international community as a whole must not go unpunished and that their prosecution must be ensured by taking measures at the national level and by enhancing international cooperation.'[140] It goes further to '[e]mphasize that the International Criminal Court established under this Statute shall be complementary to national criminal jurisdictions.'[141] The principle of complementarity,[142] in the words of Ocampo,

> represents the express will of States Parties to create an institution that is global in scope while recognising the primary responsibility of States themselves to exercise criminal jurisdiction. The principle is also based on considerations of efficiency and effectiveness since States will generally have the best access to evidence and witnesses.[143]

It is worthwhile to understand that the preambular provisions of a statute, which usually contain motives or objectives of the parties to the treaty, carry legal force and effect from an interpretative view point.[144]

There has been a series of arrest of some Boko Haram members, who are currently been held either in police custody or military detention camps without facing trial.[145] It is common knowledge that those detained by the Nigerian police often suffer protracted detention, long before they are brought before the court, which may be attributable to the country's over-stretched judicial system. The situation has probably gone worst by the current influx of Boko Haram suspects into police custody. For instance, as of 2017, the Nigerian government commenced the trials of about 1,669 Boko Haram suspects where most of them were charged with providing materials and non-violent support to the group. Surprisingly, first round of the trials, which took place in October 2017, was obscured in secrecy thereby excluding people and communities that were directly affected by the Boko Haram ferocious aggression from giving testimony or observing the legal proceedings. Further trials that took place in February and July 2018 at Wawa Cantonment, a military base in Kainji, Niger State, where over 200 Boko Haram suspects were charged for offences under the Terrorism Prevention Amendment Act 2003. At the trials, 113 of the defendants got convicted, 97 were discharged on the ground that they had no case to answer and 5 were acquitted.[146] The entire proceedings raised a lot serious concern, which was summed-up in the following words:

---

[140] Paragraph 4 of the Preamble of the ICC Statute.

[141] Ibid., Para. 10.

[142] Complementarity, as one of the basic principles of the Rome Statute system, was meant to be a comprehensive system of international justice which reinforces States Parties to investigate and prosecute international crimes. The Rome Statute of International Criminal Court thus establishes a subsidiary role for ICC and supplements the domestic investigation and prosecution of the most serious crimes of international concern. See Benzing 2003, p. 592.

[143] Cited in Schabas 2007, p. 1.

[144] Case Concerning *Rights of Nationals of the United States in Morocco(France v United States)* [1952] ICJ Rep 176, 196; *The Asylum Case (Colombia v Peru)* [1950] ICJ Rep. 266, 282.

[145] See Amnesty International 2016/2017.

[146] Human Rights Watch 2018.

The proceedings were very short, with some lasting less than 15 minutes, raising several fair trial and due process concerns. Most charges were couched in ambiguous and vague terms without the crucial information Nigerian law requires, like the specific date, place, and details of the alleged offense. Other procedural lapses included a lack of official interpreters and the use of untrained unofficial interpreters; reliance on alleged confessions; charging previously discharged defendants again for the same offenses; and unclear orders for rehabilitation for some defendants whose releases were ordered.[147]

The prosecution of suspected terrorists should be given top national priority without any undue delay considering the seriousness of their acts so that the justice system will not be seen as condoning impunity and upholding the principle of fair hearing and due process.

It is obvious that crimes against international law have been and are still being committed by the Boko Haram militant group, and the perpetrators need to be punished just as it was stressed by the judges at Nuremberg while condemning the Nazi leaders for their atrocities: '[c]rimes against international law are committed by men, not by abstract entities, and only by punishing individuals who commit such crimes can the provisions of international law be enforced.'[148] The Nigerian government should holistically undertake a full implementation of the rule of law with a robust human rights mechanism with a view to strengthening its criminal justice system to serve as a most formidable weapon against terrorism. It is of interest to note that in Cameroon, which is a neighboring State, 89 suspected Boko Haram operatives have been so far tried and condemned to death in 2015.[149] A similar story was also gathered in the Republic of Chad, where 10 men suspected to be Boko Haram members who allegedly carried out the twin attacks that killed 38 people in the capital N'Djamena in June, 2015 were all sentenced to death.[150]

When one considers the speed at which justice was delivered in Cameroon and Chad, one begins to wonder whether Nigeria is indeed willing and able to genuinely carry out the investigation and prosecution of Boko Haram suspects as required by Article 17(1)(a) of the Rome Statute. Most importantly, if one takes into consideration the notion of willingness, which presupposes that justice is speedily administered without unjustified delay; and that the trial be conducted independently and impartially, that is when the enormousness of the incentives placed on member states can be well appreciated. 'Willingness' and 'ability', according to Kleffner, 'entail important incentives for States to do everything in their power to carry out investigations and prosecutions' of international crimes within their respective jurisdiction.[151]

---

[147] Ibid.

[148] Judgment of international military tribunal for the trial of German major war criminal, Nuremberg, 30 September and 1 October 1946, Misc No 12, 1946, Cmd 6964, reproduced, *AJIL* 41 (1947): 172 (Nuremberg Judgment), 220.

[149] Vanguard 2016.

[150] Vanguard 2015.

[151] Kleffner 2008, p. 248.

Undoubtedly, although the ICC does not have the power to enforce domestic prosecution, it could, however, take over such prosecution where a State fails or unwilling to genuinely prosecute.[152]

61.6 Conclusion

Terrorist groups, the like of Boko Haram, have continuously made Muslims and non-Muslims, and including Muslim states their targets in the name of a self-declared jihad. It is high time the international community gave credence to the dictates of Islamic law with regard to acts of terrorism which is fast becoming endemic mostly in Muslim States. Islamic law, just like many international treaties, has been shown to negate whatever terrorism stands for. What is left is to rectify the 'mistake of considering such terrorist acts as Islamically motivated or permitted'[153] regardless of their unfounded claim to Islamic jihad. Boko Haram has been found to significantly contravene, not only the Nigerian Terrorism (Prevention) Act, 2011 and the conventional international humanitarian law, but also the Islamic principles of the Islamic armed conflict, which it erroneously claims to uphold. The statement of Schwartz in this regard is quite instructive that '[t]he *Shari'ah* provides a genuine, workable framework for countering international terrorism . . . Islamic law coordinates, integrates and legislates against that which Western jurists have so far failed to control. The *Shari'ah* is a resource the West must no longer overlook.'[154] Having concluded, based on the level of intensity of the violence and the level of organization of Boko Haram, which brings its activities within the threshold of an armed conflict of non-international character, by implication, the Nigerian government is, therefore, bound to fulfil obligations under municipal laws and rules under international humanitarian law. It is worthy of mention that since Boko Haram's activities have met the threshold of non-international armed conflict, and considering the phlegmatic attitude of the Nigerian government in investigating and diligently prosecuting members of Boko Haram for its criminal and terrorist activities, it is suggested that a trial of such offences would be better brought before the International Criminal Court. The four basic principles of the law of armed conflict present in international humanitarian law and Islamic law are harmonious related in the two legal regimes and the fact that the activities of Boko Haram grossly violate these four basic principles as analysed in this chapter is very clear.

---

[152] Seibert-Fohr 2003, pp. 558–559.
[153] Al-Dawoody 2011, p. 145.
[154] Schwartz 1991, p. 652.

References

Abu Dawud Sulaiman bin Ash'ath (2008) English Translation of Sunan Abu Dawud. Vol. 3, (Hadith No.2669). Darus Salam, Riyadh

Ainoko I (2017) Boko Haram: A Jihad without Religionz Vanguard, 13 August 2017. Available from https://www.vanguardngr.com/2017/08/boko-haram-jihad-without-religion/ [accessed 9 September 2018]

Al-Dawoody A (2011) The Islamic law of war: Regulations and justifications. Palgrave Macmillan, New York

Al-Dawoody A (2017) Islamic Law and International Humanitarian Law: An Introduction to the Main Principles. IRRC 99:3, 995-1018

Aljazeera (2011) Blast Rocks Police Headquarters in Nigeria. Aljazeera, 16 June 2011. Available from http://www.aljazeera.com/news/africa/2011/06/201161611451344807.html [accessed 10 May 2018]

Aljazeera (2019) Eight killed in Boko Haram Attack in Nigeria. Aljazeera News, 16 February 2019. Available from https://www.aljazeera.com/news/2019/02/killed-boko-haram-attack-nigeria-190216120448266.html [accessed 14 March 2019]

Amnesty International (2016/2017) Nigeria. Amnesty International. Also available from https://www.amnesty.org/en/countries/africa/nigeria/report-nigeria/ [accessed 12 July 2018]

Arango T (2014) Sunni Extremists in Iraq Seize 3 Towns from Kurds and Threaten Major Dam. The New York Times, 3 August 2014, https://www.nytimes.com/2014/08/04/world/middleeast/iraq.html [accessed 16 November 2021]

Arsanjani MH (1999) The Rome Statute of the International Criminal Court. AJIL 93:1, 22-43

Badawi J (2003) Muslim/non-Muslim relations: An integrative approach. J. Islamic L. & Culture 8:2, 23-48

Bassiouni M (1999) Crimes against humanity in international criminal law. Kluwer Law International, London

Bassiouni M (2008) Evolving approaches to Jihad: From self-defense to revolutionary and regime-change political violence J. Islamic L. & Culture 10:1, 61-83

Bassiouni M (2011) Crimes against humanity: Historical evolution and contemporary application. Cambridge University Press, Cambridge

Bassiouni M (ed) (1975) International terrorism and political crimes. Charles Thomas, Springfield

Bayhaqi (1414/1994) Sunan. In: Qadir 'Ata' MA (ed) Maktabah Dar al-Baz, Makkah 8

BBC Africa (2014) Chibok Abductions in Nigeria: 'More than 230 Seized'. BBC Africa, 21 April 2014. Available from http://www.bbc.com/news/world-africa-27101714 [accessed 12 May 2018]

Benzing M (2003) The complementarity regime of the International Criminal Court: International criminal justice between state sovereignty and the fight against impunity. Max Planck UNYB 7:1, 591-632

Berkebile R (2017) What is domestic terrorism? A method for classifying events from the global terrorism database. Terrorism and Political Violence. 29:1, 1-26

Blank L, Noone G (2019) International law and armed conflict: Fundamental principles and contemporary challenges in the law of war. Wolters Kluwer, New York

Boffey D (2015) Boko Haram Declares Allegiance to Islamic State. The Guardian, 8 March 2015. Available from https://www.theguardian.com/world/2015/mar/07/boko-haram-suicide-bombers-50-dead-maiduguri [accessed 10 April 2018]

Bulac A (2004) Jihad. In: Capan E (ed) Terror and Suicide Attacks. The Light Inc., New Jersey, pp 63-79

Burke J (2016) Nigeria Denies Paying Ransom and Freeing Boko Haram Leaders for Chibok Girls. The Guardian, Friday 14 October 2016. Available from https://www.theguardian.com/world/2016/oct/14/boko-haram-chibok-girls-nigeria-denies-paying-ransom-and-freeing-leaders [accessed 21 April 2018]

Comer CA, Mburu D M (2015) Humanitarian law at wits' end: Does violence arising from the 'war on drugs' in Mexico meet the International Criminal Court's non-International Armed Conflict Threshold? YIHL, volume 18, 67-89
Comolli V (2015) Boko Haram: Nigeria's Islamist insurgency. Hurst and Company, London
Dinstein Y (2016) The conduct of hostilities under the law of international armed conflict, 3rd edn. Cambridge University Press, Cambridge
Dorrie P (2015) How Big is Boko Haram? War is Boring, 3 February 2015. Available from https://medium.com/war-is-boring/how-big-is-boko-haram-fac21c25807 [accessed 13 April 2018]
El Fadl A (1990) Abkam al-Bughat: Irregular warfare and the law of rebellion. In: Johnson J, Kelsay J (eds) Islam, Cross, Crescent and sword: The justification and limitation of war in Western and Islamic tradition. Greenwood Press, Westport CT
Engeland A (2016) Islam as a religion of peace: An articulated reply to terrorism. In: Barnidge Jr RP (ed) The liberal way of war: Legal perspectives. Routledge, Oxon, pp 239-258
Esposito J (2002) Unholy war: Terror in the name of Islam. Oxford University Press, Oxford
Fitzpatrick B (2016) Tactical rape in war and conflict: International recognition and response. Policy Press, Bristol
Gardam J (2004) Necessity, proportionality and the use of force by states. Cambridge University Press, Cambridge
Gasser HP (1993) International humanitarian law: Introduction. In: Haug H (ed) Humanity for all: The International Red Cross Red Crescent Movement. Paul Haupt Publishers, Bern, pp 555-575
Goppel A (2013) Killing terrorists: A moral and legal analysis. Walter de Gruyter, Berlin
Green M et al. (2018) Religion, law and security in Africa. African Sun MeDIA, Stellenbosch
Harrison K, Ryder N (2017) The law relating to financial crime in the United Kingdom. Routledge, Oxon
Hashmi S (2003) Saving and taking life in war: Three Modern Muslim views. In: Brockopp J (ed) Islamic ethics of life: Abortion, war, and euthanasia. University of South Carolina Press, pp 1-21
Hill J (2012) Nigeria since independence: Forever fragile. Palgrave Macmillan, Hampshire
Hollingsworth M, Kemedi V (2015) Against the odds. Susquehanna Press, Leicestershire
Human Rights Watch (2017) World Report 2018: Events of 2017. Human Rights Watch
Human Rights Watch (2018) Nigeria: Flawed Trials of Boko Haram Suspects. Human Rights Watch, 17 September 2018. Also available from https://www.hrw.org/news/2018/09/17/nigeria-flawed-trials-boko-haram-suspects [accessed 21 August 2020]
Huntington S (1996) The Clash of Civilizations and the Remaking of World Order. Simon & Schuster, New York
Ibanga M, Archibong J (2018) The Boko Haram insurgency: Characterisation and implications under municipal and international law. In: Iyi J-M, Strydom H (eds) Boko Haram and international law. Springer, Cham, pp 137- 153
Ibn Ishaq (1997) *Sirat al-Rasoolullah* (Guillaume A (translator)), repr. Oxford University Press, Karachi
Ibn Qudamah (1972), *Al-Mughni*, vol. 9. Dar-al-Kitab-al-'arab, Beirut
ICC (2013) Report on Preliminary Examination Activities 2013 (November 2013), para. 215. Also available online at https://www.icc-cpi.int/OTP%20Reports/otp-report-2013.aspx#nigeria [accessed 12 December 2018]
ICC (2015) Office of the Prosecutor - Report on Preliminary Examination Activities (2015). Available from https://www.icc-cpi.int/iccdocs/otp/OTP-PE-rep-2015-Eng.pdf [accessed 13 June 2018]
Independent (2015) PMB on Small Fires Causing Large Fires. Independent, 14 June 2015. Available from http://independent.ng/pmb-small-fires-causing-large-fires/ [accessed 13 May 2018]
Inter-Governmental Action Group Against Money Laundering in West Africa (GIABA) (2010) Threat Assessment of Money Laundering and Terrorist Financing in West Africa. Available from https://www.giaba.org/reports/typologies/reports.html [accessed 24 March 2022]
International Committee of the Red Cross (ICRC) (2008) How is the term 'armed conflict' defined in international humanitarian law? Opinion paper, ICRC, Geneva

International Criminal Court (n.d.) 'States Parties-Chronological List'. Available from https://asp.icc-cpi.int/en_menus/asp/states%20parties/pages/states%20parties%20_%20chronological%20list.aspx [accessed 11 January 2019]

Iocchi A (2015) The Boko Haram franchise and the war on terror in Nigeria. Diritto & Questioni Pubbliche number:15:2, 203-214

Isioma M (2011) Boko Haram: Rise of a Deadly Sect. National Mirror, 19 June 2011, available online at http://www.nationalmirroronline.net/sunday-mirror/bigread/14548.html [accessed 1 May 2018]

Ismail M (2015) Terror on diplomats and diplomatic missions in the name of Jihād: Islamic Law Perspective. Journal of Malaysian and Comparative Law 42:1,19-42

Ismail M (2016) Islamic Law and transnational diplomatic law: A quest for complementarity in divergent legal theories. Palgrave Macmillan, Basingstoke

Jalal-u-din al-Sayuti (n.d.) Tanweer Al-hawalik, Sharh a'la Muwatta' Malik. Vol. II. al-Halabi Press, Cairo

Khan L (2006) A theory of international terrorism: Understanding Islamic militancy. Martinus Nijhoff, Leiden

Klamberg M (ed) (2017) Commentary on the law of the International Criminal Court. Torkel Opsahl Academy, Brussels

Kleffner J (2008), Complementarity in the Rome Statute and national criminal jurisdiction. Oxford University Press, Oxford

Kriel R (2017) Boko Haram Favours Women, Children as Suicide Bombers, Study Reveals. CNN, 11 August 2017. Available from http://edition.cnn.com/2017/08/10/africa/boko-haram-women-children-suicide-bombers/index.html [accessed 18 January 2019]

MacEachern S (2018) Searching for Boko Haram: A history of violence in Central Africa. Oxford University Press, Oxford

Magstadt T (2016) Understanding politics: Ideas, institutions, and issues. Cengage Learning, Boston MA

Malekian F (2011) Principles of Islamic international criminal law: A comparative research. Brill, Leiden

Mamah E et al. (2012) Boko Haram Bombs Kano Afresh. Vanguard, 24 January 2012. Available from http://www.vanguardngr.com/2012/01/boko-haram-bombs-kano-afresh/ [accessed 12 May 2018]

Mang H (2014) Christian perceptions of Islam and society in relation to Boko Haram and recent events in Jos and Northern Nigeria. In: Pérouse De Montclos M (ed) Boko Haram: Islamism, politics, security and the state in Nigeria. African Studies Centre, Leiden

Moir L (2002) The law of internal armed conflict.Cambridge University Press, Cambridge

Mullins C (2010) Conflict victimization and post-conflict justice 1945–2008. In: Bassiouni M (ed) The pursuit of international criminal justice: A world study on conflicts, victimization, and post-conflict justice. Intersentia, Antwerp

Munir M (2008) Suicide attacks and Islamic law. IRRC 90:869, 71-89

Munir M (2011) The protection of civilians in war: Non-combatants immunity in Islamic law. Hamdard Islamicus XXXIV:4, 7-39

Nafi B (2004) Fatwa and war: On the allegiance of the American Muslim soldiers in the aftermath of September 11. Islamic Law and Society 11:1, 78-116

Newman P (2013) The etymology of Hausa Boko. Mega-Chad Research Network, 1-13

Nielsen E (2011) State Responsibility for Terrorist Groups. U.C Davis J.Int'l L. & Pol'y 17:151-192

Omeni A (2020) Insurgency and war in Nigeria: Regional fracture and fight against Boko Haram. I. B. Tauris, London

Onuoha FC, Oyewole S (2018) Anatomy of Boko Haram: The rise and decline of violent group in Nigeria. Al Jazeera Centre for Studies (22 April)

Onyebuchi E, Chigozie C (2013) Islamic fundamentalism and the problem of insecurity in Nigeria: The Boko Haram phenomenon. Journal of Humanities and Social Science 15:3, 43-53

Otto R (2012) Targeted killings and international law. Springer, London

Pérouse De Montclos M (ed) (2014) Boko Haram: Islamism, politics, security and the state in Nigeria. African Studies Centre, Leiden.

Phares W (2005) Future Jihad: Terrorists strategies against the West. Palgrave Macmillan, New York

Quraish A (2000) An Islamic critique of the rape laws of Pakistan from a woman-sensitive perspective. In: Webb G (ed) Windows of faith: Muslim women scholar activities in North America. Syracuse University Press, Syracuse, N.Y.

Re D (2018) International crimes: A hybrid future? Nigerian Yearbook of International Law, Volume 2017, 173-190

Rogers P (2012) Nigeria: The generic context of the Boko Haram violence. Monthly Global Security Briefing (April 30)

Roman L (2012) Boko Haram: The development of a militant religious movement in Nigeria. Afrika Spectrum 47:2-3

Ryder N (2015) The financial war on terrorism: A review of counter-terrorist financing strategies since 2001. Routledge, London

Sandoz A et al (1987) Commentary on the Additional Protocols. Martinus Nijhoff, Geneva

Schabas W (2007) 'Complementarity in practice': Some uncomplimentary thoughts. Paper presentation at the 20th Anniversary conference of the International Society for the Reform of Criminal Law, Vancouver, 23 June 2007

Schachter O (1991) International law in theory and practice. Martinus Nijhoff, Dordrecht

Schmid A, Jongman A (2005) Political terrorism: A new guide to actors, authors, concepts, data bases, theories, and literature, 2nd edn. Transaction Publishers, Piscataway, NJ

Schwartz D (1991) International terrorism and Islamic law. Colum. J. Transnat'l L., 29:3, 629-652

Seibert-Fohr A (2003) The relevance of the Rome Statute of the International Criminal Court for amnesties and truth commissions. Max Planck UNYB 7:1, 553-590

Serralvo J (2015) Government Recognition and International Humanitarian Law Applicability in Post-Gaddafi Libya. Yearbook of International Humanitarian Law, Volume 18, 3-41

Shah N (2008) Self-Defense in Islamic and international law: Assessing Al-Qaeda and the invasion of Iraq. Palgrave Macmillan, New York

Shah N (2011) Islamic law and the law of armed conflict: The armed conflict in Pakistan. Routledge, Abingdon

Shah N (2013) The use of force under Islamic law. EJIL24:1, 343-365

Sharif M (2015) Ibn Taymiyyah on Jihad and Baghy. Penerbit Universiti Sains Malaysia, Pulau Pinang

Silverman A (2002) Just war, Jihad and terrorism: A comparison of Western and Islamic norms for the use of political violence. Journal of Church and State 44:1, 73-92

Smith D (2009) Inquiry Call after Nigerian Sect Leader Dies in Custody. The Guardian, 31 July 2009. Available from https://www.theguardian.com/world/2009/jul/31/nigeria-boko-haram-leader [accessed 5 May 2018].

Smith P (2015) The terrorism ahead: Confronting transnational violence in the twenty-first century. Routledge, London

Solis G (2016) The law of armed conflict: International humanitarian law in war. Cambridge University Press, Cambridge

Solomon H (2015) Terrorism and counter-terrorism in Africa: Fighting insurgency from Al-Shabab, Ansar Dine and Boko Haram. Palgrave Macmillan, Hampshire

Sseyonjo M (2012) Jihad re-examined: Islamic law and international law. Santa Clara J. Int'l L. 10:1, 1-33

Syed Razi (n.d.) Nahj al-Balagha (Mufti Ja'far Husain (translator and ed). al-M'iraj Company, Lahore

Tarpel F (2014) Boko Haram's Attempt to Kill Buhari Leaves 40 Dead. Nigeria Communications Week, 24 July 2014. Available from http://www.nigeriacommunicationsweek.com.ng/other-business/boko-haram-s-attempt-to-kill-buhari-leaves-40-dead [accessed 12 May 2018]

Tattersall N, Maclean W (2010) Nigerian Sect Leader Praises al Qaeda, Warns U.S. Reuters, 13 July 2010

The Sun (2015) Bombs at Mosque, restaurant in Jos kill 44. The Sun, 6 July 2015. Available from http://sunnewsonline.com/new/bombs-at-mosque-restaurant-in-jos-kill-44/ [accessed 12 May 2018]

Thomson V (2012) Boko Haram and Islamic fundamentalism in Nigeria. Global Security Studies 3:3, 46-60

Tsagourias N, Morrison A (2018) International humanitarian law: Cases, material and commentary. Cambridge University Press, Cambridge

UK Ministry of Defence (2004) The Joint Service manual of the law of armed conflict. Joint Service Publication

Urmacher K, Sheridan M (2016) The Brutal Toll of Boko Haram's Attacks on Civilians. The Washington Post, 3 April 2016. Available from https://www.washingtonpost.com/graphics/world/nigeria-boko-haram/ [accessed 5 June 2018]

Vagts D (2003) Which courts should try persons accused of terrorism? EJIL 14:2, 313–326

Vanguard (2015) Chad Executes 10 Boko Haram Suspects by Firing Squad. Vanguard, 29 August 2015. Available from http://www.vanguardngr.com/2015/08/chad-executes-10-boko-haram-suspects-by-firing-squad/ [accessed 30 March 2019]

Vanguard (2016) Cameroon Sentences 89 Boko Haram Suspects to Death. Vanguard, 19 March 2016. Available from http://www.vanguardngr.com/2016/03/cameroon-sentences-89-boko-haram-suspects-death/ [accessed 30 March 2019]

Vanhullebusch M (2015) War and law in the Islamic world. Nijhoff, Leiden

Varin C (2016) Boko Haram and the war on terror. Praeger, CA

VOA News (2018) Amnesty Calls on ICC to Fully Probe Boko Haram Conflict Atrocities. VOA News, 10 December 2018. Available from https://www.voanews.com/a/boko-haram-icc-probe/4693811.html [accessed 14 February 2019]

Wa Baile M (2011) Beyond the clash of civilizations: A new cultural synthesis for the Muslims in the West. iUniverse, Bloomington

Walker A (n.d.) What is Boko Haram? United States Institutes of Peace Special Report. Available from http://www.xtome.org/docs/groups/boko-haram/SR308.pdf [accessed 1 May 2018]

Zirker D (2015) Forging military identity in culturally pluralistic societies: quasi-ethnicity. Lexington Books, London

Muhammad-Basheer A. Ismail is a lecturer in law at the School of Law, University of Hull, England. He holds the degrees of LLB (Islamic and Common Law), Bayero University, Kano; LLM, Obafemi Awolowo University, Ile-Ife; and PhD in international law, University of Hull, England. He was admitted to the Nigerian Bar in 1992 and became a Solicitor and Barrister of the Supreme Court of Nigeria. He researches international diplomatic law, law of terrorism, international human rights law and Islamic law. He is the author of Islamic Law and transnational Diplomatic Law: A Quest for Complementarity in Divergent Legal Theories (Springer, 2016).

Chapter 62
Accountability of Religious Actors for Conflicts Motivated by Religion

Nicolás Zambrana-Tévar

Contents

62.1 Introduction: The Responsibility of Religion and the Responsibility of Religious Actors	1422
62.2 Religious Authority as a Central Factor in the Attribution of Responsibility to Religious Actors	1425
62.3 Responsibility of Religious Actors under Municipal and International Law	1429
62.4 The Catholic Church and Islam as Accountable Religious Actors	1431
62.5 Religious Authority in the Catholic Church: The Holy See and Local Churches	1434
62.6 Religious Authority in Islam: The Central Role of Sharia Scholars	1436
62.7 Conclusion	1439
References	1440

Abstract There is an enormous body of literature highlighting the relevance of religion and religious actors in international relations, as well as their potential as a catalyst for peace and conflict. However, the responsibility and accountability of religious actors for the wrongful acts of their members has not received so much attention. The degree of institutionalization of the religious group, as well as religious authority and relations of authority within the group is an element to which courts and law operators are giving an increasing importance in order to evaluate that responsibility and accountability of the religious organization, as evidenced by civil litigation for sex abuse by clergy. However, it must be taken into account that religious authority and religious organizational structures depend heavily on the beliefs of the community. Therefore, those beliefs must be examined closely.

Keywords Catholic Church · conflict · Islam · religion · religious actors · responsibility

---

N. Zambrana-Tévar (✉)
School of Law, KIMEP University, Almaty, Kazakhstan
e-mail: n.zambrana@kimep.kz

© T.M.C. ASSER PRESS and the authors 2022
S. Sayapin et al. (eds.), *International Conflict and Security Law*,
https://doi.org/10.1007/978-94-6265-515-7_62

62.1 Introduction: The Responsibility of Religion and the Responsibility of Religious Actors

The relationship between religion and conflict has led to abundant academic literature addressing religion and religious actors as potential sources, catalysts or enhancers of conflict, on the one hand and, on the other hand, their potential for peacebuilding and reconciliation.[1] For some, non-state actors—including religious actors—are in a privileged position to facilitate the enforcement of human rights in situations of conflict and natural disasters but, at the same time, they should also consider their own behaviour and accountability.[2]

General theories of religiously motivated violence provide psychological or sociopolitical explanations which draw on historical, cultural or theological factors. Nationalism and the way religion and nationalist movements and ideas may reinforce and influence each other has also been the object of much research. Studies on religious fundamentalism deal with religious movements which, often in opposition to state imposed secularization, provide literal interpretations of their faith or of religious texts and propose a return to a mythical time where religion was practiced more purely. Religion may also be a powerful component and resource of a wide range of violent or peaceful social and political movements. There may also be more specific and contingent reasons for religious conflicts such as contested sacred spaces. Although much of the research has centred on Islam since the early years of the 21st century, there are historical as well as recent examples of religiously motivated conflicts in all the major world religions, even in those which, like Hinduism or Buddhism, are believed to be essentially pacific.[3]

Religious ideas may cause violence to the same extent that political ideas without any supernatural component. The reason why religiously motivated conflicts may be more savage is because ethical or political ideals derived from religious beliefs deal with the absolute and the ultimate and, therefore, may provide less room for negotiation and compromise. Religion may also be a form of identity or one of the most important identifying characteristics of a human group, which may lead to conflict against other human groups signalled as "the other". Universal and transnational religions may also bring the positive or negative potential of religious beliefs to an international plane, aided by the different communication processes involved in globalization. In this regard, religious groups may operate locally or transnationally in different forms and structures: as loosely bound communities such as some Protestant denominations like the Lambeth Conference of the Anglican Church; as well structured and active non-state actors such as the Holy See, as the highest governing body of the Catholic Church; as confessional states like Saudi Arabia; as international organisations like the Organisation of Islamic Cooperation; or as violent and non-violent religious factions with ties to sovereign states, such as Hezbollah and

---

[1] Juergensmayer et al. 2013, p. 1; Omer et al. 2015, p. ix, Preface.
[2] Davis 2007, p. 5; Clapham 2009, p. 7.
[3] Jerryson 2018, pp. 453–478.

certain Muslim charities and associations. Religions are not a threat to states nor to the international system of states. However, in recent decades they have successfully posed a challenge to state imposed secularism and to the international system that enables it.[4]

Although the collective and institutional dimension of religion is not absent in the analysis of the relationship between religion and conflict, the focus of academic research is often on the responsibility of religious beliefs and not so much on holding religious actors accountable, let alone any concrete responsibility of religious actors under municipal or international law.[5] Sociologists and political scientists seem mostly interested in explaining and predicting the behaviour of believers, i.e. to what extent individually and collectively held religious beliefs might lead to conflict or, more specifically, to violence. There is an increasing interest in the obligations of NGOs and armed groups under international humanitarian law and international human rights law.[6] but maybe not so much concerning the incidence that the peculiarities of religious non-state actors have in those two areas of the international legal system.

The emphasis may thus be on the study of harmful or beneficial beliefs or, alternatively, on harmful and peaceful believers. The degree to which religious communities, groups or entities *qua* entities are liable for religiously motivated conflict may not have received so much attention. This is understandable because social sciences are descriptive, whereas the law and legal sciences are not interested in describing social phenomena but in subsuming facts into norms, in order to ascertain the legal consequences provided by such norms.

The domestic or transnational component of religion and religious groups is also relevant for accountability. To the extent that a religious group is incorporated in a given jurisdiction or to the extent that the legal system and enforcing mechanisms of that jurisdiction are sufficiently developed to address issues of collective responsibility in the absence of legal personality, the accountability of religious groups may not be a problem at the domestic level.

However, many religions and many religious groups are transnational by nature or by necessity. Their beliefs—even their core beliefs—lead them to spread their message, practices and rituals around the world. Alternatively, some believers may simply move from one country to another for economic reasons or because they are persecuted. Often, believers may bring with them to their new home the same or similar organizational structures which may or may not be wholly independent from the religious organizational structures and religious authorities of the country of origin. Depending on the internal organization and relations of authority, this kind of migration may make the religious group to be in practice a transnational force which operates with a degree of coordination. This transnational element may make religious actors more difficult to police or to hold accountable.

---

[4] Thomas 2000, pp. 20–21.

[5] Cismas 2014, p. 9.

[6] Lindblom 2010, pp. 343–354.

In the analysis of the relationship between conflict and religiously motivated behaviour and of the accountability and liability of religious actors, freedom of religion also plays an important role. First of all, in the context of religious conflict or conflict exacerbated by religion, freedom of religion might be one of the first casualties because victims of religious conflicts may be prevented from practising their religion, forced to convert or deprived from sacred spaces which are essential to their faith.

In the second place, the human right or constitutional right to freedom of religion may sometimes lead to exemptions from the general obligation to abide by state laws, even where those laws protect certain individual and/or public interests. This may lead to a real conflict between the wish or need to follow a religious mandate and the mandates of the state. There may also be a real conflict between the right to practise religion and the rights of others, which may be curtailed if freedom of religion is accommodated. Such conflicts are well known in labour and employment law, in family law or in laws dealing with festivities, personal attire, dietary restrictions and treatment of animals.[7]

In the third place, religious beliefs always have a collective dimension and protecting religious freedom implies protecting that collective dimension. Believers do not only form religious communities; the very existence of a religious community is often one of the most crucial beliefs of its members and so are some of the characteristics of that community. Therefore, accepting and protecting religious beliefs without protecting the existence and structure of the community which holds those beliefs may be a violation of freedom of religion.

One manifestation of this respect for the autonomy of religious groups is the recognition of the relations of religious authority, which are internal to the group, for example, in those cases where a court respects a decision to dismiss a clergyman or a church employee on religious grounds which may not be justifiable in a non-religious context.[8] However, that same respect for autonomy also implies that courts and other state authorities do not see religious authority and relations of authority where there are none. Doing otherwise would disregard the autonomy that religious groups have to organize themselves in accordance with their beliefs and ideals and, in practice, would prevent them from doing so.[9]

As explained below, this has many implications for the attribution of responsibility to a religious group or entity because the more institutionalised, structured and hierarchical is the group and the abovementioned relations of authority, the easier it will be to attribute responsibility to the group for the wrongful acts of some of its members, committed in a religious context. However, freedom of religion should prevent state authorities and human rights enforcing mechanisms from attributing to the religious group characteristics which the group does not actually possess.

---

[7] Witte 2016, p. 253.
[8] Witte 2016, p. 222.
[9] Schouppe 2015, pp. 279–282.

62.2 Religious Authority as a Central Factor in the Attribution of Responsibility to Religious Actors

There may be cases where a strong cause and effect nexus can be established between a crime or wrongful action and a religious belief or mandate. Such religious mandates may be issued by those members of a religious group who hold religious authority. The resulting wrongful action may have also been committed following a certain interpretation of a religious text or of a religious doctrine transmitted by the holder of religious authority, without express instructions to cause harm to others. In all these cases, the question may be posed as to the responsibility of religious authorities in the group, for the acts of the actual perpetrator. An example of the above might be the responsibility of an *ulema* who preaches violence or who issues a *fatwa* against a certain individual, provided that somebody commits a wrongful act as a result of that preaching or ruling.[10]

There might also be cases where the holders of religious authority have certain organisational control over members of the religious group and the duty or the capability to supervise their behaviour. Whenever a wrongful act is committed by a member, which could have been avoided if diligent supervision or disciplinary measures had been in place, the question might also arise as to the responsibility of religious—i.e. supervisory—authorities. This might be the case of some Christian entities such as congregations, dioceses or religious orders, which have been made responsible for the acts of sex abuse by clergy.[11]

Obviously, an act of violence might not be or be only partially motivated by religion or by a desire to follow a religious mandate. A religious group or entity might also be responsible for an omission where, for instance, it had a duty to exert its positive influence on a community and it did not. As an exceptional case, the UN Committee on the Rights of the Child once censured the Holy See, conscious of its moral authority, urging it to change its doctrine on homosexual relationships in order to fight discrimination of homosexual children.[12] However, for the attribution of responsibility to a religious actor in these cases it would probably be necessary to verify to what extent the harm could in fact have been avoided by the positive influence of that religious actor.

The common denominator of these examples is the exercise of religious authority as the main factor for the attribution of responsibility to a religious leader or to a religious group or entity, for the wrongful acts committed by members of the group. Someone with the power to make others follow their mandates or to prevent them from doing something might intuitively be attributed a degree of responsibility for the use made of that power.

In Weberian terminology, power is imperative control and authority imperative legitimate control. In both cases, power and authority are the capacity to make others

---

[10] Winston 2014, p. 1.
[11] Lytton 2008; O'Reilly and Chalmers 2014.
[12] United Nations (CRC) 2014, para. 25.

follow a mandate issued by whoever holds authority, without him having recourse to coercive power. In the case of religious authority, such capacity is basically meant to define the right beliefs and practices (orthodoxy and orthopraxy) of a community.[13] Religious authority might have an element of organisational control within that community and in its relations with others. Now following Durkheim, no community can exist without order, including religious communities, and authority is a major element in any social order.[14] Thus, religion may be the basis or one of the possible justifications for authority in a human community but religious communities *qua* religious communities also need some sort of authority to legitimise the authoritative teaching and interpretation of doctrine, the organisation of charity work, the correct way to perform rituals, as well as correct individual behaviour and social mores.

Nevertheless, religious control and the enforcement of religious norms and mandates entail difficulties that may not be present in the case of non-religious organizations because religious groups do not usually have recourse to financial incentives, as in business, nor to physical sanctions, as in the case of states. These difficulties also exist with respect to religious "managerial control", i.e. control of clergy, ministers and Church employees by hierarchical superiors, where religious groups have to rely on peer control and identity-based control.[15]

Religious beliefs may determine the type and the scope of religious authority and who holds it. This may in turn determine the type of organization that the religious group adopts—e.g. hierarchical or congregational –, as well as its internal and external relationships. Religious authority may also be institutionalized to different degrees. It may reside in a charismatic holy man or preacher or in the institution to which the preacher belongs and which has ordained him or given him training and specific pastoral tasks. However, in the same way that religions evolve, religious authority might also have different contents and scope or be held by different persons or institutions in the course of history.[16] In this regard, religious authority in the Muslim world is no longer held by the Sultan and the kind of authority that the Pope has held in the Catholic Church has also been understood in significantly different ways.

The sources of religious doctrine and authority may be found in oral or written texts which are believed to have been revealed and communicated by the divinity or whose undoubted truth may be based in its perceived antiquity, as a reflex of tradition. In addition to such appeals to tradition and to a remote past, religious authority may take the form of references to nature, to an order found or perceived to exist in the universe and in everyday events, from which principles or norms for individual and communal behaviour may be derived. Finally, those in charge of establishing the official canon of texts or of interpreting and teaching those traditions and texts may

---

[13] Bartholomew 1981, pp. 119–120.
[14] Bartholomew 1981, p. 128.
[15] Tracey 2012, pp. 110 and 122.
[16] Gifford 2009, p. 397.

also be powerful religious authorities.[17] Thus, religious authority may be said to reside in a person, an office, an institution or a text.

Religious leaders (e.g. priests, scholars, judges, *gurus*, etc.) may hold a position of religious authority because of their thorough, professional training and expertise, their accepted charisma or perceived spiritual gifts, their religious virtues and authenticity, the belief that they are in closer contact with the sacred.[18] or for having received an appointment or ordination from another religious or secular authority. Finally, religious authority may also be vested to some extent in the religious group as a whole, as in the specific meaning given to tradition and the *sensus fidelium* in Catholicism or in the importance of the consensus of the *umma* in Islam.

The scope of clergy's authority might also vary, depending on a number of factors. Clergy may only hold authority with respect to teaching doctrine, celebrating rituals and administering intra-church life. In some cases, clergy may have also become essential figures in society or even officials of the state. In these cases, they may also have some socially or even officially acknowledged authority in secular and political areas or in areas which are only indirectly affected by religious or moral beliefs.[19]

On the other hand, any degree of responsibility, as well as the modes of attribution of responsibility to the religious leader or religious group or entity may vary greatly, depending on the kind of norm or legal system that is being discussed or applied. Thus, in a national legal system, a religious leader might be held criminally liable as instigator or accomplice of a religiously motivated crime or simply as a member of what is considered a criminal organisation he is part of. The religious leader or religious group might also or alternatively be held liable in tort under rules of direct liability in negligence if they fail to supervise their members or, under the rules of vicarious liability, if there is evidence of enough organisational control.[20] In this regard, the idea that human rights violations can also be civil wrongs and that human rights obligations can be enforced through tort law is nothing new, as exemplified by the abundant literature on the Alien Tort Claims Act and human rights litigation.[21]

Regulations and administrative law norms might also lead to fines, prohibitions or even to the dissolution of the religious group or at least to the withdrawal of its legal personality.[22] Religious actors, especially those established as legal entities, may also have obligations derived from tax laws, norms for the protection of cultural patrimony, norms on educational and health establishments, municipal ordinances on zoning, use of public spaces and public order, as well as, for instance, banking and financial regulations with respect to the assets collectively owned by those religious actors. Under the international law of human rights, even non-state religious actors might have certain positive and negative obligations to use their religious influence in such a way that human rights are promoted or, at least, not infringed.

---

[17] Gross 2003, pp. 235–241.
[18] Carroll 1981, p. 102.
[19] Carroll 1981, pp. 104 and 108.
[20] Lytton 2008, pp. 55 et seq.
[21] Joseph 2004, pp. 21 et seq.
[22] Council of Europe, Venice Commission 2014, p. 10.

The obligations of religious groups and entities under domestic and international law are nothing but the reverse of the coin of the collective rights that they might have in order to assemble in meetings, organise religious activities, hold property or enter into contracts. For instance, if a bishop can buy land in the name of the diocese and not necessarily in his own name, so that the land can stay in the diocese centuries after that bishop is gone or dead, it is only natural that the diocese and not the bishop in his personal capacity can be held accountable in all matters pertaining to the acquisition and use of that land.

The attribution of responsibility may also depend on the nature and legal status of each religious group or entity, which may vary according to the kind of religious polity and structure, which is largely determined by the beliefs of their members, in addition to other non-religious circumstances of time and place.[23] Such polity and structure may also vary depending on the state where a religious group carries out its activities and which may simply ignore its existence or may treat it like any other private associations or legal entities. Alternatively, a state may recognise or grant a religious group legal personality and the kind of legal structure that perfectly fits its beliefs, internal relationships and needs.[24] As previously said, there might also be cases, in confessional states with established religions, where the religious group is simply part of the structure of the state and clergy have the status of state officials.

Incorporation makes the attribution of responsibility much easier because the legal entity itself—as opposed to its leaders or ordinary members—might have rights and obligations and its own patrimony with which to pay fines or damages to victims. Whether the religious group has incorporated as a private association, a foundation or a company with limited liability might also be relevant for these purposes. Where the religious group or some of its leaders and clergy are part of the structure of the state, not only public law might be applicable, rather than private law, but the state itself might be liable under municipal or international law, for wrongful acts committed by state officials or state entities. This is also in addition to the international responsibility incurred by a state which violates its duty of care for not policing conveniently any individuals or entities within its jurisdiction or to whom governmental functions have been entrusted.[25]

In all of these cases, the religious nature of religious actors, as well as the religious nature of their goals and behaviour must necessarily be taken into account for a proper determination of their legal obligations and for the attribution of responsibility in the violation of those obligations. Such determination must necessarily differ from the case of other entities such as commercial corporations or purely secular associations. Religious actors do not deserve a special treatment beyond the exemptions or accommodations provided by freedom of religion and human rights but it is common that legislators establish different consequences for the different addressees of the laws they pass. Thus, a legislator may take into account the collective nature of a religious

---

[23] Hinings and Raynard 2014, pp. 159–186.

[24] Durham 2010, pp. 3–14.

[25] *O'Keeffe v Ireland* (European Court of Human Rights, Grand Chamber, Application No 35810/09, 28 January 2014).

group, its motivations and goals, its size, how historically deep-rooted or assimilated in the rest of the community it is, etc.

However, and as previously mentioned, domestic courts and secular authorities must also be careful not to see religious authority where there is none or else individuals and groups can be made responsible for the acts of third parties on very weak grounds. Recognising and protecting the autonomy of religious groups must take into account both the existence or the absence of certain religious structures and internal relationships, without making the religious group be something that it is not. For instance, religious doctrine or religious norms may attribute certain organizational or supervisory control to the religious hierarchy which does not exist or is not exercised in practice. That doctrine and those norms may also employ certain language and terminology which is similar to terminology used in a non-religious context and this might lead to serious misunderstandings as to whether authority actually exists.

Possessing religious authority and a specific internal structure or legal personality derived from religious beliefs may therefore be two of the most important factors in determining the responsibilities of those who can kindle the flame of religious conflict but who can also work in favour of peace and interfaith dialogue with their influence, prestige and soft power. We are talking here, therefore, about the responsibilities of religious groups and religious authorities under municipal and international law, i.e. territorial entities such as dioceses, associations such as religious orders, NGOs and guilds, as well as agents or organs of states.

62.3 Responsibility of Religious Actors under Municipal and International Law

As previously said, religious actors may adopt different organizational forms, which may strongly reflect their religious beliefs and which may also determine the existence and/or exercise of religious authority within the group and the corresponding responsibility in the exercise or lack of exercise of that authority. Because of that strong link between religion, religious organization and religious authority, the three should be part of the religious freedom enjoyed by individuals and communities.

The two religions chosen in this chapter—Islam and Catholicism—are good examples of that range of possible forms of organization and of the different kinds of exercise of religious authority. Because they are successful religions with universal aspirations, they are also good examples of the transnational hard and soft power that religious actors may have. In addition to religious authority and to the existence of an internal structure and the possession of legal personality, responsibility may depend on the legal system—e.g. municipal or international—and the type of norm—e.g. civil or criminal—applied in the adjudicatory process.

Where the organizational structures of a religion may be said to be part of the state or to be heavily controlled by the state, to the extent that religious authorities are state officials, agents or entities who carry out governmental functions, the state may be responsible for the wrongful acts of those religious authorities, if not for the wrongful acts of any member of the religious group, committed in a religious context.[26]

At least one religious actor—i.e. the Holy See—may have certain human rights obligations under international law which are analogous to those of states, both because it is a sovereign entity which participates as such in multiple international fora and because it is also a party to several human rights treaties.[27] The case of the Holy See deserves some attention because the nature and scope its obligations under the human rights treaties it has entered into are unclear and because it may or may not engage responsibility, not just for its activities on the international plane but also for its peculiar governing role with respect to local Catholic churches. In this regard, even if a US diocese is not part of the Holy See, some claim that the responsibility of the Holy See could be engaged if a US bishop or priest could be said to be actually under the direct and effective religious authority of the Holy See.[28]

Additionally, some Muslim confessional states are doubtlessly sovereign entities, besides being Muslim religious actors. Furthermore, certain Muslim countries may not be confessional, properly speaking, but may incorporate Muslim clergy and Muslim religious organizational structures within its state bureaucratic apparatus, so that the acts of Muslim clergy may, to some extent, be attributed to the state, if the rules of attribution under the international law of state responsibility so indicate. These human right obligations may be territorial and extraterritorial, in the case of states and non-territorial, where the religious actor does not have a territory, as is the case with the Holy See.

Having said this, states have, under international treaties and customary international norms, negative extraterritorial obligations not to engage or to contribute to acts of torture and other kinds of cruel, inhuman or degrading treatment. Some acts of violence committed in religious conflicts, as well as other crimes committed in a religious context, such as sex abuse by clergy, may fall under such concepts. The scope of such extraterritorial obligations may vary, depending on the language of each international instrument.

Negative obligations are present whenever the potential victim is understood to be within the jurisdiction of the state, within an understanding of jurisdiction that is broader than prescriptive, adjudicatory or enforcement state jurisdiction and which is present whenever the state exercises, lawfully or unlawfully, factual control over

---

[26] Deutscher Bundestag, Wissenschaftliche Dienste 2010, pp. 1–8.

[27] UN General Assembly, Convention on the Rights of the Child, 20 November 1989, United Nations, Treaty Series, vol. 1577, p. 3; UN General Assembly, Convention Against Torture and Other Cruel, Inhuman or Degrading Treatment or Punishment, 10 December 1984, United Nations, Treaty Series, vol. 1465, p. 85; UN General Assembly, International Convention on the Elimination of All Forms of Racial Discrimination, 21 December 1965, United Nations, Treaty Series, vol. 660, p. 195.

[28] Cismas 2017, pp. 310 et seq; Milanovic 2014; New York Times, "The U.N. Confronts the Vatican" https://www.nytimes.com/2014/02/06/opinion/the-un-confronts-the-vatican.html(accessed 24 July 2020).

an area, place, individual or transaction.[29] States also have positive extraterritorial obligations to protect persons from torture and other ill-treatment. Again, these positive obligations arise whenever states are in control or can influence an area which is not the territory over which it exercises sovereignty.

The responsibility of a state may also be engaged when it fails to discharge its duty of due diligence in the supervision of individuals and private entities within its jurisdiction, which may go beyond their territory. States may also engage responsibility under international human rights law, even if the religious group or the religious authorities cannot be said to be part of the structure of the state, where the State regulates intensely the religious activities of Muslim religious authorities. The responsibility of that State could be engaged in cases of harmful acts of the religious group within its territory and, exceptionally, for the extraterritorial effects of those acts.

An international organisation such as the Organisation of Islamic Cooperation may rightfully be considered a religious actor and may also engage responsibility in the same terms as any other international organisation.[30]

Violations of these international negative and positive obligations can therefore take place through (a) acts or omissions of State organs or entities, (b) acts or omissions of private actors over which the State exercises control or influence or (c) through acts of complicity with a territorial or extraterritorial dimension.

The attribution of responsibility to a State for failure to comply with these negative and positive obligations presupposes the attribution to that State of the international wrongful acts in accordance with general rules of attribution of State responsibility for internationally wrongful acts.

To sum up, incorporated or unincorporated, domestic or transnational religious groups may engage responsibility under the civil, criminal or administrative law of the place where they are incorporated or where they operate. They may also engage responsibility under international humanitarian law or—although this is still controversial.[31]—under international human rights law—in the same way as any other non-religious individual, group, corporation or NGO.

62.4 The Catholic Church and Islam as Accountable Religious Actors

One of the most recent and useful examples of attribution of responsibility to a religious group for wrongful actions committed by some of its members are those instances where either national courts of law or international tribunals and human rights reporting mechanisms have dealt with cases of sex abuse by Catholic clergy.

---

[29] United Nations General Assembly 2015, p. 23; Wilde 2013, pp. 635-661; Schutter et al. 2012, pp. 1084-1169.
[30] Cismas 2014, pp. 239-305.
[31] Clapham 2014, pp. 531-549.

Here, Catholic entities such as dioceses, religious orders or the Holy See itself have been held liable or accountable and in all cases the perception of their religious authority over clergy and Church members has been a crucial element for the attribution of responsibility.

Catholic entities have been held liable because of the perception that (a) they had a duty and the capacity to supervise clergy and had been negligent in such supervision; (b) they had organizational control over clergy and Church activities, which made them strictly liable to the same extent that an employer may be strictly liable for wrongful acts of his employees; (c) they had appointed and ordained clergy and other church employees, conferring upon them religious authority that they could abuse, which justified holding them accountable for such abuse; and (d) they had the duty and the capacity—especially the Holy See—to foster human rights through their doctrine and had not done so.

This model of attribution of direct and indirect responsibility to religious groups and other institutions, based on authority and organizational control, is still controversial and some believe that the rules of vicarious liability have gone too far.[32] However, the model may nevertheless be tested to some extent in the case of wrongful actions other than sex abuse committed by clergy or in a purely religious context. In any case, this kind of collective responsibility on the basis of the existence of religious authority necessarily implies analysing the concept of religious authority and its existence in each specific religion and/or religious group.

The limitations of space in this chapter have prompted us to choose the Catholic Church and, by way of comparison, Islam. This choice has also been motivated by the fact that these two religions and religious groups are among the most successful in history, they both have universal aspirations and engage in proselytism although in different ways and to this end they are not confined to just one culture, territory or ethnic group.

Other significant similarities between the two are the fact that they are both revealed religions and religions of salvation, i.e. they contend that their basic truths have been communicated by the divinity and they promise relief from evil and suffering, in this life and in the next. They both preach and operate on the basis of objective moral norms, virtues and values. Islam is often described as relying heavily on the belief that moral and religious norms are obligatory because they are mandated by the divinity,[33] whereas Catholicism stresses the possibility to achieve objective moral truth solely through reason.[34] To an external observer, they both seem to share some common beliefs and values with regards to family life, sexual relationships or the limits of individual freedom, which sometimes are at odds with the secularized West and with world areas deeply influenced by the West.

However, Catholicism and Islam also have important differences. Although both are Abrahamic religions born in the Middle East, Christianity in general and Catholicism in particular acquired their present form in Europe and have left a deeper imprint

---

[32] Phillip 2011, pp. 932–961.
[33] Al-Attar 2010.
[34] John Paul II 1993 §31.

than Islam in Western civilization. Furthermore, and very importantly for the analysis of religious authority, Christian doctrine always understood that the temporal and the spiritual were two separate realities although this separation has been understood in different ways and there has always been tension between the two, sometimes spiritual authority prevailing over earthly powers or the other way round.[35] Conversely, there is no clear separation between the secular and the spiritual in Islam, which aspires to be a code of conduct for all spheres of the life of the individual and the society or state he or she lives in.[36]

Furthermore, a classic view of religious authority may lead to the conclusion that, in Catholicism, this kind of authority is conferred through the sacrament of priesthood, which sets the ordained clergy in a class apart, either metaphysically, socially or both. Besides, Catholic clergy may appear to be thoroughly organised within a centralised hierarchy, in contrast to some less hierarchical or congregational Protestant denominations and sects. In contrast, there is in principle no clergy in Islam and religious authority is held in practice by experts in Islamic doctrine, especially Islamic law. However, those who attain this level of knowledge and authority may sometimes also appear to constitute a clerical class apart from the rest of the faithful.

Importantly for the purposes of the attribution of authority, Catholic entities (e.g. dioceses and religious orders) can easily be granted legal personality by the state, thanks to their organisation and structure, which facilitates their having rights and obligations *vis à vis* other individual and entities, with whom they can establish many of the same types of relationships that are common in non-religious polities (e.g. contracts, non-contractual obligations, etc.). In fact, Canon law (i.e. Church law) greatly contributed to the birth of legal entities in Western legal systems.[37]

This level of institutionalization and polity structure may appear to be lower in Islam or at least its process of institutionalization runs along different lines. Because the separation of the religious and the secular is more tenuous in Islam than in Christianity, political structures were for centuries also the basic religious structures of this religion. However, in Islam there may also be associations and religious guilds such as *sufi* brotherhoods or Muslim associations established in Western countries around a Mosque. However, such structures are looser and not as well defined by religious doctrine and religious law as in Catholicism. At the present time and in certain countries, Islam may have been absorbed by the state to some extent and this determines the kind of Muslim polity that exists in that country.

---

[35] Sabine and Thorson 1937, pp. 224–243.
[36] Esposito 2011, p. 161.
[37] Davoudi 2018, p. 25.

62.5 Religious Authority in the Catholic Church: The Holy See and Local Churches

The Catholic Church sees any authority it has as having been delegated or bestowed upon it by Jesus Christ, its founder.[38] Such authority is therefore deemed necessary to fulfil the Church's mission of salvation through teaching, sanctifying (e.g. celebrating sacraments such as baptism, marriage or the eucharist) and governing, understood as the organisation or coordination of teaching and charity activities, as well as the celebration of the sacraments.

The Church asks its members to believe and follow the "Magisterium" of the Pope and the Bishops who "announce moral principles, including those pertaining to the social order".[39] The Church believes that its moral norms are both based on human dignity and reason, as well as have support in the Bible, its sacred scripture.[40] A conscious violation of moral norms is considered a sin and certain sins, to the extent that they affect the social dimension of the Church, may also be criminal offenses under Church law (i.e. Canon law). The consequences of a sin are only "spiritual", i.e. may not be empirically perceived. However, sanctions under Canon law do have perceptible, even patrimonial effects. For instance, two of the most serious punishments for offenses under Canon law are the loss of the clerical state, which prevents from holding positions reserved for clergy and excommunication, which prevents from receiving the sacraments.[41] Canon law norms are also morally binding but in different degrees, depending on the issuing authority and its contents. Generally speaking, purely ecclesiastical norms which are not explicitly derived from natural law principles may not be followed if they cause great inconvenience to the addressee of the norm in a specific case.[42]

As previously mentioned, "governing" in the Church makes reference to the organisation and discipline of teaching, sacraments and charity work. Such triple mission is usually referred to as the three *munus* or functions: *munus sanctificandi*, *munus regendi*, and *munus docendi*.[43] The *sacra potestas* conferred by the sacrament of holy orders grants priests a specific power to fulfil that mission. Such power can correspondingly be divided into the power of orders and the power of jurisdiction.

The power of jurisdiction is indeed granted by the sacrament of priesthood but it also requires a specific appointment (i.e. *collatio*) to carry out a specific task. This power may involve issuing norms and judicial decisions which are legally binding but such power would not properly describe the tasks of ecclesiastical authorities if it was forgotten that the *munus regendi* does not only include a rule-making power but also a role of promotion, coordination and supervision of pastoral activities

---

[38] Matthew, 16-19; Paul VI 1964, *Lumen Gentium* (LG), paras. 7 and 8.
[39] John Paul II 1993, §2032 et seq.
[40] John Paul II 1993, §1950 et seq.
[41] John Paul II 1988, can. 1331 et seq.
[42] Colom and Rodríguez Luño 2001, p. 394.
[43] Paul VI 1964, LG, no. 20.

which is to be performed through non-imperative mandates, e.g. through counselling, advice, exhortation and by setting an example.[44] In certain places and at certain times, ecclesiastics have also fulfilled other, more secular roles as state officials or as community leaders of different kinds.

Although the *potestas* and the *tria munera* are conferred through ordination, laymen and women may also have and exercise to a certain degree the power of jurisdiction and therefore can participate in the authority to teach, sanctify and govern. For instance, a layman may be appointed an ecclesiastical judge or be a member of certain ecclesiastical administrative bodies and councils at the parish, diocesan and universal level.[45] Furthermore, through the sacrament of baptism, any Catholic faithful acquires certain rights and duties with regard to the aforementioned functions and mission of salvation,[46] so that every Catholic, to some extent, may be said to exercise a degree of religious authority.[47]

Priests are considered "co-workers" of bishops[48] and owe special obedience to the bishop of the place where they are incardinated.[49] Bishops can and should exercise certain supervisory and disciplinary powers over clergy and over all the faithful.[50] Bishops enjoy a lot of autonomy in their diocese[51] although bishops' power must always be exercised in "hierarchical communion" with the Pope.[52]

The Church is often perceived as "an ultrahierarchical, rigidly controlled organization", instead of actually being "remarkably decentralized".[53] There is also a tendency to regard "the pope as the chief executive from whom the bishops receive their authority".[54] In this regard, the Pope "possesses supreme, full, immediate, and universal ordinary power in the Church, which he is always able to exercise freely" and "not only possesses power over the universal Church but also obtains the primacy of ordinary power over all particular churches".[55] However, bishops enjoy the autonomy previously mentioned and their authority does not derive from or is delegated by the Pope. Bishops exercise their power of administration over local church affairs in their own name and with the authority of the ordination granted by another bishop or bishops, not by the Pope. Bishops are commonly appointed to a specific diocese by the Holy See but in a process where local churches and episcopal

---

[44] Viana 1997, pp. 39 et seq.

[45] Paul VI 1964, LG no. 33; John Paul II, CIC can. 228 §2, can. 1421 §2.

[46] John Paul II 1988, CIC can. 208 et seq.

[47] Paul VI 1965, *Apostolicam Actuositatem*, no. 2; John Paul II, *Christifideles Laici* 1988, no. 14; Paul VI 1964, LG, no. 33.

[48] Paul VI, *Presbyterorum Ordinis*, no. 2.

[49] John Paul II 1983, CIC can. 273 et seq.

[50] John Paul II 1983, CIC can. 392.

[51] John Paul II 1983; CIC 375 et seq.

[52] Paul VI 1964, LG, 21 and 22.

[53] Allen 2004, p. 65.

[54] Reese 1996, p. 24.

[55] John Paul II 1983, CIC, can. 331 and 333; Paul VI 1964, LG, no. 22; Paul VI 1964, Christus Dominus, no. 2.

conferences are usually involved, or "can come about by legitimate customs that have not been revoked",[56] as is the case with Catholic churches in Eastern rites. In this regard, the Holy See is basically the personal office of the Pope or the Bishop of Rome, who is also the head of the Church. Under Canon law, the Roman Curia, i.e. the administrative organs which aid the Pope in his task, are also considered part of the Holy See.[57]

The Pope is a bishop himself and local bishops are in no way an inferior category of clergymen.[58] Furthermore, if the "primacy" of the Pontificate were used by a future Pope to trump the legitimate autonomy of local churches,[59] it would be contrary to the doctrine of the Church and the Pope could not expect to be obeyed in this regard.[60] Bishops themselves are also called to exercise their collective power as College of Bishops over the entire Church in institutions such as Ecumenical Councils, Synods of Bishops, the increasing importance of Episcopal Conferences, as well as in international associations of Episcopal Conferences or in the bishops' roles as officials of the Roman Curia, if they receive such an appointment. However, "the college or body of bishops has no authority unless it is understood together with the Roman Pontiff".[61]

Although authority within religious orders stems from their associative nature and not from the sacrament of priesthood—which not all monks receive and obviously none of the nuns –, superiors of religious orders have a degree of authority over ordained monks and over lay brothers alike and are often assimilated to diocesan bishops by Canon Law.[62] Where a Catholic entity has been incorporated or set up under domestic law, its internal life and any supervisory or disciplinary powers are also governed by domestic laws and regulations.

62.6 Religious Authority in Islam: The Central Role of Sharia Scholars

The Quran is by far the most important source of doctrine and religious norms in Islam. The Quran is not just a revealed text but the very Word of God and it aspires to be a complete set of rules which regulate the relationship between man and God, man and other men, private as well as community life, state life and also the relationships between the Muslim community and non-Muslim communities.[63] Thus, the autonomy of the secular with respect to the religious and the distinction between

---

[56] Paul VI 1964, LG, no. 24.
[57] John Paul II 1983, CIC, can. 361.
[58] Paul VI 1964, LG, no. 21; John Paul II 1983, CIC, can. 381.
[59] Grigorita 2011, pp. 383 et seq.
[60] Arrieta 1997, p. 92.
[61] Paul VI 1964, LG, no. 22.
[62] John Paul II 1983, CIC, can. 134.
[63] Endress 2002, pp. 55 et seq; Hillenbrand 2015, chapter 5: Law.

moral norms and religious norms is not so marked in Islam as in Catholicism.[64] Furthermore, moral, legal and political norms in Islam receive much more attention by Muslim scholars and Muslims in general than Muslim religious doctrine, theology and mysticism.

The relevance of Islamic law (*fiqh*) in Islam, as well as the entanglement between the religious and the secular, morality and law, necessarily has certain implications for the issue of religious authority in Islam. Although the Quran states that authority belongs to God, He can delegate it to some elected men who become mediators between God and humans. Traditionally, both religious and political authority were held by one person, the caliph, after the death of the Prophet Muhammad.[65] Classical Islam may nevertheless not be described as a theocracy because, strictly speaking, there is no clergy in Islam[66] and no Church in the sense of an organised structure able to present a doctrine that is binding for all Muslims.[67] Nevertheless, there are some elements of religious establishments in many Muslim countries, notably in Saudi Arabia and Iran. Still, no one is anointed or granted a special status through ordination and set apart from the rest of believers in order to establish a relationship between the community and the sacred.[68]

Access to supernatural truths is always mediated and in the case of religions which rely heavily on religious texts as mediators which convey God's will and message, such texts must be interpreted. The central place of Islamic law in the path to salvation has facilitated that Islamic law scholars (i.e. the *ulama*) take the place of clergy as authoritative interpreters of the Quran as well as of other, secondary sources of Islamic law such as the *hadiths*—record of sayings, actions and silent approvals of the Prophet. Through their interpretation of sacred texts and their institutional appeal to the infallible consensus[69] of the *umma* or community of believers, the *ulama* not only determine supernatural beliefs but define social behaviours and mores. In the absence of the powerful symbolism of Catholic ordination and priesthood, Muslim clerics derive their authority from a number of academic sources such as peer reviews, appointments to prominent academic positions and publications.[70] This has actually turned the *ulama* into a professional religious class apart from the lay faithful whose duties are cultural, missionary, legal and theological, and whose authority is a complex relationship of knowledge, conduct and charisma or academic reputation.[71]

To fulfil their mission, the *ulama* receive their pedigree as learned scholars of religious texts in institutions of higher Islamic learning, such as the influential Al-Azhar Mosque and University, in Cairo. The *ulama* also organise themselves in

---

[64] Gaborieau 2004, p. 6.

[65] Inam 2013, p. 69.

[66] Krämer and Schmidtke 2006, p. 5.

[67] Inam 2013, p. 67.

[68] Hillenbrand 2015, chapter 4: Faith: The second pillar of Islam-Prayer.

[69] Muhammad Qasim Zaman, in Krämer and Schmidtke 2006, op cit. p. 153 et seq.

[70] Nielsen 2016, p. 2.

[71] Krämer and Schmidtke 2006, p. 8.

corporations, sometimes along hierarchical lines, notably in *Shia* Islam, where the *ayatollahs* have an official relevance that *imams* and *muftis* may not have in *Sunni* Islam.

Furthermore, the *ulama* sometimes obtain a monopoly on worship instruction and on the legal system from political authorities, in exchange for their ideological support. This has also led the *ulama* to establish vast educational and charitable structures, at least in some countries like Saudi Arabia. Thus, in some Muslim and/or Islamic countries, the *ulama* may be state officials, public sector employees or somehow be under direct state control and their ministry may be regulated and supervised by a specific ministry or agency like the Committee of the Grand Ulama, in Saudi Arabia.[72] Quite understandably, this may also lead to the manipulation of Islamic authorities and Islamic beliefs by the state.[73]

Religious authority in Islam may now be experiencing a process of fragmentation, too. One significant example is the Muslim diaspora in the West, where Islam is being individualized and Muslim beliefs are increasingly subjective.[74] Furthermore, lay Muslims in Europe may be relatively disconnected from pre-existing structures of religious authority and have assumed a more preeminent role—in mosques or in Muslim associations—than the one they had in their countries of origin.[75]

Curiously, in some European countries, Muslim religious authority may be created indirectly by state authorities where these request the presence of "official interlocutors" with which to negotiate a framework for the relationship between the State and Muslim communities. On top of the theoretical absence of clergy in Islam, the diversity of religious trends and associations may make those official interlocutors little representative and therefore have little authority.[76] In the West, Muslim communities are also setting up Islamic law tribunals, especially in the field of family law, which may function under domestic mediation and arbitration laws.[77] However, this apparent democratization of the religious sphere in the West may or may not have been conducive to liberalizing changes in dogma[78] or to the acceptance of a Western understanding of human rights.

It is also remarkable how social media and the internet,[79] as well as the greater accessibility to Islamic texts, have led to the apparition of a new category of Muslim preachers and Islamic law professionals who have sometimes acquired much bigger audiences and more practical authority than their "official" or traditional counterparts,[80] as exemplified by media stars such as Yusuf al-Qaradawi and Muhammad

---

[72] Mouline 2014, p. 1 et seq.

[73] Nielsen 2016, p. 6 et seq.

[74] Volpi and Turner 2007, p. 4.

[75] Ibid., p. 10.

[76] Gaborieau 2004, p. 11; Conseil Français du Culte Musulman, https://www.cfcm.tv/ (accessed 24 July 2020).

[77] Muslim Arbitration Tribunal, http://www.matribunal.com/history.php (accessed 24 July 2020).

[78] Peter 2006, p. 108.

[79] https://islamonline.net/; https://ar.islamway.net/ (accessed 24 July 2020).

[80] Gaborieau 2004, p. 13.

al-Urayfi, who boast millions of followers in several online platforms.[81] Another example is the issue of *fatwas* or religious rulings by non-traditional institutions or even by non-specialists.[82]

Additionally, secular authorities such as parliaments and high courts staffed with secular lawyers, as well as political activists and religious intellectuals who are the product of Western academic institutions, are increasingly performing interpretative roles which were confined to the *ulama*, in the past. Finally, some violent Islamic groups despise traditional Muslim religious authorities and their leaders have assumed both political and religious authority without having gone through the official kind of training and academic channels that usually produce the *ulama*.[83]

62.7 Conclusion

This chapter has put forward the concept of religious authority as the basis for the attribution of responsibility to the holders of such religious authority, be they individuals or legal entities, religious leaders or religious communities. The individual acts of members of a religious group may be attributed to the group when they are performed following a mandate of a religious authority or when the religious authority had organizational and supervisory control over those members and those acts, executed in a religious context.

The existence of responsibility for the acts of others and the attribution of that responsibility to religious leaders or to the religious group will largely depend upon the true existence of religious authority and the specific norms which establish the existence of legal duties and responsibilities, as well as the methods of attribution under domestic or international law.

Tort law in particular, in the context of the sex abuse scandal, has revealed how control may be used in the attribution of collective responsibility for lack of effective supervision or, even in the absence of negligent supervision, because organizational control is considered the basis of strict and vicarious liability.

International human rights law may also be a rich field where to explore this kind of collective responsibility of religious actors for the acts of some of their members. In the case of the Holy See as signatory of certain human rights treaties, certain UN human rights committees have tried to attribute that responsibility because they understood that the Holy See, as governing entity of the Catholic Church under international law and Catholic doctrine, had not only the duty but also the responsibility to supervise and steer local churches in the direction of a more effective protection of human rights. However, there may be a clear misunderstanding as to the nature and effectiveness of religious authority in the Church. Furthermore, the autonomy of local churches is also an important consideration, given the fact that the Holy See is

---

[81] Nielsen 2016, p. 5.
[82] The European Council for Fatwa and Research, https://www.e-cfr.org/ (accessed 24 July 2020).
[83] Lacroix 2012, p. 5.

far from engaged in the daily supervision or day to day management of those local churches.

Finally, human rights law and the rapidly developing doctrines about the extraterritorial human rights obligations of states make such obligations largely rest on some kind of effective control over territory and over the perpetrators of human rights violations. Such control or "jurisdiction" often refers to "factual" or "effective" "control, power or authority" but also to "influence" in the "enjoyment of human rights outside its national territory". This type of control and influence may or may not be derived from any exercise of religious authority.

References

Al-Attar M (2010) Islamic ethics: Divine command theory in arabo-islamic thought, culture and civilization in the Middle East. Routledge, New York
Allen J (2004) All the Pope's men: The inside story of how the Vatican really thinks. Doubleday, New York
Arrieta J I (1997) Diritto dell'organizazione ecclesiastica. Giuffrè, Milan
Bartholomew J N (1981) A sociological view of authority in religious organizations. Review of Religious Research, vol. 23, no. 2: 118-132
Carroll J W (1981) Some issues in clergy authority. Review of Religious Research, vol. 23, no. 2: 99-117
Cismas I (2014) Religious actors and international law. Oxford University Press, New York
Cismas I (2017) The child's best interests and religion: A case study of the Holy See's best interests obligations and clerical child sexual abuse. In: Sutherland E E, Barnes Macfarlane L A (eds) Implementing article 3 of the United Nations Convention on the Rights of the Child. Best interests, welfare and well-being. Cambridge University Press, New York, pp 310-325
Clapham A (2009) Non-state actors. In: Chetail V (ed) Postconflict peace-building. A lexicon. Oxford University Press, New York, pp 200-212
Clapham A (2014) Non-state actors. In: Moeckli D et al. (eds) International Human Rights Law, 2nd edn. Oxford University Press, Oxford, pp 531-549
Colom E, Rodríguez Luño A (2001) Elegidos en Cristo para ser santos: curso de teología moral fundamental. Palabra, Madrid
Council of Europe, Venice Commission (2014) Joint Guidelines on the Legal Personality of Religious or Belief Communities, 16 June 2014, Opinion No. 673/2012, CDL-AD(2014)023 https://www.venice.coe.int/webforms/documents/default.aspx?pdffile=CDL-AD(2014)023-e. Accessed 24 July 2020
Davis A (2007) Concerning accountability of humanitarian action, humanitarian practice network. Network Paper no. 58: 1-24
Davoudi L (2018) The historical role of the corporation in society. Journal of the British Academy, 6(s1): 17-47
Deutscher Bundestag, Wissenschaftliche Dienste (German Parliament Research Office) (2010) Haftung der Kirche in sexuellen Missbrauchsfällen, 2010, WD 3 – 3000 – 144/10 https://www.bundestag.de/resource/blob/413890/2c763f7449ab65fbdd8a30f26ab94ff3/WD-3-144-10-pdf-data.pdf. Accessed 24 July 2020
Durham W C (2010) Legal status of religious organizations: a comparative overview. The Review of Faith and International Affairs, vol. 8, issue 2: 3-14.
Endress G (2002) Islam an historical introduction. Edinburgh University Press, Edinburgh
Esposito J L (2011) What everyone needs to know about Islam. Oxford University Press, New York

Gaborieau M (2004) Autorités religieuses en Islam. Archive de Sciences Sociales des Religions https://doi.org/10.4000/assr.2883

Gifford P (2009) Religious authority: scripture, tradition, charisma. In: Hinnells J R (ed) The Routledge Companion to the Study of Religion. Routledge, New York, pp 397-410

Grigorita G (2011) L'autonomie ecclésiastique selon la législation canonique actuelle de l'Eglise Orthodoxe et de l'Eglise Catholique. Editrice Pontificia Università Gregoriana, Rome

Gross R M (2003) Authority in religious traditions. In: Post S G (ed) Encyclopedia of Bioethics, Vol. I, 3rd edn. Thomson Gale, New York, pp 235-242

Hillenbrand C (2015) Islam: A new historical introduction. Thames & Hudson, London

Hinings C R, Raynard M (2014) Organizational form, structure and religious organizations. In: Tracey P, Phillips N, Lounsbury M (eds) Religion and Organization Theory. Research in the Sociology of Organizations. Emerald Group Publishing Limited, Bingley, pp 159-186

Inam H (2013) Power and authority in religious traditions in Islam. European Judaism, vol. 46, no. 1: 66-74

Juergensmayer M, Kitts M, Jerryson M (2013) Introduction: the enduring relationship of religion and violence. In: Jerryson M, Juergensmeyer M, Kitts M (eds) Oxford Handbook of Religion and Violence. OUP, New York, pp 1-12

Jerryson M (2018) Buddhism, war, and violence. In: Cozort D, Shields J M (eds) The Oxford Handbook of Buddhist Ethics. Oxford University Press, New York, pp 453-478

John Paul II (1983) Code of Canon law - *Codex Iuris Canonici* (CIC) http://www.vatican.va/archive/cod-iuris-canonici/cic_index_en.html. Accessed 24 July 2020

John Paul II (1988) Post-Synodal Apostolic Exhortation *Christifideles Laici* http://w2.vatican.va/content/john-paul-ii/en/apost_exhortations/documents/hf_jp-ii_exh_30121988_christifideles-laici.html. Accessed 24 July 2020

John Paul II (1993) Catechism of the Catholic Church. Libreria Editrice Vaticana, Vatican City http://www.vatican.va/archive/ENG0015/_INDEX.HTM Accessed 24 July 2020

Joseph S (2004) Corporations and transnational human rights litigation. Hart, Portland, OR

Krämer G, Schmidtke S (2006) Speaking for Islam. Religious Authorities in Muslim Societies. Brill, Leiden

Lacroix S (2012) Islamism and the question of religious authority. DIIS Religion and Violence papers, Danish Institute for International Studies https://spire.sciencespo.fr/hdl:/2441/3obp0eq3mp8loq5ndor929pd43/resources/islamism-and-the-question-of-religious-authority.pdf. Accessed 24 July 2020

Lindblom A-K (2010) The responsibility of other entities: Non-governmental organizations. In: Crawford J, Pellet A, Olleson S (eds) The law of international responsibility. Oxford University Press, New York, pp 343-354

Lytton T D (2008) Holding bishops accountable: How lawsuits helped the Catholic Church confront clergy sexual abuse. Harvard University Press, Cambridge, MA

Milanovic M (2014) CRC Concluding Observations on the Holy See, EJIL Talk Blog of the European Journal of International Law https://www.ejiltalk.org/crc-concluding-observations-on-the-holy-see/. Accessed 24 July 2020

Mouline N (2014) The clerics of Islam. Religious authority and political power in Saudi Arabia. Yale University Press, New Haven, CT

Nielsen R A (2016) The changing face of Islamic authority in the Middle East. Middle East Brief, no. 99, Brandeis University, Waltham, MA, pp 1-8

Omer A, Appleby R S, Little D (2015) Oxford Handbook of Religion, Conflict and Peacebuilding. Oxford University Press, New York

O'Reilly J T, Chalmers M (2014) The clergy sex abuse crisis and the legal responses. Oxford University Press, New York

Paul VI (1964) Dogmatic Constitution on the Church *Lumen Gentium* http://www.vatican.va/archive/hist_councils/ii_vatican_council/documents/vat-ii_const_19641121_lumen-gentium_en.html. Accessed 24 July 2020

Peter F (2006) Individualization and religious authority in Western European Islam. Islam and Christian–Muslim Relations, 17:1, 105-118, https://doi.org/10.1080/09596410500400165

Phillip M (2011) Distorting vicarious liability. Modern Law Review 74(6): 932–961

Reese T J (1996) Inside the Vatican: the politics and organization of the Catholic Church. Harvard University Press, Cambridge MA

Sabine G H, Thorson T L (1937) The investiture controversy. In: A history of political theory. Dryden Press, New York

Schouppe J P (2015) La dimensión institutionnelle de la liberté de religion dans la jurisprudence de la Cour européenne des droits de l'homme. A. Pédone, Paris

Schutter O et al. (2012) Commentary to the Maastricht principles on extraterritorial obligations of states in the area of economic, social and cultural rights. Human Rights Quarterly 34, no. 4: 1084-1169

Thomas S (2000) Religion and international conflict. In Dark K R (ed) Religion and international relations. Palgrave McMillan, London, pp 1-23

Tracey P (2012) Religion and organization: a critical review of current trends and future directions. The Academy of Management Annals, vol. 6, no. 1: 87-134

United Nations (CRC) (2014) Concluding observations on the second periodic report of the Holy See, 31 January 2014, CRC/C/VAT/CO/2 https://www.refworld.org/publisher,CRC,CONCOBSERVATIONS,VAT,52f8a1544,0.html

United Nations General Assembly (2015) Note by the Secretary General, Torture and Other Cruel, Inhuman or degrading Treatment or Punishment, 7 August 2015, A/70/303 https://www.refworld.org/docid/55f292224.html

Viana A (1997) Organización del gobierno de la Iglesia. EUNSA, Pamplona

Volpi F, Turner B S (2007) Introduction: making Islamic authority matter. Theory Culture and Society, vol. 24(2): 1-19

Wilde R (2013) The extraterritorial application of international human rights law on civil and political rights. In: Sheeran S, Rodley N (eds) Routledge Handbook of International Human Rights Law. Routledge, New York, pp 635-661

Winston B (2014) The Rushdie fatwa and after: A lesson to circumspect. Palgrave Macmillan, London

Witte J, Nichols J A (2016) Religion and the American constitutional experiment. Oxford University Press, New York

Nicolás Zambrana-Tévar studied law at the Complutense University in Madrid. He received an LLM degree from the London School of Economics and a PhD from the University of Navarra. He worked as a lawyer for Freshfields Bruckhaus Deringer and Garrigues Abogados. He has been a member of several research groups on Business and Human Rights. He has also published in the field of law and religion in the Journal of Church and State, the Oxford Journal of Law and Religion and Ius Canonicum.

Chapter 63
The Children vs the Church: Human Rights and the Holy See in the Sex Abuse Crisis

Nicolás Zambrana-Tévar

Contents

63.1 Sex Abuse by Catholic Clergy: Local and Global Responsibilities 1444
63.2 The Holy See before the Council of Europe 1447
63.3 The Holy See before the International Criminal Court 1448
63.4 The Holy See before the United Nations Human Rights Treaty Bodies 1449
    63.4.1 The Holy See before the United Nations Committee on the Rights of the Child 1449
    63.4.2 The Holy See before the United Nations Committee against Torture 1453
    63.4.3 The Holy See Before the United Nations Committee on the Elimination of Racial Discrimination 1455
    63.4.4 Preliminary Conclusions: The Understanding of the International Obligations of the Holy See by United Nations Treaty Bodies 1459
63.5 The Holy See in Dialogue with the United Nations Treaty Bodies 1460
63.6 Conclusion 1468
References 1471

Abstract From 2014 to 2016, several reports issued by United Nations Treaty Bodies made some very severe criticisms about what they saw as the deficient fulfilment of the obligations that the Holy See had as a party to human rights treaties. In particular, these treaty bodies insisted that the Holy See, as supreme governing body of the Catholic Church, had international obligations of an extraterritorial nature and that it had to discharge those duties making sure that local churches all over the world aligned their actions and teachings with the protection of human rights. In light of the scandals of child abuse, the Treaty Bodies argued that those extraterritorial obligations had been breached. The Holy See responded that it not only did not have such extraterritorial obligations but that its position as supreme governing body of the Church did not allow it to inappropriately interfere in the internal life of local churches and of the states where the churches were located. This chapter is a contribution to the understanding of the human rights obligations of religious actors.

Keywords Holy See · Vatican · Child Abuse · Human Rights · Extraterritorial obligations

---

N. Zambrana-Tévar (✉)
School of Law, KIMEP University, Almaty, Kazakhstan
e-mail: n.zambrana@kimep.kz

63.1 Sex Abuse by Catholic Clergy: Local and Global Responsibilities

Criminal and civil proceedings under domestic law and before domestic courts have been the two most frequent mechanisms to hold perpetrators and Church entities accountable in cases of sex abuse committed by Catholic clergy.[1] Ecclesiastical "authorities" in various countries are often perceived as not having done enough to prevent sex abuse and to have made things worse with a policy of cover up and not exercising swift "canonical" justice.[2] Some of the most important aspects of the crisis and a relevant element in the analysis of the responsibility of Church entities under domestic and international law are its governance and organisational failures: what Church authorities did wrong and what they failed to do in terms of prevention, discipline and reparation. Church organisation is highly relevant in any analysis of Church accountability because the degree of authority and "control" of higher levels of the Catholic hierarchy over clergy and the lay faithful has often determined the responsibility of members of the hierarchy and Church entities, even in the absence of any personal wrongdoing.

In the process of determining the liability in tort of Church entities for its own acts or for the acts of others, United States courts have for instance been inclined to apply principles of direct liability for fault[3] whereas courts in the rest of the world courts have oscillated between the application of principles of direct and vicarious liability, introducing elements of liability for fault, strict liability and enterprise risk in their analysis.[4]

However, for the analysis of the abovementioned degree of authority and control, as well as for determining the religious structure where that authority is exercised, it is unavoidable that courts and other state and international bodies try to understand what the Catholic Church is and how it operates which, in turn, leads to an analysis of the teachings of the Church about itself (i.e. ecclesiology), with the risk that the perception of the Church from the outside differs from the one that the Church has of itself.

United States courts, especially during the 1990s, have been especially careful not to become "entangled" in issues of religious doctrine and religious law and have often gone to great lengths to explain that they were going to look at the behaviour of Church authorities from a non-religious perspective.[5] Therefore, they tried to avoid ruling on the negligent discharge of any supervisory obligations that bishops or religious superiors may have over priests and members of religious orders, under Canon law and Church doctrine. United States courts have instead focused on general duties to act diligently and in how appropriately were the victims or their families

---

[1] Lytton 2008; O'Reilly and Chalmers 2014.

[2] Allen 2004, p. 292.

[3] Lytton 2008, pp. 55 et seq.

[4] Hoyano and Keenan 2007, pp. 216 et seq.

[5] Lupu and Tuttle 2004, pp. 1–124.

treated by ecclesiastical authorities where, for instance, the parents of the victim had reported the priest before the bishop. This "neutral" way of treating intra-Church relationships has also been the way in which United States courts have traditionally dealt with property issues involving members of any religious group.[6]

In civil law countries, the rules of 19th century civil codes do not seem to contemplate the kind of situations involved in clergy sex abuse but, surprisingly, civil law courts have had much less problem in applying with extreme flexibility their own principles of vicarious liability, with or without fault. Furthermore, civil law courts and common law courts from countries other than the United States have had little trouble quoting and analysing provisions of ecclesiastical laws—especially the Code of Canon law[7]—and Church doctrine, often reaching conclusions which depart from the usual interpretations of Canon lawyers and theologians.[8] These courts have often had recourse to what they understood to be a priest or a bishop, from a religious and/or a sociological perspective, reaching rather debatable conclusions from the point of view of Church doctrine. Again, the main issue has been whether there was sufficient control of bishops over priests—or superiors of religious orders over their members—and of priests over the lay faithful.

The most striking example of the above tendency is a line of Canadian and English cases where courts have opted for introducing some sort of "enterprise risk" rule.[9] Under this rule, priests are seen as figures of fatherly authority who, especially in small and isolated communities, are a risk to believers and non-believers alike because, afraid of that authority, victims may give in to their sexual advances or may fear to report them when they occur. Because the bishop is the one who ordained the priest and/or appointed him as pastor of the community, it is the bishop who introduced the risk in much the same way as a company may be held liable for introducing some sort of risky product in the market.

However, for the purposes of accountability in an international plane, only in a handful of cases have the Holy See, the Vatican City State or even the Pope himself been named as defendants or co-defendants before domestic courts, under some of the abovementioned principles of direct or indirect liability in tort.[10] In this regard, references to the Church in this chapter are to the Roman Catholic Church. References to the Vatican City State (VCS) are to the microstate created by the Lateran Treaty.[11] References to the Holy See are to the internationally recognized highest governing body of the Catholic Church, which is also the personal ecclesiastical office of the Pope, aided by the Roman Curia, i.e. the administrative apparatus of the Holy See, hosted by VCS.

---

[6] Witte and Nichols 2016, pp. 222 et seq.

[7] John Paul II 1983, Code of Canon law—*Codex Iuris Canonici* (CIC), can. 134 http://www.vatican.va/archive/cod-iuris-canonici/cic_index_en.html. Accessed 15 September 2020.

[8] Zambrana 2020a, pp. 2010–11.

[9] Giliker 2010, pp. 55 et seq.

[10] Martinez 2008, p. 123; Zambrana 2020b, pp. 33–46.

[11] Lateran Treaty, 11 February 1929, 23 Am. J. Int'l L. Sup. 187 (1929).

Claims that the Holy See is directly liable for its own acts or omissions include allegations that it participated in the cover up or that it did not do enough to prevent abuses through stricter world-wide regulations on the screening of seminarians, on the disciplining of priests and bishops, on the reporting to civil authorities—where it is mandatory—or even on non-law related issues such as celibacy, viewed by some as a trigger of child abuse.[12] Claims that the Holy See or the Pope are indirectly and strictly liable for the acts of local bishops, regardless of any fault of their own, would involve allegations that all priests and bishops in the world are under their control or authority, so as to make the Holy See responsible for their actions, i.e. not only for its own.

This chapter presents an overview of the recent occasions where the Holy See's responsibility and commitment to human rights has been put into question before international organisations and international tribunals. The reports issued by various organizations and human rights treaty bodies, as well as the replies of the Holy See's representatives concerning the nature of its international obligations and the degree of control that the Pope and officials of the Roman Curia have over clergy and laypersons contributes to the analysis of the responsibility of the Holy See in the sex abuse scandals but, even more importantly, contributes to the proper understanding of the Holy See as an international religious non-state actor and its obligations under international law.

On the one hand, it will be described how several United Nations Treaty Bodies, as well as the initiators of proceedings before the International Criminal Court, perceive the Holy See as being able to effectively direct the actions of Catholics all over the world, especially its clergy. These same Treaty Bodies also understand that the Holy See has assumed certain human rights obligations which, in the case of the Holy See, would be mostly of an extraterritorial nature, i.e. the Holy See would have the obligation to use all its moral and religious authority to prevent any human rights violations by Catholic clergy, such as child abuse, but also to extend the particular interpretation of human rights presented by the Treaty Bodies and which in some instances clashes against Catholic teachings. Other Treaty Bodies, as well as the Council of Europe will, in general, hold a more moderate position, in the understanding that the obligations of the Holy See may be extraterritorial but not of the same nature as those of states, which involve a kind of coercive power that a religious organization does not have.

On the other hand, the Holy See's representatives will insist once and again that the Holy See has not assumed any kind of extraterritorial obligations and that their mission as state party to human rights treaties is to a large extent to promote a worldwide culture of respect for human dignity, without interfering with the domestic policies of those states where the Church is present. Any kind of coercive power of the Holy See would actually be limited to the small territory of the Vatican City State.

The truth may as usual be in the middle of these two extreme positions and the chapter ends suggesting that the Holy See may in fact have human rights obligations but that it might be more appropriate to characterise them as having a non-territorial

---

[12] Tribunal de Justiça do Paraná TJ-PR: 8451003 PR 845100-3, Acórdão, 21 June 2012.

nature which moreover must be compatible with the kind of religious and non-coercive authority that the Church has over its clergy and lay faithful and which is very different from any kind of ordinary state authority.

63.2 The Holy See before the Council of Europe

A 2010 report issued by a committee of the Council of Europe's Parliament Assembly has been comparatively the mildest international assessment of the responsibility of the Church in the child abuse crisis, especially because it focuses on institutions in Europe at large, acknowledging that "the issue is not one of institutions related to the Catholic Church alone but concerns many other institutions, including secular ones".[13] This report is also the least helpful for the purposes of this chapter because it does not address the international responsibility of the Holy See as such. Although the Holy See has an observer, non-member state status at the Council of Europe, it is not a party to the 2007 Council of Europe Convention on the Protection of Children against Sexual Exploitation and Sexual Abuse.[14] However, the Holy See is a party to other treaties sponsored by this international organisation.[15]

The 2010 report seems to refer to the Church as a single institution, without differentiating between the liability, under domestic or international law, of the different entities involved: dioceses, religious orders and the Holy See, which is somewhat inaccurately referred to as "the Vatican". The report does mention that "[v]arious reactions at different hierarchical levels have come from the Catholic Church"[16] but does not distinguish between disciplinary proceedings against priests at the diocesan and Holy See level, simply mentioning the instances where the Pope has taken the disciplining into his own hands. Failures in Canon law and in its proper application are also mentioned, without making reference to the process of making and promulgating these religious norms at the local or universal level, although some references are made to the guidelines approved by the episcopal conferences of the different countries. The report also indicates that "the new rules do not, for example, hold

---

[13] Council of Europe, Parliamentary Assembly, Social, Health and Family Affairs Committee, Child Abuse in Institutions: Ensure Full Protection of the Victims, 20 September 2010, Doc. 12358, para 18, https://assembly.coe.int/nw/xml/XRef/Xref-XML2HTML-en.asp?fileid=12527&lang=en. Accessed 15 September 2020.

[14] Council of Europe, Council of Europe Convention on the Protection of children against sexual exploitation and sexual abuse, 12 July 2007, CETS No.: 201.

[15] The Holy See is a party to the European Cultural Convention (1954), the European Convention on the Protection of the Archaeological Heritage (1969), the European Convention on Transfrontier Television (1989), the Convention on the Recognition of Qualifications concerning Higher Education in the European Region (1997) and the protocol amending the European Convention on Transfrontier Television (1998). The Holy See is also a member of the Council of Europe Development Bank and of the European Centre for Global Interdependence and Solidarity.

[16] Ibid., para 26.

bishops accountable for abuse by priests on their watch".[17] Although this quote does not identify the source of these "new rules", it apparently assumes that someone or some entity within the Church has the authority to hold bishops accountable and that bishops are, of course, responsible for overseeing diocesan priests.

63.3 The Holy See before the International Criminal Court

In 2011, the Center for Constitutional Rights (CCR) filed a "Victims Communication" before the Office of the Prosecutor of the ICC,[18] requesting an investigation into the commission of international crimes by Catholic clergy and by other members of the hierarchy of the Church. The Communication understood that the sex abuse crisis constituted a "widespread or systematic attack directed against a civilian population", identifying any acts of sex abuse with rape and torture. The Communication understands that Church authorities facilitated the cover up of the acts of sex abuse by refusing to cooperate with civil authorities, "priest-shifting", destroying evidence and obstruction of justice, punishing whistleblowers and rewarding cover-ups.

Of interest here is the CCR's description of the "chain of command" in the Church, necessary to establish the criminal liability of Pope Benedict XVI and other officials of the Roman Curia, under international criminal law.[19] The Communication and the attached Expert Opinion understand that the Church is "monarchical in practice, with all authority leading to and ultimately residing in the Pope". Furthermore "[w]hile bishops are responsible for the clergy who serve in their dioceses, they are in turn subject to the directions and limitations imposed on them by the Pope" whose "authority and power is absolute" and can "by-pass all intermediate levels of authority". After describing in this way the allegedly limitless power of the Pope, the Communication insists that "[t]he organizational (i.e. Vatican) policy to commit such an attack was implemented by both a deliberate failure to take action in some respects and by organizational action in others". The Communication thus makes a portrayal of the Church and the relationships between the different levels of the Catholic hierarchy where the top levels must inevitably be held responsible for any wrongful actions or omissions of the lower levels.[20]

Similar unnuanced language to that of the Victims Communication can be found in some of the civil claims filed against the Holy See before US Courts. For instance, the claimants in *O'Bryan v. Holy See* asserted at first instance that the Pope had "absolute and unqualified power and control... over each and every priest, bishops, brother, sister, parish, diocese, archdiocese and instrumentality of the Church".[21]

---

[17] Ibid., para 30.

[18] ICC File No. OTP-CR-159/11, 13 September 2011, https://ccrjustice.org/home/what-we-do/our-cases/snap-v-pope-et-al. Accessed 15 September 2020.

[19] Ibid., part III.

[20] Ibid., paras 134, 136 and 183; Expert Opinion of Thomas Doyle, Exhibit A-1, paras 12, 21–27.

[21] *O'Bryan v. Holy See*, 471 F. Supp 2d 784 (W.D. Ky. 2007), part III.B.

The claimants in *Doe v. Holy See* also contended that the Pope had "complete and absolute" authority over "the entire worldwide Catholic Church".[22] The authority of the Holy See over local churches was also addressed in *Anderson v. Holy See*, where the District Court described the Holy See as "a foreign sovereign that directs the activities of the Church in the United States. Such direction includes assigning and supervising bishops who are vested with authority to oversee and remove clergy within local Archdioceses."[23] Finally, in *Roman Catholic Archbishop v. Superior Court*, the claimant also alleged that the Pope possessed "supreme spiritual authority over all Catholics throughout the world" as well as "considerable temporal control over the persons and property of clerics, religious, dioceses".[24]

However, exactly two years after the Communication was filed, a reply by the "Office of the Prosecutor "determined that there is no basis at this time to proceed" with the requested investigation".[25] The Office of the Prosecutor understood that "[s]ome of the allegations described in [the] communication do not appear to fall within the Court's temporal jurisdiction [i.e. crimes committed after the entry into force of the Rome Statute on 1 July 2002], and other allegations do not appear to fall within the Court's subject-matter jurisdiction [i.e. international crimes]". This way, the Office of the Prosecutor avoided having to delve into the question of the nature of sex abuse under international criminal law and, more importantly, the complicated question of whether authority and discipline within the Church are so tight as to make bishops, cardinals and the Pope responsible for the acts of predatory priests and mishandlings of claims at the local level.

63.4 The Holy See before the United Nations Human Rights Treaty Bodies

63.4.1 The Holy See before the United Nations Committee on the Rights of the Child

The 2014 Concluding Observations of the UN Committee on the Rights of the Child (CRC) on the second periodic report of the Holy See, about the latter's implementation of the UN Children's right convention, may be the one which has aroused more academic and media attention and an angrier reply from the Holy See.[26] The report addresses the issue of sex abuse by clergy but actually devotes more space to

---

[22] *Doe v. Holy See*, 557 F.3d 1066 (9th Cir. 2009); Expert Declaration of Thomas P Doyle, J.C.D., C.A.D.C., Docket No. 302, dated 12 March 2012, para 13.

[23] Anderson v. Holy See, 878 F. Supp 2d 923 (N.D. Ill. 2012).

[24] *Roman Catholic Archbishop v. Superior Court*, 93 Cal. Rptr. 338 (Cal. Ct. App 1971).

[25] ICC Office of the Prosecutor, Letter of 31 May 2013, OTP-CR-159/11.

[26] Cismas 2017, pp. 310 et seq; Milanovic 2014; Editorial, The U.N. Confronts the Vatican. *The New York Times*. 5 February 2014. https://www.nytimes.com/2014/02/06/opinion/the-un-confronts-the-vatican.html. Accessed 13 September 2020.

accusing the Holy See of putting children's welfare in danger due to the Catholic position on matters such as abortion, contraception and homosexual relationships, which the CRC urges it to change.

Cismas suggests that in order to understand the CRC's approach to the obligations of the Holy See and its corresponding responsibility one must took count of "judicial and doctrinal developments" in the area of the extraterritorial human right obligations of states.[27] True, such approach and the aggressive language of the CRC in 2014 were all but absent in the Committee's previous Concluding Observations. In 1995, the CRC had made only mild criticisms with regard to the reservations entered by the Holy See to the Convention, gender "discrimination" in Catholic schools and lack of guidance on "family planning" (i.e. contraception) for parents.[28] An explanation for this change of attitude might be that before 2002 less attention had been paid by all stakeholders to the serious problem of child abuse by clergy.

With respect to the kind of obligations that the Holy See had assumed and the way in which it can or must implement the Convention, the CRC in 1995 simply said that "[i]n view of the moral influence wielded by the Holy See and the national Catholic Churches, the Committee recommends that efforts for the promotion and protection of the rights provided for in the Convention be pursued and strengthened." The CRC urged the Holy See to disseminate the Convention and train voluntary workers, which seems in line with the teaching role that the Holy See basically assigned to itself in its dialogue with UN bodies, in the course of the years.[29]

Finally, in 1995 the CRC called for the best interests of the child to "be fully taken into account in the conduct of all the activities of the Holy See and of the various Church institutions and organizations dealing with the rights of the child," without explaining which are those Church institutions or the kind of connection that must exist between them and the Holy See as signatory of the treaty.[30]

In 2014, the CRC devoted more space to explaining what it expected the Holy See to do and achieve with respect to local churches and Church entities. In an initial section entitled "Specificities in the implementation of the Convention", the CRC manifested that "[w]hile fully aware that bishops and major superiors of religious institutes do not act as representatives or delegates of the Roman Pontiff, the Committee notes that subordinates in Catholic religious orders are bound by obedience to the Pope, in accordance with Canons 331 and 590 of the Code of Canon Law".[31]

The CRC therefore took the view that in ratifying the Convention, the Holy See made a commitment to implement it worldwide, as the recognised governing body of the Church under international law, through individuals and institutions "under its

---

[27] Cismas 2017, p. 311.

[28] CRC 1995, Concluding Observations on the Second Periodic Report of the Holy See, 27 November 1995, UN Doc. CRC/C/15/Add.46, paras 8 and 9.

[29] Ibid, para 11; Arsheim 2018, pp. 224–5.

[30] Ibid., para 14.

[31] CRC 2014, Concluding Observations on the Second Periodic Report of the Holy See, 31 January 2014, UN Doc. CRC/C/VAT/CO/2, para 8.

authority", and not or not only as the sovereign of VCS.[32] That is, the obligations of the Holy See are not only to exercise its temporal, state jurisdiction over the specific territory and inhabitants of VCS but to exercise the kind of authority it has as a religious institution, anywhere it exercises such authority.

This brief attempt of the CRC to define the international obligations of the Holy See in terms of who or what is the Holy See is nevertheless miles away from the unqualified description of the "direct and absolute power" attributed to it by the CCR's Victims Communication to the International Criminal Court.

The CRC sometimes roughly differentiates between what the Holy See is expected to do within the bureaucratic apparatus of the Roman Curia and "with regard to individuals and institutions of a religious nature that function under the authority of the Holy See", "church-related organizations and institutions in States parties where the Holy See has influence and impact", with respect to "children attending or involved in schools, services and institutions provided by the Catholic Church", encouraging the Holy See "to provide guidance... to disseminate such guidance to all Catholic churches, organizations and institutions worldwide", "[e]ncourage through legislation and policy" or simply "transmitting" it.[33] Again, the nature and the scope of that authority or influence is not clarified.

However, at some point the CRC departs from this less drastic, although rather superficial, description of the capacities of the Holy See and adopts the unqualified tone of the Victims Communication, urging the Holy See to ensure that victims of sex abuse are compensated because it is "the supreme power of the Church, which is legally responsible for its subordinates in Catholic religious orders under its authority".[34]

In this same belief in its worldwide power, the CRC urges the Holy See to "[e]stablish mechanisms to effectively enforce this ban [on corporal punishment] in all Catholic schools... including in the territory of Vatican City State", once again establishing a difference between the "territorial jurisdiction" that the Holy See is supposed to have over VCS and its "jurisdiction" as a religious leader. There are other references to an unexplained "full jurisdiction" of the Holy See "over child abuse cases by clerics" and to a "code of silence imposed on all members of the clergy under penalty of excommunication".[35] Regardless of these implied references to the controversial instruction *Crimen Sollicitationis*,[36] what is relevant here is the insistence on the power of the Holy See, which must be exerted over "all members of the clergy", i.e. worldwide.[37]

---

[32] Ibid., para 8.

[33] Ibid., paras 16, 17, 20, 30, 32, 63.

[34] Ibid., para 38.

[35] Ibid., paras 40 and 43.

[36] *Crimen Sollicitationis*, Holy See, Supreme Sacred Congregation of the Holy Office, Addressed to all patriarchs, archbishops, bishops and other local ordinaries also of the oriental rite on the manner of proceeding in causes of solicitation, 16 March 1962, Vatican Polyglot Press http://www.vatican.va/resources/resources_crimen-sollicitationis-1962_en.html. Accessed 15 September 2020.

[37] Ibid., para 24.

As regards the nature of the authority attributed to the Holy See, the Concluding Observations also make one reference to the Holy See's "moral authority to condemn all forms of harassment" and "to provide guidance".[38] Nevertheless, there are many more references to what the Holy See must do "through legislation and policy", i.e. through the enactment of Canon law norms or simply acting directly upon "Catholic schools" and "Catholic institutions". No attempt is really made, except in the abovementioned references to just two provisions of the Code of Canon Law, to explain if and to what extent the Holy See, in theory or in practice, has power or authority over "Catholic institutions", Catholic clergy or Catholics in general or if these really have a duty to follow such mandates.

On the same day that the abovementioned CRC report was released, this UN Committee also issued its Concluding observations with respect to the Optional Protocol to the Convention on the sale of children, child prostitution and child pornography.[39] This report basically replicates the language, criticisms and issues of the previous one. It also starts acknowledging that bishops and religious superiors are neither representatives nor delegates of the Pope under Canon law but warns that the obligations of the Holy See under the Convention have to be fulfilled, not just "within the territory of Vatican City State, but also, as the supreme power of the Catholic Church, worldwide through individuals and institutions under its supreme authority", bringing its "norms and regulations, including Canon law, into line with the Optional Protocol and ensur[ing] that the same laws apply to Vatican City State and individuals and institutions operating under its supreme authority". Again, there are no clarifications as to who those individuals and institutions are or what kind of supreme authority can the Holy See exert over them. There are no fewer than sixteen references to the Holy See's "legal", "moral", "supreme" or "worldwide" "leadership" and authority.

This second CRC report of 2014 requests the Holy See to introduce certain reporting and compensation mechanisms without sometimes specifying if such mechanisms are meant to be applied in the Vatican or worldwide. There are also calls to reform or abrogate certain ecclesiastical norms of universal application and to adopt "appropriate legal and administrative measures" including a reform of its extradition policy to ensure that extradition requests from other countries concerning charges of child abuse are granted and that the requirements of double criminality are repealed.[40] At the same time there are also more realistic references to what the Holy See can and should do, developing programmes and guidelines, disseminating information and assisting episcopal conferences in each country.

Also, on 25 February 2014, the CRC issued its Concluding Observations with respect to the Optional Protocol to the Convention on the Involvement of Children

---

[38] Ibid., paras 26 and 30.

[39] CRC, Concluding Observations on the Report Submitted the Holy See under Article 12, para 1, of the Optional Protocol to the Convention on the Rights of the Child on the Sale of Children, Child Prostitution and Child Pornography, 31 January 2014, UN Doc. CRC/C/OPSC/VAT/CO/1.

[40] Ibid., paras 26, 31, 32.

in Armed Conflicts.[41] Again, there are both references to what the Holy See must do with respect to "individuals and institutions working under its authority", as well as to the Holy See's potential to "support", "transmit", "appeal", "take all appropriate measures" and to "play a key role". Passing references to Catholic schools indicate that the CRC understands that the Holy See has the duty or the capacity to run them directly or at least influence them decisively.[42]

Interestingly, the CRC "notes that the Holy See does not have a military body or armed forces".[43] Although this reference is made with respect to the minimum age to recruit soldiers, it is significant that a body of the UN recognises that the Holy See does not have this kind of physical enforcement capacity, since case law on the extraterritorial human rights obligations of states usually refer to that type of coercive power when discussing "effective control" over territory, individuals or situations.[44]

63.4.2 The Holy See before the United Nations Committee against Torture

The criticisms and requests of the Committee against Torture (CAT) in its Concluding Observations[45] and in the Extracts for follow-up, are also relevant. The UN Committee recalls that "State authorities or others acting in official capacity or under colour of law have an obligation to exercise due diligence to prevent violations of the Convention, including by non-State officials or private actors under their effective control", which can be exercised "over persons or territory".[46]

The CAT urges the Holy See to make sure clergy do not commit acts of sex abuse but it does so indicating that "[t]he State party should ensure that Holy See officials and other public officials of the Holy See take effective measures to monitor the conduct of individuals under their effective control".[47] As previously mentioned, the expression "effective control" is commonly used by international tribunals and human rights bodies to mean, first and foremost, effective physical control,[48] usually exercised by armed forces or armed groups, but the Committee does not discuss the degree to which the Holy See has this or any other kind of control or authority.

---

[41] CRC, Concluding Observations on the Report Submitted the Holy See under Article 8, para 1, of Optional Protocol to the Convention on the Rights of the Child on the Involvement of Children in Armed Conflict, 31 January 2014, UN Doc. CRC/C/OPAC/VAT/CO/1.

[42] Ibid., paras 7, 13, 14, 17 and 18.

[43] Ibid., para 5.

[44] GA, Interim report of the Special Rapporteur on Torture and Other Cruel, Inhuman or Degrading Treatment or Punishment, 7 August 2015, UN Doc. A/70/303, para 14.

[45] CAT, Concluding Observations on the Initial Report of the Holy See, 17 June 2014, UN Doc. CAT/C/VAT/CO/1.

[46] Ibid., paras 8 and 10.

[47] UN Doc. CAT/C/VAT/CO/1, Extracts for Follow Up, para 11.

[48] Wilde 2016, pp. 635 et seq.; Schutter et al. 2012, pp. 1084 et seq.

Although the CAT tries to define "public officials of the Holy See" as both officials of the Roman Curia and Holy See diplomats serving abroad, the Committee also uses the expression "other public officials of the Holy See" and it also reminds that violations of the Convention can take place at the hands of "non-State officials or private actors under their effective control",[49] which may mean anything from bishops, clergy, monks, superiors of religious orders and those of their members who are not ordained, lay teachers or other personnel in Catholic schools or Catholic hospitals, who may not even be Catholic, and lay Catholics who may temporarily or permanently devote part of their time to parish councils, diocesan administrative bodies or even summer camps.

Illustrative are several statements of Ms Gaer, Country Rapporteur of the CAT: "[r]egarding the extent of the Holy See's effective control over Catholic Church activities occurring outside the Vatican City State, the Committee was persuaded that the Holy See exercised such significant control and was in a position to, among other things, compel perpetrators of acts of sexual abuse to cease committing them; order bishops to monitor the conduct of clerics reporting to them; and transfer, or prevent the transfer of, accused persons outside the jurisdictions in which the acts had occurred. Recalling the direct obligations of VCS officials, including Holy See officials, under the Convention, and in particular their extraterritorial obligations, she asked whether the Holy See believed that it was doing everything possible to fulfil those obligations."[50]

In another meeting of the CAT with the Permanent Observer Mission of the Holy See, a few weeks later, Ms Gaer said again that the State party's "obligation to prevent torture" applied "to all person who act, de jure or de facto, in the name of, in conjunction with ... the State party", noting that in her view the Holy See's "interpretative declaration effectively placed representatives and official members of the Catholic Church outside the scope of the Convention. The Convention should apply to the Holy See as a whole and to all the bodies placed under its authority, not only to the Vatican City State" and asked if the Holy See's interpretation of the Convention "was conducive to preventing acts of torture from being committed in all jurisdictions under the authority of the Sovereign Pontiff".[51] She did not elaborate on which those jurisdictions were nor on which individuals or bodies were under such authority, nor what that authority consisted of.

---

[49] Ibid., para 10.
[50] UN Doc. CAT/C/SR.1223, 22 May 2014, para 21.
[51] UN Doc. CAT/C/SR.1220, 23 June 2014, para 5.

63.4.3 The Holy See Before the United Nations Committee on the Elimination of Racial Discrimination

There is a world of difference between the CRC's and CAT's attitude towards the Holy See and that of the UN Committee on the Elimination of Racial Discrimination (CERD), in 2016. The responses of the Holy See to the CERD's criticisms and comments are also somehow different than the defensive attitude adopted before. Both "sides"—the Holy See and the CERD—seemed to abandon any extreme positions and to have found some common ground.

The CERD's Concluding Observations of 2001[52] had been generally quite laudatory. With respect to the obligations of the Holy See under the Convention and its capacity to discharge them, the Committee acknowledged that "the unique structure and nature of the State party may limit the directness of the measures that can be taken to fully implement" it. The CERD also "recommends that the State party implement, as appropriate, the Convention".[53] At the same time the CERD tried to address separately any acts of racism as well as the fight against racism led by Catholic establishments and Catholic ecclesiastics, on the one hand, and the Holy See and VCS, on the other. Thus, the CERD seemed to support the idea that, regardless of whether the scope of the human rights obligations of the Holy See as signatory of the treaty was limited to the territory of VCS or not, the peculiar nature of this religious actor definitely affected those obligations and their fulfilment.

However, the CERD's Concluding Observations also denote the objective difficulties in differentiating the competences and scope of the authority of the different levels of the Catholic hierarchy, as well as, maybe, a lack of sufficient effort from the Holy See to differentiate between those levels. Thus, a general reference is made by the CERD to the fact that "the laws and teaching of the Catholic Church promote tolerance" followed by an acknowledgment that the Pope had asked "for pardon for past acts and omissions of the Church", rightly assuming that the Pope can speak "on behalf of" the Church, at least for that type of declarations. There are other references to the implementation of the Convention by the Holy See itself—and not by local churches –, as when the Committee refers to the "contributions made by the Pontifical Council for the Pastoral Care of Migrants".[54]

Separately, the Committee simply asks for clarifications about the involvement of ecclesiastics in the genocide of Rwanda, without delving into whether the Holy See would be responsible for such involvement under the Convention. However, the Committee also requests the Holy See—not local Churches—to cooperate with national and international judicial authorities with respect to that involvement. Nothing is said about whether, for that collaboration, it would be enough that the Pope makes another general address about the situation in the Great Lakes or whether

---

[52] Committee on the Elimination of Racial Discrimination, Concluding Observations on the Report Submitted by the Holy See under Article 9 of the Convention, 1 May 2001, UN Doc. CERD/C/304//Add.89.

[53] Ibid., paras 3 and 9.

[54] Ibid., paras 4 and 7.

the Committee expects that the Holy See, somehow, extradites to the Hague those "operating under its authority", including clergy based in Rwanda and not in VCS. In this regard, the CERD makes a passing but meaningful request for clarification about the relationship between the Convention, Canon law and the criminal law of VCS.[55]

The 2016 Concluding Observations of the CERD[56] probably benefitted from a less tense and more fruitful dialogue with the Permanent Mission of the Holy See. However, during those meetings, it was still possible to detect, among the members of the CERD, the same kind of belief about the power of the signatory party, as when Ms Dah mentioned that "in her view, the Holy See was the most powerful of all the world powers, given its extraordinary moral authority".[57] However, this reference to "moral authority" and not to physical or coactive power, may exemplify the CERD's position about the human rights obligations and actual capacities of the Holy See to implement them. As previously mentioned, the CERD seems to be saying that the Holy See does have obligations under the Convention which extend beyond the territory of VCS but the way to discharge them has little to do with the way that other states can or must implement them.

The CERD tries to differentiate between the Holy See, VCS and local churches in a way the CRC and CAT did not. For instance, the CERD uses only once the expression "individuals and institutions that function under the authority of the Holy See" and also asks for clarification about the "prohibition of acts of racial discrimination as they apply, respectively, to citizens and officials of the Vatican City State, officials of the Holy See and officials of the Catholic Church".[58]

There are also references to the statements and activities of both the Pope and the Roman Curia, mentioning the separate "role of the Holy See and the Catholic Church in providing access to education". At the same time, the Committee seems concerned about the scope of the "jurisdiction of judicial authorities of Vatican City State in criminal matters" which after 2013 they understand to extend to "crimes committed outside Vatican City State by public officials and citizens" of VCS, e.g. Vatican diplomats.[59]

The CERD significantly notes "the State party's position that the Church as such cannot be held responsible for transgressions of its members who have acted against the precepts of evangelical law". The CERD also indicates that it is "mindful of the need to avoid interference in the domestic affairs of the States in which the Church operates" although the State party should "use its moral authority to promote the aims of the Convention". It should therefore "employ the mechanisms at its disposal

---

[55] Ibid., paras 9–13.

[56] Committee on the Elimination of Racial Discrimination, Concluding Observations on the Combined Sixteenth to Twenty-third Periodic Reports of the Holy See, 7 December 2015, UN Doc. CERD/C/VAT/CO/16-23.

[57] UN Doc. CERD/C/SR.2395, 1 December 2015, para 49.

[58] UN Doc. CERD/C/VAT/CO/16-23, paras 8 and 13.

[59] Ibid., paras 4 and 5.

to promote sensitivity among the Catholic clergy... through its Pontifical Council... providing guidance to Catholic clergy and the Catholic faithful".[60]

The CERD seems therefore to have taken note of some of the concerned statements of the state party in its previous replies to CRC and CAT, about the autonomy of local churches and the faithful and about the impossibility to exercise any state jurisdiction in countries other than VCS, because that would be an illegitimate interference into other states' jurisdiction. The Holy See, not local churches, is nevertheless the one being asked to collaborate with national prosecutorial authorities and to apply, "as appropriate" penal Canon law.[61] This also seems to take count of the Holy See's past protests about the shortcomings that penal Canon law has, as a legal system which is applied differently from state law and which is simply no substitute for the application of states' criminal laws. The CERD also seems to bear in mind that the application of penal Canon law to "canonical crimes" committed within local churches is basically a competence of local bishops and only exceptionally of the Holy See, as it happened with the enactment of the *motu proprio Sacramentorum Sanctitatis Tutelae* in 2001, after it was manifest that the inability of many bishops to discipline paedophile priests had had very serious consequences.[62]

Different interventions of members of the CERD during its meetings with the representatives of the Holy See seem to confirm this interpretation of the generally positive Concluding Observations of 2001 and 2016.[63] For instance, the Country Rapporteur declared that "the Holy See had ratified the Convention in part as an instrument through which to exercise its moral authority",[64] as opposed to the basic obligations that a state might have to implement the Convention in its own territory, with the coercive force of its state's apparatus. The Country Rapporteur also indicated that "[a]ccording to the report [of the state party], the Holy See did not consider the territorial scope of the Convention to be limited to the Vatican City State [because] [n]o interpretative declaration had been attached to the State party's ratification."[65] This acknowledgment of the CERD is very significant because the reservations and interpretative declarations of the Holy See with respect to the CRC and CAT Conventions do show the Holy See's understanding that its obligations under those specific conventions are indeed limited to the territory of VCS and, within VCS, are also subject to the peculiarities of VCS as a state and of the Holy See as a religious organization. The Country Rapporteur continued saying that "the Convention did

---

[60] Ibid., paras 20 and 21.

[61] Ibid., para 19.

[62] John Paul II (2001) Motu proprio *Sacramentorum sanctitatis tutela* by which are promulgated norms on more grave delicts reserved to the congregation for the doctrine of the faith. https://w2.vatican.va/content/john-paul-ii/en/motu_proprio/documents/hf_jp-ii_motu-proprio_20020110_sacramentorum-sanctitatis-tutela.html. Accessed 15 September 2020.

[63] UN Doc. CERD/C/SR.2394, 1 December 2015; UN Doc. CERD/C/SR.2395, 1 December 2015.

[64] CERD/C/SR.2395, para 56.

[65] CERD/C/SR.2394, para 11.

not contain express territorial limitations" and there was "no territorial limitation to the obligation to combat prejudice".[66]

Furthermore, with a view to proving that the Holy See itself accepts its extraterritorial obligations, the Country Rapporteur highlighted the activities of "promotion" of "the Pope and various Church bodies outside the territory of the Vatican City State with a view to eliminating racial discrimination throughout the world".[67] Since these activities are mostly of a diplomatic and pastoral nature, as opposed to coactive or disciplinary, the CERD seems to accept that the extraterritorial obligations of the state party under the Convention are not of the same nature and extent than those of "real" states.

The same can be noticed in the Rapporteur's acknowledgement that VCS's criminal laws are applicable within the territory of VCS and to "public officials of the State acting abroad"[68] (e.g. apostolic nuncios and legates) but not to all clergy or Catholics, "operating under the authority" of the Holy See. This same understanding, so different from the CRC's and the CAT's, can be read in the words of the Rapporteur when he manifests that "[t]he Committee recognized that the Holy See was not responsible for racist acts by Catholic priests acting in other countries. At the same time, a State party's responsibility could be engaged if it failed to take appropriate measures to redress the conduct of its citizens or others under its authority or control. As previously mentioned, the State party had ratified the Convention in part to manifest its moral authority".[69] In this regard, another Committee member defined the Holy See as "the moral and religious authority overseeing the activities of the Roman Catholic Church worldwide".[70]

The CERD also acknowledged that there were still discrepancies between the CERD and the Holy See as regards the extraterritorial obligations of the latter under the Convention. In another meeting, the Country Rapporteur also indicated that the Holy See's admission of its "extraterritorial moral—if not legal—obligations" had facilitated the dialogue.[71] Nevertheless, the expression "extraterritorial moral obligations" must be read in the light of the description that the CERD makes of the Holy See as having great moral authority to promote the Convention worldwide and to "provide guidance" to local Catholic communities and clergy to comply with it. Since the CERD also notes that the Holy See ratified the Convention to manifest "its moral authority", the CERD seems to think that the exercise of such degree of "moral authority" is one of the human rights obligations of the Holy See under the Convention.[72]

---

[66] Ibid., para 12.
[67] Ibid., para 13.
[68] Ibid., para 15.
[69] Ibid., para 22.
[70] Ibid., para 33.
[71] UN Doc. CERD/C/SR.2395, para 55.
[72] Ibid., paras 20 and 21.

63.4.4 Preliminary Conclusions: The Understanding of the International Obligations of the Holy See by United Nations Treaty Bodies

To summarize the approach taken by the CRC and the CAT, although probably not the CERD, in their reports and dialogue with the Holy See, the following ideas might be highlighted:

(a) the Holy See, as a signatory to several human right treaties, must have the same level of responsibility, implementation and obligations as the rest of signatories, regardless of its peculiar characteristics;

(b) the Holy See has territorial jurisdiction over the territory of the VCS, which it must exercise in the same way and with the same means as any other temporal sovereign, regardless of the specific nature and purpose of VCS in safeguarding the independence of the Holy See's religious mission and regardless of the peculiar nature of the laws of VCS and its capacity to enforce them;

(c) as the territorial sovereign of VCS, the Holy See also has extraterritorial human rights obligations to protect the human rights of all those who are beyond the territory of VCS but under the Holy See's "effective control". Such protection must be offered through anyone and any entity operating under the Holy See's authority; and

(d) the Holy See being not just the governing authority of VCS as a territorial state but also the "supreme power" of a worldwide religious group, it must also fulfil its human rights obligations making use of any means that such position entails.

It is appropriate to mention that the Holy See's commitment to human rights has been questioned before. After the relative diplomatic success of some of the ethical positions defended by the Holy See's delegations in the UN Conferences of El Cairo (1994) and Beijing (1995), several NGOs commenced a campaign to deprive the Holy See of its observer status at the UN.[73] However, in 2004 the UN General Assembly actually issued a resolution strengthening the Holy See's position in its midst, invoking the Holy See's active and positive participation at the UN.[74] Although the resolution made ample reference to the treaties that the Holy See was a party to and to its active participation in UN subsidiary bodies and specialized agencies, no reference was made to any specific differences between ordinary states and the Holy See, concerning the obligations arising out of those treaties and participation.

Similarly, a 2008 draft resolution of the Parliamentary Assembly of the Council of Europe concerning its observer states made an attempt to qualify the participation of the Holy See with language which referred to "[i]ts lack of democratic institutions and its position on certain human rights matters makes it a special case". Instead, the resolution finally approved simply mentioned that the Holy See "participates

---

[73] Vega Gutiérrez 2008, pp. 235–236.
[74] UNGA Resolution 58/314, 1 July 2014, UN Doc. A/RES/58/314.

according to its specific nature and mission" without delving into this complicated matter. In its comments, the Holy See mentioned in passing its "specific nature and mission" but mostly relied on how it had been an active participant in various bodies of the Council of Europe. Invited to comment on this matter, the Rapporteur for opinion of the Committee on Legal Affairs and Human Rights just wrote that "the Vatican's atypical institutional structure makes it a special case".[75]

63.5 The Holy See in Dialogue with the United Nations Treaty Bodies

Further to the above analysis of how UN Treaty Bodies regard the Holy See and its international obligations as state party to various human rights instruments, this section will describe how the Holy See sees itself in the same context.

The Holy See ratified the 1989 Convention on the Rights of the Child in 1990, including a reservation providing "c) [T]hat the application of the Convention be compatible in practice with the particular nature of the Vatican City State and of the sources of its objective law (Article 1, Law of 7 June 1929, n. 11) and, in consideration of its limited extent, with its legislation in the matters of citizenship, access and residence." It also included a declaration to the extent that "[i]n consideration of its singular nature and position, the Holy See, in acceding to this Convention, does not intend to prescind in any way from its specific mission which is of a religious and moral character".[76]

Additionally, the Holy See had signed and ratified the 1984 Convention against Torture in 2002, including a declaration in the sense that "[t]he Holy See, in becoming a party to the Convention on behalf of the Vatican City State, undertakes to apply it insofar as it is compatible, in practice, with the peculiar nature of that State".[77] Finally and as mentioned above, the Holy See ratified the Convention on the Elimination of all sorts of Racial Discrimination in 1969 and did not include any reservations or declarations.

The Holy See filed its initial report on the implementation of the UN Convention on the Rights of the Child in 1992 and the following three in 2012, two under the Optional Protocols to the Convention on the Rights of the Child on the Involvement of Children in Armed Conflict and on the Sale of Children, Child Prostitution and Child Pornography and another report under Article 44 of the Convention. It filed its initial report under the Convention against Torture in 2012 and filed twelve state

---

[75] Parliamentary Assembly of the Council of Europe, Documents Working Papers, 2008 Ordinary Session (First part), 21–25 January 2008, Volume II, Doc. 11471 – 22 January 2008, p. 25 and Addendum, Doc. 11500.

[76] Multilateral Treaties deposited with the Secretary-General, Status as at 31 December 1991, United Nations, New York, 1992, pp. 200–201; https://treaties.un.org/Pages/ViewDetails.aspx?src=TREATY&mtdsg_no=IV-11&chapter=4&clang=_en. Accessed 17 September 2020.

[77] Ibid., pp. 200–201.

party's reports under Article 9 of the 1966 Convention on the Elimination of all Forms of Racial Discrimination, from 1970 to 2014.

In all its reports and interventions, the Holy See seems to have been expecting a harsh confrontation with UN Treaty Bodies because they contain many references to the abovementioned reservations and declarations, mentioning once and again the special nature of the signatory and the alleged scope of its obligations. The Holy See seems particularly concerned with the references made by the UN Treaty Bodies concerning Church doctrine on sensitive moral issues and their approach to its alleged worldwide obligations and responsibility under international law, not just as territorial sovereign of VCS but also as a governing entity of the Church, over every single clergyman and even over every single Catholic. The Holy See believes, for instance, that the CRC was suggesting "changes in faith and morals" and "revision of ecclesial governance", which the Church should supposedly undertake in order to comply with the Convention.[78]

As previously discussed, the UN Treaty Bodies seem to consider that the Holy See has two sets of capacities and corresponding obligations: one as territorial sovereign over VCS and another as the highest governing entity in the Church. They also believe that the Holy See ratified the abovementioned human rights treaties in both capacities and it must therefore implement them in accordance with those two distinct capacities. However, the Holy See insists time and again that its internationally recognized sovereignty as head of the Church and also as territorial sovereign of VCS have never been confused and that local Catholic institutions of any kind operate autonomously and under their own authority, conferred by Canon law and Church doctrine, not by the Holy See and much less by VCS.

In the course of the years, the reports filed by the Holy See before the UN Treaty Bodies have used very similar language to describe itself, the VCS, the Church, the often baffling relationship between the three and their respective obligations. Concerning its obligations under the CRC, the Holy See would thus be "the highest organ of government of the Catholic Church", not necessarily the "supreme" organ because this may imply "absolute" power. The Holy See also has a "singular nature within the international community" and its "jurisdiction over a territory, known as Vatican City State, serves solely to provide a basis for its autonomy and to guarantee the free exercise of its spiritual mission".[79]

Such qualifications do not only intend to limit any obligations under human rights treaties to the territory of VCS but also warn that such territorial jurisdiction is of a lesser intensity than that of other sovereigns or at least of a different nature. The reason would be that VCS is only a state to the extent that it has to prevent earthly powers from interfering with the religious mission and message of the Holy See. This is the VCS's sole purpose, which would also affect its capacities and corresponding obligations.

---

[78] Verbal Note N. 4322/2014/RS of 22 September 2014 from the Secretariat of State of the Holy See: Comments of the Holy See on the Concluding Observations of the Committee on the Rights of the Child, presented by the Permanent Mission of the Holy See to the United Nations, N. 11399//2014 https://tbinternet.ohchr.org/Treaties/CRC/Shared%20Documents/VAT/INT_CRC_COB_VAT_18491_E.pdf, para 18.

[79] CRC, Initial Report of the Holy See, 28 March 1994, UN Doc. CRC/C/3/Add.27, para 1.

By implication, the authorities of VCS would not have the kind of effective physical control over the citizens and inhabitants of VCS that other states have and much less could those authorities extend such inexistent control beyond the borders of VCS.

However, the Holy See sometimes argues that it having the same kind of jurisdiction over the VCS that other states exercise over their own territory. For instance, the Holy See once affirmed that its obligations under the Convention of the Rights of the Child were "fulfilled first and foremost through the implementation of the aforementioned duties within the territory of the Vatican City State (VCS), over which the Holy See exercises full territorial sovereignty. ... Therefore, the obligations of the Convention and its Optional Protocols refer to Vatican citizens, as well as, where appropriate, the diplomatic personnel of the Holy See or its Officials residing outside the territory of Vatican City State".[80]

Despite this acceptance of its "full territorial jurisdiction" over the territory of VCS, the Holy See qualifies again its territorial power when it repeatedly explains that the law applicable within the VCS is Canon law and that it also has other legal instruments which are not canonical in nature but which must be interpreted in the light of Canon law. The Holy See insists that Canon law is very different from state law and that, for instance, penal Canon law is not enforced by force and is much more lenient in its application than state criminal law. Furthermore, "[p]enal Canon law specifically acknowledges the State's concurrent legislative jurisdiction".[81] These explanations seem to be provided in order to justify the non-inclusion of certain crimes in the Code of Canon Law, its different terminology, its benevolent punishments and maybe even the non-application of penal Canon law altogether, in some cases. The Holy See added that very few serious crimes ever take place within VCS, given its small size and population, that the laws of Italy are incorporated within the legal system of VCS and that the Holy See usually allows Italian authorities to prosecute crimes committed within VCS.

At least some of these views concerning the goals and obligations of VCS and the Holy See in accordance with their peculiar nature and mission seem to be in accordance with statements made by all the Popes who have spoken at the UN or before UN officials.[82]

Paul VI, speaking before the UN General Assembly in 1965, manifested that the Pope was "the least among you who represent sovereign States, since he possesses ... only a tiny and practically symbolic temporal sovereignty: the minimum needed in order to be free to exercise his spiritual mission and to assure those who deal with him that he is independent of any sovereignty of this world. He has no temporal power, no ambition to enter into competition with you ... you know that our mission is to bring a message for all mankind".

Also before the UN General Assembly in 1979, John Paul II made reference to "the sovereignty with which the Apostolic See has been endowed for many centuries.

---

[80] Verbal Note N. 4322/2014/RS of 22 September 2014, para 3.
[81] CRC, Second Report of the Holy See, 27 September 2011, UN Doc. CRC/C/VAT/2, para 98.
[82] https://holyseemission.org/contents/mission/past-papal-visits-to-the-united-nations-organization.php.

The territorial extent of that sovereignty is limited to the small State of Vatican City, but the sovereignty itself is warranted by the need of the papacy to exercise its mission in full freedom, and to be able to deal with any interlocutor, whether a government or an international organization, without dependence on other sovereignties. Of course the nature and aims of the spiritual mission of the Apostolic See and the Church make their participation in the tasks and activities of the United Nations Organization very different from that of the States that are communities in the political and temporal sense." Once again at the UN General Assembly in 1995, John Paul II insisted that "I come before you, as did my predecessor Pope Paul VI exactly thirty years ago, not as one who exercises temporal power."

Benedict XVI, in 2008, in a meeting with members of the UN General Assembly said that "the Church also works for the realization of these [ethical] goals through the international activity of the Holy See. Indeed, the Holy See has always had a place at the assemblies of the Nations, thereby manifesting its specific character as a subject in the international domain. As the United Nations recently confirmed, the Holy See thereby makes its contribution according to the dispositions of international law, helps to define that law, and makes appeal to it." And in another meeting with officials and staff of the UN: "[t]he Catholic Church, through the international activity of the Holy See, and through countless initiatives of lay Catholics, local Churches and religious communities, assures you of her support for your work."

Thus, the Pope, who is properly speaking the Holy See itself as the personal office of the bishop of Rome, assisted by the Roman Curia, has consistently manifested that he does not have any temporal power or state jurisdiction—apparently, therefore, not even within VCS –, that VCS is only a state to the extent that it is necessary to defend the Pope's ministry from external governmental interference and that the mission of the Holy See at the UN—and by extension, as signatory of UN sponsored human rights treaties—is mainly to disseminate and promote the moral message contained in those conventions.

With respect to the Holy See as supreme governing entity of the Church, the Holy See rejects that it has assumed any international obligations under the Convention on the Rights of the Child in that capacity. With respect to the extraterritorial obligations that it allegedly would also have, the Holy See understands that the obligations under the Convention are "*prima facie* territorial" and that the Holy See "does not ratify a treaty on behalf of every Catholic in the world and that, therefore, does not have obligations to implement the Convention within the territories of other States Parties on behalf of Catholics, no matter how they are organized". More importantly, it also warns that the Holy See "does not have the capacity or legal obligation to impose [the Convention] upon the local Catholic churches and institutions present on the territory of other states". The Holy See does not only justify this extensive limitation on its obligations because the Convention would only be territorially applicable within VCS but because doing otherwise would "constitute a violation of the principle of non-interference in the internal affairs of States", i.e. the affairs of the states where local Catholic entities are present.[83]

---

[83] Verbal Note N. 4322/2014/RS of 22 September 2014, paras 3 and 10.

The Holy See also tries to differentiate between the Pope's personal actions (e.g. speeches and apostolic visits) and those of Pontifical Councils which, as part of the Roman Curia, are also nevertheless attributable to the Holy See. These councils may issue their own doctrinal messages, manage directly certain charity works in different parts of the world or may have a role of encouragement or coordination of the work of local churches and Catholic associations. Such role may also consist in issuing different kinds of guidelines for local action which, for the most part, are just the framework for subsequent local guidelines or local Canon law legislation, issued by local Church authorities (diocesan or otherwise), making use of their autonomy under Church law and doctrine.[84]

The Holy See also mentions "the combined action taken by local Churches and by the Holy See".[85] It also consistently uses the following expression: "The Holy See encourages the activities carried out by [Catholic institutions] at the local level, according to their own authority in Canon law, and the laws of the respective States in which they operate",[86] thus highlighting its view that it cannot be responsible for what others do in their own name and with their own means in the fulfilment of their own mission or role and that not respecting such autonomy of local churches would additionally mean interference with the states where local churches are present.

Furthermore, the Holy See disagrees with the interpretation made by the CRC of the few Canon law provisions it mentions, whereby "religious obedience" would actually enable or require the Holy See to "control the daily activities of clerics, religious and laypersons, living in the territories of sovereign states". Contrary to that, "religious obedience ... concerns the unity of the doctrine of the Catholic faith", as if to say that local ecclesiastics have to follow the doctrinal texts coming from Rome, but not specific mandates dealing with the day-to-day management of their dioceses.[87]

The Holy See adds that it is the only one which can provide the authentic interpretation the abovementioned Canon law provisions, not the CRC. Such interpretative authority, in accordance with freedom of religion and international law, would derive from "the exclusive power of faith communities to organize and govern their internal affairs".[88] This makes reference to the respect for the autonomy of religious groups in human rights law, as part of freedom of religion and the separation between Church

---

[84] CRC, Summary Record of the 1852 Meeting, 16 January 2014, UN Doc. CRC/C./SR.1852, para 3.

[85] Permanent Observer Mission of the Holy See in Geneva, Presentation of the Periodic Reports of the Holy See to the CRC, 16 January 2014. http://www.vatican.va/roman_curia/secretariat_state/2014/documents/rc-seg-st-20140116_tomasi-child-rights_en.html. Accessed 13 September 2020.

[86] CRC, Second Report of Holy See, UN Doc. CRC/C/VAT/2, 22 October 2012, para 38; CRC, Initial Report of the Holy See on the Optional Protocol to the Convention on the Rights of the Child on the Sale of Children, Child Prostitution and Child Pornography, 8 November 2012, UN Doc. CRC/C/OPSC/VAT/1, para 25.

[87] Verbal Note N. 4322/2014/RS of 22 September 2014, paras 7 and 9. Accessed 26 September 2020.

[88] Ibid., para 8.

and State.[89] Such autonomy would necessarily imply a limited obligation for states to respect the organizational structure of religious groups, so that state authorities cannot impose intra-church relationships which are different from those prescribed by the doctrine of that group. This, in turn, means that if dioceses and religious orders in the Catholic religion enjoy a great degree of autonomy from the Pope, the CRC cannot pretend that Catholic doctrine and Canon law actually do not grant such autonomy.

Furthermore, a proper understanding of the relationship between the Holy See and local churches should "respect the principles of collegiality and primacy and the duties and rights in Canon law of all members of Christ's faithful".[90] This is another reference to the limits of the power of the Pope, which can neither violate the autonomy of local churches and religious orders nor forget that it does not govern the "universal Church"—as opposed to local churches—alone but together with the College of Bishops.[91] However, the Holy See does not really attempt to clarify concepts such as "collegiality" and "primacy".

Beyond the territory of VCS and with respect to the Convention against Torture, the Holy See understands that it "globally encourages basic principles and authentic human rights recognized in the" Convention and "adds a crucial moral voice in its support through its teaching", asserting that with its "various media services [...] reaches a truly international audience that makes it arguably one of the most crucial moral voices in the world for human rights".[92] Thus, the Holy See believes that one of its most important tasks under the Convention is to set a good example for other nations, by having ratified the Convention and promoting its further ratification and compliance with its principles.

The language used by the Holy See before the UN Treaty Bodies to refer to the way that it promotes human rights in general and with respect to the activities of local churches is usually the same: the Holy See "urges", "teaches", "exhorts", "advocates", "makes proposals", "promotes", "assists", "supports", "condemns", "encourages", has "formulated guidelines" and "delineated policies and procedures", "encourages States to ratify the treaty" and "disseminates teachings about moral principles".[93]

The Holy See's reports also devote a lot of space to describing the promotion and implementation of the Conventions through the activities of the Pope and the institutions of the Roman Curia, which are part of the Holy See. Such activities are basically messages and writings of a doctrinal nature but also the coordination of the efforts of the local clergy and the lay faithful, providing guidelines for local churches and encouraging their respective ministries. The Holy See would only exceptionally assume for itself the canonical jurisdiction over canonical crimes taking

---

[89] Witte and Nichols 2016, chapter 12; Schouppe 2015, chapter 5.

[90] Ibid., para 9.

[91] Granfield 1987, pp. 114 et seq.; Grigorita 2011, pp. 383 et seq.

[92] Presentation of the Initial Periodic Report of the Holy See to the Committee on the Convention against Torture (5 May 2014—Palais Wilson, Geneva).

[93] CRC, Second Report of the Holy See, 27 September 2011, UN Doc. CRC/C/VAT/2, para 5.

place outside VCS and committed by individuals who are, in principle, under the everyday canonical jurisdiction of local church authorities. This would be different from the jurisdiction over Vatican diplomats and officials who are within the reach of the VCS laws.[94]

It is nevertheless fair to say that the Holy See does not see its religious and moral mission as governing authority of the Church as being without significance in the implementation of the Conventions. It would otherwise be difficult to understand why it takes so much trouble to describe and praise the pastoral activities of the Pope and those of the Curia, its encouragement of the activities of clergy and lay persons in local churches, sometimes coordinating or providing guidelines for those activities and, exceptionally, intervening directly in their governance.

In this regard, a representative of the Holy See admitted before the CRC that "the Holy See's competence extended beyond national borders and that efforts were being made to encourage the community of believers". Still that same representative added that "the Holy See's jurisdiction was spiritual and did not take precedence over the jurisdiction of States".[95] Therefore, the Holy See does not seem convinced that its obligations under the Conventions end at the "borders" of VCS and only affect Vatican's officials and its inhabitants. A different interpretation would render such ample descriptions of the Holy See's activities meaningless. Thus, the jurisdiction of the Holy See would be in fact extraterritorial—or rather, non-territorial—but not of the kind which involves the exercise of governmental functions nor an effective control over territory, individuals or property.

However, sometimes one may also have the impression that, in terms of punishing predatory priests, the Holy See is saying that it was doing enough just by letting prosecuting state authorities do their job, even if some of the accusations of the UN Treaty Bodies involved allegations that Holy See officials or local ecclesiastics "operating under its authority" had engaged in obstruction of justice or that some Holy See officials had praised those few local ecclesiastics who had not collaborated with state authorities.

The Holy See also rejects the existence of extraterritorial obligations under the Convention Against Torture, at least in the understanding that the CAT has of such extraterritoriality, for two basic reasons: the prohibition of interference with the jurisdiction of other states within their territory and the autonomy that local churches and Catholics in general have, under Church law and doctrine. Referring to the CAT's Concluding Observations, the Holy See also rejects that the "obligations under the Convention concern both acts and omissions of public officials or other persons acting in an official capacity wherever they exercise effective control over persons or

---

[94] Apostolic letter issued *motu proprio* of the supreme pontiff Francis on the jurisdiction of judicial authorities of Vatican City State in criminal matters, 11 July 2013. http://w2.vatican.va/content/francesco/en/motu_proprio/documents/papa-francesco-motu-proprio_20130711_organi-giudiziari.html. Accessed 17 September 2020.

[95] CRC, Summary record of the 1852 meeting, 16 January 2014, UN Doc. CRC/C. /SR.1852, para 24.

territory".[96] The Holy See therefore accuses the CAT of imposing new obligations on signatories of the Convention against Torture, among them the obligation "to prevent purely private acts of violence" and including a "new definition of public official".[97]

The Holy See's 2014 report under the CERD basically makes the same qualifications as to the international obligations of the Holy See adding, with respect to allegations that ecclesiastics were involved in acts of genocide in Rwanda, that "[t]he Church as such cannot be held responsible for the transgressions of its members" and that in this regard, local bishops and religious superiors have jurisdiction to apply religious sanctions with their own authority under Canon law.[98]

Also, with respect to crimes committed by local clergy, the Holy See declares that it "exercised that same [state] authority over the inhabitants of the Vatican City State. It did not have civil jurisdiction over each and every member of the Catholic Church". "Although the Holy See had religious authority over the members of the Catholic Church across the world",[99] the "Holy See could only invoke its moral authority to urge local communities to open their doors. It was for bishops to ensure that the clergy under their charge acted in accordance with that spirit of solidarity."[100] "The Holy See directly appointed bishops after consulting the local clergy, the local community and local bishops". However, "[o]utside the territory of Vatican City State, it was the responsibility of local bishops to apply penal Canon law within the territory of their jurisdiction"; "local institutions were under the diocesan bishops" responsibility. "The Holy See did not intervene directly in management".[101] Finally and also before the CERD, the Holy See made a minor concession, admitting that its obligations under the Convention were not "strictly limited to the territory" of the VCS in the sense that it can promote the Convention worldwide, as "a moral entity with a wider impact".[102]

---

[96] Comments of the Holy See on the Concluding Observations of the Committee against Torture and Other Cruel, Inhuman and Degrading Treatment or Punishment, Nota verbale N. 2254/15/RS, 15 May 2015, para 5. https://tbinternet.ohchr.org/Treaties/CAT/Shared%20Documents/VAT/CAT_C_VAT_CO_1_Add-1_20599_E.pdf. Accessed 13 September 2020.

[97] Ibid., paras 16 and 22.

[98] CERD, Periodic Report of the Holy See, UN Doc. CERD/C/VAT/16-23, 4 September 2014, paras 33 and 34 https://documents-dds-ny.un.org/doc/UNDOC/GEN/G14/154/90/PDF/G1415490.pdf?OpenElement. Accessed 27 September 2020.

[99] Committee on the Elimination of Racial Discrimination, Eighty-eighth session, Summary record of the 2394th meeting, UN Doc. CERD/C/SR.2394, 1 December 2015, para 3 https://undocs.org/CERD/C/SR.2394. Accessed 27 September 2020.

[100] Committee on the Elimination of Racial Discrimination, Eighty-eighth session, Summary record of the 2395th meeting, UN Doc. CERD/C/SR.2395, 1 December 2015, paras 18 and 21 https://undocs.org/CERD/C/SR.2394. Accessed 27 September 2020.

[101] Ibid., paras 18 and 39.

[102] Ibid., para 9.

63.6 Conclusion

The Holy See sees itself as having a dual character. It is the *sui generis* territorial sovereign of VCS and, at the same time, the highest governing authority of the Catholic Church. In the case of the Convention on the Rights of the Child and the Convention against Torture, the Holy See insists that it has only ratified the Convention on behalf of VCS and that its obligations are basically limited to the territory of VCS. In the eyes of the Holy See, however, the peculiar nature of VCS and of its legal system would make its territorial jurisdiction more limited than that of ordinary states and this curtails its prosecutorial power even with respect to crimes actually committed in its territory or by its citizens (i.e. diplomats and officials) elsewhere.

It is therefore maybe inappropriate to talk about its extraterritorial human rights obligations as signatory of the abovementioned two conventions. The Holy See would be truly discharging such extraterritorial obligations if it tried to impose on Catholics, worldwide, the legislation and policies that are meant to be enforced and implemented only within the territory of VCS and which the Holy See has enacted as sovereign over that territory. The Holy Objects to doing this, not only because it has not assumed such obligations but because it would be against the principle of non-interference and against the autonomy that local churches have in accordance with Canon law and church doctrine.

However, if the Holy See is understood to have acquired true human rights obligations in its position as governing authority of the Catholic Church, those human rights obligations are simply "non-territorial", i.e. the Holy See cannot discharge those obligations with respect to any territory, not only because it does not have any territorial jurisdiction outside VCS and such jurisdiction would be truly in breach of the territorial sovereignty of other countries, but because any "authority" that the Church has is personal and depends on the juridical link born out of the sacrament of baptism, not necessarily the sacrament of priesthood or any religious vow.[103] Furthermore, however personal this jurisdiction over Catholics is, it cannot be assimilated to any kind of state control over state officials, state organs or state entities.

Again, because the Holy See is not a state and because any human rights obligations it has beyond the VCS are neither territorial nor extraterritorial, it would be an exercise of wishful thinking to expect from it the kind of conduct for the protection of human rights that is expected from states.

The formula used by the Holy See when ratifying the CAT and the CRC, "on behalf of" VCS may have been meant to shield the Holy See from the ordinary human rights obligations ordinary states have. However, even assuming that the Holy See and the VCS are two different entities and that the Holy See only exercises territorial sovereignty over VCS, the entity represented at the UN is the Holy See and it is logical that the UN turns its eyes towards the Holy See and not VCS to demand accountability.[104] This makes sense because the relevance of the VCS—the smallest

---

[103] John Paul II 1993, Catechism of the Catholic Church (CCC), §1213.

[104] Exchange of notes of 16 and 28 October 1957; Tomasi 2012, p. 17.

country on earth—is minimal in comparison with the huge international relevance of the Holy See.

The Holy See is allowed into the concert of nations because it is the highest governing entity of the Church and not because it is the sovereign of VCS. This should be the starting point of any discussion about the international human rights obligations of the Holy See but should also help to understand that any such obligations must take count of what the Holy See is and what it is not. In this regard, if there is an attempt to attribute to the Holy See any responsibility for the acts of clergy or the lay faithful, committed in the context of the activities of local Churches, the relationships between the Holy See and those local churches must be carefully assessed and not simply taken for granted.

Therefore, a correct analysis of the nature of religious authority and of the way that authority operates in intra-Church relationships is essential to determine the international responsibility of the Holy See and the responsibility of other Church entities at the municipal level. Neither the Holy See nor UN Treaty Bodies have done a good job in this analysis.

Despite the dramatic language used by some claimants and human rights bodies to refer to the authority of the Holy See over clergy and/or over Catholics in general—e.g. "supreme", "absolute", "worldwide"—or the insistence with which they referred to individuals and institutions "operating under the authority of" the Holy See, little or no effort has been made to explain the nature of such religious authority, how it operates, what are its scope and limits. Some references are made to the "laws and policies" of the Holy See but the raw citations of a few provisions of the Code of Canon Law and other ecclesiastical norms do little to explain if the kind of obedience requested by those norms, as well as their enforceability, is the same as or analogous to that of state legal systems.

Although many, including the Pope, have occasionally suggested that clericalism and abuse of conscience—as illegitimate forms of coercion born of a mistaken understanding of religious authority—may have facilitated acts of abuse and their cover up, no references are made to this by claimants or human rights bodies, except misplaced and unqualified statements to codes of silence supposedly imposed under threat of "damnation"[105] by certain ecclesiastical norms whose contents are never explained nor analysed.

Although some references are made by the Holy See and the UN Treaty Bodies to its teaching activities, other forms of soft power are absent such as rituals, symbols, art and music. However, the degree to which these forms of authority and control actually command obedience from the faithful is very difficult to determine and probably very uneven. Besides, such forms of soft power can and must be exercised by all members of the Church, e.g. by Catholic parents over their children, and not just by the hierarchy or by clergy in general.

Nothing is said, either, before the UN Treaty Bodies, about the fact that obedience in Catholic teaching is first and foremost a moral virtue and not a legal duty. As a virtue, it is subject to the same doctrine as all the other virtues, which forecloses any

---

[105] Victims Communication to the ICC, para 144.

kind of "blind obedience".[106] Cases of abuse of conscience in the Church are simply misrepresentations of the Catholic teaching on authority by the very teachers of that doctrine. Besides, "vows of obedience" do not increase the level of control over a Catholic clergyman. They do "increase" the religious or moral obligation to obey the pre-existing obligations that each faithful has concerning his or her position in the hierarchical constitution of the Church: lay person, clergyman, member of religious order.

The "moral authority" and diplomatic influence of the Holy See is indeed acknowledged and even praised by the UN Treaty Bodies, but one has the impression that it is not the kind of effective control and authority with which they want the Holy See to implement the measures they propose. They seem to think that the Holy See rules the Church by simple mandates down the line of the hierarchy, which makes it responsible for its actions and omissions and for the actions and omissions of lower levels of that hierarchy. Actually, the Catholic Church is far from being able to enforce its discipline over its clergy or lay faithful nor to maintain the unity of its faith among Catholics, to the extent necessary to call it a highly centralized and controlling institution. Arguably, the Holy See does not have the kind of physical control present in the concept of jurisdiction, even within the nominal territory of VCS, as the ordinary need for Italian police services may show.

It is true that, with respect to the promotion of human rights, the Holy See sees itself more as a "super-diplomat" and as a moral authority than as the entity responsible for the compliance with human rights of Catholic entities and clergy, worldwide. The Holy See believes that, concerning the promotion of human rights, its role is more that of a teacher than of a governing entity.[107]

Therefore, it may seem that, notwithstanding the existence of ecclesiastical laws and a highly developed administrative apparatus at the different levels of the hierarchy and without denying the great "influence" that the Church has, the Holy See, local churches and religious orders may have a lot of *auctoritas* but hardly any *potestas*, i.e. the kind of physical power to control which is often at the heart of any analysis of the extraterritorial exercise of state power by state organs or state officials and other individuals or non-governmental entities. However, as the Maastricht Principles indicate, state "influence", as opposed to state "power", is increasingly taken into account, at least *de lege ferenda*.[108] Whether religious authority as soft power can be more or less effective or more or less dangerous than state power is beyond this chapter but religious authority is the only one that the Holy See can wield and the only one that can be demanded of it.

---

[106] St. Thomas Aquinas, Summa Theologica, Quaestio 104, Article 5.

[107] John XXIII 1961, Apostolic Constitution *Humanae Salutis*. https://w2.vatican.va/content/john-xxiii/la/apost_constitutions/1961/documents/hf_j-xxiii_apc_19611225_humanae-salutis.html. Accessed 15 September 2020.

[108] ETO Consortium, Maastricht Principles on Extraterritorial Obligations of States in the Area of Economic, Social and Cultural Rights, January 2013, Principle 26 https://www.etoconsortium.org/nc/en/main-navigation/library/maastricht-principles/?tx_drblob_pi1%5BdownloadUid%5D=23. Accessed 13 September 2020.

References

Allen J (2004) All the Pope's men: the inside story of how the Vatican really thinks. Doubleday, New York

Arsheim H (2018) Making religion and human rights at the United Nations. De Gruyter, Berlin

Cismas I (2017) The child's best interests and religion: a case study of the Holy See's best interests obligations and clerical child sexual abuse. In: Sutherland E E, Barnes Macfarlane L A (eds) Implementing article 3 of the United Nations convention on the rights of the child. Best interests, welfare and well-being. Cambridge University Press, New York, pp 310–325

Giliker P (2010) Vicarious liability in tort. A comparative perspective. Cambridge University Press, New York

Granfield P (1987) The limits of the papacy: authority and autonomy in the church. Crossroad, New York

Grigorita G (2011) L'autonomie ecclésiastique selon la législation canonique actuelle de l'Eglise orthodoxe et de l'Eglise catholique. Editrice Pontificia Università Gregoriana, Rome

Hoyano L, Keenan C (2007) Child Abuse. Law and policy across boundaries. Oxford University Press, New York

John Paul II (1983) Code of Canon law - Codex Iuris Canonici (CIC) http://www.vatican.va/archive/cod-iuris-canonici/cic_index_en.html

John Paul II (1993) Catechism of the Catholic Church. Libreria Editrice Vaticana, Vatican City. http://www.vatican.va/archive/ENG0015/_INDEX.HTM. Accessed 15 September 2020

Lupu I C, Tuttle R W (2004) Sexual Misconduct and Ecclesiastical Immunity. B.Y.U. L. Rev. 1789:1–124

Lytton T D (2008) Holding bishops accountable: how lawsuits helped the Catholic Church confront clergy sexual abuse. Harvard University Press, Cambridge, MA

Martinez L C (2008) Sovereign impunity: Does the Foreign Sovereign Immunities Act bar lawsuits against the Holy See in clerical sexual abuse cases? Tex. Int'l L.J. 44:123–155

Milanovic M (2014) CRC Concluding Observations on the Holy See. EJIL Talk Blog of the European Journal of International Law. https://www.ejiltalk.org/crc-concluding-observations-on-the-holy-see/. Accessed 15 September 2020

O'Reilly J T, Chalmers M (2014) The clergy sex abuse crisis and the legal responses. Oxford University Press, New York

Schouppe J P (2015) La dimension institutionnelle de la liberté de religion dans la jurisprudence de la Cour européenne des droits de l'homme. A. Pédone, Paris

Schutter O et al. (2012) Commentary to the Maastricht principles on extraterritorial obligations of states in the area of economic, social and cultural rights. Hum. Rts. Q. 34:1084–1169

Tomasi S (2012) The Diplomatic Representations of the Holy See to the United Nations and Other International Organizations, in International Catholic Organisations and Catholic Inspired NGOs, Their Contribution to the Building of the International Community. The Caritas in Veritate Foundation

Vega Gutiérrez M (2008) La Santa Sede y la Organización de las Naciones Unidas, in Iglesia Católica y Relaciones Internacionales, Actas del III Simposio Internacional de Derecho Concordatario. Ediciones del Cogreso, Granada, pp. 215–247

Wilde R (2016) The extraterritorial application of international human rights law on civil and political rights. In: Sheeran S, Rodley N (eds) Routledge Handbook of International Human Rights Law. Routledge, New York, pp 635–661

Witte J, Nichols J A (2016) Religion and the American constitutional experiment. Oxford University Press, New York

Zambrana N (2020a) Tort liability and representations of religious authority in clergy sex abuse litigation. In: Blasi A, Oviedo L (eds) The Abuse of Minors in the Catholic Church: Dismantling the Culture of Cover Ups. Routledge Studies in Religion, Routledge, pp. 182–217

Zambrana N (2020b) Reassessing the immunity and accountability of the Holy See in clergy sex abuse litigation. J Church State 62:26–58

Nicolás Zambrana-Tévar studied law at the Complutense University in Madrid. He received an LLM degree from the London School of Economics and a Ph.D. from the University of Navarra. He worked as a lawyer for Freshfields Bruckhaus Deringer and Garrigues Abogados. He has been a member of several research groups on Business and Human Rights. He has also published in the field of law and religion in the *Journal of Church and State*, the *Oxford Journal of Law and Religion* and *Ius Canonicum*.

Chapter 64
The Role of International Law in the Prevention and Resolution of Possible Conflicts over Water in Central Asia: A Comparative Study with Special Reference to the European Union (EU)

Hafeni Nashoonga

Contents

64.1 An Overview: The Role of International Water Law in the Prevention and Resolution of Possible Conflicts over Water in Central Asia	1474
64.2 The Right to Water	1477
64.3 Substantive Principles Concerning the Sharing of Transboundary Water Resources	1479
64.4 How Can International Water Law Prevent and Resolve Possible Conflicts over Water?	1480
64.5 Water Scarcity, Disputes and International Law–Scarcity or Lack of Political Will: What Really Connects Water Resources to Conflicts?	1482
64.6 Agreements Governing the Management of Transboundary Watercourses in the EU	1485
64.6.1 The Rhine River Basin and the International Commission for the Protection of the Rhine (ICPR)	1485
64.6.2 The EU Framework	1487
64.6.3 The 1992 Water Convention and the 1997 Watercourses Convention	1488
64.7 Enforcement of International Water Law in Central Asia: Examples from Kazakhstani Jurisdiction	1490
64.8 Conclusion	1492
References	1494

Abstract After the collapse of the Soviet Union, water management has caused severe disputes in Central Asia. Likewise, due to competing needs and priorities between the upstream and downstream states, water continues to divide these two groups of countries. As a result, water resources have emerged not as tools for facilitating regional cooperation but as a source of conflict. Though, at present, these conflicts do not seem to threaten war, they pose a significant threat to regional stability, security and sustainable development. In view of that, if they are not addressed, they could lead to armed conflicts. This chapter explores the role of international

---

H. Nashoonga (✉)
Independent Legal Consultant, Windhoek, Namibia
e-mail: hafeni@live.no

© T.M.C. ASSER PRESS and the authors 2022
S. Sayapin et al. (eds.), *International Conflict and Security Law*,
https://doi.org/10.1007/978-94-6265-515-7_64

law in the prevention and resolution of such conflicts, with the main question here being: what is the role of international water law in the prevention and resolution of possible conflicts over water in Central Asia? To that end, the chapter takes a sneak peek into the tools in international water law to respond to water disputes. In examining the management of transboundary watercourses in Central Asia and ratification by Central Asian countries of the agreements governing the management of such watercourses, the chapter then takes a comparative approach and makes special reference to the European Union, specifically with respect to the Rhine river basin. The author posits that cooperation over shared watercourses, supplemented by treaties, can be a good tool of managing conflicts over such watercourses and that water scarcity may not be the sole cause of conflicts.

Keywords Upstream · Downstream · Transboundary · Ratification · Watercourses · Treaties · Water Law · Cooperation · Conflict · Water scarcity · Prevention · Resolution · Stability · Security · Sustainable Development

> *Water conflicts are inevitable if we continue to do nothing to prevent them from occurring. While this response may appear simplistic, it is guided and framed by the key insight that the continent's finite fresh water resources cannot continue indefinitely to support the escalating demands that we make on them.*
>
> —Peter Ashton[1]

> *And just ten years from now, 1.8 billion people will live in areas with absolute water scarcity, and two out of three people around the world could live under water stress conditions. It is little wonder that many global experts have called the "water crisis" one of the greatest global risks that we face. Here in Central Asia and far beyond, pressures on water resources are building. Yet water also has the power to connect. It can be a source of cooperation – and from that cooperation even greater good can flow. Bringing people together around how they might share a scarce and precious resource opens the door to bringing them together around wider issues of peace and security. The countries of this region are interconnected by shared water resources. It is crucial to reach consensus over the management of trans-boundary water resources in Central Asia. Further ratification by countries of Central Asia of the water conventions will create a solid framework for this.*
>
> —Ban Ki-moon[2]

64.1 An Overview: The Role of International Water Law in the Prevention and Resolution of Possible Conflicts over Water in Central Asia

Interstate water disputes are hard to manage or control. The situation in Central Asia continues to put the interstate water disputes resolution mechanisms to the ultimate test yet again. World leaders, including the former United Nations (UN) Secretary

---

[1] See Alao 2007, p. 207.
[2] Ki-moon 2015.

General Ban Ki-moon, have urged that this issue be given high priority.[3] Water has been at the center of escalating and recurrent disputes among the Central Asian states since the fall of the Soviet Union.[4] Some states in the region are short on water, while others are short on electricity. Though this may not yet be the case in Central Asia, shared resources might be used as a political tool. Water can also be weaponized by certain factions in society such as belligerents and non-state actors. In the year 2000, then UN Secretary General Kofi Annan suggested that 'fierce competition for fresh water may well become a source of conflict and war in the future'.[5] Little did the late Annan know that this statement would be partially applicable to the situation in Central Asia in the near future.

Inadequate access to safe freshwater contributes to poverty, economic and political instability, and conflict.[6] Conflicts over water, both within countries and between countries, are sharply increasing. Moreover, these conflicts are a cause for concern as they continue to pose a significant threat to regional stability and security. More importantly, if these protracted conflicts are not dealt with, they could soon elevate to the level of 'armed' conflicts and lead to an increase in political violence. And this will make them very difficult, if not impossible, to resolve. It is noteworthy that accountability for international law violations is of fundamental importance with regard to respect for the rule of law, deterrence of future violations, and the provision of redress and justice for victims.

Notwithstanding the risks that disputes over water continue to pose on the regional peace, security, stability and sustainable development, they can also lay the groundwork for regional or interstate cooperation. Hence, it is imperative that these conflicts are given the necessary attention they deserve. The situation in Central Asia is not unique, and it, too, can become a success story and a noble example for other jurisdictions if shared water resources are used as a tool for facilitating cooperation. While actual war between Central Asian nations is, at the moment, unlikely, the protracted disputes over water are still a major cause for concern. It is true that resolving conflicts takes time and requires a significant amount of resources but the crisis in Central Asia must be dealt with as a matter of urgency. Obviously, this will require a proper legislative and policy environment, something which the region does not have at the moment. But this is achievable. One of the most important principles in the international regulation of transboundary or shared watercourses is equity. It is therefore important that states who share a watercourse such as a river basin should respect and apply the existing rules of general or customary international law relating to the equitable utilization and management of the resources of such shared watercourse. In the absence of equity, water conflicts are more likely to be more imminent as competing users try to secure the shared water resource that is, in most cases, scarce.

---

[3] Ibid.
[4] Dalbaeva 2018.
[5] Jannik and Ravnborg 2004.
[6] Levy and Sidel 2008.

To overcome this, a variety of conflict resolution methods have been developed in order to create peaceful relationships among riparian states.[7]

At least 276 river basins cross the political boundaries of two or more countries and are home to about 40 per cent of the world's population.[8] Alas, roughly two-thirds of these do not have a cooperative management framework.[9] Generally, efficient and effective transboundary water sharing should be based on four guiding principles: coordination and cooperation, interdisciplinary analysis, watershed and river basin planning, and adaptive management.[10] As Draper pointed out, the goal of water sharing agreements is to create a legal framework between the parties to establish the guiding principles of effecting water sharing, essential to sustaining economic growth and prosperity while enhancing the quality of life for the citizens of the parties.[11] The substantive principles in international water law must be taken into consideration at all times.[12] The applicability of these principles is considered universal under international law. This chapter will discuss these principles in the subsequent sections. One of the key proponents of the equity principle, Wolf, argued that there is no such thing as managing water for a single purpose.[13] He goes on further to say that disparities between riparian states only add further complications to water resources management. Thus, according to Wolf, water treaties themselves are regularly seen as, inefficient, ineffective, and, occasionally, as a new source of tensions.[14] But, if countries are willing to come together and start cooperating over shared water resources, a dream of a world without water conflicts is not far from becoming a reality. Solid cooperation and acute conflict over international water courses cannot coexist.[15] The relevant literature usually concludes that water conflicts are not attributable to one single driver (e.g. scarcity), but to the weakness of the governance regime that cannot absorb major or sudden hydrological or political changes in the basin.[16]

This statement holds true for Europe where, until recently, the governance system proved just suitable to handle both the hydrological and political challenges. As regards the power asymmetries and hegemony however, studies have shown that the abundance of water in a country's territory does not assure power on the global geopolitics.[17] Studies have also shown that proactive cooperation can indeed help resolve conflicts over water and help maintain both political and economic stability. More

---

[7] Alao 2007.

[8] Sedeqinazhad et al. 2018, p. 3.

[9] International Centre for Water Cooperation (2017) Cooperation over shared waters. www.siwi.org/priority-area/transboundary-water-management/. Accessed 27 May 2019.

[10] Draper 2006, p. 3.

[11] Ibid., p. 5.

[12] Lazerwitz 1993.

[13] Wolf 2007.

[14] Ibid.

[15] Ibid.

[16] Ibid.

[17] Alan et al. 2013, p. 569.

importantly, cooperation can help prevent violent conflict and help build sustainable peace.[18] It is true that water's economic value is at its highest at the moment and this is mostly due to increasing demands and pressure that the world continues to exert on the already scarce resource, making it even relatively scarcer in some parts of the world. As Bauer postulated, 'there is belief that in regions with growing populations, unstable governments and dwindling water resources, war over water at some point is highly probable.'[19] This is the same in Central Asia where the region's population continues to increase sharply. But water scarcity is not just a problem of water quantity; it also includes issues of pollution and water quality. Lack of sufficient water of adequate quality, for whatever purposes, is a problem of scarcity. The two aspects of water management are always physically interrelated.[20] If water is not adequately planned and managed, its use may cause tensions among competing users. However, such tensions can be averted through the enactment of adequate water legislation and the establishment of an appropriate water administration. Needless to say, triumph in the development, protection and management of water resources in a country depends to a large extent on the effectiveness of its water laws and institutions.[21]

64.2 The Right to Water

International water law was recently strengthened with the adoption of the Draft Articles on the Law of Transboundary Aquifers by the International Law Commission (ILC).[22] The Draft Articles lay out rules regarding sovereignty of Aquifer States. According to the Draft Articles, 'each Aquifer State has sovereignty over the portion of a transboundary Aquifer or Aquifer system located within its territory.' Further that it shall 'exercise its sovereignty in accordance with international law and the present Draft Articles.'[23] It cannot be denied that international law underwent a process of specialization from general rules to more specialized rules of international water law. Although international water law is a relatively recent and distinct field of international law, its importance and role as well as its impact on the international plane cannot be overlooked. Against this background, let us now turn the focus on the 'right to water'. While water is the foundation of human life, is a limited and scarce resource, it can also be a common and divided resource. 'As water is fundamental for life and health, the human right to safe drinking water is considered

---

[18] Levy and Sidel 2011.

[19] Zeitoun 2008, p. 3.

[20] Bauer 2004, pp. 6–7.

[21] Nanni 2007.

[22] Report of the International Law Commission, Draft Articles on the Law of Non-Navigational Uses of International Watercourses, U.N. GAOR, 46th Sess., Supp. No. 10 at 161, U.N. Doc. A/46/10, (1991) [hereinafter Draft Articles].

[23] Ibid., Article 1.

a pre-requisite for the realization of other human rights.'[24] Likewise, while states are gifted with the right to protect territorial resources under customary international law, the human right to safe drinking water was first recognized by the UN General Assembly and the Human Rights Council (HRC)[25] as part of binding international law in 2010.[26] The right to water entitles everyone, without discrimination, to have access to sufficient, safe, acceptable, physically accessible, and, affordable water for personal and domestic use.[27]

Recognizing a human right to water in international law imposes certain obligations on states. For example, states are at least obliged to ensure that the general population has access to safe drinking water. States are also expected, albeit not at all times under an obligation, to use rivers, and other freshwater resources, in an equitable and reasonable manner. However, there has been difficulty interpreting what constitutes equitable and reasonable use, and as a result, some states have often accused other states of using more water than they should (or using it for purposes considered unreasonable) and this has led to regional disputes in many parts of the world including Central Asia. It should also be understood that fresh water is a legal entitlement, rather than a commodity or service provided on a charitable basis and that water must not be privatized. Privatization can lead to higher water rates, and the difficulty in ensuring that the new managers respect their obligation to develop the water supply in poorer areas, where consumption is lower.[28] If freshwater is a legal entitlement which all states must respect, protect and uphold, at all times, then people are rights-holders and states are duty-bearers of providing water and sanitation services. Subsequently, people being rights-holders can then claim their rights and states being duty-bearers, must then guarantee the rights to water and sanitation on an equal and, more importantly, non-discriminatory basis.[29]

States also have the obligation to refrain from interfering directly or indirectly with the enjoyment of the right to water. States are further obliged to prevent third parties such as corporations from interfering in any way with the enjoyment of the right to water.[30] Most importantly, states have an obligation to adopt the necessary measures to achieve the full realization for their citizens, of the right to water. It is therefore important that governments are held accountable in their efforts to realizing the right to water.[31]

---

[24] Barraqué 2011, p. 2.

[25] See also UN Human Rights Council resolution 15/9 of September 2010, resolution 16/2 of March 2011, resolution 18/1 of September 2011 and resolution 21/2 of September 2012.

[26] United Nations Water 2014.

[27] United Nations General Assembly, "The human rights to safe drinking water and sanitation," Resolution 70/169, U.N. Doc. A/RES/70/169/.

[28] Barilla Center for Food & Nutrition 2017, https://www.barrilacfn.com/en/magazine/food-for-all/the-pros-and-cons-of-water-privatization/.

[29] Ibid.

[30] Office of the High Commissioner for Human Rights 2003.

[31] Ibid.

64.3 Substantive Principles Concerning the Sharing of Transboundary Water Resources

As a general principle, in the absence of an applicable treaty on shared waters, countries' rights and obligations are (and must at all times be) governed by customary international law.[32] Although as a matter of formal doctrine, treaty and customary international law are coequal sources of a state's international legal obligations.[33] If we look at the historical development of international water law more closely, we will begin to understand that the codification of customary law pertaining to the rules of customary international law concerning shared freshwater have been 'codified' in the 1997 Watercourses Convention. These rules were negotiated and adopted by the UN General Assembly. Though not in force at the time (as it only entered into force in August 2014), the 1997 Watercourses Convention had already been cited as evidence of custom by the ICJ (hereinafter the Court) in one of the famous cases in the history of international water law, the Danube case in 1997.[34] Moreover, the security (whether human, environmental or political) of international basins, which host about half of the world's population, is threatened by the lack of effective mechanisms for managing such basins.

International water law has played an instrumental role not only in managing but also in resolving disputes over shared watercourses around the world. For example, in its Decision in the case concerning Gabcikovo-Nagymaros Project (Hungary/Slovakia), the Court held that Hungary was not permitted to suspend and subsequently abandon, in 1989, its part of the works in the dam project, as laid down in the treaty signed in 1977 by Hungary and Czechoslovakia and related instruments.[35] There are three main principles on water courses in customary international law, namely: equitable and reasonable utilization, prevention of significant harm, and prior notification. Equitable and reasonable utilization states that *shared waters must be used in a manner that is equitable and reasonable vis-à-vis co-riparian states*. This principle has also been recently strengthened by the Draft Articles. Article 4 of the Draft Articles requires Aquifer States to utilize transboundary Aquifers or Aquifer systems according to the principle of equitable and reasonable utilization.[36] Although this entails certain difficulties, what is 'equitable and reasonable utilization' is determined case-by-case. The principle of prevention of significant harm states that countries must do their best to prevent uses within their territories from causing significant harm to other states. This principle has also been strengthened by the Draft Articles under Article 6. Article 6(1) stipulates that, in utilizing transboundary

---

[32] Dellapenna 2011.
[33] Crootof 2016.
[34] 'Gabčíkovo-Nagymaros Project (Hungary/Slovakia), Judgment, 25 September 1997' [1997] International Court of Justice/Reports of judgments, advisory opinions and orders (ICJ Reports).
[35] 'Case Concerning the Gabcikovo-Nagymaros Project (Hungary/Slovakia) ("The Danube Dam Case") [1997] ICJ Reports 7' [1997] International Court of Justice/Reports of judgments, advisory opinions and orders (ICJ Reports).
[36] Draft Articles (n 22).

Aquifers or Aquifer systems in their territories, Aquifer States shall take all appropriate measures to prevent the causing of significant harm to other Aquifer States or other States in whose territory a discharge zone is located. The principle of prior notification is perhaps the most important one in the prevention of possible conflicts over water. The prior notification principle requires that a state must notify other states of planned activities that may adversely affect such other states who share that same watercourse. The 1997 Watercourses Convention for example further provides that an international watercourse shall be used and developed by watercourse States with a view to attaining optimal and sustainable utilization thereof and benefits therefrom, taking into account the interests of the watercourse States concerned, consistent with adequate protection of the watercourse.[37]

The Draft Articles also oblige States to cooperate. Article 7(1) of the Draft Articles, specifies that Aquifer States shall cooperate on the basis of sovereign equality, territorial integrity, sustainable development, and mutual benefit and good faith in order to attain equitable and reasonable utilization and appropriate protection of their transboundary Aquifers or Aquifer systems.[38] Watercourses States also have a general obligation to cooperate under the 1997 Watercourses Convention. Cooperating over shared watercourses is one way to prevent possible conflicts over water. Cooperation, according to the 1997 Watercourses Convention, shall be on the basis of sovereign equality, territorial integrity, mutual benefit and good faith in order to attain optimal utilization and adequate protection of an international watercourse.[39]

64.4 How Can International Water Law Prevent and Resolve Possible Conflicts over Water?

States have historically exercised absolute sovereignty over the use of rivers and other natural resources located within the State's territory, no matter what the effects of the resource use on neighboring States. The development of international water law has, no doubt, helped to change the trajectory and ultimately prevent possible water conflicts. Indeed, international water law can play an important role in the prevention and resolution of possible conflicts over water in that it provides a framework for the cooperation of states regarding their rights to, and responsibilities for, transboundary freshwater resources.[40] Cooperation is one of the general and most fundamental principles in international law which is designed to facilitate the fulfillment of obligations, especially the more specific obligations.[41] Cooperation over shared water

---

[37] See Article 5(1) of the Convention on the Law of the Non-Navigational Uses of International Watercourses (adopted 21 May 1997, entered into force on 17 August 2014) 2998 UNTS (UN Watercourses Convention).

[38] See Article 7(1).

[39] Ibid., Article 8(1).

[40] Magsig 2015.

[41] Crawford and Brownlie 2012.

resources can also assist decision-makers to reduce water conflicts. The application of cooperation has been identified in several instruments in the context of the law of international water resources. According to Bearden, who borrows from McAffrey, international water law is the body of law that reconciles the sovereign rights of riparian states in order to optimize benefits for all, while at the same ensuring adequate protection of the shared watercourse.[42] As Louka rightly put it, 'the sovereignty of a state over its natural resources is a principle frequently iterated in international treaties.'[43] Accordingly, States planning projects on international watercourses must account for international law rules requiring prior notification, equitable utilization and prevention of significant harm.[44] These rules greatly restrict the scope for purely unilateral action.[45] International law has developed a range of options in addressing issues related to conflict avoidance under the sphere of 'access' and it also offers mechanisms for resolving disputes in a peaceful manner.[46]

Under international water law, as a widely-accepted rule, a riparian state that is planning a project on international waters ought to bear in mind that such a project may not deprive co-riparian states of their right to an equitable and reasonable share of the uses and benefits of these waters. Further that the country in which the project is to be located should ensure that a Transboundary Environmental Impact Assessment (TEIA) is conducted in accordance with that country's applicable law, to establish what effects such project could have on other countries sharing the watercourse. There also needs to be a proper exchange of information between the state which is planning to embark on the project and co-riparian states as regards the impact such a project could or may have on co-riparian states. In the event that the envisaged project does not pose any real or potential and foreseeable threats on other countries sharing the watercourse, it is always good practice under international relations to notify co-riparian states. Because what is 'equitable' may change with time and conditions, a constant exchange of data and information, as well as monitoring, is essential.[47] The principle of equitable utilization of resources has been articulated in early judicial decisions regarding the sharing of freshwater resources.[48] The principle of regular exchange of data and information is also covered under Article 8 of the Draft Articles, which requires Aquifer States to exchange readily available data and information on the condition of their transboundary aquifers or aquifer systems on a regular basis.

---

[42] Bearden 2018.
[43] Louka 2006, p. 49.
[44] McCaffrey 2001.
[45] Ibid.
[46] Magsig 2015.
[47] Ibid., at 26.
[48] Louka 2006.

64.5 Water Scarcity, Disputes and International Law–Scarcity or Lack of Political Will: What Really Connects Water Resources to Conflicts?

This section examines the link between water scarcity and water disputes in Central Asia with special reference to other jurisdictions. In addition, the international agreements governing the management of watercourses in the EU are studied and compared to the situation in Central Asia with a view to establishing whether the Central Asian watercourses legal framework complies with its international (and where necessary, national) obligations. The section analyzes the major agreements governing one of the most important European river basins, the Rhine. The EU Water Framework Directive (2000/60/EC) (hereinafter the Framework)—an integrated river basin management for Europe is also critically analyzed. In the last part of the section, the Convention on the Protection and Use of Transboundary Watercourses and International Lakes (hereinafter the 1992 Water Convention), the 1997 Watercourses Convention and enforcement of international water law in Central Asia, are also critically discussed.

'In order to survive, all civilizations must have a consistent water supply.'[49] Likewise, to thrive, particularly in the presence of scarcity, a society must also have an efficient means of allocating and distributing that supply.[50] Otherwise, the struggle for control of scarce resources will result in violent conflict.[51] The demand for water continues to grow at an exponential rate. According to a 2019 UN report, global water demands is expected to continue increasing at a similar rate until 2050, accounting for an increase of 20 to 30% above the current level of water use. This is mainly due to rising demands in the industrial and domestic sectors. Additionally, over 2 billion people live in countries experiencing high water stress, and about 4 billion people experience severe water scarcity during at least one month of the year.[52] Competition for water is intensifying. 'To urge to cater for basic human needs, together with demands for general improvements in standards of living and continued economic growth, has resulted in a rapid increase in the pressure on available water resources.'[53] At the international level, laws regulating the uses and benefits of shared water resources are based on certain recognized principles, as developed through the interactions and relationships between autonomous states.[54] However, the supply is declining due to the deterioration in water quality and that 'lack of cooperation could mean more conflict ahead as climate change brings more competition for water. 'Unless there is greater regional cooperation over water then these issues might create

---

[49] Jones and Cech 2009, p. 51.
[50] Ibid.
[51] Ibid.
[52] United Nations Water 2019.
[53] Gronwall 2008.
[54] Ibid.

the next big war.'[55] As a result, countries are faced with major challenges as to the allocation and protection of water resources and disputes among neighboring water users and communities continue to multiply. Where water crosses boundaries, the stage is set for disputes between different users trying to safeguard access to a vital resource, while protecting the natural environment.[56] Societies have for centuries fought over access to water resources and water supply. In modern times, the increasing diversification in its uses has further increased the ways through which water has been linked to politics, conflict, and diplomacy.[57]

It is noteworthy that water differs from other natural resources in many ways. One of the ways in which water differs from other natural resources is the fact that, unlike other resources, water offers very limited opportunity for individual ownership or control.[58] Notwithstanding the fact that water has been privatized in some parts of the world, it still offers low opportunities for elite greed, as the predominance of the community's role in ensuring necessary regulations for its management is greater than any other natural resource.[59] Another way in which water differs from other natural resources is that water is crucial to a string of ecological, social, economic, and political issues in ways other resources are not, and for this reason, its availability generally determines the nature and extent of development, the level of food, security, and the health of populations.[60] It is also worth mentioning that water scarcity is common in regions where water is shared by several riparian states and especially where water is used for competing purposes. This is the case in Central Asia, where water is shared and used, albeit for different purposes, by and among all five states in the region.

While there is evidence that water scarcity may give rise to conflicts among the riparian states that share water basins, there is also evidence that proper arrangements among these riparian states could create a basis for cooperation. Water scarcity may lead to both interstate and intrastate conflicts. Interstate conflicts are possible when one state deprives another riparian state (or several riparian states) of water. Intrastate conflicts occur when the water scarcity becomes a local issue, such that the local populace starts fighting over this resource that they need for human consumption, agricultural and other purposes. While Central Asia is not a water-scarce region *per se*, there is still a need for cooperation between riparian states to ensure that recurrent water disputes become a thing of the past. Wolf in his article is provoking our thoughts by asking some very pertinent questions regarding conflicts and possibility for cooperation. Wolf is saying that if there is little violence between nations over their shared waters, 'What is the problem? Is water actually a security concern at all?'[61] Wolf's view may be shared in that there are a number of issues where water causes

---

[55] Arnold 2018.
[56] Alao 2007.
[57] Ibid.
[58] Ibid.
[59] Ibid.
[60] Ibid.
[61] Wolf 2007, pp. 1–3.

or exacerbates tensions. Most conflicts are usually due to the absence of the principle of equity. Equity concerns with how such rights in shared water resources can be allocated equitably, taking account of a range of relevant factors and considerations. Hence, conflict resolution methods have been developed to ensure equity and, in the long run, to create peaceful relationships among riparian states.[62]

Wolf further argued that differences between riparians states may add further complications to water resources management.[63] Moreover, failure to cooperate may lead to ineffective water management and decreasing water quantity, and quality.[64] The emergence of water disputes and conflicts are more often than not due to a lack of legal and proper policy frameworks that govern water management rather than water scarcity. While there is a growing belief that as much as water problems of our world, are a cause of tension, they could also be used as a catalyst for cooperation.

Certainly, shared waters are a good basis for cooperation. This is true especially in the EU where cooperation in water resources ranks higher than in Central Asia. The EU has cooperated on a diverse range of issues in water resources management for many decades. The EU has adopted a risk management program which is intended to regulate the flow of water especially in times of flood. This cooperation approach has been beneficial in the sense that it helps countries to mitigate flood impacts and at best they can, preventing flood-sponsored damage and improving flood warning systems thanks to international co-operation. Cooperation over shared waters in the EU is characterized by regular meetings between riparian states,[65] which lays down a strong foundation for good relations and diplomacy and also offer opportunities for cooperation in other important areas. Riparian states in the EU have also adopted a joint-action program which is responsible for ensuring water quality. Water cooperation in the EU continues to be a success story at all levels. There seems to be no prospects of conflicts and disputes around water in the EU in the foreseeable future.

Be that as it may, what is the potential for outright conflict between EU countries over shared watercourses? Water conflicts in the EU, if ever they would occur, would be driven mainly by quality rather than by quantity. This is to say, water scarcity is currently not an issue in the EU. Cooperation has largely been in the areas of water quality, river continuity and fish passage and migration. However, while there are conflicting interests among riparian states in the EU, possible conflicts over water have been easily averted, mostly through regional cooperation. Moreover, outright water conflicts are commonly triggered by a unilateral intervention by an upper riparian state that is strongly contested by a downstream riparian. However, given that large-scale immediate interventions with transboundary impacts are not permissible under both EU and international law, such situations are very unlikely to happen. Notwithstanding the aforesaid, lack of cooperation by one or more riparian states

---

[62] Abukhater 2013, p. 2.

[63] Wolf 2004.

[64] Ibid.

[65] See Article 1(4) of the Convention on the Protection and Use of Transboundary Watercourses and International Lakes (adopted on 17 March 1992, entered into force 6 October 1996) 1936 UNTS 269.

may give rise to prolonged differences among them that may eventually escalate into a full-fledged political conflict.

64.6 Agreements Governing the Management of Transboundary Watercourses in the EU

64.6.1 The Rhine River Basin and the International Commission for the Protection of the Rhine (ICPR)

The Rhine is Europe's third biggest river basin. It is shared by nine countries, consisting of 58 million inhabitants. The Rhine supplies drinking water for 30 million people. The first sign that a new spirit of cooperation was emerging on the Rhine came with the establishment of the ICPR which was established in 1950 (amended in 1963 and 1999) as the first intergovernmental body for the management of transboundary waters.[66] Within the ICPR, Germany, the Netherlands and other countries co-operate closely[67] The ICPR serves, *inter alia*, as an example of transboundary co-operation within an international river basin district. All agreements concerning the protection and management of the Rhine are by consensus. Measures taken are mostly just recommendations to countries; however countries have the obligation to report on implementation of these measures.

'The nine states and regions in the Rhine watershed closely co-operate in order to harmonize the many interests of use and protection in the Rhine area'.[68] As mentioned above, a total of 58 million people depend on the Rhine (they live in the river basin) and so drinking water supply for 30 million people has to be guaranteed directly from the river or from its banks.[69] For many years, the EU member states in the Rhine basin have desired to work towards the sustainable development of the Rhine ecosystem on the basis of a comprehensive approach. Notably, two fundamental types of cooperation in international watercourses in the EU are direct exchange of data and information and the establishment of joint development commissions. These types of cooperation have been working quite well.

The ICPR is the foundation upon which the Rhine Convention was founded. It serves as a platform for riparian states to build mutual trust which is necessary for cooperation. The ICPR's instructions derive from the Rhine Conferences of Ministers that are held every two to three years. It is at these conferences that the 'responsible ministers formulate the political goals of the Commission, and evaluate ongoing and completed activities.'[70] Indeed, the ICPR is known as the only

---

[66] Cioc 2002.
[67] Ibid.
[68] International Commission for the Protection of the Rhine 2019.
[69] Plum and Schulte-Wülwer-Leidig 2014.
[70] Verweij 2000, p. 80.

efficient existing working platform. Basin commissions have been very successful in preventing conflict by way of providing a platform of dialogue and by way of implementing projects that are mutually beneficial for riparian states. Water quality problems in the Rhine have not started recently however; they were already acknowledged in the 15th century, although a deteriorating quality of the water was not really recognized before the end of the 1960s. As a result, more and more efforts were needed to produce good quality drinking water and the Rhine had the distressing reputation of being the sewer of Europe.[71] Having established that water scarcity is not an issue in the EU, what are some of the possible triggers of water disputes in the region? Studies indicate that water disputes in the EU would possibly be triggered by failure to inform other riparian states about projects (i.e. lack of information flow), lack of cooperation (lack of working relationships), and transboundary water pollution. Hence, in order to prevent possible conflicts over water in the EU, it is important that riparian states avoid doing things which could lead to mistrust. Most importantly, the riparian states need to have good communication channels in place through which they can inform each other about project implementation, etc. Riparian states cooperating on the Rhine also need to respect the information exchange obligations as set out in the Convention on the Protection of the Rhine (Rhine Convention).[72] Article 3 (e) of the Rhine Convention requires the Contracting States to commit their efforts to "ensuring environmentally sound and rational management of water resources". This article is crucial, as it covers two most important areas in water affairs—basically, rational management of water resources while also having regard to the environment. The Contracting Parties are also obliged to 'reinforce their co-operation and mutually inform one another in particular of the measures carried out on their territories aimed at protecting the Rhine.'[73] There has been no real competition for water in the EU although this may vary due to climate change. At present the EU does not have any instrument on water quantity. Also, no real conflicts over water quantity (i.e. water scarcity) have been experienced. The disputes have mainly been about the quality of the water in the Rhine and other shared river basins. The Rhine river basin is considered one of the most international watercourses in the world, yet it is often used as a benchmark when it comes to transboundary watercourses cooperation discourses and especially when it comes to practical examples where sharing international watercourses has successfully emerged as a tool for cooperation rather than a source of conflict, so what makes cooperation over this important river basin increasingly possible?

Obviously, it is not safe to say that the existence of the Rhine Convention alone is sufficient to guarantee cooperation among and between riparian states. Poland, for instance, is not a Contracting State to the Rhine Convention; however, there has

---

[71] International Commission for the Protection of the Rhine (2013) First European River prize 2013: success on the Rhine. www.icpdr.org/main/publications/first-european-riverprize-2013-success-rhine. Accessed 28 June 2019.

[72] See Article 3(e) of the Convention for the Protection of the Rhine against Chemical Pollution (Rhine Convention) [1977] OJ L240/37-63.

[73] Ibid., Article 5(1).

been significant cooperation between the Contracting States and non-Contracting States such as Poland. The Rhine Convention, albeit having been amended twice, is at least 70 years old and it is still considered one of the fundamental instruments upon which cooperation over shared watercourses in the EU is founded. This only tells us that cooperation over shared watercourses is only possible with the existence of a proper legal and policy framework, something that the region of Central Asia does not have but which it desperately needs if the water conflicts in that region are to be resolved and, at best, prevented. It is obvious that the most important things which make cooperation on the Rhine increasingly easy are: the existence of a clear and proper legal framework, working structures, on-going and continuous exchange of data and joint activities, complemented by the riparian states' spirit of consensus and compromise. Water protection is a longstanding issue in most EU countries as they all apply very similar measures. Germany for example, has adopted an elaborate law on water protection and water resources management.[74] Germany also has in place a law on waste water management.[75] However, at the EU level, water protection is implemented through the Framework, as discussed in the following section.

64.6.2 The EU Framework

In 2000, the European Parliament and the European Council adopted the Framework for Community Action in the Field of Water Policy. This Framework is aimed at implementing comprehensive water protection in the European river districts.[76] The Framework stipulates that Member States shall ensure that a river basin covering the territory of more than one Member State is assigned to an international river basin district. Further that at the request of the Member States involved, the Commission shall act to facilitate the assigning to such international river basin districts.[77] Sustainable development is a core objective of the EU and the Framework is based on the idea that water management needs to take account of economic, ecological, and social issues and that its prime objective is the sustainable use and management of water resources.[78] Integrated river basin management adopts a holistic approach to protecting the whole body of water, its source, tributaries, and river mouth. Therefore, the river basin approach is the best way to manage water.[79]

The Framework ensures the implementation of comprehensive water cooperation by modernizing and harmonizing European water legislation. The Framework also

---

[74] Federal Water Act 1957 (GE).
[75] Waste Water Charges Act 1976 (GE).
[76] Directive 2000/60/EC of the European Parliament and of the Council of 23 October 2000 Establishing a Framework for Community Action in the Field of Water Policy [2000] OJ L327/1.
[77] Ibid., Article 3(3).
[78] Guerrini and Romano 2014, p. 55.
[79] European Commission 2019.

considers a river basin district as an entity.[80] The Framework requires transboundary, integrated assessment and management. To ensure expeditious implementation, the Framework had fixed 2015 as deadline for achieving the desired status in all European water bodies.[81] The EU has a very effective water legislation that aims to protect and enhance aquatic ecosystems and promote sustainable water use across Europe. However, much of today's transboundary water cooperation regime in the EU is based on a number of fundamental premises that may not reflect future hydrological realities. These include water pollution; water quantity management for allocation is not an issue. Nevertheless, the existing Framework is adequate to handle future water challenges and possible disputes. Likewise, water has been and will remain a key driver of interstate cooperation in the EU, but new hydrological challenges are emerging that are likely to give rise to serious differences among riparian states in the bloc.

64.6.3 The 1992 Water Convention and the 1997 Watercourses Convention

The Water Convention, adopted in 1992 and entered into force on the 6 October 1996, codifies the key principles of international water law. The 1992 Water Convention emphasizes that "cooperation between member countries in regard to the protection and use of transboundary waters shall be implemented primarily through the elaboration of agreements between countries bordering the same waters, especially where no such agreements have yet been reached."[82] The 1997 Watercourses Convention defines 'international watercourse' as a watercourse, parts of which are situated in different States.[83]

It is worth reiterating that transboundary water cooperation ranks higher in the EU than anywhere else in the world. EU member states are subject to four layers of transnational water law: the 1997 Watercourses Convention, EU law such as the Framework, basin agreements and bilateral water agreements. Because these water norms are mutually compatible and reinforcing in character, they provide a solid ground for cooperation. Aside from shared watercourses, there are other conditions which foster cooperation in the regional bloc, such as the very high level of political integration of the relevant states through EU institutions and law, high level of economic development, lack of regional hegemony, lack of intensely rising human

---

[80] See Article 2(15) of the Directive 2000/60/EC of the European Parliament and of the Council of 23 October 2000 Establishing a Framework for Community Action in the Field of Water Policy [2000] OJ L327/1.

[81] International Commission for the Protection of the Rhine 2018.

[82] Convention on the Protection and Use of Transboundary Watercourses and International Lakes (adopted on 17 March 1992, entered into force 6 October 1996) 1936 UNTS 269 (Water Convention).

[83] See Article 2(b) of the Convention on the Law of the Non-Navigational Uses of International Watercourses (adopted 21 May 1997, entered into force on 17 August 2014) 2998 UNTS (UN Watercourses Convention).

pressures, high degree of cultural homogeneity and the importance of environmental awareness. While there might not be evidence of the financial costs for noncooperation between riparian states, cooperation has been more beneficial, particularly in the areas of flood protection on the Rhine. There are robust early warning and alarm systems in place, dedicated to preventing damage and mitigating flood impacts. Needless to say, noncooperation among riparian states would lead to more flood-sponsored damage. The existing 1992 and 1997 Conventions, complemented by EU legislation, have been able to deal with such issues related to water and, as a result, any possible conflicts over water have been averted. But the EU in fact does not have a model for managing transboundary competition for water. This, nonetheless, does not reduce the values of EU's transboundary water governance regime, just a sign that, unlike many other regions of the word, the EU has not yet faced basin-wide, multilateral allocation challenges and, as such, it does not have the legal machinery to handle them. The 1992 Water Convention requires states to prevent, control and reduce transboundary impact, use transboundary waters in a reasonable and equitable way, and ensure their sustainable management.[84]

While fierce competition for fresh water may well become a source of conflict and wars in the future, the same is not true for the EU. This is because the EU has better mechanisms in place, both legal and policy-based, which ensure that disputes, if and when they arise, are handled before they can escalate to the level of conflicts. The 1992 Water Convention has been working effectively in the EU; it covers all uses that may have an impact on the protection, preservation and management of international watercourses. Also, the amount of political will from the governments of riparian states has been overwhelming. And we know that successful and effective implementation of water agreements depends largely on the political will of riparian states. The 1992 Water Convention thus provides a legal framework for regional cooperation on shared water resources. As a result, several bilateral or multilateral agreements between European countries are based on its principles and provisions.[85] The Contracting Parties must also ensure that transboundary waters are managed in a way that is rational, that they are preserved and protected, and that their use is reasonable and equitable.[86] There are, regrettably, numerous new challenges that were not foreseen when the instruments (e.g. the Rhine Convention) were adopted. These include: transboundary water allocation, adaptation to climate change, sediment transport and its legal implications, as well as groundwater protection and management.

---

[84] Bernardini 2007.
[85] Ibid.
[86] Ibid.

64.7 Enforcement of International Water Law in Central Asia: Examples from Kazakhstani Jurisdiction

Water uses in international basins, the world over, have for years been governed by a number of treaties. These treaties, and the negotiations upon which they were founded, indicate that there are principles limiting the power of states to use such waters without regard to injurious effects on riparian states. However, the same is not true in Central Asia, as there have been cases of states planning or wanting to use such shared waters (e.g. one state building a dam at the expense of co-riparian states) and in the end depriving other states of using such shared waters to the maximum benefit. Hence, what Central Asia needs is a truly level playing field between states sharing the water resources. This level playing field will only be possible if states in the region, with the support of the international community, are willing to come together and cooperate. Cooperating means ratifying existing regional and international water treaties and in the absence of such treaties, concluding new ones. Three countries in Central Asia are at least State Parties to the 1992 Water Convention, namely Kazakhstan, Uzbekistan and Turkmenistan.[87] Uzbekistan is also a State Party to the 1997 Watercourse Convention. If the 1992 Water Convention and other treaties were to be implemented after ratification, a decline in the water-related disputes in that region is guaranteed. The problem is not water scarcity, it is how water is distributed among and between users who share such water resources. Also, the problem is not the absence of treaties; the problem is non-ratification of such treaties by countries in Central Asia.

Under the Water Code, privatization of water is not allowed in the Republic of Kazakhstan as all water courses in the Republic of Kazakhstan are the exclusive property of the State.[88] Interestingly, ratification and denouncement of international treaties on the matters of regulations of water relations is under the authority of the Supreme Council of the Republic of Kazakhstan and is provided for under the same Code.[89] So this means that the Republic of Kazakhstan is endowed with the right to enter into regional and international water agreements with co-riparian states. Concluding such water agreements and ratifying them would guarantee cooperation, and cooperation, once again, is a necessary condition for equitable and reasonable utilization (as well as distribution) of water resources. According to the Water Code of the Republic of Kazakhstan, if the international treaties ratified by the Republic of Kazakhstan establish any rules other than those contained in the present Code, the rules of such international treaties prevail.[90]

---

[87] Convention on the Protection and Use of Transboundary Watercourses and International Lakes (adopted on 17 March 1992, entered into force 6 October 1996) 1936 UNTS 269.
[88] See Article 4(1) of the Water Code 1993 (KZ).
[89] Ibid., Article 7.
[90] Ibid., Article 2(2).

The present Water Code also stipulates the order and conditions of water use from interstate reservoirs which shall be determined upon the agreement between interested States.[91] Looking at this article with an international law lens, one can see that the Republic of Kazakhstan at least thought of entering into water agreements with interested states when the present Water Code was being drafted. Notwithstanding it being a 25-year-old law, the present Water Code also provides for the use of reservoirs located in the territory of several States. The Code expressly states that the use of reservoirs located partly in the territory of the Republic of Kazakhstan and neighboring States, or the States connected by the unity of water basins, is carried out in accordance with Agreements being concluded by the States concerned.[92] Again, the Republic of Kazakhstan had regard to the concluding and probably the ratification of water agreements with other States in the region (i.e. co-riparian states). The treaties governing the management of international watercourses are there, but most of them have not been ratified by the affected countries in Central Asia and are thus not legally binding on them, which makes cooperation increasingly difficult.

If the existing international water treaties were respected by Central Asian countries that have ratified them, they would have a legally binding force and, as a result, some of these water-related conflicts would be averted. The Kazakh water legislation clearly states that the solution of disputes on frontier waters are carried out on the basis of international treaties.[93] Ratifying international treaties will, in principle, also hold such States Parties to account as they will be legally responsible for the realization of the rights guaranteed under such treaties and would subsequently respect the governing principles thereof. Also, international agreements governing the management of these rivers which are old and whose provisions are no longer perceived as fair, just, equitable and reasonable under both international water law and domestic legislation by all riparian states should be reviewed and amended accordingly. At best, they could be repudiated and replaced with new treaties.

Notwithstanding the increasing range of actors and participants in the international legal system, 'states remain by far the most important legal persons'[94] and thus retain their attraction as the primary focus for the social activity of humankind and thus for international law.[95] The States in Central Asia, as sovereign States, are subjects of international law. Consequently, they are well aware that no matter the severity of their disagreements over water, the rules of international law have to be respected. These States also recognize that the rules of international law have to be enforced and upheld. Even more important, they know that escalating these conflicts especially to the level of international armed conflicts might lead to their actions constituting an element of 'international law breach', and that would be a 'reprehensible' violation of the rules and general principles of international law. The regulation of freshwater has primarily come about as a result of the conclusion of

---

[91] Ibid., Article 25(2).
[92] Ibid., Article 95.
[93] Ibid., Article 96.
[94] Shaw 2008, p. 197.
[95] Ibid., at 197.

treaties governing international watercourses.[96] The development of other distinct areas of international law such as international human rights law and international humanitarian law has also contributed to the development of the international regulation of watercourses, consequently ensuring a sound and equitable distribution of this shared vital resource.[97]

64.8 Conclusion

It is very important that we understand the causes of international conflicts over freshwater resources, and to attempt to identify the conditions under which such conflicts may be resolved or better yet, prevented. Indeed, we need to find solutions to the protracted problem of water scarcity and to water disputes in Central Asia. The recommendations provided herein are based on a study which was conducted in Europe and which corroborates the evidence in literature, i.e. that without proper legal and policy frameworks to regulate competing water users, intractable water disputes in Central Asia are more likely to become more intense and more disruptive. They are also more likely to escalate to the level of conflicts or even war if they are not addressed. Hence, the urgent need for cooperation which will ultimately lead to conflict prevention instead of conflict resolution.

In order to achieve this, international law is essential. International law seeks to achieve international peace and security and to ensure individuals' respect for the rule of law. 'The simplest games of international cooperation are those in which states have common interests.'[98] No doubt, states in Central Asia have common interests, as evidenced by the fact that they belong to the Commonwealth of Independent States. Once states have common interests, 'there is, therefore, no need to invest major resources pursuing cooperation.'[99] Since States in Central Asia are subject to the rules of international law, enforcing international water law is necessary in the prevention of possible conflicts, which is essential for the maintenance of regional peace, stability, as well as sustainable development and security. International law in general can also play an important role in the process of transforming these States into rights-respecting democracies. International water law in particular aims to avoid, manage and resolve water disputes.

Perhaps one question which is significant as regards the Central Asian situation is: when it comes to negotiations, regional agreements, signing of international treaties governing the management of transboundary or international watercourses in the EU, for example in respect of the Rhine, to what extent do power asymmetries between riparian states affect the outcomes of such negotiations, agreements or treaties? It was found that there are no power asymmetries between riparian states in the EU,

---

[96] Boisson de Chazournes 2013.
[97] Ibid.
[98] Guzman 2008, p. 126.
[99] Ibid., at 126.

especially those that are involved in or concerned with the protection of the Rhine. When it comes to voting, every state has a right to vote and decisions are mostly consensus-based. There is also a good flow of information, exchange of data and a balanced relationship among and between EU riparian states which makes cooperation over shared watercourses increasingly easy, subsequently leading to mutual agreements, and thereafter averting any potential conflicts. As regards sheer power politics, there is no real hegemony in the EU or in EU river basins in that, even in basins where the upstream riparian states are larger, they tend to be cooperative players, even drivers of basin-wide cooperation. Thus there is no indication that general power asymmetries have any influence in the development of water cooperation in the EU. However, it does not mean that upstream-downstream clashes do not play an important role. This same approach can be adopted in Central Asia.

From an international law perspective, there are still some challenges in enforcing or implementing some regulatory tools, especially the Rhine Convention and the EU Framework because decisions are not legally binding on the parties but are just recommendations. They are however politically binding, in the sense that any state which resolves to do (or not to do: commission v. omission) something and fails to do so, will be met with political pressure from other contracting states to implement (or not to implement) the decisions of the ICPR. Ministerial Conference decisions are also not legally binding but are at least necessary to exert pressure on contracting states to ensure continuous cooperation and implementation of resolutions. The Framework is however more detailed, has more legally-binding force and this makes its implementation easier. Some countries are not EU member states (e.g. Switzerland) but are nevertheless obliged to implement the Framework. The Framework obliges Member States to cooperate through holding public consultations (paying regard to the 'prior notification' principle) among themselves. Needless to say, all EU Member States are obliged to implement the Framework. Failure to cooperate is punished by way of fines. Also, the Framework is incorporated in most domestic legislations of EU Member States, which is commendable, because this approach makes it easier for such Member States to share the burden in terms of monitoring activities. There is so much that Central Asia can learn from the EU, both in terms of cooperation and adopting a working legal framework for governing the management of shared watercourses. As mentioned before, States in Central Asia need to ratify the existing international water treaties such as the 1997 Watercourses Convention, the 1992 Water Convention, and various other regional agreements as concluded between themselves after the dissolution of the Soviet Union. If the water resources distribution system worked quite effectively during the Soviet Union era, there is no reason why it should not work today, given the economic integration of the region.

To reiterate the point of the former UN Secretary General, Ban Ki-moon:

> It is crucial to reach consensus over the management of trans-boundary water resources in Central Asia. Further ratification by countries of Central Asia of the water conventions will create a solid framework for this.[100]

---

[100] Ki-moon 2015.

The rules of international environmental law, which complements the applicability of international water law, have developed in pursuit of two important principles which pull in opposing directions: the states have sovereign rights over their natural resources, and that states must not cause damage to the environment.[101] The second principle reflects customary international law. States are also required to 'ensure that they develop and use their natural resources in a manner which is sustainable.'[102] This principle is especially important in the current era as the world is moving towards achieving the 2030 Sustainable Development Goals.

References

Books, (Online) Articles and Chapters in Books

Abukhater A (2013) Water as a catalyst for peace: Transboundary water management and conflict resolution. Routledge, New York

Alao A (2007) Natural resources and conflict in Africa: The tragedy of endowment. University of Rochester Press, Rochester

Alan T, Keulertz M, Sojamo S, Warner J (2013) Handbook of land and water grabs in Africa: Foreign direct investment and food and water security. Routledge, New York

Arnold K (2018) In Kyrgyzstan, warming brings less water - and more conflict. www.reuters.com/article/us-kyrgyzstan-water-climatechange/in-kyrgyzstan-warming-brings-less-water-and-more-conflict-idUSKCN1NE0BW. Accessed 20 July 2019

Barilla Center for Food & Nutrition (2017) The pros and cons of water privatization, https://www.barillacfn.com/en/magazine/food-for-all/the-pros-and-cons-of-water-privatization/. Accessed 28 September 2020

Barraqué B (2011) Urban water conflicts. CRC Press, Boca Raton

Bauer C (2004) Siren song: Chilean water law as a model for international reform. RFF Press, Washington, DC

Bearden LB (2018) Following the proper channels: Tributaries in the Mekong legal regime. Brill/Nijhoff

Bernardini F (2007) The UNECE Water Convention: A unique framework for improved management of shared waters. www.inbo-news.org/en/file/259655/download?token=bHWb4QMa. Accessed 23 July 2019

Cioc M (2002) The Rhine: An eco-biography, I8I5-2000. University of Washington Press, Washington, DC

Chazournes LB (2013) Fresh Water in International Law. Oxford University Press, Oxford

Crawford J, Brownlie I (2012) Brownlie's principles of public international law. Oxford University Press, Oxford

Crootof R (2016) Change without Consent: How Customary International Law Modifies Treaties. Yale J. Int'l L 41 www.digitalcommons.law.yale.edu/yjil/vol41/iss2/1. Accessed 14 July 2019

Curie JH (2008) Public international law: Essentials of Canadian law. Irwin Law Inc, Toronto

Dalbaeva A (2018) End the weaponisation of water in Central Asia. www.crisisgroup.org/europe-central-asia/central-asia/kazakhstan/end-weaponisation-water-central-asia. Accessed 30 May 2019

---

[101] Sands 2000.

[102] Ibid., at 374.

Dellapenna JW (2011) The forms of international law. Working Paper Series. www.digitalcommons. law.villanova.edu/wps/art164. Accessed 14 July 2019

Draper SE (2006) Sharing water in times of scarcity: Guidelines and procedures in the development of effective agreements to share water across political boundaries. American Society of Civil Engineers, Reston

European Commission (2019) Introduction to the EU water framework directive. www.ec.europa. eu/environment/water/water-framework/info/intro_en.htm. Accessed 3 September 2009

Frijters I, Leentvaar J (2003) Water Conflict and Cooperation/Rhine River Basin, www.waterw iki.net/index.php?title=Water_Conflict_and_Cooperation/Rhine_River_Basin. Accessed 23 July 2019

Gronwall J (2008) Access to water: Rights, obligations and Bangalore situation. Linkoping University Press, Linköping

Guerrini A, Romano G (2014) Water management in Italy: Governance, performance, and sustainability. Springer, Heidelberg/New York

Guzman AT (2008) How international law works: A rational choice theory. Cambridge University Press, Cambridge

International Commission for the Protection of the Rhine (2018) European water framework directive. www.iksr.org/en/eu-directives/european-water-framework-directive/. Accessed 10 July 2019

International Commission for the Protection of the Rhine (2019) On the move –the ICPR is preparing for the future. www.iksr.org/fileadmin/user_upload/DKDM/Dokumente/Pressemitteilungen/EN/press_En_PLEN-CC19.pdf. Accessed 12 July 2019

Jannik B, Ravnborg HM (2004) From water 'wars' to water 'riots'? Lessons from transboundary water management. Danish Institute for International Studies Working Paper. www.diis.dk/files/media/documents/publications/jbo_hmr_water.pdf. Accessed 20 July 2019

Jones A, Cech T (2009) Colorado water law: For non-lawyers. University Press of Colorado, Boulder

Ki-moon B (2015) Speech at the High-Level International Conference on Implementation of International Decade for Action "Water for Life". https://www.un.org/sg/en/content/sg/statement/2015-06-09/secretary-generals-remarks-opening-ceremony-high-level-international. Accessed 20 April 2019

Kothari CR (2011) Research methodology: Methods and techniques, 2nd edn. New Age International, New Delhi

Lazerwitz D (1993) The Flow of International Water Law: The International Law Commission's Law of the Non-Navigational Uses of International Watercourses. Indiana Journal of Global Legal Studies. www.repository.law.indiana.edu/cgi/viewcontent.cgi?article=1011&con text=ijgls. Accessed 12 July 2019

Levy BS, Sidel VW (2008) War and health, 2nd edn. Oxford University Press, Oxford

Levy BS, Sidel VW (2011) Water Rights and Water Fights: Preventing and Resolving Conflicts Before They Boil Over. AJPH. www.odu.edu/content/dam/odu/offices/mun/2018/ib-2018-first-water.pdff. Accessed 20 July 2019

Louka E (2006) International environmental law: Fairness, effectiveness, and world order. Cambridge University Press, Cambridge

Magsig O (2015) International water law and the quest for common security. Routledge, Abingdon

McCaffrey S (2001) The contribution of the UN Convention on the law of the non-navigational uses of international watercourses. Int. J. Global Environmental Issues, 1 www.internationalwa terlaw.org/bibliography/IJGEI/03ijgenvl2001v1n34mccaffrey.pdf. Accessed 20 September 2019

Nanni M (2007) Principles of water law and administration: National and international, 2nd edn. Taylor & Francis, London

Office of the High Commissioner for Human Rights (2003) General Comment No. 15: The Right to Water (Arts. 11 and 12 of the Covenant). www.refworld.org/pdfid/4538838d11.pdf. Accessed 20 September 2019

Plum N, Schulte-Wülwer-Leidig A (2014) From a sewer into a living river: The Rhine between Sandoz and Salmon. Hydrobiologia 1:95–106

Sands Ph (2000) Environmental protection in the twenty-first century: Sustainable development and international law. In: Revesz RL, Sands Ph, Stewart RB (eds) Environmental law, the economy, and sustainable development. Cambridge University Press, Cambridge, p 374

Shaw MN (2008) International law, 6th edn. Cambridge University Press, Cambridge

Sedeqinazhad F, Atef SS, Devendra A (2018) Benefit-sharing Framework in Transboundary River Basins: The Case of the Eastern Kabul River Basin-Afghanistan. CAJWR 4:1–18

United Nations Water (2014) Human rights to water and sanitation. www.unwater.org/water-facts/human-rights/. Accessed 10 July 2019

United Nations Water (2019) World water development report 2019: 'Leaving no one behind. www.unwater.org/world-water-development-report-2019-leaving-no-one-behind. Accessed 30 July 2019

Verweij M (2000) Transboundary environmental problems and cultural theory: The protection of the Rhine and the Great Lakes. Palgrave Macmillan, New York

Wolf AT (2004) Regional Water Cooperation as Confidence Building: Water Management as a Strategy for Peace. Initiators of the Environment, Development, and Sustainable Peace (EDSP) Initiative Working Paper. www.citeseerx.ist.psu.edu/viewdoc/download?doi=10.1.1.132.2717&rep=rep1&type=pdf. Accessed 14 July 2019

Wolf AT (2007) Shared waters: Conflict and cooperation. Annual reviews. www.citeseerx.ist.psu.edu/viewdoc/download?doi=10.1.1.365.1656&rep=rep1&type=pdf. Accessed 14 July 2019

Zeitoun M (2008) Power and water in the Middle East: The hidden politics of the Palestinian-Israeli water conflict. I.B. Tauris & Co Ltd, London

Cases, Conventions and Other Documents

Case Concerning the Gabcikovo-Nagymaros Project (Hungary/Slovakia) ("The Danube Dam Case") [1997] ICJ Reports 7' [1997] International Court of Justice / Reports of judgments, advisory opinions and orders (ICJ Reports)

Convention on the Protection and Use of Transboundary Watercourses and International Lakes (adopted on 17 March 1992, entered into force 6 October 1996) 1936 UNTS 269

Convention on the Law of the Non-Navigational Uses of International Watercourses (adopted 21 May 1997, entered into force on 17 August 2014) 2998 UNTS (UN Watercourses Convention)

Convention for the Protection of the Rhine against Chemical Pollution (Rhine Convention) [1977] OJ L240/37

Directive 2000/60/EC of the European Parliament and of the Council of 23 October 2000 Establishing a Framework for Community Action in the Field of Water Policy [2000] OJ L327/1

Federal Water Act 1957 (GE)

Gabčíkovo-Nagymaros Project (Hungary/Slovakia), Judgment, 25 September 1997 [1997] International Court of Justice / Reports of judgments, advisory opinions and orders (ICJ Reports)

Report of the International Law Commission, Draft Articles on the Law of Non-Navigational Uses of International Watercourses, U.N. GAOR, 46th Sess., Supp. No. 10 at 161, U.N. Doc. A/46/10, (1991) [hereinafter Draft Articles].

United Nations General Assembly, "The human rights to safe drinking water and sanitation," Resolution 70/169, U.N. Doc. A/RES/70/169/

UN Human Rights Council resolution 15/9 of September 2010, resolution 16/2 of March 2011, resolution 18/1 of September 2011 and resolution 21/2 of September 2012

Waste Water Charges Act 1976 (GE)

Water Code 1993 (KZ)

Hafeni Nashoonga BA (Hons), LLM is a Legal Consultant based in Windhoek, Namibia who specializes in public health law, international criminal law, labor and employment law, public international law, immigration law, refugee law, water law, human rights law, security law (particularly in relation to counter-terrorism). In 2009 he studied conflict resolution abroad in Norway under Nobel Peace Prize nominee Steinar Bryn. In 2019 he was awarded a DAAD scholarship and conducted his research stay in Germany. He has held various research, analytical and advisory positions at the Office of the UNHCR Representation for Namibia, at the Office of the WHO Representative for Namibia, as well as in his country's public service.